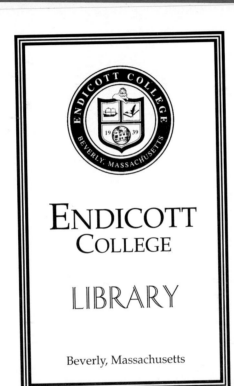

ENDICOTT COLLEGE
BEVERLY, MASSACHUSETTS
19 39

ENDICOTT
COLLEGE

LIBRARY

Beverly, Massachusetts

Encyclopedia of the
AMERICAN
RELIGIOUS
EXPERIENCE

Encyclopedia of the
AMERICAN
RELIGIOUS
EXPERIENCE

Studies of Traditions and Movements

Charles H. Lippy and Peter W. Williams, *EDITORS*

Volume III

CHARLES SCRIBNER'S SONS · NEW YORK

Copyright © 1988 Charles Scribner's Sons

Library of Congress Cataloging-in-Publication Data

Encyclopedia of the American religious experience.

Bibliography: p.
Includes index.
1. United States—Religion.   2. North America—
Religion. I. Lippy, Charles H. II. Williams, Peter W.
BL2525.E53   1987   291′.0973   87-4781
ISBN 0-684-18062-6 Set
ISBN 0-684-18861-9 Volume I
ISBN 0-684-18862-7 Volume II
ISBN 0-684-18863-5 Volume III

Published simultaneously in Canada
by Collier Macmillan Canada, Inc.

3 5 7 9 11 13 15 17 19   Q/C   20 18 16 14 12 10 8 6 4 2

Printed in the United States of America.

The paper in this book meets the guidelines for permanence and
durability of the Committee on Production Guidelines for Book Longevity
of the Council on Library Resources

CONTENTS

v

CONTENTS

CONTENTS

CONTENTS

CONTENTS

CONTENTS

Encyclopedia of the
**AMERICAN
RELIGIOUS
EXPERIENCE**

Part VII
LITURGY, WORSHIP, AND THE ARTS

LITURGY AND WORSHIP

James F. White

NO country can equal the variety of liturgical traditions—Protestant, Catholic, Orthodox, and Jewish—found in the United States; few countries can even equal the variety of worship forms that have originated here, some of which remain unique to this country. Yet within this vast assortment many common characteristics have emerged, so that one can, to a limited degree, speak of the "Americanization" of worship.

It is surprising how little scholarly research has been devoted to studying the history, theology, and phenomenology of various American expressions of worship, even though Christians generally regard worship as the church's most important activity. Each heresy or theological innovation has been tagged and cataloged, each ethical movement probed and described, but there is no comprehensive study of worship in America. Thus, in writing a survey of the subject there are few scholarly landmarks from which to get our bearings. We shall attempt to develop a comprehensive methodology for such a survey, but this article will frequently reveal vacant areas in liturgical scholarship. Someday, it is possible that enough work will have been done to enable an American production similar to Horton Davies' five-volume *Worship and Theology in England* (1961–1975). Until that time anything attempted here must have a provisional quality.

Liturgical practices can best be examined in terms of liturgical traditions. A *liturgical tradition* can be defined as an inherited body of habits and assumptions about worship as well as the actual service books and practices that reflect and reinforce those assumptions. Some liturgical traditions can be defined by the service books they use; other traditions have none to use. But all pass along common habits and assumptions that, modified by subsequent generations, tend to shape actual practice. In some cases, such as Roman Catholicism before Vatican II, remarkable consistency characterizes the tradition; in others, such as the Free Church, multitudes of deviations are produced, yet all within a common set of assumptions. Distinguishing liturgical traditions necessitates defining the common factors or dominant characteristics that unite the varieties. The *Book of Common Prayer* is an obvious common factor for Anglican worship; Pentecostal worship demands other criteria.

We shall first define the dominant characteristics of each tradition, and then trace the recognizable features in its progeny. The ethos of most traditions is defined by relative emphasis on sacraments, tendencies to uniformity or to pluralism, congregational autonomy or connectionalism, service books or their absence, abundance or lack of ceremonial, specific functions for music and other arts, and various theological, historical, and sociological factors. Many of these must be treated impressionistically, but some reliable generalizations can be made in most cases.

We shall give thumbnail sketches of ten worship traditions in America: Anglican, Free Church, Reformed, Quaker, Lutheran, Methodist, Pentecostal, Roman Catholic, Orthodox and Oriental, and Jewish. Obviously, much diversity occurs within each, and we cannot detail all variations. Still, almost all Protestant worship fits within one of the first seven traditions listed, no matter how far a group's practice has evolved from its roots.

There are many types of services within a single tradition. For Christians these usually involve rites for the Eucharist, Christian initiation, daily services, a Sunday service, various rites of passage (matrimony, burial), penance or reconciliation, ordination, healing, prayer services, sacred concerts, and various observances of the occasions of the liturgical year. Judaism has its own cycle of festivals, rites of passage, and Sabbath services. Here the focus will be the normal Sunday service for Christians and the Sabbath rites of Jews.

It must be recognized that there are ethnic and cultural styles within each tradition. Thus, there are black congregations of Lutherans and Hispanic Roman Catholic parishes in which worship still recognizably belongs to a specific tradition but is expressed in ways most natural and familiar to the group. Such differences are especially apparent in the use of music and the organization of time in the liturgical year. Cultural variety is now increasingly cherished, and efforts at indigenization have had wide appeal in recent years. Although we shall discuss only traditions of worship here, each local manifestation of a tradition is contingent upon the ethnic or cultural style of the congregation involved.

Despite the variations among liturgical traditions, they share in the American experience, and common American forces impinge on all. It is not easy to specify what is the "Americanization" of worship. One approach may be to contrast any particular tradition with its European ancestor after several centuries of separation to perceive how different is the American reality from the foreign. One common factor is the wooing away from European roots; another is mutual influence and reactions within a pluralistic society. Characteristics from one tradition slip into the use of another, while yet another tradition may reject some of its own history in order to avoid confusion with a competing group; but none exists in isolation, not even a group such as the Shakers. A third factor is the constant necessity to adapt each tradition in styles natural to the various ethnic cultures present in the United States.

A major development in America has been the overwhelming influence of the Free Church tradition on all others. Reformed and Methodist traditions, in particular, have succumbed to the pull of Free Church practice and entered its orbit, and even Quakers and Lutherans have not been able to remain aloof.

Recent decades have brought a period of ecumenical borrowing so that distinctions have somewhat blurred. Pentecostal Episcopalians have appeared, as well as Free Church congregations with a rich sacramental life. Church music and the lectionary have been shared across borders once secure from penetration. The current attitude often seems to be to seize the best available, whatever the source. Today, diversity is often as great within a tradition as it is among various traditions.

THE ANGLICAN TRADITION

The Anglican (or Episcopal) was the first Reformation tradition to make its appearance in the United States. Worship according to the 1559 *Book of Common Prayer* was celebrated at Drake's Bay, California, in 1579. The Anglican tradition is rooted in the use of the *Book of Common Prayer* (*BCP*) in its various editions. While Anglican worship has changed as a result of theological controversies, devotional shifts, and cultural changes, the *BCP* has remained a constant point of unity ever since the sixteenth century. Even the recent American prayer book (1979) retains much continuity with its predecessors.

Much of the durability of the prayer book lies in the catholicity of the sources that Archbishop Thomas Cranmer, its chief compiler, used in producing the first two *BCP*s. He blended the service books of the Sarum rites, used in his province in England, with current reform proposals from the Continent. A relative freedom in theological interpretation and the beauty of prayer-book English produced a book that English folklore came to refer to as "our incomparable liturgy," and it has been treasured just as much in America.

Colonial Anglicanism, particularly in the southern colonies, was remarkably devoid of ceremonial in line with a strong Puritan challenge to "nocent ceremonies" that had no scriptural warrant. In 1614 Reverend Alexander Whitaker, writing from Virginia, reported that the surplice was not even "spoken of" there. In northern colonies, surrounded by groups that prayed extemporaneously, Anglican worship appeared distinctive in its insistence on read prayer. On the other hand, colonial Anglicans seemed to place little more emphasis on sacramental worship than their Reformed or Free Church neighbors. Morning prayer, litany, and antecommunion was the usual Sunday-morning pattern with the Eucharist celebrated only a few times during the year. Worship centered on the reading desk and pulpit, not the altar.

The Enlightenment of the eighteenth century further diminished the sacramental aspects of worship for most Anglicans and influenced the process of liturgical revision once the revolutionary war had made an American *BCP* inevitable. A convention in Philadelphia in 1785 proposed alterations in the *BCP,* reflecting many of the liberal theological influences of the time as well as eliminating all reference to British government. The "Proposed Book," published in 1786, provoked a variety of reactions. Meanwhile, Bishop Samuel Seabury had been consecrated by bishops in Scotland in 1784 with the condition that he seek to make the liturgy in Connecticut, his diocese, conform to that of Anglicans in Scotland. The 1789 General Convention produced its own version of the *BCP,* which went into effect for the newly organized Protestant Episcopal Church on 1 October 1790. Among the American changes were the inclusion of Bishop Seabury's revision of the 1764 Prayer of Consecration from Scotland, the removal of the rubric demanding thrice-yearly communion, the disappearance of the Athanasian Creed, and the addition of a collection of twenty-seven metrical hymns, a new departure for Anglicans.

The new *BCP* lasted through a century of drastic changes in Anglican worship throughout the world, all made without producing new prayer books. The Oxford and Cambridge movements in England produced a major Catholic revival within Anglicanism, moving large segments of Anglicans around the world to restore the sacraments to centrality in worship. Vestments, crosses, candles, and much ceremonial, absent from Anglican worship for two or three centuries, reappeared despite vehement protests from those who feared creeping Romanism.

In America Bishop John Henry Hopkins, the first Episcopal bishop of Vermont, was one of the clergymen who defended the changes in worship. The short-lived New York Ecclesiological Society, begun in 1848, encouraged the building of "correct" Gothic churches with long chancels. Many fought for or against change in worship. Such now-common practices as candles on the altar table brought vehement reaction from bishops who opposed such symbols of "popery." Much of the enthusiasm for things medieval and highly clerical is hard to understand in the midst

of Jacksonian democracy. Yet, from the 1840s onward, Anglican worship in many areas of the United States moved steadily in the direction of a fuller sacramental life and more elaborate ceremonial.

Concrete manifestation of change became evident in 1871 in the first full *Hymnal,* reflecting the current recovery of hymn singing in the Church of England. Slightly changed in 1874, a larger edition appeared in 1892, which gave way to the 1916 *Hymnal.* The *Hymnal 1940* became the longest lasting, yielding finally to *Hymnal 1982.* Metrical hymnody had replaced the stilted repertoire of metrical psalms, and service music had become a normal part of Anglican worship.

The first American BCP was revised in 1892, which was then revised in the 1928 BCP. Each represented the perceived needs of the time, growing liturgical scholarship, and the desire to appropriate a wider Christian tradition.

Meanwhile, in many dioceses frequent Eucharist came to be more and more a part of parish life, with an early Sunday-morning Eucharist becoming common, followed by morning prayer and a sermon. American cathedrals began to be built in the 1860s; the first designed on a large scale was consecrated in 1884 in Albany, New York. The cathedrals often took the lead in developing their own offices and in influencing parishes, especially in church music. The advent of communities of religious brought new liturgical needs, especially in the liturgy of the hours.

The twentieth century has seen the impact of the liturgical movement, a movement seeking a richer liturgical life, especially as mediated through the Church of England and Roman Catholicism. Associated Parishes has been the most persistent agent in promoting liturgical renewal, assisted by teachers in several of the seminaries. The process of liturgical revision, initiated by the 1949 General Convention, reached a crescendo once the Second Vatican Council (1962–1965) had mandated changes in Roman Catholic worship. The Standing Liturgical Commission produced twenty-nine volumes of *Prayer Book Studies* (1950–1976), leading to the adoption of a much-revised and expanded *BCP* in 1979.

The new prayer book shows the widening worship life of Episcopal parishes in its acceptance of liturgical pluralism as a basic given. Alternate texts are provided for morning and evening prayer, the Eucharist, and burial of the dead. Many options are provided throughout, including eight Eucharistic prayers instead of the invariable one. The ecumenical Sunday lectionary (list of lessons) and daily lectionary have replaced the old one-year lectionary. Major changes have occurred in the process of Christian initiation. Liturgies for special days have been added, the pastoral offices have expanded and been revised considerably, and ordination has recovered many early Christian features.

In parish life there has been a steady move in many areas to the Eucharist as the main service on Sunday morning. And a new concern for cultural pluralism is reflected in hymnals designed especially for blacks (*Lift Every Voice and Sing*) and Hispanics (*El Himnario Provisional*).

THE FREE CHURCH TRADITION

The Free Church tradition includes the largest segment of American Protestantism, especially Baptists and Congregationalists from the colonial period, and the Christian Church (Disciples of Christ) and Mormons from the nineteenth century. It also encompasses a large number of smaller bodies: Brethren, Mennonites, Adventists, and many independent churches.

The Free Church tradition is distinguished by congregational autonomy in the ordering of worship. This means freedom to follow fixed formularies, when desired, but also the freedom to ignore them, to the extent of even rejecting use of the Lord's Prayer and the creeds. Prayer is usually extempore and often the only service book employed is a hymnal.

The origin of the Free Church tradition lies in the desire to follow God's word alone in worship. All practices that developed in the course of church history were rejected as human invention; that is, without scriptural warrant. The result usually meant the abolition of liturgical texts of any kind, including fixed prayers, in order to achieve worship devoid of any practices that are without divine sanction.

Three groupings of the Free Church tradition are prominent in America: the continental Anabaptists, the descendants of English Puritanism, and those bodies originating on the American frontier.

In Europe the Anabaptists originated underground churches in resistance to state churches that had not, in their estimation, completed the work of reformation. Rather than be hampered by "dregs of popery," they attempted to reform worship according to God's word, eliminating practices such as infant baptism, for which they could find no clear scriptural warrant, abolishing liturgical texts (although Balthasar Hubmaier, a Swiss reformer, did produce such texts), and developing strict standards as to whom they would allow as part of their worshiping company. Many of them developed fervent hymnody, often reflecting the witness of their martyrs.

Representatives of various Anabaptist groups emigrated in the eighteenth and nineteenth centuries, especially to Pennsylvania. The worship of some Mennonites has become similar to that of most American Free Churches except in unaccompanied hymnody and believers' baptism by pouring. The Hutterites have been the most conservative, even retaining sixteenth-century sermons.

Far more common are the liturgical descendants of English Puritanism. Inspired by the Reformed tradition, English Puritans eventually persuaded themselves that although John Calvin and John Knox had pursued reformation further than the Church of England had, there was still need to go beyond both the Anglicans and the Reformed if worship was to be purified according to God's word. Not only were vestments and much surviving ceremonial without scriptural warrant, but some even felt that Calvin's use of a liturgy could lead to the "vain repetition" condemned by Christ.

New England provided a convenient laboratory where liturgical experimentation could take place in truly reformed worship. In the seventeenth century John Cotton flaunted Boston's practices as containing no "prescribed form of prayer, or studied liturgy." Opening prayers were followed by sung psalmody, the reading of Scripture was accompanied by expounding it as read, and then came the sermon, which was subject to further exhorting and questioning by the congregation. Baptism was accorded to "Disciples and . . . their seed" and the Lord's Supper was celebrated "once a month at least" without "any set forms prescribed to us, but conceived by the Minister. . . . Ceremonies we use none, but are careful to administer all things according to the primitive institutions."

But God's word, it turned out, was not all that

clear. Divisions soon arose as some became persuaded that children were not to be baptized, not even the children of believers. Baptists increased in numbers, baptizing believers only, at first with the laying on of hands and eventually developing an insistence on immersion as the only acceptable mode. The Great Awakening of the eighteenth century brought even more changes. Preaching for conversion became prominent, and preachers traveled to other congregations. Another major development was the gradual infiltration of congregational hymnody. Isaac Watts popularized hymns of "human composure," a practice resisted by most Congregationalists of his time, who preferred the inspired texts, if not paraphrases, of psalmody.

English Puritans and Scottish Presbyterians had not waited for New England to show the way. The *Westminster Directory* (1644) was an attempt to reform the national churches by substituting a book of rubrics for a book of liturgies. It heralded the triumph of the Free Church tradition over the Reformed and led to the abandonment of the 1556 *Book of Common Order* in Scotland. The *Directory,* though providing "some help and furniture" to ministers, essentially left the ordering of worship to the local congregation within certain basic patterns "agreeable to the general Rules of the Word of God." In America the *Directory* became the foundation of both Free Church and Reformed worship. Preaching, psalmody, and prayer stood out as the chief characteristics.

Currents of the Enlightenment brought major changes in the sacramental life of many Free Church congregations. The sense of the sacraments as gracious acts of God's self-giving, mediated from the medieval tradition by John Calvin, was lost. The belief, so strong in Calvin, that God conveys spiritual blessings through material objects tended to be thought of as embarrassingly crude. Yet clearly baptism and the Lord's Supper were divine commands if one took Matthew 28:19 and I Corinthians 11:24–25 in a literal sense. Increasingly, justification for the sacraments was found in a moralistic way. Typical is the later statement by Ralph Waldo Emerson about the Lord's Supper: "The whole end and aim of this ordinance is but this, to make those who partake of it better." Such a moralistic function could be served by other means, notably preaching, and so frequent communion came to be regarded as less and less necessary.

In 1832 Emerson himself became convinced that the Lord's Supper was not necessary and resigned as pastor rather than administer it. Without much controversy, a massive desacralization occurred in the Free Church tradition, a shift of enormous consequence for the future of worship in America. The Lord's Supper came to be seen as only a human act of remembrance and an urging to good behavior. Consequently, infrequent celebrations seemed sufficient.

The early nineteenth century saw the beginnings of a third variety of Free Church worship. The revivals of the frontier, especially in Kentucky, led two Presbyterian clergymen, Barton Stone and Alexander Campbell, to found the Christian Church (Disciples of Christ) in 1832. As early as 1811 Campbell had become convinced that when weekly communion is missing "there New Testament worship ceases." Weekly communion came to be characteristic of Disciples (and eventually of Churches of Christ as well). Ordained clergy were at first deemed unnecessary, and even today, lay people still preside at the Lord's Supper, using an improvised Eucharistic prayer and minimal ceremony. Pew communion is usual, and frequently the sermon follows. Immersion of believers has come to be the accepted baptismal practice.

Enormous impact was made on Free Church worship by the revival system of the nineteenth century. Originating in frontier camp meetings, revival techniques spread eastward. The great apostle of these techniques was Charles Grandison Finney, who finally identified with Congregationalists. Finney's new measures focused on inquiry meetings, protracted meetings, and the anxious bench, all in the context of preaching for conversion. Worship came to focus on producing conversions, thus shifting worship toward the pragmatic direction of making converts rather than rejoicing in the orderly recital of God's works. Worship became a means rather than an end. Individualism came to the forefront, reflected in the heavily subjective gospel song.

The "Free" of Free Church had undergone a marked transformation from freedom to follow the word of God to being free to do what worked. So attractive and effective did such an attitude appear that it overwhelmed many remnants of the Methodist and Reformed traditions and even affected Quakers and Lutherans.

The usual service had three parts: a time of warm-up with music prominent, evangelistic preaching for conversion, and a harvest of those savingly wrought upon. This is still the dominant pattern of much of American Protestant worship and is the format of most television evangelistic services.

In the twentieth century much of the Free Church tradition has moved away from the emotionalism that had characterized many congregations. Others, of course, have remained less touched by revivalism. A vague groping for something to make worship more attractive led in the years preceding World War II to an emphasis on aesthetics. Free Church aestheticism manifested itself in Gothic revival churches and trained choirs. Von Ogden Vogt, pastor of a Unitarian church in Chicago, was the most prolific writer on this topic. He saw worship as closely akin to the experience of the beautiful. The period immediately after World War II brought interest in lost historic roots, particularly in rediscovery of the sixteenth-century Reformation. Neo-orthodox theology encouraged the use of a prayer of confession and creeds.

Slowly the liturgical movement and the post–Vatican II Roman Catholic reforms have made their presence felt in the Free Churches. The United Church of Christ published *Services of the Church* (1969), followed by the *Hymnal of the United Church of Christ* in 1974. Further liturgical publications were under way in the late 1980s. Baptist churches have been less touched by recent changes. The most important change has been widespread adoption of the ecumenical lectionary and, as a result, a deeper involvement in the liturgical year. The desacralizing tendencies of the Enlightenment have never been overcome even among Disciples, although Free Church congregations always have freedom to appropriate a richer sacramental life.

THE REFORMED TRADITION

The Reformed tradition enters American history with several national groups: French Huguenot, Dutch, German, Scots, and Scotch-Irish. Presbyterians and various Reformed churches are the chief representatives. The Reformed tradition originated with three leaders of liturgical reformation: Ulrich Zwingli in Zurich, Martin Bucer in Strasbourg, and John Calvin in Geneva. From Geneva the Reformed tradition spread across Europe under the leadership of men such as John Knox, who mediated this tradition for Scotland and England.

Characteristic of Reformed worship is emphasis on the centrality of the word of God. A willingness to imitate the first Christian centuries of worship avoids the extreme biblicism characteristic of some Free Church groups. Fixed liturgies were usual for the first century of this tradition. Psalm singing was a prominent feature of Reformed worship and is still the only form of congregational song allowed in some Reformed churches. Didacticism characterizes sixteenth-century Reformed liturgies, as in the use of the Decalogue as a part of the Eucharistic liturgy and prayers and exhortations that tend to stress correct doctrine and strict ethics. Although it often seems the most exclusively cerebral tradition of worship, joyful psalm singing gave some emotional balance to Reformed worship.

John Calvin's Genevan rite of 1542 is the prototypical Eucharistic rite, heavily influenced by Bucer's service in Strasbourg. It included a prayer for illumination, the Decalogue, and the words of institution (read outside of the Eucharistic prayer as a "warrant"). Contrary to Calvin's wishes, the Eucharist was not celebrated weekly, even in Geneva. John Knox's version of 1556 was used in Scotland for just eighty years, eventually being replaced by the Scots' concession to the *Westminster Directory* in hope of national unity.

Many of the French Reformed immigrants became Anglicans, especially in South Carolina, although one Huguenot church in Charleston still uses an eighteenth-century Swiss Reformed liturgy. The Reformed Dutch Church retained a liturgy for the sacraments. The dominant Reformed group, the Presbyterians, increasingly were drawn into the orbit of the Free Church and Methodist traditions. Examples of this were adoption of the singing of hymns, communion received in the pews, instead of around tables, and revivalistic preaching. The sacramental seasons, events of much introspective soul-searching, also dissipated. Although Finney left the Presbyterians, much of Finney remained with them. Long forgotten was any sense that the Scots had had a *Book of Common Order* for eighty years, as much Presbyterian worship devolved into the common three-part shape: preliminaries, sermon, and harvest.

The nineteenth century witnessed some reactions against such abdication of Reformed history. A young Presbyterian minister, Charles W. Baird, published *Eutaxia,* or the *Presbyterian Liturgies,* anonymously in 1855. He took as his first premise "that the principles of Presbyterianism in no wise conflict with the discretionary use of written forms." A survey of the long-forgotten history of Reformed liturgies in Geneva, France, the Palatinate, the Netherlands, Scotland, and England concludes with his wistful hope that some "formulary" might be made available "as a lawful aid to those who may desire its use." A similar stirring appeared in the Kirk of Scotland under Dr. Robert Lee, who had the temerity to read prayers from a book until censured for it by the 1859 General Assembly.

At the same time among the German Reformed churches the Mercersburg Theology developed as a reaction to the prevailing revivalism. John W. Nevin came to concur with what Edward Irving, a Scot ministering in London, had labeled the "infidelity of Evangelicalism." Nevin engaged in various theological battles to uphold Calvin's high doctrine of the sacraments that Enlightenment trends had buried. In 1857 Nevin, Philip Schaff, and others produced for the German Reformed Church a *Provisional Liturgy.* An *Order of Worship* followed in 1866. These rites reflected Schaff's knowledge of the Irvingites (or Catholic Apostolic Church) in England plus considerable research in the authentic Reformed liturgies. The Mercersburg liturgies were produced at least a century too soon and probably caused more controversy than converts. Although the impact on American Protestant worship of these liturgies was slight, they did provide a precedent.

Another American countercurrent appeared in 1897 with the formation of the Church Service Society under the influence of two pastors, Henry van Dyke and Louis Benson. These two, with Charles Cuthbert Hall, the president of Union Theological Seminary, took the lead in preparing the 1906 *Book of Common Worship,* published with scant endorsement by the General Assembly "for Voluntary Use." In 1932 a revised and expanded edition, produced by a committee

also chaired by Henry van Dyke, led to more enthusiastic adoption by the northern Presbyterians and was approved "for the optional and selective use" of ministers by southern Presbyterians. The third edition, published in 1946, provided a much richer selection for use. The *Directory for Worship* of 1788 was finally revised by the United Presbyterian Church in the United States in 1961, and the Presbyterian Church (U.S.A.) brought out its own revision in 1963.

These paved the way for the post–Vatican II publication of the *Worshipbook* in 1970 and (with hymns and service music) 1972. A long-delayed *Liturgy and Psalms* was published by the Reformed Church in America in 1968 and was replaced in 1985. The Christian Reformed Church published its *Psalter Hymnal* in 1976. It follows Calvin in not providing a burial rite while including rites for excommunication and readmission. In 1980 the Presbyterian Church (U.S.A.) began work on a fifteen-volume *Supplemental Liturgical Resources* series that incorporates the best of late-twentieth-century ecumenical and Reformed liturgical scholarship and practice.

THE QUAKER TRADITION

The Quaker tradition is the most radical of all, having dispensed with much that even the Free Church tradition maintained: psalmody, preaching, prayer, and outward sacraments. Yet it has also been the most stable tradition, in many places changing very little in its more than three hundred years of existence. Its founder, George Fox, infuriated the Puritans by appealing to an authority even higher than the written word of God, the Holy Spirit present and active in the midst of the congregation. Inspired Scripture was secondhand when the source of inspiration was directly available to all who had ears to hear.

Robert Barclay gave the Society of Friends theological coherence and interpreted Quaker corporate mysticism with its insistence on the need to gather to hear what the Spirit had to say to the community through the voice of an individual or through silent waiting on God. Outward and visible sacraments were considered unnecessary and never intended by Christ. This possibility of access by all to the Spirit led to a radical equality among Quakers, of which the absence of clergy was a further sign. Quakers were the first in America to insist that women's concerns be heard in meetings and the first to oppose slavery.

The Quakers lost little time in coming to America, the first missionaries arriving in Rhode Island in the mid-seventeenth century. Pennsylvania soon provided a haven for Quaker worship.

The American environment brought eventual changes to some meetings. Women's concerns began to be part of every meeting rather than aired separately. (Sliding partitions had divided many meetinghouses to separate the sexes in their worship.) Many Quakers were affected by frontier evangelical movements. Joseph John Gurney, an English Quaker banker, saw much of value in the evangelicalism of the time. Gradually, he and a number of other Quakers, especially west of the Appalachians, assimilated the patterns of Free Church worship. Paid ministers became common among these "Gurneyite" Friends, as did hymn singing, choirs, and sermons, a decisive break from the traditional silent meetings. Even revivalism became a Quaker phenomenon, especially in Indiana after the Civil War, although elements of spontaneity remained despite the intrusion of prepared elements.

Even though much of Quaker worship in the Midwest was drawn virtually into the Free Church tradition (with the exception of continued rejection of outward sacraments), conservative Quakers have maintained the original "unprogrammed" forms of worship. "Recorded ministers" are sometimes recognized as those who are most frequently channels of the Spirit; that is, individuals not prone to speak from "their own will and wisdom." In recent years there has been less inclination to recognize such persons as distinct within the community. As other traditions come to value periods of silence in their worship, we find that traditional Quakers have given much to others but taken little in return.

THE LUTHERAN TRADITION

The only tradition named for an individual, the Lutheran tradition of worship stems from the reform movement that Martin Luther directed from Wittenberg in the 1520s and 1530s. Lutheranism still shows a continuing loyalty to its founder's principles. Despite wholesale denunciations of corruptions of the medieval sacramental system, Luther's liturgical reform was a conservative one. He retained much of the medieval cultus but added the vernacular, congregational hymnody, and an insistence on preaching. Luther's conservatism was retained when his reform spread beyond Germany into the Netherlands, the Baltic states, Sweden, Finland, Denmark, Norway, and Iceland. A relish for liturgical art and choral and congregational music continued to characterize worship in these lands, often in contrast to other Protestant traditions.

Lutheranism arrived in America early, with Dutch Lutherans first settling along the Hudson River (although without clerical leadership until 1657). Swedes built the first Lutheran church near Philadelphia in 1646. The majority of Lutheran settlers in the eighteenth century were Germanic. By mid-century nearly half the settlers of Pennsylvania were of Germanic origin, including Reformed, Moravians, and Anabaptists, as well as Lutherans. Liturgical leadership appeared with the arrival of Henry Melchior Mühlenberg in 1742. The organization of the Ministerium of Pennsylvania in 1748 brought adoption of a liturgy largely prepared by Mühlenberg, for which the liturgy of the Lutheran Church of the Savoy, in London, was the basis, along with some Swedish elements. Although some would have preferred different Lutheran agenda, the 1748 liturgy remained a source of consensus for most of the century. The order of public worship and communion were in German while forms for baptism and marriage were in English, taken from the *Book of Common Prayer*. The Eucharist was mandatory three times a year.

Successive agenda and hymnals appeared in Pennsylvania and other synods throughout the nineteenth century. The effects of the Enlightenment became apparent in many of these books as sixteenth-century hymns disappeared and rationalistic texts replaced sixteenth-century liturgies. Not until 1847 was a full liturgy published in English. But by mid-century a return to pure Lutheran rites, unaffected by rationalism and the Reformed tradition, was seen as desirable. Nineteenth-century immigrant groups from Scandinavia and Germany added further complexity. Most brought their own service books but eventually felt the need for English texts. Many Germans, coming to the Midwest in the mid-nineteenth century, were inclined to use the agenda of Saxony or the *Agende* of 1844 that the Bavarian pastor Wilhelm Loehe had sent for their use.

Eastern Lutherans published the *Church Book* in 1868, representing a return to the earlier Lutheran tradition and a much richer use of the church year. A constant perplexity was the degree to which German hymnody should be balanced with that of Watts and Wesley. Agreement on features of the "Common Service" by a variety of Lutherans occurred in 1888, and still more progress toward Lutheran unity was apparent in the *Common Service Book* of 1917. In 1941 the Lutheran Church–Missouri Synod published its *Lutheran Hymnal;* the *Worship Supplement* appeared in 1969. A major publishing event, again the result of growing Lutheran cooperation and mergers, was the *Service Book and Hymnal* of 1958. Although restoring historic Lutheran forms, it also ventured in a more ecumenical direction, such as the addition of a full eucharistic prayer.

A special problem of Lutheran liturgical history in America has been the abiding influence of Pietism. Moravians in Pennsylvania and North Carolina moved beyond Lutheran structures and developed distinctive forms such as the "love feast" and the "watch night." Mühlenberg, although influenced by Pietism and having taught at Halle, realized the need for liturgical texts, unlike many of his fellow immigrants. Nineteenth-century waves of immigrants, especially from Norway, found little value in fixed forms, and their worship life often resembled that of the Free Church tradition with a German or Scandinavian accent.

A Lutheran revival began to flourish in American Lutheranism, coming to full flower in the years after World War II. Arthur Piepkorn in the Missouri Synod, Luther Reed in the United Lutheran Church, the Society of St. James, the Institute of Liturgical Studies at Valparaiso University, and the Lutheran Society for Worship, Music, and the Arts—all played leadership roles. Fervent hymnody had become a Lutheran trademark, and the singing of service music for the antecommunion was common. But the legacies of Enlightenment and Pietism as well as assimilation with American Free Church worship hampered the development of sacramental life.

In the changed atmosphere after Vatican II the ground was prepared for a liturgical renewal. The Lutheran Church in America was the first denomination to have a full-time worship executive (1955). In the fall of 1966 the Inter-Lutheran Commission on Worship (ILCW) took up the task Mühlenberg had dreamed of: a single service book for all American Lutherans. The result was the *Lutheran Book of Worship* (1978), although Missouri seceded at the last moment to publish its own *Lutheran Worship* (1982). The *Lutheran Book of Worship* reflects strong ecumenical influence in the use of the ecumenical lectionary and provision of five eucharistic prayers. But it is also firmly Lutheran, especially in assuming a sung liturgy. Thus, Lutheran worship seems to be moving on two tracks that often coincide: ecumenical and neo-Lutheran. A richer sacramental life is emerging, although monthly communion still seems the norm. Several of the Lutheran seminaries have made advances in appointing trained liturgists to their teaching staffs.

THE METHODIST TRADITION

The Methodist liturgical tradition arrived in America later than the religious groups discussed so far. Although Methodists appeared in the colonies shortly before the Revolution, the movement did not become organized on a national level until 1784. Methodism's liturgical patterns are the legacy of its founder, John Wesley. Wesley was a most catholic man, uniting in one person the knowledge of a patristics scholar, the fervor of his Puritan ancestors, and Anglican piety. His Methodism challenged the prevalent Enlightenment religion of the established church. Current desacralization Wesley countered with a return to "constant communion." To the Enlightenment's distrust of enthusiasm, he brought evangelistic preaching and joyful hymn singing. To tepid rationalism and shallow moralism, he brought spontaneous testimonies at "watch nights" and "love feasts" and stringent examination of consciences at class meetings. To the prevailing stress on decency and order, he brought extempore prayer.

Wesley's younger brother, Charles, produced over six thousand hymns. In an age when Anglican church music was confined to psalmody, such hymns gave a new and dynamic possibility of personal expression in worship. Early Methodist worship combined structure and freedom. Wesley's love and use of the *BCP* was lifelong, but he saw the need to give prayer-book services relevance and immediacy with hymn singing and extempore prayer. He was enough of a pragmatist to appropriate for new use ancient forms: the ancient *agape* as the "love feast," vigils as the "watch night," and the biblical covenant renewal as the "covenant service." No Christian leader since has combined a strong sacramental and traditional piety with evangelical fervor as successfully as did Wesley.

In 1784 John Wesley sent to America the foundations of Methodist worship: *A Collection of Psalms and Hymns for the Lord's Day* and his revision of the *BCP*, *The Sunday Service of the Methodists in North America with Other Occasional Services.* The *Sunday Service* was a complete service book, largely faithful to the 1662 *BCP* but incorporating distinctively Wesleyan features: abridgment of services so as to make a weekly Eucharist more feasible, a careful reduction of the psalter by thirty-four full psalms and parts of fifty-eight others, elimination of remnants of the sanctoral cycle (commemorations of saints), removal of all reference to the British sovereign and state services, and numerous minor changes that eliminated items he found theologically objectionable, such as confirmation, absolution, and anthems. Much of this had precedents among the Puritans but other items (such as abolishing the giving away of the bride) are unique.

Wesley's 314-page *Sunday Service,* an abridgment of the *BCP,* was little loved or used by his American followers. They received three subsequent printings of it during Wesley's lifetime, but a year after Wesley's death in 1791 it quietly became a thirty-seven-page section of the *Discipline,* which contains the doctrines and constitution for governing Methodist churches, institutions, parishioners, and ministers. This section, eventually named "The Ritual," includes frequently revised services, such as baptism of infants, baptism of adults, the Lord's Supper, marriage, burial, and the three ordination rites. In 1864 services were added for receiving persons into church membership and for laying a corner-stone and dedicating a church. For the most part these occasional services seem to have been followed rather faithfully.

Methodism's great growth on the frontier tended to obliterate the structured services of prayer and the frequent celebration of the Eucharist that Wesley expected. No service materials appeared in the hymnals until 1896. The *Discipline* requires only that worship consist of "singing, prayer, [lessons for both testaments] . . . and preaching." Sunday-evening services tended to be still more informal and Wednesday-evening prayer meetings, devoted to spontaneous prayer by all present, were common.

Frontier styles of worship eventually had an impact on the more staid churches of the East. For all practical purposes, except in the sacraments, Methodists, like the Reformed, joined the Free Church tradition. In practice almost everything was left to the discretion of the local congregation. Such liberty meant that the pastor could order worship as he saw fit or, rather, thought worked best. Yet standard patterns evolved, especially the three-part order, consisting of preliminaries, sermon, and harvest, that is still prevalent in Methodist churches in the South. Methodism contributed a style of preaching and hymnody to the Free Church tradition and received in return a new structure of service.

Significant debates occurred throughout the nineteenth century as Methodists defended infant baptism (which was opposed by Baptists). Wesley's strong doctrines of Eucharistic presence and sacrifice were largely forgotten and his 166 Eucharistic hymns scarcely remembered, partly as a reaction to the Oxford Movement and its American counterparts. Increasing numbers of blacks adapted Methodist worship in their own style. Charles Tindley and Thomas Dorsey brought the gospel hymn to its height. Suggestions for a return to a more "Wesleyan" style of worship occurred under the leadership of Thomas O. Summers, dean of Vanderbilt Divinity School and publishing agent for the southern church. An order of worship was approved by the northern Methodist Episcopal Church in 1892 and 1896 and became a part of the 1905 *Methodist Hymnal* shared by northern and southern churches despite the objections of some to such "formalism" after more than a century of no official order.

The twentieth century saw growing affluence

and higher educational standards reflected in a move to aestheticism. Elbert M. Conover, director of the Interdenominational Bureau of Architecture, successfully encouraged Methodists to imitate Episcopalians by building Gothic churches with divided chancels for robed choirs. After World War II a greater interest in Wesleyan forms was made concrete in the 1944 and 1964 *Book of Worship.* New hymnals in 1935 and 1966 show the drift toward more structured worship.

The post–Vatican II era took Methodism by surprise. Suddenly it found itself the last church to have revised a service book in Elizabethan English (1964) and possibly the last to adopt and defend such medieval practices as the term *confirmation* (1964). Many congregations indulged in a period of experimentation in the late 1960s and early 1970s, usually without much concern about theological foundations.

A new era began in 1972 with the first professionally staffed Section on Worship Office and the inauguration of a new series of service booklets, the *Supplemental Worship Resources* series. Unlike the 1964 *Book of Worship* these are not revisions of Methodist-Anglican materials but are based on early church patterns in current ecumenical use, written in contemporary language, and grounded in solid theological scholarship both Wesleyan and ecumenical. Methodists have made the greatest progress in seminary teaching of worship among American Protestants. Adoption of the ecumenical lectionary (and calendar) has been widespread and a common feature is the move to more frequent celebrations of the Eucharist. In joining a broader Christian tradition, Methodism has also come closer to John Wesley.

THE PENTECOSTAL TRADITION

The Pentecostal tradition is the most recent, its advent coinciding with the opening of the twentieth century. Not only are its origins uniquely American, but its early leaders included both whites and blacks, men and women. The roots of Pentecostalism are in the Holiness movement of the late nineteenth century, itself the child of an emphasis on sanctification in various Methodist groups. Flourishing in various Assemblies of God, Pentecostal, and Holiness churches, the movement has become worldwide.

Liturgically, Pentecostalism seems closest to the Free Church tradition or the spontaneous Methodist prayer meeting. The black style of worship in both traditions was crucial in the formative years of Pentecostalism. The links one might expect to the Quaker tradition do not seem to exist, although there is certainly the same stress on the Spirit-filled community. The differences from the Quakers are significant: Pentecostals retain visible sacraments, hymn singing, and preaching. Differences from the Free Church tradition are equally important. The freedom of the Free Church tradition largely consists in allowing the minister to order worship as desired by creating a definite structure, usually dominated by the clergyman.

Pentecostal worship seems best characterized by the unexpected possibilities inherent in worship led by the Spirit in which the whole congregation participates. Speaking in tongues ("the gift of glossolalia") is the most graphic example of a charism but by no means the only gift. Interpretation of tongues, spontaneous singing and prayer, and preaching are gifts granted to any worshiper. Thus the concern is not with following organized order of worship but with following the lead of the Spirit, which blows where it will. Certain perdurable patterns emerge in each congregation but a sensitive minister soon develops the skill of flowing with the moment. When one recognizes that there is a definite recurring pattern to such worship, complete informality becomes possible and sequential ordering of worship unnecessary.

A variety of practices characterize various Pentecostal groups. In general, only believers receive water baptism. Early Pentecostalism was split by those practicing a "Jesus only" form of words for administering water baptism instead of Trinitarian. Far more important than water baptism is baptism of the Spirit, in which possession by the Spirit becomes manifest, especially through the gift of tongues. This can appear in anyone, and the number of women leaders in this tradition is significant. In many groups healing has become a major gift of ministry. This newest tradition often resounds with gifts such as glossolalia and interpretation familiar to the apostolic church, and fear of the disappearance of these is an ongoing concern.

In recent years Pentecostalism, or the charismatic movement, has had major impact on many of the mainline Protestant churches and on Roman Catholicism. "Neo-Pentecostals" (in the mainline churches, as distinguished from "Classical Pentecostals" in Pentecostal churches) often share their gifts in separate services within a congregation of Methodists, Episcopalians, Reformed, or Roman Catholics. After an initial period of suspicion many of these groups have shown openness to Neo-Pentecostals and have encouraged such worship as a supplement to their tradition's familiar patterns. In addition, many of the mainline churches have tried to accommodate elements of spontaneity, particularly intercessory prayer, within their customary worship. At the same time affirmation of some of the values of decency and order may have more appeal today to traditional Pentecostals.

THE ROMAN CATHOLIC TRADITION

Although comprising the greatest variety of nationalities and cultures, Roman Catholic worship has shown great consistency in America. The diversity of nationalities represented in American Roman Catholicism is most apparent in the various cults of saints and the calendars of festivals. The Feast of the Three Kings is significant to Hispanics; St. Patrick's Day appeals to the Irish. Various pieties and devotions appeal to diverse groups, such as the Good Friday rites of the Penitentes in New Mexico.

Much of the consistency of Roman Catholic worship in American is due to the policies of Rome, which, in the sixteenth century, came to see uniformity as desirable in worship and demanded strict observance worldwide of all Latin rites with only minor exceptions. The Congregation of Sacred Rites was set up in 1588 to regulate the liturgy and it did so very effectively. The official Latin texts appeared in the years after the Council of Trent (1545–1563): *Roman Breviary,* 1568; *Roman Missal,* 1570; *Roman Martyrology,* 1584; *Roman Pontifical,* 1596; *Caeremoniale Episcoporum,* 1600; and *Roman Ritual,* 1614. Except for occasional changes in the calendar and some revisions in the *Roman Breviary* in 1911, these books remained the basis for Roman Catholic worship for nearly four hundred years. Architectural and musical styles changed drastically but the rites scarcely at all.

The uniformity of rites in Latin led most congregations to occupy themselves during mass with various devotions such as the rosary. John Carroll, appointed the first American Roman Catholic bishop in 1790, desired a vernacular liturgy, since he felt Roman Catholicism could not grow in America without it. It was nearly two centuries before his wish was fulfilled. Numerous extra-liturgical devotions such as benediction, novenas, the rosary, and stations of the cross supplemented the mass. Clergy and religious read the breviary daily or participated in the daily office when living in community.

The seeds of liturgical change were slow in sprouting. The liturgical movement, whose beginnings are often traced to Dom Prosper Guéranger in nineteenth-century France, took nearly a century to reach the United States. The first visible changes came through Dom Virgil Michel of the Benedictine Abbey of St. John's in Minnesota. Having encountered the liturgical movement as a student in Europe, Father Virgil began the publication of *Orate Fratres* in 1926 (since 1951 called *Worship*). He enlisted most of the early proponents of liturgical renewal as contributors, displaying a keen sense of the connection between liturgy and social justice. Godfrey Diekmann took over editorship of the magazine after Dom Virgil's death in 1938, and a series of sympathetic abbots made St. John's the center of the American liturgical movement.

Long associated with *Worship* was H. A. Reinhold, who escaped Nazi Germany to become a diocesan priest and a prolific writer in America. At the University of Notre Dame in 1947 Michel Mathis, C.S.C., began a liturgical studies program, importing distinguished visitors from Europe. In 1966 this became the Graduate Program in Liturgical Studies. Maurice Lavanoux devoted his life to the Liturgical Arts Society and its periodical *Liturgical Arts* (1931–1972). Gerald Ellard, a Jesuit scholar, Martin Hellriegel, a parish priest in St. Louis, and many others devoted themselves to the liturgical apostolate.

The fruits of such labors in North America and Europe became manifest in Vatican II's *Constitution on the Sacred Liturgy* (1963). This marked the beginning of enormous change for Latin-rite Catholicism. All services are now in the vernacular, many of the rites have been greatly simplified, various options have become available for local situations, communion at mass has increased while confessions continue to decline, and the pastoral offices have become much more adaptable. Most important of all, "full, conscious, and active participation" of the laity has been made a major goal of worship. The amount of Scripture reading at mass has increased greatly as a result of the ecumenical lectionary, now also used by many Protestants. Sermons at Sunday mass have become mandatory. Only minimal success has been achieved in introducing the liturgy of the hours (daily prayer services) to the laity, although reforms here brought major changes to the worship life of religious communities. Many private devotions have disappeared in recent years in favor of a more liturgical piety.

Revision of the liturgical books and their translation into English have taken nearly twenty years. Now, problems of cultural adaptation remain to be faced. The connection between liturgy and justice, so clear to Virgil Michel, is being recovered. After two decades of vigorous liturgical change, American Roman Catholics in the 1980s have begun to consolidate change by seeking better understanding of the reformed rites.

THE ORTHODOX AND ORIENTAL TRADITION

Most, if not all, branches of the Orthodox churches of the world, such as the Russian and Greek churches, are represented by worshiping congregations in this country. The Armenian Apostolic Church, Syrian Jacobites, and other Oriental churches are also represented. Many different Eastern-rite or Uniate Roman Catholic communities such as Melchites and Chaldeans are also present. Some cities, such as Pittsburgh, can boast several hierarchies of both Orthodox and Roman Catholic varieties.

Ever since Russian Orthodox traders settled in Alaska and ventured down the coast to California, Orthodox worship has been present in North America. An Alaskan diocese was established in 1799. Massive emigration from Eastern Europe in the early twentieth century swelled the numbers of Russian Orthodox. Arriving later (the first parish, in New York, was formed in 1891), Greek Orthodox believers came to outnumber the Russians. For both Russians and Greeks the ancient Byzantine liturgy, attributed to Saint John Chrysostom, continues to be the main rite except when replaced by that of Saint Basil on a few occasions each year, especially in Lent.

In theory Orthodox worship has not changed; in fact much has changed, with the exception of texts. In many cases the rites have been translated from Old Church Slavonic or Greek into English. Pews have been added where there were none in Europe and even the Western innovations of stained-glass windows and pipe organs have found their way into Orthodox churches. Men and women sit together. Yet much of the original ethos persists: freedom from the time-harried limitations of Western worship, worship amid the splendors of heaven itself reflected in domes and images of the saints in glory, and the ancient texts scarcely changed since the eighth century. Translation represents an enormous change but is hardly unprecedented.

Similar issues have confronted the ancient Oriental churches of Nestorian or Monophysite background. They have had to try to accommodate Western culture without losing something essential in their worship. Ancient liturgical families have been transplanted to this soil, bringing with them the old Julian calendar.

Some ancient Eastern churches that are connected to Rome use rites other than that of the Latin West. They have not been affected by the changes Vatican II mandated for the West and in many ways parallel the worship of other Orthodox or Oriental expatriates. Many of these churches, such as the Melchites and Chaldeans, have translated their liturgies into English and most have acculturated in some ways in their use of music and architecture. But much of the iconography, ceremonial, calendars, and chant has been preserved. The presence of Eastern-rite churches has had a healthy influence in challenging the normativity of the Latin rite in Roman Catholicism. Often, the eastern rites testify to practices older than those common in the West, many of which were evolved in the late Middle Ages.

All in all, the many varieties of Christian worship existing in America side by side have had much influence on one another. Except for the Orthodox, Oriental, and Uniate churches, the post–Vatican II era has been one of mutual borrowing and sharing. The exploration of present concerns such as sexism, indigenization, and liturgical arts can be undertaken together rather than compartmentalized in separate traditions. Indications are that the Americanization of worship will proceed at an accelerated pace as the churches continue to assimilate each other's patterns.

THE JEWISH TRADITION

Jewish worship in America has faced many problems of adaptation to a new world and a new culture. Judaism was but a minor presence in the colonial period, there being no rabbis and few congregations in America before the Revolution. But in the first half of the nineteenth century there were major immigrations, mostly from Germany. Among these emigrants adaptation of law and custom to the circumstances of modern life was already under way, leading to what eventually became known as Reform Judaism. The 1840s saw the swelling of more liberal ranks as Ashkenazic Jews from Germany came to outnumber the more traditional Sephardic Jews already present in America.

Reform Jews in the United States demanded liturgy and hymns in German or English instead of Hebrew, together with alteration of the traditional *Siddur,* the prayer book that contains the daily and Sabbath liturgy. Such stirrings were already prevalent in Germany. Since "public worship for Jews is the recitation of a fixed liturgy" (Hoffman, 1977), the stage was set for the revision of the liturgical books. Rabbi David Einhorn pioneered in the production of a service book, the *Olat Tamid,* in German and Hebrew for Reform Jews in 1858. In the previous year Rabbi Isaac Wise had published his more conservative *Minhag America (American Ritual).* The Pittsburgh Platform of 1885 gave expression to a new form of Judaism that had little use for references to Jews as still living in exile, to a personal messiah, or to prayer for the restoration of the Temple and animal sacrifice. Rabbi Einhorn's prayer book and the Pittsburgh Platform were reflected in the *Union Prayer Book I and II* of 1895–1896. This moved Reform Judaism to more restrained total decorum with rubrics designating everyone's role. Of the prayers removed from the *Sid-*

dur, most had been among the last to be added. In early editions Hebrew was almost eliminated. Further changes came to Reform worship in allowing men and women to sit together, and in adding organ and choir music to the service.

A new current ran from the late nineteenth century to the legal close of immigration to America in 1924. During this time thousands of Jews from Eastern Europe, fleeing persecution, came to North America. Their intellectual milieu was different from that of the German Jews, who had appropriated modern scientific learning. The Orthodox Judaism of these immigrants included worship largely in Hebrew, the absence of roles for women, and rather boisterous and noisy behavior during worship. The modified religious practices of their Reform neighbors seemed to the Orthodox heedless capitulations to American culture. The Orthodox continued to pray for the return of the Temple and for the coming of the Messiah.

A third movement, Conservative Judaism, came into prominence in the twentieth century. It accepts some of the liturgical "reforms," especially the changed role of women, pipe organs, and mixed choirs, but prefers to retain a Hebrew liturgy. Participation in the high-holiday services (in observance of Rosh Hashanah and Yom Kippur) remains strong although attendance at daily and Saturday-morning services has declined. Friday-evening worship has become popular partly because lack of knowledge of Hebrew is less of a barrier then (since it's less used), preaching is more prominent, and familiar traditional Hebrew music—that is, with cantor and without organ—is employed. Prayer books with both Hebrew and English texts are used. Social gatherings usually follow. The role of women has expanded in Conservative worship, decorum has been greatly sought with more restraint, and fund-raising has been downplayed during services. While daily and Saturday-morning worship remain close to Orthodox practice, high-holiday and Friday-evening services allow more use of the vernacular, congregational song, and participation.

The Reconstructionist movement, under the leadership of Mordecai Kaplan, pioneered some changes in worship, apparent in the *Sabbath Prayer Book* (1945). The movement reflected the difficulty that many Jews have in praying for the

Temple, sacrifice, and the coming of the Messiah. Prayers in English and Hebrew also tend to omit reference to the subordination of women and physical resurrection. Sometimes, portions that might offend are left in Hebrew and other parts done in English. The 1945 prayer book combines continuity with tradition, relevance, and intellectual integrity.

Recent years have seen further changes in both Conservative and Reform worship. Subsequent editions of the *Union Prayer Book* added more Hebrew. Since the 1960s, serious concerns about sexism have come to the forefront, especially in Reform Judaism. Liturgical scholarship has flourished. Reform Judaism has tended to be somewhat more firm in asserting its Jewish roots while insisting on continuity with normal life in American society. A notable product is the 1975 publication *Gates of Prayer: The New Union Prayerbook,* widely admired for its poetic contemporary language. It is matched with *Gates of the House: The New Union Home Prayerbook,* a collection of prayers and readings (1977), *Gates of Understanding* (1977), an interpretative volume, and *Gates of Repentance* (1978) for high holidays. These volumes express Reform Judaism in its maturity. Similar work is in process in Conservative Judaism with a new volume under way to replace the 1946 prayer book. All branches seem to have survived the experimentation of the 1960s, having found a new freedom, yet retaining a devotion to abiding tradition. Jewish worship seems to be becoming both more deliberately Jewish yet more confidently American. The ability to sing the Lord's song in a new land seems to flourish today as in centuries past.

BIBLIOGRAPHY

Doug Adams, *Meeting House to Camp Meeting: Toward a History of American Free Church Worship from 1620 to 1835* (1981); Sydney E. Ahlstrom, *A Religious History of the American People* (1972); John Bishop, *Methodist Worship in Relation to Free Church Worship* (1975); John C. Bowmer, *The Sacrament of the Lord's Supper in Early Methodism* (1951); G. J. Cuming, *A History of Anglican Liturgy* (1969; 2nd. ed., 1982); Horton Davies, *The Worship of the English Puritans* (1948) and *Worship and Theology in England,* 5 vols. (1961–1975); Howard G. Hageman, *Pulpit and Table* (1962); Francis B. Hall, ed., *Quaker Worship in North America* (1979).

Robert T. Handy, *A History of the Churches in the United States and Canada* (1976); Marion J. Hatchett, *The Making of the First American Book of Common Prayer, 1776–1789* (1982); Lawrence Hoffman, ed., *Gates of Understanding* (1977); Walter J. Hollenweger, *The Pentecostals: The Charismatic Movement in the Churches* (1972); Ernest B. Koenker, *The Liturgical Renaissance in the Roman Catholic Church* (1954; rev. 1966); Bernard Martin, ed., *Movements and Issues in American Judaism* (1978); Paul B. Marx, *Virgil Michel and the Liturgical Movement* (1957); Kilian McDonnell, *Charismatic Renewal and the Churches* (1976).

Julius Melton, *Presbyterian Worship in America* (1967); Clifford Nelson, *The Lutherans in North America,* rev. ed. (1980); James Hastings Nichols, *Corporate Worship in the Reformed Tradition* (1968); J. Ernest Rattenbury, *The Eucharistic Hymns of John and Charles Wesley* (1948); Luther Reed, *The Lutheran Liturgy,* rev. ed. (1960); Marshall Sklare, *Conservative Judaism: An American Religious Movement* (1955); Von Ogden Vogt, *Art and Religion* (1921).

[*See also* HISTORY OF PREACHING IN AMERICA; MATERIAL CULTURE AND THE VISUAL ARTS; RELIGIOUS ARCHITECTURE AND LANDSCAPE; *and* RELIGIOUS MUSIC AND HYMNODY.]

RELIGIOUS MUSIC AND HYMNODY

Paul Westermeyer

FOUR themes with symbolic mid-century points of reference serve to summarize the development of American religious music and hymnody. In 1640 the Puritans published the *Bay Psalm Book*, which signaled the importance of psalmody for America's early settlers. A century later the question was whether hymns could be sung, for by then the hymns of Isaac Watts were being printed in Boston, Philadelphia, and New York. By 1840, though Watts was dominant, revivalism was generating a simpler hymnody with lively choruses and more immediate popular appeal; Joshua Leavitt's *The Christian Lyre* of 1831 fit this mold. Yet another century later *The Hymnal 1940* of the Episcopal church epitomized what at least eight other denominations were doing—publishing hymnals in their own traditions, but with a cross section of ecumenical materials from the breadth of Judeo-Christian history.

Psalmody, hymnody, revivalism, and ecumenicity serve, then, as leading themes in the story of America's hymnic and religious musical history. We will examine those themes presently along with other complementary motifs, but first some early Catholic initiatives must be noted.

When Christopher Columbus and his fellow explorers came to America, they brought with them their Spanish Roman Catholic culture and its music. A choir of sorts sang a mass in San Domingo in 1494. A Dominican cathedral with a singer and organist was approved in 1512. In 1524 the Franciscan Father Pedro de Gante organized a school at Texcoco to train native musicians. Many similar training schools sprang up in the next two centuries. During the sixteenth century the cathedral in Mexico City boasted polyphonic choral music by Palestrina, Lassus, Victoria, and other Renaissance composers, and

Gregorian chant, performed by Europeans and Indians. In 1539 a printing press was established in Mexico City, and in 1556 it printed the *Ordinary of the Mass,* the first printed American book with music.

Within what was to become the continental United States, Father Cristóbal de Quiñones installed an organ and taught the San Felipe Indians the music of the liturgy at the San Felipe Mission in New Mexico between 1598 and 1604. The Indians also developed vernacular folk hymns called *alabados* along with medleys of Gregorian chant, Spanish, and Indian melodies. These, as well as some four-part masses, became part of the culture.

Roman Catholicism and its musical heritage left some mark in southwestern portions of the United States, but the mainstream can be traced to the Reformed movement within the Protestant Reformation in Europe.

PSALMODY

The sixteenth-century Reformation brought with it an outpouring of congregational song that took two basic forms, one Lutheran and one Reformed. Martin Luther and his followers composed new hymns, called chorales. They welcomed instruments, contrapuntal settings of chorales for choirs, and the whole Catholic heritage of chant and polyphony. All this they worked into a slightly modified form of the mass. John Calvin, the father of the Reformed churches, took a quite different position. He and his followers permitted only rhymed versions of the psalms to be sung in unison without instruments or contrapuntal settings or choral music separate from the congregation's singing. The

Reformed churches therefore produced many metrical psalters. Since Calvin threw out much of the liturgical inheritance of the West, unison unaccompanied psalm singing virtually became the "liturgy" of Reformed congregations. (Harmonized or polyphonic psalm settings were for use at home, not at church services.)

Psalm singing graced America's shores almost as early as Catholic chant and polyphony. The Huguenots who came to South Carolina and Florida between 1562 and 1565 brought French metrical psalms and tunes with them. The Indians learned snatches of these and continued to sing them after Spain had laid waste the Huguenots. The Indians were also attracted to the psalm singing of Sir Francis Drake and his men, who brought English psalms to the coast of California in 1579. Early in the seventeenth century the Jamestown settlers also carried English psalms and tunes with them.

Neither the Huguenots nor Drake nor the folk in Jamestown made a lasting impression on American church music. Two other groups of Calvinists did. We call them Pilgrims and Puritans.

The Pilgrims who landed at Plymouth, Massachusetts, in 1620 were English Separatists; that is, they wanted to "separate" from the Church of England to get on with the Reformation. They regarded the Bible, not prayer books, as a sufficient guide for worship, and they viewed religious experience as direct and immediate—not "mediated" through previously written words in a prayer book that they called "set forms."

This view of worship led some Separatist groups to reject any congregational singing "with conjoint voices" because it fit the category of "set forms" and therefore "quenched the Spirit." The Pilgrims did not share this radical opinion. They followed the more moderate Calvinist course and sang psalms. But they wanted their psalms in as literal a translation as possible, with every nuance of the Hebrew original carried over into English.

The first complete English metrical psalter, published in England in 1562 as *The Whole Book of Psalmes* and known as "Sternhold and Hopkins" for its chief authors, did not preserve the original meaning of the psalms closely enough for the Separatists. After they fled England, therefore, and were exiled in Holland, Henry Ainsworth—one of their teachers and biblical scholars—prepared a more literal metrical psalter. It was published in Amsterdam in 1612 and brought on the *Mayflower* to Massachusetts. Ainsworth's literal concern and his awkward rhymes militated against beauty of language. Yet the psalter was used in Plymouth and later in Salem. Henry Wadsworth Longfellow tells us as much in *The Courtship of Miles Standish,* when he refers to the "psalmbook of Ainsworth" on Priscilla's lap as "well-worn."

While the Pilgrims endured the hardships of the New World by "showting" their psalms "to Jehovah with singing-merth," as they sang Psalm 100, another group decided they too would have to leave England. We refer to them today as Puritans. Since they wanted to reform the Church of England from within they are called "non-Separatists."

When reform of the church from within became a dim prospect after 1625, many non-Separatists established an outpost at Salem, Massachusetts. Between 1630 and 1640 more than 20,000 of them formed the Massachusetts Bay Colony. They brought with them "Sternhold and Hopkins," for in good Calvinist fashion they too sang metrical psalms. Since these were not literal enough for them either, in 1636, the same year the Puritans founded Harvard College, they appointed thirty ministers to translate and versify the psalms. Four years later Stephen Day completed the printing of the finished psalter on a hand press in Cambridge. Titled *The Whole Book of Psalmes,* it is usually known as the "Bay Psalm Book." It was the first book printed in North America for the English-speaking colonies.

The new psalter found an eager audience, but like Ainsworth's *Psalter* it was not a literary masterpiece. The preface made that clear: "If therefore the verses are not always so smooth and elegant as some may desire or expect; let them consider that Gods [*sic*] Altar needs not our polishings." The people still required singable psalms, however. To employ "a little more of Art," Henry Dunster, president of Harvard College, revised and refined the translations. His edition of 1651 became the commonly used form of the "Bay Psalm Book."

The Puritans could have used the Pilgrims' *Psalter* by Ainsworth. It was literal enough and was adopted at Salem very early. Curiously, however, the more aristocratic Puritans found Ainsworth's choice of tunes and meters too varied and difficult. The Pilgrims themselves lost their expertise in music within a generation or two, so they abandoned their own Ainsworth psalter for the "Bay Psalm Book."

Ainsworth had fifteen meters and thirty-nine tunes, including OLD 124TH, OLD 100TH, and WINDSOR, that are still in use today. The "Bay Psalm Book" reduced the number of meters to six, favoring Common Meter; in the 1698 edition, when tunes were first included, only thirteen were given, among them OLD 100TH and WINDSOR. Sources for additional melodies were available and probably were used, but the reduction in number and variety from Ainsworth to the "Bay Psalm Book" does represent the trend of the times.

"Lining out" was an expedient adopted in England "for the present" by the Westminster Assembly of 1644 to make possible the singing of psalms even if people could not read or did not have books. It refers to a practice in which one person—minister, clerk, precentor, elder, or deacon—sang or read a psalm line by line, followed in each case by the people singing the same line, usually in an elaborated version. Though lining out began as a practical expedient, it became widespread in England, Scotland, and New England. When German immigrants came to America, some of them even adopted the custom. Its use can be traced in Pennsylvania well into the nineteenth century, and some rural southern congregations still follow the practice today.

Lining out interrupted both the textual and musical flow of a psalm, thereby fragmenting it. Simultaneously it generated a new call-response pattern that did not rely on the printed page, but lived in the ear of the people as a folk idiom. It gathered a life of its own.

The Pilgrims and Puritans did not line out their psalms. They enjoyed their psalm singing whole, at a vigorous, perhaps peppy pace. The stern and negative press Puritans receive today is not totally justified if psalm singing is any indication of their common life. John Cotton, in his *Singing of Psalmes a Gospel Ordinance,* tells us that detractors called metrical psalms "Genevah jigs" and "scoffed at Puritan-ministers, as calling the people to sing one of *Hopkins jigs,* and so hop into the pulpit."

But the vigor declined. The second and third generations did not share the spiritual zeal of the early settlers. Some did not "own the covenant" when they reached maturity, and a compromised "Halfway Covenant" was worked out. Simultaneously people forgot some tunes, the number of tunes in common use diminished, and the pace of singing slowed. Pioneer hardships did not encourage time or energy for the cultivation of music. Where people did not know the psalms from memory and where no books were available, lining out was adopted. The traditional shape of a psalm was thereby broken. To fill the vacuum congregations began to supply their own interest. The slow tempo allowed them to improvise turns and flourishes. To keep afloat in this drifting sea, people had to sing loudly. Presently a grand and glorious cacophony resulted, with everyone belting out unique versions of the melody and no two people singing the same thing at the same time. The singing grew so slow that people paused twice in one note to take a breath.

Not everyone took kindly to this state of affairs. Several ministers, generally the most progressive and educated group in the society, began to fight it. Thomas Walter said it sounded like "five hundred tunes roared out at the same time." He called it "an horrid medley of confused and disorderly sounds" and "something hideous and beyond expression bad." He argued for a return to singing "according to the rules of music" and in 1721 authored *The Grounds and Rules of Music Explained.* Several years earlier John Tufts wrote *A Very Plain and Easy Introduction to the Singing of Psalm Tunes.* Thomas Symmes entered the fray in 1720 with *The Reasonableness of Regular Singing, or Singing by Note.*

The ministers who argued for "regular singing" correctly perceived that it was the practice of the early New England settlers, but that did not matter to the people. After a couple of generations "singing by rote" had become a folk tradition and was perceived by the people as the old way. The ministers were therefore regarded as the innovators. They were not always charitable, as is often the case with reformers, and the people were not of a mind to be convinced. The result was a standoff. The decline and fall of lining out and singing by rote came to be controlled more by sociology than by debate. Urban churches were first to adopt and then dispense with lining out. The progressive Brattle Street Church in Boston had abandoned it already in

1699. At about the same time more rural churches were first adopting it. It rose in popularity until the middle of the eighteenth century and died out in New England by 1800. It then moved south and west with the frontier. That is how it migrated to places like Blackey, Kentucky, where Old Regular Baptists still practice it today.

The "regular singing" reformers did have a long-term influence. Their concerns generated singing schools that became established institutions after the mid-eighteenth century and important cultural forces in New England, Pennsylvania, and other areas well into the nineteenth century.

Singing schools were often organized by ministers or laypersons of a church. They found patrons to underwrite costs, hired a teacher, and secured a meeting place that could be a room in the church or the church basement or a private house or even the village tavern. The teacher instructed the students in the rudiments of musical notation and singing so they could sing the psalms. Students usually paid a fee and were expected to bring a candle, an instruction book, and a board to hold those items. Singing schools sometimes were sponsored by churches on a more or less long-term regular basis, but usually they lasted for a specified period of fewer than twenty-four evenings.

Singing schools exerted a considerable influence on America's musical and cultural life. First, they generated hundreds of instruction books, or "tunebooks," that by the end of the eighteenth century were printed in their characteristic oblong shape. These books almost invariably contained an introduction to the rudiments of music followed by an anthology of musical examples. The anthology came to include not only metrical psalms; hymns, fuguing tunes, and anthems were also included as the repertoire expanded beyond psalmody.

Second, singing schools and their tunebooks stimulated Americans to move well beyond psalms to newly composed hymn tunes and somewhat more complex choral music. The tune CORONATION, for instance, still used for "All Hail the Power of Jesus' Name," was composed by Oliver Holden and first appeared in 1793 in his tunebook *Union Harmony.*

Third, singing schools stimulated the development of choirs. Singing-school classes often became the church choir or the church choir nu-

cleus in the sponsoring parish. That set the stage for the development, especially in urban centers, of larger choral societies. These were less closely affiliated with one parish and tended toward the performance of high art music from Europe. The Handel and Haydn Society of Boston, founded in 1815, is an example. The singing schools did not only stimulate high art, however. As they followed the frontier to the Midwest and South, they provided for a type of communal song that Gilbert Chase calls "home-spun hymnody," to be discussed below.

Fourth, singing schools often used a pitch pipe and bass viol. Church choirs composed of the singing school class naturally took these instruments with them into worship services. They often met with opposition because the Reformed practice of psalm singing did not permit instruments. Churches were sometimes divided, therefore; some people left services when instruments were used, and churches with bass viols were dubbed "catgut churches." But by the end of the eighteenth century and well into the nineteenth the bass viol came to be the usual accompaniment for singing in many places. Some churches and towns even bought their own pitch pipe and bass viol. This new practice obviously modified the Calvinist stricture against instruments in worship and paved the way for the introduction of organs.

Fifth, by the middle of the nineteenth century singing schools had produced itinerant teachers, or "singing school masters." They went from community to community organizing students into schools. The going rate was about fifty cents a lesson for some thirteen lessons.

Finally, though singing schools started for instructional reasons—to learn psalms—recreational interests were never absent. The schools were partly social gatherings, a place to see friends, a place for courtship, and a place to sing together. The recreational aspects gradually became more important than the instructional ones; toward the end of the nineteenth century "singing schools" in Pennsylvania functioned primarily as social occasions or even parties.

HYMNODY

Singing schools have led us ahead of the story, so we must now back up to trace the transition to hymnody. In the eighteenth century Isaac Watts proposed to renovate psalmody toward hymnody. Watts was an English Independent (or Congregational) minister who argued for evangelical, freely composed hymns that would express the thoughts of the singers. Yet he did not want to forget psalmody. He wanted instead to "Christianize" and contemporize the psalms; that is, paraphrase them more freely, but also add to them newly composed hymns. He carried out his proposals most notably in his *Hymns and Spiritual Songs* (1707) and *Psalms of David Imitated in the Language of the New Testament* (1719). "Our God, Our Help in Ages Past," "Joy to the World," "Jesus Shall Reign Where'er the Sun," "Before Jehovah's Aweful Throne," and "When I Survey the Wondrous Cross" are among his hymns.

Watts was a prolific writer and theologian. His *Logic* was used at Harvard, and he carried on a large correspondence with New England leaders, including Cotton Mather. His psalms and hymns were known and welcomed in New England as devotional literature, but at first nobody thought of introducing them into worship services, where the received metrical psalmody remained unquestioned.

Watts also became known outside New England. In 1729 Benjamin Franklin reprinted his *Psalms* in Philadelphia. It did not sell for several years, and Franklin did not reprint until 1741. Between 1739 and 1752 the work was also printed in Boston and New York.

In 1735 John and Charles Wesley came to Georgia as missionaries of the Church of England. This was the well-known voyage during which they encountered Moravians on board ship and were introduced to their hymn singing. The Wesleys brought with them Watts's psalms and hymns. They did not remain long in Georgia, but while he was there John compiled a hymnbook himself. Published in Charleston, South Carolina, in 1737, it was called *A Collection of Psalms and Hymns.* This was the first hymnbook, as distinct from a psalmbook or psalter, to be printed in America. Half of its contents came from Watts, the rest from various writers including five translations from the German by John Wesley. Charles Wesley, who was to become the prolific hymn writer of the Methodist movement, was not represented at all.

Charles Wesley would eventually write over 6,500 hymns in many different meters, as opposed to Watts, who wrote about 700 hymns and psalms in a few psalm meters. Wesley's hymns combine his Anglican heritage with a joyful and sometimes passionate emphasis on conversion. "O for a Thousand Tongues to Sing," "Come, Thou Long-Expected Jesus," "Christ the Lord Is Risen Today," "Hark the Herald Angels Sing," and "Love Divine, All Loves Excelling" are typical of his work.

The beginning of a repertoire of English hymns was now available to the American churches, but these hymns needed a new zeal to be adopted in worship. The Great Awakening provided that zeal, and even then hymns met resistance. When George Whitefield, the great eighteenth-century English preacher, came to the American colonies in 1739 and bound together the incipient spiritual awakening into a movement, he brought with him John and Charles Wesley's *Hymns and Sacred Poems* of 1739. It was reprinted in Philadelphia in 1740. Soon Whitefield began to protest Wesley's Arminian position, so he abandoned use of Wesley's hymns. Though Whitefield was not in complete agreement with Watts either, he nevertheless admired Watts's psalms and hymns. In churches where Whitefield was admitted, he and other preachers usually stimulated an evangelical fervor that required a hymnic response. Watts's hymns met the demand and opened the way to those of Wesley and others. The theological disputes between George Whitefield and John Wesley ultimately lost their force as far as use of hymns was concerned.

At First Church, Northampton, Massachusetts, Pastor Solomon Stoddard had favored regular singing. Stoddard's grandson Jonathan Edwards joined him as assistant and became the pastor at Stoddard's death. Edwards championed both revivals and hearty congregational singing. From about 1734 his preaching stimulated the Great Awakening in New England. Upon his return to Northampton after a trip in 1742, he found that his congregation had substituted Watts for metrical psalmody. Edwards approved the presence of Watts, but not the absence of psalms. A compromise was arranged so that both Watts and metrical psalms were used.

Not all Congregational churches and leaders approved of Whitefield, revivals, or the use of Watts. As was to become characteristic of American church history, revivals generated heated conflicts. The pastor at First Church in Boston, Charles Chauncy, for instance, vigorously opposed what he regarded as the excesses of the Great Awakening. Among these he attacked "singing through the streets and in Ferry-Boats," a phenomenon in which Watts's hymns were sung by groups of people as a kind of recreation outside the churches.

Little by little, as at Northampton, New England's Congregational churches tentatively took steps to adopt Watts. In what was to become an American pattern, congregations compared Watts and Tate and Brady's "New Version" of 1696 with the "Bay Psalm Book," made trials, voted, referred the matter to committees, worked out compromises, and gradually introduced Watts in some way or other. It was not until after the Revolution, however, that New England Congregationalism generally used Watts's psalms and hymns. Then, because Watts's "contemporizing" of the psalms had made the psalmist speak like an eighteenth-century English patriot ("Judah and Israel may be called England and Scotland," said Watts), his work had to be altered for American use. This gave rise to numerous publications that were conveniently called by their editor's name, like "Barlow's Watts" and "Dwight's Watts."

The Presbyterians, who engaged in the fiercest dispute over the introduction of hymns, were first organized from scattered Puritan congregations in New England. Scotch-Irish immigration augmented the denomination and changed the ethnic balance by the early eighteenth century. Disputes over organization and doctrinal standards were exacerbated by the Great Awakening. In 1741 the more experientially oriented revivalist "New Side" party and the more orthodox "Old Side" party split into separate groups. The "Old Side," mostly Scotch-Irish, clung to the *Psalmes of David in English Meeter,* originally prepared by Francis Rous in 1643, or used William Barton's psalter from 1644. The "Old Side" resisted Tate and Brady's 1696 "New Version" of the psalms and Watts, while the "New Side" argued for their use. Gradually, after the Revolution and on into the nineteenth century, Presbyterians did adopt Watts and other hymns, but in the meantime fierce controversy arose and involved considerable dissension and schism. The most intense partisan was probably the Kentucky pastor Adam Rankin, who vigorously opposed hymns and led some congregations into the Rankinite Schism.

Baptists, who originally objected to congregational song because it required "set forms" and forced believers and unbelievers to sing together, through the efforts of Benjamin Keach in England and his son Elias in the United States gradually began to sing both psalms and hymns. The Great Awakening influenced the Baptists as much as or more than other denominations, and just over a decade prior to the Revolution American Baptist hymnals began to be published. These included not only Watts, but the English Congregational minister and hymn writer Philip Doddridge and the English Baptist Anne Steele. A number of English Baptists in this period wrote hymns that found their way to the American colonies. Since the Baptists adapted easily to the American frontier and gained new adherents quickly, their hymnody had a wide influence.

Methodist societies in the United States began to form by 1766. They had available to them the 1740 Philadelphia reprint of John and Charles Wesley's *Hymns and Sacred Poems* and other English hymn publications of the Wesleys. In 1781 Melchior Steiner of Philadelphia collected three of these into a single volume, probably for the use of St. George's Church in Philadelphia, then the largest Methodist church in the United States. In 1784 John Wesley himself prepared two publications for his American followers: an abbreviated revision of the Anglican *Book of Common Prayer* that provided more time for preaching, extemporaneous prayer, and hymnody; and *A Collection of Psalms and Hymns for the Lord's Day* selected from his and Charles Wesley's *A Collection of Psalms and Hymns* of 1741. (Wesley used the same title for similar books in 1737, 1738, and 1741.) John Wesley intended a liturgical worship life for the Americans with high standards of hymnody. The American Methodist bishops, following his lead, required preachers to "sing no hymns of their own composing." Wesley saw the potential for a low quality of hymnody on the excitable American scene, and he aimed to guard against it. His "followers" did not always follow his wishes in this regard.

During the latter half of the eighteenth century native American composers began to appear. They were stimulated partly by the trend toward hymnody, but also by the continuing psalmody and singing schools, the rise of choirs, and the birth of the nation. William Billings, perhaps the most colorful of these composers, epitomizes them.

Billings was a tanner by trade, but music consumed him. Not very tall, with one leg shorter than the other, one eye, and an unkempt mien, Billings made up in energy and personal force what he lacked in appearance. He tirelessly taught, composed, conducted, published, and promoted music—in a fiercely independent way. He had no formal schooling after the age of fourteen, studied music on his own, and argued that "Nature" is the best foundation for the musical art. He published six collections, the best known of which is probably *The Singing Master's Assistant* (1778). His music was rough and rugged, characterized, as Harriet Beecher Stowe said in *Poganuc People* (1878), by "a grand, wild freedom, an energy of motion."

Billings is perhaps best known for his fuguing tunes, though he was not their inventor nor their only composer. Fuguing tunes can be described as psalm and hymn tunes, a bit too elaborate for congregations and characteristic of the last half of the eighteenth century. Irving Lowens, who surveyed this phenomenon, found that they are in three or four parts, begin with homophony (chordal texture), then break into strict or free polyphonic imitation (each voice is independent), and finally return to a homophonic conclusion.

Billings and his contemporaries did not restrict themselves to psalm and fuguing tunes. They composed numerous anthems in which solos alternated with chorus. For their texts they chose biblical passages as well as the poetry and hymnody of Watts and others.

Some of the New England composers who fit Billings' rustic and independent mold included the tavern keepers Supply Belcher and Jeremiah Ingalls and the comb manufacturer and bank stockholder Daniel Read. There were other composers who considered this music crude and looked with disdain on the jiglike frivolity of the refrain to William Billings' "A Virgin Unspotted" or the less than dignified hymns they heard in the churches. Much like the "regular singing" reformers of the early eighteenth century these men sought to improve musical standards and practices. They included Andrew Law, minister and grandson of a Connecticut governor who

provided tunes for the Philadelphia version of Watts's hymns in 1781 and who in 1803 produced a method of shape notes to teach music more easily; Oliver Holden, a carpenter, real estate operator, and composer of the tune CORONATION; and Samuel Holyoke and Oliver Shaw, who were interested both in high church music standards and in instrumental music. Shaw is another of history's numerous blind organists. All of these men led to Lowell Mason, a dominant force in nineteenth-century church music and hymnody whom we will discuss below.

Since Puritan psalm singing permitted no instruments in worship, seventeenth-century New England churches had no organs. Instrumental music was perfectly acceptable at home, however, and at least by 1711 the wealthy Bostonian Thomas Brattle had imported an organ for his house. When he died in 1713 he left the organ to his Brattle Street Church. Though the church was progressive, even that congregation could not make a move so bold as to accept an organ. They rejected the gift. Brattle, anticipating their action, had provided in his will that if his church refused the organ, it was to go to the Episcopal King's Chapel. Since the Episcopalians did not share the Puritans' scruples against instrumental music in church, they accepted the organ.

Brattle's instrument, the first permanent organ installation in a New England church, was not the first organ used in a North American church. The Wissahickon Pietists and Swedish Lutherans (both discussed more fully below) probably hold that distinction. Lacking pastors, the Swedish Lutherans in America received permission to ordain Justus Falckner, a native of Saxony who had studied for the ministry at Halle. The ordination took place in 1703 at the Swedish Gloria Dei Lutheran Church in Philadelphia. "Jonas the organist" and the Wissahickon Mystics (or Pietists) supplied the music, according to Julius F. Sachse, a writer on the history of the German sects in Pennsylvania. Sachse's account is not without its problems, and where the small organ came from is not clear. This is the first reference to organ music in the colonies, however, and the organ's presence is at least probable.

Several organ builders were active during the eighteenth century, the most famous and able of whom was David Tannenberg. Tannenberg was a Moravian who came to the United States in

1749 and built organs largely for Moravian, Lutheran, and German Reformed churches in Pennsylvania and neighboring states.

The first Puritan New England church to have an organ was First Congregational in Providence, Rhode Island, which, after much debate, acquired the instrument in 1770. By 1800 there were about twenty organs in New England, but most were in Episcopal churches. Puritan scruples against instrumental music and organs continued well into the nineteenth century.

The most typical nineteenth-century organ in American churches was a reed or pump organ. These were first manufactured as harmoniums or melodeons in Bavaria and France after 1800 and in the United States by 1820. American ingenuity reversed the flow of air and developed reeds. Around 1860 the instrument was renamed the "cabinet organ." Emmons Hamlin and Henry Mason, brother of Lowell Mason, founded Mason and Hamlin in 1855 to manufacture these organs. The Estey Organ Company in Brattleboro, Vermont, also produced reed organs, which became common in many American homes and churches. They could be found in rural churches as late as the 1940s.

Developments in traditional organ building during the first half of the nineteenth century paved the way for organs in which pneumatic levers and electric currents replaced mechanical action. Toward the end of the century and during the first part of the twentieth century these developments gave builders the means to imitate the sounds of an orchestra and to create romantic effects. Organs became less and less like classic organs until in 1906 Albert Schweitzer and later others called the instrument back to some integrity and roots. The classic organ movement was felt in the United States and Canada from the 1930s onward, as many companies voiced their instruments more boldly and even returned to building mechanical, or tracker, action organs.

Simultaneously with the classic organ movement, electronic organs were also being developed. Very popular in many churches, they point to the diversity that is so characteristic of the twentieth century.

Again, we have gotten ahead of the story with the excursus on organs. The Wissahickon Pietists and Swedish Lutherans just mentioned call us back to the earlier period and remind us that groups other than English Pilgrims and Puritans, each with their own musical practices, also came to North America. They did not dominate the landscape, but they began to add to it the rich variety that became so characteristic.

Swedish Lutherans settled along the Delaware in 1638. They maintained the sung liturgy of the Church of Sweden, including matins and High Mass on Sunday and sometimes matins and vespers daily. Within two centuries, however, this community had disappeared as one by one the Swedish Lutheran churches joined the Episcopalians.

Some of the followers of Menno Simons, a group of Anabaptist pacifists that sprang from the sixteenth-century Reformation in its more radical form, began to migrate to Pennsylvania and farther west from 1683 onward. In the eighteenth and nineteenth centuries a more radical group with even greater social cohesion, followers of Jakob Amann, also migrated to the United States. Named Mennonites and Amish after their leaders, these people employed a hymnal called the *Ausbund* that dates from the sixteenth century. The hymns are by Anabaptist writers, sometimes composed in prison or under persecution. The music for these texts was drawn from sixteenth-century folk melodies or Lutheran chorale tunes and was sung without accompaniment. Mennonites used the *Ausbund* until the nineteenth century. The Amish still use it today.

A group of pietistic millennialists with esoteric theosophical and mystical tendencies came to America in 1694 and settled near Philadelphia on the Wissahickon Creek. Led by Johann Kelpius, this group came to be called the Wissahickon Pietists. Kelpius was a student of Jacob Boehme and a graduate of Altdorf University. He mastered several languages, loved music, and compiled a musical manuscript called "The Lamenting Voice of the Hidden Love at the Time When She Lay in Misery and Forsaken." It contained ten Baroque melodies from German sources, some with figured bass (a Baroque convention in which numbers given with the bass line implied chords for a keyboard player to "realize"). The Wissahickon Pietists played instruments, sang, attracted considerable attention, and exerted an influence beyond their numbers on the community that surrounded them.

The Wissahickon Pietists and their music died out within a generation: Those who came from

RELIGIOUS MUSIC AND HYMNODY

Europe to replace those who died, in an attempt to keep the membership at the perfect number of forty, found the discipline too harsh and left. After Daniel Falkner, one of the leaders, married, he and others involved themselves in the civic and political life of the surrounding township and found less time for spiritual matters. Kelpius, whose health was frail, died in 1708. In 1736 August Spangenberg, a scout for the Moravians, reported that the survivors of the community were living austere lives as "Separatists." Conrad Beissel and the Ephrata Community represent the spiritual successors to the Wissahickon Pietists.

Beissel, like Kelpius, came from Germany. Converted in the Palatinate, he tended toward pietistic and ascetic views. Apprenticed to a baker who also taught him the violin, he joined with the Church of the Brethren in Germany and in 1720 came to Germantown, Pennsylvania. There he was baptized by the Brethren leader Peter Becker. His ascetic tendencies drove him to withdraw to the wilderness. In 1732 he gathered a group that became the Ephrata Community in Lancaster County, Pennsylvania, where the seventh-day (Saturday) Sabbath, celibacy, separation of the sexes, and sharing of property were observed.

The Ephrata Community sang German chorales and pietistic hymns, but they also composed their own texts and music. Beissel especially, but more than fifty other brothers and sisters as well, wrote numerous hymn texts. They —again, especially Beissel—also wrote hymn tunes and other musical compositions that varied in complexity and length and that employed two to eight parts. Beissel also composed music for whole sections of the Old Testament and two settings of the Song of Songs. His music eschewed dissonances and employed many parallels. It is naive to modern ears, but it imprinted itself on the Ephrata Community. Members transcribed it into beautifully illuminated manuscripts and sang it as an ethereal foretaste of heavenly harmony. Women were the core of the choral group, and rehearsals under Beissel lasted four hours each night. Visitors were usually amazed at the contemplative and spiritual qualities of the singing.

The Ephrata Community lasted longer than the Wissahickon Pietists, but by the end of the eighteenth century only nineteen brothers and sisters were left. The spiritual fervor, the mysticism, and the choir were things of the past. In 1814 only four members remained, and the trustees took over the administration of the property. But the Ephrata Community was a rather remarkable experiment with tremendous inertia. Betty Jean Martin points out that "the 'spirit' of Ephrata died slowly." There was a love feast in 1871 and services in 1872. The congregation itself did not come to an end until 1934. In 1941 the buildings and grounds were deeded to Pennsylvania, and they are now a tourist attraction.

The Moravians, or Unitas Fratrum, another group of Pietists, were much closer to the Protestant mainstream and exerted a considerably greater influence. Tracing their origins to John Huss, but renewed by Count Nickolaus von Zinzendorf on his estates in Saxony, they first journeyed to Georgia in 1735 and founded Bethlehem, Pennsylvania, in 1741.

These folk had an intense interest in music. They boasted a number of able composers and organ builders and carried on a high quality of choral singing and instrumental playing that they carefully integrated into their worship services. They founded a Collegium Musicum as early as 1744. By 1800 it was performing choral and instrumental works of Bach, Haydn, and other contemporary composers. Moravians have exerted a potent influence on American music right up to the present, including, but not limited to, their famous "trombone choirs."

Anglicans (called Episcopalians in the United States) struggled to organize and to keep a regular schedule of worship alive in the face of widely scattered parishes and a severe shortage of clergy in the South. Nonetheless, there were pockets of musical activity. In Virginia psalms were sung, singing schools were inaugurated by 1710, and masters and slaves played instruments. In Bruton Parish Church in Williamsburg, Virginia, where Philip Pelham became organist in 1755, by the last quarter of the eighteenth century singing and playing of four-part hymns and anthems overflowed from church into home as a diversion.

Charleston, South Carolina, took the lead in southern Anglican musical activity. Citizens there imported and cultivated organs, organists, bells, printers, and composers. Charles Theodore Pachelbel, for instance, son of Johann Pachelbel, was organist at St. Philip's from 1737 to

1750. He not only played the organ, but also composed for and played the harpsichord. St. Michael's had a Johann Snetzler organ and a congregation that sang hymn and psalm tunes composed by their organists.

REVIVALISM

In 1800, when Watts's tunes were firmly entrenched along with eighteenth-century English tunes and those of American composers like William Billings, an evangelical revival was brewing. This Second Great Awakening led to a more immediate, emotive hymnody and music.

Revivals began in two centers. One started at Yale under the school's president, Timothy Dwight. Dwight was one of the editors of Watts, and his *Dwight's Watts* (1800) was the most popular hymnal for Congregationalists and Presbyterians during the first quarter of the nineteenth century. Dwight fostered hymn singing and with Lyman Beecher and others sponsored a revival that opposed deism and simultaneously stressed good morality and good government.

On the western frontier a more emotional and less intellectual revivalism developed. The camp meeting in 1801, at Cane Ridge, Kentucky, symbolized this movement. More than 12,000 people came to the gathering, which was jointly sponsored by Methodists and Presbyterians. It lasted several days and involved the converted in sighs, moans, jumping, jerking, trances, and similar physical manifestations. Revivalism with these tendencies quickly spread throughout the Midwest. It obviously did not lend itself to psalm singing or hymn singing of the type a small group of worshipers might do who gathered regularly with known texts or hymnals. Instead it stimulated an immediate emotive response. This took the form of choruses fashioned from Watts or others that throngs of persons could learn and remember easily and quickly. As Henry Wilder Foote points out, many anonymous publications appeared that were barely above the level of doggerel.

Revivalism and evangelistic services became part of the nineteenth-century religious landscape. Sensing the need for a hymnal that would serve this type of worship, the evangelist Asahel Nettleton assembled *Village Hymns for Social Wor-*

ship (1824). The subtitle, "Designed as a Supplement to the Psalms and Hymns of Dr. Watts," shows how firmly Watts had taken hold. Nettleton's hymnal was not formally adopted by any denomination, but was used widely by both Congregationalists and Presbyterians and exercised considerable influence on other groups as well. The hymnal contained 600 hymns. Nettleton, says Foote, "rejected the cheaper type of revival hymn." He included hymns by Charles Wesley, James Montgomery, Anne Steele, some from the evangelical *Olney Hymns* published in England in 1779 by John Newton and William Cowper, and some from American writers. In 1824 Nettleton also published a tunebook called *Zion's Harp* to accompany *Village Hymns.* He avoided the excesses of revivalism, but still moved American hymnody in a more emotive direction.

Charles Grandison Finney's work moved hymnody even further in that direction. Finney forsook his law practice and pursued the evangelist's role with new extremes. He introduced the "anxious bench" in the front of churches, where individual sinners were called and addressed or prayed for by name. His campaigns needed an even more immediate hymnody than Nettleton's *Village Hymns,* and in 1831 the Congregational minister Joshua Leavitt prepared *The Christian Lyre* to meet this need. On a lower literary and musical level than *Village Hymns,* it included many "choruses" and printed the tune opposite the words; twenty-six editions were published by 1846.

Waves of emotional response greeted Finney's campaigns, and even portions of the German Reformed and Lutheran bodies of Pennsylvania were carried along as they adopted English. Their hymnody and hymnals lost their Germanic roots and began an almost wholesale embrace of Watts and materials like those in Nettleton's *Village Hymns* or even Leavitt's *The Christian Lyre.* But this was short-lived.

Finney's revivals brought with them violent disagreements and even schisms. They also stimulated confessional renewals in some denominations from midcentury on, along with a high quality and quantity of hymnological research. John Williamson Nevin and especially Philip Schaff worked on hymnody for the German Reformed, and Frederic M. Bird did the same for the Lutherans. Both denominations split into confessional and revivalistic factions that fought bitterly with each other. The confessional wings sponsored the hymnological research along with some remarkable liturgical study. Especially for the Lutherans, musical matters were included. By the end of the nineteenth century the Lutherans had recovered not only their hymnody, but their liturgy and music as well. Chorale melodies, German and Latin motets, and sometimes even Gregorian chant found their way into print and usage.

Leavitt's *The Christian Lyre* generated another typically American response for better quality. Lowell Mason, a Congregational layman, led this movement. After working in Savannah, Georgia, as a bank clerk and choirmaster-organist, he returned to his native Massachusetts and in 1827 became choirmaster at Lyman Beecher's Hanover Street Congregational Church in Boston. In 1832 he helped organize the Boston Academy of Music to teach children and later the New York Normal School to train teachers. In addition to introducing music into the public schools of Boston (the first official public school music program in the United States), he edited numerous collections of church music and composed many hymn tunes. Today they often seem a bit sentimental or trite and little better than what he opposed, but some of them are still in use, like BETHANY for "Nearer, My God, to Thee," MISSIONARY HYMN for "From Greenland's Icy Mountains," and OLIVET for "My Faith Looks Up to Thee."

Mason was an extremely important musical figure who often joined forces with others. One of these men was Thomas Hastings, with whom he produced *Spiritual Songs for Social Worship* in 1832 to counteract *The Christian Lyre*. Hastings was a New York choirmaster and composer who is today best known for his tune TOPLADY, used often for "Rock of Ages" (by the English Calvinist Augustus Toplady). Another colleague and student of Mason, William B. Bradbury, wrote tunes as bad as anything Mason objected to. He produced the sentimental, stagnant harmony of SWEET HOUR and ground out "light tripping" Sunday-school music in endless profusion. This appeared in books aptly named *Golden Chain, Golden Shower,* and *Golden Censer*. He is important in the development of the gospel hymn, to which we shall return.

Black Song. The "American dilemma" of enslaved blacks created not only a societal cancer for American civilization, but a separate strand of church life as well. Because of laws that restricted slaves' freedom of assembly, by 1790, when the slave trade reached its height, local churches in the South were made up of blacks and whites with the blacks restricted to a separate section for worship. But an invisible black church also took shape long before there were separate black churches, and clandestine "praise houses" in the woods even developed. As Portia K. Maultsby points out, two distinct musical and hymnic traditions evolved. The one tried to imitate the customs of the larger white society; the other was different from its white Protestant surroundings.

Black preachers were often song leaders as well. Their sermons pushed speech to an elated state of chant and improvised melody that called forth responses by the congregation. The style of response derived from West African roots. It included moans, shouts, groans, slides, and spoken interjections, combined with energetic bodily movement, hand clapping, foot stamping, and dancing. The repertoire included African songs as well as white Protestant psalms, hymns, and revival songs—all filtered through the African tradition so that melodies, rhythms, and texts were altered.

Black music in the seventeenth and eighteenth centuries has been described by Wyatt Tee Walker as the moans, chants, and cries for deliverance that he classifies as slave utterances. This oral tradition resulted in "spirituals." So called from the reference to "spiritual songs" in Ephesians 5:19 and Colossians 3:16, spirituals can be defined as religious folk songs that grew out of the American environment and developed between the middle of the eighteenth and the end of the nineteenth centuries. Black spirituals combine African and American elements. They are characterized by simple verses and refrains sung alternately between soloist and people, an African call-response form that related easily to lining out. The form invited extensive improvisation in which slides and turns abounded, no two people sang the same thing while not however singing in parts, pitches were shaded to the flat side of the Western norm, and syncopation shifted accents before or after their anticipated point of arrival. Black spirituals could be exceed-ingly sorrowful, like "Nobody Knows the Trouble I've Seen" or "Sometimes I Feel Like a Motherless Child." They could also be highly jubilant, like "In That Great Gettin' Up Morning" or "Didn't My Lord Deliver Daniel," related perhaps to plantation "ring shouts"—a circular dance accompanied by clapping and chanting.

In the 1870s the Fisk Jubilee Singers of Fisk University in Nashville, Tennessee, sang choral arrangements of black spirituals and successfully toured the United States and Europe with them. The Fisk Singers popularized spirituals and moved them out of their native liturgical environment, introducing them to a wide audience that eventually spanned the globe. Since their tours, both black and white high school, college, and professional choirs have regularly incorporated black spirituals and Europeanized arrangements of them into their programming. Harry Burleigh's arrangement of "Deep River" in 1916 provided a model that Nathaniel Dett, William Dawson, and others have followed, thereby creating a rich choral repertoire.

Prior to the popularization of spirituals, they served the black community not as concert pieces (there were no concert halls on slave plantations), but as communal liturgical vehicles in which entire congregations of slaves could worship in their praise houses. What did the spirituals express? There are those who take them at face value and argue that they expressed the faith and hope that Christians of all races have sung about. Others argue that they were coded protest songs dressed in a form the white culture would interpret as harmless. Both interpretations are probably correct, and they need not exclude one another. Blacks, as the oppressed, understood the central Judeo-Christian motifs of liberation and freedom from bondage far more fully than their white oppressors, who were blinded by their position. Blacks sang those motifs as Jews and Christians have always done. The song, then, was obviously protest and struggle for survival, logically folded into the overriding Christian faith and hope.

Blacks have not only sung spirituals. In the early nineteenth century, as literacy increased, they began to adopt the hymns of Isaac Watts. These are called "Dr. Watts hymns," or meter music, the latter because the text is in a metrical form. These hymns were integrated into the oral tradition by lining out and they were "blackened" so that the rhythmic, melodic, and other performance characteristics of spirituals became evident in them. Meter music developed over the years and reached its peak around 1875 without ever displacing spirituals.

Black congregational song was at first unaccompanied by instruments. Organs were introduced into black Episcopal churches in the 1820s and thereafter, with opposition, into independent black churches. This introduction reflected white acculturation. More native hand clapping, foot stomping, and spoken interjections provided a percussive frame, however, to which tambourine, drums, and other percussion instruments were easily added. Wind instruments, piano, and eventually the Hammond organ were gradually introduced, providing the instrumental resources that black gospel music employed in the twentieth century.

Black gospel music appeared at the end of the nineteenth century at the same time as ragtime, blues, and jazz. It is essentially an intense form of black congregational hymnody that began in the independent Holiness churches as an oral, communal creation. At first white tunes in the Lowell Mason tradition were "blackened" by syncopating the rhythms.

The style was influenced by the highly emotional services of the newly forming Pentecostal churches, typified especially by the prolonged Azusa Street Revival in Los Angeles that ran from 1906 to 1909. It reached a composed state and entered mainstream black churches after 1900, when the Methodist minister Charles A. Tindley began setting hymns. Thomas A. Dorsey, Baptist jazz pianist and accompanist for Mahalia Jackson and Bessie Smith, developed Tindley's beginning by using blues and ragtime melodic and harmonic patterns.

Black gospel became widespread in many black churches by World War II and continued to spread even to black Catholic parishes in the 1970s. Dorsey's very popular "Precious Lord, Take My Hand," composed in 1932, illustrates the importance of gospel music for the black community. Like gospel music generally, it can be sung by individuals, duos, trios, quartets, choirs, or whole congregations. The vocal quality, at least for much of this century, has been forced, rough, even raspy, utilizing high registers and vibrato to be heard over instruments or loud-shouting congregations. The advent of amplified sound has lessened this necessity. It is generally sung in a slow or moderate tempo with ample time for improvisation.

White Spirituals. Black spirituals and their jazz relatives grew out of intense suffering, but paradoxically they are probably America's unique musical gift to civilization and are therefore widely known. They are not, however, the only spirituals America has produced. Hidden away in rural areas, white spirituals have also tenaciously contributed their haunting contours to America's music. George Pullen Jackson did the pacesetting research that introduced this part of America's heritage to many Americans and to the rest of the world.

Singing schools and singing school masters employed a system in which pitches were described by four syllables: fa (or faw), sol, la (or law), and mi. Since the diatonic scale involves more than four pitches, these syllables were repeated as follows: fa, sol, la, fa, sol, la, mi, fa. In 1801 William Smith and William Little published a book called *The Easy Instructor* in which they applied shapes to the syllables. Fa was given a triangle (▷), sol a circle (◗), la a square (◹), and mi a diamond (◇). *The Easy Instructor* was first published in Philadelphia, then in New York, and went through numerous editions in Albany from 1805 to 1831. It became popular throughout the country, and its system of shape-note notation took hold, especially in rural areas and among those who emigrated to the South and West. This system is often called "fasola" solmization. (Solmization means naming pitches by syllables rather than letters.)

Nineteenth-century urban centers tended to be more influenced by European do-re-mi solmization. They were embarrassed by singing schools, self-educated singing school instructors who were also cobblers or carpenters, and "buckwheat" or "dunce" (shape) notes. Lowell Mason, his brother Timothy, and others set out to make a "scientific improvement" on American musical culture by attacking and attempting to rid the country of the fasola system and shape notes. In its place they substituted do-re-mi solmization and European models of propriety. Two cultural modes resulted, one looking over its shoulder to Europe, the other with an indigenous American cast.

The indigenous American material came largely from the British Isles and was filtered through the early New England singing school instructors. It was an oral tradition in which composers and compilers used old tunes, altered old tunes, or composed new tunes in the same idiom. Contemporary copyright issues and concern for who composed what were unimportant. The living tradition took precedence over individual contributors to it. The pentatonic tune NEW BRITAIN, associated with John Newton's text "Amazing Grace," is a good example. Its origin is unknown, and it appears in many fasola books with no composer indicated.

The tunes in this tradition often employed "gapped" features and appeared in the tenor voice. The most natural setting was for three parts, though four were often employed. Traditional Western rules of "correct" harmony were not observed: parallel fifths, octaves, and unisons, for instance, were permitted; dissonances did not have to be prepared or resolved; and voices were allowed to cross. The result was a haunting, rustic, and rugged music without the thick harmonic palette of the nineteenth-century European tradition. It has therefore attracted twentieth-century composers and even congregations that do not have a fasola heritage.

A number of songbooks in the oblong tradition printed white spirituals and fuguing tunes in the nineteenth century. Examples are John Wyeth's *Repository of Sacred Music, Part Second* (1813), Ananias Davisson's *Kentucky Harmony* (1816), William Walker's *Southern Harmony* (1835), and Benjamin F. White's and E. J. King's *Sacred Harp* (1844). *Sacred Harp,* in print yet today, is still used at Sacred Harp "singings" that continue to be held in southern portions of the country.

The shape-note tradition found its home primarily among English-speaking white Baptists and Methodists. But it influenced other groups as well, including German-speaking Lutheran and German Reformed bodies in Pennsylvania. In 1810 *The Easy Instructor*'s title was translated into German in a book by Joseph Doll called *Der leichte Unterricht.* This work and others that followed it combined Smith and Little's shapes with German texts and elements of the German chorale tradition. This strange mixture achieved some popularity among the less revivalistic German groups.

The more revivalistic German groups that dated from the Second Great Awakening, like the United Brethren, the Evangelicals, and the Church of God, did not employ shape notes. They sang chorus-type gospel songs in the Pennsylvania Dutch dialect without the use of books. Don Yoder researched this tradition and labeled it Pennsylvania spirituals. Pennsylvania spirituals make a third set of American spirituals in addition to the white English-speaking and the black ones.

The Shakers produced yet a fourth American "spiritual." The group, of English Quaker origin, was led by Mother Ann Lee, who brought eight followers with her to Watervliet, New York, in 1774. Some increase in membership came during the Revolution, but it was the Second Great Awakening that stimulated groups in Massachusetts, Connecticut, Kentucky, Ohio, and Indiana, as well as in New York. The Shakers flourished throughout much of the nineteenth century, but gradually declined toward the century's end and by the mid-twentieth century they had virtually disappeared. They lived in spotless celibate communities characterized by common property, faith healing, and separation from the world. They viewed Mother Ann Lee as a feminine incarnation and the Second Coming of Christ.

The Shakers, or "shaking Quakers," were so named because they employed group dancing in their worship. It could reach frenzied heights and sometimes included complex configurations and movements. The songs came out of an Anglo-American folk tradition, and, at least until the mid- to late nineteenth century, Shakers eschewed instruments and harmony. While they at times employed shape notes and used music that bore some relation to the music around them, essentially they isolated themselves musically as well as communally. They devised their own arcane notational systems, sometimes sang with vocables in "unknown tongues," and considered many of their compositions "inspired." "Simple Gifts," popularized by Aaron Copland in his suite "Appalachian Spring," is perhaps the best-known Shaker spiritual. Daniel W. Patterson has carefully compiled and discussed several hundred of the Shaker songs out of the more than 8,000 that were produced.

Mormons. The Mormons, or Church of Jesus Christ of Latter-day Saints, founded by Joseph Smith, grew out of nineteenth-century revivalism into an aggressive missionary body in the twentieth century. For music and hymnody Mormons have employed much of the Protestant heritage. The famous Mormon Tabernacle Choir at Salt Lake City, Utah, and their radio programs have popularized good choral music as well as fine organ music. The Mormons' westward trek to Utah stimulated the hymn "Come, Come Ye Saints" by William Clayton. Sung to the tune ALL IS WELL, it symbolizes Mormonism, but has occasionally passed to other denominations in altered form.

Gospel Hymnody. The throngs who came to the camp meetings around 1800 did not come with hymnals in their pockets. The context required something simple and emotional that could be learned quickly. Refrains, often improvised and with much internal repetition, worked well for this purpose and were used either separately or as attachments to hymns people knew or a soloist sang.

Charles Grandison Finney often called for musical help from Thomas Hastings, a colleague of Lowell Mason and author of TOPLADY. William Bradbury, a student of Mason and composer of the tune SWEET HOUR for the text "Sweet Hour of Prayer," took the characteristics of camp meeting songs—catchy tunes with simple rhythms, simple harmonies, and the usual refrain—and introduced them in the 1840s as Sunday-school hymns. When adults began to sing these along with or in place of their children, this style became known as the gospel song or gospel hymn. Gospel hymns have ever since been associated with revivalists and their campaigns.

Dwight Moody, shoe salesman turned evangelist, began his revivalist activities in Chicago and eventually went to England with successful campaigns. The Moody Church and Bible Institute resulted from his labors. Ira D. Sankey joined Moody in 1870 as his song leader and accompanied Moody to England; he accounts for much of Moody's success. Moody and Sankey together made gospel songs popular.

In 1875 Sankey and another gospel hymn writer, Philip P. Bliss, together published *Gospel Hymns.* In the next twenty years Sankey was joined by James McGranahan and George C. Stebbins, who continued to produce gospel hymns until 1895, when *Gospel Hymns Nos. 1 to 6 Complete* was published with 739 entries. Much of this activity centered around Chicago and what became the Moody Bible Institute.

One of the important gospel hymn writers not

directly associated with Chicago was Fanny Crosby, who, blind almost from birth, studied and taught at the New York City School for the Blind. At the age of forty-four, she began writing gospel hymns, and by the time she died in 1915 she had created more than 8,500, including "Jesus, Keep Me Near the Cross" and "Rescue the Perishing." Her texts were set by gospel tune writers and published by Biglow and Main, of New York and Chicago, which became the largest nineteenth-century publisher of gospel hymnody.

Gospel hymnody employed numerous repetitive refrains, exploited triplicate and dotted rhythms, and utilized simple melodies and harmonies. W. Wiley Hitchcock has described it, in his introduction to the 1972 reprint of *Gospel Hymns,* "at its best as a kind of religious pop art almost irresistible in its visceral appeal; at its worst, an embarrassingly trivial sacred counterpart of the sentimental 'songs of hearth and home' of the same era." Donald P. Hustad, a musician who directed music at the Moody Bible Institute from 1950 to 1963 and who served as organist for the Billy Graham Crusades, writes with great understanding of evangelism and gospel hymns. He argues that the "chief pitfall" was to "canonize them as the norm for regular worship."

Throughout the twentieth century gospel hymnody has often been so canonized even by some mainstream churches. It has found its way into denominational hymnals or hymnal supplements. And it has continued to accompany revivalism, its natural habitat. Homer Rodeheaver, as solo singer and trombone player, used it with the evangelist Billy Sunday. Charles Alexander, songleader for R. A. Torrey and J. Wilber Chapman, developed mass choirs who sang gospel music, sitting behind the preacher, and became a regular feature of revivals. Gospel hymns have accompanied Billy Graham's crusades as led by song leader Cliff Barrows or sung by soloist George Beverly Shea.

Other Nineteenth-Century Hymnic Currents. In addition to Lowell Mason and the revivalist gospel coalition of hymnic forces in the nineteenth century, there were other currents as well. One was the confessional impulse, best symbolized by the Oxford movement in England and the Lutheran confessional movement around Wilhelm Loehe in Germany. The Oxford movement stimulated translations of Greek, Latin, and German hymns that were used by Episcopalians and others in the United States. The confessional Lutheran movement brought with it a renewed interest in rhythmic Lutheran chorale tunes and sixteenth-century Lutheran texts. Lutherans who had been in the United States and were already Americanized were responsive to this, but when the Saxon Lutherans emigrated in the nineteenth century to become the Lutheran Church–Missouri Synod, the confessional Lutheran force became stronger. Eventually English translations were produced, and in the twentieth century virtually all Lutherans in the United States have been affected by them and by the rhythmic chorale.

Several other currents formed a cluster: high art, social-ethical concerns, and patriotism. These often came from Unitarian or nondenominational sources. John Greenleaf Whittier, a Quaker poet, did not actually write hymns, but hymns have been derived from his poems. "Dear Lord and Father of Mankind" and "O Brother Man, Fold to Thy Heart Thy Brother" are perhaps among the best-known of his "hymns." "O Brother Man" illustrates not only a poetic approach to hymnody, but a social-ethical concern as well—loving the other, feeding the widow, seeking peace.

Samuel Longfellow, Unitarian poet and brother of Henry Wadsworth Longfellow, wrote a number of hymns still in use today, including "God of the Earth, the Sky, the Sea" and "Holy Spirit, Truth Divine." James Russell Lowell, a poet and essayist who was not a member of any church, but was virtually a Unitarian, in 1845 wrote the antiwar poem "The Present Crisis." From it the hymn "Once to Every Man and Nation" was extracted. It found its way into many hymnbooks and services of worship. Worshipers found themselves applying it to whatever crisis the church or nation faced.

Several patriotic hymns from the nineteenth century have proven rather durable. Samuel F. Smith, a Baptist pastor from New England, wrote "My Country, 'Tis of Thee." Julia Ward Howe, the abolitionist and Unitarian, penned "Mine Eyes Have Seen the Glory of the Coming of the Lord," better known for its tune name, THE BATTLE HYMN OF THE REPUBLIC. Katharine Lee Bates, who had no church affiliation herself, but was the daughter of a Congregational minister, wrote "O Beautiful, for Spacious Skies" after she visited the Rocky Mountains in 1893. Whereas Smith's hymn reflected New England's scenery,

Bates responded to the wide expanses of the West.

Quartets and Choirs. Singing schools had generated choirs, and here and there a southern Episcopal choir of men and boys followed the English tradition. But the nineteenth century also saw the development of quartets, or "quartet choirs," which most often replaced choirs.

Volunteer choirs were often augmented by a quartet of paid professional singers. These singers "led" their respective sections and sang solos. Since they seldom blended with the rest of the choir, the result was not genuinely choral. When churches tired of the struggle to motivate and discipline amateur choristers, they abandoned choirs altogether and hired quartets to fill their vocal needs.

Professional quartets were often composed of singers with operatic interests and little sensitivity to worship. They characteristically performed for the congregation as if it were an audience. By the 1890s churches, especially leading urban Presbyterian ones, were even designed to stimulate this. A narrow choir loft, suitable for four singers, was built in the front of the church high above a central pulpit and chairs for the clergy. A velvet curtain could be drawn to conceal the quartet when they sat, but when they stood they looked directly at the congregation from above the curtain. The organist sat just behind the quartet. Organist and quartet performed for the people, but were not conceived as leaders in worship. Objections were raised from the mid-nineteenth century onward, but the quartet became a staple of many mainstream Protestant churches and did not diminish in popularity until after World War I.

Liturgical Reaction. The contradiction of professional quartets and worship was most apparent in liturgical churches like the Episcopal, but the alternative of boys' choirs wearing vestments was virtually nonexistent in the early nineteenth century. In 1828 William Augustus Mühlenberg, an Episcopal priest who was the great-grandson of the Lutheran patriarch Henry Melchior Mühlenberg, organized a boys' choir on Long Island.

The Oxford and Cambridge movements in England, usually dated from 1833, brought with them a liturgical renewal and sung services. They influenced Episcopalians in America and stimulated the growth of vested choirs of boys and men. Parishes with these choirs increased throughout the nineteenth century and into the twentieth, occasionally with parochial schools for the boys. These choirs did not decline until the period around World War II, when extracurricular activities in the public schools crowded out choral rehearsal time.

The liturgical movement was not limited to the Episcopal church. In the twentieth century virtually all American churches, especially mainstream Protestant ones, adopted choirs whose members wore vestments of some sort. Though worship was not everywhere conducted with the choral services of the Anglican tradition, even the so-called nonliturgical churches began to employ sung responses by their choirs.

Theatrical and operatic music flourished in Europe in the Roman Catholic church during the nineteenth century. When poor German, Italian, or Irish congregations in America could afford it, they hired soloists and quartets to sing what they had heard in Europe. The Jesuit Church of St. Francis Xavier in New York City was one of the few exceptions that had a boys' choir.

John Baptist Singenberger, a Swiss immigrant and conductor, took measures to turn this situation around when he founded the Caecilian Society in 1873 in St. Francis, Wisconsin. He held meetings in Wisconsin and Ohio and began to publish the magazine *Caecilia* in 1874. *Caecilia,* printed in German, influenced German Roman Catholic parishes in Chicago, Cincinnati, Milwaukee, and midwestern states. The Caecilian Society attempted to reintroduce and reform Gregorian chant, to revive polyphony in place of operatic music, and to encourage congregational song. Gregorian chant and polyphony were also nurtured by St. John's Abbey in Collegeville, Minnesota, a Benedictine house founded in the middle of the nineteenth century. Its salutary influence has continued to the present time.

ECUMENICITY

By the twentieth century psalmody, hymnody, and revivalism had left strong marks and ongoing traditions. In addition, more and more groups outside the central Puritan mold gradually began to form a rich ecumenical mosaic. The confessional movements of the nineteenth century and the increase in scholarly "scientific" pursuits generated research and a breadth of historical knowledge and perspective. All this combined to make the twentieth century a time of ecumenicity in hymnody and church music.

Societies began to form. Some of these had relatively narrow interests; examples are the Methodist Church Music Society (founded in 1935), the American Guild of English Handbell Ringers (1954), and the Moravian Music Foundation (1956). But the most influential societies were founded earlier and were broadly ecumenical.

The American Guild of Organists (AGO) began in 1896 "to advance the cause of organ and choral music" and "to improve the proficiency of organists and conductors." It is organized by chapters, each of which usually meets monthly. Regional and national meetings are also held, with an ecumenical array of topics, concerts, recitals, and services. The AGO conducts examinations and offers certificates. It has consistently pressed for high quality and has been a positive force in American church music.

The Hymn Society of America (HSA) was organized in 1922 with a more precise concern for congregational song. Both a scholarly and practical society, it has published hymnological studies and promoted indexing as well as sponsored hymn festivals and new hymn projects. Both the AGO and HSA have journals, *The American Organist* for the AGO and *The Hymn* for the HSA.

Schools represent a second instance of ecumenicity. Shortly after Peter Christian Lutkin became dean of the School of Music at Northwestern University, Evanston, Illinois, in 1896, he established a Department of Church Music that reached beyond the Methodist roots of Northwestern and the geography of the Midwest.

The School of Music at the Union Theological Seminary in New York is one of the strongest illustrations of ecumenicity. Clarence Dickinson, a founder of the AGO, became professor of music at Union in 1912. In 1928 he established the School of Sacred Music, which reflected a wide denominational spread in its practice, scholarship, and student body. It served church musicians from all over the country and utilized the breadth of ecumenical opportunities that New York City provided.

Westminster Choir College was founded by John Finley Williamson in 1926. It grew out of his work at Westminster Presbyterian Church in Dayton, Ohio, and represented his approach to revitalizing choral music. It involved choirs for all age groups and a big, dark choral sound. Westminster was not nearly as eclectic as Union, but it was not limited to its Presbyterian roots. It appealed largely to the "nonliturgical" Protestant mainstream.

Several liturgical counterparts to Westminster emerged with more limited denominational ties. One was Trinity School of Church Music for the Episcopal church. It operated in New York from 1912 to 1918. Another was the Pius X School of Liturgical Music, founded in 1918 at Manhattanville College of the Sacred Heart. It and the Gregorian Institute of America, founded in 1941 with correspondence courses, primarily served Roman Catholics.

A third illustration of ecumenicity can be seen in hymnals. The nineteenth century produced the models. In 1855 John Zundel and Charles Beecher edited *The Plymouth Collection*. Zundel was organist at Plymouth Church in Brooklyn, where Henry Ward Beecher championed congregational singing. *The Plymouth Collection* fit the evangelical climate and is not especially noteworthy for texts apart from Harriet Beecher Stowe's contribution of "Still, Still with Thee." However, this was the first American church hymnal to print text and music together. The tune was printed above the text, one verse interlined with the music. This paved the way for the twentieth-century American practice.

In 1861 *Hymns Ancient and Modern* appeared in England, largely as a result of the Oxford movement. *Hymns Ancient and Modern* brought together a broad ecumenical cross section of hymns from the entire history of the Christian church. This became the model of a modern hymnal.

American denominations became increasingly ecumenical in their hymnals from the late nineteenth century onward. They represented the concerns of their individual traditions, but included a cross section of other hymnic materials as well. *The Hymnal 1940* of the Episcopal church, a classic production that appeared in 1943, is probably the best illustration of this pattern, but a spate of publications by other denominations points to the same conclusion: *The Methodist Hymnal* (1935); *Hymns of the Spirit* for Unitarians and Universalists (1937); *The Mennonite Hymnary* (1940); *St. Gregory Hymnal* for Roman Catholics, *Christian Worship* for the

Northern Baptist Convention, the Evangelical and Reformed *Hymnal* and *The Lutheran Hymnal* for the Lutheran Church–Missouri Synod (all 1941); and the *Mennonite Youth Hymnal* (1942).

Composers and Leaders. Probably the most important of America's native-born and trained composers of religious music in the late nineteenth and early twentieth centuries was Charles Ives. Ives took the musical materials of American Protestantism and wove their themes together with techniques that were to be typical of important twentieth-century composers. David Ewen points out that Ives worked with polyrhythms before Stravinsky, dischords before Bartok, polytonality before Stravinsky and Milhaud, atonality before Schoenberg, quarter tones before Hába, tone clusters before Cowell, and chance music before Boulez. Until 1902 Ives worked as a church organist in New England and New York City; he quit because he realized the worshipers had rights that his stacks of thirds and consecutive dissonances tended to negate. He became an insurance man so he would be free to write his kind of music, a uniquely American civil religious product. With Protestant hymn tunes as a storehouse for melodic quotations and with the freedom of the individual composer never compromised, Ives and his music celebrated both America's "sacred" events, people, places, and festivals and America's "faith" in progress and the ultimacy of a broad consensus.

Other American composers were not so innovative, but still quite important. Horatio Parker, an organist-choirmaster and professor of music at Yale University, wrote the oratorio *Hora Novissima* in 1893 on a text by Bernard of Cluny. T. Tertius Noble, an Englishman, came to St. Thomas' Church in New York, developed a boys' choir, and is known for his free harmonizations of hymn tunes. Healey Willan, another Englishman, came to Toronto in 1913 to St. Paul's Church and the Toronto Conservatory. From 1921 he served the Church of St. Mary Magdalene with a rich use of plainsong, polyphony, and his own organ and choral works. Leo Sowerby was born in Grand Rapids, Michigan, but made his home in Chicago, where he taught at the American Conservatory and served at St. James Episcopal Church from 1927. He stood in the romantic tradition with Parker, Noble, and Willan, but utilized more dissonance and less traditional progressions.

Other musical personalities from the first half of the twentieth century, though they may have composed, left their mark on American church music for other reasons. W. Lynnwood Farnam, born in Sutton, Quebec, worked in Montreal, Boston, and New York as an organist. An unusually gifted recitalist and teacher, Farnam moved the organ to a dignified role in worship and helped it become an important recital instrument. Charles Winfred Douglas, an Episcopal priest and musician, led in the restoration of plainsong and research in musical and liturgical matters. F. Melius Christiansen, a native of Norway, developed the famous St. Olaf Choir in Northfield, Minnesota, with his romantic editions of Lutheran literature.

Each of these strong personalities, along with others like Williamson and Dickinson whom we encountered earlier, influenced and trained numerous men and women. These students came to serve churches and schools across the American continent. They represent an ecumenical array of theory and practice in which many traditions live side by side, often nourished by one another.

Pluralism. Ecumenical begins to describe the twentieth century, but the landscape also broadened into pluralism. Pluralism, of course, was inherent in the American experience from the moment separation of church and state was made constitutional. It was always present to some degree, as William Penn's Pennsylvania testifies. By the mid-twentieth century, however, it had become the dominant reality, replacing the previously pervasive Puritan mentality.

One manifestation of this pluralism in American religious music at mid-twentieth century was the presence of so many different religious bodies, both Christian and non-Christian. Somewhere in America one could probably find almost every ethnic religious music the world knew. Much of this had little impact on the society as a whole, but it formed part of the mosaic.

Eastern-rite groups have made an impact. Less ecumenical than Western Christians in America, they have been numerous enough to form congregations in most urban centers. They have sometimes maintained their rich unaccompanied choral tradition, particularly among Russian Orthodox, where nineteenth-century romantic influence is also present. But, especially in Greek churches, they have also been influenced by Western practices and electronic organs. This loss was offset by the gain of a lapsed Russian Orthodox composer named Igor Stravinsky, who came to the United States at the outbreak of World War II. His return to the Orthodox faith stimulated his *Mass,* which, though written in the tradition of Western masses, is nonetheless a monument of twentieth-century religious music, as is his *Symphony of Psalms.*

Jewish groups have also made substantial contributions to America's religious music. Jews first came from Spain and Portugal, but these groups were small and their Sephardic musical tradition has had little influence. Larger waves of Jewish immigrants came to the United States from Germany, Austria, Poland, and Russia at the end of the nineteenth century; their Ashkenazic tradition has therefore been much stronger.

Not all Jews maintained their Ashkenazic synagogue and cantorial traditions in America. Many were influenced by the Reform movement, which adopted organs, choirs, and even Protestant-style hymns. Professional organists and singers often found themselves playing and singing in Jewish temples on Friday evening and in Christian churches on Sunday morning.

Jews have contributed in other ways to the American musical religious culture. Hebrew Union College in Cincinnati, Ohio, has assembled a fine library that includes Jewish musical materials. The Hebrew Union School of Sacred Music, founded in New York in 1948, both reflected the concern of Jews for their musical traditions and contributed to the American musical scene. Ernest Bloch, a Swiss Jew who came to the United States in 1916, created his *Sacred Service* for the synagogue. It has had an appeal well beyond that.

POST-PURITAN HYMNODY

Sydney Ahlstrom has called the 1960s "post-Puritan." By that he means that Reformed and Puritan impulses no longer functioned as the dominant forces to which everyone had to relate. The 1960s were a turbulent period: the assassinations of President John F. Kennedy and Martin Luther King, Jr., the Vietnam War, and unrest manifested in demonstrations and marches. A dream died, expressed by Don McLean's popular song "American Pie."

Religious music did not go unscathed. Coalitions and financing came apart. The School of Sacred Music at the Union Theological Seminary, long the leader for training church musicians of all denominations, closed its doors in 1973. Even though the school moved to Yale as the Institute of Sacred Music, that closing symbolized a new period. After the Second Vatican Council finished its deliberations in 1965, American Roman Catholics, for example, lived in a new world. Latin masses were replaced by English ones, and there was a scramble to set the new, hastily devised English texts to music. Guitar masses, ground out in great profusion, reflected the haste in their substandard quality and lack of durability. Protestant denominations were influenced by guitars as well. Protest songs, guitar chords, choruses, and melodic lines without substance or durability all entered much of America's worship. Organs were turned off or used less.

Geoffrey Beaumont, an Anglican priest who had written songs for the "Footlights" as an undergraduate at Cambridge University, while he was chaplain at Trinity College, Cambridge, published *Twentieth-Century Folk Mass* in 1956. A musical setting for the Eucharist of the Church of England in a "popular" style, composed simply enough for the people to sing, it became popular in England in the 1960s, as did other sacred music with a "pop," folk, or even "rock" character. This was picked up in the United States very quickly; mainline churches felt its influence the most. At first some voices considered it too secular, but gradually it found acceptance. Congregations quickly discovered, however, that they had to sort out what was for entertainment and what was for participatory congregational use in worship. For instance, *Jesus Christ Superstar,* a modern Passion setting in a popular style, functioned basically as an entertainment.

Hymnody also underwent some changes. King James English was updated so that *thee* became *you, thy* became *your,* and outmoded words and phrases were avoided. Sexist language created ferment. Though the English language uses *man, his,* and similar words in a generic sense, many persons were offended by this usage. Sexism became even more controversial when the use of masculine images or pronouns with reference to God—Father, King, Son, Lord, His—was questioned. These hymnic issues caused consternation not only for hymn writers, but more especially for hymnal editors, who had to decide how much to tamper with past texts.

Twentieth-century hymnody has also been influenced by issues related to social justice, ethics, and peace. New translations of old texts with traditional words of praise and prayer have not been absent, to be sure, but concerns for ethics and justice have become far more dominant than ever before. One can find them early in the century in William P. Merrill's "Not Alone for Mighty Empire," written in 1909, and in Harry Emerson Fosdick's "God of Grace and God of Glory" of 1930. More recently Fred Kaan, a Dutchman who has spent much of his life as a United Reform minister in England, has written hymns with consciously abrasive social action lines. Not universally accepted, Kaan nonetheless is the largest single contributor to *The Hymn Book of the Anglican Church of Canada and the United Church of Canada,* published in 1971. Other writers are less abrasive and more potent. For instance, Martin Franzmann, a Lutheran hymn writer, in "O God, O Lord of Heaven and Earth" highlights ecological consciousness in the context of God's redeeming purposes. Fred Pratt Green, another Englishman whose hymns have become very popular in America, reflects depth and breadth along with a social concern.

The turbulence of the 1960s was short-lived. By the mid- to late 1970s organs were back in full use and guitarists hard to find. A new stability was quickly achieved in which denominations simply expanded their ecumenical horizons to include a multiplicity of styles. Their new hymnals, symbolized by the first-rate *Lutheran Book of Worship* of 1978, embraced their own traditions plus white and black spirituals, materials from other cultures, some hymns with guitar chords, hymns and tunes of twentieth-century Americans, and psalm singing. The revival of psalms usually involved remarkably successful chantlike experiments, not metrical psalmody. Cross-denominational supplements also appeared that represented both the range and the quality of materials. Hope Publishing Company's *Ecumenical Praise* (1977) and Hinshaw Music's *Songs of Thanks and Praise* (1980) are two examples. Choral material of virtually any style one could desire also was available.

Twentieth-century American hymn writers who have found their way into recent publications are numerous. A few should be mentioned: F. Bland Tucker, an Episcopal priest; Richard Wilbur, a leading American poet whose "A Stable Lamp Is Lighted" alone makes him important; Jaroslav Vajda, a Lutheran pastor, translator, and hymn writer, probably best known for "Now the Silence"; and Gracia Grindal, a Lutheran translator, English professor, and thoughtful writer about hymnic and poetic issues. Twentieth-century American tune writers are even more numerous than writers of texts. They include Alec Wyton, who served as organist-choirmaster at St. John the Divine Episcopal Church in New York City; Richard Dirksen, who held a similar post at the Washington Cathedral in Washington, D.C.; Richard Proulx, organist and choirmaster at the Roman Catholic Holy Name Cathedral in Chicago; Carl Schalk, a Lutheran college professor and writer; and Calvin Hampton, whose tunes sometimes exceed congregational limits. A few people have written both texts and tunes, among them Erik Routley, one of the foremost twentieth-century hymnologists.

In 1640 a visitor to New England's settlements would have found psalm singing the essence of religious music. In 1980 a visitor to an urban American center would have been bewildered by a multiplicity of practices. Between those dates the metrical psalmodic underlay, the hymns of Watts and Wesley, the revivalism of the nineteenth century, and the ecumenicity of the twentieth give shape to a story of rich development. The story includes some important individuals, but mostly it involves the gradual addition of tradition after tradition. There have been squabbles, especially within denominations. By and large, however, the various traditions have learned how to live together and how to learn from one another. American religious music and hymnody represent a rich diversity. They allow the common life of individual communities to flourish and they give the scholar an amazing laboratory to study.

BIBLIOGRAPHY

William H. Armstrong, *Organs for America* (1967); Louis F. Benson, *The English Hymn: Its Development and Use in Worship* (1915; repr. 1962); Gilbert Chase, *America's Music* (1955; rev. 1966); James Robert Davidson, *A Dictionary of Protestant*

Church Music (1975); Leonard Ellinwood, *The History of American Church Music* (1953); Henry Wilder Foote, *Three Centuries of American Hymnody* (1940; repr. 1968); Nathaniel Duren Gould, *Church Music in America* (1853); Donald P. Hustad, *Jubilate! Church Music in the Evangelical Tradition* (1981); George Pullen Jackson, *White Spirituals in the Southern Uplands* (1933).

Irving Lowens, *Music and Musicians in Early America* (1964); Hamilton C. MacDougall, *Early New England Psalmody* (1940); W. Thomas Marrocco and Harold Gleason, *Music in America: An Anthology from the Landing of the Pilgrims to the Close of the Civil War, 1620–1865* (1964); Betty Jean Martin, *The Ephrata Cloister and Its Music* (Ph.D. diss., Univ. of Maryland, 1974); Portia K. Maultsby, *Afro-American Religious Music: A Study in Musical Diversity* (n.d.); Frank J. Metcalf, comp., *American Psalmody or Titles of Books Containing Tunes Printed in America from 1721 to 1820* (1968); Orpha Ochse, *The History of the Organ in the United States* (1975); Daniel W. Patterson, *Shaker Spirituals* (1979).

Albert G. Rau and Hans T. David, *A Catalogue of Music by American Moravians, 1742–1842* (1938; repr. 1970); Julius F. Sachse, *The German Pietists of Provincial Pennsylvania* (1895); Sandra Sizer, *Gospel Hymns and Social Religion* (1978); Robert Stevenson, "Protestant Music in America," in Friedrich Blume, ed., *Protestant Church Music* (1974); Wyatt Tee Walker, *"Somebody's Calling My Name": Black Sacred Music and Social Change* (1979); James Warrington, *Short Titles of Books Relating To or Illustrating the History and Practice of Psalmody in the United States, 1620–1820* (1898; repr. 1970); Edward Wolf, *Lutheran Church Music in America During the Eighteenth and Early Nineteenth Centuries* (Ph.D. diss., Univ. of Illinois, 1960); Don Yoder, *Pennsylvania Spirituals* (1961).

[*See also* HISTORY OF PREACHING IN AMERICA; *and* LITURGY AND WORSHIP.]

THE HISTORY OF PREACHING
IN AMERICA

William B. Lawrence

IN April 1630, after a farewell sermon by the Rev. John Cotton, four ships left England for America. Aboard were English Puritans who had covenanted together under divine providence to found a community free from the secularizing pressures of England. In their Massachusetts Bay Colony, founded in 1629, they planned to organize a civil and religious order in accordance with God's law. They hoped ultimately to transplant this model Christian society back to England for its reformation.

Aboard the lead ship *Arbella* was John Winthrop, the governor of the colonists. During the Atlantic crossing, Winthrop delivered to his fellow travelers a declaration about the mission they were undertaking. His "Model of Christian Charity" exalted the role of divine providence in their enterprise. He pointed out that God had decreed the terms of the human condition: some persons are rich and others poor; "some high and eminent in power and dignity" and others destined to live "in subjection." The English Puritans were dismayed by their lack of success in reforming England according to their doctrines. A new colony offered a fresh start, an opportunity to build their social order on a foundation of true faith. Then, having built their "city on a hill," they planned to export it back to England, with proof that a community in covenant with God would be the proper earthly home for the saints. But should they fail, Winthrop argued, the wrath of God would descend upon them.

Winthrop's sermon was a typically Puritan exhortation, rich in biblical allusion and rigid in its conception of the orders of creation that God had decreed. It was, in short, a sermon proclaiming the Lord's word about the Puritans' mission (or "errand" on God's behalf) into the wilderness.

> The end is to improve our lives to do more service to the Lord . . . that our selves and posterity may be the better preserved from the common corruptions of this evil world; to serve the Lord and work out our salvation under the power and purity of his holy ordinances.
> (Smith, Handy, and Loetscher, 1960–1963, vol. 1, p. 100)

Massachusetts Bay Colony became New England's largest and most influential settlement. The Great Migration that followed in the 1630s, bringing upwards of 20,000 settlers by 1643, included many others who were ready to join the covenant, among them John Cotton, who had bidden the *Arbella* farewell with his homily.

Given the crucial place of preaching in this migration, it might be said that American history began not with a political Declaration of Independence but with a homiletical declaration of dependence on divine sovereignty. In other words, perhaps American history began not with a manifesto but with a sermon. Indeed, the line between preaching and other forms of oratory, such as political rhetoric, has not always been clear in America. Winthrop's image of a "city upon a hill," for instance, has endured long enough to become the theme of a keynote address at the Democratic party convention in 1984. From the beginning, then, preaching has been enmeshed with great civil and social events in America. The sermon has always been part of the nation's cultural drama, from the *Arbella* to the 1963 March on Washington and the address of Martin Luther King, Jr. American preachers have prophesied, and the nation has been formed and reformed as a result.

From Cotton Mather, who was ordained in the 1680s; to Francis Asbury, whose power emerged in the 1780s; to Henry Ward Beecher, the celebrity preacher of the 1880s; to Jimmy Swaggart, whose electronic evangelism spans the nation in the 1980s, the sermon has functioned as a critical American cultural phenomenon. In Mather's New England there was never an election without an election day sermon. In Asbury's time preaching played an important role in the opening of the frontier. Beecher's sermons were literary and journalistic events, with the full text of his homily appearing in Brooklyn newspapers every week. Swaggart's sermons, with his own entertaining music and tearful appeal for funds, could reach nearly every home in America on any Sunday.

But preaching in America is not merely a tangent to secular or civil history. Preaching itself has a history. It includes both the intellectual endeavors of Jonathan Edwards, whose sermons enumerated the score of principles in the Scriptures about the love of God, and the antics of Billy Sunday, who quit playing professional baseball to become a preacher, and might slide into the pulpit as if it were home plate or carry a baseball bat as he preached. It includes seminary classmates who went on to preach on opposite sides of the slavery question. It includes the demand by some synagogue trustees that their rabbi's sermon manuscripts be screened for doctrinal errors before delivery. And it includes Peter Cartwright's declaration that preachers who drafted careful, thoughtful sermons were a hindrance rather than a help in the work of God: "the illiterate Methodist preachers were setting the world on fire," he said, while the educated ones "were lighting their matches" (Ahlstrom, 1972, p. 438).

The history of preaching in America also involves the emergence of a new office for some religious groups. After the Civil War, many limitations still prevented blacks from receiving professional education. The church often stood as the only institution in which blacks could freely exercise social leadership—if not within the predominantly white congregations where they worshiped, then within black congregations that they could establish. The ministry offered them a professional opportunity without prejudice against meager academic credentials. The black preacher thus became the leading political and cultural figure in the community. "The Preacher," said W. E. B. Du Bois, "is the most unique personality developed by the Negro on American soil" (Ahlstrom, 1972, p. 711).

Among Jews who came to America from European cultures, there was no role for a preacher in the Protestant sense. Sermons had been delivered since ancient times, and a legacy dating back to Moses and the prophets recognized a role for one who could declare the word of the Lord. But the rabbi was seen principally as a teacher and judge of the Torah and its applications. The sermon was associated with folktales and casuistry and was irregularly performed, often by the laity, either local residents or itinerants. But in America, Protestant preaching affected even this tradition and gave to the synagogue the new office of "preaching minister," conferred by some congregations. In others, the office was held by one who retained the title "rabbi."

In short, while preaching in America has a history, the history is a complicated one. The first American sermon may have been the work of a New England Puritan, but preaching did not remain an exclusively Puritan device for long. Nor did it remain aloof from the social, cultural, political, and economic forces that were changing the shape of America. The sermon became less a sectarian preserve and more a secular presence as the American experience grew.

Christians in general and Protestants in particular tend to think of preaching as peculiar to their religious traditions. The roots of that prejudice probably lie in the Protestant Reformation. John Calvin, the founding theologian of the Puritan tradition, developed a theology of preaching that claimed the Holy Spirit worked through a preacher to restore the word of God to its original form as oral proclamation. Preaching, then, was quite literally defined as presenting the person and work of Jesus Christ to a body of believers.

Linked to this conviction was the Protestant principle which stressed that all adherents to the faith had direct access to God, without the need for a priest as intermediary. This was called the "priesthood of all believers." Historian DeWitte Holland says this made preaching "a spiritual exercise attributing choice and dignity to its hearers." People were encouraged to read the Bible for themselves, to judge whether a given preacher did in fact have God's spirit at work during a sermon. A dimension of personal freedom thus was integral to Protestant doctrine. And as preaching exalted individual choice and personal freedom, it complemented the developing political theories that led to declarations of inalienable human rights.

So, beyond sectarian doctrine, preachers who were attributing dignity and freedom to listeners were offering an apt vehicle for use by non-Protestants and non-Christians in their search for freedom. Whether it was freedom from an English king, or freedom from economic bondage, or freedom from racial bigotry, the sermon since Winthrop and the *Arbella* has inspired new appreciation for liberation as central to the American experience. To many living in America, life here was the equivalent of liberation. And preaching in America could become the preaching of America. The Mormons arose with the quintessential statement of that conviction in their Book of Mormon, which purports to tell the prehistory of events on the American continent and declare the confidence that God has "given this land for their inheritance" (3 Nephi 21:22) and that "a New Jerusalem shall be built upon this land" (Ether 13:6), namely, the North American continent.

And one Jewish preacher, Isaac Leeser, concluded that Jews had found the promised land when they arrived in America.

PREACHING IN COLONIAL NEW ENGLAND

In America's beginnings, of course, preaching was held in highest esteem by the Puritans. The New England preacher was a formidable presence. He (for only men qualified) not only held forth in his pulpit on Sundays and special occasions, but also headed the dominant social institution in the community, the church. He determined eligibility for public office, because only church members could be chosen, and he controlled the membership rolls. He was likely to be the best-educated person in the community, the arbiter of intellectual and moral values, and the principal interpreter of God's will.

One of the outstanding early ministers was

John Cotton. In 1633, three years after he delivered the embarkation sermon for the *Arbella*, Cotton himself left for New England. Behind him lay a twenty-year ministry in an English church, and ahead lay seventeen years as the preacher at the First Church, Boston. He wrote fifty books (the most important of which was *The Way of the Congregational Churches Cleared*, published in 1648) and thousands of sermons exalting the sovereignty of God. His preaching emphasized the covenant by which God and the people of God are bound to each other: a covenant established by the grace of God alone, into which the Lord brings those whom he has determined to save and whose place in the covenant becomes manifest by the signs of the movement of the Spirit within them.

Cotton believed that the covenant was perpetual and irrevocable and that it functioned only by the action of God, not by the effort of humanity. Not even a stalwart believer could enter into the covenant without some inner experience of faith that could be read as evidences of grace. "The Lord hath drawn thee to make this everlasting covenant," Cotton told his parishioners, "thou didst not take it upon thy own accord." Nor can one enter the covenant simply by nurturing one's family under the influence of Christian educators: "if the Lord doth not cut thee off from all thy good education, believe it, thou art not yet in Christ" (Holland, 1971, pp. 39, 40).

Cotton sought to instill the experience and evidence of personal regeneration through his preaching, for such regeneration was to him the sign of one's entrance into the perpetual covenant of faith. In effect, Cotton proclaimed the promise of eternal freedom: a promise that meant clean hearts and comfortable souls, through "an Everlasting Covenant with you that shall never be forgotten" (Holland, 1971, p. 43).

Cotton's doctrine enabled him to fence off the church, admitting to membership only those who showed signs of belonging to the covenant. Since civil leadership hinged on church membership, Cotton was also able to preach that the magistrates order the community according to his version of pure religion.

This position had its adversaries, notably Roger Williams, whose conception of freedom was broader than Cotton would allow. Williams had arrived in Massachusetts in 1631 while still in his twenties. He was called to minister to the

Boston church, but declined the position on the grounds that it was still not separated from the Church of England. He spent brief periods in Salem and Plymouth before being ordered in 1635 to leave Massachusetts. The next year he made his way to Rhode Island, where he officially founded Providence in 1638 as a sanctuary of freedom.

Williams preached the freedom of conscience and the separation of church and state. He opposed the intrusions of civil authority on behalf of the church into the lives of those deemed unfit for membership in the church. He preferred a civil democracy to the magisterial theocracy of Massachusetts Bay Colony. On that point, especially, Williams and Cotton differed. Williams insisted that civil authorities could not enforce the "First Table of the Law," that is, the first five of the Ten Commandments. And he opposed the right of the English king to issue charters to Indian lands. After helping found the First Baptist Church of Providence (which was also the first Baptist church in America), he left the Baptists and became a Seeker. Too restless to be at home in any denomination, he roamed around on the left wing of American religious life. His main work, *The Bloody Tenent of Persecution for Cause of Conscience* (1644), set out his line of argument against Cotton.

Each of the two philosophies prevailed in its own territory. In the long run America's thirst for freedom was quenched more by Williams' views than by Cotton's. But in the near term, Cotton had the greater influence. Most notably, it came in the best-known of New England's early preachers, Cotton Mather. When John Cotton died, his widow married another Boston divine, Richard Mather, who had lost his wife. Mather's son Increase courted Cotton's daughter Maria (now a stepsister in the same household) and they married in 1662. The next year, a son named Cotton Mather (in honor of both family lines) was born. In 1685 the son became the assistant minister to his father at Boston's Second Church, where Increase had been called the year before Cotton's birth. The two shared that pulpit until Increase died in 1723. Cotton succeeded him until his own death five years later.

The name Cotton Mather resonates with grim memories of New England life, including his consent to the burning of witches in Salem and his grief over the delinquency and death of his son Cressy, who joined a juvenile gang in Boston's streets, then ran away to a life at sea, and eventually drowned in a storm.

Mather's career was tumultuous, both in his personal crises and in his professional career. He feared for the decline of New England. A prolific preacher, he delivered sermons on Sunday mornings and evenings as well as during the middle of the week. He wrote enormous quantities of material, ranging from devotional tracts for his parishioners to voluminous histories of the acts of God. His magnum opus, the *Biblia Americana,* has never been published. His largest publication was the *Magnalia Christi Americana,* which runs to 1,400 pages reviewing the history of the age and the warning that time was nearing its end. His most influential works may have been the *Manuductio ad Ministerium,* a manual for training young ministers that was used well into the nineteenth century, and *Bonifacius: An Essay to Do Good,* from which Benjamin Franklin said he derived his inspiration to enter public service. In *Magnalia Christi Americana,* he described John Winthrop as the American Nehemiah, who built on a hill the city of God by prophetic vision and prodigious faith. And in sermons that scholars have called "jeremiads," he yearned for a repentant embrace of the divine covenant, the old piety, the eternal freedom that only a sovereign God could bestow, and pleaded for rededication by his own generation.

On Sunday mornings he preached to about 1,500 persons at Boston's Second Church. But except for the final five years of his life, Mather worked under the aegis of his father and was tied to the yearnings of an older generation, the dreams of his father and grandfathers. By the end of his ministry New England was no longer under the Puritan domination that had once prevailed. Nor could the name Mather direct church affairs as had once been the case.

In the late 1730s a new wind was blowing. Jonathan Edwards, a man forty years younger than Mather, had for two years served with and then in 1729 succeeded his grandfather, Solomon Stoddard, as pastor at Northampton, Massachusetts. Stoddard had sought a revival of preaching and conducted spiritual renewal services called "seasons of harvest." He had been opposed in these endeavors by Cotton Mather. But Mather died in 1728. Stoddard lived a year longer and prepared the ground for the remarkable revivals over which his grandson presided in the following years.

A philosopher rather than a pastor, Edwards was more comfortable in the confines of his study (where he said he spent thirteen hours a day) than in his parishioners' homes or even in his pulpit. His diligently prepared sermons were delivered nervously, as Edwards either read carefully from the manuscript or stared at the bell rope in the rear of the church.

A man of reason rather than emotion, he did not strive with any excess for enthusiastic response to his sermons. So he was surprised when signs of conversion began to appear in his congregation. He observed, chronicled, and analyzed them, and increasingly preached as if trying to provoke them. These "religious affections" included loud cries, fainting spells, convulsions, and other physical phenomena. One wave of revival swept Northampton in the late 1730s, another in the early 1740s.

Collectively known as the Great Awakening, these revivals prompted Edwards to analyze the outpourings of regeneration. He published four commentaries on the revival: *A Faithful Narrative . . .* (1737), *The Distinguishing Marks . . .* (1741), *Some Thoughts . . .* (1742), and *A Treatise Concerning the Religious Affections* (1746). The commentaries show him to have been skeptical of claims that physical "marks" could be direct symptoms of the movement of grace. He defined conversion instead as the indwelling of the Holy Spirit, which gave the believer a new sense or inward perception of the reality of God and a new style of behavior that could include physical evidence of conversion.

Edwards' most famous sermon was clearly pointed toward conversion. It was delivered not only from his Northampton pulpit but also outdoors at Enfield, Connecticut. Edwards, long an analyst of empirical data, had been a close observer of spiders in his childhood. At Enfield in 1740, in "Sinners in the Hands of an Angry God," he illustrated the plight of the unrepentant by an analogy to that of certain spiders: as if "by a thread," he declared, sinners are suspended over the pit of hell, dangling above the fires, and preserved from the flames only by the grace of God, who could sever the thread at any point and consign the sinner to fiery damnation. Should God's wrath be unleashed, if only for a moment, the wicked one would be lost. Thus

could Edwards rhetorically inflict terror upon his listeners as a way of awakening them to the grace of God, which was their only protection.

In 1727, about the time that Edwards was assuming his pulpit in Northampton and Mather was departing from his at the Second Church, Boston, Charles Chauncy was ordained into the ministry at the First Church, Boston. Where Edwards was passionately rational in his appreciation for "the surprising work of God" among the converted, Chauncy found passion and reason to be adversaries and elevated the divine gifts of reason and understanding. Preaching against the "disregard" that "enthusiasts" had for "the dictates of reason," Chauncy asserted that faithfulness to the Scriptures was what separated true believers from "mere pretenders to the immediate guidance and influence of the Spirit." To Chauncy, the revivalists had swamped the Scriptures with waves of emotional excess. The excitement of it all had become their standard of faithfulness, he argued. Where the Bible teaches charity, Chauncy declared, the enthusiasts exercise judgments against clergy and laity whom they consider unregenerated by the Spirit. "Keep close to the Scripture," he said, "and admit of nothing for an impression of the Spirit, but what agrees with that unerring rule" (Holland, 1971, p. 117).

Although Chauncy's voice heralded the liberal age in New England, proclaiming freedom from what he saw as the tyranny of false and affected spirituality, for the time being the "affections" of the converted drew more popular attention, both in Northampton and far beyond.

An English preacher named George Whitefield stepped onto center stage. Famous for his open-air preaching at home, Whitefield journeyed seven times to the colonies on preaching missions that often reached thousands of listeners in a single session. He was truly a celebrity preacher, one of the few who enjoyed fame from north to south. He could preach from one hillside overlooking a valley to a crowd of 5,000 assembled on the other side. In his lifetime, it is estimated that hundreds of thousands heard him preach. He traveled from New England, spending at least one weekend with the Edwards family, to the Carolinas and ignited evangelistic fires wherever he stopped. He was the most renowned and effective evangelist of his day, if effectiveness is measured by the number of persons who claimed a sense of spiritual freedom upon hearing his voice. It was said, and reported with sarcasm by Perry Miller, that he could convert sinners simply by his resonant pronunciation of the word "Mesopotamia." Despite Whitefield's importance in the history of preaching in America, his movement scarcely endured beyond his death in 1770.

PREACHING IN THE NEW NATION

For the most well-traveled preacher in America, Francis Asbury, an institutional legacy did survive his preaching. Less widely remembered as a homilist than as an organizer of Methodism in the new nation, Asbury came to the colonies in 1771 as a young lay preacher commissioned by John Wesley. In 1784, on successive days at a Christmas conference in Baltimore, he was ordained deacon, then made elder, and finally consecrated bishop of the fledgling Methodist Episcopal Church. For thirty-six years he rode the preaching circuits of the nation, covering up to 6,000 miles a year astride a horse or aboard a wagon. He left no full sermon manuscripts, but seems to have preached several thousand times from a few hundred sermon outlines. Simple and direct rather than dramatic in his style, he was primarily an expositor of texts. His sermons instructed rather than moved.

Not all of the Methodist preachers he superintended, or their successors in the Methodist movement, adopted that model of simple, direct homiletical exposition. Asbury was a conservative: unimaginative in his preaching, rigidly self-disciplined, celibate, slow to embrace changes other than those he instituted, and reluctant to support the American Revolution until after it was decided in the colonies' favor.

Others who brought sermons to the frontier, notably Peter Cartwright, were more flamboyant. Cartwright used many tactics to deliver the Gospel, Methodist style, with vigor and vitality. He was one of the traveling preachers who moved from point to point in a defined circuit. These circuit riders were typically short on theological training and long on enthusiasm for their work. Often he considered the Baptists as much his foes as the devil, and he was not above invading their territory. Once while itinerating in Virginia, he kept a preaching appointment in Stock-

ton Valley and proclaimed the Gospel in a run-down Baptist church. Twenty-three conversions resulted, whereupon the Baptists sent some preachers of their own to reconvert those who had been lost to Cartwright. The Methodists, in turn, asked him to come back. When he arrived, he used a ruse to demonstrate that infant baptism as well as believer's baptism can be legitimate. Cartwright presented himself as a candidate for baptism, told the story of his journey to salvation, was accepted by the preacher for immersion in the waters, and then announced his commitment to infant baptism. The Baptist preacher had no choice but to decline to baptize Cartwright, who then led the twenty-three converts to Methodism away from the creek.

While the history of preaching in America is filled with similar episodes of "retail" evangelism, in the nineteenth century a new device—the camp meeting—was developed to evangelize wholesale. In the summer of 1801 more than 25,000 people gathered at Cane Ridge, Kentucky, for a week-long extravaganza of preaching, prayer, and song. The usual physical gyrations and cries were observed among the converted, but beyond that, a new form of preaching had been invented. The gathering developed into a forum for sermonizing, with a number of ministers preaching simultaneously. The camp meeting became the superior means for spreading frontier evangelism.

Preeminent among the evangelists of the nineteenth century was Charles Grandison Finney, "the father of modern revivalism." The epithet serves both as a tribute to his success and as a critique of his style, for Finney was the man most responsible for the packaged approach to preaching. To him, a revival was not simply a sign of the miraculous work of God but also the result of effective management. He instituted various "means" or "measures" whose goal was to produce an energetic spiritual renewal. Working mostly in upstate New York, Finney conducted crusades in the late 1820s in such places as Rome, Utica, and Troy, as well as in Delaware and Pennsylvania. He began a revival in Rochester in 1830 and another in Boston the following year. He was untrained in the academic discipline of theology and thus ran afoul of others who were eager to guard true doctrine.

But he was pleased to function in popular rather than scholarly circles. Unlike Edwards, who terrorized listeners with the image of a single thread called God's grace that alone saves them from the flames of hell, Finney used structured means to exhort voluntary efforts to avoid sin; that is, human efforts in addition to holy grace could keep away the fires of judgment. If that seemed grossly un-Calvinistic to some, such as Lyman Beecher (who later endorsed Finney), it was appealing enough to the masses.

Finney's technique involved, among other devices, an innovation called "the anxious bench." Those who were almost ready to volunteer to be saved would be seated at the front of the church, where they could feel the most direct impact of the preacher's fiery words. Finney would pray for sinners by name, preach against their depravities specifically, and summon them to holy lives. As an instrument of psychological pressure, the anxious bench was enormously successful.

From 1832 to 1835, Finney held a succession of pulpits in New York City, but he still applied the new measures he had devised. In 1835 he joined the faculty of Oberlin College and then was its president from 1851 to 1866. His influence made Oberlin a center for his theological and homiletical principles.

In the early 1840s a serious (if isolated) critique arose against Finney. It came from a preacher and professor who was distressed to find his quiet Reformed congregation being overtaken by the new measures of Finney's crusades. Provoked to action, John Williamson Nevin published in 1844 *The Anxious Bench,* in which he deplored the emotional conversions that seemed to substitute an instantaneously aroused human spirit for the gracious, nurturing power of the Holy Spirit. Nevin was a church historian who believed that doctrinal questions should not be ignored, not even by preachers with impressive records in achieving conversions. He repudiated the evangelical contrivances of his day, saying they promoted justification by feeling instead of by faith. He saw no credibility in Finney's popular success; the anxious bench, Nevin declared, was actually a hindrance to the work of the Holy Spirit, threatening the life of the church by frustrating the power of the catechism, which was the historic extension of the incarnation of Christ.

But Nevin's outrage was an anomaly. He was fighting not only a radical religious populism, but also certain homiletical trends that had been emerging in America for a long time. Ever since generations of New England preachers had bewailed the decline of faith among the people of God, the cultus of the nation had begun to emphasize affections (emotions) as impressive displays of regeneration, skills in managing successful camp meetings, and programmatic revivals in settled parish churches. Nevin's was the first substantive critique of this newly evolved form, for he sought to return preaching in America to its traditional role and context within the church. Revival, he believed, would come not from the "quackery" or gimmicks of contrived evangelism, but from a reawakened commitment to that nurturing mother, the church. Preaching was not to be the dramatic, emotion-provoking rhetoric of a merchant of salvation, but part of the work of an ordered ministry that God gave to the church, and to which special persons were called.

Although Nevin presented his arguments with impressive force and clarity from his platform at Mercersburg Seminary, a German Reformed Church theological school in Mercersburg, Pennsylvania, in the end his work became little more than an important footnote to the history of preaching in America. Besides going against the current of contemporary preaching, Nevin was suspected of being unusually sympathetic to Roman Catholics. His views seemed to have an appreciation for the continuity of church traditions that Evangelicals found unnecessary and Roman Catholics were thought to treasure. It was the catechism that shaped Christians, he insisted, not revivalist conversions; and it was Christ's real presence during the sacrament of the Lord's Supper that brought salvation's power, he taught, not some emotional overture. Protestants of Nevin's time tended to take offense at such hints of Romanism; in the middle of the nineteenth century, American Protestants harbored grave suspicions about Catholicism.

The dilemma in which Nevin found himself was made worse because Catholics and Protestants had followed different styles of expansion in America. The incentive for Calvinist preaching was to summon the elect of God to affirm their chosen status and rejoice in God's grace. The motivation for Arminian preachers was to rouse sinners out of their indifference to God and into a willing acceptance of the grace of Christ that waits for human response. Among all Protestants, in other words—liberals and conservatives, Calvinists and Arminians—there was at least a common understanding that the sermon had supplanted the liturgy as the means of grace. But America's Catholics had never surrendered the principle that the central event of Christian life was the mass, not revival preaching—which may help explain why the shorter, simpler "homily" so typical of Catholic preaching seemed to evolve differently from the generally longer, more fully developed oratory of the Protestant pulpit. Though the words *homily* and *sermon* are essentially synonymous, in practical use they have served to identify the different lines along which Catholic and Protestant preaching in America developed.

This is not to say that Catholics were unaffected by the religious movements sweeping the new nation, or that they did not develop new forms of church life. Bishop John Carroll's first sermon in Bardstown, Kentucky, in 1790 was an open-air proclamation. And at a 1791 synod in Baltimore, he directed his priests to preach regularly to encourage their parishioners to live holy Christian lives. Bishop John England of Charleston, early in the next century, traveled extensively on preaching and sacramental missions.

The American situation continued to shape Roman Catholicism. One example is Isaac Hecker, who converted from Methodism and was ordained to the Catholic priesthood in 1849. He and the Paulist Fathers, which he founded in 1858, waged successful efforts at converting Protestants to Catholicism. Centered in a New York City parish, and working with the authorization of Archbishop John Hughes, the Paulists circulated tracts throughout America. Eventually, however, the techniques of American revivalism that had crept into this ambitious work earned a rebuke from the Vatican in 1899 that such "Americanism" was unacceptable. The notion that the Holy Spirit could touch individuals apart from the sacramental system of the church did not please the Curia any more than it had pleased Nevin.

Notwithstanding any official church efforts to restrain the trends, America was finding new ways to enjoy the meaning of freedom. And preaching in America, in every denominational group, was helping to discover greater dimensions of freedom. Liberation from authorities, even ecclesiastical ones, became a standard element of American religious life.

Perhaps the failure of the Roman Catholic church to yield entirely to the pursuit of freedom was what prompted some prominent Protestant voices to see in it nothing but treachery. Lyman Beecher, for instance, found Catholic expansion to be a demonic force in conflict with the real movement of the Spirit in America. Beecher was a revivalist and moral reformer who held pastorates in Presbyterian and Congregational churches on Long Island, in Connecticut, and in Boston, during the first quarter of the nineteenth century. He became president of Lane Theological Seminary in 1832. Continuing the vision of the early New Englanders that God would establish his kingdom in America, Beecher saw a Catholic threat to this vision. He complained of a Catholic conspiracy to dominate America by flooding it with Catholic immigrants who would undermine the godly democracy of the nation. His sermons had their effect: in 1834 an anti-Catholic mob burned a convent and a girls' parochial school in Charlestown, Massachusetts.

Leaders of America's Catholics responded not alone with sermons. In the 1840s Bishop Hughes made public schools the battleground, demanding that a portion of state money be designated for parochial school education, and deploring the Protestant domination of the public schools. The gospel of freedom in the country had come to mean more than just the constitutional toleration advocated by Bishop Carroll in the early days. Now it meant a full taste of America's liberties.

The developments in American preaching were merging in various ways with concepts of social and political freedom. Sermons exalted forms of liberation that transcended narrower ecclesiastical or spiritual goals. Protestant preachers were letting their social agendas for the nation shape their sermons. Roman Catholic preaching caught the American spirit of freedom as well. And the influence of American values had, if anything, an even greater impact on Jewish preaching. Within American Judaism, several transitions occurred: preaching became a regular part of the liturgy, sermons became a rabbinical prerogative, homiletical ability became a valued talent, and the American rabbi came to be perceived as a Jewish preaching minister.

At the time of the American Revolution, there was not one ordained rabbi in the country; in fact, none arrived until the 1840s. But preaching preceded the coming of the rabbis. In 1829 Isaac Leeser was elected cantor of the Sephardic congregation of Philadelphia, Mikveh Israel. He introduced a startling and controversial innovation by preaching regular sermons. The practice was frowned upon at first, according to historian Leon Jick, and was not officially accepted by the congregation until fourteen years later.

In part what made Leeser's actions possible was the decentralization of Jewish organization. Every congregation was free to structure itself in its own way, with its own officers, spiritual leaders, and rules of governance. Leeser managed to rewrite most of the rules: he preached and wrote in English, compiled a Jewish "catechism," and, using the role of pastor-preacher, Americanized the synagogue on the model of the Protestant congregation. He was not alone. Isaac Noah Mannheimer, who was born in 1793 in Denmark, moved to a Vienna pulpit from which he became recognized as the most outstanding Jewish preacher of the nineteenth century. He believed strongly in moderate reforms of orthodox practices. Yet he said that Jewish preaching had been around for only a short time and that its practitioners had to learn from the Protestant masters. The outcome of this influence was the emergence of a new religious professional, the rabbi-pastor-preacher, whose roots were in the Jewish community but whose role was shaped by the Protestant clergy.

By the time the first rabbi did arrive in America, his place had been usurped by the Jewish minister. After Rabbi Abraham Rice arrived in Baltimore in 1840, he found himself in constant conflict with his congregation. Since one of his "shortcomings" was that he preached in German, the congregation voted to add Samuel Isaacs to the staff, keeping Rice as rabbi but naming Isaacs (who spoke English) as preacher. Isaacs declined the invitation. Nevertheless, before the end of the decade, Rice resigned and opened a dry goods store, wondering aloud "if it is even permissible for a Jew to live in this land."

Isaac Leeser did not share Rice's doubts. "In America," he said, "the children of Jacob have received a new home." However, it became increasingly clear that the traditional rabbi was not welcome. In 1845 Leo Merzbacher became the second rabbi to arrive in America. His free use of the pulpit, especially on controversial topics

such as slavery, led the officers of the congregation to try regaining control of the sermon. In 1855 the trustees ordered him to write out his sermons in full and have them on the pulpit during delivery, so that they could search for any doctrinal errors. The concern for theological purity was one matter. That this rabbi could not preach in English was another. Within a year the trustees voted to hire an assistant minister who could preach in the common American tongue.

One traditional rabbi who met with success, though, was Isaac Mayer Wise. He succeeded largely because he was able to reach both traditional Jews and Americanized ones. In his trial sermon before a Cincinnati congregation in 1853, by his own admission, he "said not one word about principle" but instead "scattered so many blossoms and flowers upon the congregation from the pulpit . . . that there were enough bouquets to go around and everyone went home bedecked." Wise openly advocated Americanization. He was eager for the American synagogue to be free from the confines of its European heritage. He wanted Judaism to establish a home in the midst of America's emerging culture and to find ways for Jewish worship to be compatible with the American social experience. He scheduled two services every week, one in German, the other in English. Wise's experience was just one more example of freedom finding new forms in the American pulpit.

In 1785 Francis Asbury invited a young, unordained black preacher named Richard Allen to accompany him on a preaching tour, as another companion, "Black" Harry Hosier, had done. Hosier had served as Asbury's assistant, substituting for the bishop at an occasional preaching appointment and often preaching on his own to integrated groups. To Allen, Asbury explained the practical circumstances of such a trip: in the South Allen would be forbidden to mix with slaves and would be unable to sleep in the homes of whites or at inns. Allen declined to make the trip, choosing instead to settle and preach in his native Philadelphia.

Black Methodists lived and worshiped under certain racial constraints in Philadelphia, too, but they were able to function openly within the life of the oldest Methodist congregation in the city, St. George's Church. As the congregation grew, however, a controversy brewed over seating arrangements. And after a remodeling project was completed, the matter reached a crisis. Allen and his friends arrived for a service and were directed to the gallery. Just after the prayers had begun, and while all the worshipers were on their knees, a trustee tried to pull one Absalom Jones up from his prayers, claiming that blacks were not to be accommodated in that particular place. Jones asked that he be allowed to finish his prayers first, but the trustee refused and sought help in removing the blacks to another section. When the prayer ended, the entire group of blacks walked out of the church together. Allen commented that "they were no more plagued with us in the church" (George, 1973, p. 55).

This episode resulted in the establishment of a new denomination, the African Methodist Episcopal Church, of which Allen became a bishop. The emergence of such independent black churches, together with that of certain individuals like Harry Hosier, afforded blacks a special place in the history of preaching in America. Pulpit oratory quickly provided a vehicle for transcending the limits of status imposed by slavery and segregation. Black preachers were perceived as social and moral leaders. Their sermons tended to be the centerpiece of Sunday worship, with a preacher's effectiveness measured by the size of the crowds he drew and by the intensity of his interaction with the congregation, as his listeners became visibly and audibly involved with the sermon.

Allen, and most who followed him, preached extemporaneously. Sermons were more likely to be responses to a situation, such as a lynching, than expositions of texts or explanations of doctrines. Teaching was typically done through emotionally charged persuasion rather than through closely reasoned presentation. And the theme of freedom was direct and precise: God had liberated the Israelites from slavery in Egypt; God would liberate the Africans from captivity in America.

That message was spoken and shared widely beyond the black community, both among Christians and Jews. But it was also a divisive factor in American preaching. In the 1830s Theodore Parker and James Henley Thornwell were classmates at Harvard Divinity School. Parker became an active abolitionist minister after completing his studies, preaching widely in the antislavery

cause. Thornwell, on the other hand, after being ordained as a Presbyterian, became a college and seminary professor in South Carolina and in 1850 preached a widely influential sermon justifying slavery, "The Rights and Duties of Masters."

Roman Catholics were divided as well. In 1839 Pope Gregory XVI issued an apostolic letter that was interpreted in some circles as an endorsement of abolitionism. Bishop John England responded that the pope had indeed condemned the slave trade but not the institution of slavery as such. He surveyed the history of Catholic doctrine and asserted that the church had always accepted slavery. Confessing that he was personally opposed to it, he said there was no way to abolish it entirely. And in any case he believed that the issue was one to be resolved by civil rather than ecclesiastical authorities.

American Jews were also entangled in the controversy. In 1861 Morris Raphall, rabbi of B'nai Jeshurun Synagogue in New York, preached on "The Bible and Slavery," arguing that nothing in the Bible prohibits slavery. Like Thornwell, he said it was sanctioned by God. But when David Einhorn, a German native who had served in Budapest, was invited to be the rabbi at Baltimore's Har Sinai in 1855, he used the pulpit to preach aggressively against slavery. His denunciations of slavery provoked mobs to attack him. Within six years he had to leave his pulpit because of this outspokenness. When the synagogue trustees invited him to return, subject to the condition that he avoid controversial issues in his preaching, Einhorn, an advocate of Jewish reform, who called slavery a "crime against God," declined and fled from Baltimore for his personal safety. He served congregations thereafter in Philadelphia and New York, speaking effectively for Reform causes.

Henry Ward Beecher, son of Lyman, at least had the freedom of his pulpit in Plymouth Congregational Church, Brooklyn. He preached on a variety of social topics, notably the evils of slavery before the Civil War and the judgments of God on former slaveowners after the war had ended. When the struggle over whether Kansas was to be "slave" or "free" was boiling, Beecher used his pulpit to raise funds for the purchase of rifles ("Beecher's Bibles," they were called) to do battle against the proslavery factions. He also brought slaves before his congregation, "auctioning" them for a price sufficient to buy their freedom.

By the time of the Civil War, preaching in America had developed beyond its denominational peculiarities and sectarian limits. The sermon was sharing a point of interest with the American image of itself, as an example of freedom. The eagerness for liberation became a powerful influence, shaping the work and words of the nation's pulpits: freedom from older languages and older images of rabbinical responsibilities among Jews; freedom to provide a rationale for slaveholding or for abolitionism across the nation; freedom to establish a uniquely American Catholic church within the structures of Roman Catholicism; freedom to merge the doctrines of the faith with the dreams of the nation. The sermon in America had become a metaphor for the culture of America. It was, after all, a preacher named John Winthrop who had set the tone for the American dream aboard the *Arbella* in 1630; and it was a preacher named Father Mapple, in Herman Melville's 1851 novel *Moby-Dick,* whose sermon offered the central theme of that entire story.

In the period following the Civil War, preaching carried the meaning of freedom into more profound communion with the culture. America arrived at two profound convictions about itself: an ideology of individualism seized the nation's psyche and a sense of optimism nourished the nation's soul. People felt free to engage in bold new business ventures. Progress seemed both inevitable and boundless. Poor immigrants sought and, occasionally, found their fortunes. Commercial entrepreneurs prospered. New industries in steel and on rails were forged. Electricity fostered invention. Automobiles were made and marketed. And Christians spoke boldly about sending missionaries from America to evangelize the whole world in the next century: the city set on a hill might yet shed its light over the earth.

To believers, freedom meant more than it ever had. Women looked for liberation from the limits placed upon them. They sought credentials as preachers in the churches. In 1869, when male leaders of the Methodist denomination refused to authorize female missionaries for their global evangelistic enterprise, women established their own independent foreign missionary society.

Preachers increasingly cherished a sense of freedom from doctrinal and denominational limits. They shared the optimism of the nation and individually found ways to make the free exercise of religion a free enterprise as well.

Henry Ward Beecher was one of the preeminent pulpit figures in the second half of the nineteenth century. Upon coming to Plymouth Church in 1847, he simplified the furnishings for worship to a bare minimum, leaving only a preaching desk. He insisted that there be no doctrinal requirements for membership in the church, asking only that those seeking to become members express their personal commitment to Christ. For four decades he used the Plymouth pulpit as his platform. He addressed burning social questions such as women's rights and political corruption. He endorsed modern critical study of the Scriptures. He accepted the theory of evolution. Beecher's critics within the Congregational fold attacked him for such openness. And in 1882, after thirty-five years at the church, he left the denomination and took his congregation with him, declaring that he was a free man.

His sermons were widely circulated and were published in their entirety in city newspapers. From his platform of prestige (he had a national following) and personal wealth (due to the generosity of his parishioners and the general public), Beecher addressed nearly every social issue of his day.

Beecher's only equal for acclaim was Phillips Brooks of Boston. From the pulpit of Trinity Church, where he served from 1869 to 1893, and also (from 1891) as Episcopal bishop of Massachusetts, Brooks delivered thoughtful, scholarly sermons. His influence on preaching in America is almost immeasurable. While Beecher was the first to deliver the Lyman Beecher lectures on preaching at Yale (he in fact delivered them the first three years they were offered, 1872–1874), Brooks probably gave the best of them in 1877. Brooks defined preaching as the proclamation of truth through personality, and no better description has been offered since.

In Brooks's view, the truth of the Christian gospel is abiding and unchanging, yet its proclamation is expressed through the unique individuality of the preacher. The Gospel acquires form from the personality in the pulpit, whose experiences and study and goals and dreams offer the vehicle by which the truth of God's word reaches an audience.

At the same time, if the freedom of the American pulpit had elevated Brooks (and Beecher) to such national prominence, it also held them in a strange captivity. They were, in a sense, creations of the culture at the time. Imbued with the optimism of the nation's growing prosperity, they were captivated by the spirit of the age. For all his pastoral sensitivity and articulate handling of biblical texts, Brooks lacked a deep appreciation for what was happening in the society in the late nineteenth century. Industrial progress was providing the wealth that could at last build a rather impressive city on a hill, but it was being built at a price, and the price was being paid by the urban poor, who suffered low wages, inadequate housing, and very little if any health care.

Certain preachers unabashedly allied the cause of the Protestant church to the cause of American prosperity. Russell Conwell, a Philadelphia Baptist who founded Temple University, delivered his sermon "Acres of Diamonds" at least 5,000 times in the last decades of the nineteenth century, announcing that money is power and that people should get rich in order to do good things with their wealth. In 1900 William Lawrence, successor to Brooks as Episcopal bishop of Massachusetts, declared that wealth comes "only to the man of morality" and insisted that riches were making the national character "sweeter" and "more Christ-like."

This was the gospel of wealth, the merger of American church life with the prerogatives of the social and industrial elite. Brooks and Beecher preached to this elite each week. Conwell and Lawrence cultivated them. In the opinion of Ralph Henry Gabriel, the gospel of wealth was "a Protestant stratagem to retain for itself a place in the new social order, to provide itself with a function, in short, to save itself as a significant social institution" (*The Course of American Democratic Thought,* 1940, p. 157).

However, preaching in America found alternate strategies to address the new crisis in urban America. One approach was typified by Dwight L. Moody, an example of the growing economic prosperity in his own right. Moody was a shoe salesman, untrained in theology but profoundly moved by his own religious experience in 1856 to help the poor. He rented several pews in his church and gave the space to any poor persons he could find on Chicago's streets every Sunday. He ran a mission Sunday school for drifters and street people, who numbered about 1,500 on his membership rolls. Teamed with music director Ira Sankey in 1870, he sought to save the souls of the lost and to improve the situation in the cities by converting individual sinners. In 1871 Moody experienced a further spiritual renewal. With his preaching and Sankey's music, the pair traveled across the nation and over to Europe. His optimism was characteristic of the liberal age: the power of personal salvation would be enough to bring economic freedom for all.

Another approach—the Social Gospel movement—came in direct response to the gospel of wealth. While even Beecher and Brooks believed that social degradation was essentially the consequence of the sins of those who suffered it, other pulpit voices rose to question that belief. One of the first was Washington Gladden, a native of Owego, New York, and minister for nearly thirty years at the First Congregational Church, Columbus, Ohio. He became a severe critic of American free enterprise and demanded that churches devote themselves vigorously to issues of social justice. But at the forefront of the Social Gospel movement was Walter Rauschenbusch, for eleven years the pastor of a German Baptist congregation in the Hell's Kitchen neighborhood of New York City. His preaching was part of a ministry that included building public parks and improving urban housing. Rauschenbusch believed himself a preacher of the good news that the day of the Lord had come: now believers in Christ had to break the "bonds of evil" of society and control the social forces that were preventing the last barrier, poverty, to human perfectibility from falling. Rauschenbusch's was a new vision of the city that John Winthrop had prophesied from the deck of the *Arbella.* The Social Gospel involved preaching the word of freedom that would liberate the poor from their social captivity.

Other preachers shared the same vision, even if they expressed it in more modest terms. Henry Sloane Coffin, for instance, learned when he became pastor of the Madison Avenue Presbyterian Church in New York City that the congregation operated two Sunday schools: one for the elite on Park Avenue and westward, the other for the tenement-dwelling immigrant families in a mission building on Third Avenue. Coffin unified the schools and forced the church to shake its aristocratic self-image. He was undeterred by claims from some parishioners that the old forms of reverence, such as requiring ushers to wear morning coats to worship, were passing away with the arrival of other influences. In Coffin's preaching, the message was that the church should, if necessary, work to improve the housing and education and wages of the people in the neighborhood. But the main role of the church was to offer ideals and motives for individuals to accomplish those improvements through their businesses and their nondenominational benevolent societies.

There remained by the turn of the century no lack of optimism about the future. With a national economy surviving various setbacks only to expand more vigorously, a confidence endured that the only problems which remained were those to which not enough energy or ingenuity had yet been dedicated. The Social Gospel movement left a permanent stamp on the American religious experience. Social problems could never again be excluded from the field of vision of the nation's pulpits. But the specific forms of service that religious institutions should render remained open to debate. And the boundless optimism that the problems would be solved eventually came to be questioned.

PREACHING IN THE TWENTIETH CENTURY

Washington Gladden and Walter Rauschenbusch both died as World War I was drawing to a close. From the other side of the sea, America's preachers were beginning to hear a new version of the old orthodoxy: that the responsibility for social activism should not be taken to imply continuous social improvement. Reinhold Niebuhr, a pastor in Detroit, heard the Neo-Orthodox message more clearly than anyone else in America and began preaching it forthrightly.

Niebuhr was a product of the German Evangelical Church, born in 1892 and educated (like his brother H. Richard) in denominational schools and at Yale. For thirteen years Reinhold held a Michigan pastorate, serving auto workers and others among the inner-city residents of De-

troit, before moving to the faculty of Union Theological Seminary in New York City in 1928. But by 1915 he had begun to lose his optimism about the progress that could be accomplished through religious education and social change. He became an advocate of "Christian realism," the position that took seriously the inability of social institutions to progress toward good and noble ends. An individual may uphold moral values and pursue righteous goals, he argued in his most important work, *Moral Man and Immoral Society* (1932), but groups within society (such as businesses, labor organizations, and governments) are inherently unable to serve such ends. Niebuhr's words offered a realistic assessment of the optimism whose torch so many preachers had carried.

But nineteenth-century notions did not end abruptly. The gospel of wealth and the Social Gospel both endured into the twentieth century and found a new synthesis in American preaching. Harry Emerson Fosdick was born in 1878, a child of nineteenth-century optimism and conventional revivalist piety, which used emotional appeals to provoke sufficient guilt over the state of one's soul, in order that a swift spiritual rebirth might occur. He was also the victim of a crushing psychological crisis that erupted in a suicide attempt. His religious background and his own personal crisis became for him the context of a creative and powerful ministry that made him the foremost pulpit figure of the first half of the twentieth century.

Fosdick's liberal thought had been developing since his college and seminary days. He jettisoned the revivalist piety of his youth and allied himself with causes ranging from the renunciation of war to evolution to birth control.

There was scarcely a major controversy in his time that did not bring Fosdick to center stage. As a Baptist pastor in Montclair, New Jersey, during the decade before World War I, he was drawn into a labor union controversy. Later, while preaching at First Presbyterian Church in New York, he became involved in a test of strength between Fundamentalists and Modernists within and beyond that denomination. In general, the debate raged over the work of biblical scholars that called into question such tenets as the inerrancy of Scripture, the proposition that the Bible is the literal, inspired word of God and is accurate in every detail.

Fundamentalists insisted that if there was no biblical inerrancy then there was no biblical authority. Modernists rejected the argument that to retain scriptural authority one had to ignore the conclusions of modern scholarship about the date of composition of biblical materials, the historical settings in which they were composed, and the examples of self-contradiction within the Bible itself about matters of fact—such as the names and numbers of the persons who arrived at Jesus' tomb on Easter. But the controversy seemed to crystallize around one issue—evolution. Fundamentalists said that evolution must be rejected because it contradicts the creation story in Scripture. Modernists were willing to see the value in myth, symbol, poetry, and story in the biblical account of creation without any need to reject the discoveries of science regarding species' evolution.

In a famous sermon titled "Shall the Fundamentalists Win?" Fosdick attempted in 1922 to cool the dispute. Instead, partly because a publicist named Ivy Lee printed the sermon for wide circulation, the debate exploded. Two sessions of the Presbyterian General Assembly fought over Fosdick's views and over his status as a Baptist preaching in a Presbyterian pulpit. In 1924 he resigned his post rather than accept an offer to become a Presbyterian, for he surmised that his acceptance would require either his doctrinal surrender to the Fundamentalists or his submission to a heresy trial since his Modernist views were anathema to the reactionary forces dominating the Presbyterian church.

A year after his resignation from the Presbyterian pulpit, he became pastor of the Park Avenue Baptist Church in New York City, whose leading member was John D. Rockefeller, Jr. Before accepting this new position, the preacher agreed with his patron upon several stipulations of the call, among them that a new church would be built somewhere away from the existing (and nearly brand-new) facility in "the swankiest neighborhood in the city," as Fosdick described it. Moreover, he wanted that new church to provide a comprehensive ministry, offering recreational, educational, nutritional, and other human services, seven days a week. The new site was chosen on Riverside Drive, near Columbia University and Harlem.

Since the Rockefeller resources were to bear a large responsibility for this construction, Fosdick's foes saw in the whole arrangement an unholy alliance between wealth and liberal Christianity. John Roach Straton, pastor of Calvary Baptist Church in New York City, had been Fosdick's adversary on many issues: he called him a "Baptist bootlegger," for having abandoned his Baptist pulpit in the past in order to preach to the Presbyterians, who had more money; he carried the banner of Fundamentalism into battle against Fosdick and the Modernists; and now he suggested that the new, and as yet unnamed, church on Riverside Drive be identified by a neon sign above the steeple and that it be called the Socony church in honor of the oil company from which the Rockefellers received their billions. But Fosdick, instead of using his new pulpit at "The Riverside Church" to preach the gospel of wealth, shaped it into a witness for pacifism, personal counseling, and social improvement.

There were other "pulpit princes" in this period who proved themselves able to shape their congregations around their own personalities, while at the same time building a commitment to mission that transcended their own individual personalities.

In the Jewish community there was Stephen S. Wise, an early advocate of Zionism as well as social reform causes, including housing improvements and public education. He was frequently in conflict with his congregation, including a noteworthy episode when he was being considered for the post of rabbi of Temple Emmanu-El in New York. The president of the congregation expressed the view that controversial matters in the pulpit, regarding doctrinal orthodoxy, political issues, or social reform causes, should be controlled by the trustees. Wise declined to be bound by such conditions and instead in 1907 founded the Free Synagogue to uphold pulpit liberty. Eastern European Jews, who retained the traditional view of the rabbi's role in teaching and judging the implications of the law in specific cases, found issues like those pressed by Wise irrelevant for Judaism. Zionism was a creature concocted by secularized, Western Jews, they said; and the concept of freedom in the pulpit was a Protestant problem, not a Jewish one.

Nevertheless, in the new office of preaching minister that American Judaism had devised to supplement—and eventually supplant—the traditional office of rabbi, Wise was simply establishing a few additional ground rules that applied the principle of pulpit freedom. It was a further indication that American Jewish preaching shared the tendencies of the other pulpits in the nation. Each religious tradition or denomination was finding a way to discover new forms of freedom. For Wise, it meant being free from the constraints of traditional Hebrew language and doctrine. He openly forged a secular image for his synagogue, dedicated to noble ethical ideals and social reform, in pursuit of the highest aspirations of freedom and justice for all in America. This lends support to the judgment of one historian, Arthur Hertzberg, who described the secularized rabbi in twentieth-century America as a creature of the culture rather than the heir of a tradition.

In *American Judaism: Adventure in Modernity* (1978) Jacob Neusner describes the role of the modern rabbi:

> The rabbi in America today is a cross between a pastor or parish priest and the leader of an ethnic group. The East European . . . tradition produced, at its very end, two images of a proper spiritual leader: either that of the Lithuanian tradition—profound learning—or that of the Hasidic tradition—holiness. The American rabbi today is rich in eloquence, organizational talent, and practical achievement; the American scene has evoked neither intellectual endeavor nor transcendent piety, but it has not done so in American Christianity either. The most Jewish figure on the American scene, the rabbi, is thus in many senses the most American.
>
> (p. 121)

The American scene also produced another identifiably ethnic creation, the black preacher. In some ways, the representative figure for the early-twentieth-century black church may be Charles Albert Tindley. Tindley was born in the 1850s, the son of slaves, in Delaware. As a young man, he married and moved to Philadelphia, where he worked as a construction laborer and church sexton while attending school at night. In 1885 he was admitted as a minister on trial, following the Methodist polity; and in 1889 he was ordained elder.

In a series of pulpits to which he was appointed early in his ministry, Tindley either stopped the decline of membership and congregational spirit, or he fostered new growth, or

both. But his greatest triumph was in Philadelphia. The East Calvary Methodist Episcopal Church increased its membership during his tenure to the point that the 900 spaces in its auditorium were woefully inadequate. In fact, for festival services the congregation rented an arena that seated 5,000 and had to turn people away from that. Tindley cut an impressive figure. At six-foot-three, with a rich baritone voice, he was a commanding presence. Besides being a dynamic preacher in the black church tradition, he was one of the ablest musicians of his time. His sermons became events, with the spoken words often illuminated by a hymn he would sing. Some of the hymn tunes were familiar gospel songs known to the congregation, while others were his own new compositions, which he eventually published.

Beyond his words and his music, he developed lines of influence that far exceeded the usual pastoral impact. For he was recruited by political leaders and courted by commercial enterprises in need of contacts within the black community. His friend and patron was John Wanamaker, marketplace magnate and philanthropist, who gave generously to the building fund of Tindley's church, and who saw in Tindley a helpful contact with the black community.

His sermons dealt with broad biblical themes like love and justice and peace, but typically were illustrated with poetic imagery and practical examples of believers caught between suffering and hope. His most frequently repeated sermon was probably "Heaven's Christmas Tree," which begins with an extended narrative that identifies Jesus as God's Christmas tree laden with gifts of hope, help, home for the homeless, friendship, and peace. They were themes that carried a message of freedom from racial captivity which the members of his congregation experienced daily.

Crowds assembled wherever he preached, and it was common for all 3,200 places in his new church, which opened at Christmastime 1924, to be filled for services on Sunday mornings and evenings. But in the community he was more than a preacher. Philadelphia's mayors consulted him, labor leaders sought his opinions, politicians were conscious of his influence among the city's black population. A family in his parish that discovered its supply of coal running low might, after informing the pastor, find a fuel delivery arrive unexpectedly, because Tindley could place a word in the ear of some important political operative. This social status was not uncommon for black preachers in Tindley's day. But until his death in 1933, he towered above the rest.

Yet it was indicative of the racial separation of the era that Tindley's stature was generally unrecognized by the white majority, who were discovering their own pulpit celebrities. The voice that seemed to be heard as widely as any belonged to a preacher of self-confidence and individual optimism.

In 1932 Norman Vincent Peale came to Marble Collegiate Church in New York City from a Methodist congregation in Syracuse. A contemporary of Fosdick's, Peale functioned with a similar definition of preaching: "pastoral counseling on a group scale," Fosdick called it. But Peale's message was more specifically focused on mental or emotional health, whereas Fosdick pointed to social, cultural, and political health as well. A typical Peale sermon consists of anecdotes in which people triumph over their tragedies by "the power of positive thinking." Published under that title in 1952, Peale's book provided a version of the Gospel that became widely known. Two million copies of the book were sold, and the title phrase became a monument to the man himself. Like Fosdick, Peale found radio to be an effective medium for his message and transformed his pulpit into a presence in millions of homes. Anyone of any faith could discover the power of confident, positive thinking, Peale believed.

Nor was Peale's point of view unique. Rabbi Joshua Loth Liebman's 1946 book *Peace of Mind* touted the same sort of personal happiness as the great goal of modern life. The message was an essentially secularized version of spiritual confidence that fed a longing for individual contentment with an optimism that it could be had by anyone, without restriction to a particular dogma. It was a message not to a religious community but to a national ethos. It was a message of freedom from self-doubt, delivered by preachers who were themselves examples of freedom from any theological tradition. It came from the Protestant Peale and from the Jewish Liebman.

And from the Roman Catholic establishment came Rochester's Bishop Fulton J. Sheen, whose preaching style seemed to be just the right blend of ecclesiastical prestige and personal charm, as he floated into America's living rooms through the newest medium, television.

By the middle of the twentieth century, the gospel of freedom had been mellowed into a mild, middle-class dream of deliverance from anxiety, emotional distress, and psychic pain. And a new doctrinal orientation could be clearly identified: Will Herberg, a sociologist of religion, identified the secularized, nonsectarian faith of the age in his 1955 book *Protestant, Catholic, Jew* and called this new religion "the American Way of Life." It had become evident to Herberg that an American civil religion had supplanted the separate theological convictions of the nation's several religious communities. Religion had reached the full freedom not to be religious any longer. It had evolved into a secular phenomenon that expressed the values of the prevailing culture.

The voices of pulpit-pounding evangelists were scarcely silent, of course. Billy Graham emerged in the late 1940s as the widely popular heir of the techniques developed a century earlier by Finney: a smoothly organized, coolly efficient, carefully managed system of crusades gave Graham the means to offer a passionately proclaimed word that freedom from personal or social captivity required individual salvation. If one were ill or ill-housed, depressed or economically deprived, the first step to hope required spiritual renewal. An individual had to accept Jesus Christ as his or her personal savior. And in the customary revivalist style, Graham's sermons describing the world's wickedness and doom concluded with intense appeals for repentance and regeneration.

Not every form of captivity, however, can be erased by an individual's decision to repent of personal sinfulness and be born again. As Niebuhr had realized early in the twentieth century, even a moral person can be overpowered by an immoral society. And in the late 1950s a young black preacher emerged with new ways to tell America so. Martin Luther King, Jr., the son of an Atlanta preacher, earned his doctorate at Boston University. With unsurpassed eloquence and an ability to find radically direct means to assert the Gospel's claim of freedom, King quickly became the messenger of hope for a captive people. He identified and employed methods of protest that could attack racial injustice, expose it publicly, and arouse wider public support for his cause.

King's sermons on peace and love were the inspiration for thousands to march, to boycott, to sit-in, and to face martyrdom in the cause of black freedom in America. His was a different version of open-air preaching: sometimes done in the streets, sometimes in massive rallies, and sometimes in sweaty church auditoriums that spilled over into sidewalk protests using "non-violent direct action." King was the embodiment of the best black preaching traditions. A prophet like Moses, he was a political figure whose prestige and power could never be separated from his preaching. He could sway a congregation with the rhythmic cadence of well-spoken phrases. He could merge the biblical stories of captivity and freedom with the personal experiences of black people. He could illustrate the principles of his preaching by taking to the streets, confronting those in authority, and surrendering to their jails. In captivity he led the way to freedom.

Nor could he be confined to a pulpit. By the middle of the twentieth century, that freedom seemed to be one of the clear trends in the history of American preaching. The Mathers and their colleagues in New England were men of the pulpit, whose stature and service were derived from their primary roles as preachers to a congregation. Such ministries as they extended to the larger community were expressions of their sermons, which were delivered to a congregation of the elect, whom God had chosen to be saints in the world, gathered in settled communities. Francis Asbury managed a movable pulpit, for himself and for the preachers he deployed to reach people wherever they gathered. Charles G. Finney tested his pulpit techniques on the frontier but took them—personally and by his influence upon others—into houses of worship where Christians gathered. Henry Ward Beecher did everything from running guns to freeing slaves from his pulpit. Stephen Wise made the pulpit the sacred ground of freedom. Harry Emerson Fosdick did his counseling from his pulpit. In nearly every case until the middle of the twentieth century, no matter how widely extended their ministries became, preachers worked from and for a base in a worshiping congregation.

The electronic age may have changed that entirely. Robert Schuller, a preacher whose message focuses on "possibility thinking," a version of Peale's message, built a base of operations at his Crystal Cathedral. The glass house of worship was constructed not with congregational funds alone, but with resources raised through television appeals, and it represents, as a structure, the accessibility and wide range of Schuller's ministry through television.

More illustrative of the point, perhaps, is Jimmy Swaggart. Heir to Finney in his emotionally provocative devices for making revivalist appeals, heir to Lyman Beecher in his anti-Catholic venom, and heir to Peter Cartwright in his conviction that education may be a hindrance to the proclamation of the Gospel, Swaggart exploits the electronic age. His ministry is that of a preacher to the nation, and his pulpit is present wherever there is a television screen or a phonograph.

Or again there is Jerry Falwell, who as pastor of Thomas Road Baptist Church in Lynchburg, Virginia, operates from a pulpit that not only fails to contain him, but is almost an auxiliary to his larger sense of ministry. He sees himself laboring on behalf of the moral and military defense of the American nation, preaching the message that freedom is to be found within the American way of life.

These preachers in the late twentieth century seem convinced that freedom has already been achieved in the nation, and the role of the society is to protect that freedom against any threat, at any cost. For some of the most popular preachers in America, the city set on a hill has been established and now must become a fortress. But that is only one form of freedom. There are preachers of liberation who can carry the vision of Gladden and King into the late twentieth century. Convinced that freedom has yet to be found, they preach to an age that is reluctant to let go of its civil religion and its secular salvation. There are, as well, differences among preachers about the relationship between freedom and the heritage of their separate traditions. Some resist the disappearance of doctrine and dogma into secular civility, insisting that true freedom can be found only within the contours of theological commitment.

So, the message in the history of American preaching finds new forms. What remains is the pursuit of freedom. But perhaps the culture, rather than the dogma of faith, now defines what that freedom means.

BIBLIOGRAPHY

Sydney E. Ahlstrom, *A Religious History of the American People* (1972); Emory Elliot, *Power and Pulpit in Puritan New England* (1975); Solomon Bennett Freehof, *Modern Jewish Preaching* (1941); Carol V. R. George, *Segregated Sabbaths: Richard Allen and the Rise of Independent Black Churches, 1760–1840* (1973); Nathan Glazer, *American Judaism* (1957); DeWitte T. Holland, *Sermons in American History: Selected Issues in the American Pulpit, 1630–1967* (1971) and, as ed., *The Preaching Tradition: A Brief History* (1980).

Leon A. Jick, *The Americanization of the Synagogue, 1820–1870* (1976); Phyllis M. Jones, *Salvation in New England: Selections from the Sermons of the First Puritans* (1977); Ralph H. Jones, *Charles Albert Tindley: Prince of Preachers* (1982); Henry H. Mitchell, *Black Preaching* (1970); Jacob Neusner, *American Judaism: Adventure in Modernity* (1972); H. Shelton Smith, Robert T. Handy, and Lefferts A. Loetscher, *American Christianity: An Historical Interpretation with Representative Documents,* 2 vols. (1960–1963).

[*See also* LITURGY AND WORSHIP; MASS COMMUNICATIONS; PASTORAL CARE AND COUNSELING; PROFESSIONAL MINISTRY; *and* WOMEN AND RELIGION.]

RELIGIOUS ARCHITECTURE
AND LANDSCAPE

Peter W. Williams

FROM the beginnings of the European colonization of the New World, the diversity of attitudes toward the religious significance of place,
space, and structure, which continues into the
present, was manifest in the variety of sites for
worship devised by both aboriginal inhabitants
and newcomers. Catholic and Protestant, Puritan and Anglican, Aztec and Algonquian, each
had a distinctive approach to the question of
where and in what structural context worship
might best be conducted. The interaction of
these groups in the ferment introduced into the
"virgin land" by the European intruders, who
were confronted with seemingly endless and
open space and a whole new range of physical
environments, added the issue of adaptation and
mutual relationship to the diverse heritages already present or then undergoing transplanta-
tion. Continuing contact over the centuries with
European development and the growth of indigenous American religious movements all added
to the complexity, as did the ongoing interplay
between secular and sacred architectural development. The study of this endlessly rich and
complicated dialectic provides an insight into the
history of the American religious experience
based on geographical and material rather than
purely verbal evidence and thus is a provocative point of departure for understanding that
experience.

The "Indians" whom the French, Spanish,
English, Dutch, and African newcomers encountered in the New World were by no means homogeneous in their religious cultures. One major
difference, which had profound implications for
worship sites, was between the settled, agriculturally oriented tribes of the South and Southwest and the hunters and gatherers of the northern forests and plains. Temples, such as the

monumental pyramids of the Aztecs, were characteristic of the settled peoples and exhibited
structural characteristics that resembled those in
a variety of other cultures. (Similar structures
were also erected by the early inhabitants of the
lower Mississippi Valley.) Among other tribes,
such as the Pueblo, that had fixed dwellings,
those dwellings themselves exhibited a religious
character in their deliberate design as microcos-
mic representations of the larger cosmos. "Religion" as it was known to Europeans, as a separable aspect of cultural activity, was a foreign
concept to Amerinds, who lived in a sacred manner. Among more mobile hunters and gatherers,
aspects of the land took on symbolic dimensions
of cosmic orientation, and sites could become
temporarily sacred for the duration of rituals
performed as the tribe moved from place to
place.

For the vast majority of European colonists,
the notion of movable sacred places and
the absence of a concept of private property
were incomprehensible, and this incomprehen-
sion helped to precipitate a cultural clash that
would ultimately end in the displacement or an-
nihilation of the aboriginal inhabitants. The notion of religious dwellings as spatially orienting
and even as microcosms, however, was not completely alien. Christian churches had traditionally been designed so that their most sacred part,
the sanctuary, faced the east, and Gothic cathedrals have been interpreted as symbolically re-
creating the entire Christian cosmos in their statuary programs. Cathedrals in Europe were often
erected on the most prominent physical sites
available, so that they overshadowed and dominated the towns in which they were situated; parish churches, though less obtrusive, fulfilled a
variety of secular functions and gave an ontologi-

cal as well as a social focus to a community. These symbolic functions were frequently recapitulated in the New World, although significant differences were beginning to emerge among the recently divided branches of Christendom, and reflected in the different colonial enterprises.

The colonization of New Spain, part of which now forms the southwestern portion of the United States, is a good illustration of the importation of European attitudes toward religious space and building and their adaptation to the circumstances of a new social and physical environment. The mission churches erected from Texas to California by the friars, primarily Franciscan, were inspired by the architectural ideas of the Spanish Renaissance and Baroque styles, but were often built by Indian workers using indigenous techniques of construction and materials, especially adobe.

The churches followed in their basic plans the traditional Catholic scheme; that is, a rectangular nave with the far end reserved for the altar, the focus of worship. In later churches, which were inspired by Baroque ideals, special lighting effects were employed to accentuate the altar through the play of light against dark spaces. In Texas, especially, the importation of European craftsmen resulted in churches, such as Mission San José y San Miguel de Aguayo in San Antonio (1720–1731), that utilized vaulting and domes never attempted by Indian workers and an elaboration of carving in the facade approaching that of the spectacular creations of the Mexican Churrigueresque style. None of the mission churches in these areas, however, ever equaled the sophistication that was achieved farther south or in the mother country, and the missions of California, the best known but last to be built (San Carlos Borromeo in Carmel, for example, dates from after the American Revolution), were quite simple and primitive compared even with those of Texas.

Just as mission architecture consisted of simplified, even crude (though often dramatically effective) adaptations of Spanish styles to colonial circumstances, the settings in which they took their place also reflected European conceptions much more than those of the original inhabitants of the land. Missions were erected for the conversion of Indians not only to Christianity but to settled, routinized patterns of existence,

and the mission compound gave a visual and material focus to the lands that the missionaries attempted to teach their charges to cultivate.

In larger new communities where the Spanish themselves planned to live, a similar preoccupation with order and hierarchy was reflected in the spatial arrangements. Towns in northern New Spain were laid out on strictly rectilinear grids so far as possible, and their center was a *zócalo,* or plaza, flanked by governmental buildings on one side and ecclesiastical structures on the other. Church and state were to be the twin foci of a stable European society, and the size, style, and siting of a town's principal structures reinforced this social model both functionally and symbolically. Beyond the town lay wilderness, the proper realm only of un-Christianized savages.

In the other Catholic regions of the North American colonies, a similar process of adaptation of Old World traditions to New World circumstances took place, though on a smaller scale and with virtually no influence from the less populous indigenous peoples. In the English Catholic colony of Maryland, which rapidly succumbed to Anglican control, Catholic worship could only take place in private structures, so that priestly residences functioned as "mass houses" as well. Private chapels or dwellings took the place of churches and were often the houses of the Jesuits, who maintained sizable plantations. In New France, parish churches reflected the modes of the period in the old country, and the fusion of late-medieval techniques with some of the new classical ornament of the Renaissance appears similar to contemporary vernacular developments in the Île de France.

Whether French, Spanish, or English in flavor, Catholic worship throughout the colonies reflected a characteristic attitude toward liturgical space. The church was a distinctive spatial realm, set off from the profane world by a series of gradations, each of which came increasingly closer to the locus of sacred power. The vestibule, or narthex, marked an area of transition, a *liminal* space, between outside and inside. The nave, in which the laity sat or stood, was the beginning (and largest part) of the church itself and was usually entered only after a ritual purification from the holy water stoup at its entrance. The chancel was divided into two parts: the choir, originally the place of monks who chanted the office, and the sanctuary, the place where the officiating priest conducted the sacrifice of the Mass at the altar. The altar itself was the focus of the entire church and was fixed in the holiest of ecclesiastical space. Some modification of this scheme took place with a Baroque accentuation of the altar by creative use of lighting or the erection of preaching halls adjoining the church for the use of Franciscan or Dominican friars focusing on the Word rather than the sacrament, but the idea that the church was a sacred space, hierarchically divided and dominated by the clergy, remained a constant.

The polar extreme to this notion of liturgical space was carried to the New World by the English Puritans, who were direct descendants of the Reformed tradition that had originated in the Switzerland of Calvin and Zwingli. Reformed influence rapidly spread through France, the Netherlands, the British Isles, and ultimately to New England in the 1620s and the following decades. Here the focus of worship was no longer the sacraments but rather the proclaimed and preached Word of God. Although the idea of the Real Presence of Christ in the Eucharist was not rejected by Calvin and his followers (who did not follow the more radical course chosen by Zwingli), the altar of Catholic tradition was displaced by the less conspicuous table, and the pulpit became the major focus of liturgical interest. In addition, the whole Catholic notion of the church as creating a sacred space was abandoned. The physical setting for worship was no different from any other secular space and only had to provide an appropriate setting for the preached Word.

The Calvinists clearly rejected the Old Testament notion of the temple, but did follow the Hebrew tradition in their iconoclastic prohibition of all religious figures and scenes as idolatrous. Calvinism, in short, favored a neutral, functional, unornamented place as normative for the proper setting for Christian worship, an ideal diametrically opposed to what had heretofore prevailed throughout both Eastern and Western Christendom.

Whether on the Continent or in the British Isles, however, the Reformers had little opportunity to create new houses of worship designed and built according to their own specifications. Where they were an illicit minority, as they were at different periods in England and France, they followed the early Christian pattern of worshiping covertly in private houses, barns, or other secular structures. When they were recognized as legitimate or had attained power, they generally contented themselves with adapting already existing medieval churches by destroying the statuary and other ornaments and rearranging the liturgical fixtures to suit their new needs.

In the wilderness of New England, such constraints no longer applied, and the Puritans of Plymouth, Massachusetts Bay, and later colonies were free to erect structures according to their own needs, tastes, and resources. Their task was rendered both more creative and more problematic by the fact that, just as they had no constraints, they also had no precedents. Their solution was to create an essentially new form of house of worship, the meetinghouse. This was a building distinguished not so much by a fixed shape but rather by a distinctive function or set of functions. In both design and conception it probably had roots in the English town halls of the Middle Ages, which served a variety of secular purposes of commerce and governance, as well as in Dutch and British Reformed worship. These new meetinghouses similarly combined a variety of functions and were utilized not only for worship but also as forts, courthouses, schools, and sites for what would become the New England town meeting. Most of these functions were later removed to separate structures as society became increasingly complex and differentiated, but the idea that the house of worship was intrinsically sacred and ought to be distanced from the common round of secular activity was clearly rejected in practice as well as theory.

The earliest Puritan worship in New England was conducted in private homes or in crude meetinghouses that seldom stood for very long. As the settlements grew more populous and prosperous, a general type of meetinghouse began to emerge. It was square or rectangular, with a hipped roof, and had its main entrance located on one of the long sides when the building was rectangular. Inside the focus was on an elevated pulpit, which was located directly opposite the entrance in the center of the opposing long side. Pews were of the box type, and pew ownership was directly based on social status, with those belonging to the most prestigious individuals of the community closest to the pulpit. The Old Ship Meetinghouse in Hingham, Massachusetts, built in 1681, is the only surviving example of a seventeenth-century meetinghouse. It is currently known as First Parish–Old Ship Church.

The furnishing and decoration of these meetinghouses followed the Reformed rejection of the notion that the structure was in any way sacred. The term *Puritan plain style* has often been used to describe this iconoclastic austerity, although its accuracy has been questioned on the grounds that nonpictorial wood carving and other ornaments were frequently quite elaborate. (A parallel with Islamic art seems quite clear here.) All of the material apparatus connected with worship, especially the Lord's Supper, was purely functional in design and conception. Where the Catholic church had developed an elaborate set of accoutrements of cloth, metal, and wood with Latinate names to be employed in the consecration and distribution of the elements, the Puritans simply used a long table, bread plates, and an assorted collection of cups and flagons, all of domestic provenance, as their only material aids. The pulpit, the visual and symbolic focus of the interior, was often elaborately carved and of fine wood, but bore no pictorial representations of religious subjects.

The site of the meetinghouse also held symbolic significance, one that was more in continuity than disjunction with its medieval predecessors. Just as the cathedral or parish church had functioned as a symbolic and social center for its community, often distinguished by its location on a hilltop or other conspicuous place, so was the meetinghouse deliberately placed at the center of each new Puritan settlement, with civil and ecclesiastical functions deliberately combined. The phrase *meetinghouse hill* entered the New England vocabulary as a synonym for the town's focal point. Together with an adjacent training ground, town common, graveyard, and parsonage, the meetinghouse in the earliest years of settlement marked the center of each newly covenanted community, and social rank was discernible from the proximity of a citizen's holdings to that center. This ideal was by no means consistently adhered to as the years rolled on and society diversified; in its pure form, however, it combined the continuity of the New England settlers with ancient medieval settlement patterns and an emphasis on the meetinghouse as the locus in which social and religious unity were manifested in tandem, separate but cooperative

forces freely intermixing in this new definition of religious space.

In its earliest manifestations in the American colonies, Anglicanism also expressed itself as a fusion of the old and new. St. Luke's Church in Isle of Wight County, Virginia, usually dated 1632, is very similar to the parish churches of New France in its combination of a handful of Renaissance (neoclassical) decorative elements on Gothic form. This appears to be a genuine survival, a carryover of a time-honored popular building tradition with just the barest hints of awareness that an architectural revolution was in the offing. The Anglicanism of the period was characterized by more tensions than simply those of form. From its beginnings, the Church of England was in an almost continual state of ferment over the proper architectural setting for worship conducted according to the *Book of Common Prayer*. The Protestant party, which would eventually develop into the Puritan movement, insisted on the elimination of traditional "popish" forms and the substitution of the iconoclastic, preaching-centered Reformed ideal. What would eventually become the Laudian "High Church" party, on the other hand, disliked the Puritan insistence that the secular term *table* definitively replace the traditional *altar* and promoted a liturgical arrangement that would focus on the celebration of the Eucharist.

A typically Anglican compromise began to emerge in the work of Christopher Wren, who was commissioned to replace many of the churches that had been destroyed in the great fire of London in 1666. For Wren, the ideal church was "auditory" in character, one that made it possible for all the assembled congregants to hear the preached Word clearly. His churches were centralized in design and were usually undivided rectangular rooms that lacked the altar screens which had symbolically and physically separated the sanctuary, the domain of the clergy, from that of the laity. The pulpit did not eclipse the table (or altar); rather the primary "liturgical centers"—font, altar/table, pulpit, and reading desk—were arranged in a harmonious balance. After the Restoration in 1660, the "three-decker" pulpit, which combined the reading pew and clerk's seat with the preaching center, became popular and was a familiar feature in colonial as well as English churches.

RELIGIOUS ARCHITECTURE AND LANDSCAPE

This liturgical ideal, expressed in buildings in the neoclassical or Georgian style, became the normative setting for colonial Anglican worship, although its actual expression varied considerably according to local tastes and circumstances. Since Anglicanism was the official religion of the mother country, it was more widely distributed along the Atlantic seaboard than virtually any other group, such as the Puritan Congregationalists of New England, the Quakers of Pennsylvania and New Jersey, or the Maryland Catholics. In the South, where it was universally established, it attracted an aristocratic clientele that could follow its written prayer-book services and travel to the scattered and isolated churches that were accessible primarily by water. (Much of the southern Tidewater was oriented around plantations, and cities or even villages were unusual.)

Most of the surviving colonial Anglican churches of the South were built of brick in rectangular or cruciform shape and were ornamented with Georgian embellishments according to the wealth of the congregation. Christ Church in Lancaster County, Virginia, endowed by the wealthy Robert "King" Carter in 1732, was a model of elegance for its time and place, while others, such as Merchants' Hope Church in Prince George County (ca. 1715), were considerably less pretentious. Many of these structures lacked towers and spires and resembled more the domestic models of New England than the classic Wren church that their northern counterparts reflected.

Anglican churches in the middle and northern colonies varied considerably in architectural form, but after 1720 frequently followed what was then emerging as the classic Wren church, which would be so influential in American design for many denominations. These churches, which rose more frequently as the distaste for Anglicanism began to wane in many northern areas (especially New England), were characteristically rectangular in shape, with a "long" pitched roof rather than a hipped one. They were liturgically oriented along the long axis, with the altar or table at the east end opposite the main entrance; had one or more rows of windows, the uppermost round topped; and were finished with a bell tower and spire, cupola, or steeple. In New York and New Jersey they were frequently constructed of brownstone, while wood prevailed in New England, especially in rural areas. Anglicanism in the North usually flourished in the more cosmopolitan urban areas, which provided sufficient wealth and taste to sponsor some of the most sophisticated buildings of the period and which soon aroused the emulation of their more "evangelical" neighbors.

Although the earliest Anglican churches in New England had looked much like the dominant Puritan meetinghouses, the turn of the eighteenth century brought about a reversal of this line of influence. Christ Church (Old North) in Boston of revolutionary war fame, built in 1723, was the first of these Wren-style churches, and was soon reproduced in general outline in nearby Congregational Old South Meetinghouse in 1729. The combination of tower and spire, which in later centuries would be an almost inextricable part of the American image of what a church (especially a New England church) ought to look like, was irresistible in its elegance and vertical thrust to all but the Friends, who persisted in their domestic, plain-style, pulpitless meetinghouses indefinitely. It rapidly displaced the Puritan ideal among Baptists as well as Congregationalists, even when a tower had to be tacked to the side of a meetinghouse with its main entrance on the long side (as was done, for example, by Congregationalists in Farmington, Connecticut).

Once this basic form had become established and widely accepted, American versions began to reflect changes of taste and form in the mother country in successive waves. James Gibbs replaced Wren as England's premier architect, and his work became well known in the colonies through pattern books. Imitations and adaptations of St. Martin-in-the-Fields, with its massive classical porch and many-storied steeple, soon appeared from Boston (King's Chapel, 1749) to Providence (First Baptist Meetinghouse, 1774–1775) to Philadelphia (Christ Church, 1727) to Charleston (St. Michael's, 1752–1761).

After 1800, the more delicate Adam style (named for Robert Adam, the great British architect) was translated by Charles Bulfinch and others into the Federal style in the new republic and was manifested in such fine houses of worship as Bulfinch's Lancaster, Massachusetts, meetinghouse of 1816–1817. These styles were then carried west by New Englanders moving into Ohio's Western Reserve and points beyond, as illustrated by the "typical New England church" designed and built by Connecticut-born Lemuel Porter in 1821 on the town green of Tallmadge, Ohio.

Bulfinch's work marked a transition within the now firmly established tradition of classicism from a free adaptation of classically inspired forms to a stricter adherence to the canons of the Greeks and Romans, especially as archaeological investigations of the late eighteenth century were providing more accurate information about those canons. Besides their aesthetic and historical appeal, both Greek and Roman styles attained a special popularity in the new American nation because of their ideological resonances. The new republic craved a distinctively republican style of architecture, and these were the most obvious and attractive models at hand. (In the South, the alternate association of Greek buildings with a slave-holding aristocracy added another iconic dimension to the architecture of the period.)

Roman and Greek forms were adopted not only among the Evangelical denominations, but also by a wide range of other religious groups, from Swedenborgian to Roman Catholic, that were beginning to thrive and multiply in the heady new atmosphere of religious pluralism. Archbishop John Carroll of Baltimore, for example, was presented by his architect, Benjamin Latrobe, with a choice of Gothic and Roman models for his new cathedral and somewhat surprisingly, perhaps, elected the latter. The great domed structure (1804–1818) that resulted no longer serves as the Baltimore cathedral but remains a great monument to the taste of the period, as does the Greek-modeled St. Peter-in-Chains Roman Catholic cathedral in Cincinnati (1845). Examples of the Greek revival on a smaller scale include the Congregational Church in Madison, Connecticut; the Swedenborgian Church in Bath, Maine; and the African Methodist Episcopal Church in Oxford, Ohio, all built from the 1830s to the 1850s.

A distinctive American ecclesiastical style—or, perhaps more accurately, a cluster of related styles all based on classical precedent—was thus emerging as the preferred option for a wide variety of religious groups. The Sephardic Jewish congregation of Newport, Rhode Island, commissioned Peter Harrison, America's first professional architect, to construct an appropriate house of worship. The result was the splendid Touro Synagogue, which was executed in the neoclassical mode between 1759 and 1763. Most of these buildings were erected by congregations or bishops of relative wealth and taste.

Another cluster of forces that would have a very different impact on American notions of religious space had its origin in the Great Awakening of the 1730s and 1740s, a movement that reflected both the impact of the frontier and a deep-seated resentment of "establishment" in its various senses. The main significance here of the Great Awakening was not so much architectural as geographical. One of the principal ways in which its proponents offended the establishment was in their repudiation of the "parochial principle," the notion shared alike by Anglicans, Puritans, and Catholics that each social and geographical unit was to be served by one single church and by that church only. The violence done to this principle by the awakening is illustrated in material form to this day by the two Congregational churches that stand side by side only a few yards from one another on the New Haven, Connecticut, town green. When the First Church was split on the question of the revival, the schismatics defied the notion that they were obliged to attend the parent church by founding a rival one, United Church, next door. This repudiation of establishment and parochiality eventually helped to prevent or bring to an end the establishment of religion at both federal and state levels, and resulted in a new division of religious space where the rival "turfs" of competing denominations overlapped one another. The traditional medieval pattern of neat geographical division with religious, social, and political space each coextensive with the other was banished forever; it could now be achieved only by such denominations as the Roman Catholic, which enforced the principle within its own polity and at times attained an overwhelming numerical superiority in neighborhoods or regions.

Another result of the Great Awakening was the stimulation of evangelical and revivalistic activity among the newer denominations such as the Methodists and Baptists, which had their own distinctive approaches to the question of religious space. For each, functionalism rather than aesthetics was the dominant principle. John Wesley, Methodism's founder, retained the Anglican commitment to both preaching and sacraments, and favored an octagonal form for churches as most conducive to the hearing of the preached Word. His American followers tended to downplay the sacramental and adapted their buildings to the needs and resources of a young and aggressively evangelical denomination.

American Methodism's legendary contribution to American religious life, the circuit-rider system, dispensed with buildings entirely, although churches rapidly began to dot the villages and crossroads of the frontier as congregations became settled. This Methodist propensity for carefully controlled expansion and organization stood in sharp contrast with the fiercely localistic genius of the frontier Baptists. Where their Rhode Island forerunners had erected meetinghouses in the Wren and Gibbs styles, the farmer-preachers of the South and West spread their message from any platform that presented itself and baptized their converts in the closest river or creek.

Religious building on the ever-expanding frontier followed in general pattern, though not in detail, the experience of the early French and Spanish missionaries in the far North and the Southwest. Missionaries or, more likely in the case of American Protestants, congregations and individual members of the laity carried with them images of what a church should look like derived from their early experiences in the East or in Europe. Their earliest churches were log cabins or, on the prairies, sod huts, quickly and cheaply erected from available materials to provide rudimentary shelter. After settlement was sufficiently advanced to allow the building of more permanent structures, memories of church form melded with available materials and human skills to produce small churches (or temples or synagogues) reflecting in stylized ways this ad hoc merger of distinctive shape and ornament with simple, even crude frameworks, usually of the readily available wood. (Stone and brick were out of the question in most cases.) Distinguishing features varied from Russian Orthodox onion domes to Greek-revival temple fronts, each providing a clue to the congregation's particular identity or, as in the case of the increasingly popular Gothic revival, simply identifying it as belonging to some denomination of Christianity.

Established denominations with Old World or colonial lineage were not the only religious groups attracted to the opportunities of the fron-

tier. From the beginning the American land itself had acquired a symbolic character for new settlers, ranging from the vision of earthly paradise of the Spaniards to the biblical images of exile, or errands, in the wilderness evoked among the Puritans by the bleak but subtly attractive New England landscape. With the founding of the new nation, a Jeffersonian vision of virgin land in the Mississippi Valley and yet farther west presented this territory as a great tabula rasa upon which the visions of an egalitarian and agriculturally based democracy could be fashioned through readily available, rectilinearly plotted farmsteads. Small sectarian groups such as the Hutterites continued to migrate from Europe to seek freedom to pursue unconventional ways undisturbed by the conventions and biases of overly inquisitive and censorious neighbors. Images of Eden and Jerusalem abounded in the rhetoric of the time, giving the land itself a religious meaning.

The period from roughly 1820 to the Civil War was a hotbed of what Alice Felt Tyler has called Freedom's Ferment, a time when the past seemed to have lost its grip and the vision of unbounded land and free institutions held out the promise of experiments in social organization that would put an end to the vicissitudes of history and help to bring in the millennium, which a century earlier Jonathan Edwards himself had envisioned as beginning in the New World. Utopian communities of the most fantastic variety, ranging from rationalistic socialism to the most authoritarian theocracies, began to spread from New England increasingly farther west, until the coast of California marked an end to the possibilities of further expansion.

The Shakers, who in their heyday established nineteen permanent settlements ranging from Maine to Kentucky, were among the most successful in establishing a new self-contained social order that would endure, if not for a thousand years, at least for more than a century. Even more successful in quantifiable terms were the Mormons, or Latter-day Saints, who succeeded in creating what for a time was a virtual empire in the hitherto barren salt flats of Utah, and who would endure, after making necessary compromises with political and social reality, as one of America's major distinctive religious subcultures.

Both Shakers and Mormons committed themselves not simply to particular beliefs but to patterns of life that required highly specialized geographical and architectural settings for their successful realization. For the Shakers, reality was divided into two realms. The visible was that in which the millennium was being realized through the communal efforts of highly disciplined, ascetic, and celibate believers for whom every mundane activity was an act of dedication. The architectural expression of this aspect of life took the form of what might be called a sanctified intentional vernacular, where the American tradition of wood and metal craftsmanship, simplicity of line, and subordination of form to function received a theological legitimation. On the other hand, the transcendent dimension of Shaker spirituality received expression in their highly ornate "spirit drawings" and the ecstatic dances that were conducted in the "heavenly space" of the "New Jerusalem," the imagined realm of the world beyond. Worship took place in a meetinghouse that, though externally domestic in appearance, was revealed upon entrance to be a large, bright, and dazzling space symbolic of the release from discipline and regimentation in the realized millennial kingdom. Another noteworthy dimension of Shaker building was its symmetry, in which the side-by-side entrances into communal dwellings for each sex reflected the distinctive theology of founder Mother Ann Lee.

The architectural evolution of the Mormons also reveals their roots in American vernacular culture, but their patterns of spatial organization demonstrate an adaptation to that culture very different from that of the Shakers and other more radical communitarians of the era. The first Mormon settlement in Kirtland, in northeastern Ohio, was characterized by a short-lived experiment in communality of goods, and a temple (the first of many) based on the by now traditional New England church plan circulated in Asher Benjamin's pattern book. Onto this basic frame were grafted Gothic-style pointed windows, coigning at the corners, and other highly eclectic ornamental features, giving the overall design a slightly exotic and rather awkward appearance. Internal arrangements were even more singular in their adaptation to the emergent Mormon liturgy and included opposed sets of pulpits for the two priesthoods and reversible pews to permit the focusing of attention on the

different centers. A second floor provided space for the instruction of proselytes, while an attic was subdivided into meeting rooms and offices.

Further peregrinations eventually brought Joseph Smith and the Mormons to Nauvoo, Illinois, where the prophet was soon to meet his death. Before that traumatic occurrence, he attempted to construct a new city based on a grid plan that combined the pastoral symbolism of Eden in neatly arranged single-family dwellings with attached garden plots and a new urban Zion focused on a Nauvoo Temple and Nauvoo House, the latter for the use of the prophet and as an accommodation for visitors. The temple continued the patterns of its Kirtland predecessor on a grander scale, and its capitals were topped with celestial symbols constituting a new "Mormon order." Similar symbolic innovation based on biblical and Masonic themes also began to emerge in the baptismal font and other accoutrements designed for new liturgical functions. Inadequate planning, land speculation, and the encroachment of Gentiles ultimately culminated in the experiment's violent failure; and the journey west under Brigham Young's leadership in which the climactic phase of Mormon development would take place soon commenced.

Once the Mormons had reached the Great Salt Lake after their epic trek across the plains, the vast task of erecting a whole society on barren ground rallied them into an effort of community building of almost unprecendented magnitude. Irrigation turned the desert literally into a garden, and grid-based planned communities proliferated throughout what would eventually become the state of Utah. The most distinctive architectural achievement was the Salt Lake City Temple, built over a forty-year period under Young's direction and combining a highly disparate and at times original blend of features into the Mormon counterpart of a Gothic cathedral. Ordinary worship was conducted in more modest structures, also eclectic in character. With success came eventual expansion back eastward, as the gleaming white windowless towers and soaring needlelike spires of the Washington, D.C., temple bear witness.

While westward expansion was affecting the fortunes of "orthodox" and religious innovators alike, a revolution in ecclesiastical architecture was taking place that would rapidly have major consequences for church building across the entire nation and may be characterized without exaggeration as the most significant "paradigm shift" since the introduction of the Wren church. The Gothic revival had its genesis in that diffuse cultural movement known as romanticism, and its sources and expressions are nearly as varied as those of its literary counterparts. Early interest in Gothic manifested itself playfully in eighteenth-century England in Horace Walpole's Strawberry Hill and other dilettantish experiments of the era. Early in the nineteenth century, this enthusiasm for Gothic as a style of ornament featuring pointed arches, crenellations, pinnacles, and flying buttresses began to influence the design of American churches as well as secular buildings. Such ornament found its way onto the neoclassical churches by such major architects as Benjamin Latrobe (Christ Church, Washington, D.C., 1808) and even Charles Bulfinch, whose Federal Street Church in Boston (1809) accommodated the great Unitarian William Ellery Channing's fancy for romantic medievalism. John Henry Hopkins, the Episcopal bishop of Burlington, Vermont, gave ecclesiastical sanction to Gothic design in his *Essay on Gothic Architecture* (1836), but his knowledge and rationale were basically superficial. Ithiel Town's Trinity Episcopal Church on the New Haven Green (1814–1817) demonstrated a more sophisticated and sympathetic knowledge of Gothic design, but the basic shape of the church proclaimed its continuity with the New England colonial tradition.

The most important religious impetus to the Gothic revival also had its origins in England. At the time when the Oxford movement was promoting a more "Catholic" understanding of the nature of the Church of England and reappropriating the theological legacy of past ages to these ends, another group at Cambridge led by John Mason Neale and Benjamin Webb was advocating a similar recovery of the material religious heritage of the Middle Ages. Adherents of this Ecclesiological or Cambridge movement believed that they had discovered the key to true Christian symbolism in the work of Durand de Saint-Pourçain, a medieval French bishop, and identified one form of Gothic, the second or "Decorated" phase that flourished in England between 1260 and 1360, as the purest and most essential manifestation of that "most Christian of

styles." Their organization, the Cambridge Camden Society, promoted these views avidly and dogmatically in the periodical *Ecclesiologist* (commenced 1841) and achieved enormous influence at a time when the government was engaged in constructing hundreds of new churches and when many medieval buildings were being restored.

Their Roman Catholic counterpart, the architect Augustus Welby Pugin, added further polemical fuel to the flames through his *Contrasts* (1836), in which modern society and architecture were compared most unfavorably with the medieval past, and *The True Principles of Pointed or Christian Architecture* (1841), in which he demonstrated both a profound architectural knowledge of Gothic and a philosophical interpretation of it that anticipated what would be articulated and popularized on both sides of the Atlantic by John Ruskin in subsequent years. For both Pugin and Ruskin, Gothic was a "moral" style, and Christians were ill-advised to build in any other.

This architecturally more sophisticated and theologically informed phase of the Gothic revival found its way to the United States through a number of avenues. St. James-the-Less, an exquisite stone parish church, was built near Philadelphia between 1846 and 1848 through the efforts of a Philadelphia merchant according to plans supplied by the Cambridge Camden Society. The New York Ecclesiological Society, founded in 1848, set to work approving architects whom they felt were in sympathy with their own distinctively American version of the movement's philosophy. The most important conduit, however, was the English-born Richard Upjohn. Upjohn shared the High Church and Gothic sympathies of the movement, although he occasionally found himself at odds with its spokesmen over various points of contention. On the whole, however, he was in agreement with such basic liturgical premises as that a church's sanctuary was a holy place that should be visually and structurally distinguished from the nave. He also exhibited great sensitivity to such more general emphases of the mature Gothic revival as the idea that form should express function, that materials should be chosen and worked with respect for their essential integrity, and that a Gothic church should evoke a sense of mystery and solemnity as opposed to the lucidity of the neoclassical tradition. His Trinity

Church in New York (1839–1846) was a major advance in recapturing the spirit of medieval England, even though he was forced by circumstances to forgo the traditional vaulting methods he preferred. St. Mary's Church in Burlington, New Jersey (1846–1848), demonstrated his capacity to work in stone on a smaller and more intimate scale, as did numerous other suburban parish churches, mostly Episcopal, whose vestries rushed to bestow commissions upon him.

Upjohn was also instrumental in spreading the Gothic mode though the board-and-batten churches, a uniquely American adaptation that spread throughout the entire nation, rapidly gaining the nickname Carpenter Gothic. This method of construction and use of Gothic ornament had been popularized in the rural cottages designed by Alexander Jackson Davis, Andrew Jackson Downing, Calvert Vaux, and others as the quest for "picturesqueness," a popular version of the romantic movement, captured the imagination of the middle classes. Upjohn adopted this style for churches, both Episcopal and others, and his pattern book of 1852, *Upjohn's Rural Architecture,* which contained designs for a church and a chapel, inspired countless rural churches ranging from the "cute" to genuine works of art.

The result of the work of Upjohn, the New York Ecclesiologists, and their associates was the contribution of a new form to the American imagery of what a church should look like that would endure well into the twentieth century. On the exteriors, churches would boast buttresses, pinnacles and crockets, and pointed-arch windows, whether these were in conformity with the general style of the church or not. For Episcopalians especially, the effect on the interior spatial and decorative arrangements was even more definitive. Nave and sanctuary were differentiated by the elevation of the latter by several steps; the congregation sat in rows of slip pews while the clergy performed their functions; and the choir, at first only of men and boys, sat facing one another in the forward part of the chancel, perpetuating another Victorian innovation of two men with the Dickensian names of Jebb and Hook.

The "Gilded Age" that followed the upheavals of the Civil War witnessed a new direction in American social and demographic expansion which was centripetal, and the frontier's centrif-

ugal force began to dissipate as the century approached its conclusion. The city was now emerging as the major form of American social organization, and vast numbers of immigrants, few of them Protestant, arrived in the cities and toiled in the new industries that helped to generate urban growth. Churches that had once been suburban or even rural in their siting now found themselves surrounded by houses, stores, and factories, and the creeds that they represented were not attractive to the Catholics, Jews, and Eastern Orthodox who were transforming the nation's social fabric. A new era of church building thus commenced to meet these changes and challenges.

For Protestants, especially those in the wealthier and socially prominent classes, the new urban church would provide a monument to their status and a home for the "Princes of the Pulpit" whom they supported. The archetype of both church and man was H. H. Richardson's Trinity Church at Copley Square, Boston, which was built initially as a setting for Phillips Brooks, preacher extraordinary and later Episcopal bishop of Massachusetts. Trinity, perhaps the greatest example of the style that would come to be known as Richardsonian Romanesque, combined early medieval features with fine, warm stone, monumental massing, and intricacy of detail in a way that seemed at once elegant, traditional, and uniquely American. Its general features were subsequently diffused throughout the country in countless city halls, public libraries, college classroom buildings, and as facades for any number of "mainline" urban Protestant churches whose liturgical needs had not the slightest affinity with the tradition represented by the Romanesque. Richardson also helped to popularize the less monumental and more domestic "shingle style," which was taken up in a most creative way in the San Francisco Bay area in the churches of the English-born architect Ernest Coxhead.

Protestant response to the new urban context took a number of other forms. Evangelists such as the great Dwight L. Moody erected temporary "tabernacles" that were vast, rather shapeless halls constructed for his revivals and frequently converted later to secular uses. Emphasis was entirely on the function, and the form held no significance as long as vast throngs of listeners were able to hear the evangelist, participate in communal singing, and "hit the sawdust trail" easily. Even in Protestant churches unaffected by urban revivalism, the internal arrangements generally gave increasing prominence to the preacher, and platforms that could accommodate visitors and choirs supplanted the colonial pattern early in the century in many eastern cities. The "institutional church," which combined educational and recreational facilities with those for worship, was another adaptation of the time and resulted in major enlargements of the urban church's "plant."

The development of the Sunday school as a major component of the evangelical Protestant program during the early nineteenth century also led to structural change. As James F. White has noted, churches after 1830 frequently had an elevated "sanctuary," with the lower (ground) level given over to classroom space. Perhaps the most significant innovation of the period was the enormously successful Akron Plan, popularized by Ohio architect George W. Kramer and Lewis Miller, a Methodist minister in the city from which it took its name. The exterior could take almost any form, and many of the churches built by Kramer and others for Methodists, Baptists, and other mainline denominations that adopted the plan were in the Gothic, Romanesque, or classical revival styles popular at the time. Its distinctiveness was expressed in its interior arrangements, which were devised to accommodate both the traditional Protestant emphasis on preaching and, more specifically, large numbers of Sunday-school classes.

Akron Plan churches therefore consisted of adjoining church and Sunday-school auditoriums, the latter of which could be easily subdivided into small classroom units, so that the same space could be utilized for both collective opening exercises and the conduct of graded classes. When necessary, the two large spaces could be combined to accommodate especially large congregational assemblies. The seating layout was curved, with the pulpit platform in the center or a corner of the church auditorium, and opera-style seats were frequently utilized rather than pews. The resultant structures thus resembled "traditional" churches on the outside while appearing more like theaters within. With the rise of the departmentalized Sunday school early in the twentieth century, the Akron Plan rapidly declined in popularity.

The late nineteenth and early twentieth centuries were an age not only of Protestant migration from country and town to the city but also of the extremely rapid growth of the urban Catholic church. Enormous resources were channeled into the erection of Catholic churches as well as complete parish plants, since the Third Plenary Council of Baltimore in 1884 had established a mandate for the primary education of all Catholic children in parochial schools. Schools were thus often erected prior to the building of the church itself, and their auditoria served as places for worship until resources could be mustered for the church proper. In addition to the school and church, space was also necessary for the housing of the clergy and teaching sisters, and a rectory and convent were usual adjuncts.

Since the Catholic church clung tenaciously to the parochial principle, which had been abandoned long since as a formal desideratum by most Protestants, the geographical spread of Catholicism was uniform, and building programs were directed and coordinated from episcopal headquarters. In many predominantly Catholic neighborhoods, especially those where immigrants from Catholic lands had recently settled, the parish plant acquired the same function of spatial and social orientation that churches had traditionally exercised in ages past. Congregations sometimes numbered in the thousands, and churches were frequently constructed in monumental form to express their importance for their constituency and perhaps to impress the outside world with the Roman Catholic presence on the American scene as well.

Stylistically, the Catholic church had a wealth of tradition upon which to draw, and clues as to the ethnic composition of a congregation were often provided by a church's style. Romanesque, Gothic, and Renaissance in their various national varieties were the most popular, although Byzantine, Spanish Mission, and other forms appeared periodically as well. Other structures, such as high schools, colleges, seminaries (both minor and major), motherhouses for orders of sisters or nuns, hospitals, orphanages, and other "total institutions" were also prominent features of the Catholic religious landscape and were generally erected in the eclectic, monumental fashion of the Victorian era. Frequently mansions built for private use were donated to or purchased by the church, then converted into episcopal residences, convents, or college dormitories, thus adding an air of opulence to the Catholic presence. Finally, cemeteries specifically set apart for Catholic use completed the sacramental program of the church's geography, since burial was expected to take place in consecrated ground. (The "garden cemetery" movement of antebellum days, which had promoted landscaped, parklike urban grounds such as Cambridge's Mount Auburn and Cincinnati's Spring Grove, had already established a prototype for a distinctively urban mode of burial.) In most cities of the North, Midwest, and Southwest, it was difficult to escape continual notice that the Catholic church was rapidly becoming an integral part of the American city.

The great waves of immigration of the era also brought to America millions of Jews from Eastern and Central Europe, who were confronted with a very different problem in providing suitable houses of worship for themselves. Where Catholics had a rich set of architectural models upon which to draw, a distinctively Jewish style had never emerged during the centuries of diaspora in Europe, the Middle East, and North Africa. Jews had generally contented themselves with erecting synagogues in styles borrowed from "host" cultures, and the same strategy prevailed in America from the days of the Touro Synagogue. Some historical affinity was felt for the Byzantine and Moorish or Venetian Gothic styles more than others, as manifested in the latter case in the Isaac Meyer Wise Temple erected across from Cincinnati's Catholic cathedral in 1865 by Congregation B'nai Yeshurun. Early Eastern European congregations on New York's Lower East Side and elsewhere were usually both Orthodox and poor and had to content themselves with storefronts during their early days. With the eventual movement of large numbers of second- and third-generation Jews to the suburbs in the twentieth century, contemporary styles were readily adapted to the requirements of Jewish liturgy. Among Reform Jews, especially, services had come to resemble those of their liberal Protestant counterparts more than those of their Orthodox contemporaries. Eastern Orthodox Christians, the other major component of the great immigration, usually built in the traditional Byzantine-derived styles of Greece and Russia.

The final aspect of the religious dimensions of urban expansion in the era that came to an end with the Crash and the Great Depression was the last major phase of the Gothic revival. The Episcopal church had emerged in the post–Civil War period increasingly as that preferred by urban men and women of wealth and status, and an extraordinary financial reservoir was available for the undertaking of major building programs. The architect who emerged to direct this "campaign" was Ralph Adams Cram, a New Englander of Unitarian background who had become converted as a young man to High Church Anglicanism. Cram produced not only buildings but countless books and essays in which he argued that the Gothic was the only appropriate style not simply for correct Christian worship but also as an antidote to the cultural wasteland that had resulted from the combined onslaughts of Protestantism, rationalism, and the industrial revolution. Cram rejected not only such "un-Christian" styles as the fashionable Beaux Arts classicism (favored especially by the then new Christian Scientists), but also the eclectic polychromed Gothic that characterized such High Church structures as Boston's Church of the Advent. Instead he returned to the program of medieval restorationism that Upjohn had earlier begun, though substituting a preference for the English Perpendicular over the "Decorated" Gothic favored by his predecessor.

Both talented and persuasive, Cram received commissions for projects ranging from the suburban Boston parish church of All Saints, Ashmont, to the Cowley Fathers monastery in Cambridge, to the monumental Cathedral of St. John the Divine in Manhattan, allegedly conceived to meet the Roman Catholic challenge presented by James Renwick, Jr.'s, St. Patrick's Cathedral on Fifth Avenue. Cram also occasionally (and rather reluctantly) accepted commissions from other denominations (including the Swedenborgian Cathedral in Bryn Athyn, Pennsylvania, and the Princeton University Chapel), but was most comfortable when designing Episcopal churches, chapels, and cathedrals in the English Gothic mode. His buildings (many designed in collaboration with his sometime partner, Bertram Grosvenor Goodhue) remain as monuments not only of the final and most elaborate phase of the Gothic revival, but also as virtual museums of the "minor" arts of wood and stone carving and stained glass design. New York's St.

Thomas', designed in 1911 by Cram and Goodhue together, is a splendid example of this concern for detail, manifested especially in the elaborate reredos executed by Lee Lawrie. Although Cram was the most prolific architect in this movement, the English-born Henry Vaughan also deserves mention as a principal designer of the National Cathedral in Washington, D.C., another example of the Episcopalian campaign after the Civil War to erect a truly monumental ecclesiastical architecture that aimed to provide the entire nation with a visible religious focus.

Until the early twentieth century at least, the leadership in innovative religious architecture came primarily from the Northeast through such dominant figures as Richardson, Cram, and Goodhue, who worked primarily within the framework of the medieval revival. The South in general remained even more conservative. As the Evangelical denominations began to become more established as middle-class and urban churches, Methodists and Baptists built largely within the Greek-revival and Gothic modes (with internal arrangements freely interpreted to accommodate a "non-liturgical" style of worship), while Presbyterians often favored variations on the Georgian. Resistance to adoption of the more ornate revival styles gradually yielded to the desire for monumentality, just as indoor baptistries replaced the traditional rural Baptist custom of locating near a river or spring for outdoor rites of initiation. With some exceptions, such as the persistence of Spanish Mission influence and an occasional example of innovative excellence such as Bernard Maybeck's First Church of Christ, Scientist, in Berkeley, California (1909–1911), the West also tended to follow the lead of the East.

Although the Midwest was in many ways characterized by a conservative and even derivative bent in the realm of religious architecture, the roots of the last major "paradigm shift" in American church building were more directly located in this region than in the more sophisticated East or the culturally tolerant West. On the one hand, the movement that would come to be known across denominational lines as Liturgical Renewal had its origins among the Roman Catholic Benedictine order of monks, especially in the leadership of Virgil Michel of St. John's Abbey, Collegeville, Minnesota. Michel, who founded the journal *Orate Fratres* (later *Worship*) in 1925, helped to promote within the Catholic community the notion that liturgical celebration was a communal rather than a private act and that it had implications for both the life of the individual and the social realm. The great abbey church designed by Marcel Breuer some years after Michel's death remains a major monument to the impetus of the Liturgical movement's compatibility with progressive forces in architecture that would ultimately result in a vastly enlarged set of possibilities for Catholic and Protestant church building alike. The influence of modern European architects such as Breuer, Rudolf Schwartz, and Le Corbusier, and the actual design of many American churches by Europeans, were symbolic of the increasing cosmopolitanism of religious building as well as thought among American Catholics.

The other major midwestern impetus to change came from the thought and work of Frank Lloyd Wright, the son of a Wisconsin Unitarian minister. Although Wright's practice focused on houses and commercial structures, the few churches he designed, such as Unity Temple (1904–1906) in Oak Park, Illinois, demonstrated graphically the potential of the Prairie school for houses of worship. The temple, a Unitarian church, exhibited the possibilities of new building materials such as textured poured concrete, indirect access, horizontal rather than the traditional vertical lines of flow, de-emphasis on ornamental detail in favor of a rugged simplicity, and a commitment to the Wrightian philosophy, derived from that of Horatio Greenough and Louis Sullivan, that form ought to follow function.

It is perhaps needless to say that such radical new ideas did not triumph immediately among either Catholics or Protestants. At least until World War II, Catholics with sufficient resources preferred the creative but still traditional work of such firms as Maginnis and Walsh, which promoted Lombard Gothic as the most appropriate style for American circumstances. Protestants during the years between the world wars were beginning to organize denominational and ecumenical bureaus to provide advice on church architecture and construction, but such spokesmen as Elbert M. Conover, director of the Methodist Episcopal church's Bureau of Architecture from 1924 to 1934 and the author of innumerable books and pamphlets, promoted the Gothic as most appropriate for a Protestant worship now increasingly influenced by the principles of the Oxford and Cambridge movements. Similar arguments in favor of traditional forms were disseminated in the writings of the liberal Protestant Von Ogden Vogt and, of course, the indefatigable Episcopalian Ralph Adams Cram.

Even though the Georgian and even the Gothic persisted into the massive campaign of new and largely suburban church construction that followed World War II, a consensus was emerging among the theological and liturgical leaders within both Catholicism and mainline Protestantism that such an archaeological approach was simply not appropriate for their respective traditions' increasingly convergent understanding of the appropriate setting for Christian worship. A revived interest in history and especially in biblical studies made it clear that the heretofore favored revival styles were the products of specific cultural circumstances and certainly did not reflect the practice of the early church, which was coming to be widely regarded as normative for worship. European-born architects on the American scene, such as the Saarinens, and others of Asian extraction, such as Minoru Yamasaki and I. M. Pei, expanded the range of possibilities considerably, as did continuing technological advances that had begun with the appropriation of reinforced concrete and structural steel for ecclesiastical as well as secular building. A handful of architects, such as the Minnesota-based Lutheran E. A. Sovik, combined theological and technical expertise. Sovik helped build innovative churches for Catholic and Protestant alike, reflecting on the significance of his work in books such as *Architecture for Worship* (1973).

Leadership in the field of religious architectural innovation came from a number of fronts. Roman Catholics, as we have seen, had been prepared by the Liturgical movement and the subsequent ratification of its premises by Vatican II to commission such dramatic new ventures as Pietro Belluschi's St. Mary's Cathedral in San Francisco (1963), which utilized the hyperbolic paraboloid form to achieve a dazzling sense of lightness and verticality. Unitarians and Reform Jews, both free from an overpowering sense of tradition, also employed such progressively oriented architects as Louis Kahn (First Unitarian Church, Rochester, New York, 1958) and Philip Johnson (K.T.I. Synagogue, Port Chester, New York, 1956) to experiment with new possibilities of structure and design.

Liturgically oriented Lutherans and Episcopalians were probably the most likely to depart from traditional ways despite the seeming paradox of their deep roots in tradition, though examples of contemporary design can be found in virtually every denomination. Even Missouri Synod Lutherans, noted for their often extreme theological conservatism, have frequently placed themselves in the architectural vanguard (as with Christ Lutheran Church in Minneapolis).

Generalizations about "modern" or "contemporary" church architecture are more difficult to make than about, say, the revival styles of the nineteenth century, since variety and innovation are characteristic of this approach to building. Negatively, all such design rejects an explicit reliance on traditional forms, although a concern with symbolism (e.g., that of light and darkness) is common among all denominations. The use of steel, concrete, and other new materials has made possible a vast range of experiments in lighting, ranging from the completely windowless Episcopal Church of Saint Clement in Alexandria, Virginia (Joseph H. Saunders, 1948), to Philip Johnson's dazzling "Crystal Cathedral," built for television preacher Robert Schuller in Garden Grove, California, in 1979–1980. In general, however, modern churches have featured simplicity of line, directness of expression focusing on liturgical function, and an adaptability of space that permits expensive structures to be utilized for a variety of purposes in addition to the traditional Sunday-morning worship service.

All religious groups, however, are not willing and able to follow these trends, even as the twentieth century draws near a close. Black congregations in inner-city neighborhoods seldom are able to afford their own new structures and instead adapt either storefronts or formerly white churches whose congregations have left for the suburbs. Many urban Catholic churches have seen their constituency shift from Irish, Germans, or Poles to blacks and Hispanics, and have adapted the customs and uses of their worship and plants accordingly.

Another sort of problem posed by urbanization and demographic change has manifested itself for two of New York's monumental Episcopal churches, Cram's Cathedral of St. John the

Divine and Goodhue's St. Bartholomew's on Park Avenue. The cathedral, which has long been known as "St. John the Unfinished" after a decision was consciously made following World War II to suspend construction and divert resources to a social ministry in an increasingly poor neighborhood, reversed its policy and resumed construction in 1983, employing master craftspeople to train local youth in skilled trades. St. Bartholomew's in the 1980s was embroiled in a complicated congregational and legal dispute involving the sale of part of its parish house (designed by Goodhue) and air rights for the construction of a skyscraper, which would produce ample revenue for good works but which critics (including roughly half the congregation) maintained would detract from the human scale that the church and its grounds provide in the midst of an "urban wilderness." Both these churches, as well as the once towering St. Patrick's Cathedral, have also been displaced in their monumentality by the forest of high-rise buildings that surround them, an alteration in the cityscape of great potential symbolic import.

Finally, the major alteration in the religious landscape of the late twentieth century has been produced by the rapid growth of Evangelical and Holiness-Pentecostal denominations since the end of the Vietnam era. This growth has frequently resulted in the abandonment of these groups' formerly rather humble churches for new plants in massive scale and striking geometrical designs, often situated at the nodes of interstate highways and other major routes and flanked by vast fleets of buses for transporting Sunday-school students and worshipers from a wide surrounding area. Smaller versions of these same churches in rural areas are more traditional in design, usually featuring a conspicuous roadsign and a "Georgian" structure with a vestigial belfry on the top. These denominations thus reflect a certain ambivalence in their symbolic expression: when small and poor, they manifest an alignment with the American colonial tradition, correlating with the nationalistic politics of many of their members and clergy; when more successful, they demonstrate an independence of tradition perhaps appropriate to their origins in the Radical Reformation (the Anabaptist movement that rejected churches as worldly) and the American frontier. In any case, they represent well the mixture of traditionalism and innovation that has for nearly four centuries characterized the development of religious architecture in America.

BIBLIOGRAPHY

G. W. O. Addleshaw and Frederick Etchells, *The Architectural Setting of Anglican Worship* (1948); Laurel B. Andrew, *The Early Temples of the Mormons* (1978); Architectural Record, eds., *Religious Buildings* (1979); Peter Benes, ed., *New England Meeting House and Church: 1630–1850* (1979) and, with Phillip D. Zimmerman, *New England Meeting House and Church: 1630–1850* (exhibition catalog) (1979); Albert Christ-Janer and Mary Mix Foley, *Modern Church Architecture* (1962); Clifford E. Clark, Jr., "American Architecture: The Prophetic and Biblical Strains," in Giles Gunn, ed., *The Bible and American Arts and Letters* (1983); Ralph Adams Cram, *My Life in Architecture* (1936); John De Visser and Harold Kalman, *Pioneer Churches* (1976); Marian Card Donnelly, *The New England Meeting Houses of the Seventeenth Century* (1968); Stephen P. Dorsey, *Early English Churches in America, 1607–1807* (1952).

Donald Drew Egbert, "Religious Expression in American Architecture," in James Ward Smith and A. Leland Jamison, eds., *Religious Perspectives in American Culture* (1961); Anthony Garvan, "The New England Plain Style," in *Comparative Studies in Society and History*, vol. III (1960); Alan Gowans, *Church Architecture in New France* (1955); Dolores Hayden, *Seven American Utopias* (1976); Henry-Russell Hitchcock, *The Architecture of H. H. Richardson and His Times* (1966); Roger C. Kennedy, *American Churches* (1982); George Kubler, *The Religious Architecture of New Mexico* (1972); William Morgan, *The Almighty Wall: The Architecture of Henry Vaughan* (1983); Robert Muccigrosso, *American Gothic: The Mind and Art of Ralph Adams Cram* (1979); Richard Oliver, *Bertram Grosvenor Goodhue* (1982).

William H. Pierson, Jr., *American Buildings and Their Architects*, 4 vols. (1970–1978); Harold W. Rose, *The Colonial Houses of Worship in America* (1964); John Knox Shear, ed., *Religious Buildings for Today* (1957); Edward A. Sovik, *Architecture for Worship* (1973); Phoebe B. Stanton, *The Gothic Revival and American Church Architecture* (1968); John R. Stilgoe, *Common Landscape in America, 1580 to 1845* (1982); Paul Thiry, Richard M. Bennett, and Henry L. Kamphoefner, *Churches and Temples* (1953); Douglass Shand Tucci, *Church Building in Boston* (1974); Harold W. Turner, *From Temple to Meeting House* (1979); James F. White, *The Cambridge Movement* (1962) and *Protestant Worship and Church Architecture* (1964).

[*See also* LITURGY AND WORSHIP; *and* MATERIAL CULTURE AND THE VISUAL ARTS.]

RELIGION AND FILM

Henry Herx

IT is not difficult to understand why the medium of film attained a dominant place in the popular culture of the twentieth century. Film began as the century began—the ideal mass medium for the burgeoning industrial society of the United States. As the century progressed, its technological culture increasingly valued the image over the word and immediate experience over reflective thought. Television became the mass medium of the home midway through the century and forced film into other, more specialized directions. As the twenty-first century approaches, film faces new challenges from the younger electronic media, whose advances threaten to displace the celluloid world entirely.

Whatever the future of film holds, its contribution to contemporary culture remains indisputable, for it developed a new medium for narrative, the medium of moving pictures. It was the power of these moving pictures to affect and influence large numbers of people that concerned religious groups earlier in the century. Except for Britain, West Germany, and Japan, in most countries of Eastern and Western Europe, Latin America, Africa, and Asia, government has assumed the burden of safeguarding public morality by setting the standards of screen content. In contrast, the American film industry has always relied on self-regulation and has attempted to balance the demands of a profit-making business with, on the one hand, the right of free speech and, on the other hand, the good of society. Wary of the industry and believing it lax in self-regulation, religious groups have more often than not taken a negative rather than a positive role in the development of American film culture.

Beginning in the late 1950s, cultural critics and religious educators began looking at film as something more important than escapist entertainment. Indeed, during the 1960s some American movies were exploring the nature of human relationships and probing into the deeper causes of social injustice as never before. A number of these films were seen as having theological implications far beyond such moralistic concerns as the amount of skin exposed in a particular shot or the potential danger of a morally ambiguous scene.

Individual churches and temples began showing and discussing films by such foreign directors as Ingmar Bergman and Federico Fellini, and, closer to home, by John Ford and Fred Zinnemann. National Protestant and Catholic organizations such as the National Council of Churches and the U.S. Catholic Conference supported such film study efforts, but this interest in film as a serious art form never developed a broad-based constituency among religious groups, let alone among Americans in general. Instead, at the end of the 1970s religious groups found themselves preoccupied with their older concerns about film but now posed in terms of safeguarding the morals of those watching television and home video.

ORIGINS OF FILM

The history of film began during Christmas week 1895 when the Lumière brothers, Auguste and Louis, presented the first public exhibition of motion pictures for a paying audience at the Grand Café in Paris. Each of the films on the program ran under a minute in length and offered simple views of everyday life—a train arriving in a station, strollers walking along a Paris boulevard, workers leaving a factory at the end of a day.

This first audience, and those that followed, were astounded by the experience. Crude as the quality of early film images may appear to us today, the spectators of the time were awed by seeing something they had never seen before—pictures that moved realistically on a screen. In their excitement and enthusiasm was born a new entertainment industry that eventually came to be regarded as a serious art form and as a vital medium of communication.

The Lumières by no means invented the technology of moving pictures. They were but two among the many who contributed to its technical evolution through the nineteenth and twentieth centuries. However, the brothers were the first to demonstrate the potential of movies as a medium of exhibition in theaters rather than on the Kinetoscope, a peepshow device patented by Thomas Edison in 1891. Moreover, they did so by relying solely on subjects of reality, and out of their attempts "to catch nature in the act," in the words of a contemporary French journalist (quoted in Siegfried Kracauer, *The Theory of Film*, 1965), came the documentary tradition, one of the twin pillars upon which all cinema rests.

The other pillar is the fantasy tradition, pioneered by Georges Méliès, a trained magician and a contemporary of the Lumière brothers, who discovered that the camera could do considerably more than record reality. It could make things disappear and reappear, speed up action, slow it down, or even reverse it. Using film to create its own reality, Méliès produced a series of short fantasies that delighted audiences around the world and inspired a host of imitators after the turn of the century.

The use of the camera to tell a story gave the new medium its own language and unique identity. The first notable movie said to depend solely on camera-created narrative links rather than on staged tableaux explained by subtitles was Edwin S. Porter's *The Great Train Robbery* (1903). Yet, like film technology, film language was not the creation of any single individual but evolved through the trial and error of many until the cut and the fade, the crosscut, and the close-up became commonly accepted as narrative conventions.

While the filmmakers experimented with the form and content of movies, exhibitors explored places to screen them. At first this meant using already existing facilities, such as vaudeville houses and fairgrounds. By 1910, storefront theaters called nickelodeons had become an urban phenomenon, and they soon spread from the poorer neighborhoods to all corners of the metropolis and beyond. For the poor and the non-English-speaking masses who flocked to the United States at the turn of the century, the nickelodeon offered an inexpensive way to escape the harsh realities of working-class life. Available to any who could afford the nickel admission, movies were looked down upon by the middle and upper classes as vulgar entertainment for the poor and undereducated. Film content, however, had not yet come under official scrutiny. Most local administrators were concerned more with the hygienic conditions within the storefront operations than with what was being shown.

When the nickelodeons expanded to the better parts of town, the middle class responded with as much enthusiasm as had the tired day laborer and sweatshop seamstress. As the demand grew, production boomed, resulting in a diverse hodgepodge of one-reelers (approximately twelve to fourteen minutes in length, a variable dependent upon the dexterity of the operators of the hand-cranked cameras and projectors). These early silent entertainments, few of which survive except as titles in a distributor's catalog, reflect a world of relative innocence compared to the moral complexities of contemporary life. These pre–World War I films were grounded in the sensibilities and mores of the nineteenth century: good triumphs in the end, virtue prevails, and faith in God is the norm. These cultural values were shared by both the filmmakers and the audiences of the day.

The typical objection to these simple entertainments had less to do with immorality than with their crudeness of expression and their appeal to the emotions rather than to the intellect. Indeed, intellectuals dismissed film as a banal, passing novelty that hardly merited attention. Others feared that movies would dull the inclination of the unskilled and uneducated masses to better themselves and thus inevitably lower the standards of society. Among those who took offense at such sights as Wild West shoot-outs, slapstick violence, and on-screen kisses were public officials, civic and religious leaders, educators, and representatives of competing commercial entertainments. Often characterized as "bluenoses" and "do-gooders" by an industry fearful of censorship, there was little unanimity within these groups, let alone among them.

The religious community, in particular, was divided in its response to the new medium. Conservative Protestants disdained moving pictures as worldly amusement, of questionable morality and certainly unsuitable as Sabbath activity. Roman Catholics, whose church served largely poor immigrant congregations, were concerned more about the possible offenses in individual films than about the medium itself.

From the first, movie producers had noticed that religious subjects could draw large audiences. One of the earliest movies based on a religious theme was a version of the Oberammergau Passion play produced in France in 1897. Made by a religious book company, La Bonne Presse, it proved so successful that the firm turned from publishing to full-time movie production. For more than a decade, other European and American versions of the Passion play were filmed, each a little longer and grander than the last, until other more imaginative approaches to the Gospel story gained popularity. One of them was *The Illumination,* produced by Vitagraph in 1912. Set in Palestine at the time of the Resurrection, the film concerns two couples, one Roman and the other Jewish, affected by the risen Christ, portrayed only by means of the light shining across the faces of those at his tomb.

A more ambitious project was *From the Manger to the Cross,* a six-reel epic released by Kalem at the end of 1912. A straightforward, reverential retelling of the Gospel narrative, it was remarkable for its filming on location in the Holy Land. Both secular and religious critics were impressed, and an English bishop was quoted as saying, "A new art has been turned to a noble use with wonderful success" (in Anthony Slide, *Early American Cinema,* 1970). But it was a series of films made in Italy that set the pattern of religious productions and shaped the future of the industry itself. These feature-length spectaculars included Enrico Guazzoni's *St. Francis* (1911), *Quo Vadis?* (1912), and *Fabiola* (1913); Giovanni Pastrone's *Cabiria* (1914); and Giulio Antamoro's *Christus* (1914). When the nine-reel *Quo Vadis?* opened in a Broadway theater with a ticket price

of \$1.50, the nickelodeon and its program of two-reelers were finished.

The first to recognize the artistic potential of the feature form and to take full advantage of it was D. W. Griffith. A stage actor who quickly learned the film craft, Griffith directed almost five hundred one-reelers for Biograph from 1908 to 1913. When the company refused to release Griffith's four-reel biblical epic *Judith of Bethulia,* he left to pursue his vision of what could be accomplished in longer films. Risking all the money he possessed and could borrow, Griffith produced and directed *The Birth of a Nation* (1915), considered a breakthrough for the feature film in its quest for recognition as the equal of the older dramatic arts. Rereleased many times over the years, it was regarded by many in the industry as having made more money than any other motion picture until overtaken in 1977 by *Star Wars.*

Based on *The Clansman,* a novel by the Reverend Thomas Dixon, Jr., the film begins on the eve of the Civil War and ends with the rise of the Ku Klux Klan. Described by President Woodrow Wilson as "like writing history with lightning," the movie remains a masterpiece of narrative cinema. Part family chronicle (it focuses on two families, one southern and the other northern) and part war epic, *The Birth of a Nation* is both visually compelling and emotionally convincing. The film's viewpoint, however, romanticized the cause of the South and portrayed the Klan as a courageous band protecting the rights of white society. Its depiction of the emancipated Negro as an inferior race was no less controversial during the pre–World War I era than it is now. When riots erupted during the film's exhibition in northern cities, Griffith's defenders argued that his work and motives had been misjudged. They pointed to the film's allegorical conclusion in which the figure of Christ is depicted ending war and uniting all peoples in peace and brotherly love.

Griffith's own response to his critics was to undertake an even more ambitious work, *Intolerance* (1916). The film presents four interlinked stories: "The Fall of Babylon"; "The Nazarene," which recounts Christ's crucifixion; "The Medieval Story," which depicts the massacre of French Huguenots in Paris on Saint Bartholomew's Day 1572; and "The Mother and the Law," a modern story of injustice. Using the image of a woman

(Lillian Gish) rocking a cradle to interlink the various episodes, Griffith created a complex film that shifted from one story to another, with rapid cross-cutting at the climax.

The story of Christ, the best-known and the least-developed section of *Intolerance,* serves to underline elements in the other stories. For instance, after a sequence with the hypocritical law enforcers in the modern story, the film cuts to the wedding feast at Cana, where the Pharisees grumble about the miracle of turning water into wine as "too much pleasure-seeking." Inevitably, the sequences with Christ lead to his trial by the Roman procurator, condemnation, and crucifixion on the Hill of Calvary. The only story that does not end in tragedy is the modern story, in which the gallows is cheated at the last moment. As in *The Birth of a Nation,* the concluding scenes are an allegory showing a world transformed by divine peace and justice.

Intolerance is one of the screen's great accomplishments, still studied today for its brilliance of narrative structure and dramatic camerawork, but it was a commercial failure in its own day. Ahead of its time technically, and released as America prepared to enter World War I, the film was rejected by a public more interested in pro-war films than this plea for tolerance among humankind.

Griffith's great postwar achievement was *Broken Blossoms* (1919), the tragic story of two outcasts who are destroyed by the indifference of society. The touching performance of Lillian Gish as a downtrodden child of the slums complements the convincing portrayal of Richard Barthelmess as a Chinese youth who, after witnessing brutality by American sailors on shore leave, becomes a Buddhist missionary intent on introducing the peace of Eastern religious beliefs to the violent West. Arriving in London, his good intentions are discouraged, and he slips into the oblivion of opium addiction. He redeems his original sense of purpose by sacrificing his life to stop a drunken killer. This tragic Oriental hero wins our sympathy and makes some amends for the racial stereotyping in *The Birth of a Nation.*

Although Griffith continued to expand the repertory of film techniques, his stories and their treatment increasingly became regarded as old-fashioned, melodramatic, and moralistic. The traditional values reflected in Griffith's films (his last was an unsuccessful 1931 sound film about the evils of bootleg liquor) found a diminishing response in the new prosperity and broadened horizons of postwar America.

FILM IN THE TWENTIES

During World War I Hollywood became not only the center of the American film industry but also the central source of product for European cinemas, since the warring countries of Europe produced few films. The glamor, romance, and vitality that characterized the Hollywood version of movie entertainment in the 1920s came to dominate the silent screens of the world.

One of the founders of the movie capital was Cecil B. DeMille, who made his mark with a series of social comedies and melodramas about the loosening code of sexual conduct during the Jazz Age. In such films as *Male and Female* (1919) and *Why Change Your Wife?* (1920), DeMille discovered that audiences were prepared to accept provocative sexual content provided it conformed to the moral standards of the time.

Having mastered this technique, DeMille applied it to *The Ten Commandments* (1923), a movie that was half biblical spectacle, half modern melodrama. The film begins with a majestic prologue portraying Moses (Theodore Roberts) leading the Israelites out of Egypt through the parted Red Sea to Sinai, where he receives the clay tablets with the Law. The main section of the film focuses on two brothers, the righteous John (Richard Dix) and the immoral Dan (Rod La Rocque). Dan breaks all the commandments, with each transgression spelled out in the titles, until he is killed in the collapse of a cathedral constructed with defective building materials for which he had overcharged. Here was an exotic mixture of sin and piety that fascinated audiences of the day and became DeMille's specialty. His 1956 remake of *The Ten Commandments,* with Charlton Heston as Moses, was strictly a costume affair. Although the movie was made on a far grander scale and with more sophisticated special effects (the parting of the Red Sea in particular), its fictional story elements do little except pad out the biblical account.

DeMille's last silent film, *King of Kings* (1927),

depicts the life of Christ. A work of considerable visual force, it is also replete with melodramatic clichés and takes broad liberties with the Gospel narrative. Notable among these is the invention of a convoluted sexual motivation for the betrayal of Jesus by Judas, who resents his former love, Mary Magdalene, for following the Nazarene. Creative license notwithstanding, this silent film won the respect of the American religious establishment. Scholars of various faiths were consulted during the scripting, and two clergymen were on hand during the filming. It proved a resounding success in theaters across the country and abroad. Indeed, the film later was used by missionaries in far-off corners of the world, where its lack of dialogue was a decided advantage for non-English-speaking viewers.

During the sound era DeMille continued to be identified with historical epics, only a few of which were religious. Notable among these was *The Sign of the Cross* (1932), reissued in 1946 with a prologue about an American bombing crew flying a mission over the Eternal City. (The latter version is the one most often shown on television.) Fredric March plays a Roman officer who joins the martyrs in the arena because of his love for a chaste Christian maiden (Elissa Landi). Distracting the viewer's attention from the religious story, however, is the alluring Claudette Colbert as a sensual Poppaea and Charles Laughton as a wicked Nero. Because some scenes of Roman excess included nudity, various church groups loudly protested the film. This time the pious mixture of vice and virtue aroused so much controversy that DeMille did not return to a religious subject until after World War II.

The silent era produced a number of biblical features, many of which have not survived. Among those that still merit viewing is *Salome* (1922), a stylized production patterned after the eccentric illustrations of Aubrey Beardsley. Featuring Alla Nazimova as the young woman who dances for the head of John the Baptist, the film is almost surrealistic in its staging. Its emotionally charged imagery expresses the conflict between the freedom of the spirit and the decadence of worldly riches.

Fred Niblo's *Ben-Hur* (1926) was as great a success in its day as was William Wyler's sound version in 1959. The title character (Ramon Navarro) is a contemporary of Jesus, and their paths cross on various occasions, but the plot focuses on sea battles and chariot races. The figure of Christ is suggested by shots of an actor's back, hands, or feet, but never his face.

One of the last of the silent biblical epics was *Noah's Ark* (1929), directed by Michael Curtiz. Overtaken by the sound revolution midway in production, the studio inserted some dialogue scenes and released it as a "part talkie," but audiences bypassed it in favor of all-talking pictures. Made by one of the screen's great action directors, the film deserves more recognition than it has received.

Clearly, the religious spectacle had become accepted as a distinct genre of Hollywood movies. But religion also appeared in other types of silent films. For instance, in most Westerns, the frontier parson was a standard character. William S. Hart combined religion with the code of the West in *Hell's Hinges* (1916), the story of a weak-willed minister from the East whose sister converts a gunman who has been hired to run them out of town. When the outlaws kill the minister and burn down the church, the converted gunman (played by Hart) corners them in a saloon, shoots the ringleader, and sets the saloon ablaze. Perhaps Hart's best Western, the film revolves around the moral question of using violence in a righteous cause. It was all quite convincing then and is still of interest today.

Hart's lead was quickly followed by John Ford in his film *The Soul Herder* (1917), remade by King Vidor in 1921 as *The Sky Pilot*. In both movies Harry Carey plays a cowboy who assumes the garb of a murdered minister and reforms a lawless town. Often clergymen were simply part of the background. For instance, the padres of the southwestern missions functioned in this way in Douglas Fairbanks' *The Mark of Zorro* (1920) and other films set on the Mexican-American border. One recent exception is Robert Aldrich's *The Frisco Kid* (1979), an indifferent comedy about a Polish rabbi (Gene Wilder) traveling across Indian territory to reach his San Francisco congregation.

Religion became a standard part of the iconography of the Western, with the church representing a civilizing influence on the life of frontier settlements. Churchgoers might prove hypocritical, as in *High Noon* (1952) when they refuse to help a marshal fight off a gang of outlaws, but most often they were seen as part of the bedrock of American society. John Ford made religion the lifeblood of his frontier communities, celebrating how the settlers' faith in God and country contributed to their taming the wilderness. But at the same time Ford seemed to mourn the loss of the frontier's rugged individualism to the moral conformity of organized religion.

Early comedy films frequently depicted men of the cloth or religious imposters, from hypocritical do-gooders and venal schemers to long-winded preachers and impractical innocents. But as its audience became predominately middle-class, silent comedy grew more sophisticated and producers more cautious about giving possible offense to clergy and faithful.

Like other silent comics, Charlie Chaplin made his share of slapstick farces in which churchmen were figures of fun. For example, in *Easy Street* (1917) the Little Tramp helps save a slum mission run by well-intentioned but sanctimonious reformers. Spunky and aggressive, Chaplin uses every means, whether fair or not, to intimidate the thugs terrorizing the area. By 1923, however, Chaplin had mastered his art and had little need for comic stereotypes. In that year he produced *The Pilgrim,* a classic comedy about an escaped convict (Chaplin) who, disguised as a minister, stops in a town awaiting the arrival of a new pastor. Unable to tell the townspeople the truth, Chaplin does his best to live up to their expectations. Just as his real identity is discovered, he recovers the stolen church mortgage fund. The film's most notable sequence occurs when Chaplin uses mime to preach a Sunday sermon on David and Goliath, acting out the story by bobbing up and down in the pulpit. The result is a tour de force that renders the struggle between might and right as transcendental comedy.

If DeMille was the director who invented the American form of pious but titillating entertainment, it was the Danish director Carl Dreyer who realized film's potential for probing the spiritual depths of the human being. His first successful feature, *Leaves from Satan's Book* (1920), shows the devil at work in four periods of history. Although directly influenced by Griffith's *Intolerance,* Dreyer did not attempt simultaneous and parallel narratives but presented his stories in

sequence, beginning with the devil disguised as a Pharisee tempting Judas to betray Christ. Dreyer's personal style developed further with *The Parson's Widow* (1920), a sixteenth-century story about a young minister who marries a pastor's widow in order to get the deceased's parsonage. When Dreyer discovered during production that Hildur Carlberg, the Swedish actress playing the widow, was actually dying, he changed the film into a study of the loneliness of an elderly woman facing death. Succeeding films continued Dreyer's interest in themes of loneliness and suffering. *Love One Another* (1922) sets the love story of a Jewish maiden and a Christian youth in the midst of the terrors of a Russian pogrom. *Michael* (1924) is a character study of an old artist, deserted by a cherished protégé, slowly withering away alone among the trappings of material wealth. *Master of the House* (1925), Dreyer's first popular success, tells of a tyrannical husband whose timorous wife is saved from a nervous breakdown by the intervention of a resourceful housekeeper.

All of these films anticipated Dreyer's masterpiece, *The Passion of Joan of Arc* (1928), considered by many to be one of the greatest films of all time. Made at the end of the silent era, it remains that period's greatest achievement. Instead of limiting the viewer's experience, the absence of sound helps create the concentrated intensity of the film's interior reality. The central trial sequences are filmed almost entirely in close-ups, especially of Maria Falconetti, the actress portraying Joan. Hers is a supreme performance, every facial nuance a revelation. (Supposedly exhausted by Dreyer's insistence on expressing the reality of Joan's feelings, Falconetti never acted again.) The camera records both her anguish at the hands of her tormentors and her total confidence in her inner voices, making concrete her conflict between the vulnerability of the flesh and the transcendence of the spirit. There is not the slightest doubt of Joan's victory over the flames of her pyre.

In *Day of Wrath* (1943), made during the Nazi occupation of his native Denmark, Dreyer explores the dark night of the soul. Set in the seventeenth century, the film centers on a harmless old woman accused of witchcraft, who is tortured to reveal the names of her accomplices and sentenced to be burned at the stake. Filled with a sense of fear and anguish, *Day of Wrath* is stark and unforgiving about the evil nature of total power wielded by any institution, whether church or state. Before the Nazi censor realized its political significance, Dreyer had fled to Sweden.

The most challenging of all Dreyer's works is *Ordet* (1955), a film in which a dead woman is brought back to life by the faith of a young child. The real miracle, however, is the strong bond of love shared by a family of good and simple people. *Ordet* was one of only fourteen features made by Dreyer, because he refused to compromise his vision and independence by making commercial films. Yet perhaps no other director has left such a significant legacy of films exploring the mysteries of the human soul.

With the exception of Dreyer, European directors in the 1920s found religion only of interest in connection with horror fantasies, such as Paul Wegener's *The Golem* (1920), the legend of a clay monster summoned to protect the Jews of medieval Prague. Another example is Benjamin Christensen's *Witchcraft Through the Ages* (1922), a wildly imaginative presentation of black magic and devil worship. It focuses on the witch-hunts of the late Middle Ages and ends with an explanation of women's victimization through history by the unenlightened male's dominance of society.

Religion also played a key part in Fritz Lang's *Metropolis* (1926), a futuristic film set in the year 2000. Oppressed workers gather secretly in the catacombs beneath a great city to be inspired by Maria, a holy woman preaching love and forbearance. However, a robot made in Maria's likeness incites the workers to revolt, resulting in chaos until all is resolved on the steps of an aboveground cathedral, where the representatives of capital and labor are united. Although an impressive visual metaphor, the film makes little literal sense of the reconciliation.

AMERICAN FILM AFTER 1930

The sound era began tentatively with some songs and a few bits of dialogue in Alan Crosland's *The Jazz Singer* (1927), a film about a cantor's son (Al Jolson) who, against his father's wishes, makes good as a musical-theater star.

The public wanted more and better sound films, but it took several years before the studios and theaters had all the necessary equipment in place to produce them.

One of the first great American sound films was King Vidor's *Hallelujah!* (1929). Telling the story of a black couple in the South, the film is remarkable for its on-location recording of rural life as centered on the local church. Like the spirituals and folk songs on the sound track, the simple faith of these people, mostly portrayed by nonprofessionals, possesses a documentarylike authenticity. Certainly the story—a young farm lad intrigued by a city girl—is old-hat melodrama, but the film's virtue lies in its attempt to show for the first time the black religious experience. Although the film was not completely free of stereotyping, it was made with sympathy and a sense of integrity; causing controversy at the box-office and not showing the progress blacks had achieved, the film made Hollywood and some blacks uncomfortable.

Another remarkable film centered in the black religious heritage was *Green Pastures* (1936), directed by William Keighley. Beginning with a Sunday-school class about Genesis, the film imagines heaven as an eternal fish fry with a heavenly host of southern blacks presided over by "De Lawd" (Rex Ingram). This was Hollywood's version of a popular Broadway play by Marc Connelly, a white dramatist. Although some viewers criticized its patronizing attitude, *Green Pastures* was warmly received by both blacks and whites. The film has since been praised for its showcasing of talented blacks, few of whom had much opportunity to appear on the screen other than in the few black-produced films. In 1943 Hollywood produced another all-black film of some religious interest: Vincente Minnelli's *Cabin in the Sky*, a musical about the devil's struggle to win the soul of a good man (Eddie "Rochester" Anderson).

Frank Capra's early sound films contained little of the sentimentality that characterizes his later work. In *The Miracle Woman* (1931) he looks at the far reaches of religion in a story about a woman evangelist (Barbara Stanwyck) whose cult grows wealthy through the use of show-business techniques but who, in the final reel, finds love and true piety. Except for its trite ending, the film convincingly portrays the exploitative nature of commercialized religion. Not wanting to offend the religious sensibilities of any viewer, Capra carefully avoided any indication of whether the evangelist (modeled on Aimee Semple MacPherson) was sincere but misguided or just an outright charlatan. This ambiguity about the central character's quality of faith was an evasion that did not help the film at the box office or save it from the charge of irreverence. It was the only film to lose money for Columbia Pictures that year.

United Artists fared little better with Lewis Milestone's *Rain* (1932), the story of a missionary (Walter Huston) who tries to convert a South Seas island lady of pleasure (Joan Crawford) but instead yields to temptation himself. This Somerset Maugham story had been tried in 1928 with Gloria Swanson. A third version, *Miss Sadie Thompson* (1953), starred Rita Hayworth. None succeeded at the box office.

In 1936 Spencer Tracy became the first in a long line of folksy clerics with his warm and engaging portrayal of a likable, down-to-earth priest in *San Francisco,* W. S. Van Dyke's account of the devastating 1906 earthquake. Tracy gave the same kind of winning performance as Father Flanagan in *Boys' Town* (1938) and *Men of Boys' Town* (1941). Toward the end of his career he was cast as an irascible missionary trying to save a group of leper children from a volcanic eruption in *The Devil at Four o'Clock* (1961), a sad parody of his earlier roles.

Pat O'Brien's Irish geniality led to his being cast as a Catholic clergyman in such films as *Angels with Dirty Faces* (1938), *The Fighting 69th* (1940), and *Fighting Father Dunne* (1948). But the most successful of the "lovable priest" films was Leo McCarey's *Going My Way* (1944), featuring Bing Crosby's crooning curate and Barry Fitzgerald's crotchety old pastor. Held together by Crosby's relaxed persona and McCarey's comic talent, the film was essentially a sentimental confection that wartime audiences found entertaining, if not inspirational. McCarey's sequel, *The Bells of St. Mary's* (1945), repeated the same formula, except this time Crosby was the new pastor and Ingrid Bergman was the nun in charge of the parish school. Sentimentality once again took the upper hand, although this time the mawkishness was quite transparent. A low-keyed attempt to humanize clergymen had been made in the beginning of the decade by Irving Rapper, whose

One Foot in Heaven (1941) was a refreshing look at a minister (Fredric March) and his work in a poor urban parish in the 1920s. His warm relationship to wife and family added to the human dimension of a modest but uplifting story.

The sole exception to this genre of pious clerics was John Ford's *The Fugitive* (1947), based on *The Power and the Glory* (1940), Graham Greene's novel about a "whiskey priest" who is hunted by an antireligious government following the Mexican Revolution. Ford's direction heightened the Christlike aspects of Henry Fonda's performance, eliminating much of Greene's paradox of human weakness as an instrument of the divine. Still, the film is so extraordinarily rich in its Christian iconography that, whatever its dramatic shortcomings, it deserves recognition for attempting to move beyond the narrow boundaries of Hollywood's surface treatment of religion.

Nevertheless, audiences continued to respond to films about clergymen who were like other people except that they wore a Roman collar. This image of the cleric as a "regular guy" was summed up in the role played by Karl Malden in *On the Waterfront* (1954). After facing down some thugs in a barroom encounter, Malden turns to the bartender and says, "Gimme a beer."

The next year, however, an entirely different clerical image appeared in Charles Laughton's *The Night of the Hunter* (1955), starring Robert Mitchum as an itinerant preacher who is also a psychotic killer. The film is an artful thriller in which the fanatic marries and kills a woman (Shelley Winters) for her money, then pursues her two children, who are saved by a God-fearing woman (Lillian Gish).

As Hollywood struggled in the 1950s and 1960s to pull viewers away from television sets and into theaters, it turned to increasingly controversial subject matter and treatment. For instance, Richard Brooks's *Elmer Gantry* (1960), starring Burt Lancaster, details the rise and fall of a Bible Belt revival preacher who exploits the willingness of simple folk to contribute to a religious cause. The next year Paul Wendkos directed *Angel Baby,* a simpler and more credible film than *Elmer Gantry.* in which Salome Jens plays an evangelist being manipulated by others. The genre reached its nadir in 1980 with Marty Feldman's unfunny satire *In God We Trust,* about a monk who leaves his monastery to raise some money. In an instance of life imitating art, the 1972 documentary *Marjoe* examines the career of a former child evangelist who smugly talks about "the tricks of the trade."

Nuns did not take center stage in Hollywood films until the 1940s. Before then, sisters had appeared only as background figures running convent schools or offering refuge to women with broken hearts, for which the prototype was *The White Sister* (1924, with Lillian Gish, and 1933, with Helen Hayes). In 1945 *The Bells of St. Mary's* initiated a genre of pictures about nuns that became more popular than those about priests. Most were conceived simply as star vehicles and paid more attention to the women themselves than to the religious significance of the subject. The following list evidences the durability of this genre: Loretta Young and Celeste Holm in *Come to the Stable* (1949); Deborah Kerr in *Heaven Knows, Mr. Allison* and Joan Collins in *Sea Wife* (both produced in 1957 and both about a nun marooned on a Pacific island with a man); Lilia Skala in *Lilies of the Field* (1963); Debbie Reynolds in *The Singing Nun* (1966); Rosalind Russell in *The Trouble with Angels* (1966); Mary Tyler Moore in *Change of Habit* (1969); and Glenda Jackson, Melina Mercouri, Anne Meara, and Sandy Dennis in *Nasty Habits* (1977).

Even though a 1947 British film, *Black Narcissus,* had demonstrated the potential for serious drama in its story about an Anglican community of nuns, it was not until more than a decade later that American filmmakers tried to come to grips with a woman's devotion to religious life. In Fred Zinnemann's *The Nun's Story* (1959). a young Belgian woman who has joined a strict nursing order is sent to the Congo, where she resists her feelings of love for the doctor with whom she works. She returns to Belgium and, after struggling with the routine of convent life, leaves for the world beyond the wall. Based on a true story, the film focuses on the interior conflict between the nun's idealism and her growing sense of her own needs. With Audrey Hepburn in the title role, *The Nun's Story* is convincing in its portrayal of religious life as a vocation to which few are called.

The biblical epic so popular in the silent era did not find its counterpart in sound films until the postwar remakes of *Quo Vadis?* (1951), *Ben Hur* (1959), and *King of Kings* (1961). An exception of minor interest was *The Last Days of Pompeii*

(1935), a small-budget costume film that contrasts the idealism of the early Christians with the corruption of the Romans. Starting off the new biblical cycle was Cecil B. DeMille's *Samson and Delilah* (1949), which featured little of the scope and vitality of his earlier efforts. Henry King's *David and Bathsheba* (1951), Richard Thorpe's *The Prodigal* (1955), King Vidor's *Solomon and Sheba* (1959), and Robert Aldrich's *Sodom and Gomorrah* (1961) were all critical and commercial disappointments.

The cycle culminated in John Huston's *The Bible . . . In the Beginning* (1966), which retells Genesis up to the story of Abraham and Isaac. It is chiefly of interest as a curious and wrongheaded attempt to present a completely literal visualization of Scripture on the big screen. The result has its moments of imagination and grandeur, but the massive sets too often distract from the narrative.

New Testament stories that reached the screen included Henry Koster's *The Robe* (1953), Frank Borzage's *The Big Fisherman* (1959), and Richard Fleischer's *Barabbas* (1962). The last and best life of Christ in the old Hollywood tradition of the big-budget epic was *The Greatest Story Ever Told* (1965), directed by George Stevens. Although scorned by the critics and a disaster at the box office, the film has more religious substance than pious sentimentality, and Max von Sydow's portrayal of Christ is arguably the finest the screen has essayed.

More than anything else, the public's rejection of Stevens' film reflected the changing expectations of many filmgoers. American filmmakers now not only had to lure one-time movie enthusiasts away from their television sets, they had to compete with innovative foreign films that were finding a growing audience among an American public tired of Hollywood conventions. In the struggle for a diminishing, highly selective audience, almost nothing was sacred. For instance, in Mike Nichols' *The Graduate* (1967), the hero (Dustin Hoffman) stops a church wedding by seizing a cross and using it to block the path of his pursuers. Few moviegoers objected to the scene because in the context of the story guests at the wedding are materialistic hypocrites who richly deserve their chastisement.

Notable also was a brief period of religious musicals, the best of which remains David Greene's *Godspell* (1973). It is zestful but simple, the parables are fun, and the film still plays well with audiences. Norman Jewison's *Jesus Christ Superstar* (1973), filmed in Israel, was ponderous and overproduced. Also shot in the Holy Land but much less pretentious was *The Gospel Road* (1973), a truly Americanized version of the Gospels, with Johnny Cash retracing the steps of Jesus, accompanied by appropriate down-home country songs.

A more realistic cycle of horror films emerged at this time, beginning with *Rosemary's Baby* (1968), *The Exorcist* (1973), *The Omen* (1976), and their sequels and imitators. Unlike earlier Hollywood horror films, these films attempted to make religious ritual as authentic as possible in order to heighten the sense of the supernatural. But such films inevitably trivialized both religion and the supernatural since they gave literal renderings of theology as ancient rituals and of evil as special-effects horror.

In a lighter vein *Oh, God!* (1977) and its sequel *Oh, God! Book II* (1980) centered on the appearance of the deity in the form of comedian George Burns and satisfied audience demand for pure entertainment. Conceived by TV producer/writer Larry Gelbart and directed by Carl Reiner, the films are one-note jokes that could just as easily be television movies. Interestingly, one is more likely to see serious treatments of religious subjects and issues on television through documentaries and news stories than in movie theaters today.

In the 1980s films like Ulu Grosbard's *True Confessions* (1981) and Sidney Lumet's *The Verdict* (1982) have tended to concentrate on the sociological aspects of religious institutions and their representatives rather than on the values of religious beliefs and works. Unlike *The Nun's Story*, *Agnes of God* (1985) never achieves a credible frame of reference for convent life and substitutes ambiguities for the mystery of psyche and spirit.

A serious film such as Daniel Petrie's *Resurrection* (1980), in which a woman (Ellen Burstyn) returns from the brink of death with miraculous powers of healing, was not even given a chance to find its audience. In a marketplace defined by the quest for one or two large-grossing films and not a number of small but profitable ones, the only films with a significant religious dimension that have been financial successes are two British blockbusters: Hugh Hudson's *Chariots of Fire*

(1981) and Richard Attenborough's *Gandhi* (1982). The former partly concerns a Christian athlete's desire to race in the Olympics in order to demonstrate the talents he has received from God. The latter shows the complex blending of Western pragmatism and Hindu mysticism that made the founder of modern India such a successful leader.

EUROPEAN FILM AFTER 1930

Europe lagged several years behind America in the development of talking pictures. During the 1930s there were few religious features, none of which was considered of sufficient worth to be imported into the United States. Following World War II, however, a number of notable films appeared, beginning with Jean Delannoy's *La Symphonie Pastorale* (1946). Based on the André Gide novel (1919), the film is about a Swiss pastor who devotes himself to helping a young blind woman (Michèle Morgan) but comes to love her with a passion that destroys his wife and family. Delannoy uses the situation to explore the development of spiritual blindness within the pastor and the growing insight of the blind woman who eventually regains her vision. Considered by some at the time as irreligious and by others as political allegory, the film is still of interest today.

Delannoy followed this with a film of even more religious substance and contemporary relevance. *God Needs Men* (1950) takes place on an island off the French coast, whose primitive economy is supplemented by the shipwrecks caused by blacking out the lighthouse during storms. When the islanders refuse to stop this practice, the bishop withdraws their curate, and the parishioners force the sexton (Pierre Fresnay) into serving as their priest. A marvelous film that posed many questions about the need and function of religion in everyday life, it unfortunately had a limited release in the United States and was withdrawn from circulation in the late 1950s.

Popular on both sides of the Atlantic, and still in circulation, is Maurice Cloche's *Monsieur Vincent* (1947), about the life of the seventeenth-century Catholic saint Vincent de Paul. With Pierre Fresnay in the title role, Vincent is convincingly portrayed as a man whose compassion meets the needs of his own troubled age, a reassuring figure for a world trying to rebuild after a devastating world war. Notable also are Jules Dassin's *He Who Must Die* (1957), in which the Passion play parallels the 1921 persecution of Greeks by the Turks on Crete; Anselmo Duarte's Brazilian film *The Given Word* (1962), in which a peasant's vow to place a cross in the local church is refused because the vow was made during a voodoo ceremony; and Kon Ichikawa's *The Burmese Harp* (1956), a Japanese film about a soldier who escapes capture by dressing as a Buddhist monk but who then devotes his life to finding and burying the remains of those who died in the jungle warfare of 1944–1945.

However, the only filmmaker to follow Carl Dreyer's search for the absolute within the human soul has been Robert Bresson. More austere and disciplined than even Dreyer, Bresson has created a small but exceptional body of work that stands above the passing trends of film convention and audience expectation.

Bresson's first feature as a director was *Les Anges du Peche* (1943), the story of two novices in a Dominican convent. The salvation of the one through the sacrifice of the other avoids sentimental piety by immersing the film in the lofty aspirations as well as the petty failings of this community of women religious. The film's translucent photography was by Philippe Agostini, who was to co-direct (with R. L. Bruckberger) the remarkable *Dialogue des Carmelites* (1960), based on a true incident in which a group of nuns were martyred during the French Revolution. Also concerned with the struggles and feelings of women was Bresson's *Les Dames du Bois de Boulogne* (1944), adapted from a Denis Diderot story about a woman's revenge on her ex-lover. Once again, it is the story of a woman's transformation, this time from sin to respectability.

Considered by many to be Bresson's masterpiece, *Diary of a Country Priest* (1950) was based on an acclaimed novel by Georges Bernanos about a young curate whose hopes for renewing the spiritual life of his poor parish are ground down by the apathy of those he seeks to serve. Disappointed, lonely, and suffering from an ailment eventually diagnosed as stomach cancer, he visits a former priest, a friend from his seminary days. Here he collapses, is cared for by his friend's mistress, and dies with his final thoughts on the mystery of grace. Through the device of the diary, the film provides an intimate account of a man's inner struggles with himself and his faith. It is the film's images, shot on location with a mostly nonprofessional cast, that give credibility to this record of psychic suffering. Bresson shaped the film's physical reality into a kind of battleground of the spirit, resulting in an agony of the soul comparable in a religious sense only with that of Dreyer's Joan.

Two of Bresson's films from the late 1950s present portraits of very different men. *A Man Escaped* (1956) was based on the actual story of a Resistance leader who escaped imprisonment just before execution. Until the final reel's successful getaway, the film is a meditation on an individual's isolation and need to believe in something beyond himself. Conversely, the protagonist of *Pickpocket* (1959) prefers going to prison over giving up crime. He has plenty of chances to reform, but is uninterested in the alternatives.

Bresson's *The Trial of Joan of Arc* (1962) is stripped down to the bare essentials of the maid's court interrogations and execution. Lacking the emotional purity of Dreyer's silent version, Bresson's film makes Joan no less vulnerable a victim yet projects the cold inevitability of history. However, some critics see *Balthasar* (1966) as more central to Bresson's spiritual message than *The Trial of Joan of Arc*. The film's title is the name of a donkey, a beast of burden who ultimately pays the price for all the evils visited upon it by humans. Seen as an allegory of Christ's suffering for mankind, the film contrasts natural innocence with the corruption of human nature. Like *Mouchette*, a Bernanos film made the same year about a young girl who kills herself because of the world's depravity, *Bathasar* has little meaning outside the context of this Christian interpretation.

Of Bresson's work after 1970, mostly adaptations from literary classics, only *Lancelot du Lac* (1974) stands out for its anthropological interpretation of a newly Christianized society just emerging from barbarian times. His other films have become increasingly somber, withdrawn, and pessimistic about the human condition.

In the United States Bresson never achieved the recognition and popularity afforded Ingmar Bergman, the son of a Lutheran clergyman whose use of Christian symbolism and references has continued to fascinate secular audiences and film critics. With some experience in stage direction, Bergman began making films in the late 1940s, mostly romantic melodramas for distribution in his native Sweden. In 1955, however, he received international attention by winning an award at the 1956 Cannes Film Festival for *Smiles of a Summer's Night,* a sophisticated sex comedy with considerable wit and charm. In the wake of this success his Swedish producers exported an earlier film, *Sawdust and Tinsel* (1953), whose central character was a clown in a traveling carnival who could be seen as a kind of Christ figure.

It was *The Seventh Seal* (1957), however, that caught the interest especially of religious viewers. The story concerns a knight who hopes to gain some knowledge before he dies by challenging Death to a game of chess. At the climax, the knight tricks Death in order to save a small family of traveling players, who symbolize the holy family. The film's allegorical allusions are a natural part of its medieval setting, which is rendered so convincingly that viewers are easily drawn into Bergman's exploration of the mysteries of faith, grace, and redemption. Bergman followed this with *Wild Strawberries* (1957), the work many critics consider his masterpiece. The film is an evocative study of an old man whose dreams are troubled by images of mortality but who finds peace in recalling the innocent joys of his youth. Adding to the movie's poignancy, *Wild Strawberries* marked the last film appearance of the venerable Swedish actor and director Victor Sjöström, who died in 1960.

After several minor works, Bergman again confronted religious themes in *The Virgin Spring* (1960). Based on a medieval ballad, the story concerns the rape and murder of a young woman whose father avenges her in an act of terrible wrath. Purging this crime, however, is a spring that miraculously flows from the site of her death. Bergman's major statement on faith and the contemporary world is to be found in his trilogy of films beginning with *Through a Glass Darkly* (1961), a work that ends in a quiet affirmation of divine existence and the redeeming power of love. This was followed by *Winter Light* (1962), a coldly relentless exposition of a pastor's dark night of the soul, exposing the spiritual pain of a man of God living without hope in a stark and sterile world. The final film of the trilogy, *The Silence* (1963), follows the jour-

ney of two women in a foreign country where they cannot speak the language. The inability of the women to understand what is being said or to make themselves understood represents Bergman's most ambitious attempt to deal with the themes of absence of communication, isolation, and alienation. An existential vision of life in an impersonal universe, *The Silence* disappointed many; one religious group, the Catholic National Legion of Decency, condemned it as "dangerously close to pornography."

Although Bergman continued to do interesting work, it was never of the same caliber as his earlier films. His nadir was his attempt at an English-language production, *The Touch* (1971). With the lightweight comic actor Elliott Gould in the lead role, the film was an embarrassment and showed how much Bergman depended upon the skill of his stock company of actors and crew. *Cries and Whispers* (1972) was Bergman's last work having deeply felt religious resonances. It is about death and dying, but, unlike *Wild Strawberries,* it confronts this subject directly and with anguish.

If Bergman was an agnostic open to the theology of belief, Luis Buñuel was a firm nonbeliever obsessed with the absolute. Whereas Bergman's films focus on the conflict between reason and emotion and at times temper the theme with a bit of Nordic mysticism, Buñuel's works revel in the contradictions between human nature and conventional society and are often surreal in the absurdity of their juxtaposition.

Buñuel's first two short features, *An Andalusian Dog* (1928) and *The Golden Age* (1930), made in France with Salvador Dali, were dadaist attacks on bourgeois institutions and morality. They furnish an arsenal of subversive confrontations with the accepted social order through such images as a close-up of a woman's eye being slashed by a razor; a mutilated hand from which swarms a nest of ants; a man dragging behind him a pair of pianos, priests, and dead mules; and a monument being dedicated to the sounds of a flushing toilet. Abandoning this approach, Buñuel made a documentary, *Land Without Bread* (1932), whose images of incredible poverty in a Spanish mountain community might have come from a nightmare. Here reality is shown as more surreal than anything imagined in his two previous films.

With the Spanish Civil War raging at home, Buñuel went to Hollywood and then to New

York in 1938. After World War II he moved to Mexico, where he made *Los Olvidados* (1950), an international success about the dehumanizing effects on young people of living in the slums of Mexico City. Unlike other neorealist directors of the period, Buñuel conveyed not only the physical conditions of poverty but also the brutalization of the human spirit. Although he became a successful director of Mexican romances and melodramas, noted for conveying stories in a straightforward manner, Buñuel was adept at weaving iconoclastic subtexts into his films. He did this with *Nazarín* (1958), the story of a pious priest who is ridiculed and imprisoned for living according to a literal interpretation of the Gospels.

In 1961 Bunuel was invited to Spain to make *Viridiana,* in which a novice about to take her vows visits her uncle, tries to run his estate on Christian principles, and becomes totally disillusioned about both God and man. It was the beginning of a remarkable series of works that grew more and more confident in their mixture of realism and the surreal. These include *The Exterminating Angel* (1962), which focuses on a roomful of affluent people who are reduced to the level of primitive savages when some supernatural force prevents them from leaving after a dinner party; *Simon of the Desert* (1965), which depicts the temptations of a stylite (a desert hermit perched on a pillar) who ends by being transported by the devil to a New York nightclub; and *The Milky Way* (1968), which tells of the strange adventures of two men making a pilgrimage to the shrines of medieval Europe.

In *Tristana* (1970) Buñuel reconciled his determined anticlerical and antireligious convictions with his idealization of individual freedom and personal morality. His remaining works are the playful exercises of a master, a kind of coda for his career and a recapitulation of themes that interested him, best summed up in his remark to an interviewer: "I am still, thank God, an atheist."

Other postwar European directors were interested in religion, but only as one of many other subjects of contemporary life. Such was the diverse group of Italian directors called neorealists. They shot their films on the streets rather than in studios, used nonprofessional performers, and probed the problems of ordinary people instead of telling polished stories with happy endings. The first neorealist film to appear in the United States was *Open City* (1945), directed by Roberto Rossellini. In its exploration of the brutal Nazi occupation of Rome, the film centers on a priest who is human rather than a plaster-of-paris saint.

In 1948 Rossellini made *The Miracle,* about a retarded peasant woman (Anna Magnani) who is seduced by a traveler (Federico Fellini) she believes to be Saint Joseph. When the woman announces to the village that she is to be the mother of the Messiah, she is cast out and bears her child in an empty church. In the United States the film caused considerable protest and litigation ending in a ruling by the Supreme Court that a film could not be censored on the grounds of blasphemy. *The Flowers of St. Francis* (1949) is Rossellini's retelling of the story of Saint Francis of Assisi. It captures admirably the spirit of simplicity and joy with which this early medieval saint lived and inspired others to join him. A sincere celebration of the basic goodness of simple, unassuming people, the film is among Rossellini's best.

By 1953 neorealism was no longer attracting people to the box office, so directors turned to other approaches and more popular subjects. Federico Fellini developed a more personal style of realism with such films as *La Strada* (1954), *The Nights of Cabiria* (1957), *La Dolce Vita* (1960), *8½* (1963), and *Juliet of the Spirits* (1965). Made in Fellini's prime, these films are filled with Christian iconography and religious themes, depicting life as a pilgrimage (through processions and journeys), agape in celebrating the joy of life, and most of all, moments of grace in which characters evidence a sense of mystery, of something beyond physical reality. These themes, however, serve more as a cultural context for his characters than as subjects in themselves.

One other Italian director who merits discussion is Pier Paolo Pasolini, a Marxist who tried to integrate Christian concepts into several of his works. The most direct of these is *The Gospel According to St. Matthew* (1964), a stark visualization of the Gospel narrative, epic and yet poetic in its style, but insistent on the revolutionary nature of the Messiah. *The Hawks and the Sparrows* (1966) contrasts the simplicity of Saint Francis and his followers with the pomp and panoply of the Vatican and the Italian Communist party. Pasolini's *Teorema* (1968), an ambiguous film that found some favor with a handful of critics, tries to identify profane love with the Christian concept of agape.

The films of the French New Wave, starting with Jean-Luc Godard's *Breathless* (1959), rarely explored religious matters. Among the exceptions, the most successful was Eric Rohmer's *My Night at Maud's* (1969), a wry moral tale about matching physical attractions with spiritual affinities, in which a young man spends a night in a woman's apartment arguing a philosophic point about belief in God.

One of the few 1980s films to deal directly with a religious subject is Godard's *Hail Mary* (1985), which tells the story of the virgin birth in contemporary terms. Depicted as the daughter of a gas-station owner, Mary is an independent young woman who knows that her pregnancy is of divine origin because she had refused to let any man, including her boyfriend, Joseph, even touch her. Although the film contains nudity and a few profanities, critics for some religious publications, including Richard Blake in *America* and Jean-Maurice de Montremy in *National Catholic Register,* have defended it against charges of blasphemy. Most secular critics found it uninteresting and further evidence of Godard's artistic decline. Yet the film attracted pickets to many of the houses in which it played, the first film in recent years to have stirred such controversy on the part of religious, mostly Catholic, groups.

FILM CENSORSHIP

Such protests were common in earlier days, when movies were believed to have a potentially evil influence over the mass audience. Part of the reason for this assumption was that Hollywood after World War I had become one of America's biggest businesses. The very wealth of the industry and the high salaries paid to those who worked within it isolated the Hollywood community from the average movie patron.

Then, in the early 1920s, a series of major scandals rocked the industry. Fatty Arbuckle, a leading comedian, was arrested in the mysterious death of a starlet in 1921. The next year, director William Desmond Taylor was shot to death in an unsolved murder involving several popular actresses, and in 1923 handsome mati-

nee idol Wallace Reid died of drug addiction. Citing these front-page stories as evidence of cinema's moral depravity, reformers spoke from pulpits, editorial pages, and legislatures across the country. Fearing possible government controls, Hollywood responded in 1922 by forming the Motion Picture Producers and Distributors of America (MPPDA), an organization of self-regulation.

Will H. Hays, postmaster general in President Warren G. Harding's cabinet, became the first MPPDA president. Hays's first challenge in his new role as industry spokesman came in November 1922, when Massachusetts held a referendum on establishing a state movie censorship board. Mounting a free-speech campaign, Hays helped defeat the referendum handily. He turned next to disarming the industry's critics among the public. Holding a conference attended by some two hundred representatives of religious, civic, educational, and family organizations, Hays persuaded participants to join in helping the industry to reform itself. The result was the formation of a Committee on Public Relations, composed of representatives of such organizations as the Boy Scouts of America, the National Council of Catholic Women, and the Daughters of the American Revolution, and headed by Lee F. Hammer, director of recreation for the Russell Sage Foundation. Colonel Jason S. Joy, former director of the American Red Cross and a prominent Methodist layman, was appointed executive secretary. The committee's purpose was to serve as a liaison between the industry and public groups, keeping each aware of the concerns of the other.

Four years later, in 1927, a formal document became available to producers listing eleven items that should not be filmed (including profanity, nudity, or ridicule of the clergy) and twenty-five subjects (such as arson, rape, and murder) that should be handled with special care. This new code was completely advisory because the MPPDA had set up no means of enforcing compliance with its strictures. No sooner had the MPPDA regulations been formulated than talking pictures caused the industry not only to retool its technology but also to raid the Broadway stage for actors who could put across dialogue scenes and for playwrights who knew how to write such scenes. The coming of sound brought language that many found offensive and adult themes unsuitable for family audiences.

Hays foresaw a new wave of public protests and in 1930 had the MPPDA ratify a revised and strengthened code written by Martin Quigley, the Catholic publisher of a major industry journal, *Motion Picture Herald,* and Father Daniel Lord, a Jesuit who had served as a technical advisor on *King of Kings.* As per an agreement with the Association of Motion Picture Producers (AMPP), a Studio Relations Committee viewed every film before it was sent to the laboratory for printing. Films that failed to meet the standards of the new Motion Picture Production Code could not be released unless appropriate changes were made. However, an appeals board had the power to overrule decisions of the Studio Relations Committee, weakening the rigor with which the code was applied.

So it was not surprising that a number of groups and individuals were offended by what they saw on the screen. The gangster films that flourished in the 1930s were assailed for using excessive violence and for glamorizing crime. A new generation of movie sirens—typified by Mae West, a master of the sexual innuendo and the double entendre—sparked demands for censorship from outraged moralists. Seeking to demonstrate that movies exerted a dangerous influence on young people, the Reverend William H. Short, head of the pro-censorship Motion Picture Research Council, got a two-hundred-thousand-dollar grant from a private foundation, the Payne Fund. The importance of these studies cannot be overestimated. As the first interdisciplinary attempt to scientifically measure the effects of a modern medium of communication, the studies involved testing models and procedures that have become standard in many areas, especially in television research. Their approach was seriously flawed, however, because the researchers were unable to separate the influence of movies from that of other forms of communication or actual life experiences.

After four years of testing and research projects by a team of psychologists, sociologists, and educational specialists, nine volumes of the Motion Picture Research Council's reports were published in 1933. Although the authors carefully limited their conclusions, the writer chosen by Short to provide a popular summary of the studies saw no need to avoid broad generalizations. *Our Movie-Made Children* (1933), written by journalist Henry James Forman, presented the research findings as scientific evidence that Hollywood was a corrupting influence on America's youth and needed to be brought under control. In this atmosphere cries for censorship grew, culminating in November 1933 with the establishment of the National Legion of Decency, an organization set up by a committee of Catholic bishops. A bishops' Committee on Motion Pictures was appointed to oversee the activities of the legion, which in April 1934 called upon Catholic dioceses to administer in their parishes a pledge against patronizing "indecent and immoral films." Other religious and civic groups, including the Federal Council of Churches, the United Presbyterian General Assembly, the National Conference of Christians and Jews, and the Massachusetts Civic League, joined in the growing movement to boycott offensive movies.

The MPPDA responded to this threat by ending its voluntary approach to self-regulation and creating the Production Code Administration (PCA), which had the authority to bar any member from releasing a film without the Motion Picture Production Code seal of approval. Under the direction of Joseph Breen, a former publicist and devout Catholic, the PCA wielded enormous clout, overseeing films from conception to completion. Indeed, many producers felt that it was better to consult the PCA about a script than to make changes in a finished film in order to get the required seal. Without PCA approval there were few theaters that would show a film.

In order to comply with the Legion of Decency's directive, various dioceses initiated their own local systems of categorizing movies, until the legion began issuing national classifications in February 1936. There were four categories: A-I (morally unobjectionable for all); A-II (morally unobjectionable for adults); B (morally objectionable in part for all); and C (condemned). One may gauge the success of the legion by the fact that no major studio issued a C-rated film until MGM's *Two-Faced Woman* (1941), Greta Garbo's last movie (a revised version was re-rated as B).

Most of the films that received a C rating before the 1950s were foreign imports, some of them quite notable examples of film art, such as

The Blue Angel (1930), *Carnival in Flanders* (1935), and *The Private Life of Henry VIII* (1933). No matter what a film's artistic merit, the Legion of Decency determined its ratings according to the material presented on the screen. Viewing films primarily as a medium of escapist entertainment for the family audience, the legion slapped a C rating on any film that featured nudity, objectionable language, or immoral behavior.

Although today such an attitude seems patronizing, the film industry thrived in spite of— some believe because of—the constrictions imposed by the legion and the PCA. Regarded by many as the jewels of Hollywood's Golden Age, the movies of the Depression era and World War II were enjoyed by ninety million Americans every week and still command an audience when shown on television today. One reason given for their popularity is that films made during the 1930s and 1940s had to comply with the detailed codification of morality and taste spelled out in the Production Code and by the members of the Legion of Decency. Working within such a clearly defined framework of conventions, filmmakers were free to focus their creative energies on improving the quality of other aspects of their work. Some, like Ernst Lubitsch, found ways to circumvent the code by suggesting forbidden behavior rather than directly showing it. For example, in *Trouble in Paradise* (1932) a woman visits a man in his hotel room, they embrace, and a light casts their shadow onto a double bed, which then fades to the next day.

In 1945 Will Hays was succeeded by Eric Johnston, president of the U.S. Chamber of Commerce, who soon changed the name of the industry organization to the Motion Picture Association of America (MPAA). The change in leadership and name could not avert the upheavals that the postwar world brought Hollywood. Inflation, foreign competition, blacklisting, changing mores, and the financially painful separation of theaters from studio ownership were fundamental problems. Even worse, television began displacing movies as the American family's favorite form of entertainment.

In attempting to do things television could not do, Hollywood in the 1950s increasingly turned to adult subjects that brought it into direct confrontation with the PCA and the Legion of Decency. One of the first films to test the waters was Otto Preminger's *The Moon Is Blue* (1953), a mild romantic comedy that used words then considered unacceptable in screen entertainment, such as "pregnant" and "virgin." Condemned by the legion and refused the PCA seal of approval, the film received only limited showings.

The turning point for the industry and the legion came a few years later with Elia Kazan's *Baby Doll* (1956), adapted from two Tennessee Williams stories of southern decadence and corruption. Released by Warner Brothers, the film was vigorously condemned by the Legion, which called it "morally repellent both in theme and treatment." Besides objecting to its "carnal suggestiveness," the Legion stated that *Baby Doll*'s "unmitigated emphasis on lust and the various scenes of cruelty are degrading and corruptive." Several bishops forbade Catholics in their dioceses to see it. Although *Baby Doll* made a modest profit, the film secured only one-quarter of its potential bookings because of the controversy.

Without abandoning its mandate to condemn films that were "seriously offensive to Christian and traditional standards of morality and decency," the Legion took some new initiatives. One was to broaden its classification system in 1957 by adding a new adult rating, the A-III, and changing the A-II category to include adolescents. This, in effect, acknowledged that Catholic adults were not incapable of understanding morally complex films.

Such films, often imported from Europe, had already appeared. The film that perhaps demonstrated most forcefully the need for the Legion rating system to recognize movies as more than passive general entertainment was Fellini's *La Strada* (1954), a parable about the universality of love set in the midst of a seedy traveling carnival. Highly praised by religious and secular critics in Europe, *La Strada* was rated B, with the objection: "Tends to arouse undue sympathy for immoral characters." Originally thought suited only for the small art-house circuit playing foreign-language films, it proved so successful that it was dubbed into English and played in neighborhood theaters across the country.

The Legion, fully aware that Catholics were part of the audience for *La Strada* and that a declining number of parishes were taking the annual pledge, added one more classification in 1963, the A-IV, "adults, with reservations," meaning a film of some complexity that might not be accessible to all adults. Moreover, the Legion began to turn toward a more positive engagement with the medium, taking notice of the parish film study clubs in European countries.

In the United States religious groups began to show theatrical movies in parish schools, church basements, and synagogue meeting rooms. The features selected were usually not films about religious subjects but rather secular films that grappled with issues of social justice and personal dignity. In discussing these movies, the object was to plumb their spiritual dimension and mine their religious significance. Although some have argued that any film can be analyzed for theological content—for example, good versus evil—most movies are too superficial to merit the effort. The film study movement was posited on the notion that in order to understand a film's moral significance, one has to appreciate aesthetic coherence; that is, moral judgments about a film's content and treatment have to be considered within the context of its artistic intentions and accomplishments.

In 1964 the Center for Film Study, a division of the Catholic Adult Education Center in Chicago, was designated by the Legion of Decency as its educational affiliate. In addition to preparing discussion guides for use in parish film series in the Chicago archdiocese, the center provided the legion with a monthly publication, the *Catholic Film Newsletter,* which reviewed the best of the new films, critiqued books about film, and commented on aspects of film culture. In 1969—three years after the Legion of Decency became the National Catholic Office for Motion Pictures (NCOMP)—the newsletter was expanded to review all new films and was issued twice monthly. Renamed the *Film and Broadcasting Review* in 1976 with the addition of television reviews, it was published until 1980.

In the early 1940s, the Federal Council of Churches (FCC) established a Film Commission with offices on both coasts. The East Coast office was given the responsibility for coordinating the production of educational films for use in churches. The West Coast office was to maintain a liaison with the Hollywood industry, primarily through consultation with producers interested

in accurately portraying the religious aspect of films they were making. When the FCC became the National Council of Churches in 1950, its Film Commission was merged with the Protestant Radio Commission and renamed the Broadcast and Film Commission (BFC), with television as a major new priority. As movies grew in depth and maturity, the BFC undertook a program of film awards in 1964, disbanding its West Coast office soon afterward. The National Catholic Office for Motion Pictures began its own award program in 1965. Not surprisingly, there was a discernible correlation in the films chosen by both groups. Some films honored by both organizations include *A Man for All Seasons* and *The Battle of Algiers* (1966), *In the Heat of the Night* (1967), *The Heart Is a Lonely Hunter* and *Rachel, Rachel* (1968), *Z* (1969), and *I Never Sang for My Father* and *Kes* (1970).

In 1971 the BFC, NCOMP, and Committee on Films of the Synagogue Council of America joined together in an interreligious film award program. That year the awards went to *Fiddler on the Roof, One Day in the Life of Ivan Denisovich,* and *The Garden of the Finzi-Continis.* In making these awards, the three groups hoped to encourage the production of artistic films that expressed a substantive moral dimension. Although the awards were presented on a national television broadcast, they occasioned little recognition in the religious, let alone the secular, press and did not increase the audience for the winners by any appreciable degree. Unfortunately, this award process was abandoned under the pressure of other priorities facing the small staffs of the three organizations involved. The list of films singled out for recognition by these representatives of the religious community includes some remarkable works testifying to the high aspirations of the medium.

In addition to its award program, the BFC began publishing a monthly newsletter, *Film Information,* in 1970. Unlike the *Catholic Film Newsletter,* whose reviews were prepared by NCOMP staff and reflected an official viewpoint, the reviews in *Film Information* were written by professionals providing knowledgeable but personal opinions on the relative merits of the films under scrutiny. In an effort to promote films of substance, *Film Information* developed detailed discussion guides with background information and suggested questions and resources, issuing them as supplements to subscribers and interested church groups. After a decade of service to the religious community, *Film Information* ceased publication in 1978.

Although the National Council of Churches Communication Commission (formerly BFC) reinstituted its film award program in 1979, and the U.S. Catholic Conference Communication Department (formerly NCOMP) continued to distribute its film classifications and reviews through the National Catholic News Service, the religious interest in theatrical motion pictures was on the decline. Part of the reason for this was that a decade earlier the film industry had replaced the Production Code with a four-category rating system ranging from G (all ages admitted) to R (no one under seventeen admitted). Freed from the restrictions of the code, filmmakers began peppering their movies with increasing amounts of violence and sex, thus changing the nature of films from family-oriented entertainments to diversions for young adults.

The 1950s and 1960s had proven the highwater mark for the religious engagement with film as a means of spiritual enlightenment. Besides supporting the film study movement, various denominations had tried to produce films for the theatrical market, the best example of which is the Lutheran Film Associates 1953 production, *Martin Luther.* For the most part, however, the churches saw film as an audiovisual tool for their religious education needs. Increasingly, Protestant denominations and Catholic religious communities turned from short educational films to formats more adaptable to television and cable and to the new possibilities of video and videocassette players.

The religious community has come full circle in its concern about the medium of the screen. Using much the same arguments as had been used earlier in the twentieth century, religious groups are decrying the dangerous influences of "immoral" television programs and movies (especially pornographic films). Battle lines are being drawn, as in the September 1985 report of the National Council of Churches on the social impact of the sex and violence depicted on film and television. The report concludes that both government regulation and public boycotts may be necessary to change the situation. Whether a new crusade for "screen decency" will be effective remains to be seen.

BIBLIOGRAPHY

Peter Bondanella, *Federico Fellini: Essays in Criticism* (1978); Ivan Butler, *Religion in the Cinema* (1969); Richard Corliss, "The Legion of Decency," in *Film Comment* 4:4 (1968); Jorn Donner, *The Films of Ingmar Bergman* (1969); Raymond Durgnat, *Luis Buñuel* (1967); Arthur Gilson, *The Silence of God: Response to the Films of Ingmar Bergman* (1969); Ronald Holloway, *Beyond the Image: Approaches to the Religious Dimension in the Cinema* (1977); Robert G. Konzelman, *Marquee Ministry: The Movie Theater as Church and Community Forum* (1972); Anthony Schillaci, *Movie and Morals* (1968); Robert Sklar, *Movie-Made America: A Cultural History of American Movies* (1975); Robert Stanley, *The Celluloid Empire: A History of the American Movie Industry* (1978); Edward Wagenknecht, *The Movies in the Age of Innocence,* 2nd ed. (1971).
[See also JEWISH LITERATURE AND RELIGIOUS THOUGHT; MASS COMMUNICATIONS; and RELIGION AND LITERATURE.]

MATERIAL CULTURE AND
THE VISUAL ARTS

John W. Cook

THE attitudes and values of a culture are expressed in its material objects and works of
art, which provide primary evidence for a serious
study of that culture. Therefore a thorough
study of the American religious experience must
necessarily include scrutiny of the religious aspects of material culture and the arts. The primary task of material culture studies, a relatively
young discipline in America begun around 1876,
has been "to analyze the artifact as a concrete
manifestation of cultural history" (Schlereth,
1982, p. 4). Artifacts of religious culture are
available for investigation that antedate recorded verbal histories of the territory that became the United States of America.

EUROPEAN MODELS

The European immigrants who settled the
shores of this nation in the seventeenth century
considered the land to be a gift from God for the
purpose of religious liberty and an instance of
the kingdom of God on earth. The English Puritans created a colonial ethos in which the New
World had, in part at least, a religious significance. Materialism generally and the arts specifically were undervalued or discouraged by the
Puritans, for the most part on religious grounds,
since they were direct descendants of that aspect
of the Reformation which criticized religious expression in the arts as potentially idolatrous, pa-
pist, or ostentatious. Nevertheless, the Puritans
produced functional, well-crafted material objects for everyday life and worship that constitute folk-art evidence of deeply felt religious
convictions.

Their earliest religious artifacts include paintings, books, handicrafts, engravings, grave mark-

ers, and Bible boxes. A Bible box was a simple
wooden container, generally two to three feet
square by eight to ten inches deep, with hand-
carved patterns on the exterior. It was used
to store and protect the family Bible, a valued
possession.

Puritan iconoclasm did not eliminate the practice of portrait painting. The tradition of creating portraits of European Protestant leaders had
thrived since the sixteenth century. In seventeenth-century America preachers' portraits signified veneration. Some of these early American
portraits appear as flattened forms with masklike
austerity, primitive versions of English and
Northern European Reformation portraiture.
Examples include portraits painted in the style of
Anglo-Dutch realism, such as those depicting Dr.
John Clark (1664) and John Wheelwright (1677),
and John Foster's woodcut of Rev. Richard
Mather (1670). These somewhat rare paintings
and prints constitute a body of popular religious
imagery suggesting that the Puritans accepted
representational art which reflected their own
backgrounds, values, and leadership.

Puritanism was made up of many Protestant
movements in the New World, the more prominent reflecting strict Calvinist teachings that emphasized the authority of Scripture and morality.
These Puritans objected to the use in worship of
rites and vestments prescribed in the Anglican
Book of Common Prayer. Their attitudes toward
material goods and the arts were shaped by
strict teachings on piety, industriousness, and
austerity.

Nevertheless, Puritan communities produced
artifacts and handicraft items of great aesthetic
sensitivity, quality, and usefulness. Puritan families made furniture, kitchen utensils, linens,
quilts, and items of clothing that exhibited sim-

ple elegance while avoiding the appearance of materialistic pride.

At the same time, in the Southwest and West, another kind of religious and cultural awakening was finding expression in objects used for Roman Catholic worship and public piety. Whereas British and European Reformation notions of the arts shaped Puritan thought and practice, no similar influences shaped Mexican and Native American Catholic practice of the seventeenth century. On the contrary, Southwest American Catholicism produced a rich heritage of artworks that illustrates an indigenous and often primitive appropriation of European Roman Catholic Baroque styles.

The Roman Catholic church in Europe had explicitly approved the use of the arts in religious life in the Council of Trent (1545–1563), which sought to reform and strengthen the church in the face of internal pressures and external Protestant reform movements. Baroque art and architecture became the visual vocabulary of the Roman church in the Counter-Reformation of the sixteenth century. The church in Spain disseminated the Baroque style as it spread its political and religious influence around the world. Baroque art was introduced in South America by the Spanish conquistadors, and Spanish missionaries in the American Southwest introduced the style in architecture. For instance, Mission San José y San Miguel de Aguayo (1768–1782) in San Antonio, Texas, is considered the best example of a Spanish Baroque church in the United States.

The art of the Catholic communities was integrated more fully into daily life than that of the East Coast Puritans. "Spanish colonization of the Southwest and the period that followed produced perhaps the most distinctive religious folk arts in North America" (Dewhurst, MacDowell, and MacDowell, 1983, p. 5). This art was introduced into the region as early as the beginning of the seventeenth century, when Franciscan missionaries imported religious paintings and statuary. This tradition was not simply copied, the way Anglo-Dutch painting was assimilated into the culture of the Puritan colonies. In the Southwest an indigenous religious folk art emerged in stages of interaction and conflict with Spanish art until unique and primitive work like the *santos,* religious figures from colonial New Mexico, appeared. Local communities in New Mexico produced their own versions of holy objects, *retablos* (panel painting), *bultos* (carved figures of the Crucifixion), and liturgical articles that displayed complex sets of symbols. These richly decorated, highly colored objects are especially notable for their death imagery. This tradition is best illustrated in the ritual objects— e.g., candelabra, lanterns, wooden clackers, drums, and whips—found in the chapels and meeting rooms of the Penitente Brothers in New Mexico and Colorado. Especially poignant are the large crosses and death carts. Death carts, originally used during the Middle Ages to transport corpses to burial, are three- or four-wheeled carts, sometimes holding the figure of a skeleton, that were rolled through the streets ceremoniously to remind onlookers of impending death and judgment.

The legacy of Spanish and Indian Catholic artifacts continues into the twentieth century. Following essentially the format of its late-seventeenth-century antecedents, chapel architecture with *retablo* paintings, *bulto* carvings, and folk liturgical objects has persisted in the Southwest. In the twentieth century a new appreciation for religious folk art has led major museums to preserve this material culture. Academic interest among sociologists and cultural and art historians has resulted in an impressive and expanding bibliography.

As the two European traditions, Protestant and Catholic, established their contrasting religious practices in the East and Southwest, respectively, they came in contact with Native Americans, who had expressed their own natural religion in material objects venerating the earth, the sky, and their ancestors. Native American artifacts dating from 7000 B.C. and A.D. 1500 have been preserved. Functional pieces depicting ritual acts, fertility motifs, and shapes in nature are evidence of multiple cultural units across the country for whom no distinction was made between folk art and religious art. "Perhaps this inability to separate the sacred from the secular was the most common trait of Native American religious material culture" (Dewhurst et al., p. 2). Some Native American tribes developed graphic symbols that were painted or woven into skins and textiles. These symbols also expressed religious notions toward people, animals, and the natural environment in general.

Protestant settlers in the East avoided integration with the Native American population, and the Puritans borrowed almost none of the styles and art forms of Native American cultures. In the Southwest, however, Catholic religious art integrated indigenous elements of Native American culture with European styles.

Two folk-art forms popular in the Puritan tradition, namely needlework and gravestone carvings, illustrate the quality and productivity of religious folk art on the East Coast in the eighteenth century. Biblical subjects were popular as reflections of personal piety. These works are evidence of women's religious expression from a time when religious instruction and a proper familial role of women was particularly stressed. Quilts, samplers, and hangings created primarily by women served as didactic and devotional reminders for religious home life.

Gravestone carvings produced in the late seventeenth and throughout the eighteenth century display imagery concerning the inevitability of death and the promise of an afterlife. This form of carving is the earliest expression of a national sculptural tradition. Among the earliest known carvers was Joseph Lamson, who worked in Charlestown, Massachusetts, in the eighteenth century. Carved stones were normally located in graveyards near church buildings or in private family plots. Recurring subjects included the death's-head, scythe, hourglass, snuffed candles, the angel of death, and symbols of judgment. The types of stone most often selected were slate, mica schist, sandstone, and marble. After the mid-nineteenth century burial parks were introduced and more ambitious grave markers based on European sculptural models were designed.

ETHNIC CULTURES

Prior to 1800 the black American religious experience and non-Christian ethnic religious art, especially that of Jewish communities, made little or no impact on the dominant culture. Black slave communities, which existed as early as 1680, remained only marginally Christian, if at all, until the eighteenth century and the impact of the Great Awakening. Black religious folk art seemed modest and mysterious to the dominant New World culture, as it was rooted in African ritual life. Cultlike assemblages such as sticks,

vessels, stacked stones, bones, or fur at gravesites reflected African tribal customs; they constitute significant religious material culture of black slaves prior to the nineteenth century.

Although evidence suggests that the first American synagogue was founded as early as the seventeenth century in New Amsterdam, the Jewish population remained relatively small, perhaps 2,000 to 3,000 individuals, until the nineteenth century. Jewish material culture made no significant impact since art was created primarily to serve synagogue worship in the form of manuscripts, liturgical objects such as Torah shrines, and seasonal decor such as banners. Yet study of the liturgical arts of all religious traditions in the United States provides a significant body of material culture.

THE NINETEENTH CENTURY

The first major shift in the medium and subject matter of American religious art followed the American Revolution. Prior to the Revolution the leading figures of "high" art (that is, those professionally trained artists who were regarded as artists by the general public) included such outstanding painters as John Smibert, Gustavus Hesselius, Joseph Badger, Robert Feke, Benjamin West, John Singleton Copley, and John Trumbull. Portraiture was a major form, and many clergy portraits were painted. In their treatment of religious subjects these artists adapted European styles, especially that of Baroque painting. Notable are Hesselius' use of Rembrandt, West's relation to Nicholas Poussin, and Trumbull's visual references to Peter Paul Rubens. The shift is best illustrated in the works of West, who spent most of his professional life in England and was one of the first American-born artists to paint large canvases of religious subjects that were acquired by collectors and not intended for liturgical use. By the end of the eighteenth century European aestheticism, as expressed by the leading painters in Europe and America, resulted in works on religious subjects that thrived as high art separate from the liturgical and folk art, which reflected a deep, communal piety.

Religious Sects and Art. During the Revolution church attendance dropped dramatically, but shortly after the Revolution an increase in the immigrant population brought variety to the religious character of the nation. The number of Protestant groups increased in the nineteenth century, while the immigrant influx changed the nature of American ethnic and religious identity nationwide.

A small, strong, and socially active sect, the Society of Friends, or Quakers, produced simple material evidence of their religious outlook. Their meeting places, large rectangular rooms with no overt architectural style or decorative surfaces, their austere, practical clothing, and the objects they produced for daily living demonstrate what became known as the "plain style." The plainness of their material culture dates to their English origins in the mid-seventeenth century. In 1702 they were described as people who practiced abstinence and self-denial. They wore simple, coarse clothes and the women wore "no lace or superfluous ribbons" (Chamberlayne, 1708, p. 259). Even today, although more complex in their practices, the Quakers continue to express themselves in a plain style of material culture.

The Shakers, on the other hand, while also embracing simplicity and austerity, created one of America's richest legacies of religious material culture. Their official name was the United Believers in Christ's Second Coming. They came to the United States from England in 1774 under the guidance of Mother Ann Lee. The teachings of Ann Lee, including the injunction to celibacy, inspired the formation of eighteen communities with approximately 6,000 members by the mid-nineteenth century. Their clothing, furniture, textiles, boxes, stoves, and tools, as well as their inspirational drawings, embody the Shakers' religious attitudes. Distinctive but unencumbered designs and quality material indicate the Shakers' respect for human productivity, functional beauty, and the life of the Spirit; they produced some of the most beautifully crafted American folk art.

While the Shakers have been studied and their work exhibited extensively, the culture of the Northern Europeans who clustered in Pennsylvania, Michigan, Missouri, Texas, and the West has not been so well documented. By 1790 Moravians, Mennonites, Dunkards, Quakers, Evangelical Lutherans, Calvinist Reformers, and Schwenkfelders made up one-twelfth of the American population. Their aesthetic notions were born out of their European background in the Evangelical and Reformed traditions. While on the one hand they brought Luther's openness to the arts and music in the culture to bear in their daily lives, in worship many remained strictly Calvinist in their attitude toward the liturgical arts. In a general sense, this division contributed to a contemporary American tendency to equate enjoyment of the arts with leisure activity. The arts were relegated to the secular realm. Confusion concerning the role of the visual arts in Christian worship and life emerged as the arts were recognized as being capable of religious expression, which some religious traditions, on theological grounds, would not allow them to do.

Art and Religion. The so-called classical taste in religious art and architecture lingered longer in America than in Europe because in the new country classical forms, borrowed from the traditions they expressed in Europe, took on symbolic value and were equated with notions of Christian virtue and good. For example, in architecture the meetinghouse form acquired a classical portico facade such as in the First Congregational Church at Litchfield, Connecticut. Church building design appropriated classical elements with an intensity suggesting that the forms themselves connoted authority. Although artists who painted religious subjects based their aesthetics on Joshua Reynolds' *Discourses on Art* (a series of discourses delivered to the students of the Royal Academy, the final one in 1790), they based their theology on the power of the pulpit in American culture.

In the early nineteenth century, between the polarities of European taste and American Christian piety, a romantic alternative was introduced by artists such as Washington Allston, who created an art that equated spirit and form, that implied a painting could have spiritual qualities. American art emerged in a new sense as a vehicle of religious experience. Allston, a well-educated and traveled artist, treated nature in his paintings *The Deluge* (1804) and *Classical Landscape* (1821) as studies of mood and as the projection of his own vision. He became the embodiment of the spiritual artist to a whole generation of painters. For Allston, art was the great mediator between spirit and matter, freeing the sensuous or purely physical response from its earthly bonds.

According to Joshua Taylor, a twentieth-century historian of American art (and former director of the National Collection of Fine Arts in the Smithsonian Institution), artists in Europe and America adapted the doctrinal position of Emmanuel Swedenborg, who taught that heaven and hell exist within each person, that hell is a disruption of the harmonious functioning of the universe, and that heaven is the creation of harmony—a harmony that coordinates divine love and divine wisdom. Artists drew from this the notion that matter could be elevated to the realm of the spirit and that the artist's highest calling was "to catch those perfect moments when a physical manifestation gives way to spiritual awareness" (Taylor, 1972, p. 6).

Swedenborg's ideas especially influenced the painters William Page and George Inness. In 1860 Page painted a portrait of his wife standing before the Colosseum. Page had lived and worked in Rome for many years, and in this painting he not only captures a personal likeness but creates a composition that suggests mystery and timelessness. The figure's expression of inner consciousness connotes spiritual awareness. Inness painted scenes in nature that suggest an atmosphere laden with spiritual meanings. His *Home of the Heron* (1893) creates by virtue of brushstrokes and color combinations a dark and brooding landscape of a mysterious nature.

Images of the Sublime. Simultaneously there were painters who became preoccupied with expressing the sublime in natural scenery. In the 1820s some began to consider the relationship between landscape and mind, influenced by the currents of European romanticism. The most American expression of this relationship is seen in the Hudson River school of the first half of the nineteenth century.

Thomas Cole, for instance, was one devoted to the expression of the panorama of nature as the theater of human knowing. The small figures in Cole's paintings, dwarfed by vast natural phenomena, express the vulnerability of humanity, which is at the mercy of the natural order and the spirit behind it. According to Taylor, Cole "more nearly approaches an expression of the doctrine of predestination than any other major American painter" (p. 18).

Following Cole, many painters, such as Thomas Doughty, Asher B. Durand, and John F. Kensett, believed that nature had spiritual value

in itself. Their position is summarized by E. L. Magoon: "A majestic landscape, often scanned and truly loved, imparts much of its greatness to the mind and heart of the spectator. In viewing magnificent scenes, the soul, expanded and sublimed, is imbued with a spirit of divinity and appears, as it were, associated with the Deity Himself" (1852, p. 380). For instance, in contemplating Cole's *Departure and Return* (1837) or *The Voyage of Life* series (1840), the viewer assumes the position of a minuscule observer in a vast expanse of mysterious natural beauty. In the aesthetic response of awe and ecstasy the soul is "expanded and sublimed," according to mid-nineteenth-century ideals.

Images of Civil Religion. From the time of the Revolution to the present, the arts have expressed an aspect of American culture referred to as its civil religion. For those artists who believed that America was divinely elected (manifest destiny) or a "redeemer nation," public heroes and events were subject to religious interpretation. John Trumbull's famous painting *Declaration of Independence* (1818) captures a significant moment in the nation's history. A gathering of civic heroes is seen enacting civil religion at Independence Hall: a political act is depicted as an event that reflects the highest aspirations for a society living under God. Many artists painted national heroes—for instance, Robert W. Weir, *Embarkation of the Pilgrims* (1840), and John Gadsby Chapman, *The Baptism of Pocahontas* (1847)—who had gained mythological status. Among the many works that portrayed the "saints" of the redeemer nation's history, Trumbull's illustrating the American scene during and immediately following the Revolution are usually cited as the best.

From the Sublime to the Medieval. After the middle of the nineteenth century artists with specifically religious interests turned from a preoccupation with nature and historic events to references taken from the history of painting, especially the medieval period. Influenced in part by the Pre-Raphaelite Brotherhood of England, artists such as John LaFarge emphasized medieval modes of expression as though their association with historic tradition suggested spiritual truths. LaFarge, a pioneer muralist with an interest in medieval art and stained glass, was given many ecclesiastical commissions. His famous murals for Trinity Church, Boston, done in

1876, helped shape liturgical art in the nineteenth century and introduced a note of internationalism to the American art scene.

In architecture a recapitulation of medieval themes appears in Ralph Adams Cram's design for the Cathedral of St. John the Divine in New York City and St. Paul's Church in Detroit, Michigan. Bertram G. Goodhue joined the firm of Cram in Boston and extended the so-called "Gothic manner" in nineteenth-century church architecture in his designs for the churches of St. Thomas and St. Bartholomew in New York City.

After the 1870s the painter John LaFarge, joined by Elihu Vedder and Albert Pinkham Ryder, relied heavily on historicizing subject matter, insisting that truth lay within the individual's experience of the past. The dramatic presentation of figures in colorful historical settings was a preoccupation of late-nineteenth-century American art, and of liturgical art in particular. Highly stylized figures represented personifications of emotional states or cherished values. Figures depicting fear or joy and images of the muses decorated public spaces. Note, for instance, the intense interest in mood and visual impact in Henry Ossawa Turner's *The Annunciation* (1898), where the appearance of the angel as a brilliant column of light floods the room and yet leaves the enigmatic Mary as a seemingly moody and depressed figure.

Generally, American art in the nineteenth century emphasized the quest for the divine that took place outside the structures of religious organizations. Early in the century, narrative art emphasized heroic action and inspiration. By mid-century, the notion of the sublime implied that truth could be discovered in the experience of nature. In the latter half of the century, historicizing continued with an added stress on the personal experiences of the figures in the compositions. Paintings emphasized the notion that experiential religion led toward salvation.

THE TWENTIETH CENTURY

Within the development of the visual arts in the twentieth century, religious art became radically individualized. Mainstream movements—expressionism, cubism, surrealism, pop art, abstract expressionism—emphasized the identity and interior vision of individual artists. If present at all, religious subject matter expressed the private religious feelings of the artist.

Where traditional religious iconography appears, it is often presented more as an expression of personal experience and choice than as a work in the service of a traditional religious community. For example, Marc Chagall's *White Crucifixion* (1938) is a poignant reference to Jewish experience in Russia in the first quarter of the century. Chagall, a Russian who lived in France and the United States, showed a lifelong preoccupation with biblical stories in his paintings, engravings, and stained-glass windows. George Segal's life-sized figures of *Abraham's Sacrifice* (1973) constitute his personal response to modern American history and the Holocaust.

Twentieth-century Catholic and Protestant art has also emphasized individuality, albeit in different ways. The Second Vatican Council (1962–1965) provided guidelines on the arts and liturgy that encourage the arts in service to the full life of the church. Since then populist mentality has encouraged vernacular expression, folk art, and folk music in Roman Catholic life. Protestant interest in liturgical forms and in greater artistic expression has increased. Liturgical art, furnishings, and vessels are common to both traditions.

In this century visual art and liturgical paraphernalia designed and produced exclusively for religious communities have been provided to a large extent by supply houses whose catalogs are repositories of contemporary American religious material culture. Mail-order objects separate the individuality of the artist and the vitality of the created symbol from the community. Vestments and liturgical objects, such as standing altar crosses and vessels, have become standardized due to their easy availability and relatively low cost. Catalogs that offer for sale anonymously mass-produced religious objects constitute a commentary on American religious values. Copies of Warner Sallman's *Head of Christ,* sold through religious outlets and catalogs, saturate the American Christian public; in fact, Salman's is the dominant contemporary image of Jesus.

Sacred Objects in a Secular Age. From the late nineteenth century to the late twentieth century, the coincidence of national holidays and liturgical celebrations has produced a material culture that is principally economically motivated. Christmas is the most visible example of a nationwide secular holiday based on a religious tradition. The free enterprise system attests to the significance of the Christmas season by producing many items of material culture that reflect popular religious and social notions, e.g., Christmas commercial art, greeting cards, and decorations. Religious objects appear alongside objects of a secular and socially popular nature. For instance, a Nativity scene, Santa Claus, and a red-nosed reindeer may have equal billing; sacred and secular subjects are reduced to the service of holiday decor.

A functionalist perspective is reflected in the usage of some twentieth-century religious objects and symbols. During World War II small copies of the New Testament were bound with metal covers to serve as bulletproof objects when carried in a shirt pocket. Plastic images of saints stuck to automobile dashboards are meant to protect occupants against physical harm. The Star of David, used by Nazi regimes in Europe as a negative public symbol to identify Jewish citizens, has become an image of pride in the United States and elsewhere.

While some religious imagery in the United States has become diluted or more secular in character, some has remained more strictly sacred and potentially controversial. First, the power of certain readily identifiable religious symbols is not diminished. The Menorah, the seven-branched lamp of the sanctuary in the wilderness (see Exodus 25:31–40) that became a standard liturgical object in Jewish worship, and the Christian cross, the symbol of Christ's Crucifixion, maintain their cultural impact and integrity because they hold a central place in the liturgical and private lives of the faithful. American government agencies strenuously avoid the use of explicit religious symbols because the separation of church and state is a basic tenet of the Constitution. Communities battle in public and in the courts over the placement of, or priorities given to, religious symbols, such as Nativity scenes in public parks or the Menorah or Star of David in a public area.

Second, certain other powerful images continue to serve large religious constituencies. Since World War II Holocaust monuments have appeared in cities across the United States. They serve as memorials to the millions who died under Nazi rule in Europe. Another instance is the statue of Our Lady of Guadalupe in Mexico. Based on a vision a Christianized Indian had of the Virgin Mary on a hillside northwest of Mexico City on 9 December 1531, the statue has for more than four centuries attracted thousands of pilgrims annually, who come to venerate the miraculous image. Pope Pius XII in 1945 called Our Lady of Guadalupe the "Queen of Mexico and Empress of the Americas" and said that her statue had been painted "by brushes that were not of this world." The statue's fame had spread so far by the mid-eighteenth century that its patronage was acknowledged for all of New Spain, from upper California to El Salvador. Small statues of her image, "holy card" pictures, and related souvenirs constitute material culture associated with supernatural powers of healing and protection. She is a major figure in the contemporary mosaic decoration in the Shrine of the Immaculate Conception in Washington, D.C.

Assimilated Traditions. Two sources of religious objects produced by immigrant traditions in the twentieth century illustrate the contributions of subcultures to the material culture of the United States: voodoo objects from the Caribbean islands and Buddhist images and artifacts inspired by Far Eastern cultures, especially those of Southeast Asia.

The religion of *santería,* from Cuba, combines African tribal customs with Roman Catholicism. There are available in some American supermarkets today mass-produced glass candle-holders on which are images of the *santería,* i.e., symbols of the Crucifixion juxtaposed with figures of tribal deities. Recent Haitian immigration has added voodoo practitioners and their religious objects to American culture.

In the 1960s American youth and some of their leaders created a renewed interest in Eastern religions. Buddhist teachings and practice were adapted by those who sought a nature-oriented or spiritual religion. Zen Buddhism was popularized and meditation was marketed. There was an increased interest in Eastern art, especially prints of mandalas, figured circles that serve to focus the mind during meditation.

In the late 1970s Buddhists from Vietnam and Cambodia came to America, joining established Buddhist traditions. Recent celebrations of the Buddha's birthday have introduced liturgical objects. For instance, figures have appeared in the 1980s depicting the baby Buddha as an infant with a lighted halo and flowing ribbons around the waist, an image borrowed from Western figures of the New Year. Buddhist temple architecture is under construction nationwide, especially in California, Colorado, and Connecticut, where the larger Buddhist communities have settled.

Conclusions. Religiously significant material culture has been produced in every phase of American religious life since prehistoric times, providing primary evidence for the study and understanding of this religious history. The various traditions have produced material culture reflecting their beliefs and practices.

In the modern era, especially in the twentieth century, American religious material culture and visual arts fall into five categories different from denominational or traditionally religious categories. First, a vast amount of religious material culture is commercial. For instance, much jewelry includes religious symbols of various traditions, e.g., the cross, the Star of David, and the crescent.

Second, certain mass-produced objects, vessels, and artworks serve the institutional needs of the main religions. The majority of liturgical vessels, objects, vestments, and printed materials, for example, are ordered from catalogs.

Third, the priority given to radical individuality in the society shapes religious art. When a religious community commissions an artist or architect, his personal style shapes the end result, i.e., the material culture. The result is more likely to reflect the individual artist than the commissioning institution.

Fourth, the inherent power of some religious symbols appears stronger in the twentieth century than in the past. The public display of symbols that appears to give priority to one religious tradition over another creates social friction and controversy. Although some religious material culture has lost its religious impact in a post-Christian pluralistic age, some remains highly charged as specifically religious. Misplaced religious symbols can become politicized and create conflicting constituencies.

Fifth, American religious pluralism has increased as ecumenical dialogue achieves mergers of denominations as well as cooperation among religions. This expanding pluralism expresses itself in the material culture of subculture religions such as Buddism and *santería.*

Beyond these five categories American culture shows a tradition of authentic works and objects—high art, folk art, and functional pieces —that serves established religious communities. Religious material culture continues to be produced in order to meet needs and to express perspectives of religions old and new.

BIBLIOGRAPHY

Sydney Ahlstrom, *A Religious History of the American People* (1972); Edward Chamberlayne, *Magnae Britanniae Notitia; or, The Present State of Great Britain* (1708); Fray Angélico Chávez, "The Penitentes of New Mexico," in *New Mexico Historical Review,* 29 (1954); C. Kurt Dewhurst, Betty MacDowell, and Marsha MacDowell, *Religious Folk Art in America: Reflections of Faith* (1983); John Dillenberger, *The Visual Arts and Christianity in America: The Colonial Period Through the Nineteenth Century* (1984); Samuel M. Green, "English Origins of Seventeenth-Century Painting," in Ian M. G. Quimby, ed., *American Painting to 1776: A Reappraisal* (1971).

Allan I. Ludwig, *Graven Images: New England Stonecarving and Its Symbols, 1650–1815* (1966); Elias L. Magoon, *Westward Empire of the Great Drama of Human Progress* (1852); Pope Pius XII, "Our Lady of Guadalupe," in *New Catholic Encyclopedia,* vol. 6; Joshua Reynolds, *Discourses on Art,* Robert R. Wark, ed. (1959); Leland M. Roth, *A Concise History of America in Architecture* (1979); Thomas J. Schlereth, ed., *Material Culture Studies in America* (1982); Joshua Taylor, "Introduction," in Jane Dillenberger and Joshua Taylor, eds., *The Hand and the Spirit: Religious Art in America, 1700–1900* (1972); Maurice Tuckman et al., eds., *The Spiritual in Art: Abstract Painting, 1890–1985* (1986).

[*See also* LITURGY AND WORSHIP; *and* RELIGIOUS ARCHITECTURE AND LANDSCAPE.]

Part VIII
RELIGION AND THE POLITICAL AND SOCIAL ORDERS

CHURCH AND STATE

Glenn Miller

THE history of church-state relations in the United States includes more than constitutional provisions, legislative acts, and court decisions. The interaction of religious institutions and government has developed in conjunction with the religious customs and social patterns of the nation and can be regarded through anthropological, religious, sociological, and legal perspectives. In fact, American courts and legislatures have used national tradition (consciously or not) as one basis of legal directives.

THE COLONIAL PERIOD

The South. The first lasting English settlement was established at Jamestown, Virginia, in 1607. While the new settlers brought a chaplain with them, the Reverend Robert Hunt, the status of the church in Virginia was not clear from the colonial charters and, despite laws relating to establishment (such as those defining parish boundaries, setting stipends for clergy, and providing for vestries), was never completely clarified in the colonial period. Although the bishop of London assumed, for example, the right to ordain clergy for Virginia and the other Anglican colonies, Parliament never granted him the authority to do so.

What was true of Virginia was true of the other southern colonies. After a colony had survived its early years, various laws were enacted in the legislature to create an establishment similar to the Church of England. The legislatures believed that religion was a necessary part of life and saw the laws as securing the best faith for the people. The establishment laws reflected a belief in one people organized into two coordinate bodies: church and state.

The exception to the usual southern pattern of establishing Anglicanism by charter and early legislation was Maryland. The colony, a private venture of Cecil Calvert, Lord Baltimore, was designed to be a refuge for wealthy Catholics who were suffering under the anti-recusant laws of England that deprived English Catholics of most civil rights. The flaw in Baltimore's plan, however, was that the colony's Protestants (who had originally immigrated as servants) prospered and multiplied. The Protestants were no longer willing to be in a subservient position and demanded their rights as Englishmen, which at the time included Protestant churches.

When the Glorious Revolution of 1688 removed the Catholic James II from the throne and revived Protestant self-assertiveness, the Protestants began their attempt to establish the Church of England in the colony. Just as Catholic power had been forced to retreat in England before a determined Protestant opposition, so the colonial Protestants hoped to transform Maryland into a Protestant colony. The colonial legislation creating the Church of Maryland was approved by London in 1702. Ironically, Maryland adopted laws against Catholicism modeled on the various anti-recusant laws of England. Although these laws were never completely enforced, the Roman Catholic church was forced to practice a private ministry, often conducted by itinerant priests in the homes of wealthy Catholics. Individual believers lost valuable civil rights as a result of these laws, including the right to vote and to hold office.

The attempt to transplant the Church of England to southern soil involved many difficulties. Like other European churches, England's state church was governed by a combination of tradition, statutes, and legally binding customs. A comparison between the methods of appointing and maintaining clerics in the Old and New World may illustrate some of the problems.

A young English cleric received his living after he was graduated as A.B. or A.M. from a university, ordained by a bishop as deacon or priest, nominated by a patron (usually a great landowner), and installed according to canon law. Once these conditions were met, the benefice (literally, the good thing granted; a term used to describe an individual's right to tithes and other ecclesiastical revenues) was a freehold (literally, real property held without financial obligation to another) to which the incumbent cleric had a legal claim for life. In the event of sickness or the press of duties (many clergy possessed several livings), the minister might hire a curate to read the services. His income, were he a country parson, came from tithes on agricultural products and earnings of the parish farm, or glebe. In urban areas, where there were no tithes, the income came from investments, rents, or voluntary gifts. Since the parish priest was a professional, he often supplemented his funds by such means as surveying, medical practice, or secretarial works.

The social order of seventeenth- and eighteenth-century Virginia did not permit such an elaborate system. The key to appointment in the colonies was the vestry. In England the vestry was an insignificant lay committee, concerned with maintaining the fabric of the parish (the various physical aspects of a church, including buildings, pews, altars, the cemetery, etc.) and the determination of poor rates (taxes for social maintenance) in it. In America the vestry often functioned like a parish board, calling and dismissing priests at will. Although in theory the governor of an Anglican colony was the patron of the church and charged with an individual's formal induction into a parish, the vestry often functioned like a modern parish board, calling and dismissing priests at will. Only a few priests, not all, managed to secure the freehold ownership of their livings and the attached glebes.

One of the most dramatic changes from Old World practice in the New World was in the method of payment. The colonial Virginia clergyman was paid a predetermined salary in pounds of tobacco raised by a tax on the property of his congregation. Since the price of tobacco varied and the Virginia planters tended to overestimate the market, the salary was always less than its hypothetical value. A 1758 law in Virginia attempted some relief for the ministry by establishing the cash value of a parish, but the Parson's Cause, in which the famed Patrick Henry was the most important attorney, found the new arrangement contrary to law in 1763.

In England parishes were small geographically, and the priest could walk around the boundaries in a day. (Canon law required a minister to do this once a year.) In contrast, New World parishes were huge, and no single individual could provide the level of pastoral care possible in the Old World. Catechism classes were frequently not held, and many people, unable to travel the distance to the parish church (which could be as much as fifty miles), lost the discipline provided by the regular reading of the *Book of Common Prayer.* As a result, many people, although they retained a warm regard for Christianity, lost the subtle Anglican expressions of the faith. In the eighteenth century, when new denominations flooded the southern countryside, these nominal Anglicans were easy targets for conversion.

James Blair, a commissary of the bishop of London, founded the College of William and Mary in 1693. Like the great English universities of Oxford and Cambridge, the school symbolized the commitment of the colony's government to educate the "public" (the 10 percent of the population that ruled in church and state). The ideal of the school was that a common program in arts would forge habits of cooperation between the future rulers of church and state necessary to the smooth functioning of a Christian commonwealth.

An equally significant step in strengthening the southern establishments was made by Thomas Bray, commissary of Maryland, who was instrumental in the founding of two missionary societies: the Society for the Propagation of the Gospel in Foreign Parts (S.P.G.) in 1701 and the Society for the Promotion of Christian Knowledge (S.P.C.K.) in 1698. The purpose of both was to strengthen the ministry, the former by enlisting young English clerics to serve in the colonies, and the latter by providing libraries for ministers. Possession of a library provided ministers with the resources needed to prepare young men for university and, hence, with the opportunity to raise extra money by conducting an informal school.

New England. The Holy Commonwealths of

Massachusetts Bay (including Maine), Connecticut, and New Hampshire possessed a common history. Despite slight variations, these colonies conceived of and treated the relationship between church and state according to the same general principles.

The motives for establishing the first successful New England colonies of Plymouth and Massachusetts Bay were complex. The Puritans, a sect in the Church of England advocating a more Reformed (a term commonly applied to those churches that traced their heritage to Zwingli and Calvin) style of church, experienced increased pressure to conform to the worship and polity established by law during the reigns of Elizabeth I, James I, and Charles I. Although a primary reason for the new settlements was to escape persecution at home, the Puritans did not advocate religious liberty. Their vision of the New World was shaped by biblical eschatology and a fervent belief in the righteousness of their cause. The New World was to be the consummation of God's acts in history and the place where Antichrist was to be defeated decisively. The Puritans wanted nothing less than a "new" England that, by means of its purity in faith and morals, would spur old England to repentance.

The character of the New England dream demanded much fidelity to the traditions of the old country. As in the southern colonies, the model for church and state was English. The commonwealth was composed of two coordinate spheres, ecclesiastical and political, that interacted with each other to provide for the common good. Education was the meeting place of the two spheres, and Harvard College, established in 1636, educated gentlemen for service to both church and state.

Despite adjustments in church polity, the parish system of England remained the model for church life. Each colony was carefully divided into towns, similar to the towns and villages of England, and each town was served by one pastor. As in the South, the lack of traditional sources of revenue meant that taxation (outside of Boston, where ministers were supported by individual contributions) was the primary means of clerical support, although most ministers also received manse and glebe. The salary was about £100 a year, close to the average in England. In line with their understanding of church-state relations, buildings were provided by the towns. Most often the actual construction was done by

the male population, who were rewarded with rum for their efforts. The materials used in construction and the furnishings were often donated by pious individuals who wanted to glorify God, although the actual raw lumber might be cut on town lands.

New England differed from the Old World in the complex theory and practice of church government that the Puritans developed from a synthesis of European Reformed theology, their experience in England, and the colonial context. In theory a clear line separated the church from the parish or society: the church was composed of all those who had had a conversion experience and were eligible for full communion, while the society was everyone living in the town. The church called the pastor and established doctrine; the society paid the pastor and other religious expenses. Since those who paid the pastor and those who selected him were different, there was always the danger of a disagreement between church and town, and in fact the system never worked well. By 1670 some localities had blurred the lines between church and town; by 1690 a few had completely abandoned it. The full rigors of the New England Way (the combination of polity, theology, and legal tradition in the region), ironically, became an issue in the Great Awakening of the 1740s, when a dramatic increase in the number of converts seemed to make the system possible. Reformers, including Jonathan Edwards, believed that saints who had experienced dramatic conversions were now so common that congregations could again limit their membership to those who met the higher requirement without destroying the underlying unity of congregation and town.

New England was never a theocratic government. Although ministers were honored and invited to preach on such occasions as government elections, power was firmly in the hands of the magistrates. Technically, the church could enforce no civil penalties and was restricted to ecclesiastical excommunication. New England was not a uniquely "biblical" commonwealth. While the laws of the Old Testament had an effect on the enactments of the various Puritan legislatures, biblical precepts were also honored in the common and statute laws of England. Provisions against common sins such as adultery tended to be similar in old and New England, as were other laws regulating private behavior.

Puritan theology was a mosaic of Scripture,

reason, and experience, held in careful balance by paradoxes and dichotomies. An unskillful practitioner of the divine art stood in danger of losing the symmetry of the whole and falling into one heresy or another. Nonetheless, when the intricate pattern was distorted, the Puritan state attempted to set it aright by persecuting the offenders.

The most notorious case of persecution was that of Anne Hutchinson of Boston. She had immigrated to the New World to sit under John Cotton, her former pastor in England. In good Puritan fashion her home became the center of a prayer group, originally female, that met to discuss the sermons presented on Sunday. The prayer group evolved to include men as well as women (which violated the strongly held patriarchal sensibilities of many New Englanders) and, more seriously, began to criticize the sermons of John Wilson, Cotton's senior pastor at the First Church. After some skillful maneuvers by Hutchinson's enemies, Cotton was persuaded to desert his protégée, and Hutchinson was convicted of heresy and banished from the colony in 1637.

A similar fate befell Roger Williams, a young and promising minister who came to New England in 1630. Williams believed the Gospel demanded that the Puritans separate completely from the Church of England and that the Indians be compensated for the loss of their lands. The first charge struck at Massachusetts Bay's sense of its religious mission; the second, at its economy. Williams was banished and fled south to the area around present-day Providence, Rhode Island.

The relatively mild treatment given to Hutchinson and Williams was not extended to the Quakers. The early Society of Friends was believed to be especially dangerous in New England because it developed the Protestant doctrine of conscience to the point that the "inner light" was said to have an authority of its own. At first the Quakers were warned away from New England, but when their evangelistic zeal led them to return, the Puritan magistrates ordered executions under laws that Massachusetts had recently passed outlawing the sect. Between 1659 and 1661 William Robinson, Marmaduke Stephenson, Mary Dyer, and William Leddra were hanged on Boston Common. The executions stopped only when London demanded that all cases involving Friends be sent to England for trial.

The strange affair of the Salem witch trials in 1692 called into question the Puritan leadership of New England. Trials and executions of witches were common in seventeenth-century Europe and were based on the belief that magic involved an alliance with Satan and endangered the community. When the original fires of Puritan piety began to die down, however, witches came to be seen as evidence of the truth of the Christian religion, and the clergy (especially, Increase and Cotton Mather) searched earnestly for signs of the invisible realm. Although the clergy had little to do with the course of events in Salem village and warned against the use of improper evidence, the executions and accusations weakened the church establishment.

At about the same time as the trials, great changes were occurring in the government of Massachusetts Bay. The colony (which had been semi-independent of England) was rechartered as a royal colony with a governor appointed by the king. Although the dire consequence predicted by the clergy did not occur, the loss of its former charter forced Massachusetts to adopt a limited toleration of non-Puritan churches, and the other Puritan colonies followed its example.

Utopian Religious Experiments. The vast American spaces permitted the construction of what might be called utopian experiments. The earliest of these were Rhode Island and Providence Plantations. When Roger Williams was forced into exile in 1635, he went south and purchased land from the Indians. The area around Narragansett Bay attracted other deviants from the New England Way. Williams persuaded the earliest settlers to create legal structures protecting the colony's diversity. During the Puritan Revolution in England, he secured a charter that promised full religious freedom.

The passions raised by Williams' experiment in freedom were evident in the debates over the charter. Williams published *The Bloudy Tenent of Persecution for Cause of Conscience,* one of the classics of early American political theory, in 1644. John Cotton of Boston responded with the *Bloudy Tenent Washed and Made White In the Bloud of the Lambe,* followed by another blast from Williams, *The Bloudy Tenent Yet More Bloudy.* John Clarke, a less-well-known but important Baptist spokesman, provided practical evidence to support Williams' theory. In his *Ill-News from New-England,* Clarke detailed the persecution of dissenters in Massachusetts.

The best argument for Rhode Island's freedom was not intellectual but pragmatic: religious liberty worked. Not even the arrival of the Quakers, feared as sources of disorder elsewhere, weakened the colony's economic and social prosperity. The different groups learned to work, bargain, and govern together. If many New Englanders believed that Rhode Island was the sewer of the region, others found the freedom of the colony exciting. A thriving Congregational church was among the many churches that dotted Newport, and Jewish merchants entered the area at an early date. The College of Rhode Island (founded in 1763), although sponsored by Baptists, had members of different denominations on its governing board.

William Penn, the Quaker son of an English admiral, was another visionary, who, in 1681, received a royal grant to a large area west of the Delaware, which the king named Pennsylvania. Penn saw the grant as an opportunity for a holy experiment. He believed, as did other Friends, that God had implanted in all humanity an inner light which provided the individual with guidance. No established church was needed, consequently, to secure harmony and order. Much like the early Puritans, Penn hoped that his colony would prove to the world the truth of his convictions. Pennsylvania's Frame of Government, although not as liberal as that of Rhode Island, provided that residents need only believe in God, although magistrates had to profess belief in Jesus Christ as Savior.

Penn seemed to know that pluralism made freedom a practical as well as a theoretical necessity. He made land available to people of various backgrounds, securing a diversity of religious opinions among the population (and, of course, enriching the proprietor). After the tolerant Quakers had nursed the colony through its early stages, they were able to share political power without weakening its commitment to religious freedom.

Pennsylvania was important in the evolution of the characteristic American form of Christianity: the denomination. Unlike the traditional European churches, the denomination does not claim to be coterminous with the population as a whole; it is only part of the larger whole and has to be named (nominated) to be distinguished. The denomination is not a sect that withdraws from the world but rather an active body, evangelizing, advocating its own perspectives, and

having a corporate status of its own. Many religious groups developed important features of their respective polity and self-understandings in Pennsylvania: Anglicans learned to function without governmental support and to cooperate with other religious groups in the government of the college of Philadelphia. Baptists organized their first association in the Philadelphia area and used it as a basis for missions and education. Presbyterians likewise developed many of the American features of their polity in the colony's free atmosphere.

Not all of the groups in Pennsylvania became denominations, although as a rule the larger ones did. The German sects, including the Brethren, the Mennonites, Moravians, and the radical Pietists at Ephrata, were small and often settled in remote areas. Their tight communities and comparative geographic segregation enabled them to retain their characteristic practices and attitudes.

A Great and General Revival. From 1720 to 1770 a series of revivals occurred in British North America. Present to some extent in all of the colonies, the revival was strongest in New England, New Jersey, and after 1760, in Virginia and the Carolinas. Although historians disagree about the extent of the revival, the new movement increased the size of the churches, created a widespread interest in religion, and often led Americans, clerical and lay, to define faith in terms of an experience of conversion.

The most prominent early leaders of the revival were members of either an established church or a church that had a long history of establishment (such as the Presbyterians, who were established in Scotland, and the Dutch Reformed, the official church of Holland). Their message was intended to revive the existing churches and not to introduce any innovations into piety and worship. They wanted to revive or reenliven the faith once delivered to the saints. The revivalists, including Jonathan Edwards, devoted much effort to demonstrating that the Awakening was a renewal of traditional theology and piety. Despite such claims, the revival changed American religion institutionally and theologically.

The awakeners, on fire for the salvation of souls, were not respecters of the parish system. The most noted revivalists were itinerant or traveling preachers, a practice that spread to the smaller denominations. Such leaders as Theodore Frelinghuysen, Gilbert Tennent, and George Whitefield urged their hearers to flee from the preaching of "unconverted" men to the ministry of those who were able to evoke the desired conversion experience. The choice of where to worship and whom to hear became an intensely personal matter that was not to be trusted to an established church or the judicatories (church officials) of churches independent of the state.

Opponents of the movement, called Old Lights among the Congregationalists and Old Sides among the Presbyterians, noted the theological radicalism of this new perspective. If all ministers were not held equally capable of providing adequate spiritual direction, then the belief that agreement in doctrine and practice was sufficient to secure the unity of the church was defective. Since that belief provided the underpinning of European Christendom, the Great Awakening weakened the religious establishment in America.

One problem not anticipated by the first awakeners was the tendency of the revival to change patterns of church affiliation. While many of those converted remained within their traditional denominations, others sought new affiliations. The Baptists, who would be among the most determined American opponents of an established church, were a small denomination when the revival began, but by 1800 they were among the five largest denominations, with strong congregations in every state.

In some ways the Awakening also contributed to the American Revolution. In 1740 the colonies were isolated from each other and had almost no awareness of continental issues. The Awakening helped them to see themselves as having common interests. The career of George Whitefield, a famous evangelist, was avidly followed by people throughout British North America, and the periodic publication of portions of his *Journal* helped to create awareness of a common culture. The revivalists, further, espoused a theology that interpreted America as the beginning of the fulfillment of the promises of Scripture, especially the coming of the kingdom of God. This theology, often called postmillennialism, laid the foundations of a new American patriotism that was easily transformed into nationalism when the Revolutionary crises began. The patriotic sermons of Samuel Davis

and Aaron Burr, two of the most effective revivalists, during the French and Indian Wars, were models for later preaching during the Revolution.

THE ENLIGHTENMENT

The late seventeenth and early eighteenth centuries were a period of rapid intellectual change. The new physics, pioneered by Copernicus and Galileo, was completed by Sir Isaac Newton, who formulated scientific laws summarizing the discoveries of two centuries. The change wrought by the popularization of the new science was not merely a change in cosmology, it was a change in the methods and procedures constitutive of knowledge itself. Slowly—but surely—European peoples were adopting a new understanding of the world.

The new style of knowing admitted no inherent boundaries. The success of mathematical physics convinced people that progress could be made in other areas, and philosophers sought new understandings of all areas of nature and experience. Neither humankind nor religion was spared such examination.

The effects of this reevaluation of religion were manifold. The outward manifestations of religion came to be seen as far less important than the inward. For many, religion became synonymous with conscience or a matter of conscience. Since no government was believed to be able to control the interior life of humankind, it followed that religion was inherently free.

Theological changes among Christians also indicated a significant change in the apprehension of faith. For deists the Christian doctrine of a supernatural God who intervened in space and time was dated. In its place the deists proposed a God who was totally beyond the realm of ordinary experience. This God had created the world and left its governance to nature's orderly processes.

Less radical thinkers felt obliged to retain more of the traditional belief in God and Christ, although they also believed that these doctrines needed revision. The miracles of Christ, for example, were cited as evidence for his unique role in Christian theology. They had value as evidence partially because most educated people had surrendered belief in the everyday occurrence of supernatural events. John Locke, whose analysis of knowledge was widely influential, was typical of this more moderate reinterpretation of Christianity. Like others, he interpreted the claim that Jesus was the Messiah as primarily related to the universality of his teachings and had serious private doubts about the divinity of Christ and the doctrine of the Trinity.

Even conservative religious leaders adjusted traditional doctrine to some extent. Most often the results of moderate or radical philosophy were added to existing systems of thought, more or less as an introduction to the received doctrines. Thus, religious conservatives, including Archbishop John Tillotson, Bishop Joseph Butler, and John Wesley, spoke as often of natural religion or the God of nature as did their more radical counterparts.

A century of theological change had the effect of creating a shared language about faith that included belief in Nature and Nature's God and Providence. While Christian in origin, it was separable from its origin. This new religious language allowed diverse individuals to speak across traditional boundaries of denomination or even religion. Enlightenment philosophers and divines assumed that Protestants, Catholics, and Jews shared a common religious understanding (at least in regard to general categories) and, hence, that appeals could be made to all men of good will.

In English-speaking areas the new philosophy of religion acquired various shades of English Whig political philosophy. In the 1680s the Roman Catholic faith of England's James II came to be seen as politically dangerous. Louis XIV of France was the dominant power on the Continent and had considerable influence on the English court. Further, Louis was actively suppressing his own Protestant minority and, in 1685, revoked the Edict of Nantes, which had provided Protestants with some legal protections.

James II was overthrown in a political coup—the Glorious Revolution—that brought William and Mary to the throne. To secure the loyalty of the "dissenters" (Protestants outside of the national church) an Act of Toleration was passed in 1689. Philosophers such as Locke rushed to defend the Glorious Revolution. They saw government as based on a covenant between ruler and subjects in which the subjects exchanged certain liberties for certain protections. This social con-

tract was, however, limited in that citizens could not be asked to surrender such natural rights as those to life, liberty, and property. When government infringed on those areas, the people had the right to change the government. So to speak, the existence of tyranny justified actions on the part of a nation's citizens that might return the nation to a state of nature and thereby allow them to begin the reconstruction of political life on new constitutional principles.

The conjunction of the Glorious Revolution and the Act of Toleration meant—especially for the more radical—that religious liberty was one area necessarily excluded from the social contract. No person could be made to surrender the control of his conscience to another, and attempts to force him to do so were violations of the social contract. Nonetheless, most of those who supported the new Whig political philosophy and who had helped to remove James II continued to believe in the need for a church established by law as part of government, although they refused to give that church exclusive status.

Tracing the movement of ideas from England to the provinces is difficult. By 1730 the new philosophy was known in Edinburgh and in Boston and Philadelphia. Thereafter its spread among the elite was rapid. The colonial colleges, especially Harvard, William and Mary, and the College of New Jersey (later Princeton), became centers of a moderate interpretation of Enlightenment philosophy that accepted the new scientific epistemology, some of its theological implications, and much of the Whig philosophy of government. John Witherspoon, the Scottish cleric and educator who served as president of the College of New Jersey, was particularly important in this process as he was one of the most active advocates of Scottish commonsense philosophy. Common sense was an easily understood, intensely moral interpretation of the Enlightenment, well suited to the pulpit. Commonsense philosophers argued that scientific method was only the careful application of common sense and experimental verification to the external world; religion (as it was for many other Enlightenment schools) was rooted in an inherent moral sense that informed all persons of the rectitude of their actions.

Not all Americans interested in the new philosophy followed the moderate course pursued by the colleges. Benjamin Franklin learned about deism while in England and shared his perspective with close friends. Thomas Jefferson, a graduate of William and Mary and a passionate reader, seems to have learned his deistic critique of Christianity from his own program of reading, as did such leaders as George Washington. Washington, who was always cautious about his public expressions of his religious views, remained a non-communicant throughout his life and appears to have shared much of the deism common to the Masonic lodges of the period.

Other Americans encountered Enlightenment ideas in more conservative form. The Baptist Isaac Backus, who experienced the repressive New England laws demanding the payment of set taxes for the maintenance of the legally installed pastor and whose coreligionists were often arrested and convicted under laws prohibiting itinerant preaching, mastered Locke's arguments for toleration in order more effectively to write and preach for complete religious liberty in New England. Other Baptist exhorters, such as John Leland, who ministered in both Massachusetts and Virginia, followed him in the use of Locke's appeals for tolerance. Revivalists of all denominations found appeals to individual conscience and its freedom useful in their preaching.

By 1760 the leadership of British North America as well as many of the people had adopted various forms of Enlightenment philosophy. The Enlightenment was part of the intellectual coin of the realm, and its ideas were familiar enough not to require explication. When the imperial crisis between England and the colonies deepened, the colonists drew on the philosophical and religious language of Enlightenment philosophy to buttress their arguments.

THE REVOLUTIONARY PERIOD

From the end of the French and Indian Wars in 1763 to 1776, tensions between Great Britain and the colonies increased. The problems began, ironically, with one of the most successful joint endeavors of the empire: the exclusion of French political power from the North American continent. The victory left such issues as the retirement of the war debt, joint financing of the empire, and the role of colonial legislatures in the governance of the empire unresolved. Other

issues, including the question of whether Catholicism would receive legal and financial support in the areas of Canada ceded to Britain, were minor, but real, irritants.

At the same time the colonies themselves had internal problems that promoted unrest: struggles between East and West for political power and prestige, sporadic persecution of Baptists in Virginia and New England, competition between Anglicans and Calvinists for members and educational institutions, chronic economic problems related to the lack of hard currency, and the desire to move the boundaries of white settlement farther west. There were also minor problems, such as the difficulty of chartering educational institutions, that affected certain portions of the population.

By 1776 the internal and the imperial crises had merged in the popular mind, and a major segment of the colonial elite had resolved on independence (and, hence, war) as the solution to their problems at home and abroad. Naturally, as armed conflict became more imminent, Revolutionary leaders promised various factions what they wanted to enlist them in the cause. The promise of religious liberty, for example, was very important in enlisting Baptist and Presbyterian support in Virginia. Where the established churches were relatively popular, as in Massachusetts, the promises with respect to religion were much more circumspect and the present toleration of the system stressed.

The issue of the war revealed the rich and complicated religious pluralism of British North America. Calvinist ministers often seemed to form a "black regiment" (the phrase was, of course, metaphorical) because their sermons openly espoused the Revolutionary cause, encouraged Americans (in and out of the army) in the face of defeat, and were generally helpful in maintaining morale. They were, in effect, propagandists. In contrast, the Anglican church (especially in the North but also in the South to a lesser degree) was increasingly opposed to the struggle. Many Anglican clergy and devoted laity were imprisoned by the patriots, and a large percentage were forced into exile. The Church of England lost more than half of its American priests in the struggle, largely through flight to England.

The historic peace churches, including the Quakers and Mennonites, were in a serious position. For them, British government had not been slavery; on the contrary, it had secured their liberties against attacks by other Americans. Many, although pacifists, secretly favored the imperial side of the struggle, and the patriots tended to treat them as enemies.

CHURCH AND STATE AFTER THE REVOLUTION

Even before military hostilities ceased, Americans were struggling with the question of the meaning of the Revolution for their corporate life. The Declaration of Independence established a national commitment to religious freedom, but practical issues remained. Changes were needed in such areas as the relationship between church and state; the question was what changes had to be made. The various states attempted different solutions to this problem.

The South. The religious clashes of the war years were very important for the constitutional changes that followed. Throughout the South the popular identification of Anglican and Tory encouraged legislatures to terminate the union between church and state. In most of the South this process was smooth. States such as Maryland, South Carolina, and North Carolina repealed their laws establishing one denomination of Christians, although the Anglican church was permitted to retain its property and its status as a legal corporation.

Proposals to establish all Protestant churches equally were eventually defeated in all southern states, although South Carolina had such a system for a few years. These defeats did not mean the new states ignored the churches in their legislation. All churches received substantial legal benefits, including the right of incorporation, the right to hold real property as corporate bodies, to sue and be sued, and the right to own and operate schools and colleges. Further, many laws regulating moral behavior, which were rooted in Christian doctrine and practice, were enacted, as were laws prohibiting blasphemy and sabbath desecration.

Virginia. Virginia was unique among the colonies. Although conservative in its social structure, the aristocracy commonly accepted the more radical religious ideas of the Enlightenment. Many planters were deists, often members

of Masonic lodges, and others inclined toward Unitarianism. For some, hatred of traditional Christianity amounted to a crusade. Other members of the ruling class, including the fiery orator Patrick Henry, were equally devoted to the maintenance of Christian civilization.

The first steps taken in Virginia were moderate. A law affirming liberty of conscience was passed in 1776, along with a law—to be renewed annually—suspending payments to the established clergy. The latter law was made permanent in 1779. The theology faculty at William and Mary was terminated by Thomas Jefferson. The result of this first wave of legislation was to create a church that had privileges (including legal incorporation), considerable influence on the laws, and a traditional parish structure. These acts toward disestablishment were in line with common southern practices.

In 1784 Patrick Henry and other (largely eastern) political leaders, shocked by a perceived rise in crime and immorality, began a political campaign to clarify the status of Protestantism in Virginia. Bills were introduced to reincorporate the church and to provide some financial support for all Protestant teachers of religion. The first of these (called General Assessment) probably had popular support. James Madison believed the debate over a second proposal opened the way to pass Thomas Jefferson's radical Bill for Establishing Religious Freedom, which had been before the legislature since 1779.

In order to rally support to defeat the General Assessment, Madison published his *Memorial and Remonstrance,* one of the classic statements of American liberalism. He argued that if religion was, as all assumed, a matter of conscience, then the Lord of the conscience would ensure that each individual knew enough to be judged by him. There was no need for the state to undertake to teach that which was, at least in its essentials, already known. In fact, Christianity had flourished in its first few centuries when it lacked state support and was aided directly by God. Madison further maintained that human rights are of a unitary character. If the state weakens to any degree one right, all other rights are weakened as well. In time the assault on one freedom would prove to be preparation for an assault on all freedoms. The only guarantee of liberty was still liberty.

Madison's arguments proved convincing, and

they were supported by careful political organization. As he had hoped, the Baptists and Presbyterians campaigned actively against the law to compensate teachers of religion, and by 1786 the legislature passed Jefferson's radical bill, which sought to build a wall between church and state.

During the next fifteen years Virginians attempted to separate the government from all connection with the church. The Episcopal church was stripped of incorporation in 1787, the glebes were sold in 1802 as state property, and the University of Virginia (chartered in 1819) was founded in part to combat the remaining Episcopal influence at William and Mary. All churches were reduced to the legal status of private clubs.

There was no formal persecution of the former establishment, but informal harassment of Anglicanism was common. The ruling elite of the state became outspoken in their opposition to traditional faith, and such formerly flourishing churches as Williamsburg's Bruton Parish found themselves without members or support. Ordinations of members of the upper class were treated as extraordinary (and humorous) events in the press.

The wall of separation was carefully maintained in Virginia for more than forty years. The legislature was reluctant to charter church-related schools, especially those that trained ministers. Baptist Richmond College (present-day University of Richmond), chartered in 1833, for example, was prohibited from teaching theology, and the Virginia Episcopal Seminary at Alexandria remained unincorporated until 1859. Other churches had similar problems in securing charters for new institutions.

Nonetheless, there were a few cracks in the wall. The oath was retained in court cases, and much of Christian morality remained as law, partially because the legislature assumed (incorrectly) that such laws were the product of human nature or reason and not of historical development.

The legal position of the churches gradually changed in Virginia over the years 1800 to 1859 for a number of reasons. The churches, despite predictions, did not weaken but grew in numbers and political influence; the aristocracy came to see the church as an ally in the maintenance of slavery; and romantic philosophy (which stressed the role of feeling and tradition as a way of relating to the world) replaced Enlightenment rationalism. Public profession of Christianity came to be seen as respectable and, indeed, almost a requirement for a gentleman. By the Civil War, Virginia's laws were similar to those of other states.

The Middle States. The legislation adopted in much of the South was similar to that adopted by Pennsylvania, New York, and New Jersey. In these colonies the laws governing religion evolved from the colonial practice of toleration, which was rooted in social pluralism. There were, to be sure, some religious problems. During the war, for example, William Smith, the Anglican rector of the College of Philadelphia, was forced to flee Pennsylvania, but when emotions cooled he was permitted to return to his post. By and large, the Revolution marked no sharp break with the past in this area.

New England. The established New England clergy had supported the Revolution and, after the first few battles had been fought, there were no British forces on New England soil. Consequently, the war had little immediate impact. The establishments were continued in a more moderate, but still effective, form. Each town elected its own teacher of religion, and few restrictions were placed on that position. In Connecticut, where there was a strong Anglican church, a grant to the Bishop's Fund was made every year by the legislature. Those who elected not to support the official church found exemptions from taxation easy to obtain.

Eventually, the New England establishments were discontinued. In part they were abolished because increasing religious pluralism made them obsolete. But political action was also a factor. The popularity of the Democratic-Republican party (the Jeffersonians, who were strongly committed to separation) coupled with the decline of the Federalists (the principal supports of the standing order) made the end of state-supported Congregationalism all but inevitable. New Hampshire discontinued its establishment in 1816; Connecticut, in 1818.

Disestablishment in Massachusetts was a more complicated matter. The state's dissenters held different views of what they hoped would replace the standing order and hence were politically less effective than in the other New England states. In the eastern part of the state, for example, the Baptists—the largest dissenting denomination—were primarily descendants of the Separate Congregationalists. They envisioned a strongly Christian state that would provide religious instruction in schools and support churches by various laws. In contrast, in the western part of the state, the dissenters (most of whom were also Baptists) were more radical. They hoped for a "wall of separation" between church and state that would keep each in its own sphere.

Disestablishment came partly as a result of a controversy between conservatives and liberals in the established (Congregationalist) church. As early as the 1740s many of the more radical theological ideas of the Enlightenment had begun to be accepted by the more sophisticated pastors, and by the first decade of the nineteenth century the new theology was dominant in the Boston area.

William Ellery Channing, reacting to more than a decade of theological controversy, sought to define the new liberalism in his Baltimore sermon "Unitarian Christianity," preached in 1819. The essential points of the new creed were an emphasis on the benevolence of God, obedience to Jesus and imitation of his life, and immortality. But, as important as these affirmations were, Channing and his friends also made some important denials, disclaiming the traditional doctrine of biblical inspiration, the substitutionary atonement, and the traditional doctrine of the Trinity. Despite their own differences, orthodox Congregationalists were shocked by these denials, which they believed were heretical, and they reasserted the principal points of orthodoxy all the more vigorously.

What provoked the actual schism was the Dedham case (1820). The town had elected a Unitarian as its pastor, and those who were members of the Congregational church sued. The original deed had specified that the church follow the Cambridge Platform, a statement of faith adopted by a synod of Massachusetts pastors in 1648, and New England custom had granted to the church the right to veto an election. The court, reading literally the establishment laws, argued that every citizen who had not presented a certificate of exemption (a sworn statement that one was not a member of the established church and supported another denomination) had an equal right in the determination of church property and theology. In other words,

the establishment of religion did not mean that a particular form of religion had legal sanction. The orthodox, old-line Congregationalists, consequently, lost their suit, and the Unitarian pastor was legally installed.

The orthodox, who believed that the churches had been established to protect the traditional faith of the Puritans, were outraged, and after more than 120 churches declared themselves Unitarian, they faced the problem of constructing non-established (free) churches in the Unitarian towns. Many orthodox became active in the battle for disestablishment on the grounds that faith should not be adjudicated by those who were not committed to it. By 1833 Massachusetts was ready to join the rest of the nation in ending its religious establishment.

THE CONSTITUTION, RELIGIOUS FREEDOM, AND PLURALISM

By the end of the War of Independence many thoughtful Americans believed that a more powerful central government was needed, and in 1787 a national convention was called in Philadelphia to revise the Articles of Confederation (the frame of government that various states adopted in 1781 to unite them in certain common actions). However, once assembled, the convention decided that a new frame of government was needed. Dominated by gentlemen of property and standing, the debates in the new body were primarily concerned with such issues as the protection of commerce, the status of slavery, the balance of power between states, and foreign affairs. After many arguments and compromises, a new constitution was accepted by the delegates in 1787 and recommended to the states for ratification.

The most remarkable fact about the Constitution was that religion was mentioned only once, and then indirectly, in the oath prescribed for the president. God was not held to be the founder of the government, his aid was not invoked to guide the nation, nor was he named as its protector. The document was one of the most secular in history. Political power came from the people and served their earthly purposes.

The Constitution did not mention an established church or religious liberty for a simple reason: constitutional theory was that the central government had only the powers explicitly enumerated. However, in the heated battles over ratification, many became uneasy over the lack of formal restraints on federal power. There was a widely expressed desire for a Bill of Rights, similar to the lists of privileges in the various state constitutions, to serve as a protection from arbitrary power.

The First Amendment's provisions were drawn carefully: "Congress shall make no law respecting an establishment of religion or prohibiting the free exercise thereof." In its original form the purpose of the amendment was to assure the citizens of various states that their own handling of religious matters was secure. The citizens of Virginia did not have to fear that Massachusetts or Connecticut would extend their establishments, nor did the citizens of Massachusetts—who were deeply suspicious of Jefferson and the other Virginia radicals—need to fear that their establishments would be ended by court action. Religion was simply out of the sphere of federal action.

The most significant part of the amendment was the provision for free exercise, which meant that the government could not interfere with religious practices in any area. If the people elected forms of worship, then those forms were to be respected. Ironically, the one phrase that would have strengthened the amendment's power, "nor shall the rights of conscience be abridged," was omitted from the version submitted to and ratified by the states.

For several reasons few court cases were brought under the First Amendment before 1920. First, it was not clear exactly how the amendment applied to the states (which often had stronger provisions in their own constitutions) or to various traditional federal actions. Second, the Civil War Amendments (the Fourteenth and Fifteenth)—passed to protect the freedmen (former slaves)—had been either interpreted in terms of concrete matters of legal procedure or ignored. In the twentieth century those amendments were reinterpreted as guarantees that the various states would not infringe upon individual liberties.

The courts' expansion of the scope of the Bill of Rights required a difficult adjudication of the meaning of the First Amendment. The courts interpreted it as having two clauses—a prohibition of establishment and a guarantee of free exercise—and tried to balance the protection given to religion in the latter against the prohibition of state support or control in the former. The balancing act has proven to be almost impossible as the courts have been drawn first to the one and then to the other provision.

Throughout the nineteenth century traditional Christianity, although not in its denominational forms, was seen by many state judges as part of the common law of their states—as it was part of the common law in England—and was favored in legal decisions. Protestant piety was encouraged in the schools through school prayers, the reading of the King James Bible, and such didactic literature as McGuffey's Readers, which openly taught Protestant virtue. Public occasions—such as the opening of Congress or a state legislature, the inauguration of the president—were accompanied by Protestant religious leaders reciting prayers, reading Scripture, and occasionally preaching.

Until 1914 the United States saw itself as a Christian (and predominantly Protestant) power in world relations and acted accordingly. American missionaries played an important role in the imperial expansion of the nation into Oregon and farther west to Hawaii. The Spanish-American War (1898) was fought in large measure as a reaction to the perceived evils of Catholic Spain, and the churches met before the war to divide the missionary territories.

The informal establishment of Protestant Christianity seemed to many to offer the best of all possible worlds. The United States had a religious foundation, its laws were informed by morality that had religious sanctions, including the threat of penalties in this world and the next, and yet the individual was free to belong to any church or to no church at all. To many it seemed that Christianity had been purified of its tendency to persecute and returned to the supposedly happier state of the New Testament. As late as 1931 the Supreme Court declared: "We are a Christian people, according to one another the equal right of religious freedom" (*U.S.* v. *Mackintosh*).

The informal Protestant establishment was unable to maintain itself. As early as 1880 American Protestants were losing internal unity, despite a rising ecumenical consciousness. One major line of dissent divided those who accepted such aspects of modernity as biblical criticism and were open to new trends in sociology and psychology and those who rejected these developments on theological grounds. Other divisions also existed, including conflicting views of the role of the church in the social order, a tendency of Protestant denominations to serve particular classes and races (middle-class people of British descent), and regional differences. If "evangelical" or "Protestant" had a clear meaning in the nineteenth century (or was believed to have such a meaning), it had lost that meaning by 1930. To say that the United States had a Protestant majority was to say little or nothing specific.

The primary reason for the decline of the informal Protestant establishment was immigration. During the nineteenth and early twentieth centuries, immigration from Europe changed the religious as well as the ethnic composition of the United States. This immigration created a society in which Catholics made up approximately 25 percent of the population and Jews about 3 to 4 percent. The nation ceased to be overwhelmingly Protestant, and the laws and customs of the people gradually changed to reflect the actual demographics. One mark of the new understanding was the tendency to use such phrases as "Judeo-Christian tradition" for the religious heritage or common morality of the nation.

The older Anglo-Saxon concept of religious liberty influenced this development by encouraging diversity. A comparison with Latin America, where a different understanding of the relationship between church and state existed in the nineteenth century, indicates that the United States received a more religiously diverse body of new settlers than, for example, did Argentina or Brazil. The immigrants to those countries tended to be from Catholic Europe and to desire to live in a Catholic society. But one must be careful not to attribute too much power to the ideal or the constitutional tradition. If the laws made non-Protestant immigration possible, non-Protestants made the country pluralistic.

The process of the country's transformation by immigration began anew in the post–World War II period and has accelerated in the 1970s and 1980s. The first wave of new immigrants were displaced persons who had suffered from the clash of dictatorships in Europe, while the second wave has been composed of settlers from Latin America and, particularly, from Asia. The changes brought about by these new Americans are not yet evident, although many large cities now have Muslim, Buddhist, and Hindu places of worship, but one may predict (cautiously) that talk about Judeo-Christian roots will be replaced by talk about all the world's religions in the future.

JUDAISM

Although many Jews had resided in the United States before 1800 and one, Haym Salomon, had been a hero of the Revolution, the process of integrating Jewish citizens into the new republic took almost a century. In part the process was legal. In some states Jews were not citizens when the Revolution ended and did not have the right to vote or to serve on juries. Maryland did not pass its "Jew" Bill (granting Jews full civil privileges, including the right to vote and hold office) until 1825, North Carolina until 1868, and New Hampshire until 1878. General Ulysses S. Grant felt justified in issuing his infamous General Order No. 11 (1862), which expelled the Jews from the area his army had conquered. This order was repealed by Lincoln only after considerable political pressure.

Anti-Semitism was widespread. Jews were pictured in schoolbooks as greedy, untrustworthy, and as the power behind the throne in many European states. By the 1870s, Jews were often discussed as belonging to a different race from other white Americans. The increase in Jewish immigration in the 1880s and 1890s came just as this new anti-Semitism was reaching its high point of influence, and the poor conditions in which those Jews lived reinforced popular misconceptions.

In the 1920s and 1930s some American conservatives attempted to use the Jews as scapegoats for the nation's ills. In that period the Ku Klux Klan assaulted Jews as well as blacks, and Henry Ford, the nation's premier industrialist, contributed to the publication of the *Protocols of the Elders of Zion*, a violently anti-Semitic tract. Other Americans, including Charles Lindbergh, were admirers of Adolf Hitler, although not openly anti-Semitic. There was also a polite anti-Semitism that was revealed in social discrimination, including restrictions in the membership of clubs, covenants against the sale of property to Jews, and the like.

Jewish response to discrimination has been varied. In traditional European societies, the price for full admission was baptism. In countries such as the United States, where Enlightenment influence was strong, the demands were more subtle. There was little objection to the pure ethical monotheism of the Hebrew Bible, but the various ceremonies, the careful following of the traditional rabbinic law, and Jewish customs caused much concern. The Enlightenment seemed to promise something similar to what traditional Christianity had promised: Jews could be accepted—if they ceased to be Jews.

Reform Judaism in Europe and America attempted to conform Judaism to Enlightenment standards. Judaism was defined as a religion, not tied to a historical community. Hebrew was eliminated from worship; non-ethical matters, such as restrictions on food or kosher dishes, were seen as no longer binding; and such Protestant customs as organs, choirs, and sabbath schools were introduced. America (or the land a particular Jew lived in) was seen as the holy land, and hope for a messiah who would restore the Jews to Jerusalem was explicitly rejected. In general Reform Judaism did succeed in creating a denominational form of the tradition that seemed little more distinctive to its neighbors than Unitarianism.

Reform Judaism did not satisfy all people who were born Jews. The first major wave of Jewish immigrants to the United States were from Germany, where Reform faith was strong; the second came from eastern Europe, where Judaism was strongly Orthodox. The eastern European Jews insisted, at least at first, on the full observation of the laws and customs. Reform Jews initially feared that the new immigrants would weaken their position in their communities, but in time came to see the newcomers as valuable fellow religionists and allies. Other Jews drifted far from an organized form of religious life and maintained only a tenuous connection to Judaism.

The persistence of prejudice led many Jews to an active defense of their rights. In the 1920s they began to form organizations to combat the anti-Semitism in the culture and to assert Jewish perspectives. The Anti-Defamation League of B'nai B'rith and the National Conference of Christians and Jews are the best known of these.

The horrors of Nazi Germany and the subsequent establishment of Israel infused a new dedication into the American Jewish community. Jewish leaders had been unable to convince political or church leaders of the magnitude of the German attack on the Jews during the conflict, and they were determined to present a united front on the issue of Israel's survival. Further, the fact that the Holocaust had taken place in Germany—the center of high Jewish culture in the nineteenth century—convinced American Jews that they needed to become stronger advocates of religious (and other civil) rights at home. If such things could happen in the most educated state in the world, then they could happen in America as well.

The political issues surrounding the state of Israel became more important in separating American Jews from their fellow Americans in the 1970s. As it became clear that in meeting its energy needs the United States was dependent on the Arab world, many Americans believed that the nation's foreign policy ought to change from its generally pro-Israel policy to a more evenhanded approach to the region. The continuing problems of the Israeli occupation of the West Bank and intervention in Lebanon, both of which are generally supported by American Jews, have intensified criticism of Israel by non-Jews.

Jewish leaders have been correct in detecting elements of traditional anti-Semitism in some of the reactions to Israel. Clearly Israel was judged, not as a democracy struggling to live in a threatened world, but in terms of such traditional anti-Semitic types as the "grasping Jew" (Shylock) or the "Wandering Jew," driven mad by centuries of persecution. Lack of vigorous reaction to domestic anti-Semitism (including the occasional painting of swastikas on synagogues) has reenforced the fear of a new anti-Semitism.

Anti-Semitism persists in the 1980s. While most of the legal and social forms of discrimination have passed, the attitudes that sparked those laws and practices remain. Unfortunately, the constructive period of dialogue and exchange that followed World War II appears to have passed. Although some Jewish-Christian dialogues remain, these conversations do not appear as central to American religion as they once were.

CATHOLICISM

The first settlers of British North America arrived shortly after the defeat of the Spanish Armada by Elizabeth I, and they were deeply influenced by the English anti-Catholicism of the seventeenth century. The Glorious Revolution, which removed James II from the throne in 1688, was largely motivated by the desire to secure a Protestant succession to the English throne, and this contributed to a revival of colonial anti-Catholicism. In Maryland, where Catholics were most numerous, one result of the Glorious Revolution was the passage of penal laws restricting the civil rights of the Catholic minority.

At the time of the American Revolution there were about 25,000 Catholics in the United States. These Catholics believed that the Revolution offered them substantial chances for greater freedom, and they supported it strongly. After the war the Catholic church in the United States was organized under John Carroll, bishop of Baltimore. The establishment of a formal hierarchy occurred on the brink of a century of steady emigration from Catholic Europe. By 1833 Catholics were the largest single denomination in the nation, and they continued to expand for the next 150 years as new immigrants, first from Ireland and Germany, then from southern and eastern Europe, and finally from Latin America, entered the country.

The nineteenth century was a period of reaction for European Catholics. Following the defeat of Napoleon, the church attempted to wall itself off from any contact with the Enlightenment ideas believed to have contributed to its debacle in the French Revolution. The popes, particularly Gregory XVI and Pius IX, issued declarations in which they opposed the separation of church and state and denounced democracy, religious freedom, socialism, and freedom of the press.

This political hard line was accompanied by similar movements in theology. St. Thomas was seen as the normative interpreter of doctrine, the Immaculate Conception was proclaimed as dogma, and the pope was declared to be infallible in his teaching of faith and morals (when speaking explicitly *ex cathedra* or in his sacred office).

These political and theological perspectives provoked struggles between church and state in Germany, France, and Italy. The struggle in Germany might be seen as a draw: Bismarck allowed the formation of a Catholic party and the education of priests in church seminaries in exchange for Catholic political support. In France, where a secular state was founded, Catholicism was disestablished. The unification of Italy left the popes self-proclaimed prisoners in the Vatican until the 1920s, and Catholics were urged not to vote in elections. Non-Catholic Americans, following events in Europe, were concerned that similar problems might arise in the United States if the Catholic church were ever to acquire political power.

The nineteenth-century American Catholic minority tended to be poor. As new immigrants arrived, they often settled in the same area of a city, where life came to revolve around the parish church and school. Despite the efforts of the church, these communities, like other ghettos, became centers of vice, drunkenness, and crime. As the earlier arrivals moved up the economic ladder and out of the ghettos, new immigrants entered these areas or created new ghettos. Despite their poverty, these communities formed the bases of the big-city political machines that played an important political role in American life.

Catholic attitudes toward Protestantism were shaped by the competition between the two movements since the Reformation and, especially, the European struggles of the nineteenth century. The Counter-Reformation had pictured Protestants as rebels and traitors against God, and this attitude persisted in nineteenth-century Catholic literature.

Many Catholics feared that something similar to the struggles between church and state in Europe might erupt in the United States, and some believed union between church and state on the European models would be their best protection. Among German-American and Polish-

American Catholics there was a strong sense of a link between religion, language, and ethnicity that stressed the need for strict separation from the Protestant majority in order to preserve the Catholic character. Just as Protestant papers denounced Catholics as bars to political and social reform, many Catholics denounced reforms as atheistic or as anti-church.

Considering the depths of animosity between Protestants and Catholics in the nineteenth century, it was remarkable not that anti-Catholic incidents occurred, but that they were not more disruptive. American anti-Catholicism was, in fact, mild for several reasons.

First, the Catholic church was careful to provide open and explicit support for American institutions. In the early nineteenth century Bishop John England of Charleston combined a vigorous patriotism with open support of American liberties. Like many other Irish Catholics he used the fact of Ireland's sufferings under British rule to suggest a Catholic counterpart to the escape of the Puritans from Archbishop William Laud. Thus, Catholic immigrants were presented as participating in the American epic of establishing a refuge for civil and religious liberty.

In the twentieth century the Jesuit John Courtney Murray further developed the American Catholic theology of the state. While Murray asserted the supremacy of the spiritual over the political, he maintained that such superiority was not a matter of hierarchical power. Rather, it was part of the nature of the relationship between spirit and matter. Like other such relationships—husband and wife, parent and child—the rule was one of love. While decrying the secular European states, Murray found much to praise in the American situation.

Second, for most of the nineteenth century the Vatican was very careful to avoid explicit criticism of the United States or of the condition of the Catholic church there. When the clash came in the "Americanism" controversy—a complex battle that was as concerned with events in France as with the American church—Rome contented itself with stating that the situation of the church in the United States was not ideal and that the American Catholic church would benefit from the support of the nation's laws.

Third, as anti-Catholic as many Protestants were, the American tradition of religious toleration nonetheless usually prevailed. The nineteenth-century minister Lyman Beecher, for example, while willing publicly to decry a feared Catholic domination of the Midwest, still believed that Catholics could be opposed only by persuasion.

Although usually restrained (there were some anti-Catholic riots in the nineteenth century), American anti-Catholicism was often expressed in pamphlets and books, as it continues to be. Anti-Catholicism was also reinforced by conspiracy theories. Such prominent Americans as Samuel Morse and Beecher believed that Catholics were plotting to secure a majority in the Midwest and planning to move the pope to that region after his power declined in Italy. Such theories were often combined with ancient Protestant polemics that identified the pope with the Antichrist and his fall with the beginning of the millennium.

Anti-Catholicism has also taken political form and emerged at significant points in the nation's development. As the nation drifted toward the Civil War in the 1840s and 1850s, a vigorous but small American, or "Know Nothing," party emerged that influenced many state elections. The party believed that Catholics were about to take over the country and advocated laws to preserve a Protestant America. In the 1920s anti-Catholicism was often part of Ku Klux Klan activity in the North.

Political anti-Catholicism was, however, largely ineffective. One reason for this was the pattern of Catholic settlement. The large cities of the East and Midwest, where many Catholics lived, were spread out over a wide area. Immigrants were able to settle in compact enclaves and create their own institutions. Such Catholic areas, often as large as a city ward and occasionally as large as a congressional district, enabled the immigrants to elect representatives to governing bodies. Actual power was the best antidote to discrimination.

Political discrimination functioned most significantly with respect to the presidency. It was widely believed that a Catholic could not serve as president. Like all prejudices, this had many roots: traditional Protestant distrust of Catholics, fear that a Catholic leader might be subservient to Rome, and perhaps the feeling that the president, who has often served as quasi-religious leader for some Americans, ought to be a member of the religious majority. In 1928, when

Democrat Alfred Smith ran for that office, Protestant clergymen actively campaigned against his election, and for the first time since the Civil War, Republicans dented the solidly democratic South, where Protestant ministers, breaking the region's long-standing taboo against ecclesiastical involvement in politics, campaigned long and hard for his defeat. It is important to note, however, that Smith's advocacy of the "wet" position on Prohibition and the popularity of his opponent, Herbert Hoover, may have had as much impact as his religion on his loss of the election.

The election of 1960, in which John F. Kennedy opposed Richard Nixon for the presidency, saw a reversal of the accepted wisdom. Although Kennedy's religion was an issue, especially in the South, it does not appear to have affected the race adversely. Kennedy, curiously enough, may have gained more votes in the crucial urban states, including Illinois, than prejudice against his religion cost him. In these states, Catholics were numerous and presumably were inclined to favor a fellow church member.

Kennedy's election came at a favorable time for a Catholic to hold high office. Pope John XXIII had called the Second Vatican Council (1962–1965). In terms of church and state relationships, this council was the most important in recent Catholic history. The church's belief that religion ought to be allied with the existing government, which had been held since the time of the Roman Emperor Constantine, was substantially modified, if not repudiated.

The combination of a popular president and a progressive council buried American political anti-Catholicism, except for certain fringe groups. From the 1960s to the 1980s conservative Protestants and Roman Catholics, traditionally political rivals, began to find common cause in a number of areas, including anti-abortion and aid to private schools. In 1984 this alliance contributed to Ronald Reagan's reelection.

RELIGION AND EDUCATION

In the early nineteenth century, the Friends of Education, a movement largely composed of Protestants, began a program of educational reform. Although the original objective was for free public education to replace the early system of schools maintained partly by private tuition,

that objective was expanded into a drive for universal, compulsory education. Although such an objective can be (and since has been) secularized, it had religious overtones in the nineteenth century. Protestant educators believed that schooling should form character, and they selected books in such areas as history and literature that affirmed the nation's Protestant heritage. One purpose of the schools was to assimilate immigrants to American life, and religion was one means of assimilation.

Protestant interest in education intensified as the nineteenth century progressed. As an experience of conversion became less important for many Protestants, a major emphasis came to be placed on education. In his classic work *Christian Nurture* (1847), Horace Bushnell argued that a child raised in a Christian atmosphere generated by nation, town, church, and school would never know himself as other than Christian. His followers often used the phrase "Christian civilization" for this matrix of shaping institutions.

Catholics had no objection to a system of education that combined religion and education. The ideal of Catholic theology was a synthesis of religion and reason in which Christian doctrine completed the theological truths (such as the existence of God and immortality) taught by nature. The problem was that the public schools were Protestant. The church's response, in line with its practice in Europe, was to establish a system of Catholic schools. Although the plan was ultimately unattainable, the church hoped to have a school in every parish and to have all Catholic children enrolled in their own parochial schools.

Early-nineteenth-century Catholic leaders hoped that public funds available for education might be proportionally shared with Catholic schools, and this remained one of the church's hopes well into the twentieth century. For Catholics such a sharing of funds was simple justice. They were paying taxes for an educational system that was hostile, at least implicitly, to their beliefs, and they believed that they should receive aid in providing what they maintained was best for their children. Protestants disagreed and maintained that the schools were secular, supporting no specific religious position, and should be seen as a public service, available to all who wanted it.

Many of the Supreme Court decisions from

1930 to 1986 on church-state issues have revolved around attempts to adjudicate this issue. In such decisions as *Cochran* v. *the Louisiana Board of Education* (1930) and *Emerson* v. *Board of Education* (1947), the Court permitted considerable aid to students attending parochial schools in the form of textbooks and bus transportation. Attempts to expand such aid to include more direct subsidies were struck down in *Lemon et al.* v. *Kertzman et al.* (1971), *Lemon* v. *Dicenso* (1971), and *Committee for Public Education and Religious Liberty* v. *Nyquist* (1973).

The Court's willingness to prohibit aid to Catholic schools has carried with it a commitment to the secularity of the system. In landmark decisions (*Engel* v. *Vitale,* 1962; *Abington School District* v. *Schempp,* 1963; and *Murray* v. *Curlett,* 1963) Protestant devotional practices, such as the recitation of the Lord's Prayer and daily reading from the Scriptures, were held to be unconstitutional infringements of the anti-establishment clause. While teaching *about* religion, such as might occur in a history or geography class, was permitted, the teaching *of* religion was prohibited. Other religious practices, by extension, were also prohibited.

The 1963 school prayer decision shifted the traditional Protestant-Catholic debate over public and church education to a different arena. Conservative Protestants began to see in the secularization of education a threat to their faith and practice. Other issues were also important: the secular character of sex education (where available), the apparent inability of administrators to keep order, and the increase in student drug use.

While some conservative Protestants joined campaigns to restore—by constitutional amendment, if necessary—prayer to public schools, others began organizing their own private schools. These schools frequently found themselves in conflict with various state authorities over such matters as certification of teachers and standardized testing of students. Like the earlier Catholic system, this one also experienced pressing financial problems. By the election of 1980, hard-pressed conservative Protestants had joined Catholics in demanding some financial support, direct or indirect, for their institutions, and Reagan had made such relief (in the form of tax credits) part of his announced program. The

Supreme Court in the 1980s has indicated a new openness to such aid as well.

Another approach to the provision of some formal religious instruction in the context of public education was rooted in the traditional belief in the coordination of church and state. The public schools were to educate the students in secular subjects with the state permitting some time, from an hour to two hours a week, for the students to study religion under their own teachers in a non-public environment. Many factors went into the discussion of "released time." Its advocates argued that any religion with a strong doctrinal basis needed time to present its heritage adequately to its children. Since public schools demanded so much of the students' time and effort, the best way for this religious instruction to be provided was for the state to relinquish some of its control over the lives of the students. Opponents have been equally insistent that such "released time" constitutes an informal establishment of religion and that all such instruction must be done after school hours. The courts' attempts to adjudicate the issue have been confusing. In *Zorach* v. *Clauson* (1952) the Supreme Court argued that such programs are legal, provided that the classes are held away from the school grounds, and this distinction has held in a number of subsequent cases.

Another issue in education concerning the relation of church and state has been evolution. The publication of Charles Darwin's *Origin of Species* in 1859 marked the advent of a new era in the understanding of the biological sciences, and by 1900 Darwin's theories as modified by continuing research had become foundational for scientific study as well as intellectually and ideologically widely pervasive.

Yet Darwinism was also threatening to people with traditional religious understandings. Despite the explanations of the nation's leading theologians, including Newman Smyth in *Through Science to Faith* (1902) and William Newton Clarke in *What Shall We Think of Christianity* (1899), it seemed to undercut the first chapters of Genesis and to lead, intentionally or not, to a moral relativism. By 1920 there was a concerted effort to ban the teaching of evolution in the public schools.

The crusade had limited success. In a few states laws were secured demanding that evolution not be taught, but these were ordinarily ignored in the classroom. Nonetheless, a test case was inevitable. In Tennessee a young biology teacher, John Scopes, was accused of breaking the law. The resultant trial, held in 1925, became a national event. Clarence Darrow, the great Chicago lawyer and civil libertarian, argued for the defense, while William Jennings Bryan—one of the abiding symbols of conservative Protestantism—was invited to plead the state's cause. The decision of the court went against Scopes. Yet the widely followed trial convinced most Americans that the attempt to pass laws restricting scientific knowledge was absurd, and the anti-evolution drive stalled and was finally laughed off the stage.

Although the issue seemed dead, it re-emerged in the 1970s as a major church-state controversy. The question was whether or not school textbooks had to give equal time to "scientific creationism" as well as to evolution. As the matter was presented, serious scientific questions existed about the validity of neo-Darwinism that were seldom included in the nation's schoolbooks. In the interest of fairness and, indeed, of scientific method, did not the anti-evolutionary perspective have to be included as well as scientific orthodoxy?

Had the new anti-evolutionary crusade not been conjoined with a number of other textbook issues, it would have probably been ignored. However, many parents were making contradictory demands on the nation's publishers. Advocates of women's liberation, for example, believed that the books ought to include pictures of successful women outside the home, while advocates of traditional roles believed that such portraits degraded those who elected to stay at home and who hoped that their daughters would do the same. The related issues of racism and of providing appropriate role models for blacks and other minorities in textbooks were also hotly debated. The conservative position was presented as an extension of these broader issues: If one granted black parents and feminists power over the content of texts, should not religious conservatives expect the same?

Although the courts, supported by the opinions of an apparent majority of Americans, have silenced the "scientific creationism" arguments, some observers believe that the political pres-

sure brought by religious conservatives has modified the type and style of books purchased by some school systems. If so, the late 1980s and 1990s will probably see a number of cases attempting to disentangle political influence (always considered legal) from informal establishment (of dubious legality).

LEGAL ISSUES: CIVIL RIGHTS, MORAL LAWS, AND PLURALISM

One of the most significant recognitions of the 1970s and 1980s was that religious and civil liberties might be in conflict. American law, for example, makes it clear that persons are to benefit from the law equally, regardless of race, sex, or national origin.

Any nonprofit corporation with tax-exempt status receives a benefit from the state. But what if that organization believes that the laws securing equality are wrong from a religious standpoint? This happened with Bob Jones University, a Fundamentalist school in Greenville, South Carolina, that prohibits interracial dating because it is believed to violate the Scriptures.

In 1985 Bob Jones University lost its tax exemption on broadly based civil rights grounds. The case, and the issue it represents, sparked a new round of intense debate; there is an ongoing campaign to have the decision reversed. Many conservative churches do not believe that women ought to be ordained to the pastoral ministry, and some do not believe that they should serve in any leadership position. Are such churches in violation of federal law and, if so, should they be deprived of their right to nonprofit status? What will happen to their schools, which have legal charters giving them the privilege of granting degrees?

During the 1960s and 1970s the courts demonstrated a willingness to decide many cases that apparently involve issues which seemingly raise conflicts between the establishment clause of the Constitution and its equally clear mandate of no interference with free access on the clearer grounds of the Constitution's protection of free speech. The debates have centered on the legal phrase "a public forum." In a public forum, individuals have the right to present and argue their points of view provided their behavior does not cause disruption or harm others. Thus, student religious meetings at universities and to some extent in high schools have been protected as "free speech," although their opponents have claimed that the use of such facilities constitutes aid to religion (*Widmer* v. *Vincent*, 1981).

For the eighteenth century, the separation of church and state was possible, at least in part, because the conventional wisdom held that morality was taught by a natural law, available to all, and not by historical institutions. This view was seriously damaged by subsequent research showing moral life to have complex roots in matters such as family life, childhood experiences, and culture. One learns *a* morality rather than morality itself.

The problems of morality became legal problems when the United States became more religiously diverse. American descendants of the British colonists who had originally settled the country, for example, were deeply offended by the new immigrants' "continental sabbath" (the practice, common in Europe, of using Sunday as a day of recreation) and sought to pass local "blue laws" prohibiting business on Sunday. Fears of weakening family ties in the cities also contributed to a number of laws in the late nineteenth century, including a postal regulation that prohibited the mailing of information about birth control.

The great crusade for Protestant morality was the battle for Prohibition, which climaxed in the adoption of the Eighteenth Amendment (1919) to the Constitution. The motives behind the drive were complex. Many Protestants believed that alcohol could not be used responsibly in a modern society; others that the Bible prohibited its use; and yet others that liquor was the cause of poverty in the great cities. These openly stated reasons, while sincerely held and strenuously argued, may have been part of a larger battle for Anglo-Saxon supremacy over the immigrants or for the values of the small town over those of the city.

Prohibition failed for a number of complex reasons, although not as dramatically as its enemies supposed. These included the difficulty of enforcement, the persistence of alcohol use among the wealthy, the religious depression of the 1920s (when Protestant church attendance, contributions, and political influence waned),

and President Franklin Roosevelt's need for revenues to fight the nation's economic depression in the 1930s. Perhaps most basic, Americans simply decided that they did not want the law or the type of control of personal decisions it implied. With the repeal of Prohibition (1933), a process of separation of personal morality and law began that has continued throughout the twentieth century.

The slow repeal of laws relating to Protestant morality did not attract much attention in the 1950s and 1960s. Laws relating to divorce and family life were liberalized or simply ignored. When such laws were defended, it was by the Catholic church, and many Americans came to see divorce and anti–birth-control laws, ironically, as examples of Catholic power.

The 1970s and 1980s have seen an acceleration of the process of dismantling the older laws restricting personal morality. The laws regulating sexual relationships between consenting adults, for example, were either repealed or became dead letters. And some jurisdictions enacted (often with liberal Protestant support) laws protecting the civil rights of homosexuals.

The most dramatic change came, however, with the Supreme Court's decision in *Wade* v. *Roe* (1971), which not only declared abortion to be legal, but declared that a woman had a right to seek such an operation in the early stages of pregnancy. At first, opposition to the decision was primarily raised by Roman Catholics, who had traditionally regarded abortion as murder, but by 1976 conservative Protestants were active in the cause as well, and anti-abortion sentiment has expanded rapidly since that time. The issue has played a major role in many local races for political office and was a factor in the 1980 and 1984 races for the presidency. No issue of personal morality has attracted such prolonged debate since Prohibition.

Despite all attempts to define the anti-abortion issue in the popular language of civil rights, the case against abortion rests primarily on traditional Christian moral teaching on the sanctity of life and the family. The question of whether such values have or ought to have legal sanction in the United States is the primary one. Does the separation of church and state mean that the laws of the nation must have their foundation in a nonreligious consensus or may the consensus informing the laws be that of a particular community of moral discourse? A constitutional amendment prohibiting abortion would have implications beyond the issue at hand. Implicitly, such an amendment would grant Christian morality (Catholic and Protestant) a status in constitutional law similar to the status that it held in English common law (and still does) or the statutes of the various states in the nineteenth century, and such an amendment would thus change the fundamental rules relating church and state on the federal level.

Opposition to war has deep roots in the Christian tradition. For the first three centuries of Christian tradition, military service was considered a barrier to church membership, although there are indications of exceptions. After A.D. 325, when Constantine established the church, military service was interpreted as a permitted Christian occupation, and the taking of life in a just war was not considered sinful. This has remained, until the present, the main Christian tradition. However, in the sixteenth century, the Continental Anabaptists renewed the opposition to war, and their protest was echoed by the Society of Friends (Quakers) in the next century. The United States has never been without objectors to military service.

The authors of the First Amendment, perhaps because of the recent experience of the Revolution and the pro-British sympathies of the historic peace churches, carefully avoided blanket protection for the rights of conscience, and both the federal and state constitutions called for a well-regulated militia. In theory all male citizens were part of the militia and could be called upon to preserve the peace or to fight enemies, domestic and foreign.

During the Civil War, conscription—a relatively new technique in the history of warfare—was resorted to by both sides with the curious provision that a draftee might hire a substitute to serve in his place. The Union Draft Law of 1864 was the first to exempt those whose religious traditions prohibited armed participation in conflict. This law was the basis of later ordinances until 1940, when the requirement of membership in a recognized religious body was replaced with a requirement of "religious training and belief." In 1965 the Supreme Court (*U.S.* v. *Seeger*) expanded this to include any belief that held

the place of religion in the life of an individual. In *Welsh* v. *United States* (1970), the same protection was extended to those who opposed war on humanistic grounds.

St. Augustine and other Christian moralists had long debated the issue of whether a believer might participate in a war that was unjust. However, despite the technical distinctions, the American churches refrained from declaring particular wars unjust and tended to see the causes of their own nations as just. Hence, the issue was mute before the Vietnam conflict. Widespread popular dissatisfaction with the war, serious ethical questions about its goals and aims, and the lack of defined objectives encouraged many to argue that they should be allowed the privilege of selective conscientious objection. The Supreme Court rejected this position in *Gillette* v. *United States* (1971).

Legal provisions have not softened the popular reaction to conscientious objection. Despite the provisions for alternate service and despite the fact that such service was often dangerous and unpleasant, popular opinion has not kept pace with the law. Americans have often subjected conscientious objectors to public opprobrium, and considerable pressure is brought on individuals to shift their position.

The relationship between government and religion in the United States has rested on a broad consensus about what religion ought to be and how it ought to function in the life of individuals. American pluralism and American law have rested on that agreement, and even the most striking reversals of traditional positions—such as the school prayer decision—have been within that framework.

The booming confusion of American religion, with its many denominations, sects, and cults, has refused to stay within boundaries. There have been religious movements so distant from the understandings of most Americans as to put the underlying national consensus about religious toleration to the test.

The first of these were the Mormons, or Church of Jesus Christ of Latter-day Saints. Founded by Joseph Smith in the first half of the nineteenth century, the Mormons claimed prophetic inspiration for their leaders. In addition to claiming new Scriptures, the early Mormons supported such ideas as shared economic responsibility, secret services, and theocracy. The group was driven by mob action from such areas as Kirkland, Ohio, and Far West, Missouri. Just when it appeared that they had found a home in Nauvoo, Illinois, rumors of the practice of polygyny—which Smith claimed had been revealed to him by God—contributed to further rioting. Smith was killed, and his followers began a long journey to Utah, where they established the semi-independent state of Deseret.

Relations between the Mormons and the nation that surrounded them were not peaceful. The United States exerted its military authority, and the Mormons were forced—by statutes, court action, and politics—to abandon polygyny. Laws prohibiting polygyny were upheld by the courts in 1878, and Utah's statehood was finally made conditional on the ending of the practice and the state's agreement to suppress it.

The provision for continual prophecy has allowed the Mormons to avoid further conflicts with their "gentile" neighbors. In general when an area of Mormon practice has been too controversial for contemporary American opinion, the prophets have received revelations permitting changes in the practice. Over the years such accommodations have narrowed the distance between Mormons and other Americans.

The Jehovah's Witnesses, a radical apocalyptic denomination founded by Charles Taze Russell in the latter half of the nineteenth century, and later developed by Joseph Franklin Rutherford, have further tested the limits of American tolerance. Although the Witnesses have experienced some difficulties because of their pacifism, it is their evangelism, refusal of blood transfusions, and refusal to salute the flag that have created great controversy.

In general, the Supreme Court has held that however offensive their evangelism might be to other Americans their rights in this area must be protected (*Lovell* v. *Griffin*, 1938; *Schneider* v. *Irvington, New Jersey*, 1939; and *Cantwell* v. *Connecticut*, 1940). Likewise, the right of Witnesses to refrain from saluting the flag has been given legal protection. On such issues as the Witnesses' refusal of transfusions and other medical treatments, the federal courts have consistently refused to review state court decisions placing sick children under the care of the state. In this sense, while protecting the rights of adult Witnesses, the courts have seen the state's duty to protect its citizens above the rights of parents to direct their children's life. A similar pattern of governmental action has been followed in regard to the children of parents of other denominations that reject (in whole or in part) present-day medical practice.

The decisions in the Witness cases continued to be significant in the 1960s and 1970s, when a number of new religions came into being in the United States. In general, the protections extended to the Witnesses have been extended to such groups as the Unification Church ("Moonies"), the Hare Krishna sect, and others.

Certain fundamental aspects of the relationship between church and state in the United States appear to have remained almost constant over the centuries. First, American religious liberty rests primarily on a social consensus that as full a religious freedom as possible ought to exist. The laws and judicial decisions reflect this deep commitment to freedom.

Second, pluralism, or religious diversity, has been the primary factor in the development of the American system of church-state relations. In the colonial period no one Protestant denomination was able to secure uniformity in a particular area over a significant period of time. Even in those colonies where establishments existed, the tendency was for minorities to secure and defend political rights that guaranteed their religious rights. The wide spectrum of religious belief in America has forced an increasing distance between the government and any particular religious tradition.

Third, the Supreme Court has acted to preserve America's religious liberties by deciding those issues, often dealing with hard-to-resolve technicalities or conflicts, that arise whenever a government is committed to democracy and to personal liberty. At times, Court cases have attempted to resolve ambiguous areas in American life. For example, in the area of religion and education, many Americans have wanted contradictory actions from the government; the schools are to both preserve basic values, which have a religious component, and the schools are not to teach religion. Interpreting the Constitution in such a way as to recognize the problems inherent in such positions has not been easy, and what has been remarkable about the Court's decisions is that despite the controversy some of its decisions have aroused, as in the case of school prayer, Americans have never resorted to constitutional amendment to overthrow or modify its decisions. Basically, the courts, public opinion, and tradition have been on a parallel course.

Fourth, American law, whether federal or state, has progressively moved away from the regulation of personal morality in such areas as marriage and sexual behavior. Although not initially controversial, this trend became deeply so in the years since the Court's ruling on abortion in 1973. What will happen in this particular dispute is far from clear.

Finally, no simple formula has ever expressed the nature of church-state relations in the United States. At the very time that Jefferson was erecting a wall of separation between church and state in Virginia (or trying to), most of the nation was devising methods of positively assisting the church in its mission. Similar ironies can be found in all areas of the history of this relationship. Baptists, for example, were among those most favoring legal disestablishment and yet often have been among those most vigorously demanding informal Christian establishment.

The course of American history has not been smooth, and while one might hope that a simple principle or rational argument might be found to chart the future, no such predictor is on the horizon. If our past is any guide, we will not find any single answer in our quest for what the Founding Fathers called "liberty, civil and religious." But that may be the best evidence for the reality of American freedom. To speak of the predictable course of the history of liberty would be a contradiction in terms.

BIBLIOGRAPHY

Joseph Blau, ed., *Cornerstones of Religious Freedom in America* (1965); Lynn R. Buzzard and Samuel Ericson, *The Battle for Religious Liberty* (1982); Mark DeWolfe Howe, *The Garden and the Wilderness: Religion and Government in American Constitutional History* (1965); Philip B. Kurland, ed., *Church and State: The Supreme Court and the First Amendment* (1971); Franklin A. Littell, *From State Church to Pluralism: A Protestant Interpretation of Religion in American History* (1962).

Glenn Miller, *Religious Liberty in America: History and Prospects* (1976); William Miller, *The First Liberty: Religion and the American Republic* (1986) and, with Charles Cureton, as eds., *Supreme Court Decisions on Church and State* (1986); Frank Sorauf, *The Wall of Separation: The Constitutional Politics of Church and State* (1976); Anson Phelps Stokes and Leo Pfeffer, *Church and State in the United States* (1964).

[*See also* CIVIL AND PUBLIC RELIGION, MILLENNIALISM AND ADVENTISM; *and* WAR AND PEACE.]

CIVIL AND PUBLIC RELIGION

Donald G. Jones

FIRST referred to in the eighteenth century by Jean-Jacques Rousseau as the religious dimension of public life, civil religion is regarded as a common public religion in society, different from and transcending particular faiths. Only in the past thirty years has civil religion come into its own as a topic of formal discussion and study. Though uncertainty remains as to what the term actually means, it nevertheless appears that the concept of civil religion is here to stay as a means of describing certain aspects of a society's life.

Traditionally, the term *American religion* evoked images of chapels, synagogues, circuit riders, priests, Bibles, pilgrims, and stained glass. Now when scholars think of American religion, they may also conjure up certain other images, such as Memorial Day celebrations, a president's funeral ritual, George Washington, the American flag, the Constitution, or an inaugural address proclaiming a providential national destiny. Such symbols, rituals, or sentiments, held in reverence by most Americans regardless of faith, are all entailed within the concept of civil religion.

The concept was not formally discussed until 1955, when Will Herberg used the term *civic religion* in his influential work *Protestant, Catholic, Jew* to identify a common religion in American society. Calling civic religion the "American Way of Life," Herberg wrote that it is "at bottom, a spiritual structure, a structure of ideas and ideals, of aspirations and values, of beliefs and standards; it synthesizes all that commends itself to the American as the right, the good, and the true in actual life" (p. 75).

While there are ample grounds for crediting Herberg with starting the formal discussion, it was Robert Bellah who popularized the term. His "Civil Religion in America," published in the 1967 issue of *Daedalus,* created an explosion of

comment, literature, conferences, and intense debate. In that article, which later appeared in a number of anthologies, Bellah suggested that what Rousseau had envisioned for eighteenth-century France was a fact of American history and contemporary American society.

Although there are some differences in their definitions, both Herberg and Bellah agree that there was, and is, a public religion that exists alongside, and perhaps within, particular traditional religions. That there actually is an American civil religion is also the conclusion of most historians and sociologists of religion. Martin Marty, in *A Nation of Behavers* (1976), identifies civil religion as one of six types found in America. The others are mainline religion, Fundamentalism, Pentecostal-charismatic religion, new religions, and ethnic religion.

Even though most scholars involved in the civil religion discussion would agree that it should be identified as a distinct type of religion, the field of study is so new that the term cannot be taken for granted. Because of its omission from major reference works and scant mention in specialized references, it is known only to certain scholars, members of the clergy, and some politicians. Describing the embryonic stage of the civil religion discussion, Marty writes:

> The term "Civil Religion" appears only in books, articles, or reports of theologians, sociologists, historians, and social critics. The term would inspire only bemusement and puzzlement in the neighborhood tavern, St. Boniface Parish, or a meeting of the American Legion. The absence of awareness on the part of the majority . . . indicates that in the first ten years of debate the entire issue formally has been in the hands of elites. Almost no empirical studies of the people's involvements with Civil Religion

exist. The discussions have had to do with intel-lectual-theological, institutional and political themes and methods of study and almost never with behavioral observation . . . of how Civil Religionists act or what the meaning of their rituals might be.

(pp. 182–183)

Since 1976, when Marty made those observa-tions, there have been several good empirical studies, conceptual analyses, and the first full-length book offering a rigorous and systematic treatment of the subject, John F. Wilson's *Public Religion in American Culture* (1979). Wilson ad-vanced the discussion considerably by providing historical data, new perspectives, and termino-logical precision. His preference for the term *public religion* over *civil religion,* however, has not gained acceptance. Virtually everyone has fa-vored Rousseau's phrase.

Frequent references to the civil religion de-bate have been made in the literature of the field. The debate has centered around five key issues that merit greater clarity and consensus. This essay is organized around the following ques-tions, with an emphasis on American civil reli-gion: (1) What is an adequate definition of civil religion? (2) What is the intellectual and historic background of civil religion? (3) What are the different modes of analysis? (4) What are the social and institutional expressions of civil reli-gion? (5) Is civil religion desirable?

DEFINITION

The concept of civil religion combines two ordinary terms: a civil order and a religious order. The word *religion* can be, and has been, connected to other terms. There can be black religion, Native American religion, natural reli-gion, romantic religion, new religion, or mystical religion. In like fashion, the word *civil* has been linked to other words, such as civil rights, civil liberties, civil service, or civil war. Since under-standing the meaning of any one of these con-cepts requires an understanding of each term, it follows that a definition of civil religion logically flows from a definition of the two linked words *civil* and *religion.*

While there is some debate as to the meaning of the word *civil,* and greater debate about a definition of *religion,* it is possible to arrive at a broad definition of civil religion, one that in-cludes the widest range of issues. *Civil* refers to the social order or public life of a people. Derived from the Latin *civilis,* the term classically refers to the nation or state, its citizenry, and its laws. The Latin term for the noun form of *civilis* is *civitas,* meaning political society. Political soci-ety, as a synonym for social order or civil order, encompasses more than a citizen's direct ties to the state. The term includes the culture, public behavior, and institutional arrangements that give a sense of meaning, identity, belonging, and order to a people. This definition also makes it possible to discover a religious dimension in so-cial locations not directly tied to government or laws, such as rituals at athletic games, beauty pageants, or Boy Scouts' events.

Religion refers to a sacred order, a being, power, or authority transcending human or nat-ural reality. While there are other features to an adequate definition of religion, a notion of the sacred is the central one.

There are three approaches to defining reli-gion—institutional, functional, and substantive. Scholars in the field of social history put empha-sis on religion as a historical institution. Sociolo-gists and anthropologists tend to define it in terms of its functions. Those in fields of theol-ogy, phenomenology of religion, and history of religions define religion in terms of its substan-tive feature—the sacred. These three ap-proaches need not be mutually exclusive, but, in practice, the different orientations and meth-odologies with which they are associated have created much of the confusion surrounding the concept of civil religion. While this essay as-sumes the prominence of the sacred in any defi-nition of religion, it is important to consider all three approaches to understand the disagree-ment over how the term *civil religion* should be defined.

The most common way of understanding reli-gion is in its differentiated, historical, and institu-tional forms. For instance, it is natural to con-trast Buddhism and Christianity in terms of their different histories and such institutional features as beliefs, rituals, sacred figures, codes, and com-munal arrangements. Is this the way we should think about civil religion—as an institutionally differentiated religion? This question is one of the most debated in the civil religion discussion.

CIVIL AND PUBLIC RELIGION

Robert Bellah claims that there is "clearly differentiated from the churches an elaborate and well-institutionalized civil religion in America." Will Herberg, in "America's Civil Religion: What It Is and Whence It Comes" (Richey and Jones, 1974) makes almost the same claim: civil religion is "fully operative in a familiar way, with its creed, cult, codes, and community."

In "The Status of 'Civil Religion' " historian John Wilson, skeptical of such claims, goes beyond the four institutional features mentioned by Herberg to suggest that a more complex set of conditions must be met in order to qualify as institutional religion:

> (1) Cultic aspects to the phenomena, i.e., . . . (frequent) ceremony or ritual . . . ; (2) Recognized leadership offices invested with effective authority; (3) Explicitly defined means of participation in the religion . . . ; (4) At least implicit delineation of beliefs—if not correct belief; (5) Influence upon behavior . . . ; (6) Finally, and perhaps most important, a coherence of the above in order for the conception of religion to be applicable.
>
> (1971, p. 12)

Critics of such an approach charge that defining religion in these institutional terms does not do justice to the core of religious experience, for neither the individual nor for the various social expressions of religion in society, that might clearly exist in a nonformal and noninstitutionalized fashion.

Another way of defining religion—a source of confusion in the civil religion debate—is the functional approach, where the focus is on what religion does for people. There are three major functional theories of religion. The first, following the tenets of Karl Marx and Sigmund Freud, is the deprivation theory, where religion functions as an opiate or as an escape mechanism, helping people to cope with the afflictions of life. The second, following Max Weber, emphasizes the meaning function of religion. The third, following Émile Durkheim, stresses social identification and communal cohesion.

The three theories are not mutually exclusive; on the contrary, they may be detected as complementing and reinforcing one another in numerous analyses of American civil religion. For instance, in Charles Reagan Wilson's 1980 study of the religion that emerged in the South after the Civil War, in what he refers to as "religion of the lost cause" it becomes clear that a new form of public religion was born out of deprivation. It provided meaning in the face of perplexity and gave southern celebrants a sense of social solidarity and social identification with a sacred past.

Bellah, Thomas Luckmann, F. O. Wallace, Gail Gehrig, Clifford Geertz, and many others have adopted the functional approach in defining religion. Critics of functional definitions point out that almost any cultural system—such as a workplace organization, a political group, or a family system—could, in fact, furnish the basic human needs identified by sociologists of the functional theory. The emphasis on function, they claim, leads to such a broad and vague notion of religion that it could make civil religion nothing more than a synonym for political culture. Marty has said that some anthropologists and sociologists define religion so broadly that nothing can escape it, noting that "if everything is religious nothing is religious."

Peter Berger, Rodney Stark, and Mircea Eliade represent a substantive approach, which they claim avoids the tendency to reduce religion to purely human or natural terms, in contrast to an institutional or functional approach. Ellis M. West summed up the emphases of substantive definitions of religion by declaring:

> The object of the religious attitude is the sacred, holy, or divine, by which is meant a mysterious, extraordinary, awesome . . . power. . . . The essential characteristic of the sacred is its transcendence; i.e., it is always apprehended as other than man and nature.
>
> (1980, p. 35)

Opting for the narrower substantive definition, without seeing it as exclusive of the two other approaches, seems justified. Defining civil religion this way, of course, does not limit it to Western theistic notions of the sacred. The phenomena of the sacred as transcendence may be discerned in Japanese Shinto just as it may be discovered in American civil religion. Thus the existence of a civil religion may be a possibility in all societies.

In light of the above definitions of *civil* and *religion,* it may be said that a civil religion exists whenever a majority of the people of a nation or region ascribe ultimacy to aspects of their political society, such as their social ideals or means of governance; when they envision a transcendent goal to the political process; when they believe that a sacred reality is the source of meaning for their history and social order; and when these convictions are expressed through public rituals, myths, symbols, and a set of sacred beliefs.

This definition avoids the issue of whether civil religion must be structurally differentiated from the political community and traditional religious communities. It allows for a civil religion to provide legitimation or criticism of the status quo. It contains no ethical judgments as to the desirability of civil religion and says nothing about its being inevitable or not.

INTELLECTUAL AND HISTORIC BACKGROUND

The idea of civil religion comes from the classical world of ancient Greece and Rome, where there were two types of religion—the domestic and the public cult. The domestic cult was the religion of the family, which centered around a private altar and the hearth at the center of the house. Just as the sacred acts of piety, around altar and hearth, held a family together, so a public altar, enclosed within a temple and with its sacred fire, was the uniting center for civic life. Every city had its gods, and just as the rituals of the domestic cult were private, the ceremonies of the public cult were closed to all outsiders. Only a citizen could take part in the sacred ceremonies, and this public worship became the source of civic duty, identity, order, and the social bond of a citizenry.

Just as American civil religion has been seen as closely tied to the political life of our society, so was the Greek and Roman religion closely interconnected with politics. As in modern America, where a city council meeting, a football game, or the sessions of a court of justice or the U.S. Senate commence with a prayer, so it was with their counterparts in ancient Greece and Rome. There were no acts of public life in which religion was not present. The popular assemblies always took place in a sacred place. In Rome, it was the temple; in Greece, the "hall," containing an altar and sacred fire. Each assembly opened with prayers and acts of sacrifice.

By the time a popular assembly took up the "profane things," it is clear that the profane was infused with the sacred. Practical politics was penetrated by transcendence. The result of such a fusion of religion with public affairs was the common belief of citizens of a particular city that they were in special favor with the gods and that if they obeyed the oracles, exhibited public virtue, and maintained civic piety, they would have a special destiny. This is not unlike the belief many Americans have that God "smiled on their beginnings" and chose America for a special destiny, a prominent theme of American civil religion.

Because the public cult of the ancient world produced a religio-political order of powerful social cohesion and motivation for civic duty, it can be said that Rousseau's vision of civil religion did exist in the ancient world. Even though Rousseau believed ancient religion was based on error, he approvingly described how "every religion, then, was uniquely associated with the laws of the state." And in describing the Roman state cult, he gives us reason to believe that early Roman civic religion was close to his ideals of social unity and tolerance.

Unlike Christianity, which Rousseau thought divided a citizen's loyalty between the political order and the spiritual order and which was a religion of intolerance toward other religions, Roman religion was applauded for uniting divine and civic obligation, and for allowing the existence of particular religions, as long as they accepted the state cult. Writing about the spread of Rome's religion through the empire, Rousseau observed that the "Romans adopted the gods of the vanquished peoples—admitting them, gods, and people alike, to the freedom of the city." The result was a single "homogeneous religion," the central focus of which was the emperor, who was at once the chief priest of the state cult and, increasingly, after the first century A.D., an object of worship.

Pertinent to the American civil religion discussion is what happened when Roman religion came into contact with early Christianity. It is pertinent because a point of contention in the civil religion debate is whether or not, from a Christian perspective, a civil religion should be tolerated. Recalling how this new religion of a jealous god could not adapt to Rome's civil religion lends support to Rousseau's judgment that early Christianity did subvert the religio-political order.

The persecution of the early Christians should be seen in light of the trials for impiety that were common in the classical world of Greece and Rome. It should not be forgotten that the charges against Socrates in 399 B.C. were in terms of impious acts. Not to worship the gods in the correct way was the worst form of civic crime. It is not at all surprising that when the Christians refused to sacrifice to Caesar in the accepted way of the public cult, they were considered enemies of the state and guilty of treason. Rome, as Rousseau pointed out, allowed new and different religions, as long as there was at least nominal acceptance of the state cult.

Rome's attempt to absorb Christianity never worked, and, in fact, its attempt to maintain an imperial civil religion was increasingly frustrated. Although the strong public cult of the ancient world became increasingly weaker after the first century A.D., in all its forms—strong, weak, and variant—we find the historical source of Rousseau's concept as well as the current notions of civil religion.

In Book IV of *The Social Contract* (1762), Rousseau describes three kinds of religion—the pagan religion of Greece and Rome, evangelical Christianity, and the Roman Catholic church. Rejecting evangelical Christianity (Protestantism) as a religion without "any assignable point of contact with political society" and the Catholic church because it created a conflict of loyalties between the civil and spiritual realms, he clearly preferred paganism because it "was uniquely associated with the laws of the state." But he formally rejected paganism because, from an Enlightenment perspective, it was based on error.

It is fair to say that Rousseau did not invent civil religion; rather, he proposed an Enlightenment version of the civil religion he saw in antiquity. After a complex projection of a political society based on the consent of the governed, in which individual liberty would be reconciled to the public good, he proposed a civil religion that would provide the social bond to make this possible. Civil religion was also the answer to the issue of religious conflicts and wars, which were so vexing in the sixteenth and seventeenth centuries, for it provided overarching commonality for the achievement of social peace.

While Rousseau's concept of political society

in *The Social Contract* was extensively elaborated, his closing section, entitled "Civil Religion," was brief and his definition of the concept, short: "each citizen must have a religion requiring him to cherish his duties." These dogmas are of concern to the state "only in so far as they relate to morality or to the duties the faithful are enjoined to discharge toward others."

He thought the sovereign was entitled to fix the tenets of a purely civil creed, "but that this profession of faith would not be, strictly speaking, dogmas of a religious character, but rather sentiments *deemed indispensible* for participation in society, i.e., sentiments without which no man can be either a good citizen or a loyal subject." The dogmas of this civil religion were to be simple and few, such as belief in God and the life to come, the blessedness of the just, the punishment of the wicked, and "the sanctity of the social contract and the laws." Added to this short list is one negative tenet—the prescription against "intolerance."

In sum, Rousseau defined civil religion as a political instrument functioning to engender loyalty among citizens and to secure social order. The key feature of this civil religion was a social morality articulated in terms of civic duty. The emphasis was not on objective beliefs or on a transcendent realm; rather, it was on the "social sentiments" of the faithful.

Another aspect of Rousseau's view of civil religion, not apparent in his brief definition, but apparent in the framework of his social thought, was that civil religion had its personal side. His idea that civil religion provides social cohesion and produces good citizenship was not a new notion of how religion functions in society. The public face of traditional established religions, such as the Roman Catholic church in Italy, the Lutheran church in Norway, and the Anglican church in England, was thought to have done the same. What is different in Rousseau's Enlightenment version of civil religion is that political society itself was redemptive, an idea similar to Aristotle's conviction that spiritual fulfillment occurs only in the polis. In the words of historian Louis J. Voskull, Rousseau's civil society "becomes the solution for man's religious quest. There man first becomes a moral and rational being; there he finds secure freedom. In short, he becomes a *New Man*" (1975, pp. 21–22).

On the American scene, during the time of

nation building in the eighteenth century, the role of religion in public life received much attention. And while there was no systematic discussion of civil religion in Rousseauian terms, there is ample evidence that the Founding Fathers assumed religion would play a formative role in the new American society. John Wilson suggests that Benjamin Franklin may have been the earliest "to advocate serious attention to the public import of religion," when in his 1749 "Proposals" he "urged the founding of an academy in Philadelphia for the education of youth," taking special note that the study of history would be one of the most important disciplines because it would "afford frequent Opportunities of showing the Necessity of a *Publick Religion*" (1979, p. 7).

There was nothing novel in believing that a public religion was necessary because of its usefulness to the social order. The common assumption of the time was that government could not survive without an established religion and that religion could not survive without the support of government. But what would happen to that common assumption when the Founding Fathers erected a formal wall of separation between organized religion and the state?

Thomas Jefferson and other advocates of Enlightenment religion believed that in a pluralistic culture a common rational religion would emerge as a commonly held public religion. Evangelical Protestants believed that disestablishment of religion provided an opportunity to Christianize American society and to make Protestant Christianity the public religion. The civil religion that emerged in the nineteenth century, according to most scholars, was a combination of Enlightenment religion and evangelical Christianity—some called it republican Protestantism.

The importance of religion in nineteenth-century American public life was observed by many foreign visitors, most notably by Alexis de Tocqueville. Unlike Rousseau, who developed an abstract definition of civil religion, Tocqueville observed, firsthand, what he termed republican religion during his tour of America in 1831. He discovered a unique form of civil religion that developed out of religious pluralism and voluntarism. It was a fusion of democratic values and generalized Protestant beliefs that influenced politics and cultural mores, without being tied to any sect or denomination. He called religion "the first of American political institutions." He saw the function of religion in America to be a public one—"its chief aim being the making of citizens."

Tocqueville's contribution to the intellectual background of the civil religion discussion is significant because his was the first description of a generalized republican religion—or what is now called civil religion—that was structurally and functionally independent of religious and political institutions.

James Bryce, a visitor from England toward the end of the nineteenth century, found that contrary to the predictions of many Europeans, not only did Christianity survive, but it appeared to be an established religion. He recorded that each house of Congress "has a chaplain" and, like all of the state legislatures, its proceedings open "each day with prayers." The army and navy have "religious services, conducted by chaplains of various denominations," and in most "States there exists laws punishing . . . swearing by the name of God" and laws "forbidding trade or labour on the Sabbath." Bryce then summed up his impressions:

> Christianity is in fact understood to be, though not the legally established religion, yet the national religion. . . . They deem the general acceptance of Christianity to be one of the main sources of their national prosperity, and their nation a special object of Divine favour.
> (*The American Commonwealth*, 1893, pp. 769, 770)

Twentieth-century historians of American religion have, through numerous studies, confirmed what these and other foreign visitors observed firsthand. Franklin's assumption that public religion was a necessity was confirmed in the American experiment. The debate over whether this American civil religion is rooted primarily in the Enlightenment or in evangelical Protestantism goes on. Most have been convinced that it is an amalgam of both, with evangelical Protestantism the dominant force, at least in the nineteenth century.

Historians of American religion have critically discussed the emergence of this unique kind of national religion with its strong Protestant coloring, described by Tocqueville, Bryce, and others. Numerous books support its influence in American history: Ernest Lee Tuveson, *Redeemer Nation* (1968); Winthrop Hudson, *Nationalism and Religion in America* (1970); Martin Marty, *Righteous Empire* (1970); Conrad Cherry, *God's New Israel* (1971); Robert Handy, *A Christian America: Protestant Hopes and Historical Realities* (1971); Sidney Mead, *The Nation with the Soul of a Church* (1975); and John Wilson, *Public Religion in American Culture* (1979).

In addition, there have been numerous other books, monographs, and articles by historians who have contributed significantly to American civil religion studies. Daniel Boorstin, Ralph Gabriel, Richard Hofstadter, and Yehoshua Arieli, in different ways, delineated the religious dimension of American nationalism, patriotism, the American creed, and the democratic faith. Much of their work, as well as that of other historians, took place before, or at least independent of, the civil religion proposal by Bellah in his 1967 *Daedalus* article, where he wondered why something so obvious as civil religion had escaped the attention of scholars. A review of the literature shows that the sociologists were far less ready to entertain the idea of a common religion in America than were historians and theologians, and that a number of books and articles had already been written pointing to the phenomenon Bellah labeled civil religion.

As mentioned earlier, the most important study predating Bellah was Herberg's *Protestant, Catholic, Jew,* in which he identified a functionally and structurally differentiated civic religion that he called the "American Way of Life." His study focused not so much on the history of public religion, but on its mid-twentieth-century expression. He believed that civic religion, shaped by the contours of American Protestantism, especially the Puritan dream of a new "Israel" and a new "Promised Land," was a kind of "secularized Puritanism," the content of which was shared by both Catholics and Jews. Herberg relied on such prior studies as Robin Williams' chapter "Religion in America" in his book *American Society* (1951) and J. Paul Williams' *What Americans Believe and How They Worship* (1952). Robin Williams pointed to a "common faith" of Americans, while J. Paul Williams observed a "societal" religion he called the "democratic faith," which was different from denominational religion.

Following Herberg's study there appeared a spate of books that further identified a public religion in America. Martin Marty, in *The New Shape of American Religion* (1959), called American public religion "Americanized State Shinto" and "Religion in General." Peter Berger, in *Noise of Solemn Assemblies* (1961), referring to "Culture Religion" and "Religion of Democracy," likened the American public religion to the Roman imperial cult. A. Roy Eckardt's *The Surge of Piety in America* (1958) contained an analysis of a "Folk Religion," existing alongside and within traditional faiths. In "Constitution and Court as Symbols," written in 1947, Max Lerner alluded to the emergence in American history of what amounts to a "state church," the study of which would produce the "real religious history of America," in contrast to a narrowly misguided focus on "formal churchgoing religion."

Because many scholars advanced the scholarship of a public religion, or what has now come to be called civil religion, Bellah's claim to discovery is unfair. The public cults of antiquity, the imperial cults of Rome, the public religion of Franklin, and the civil religion of Rousseau and Herberg all received attention before the Bellah article. In another sense, Bellah is right, for scholars had been without a commonly accepted concept as a basis on which description, analysis, interpretation, and evaluation could proceed. Scholars awaited a more refined concept. Bellah's civil religion has become that concept. It has brought together sociologists, historians, and theologians to a more refined, coherent, and common discourse. It renewed the discussion in the late 1960s and 1970s, engendering scholarly publications, numerous conferences, and considerable press coverage, especially as the peak of the discussion took place during the 1976 bicentennial celebration. While a consensus as to what civil religion is, how it should be studied, and whether it is desirable has not yet been achieved, these are goals receiving serious attention in the mid-1980s.

MODES OF ANALYSIS

Much of the confusion in the civil religion discussion results from the variety of ways civil religion has been understood and analyzed. In their 1974 essay "The Civil Religion Debate," Russell E. Richey and Donald G. Jones sort out five ways civil religion has been interpreted. This fivefold typology has been used by other scholars to organize the literature and has instigated some discussion as to which type should be developed as the normative conceptual scheme for civil religion studies. The five characterizations are: folk religion, transcendent universal religion of the nation, religious nationalism, the democratic faith, and Protestant civic piety.

The idea of civil religion as folk religion emphasizes the actual common religion emerging out of the life of the "folk." Will Herberg, Robin Williams, Lloyd Warner, Martin Marty, A. Roy Eckardt, Peter Berger, and Andrew Greeley represent this category by looking not at historical texts and speeches, but at the actual life, ideas, values, rituals, symbols, and loyalties of a people. The starting point is not a normative view of what civil religion is at best—the starting point for both Rousseau and Bellah—but rather what it actually *is,* based on empirical studies, surveys, polls, and phenomenological investigation. This approach is the most amenable to behavioral analysis.

One of the most notable studies cited as evidence for the existence of civil religion, and as representative of this mode of analysis, is Lloyd Warner's Yankee City series. In this study of social systems in a New England town, he provides an analysis of "An American Sacred Ceremony," a Memorial Day celebration. By observing the phases before, during, and after the celebration, he discerned beliefs in intricate fashion and the commingling of sacred and secular symbols. He concludes that these symbols and beliefs functioned to organize and integrate various religious, national, and class groups into a sacred unity. Memorial Day is a cult of the dead evoking images of the sacrifices soldiers made for the living, and the concomitant obligation of the living to sacrifice their individual purposes for the good of society, "so that they too can perform their spiritual obligations" (Richey and Jones, p. 91).

The other study most often cited as representing civil religion as folk religion is Herberg's *Protestant, Catholic, Jew,* which analyzes the religious dimension of the American folkways. Relying on surveys, polls, and prior studies concerning beliefs and values of Americans, Herberg concludes that Americans do have a "common" religion and that "religion" is the system famil-

iarly known as the "American Way of Life." It is this American Way of Life, he believes, that supplies American society with an overarching sense of unity amid conflict.

A summary of the values and beliefs of the American way reveals that, on the spiritual side, Americans place an extraordinarily high valuation on religion itself, with belief in a supreme being nearly a must. On its political side the American way means "democracy" and the Constitution; on its economic side, "free enterprise"; on its social side, the American way is pragmatic, dynamic, and optimistic, with a fervent belief in the supreme value of the individual. Culturally, the American way exhibits intense faith in education and an extremely high valuation of sanitation, where cleanliness is not merely next to godliness, but "virtually on the same level, as a kind of equivalent." Morally, Americans are idealistic, needing to justify political causes and materialistic pursuits in "higher" terms—in terms of a crusade, in terms of service or stewardship.

Even though Warner stresses the importance of symbols, while Herberg emphasizes values, they both share Durkheim's assumption that every society has a common religion which functions as a social bond. Such a common religion can be investigated in America the way a folk religion in an undeveloped village can be studied. They also assume, along with Durkheim, that aspects of society—or the society as a whole —become sacred. For Herberg, in American civil religion, "national life is apotheosized, national values (such as sanitation) are religionized," and national history is experienced as "a *Heilsgeschichte,*" a redemptive history.

Civil religion discussed in this way functions to integrate a widely diverse American society; it provides identity and meaning. Finally, it is capable of being a source of limited judgment on society, because of the idealized content of American values, and a transcendent dimension in the sacred symbols that may evoke guilt or motivate effort toward the public good.

The second meaning of civil religion has been categorized as the transcendent universal religion of the nation. This is the categorization of Sidney E. Mead, who preceded Bellah by several years in articulating a "religion of the republic" that is a real, universal, and transcendent religion, hovering over folk religion and church religion. He describes this transcendent "cosmopolitan" religion in terms of Enlightenment faith, similar to Rousseau's concept. He evaluates this public or civil religion as superior to particular sectarian religion because unlike church religion, which divides, the religion of the republic unites precisely because of "a universal principle which is thought to transcend and include all the national and religious particularities" (*Church History,* 36, 1967).

In like fashion, Bellah describes a civil religion that exists alongside of and transcends the American Way of Life and church religion. He then makes a normative claim that American civil religion is a "genuine apprehension of universal and transcendent religious reality," which is "revealed through the experience of the American people," but not to be identified with American folkways. And, like Mead, Bellah advocates this civil religion "at its best" as a source of judgment and redemption for America in a time of "trial" and "crisis." Because of its transcendent universality, Bellah entertains the possibility that American civil religion could become "simply one part of a new civil religion of the world." In his pivotal 1967 essay, he concludes: "A world civil religion could be accepted as a fulfillment and not a denial of American civil religion." Such an outcome, he believes, has been the hope of American civil religion from the beginning. "To deny such an outcome would be to deny the meaning of America itself." In *Varieties of Civil Religion* (1980), Bellah and Phillip E. Hammond struck the same note. Thinking about a troubled world facing the possibility of nuclear holocaust, they wrote:

> American civil religion with its tradition of openness, tolerance, and ethical commitment might make a contribution to a world civil religion that would transcend and include it. . . . It is time that we raise our sights to consider the relation of religion and politics in a global order of civility and justice.
>
> (p. xiv)

As representatives of the folk religion approach, Warner and Herberg are not interested in such global considerations. They focus, rather, on the religion of a particular people and attempt to discern how values and ritual behavior function to achieve social unity and spiritual meaning for a specific nation or culture. In con-

trast, Mead and Bellah are less concerned with the culture-specific expressions of civil religion and more concerned with a theoretical framework of symbols, beliefs, and ethical norms that point to a transcendent deity acting upon the civil order in judgment and redemption. According to this approach, there is a notion of heresy, idolatry, and profanation. When symbols are misused for narrow political purposes or national self-aggrandizement, or when the god of civil religion becomes identified with cultural values, civil religion is reduced to an apostate status. In this sense, it is possible to see that in the transcendent universal religion of the nation model, there can be an apprehension of folk religion. Some, such as Gail Gehrig and John Wilson, believe that because this mode of analysis is more comprehensive, it has more promise as a functioning concept for further studies in civil religion. The problem for followers of Mead and Bellah is that of objectivity. It is difficult to study a common religion of the people with fairness and scholarly openness when the version being studied represents a violation or banalization of the normative religion of the investigator. In spite of this problem, this transcendent universal model of civil religion has, in Gehrig's words, "stimulated the greatest amount of contemporary inquiry."

A third meaning of civil religion is indicated by the phrase *religious nationalism.* In this usage the nation itself takes on a sacred and self-transcendent character, becoming the object of reverence. Religious nationalism implies fervent patriotism, glorification of national heroes, and sacralization of national purposes—real or pretended.

Some have called this kind of civil religion the religion of patriotism. In the late nineteenth century, articulating a strong religious nationalism typical of his time, Archbishop John Ireland said that the "religion of patriotism is not sufficiently understood," and yet, he believed, that it was "this religion that gives to country its majesty, and to patriotism its sacredness and force." Elton Trueblood (*The Future of the Christian,* 1971) claims that patriotism inherently involves a religious dimension because sacrifice and dedication are its powerful ingredients. Thus it is not uncommon when a traditional faith, with themes of sacrifice and dedication, gets blended into patriotism during or after times of war.

The sanctification of the nation and the fusion of religious fervor and patriotism are common themes in civil religion studies. For instance, Charles Henderson's 1972 treatment of Richard Nixon's theology shows how the concept of "a nation under God" can easily shift to the notion of a nation becoming godlike, as when President Nixon took sacred language and applied it chiefly to his personal vision of the nation.

The analysis of civil religion as religious nationalism also figures in assessments by James Smylie, Conrad Cherry, Martin Marty, Herbert Richardson, and Carlton Hayes, all of whom make the point that when traditional religions move out of the civil order, the nation moves in and assumes functions normally associated with church religion. One of the major themes of this type of analysis is that nations can be seen as the primary agent of God's activity in history, which, from the standpoint of traditional religion, inevitably leads to idolatry; that is, a sacralizing of the nation and politics.

The analysis of civil religion as religious nationalism focuses on elements that are analogous to traditional religions, such as holy days, parades, pilgrimages, solemn feasts, relics, and shrines. The flag receives attention as the most sacred symbol of fervent nationalism; presidents are studied as high priests; national documents, such as the Declaration of Independence, the Constitution, and the addresses of Washington and Lincoln, are called "holy scriptures" and sources of national "theological doctrine."

For political society, nationalism achieves a sense of unity and grand mission. To individual citizens, it gives an emotional lift and meaningful identity. However, unlike transcendent universal civil religion, religious nationalism is tribal and exclusive, representing a reaction against notions of universality. Moreover, it elicits sacrifice and dedication for narrow national interests, and it tends not to encourage a sense of universal justice and benevolence. Many interpreters view religious nationalism as fundamentally intolerant and with an inherent predisposition for war. Hence, there are those who do not think civil religion is a good thing when it is defined as religious nationalism, which is the extreme expression of folk religion and the exact opposite of the transcendent universal civil religion of Bellah.

A fourth meaning of civil religion has been designated as the democratic faith. This model is represented in the writings of humanistic scholars who have a stake in promoting democracy or "republican virtue" as a unifying common faith. The humane values and ideals of freedom, equality, benevolence, fraternity, and justice, without necessary reference to a transcendent god or a spiritualized nation, represent the core of a civil religion creed according to this model.

Democracy as a religion has been consciously promoted by a number of thinkers in twentieth-century America. J. Paul Williams said that Americans must look upon the democratic ideal "as the Will of God" and must be brought to the conviction that "democracy is the very law of life." He believed that the government, through the public school system, should teach the democratic ideal "as religion." Horace M. Kallen, in referring to the "communicants" of the democratic faith, said that they were believers in the religion of religions, where, despite particular faith commitments, "all may freely come together in it." The "common faith" of John Dewey and the "public philosophy" of Walter Lippmann are classic examples of democratic faith.

According to this model, the democratic faith encompasses these beliefs: that individuals are born to be free and equal; that human rights are universal; that justice is the animating principle of politics; and that benevolence and loyalty are duties of citizenship. Thus its main function is to produce civic virtue and public cohesiveness.

This concept of civil religion is similar to Rousseau's vision. Rousseau eschewed chauvinistic nationalism, was not concerned with shared cultural values, was not interested in rituals and symbols, and did not emphasize a transcendent god as a source of judgment on national life. He was concerned with civic virtue, rights, duties, and the principles of democracy.

This fourth model represents a civil religion tied to a particular society and applicable only as a theoretical construct to democratic societies. The underlying assumption of this model is that a differentiated set of beliefs, loyalties, and behaviors can be recognized, analyzed, and studied as constituting one type or expression of civil religion. This type may be included in all of the other types. Indeed, it does appear in Herberg's folk religion analysis and Bellah's transcendental universal civil religion, but it is distinct and does not require any of the other models to study civil religion effectively.

The fifth meaning of civil religion has been called Protestant civic piety. It is applicable as a model only to the United States, because the literature representative of this type concerns the Protestant origins of, and influence on, American civil religion. Catherine Albanese uses the term *public Protestantism* in discussing how dominant Calvinistic Protestant religion was in the public domain during colonial America. Yehoshua Arieli calls the nineteenth-century blend of Christianity and public life "Protestant nationalism" (*Individualism and Nationalism in American Ideology*, 1964). Denis Brogan, in agreeing with Bellah that there is a civil religion in twentieth-century America, says that it is not wrong to call this country a "Protestant country," and that the "public civil religion is Protestant" (*The American Character*, 1944).

Historians such as Robert Handy, Winthrop Hudson, James Smylie, James Maclear, and Robert Michaelson, among others, emphasize the fusion of Protestantism and nationalism, and the pervading Protestant coloring of the American ethos. Herberg employs the concept of Protestant civic piety when he says, "America's civil religion is compounded of the two great religious movements that molded America—the Puritan way, secularized; and the Revivalist way, secularized."

Scholars who emphasize Protestant moralism, individualism, activism ("deeds not creeds"), hard work, religious liberty, democratic equality, the quest for simplicity, and the grand motif of "missionizing" the world as characteristics of American civil religion are representative of this type. Also, those who stress the importance of such national self-images as the "New Israel," the "Chosen People," the "Promised Land," and this nation as a "Light to the World," both in terms of tracing the origins of civil religion in America and the ongoing self-understanding of the American people, are emphasizing themes that flow out of the Protestant concept of civic piety.

While this model is a less comprehensive characterization of civil religion, what it loses in general applicability it may gain in historical and sociological precision. For instance, it may be useful in understanding the differences and commonalities of northern and southern civil religion during the Civil War, certain aspects of public religion in frontier America, and elements of common religion in rural and suburban America from the 1950s through the 1980s. The categorization also may be particularly apt for understanding the blend of evangelical Protestantism and Americanism in the Moral Majority movement of the 1980s. One way of viewing this group is to see that it wants a return to a Protestant public religion. The model helps to illuminate an ongoing, albeit changing, Protestant coloring in the American experience by emphasizing the historical role Puritanism and revivalism have played in shaping aspects of the American culture.

All of the aforementioned models may encompass assumptions, themes, and the distinct focus of this fifth type. While there is some overlapping of categories with the other four meanings of civil religion, Protestant civic piety, as a distinct theoretical framework, has made its unique contribution.

The main problems still confronting scholars of civil religion relate directly to the diversity of conceptualization illustrated by these five types. The diversity expresses also the complexity and pioneer nature of the subject.

SOCIAL AND INSTITUTIONAL EXPRESSIONS

According to Durkheim, religion must have social and institutional expressions. He says that in all history there has never been a religion without a church. A virtual consensus exists among scholars that Durkheim is right: religion, by definition, is social in nature. Theorists of civil religion take for granted this proposition, but disagree whether there is such a thing as a "clearly differentiated" civil religion, as proclaimed by Bellah in "Civil Religion in America." John Wilson, in his seminal study *Public Religion in American Culture*, concludes that the case for a developed and differentiated civil religion in American history is highly questionable, but that it is possible to identify a religious cultural reality in various social structures which may be identified as civil religion. While the issue of a "clearly differentiated" civil religion has not been settled, its social and institutional expressions have been investigated, mainly in these seven social locations: organized religion, public school systems, legal institutions and traditions, presidential speeches, patriotic rituals and symbols, patriotic voluntary societies, and sports.

That American civil religion had its beginnings in Protestant Christianity and continues to be expressed in various formal religions is a commonplace notion. Civil religion has even been located in a new religion, the Unification Church of Sun Myung Moon. One of the major themes of Herberg's *Protestant, Catholic, Jew* is that these three main faiths embody and maintain the American Way of Life as a common religion, that to be religious is considered a patriotic duty, and that patriotism is a fruit of religious piety.

There are many examples of how the civil order and formal religion become intertwined and function as agents for each other: religious leaders of inaugural ceremonies; prayers for public figures; chaplains in the military and the Congress; celebration of religious holy days in public life; religious marriages accepted in lieu of civil services; and the blend of nationalistic and religious language in both patriotic and religious hymns. A complete explication of these and other similar connections between formal religion and the civil order makes a compelling case for the existence of a civil religious dimension, maintained and elaborated by formal religion.

The public school system is a place where Americans for a long period of time experience civil religion. Some have even said the public school system functions as "the church" of American civil religion. In the nineteenth century, public schools were not only in the business of inculcating patriotism, the American way, and reverence for national heroes, but also of promoting what has been called "practical Protestant morality." This combination of nationalism and Protestant piety has become the central spiritual structure of American civil religion, according to Herberg and others.

Democratic ideals and democratic practice (as in student government activities) are reinforced by pictures of George Washington and Abraham Lincoln, recitation of the Pledge of Allegiance, the presence of an American flag, and celebrations of national holidays. There have been many advocates of the idea that schools should promote a common faith. Most notable have been John Dewey, Horace Kallen, Luther Weigle, and

J. Paul Williams. Weigle, former dean of the Yale Divinity School, believed that public schools should self-consciously promote the "common religious faith" of democracy. The future of civil religion and the public schools remains uncertain, but it seems clear that in the past they have been "temples of the democratic faith," to use Williams' phrase.

If free public education has been a vital force in orienting masses of people to this religion, legal institutions and traditions have functioned to adjudicate the right and wrong of its moral substance. Philip Hammond and John Wilson emphasize this area as an important social location of civil religion in America. Because Americans believe in God-given, natural rights and because the Constitution and the court system represent the highest criterion by which rights are to be judged, judicial structures, procedures, and persons take on a sacred quality.

Max Lerner is the most famous of those who have observed that Americans tend to see a religious dimension in the legal system, regarding the Constitution as holy writ, the Supreme Court as a temple, and the justices as high priests. In "Constitution and Court as Symbols" (1937), Lerner says that for Americans the "Constitution and Supreme Court are symbols of an ancient sureness and a comforting stability." He points out that the Court as a sacred symbol goes hand in hand with the Constitution as a sacred symbol. Since the Supreme Court exercises a guardianship over the Constitution, the result "has been to invest the judges of the Court with all the panoply of sanctity with which the Constitution has itself been invested."

Lerner's conclusion that Americans actually worship the Constitution and the Supreme Court suggests that these judicial entities may be important institutional locations of American civil religion. Hammond's suggestion, following an appreciative interpretation of Lerner's thesis that law, in general, might be perceived as having sacred functions, has received positive responses from civil religion theorists. Though the study of civil religion focusing on legal institutions and traditions is undeveloped, enough has been done to encourage further investigation.

Another location of American civil religion is the presidential address, with special emphasis on the rhetoric of presidents on Inauguration Day. Bellah triggered the whole discussion by claiming that a civil religious dimension could be found in inaugural addresses. He analyzed President John F. Kennedy's 1961 inaugural speech and commented on addresses by Washington, Jefferson, Lincoln, and Johnson.

Bellah's method was to look for specific references to a deity (e.g., Almighty God, the hand of God, God's work, almighty being, providence of God), religious metaphors and images (sacred fire of liberty, invisible hand, sacrifice, chosen people, promised land), and civic virtue (struggle, sacrifice, loyalty, justice, liberty). Bellah and Conrad Cherry both suggested that four major themes can be discovered in the civil religion rhetoric of presidents: the language of patriotic sacrifice, American destiny under God, exodus from the Old to the New World, and America as an international example.

Cynthia Toolin, in a 1983 study of forty-nine inaugural addresses, tested this hypothesis and discovered ample evidence of a civil religion. Most of the addresses refer to a deity, civic virtues of duty and freedom are espoused, and numerous religious metaphors and images are taken from the Judeo-Christian tradition. However, she also discovered that the Constitution, the Revolution, and George Washington—all representing a grand past—were dominant themes. This study also revealed that the exodus and sacrifice themes were minor. The most important themes pointing to a civil religious dimension were American destiny under God and international example.

Patriotic rituals and symbols—such as Memorial Day, the Fourth of July, Thanksgiving Day—and various ethnic day ceremonies, such as Columbus Day, represent another type of institutional expression of civil religion. The symbol of the unfinished pyramid under the all-seeing eye of God, which appears above the phrase *novus ordo seclorum*—a new order of the age—on the Great Seal of the United States, reflects the central theme of American civil religion. God chose America for a special destiny. That symbol receives added force from the slogan In God We Trust, found on all American coins and paper currency (mandated by an act of Congress in 1955, though it had appeared on select coins since 1873). The addition of the phrase "under God" in the Pledge of Allegiance by an act of Congress in 1954 is further evidence of the continuing notion that God has smiled on America.

It is no wonder that the vast majority of Americans believe that national leaders should affirm their belief in God.

One ritual, which seems to be unknown in most Western countries, is that of flag worship in America. Surveys have revealed that the majority of Americans believe the flag is sacred. The British historian Denis Brogan said the "rabbinical rules" about raising and lowering the American flag are "unknown in Britain, where most people neither know nor care, and so innocently offended Americans in England during World War II by treating Old Glory as casually as they treated the Union Jack" (*Religious Situation*, 1968, p. 359). These public symbols and rituals are just a few among the many that function to maintain and express civil religion.

The most direct and explicit expression of civil religion in America is rendered in patriotic voluntary societies and lodges. At least five kinds of organizations are identified as agencies of civic piety. First are the veterans' organizations, such as the Grand Army of the Republic (1866), the American Legion (1919), and the Veterans of Foreign Wars (1913). Second are hereditary organizations, where membership is passed down through family or ethnic ties, such as Sons of the Revolution, Daughters of the American Revolution, Colonial Dames of America, and Society of Mayflower Descendants. Third, fraternal orders, like the Masons, Odd Fellows, Elks, and Rotary, freely mix aspects of traditional religion with civil religion. Fourth, scouting groups, which have God language and patriotism commingling in the socialization process, are very important agencies for citizenship training. Finally, there are the nativist groups (among them, the American Protective Association, the Supreme Order of the Star Spangled Banner, and the Ku Klux Klan) that were hostile to certain immigrant groups in the late nineteenth and early twentieth centuries. In recent years, white supremacist groups like the Ku Klux Klan and various groups hostile to communism qualify as analogues to the earlier nativist groups. What is common to most of these is the belief that America is a sacred society, deserving of good citizenship and ultimate loyalty.

Sports in America and many other countries are candidates for the social and institutional expressions of civil religion. In the United States, sports used to be primarily a male activity. With cultural and legal changes, sports increasingly have become a central meaning system in popular culture for men and women alike.

Hammond was the first to identify sports as a channel of civil religion, when he suggested that in America, God's will is known "through majority vote, fair play, or some such enabling rules." The greatest glory, highest honors, and rewards of satisfaction go to those who have played hardest and fairest within the rules. This promise is central not only to the ethics of American sports, but to the common faith of Americans, according to those who see sports as a social structure for the transmission of that faith.

The ritualistic expression of this ethic and belief is found in the prayer before the game, which emphasizes sportsmanship, protection from injury, and competitive excellence. A common prayer that has been used before high school football games all over the country states: "Dear God, may this be a fair game, may no one get hurt, and may the best team win. Amen."

Not all teams pray, and not all teammates who pray are true believers, but the outward piety of American sports events is remarkable. At a typical Super Bowl football game, one finds American flags, patriotic bunting, clergy prayers, the national anthem, and sometimes military jets flying in formation overhead. Going to a stadium can be like going to a high mass or political rally.

The notion of sports as a civil cult goes back to Greek antiquity, when the gods and the state were honored at the Olympic Games festivals. This classic role of sports in bringing together the civil order and the religious order continues to this day.

The best contribution to the study of sports as a civil religion comes from Michael Novak, who insists in his 1976 book *The Joy of Sports* that in addition to the emphasis on rules, fair play, and outward rituals, sports are inherently religious, driving people "godward." He sees sports as a natural religion, with liturgies, organized institutions, and disciplines that "teach religious qualities of heart and soul." Because they speak a universal language, they function to bind a diverse nation together much as do other structures of civil religion.

All of the expressions and structures of civil religion in America, when taken together, provide strong evidence that it does exist in public life, but that the claim of a clearly differentiated and well institutionalized civil religion remains questionable. Of all the expressions or structures of civil religion, sports probably come closest to being a differentiated civic cult. But at this point in the study, it is more accurate to acknowledge the existence of civil religion as more diffused than differentiated, and to say that it finds expression in a variety of social locations in episodic fashion.

DESIRABILITY OF CIVIL RELIGION

One of the most debatable questions is: Should civil religion be regarded as desirable? The answer depends on the definition of civil religion and the ideological assumptions brought to the discussion. In a general sense, both liberal and conservative camps can be identified with a large pluralistic group in between. There are three answers to the question: yes, no, and yes-and-no.

Those who think civil religion is a good thing represent two different types in definition and attitude. When defined as the transcendent universal religion of the nation, Sidney Mead, Robert Bellah, and others applaud civil religion as an authentic and positive dimension of political society. When defined as democratic faith, devotees of John Dewey think civil religion is not only a good thing but also a necessary feature of a democratic society. These positions represent the liberal camp.

On the right are those more identified with evangelical Protestant and conservative causes, who strongly endorse civil religion when expressed in terms of a Protestant civic piety. Though they may not use the language of academicians, they do promote vigorously a form of public religion that contains many of the features of religious nationalism, American folk religion, and, of course, Protestant civic piety. Representatives of this favorable view of civil religion are members of the American Legion, the Moral Majority, and some but not all Evangelicals and members of mainline religion in America. The themes *returning to traditional values, bringing prayer back in schools,* and *getting back to God in our national life* are expressions of this positive view of civil religion.

The question of civil religion's desirability is answered negatively in a variety of ways. What is approved by the conservatives is precisely what is denounced by the liberals. If civil religion is expressed as a common denominator, folk religion, nationalism, or Protestant piety, then the liberal camp is repelled. In like manner, when civil religion is defined as democratic faith, in John Dewey's terms, or as a religion transcending and encompassing traditional religions, as with Mead and Bellah, it is rejected as a form of liberal humanism by evangelical conservatives.

Another large pluralistic group that cannot be neatly categorized thinks civil religion is undesirable. The main charges against it are that it vitiates and trivializes traditional religions. It hurts the body politic by becoming a substitute for rational and ethical approaches to public life. And it is fundamentally idolatrous from the point of view of particular faiths.

Evangelical Protestants, such as Sen. Mark Hatfield, have opposed civil religion in no uncertain terms. In the midst of the Vietnam War, in 1973, Hatfield deplored the use of civil religion to sanctify the war effort, as though "it were spiritually ordained." He said that the God of American civil religion is a small and private deity and an "exclusive defender of the American nation." In contrast, he said, authentic faith must be in the "biblical God of justice and righteousness who is revealed in the scriptures and in the person of Jesus Christ." For Hatfield, it made no difference how civil religion was defined; it was not a good thing.

Many other clergy, theologians, and lay people, from various confessional standpoints, have seen civil religion, however defined, as a competing faith to be rejected. Mary Schneider, a Catholic, comes out against civil religion, as currently defined, because of its strong Protestant coloring and link to American nativism. Drawing on Thomas Aquinas, Schneider proposes an approach to civil religion that would link it to natural law and a universal moral order, allowing for active patriotism, political loyalty, and national reverence without blending traditional Catholic faith with Americanism. She does open the way for a Catholic acceptance of civil religion by her own proposed definition.

Finally, there are holdout groups that oppose American civil religion. Most of the new religions are against civil religion, with the exception of the Unification Church. Minority religions such as the Amish, Jehovah's Witnesses, and Hutterites would also fit into this classification. Some feminists think civil religion is just as sexist as traditional religions, and many blacks and other minorities consider civil religion another racist structure. Such groups either oppose civil religion or call for its reform.

Among those who give a yes-and-no answer to the question, Is civil religion desirable? is Martin Marty, with his balanced, appreciative, and at the same time skeptical descriptions of civil religion. Many others want to say yes to some elements and no to others. Will Herberg represents the middle dialectical position more dramatically than any of the others. For him, the normative evaluation of civil religion depends on the social role from which one speaks. As an ordinary citizen, he praises American civil religion as a "noble" religion and perhaps the best ever to appear in a mass society. As a theologian, working out of the traditional biblical faith, the claims to ultimacy of civil religion have to be absolutely rejected as idolatry. For him, the good citizen and faithful believer must live with this tension and paradox:

> I . . . regard America's civil religion as a genuine religion; . . . The fact that . . . America's civil religion is congruent with the culture is no argument against it; . . . America's civil religion . . . strikes me as a noble religion, celebrating some very noble civic virtues. . . . I would regard the American Way of Life . . . the social face of America's civil religion, as probably the best way of life yet devised for a mass society. . . . So I certainly would not want to disparage America's civil religion.
>
> ("America's Civil Religion," in Richey and Jones, 1974, p. 86)

Herberg then registers a resounding no to the civil religion concept. Because Judaism and Christianity serve a jealous God who transcends and judges all human structures, claims to ultimacy in civil religion cannot be allowed: "To see America's civil religion as somehow standing above or beyond the biblical religions . . . as somehow including them and finding a place for them in its over-arching unity, is idolatry" (p. 87).

Not many scholars have been this overt in holding together civil religion and biblical faith in paradoxical tension, but it may not be wrong to assume that a host of Americans covertly are holding together traditional religion and civil religion in either tension or harmony.

While the debate about the desirability of civil religion continues, there are some scholars of American society who are still not sure there is such a thing. Some, like the historian Sydney Ahlstrom, allow that, while it may have existed once, civil religion did not survive the turbulent 1960s. Even Bellah now characterizes American civil religion as an "empty and broken shell."

What clearly has survived is the concept of civil religion and the conviction that it does describe a dimension of public life that cannot be equated with particular organized religions. Although this concept has been applied to other countries—South Africa, Mexico, Japan, and Sri Lanka, among others—the study of civil religion remains primarily an academic venture of a select group of American scholars with a focus on American history and contemporary culture.

BIBLIOGRAPHY

Catherine L. Albanese, *Sons of the Fathers: The Civil Religion of the American Revolution* (1976); Robert N. Bellah, "Civil Religion in America," in *Daedalus*, 96 (1967), *The Broken Covenant: American Civil Religion in a Time of Trial* (1975), and, with Phillip E. Hammond, *Varieties of Civil Religion* (1980); Henry W. Bowden, "A Historian's Response to the Concept of American Civil Religion," in *Journal of Church and State*, 17 (1975); Conrad Cherry, *God's New Israel* (1971); William A. Cole and Phillip E. Hammond, "Religious Pluralism, Legal Developments, and Societal Complexity: Rudimentary Forms of Civil Religion," in *Journal for the Scientific Study of Religion*, 39 (1978); Donald R. Cutler, ed., *The Religious Situation: 1968* (1968); Gail Gehrig, *American Civil Religion: An Assessment* (1981); Phillip E. Hammond, "The Sociology of American Civil Religion: A Bibliographic Essay," in *Sociological Analysis*, 37 (1976); Will Herberg, *Protestant, Catholic, Jew* (1955; rev. 1960).

Max Lerner, "Constitution and Court as Symbols," in *Yale Law Journal*, 46 (1937); Robert D. Linder, "Civil Religion in Historical Perspective: The Reality That Underlies the Concept," in *Journal of Church and State*, 17 (1975); Charles H. Lippy, "The President as Priest: Civil Religion and the American Presidency," in *Journal of Religious Studies*, 8 (1980); Martin Marty, *A Nation of Behavers* (1976); Sidney E. Mead, *The Nation with the Soul of a Church* (1975); Robert Michaelson, *Piety in the Public School* (1970); Michael Novak, *The Joy of Sports* (1976); Russell E. Richey and Donald G. Jones, eds., *American Civil Religion* (1974); Jean-Jacques Rousseau, *The Social Contract and Discourses* (1893); Mary L. Schneider, "A Catholic Perspective on American Civil Religion," in Thomas M. McFadden, ed., *America in Theological Perspective* (1976); Elwyn A. Smith, ed., *The Religion of the Republic* (1971).

Cynthia Toolin, "American Civil Religion from 1789 to 1981: A Content Analysis of Presidential Inaugural Addresses," in *Review of Religious Research*, 25 (1983); Louis J. Voskull, "Jean-Jacques Rousseau: Secular Salvation and Civil Religion," in *Fides et Historia*, 7 (1975); William Lloyd Warner, *American Life: Dream and Reality* (1953); Ellis M. West, "A Proposed Neutral Definition of Civil Religion," in *Journal of Church and State*, 22 (1980); J. Paul Williams, *What Americans Believe and How They Worship* (1952; rev. 1962); Charles Reagan Wilson, *Baptized in Blood: The Religion of the Lost Cause, 1865–1920* (1980); John F. Wilson, "The Status of 'Civil Religion,' " in Elwyn Smith, ed., *The Religion of the Republic* (1971) and *Public Religion in American Culture* (1979).

[*See also* BIBLE IN AMERICAN CULTURE; CHURCH AND STATE; IMPACT OF PURITANISM ON AMERICAN CULTURE; THEOLOGICAL INTERPRETATIONS AND CRITIQUES OF AMERICAN SOCIETY AND CULTURE; *and* WAR AND PEACE.]

WAR AND PEACE

Melvin B. Endy, Jr.

THE DEVELOPMENT OF JUDAEO-CHRISTIAN ATTITUDES THROUGH 1700

The roots of the predominant American attitudes toward war and peace are the Jewish and Christian Scriptures. While the justifications for war and pacifism developed in the Christian tradition, the Hebrew Scriptures contain all three of the major religious attitudes toward war; namely, pacifism, the holy war, and the just war.

In Genesis 6:13 it is the violence of the fallen creation that God especially despises and that makes God want to destroy the world. The prophets portray the kingdom toward which God is driving creation as above all a kingdom of peace, distinguished from this world by the lion's companionship with the lamb and the beating of swords into plowshares. By contrast, the central thread of the Torah, or Pentateuch, is the selection of Israel as God's militant chosen nation or holy people. Israel's establishment as a politico-religious nation destined to lead the creation to the realization of God's saving purposes in history is said to have come about through a war of conquest that in turn became the paradigm for later Jewish and Christian conceptions of a holy war or crusade. Both religious communities have seen themselves as the chosen people called by God. This belief is the basis both for the Jewish teaching that a war in which the very existence of Israel is threatened is a "commanded" war or a religious honor and duty and for the assumption by some Christians that the propagation and defense of the one true faith is the supreme duty placed on Christian nations by God.

Jewish and Christian thinkers have also found in the Hebrew Scriptures a conception of war that is more appropriate for fallen creatures and that is applicable to all of humanity. According to this conception, men and women are called on to preserve what semblance of justice and order they can in a fallen world and to express their love for God and their fellow creatures by defending persons unjustly attacked against violence and threats to their essential rights to life and liberty.

Although early Christians assumed that Jesus would soon return for the final conquest of evil, they understood him to be a "Prince of Peace" who had conquered evil by submitting to deadly violence and who had taught his followers to avoid the violent ways of the fallen world and to love their enemies. There is no evidence of Christian participation in war until the late second century, 150 years after the birth of the Christian communities. Although some Christians took on military responsibilities in the course of the third and fourth centuries, Christian officials and theologians insisted that Christians were not to shed human blood on pain of excommunication.

As Christianity became first a licit religion, in 313, and then the official religion of the Roman Empire, in 380, Christians accepted full political and military responsibility. By the end of the fifth century only Christians could serve in the Roman armed forces. Among the thinkers providing justification for the new attitude, Augustine was the most cogent and persuasive.

Augustine is considered the source of the Christian just war concept because he discussed war primarily as a political remedy for disorder and injustice rather than as a way of achieving such religious purposes as the glorification of God, the spread of the church, or the establishment of God's rule on earth. He did not distinguish clearly between just and holy wars. The

Old Testament, with its record of holy wars of conquest, was an important influence on his thought, and he understood the righteous use of political power as a punishment of sin and an upholding of divine honor. Until the twelfth and thirteenth centuries wars by Christian states were justified primarily by biblical and theological rationales rather than by reference to the general or natural human right to protection from unwarranted attack on life and liberty.

The Western church's attempts between 1095 and 1250 to reconquer the Holy Land and to defeat Turkish Muslims, Moors, and Christian heretics gave rise to a new and more clearly defined kind of holy war, the crusade. A crusade was a religious war against enemies of the faith that was declared and authorized by the papacy to accomplish a religious goal, with religious orders engaged in preaching campaigns to gather soldiers and money and with soldiers promised both release from the purgatorial penalties for their sins and, should they die in battle, a martyr's crown.

Yet the very elaboration by canon lawyers of specific forms of religious, as opposed to political, wars was indicative of developments in the medieval period that by the fourteenth and fifteenth centuries led to a clearer differentiation between the political and religious realms. This process took a large step forward with Thomas Aquinas and the reintroduction to Europe of the Aristotelian conception of natural law. Applying natural law analysis to wars, the Spanish theologians and ethicists Francisco Suarez and Francisco Vittoria in the fifteenth and early sixteenth centuries and the Dutch Protestant Hugo Grotius in the 1630s and 1640s developed comprehensive and systematic approaches to just war thought.

To be sure, these thinkers allowed for war in defense of religion. Taking Christianity for the one true faith, they at times implied that war in defense of true religion had a special legitimacy and gravity. Nevertheless, Suarez and Vittoria, followed by Grotius, saw themselves as elaborating the conditions for just wars, not holy wars; they elaborated a comprehensive set of limiting conditions for warfare between political communities and saw religious wars as legitimate only when fought for the universal right to religious liberty or against those sinning most heinously against natural law. Suarez and Vittoria, in particular, argued against the legitimacy of Christians forcibly subjugating, converting, or taking property from pagans, whether Muslims in the Middle East or Native Americans in the New World.

The essentially secular just war theory, developed in the late medieval period, provided for the defense of political communities against aggressors contravening the law of nations. The theory authorized rulers to defend the communal and individual rights of those unjustly attacked in order to retain the status quo. Just cause included the defense of individual and communal rights to life, liberty, and property; the recovery of unjustly taken possessions and rights; and the punishment of transgressors against the law of nations. Such causes—essentially defensive—legitimated warfare when the injustice was grave enough to outweigh the costs, when all other means of redress short of war had been tried, and when there was a reasonable chance of success.

Early modern theorists, led by Vittoria, Suarez, and Grotius, imposed limitations on the means of warfare by the application of the principles of proportion and discrimination. The legitimacy of damage inflicted in a particular campaign depended upon whether it was proportionate to the value of the campaign to a successful outcome of the war. Damage, moreover, was to be inflicted intentionally only on those materially involved in the unjust military effort, and even unintentional damage was to be retrospectively subjected to the principle of proportion. In practice, however, the early modern theorists did not hold just war belligerents to high standards in evaluating means of warfare.

The Protestant Reformation and its effects on attitudes toward war form the immediate backdrop for understanding American religious thought on war and peace. Although the warfare of the sixteenth and seventeenth centuries was in no simple sense religiously motivated, the mere existence of religious schism on a broad scale, along with the assumption by virtually all Christian religious and political authorities that political and religious borders had to coincide, brought many Christians to the conclusion that the very existence of the true faith, at least in their country, state, or province, was at stake in the military struggles between Catholics and Protestants. Moreover, the Reformation gave

Protestants—especially those influenced by Huldrych Zwingli and John Calvin—the conviction that God was at work in and behind the scenes of human history, incorporating the struggles among the nations into salvation-history and bringing about the eschatological culmination of history in the kingdom of God. This sense of religious destiny was most prominent among Calvinists, and national consciousness in England was affected by this sentiment to a unique degree.

In the eyes of many English Puritans, England was to become a model Christian social order, the paradigmatic power by which the kingdom of God would imprint itself on human history. Some Puritan supporters of the English Civil War of the 1640s espoused a renewed version of the holy war, including God's eschatological call to arms, the belief that the purpose of the war was the beginning of the final chapter in the history of salvation, the conviction that God's saints were pitted against demonic powers, and the zealous sense that fighting for God's cause was not a mournful duty but a unique privilege.

Although the Protestant Reformation, along with a developing nationalism in Europe, renewed holy war thought among Catholics and especially among Calvinists, it also led over time to a more secular approach to war and to a clearer division between just and holy wars, especially in the period from 1650 to 1789. With Roman Catholics and a variety of doctrinally incompatible Protestants facing each other across borders and within societies, as in England, the Netherlands, and the Germanic provinces, and with Europeans having more or less regular contact with Native Americans in the New World, some Christians began to learn that they could live with other Christians of fundamentally opposed theological beliefs as well as with pagans and that all human beings seemed to possess knowledge of the moral law. As a result there developed in Europe, especially in England, the Netherlands, and Germany, the beginnings of a pluralistic mentality that left some Christians less certain that they possessed the whole of religious truth and therefore less likely to fight wars on its behalf. Although the holy war mentality associated with the Protestant-Catholic struggles was especially prominent in England in the 1640s, the shifting fortunes of various Protestant authorities in England in the 1640s and 1650s, as well as the proliferation of religious sects spawned by the Interregnum, the period between the death of Charles I in 1649 and the restoration of the Stuart monarchy in 1660, with its Anglican establishment, made the secularization of politics especially important to dissenting English Christians by the latter part of the seventeenth century.

The Reformation led to a resurgence of Christian pacifism as well as to the further development of holy war and just war thought. The Southern German, Swiss, and Dutch sectarians known as the Radical Reformers, such as the Mennonites and the Swiss Brethren, believed that they were carrying to completion the Lutheran and Calvinist reformations by imitating as far as possible the primitive church described in the New Testament. True Christians were to be set apart from the world and to follow as a new law the teachings of Christ, including the Sermon on the Mount. Although governmental authority was necessary in a fallen world to restrain evildoers and to maintain order, and hence was to be obeyed and supported by Christians unless such authority was used in a manner contrary to the law of Christ, Christians restoring the purity of the primitive church were to stand apart from active participation in political life and were not to resist evildoers, whom God would use to accomplish his ends in spite of their fallenness.

Influenced by strains of Radical Reformer thought in England that filtered through the radical wing of the Puritan movement, the Quakers, or Society of Friends, arose in the 1650s to espouse a less separatist form of pacifism than that of the Radical Reformers. Although affected by the New Testament witness, the Quakers' sense of obligation to return good for evil and love for violence stemmed less from a biblical literalism than from their purported possession by the spirit of Christ, or Inner Light. Since all people had the divine light within them, Quakers believed that their nonviolent witness would speak to "that of God" in their attackers and would gradually overcome sin and lead to the transformation of the world.

Thus by the time of the founding of the European colonies in the New World there were in Europe prominent proponents of all three primary Christian attitudes toward war. The major Christian tradition that emerged in the medieval period—namely, that of the just war—had been developed into a comprehensive set of criteria for determining when war was just and how it was to be fought. The responsibility of governmental authorities and their armies was to restrain and punish those using force unjustly to deprive a people of its natural rights. At the same time, Roman Catholic expansionism after the expulsion of the Moors from Europe in 1492, combined with the rise of Protestantism, led to a series of wars in Europe and the New World in the sixteenth and seventeenth centuries that found the rival Protestant and Catholic forces interpreting their struggles as religious battles against the minions of Antichrist. Many Calvinists in England and on the Continent came to believe that their national destiny was to defeat finally the Roman Catholic Antichrist and bring the history of God's creation to its foreordained conclusion in the kingdom of God. Those Protestants who carried the Reformation further than Lutherans and Calvinists believed that their "reform" necessitated a return to the ways of the primitive church, including a refusal to shed blood.

WAR AND PEACE IN COLONIAL AND REVOLUTIONARY AMERICA

The colonial period of American history was a time of brutal violence and almost constant warfare involving first the conquest of native peoples, then a great imperial struggle between Protestant England and Catholic France with its "heathen" Indian allies, and finally a colonial victory over English religious and political tyranny. Given this setting, it is not surprising that at times both Catholic and Protestant settlers saw themselves as warriors of the Lord engaged in holy wars. The papacy divided the New World among its Catholic nations and at times exercised its sovereign right, as the one true religious authority in the world, to legitimate conquests by Spanish, French, and Portuguese Catholic powers and thereby to spread the faith in disregard of the natives' natural rights. The Spanish rulers, for the most part, adopted that perspective, justifying their conquests, when they bothered to justify them, as the work of religious crusaders.

Although the English settlers usually sought a legal pretext to displace the natives, many of them also believed that they were on a divine errand into the wilderness to accomplish in the New World what had seemed impossible in the Old; namely, the establishment of a truly Christian religious and social order as a model and goad for the establishment of the kingdom of God throughout the world. The Puritans were steeped in the Old Testament and saw striking parallels between Israel's exodus from corrupt Egypt and conquest of the Holy Land and their own exodus from England and wresting of the New World from heathen natives. They could not resist at least speculating on their place in salvation-history, and some of them plainly saw their wars against Catholic and heathen enemies and then against England as part of that history.

Despite the crusading aura of the New World conquests and the interpretations and justifications of political leaders and their followers, neither Catholic nor Protestant theologians and religious leaders developed holy war rationales for the colonial wars. Vittoria applied his just war theory, based on natural rights, to the New World, and the Catholic church gave its blessing in the Requirement of 1513. (According to it, the natives were not to be converted by force or killed if they rejected the Gospel, but they could be fought if they denied the natural right of travel through their territory or the preaching of Christian missionaries, or if they refused to acknowledge the church as the ruler of the world and Spain as its representative.) This insistence on a universal ethic of war and on fairness and compassion for the Indians fit the spirit of the large majority of the many Catholic missionaries who labored in the Spanish and French New World empires.

More influential by far on later American religious attitudes toward war were the Protestant colonial religious leaders, especially the Puritan ministers of New England and the Presbyterians of the Middle Atlantic region. There was, to be sure, a good deal of holy war sentiment among the American clergy of the colonial era, and it came to the fore in the 1640s and 1650s when colonial leaders were attempting to justify their exodus from England, at various times during the struggle against the French and Indians from the 1680s through 1763, and during the revolutionary war, which some saw as fraught with millennial significance. Nevertheless, in their preaching and their relatively few ethical and theological treatises the great majority of the American colonial clerics—whether Congregationalists such as Samuel Willard, Presbyterians such as Gilbert Tennent, or Baptists such as Isaac Backus—encouraged the militiamen and analyzed the colonial wars primarily in terms of the just war tradition that incorporated the restraints natural law imposed on all of fallen humanity. The ministers associated crusading warfare with Rome, viewing it as offensive warfare that disregarded natural rights and hence unjustifiable. Even when the colonies appeared to be engaging in offensive warfare, as in the Pequot War of 1637 or King Philip's War of 1675–1676, the ministers insisted that these were defensive wars on behalf of basic rights. What holy war themes one finds in the sermons and treatises originated in moments of excitement and war fever, not in reasoned theological or ethical treatises or summonses.

The number of colonial treatises devoted to the comprehensive development of ethical thought on war of any kind is surprisingly small, considering the prominence and persistence of war throughout the period. In their discussions of legitimate authority for war, the colonial religious leaders assumed that political authorities supporting the rights of their subjects, as outlined in Scripture and as discovered by reason in the law of nature, could call on their subjects to defend the community, as well as neighboring colonies, against unjust aggression. They at times made clear—implicitly until the 1760s and then explicitly—that subjects whose rights were attacked by a tyrant could also make revolutionary war to reestablish legitimate authority. In times of war New Englanders turned to the Lord for guidance in prayer, as did all Christians, and they often received assurance regarding their cause or campaigns in the form of deliverance from defeat by storm or against great odds, but there were no claims that the "commanded" holy war of the Old Testament tradition—which was in principle still a possible part of God's providential arsenal—served as the justification for particular wars or campaigns. While New Englanders spoke and wrote a great deal about their New Israel, they apparently did not see themselves as a unique people in strict parallel with ancient Israel, but as one of the more thoroughly reformed of the several "professing peoples" of the latter-day Christian dispensation.

In discussions of the just causes of war, the clerical writers were content to pass on the early modern understanding of just cause, which legitimated only defensive war for purposes of self-defense, recovery of property, and punishment of unjust aggressors. They believed that the legitimacy of war was evident from its divine institution and use in events recorded in Scripture and from the right to self-defense that reason discovered in the natural law. The colonial writers also followed the developed political tradition in stating that the just cause must be grave enough to justify the evils brought by war and that war was to be undertaken only as a last resort after alternative resolutions had been tried. They also cited the criterion of reasonable chance of success, but their Calvinist conviction that the sovereign Lord of history was in support of just causes prevented this criterion from achieving prominence in their thought. Although they believed that God might be using a particular conflict to push forward his plan of history, the colonists did not use this belief to escape traditional restrictions against initiating wars. One of the reasons for maintaining military preparedness was the possible necessity of fighting the eschatological battle, according to late-seventeenth-century writers such as Increase Mather, but the call to battle was never received.

Military camp sermons often pitted the godly soldiers of Christ against heathen or Roman Catholic—or, in the Revolution, British—demons of Antichrist. This perspective, as well as the heavy reliance upon the militaristic God and sagas of the Old Testament, at times produced a more zealous and less mournful mood than usually associated with proper intention and attitude in the just war tradition. But the ministers generally addressed the assembled militiamen as Christians exercising their general calling in a political or secular duty regarded as honorable by Jesus himself, not as inspired saints carrying out a divine mandate. As Christians sure of their salvation, they would fight more valiantly than other men; death in battle would send those already saved to heaven faster and might even be the final testimony to their political and personal virtue, but only in that restricted sense was their military service of religious significance. Their military activity was not a means to righteousness before God or a sacred action. As a secular duty, war was seen as a necessary evil and was not glorified in colonial or revolutionary times.

With regard to the means of warfare, the ministers had relatively little to say. The New Englanders' indiscriminate slaughter of men, women, and children among the Pequots at Mystic, Connecticut, in 1637 and the Narrangansetts in 1675–1676 is well known, and there were many less-well-known incidents. The colonists' sense of righteousness and holiness may well have served to loosen their restraints when fighting what they perceived to be demonic idolaters, but they rarely justified their warfare in these terms or pointed out the parallels in Israel's wars of conquest. In any case, although colonial writers spent little time lamenting their indiscriminate acts of warfare, they normally assumed that their warriors were bound to the just war criteria. Actions that contravened these were seen as aberrations possibly explained by the colonists' extraordinary situation in the "howling wilderness."

English settlers formed up to 90 percent of the colonists up to the time of the Revolution, and a large majority of them were influenced by the Puritan movement and its attitudes toward war. Anglicans who migrated to the New World were often influenced by the movement to purify their church, but they—along with the Lutherans and, to an extent, the Dutch and German Reformed—perceived a greater separation between God and the world than did the Puritans and understood participation in war in even more clearly secular terms. Christians, who live in two kingdoms, were to support their government's military defense as part of their secular calling.

As a result of the Great Awakening in the 1740s, the colonists increased their communication across colonial borders and their developing sense of unity, and the Puritan version of colonial religious and political history began to spread. By the time of the Revolution increasing numbers of Anglicans, Lutherans, and Reformed Christians suspected that God might be working behind the scenes of American history to support the Revolutionary cause. Still, they were less likely than other Americans either to protest against tyranny or to give war a sacral tinge.

The pacifism of the Radical Reformers was represented in the colonies by the Mennonites of Pennsylvania, who crystallized in two main forms out of the South German, Swiss, and Dutch Anabaptists—namely, the followers of Francis Daniel Pastorius and the more conservative Amish; the Dunkers or Church of the Brethren in Pennsylvania, New Jersey, and Maryland; the Moravians in Pennsylvania and North Carolina; and a few

Schwenkfelders in Pennsylvania and Shakers in New York. Never totaling more than 10,000, the pacifists lived largely withdrawn from other colonists and maintained their pacifist stance, which was based on the teachings of Jesus in the Sermon on the Mount against resisting evil and on the witness of the primitive church.

A more significant influence on developing American religious attitudes toward war came from the many Quakers who immigrated to the English settlements. Although English Quakers had begun to realize by 1700 that their witness would not transform the world, William Penn founded Pennsylvania as a "holy experiment," a model Christian social order based on love and on largely noncoercive approaches to achieving justice. This haven induced more than 50,000 Quakers to come to the New World, and their presence and witness made a mark throughout the colonies. As the imperial struggle between England and France brought increasing fears and militia requirements to the colonies, the Quakers in most areas ceased to attract new followers and became more withdrawn. Pennsylvania's increased need for a militia and for war taxes brought a crisis to the Quaker government, and most Quakers withdrew from public service in 1756, when the French and Indian War broke out, rather than retain their influence at the expense of their peace testimony.

The Revolutionary era was the first significant time of trial for pacifists in America. Although odd inhabitants in a wilderness empire on a military frontier, pacifists often went largely unnoticed in the early colonial period because communal sentiment rarely went beyond the local, but they stood out more clearly in the 1760s and 1770s. With regard to legal provisions for "nonresistants" or "non-combatants"—the terms for religious objectors to war until "conscientious objection" came to be used in World War I—the colonies amounted to a "statutory mosaic of alternative service schemes, fines, conditional exemptions of varying rigor, provisions for distraint, and simple disregard of the whole issue" (Renner, 1974). The Mennonites and Brethren were willing to purchase exemption from military service and to perform war-related service if required, and they paid war taxes. Although their hope of transforming the world in their image induced a small group of Quakers to join the Continental Army, most Quakers differed from other pacifists in refusing to purchase exemption, serve in war-related work on government demand, or pay war taxes. Some even refused to use continental currency. Both Quakers and the sectarians refused any oaths of allegiance demanded of them. Those whose witness in whatever form provoked the ire of colonial officials suffered imprisonment or, more often, distraints of possessions or the pillaging of their property by troops. Some were corporally punished or publicly disgraced, and a handful were executed by mobs.

THE NINETEENTH CENTURY THROUGH WORLD WAR I: THE CRUSADING ERA

1787–1865. The United States began its national life with an ambivalent, if not paradoxical, attitude toward war. On the one hand, the Radical Whig natural rights ideology that had fueled and justified the revolution against Old World tyranny in 1688 and that reigned supreme in the new nation had a strong antimilitarist component. Of all of Britain's crimes, the stationing of a standing army in the colonies had seemed the most heinous, since standing armies were known to be the inevitable precursor of tyranny. On the other hand, the nation had been born in the crucible of war, and the myths, rituals, heroes, and values engendered in that virtuous violence became central to American national identity. Moreover, although the ideology of the Revolution was a natural rights ideology placing the Revolution in a political context as a just war, it became embedded in a virulent religious nationalism that shed an aura of sanctity over American violence. Filled with the heady wine of an extraordinary victory against great odds, Americans turned what had been pious hopes about their role in salvation-history into the conviction that their exodus from the corrupt Old World and their destined conquest of the continent—begun in the Indian wars of the 1790s—established them as God's New Israel. Crystallized in war, the new faith fed on a series of wars that were increasingly understood in holy war terms through World War I.

The prominence of antimilitaristic sentiment and pacifism among mainstream Protestants, along with the pacifist witness of sectarian and Quaker Christians, gave credibility to the hope that the new nation would help banish warfare from the earth. With a few dozen peace societies forming in the first decades of the nineteenth century, antiwar sentiment kept the Americans, under Thomas Jefferson's leadership, from responding to British interference with American trade with France and British impressment of American seamen. When the British actions stirred old fears of entanglement in Old World tyranny and war was finally declared in 1812, the congressional vote showed a deeply divided nation.

The religious communities also held widely differing views of the War of 1812. Methodists and Baptists supported it; Congregationalists opposed it; Presbyterians were divided; and Episcopalians and Roman Catholics kept a low profile. There was some regional political basis for the polarity, but the religious divisions crossed regions and pointed to differences in religious understanding of the war as well. The Methodists and Baptists saw the war as a continuation of the Revolutionary struggle against British religious and political tyranny. They revived the Spirit of '76 with more clear-cut salvation-history overtones and a strong and crusading expansionist imperative. For their part, the Congregationalists' opposition to republicanism and to the war contained a religious thread. Their social and national model was still that of a hierarchical society with a Protestant Christian ideology and a government controlled by Protestants and favorable to Protestantism. As such they championed the cause of England and opposed the war; Jeffersonianism, in its alliance with postrevolutionary France, represented a godless government and nation. Nevertheless, although the pro- and antiwar rhetoric became rather heated, it remained primarily political rather than religious. Despite the war's unpopularity in some quarters, the American victory after near defeat and against great odds contributed to the American myths that had taken root in the Revolution.

The peace reform movement arising partly from the Second Great Awakening in the 1790s and 1800s included a whole spectrum of what were called pacifists in the nineteenth century, even though many of them refused to renounce all recourse to war. Most were products of a form of evangelical Christianity that embraced Enlightenment hopes. They all agreed that war was a barbarous anachronism that subverted human liberty and ensnared people in vice, intemperance, and Sabbath-breaking. They agreed, moreover, that it was their responsibility to enlighten their fellow citizens about the evils of warfare through tracts and speeches and that it was necessary to develop international law and a congress of Christian nations to resolve disputes.

Under the leadership of William Ladd and George C. Beckwith, the American Peace Society (APS), formed in 1828, attempted to exert a broad influence by muting differences over defensive war and avoiding strict pacifist stands that might alienate some current and many prospective members. William Lloyd Garrison, a Baptist with a tinge of Quakerism, became convinced that governmental coercion, as well as defensive war, was out of accord with the true Christian witness and embraced nonresistance. In 1838 he and his followers left the APS to form the New England Non-Resistance Society.

A group of followers of Elihu Burritt, the "Learned Blacksmith" social reformer of Connecticut, also pressed their fellow APS members to reject all violence and to support "the sanctity of human life in all circumstances," but without rejecting all of the coercive functions of government. Burritt and his allies resigned from their positions within the APS and formed the League of Universal Brotherhood in 1846.

The Mexican War (1846–1848) found the sentiments of the religious community as divided as they had been during the War of 1812, and the pattern of division was similar. Those Christians living in the South and West, mostly Baptists and Methodists, supported the expansionism of the administration of President James Polk. The Congregationalists and Unitarians of the Northeast were opposed. Northern Baptists and both northern and southern Presbyterians were divided. Episcopalians, Lutherans, Roman Catholics, and ethnic Reformed Church members supported the government in accord with their understanding of civic duty but without relating the war to their religious beliefs. But if Christians were divided, their churches, for the most part, either refrained from official pronouncements and journalistic discussion of the war or condemned it as an unjust offensive war.

If church leaders were more silent or opposed to this war than to earlier American wars and their followers substantially divided, many devout Christians and more secular Americans of all sections of the country were caught up in war fever. It fed on the conviction that the United States was divinely destined to spread its model religious and political order from sea to shining sea. This "mission of Christian civilization" called Americans to follow higher laws than those determining boundary lines between nations, especially when the nation on the other side of the boundary was a corrupt Roman Catholic one such as Mexico. Even those who opposed the war, including the radical and moderate pacifists of the peace reform movement, tempered their criticism because they believed that the vigor and virtue of this rising Christian republic would before long legitimate its expansion at the expense of Mexico.

The conclusion of the Mexican War, like that of the War of 1812, left most Americans more convinced than ever that violence had its virtues. Even members of the peace reform movement found themselves increasingly unable to sustain their antimilitarism. Most of them were abolitionists. As the issue of slavery moved to the center as a national concern, most of the reformers grew increasingly appreciative of the righteous uses of government coercion.

In both the North and South supporters of the Union and Confederate causes in the Civil War had a variety of motives. Nevertheless, on both sides the ideology by which the war was justified had strong religious strains, and the nation's religious communities played significant roles in developing and purveying the ideologies. Opposition to slavery was strong in the northern churches of Puritan heritage. Still, most northern Christians in active support of the war effort agreed with President Abraham Lincoln that the abolition of slavery was not the purpose of the war. Since slavery was allowed in the Constitution, its demise would come in God's good time and by the inevitable march of salvation-history, and it would be the engine of the Christianization of Africa through the colonization movement, which raised funds to remunerate slave-owners and send the former slaves back to Africa to Christianize the continent. Preservation of the Union was the need of the hour; it would prove the viability of God's latter-day chosen nation, the American democracy, and enable the nation to continue its destined spread across the continent.

The churches found it easier to make official pronouncements on the Civil War than they had on the Mexican War. In both the North and the South, in the Episcopalian, Lutheran, Roman Catholic, and Continental Reformed traditions, they either affirmed their loyalty to the government and the justice of its cause, or, as with the Methodists and the descendants of the Puritans, added justifications giving a more sacred significance to the war effort. The necessity of preserving what Lincoln himself termed "God's last, best hope of earth" became for many Christians not simply a speculative hope reinforcing their sense of the justice of the cause but an overriding consideration rendering irrelevant any scruples about the political justice of the northern cause.

So prominent was the northerners' conviction about the sacredness of their cause that it also led to a holy war conception of legitimate authority, participants, and means. Those caught up in the crusading religious nationalism believed that the divine right of kings had been replaced by the divine right of the people in the sense that God's will for his chosen nation was expressed in majority rule. Since that majority had elected Lincoln knowing his opposition to the spread of slavery, those who would not accept that verdict were opponents of God. Those who upheld it were God's agents.

Union supporters among the crusading clergy also tended to paint the activity of God's warriors in less mournful hues than their predecessors and were quick to justify the extreme measures resorted to by the government in stifling dissent, such as the suspension of habeas corpus and restrictions on freedom of the press. After three successful wars, Americans were ready to believe that God's arsenal included war as well as the distribution of Bibles and tracts, voluntary reform societies, and missionary efforts. Indeed, led by the eloquent and influential Horace Bushnell, the Connecticut Congregationalist, many ministers described the war as an indispensable, ennobling experience for melding Americans, who had previously simply kenneled together under the Constitution, into a true folk. That which ideas about life, liberty, and the pursuit of happiness had not been able to perform, bloodletting between Americans would: the fusing of Americans into a chosen race capable of carrying out their unique mission. It is not surprising that in this setting the religious spokesmen found themselves imbued with a vengeful spirit and willing to justify virtually any means.

It was altogether fitting and proper that Lincoln's assassination became the symbol of vicarious self-sacrifice that pushed American civil religion, the myths and rituals by which the public realm was sacralized, from its Old Testament to its New Testament phase. For Lincoln's approach to the meaning of America and the interpretation of the war was identical in most respects to that of the crusading Calvinists. However humble about his own righteousness and that of Union supporters, and however conciliatory toward the southerners, Lincoln was absolutely convinced of the divinely guided righteousness of the northern cause and of the demonic nature of the Confederate cause. As the elected leader of a chosen people whose God revealed his will through the expressed political will of the electorate, Lincoln found it natural to expect divine guidance in the midst of the supreme national crisis.

However crusading the approach to the war by religious and national leaders, the attitudes of those called to participate in the Civil War as soldiers and of those who, as pacifists, refused to participate indicate that the crusading spirit was not all pervasive. Since colonial days Americans had assumed that each military regiment should be accompanied by a chaplain representing the faith of the soldiers. Throughout the colonial and Revolutionary periods most regiments were made up of people of the same Christian denomination, who simply appointed a local minister to serve them as chaplain. By the first half of the nineteenth century the armed forces were appointing and commissioning chaplains for federal units. Although it is reasonable to assume that some of the more crusading ministers managed to be appointed as military clergy, denominations took little initiative in this regard whatever their convictions about the holiness of the cause, and the armed services were more interested in seeing the personal religious needs of soldiers served than in tutoring them in civil religion to inspire them as crusaders.

In addition to ministering to the wounded and

dying, the chaplains and their many local volunteer clergy and laity served a variety of religious and humanitarian purposes. Great revivals occurred in both the northern and southern armies, and it is estimated that between 100,000 and 200,000 soldiers experienced a spiritual rebirth in the course of the war. Although it is no doubt true that some of the slain soldiers were hailed as martyrs, those clergymen who preached to bewildered recruits in the carnage of battle were largely preoccupied with giving solace and sustenance. They seem to have left to their silver-tongued colleagues in safe sanctuaries most of the rhetoric about biblical parallels and coming kingdoms.

Those who refused the call to battle were largely Quakers and sectarians such as Mennonites, Brethren, and other smaller sects, supplemented by a remnant of the more radical peace reformers, some Disciples of Christ, a few other mainstream Protestants, and a new type of pacifists called Adventists. The Quaker and sectarian witness against war had held steady during the first half of the century. There was no federal conscription during the War of 1812 and the Mexican War, but during these wartime periods members of the peace churches were called to militia musters and, in most cases, were expected to provide a substitute or pay a fee in order to be exempted. At these times war taxes were imposed and oaths of allegiance might be required. Since Quakers were in general more concerned than Mennonites and Brethren with such taxes and oaths, and were also less impressed with the biblical injunction to obey established authorities wherever possible, they suffered more than others for their witness.

For the first two years of the Civil War the Federal Militia Act left enrollment of soldiers in the states' hands with the understanding that the federal government could intervene if necessary. That necessity brought about the Union Conscription Act of 1863, according to which those who chose not to participate could provide a substitute conscript or pay a $300 commutation fee to secure one. In response to Quaker requests in 1864, the government provided alternatives for those who could present a certificate of membership in a peace church. Their commutation fee could be used for the benefit of sick and wounded soldiers, or, in place of the fee, they could work in hospitals or care for those recently freed from slavery. The Confederate Conscription Act of 1862 allowed conscripts to furnish substitutes. In response to a petition from Quakers, Brethren, and Mennonites, in October 1862 Confederate authorities allowed members of these three peace churches to pay a commutation fee of $500.

The large majority of Quakers refused to provide substitutes or to pay either commutation fees for substitutes or war taxes. Most Friends found the federal law of 1864 acceptable, but some extremists refused to recognize the right of the state to exact penalties or to demand service in exchange for permission to follow one's conscience. As a result they were drafted, imprisoned, or penalized by distraint of goods. Beginning in 1863 Lincoln's secretary of war, Edwin M. Stanton, who shared Lincoln's appreciation of Quakerism, began to furlough or parole indefinitely noncooperating Quakers who had been drafted, and from the end of 1863 he prevented their being inducted. Many of the several thousand Quakers in the South, mostly in North Carolina, Virginia, and Tennessee, suffered imprisonment or fines and distraint.

Mennonites and Brethren fared better than Friends. A significant minority had been partially acculturated by the time of the Civil War and were willing to be conscripted. Most of these were "disfellowshipped" (purged from membership) by their churches. The majority of those abiding by the testimony were willing to pay a commutation fee, even if it was used to hire a substitute, though direct provision of a substitute was frowned on by both churches. Since in their view money belonged to Caesar, few had difficulty paying special war taxes. Mennonites and Brethren in the South, who lived a more separate existence than their northern counterparts, generally adhered to their pacifist testimony more fully than those in the North.

In addition to the numerically insignificant pacifist witness of the Rogerenes, German-speaking communitarians, Shakers, Hopedale Community, and the Bible Christian Church of Philadelphia, the major additions to the pacifist cause were some Confederate Disciples of Christ and various Adventists. The Disciples' founder, Alexander Campbell, opposed participation in war on the grounds of a literal reading of the New Testament. But throughout the North there were no known conscientious objectors among the Disciples, and many of their clergy served as army chaplains. More distinctive and more significant because of their numbers during later wars were the Adventists. The Second Adventists and Seventh-day Adventists believed that the eschatological era had arrived and that, as a result, they belonged primarily to Christ's kingdom rather than to any worldly realm. In addition, according to the teaching of Seventh-day leaders James S. and Ellen G. White, service in the military prevented absolute adherence to the Fourth Commandment respecting the Sabbath and the Sixth respecting killing. The government's acceptance of their petition for consideration as a peace church was accepted in 1864, and most drafted Seventh-day Adventists performed alternative service.

1865–1919. At the end of the Civil War many Americans were more convinced than ever of the necessity of a strong national armed force. Moreover, the twenty years following the war found American forces tested more consistently and harshly than before in continual struggles against Native Americans. Not until the 1880s were the Sioux and Cheyennes defeated in the Great Plains, the Apaches in Arizona and New Mexico, and the Modocs, Nez Perce, and other tribes in the Northwest.

The peace reform movement that had retreated from both its radical pacifist position and its antimilitarism in the face of the Civil War remained somewhat in abeyance until the 1880s. When it did resurface, it lacked a strict pacifist wing. With war sanctified and nationalism strong, the movement aimed at humanizing war and gradually bringing peace through world order. It focused on five goals: arbitration of international disputes, arbitration treaties and clauses, development of international authority, codification of international law, and disarmament. Under Frances Willard's leadership, the Women's Christian Temperance Union became active in the peace movement in the 1880s. The American Peace Society's auxiliary in Pennsylvania became the Christian Arbitration and Peace Society in 1886 under the Baptist Russell Conwell's leadership. The Quakers Robert Treat Paine and Benjamin Trueblood helped the American Peace Society make an Anglo-American arbitration agreement its top priority.

Although they had ignored the American violence against the western Indians and the violence of industrial strife, the peace reformers were at least momentarily distracted by the Spanish-American War in 1898. Political and religious leaders, such as Josiah Strong, author of *Our Country* (1885), had drawn the religious nationalism of the Civil War era in a Social Darwinistic direction by arguing that America's destiny now was to spread beyond the continent to implant Anglo-Saxon civilization wherever backward people labored in ignorance and especially where an oppressed people needed liberation from Roman Catholic thralldom. When journalist William Randolph Hearst's newspapers began spreading stories of atrocities supposedly committed by the Spanish against Cuban insurrectionaries and the battleship *Maine* was sunk by the Spanish while on a mission of mercy, the nation was poised for war. Whether because or in spite of heavy Roman Catholic immigration, national political and religious leaders were even more insistent on the Protestant roots and universal mission of the nation. They portrayed the struggle against Catholic Spain as a holy war. President William McKinley prayed for divine guidance and received it: the nation's calling was to educate, uplift, civilize, and Christianize those oppressed Cubans for whom Christ had died.

Although many of the nation's religious leaders had called for restraint in the face of the Hearst stories and the *Maine* incident, those who had helped foster American religious nationalism quickly became convinced that the war was an Anglo-Saxon Christian missionary effort to bring political and religious enlightenment to the former Spanish empire. Following the feverish lead of fervent nationalists, Methodists, Baptists, Congregationalists, Unitarians, Presbyterians, and Disciples of Christ, forgetting their pre-1898 restraint, interpreted the war as a holy war. As in the past, Lutherans, Roman Catholics, and Episcopalians supported the government's call to arms but as a political rather than a religious duty. After the war American Christians engaged in significant missionary activity in the lands ceded by Spain; namely, Guam, Puerto Rico, the Philippines, and Cuba. Although some religious leaders voiced concern about the American war against the Philippine struggle for independence, most American Protestant Christians were convinced that Protestant republicanism must triumph even over movements of national independence.

As in the Mexican War, the peace reformers expressed opposition to and "intense disappointment" over this imperial struggle (in Elton Trueblood's words), but the main body of reformers took heart from the conviction that the war was only a temporary interlude in the march of peace to inevitable triumph. The more radical wing of the movement was more disturbed. It included the Universal Peace Union and a number of important Americans influenced by Leo Tolstoy's Christian anarchism, including Jane Addams, Clarence Darrow, and William Jennings Bryan. These were joined by some industrialists—including Andrew Carnegie—clergy, reformers, educators, urban reformers, labor leaders, and blacks in the Anti-Imperialist League, an attempt to dissuade the American government from seizing the Philippines.

The mainstream of the peace reform movement, having regained its stride by 1900, grew in prominence and power from 1900 to 1914. People of status in the business, legal, governmental, religious, and educational worlds formed forty-five new peace organizations in that period. Two figures who gave the movement a level of prominence and power not previously reached were Andrew Carnegie and Elihu Root. Carnegie became president of the New York Peace Society in 1906, formed the Carnegie Endowment for International Peace in 1910, and provided the funds for the major peace activities among Protestants. Carnegie's associate Frederick Lynch, with Charles MacFarland, convinced the Federal Council of Churches of Christ (one of eight agencies that merged in 1950 to form the National Council of Churches) in 1911 to form the Commission on Peace and Arbitration. Lynch also got $2 million from Carnegie for the formation of the Church Peace Union in 1914, which became the American branch of the World Alliance for International Friendship through the Churches.

When World War I broke out in 1914, the peace reformers agreed with President Woodrow Wilson's assessment that this was an Old World squabble. The mission of the United States was to bring peace to the world. To be in a position to accomplish that, the United States had to hold its beacon high and remain unsullied by this military result of tyranny and traditionalism. Nevertheless, the Anglo-Saxon ideology that had surfaced in the Spanish-American conflict encouraged very strong ties to Britain, which Protestant Americans considered to be the second of the two major representatives of the highest form of Christian civilization. When Germany declared unrestricted submarine warfare in 1917, Wilson became convinced that the United States had to enter the conflict in support of the more just and civilized side. Moreover, he believed that the nation's involvement would shorten the bloodletting and enable it to exert its influence in favor of a just and lasting peace.

The declaration of war received the full support of the peace reformers and of the vast majority of the American churches. Even Irish American and German American Catholics, pro-German before the war, quickly came around. They believed that peace would triumph through law and order, which would come from the extension of Anglo-American power. The Carnegie Endowment for International Peace called for "peace through victory," and the American Peace Society instituted a campaign for "justice and humanity" through force of arms. Church leaders in the Federal Council of Churches of Christ and the Church Peace Union formed the National Commission on the Churches and the Moral Aims of War. Opposition to the war was limited to antiwar socialists and to the Fellowship of Reconciliation, an organization formed by some forty Christian pacifists in 1915.

Within two months of entry, the country was engulfed in a war fever virtually unparalleled in American history. The German enemy was soon being portrayed in demonic tones, and German-born Americans and other aliens as well as pacifists became objects of suspicion and attack. Religious leaders set a similar, if less frenzied, example to that of Congress, which passed legislation encouraging the stifling of dissent. The Espionage Act provided incarceration for anyone obstructing recruitment or causing insubordination among the armed forces. The Sedition Act forbade disloyal, profane, or scurrilous remarks about the government, flag, or uniform of the United States. Virtually all of the clergy were convinced that Wilson's reluctant decision to enter the war was correct. Many withstood the impassioned chauvinism that quickly developed all around them. Nevertheless, most of the leaders of the religious press and the large majority of the clergy in general set the just cause in the context of the mission of Christian civilization. All of the elements of the crusade were present: the God of salvation-history was calling to battle; the cause was the final triumph of Christian civilization; and participants were what Wilson called "disinterested champions of right" against the minions of the devil.

As Lincoln had represented the Union mind in the Civil War, Wilson now represented the national mind. Although both presidents saw themselves as political leaders of a just cause, their religious nationalism led each to make claims for the nation's war effort that fit a holy war rationale and that fed the crusading spirit among their followers. Whereas Lincoln had stood apart from the churches and questioned their self-righteousness and had conceived of the national mission in religious terms that were not distinctly Christian, Wilson was the epitome of the Protestant establishment. Moreover, whereas in earlier eras Christian reform efforts were understood to follow the individual's conversion and to aim at a model and beacon for the world to see, by the early twentieth century "salvation" had come to mean for the Protestant establishment the salvation of the world. America was the Gospel incarnate. This meant both that only in democracy could the immanence of the Christian God be expressed in terms of human experience and that the American mission was to spread Christian civilization throughout the world.

Another difference between Lincoln and Wilson points toward an understanding of the crusading frenzy of World War I. Ironically, Lincoln, like the deist Founding Fathers whose inspiration he was attempting to revive, had a healthy sense of the pervasiveness and cancerousness of human sin. Although Wilson spoke and on occasion wrote as if he knew the power of human sin, as in his fear of an American descent toward brutality in the war, he was a man of his time in his easy conviction about American innocence: "We have no selfish ends to serve. We desire no conquest, no dominion. We seek no indemnities for ourselves, no material compensation for the sacrifices we shall freely make. We are but one of the champions of the rights of mankind" (Bailey, 1963 p. 20). History was the scene of salvation wherever America was present; the myth of New World regeneration had finally sapped the sense of sinfulness that had limited American pretensions. Whereas Lincoln

had seen war as tragic, Wilson saw it as an ennobling event—for Americans, at least—that would end war.

As in the Civil War, the soldiers and their military and religious officers were more interested in getting a dangerous and nasty job done than in saving the world. The armed services had continued since the Civil War to regularize the process by which chaplains were selected and to bring uniformity to the understanding of their duties. When, in 1889 and 1901, the army and navy, respectively, were required to appoint as religious officers only clergy who had been officially endorsed for the status by their denomination, the denominations began for the first time to set up agencies to deal with this need. In addition to increasing denominational control of chaplains, the armed services also made certain that chaplains agreed to serve in pluralistic fashion the religious needs of all servicemen. This was done primarily through the use of local clergy of different denominations or faiths and the deputizing of laity rather than through the imposition of a common theology on chaplains.

The military camps were no longer scenes of major revival efforts, but Protestant, Catholic, and Jewish organizations were very active in serving the religious and secular needs of the soldiers and sailors. In addition, over 11,000 civilians accompanied the soldiers to Europe, and many more met their various needs at stateside camps. Religious, literary, recreational, health, sanitation, and other services were provided. For Protestants, the General Wartime Commission of the Federal Council of Churches of Christ, with its Committee of One Hundred, coordinated efforts. The National Catholic War Council and the Knights of Columbus served Catholics, and the Jewish Welfare Board and Young Men's Hebrew Association provided significant non-Christian wartime services for the first time.

The Selective Service Act of 1917 provided exemption for ordained clergy as well as for those studying to become clergy, and members of existing peace churches were exempted from combat duties. Of the 64,000 young men claiming conscientious objection, 57,000 were granted it by local draft boards, indicating that primarily members of peace churches applied for the status, in accord with the intention of the law. Still, although no reliable figures are available, it is clear that significant numbers of mainline Christians, including some Roman Catholics, applied for the status for the first time.

Of the 57,000 granted conscientious objector status, 21,000 were inducted. Only 4,000 actually used their Certificate of Exemption from Combatant Service. The armed forces pressured all conscientious objectors to accept noncombatant service in the Medical Corps, Quartermaster Corps, or Engineer Service; 1,300 complied. The rest were kept in military camps doing such chores as cleaning and cooking until March 1918, when draftees were allowed to be furloughed to civilian work.

That only 4,000 of 21,000 conscientious objectors insisted on using their certificates indicates widespread defections among members of traditional pacifist churches. The harshly judgmental attitude expressed by many Americans toward any citizens of draft age who refused to become crusaders no doubt accounts for some of this falling off. The decline in the witness of pacifist Christians was also in part attributable to religious stagnation and to patterns of acculturation taking place between the Civil War and 1917. These twin processes of stagnation and religious acculturation were especially strong in Quakerism and among the Brethren. Probably a majority of those drafted from both sects served in the armed forces.

Liberal Quakers' affinities with other Christians also helped produce a more activist spirit that made some Quakers influential in the peace reform movement and caused others to lead their coreligionists in a bold new direction in World War I. Rufus Jones was the leading founder of the American Friends Service Committee in 1917. This new Quaker organization provided guidance and support for Quakers and other pacifists. It also sent Quakers and others to Europe to perform humanitarian service among those of both sides who had been ravaged by the war. A large majority of the Brethren draftees seem to have shouldered rifles. The Mennonite story was more positive, with a majority sticking to their peace testimony.

Although some of the dwindling pacifists of earlier wars died out between 1865 and 1917, their place was more than made up for by the continuing growth of the Adventist movement—represented mainly by the Seventh-day Adventists and the International Bible Students—and

by a new pacifist strain among the radical Holiness and Pentecostal churches, including the Assemblies of God and the Missionary and Christian Alliance. The Seventh-day Adventists accepted noncombatant service, whereas the International Bible Students—who later became the Jehovah's Witnesses—were absolutists who insisted on exemption as clergy and refused to accept conscientious objector status.

1919 TO THE PRESENT: RESURGENCE OF PACIFISM AND THE JUST WAR

1919–1945. America's intervention accomplished the immediate goal of ending World War I quickly, but almost as quickly it became evident that a new world order was not in the offing. A coalition of lawyers, progressive activists, educators, feminists, and liberal Protestants continued to urge support for the League of Nations and the World Court, praised the armaments agreement of 1921 and the Kellogg-Briand pact in 1928, and took hope from the disarmament conferences of 1927, 1930, and 1933. Protestantism lent support to the peace reform movement and took the lead in urging the peace reformers to remember the movement's earlier antimilitarism and even to renounce war as an instrument of national policy. Roman Catholics too began to question the justice of modern war in the Catholic Association for International Peace, formed in 1927.

The 1920s also saw the beginning of a resurgence of Christian pacifism, which spread from sectarian groups to the point where it became a significant and abiding presence in mainstream Christianity. By the late 1920s and early 1930s surprising numbers of Protestant ministers became pacifists. In the course of the 1930s the Fellowship of Reconciliation (FOR) gained a membership of 12,000. Most of the major Protestant denominations for the first time developed support structures to give counsel and general assistance to conscientious objectors.

Pacifism spread in the 1930s because of events in Europe as well as new perspectives on American society developing among socialists in the 1920s and spreading after the economic depression began in 1929. Events abroad made inescapable what many had feared; namely, that World War I, rather than ending war, had sown the seeds for its repetition. Pacifism also fed on the insights of Social Gospel Christians, who stressed the necessity of Christianizing the social order. The Fellowship for a Christian Social Order, founded by Kirby Page and Sherwood Eddy in 1921, merged with the FOR in 1928 and brought to pacifists a greater awareness of capitalism's need for the profits of war and its reliance on the suppression of workers. At the same time Quakers, Mennonites, and Brethren gained an appreciation of the Social Gospel and moved closer to mainstream pacifists in perspective, swelling their numbers and influence.

Many of the Christian pacifists of the 1930s retained something of the transformationist hope that history could gradually receive the imprint of the kingdom of God. Since modern war had shown its destructiveness and divisiveness, overcoming it simply *had* to be possible. The nonviolent campaigns of Mohandas Gandhi in India got some Western pacifists thinking about nonviolent social reforms and forms of national defense. The most widely read application of Gandhi's approach was Richard Gregg's *The Power of Nonviolence* (1934).

Some American pacifists, despite their greater realism about the United States, began to suspect nevertheless that the greatest contribution available to Americans was to stand aside from the development of Old World conflict. The Emergency Peace Campaign was formed in 1935 to promote economic justice and to keep America out of wars. The No Foreign War Crusade of 1937 and the "Keep America Out of War" Campaign in 1938 found the peace reformers and pacifists increasingly allied with conservative isolationists.

As pacifism became more supportive of the campaign for American neutrality, other peace reformers and pacifists more disillusioned about the United States began to question the usefulness of their pacifism. Reinhold Niebuhr, a leading member of the FOR, became convinced that most of the Christian pacifism of his day was "an unholy compound of gospel perfectionism and bourgeois utopianism." Restrained by self-interest and a sporadic sense of obligation and loving concern in its personal relationships, fallen humanity poured out its pent-up lusts in its collective political behavior, Niebuhr argued. This meant that only force could restrain collective aggression and that Americans should reject the naiveté and hypocritical self-righteousness that might tempt them to stand above the fray.

Before the attack on Pearl Harbor virtually all of the American denominations opposed American intervention in another European war. Japan's sudden direct attack on the American base in December 1941 made a declaration of war a foregone conclusion in the view of the churches. The general mood of the religious community was one of a reluctant and penitent sense of obligation, but those churches long accustomed to a crusading approach included a holy war tinge in their initial pronouncements. Still, the religious press and pulpit generally helped Americans to see the righteousness and necessity of opposing fascism without making the war other than a necessary evil. The perspective and mood of the just war prevailed. The attitude was that of many Lutherans and Episcopalians during earlier wars; namely, that there will always be wars in a fallen world and that religious people will always be called on to join with others in the secular struggle for order, however flawed, in human affairs. The peace reformers of the interwar years understood Adolf Hitler as a product of Allied vengeance as well as of German madness. They and other Americans were even more acutely aware of the questionableness of an alliance with Russian communists.

If modern war meant "total war" at home because of the extent of economic mobilization required, it also meant "total war" abroad in the sense of unrestrained campaigns against enemy societies. The preponderance of religious opinion in the pulpit and the religious press did not protest against the American war effort, with its saturation bombing, torture, and concentration camps for Japanese-Americans, but it is noteworthy that most American religious leaders who commented on these developments did not so much justify such phenomena as come to terms with them on the grounds that they would end the war more quickly. Still, there was steady, if scattered, opposition from the religious press. With the dropping of the atomic bomb in August 1945, criticisms became more marked. Several church leaders said that the atomic bombings were morally indefensible acts for which penitence by all Americans was appropriate. When Pope Pius XII condemned the bombings as well, Catholic voices were raised. Nevertheless, there is little evidence that these pronouncements by religious leaders made much of a dent in American public opinion or even in the views of churchgoers.

Americans supported their servicemen with the same extensive array of services that had been provided for volunteers and draftees in World War I. The churches took a more active role in the provision of chaplains through the General Commission on Army and Navy Chaplains. In addition, many denominations set up their own organizations to publish literature for the soldiers, provide them with altar kits, and meet a variety of religious needs.

In response to religious requests, the Selective Training and Service Act of 1940 provided for conscientious objector status for those of any religion or denomination who "by religious training and belief" objected to participation in all warfare. Those willing to accept noncombatant service were assigned a 1-A-O classification; those opting for alternative service involving "work of national importance under civilian direction" were to serve without pay and classified 4-E. The law made no provision for nonreligious objectors. Selective Service records indicate that over 72,000 were given conscientious objector status. Of these 25,000 were given noncombatant status, 12,000 alternative service, and 1,600 were convicted for failing to report. Nearly 14,000 were "reclassified from 1-A-O or 4-E as not available," and 20,000 were never classified. No doubt the figures were actually higher for each category, since the records are incomplete. Over 6,000 young men were imprisoned. The average imprisonment was between three and four years, with Jehovah's Witnesses, who constituted three-quarters of the imprisoned, often given four years.

Those performing alternative service were assigned to a Civilian Public Service camp run by the Mennonites, Brethren, or Quakers. Selective Service provided sites and equipment and asked the churches to run camps for them, with the conscientious objectors doing soil conservation, forestry, or related work. About 40 percent of those performing alternative service were Mennonites, and they made up the vast majority of those assigned to Mennonite camps. Brethren camps were populated mainly by Brethren inductees, who constituted 11 percent of the total of 4-E's. Quakers, only 7 percent of the 4-E's, ran the camps for the 40 percent of the 4-E's who

were not members of peace churches. Most were antiwar radicals and nonreligious or selective conscientious objectors. In all there were 151 camps costing the peace churches $7 million. Mennonites and Brethren continued to run them until they were abolished in March 1947, whereas the American Friends Service Committee stopped cooperating in 1946.

The pattern of response to the war by inducted members of the historic peace churches was similar in World War II to that of World War I. Mennonites were by far the largest group of religious conscientious objectors, and they also had by far the highest percentage of inductees who claimed the status; namely, 60 percent. Brethren inductees continued to demonstrate the extent of Brethren acculturation. Of 24,000 called, only 2,500 claimed conscientious objector status; half of these accepted noncombatant status. Acculturation continued among the Quakers as well: 75 percent of those inducted agreed to serve in the armed forces. No more than half were disowned by their meetings, and the figures may well be lower. The Quaker peace witness in war-torn Europe and Asia was impressive, however. In 1947 the American Friends Service Committee, along with the British Council of Friends, was awarded the Nobel Peace Prize for its humanitarian relief work among the suffering of both sides throughout Europe and in China and India.

For the first time in American history conscientious objector status became a legitimate option for members of mainline Protestant churches. Most Protestant churches called on the government to grant the status to those of their members claiming it and provided organized support for them within the denomination. Methodists and Baptists produced the largest numbers.

The 162 Catholics in Civilian Public Service included some "evangelical" objectors influenced by the Catholic Worker Movement, with its advocacy of a return to the practices of the New Testament church; some were selective conscientious objectors who believed that this was not a just war; some simply believed that in the modern technological era no war could be just. About fifty Jews joined the Jewish Peace Fellowship, primarily in New York, Philadelphia, and Los Angeles, and enjoyed the support of a few rabbis. Most Jews, however, regarded them as traitors to their people because of the Nazi treatment of Jews, which turned this war into a "commanded" or holy war in which the very existence of Israel was at stake, and because of the strong conviction among Jews that pacifism, a position associated with Christianity, was not in accord with Jewish insistence on defending human rights and thwarting aggression.

Two other religious groups were more prominent among conscientious objectors and religious objectors than they had been in past American wars. The Seventh-day Adventists comprised between one-quarter and one-half of the noncombatants. More difficult for the draft system to deal with were the Jehovah's Witnesses. Although they adhered to no theoretical compunction against taking human life, they believed that they should fight only when directly commanded to do so by God and that God had not so commanded since the wars of the Old Testament. They admired the ancient Israelite warriors of the Lord and believed that they were living in the eschatological era and would soon be called to the battle of Armageddon. Although all Witnesses claimed exemption as ministers, at first their claims were rejected. Since they could not qualify as objectors to all forms of war and were uncooperative, large numbers of them were imprisoned. In 1942 Selective Service ruled that they could receive 4-D classification and be exempted as ministers if they worked on ministerial duties over eighty hours a month, but many boards continued to refuse them the status.

1945–1986. The United States entered the postwar period with renewed confidence in war and a strong commitment to the use of force in international relations. With the memory of "the good war" firmly in mind, as well as the Soviet Union's drawing of an "iron curtain" across Eastern Europe, the nation easily accepted a policy of containment and assumed the role of defender of the free world virtually without national discussion. Antimilitarism was nowhere in evidence.

Although Protestant denominations did not renounce the legitimacy of pacifism as a Christian form of witness, many American Christians understood their nation as the major Christian defender against "godless communism." They accepted the first peacetime conscription in the nation's history because of their belief that the newest vocation of God's latter-day chosen nation was to lead the forces of good against the minions of evil in a worldwide struggle now being carried on at an economic and diplomatic level. The Korean War from 1950 to 1953 fit this world view. Although few churches made pronouncements on the war, American religious communities regarded it as an undeclared just war fought by an international force to preserve the status quo against clear communist aggression. With the Korean War abroad and the anticommunist crusade of Sen. Joseph McCarthy at home, peace reformers and pacifists in general kept a low profile in the early 1950s.

The peace movement started to awaken by 1955. With both the United States and the Soviet Union testing larger nuclear weapons and with fear of fallout spreading, liberal church leaders joined scientists represented by the National Committee for a SANE Nuclear Policy (SANE) in questioning the validity of modern war from the perspective of Christian ethics. In 1955 nonviolence as a political and religious weapon returned to American consciousness when Rev. Martin Luther King, Jr., applied it to the Montgomery, Alabama, bus boycott. King believed that Gandhi had provided a political technique through which Christian love could become an effective force for political and social reform as well as for religious renewal. For the next decade nonviolence touched the lives of many Protestant, Catholic, and Jewish religious leaders and entered the consciousness of many more Americans through the civil rights movement.

The civil rights movement helped strengthen the peace movement in the period of the Vietnam War, from 1963 to 1973. Church support was reasonably strong for the war effort in the early years. A moderate Roman Catholic Democrat, John F. Kennedy, who had captured the imagination of young idealists with the Peace Corps, interpreted Vietnam as the decade's just war to contain communism and protect Vietnamese independence. But the war quickly developed all the signs of the indiscriminate, technological slaughter that had sobered Americans even when carried on during World War II. When the lottery draft replaced educational deferments in 1969, increasing numbers of American draft-age youth applied for status as conscientious objectors or fled underground or to Canada.

Protest against the war mushroomed in the late 1960s. From 1965 to 1970, it is estimated, some 4 million Americans joined 560 antiwar organizations. There were three major advocates of the anti-Vietnam protest movement: liberal internationalists represented by such organizations as SANE and by moderate peace reformers including many Jews and Christians; traditional pacifists represented by the Fellowship of Reconciliation and Women's International League for Peace and Freedom; and radical pacifists such as the Committee for Non-Violent Action and the War Resisters' League. Religious leaders were prominent in the first two.

The antiwar movement also contained some new religious elements. In many respects the Roman Catholics were the earliest and most vigorous religious opponents of the war. Many had been influenced at some point by the Catholic Worker Movement, whose founder, Dorothy Day, had insisted that prayer, the sacraments, and the Christian love released by them were able in the long run to overcome whole armies and all the world's hatred. Also influential was Thomas Merton, the adult convert who became a Trappist monk and whose pen continued to speak more eloquently even than Trappist silence. Leading members of the Catholic Peace Fellowship, including Daniel and Phillip Berrigan, Eileen Egan, James Forest, and Gordon Zahn, expressed their opposition to the war and to the premises of modern defense systems by destroying and pouring blood on draft files and by other open acts of civil disobedience intended to awaken the conscience of the nation.

The main vehicle of Protestant and Jewish protest against the war was the organization Clergy and Laymen Concerned about Vietnam (CALCAV), founded in 1965. King's opposition to the war in 1965 made evident his increasing conviction about the roots of American violence and the importance of the nonviolence of the civil rights movement in reawakening American antimilitarism. CALCAV participated in marches against the war and sporadic acts of civil disobedience. Especially prominent in the movement were William Sloan Coffin, then chaplain of Yale University, Robert McAfee Brown, Presbyterian leader and theologian, and Abraham Heschel, the Jewish mystic and theologian. Most Christian and Jewish religious bodies were on record as opponents of the war to varying degrees at least by the early 1970s.

Many opponents of the war could not in good faith claim opposition to war in all forms but insisted on their right to be exempted. Some draft boards accommodated them, but most did not. Late in the war and in the years since, many churches have taken stands in favor of an exemption for those convinced that the war they are called to fight in is unjust. Many Vietnam War objectors also had difficulty demonstrating that their opposition was based on religious training and belief, and religious bodies have come to their support as well, arguing that the rights of conscience extend to all human beings. When the law was tested in court by conscientious objector claimants, the Supreme Court broadened the understanding of "religious training and belief" in *Seeger* v. *United States* in 1965. In *U.S.* v. *Welch* in 1970, the Court argued that the law exempts all persons "whose consciences, spurred by deeply held moral, ethical, or religious beliefs, would give them no rest or peace if they allowed themselves to become a part of an instrument of war."

In the period between 1973 and 1986 religious leaders turned their attention to nuclear warfare and the defense strategies of nuclear powers. Especially since 1978 the religious communities of the United States have developed a wide-ranging critique of nuclear weaponry and of American defense strategies. The first American religious thinker to devote serious systematic ethical thought to the subject of nuclear war was Paul Ramsey, who believed that a defense posture employing nuclear weapons is the only credible way of deterring and defeating unjust aggression and hence that a morally defensible approach to nuclear warfare must be found. Ramsey argued that counterforce warfare, which was directed against military targets, as opposed to countercity warfare, which was directed against a whole population, was the upper limit of justifiable defense. He pronounced immoral the defense posture that had been the American policy for most of the nuclear era; namely, mutual assured destruction.

James T. Johnson has used a similar posture to argue that the most moral defense in the nuclear age is a flexible one relying first and in most situations on a large and well-equipped conventional set of forces and then escalating, as necessary, to the level of "clean" tactical weapons against military targets. Johnson argues that such weapons developments as cruise missiles, the neutron bomb, and defense systems for lower space are desirable attempts to develop deterrence strategies relying on cleaner and more controllable weaponry.

Although it is probably the case that the vast majority of American Christians still support American policies, the Roman Catholic bishops and the moderate, as opposed to Evangelical or Fundamentalist, Protestant denominations, as well as the main Jewish bodies, have developed a more critical stance than that of Johnson and Ramsey. In calling for a new evaluation of war, the Second Vatican Council of 1962–1965 declared immoral countercity nuclear warfare. Since then a Catholic peace movement, associated most prominently with the organization Pax Christi, USA, has become prominent through identification with about one-third of the 280 American bishops. The representatives of Pax Christi came very close to having their nuclear pacifism prevail in the Bishops' Pastoral Letter on War and Peace of 1983. The bishops opposed countercity warfare, first use of nuclear weapons, the development and employment of destabilizing weapons, policies allowing proliferation, and the development of weapons control systems eliminating human choice from the response to nuclear attacks. Although the bishops avoided calling for massive unilateral disarmament, tax refusal, and resignation from defense industry jobs, their position amounted to elevating nonviolence to a level at least on a par with just war thinking and made it seem the normative position of the future.

The Protestant church bodies affiliated with the National Council of Churches have taken similar stands in the 1980s. Like the Catholic bishops, these bodies have largely opposed the direction of the Reagan administration's defense policies, including the increase in defense expenditures and the development of destabilizing weapons such as the Trident, the MX, the cruise missile, and the Strategic Defense Initiative (or Star Wars) programs. The United Methodists, the American Baptist Convention, the Disciples of Christ, the two main Presbyterian churches, the Episcopalians, the United Church of Christ, the Reformed Church in America, and the Lutheran Church in America and the American Lutheran Church (these two groups have since merged) have agreed in denouncing Ronald Reagan's rhetoric of "fighting" and "winning" a limited nuclear war, as well as many of the administration's defense policies. They have also agreed in endorsing a nuclear freeze and disarmament initiatives by the United States and a promise by the United States not to resort first to nuclear weapons in any conflict. They have all gone so far as to raise grave questions about the legitimacy of nuclear defense for the long run and have either assumed the position of nuclear pacifism or argued that nuclear deterrence is moral only if assumed to be a limited and temporary strategy while the nation actively searches for alternatives.

After a colonial period marked by violence and warfare, the American nation began its existence flushed with victory over a great military power. Although determined to avoid the violence of the Old World and to lead the world into an era of peace, the First New Nation was engaged in and won a series of wars in the course of the nineteenth century. Gradually the American ideology, marked by a just war mentality in the colonial and Revolutionary periods, became a crusading religious nationalism. Stung by the nation's failure to end war forever by its victory in World War I, many of the nation's religious leaders turned toward the pacifism that Quakers, Mennonites, Brethren, and others had witnessed to throughout American history. Unable to avoid further military violence, the American religious community interpreted World War II and its sequels in Korea and Vietnam in just war terms. Faced with modern nuclear weapons that many believe make a just war impossible, the nation's religious leaders have in the 1980s espoused a nuclear pacifism that amounts to a more extensive critique of American military policy than has ever before surfaced.

BIBLIOGRAPHY

Ray H. Abrams, *Preachers Present Arms* (1933; rev. ed., 1969); Jon A. T. Alexander, "Christian Attitudes Toward War in Colonial America," in *Church and Society*, 64 (1974), and "The Twig Bent: Instruction on the Taking of Life Provided in Catechisms Printed in America Before 1800," in *Peace and Change* (1975); Albert S. Axelrad, *Call to Conscience: Jews, Judaism, and Conscientious Objection* (1986); Thomas Andrew Bailey, *Woodrow Wilson and the Lost Peace* (1963); Roland H. Bainton, "The Churches and War: Historic Attitudes Toward Christian Participation," in *Social Action* (1945), and

Christian Attitudes Toward War and Peace (1960); Ken Booth and Moorhead Wright, eds., *American Thinking About Peace and War* (1978); Beth Ellen Boyle, ed., *Words of Conscience: Religious Statements on Conscientious Objection* (10th ed., 1983); Darrel E. Brigham, *American Christian Thinkers and the Function of War, 1861–1920* (1971); Peter Brock, *Pacifism in the United States from the Colonial Era to the First World War* (1968) and *Twentieth-Century Pacifism* (1979).

Charles Chatfield, *For Peace and Justice: Pacifism in America, 1914–1941* (1971); Conrad Cherry, ed., *God's New Israel: Religious Interpretations of American Destiny* (1971); Merle E. Curti, *Peace or War: The American Struggle, 1636–1936* (1936; repr. 1972); Donald L. Davidson, *Nuclear Weapons and the American Churches: Ethical Positions on Modern Warfare* (1983); Charles deBenedetti, *The Peace Reform in American History* (1980); Clayton Sumner Ellsworth, "The American Churches and the Mexican War," in *The American Historical Review*, 45 (1940); Melvin B. Endy, Jr., "Just War, Holy War, and Millennialism in Revolutionary America," in *The William and Mary Quarterly*, 42 (1985); William Gribbin, *The Churches Militant: The War of 1812 and American Religion* (1973); Lewis Hanke, *The Spanish Struggle for Justice in the Conquest of America* (1949); Richard G. Hutcheson, Jr., *The Churches and the Chaplaincy* (1975).

James T. Johnson, *Ideology, Reason, and Limitation of War: Religious and Secular Concepts, 1200–1740* (1975), *The Just War Tradition and the Restraint of War: A Moral and Historical Inquiry* (1981), and *Can Modern War Be Just?* (1984); Peter Karsten, *Soldiers and Society: The Effects of Military Service and War on American Life* (1978); Esther J. MacCarthy, *The Catholics Periodical Press and Issues of War and Peace, 1914–1946* (1980); Ralph L. Moellering, *Modern War and the Christian Churches* (1956); James H. Moorhead, *American Apocalypse: Yankee Protestants and the Civil War, 1860–1869* (1978); Philip J. Murnion, ed., *Catholics and Nuclear War: A Commentary on the Challenge of Peace* (1983); Mark A. Noll, *Christians in the American Revolution* (1977); Russell B. Nye, *The Almost Chosen People: Essays in the History of American Ideas* (1966).

William V. O'Brien, *The Conduct of Just and Limited War* (1981); John F. Piper, Jr., *The American Churches in World War I* (1985); Paul Ramsey, *War and the Christian Conscience: How Shall Modern War Be Conducted Justly?* (1961) and *The Just War: Force and Political Responsibility* (1968); Richard W. Renner, "C.O. and the Federal Government, 1787–1792," in *Military Affairs*, 38 (1974); Steven Schwarzschild et al., *Roots of Jewish Nonviolence* (n.d.); Thomas A. Shannon, *What Are They Saying About Peace and War?* (1983); James W. Silver, *Confederate Morale and Church Propaganda* (1957); Michael Walzer, *Just and Unjust Wars: A Moral Argument With Historical Illustrations* (1977); Ronald W. Wells, ed., *The Wars of America: Christian Views* (1981); Charles R. Wilson, *Baptized in Blood: The Religion of the Lost Cause, 1865–1920* (1980); Lawrence S. Wittner, *Rebels Against War: The American Peace Movement, 1941–1960* (1969).

[*See also* CHURCH AND STATE; CIVIL AND PUBLIC RELIGION; SECTS AND RELIGIOUS MOVEMENTS OF GERMAN ORIGIN; *and* SOCIETY OF FRIENDS.]

SOCIAL REFORM FROM THE COLONIAL PERIOD THROUGH THE CIVIL WAR

Mary K. Cayton

REFORM in its modern sense might be defined as a conscious attempt to promote change in social institutions and behavior through organized movements. By this definition Anglo-American reform was a rare phenomenon prior to the late eighteenth century. Benevolence, charity, and religious revivals sometimes produced significant social change in an indirect fashion, but collective action motivated by the *intent* to promote social change emerged only during and after the American Revolution. It was then that the majority of Americans first began to adopt religious and political views that saw individuals as the primary agents of change within society. In the first half of the nineteenth century this emphasis on the potential of both individuals and society to progress and to improve became such a prominent cultural theme that the period from 1800 to 1860 might justly be characterized as the Age of Reform.

THE COLONIAL PERIOD

The major heirs of the Reformation in the colonies, the Calvinists, the Anglicans, and (rather indirectly) the Quakers, all shared a common point of view on the nature and sources of social change. God himself was the source of all legitimate social power and order, and he had empowered a civil magistracy and a clergy to maintain the good order of society. Significant social change emanated from only two sources: God himself, whose ways were inscrutable, or his agents in the world, the civil or religious authorities, who acted on his behalf to maintain social order and justice. Only when magistrates or min-

isters failed to carry out their mission was direct action by those outside the recognized circles of power legitimate. In religious revivals such as the one that occurred in parts of New England in the 1730s and 1740s, for example, the spirit of God was seen as moving in mysterious ways to revivify faith and, almost as an unintended side effect, to motivate individuals to challenge the standing order in religion and in secular affairs. For instance, Connecticut "New Lights," or spiritually awakened, challenged the hegemony of the Congregational establishment in order to secure their right to an independent polity as separatists. Accustomed to challenging authority in ecclesiastical matters, a New Light polity went on to challenge "Old Light" policy regarding itineracy, toleration, paper money, and outmigration to newly opened lands. Economic and religious radicalism emerged in tandem, not because New Lights saw themselves in rebellion against duly constituted authority but because they felt justified by the revivals in searching for pietistic values that a corrupt magistracy had abandoned. Far from seeing their movement as a "social reform," the New Lights viewed their dissent from the practices of the standing order as a reinvigoration of the church that God himself had initiated.

Similarly, the New England clergy or civil magistracy might issue a call for reformation when they perceived people growing too conspicuous in their use of material goods, too greedy, too litigious, and lax in their piety. Frequently, periods of rapid commercial growth or political turmoil resulted either in outbursts of jeremiads, sermons designed to call the community back to its original purpose and to "reform" itself, or in pleas for prayer and fasting. In general, those whom God had appointed to oversee the welfare of the entire society took the initiative in describing social ills and prescribing cures.

Movements instigated by ordinary people for explicit social reform, however, did not flourish. Most people in colonial America believed, as John Winthrop, the first governor of Massachusetts Bay, had put it in his sermon to the colonists aboard the *Arbella,* "God Almightie in his most holy and wise providence hath soe disposed of the Condicion of mankinde, as in all times some must be rich some poore, some highe and eminent in power and dignitie; others meane and in subieccion." Given this acceptance of God's immanent power in the world, benevolence and charity could be exercised in various forms of poor relief, but neither the benefactors nor the beneficiaries saw such efforts as ways of transforming society. Rather, the plight of the widow and the orphan, the sick and the aged, the infirm or the individual who had suffered an economic setback was an occasion for gentlemen and their wives to practice the principle of "stewardship." By acting as God's agents in administering the material wealth of the world for the relief of the unfortunate, the colonial gentry performed both a pious act and a social duty. But no one expected to improve the human condition in any fundamental way.

In Puritan New England and the Anglican South, the poor were principally the responsibility of either the local parish or the pertinent civil jurisdiction. In Quaker Pennsylvania, the English precedent of geographically related poor relief was less easily replicated; as a dissenting group, English Quakers had not held the primary responsibility for administering parish poor relief. Instead, a tradition of mutual aid in matters both spiritual and material grew up among Quakers, despite the efforts of John Bellers, an English Quaker and contemporary of William Penn, to persuade his coreligionists that social service would be a formidable evangelizing device.

Nevertheless, Quakers became the first American religious group to move from mutual aid and stewardship toward a humanitarian model of benevolence that presaged much of nineteenth-century reform, including movements to better the condition of the poor, the enslaved, the Indians, and the imprisoned. The watershed year for the transformation of the Quaker ideal from mu-

tual aid to benevolence was 1755, when pacifist Quakers refused to cooperate with colonial supporters of the British war effort on the frontier. Many of the wealthiest and most powerful members of the Pennsylvania assembly were Quakers, and the war issue split Quakers into those who were willing to support military action and those who saw any compromise with civil authority as undermining William Penn's "Holy Experiment." As the Quaker pacifists increasingly came under attack, they began to encourage a religious revival within Quakerism that led to a more stringent definition of religious purity, including a willingness to labor to rid civil society of various evils. Movements to relieve the poor, improve education and prisons, and better the condition of the Indians allowed pacifist Quakers to continue to play a major role in community life, although deprived of their dominant role in government.

Quakers were also among the first to raise the temperance banner and, perhaps most significant, to institute measures of church discipline for slaveholders and slave traders. Three-quarters of the membership in the first twenty-five years of the Pennsylvania Abolition Society, founded in 1794, were Quakers, as were half of the members of the New York Manumission Society, an antislavery group founded in 1785. Indeed, in all states except Connecticut and Kentucky, Quakers were the chief organizers and agents of the earliest antislavery societies.

Besides the Quakers' efforts, there were only two other proto-reform movements of note in colonial America. Within Boston Congregationalism, Cotton Mather began forming a number of "reforming societies" to promote piety and suppress disorder in 1702. These continued to meet for two and a half decades. Among Anglicans, the Society for the Propagation of the Gospel in Foreign Parts was founded by Rev. Thomas Bray in 1701 to convert slaves and Indians to Christianity. Although both share the reforming impulse of nineteenth-century movements, both were also typical of their time in emphasizing the role of civil or religious authorities in maintaining social order. Of Mather's societies, for example, those oriented toward prayer and personal piety were the more successful, reflecting the disposition of individuals in that culture to look toward conforming themselves to well-defined standards of attitude and behavior rather than changing the social structure as a whole through reforming action. Moreover, the Societies to Suppress Disorders were composed almost exclusively of civic leaders and magistrates, whose purpose in forming such organizations was to gain additional control of social irregularities such as profane language and prostitution. Mather's societies might not have emerged at all had not the authority of Massachusetts civil government been shaken by the British dissolution of the charter in 1684, the subsequent establishment of the Dominion of England with its royal governor in 1686, and its demise in 1689.

The Society for the Propagation of the Gospel, for its part, evolved into an effort to strengthen the position of the Anglican religious establishment in places where the church enjoyed official legal status but little popular support and to extend the establishment to those colonies where it did not yet exist. In addition to its efforts to convert slaves and Indians, the society became in several colonies an agency for bringing into line both non-Anglicans and Anglicans who were straying from the faith.

Thus, movements for social change hardly existed in colonial America. In a world in which the hand of God was seen in every human activity, there was little demand for organized reform movements. A dramatic change in people's notions of human power and perfectibility was the prerequisite for efforts to improve the human condition, given the pietistic bent of revival activity. Ironically, the New England Awakening of the 1730s and 1740s was an important precipitant of such a shift. It transformed colonial society in several profound ways, the most important of which was to justify individual or popular action against religious and secular orders found lacking in piety and moral authority. This argument was later used to justify rebellion against the king's ministers and finally revolution against the king himself. Most significantly, the ultimate arbiter of when magistrates and ministers had lost their legitimacy was increasingly no longer God but the conscience of individuals.

THE BENEVOLENT EMPIRE

Reform movements became the principal avenue through which social protest occurred in the first half of the nineteenth century. Three major shifts in ideology occurred in order for this to have happened. First, individuals began to see themselves as capable of effecting significant change in their environment through their own efforts. Second, they began to employ a theological language in which personal piety was tied to social action. Third, individuals began to see the keeping of social order as each person's responsibility rather than as the job of higher authorities; that is, they saw themselves rather than an external authority as the locus of political power. All three shifts occurred in New England, the cradle of reform movements, in the late eighteenth century.

Although it would be difficult to say when Enlightenment rationalism began to dominate American thinking, certainly by the mid-eighteenth century its tenets colored educated Americans' views: God had created the world in a rational way, so that the world was transparent to human reason; the discovery of natural laws through rational investigation enabled man to exert power over and to be the agent of progress in the world.

Rationalism in religion led to an emphasis on the human role in redemption and the importance of ethics and a deemphasis of doctrine and tradition. Posing a major threat to Congregationalist doctrines of the utter depravity of humankind, the justification of human beings by faith alone, and the total sovereignty of God, rationalism forced mainstream Calvinism to modify doctrine in response to the new strains of philosophical thought. Most significant of these revisionists was Jonathan Edwards, who incorporated what he had learned from reading John Locke into a corpus of theology that revivified New England Calvinism by reinterpreting traditional theology in light of the discoveries of rationalism. He demonstrated the necessity of utter reliance on God, exploring in rationalist language how human beings are determined to remain in their own depravity and in a state of moral paralysis unless God intervenes in their experience and determines otherwise.

Perhaps the most significant theological innovator preparing Calvinists to welcome social reform as a form of personal piety was Samuel Hopkins. Hopkins, a Yale-educated follower of Edwards, whose theology formed the basis for the Hopkinsian, or "New Divinity," school, argued that although the Holy Spirit alone could initiate and complete the work of "regeneration" in the individual soul, individuals exercised the control over volition. The exercise of the will in pursuit of righteousness following regeneration was "conversion." Hopkins' most memorable proposition, that sin and self-love were the same, led to his preaching the doctrine of "disinterested benevolence": that true virtue consisted in actively moving away from self-love through selfless action, even to the point of being willing to be damned for the glory of God. This doctrine prepared the way for a legacy of organizations interested in "disinterested benevolence" as a means for furthering personal piety.

With the American Revolution, Americans increasingly came to see the maintaining of social order as their own responsibility. Neither a king nor a magistracy who received public charge on the basis of social position could properly wield power. If power remained with and emanated from individuals, however, people could no longer view the mission of maintaining a moral state as that of divinely appointed agents. Rather, the people had to dedicate themselves individually to God, for authority no longer flowed from the top down; only the conversion and commitment of all the people to the keeping of morality and good order in the community would ensure its survival. From this realization flowed both the revivals known as the Second Great Awakening (from the 1790s to the 1830s) and the reform movements that became known as the Benevolent Empire.

The Second Great Awakening formed the basis for spiritual renewal in New England in the period following the Revolution, while the Benevolent Empire was the name given to the cluster of reform organizations that took advantage of the spiritual energies of revival in the service of social change. Led by such preachers as Timothy Dwight, Lyman Beecher, and Asahel Nettleton, the Awakening spread mainly to colleges and parishes of New Divinity men from about 1800 to 1820. It sparked a renewal of religious fervor and piety, but without the highly emotional displays and disruptions that would characterize later phases of the Awakening elsewhere, especially in upstate New York in the 1820s. Out of this ardor, Congregationalist religious leaders such as Jedidiah Morse and Beecher formed religiously inspired societies whose aim was twofold, much as Mather's had

been: to promote personal piety by encouraging prayer and devotion and to prevent the spread of disorder in society by organizing individuals to eradicate it. Like the Quaker humanitarian efforts of the late eighteenth century, these Congregationalist reform groups organized in an atmosphere where secular influences (including commercialism and rationalism) threatened to dislodge the strict morality of the group as the controlling vision for the society. As both Congregational theology and its ideals of social order and piety seemed in danger of losing hegemony within the culture, Congregationalists, like the Pennsylvania Quakers, mounted a movement to purify the church, increase the stringency of its standards, and find extragovernmental ways of extending its influence. In this effort to make more definite the boundaries and ideals of Congregationalism, the nineteenth-century reform impulse was born.

The first religious voluntary organizations within the Benevolent Empire arose out of the concern of New England Congregationalists that emigrants to the frontier areas of Vermont, New Hampshire, Maine, Pennsylvania, and New York would be without the consolation and moral check of religion. Ministerial associations dominated by Hopkinsians, whose aim was to settle pastors over churches in the new areas, established Missionary Societies in Connecticut in 1798, in Massachusetts in 1799, and in New Hampshire in 1802. Following these were societies established to convert Indians and Women's Missionary Societies. The latter included Female Cent Societies and Women's Auxiliaries, whose purpose was to encourage women to band together to increase their piety through prayer and monetary contributions (in the case of the Cent Societies, a cent a week) to missionary activities.

In Andover Theological Seminary, founded in 1808 as the alternative of Trinitarian Congregationalists to what they perceived as the heresies of rationalist, Unitarian Harvard, conservative and Hopkinsian Congregationalists and Presbyterians set up an institution to promote piety through evangelization. Its purpose was to train a ministry who would preserve a Christian moral tenor for American society as a whole by preaching Congregational Trinitarianism, in contradistinction to the rationalist or atheistical philosophies spreading in New England in the wake of the Revolution. Concerned that a disregard for the truth of human depravity and a denial of divine sovereignty could lead to nothing but moral torpitude and social chaos, Trinitarian Congregationalists mounted a campaign to combat the humanistic optimism that began to manifest itself within Unitarianism, Universalism, and deism. The home mission effort inspired Samuel J. Mills, Jr., a student first at orthodox Williams College and later at Andover Theological Seminary, to contemplate calling "orthodox" Americans to apply the model of evangelization on the frontier to foreign lands. In 1810, with the support of some other students and the General Association of Congregational Ministers in Massachusetts, he founded the American Board of Commissioners for Foreign Missions. Beginning with its mission to India in 1812, it sponsored missions to the Pacific Islands, the Middle East, and the Far East. The American Board of Commissioners was technically interdenominational, but most of its members and supporters belonged to either the Congregationalist or Presbyterian denominations, which had together drawn up a Plan of Union for the evangelization of the West in 1801. Most Benevolent Empire members or supporters were drawn from these two denominations.

From the turn of the century local societies to raise money to subsidize poor students through academies, colleges, and seminaries sprang up. A larger Congregational organization, the American Education Society, was founded at New Haven in 1814–1815 to recruit and fund students for the seminary at Andover. In 1826 the National American Education Society brought the local societies together. Like the American Board of Commissioners, this new umbrella organization was officially interdenominational but consisted mainly of Congregationalists and Presbyterians dedicated to the spread of their theologies.

In conjunction with efforts on the American and foreign frontiers, a number of Congregationalists and Presbyterians also undertook to restore what they took to be crumbling moral standards in already well-established regions of the country through organizations for the general reformation of morals, as well as Bible, tract, and Sunday-school societies. As leaders such as Rev. Lyman Beecher, chief revivalist of the day and a New Divinity man, gradually recognized that common agreement on religious or moral standards no longer existed in the nation, they shifted the major work of reform from establishment of new churches to agencies for suppressing disorder and societies for the education (or reeducation) of those they took to be heretical and impious. Most of this evangelization through education took place in those areas most lacking in cultural cohesion—in the cities and on the frontier.

As part of a revival of religion led by President Timothy Dwight, students formed a secret Yale Moral Society in 1797 to promote order and morality. In 1813 Beecher's Connecticut Society for the Reformation of Morals adopted the students' voluntary organizational approach to reform, extending the project to local communities throughout the state. Members were pledged to watch out for and combat instances of immorality such as Sabbath-breaking, profanity, and intemperance as well as to block the inroads that liberals and democrats were making on the good order of the community through the spread of an insidious rationalist philosophy. In Massachusetts a similar organization, the Massachusetts Society for the Suppression of Intemperance, led by Jeremiah Evarts, a lawyer involved in the missionary effort, was founded in 1813.

The first major project of the educational reformers was the distribution of Bibles. The idea was borrowed from the English evangelical churches, which organized societies for establishing missions and Sunday schools as well as distributing Bibles and tracts between 1790 and 1805. The first Bible society in the United States was founded in Philadelphia in 1808; the idea spread to Connecticut, Massachusetts, Maine, and New York in 1809. By 1815 over 100 local Bible societies existed, the strongest of which was in New York City. In 1816 a convention meeting in New York created a national organization by renaming the New York Bible Society the American Bible Society and by organizing other local and state organizations to function as its auxiliaries.

Tract societies, which in many ways resembled Bible societies, originated among the ministers of Andover Seminary, most notably Ebenezer Porter and Justin Edwards. To them the rise in support for Republicanism and Unitarianism, at odds with the Federalism and Trinitarianism heretofore dominant in Massachusetts, seemed evidence of the decline of religion. In 1814, in response to this perceived threat, they formed a society to publish moral and religious tracts.

Tract societies differed slightly from Bible societies in that the Bible societies sought to convert mainly the poor and those without religious instruction, while the tract societies also reached out to relatively well-educated groups of rationalists (such as Unitarians) or members of radical sects (such as Universalists) whose religious beliefs were deemed nearly as dangerous to moral order as unbelief itself. By 1823 there were tract depositories (as auxiliaries of the New England Tract Society were known) in every state and by 1824 the New England Tract Society had published 167 different pamphlets encouraging piety and religious life. In 1825 the local tract societies merged into a national one, the American Tract Society.

The American Sunday School Union, organized as a national organization the year before the American Tract Society, drew on the model of English evangelical churches, whose aim was to teach poor children to read and write. An interdenominational Philadelphia group headed by Benjamin Rush, the First Day or Sunday School Society of Philadelphia, had set up an organization with similar aims in 1791. The New York Sunday School Union was formed in 1816 on the Philadelphia model by Divie Bethune, who had also been instrumental in forming the New York Tract Society. Bethune's innovation was to introduce unpaid volunteer teachers, and in 1817 the Philadelphia Sunday and Adult School Union reorganized on the voluntary principle, limiting its educational mission to instruction on moral and religious topics and thereby transforming the school into an instrument for evangelization. By 1825 related groups contained 5,000 students in seventeen states, the name of the Philadelphia umbrella organization having changed in 1824 to the American Sunday School Union.

By 1830 the network of evangelizing organizations that came to be known as the Benevolent Empire, mostly Congregational and Presbyterian in character, included five major national benevolent societies: the American Sunday School Union, the American Education Society, the American Home Mission Society, the American Bible Society, and the American Tract Society. In addition, a number of denominationally controlled societies, such as the American Baptist Board of Foreign Missions, the Reformed Dutch Missionary Society, and the Presbyterian Education Society, carried out missions similar to those conducted by the Plan of Union denominations. The governing boards of the major reform societies directed the activity of hundreds of local societies, auxiliaries, and agents and drew on a combined income of half a million dollars. Although the various organizations were separately chartered, the same men frequently served on many of the executive committees and boards of managers. For example, Arthur Tappan, who, along with his brothers Lewis and John, was involved in a wide variety of evangelical causes, either served on the managerial committee of or contributed money to nearly every Benevolent Empire cause. By the early 1830s voluntary societies for reform, headed by prominent northeastern merchants, lawyers, and clergymen, had become one of the principal instruments for social change in the United States. By then the impetus had shifted from renewing individual piety and maintaining group solidarity to extending the hegemony of orthodox Trinitarian religion. As the local organizations merged into interlocked regional and national ones, the goal of the Benevolent Empire became nothing less than the national predominance of its religious ideology, as well as of its attendant ideal of social order and piety.

One other notable current of New England reform during this period, Unitarian humanitarianism, was also inspired by post-Enlightenment concern with ethics and human capability. As the embodiment of religious rationalism in America, Unitarian reformers mainly concerned themselves with efforts to better the condition of others as the most legitimate form of piety. Prominent Unitarian reformers included Joseph Tuckerman, whose ministry to the poor of Boston was sponsored by the Benevolent Fraternity of Churches in that city; Horace Mann, who as secretary to the Massachusetts Board of Education from 1837 to 1848 played a major role in the birth of the common school; Dorothea Dix, whose work on behalf of the mentally ill resulted in legislation to improve Worcester Hospital for the Insane in 1843; and Samuel Gridley Howe, who pioneered work in education of the blind and the deaf-blind.

PERFECTIONIST REFORM

As Benevolent Empire reform reached its zenith in the late 1820s and early 1830s, a second kind of reform began to emerge that diverged from the more conservative bent of the organizations dominated by New England and New York New Divinity men. One of its sources was a new theology of perfectionism and holiness preached by Charles Grandison Finney, a Presbyterian revivalist whose work in upstate New York, beginning in 1824, led to new outpourings of communal energy in the area along the newly constructed Erie Canal. Finney, formerly a New York City lawyer, claimed to have received a spiritual "retainer from the Lord Jesus Christ to plead his cause" in an emotional conversion in 1821. In the space of a decade, he succeeded in lighting revival fires on the western New York frontier, and later pleaded the Lord's cause in Pennsylvania, Delaware, New England, and New York City, before finally accepting an appointment as professor of theology in 1835 at Oberlin College, of which he later became president.

Finney's appeal lay not only in his charisma but in his theology. Advocating "new measures" for bringing about revivals through a calculated arousal of listeners' emotions, he preached Arminianism, asserting the power of individuals to assist in bringing about their own conversions. Claiming that sin was avoidable and holiness possible for humankind, Finney connected rebirth in the spirit to social activism. During his tenure at Oberlin, the faculty there proclaimed in the pulpit, in the classroom, and in print a gospel of Christian perfectionism as the necessary accompaniment of spiritual conversion. This new emphasis on the perfectibility of the individual soul led to outpourings of social activism that fueled reform movements, principally those promoting peace, temperance, and antislavery.

Although the national organizations for these three movements, which came to take on a distinctly perfectionist tenor, date from the time of the formation of the Benevolent Empire, the impetus for these reforms was present in the humanitarian movement of eighteenth-century Quakers. For example, Anthony Benezet, a Pennsylvania Quaker, crusaded against war, slavery, and spiritous liquors, claiming them to be opposed to the spirit of Christianity. In 1760 the New England Yearly Meeting ruled slave importers subject to discipline, and in 1774 the Philadelphia Yearly Meeting threatened those buying or transferring slave property with disownment. However, little direct connection seems to exist between the organization of these (and other) Quaker benevolent efforts in the Revolutionary era and the formation of peace, temperance, and antislavery societies among New Yorkers and New Englanders from 1810 to 1820, except insofar as both represented efforts to revivify locally dominant religious groups under siege by outsiders.

In 1815 the first organized peace societies were founded. In New York, David Low Dodge, a prosperous Presbyterian merchant and philanthropist, founded the New York Peace Society, its thirty or forty members representing several religious denominations. In Massachusetts, the publication of Rev. Noah Worcester's *A Solemn Review of the Custom of War* in 1814 led to the formation of the Massachusetts Peace Society. It attracted substantial Boston merchants and ministers, among them William Ellery Channing, the prominent liberal minister who had been a parishioner of Samuel Hopkins in his youth. Although both societies were undoubtedly aided by antiwar sentiment arising during the War of 1812, both were ostensibly apolitical, dedicated to the eradication of war on moral principles. Following the pattern of the Benevolent Empire societies, local societies merged at a convention in New York in 1828 to form the American Peace Society. It dedicated itself to a discussion of the evils of war and the establishment of a "Congress of Nations" to avert it.

The cause of temperance was championed in New England by those who advocated Societies for Good Morals and by the Andover faction. Beecher's Connecticut Society for the Reformation of Morals included temperance reform as part of its program; the Massachusetts Society for the Suppression of Intemperance (1813) united many persons connected with the foreign mission cause on the local auxiliary model to demand total abstinence; and in 1814 the New England Tract Society issued its seminal temperance pamphlet, *Tract No. 3*. In 1826 ministers and merchants prominent in other missionary and moral reform movements came together in Boston's Park Street Church to form the American Society for the Promotion of Temperance, uniting Massachusetts temperance organizations. In 1829 its Connecticut counterpart was formed. By 1830, the 172 branches of the Connecticut organization included 22,000 members.

The first antislavery society, the American Colonization Society, originated in 1816 among a varied constituency of politicians, merchants, southern planters, and evangelical reformers. Its appeal was mainly to individuals motivated by self-interest in the upper South and the middle states to rid themselves of the slavery problem altogether in a gradual way; its purpose was to raise funds to send liberated slaves to a colony in Africa established for them. As a solution to the slavery dilemma in the United States, colonization was from the beginning a hopelessly impractical scheme. Nevertheless, in 1820 the first group of eighty-eight colonists, sent as the vanguard of Christianity in Africa, sailed to Liberia, the area designated a homeland for freed slaves. During the 1820s the society attracted the support of many of the trustees of the Benevolent Empire.

Beginning in the 1830s, however, the neat synthesis between these three single-cause reform efforts and the Benevolent Empire societies began to disintegrate. As the perfectionist theology began to spread among Protestant denominations, many individuals came to connect personal piety with an active effort to eradicate sin, while the Congregationalists and Presbyterians, who had dominated the cause of reform in the United States, were interested more in promoting personal piety and theological orthodoxy than in undertaking what they took to be the impossible task of eradicating sin. For Benevolent Empire adherents, reform was a means to an end; for perfectionists, reform became an end in itself.

The first dissension in the ranks between perfectionists and conservative reformers in the 1830s occurred when the abolitionist movement emerged out of the humanitarian movements that had intended merely to better the condition of slaves. Abolitionism, the movement to abolish slavery immediately regardless of political consequences, had numbered scattered advocates in the South since the mid-1810s, of which many had been Quakers. The printer/publisher who harnessed the perfectionist impulse in the service of the abolitionist cause was William Lloyd Garrison, whose mother was a pious Baptist woman from Newburyport, Massachusetts. An early temperance advocate, Garrison was influenced by Benjamin Lundy, a Quaker abolitionist, for whose antislavery Baltimore newspaper, the *Genius of Universal Emancipation*, he went to work in 1829. He was arrested for libel, found

guilty, and bailed out by Arthur Tappan, the wealthy New York merchant and partisan of reform. Garrison then moved to Boston, where he began to speak against slavery and publish his own abolitionist newspaper in 1831, *The Liberator*. The antislavery cause among Garrisonians came to resemble the process of conversion itself: just as conversion was sudden and involved a complete dedication to the eradication of sin in one's life, so too to the Garrisonians did the cause of antislavery entail a dedication to rid the nation of the curse of slavery immediately and by whatever means necessary. They saw the African colonization movement as compromised by its willingness to tolerate the sin of slavery. In December 1833, following the British Parliament's emancipation of the West Indian slaves, the members of Garrison's New England Antislavery Society (1831) combined with the group of wealthy New Yorkers who had recently founded the New York City Antislavery Society to form a national organization, the American Anti-Slavery Society.

The rise of immediatism in the antislavery movement presaged the radicalization of the temperance and peace movements as well. Undoubtedly the new interest in temperance was in part a response to the danger intoxication posed to the good order of society, especially on the frontier and in the cities, as the consumption of spiritous liquors reached an all-time per capita high in the United States about 1830. Increasingly, however, the pledge of total abstinence, not simply moderation in drink, became for many of a perfectionist inclination the visible sign of the total dedication of the converted to living an uncompromised existence. As early as 1826 the Society for the Promotion of Temperance had condemned the use of all intoxicating liquors; but finding public support for such a measure not yet strong enough, within two years the society backed off to condemn only distilled liquor. By the early 1830s, however, interest in temperance had spread nationwide. An 1833 Philadelphia convention combined the officers of the Society for the Promotion of Temperance and a number of state and local organizations into the United States Temperance Union. The new organization condemned the use of all alcoholic beverages, not only hard spirits, and triggered a wave of resolutions by state organizations denouncing all intoxicating liquors.

SOCIAL REFORM THROUGH THE CIVIL WAR

Continuing controversy provoked another convention in August 1836, in which debate centered on the question of whether the temperance crusade was a matter of expediency or sin. Was abstinence an aid to the development of piety and moral character, or was it an absolute necessity for the Christian determined to avoid sin? Advocates of the latter position formally organized the American Temperance Union, dedicated to total abstinence and a campaign for the legal means to enforce it. Local option laws were passed in a variety of areas in the 1830s and 1840s, and the first statewide prohibition was passed in Maine in 1846.

While temperance reformers debated their purposes and goals, abolitionists continued to polarize antislavery ranks with the perceived extremity and growing rigidity of their position. In October 1833 violence against abolitionists broke out, as a crowd attempted to disrupt the first meeting of the New York Antislavery Society. In May 1834 the abolitionist celebration of an antislavery week in New York led to mob threats and the razing of Lewis Tappan's home, while in the following fall, an angry mob destroyed a school for black girls in Canterbury, Connecticut, operated by Prudence Crandall, a Quaker. Dissension over abolitionism came to a head in Cincinnati with controversy over the slavery issue at Lane Seminary. It was triggered by Theodore Dwight Weld, the son of a prominent Congregational minister, who had been converted to perfectionist evangelical fervor when he heard Finney preach in Utica, New York. While at Lane, Weld was converted to the cause of abolitionism, believing that colonizationists avoided the change of heart necessary for holiness. The abolitionism of a group of Weld's followers at Lane began to rankle the Cincinnati community when the group sought to establish religious and secular schools among the city's free blacks. An eighteen-day series of debates over immediatism and colonization in February 1835 led to faculty condemnation of these Lane students and signaled the beginning of a formal rift between the church and the abolitionists. Although Weld decided to strike out on his own as an antislavery orator, most of the Lane rebels flocked to Oberlin College, where Finney had become head of the theology department.

The contagion of abolitionist perfectionism spread to the small American Peace Society as well. In their disappointment over public refusal to deal with the slavery issue, many Garrisonians came to believe that an evil state apparatus lacked the moral authority to induce individuals to reform. They looked to the American Peace Society as an adjunct to their antislavery crusade. In September 1837, however, Garrison drew comparisons in the pages of the *Liberator* between the halfway measures of the American Colonization Society and the refusal of the American Peace Society to condemn defensive along with offensive warfare. The moderates of the American Peace Society, solid citizens and merchants who were not at war with the status quo but instead sought minor changes, became increasingly alarmed at the radicals' rejection of all man-made law and civil government as hindrances to perfection. The bitter argument about goals resulted in an 1838 split between the perfectionist Garrisonians, who formed their own New England Non-Resistance Society, and the moderates, mostly Congregational ministers and businessmen, who remained within the parent organization.

In the continuing controversy over goals, strategy, and tactics, the American Anti-Slavery Society itself split by 1840 into perfectionists and those of a more moderate bent. The ostensible trigger for the split was the question of whether women ought to be accorded public roles in the antislavery crusade and be accepted as speaking and voting members of antislavery organizations. Women had first organized themselves into Female Anti-Slavery Societies in Boston in 1832. By 1836 many had become heavily involved in the movement, and some had begun speaking in its behalf in public. In 1837 the ministers of the Congregational General Association of Massachusetts spoke out against the Garrisonian practice of encouraging women abolitionists to speak to mixed assemblies. They were particularly disturbed by Sarah and Angelina Grimké, Quaker sisters from South Carolina, who had begun addressing crowds publicly and defending women's right to do so. In 1838 Garrison's own organization, the New England Anti-slavery Society, accepted women as members, prompting a number of anti-Garrisonians to secede in 1839 to form the Massachusetts Abolition Society.

The "woman question" represented, more than a simple issue of the appropriate behavior of the sexes, a larger philosophical difference that became a stumbling block between Garrisonian "ultraists" and more moderate advocates of antislavery. Was reform an occasion to call into question the legitimacy of all aspects of the standing order, as the Garrisonians seemed to contend, or was it rather a way of bolstering individual morality and piety within a standing order whose legitimacy remained unquestioned? Within the abolitionist cause, schism spread to the national level in 1840, when a minority seceded from the parent American Anti-Slavery Society over the question of whether women might be officers. The new American and Foreign Anti-Slavery Society carried with it most of the parent society's clerical members as well as many of those who had come to the antislavery crusade from Benevolent Empire reforms. They were disturbed by the increasingly anti-institutional tenor of Garrisonian perfectionism and its tendency to spill over into areas beyond the antislavery crusade.

The "woman question" within antislavery, for its part, blossomed into a full-blown movement for women's rights in the 1840s. Women who had been tutored in the cause of reform through membership in the church societies that supported missionary activity and antislavery applied what they knew about the restricted condition of the slaves to their own condition. In 1848 reformers led by Elizabeth Cady Stanton and Lucretia Mott (both abolitionists) gathered in Seneca Falls, New York, for a Women's Rights Convention that issued a declaration of women's disabilities. This meeting was the first of the conventions that met annually from 1850 to 1860, except 1857. The women's rights cause was supported by a few male abolitionists, notably Garrison and Frederick Douglass, although most remained opposed to the cause.

As abolitionists came to define immediatism as the test of morality, the American churches increasingly came under fire for their reluctance to act on this issue. In 1836 the Presbyterian General Assembly rejected a report calling for the censure of slaveholders; in the same year the Methodist General Conference rejected petitions to review church policy regarding discipline toward slaveholders. The Congregational leadership in New England did not endorse antislavery, and Unitarians endorsed gradualism,

compensation, and colonization. Baptists, organized only locally, lacked a general church policy toward slavery, while the Disciples of Christ (or Campbellites) denied that perfectionistic standards of behavior could be demanded before Christ's Second Coming. The liturgical denominations—Lutherans, Episcopalians, and Roman Catholics—attempted to remain officially neutral on all social issues of the day, a result perhaps of the existence of separate dioceses or synods adapting themselves to local conditions or, as was the case with Episcopalianism, of the social conservatism of the denomination.

The result was that the Garrisonians, initially drawn from the ranks of evangelical perfectionists and liberals such as the Unitarians and the Quakers, began increasingly to denounce church membership. "Comeouters," seeking to escape the contamination of evil influences within the church, chose to obey the biblical injunction and to "come out," leaving established churches by renouncing fellowship individually or forming new denominations of their own. By the mid-1850s six major comeouter sects existed: the Wesleyan Methodist Connection, the American Baptist Free Mission Society, the Free Presbyterian Church, the Frankean Evangelical Lutheran Synod, the Indiana Yearly Meeting of Anti-Slavery Friends, and the Progressive Friends. In upstate New York and New England in the 1830s and 1840s some Christian abolitionists sought to create a unified sect, the Union Church, that emphasized complete separation from sinners, especially slaveowners.

Perfectionist concern for reform from the 1820s to the 1840s also manifested itself in the form of separatist, autonomous reform movements whose goal was to create utopian societies as models for universal reform. Utopian communitarians believed that their exemplary way of life would redeem the corrupt society and pave the way to a new millennial age. These utopian experiments included endeavors both sacred and secular in character. The chief secular experiment, the communitarian settlement at New Harmony, Indiana, was established in 1825 and translated Robert Owen's belief that human character was a result of environmental factors into a vision emphasizing socialism in economy and cooperation in living. Communities such as George Ripley's Transcendentalist experiment at Brook Farm (1841–1847), Adin Ballou's "miniature Christian republic," Hopedale (1840–1845), and Bronson Alcott's Fruitlands (1843–1844) sprang up as adjuncts of Transcendentalism, romantic perfectionism, or both. They attempted to preserve the autonomy and spiritual integrity of the individual within a communal work environment, experimenting with new approaches to the family, labor, diet, education, and sex roles in a protest against modernization. Finneyite perfectionism also indirectly gave impetus to a number of utopian experiments, including John Humphrey Noyes's Oneida Community and the several Shaker communities that flourished during this time.

INSTITUTIONAL REFORM: 1840–1860

If radicals grew disturbed at the churches' reluctance to act on important moral questions, there was good reason: as a group, the American churches remained decidedly lukewarm on the slavery issue until the eve of the Civil War. To be sure, the liturgical denominations had always remained neutral on social issues. Others, though voicing antislavery sentiments in the late eighteenth and early nineteenth centuries, rapidly backed off from the issue as it threatened to polarize or alienate large portions of their membership. Methodists, for example, instituted measures to exclude slaveholders or dealers from membership in the 1784 conference that gave rise to the denomination in America; as Methodist southerners rose in social standing, however, such restrictions were relaxed or forgotten altogether. The same was the case with all Baptists but the Freewill sect, which since its inception had barred slaveholders from church membership. Universalists also called for abolition at their first national convention in 1790 but provided no means for enforcing their policy. Only the Quakers and a few small Scottish Presbyterian sects uniformly maintained prohibitions against slavery among their members.

As antislavery sentiment grew nationally in the 1840s and 1850s, sectional schisms resulted among Baptists and Methodists over the issue of church discipline to slaveholders. In an effort to avoid open conflict, the Methodist quadrennial

General Conference rejected all antislavery petitions in 1840 only to find a splinter-group minority led by Rev. Orange Scott seceding to form a comeouter sect in 1842, the Wesleyan Methodist Connection. In 1844, the "irrepressible issue" resulted in a complete break with southern members who were upset over the General Conference's suspension of a southern bishop who was also a slaveholder. In 1845 Baptists also divided along sectional lines, over demands that missionary societies and publications of the denomination repudiate ties with slaveholders.

As antislavery sentiment crystallized into party organizations, political participation became an increasingly acceptable way for moderate northern churchmen to advance the antislavery cause. The Free Soil and Republican parties encouraged church members to see the voting booth, not an "ultraist" organization based on perfectionist principles, as the place where true moral choices were to be made. The suggestion that slaveholding was a sin remained offensive to most northern clergy; nevertheless, the platforms of the new parties opposed to extension of slavery into the territories meshed with their philosophy of eradicating slavery through gradual measures. "Christian Anti-Slavery Conventions" became the chief vehicle through which immediatist sentiment was kept alive within the churches through the 1850s; these coalesced at the end of the decade into a permanent organization, the Church Anti-Slavery Society.

Nevertheless, by this time the reform issues of the first decades of the century had irrevocably been telescoped into a single issue, slavery, and it was the new political parties, not the churches, that were the institutions charged with the moral mission of dealing with it. The Civil War represented not so much the apogee of Finneyite/Garrisonian perfectionism as a last-gasp attempt at renewal and reform of the national purpose and character, at once both sacred and secular in character.

Most northern denominations supported the Civil War, but most did not support the abolition of slavery. What they did support was the ideal of a chosen nation destined by God for holiness and greatness, a dream that the southern secession threatened to destroy. In time many would convince themselves that they had fought the war to rid the nation of slavery. In fact, however, insofar as they fought in defense of an idea at all, most fought to preserve the myth of their identity as a covenanted people, much as their Revolutionary forebears had. In that troubled age of civil strife, the great majority of citizens feared change more than they welcomed it.

BIBLIOGRAPHY

Robert H. Abzug, *Passionate Liberator: Theodore Dwight Weld and the Dilemma of Reform* (1980); John R. Bodo, *The Protestant Clergy and Public Issues, 1812–1848* (1954); Carl Bridenbaugh, *Mitre and Sceptre: Transatlantic Faith, Ideas, Personalities, and Politics, 1689–1775* (1962); Peter Brock, *Pacifism in the United States from the Colonial Era to the First World War* (1968); Richard L. Bushman, *From Puritan to Yankee: Character and the Social Order in Connecticut, 1690–1765* (1967); David Brion Davis, *The Problem of Slavery in the Age of Revolution, 1770–1823* (1975); Louis Filler, *The Crusade Against Slavery, 1830–1860* (1960).

Clifford S. Griffin, *Their Brothers' Keepers: Moral Stewardship in the United States, 1800–1865* (1960); Joseph R. Gusfield, *Symbolic Crusade: Status Politics and the American Temperance Movement* (1963); Nathan O. Hatch, *The Sacred Cause of Liberty: Republican Thought and the Millennium: Revolutionary New England* (1977); Sydney V. James, *A People Among Peoples: Quaker Benevolence in Eighteenth Century America* (1963); Aileen S. Kraditor, *Means and Ends in American Abolitionism: Garrison and His Critics on Strategy and Tactics, 1834–1850* (1969); Richard F. Lovelace, *The American Pietism of Cotton Mather: Origins of American Evangelicalism* (1979).

Donald G. Mathews, "The Second Great Awakening as an Organizing Process, 1780–1830: An Hypothesis," in *American Quarterly*, 21 (Spring 1969), and "Religion and Slavery—The Case of the American South," in Christine Bolt and Seymour Drescher, eds., *Anti-Slavery, Religion, and Reform: Essays in Memory of Roger Anstey* (1980); John R. McKivigan, *The War Against Proslavery Religion: Abolitionism and the Northern Churches, 1830–1865* (1984); William G. McLoughlin, *Revivals, Awakenings, and Reform: An Essay on Religion and Social Change in America, 1607–1977* (1978); Perry Miller, "From the Covenant to the Revival," in *Nature's Nation* (1967).

W. J. Rorabaugh, *The Alcoholic Republic: An American Tradition* (1979); David J. Rothman, *The Discovery of the Asylum: Social Order and Disorder in the New Republic* (1971); Timothy L. Smith, *Revivalism and Social Reform in Mid-Nineteenth-Century America* (1957); John L. Thomas, "Antislavery and Utopia," in Martin Duberman, ed., *The Antislavery Vanguard: New Essays on the Abolitionists* (1965), and "Romantic Reform in America, 1815–1865," in David Brion Davis, ed., *Ante-bellum Reform* (1967).

[*See also* GREAT AWAKENING; NEW ENGLAND PURITANISM; NINETEENTH-CENTURY EVANGELICALISM; SOCIAL REFORM AFTER THE CIVIL WAR TO THE GREAT DEPRESSION; SOCIAL REFORM SINCE THE GREAT DEPRESSION; *and* SOCIETY OF FRIENDS.]

SOCIAL REFORM AFTER THE CIVIL WAR TO THE GREAT DEPRESSION

John A. Mayer

THE topic of religion and reform from 1865 to 1930 requires an attempt at definition, since it is too large to cover in detail or with a denomination by denomination survey. Major movements, events, and trends will be covered. (The exception is the Social Gospel movement, which is treated elsewhere in this encyclopedia.) Reform efforts that are expressly religious in motivation or in terms of organizational affiliation, as well as some reforms having only a partial or indirect religious connection, constitute one aspect of the topic to be covered; opposition to reform on a similarly religious basis also needs to be noted.

Reform has historically meant several things. Since the French Revolution, attempts to increase equality of opportunity and/or of condition have been seen as reforms, as have attempts to increase political liberty. Anything not commercially motivated and seen as an improvement over past or present conditions is also part of the definition of reform, though this is highly subjective. Any effort that entails a loss of equality, that increases inequality, even if it is seen by its supporters as an increase in liberty or an improvement upon the past, cannot be considered a reform. Thus, some of the American Protective Association members, and most certainly some Ku Klux Klan members, have seen themselves as reformers from a redemptive perspective, but the promotion of privilege that they wished to effect disallows such efforts from being considered as reforms.

GENERAL TRENDS

During this period, several trends are discernible. Beginning in the 1880s and then accelerating rapidly with the Social Gospel movement, churches became increasingly involved with social concerns and problems, and their outreach and reform efforts multiplied; by the 1930s most mainline churches and religions had ongoing and active programs for dealing with social conditions. (The Social Gospel movement was an attempt by numerous and varied preachers, theologians, and concerned laymen to emphasize the prophetic and social justice aspects of Christianity. They specifically sought to respond to conditions brought about by the rise of industrial capitalism, such as unhealthy and crowded urban housing, exploitation of children as laborers, corruption of political processes, and growing class segregation, by emphasizing the concept of social, rather than simply individual, sins and by seeking appropriate reforms.) At the same time, however, the social activism of Christian churches was blunted by a number of factors. Division within and between denominations and churches weakened any unified social vision. The largest evangelical Protestant denominations remained unreconciled after the Civil War, and northern churches experienced theological controversy. Fundamentalists staked out positions on the right while liberals, social gospelers, and Christian socialists followed modernism to the left. Both sides tried to contest for the more moderate center. On the right, autonomous religious agencies unconnected to any denomination proliferated, and fundamentals of the faith were penned to separate the sheep from the goats; hence the name Fundamentalism. Those who did not assent to these fundamentals of the faith were considered to be misguided, or misled, or not truly Christian at all. On the left, secular explanations derived from a social scientific paradigm became more socially powerful than theologically derived explanations, and a civic vision arose to coexist alongside a uniquely American Protestant evangelical one.

The Second Great Awakening (1800–1830) had imbued nineteenth-century evangelical Protestantism with a vision of a unified Christian nation. Theological division, growth of materialist and historical perspectives in academia, and the increased immigration of Catholics, Orthodox nationals, Jews, Buddhists, and socialists rendered this vision increasingly unfeasible, although it did remain powerful both in mainline Protestant denominations and on the religious right. But the growth of universities and particularly the social sciences provided an alternative civic vision that was pluralistic and that relied on utilitarian rather than theological justifications.

In short, the vision of mainline evangelical Protestantism for America was overtaken by historical developments and became outdated during the years from 1865 to 1930. Those who remained with that nineteenth-century perspective lost power for influencing the direction of social reform, and they not infrequently stood opposed to reform efforts. Those who moved to a generalized civic reform vision and who used social scientific explanations and utilitarian justifications gained power—they could unite diverse groups in common causes. They sought to improve society by directly reforming social conditions, unlike the evangelical emphasis on improving society by improving the moral behavior of individuals through persuasion and legal coercion. They could also more easily utilize the authority of specialized expertise being generated by the large universities during this period. Consequently, by the end of the period, autonomous secular reform agencies such as settlement houses and specialized social service organizations had become significantly more important than churches in promoting and controlling the direction of social betterment efforts. The main direct religious connection with this pluralist and civic outlook was the Social Gospel movement.

Perhaps the most significant reform drive in terms of number of people involved and long-range effects was the expanded role women established for themselves. They gained increased rights within a number of churches and they established numerous autonomous organizations and agencies. Women had, of course, been extremely active prior to the Civil War in mission and benevolent work, the women's rights move-

ment, and abolitionism. The postwar era continued to expand on these themes (minus abolitionism), but it was most memorable for the increased political power that women gained for themselves, both within denominations and outside of them.

RECONSTRUCTION

During and following the Civil War, the education and relief of southern freedmen became a primary mission field for northern Protestants. The ties between the federal government, northern evangelical denominations, and religiously staffed private agencies were extremely close. Gen. Oliver Howard, head of the Freedman's Bureau, was a New England Congregationalist who worked closely with the American Missionary Association (AMA). The latter's core membership were Boston abolitionists and, although officially nondenominational, Congregationalists dominated. The AMA considered its teachers to be missionaries, and their approach was evangelical. Howard, instructed by Congress to cooperate with private agencies, went beyond that and provided direct aid from the Freedman's Bureau to private agencies; he favored the evangelical approach of the AMA. The teachers had to profess their Protestant Christianity (the AMA would not support Roman Catholics), and for texts they most frequently used Bibles, catechisms, and American Tract Society products.

Although the AMA was the largest agency and the one most favored by the federal government, the field was a crowded one. During the immediate postwar years, numerous ad hoc groups arose to provide relief to southerners, among them the Ladies' Southern Relief Associations of Baltimore and New York City and New York City's Southern Famine Relief Commission. The executive committee chairman of the Southern Famine Relief Commission was Archibald Russell, a lawyer active in both the American Bible Society and the wartime United States Christian Commission. General relief agencies such as these provided aid to white southerners, while freedman's aid societies focused upon freedmen. Every mainline Protestant denomination in the North established freedman's aid associations, and independent societies existed in numerous cities, including New York, Philadelphia, and Boston, with evangelical Protestants and abolitionists as prominent members. At the peak of benevolent activity in 1869, approximately 5,000 northerners were teaching freedmen. Three-quarters of them were single women, and half of the total came from New England. When combined with southerners, there were roughly 9,000 persons in all who were teaching freedmen.

Given this welter of groups, organizational rivalry was perhaps inevitable. The teachers for Freedman's Bureau schools were supplied through freedman's aid societies. Howard's bias toward evangelical agencies was reflected by his director of finance and schools, John W. Alvord, formerly secretary of the American Tract Society, a Congregationalist minister, and a member of the first graduating class at Oberlin. Oberlin College, founded in 1833, became an abolitionist school in 1835, as a part of the reform fervor generated by evangelical revivalism. It was the first male college in the country to admit blacks and women. Alford therefore represented a very direct connectedness to evangelical reformers and agencies.

The American Freedman's Union Commission (AFUC) resented the AMA's dominance. The AFUC was more secular in its approach and included Unitarians and Universalists; they did not consider their teachers to be missionaries. The rivalry also had roots in earlier conflict: the AFUC emerged from a New York City–Garrisonian abolitionism as opposed to the AMA's Bostonian abolitionism. At its peak in 1866 the AFUC provided 775 teachers to over 300 schools.

The freedman schools' educators aimed to teach freedmen not just literacy, but the meaning of freedom. As such, they formed a core of support and advice for political action and for assertion of civil rights in matters such as labor contracts in the face of southern white hostility to blacks' freedom. They also taught capitalism and the particular moral values they thought necessary to succeed in a marketplace world. An attempt to assist freedmen to become small-scale capitalists originated with Alvord. Supported by the AMA, he persuaded Congress to charter the Freedman's Savings and Trust Company, designed to help freedmen accumulate savings. Unfortunately it failed in the panic of 1873, teaching a lesson quite different from the intended one.

One of the long-lasting legacies of the aid so-cieties were black normal schools, which provided teachers for the primary schools. At least one was established in every southern state; Howard, Atlanta, and Fisk universities so originated. The AMA, in addition to the Congregationalist, Methodist, Baptist, and Presbyterian churches, supplied these normal schools as well as secondary schools with regular financial aid. The financial aid from northern churches, and later from education foundation money such as the Peabody and Rosenwald endowments, allowed the construction and maintenance of a larger educational structure for southern blacks than would otherwise have been possible. It also made southern black education dependent upon white philanthropic goodwill, and during the heightened racism of the 1880s–1930s, white donors encouraged black educators to acquiesce to segregation and racial conservatism.

BLACK CHURCHES

Following the Civil War, freedmen formed separate churches. A minority joined the separate institutions southern whites established as affiliates of the Methodist and Baptist churches. But the majority of churchgoers formed independent black Baptist churches, while others flowed into the African Methodist Episcopal Church (AME) and the African Methodist Episcopal Zion Church (AME Zion), both having originated in the North prior to the Civil War. In all, Methodists and Baptists accounted for 90 percent of black church membership, with Presbyterians accounting for another 5 percent.

The black church collectively became the major organizing institution of black social life. Its preachers were recognized community leaders and spokesmen, and they tended toward racial conservatism, as did black educators. Unlike the schools, however, black churches were self-financed and thus somewhat free from the pervasiveness of white control mechanisms. Being the only major autonomous institutions, they played an important role in defining, maintaining, and regulating a black cultural perspective. The black church was also a major social center whose meetings established a sense of community and connectedness among the individual members.

The sense of connectedness became manifest in the financial activities of the individual churches. Raising funds to construct or improve the church building was a communal activity. Mutual-benefit societies were most often lodged in churches. For example, of the nine benefit societies for blacks in Atlanta in 1898, six were church affiliated. Among the poorer rural churches, sickness and burial societies predominated. Churches also raised money to support black schools, both public and private, and several Methodist denominations (the AME, AME Zion, and Colored Methodist Episcopal) established their own colleges for the purposes of clerical education.

The black church has continuously been a source of leadership for the black community. During Reconstruction ministers often served as local political leaders, and two of the congressmen and one of the senators elected to national office were clergy. After Reconstruction the rural churches adopted an otherworldly and conservative perspective, but the black urban church, particularly in the North, continued to provide political leadership that criticized racial discrimination and pressed for reform. Church women and men challenged, for example, the segregationist policies of the YWCA and YMCA respectively in the 1880s and 1890s.

Henry M. Turner had served as a state legislator during Reconstruction; after Reconstruction was overthrown, he devoted his political energies to the AME Church, where he rose to become a bishop. In the 1870s and 1880s he advocated African nationalism for American blacks while continuously attacking racial discrimination. In 1893 he founded an Equal Rights Council. In doing so, he was opposing the accommodationist tactics of Booker T. Washington. Washington's program, laid out in the mid-1880s, proposed acquiescing to the South's program of disenfranchising black males and establishing a pervasive system of segregation. Washington hoped through acquiescence to lessen the racial hostility and the endemic violence that whites were inflicting upon blacks. He urged self-help and uplift through black institutions, such as his own Tuskegee Institute, arguing that when blacks had raised their economic and their moral levels, whites would come to respect them. Other black clergy who rigorously attacked racial discrimination were Jabez Campbell, also of the AME Church, Francis Grimke, a Presbyterian, and Alexander Crummell, an Epis-

copalian. The Presbyterians and Episcopalians were the favored denominations for significant numbers of the urban black middle class.

Urban black churches engaged in a variety of social service and reform activities on the local level. Black YMCAs and YWCAs were founded in most large urban centers. Black churches also engaged in work with juveniles and supported drives for temperance, Sunday closing laws, and shutting down red-light districts. These areas of coverage also indicate the extent to which black social service often represented the segregated branch of the larger and better-financed white endeavors.

Black clergy served their constituents more distinctively in their pursuit of equal justice. Some churches, such as St. Philip's Protestant Episcopal Church in New York City, led by Hutchens C. Bishop, became centers for the local chapters of the National Association for the Advancement of Colored People (NAACP) and the Urban League. Clergymen also organized protests against expanded Jim Crow laws, such as the one led by the Reverend R. H. Boyd, a banker and general secretary of the National Baptist Publishing Board, boycotting Nashville's newly segregated streetcars in 1905–1906. A combination of black clergy and blacks educated at Reconstruction-era colleges was particularly active in protesting the American cultural institution of lynching. Ida B. Wells-Barnet had gone to Rust and Fisk universities and had been encouraged by the president of the National Baptist Convention, the Reverend William J. Simmons, to enter journalism. In 1892 three men who were friends of hers were lynched. She launched a one-woman crusade against lynching and was driven from the South by mob violence. Her work laid the foundation for a mass protest of the 1898 lynching of Frazier B. Beker, a black postmaster in South Carolina. This led to a mass meeting in Chicago, the founding of the National Afro-American Council, and a trip to Washington for an audience with President William McKinley. Bishop Alexander Walters of the AME Zion Church became head of the council, and both Booker T. Washington and W.E.B. Du Bois belonged.

While the Beker case provoked national organization, similar protests occurred on local levels. For example, the New York City police's brutality toward blacks in a 1900 race riot led to a protest organization, the Citizen's Protective

League, headed by the Reverend William Henry Brooks of St. Mark's Methodist Episcopal Church.

Washington and those who followed his tactics took control of the National Afro-American Council in 1903. The faction led by Du Bois opposed Washington's program. They felt segregation should be resisted, equal treatment should be pursued, and, in education, an intellectual elite, whom Du Bois characterized as "the talented tenth," should receive emphasis. The Du Bois faction reemerged in the Niagara Movement of 1905, which, following race riots in Brownsville, Texas, in 1906 and later in Springfield, Illinois, led to the founding of the NAACP in 1909. Among the founders were the black clergymen Alexander Walters, Adam Clayton Powell, Sr., William H. Brooks, and Francis Grimke. The first executive secretary, James Weldon Johnson, was a graduate of Atlanta University as was his assistant and successor, Walter White.

The NAACP became the major organization for advocating equal justice and for protecting and trying to expand civil rights for blacks. It continued to push for a federal antilynching law as well as to try cases that would set precedent for expanded civil rights. This research-oriented, legal, secular approach, however, distanced the NAACP somewhat from the moral and spiritual concerns of the churches. Supported by numerous clergymen and congregants, the organization came to dominate the drive for black civil rights in the 1920s and 1930s. The transcendent concerns for a just world and the moral imperatives of righteousness were kept alive, though usually dormant, in black churches, however, awaiting the right moment and the right leadership to call them forth in a mass crusade for equal justice.

WOMEN AND REFORM

One of the broadest and most deeply sustained reform movements of the nineteenth and twentieth centuries was the effort of women to expand their role in American religious and public life. Involving millions of women, it was a battle fought on many different fronts. It included attempts to expand women's role within church polities as well as to establish autono-

mous women's organizations, religious and secular, that worked for the visions held by women of a more perfect society.

Women had, of course, been intensively involved in religious and reform activity prior to the Civil War. Women's benevolent, missionary, suffrage, and reform activities had been wideranging. Yet, up to the Civil War the women's rights movement had made only very limited legal gains, and women missionaries were generally the wives of, or "female assistant missionaries" to, males, and, in spite of the precedents of Antoinette Brown Blackwell's 1853 ordination in the Congregational church and Phoebe Palmer's revival preaching and writing within the Holiness movement that arose out of Methodism, nearly all churches refused women the right to officially participate in church politics or to be ordained. The Quakers, Unitarians, and Universalists were the main denominations amenable to the concept of women's equality in church polity.

Several factors of the era helped women to expand their roles. One was that women constituted the majority of membership in most churches; they were the lay members who labored most diligently in the efforts to maintain and support the churches. Secondly, the ideology of separate spheres, while severely delimiting women's role by prescribing wife and mother as the only ones nature intended, at the same time also ascribed to woman's nature a greater proclivity to religious sentiment, intuition, purity, and spirituality. This latter provided a conveniently high moral platform for women to stand upon while making claims for greater influence in church and public life.

The Civil War led to increased volunteer activity by women. In both the North and the South aid societies to support soldiers multiplied rapidly. Women gained administrative and organizational experience in their work for the Christian Commission and the United States Sanitary Commission in the North, and in the administration of plantations and hospitals in the South. Women also gained the right to new occupations, particularly as nurses and as government clerks in the North. And, as we have seen, single women teachers worked in freedman's schools throughout the South during Reconstruction.

The immediate postwar era heralded only limited advances for women, however; women clerks were displaced from their federal government jobs, and the women's rights movement lost force when it split apart over tactical and ideological differences. One faction, led by Elizabeth Cady Stanton and Susan B. Anthony, advocated inclusion of women's suffrage in the Fifteenth Amendment to the Constitution. Other leading figures, such as Lucy Stone and Julia Ward Howe, argued that this was "the Negro's hour" and that to push for women's suffrage would endanger passage of the amendment. The Stanton-Anthony faction also came to believe that the women's rights struggle should be led by women, whereas the New England–centered Stone-Howe faction continued to include men as leaders. Two separate organizations resulted, the National Woman Suffrage Association, with Stanton as first president, and the American Woman Suffrage Association, with Henry Ward Beecher as first president.

Aside from the significant attempt to expand rights for blacks during Reconstruction, the postwar period was conservative in tone, and the growing dominance of Victorian morals and manners placed limits on the possibilities of radical change in gender politics. Yet the conditions for change continued to exert their forces. The organizational experience many women gained during the Civil War, the continued decline in the birth rate, the increased numbers of educated women aware of public affairs, the growing numbers of urban middle-class women, and the numerous networks of women that existed in churches and in benevolent societies boded well for breaking the bonds of women's restricted sphere.

The first great burst of expansion occurred in the church mission field. Between 1868 and 1884 the following missionary societies were formed in the North: Woman's Board of Missions (1868, Congregational); Woman's Foreign Missionary Society (1869, Methodist Episcopal); Woman's Foreign Missionary Societies of the Presbyterian Church, U.S.A. (1870); Woman's Auxiliary (1871, Protestant Episcopal); Woman's Baptist Foreign Missionary Society (1873); Woman's Parent Mite Society (1874, African Methodist Episcopal Church); Christian Woman's Board of Missions (1874, Disciples of Christ); Woman's Board of Foreign Missions of the Reformed Church in America (1875); Woman's American Baptist Home Missionary Society (1877); Woman's Executive Committee for Home Mis-

sions (1878, Presbyterian, U.S.A.); Woman's Missionary Society of the Evangelical Lutheran Church (1879); Congregational Woman's Home Missionary Association (1880); Woman's Home Missionary Society (1884, Methodist Episcopal). In the South, the Woman's Board of Foreign Missions (1878, Methodist Episcopal), Woman's Missionary Union (1888, Southern Baptist), and the Woman's Auxiliary (1912, Presbyterian, U.S.A.) were formed.

These societies supported women missionaries and by 1882, 694 single women had been sent out. They also built and supervised the operations of such service institutions as hospitals, schools, dispensaries, and orphanages, which in turn provided jobs for nurses, women physicians, and teachers. Most established denominational seminary programs for missionary training excluded women, but the women's societies had established 60 such schools of their own by 1916. Two such Methodist schools were the Chicago Training School (1885) and the Scarritt Bible and Training School (1887), originally in Kansas City but moved to Nashville in 1924. By 1880, 57 percent of foreign missionaries were women—a figure that increased to 60 percent by 1893.

Women in local churches and women home missionaries engaged in myriad endeavors in the 1880s and 1890s. They established mission shelters for homeless women, rescue homes for "fallen" women, day nurseries for the children of working women, "industrial" (i.e., sewing, domestic service) training schools for girls, Sunday schools, mothers' clubs, children's clubs, free kindergartens, and visitation programs to juvenile and adult women prisoners. Lay women and home missionary women also worked for public temperance laws. The temperance drive led to the first nondenominational mass women's organization, the Woman's Christian Temperance Union (WCTU).

Founded in 1874, the WCTU worked only for temperance and did little political lobbying until the pro-suffrage and social activist Frances Willard wrested the presidency away from Annie Wittenmeyer at the 1879 national convention. The temperance issue united women at a time when suffrage remained a divisive issue. (Many, if not most, women continued to believe that political activity was outside of women's proper sphere of activities, which should, they thought, be centered on the home and the church.) Temperance could easily be seen as an extension of women's religious work, and it drew upon women's solidly established church and mission activities as a base for further activism. With drinking outside the home almost exclusively a male preserve, temperance symbolized for women the defense of the home and of the values that the home symbolized. The liquor issue also dramatized women's subservient legal status. As late as 1900, 37 states still adhered to the doctrine of coverture, which gave the husband property rights to all his wife's possessions as well as the custody of children if husband and wife separated. The drunken husband thus became a powerful symbol of women's powerlessness and of the insignificance attached to the domestic sphere in public policy.

Led by Willard, the WCTU served its evangelical Protestant women members as a "base for their participation in reformist causes, as a sophisticated avenue for political action, as a support for demanding the ballot, and as a vehicle for supporting a wide range of charitable activities." The policy of making national convention positions and programs nonbinding for locals allowed the national WCTU to pursue social reform activities that might otherwise have been divisive. Although temperance probably remained the central focus for many members, Willard's policy of "Do Everything" soon led to a diversified and multifaceted reform program that encompassed issues as wide-ranging as labor reform and jail reform. The common thread of purpose became women for other women, in addition to the attempt to integrate women's moral outlook into the public policy arena.

Local branches of the WCTU engaged in activities similar to those that churches and home mission societies were already establishing, such as day nurseries and rescue homes. In the 1880s they also established free medical dispensaries and low-cost restaurants. The national office's campaigns for reform were the most important facet of the organization, however. They drew into the political arena middle-class Protestant women who were not feminists and who rejected the concept of total civil equality.

The following represent some of the reforms the national office advocated between 1879 and 1892: in the area of corrections, better prison and jail facilities for women, police matrons for women prisoners, women police, halfway houses for released women prisoners, women heads for women's prisons, and the appointment of women to state correctional boards; in education, free public kindergartens and day nurseries for children of working mothers, federal aid for public elementary education, free school lunches, free technical education, and opposition to military training in public schools; as part of the purity crusade, raising the age of consent (which in most states was between seven and ten years of age in 1887), making patronage of a brothel a felony, giving mothers advice on sex education, and opposing the double standard (which accepted pre- and/or extramarital sexual relations for men, but not for women); in the area of labor conditions, a five-and-a-half-day, eight-hour-per-day work week and support for the Knights of Labor (a national labor union of the 1880s and early 1890s that sought better conditions for workers and more cooperative forms of production); as to women's rights, the appointment of women to state boards of charity, women's right to child custody, women's right to income from a husband, women's right to vote, and women's right to full participation in the political process. Anna Howard Shaw served as superintendent of the WCTU's Franchise Department from 1888 to 1892, after which she became vice president and then president of the newly formed National American Woman Suffrage Association.

Willard herself moved considerably ahead of the majority of her followers when she converted to socialism in 1889 after having read Edward Bellamy's *Looking Backward,* an influential utopian socialist novel published in 1888. She then came to advocate municipal or national ownership of railroads, utilities, and factories. She was also out in front when she switched from a moralistic to a social scientific explanation of alcoholism; rather than simply seeing it as a sin, Willard called it an environmentally related disease, with poverty more a cause than an effect of drinking.

A campaign more relevant to her followers was her espousal of church polity rights for women. The success of women's missionary boards had established a position of some autonomous power for women within the churches, but women were still excluded from political power within the church proper. For example, the Methodist Episcopal Church Conference refused to ordain Anna Oliver and Anna Howard Shaw as ministers in 1880. Oliver continued to seek ordination, but her congregation collapsed in 1883 and her health then failed. Shaw turned to the smaller Methodist Protestant Church and was ordained, but the struggle embittered her and she soon left for new challenges in the suffrage movement.

Women also sought lay political rights during this period. At the 1888 Methodist Episcopal General Conference, Willard as well as four other women who had been elected to represent their local conferences were denied seats. In northern evangelical churches, laity rights eventually were extended to women. For example, the same Methodist Episcopal Church that had denied Willard did vote in 1904 to seat women as lay delegates. In the South the Presbyterians granted women voting rights within the church in 1918, but the much larger Baptist and Methodist churches continued to deny such rights to women. However, Lottie Moon, a Southern Baptist missionary in China, became a heroic figure to Southern Baptist women in part because she forced acceptance of the rights of women missionaries to vote in mission meetings. On the other hand, back home at the Southern Baptist General Convention the head of the Women's Missionary Union, a society founded in response to Moon's call for such an organization, could not make her report directly to the convention until 1929, and even then, it had to be given after moving the convention to the host church's Sunday school rooms so as to not have a woman speaking in the church proper. The women of the National Baptist Convention (formed in 1895 of constituent black churches) responded to the exclusion of women by forming their own Woman's Convention in 1900. In 1915 they issued a report that graded the denomination's clergymen.

Men responded to women's rising voice in the churches in several ways. Organizationally they took over political supervision of the women's mission societies by placing them under male-dominated boards. Ideologically they put forth a specifically masculine version of Christianity; the Men and Religion Forward Movement drew on this version of what has come to be called muscular Christianity. It asserted that Western culture's historic definition of masculinity was both compatible with and a true expression of Christianity. Partly an attempt to draw more men into the churches, it also suited the militaristic needs of the period's imperialistic nationalism. An earlier junior version of muscular Christianity recruited boys from Sunday schools into the semimilitaristic Boys Brigades of America, modeled after drill corps. The Methodist version of these forerunners of the Boy Scouts was called the Epworth Guards. Presented as worthwhile juvenile work designed to attract boys, their underlying military message led the WCTU to oppose such organizations.

The mainline Protestant churches also ended the autonomy of women's mission societies and training schools during the Progressive era. The avowed goal was greater efficiency through centralized administration, but men's uneasiness about women's gaining an autonomous base of power in the church was also quieted through these bureaucratic reorganizations. The women's missionary training schools were absorbed into the denominational seminaries, and the women's mission societies were reabsorbed into the denominational and male-controlled mission boards. Thus, in 1906, for example, the Southern Methodist's Woman's Home Mission Society was forced to merge with the more conservative Woman's Foreign Mission Society, and the combined mission society was placed under the general Board of Missions. In the northern Presbyterian church the Woman's Board of Home Missions, which had only won its autonomy in 1915, was also merged with the general Board of National Missions in 1920. Women's financial support for missions usually dropped precipitously following such mergers.

While the majority of the male leaders in mainline Protestant churches remained conservative with respect to both social reform and women's role in the church, women were finding new opportunities outside the denominational church. Women preachers, such as Alma White, Mary Cole, Amanda Smith, Mary Woodworth-Etter, and Florence Crawford, found acceptance in nondenominational revivalist and Holiness circuits. Women were also active in founding their own denominations. Mary Baker Eddy's founding of Christian Science, which paired male and female officials and which conceived of

God as mother and father, evolved into a denomination and is therefore the most important. White (Pillar of Fire Church, 1901), Crawford (Apostolic Faith, 1908), and Aimee Semple McPherson (International Church of the Foursquare Gospel, 1920s) also founded churches. The nondenominational Salvation Army also practiced gender equality, of which Catherine Booth, a cofounder, was a strong advocate. (Maud Charlesworth Booth, Emma Moss Booth-Tucker, and Evangeline Cory Booth served as commanders in the Salvation Army from 1887 to 1896, 1896 to 1903, and 1904 to 1934, respectively.) Aside from the Salvation Army's charitable endeavors, however, these groups rarely involved themselves in social reform measures.

For women interested in reform in the 1890s and 1900s, new opportunities opened up rapidly in the relatively new and newly professionalized fields of social work, public health, corrections, and settlement houses. Professional education became available to women in the land-grant universities established after the Civil War, as well as in prestigious private schools such as the University of Chicago. The universities adopted a secular, social-scientific, and disciplinary explanatory paradigm, and both the universities' faculties and their graduates, as academic and professional experts, sought power to shape public policy.

This cultural shift was an integral part of the Social Gospel movement, as men such as Graham Taylor, Albion Small, Charles Henderson, and Richard Ely sought to capture the intellectual and political power of the new disciplines for reform purposes. Their personal motivations derived from their evangelical Christianity, but their methods and arguments became secular, and their outlooks developed an acceptance of cultural and religious pluralism.

Women found opportunities to utilize their competence and to gain independent status in these new fields. Comparable opportunities, outside of becoming a foreign missionary, were lacking within the major denominations. Women's engagement in reform endeavors thus took a rapid turn away from the evangelical approach of the WCTU. In 1892 the WCTU had had 150,000 members, as opposed to the General Federation of Women's Clubs' 20,000, and the National American Woman Suffrage Association's 13,000.

A decade later the WCTU not only was smaller than the other two, but its power to affect policy had been eclipsed by women in the social settlement and social work field, such as Jane Addams, Grace and Edith Abbott, Florence Kelley, and Julia Lathrop—all alumnae of just one settlement, Hull House.

As in the case of the male Social Gospelers, the motivations of a person like Addams were at least partly religious in origin, but the secularity of the reform endeavors they pursued could just as easily support secular motives, such as Kelley's socialism. Other middle-class women motivated to reform through a sense of Christian commitment were, in the first decade of the twentieth century, more likely to pursue reform through nonreligious organizations, such as woman's clubs, charity organization societies, suffrage organizations, or settlement-house work, than through an explicitly evangelical organization such as the WCTU. Even the YWCA, which had been founded in 1855 as an evangelical organization, began to be administered by social work and recreational professionals and to adopt a much more secular social service rhetoric when it was reorganized as a national organization in 1906. Thus, although women continued as the mainstay of the churches, serving their charitable and maintenance endeavors, the main locus of women's reform endeavors moved outside the church.

Vast numbers of women followed a path that led from the mission societies of the 1870s, to support for the WCTU's programs of the 1880s, to the reform endeavors of secular and autonomous agencies in the 1890s and early 1900s. These women often became suffragists along the way. An example of the move from mission society to a specialized autonomous reform organization can be seen in the case of church women's involvement in the southern interracial movement and antilynching campaign of the 1920s.

The Southern Methodist's Home Mission Society began giving support to southern social settlements in 1898 and in 1911 decided to develop a ministry to southern blacks. In 1912 it assumed financial support for a settlement house founded by the women of the Colored Methodist Church in Nashville, Tennessee. It also became actively involved with the programs and support of Bethlehem House in Augusta, Georgia. In a joint program with Fisk University and the Urban League, Bethlehem House became a training ground for black social workers. Perhaps the most radical feature of its program was its biracial staff and governing board.

Interracial contact forced the Methodist women to become more conscious of racial discrimination and more aware of the issue of lynching. Inspired by Ida B. Wells-Barnet in the 1890s, black women's clubs had formed in protest to lynching and grew into the National Association of Colored Women. In 1906, when the national YWCA was organized, black women protested its segregationist policy. A sign of the Methodist women's growing concern was the 1914 publication of *In Black and White.* Its author, Mrs. J. D. Hammond, was superintendent of the Bureau of Social Service, an organization founded in 1899 by Methodist women who wished to minister to blacks. Her book was a wide-ranging attack on nearly all aspects of the southern racial caste system.

During World War I black women such as those in the Atlanta Colored Woman's War Council protested against the treatment of black servicemen, and in 1920 they reissued a call for the desegregation of the YWCA. In response Methodist women held a conference in Memphis and, after hearing the messages of four black women speakers, formed a Woman's Department of the Commission on Interracial Cooperation. This organization had only recently been established by Will Alexander, a Methodist who had left the pulpit to pursue social reform. (He had gained his first experience of interracial cooperation at a Bethlehem House in Nashville while he had been a Vanderbilt University divinity student.) The women established interracial commissions in every southern state. The commission in Texas, headed by Jessie Daniel Ames, worked to improve the economic, medical, and educational facilities available to blacks; it also proposed a state antilynching law. (Ames's mother had been president of the local church's woman's missionary society and had been an independent businesswoman.) In 1930 Ames focused on the issue of lynching and founded the Association of Southern Women for the Prevention of Lynching. The very existence of this organization, which grew to 40,000 members, simultaneously attacked the debilitating stereotype of the southern lady who needed white male pro-

tection and the open conspiracy to maintain white supremacy violently through terrorism.

CATHOLICISM AND REFORM

The Catholic church, physically separated by the Civil War, was quickly reunited at the war's end, since it had never split organizationally. Yet internal divisions hampered the church's postwar reform efforts. The Second Plenary Conference, held in Baltimore in 1866, called for the religious care and instruction of freedmen. Yet very little was ever accomplished, particularly when compared with the work of northern Protestants. One reason was the very fact of a unified church—southern Catholics became the implementers of this decree, and they, like Protestant southerners, were little inclined to help the freedmen. Given the Democratic party preferences of most northern Catholics, the issue was not pressed with any fervor. (The Reconstruction effort to ensure equal rights for blacks was a Republican party program that the Democrats, by and large, opposed.) The church also acquiesced readily in the segregated caste system established in the late nineteenth and early twentieth centuries. By that time the church was being heavily burdened to meet the needs of the millions of Catholic emigrants to America.

The Reconstruction era points to some of the structural problems Catholicism faced in the American cultural environment. A minority church in a hostile and proselytizing Protestant-majority environment, the church reacted in a self-protective manner. At every opportunity the church asserted its essential compatibility with American society, while at the same time it constructed a parallel set of institutions to those existing in the dominant culture. The institution building in part reflected a desire to keep Catholics faithful and uncorrupted through insulating them from contact with the dominant culture. The desire to belong in America while simultaneously seeing America as a potentially corrupting influence was a deep and persistent dualism within American Catholicism. Catholics also had good reason to fear the political and social power of the Protestant majority, since anti-Catholic movements occurred repeatedly; these attacks reinforced both aspects of the dualism.

This dualism existed simultaneously for most Catholics, but some leaders emphasized the compatibility of Catholicism with American culture more than its need for protective autonomy, while others reversed these emphases. Catholics supportive of reform, such as Bishop John Ireland and Bishop John J. Keane, tended to come from the former, while the latter, such as Archbishop Michael A. Corrigan and Bishop Bernard J. McQuaid, often opposed it. Thus the church in America was often divided within itself. Such divisions were intensified by the ethnic and cultural multiplicity of the church; ethnic jealousies, such as those between the Germans and the Irish, occasionally led to conflict and rancor. Consequently, the very inclusiveness of the Catholic church often hampered attempts at reform because factionalism prevented unified support for reform endeavors.

The massive number of Catholic immigrants to the United States in the years from 1870 to World War I pressed hard upon the church, which felt impelled to meet their needs for welfare, charity, and spiritual care. When combined with the desire to establish separate Catholic institutions to serve them, this era came to be dominated by an energetic campaign of institution building. Between 1884 and 1900, 4,000 parochial schools were established for the nation's 6,400 parishes. Orphanages, hospitals, and old age homes increased from 463 in 1885 to 827 in 1900. The parish conferences (local parish charity groups) of the St. Vincent de Paul Society increased from 235 in 1883 to 402 in 1902. The Catholic University of America opened in 1889, and other Catholic universities followed. And the church showed flexibility in establishing parishes for nationalities, which often held immigrant communities together.

Institution building, however, is not necessarily reform; it need not sustain a vision of a better society, a society transformed or substantially altered, nor a vision that some new endeavor will lead to improved conditions or possibilities for people's lives. The church was quite conservative in its social attitudes throughout the period from 1870 to 1891. An attempt to colonize communities of Catholics in the Midwest was motivated as much by fear of unions as by creative benevolence; it attracted little support among the laity.

James Cardinal Gibbons' persuading the Holy See not to condemn the published works of the reformer Henry George was necessitated because other church leaders, particularly Archbishop Michael A. Corrigan, had sought such a condemnation. When Father Edward McGlynn supported the redistributive concepts and mayoral campaign of George in 1886, he was removed from his New York City pastorate at St. Stephen's parish by Archbishop Corrigan and was soon thereafter excommunicated. Catholics were split over this controversy, and Gibbons, on his 1887 visit to Rome, lobbied for lifting the excommunication. (It was lifted in 1892.) Gibbons' pro-labor stance in these matters was motivated less by any vision of economic justice than by a fear of alienating Catholic workers from the church, as had occurred in Europe. It was the pronouncement of the papal encyclical *Rerum Novarum* (On the Condition of Labor) in 1891 that secured acceptance of the labor movement by the Catholic hierarchy; prior to that, the matter stood in doubt.

The store of energies spent in the institution-building drive of the church, combined with the social conservatism of the hierarchy, the divisiveness of the labor and the Americanist issues, and the weakness of Catholic intellectual roots in America suffice to explain why no peculiarly Catholic social vision emerged prior to World War I. When Catholics did engage in reforms during this period, it was usually through a separate Catholic organizational version of an already ongoing reform movement. Thus the National League of Catholic Women, formed in 1893, modeled itself after the WCTU, and the Catholic Total Abstinence Union (1872) was similar to non-Catholic organizations already existing, such as the National Temperance Union. In charity organization, youth work, and settlements, the same imitative pattern was followed. For any broad-scale movement Catholics formed their own organizational vehicle so that Catholics could participate without leaving the embrace of Catholicism.

The strongest reform element in Catholicism prior to World War I consisted of a minority of Catholic leaders who embraced the Social Gospel movement and the social welfare wing of Progressivism. Monsignor John A. Ryan, author of *A Living Wage: Its Ethical and Economic Aspects* (1906), provided a theoretical grounding for the idea of a minimum standard of living that had been put forth in Robert Hunter's *Poverty* (1902). Its argument was consistent with the *Rerum Novarum* encyclical, stressing the dignity of the worker and the need for just and adequate wages, and, as such, represents one of the few instances during these years of a Catholic perspective contributing in a unique way to a reform cause. Throughout his long career Ryan advocated the eight-hour day, compulsory arbitration laws, unemployment relief, accident, illness, and old-age insurance, low-cost housing for purchase, public ownership of natural monopolies, regulation of private monopolies, progressive income and inheritance taxes, and control of speculation in land and at exchanges. Ryan remained a strong Progressive voice throughout the New Deal, but his Catholic supporters were a distinct minority. Ryan himself lamented that the bishops and the priests generally avoided the issue of social teaching and social works.

Two other Catholic reformers who tried to build on the church's social teachings were Father Peter Dietz and Frederick Kenkel. Dietz formed the Militia of Christ for Social Service in 1910 as an educational organization for Catholic members of the American Federation of Labor. The Militia was consistently hampered by lack of support and funds from the unions, however, Dietz hoped that American Catholic workers would coalesce and form a national Catholic movement for social reform based on the social teachings of the church, as some Catholic groups were attempting to do in Europe. While his efforts did familiarize many workers with the church's teachings, no such mass movement emerged. Kenkel had a similar concept, but his vehicle was the social bureau of the Central-Verein, a German Catholic mutual benefit society. The Verein did adopt a socially progressive program and it published a journal devoted to social issues, the *Central Blatt* (now *Social Justice Review*).

As in the case of the Protestant Social Gospel movement, the pursuit of social justice through Progressive legislation and a Progressive labor movement never attained a wide following among the laity, but nevertheless the movement did find an institutional place in the church. The American Federation of Catholic Societies, a relatively loose federation embracing a wide diversity of Catholic groups, created a Social Service Commission to promote the Progressive

program. Bishop Peter J. Muldoon served on the commission, and during World War I he served on the National Catholic War Council. When the war ended and the council became the National Catholic Welfare Conference (NCWC) at the urging of Bishop Muldoon, Monsignor Ryan wrote its social action policy statement in 1919. It called for a minimum wage, unemployment, health, and old-age insurance, child-labor laws and legal support for labor organizations, and public housing. Thus a national Catholic policy existed, signed by the bishops on the Administrative Committee, but it was only advisory and not binding on American bishops.

Unfortunately, however, the church not only gave little support to this program, but was instrumental in sabotaging a part of it. In the wake of the Red Scare, the administrative board of the NCWC attacked the growth in government that had occurred as a result of the war. Growth in the federal bureaucracy was seen as

> unconstitutional and undemocratic. It means officialdom, red tape, and prodigal waste of public money. It spells hordes of so-called experts . . . to regulate every detail of family life. . . . The press, the home, the school and the Church have no greater enemy at the present time than the paternalistic and bureaucratic government which certain self-seeking elements are attempting to foist upon us.
>
> (O'Brien, 1968, p. 43)

The state of Oregon's attempt in 1922 to close parochial schools, though struck down by the Supreme Court, had frightened Catholics of the power of government, given Catholicism's minority status. They particularly feared any extension of the state's power over children and over family matters. The church hierarchy therefore strenuously opposed the child labor law amendment in 1924 and was able to mobilize lay Catholics to action, unlike the social Progressives. Catholic opposition to the amendment was instrumental in defeating the proposal in Massachusetts, where a referendum was held, and in New York, where the threat of a referendum was sufficient to defeat it.

The continued anti-Catholicism of the 1920s, as manifested by the Ku Klux Klan and during the 1928 presidential campaign of Al Smith, put the church in a defensive posture. Instead of advocating public reforms, the Catholic Progressives turned to the rationalization and development of professional standards for the Catholic institutions that had already been established.

While a number of Catholics such as Monsignor Ryan, Bishop Muldoon, and Father Dietz joined in the Progressive crusade, Catholics were nonetheless underrepresented in proportion to their population in Progressive reform movements except for the labor union movement. The Catholic Progressives generally wished greater cooperation with other, non-Catholic agencies, and they looked to the state for beneficent intervention. They were opposed within the church, however, by those conservatives who were most concerned to preserve the autonomy of the church in a non-Catholic society.

Catholics during this era also exhibited strong gender conservatism, and were underrepresented in the suffrage movement. No movement for greater political rights for women emerged within the church as it had within American Protestantism. In fact, an outspoken woman such as Mary Theresa Elder, who indirectly criticized the male hierarchy for the church's lack of rural missions at the 1893 Columbian Catholic Congress, became highly noticeable because of her singularity.

AMERICAN JUDAISM AND REFORM

Judaism in America faced a situation in some respects similar to that of Catholicism: both were minority religions within a culture that was regularly hostile to them. The anti-Catholicism of the late nineteenth century and again in the 1920s was accompanied by an even more hostile anti-Semitism. And Jews were concerned, as Catholics were, to preserve the purity of their traditional faith. Yet Jews became disproportionately active in reform and radical causes, as opposed to Catholic underrepresentation; in fact, Jews were usually in the leadership vanguard of reform efforts during the Progressive era and throughout the 1920s.

A number of reasons account for this difference. Catholicism had been, historically, the established church in pre-Reformation Europe and remained a state church aligned with the monarchy in its post-Reformation strongholds, such as Spain, France, and Austria-Hungary. In conse-

quence, the church had, up through the nineteenth century, embraced charity but had been wary of social reform. The Jewish tradition, however, provided a cultural and ethical milieu supportive of the pursuit of social justice. As Clarke A. Chambers, a noted social welfare historian, has written:

> The support of the Jewish community for welfare measures, and the dedicated and brilliant leadership which it provided, may have derived from the tradition of social justice so deeply rooted in the protests of the Old Testament prophets, as some students have suggested; or it may have derived from the religious practice of *tzdakah,* provision for the human needs of the entire community . . . or it may have come out of the ancient ethnic instinct for survival that placed the value of the whole community above the value of particular classes or individuals.
> (1963, p. 214)

Thus the Jewish tradition's rationale for supporting social welfare measures came "not out of the charitable impulse to assist the less fortunate but as of right in answer to the claims of all men for due justice."

While within the Catholic church social reform efforts were often opposed by other Catholics who desired to preserve tradition, Judaism in American split along these lines. Secular and Reform Jews embraced reform and charitable outreach, while Orthodox and Conservative Jews emphasized looking inward with a concern to preserve tradition. So the organizational fragmentation of Judaism meant that Jews pursuing social reform measures were less likely to be opposed by their more conservative coreligionists than were Catholic reformers.

One final factor influencing Jewish support for reform efforts is that historically European Jews had been social outcasts, and the policy of Russia in the 1880s to drive Jews to conversion or emigration was another local intensification of that persecution. Consequently, Jews were less willing than were other American groups, particularly Protestants, to support policies of degradation, such as those directed at blacks or those directed at persons considered to be hereditary paupers in the 1880–1920s period. Jews were also more willing to establish programs geared to redistributing wealth to the poor and the working class.

SOCIAL REFORM TO THE GREAT DEPRESSION

The pre–Civil War Jews were primarily Germanic with a smaller Sephardic element. The German Jewish immigration followed the failures of the 1830 and 1848 European revolutions for liberal nationalism, and a number of these immigrants adhered to the romantic reform tradition. The American Jewish community rose from 15,000 in 1840 to 160,000 in 1860 and to 250,000 in 1880. The German Jews achieved great success in America; by 1890 less than 2 percent were laborers or peddlers, while 70 percent employed servants. Given their new historic situation of equal citizenship in a nation and success in its economy, the German Jews, led by Rabbi Isaac Meyer Wise, moved away from Orthodoxy and toward a version of Judaism they considered more appropriate to these new conditions. The Reform Judaism that emerged from this minimized Jewish nationalism and observance of the law. It emphasized an earthly eschaton, hoping for a "Kingdom of truth, justice, and peace among all men."

Reform Judaism was very assimilationist until the 1880s; the United Hebrew Charities of Los Angeles, for example, freely gave aid to Christian charitable enterprises. But two events shook this assimilationist perspective. One was a tide of anti-Semitism that rose from the populist farmers of the Midwest to the blue-blooded Adamses and Lodges of New England. This anti-Semitism did not abate, but had intensified by the 1920s, when it could be seen in the Ku Klux Klan as well as in the writing of William Faulkner and Ernest Hemingway.

The second shock was the massive immigration of Eastern European Jews. The U.S. Jewish population jumped from 250,000 in 1880 to nearly 3½ million in 1917 as a result of this immigration and their offspring. Their poverty, their Yiddish-speaking *shtetl*-derived culture (*shtetl* literally means village or hamlet, but it also connotes Eastern European rural settlements and the centuries-old culture that arose within them), and the influence of Hasidism and the pious Orthodoxy of the religious among them made them cultural aliens to their American Reform coreligionists. The latter felt impelled to help those immigrants in need (even if the motive for some was only that other Americans not come to resent all Jews) as well as to acculturate them if possible. The result was a panopoly of charitable and philanthropic institutions—relief societies, orphanages, old-age homes, industrial schools, etc.—often organized into a United Hebrew Charities. They also offered parallel institutions to those available in the Protestant social service realm, among them social settlements, Young Men's Hebrew Associations, summer camps, and educational and social centers such as the Educational Alliance. The Eastern European immigrants did not always take kindly to the *noblesse oblige* of the German Jews and founded their own mutual self-help and cultural organizations, such as the *landsmanschaftn* lodges (mutual aid societies organized on the basis of the home village or area) and the Educational League.

American Jews thus built one of the most complete and well-financed ethnic institutional structures of any ethnic group. Even more remarkable was the range of reform efforts in which American Jews provided numerous workers and leaders. Perhaps the leading Jewish social settlement worker was Lillian Wald, founder of the Henry Street Settlement, who advocated numerous social welfare and public health reform measures and who originally suggested to Theodore Roosevelt the need for a federal Children's Bureau. Some alumni of Henry Street were Henry Morgenthau, Jr., A. A. Berle, Jr., Sidney Hillman, and Herbert Lehman.

The new profession of social work provided careers for numerous Jews who used their positions as forums from which to push for social welfare legislation such as child-labor laws, minimum wage and maximum hours for women laws, and social insurance laws. Reform rabbis such as Rabbi Stephen Wise offered their support for such efforts. Wise also served as one of the founding members of the NAACP.

German Jews showed some sensitivity to the plight of American blacks. Julius Rosenwald, a Chicago philanthropist who gave away $63 million in his lifetime, had an assimilationist perspective as indicated by the money he provided to the YMCA and the (mostly Protestant) Chicago Bureau of Charities; but he also gave generously to the Associated Jewish Charities of Chicago and served as their head. One of his largest endowments was an educational fund for schools for southern blacks. In 1920 the Central Council of American Rabbis proposed a campaign for social justice similar to those put forth by the Federal Council of Churches and the National

Catholic Welfare Council. Theirs, however, also included advocacy of an antilynching law.

American Jews also provided intellectual leadership in the social welfare reform movement. I. M. Rubinow, author of *Social Insurance* (1913), and Abraham Epstein of the American Association for Old Age Security were leading spokesmen for social insurance. Josephine Goldmark, along with Florence Kelley, both of the National Consumer's League, provided the empirical research for the "Brandeis" brief in the 1908 *Muller* v. *Oregon* case; the brief was notable for its use of statistical data and its not relying on legal reasoning alone. The Court was influenced by this brief to uphold an Oregon law regulating the maximum number of hours women could work. Louis Brandeis, Goldmark's brother-in-law, provided the legal expertise, and when Brandeis was named to the Supreme Court, Felix Frankfurter replaced him as the social welfare reformers' leading legal adviser. Goldmark's other brother-in-law, Felix Adler, founded the Ethical Culture movement and worked assiduously for child labor and tenement house legislation.

American Jews also provided leadership in the labor movement, with men such as Samuel Gompers, long-time leader of the American Federation of Labor; Sidney Hillman, head of the Amalgamated Clothing Workers of America; and Morris Hillquit, labor lawyer. Jewish women also entered the labor movement in force, often through the International Ladies Garment Workers Union; Rose Schneiderman and Belle Moskowitz both rose from ILGWU ranks, Schneiderman to the presidency of the National Women's Trade Union League and Moskowitz to become secretary of Gov. Al Smith's labor board and, unofficially, one of his closest political advisers. Although Gompers opposed socialism, a significant number of Jewish union workers, including many affiliated with the United Hebrew Trades in New York City, were supporters of some branch of socialism, and the Socialist party in New York City was heavily Jewish. The leading Yiddish daily in New York City, the *Jewish Daily Forward*, reflected editor Abraham Cahan's socialist perspective.

The majority of Jewish women reformers, such as Schneiderman, Wald, and Goldmark, also supported women's rights. Emma Goldman was probably the most radical feminist in America until her deportation as an undesirable alien in the post–World War I Red Scare. Her anarchism and her immense effectiveness as a speaker upset the government more than her feminism, but it was probably as an outspoken feminist that she most influenced the outlooks of other Americans.

The majority of social welfare reformers came from a German and Reform Jewish background, and many of them became secular. Labor leaders and socialists were also often secular Jews and were likely to have an Eastern European background. Yet the religious, cultural, and ethnic mixture that constitute Judaism makes it difficult to separate out the influence of religion alone upon reform. Certainly the pursuit of a just and peaceful world that Reform Judaism proclaimed undergirded the reform impulses of the social welfare reformers. And the secular Jews of Eastern European backgrounds often retained *Yiddishkait*—a sense of Jewishness and respect for its traditions. Although many of the reformers themselves were secular, the considerable representation of Jews as reform leaders and the fertility of their contributions suggests that the traditions of Judaism remained a vital motivating and sustaining force to their reform impulses.

PROTESTANTISM AND REFORM

In the late nineteenth century, the mainstream white Protestant denominations—Methodists, Baptists, Presbyterians, Congregationalists, Churches of Christ, and Disciples of Christ—comprised 55 percent of all religiously affiliated persons, and 80 percent of all Protestants. The beliefs of these groups had increasingly converged during the nineteenth century to form a dominant belief system, usually cited as evangelical Protestantism, that embraced Arminianism, revivalism, the necessity of a conversion experience, and postmillennialism (the belief that Christ will return for the final judgment after a thousand-year period of perfection on earth; premillennialists believe the final judgment comes prior to the thousand years of perfection). Culturally they came to identify America with civilization and civilization with Christianity. This coincided with an evolutionary perspective of culture that lent support to nativism and manifest destiny. Sin was ordinarily viewed as a reflection of personal character and habit, and poverty tended, as Henry Ward Beecher pointed out, to reflect sin: "... no man in this land suffers from poverty unless it be more than his fault—unless it be his *sin* ..."

The postmillennial evangelicalism of mainstream Protestantism provided its adherents with a vision of a unified Christian nation that in turn would spread this unity to the world at large. Campaigns of missions and revivals would be the necessary means. To convert individuals was the key—society itself needed little change if only the individuals would change. The revivalist Dwight Moody gave up all his social relief measures in the belief that they distracted from his main goal of increased conversions: "When I was at work for the City Relief Society ... [if] I had a Bible in one hand and a loaf [of bread] in the other the people always looked first at the loaf; and that was just the contrary of the order laid down in the Gospel." Consequently he stopped bringing loaves to people.

Evangelical Protestantism thus represented a conservative force, ready to defend the status quo and the relatively privileged social position held by white Protestants. From its perspective, what most needed reform were those elements of the society that looked to be a roadblock or a threat to its particular vision of a righteous Christian nation. As non-Protestant immigration, theological modernism, and secular social-scientific viewpoints increased, this vision became increasingly unrealizable, and evangelical Protestantism gradually lost much of its immense confidence, became splintered, and grew increasingly defensive in the twentieth century.

While many churchmen were able to accommodate their Christianity to Darwinian theory and to the higher biblical criticism (grammatical and linguistic analysis of the texts, combined with historical analysis; it had developed in the nineteenth century, especially in Germany) a significant minority became strongly opposed to any such accommodation. The impact of a new biblical interpretive scheme, dispensational premillennialism, led to a Fundamentalist movement that grew steadily in strength during the early twentieth century. Its adherents tended to oppose reform, particularly since their theological enemies, the Social Gospelers, embraced it. The Social Gospel movement itself was a minority splintering away from the mainstream, emphasizing social sin rather than personal sin and

embracing scientific-based social reform rather than traditional mission and revival efforts.

Agencies outside of denominations grew in number and importance during the period 1880 to 1930. The Moody Bible Institutes became a major independent force for a conservative biblical interpretation. A revival circuit independent of denominations produced more large urban revivals during the years 1890 to 1910 than in any previous similar time. A Holiness revival movement, an autonomous city mission movement, and the growth of agencies such as the YMCA and the Salvation Army also developed their own corps of followers. Except for the latter two, each of which engaged in providing social services, these independent agencies tended to be antiliberal and antireform. In the 1920s the Ku Klux Klan emerged as a nondenominational but self-consciously Protestant organization that violently and aggressively opposed reform and cultural pluralism.

Since evangelical Protestantism represented a conservative religious majority, the reforms it fostered usually entailed attempts to get minority groups to adopt the norms of evangelicals. One example of such a reform effort is the Indian policy reform movement.

The close cooperation of the government and religious groups during the Civil War and Reconstruction led some Protestants to propose similar cooperation concerning Indian policy and administration. A combination of Quakers, former abolitionists, and evangelicals envisioned a program for Indians that, when adopted by President Ulysses S. Grant, came to be called the "peace policy." Their vision involved persuading the Indians to settle permanently on reservations where they could be converted, educated, and acculturated, after which the Indians would become property-owning Americans rather than tribal members of a "backward" pagan culture. Grant adopted this policy, although he resorted to force when tribes would not accept reservation life through persuasion. A Board of Indian Commissioners composed of denominational representatives was formed in 1869 to serve in a watchdog and advisory capacity to the Interior Department's Indian Bureau, and throughout the mid-1870s denominations were given charge of running the government's Indian agencies.

It was called the "peace policy" because reformers envisioned using peaceful means, and they thought the end result would be beneficial. The reformers conceptually opposed the military, who they thought were pursuing a policy of extermination, and secular agents, whom they saw as self-seeking and corrupt. Lobbying groups, such as Quaker Alfred Love's Universal Peace Union, Peter Cooper's (of Cooper Union) Indian Commission, and various Indian Rights Associations tried, in addition to furthering this policy, to protect Indian rights: they publicized army and government mistreatment of Indians, brought Indian spokesmen such as Red Cloud of the Oglala Sioux to Washington, protected Indian treaty rights and land, and kept the Indian Bureau from being transferred to the War Department.

Under the Rutherford B. Hayes administration (1877–1881) the agencies returned to being patronage appointments rather than denominational ones. A new group of reformers arose to pursue the vision of "Americanizing" the Indians as well as to serve as watchdogs in protecting tribes from mistreatment. The Women's National Indian Association, organized in 1883 under the leadership of Amelia S. Quinton, attempted to protect Indian treaty rights; lacking the vote, the women organized petition drives to send to the president. The most influential new group, begun by Herbert Welsh in 1882, was the Indian Rights Association, which became the leading force in Indian reform policy during the 1880s. Reformers from a variety of groups met annually at conferences at Lake Mohonk, New York, during the 1880s and 1890s, and members of the Board of Indian Commissioners also attended. These reformers had self-professed Christian motivations and belonged to various Protestant denominations. Usually one-fourth of the conference participants were clergymen or denominational representatives and their wives. The Dawes Act (General Allotment Act) of 1887 reflected the vision of these reformers and provided the means to implement it. The act gave the president the power to divide the tribal lands into individual plats, or allotments, that were to be assigned to individual tribal members. The purpose behind it was to weaken tribalism and to strengthen economic individualism, which in turn was presumed to help in making the individual Indian become virtuous and self-supporting.

While their vision was a peaceful one of Indians merging into American society as Christians and as successful individuals and while they opposed the military's and the westerner's violence and lack of sympathy toward Indians, the Protestant reformer's policy was nonetheless a repressive one. For it to succeed, Indian culture had to be repressed, and the agencies and schools were often quite ruthless in their contempt for and suppression of Indian beliefs, norms, values, and practices. One such model federal school, whose avowed purpose was to detribalize and Americanize its students (who came from a variety of tribes), was the Carlisle Indian Industrial School in Carlisle, Pennsylvania.

The reformers were also paternalist; they respected the abstract and romantic idea of the Indian as a noble savage, but Indians as real people were to be transformed, whether they wished to be or not, into property-holding Americans who adhered to a middle-class Protestant ethos. That they were to become Protestant bourgeoisie was evident in the decade-long fight the reformers waged to drive the Catholic mission schools, which constituted the majority of Indian schools, off the reservations. This effort culminated under the leadership of Thomas Jefferson Morgan, an ordained Baptist and a vociferous anti-Catholic, who served as a commissioner of Indian affairs from 1889 to 1893, and of Daniel Dorchester, an ordained Methodist, who was the superintendent of Indian schools during the same years. This anti-Catholic endeavor was never wholly successful, since Congress refused to provide the necessary adequate funding to replace the needed Catholic mission schools, and because the Bureau of Catholic Indian Missions, established in 1874, fought such attempts. In the early 1900s the Supreme Court case of *Quick Bear* v. *Leupp* resulted in a resounding defeat for the Indian Rights Association, which had brought the suit; the Court upheld the right of tribes to use treaty and trust funds to support Catholic mission schools. Following this success, the Bureau of Catholic Indian Missions campaigned, with some success, to protect the religious rights of Catholic Indians in government-run schools by having overtly Protestant materials removed from them.

The net effect of the reformers was not the happy merger of Indians into American society, as they had envisioned. Instead, cultural demoralization and intergenerational conflict within tribes resulted, as did a tremendous loss of Indian land. As a result of the individual allotment provisions of the Dawes Act of 1887 and subsequent acts concerning rights of transfer, Indian land holdings fell from 138 million acres in 1887 to 48 million by 1934.

The temperance movement similarly contained an image of a millennial future that helped to justify the need for repression in the present. Temperance, supported by the majority of evangelicals, was a much broader movement than Indian reform, and the movement's rhetoric carried a weighty symbolic content. Temperance coincided with the women's movement and was easily perceived as a pro-family and pro-women's advance. But the temperance rhetoric, particularly as it was spouted by revivalists such as Billy Sunday and spread by the Anti-Saloon League (which directed the successful political drive for national prohibition), also contained an anti-urban, anti-immigrant, and antipluralist symbolism. As Paul Boyer put it, "terms like 'the saloon' and 'the brothel' became, at times, simply code words for the larger menace of urban social change."

By 1900 cities such as Chicago were more than three-fourths immigrant stock, and Protestant missions for immigrants did not succeed in attracting and converting them. If they would not become Protestant evangelicals, possibly they could be made to participate at least outwardly in the impulse-renouncing behavior that the evangelical view of sin emphasized. So charity organization societies, "industrial" schools, club work with children, closely supervised playgrounds, and mission-oriented Sunday schools all attempted to induce self-disciplined and self-restraining behavior among the immigrants and their children.

While immigration, with its influx of Catholics, Jews, Eastern Orthodox, socialists, and freethinkers, was deeply disturbing to the very possibility of the evangelical postmillennial vision, the size, diversity, and potential for anonymity of the new giant metropolises threatened the evangelical's ability to believe that any cultural norms (and therefore social order) existed. Focusing upon sexual license and drinking, rhetorical campaigns were launched not only against saloons and brothels, but also against movies, dance halls, vaudeville shows, theaters, magazine stands and billboards, excursion boats, ice cream parlors, amusement parks, and even public parks—anything that could excite the mind or provide a modicum of privacy for couples. If behavior could no longer be regulated by small-town watchfulness and a shared evangelical ethos, then public regulation designed to put controls on individual behavior became necessary. Thus, although the final image of a liquorless society of self-disciplined individuals might have been a beneficent vision in the minds of temperance reformers, the process of getting there involved images and actions that were repressive in both intent and content. That Prohibition was felt and experienced as repression rather than as a reform is indicated by its being violated in wholesale fashion and its failure to become an established norm in the 1920s.

The peace movement, a reform movement that did not contain an element of repression, rose up in spectacular fashion prior to World War I. Several small pacifist peace societies survived the Civil War or were formed shortly thereafter. The American Peace Society (APS), formed prior to the war, was dominated by Boston moral reformers. Two Quaker peace organizations were the Universal Peace Union (UPU), which was a reflection of its leader, Alfred Love, a Quaker, and the Peace Association of Friends in North America. Except for their work for the Indian "peace policy," these groups had little influence in the postwar era, and they remained small and poorly financed. The members felt encouraged, however, by efforts being made in Europe to make war more "civilized" by developing rules of war and by the creation of a special role for the Red Cross.

Foreign trade expansion, growth of foreign missions, war with Spain, and becoming an empire all contributed to America's sense of being a world power, with its welfare inextricably linked to world events. Given America's tradition of noninvolvement in European diplomacy, its ability to affect the course of great power events was minimal. Americans increasingly sought a means to preserve a stable world order that did not require active diplomatic engagement or alignment with other great powers. The search for the proper mechanisms to preserve a social or political system, a common part of the Progressive ethos, led international-minded Americans to push for an arbitration system and a world court to settle conflicts between nations. Thus a second type of peace society, not composed of pacifists or moral reformers, arose. In 1882 the National Arbitration League was founded, and in 1886 a Philadelphia Baptist, Russell Conway, formed the Christian Arbitration and Peace Society. A Universal Peace Congress held in Paris in 1889 was attended by APS, UPU, and WCTU delegates and made Americans more aware of the existence of a peace movement. The UPU began in 1893 to hold annual summer conferences at Mystic, Connecticut, and the APS, led by Quaker educator Benjamin Trueblood, followed suit in 1895 with annual summer conferences at Lake Mohonk, New York. A National Arbitration Conference in 1896 (from which women were excluded) agreed to seek an international arbitration system and a world court, with the first step being to seek an Anglo-American arbitration treaty.

The Anti-Imperialist League, which arose in response to the United States–Filipino War (1899 to 1902) had little long-range effect on the peace movement, although it did heighten awareness of the potential costs of foreign involvement. More significant to American peace reformers at the time was the First Hague Conference (1899), which established certain rules of war and an International Court of Justice.

These events at the end of the nineteenth century created a foundation of concern from which to build, and between 1901 and 1914 forty-five new peace organizations were formed. The most salient features of this new Progressive-era peace movement were its dominance by the economic and political elite and its nonpacifist character. Presidents William Howard Taft and Woodrow Wilson and secretaries of state Elihu Root, Robert Bacon, William Jennings Bryan, and Robert Lansing were all members of peace societies. The National Arbitration and Peace Congress in New York in 1907, which was attended by 40,000 people, was organized by Andrew Carnegie, who was president of the New York Peace Society, and partially financed by John D. Rockefeller. A number of the nation's leading lawyers were members of the American Society for International Law or the International Law Association. The Church Peace Union, which aimed at involving churches, was provided $2 million by Carnegie. Several foundations designed to study the causes of war were also established by wealthy industrialists.

The elite leadership, the goals of arbitration

mechanisms, and the nonpacifistic character of the members (a number of whom lobbied for a larger navy as members of the Navy League) point to the conservative nature of the movement. Its basic goal was to try to preserve the world essentially as it was, and American elites had come to fear the potential for war that they saw embodied in Europe's militaristic nationalism. Consequently, when war came, nearly all the members (Bryan was a significant exception) of these newer peace societies fully supported America's preparedness campaign and entry into World War I.

The war itself, however, led to a new type of leftist peace organization, one that insisted social reform was necessary to establish a peaceful world. The American Union Against Militarism, founded in 1916 at Henry Street Settlement, represented this new strain of thought. After World War I, Jane Addams and the Women's International League for Peace and Freedom, the Fellowship of Reconciliation and its affiliate, the Fellowship for a Christian Social Order, supported by A. J. Muste and Norman Thomas, the American Friends Service Committee, and the War Resisters' League all embodied this new approach. They were activist pacifists, and in the 1920s they faced a hostile cultural environment. With the exception of the Quaker organization, they felt little support from churches, and both Muste and Thomas left their pulpits to pursue social reform (Muste had been a clergyman in the Reformed, Congregationalist, and Friends churches; and Thomas had been a Presbyterian minister). The war had unleashed a militaristic and xenophobic nationalism that found an institutional base in the American Legion. The vast majority of American evangelicals held views closer to those of the American Legion than to those of Jane Addams.

The perspective of nonpacifist internationalists also continued throughout the 1920s, and they continuously pressured, with some success, for greater cooperation with the League of Nations. The Foreign Policy Association and the League of Nations Non-Partisan Association represented this point of view.

The Social Gospel movement represented the reforming wing of American Protestantism, and their perspective was a minority one. The capability for churches to be reconciling agencies, however, is demonstrated by every major Protestant denomination having established an institutional home for the Social Gospel, usually in a department of labor, and in the Social Gospel's having its own institution, the Federal Council of Churches. The conservatism of the churches, though, helped to ensure that reform efforts would be undertaken primarily by autonomous and secular agencies. Although the agencies were secular, the reformers were often motivated by a personal Christian vision; this was certainly true, for example, of Jane Addams, Mary McDowell, and Norman Thomas, and of many score more like them.

No simple conclusion can be drawn from such a complex era, but several trends are worth noting. During the years from 1865 to 1930, America changed from a rural to a predominantly urban nation, from an economy of independent small-scale producers to an industrial and oligarchic economy, and from a citizenry of mostly northern European origins (neither blacks nor Indians were citizens in 1865) to a citizenry with a great variety of origins. Massive changes such as these require similarly massive adjustments; the need for reform in this country has perhaps never been greater than during the half-century from 1880 to 1930.

The role of religion in the process of reform is also complex. All major religions put forth some version of a more perfect and just society that provides a vision which motivates some individuals to try to bring their own society into closer harmony with the religious ideal. At the same time, religion as a part of a people's culture also apologizes for the way that culture operates; theological rationales are developed to justify things as they are and also to warn of the dangers of changing the people's ways. Both these phenomena—religiously based calls for change and religiously based defenses of the status quo—occurred with great intensity.

America is a nation made up of many cultures; in 1865 the culture was quite clearly dominated by white males of a northern European and Protestant heritage. This culturally dominant sector felt threatened by a number of the changes occurring around them, as well as by many of the calls for reform. Thus it is no surprise that the major white Protestant denominations became bastions of conservatism during this period. At the same time, however, that same Protestant heritage imbued numerous reformers with the

vision of a better and a more just society. And, in general, the persistence and dedication of the reformers did eventually lead to changes in numerous areas, such as women's rights, laboring conditions, urban living conditions, public health, and so on, even while other areas in need of reform, such as racism and Indian tribal rights, worsened. (Whether the specific changes are considered worthy or not depends upon one's own particular outlook, of course.) Thus, the record is, as is usual in human endeavors, a mixed one.

Perhaps the clearest visible trend during this period was the change that occurred in the discourse concerning public policy. In 1865 the language of public policy was religious in tone, even if not always explicitly theological; the Gettysburg Address can serve as an example familiar to most. This rhetoric assumed the acceptance of a common set of religious beliefs. By 1930 the rhetoric of public policy was much less clearly religious, for a number of reasons. One reason was the tremendous growth of the non-Protestant population. In trying to put together coalitions of reformers, and election victories, it became more important to speak in a language that could appeal to Catholics, Jews, and the nonreligious as those portions of the population grew. A second reason is that scientific language gained immense prestige during this period, in part because of the increases in both scientific knowledge and technological achievement. In America these advances became securely linked to the concept of progress in history, and the pursuit of such knowledge came to be housed in a new prestigious institution, the modern university.

As knowledge came to be more specialized and more technical, the informed could more easily prevail in arguments with the uninformed. Professionals gained power, in the form of knowledge and the credentialing of such knowledge, against the lay person. So, given a society that was growing more pluralistic, that respected scientific knowledge, and that gave status to professionals, yet one in which the largest religious grouping—evangelical Protestantism as a whole—was most resistant to change, it is not surprising that reformers changed from a clearly theological rhetoric to a utilitarian and pragmatic rhetoric during these years. It is significant, as a sign of this change, that so many reformers whose original motivation was religious felt obliged to leave the pulpit in order to pursue their reform visions; examples include Anna Howard Shaw, Will Alexander, Charles Henderson, Albion Small, Graham Taylor, Norman Thomas, and A. J. Muste. In short, reform and for that matter public policy in general, although still often informed by religious considerations, nonetheless became secularized during this era.

BIBLIOGRAPHY

Aaron I. Abell, *American Catholicism and Social Action: A Search for Social Justice, 1865–1950* (1960); Sydney Ahlstrom, *A Religious History of the American People* (1972); Ruth Bodin, *Woman and Temperance: The Quest for Power and Liberty, 1873–1900* (1981); James Borchert, *Alley Life in Washington: Family, Community, Religion, and Folklife in the City, 1850–1970* (1980); Paul Boyer, *Urban Masses and Moral Order in America, 1820–1920* (1978); Robert H. Bremner, *The Public Good: Philanthropy and Welfare in the Civil War Era* (1980); Clarke A. Chambers, *Seedtime of Reform: American Social Service and Social Action, 1918–1933* (1963); Norman H. Clark, *Deliver Us From Evil: An Interpretation of American Prohibition* (1976); Merle Curti, *Peace or War: The American Struggle, 1636–1936* (1959); Charles DeBenedetti, *The Peace Reform in American History* (1980).

John Tracy Ellis, *American Catholicism* (1956); Barbara L. Epstein, *The Politics of Domesticity: Women, Evangelism, and Temperance in Nineteenth-Century America* (1981); E. Franklin Frazier, *The Negro Church in America* (1964); Nathan Glazer, *American Judaism* (1957); Stephen Gottschalk, *The Emergence of Christian Science in American Religious Life* (1974); Jacquelyn Dowd Hall, *Revolt Against Chivalry: Jessie Daniel Ames and the Women's Campaign Against Lynching* (1979); Robert T. Handy, *A Christian America: Protestant Hopes and Historical Realities* (1971); Thomas Haskell, *The Emergence of Professional Social Science: The American Social Science Association and the Nineteenth Century Crisis of Authority* (1977); John Higham, *Strangers in the Land: Patterns of American Nativism, 1860–1925* (1963; rev. 1965); C. Howard Hopkins, *History of the YMCA in North America* (1951); Irving Howe, *World of Our Fathers: The Journey of the East European Jews to America and The Life They Found and Made* (1976).

Janet Wilson James, ed., *Women in American Religion* (1980); Abraham J. Karp, ed., *The Jewish Experience in America*, vol. IV: *The Era of Immigration* (1969); Leon Litwack, *Been in the Storm So Long: The Aftermath of Slavery* (1979); David I. Macleod, *Building Character in the American Boy: The Boy Scouts, YMCA, and Their Forerunners, 1870–1920* (1983); Norris Magnusson, *Salvation in the Slums: Evangelical Social Work, 1865–1920* (1977); C. Roland Marchand, *The American Peace Movement and Social Reform, 1898–1918* (1972); Robert Winston Mardock, *The Reformers and the American Indian* (1971); George M. Marsden, *Fundamentalism and American Culture: The Shaping of Twentieth-Century Evangelicalism, 1870–1925* (1980); Martin E. Marty, *Righteous Empire: The Protestant Experience in America* (1970); Henry F. May, *Protestant Churches and Industrial America* (1949, 1967).

David J. O'Brien, *American Catholics and Social Reform: The New Deal Years* (1968); David S. Patterson, *Toward a Warless World: The Travail of the American Peace Movement, 1887–1914* (1976); Francis Paul Prucha, *American Indian Policy in Crisis: Christian Reformers and the Indian, 1865–1900* (1976) and *The Churches and the Indian Schools, 1888–1912* (1979); Moses Rischin, *The Promised City: New York's Jews, 1870–1914* (1962); Ruth Rosen, *The Lost Sisterhood: Prostitution in America, 1900–1918* (1982); Seth M. Scheiner, *Negro Mecca: A History of the Negro in New York City, 1865–1920* (1965); Anne Firor Scott, *The Southern Lady: From Pedestal to Politics, 1830–1930* (1970); Herbert A. Wisbey, Jr., *Soldiers Without Swords: A History of the Salvation Army in the United States* (1955); Robert L. Zangrando, *The NAACP Crusade Against Lynching, 1909–1950* (1980).

[*See also* REVIVALISM; SOCIAL CHRISTIANITY; SOCIAL REFORM FROM THE COLONIAL PERIOD THROUGH THE CIVIL WAR; SOCIAL REFORM SINCE THE GREAT DEPRESSION; *and* WAR AND PEACE.]

SOCIAL REFORM SINCE
THE GREAT DEPRESSION

Glenn R. Bucher and L. Gordon Tait

RELIGION and social reform from the Great Depression to the reelection of President Ronald Reagan in 1984 must be viewed against the backdrop of Social Gospel Christianity, a movement between the Civil War and World War I that brought Christian principles to bear on social conditions. An evangelical response to urbanization, industrialization, and Progressivism, the movement lost its momentum in the 1920s because of the war itself, the economic situation, and convictions that the Christianizing of America was reaching completion. Whether completed or defeated, the Social Gospel created an ethos and established a legacy that outlived the movement.

In the 1920s Protestantism, at least as it was practiced in the great liberal churches, was identified closely with mainstream culture. This acculturation produced a complacency. Although there were still causes to promote, there was a loss of the sense of the whole. The country was changing and only a few Protestants knew it. Historian Robert T. Handy notes that "the belief that American civilization was basically Christian and was progressively moving toward the kingdom was becoming more and more divorced from reality. . . ." During the Depression there was no general revival of religion, even though one could spot signs of vitality in parts of the South, in cults and sects, and in shifting theological patterns.

Certainly by the mid-1930s Protestant attempts to impose a vision of a Christian America were in decline. Although Protestantism remained an influence for good, the Social Gospel vision that once inspired large-scale social reform had surely faded, if not disappeared. Those who took up the process of reform in light of religious principles in the years 1929 to 1984 did so while pursuing a variety of visions of a better America and in a society shaped by pluralism, war, and economic growth.

Social reforms were of less concern to religious groups as the stock market crashed in 1929 and economic hardship ensued. Churches and synagogues struggled to pay the bills and keep their doors open; individuals fought to make a living. The Fundamentalist-Modernist controversy of the 1920s between liberals and conservatives over ecclesiastical control, critical scholarship, and church doctrine had a lingering impact upon Protestant churches. One particular social issue, Prohibition, held the attention of the entire nation for nearly two decades. The Eighteenth Amendment to the Constitution, outlawing the manufacture, sale, or transportation of intoxicating beverages, was ratified in 1919 and rendered the United States legally "dry" until 1933, when the amendment was repealed.

Enforcement had been difficult during the 1920s, and sentiment for repeal had grown stronger, despite a vigorous Protestant defense. Even after 1933 there was continued support for outlawing "liquor traffic" in the name of pure religion and the nation's morals. The prohibitionists, who combined religious and social reform impulses, sought to impose one aspect of their religious culture upon America through the legislative process. Not until the 1960s, and again in the 1980s during the civil rights struggle and in discussions of an abortion amendment and school prayer legislation, did religious groups take a similar approach to influence social change or mobilize legislative reform.

THE ECONOMIC ORDER

Economic reform from the perspective of mainline religious groups expressed itself primarily in support for organized labor and concern for the social responsibility of corporations and resulted in a body of commonly held mainstream Protestant teaching on ethics and the economy.

During the steel strike of 1919, representatives of churches influenced public opinion by supporting the right of workers to organize in independent unions, a right later guaranteed by the Wagner Act of 1935. Church support for collective bargaining and the union movement was established in a 1932 publication of the Federal Council of Churches, "The Social Ideals of the Churches." Socialism, although never a dominant tradition in either American religious or economic thought, had the support of such major Western religious thinkers as Walter Rauschenbusch, Reinhold Niebuhr, Paul Tillich, Emil Brunner, and Karl Barth. Among minority groups in the churches influenced by socialist class analysis, like the Fellowship of Socialist Christians, it was not uncommon for Roosevelt's New Deal to be perceived as a facade for corrupt capitalism.

The economic order received ecumenical attention at the Amsterdam (1948), Evanston (1954), and Nairobi (1975) meetings of the World Council of Churches, a body formed in 1948. By the late 1960s the council was composed of more than 230 Protestant, Anglican, Old Catholic, and Orthodox churches in 90 countries and representing 400 million members. In sessions that were often chaired by religious leaders from the United States, discussions of the economic order focused on the limitations of both communism and capitalism as economic systems and on the moral responsibility of transnational corporations. That official Roman Catholicism never fully accepted the assumptions of capitalism, given its international orientation, was illustrated by *Rerum Novarum* (1891), *Quadragesimo Anno* (1931), *Populorum Progressio* (1967), and *Laborem Exercens* (1981), papal encyclicals of Pius XI, Paul VI, and John Paul II, and by the Latin American conferences at Medellín (1968) and Puebla (1979), which reflected the economic concerns of liberation theologians.

As early as 1920 the Federal Council of Churches (a confederation of Protestant denominations and a precursor of the National Council of Churches) established an Industrial Division and later a Department on the Church and Economic Life (1947) to discuss issues that divided economists, labor representatives, management, and church leaders. By 1950 the National Council of Churches (NCC) had been formed by a merger of eleven interdenominational agencies representing more than thirty Protestant and Orthodox denominations. By the late 1960s the NCC had over 40 million members. From the late 1940s through the mid-1950s these councils sponsored a series of study groups on economic ethics. Theologians, social scientists, and economists deliberated the topic of economic justice, usually assuming that poverty could be eliminated by continued growth. Later this assumption became suspect in light of a growing recognition of the limits to growth and the need to talk of resource redistribution.

In 1974 the Interfaith Center on Corporate Responsibility (ICCR) was established through the National Council of Churches. Responsible to a board composed of Protestant and Catholic representatives, the ICCR supplied information and recommended policy and action on corporate responsibility issues. Prior to the creation of the ICCR several denominations under the aegis of a freedom and integration organization known as FIGHT had brought pressure on Eastman-Kodak in connection with the company's racial policies. After 1967 churches engaged in a range of economic and corporate reform activities. During the Vietnam War the Church of the Brethren sold its stock in a number of corporations that manufactured war material. In 1971 agencies of six denominations brought action against American Metal Climax and Kennecott Copper in connection with environmental issues in Puerto Rico. Throughout the 1970s church protests were directed against Gulf Oil, Gulf and Western Industries, and Royal Dutch Shell over such issues as the breaking of oil sanctions, the full disclosure of ventures in the Third World, and the exploitation of colonial peoples.

South Africa also attracted attention from religious bodies. Opposition to such policy issues as apartheid first surfaced in 1966, primarily from students at Union Theological Seminary in New York, who protested New York banks' loans to the South African government. Subsequently, the United Methodist Board of Missions withdrew $10 million from the National City Bank; the Episcopal Church called on General Motors to cease manufacturing in South Africa; and the

Mobil Oil Corporation and the United Church of Christ reached an agreement on what information would be supplied stockholders. In the mid-1970s a loose coalition of ten American religious organizations holding stock valued at $700 million challenged twenty-two corporations doing business in South Africa, and many denominations called for more aggressive monitoring of corporate activity. During the 1970s the World Council of Churches, the National Council of Churches, and coalitions of churches in Scotland and the Netherlands sold or modified their stock holdings in companies doing business in South Africa.

In *Social Responsibility and Investments* (1971) Charles Powers, a Yale University–trained ethicist, asserts that there was no general agreement about the desirability of disinvesting, although religious groups most frequently insisted on that option. More often it was thought better policy to keep the stock and use the role of stockholder to bring pressure on the corporation to improve the position of black South Africans. The debate involved two different policies—the concern to be pure and the concern to be effective.

Protestant ecumenical thinking on economic life was a source of dispute in the 1980s. Many continued to ask what effect free market economies really had had on people and what the economy could do for the millions of Americans, mostly women, children, and minorities, who were living in poverty. On the other hand, there were those, represented by Michael Novak in his *Spirit of Democratic Capitalism* (1982), who defended the moral self-sufficiency of the market economy and the logic of its economic development. For them, economic productivity as well as political and cultural freedom were at stake. Late in 1984 the National Conference of Catholic Bishops introduced a new element into this debate with its "Pastoral Letter on Social Teachings and the American Economy," which addressed the marginalization of the poor, the feminization of poverty, and the government's responsibility to exercise its influence on behalf of economic justice.

THE POLITICAL ORDER

The Social Gospel movement before 1920 sought to redirect American life by applying Christian ethical principles to social conditions. The 1930s brought a challenge to liberal assumptions about human nature, the moral composition of society, and the process of social reform. In 1932, the year of Franklin Delano Roosevelt's election, Reinhold Niebuhr's *Moral Man and Immoral Society* appeared. The book, an unexpected critique of Progressivism, called for reconceptualizing the role of religion in social reform, a call that dominated the next thirty years of American religious and intellectual life.

Niebuhr, a Detroit inner-city pastor who joined the Union Theological Seminary faculty in 1928, was a product of liberal culture and was greatly influenced by his debates with Henry Ford and by his respect for British socialism. Niebuhr's thesis was that an ethical distinction must be made between individuals and groups (nations, races, classes) if one is to understand the nature of social change. In the pursuit of an ethical society the realistic Christian reformer will take self-interest, power, and violence seriously, said Niebuhr, and not seek to apply individualistic ethics to social problems.

He ran for Congress on the Socialist party ticket, founded Americans for Democratic Action, was instrumental in the formation of the World Council of Churches, and served on the Policy Planning Staff of the State Department. In 1941 he founded *Christianity and Crisis,* a popular bi-weekly journal of religious opinion. And in the 1960s he criticized conservative American views of communism, the Vietnam War, and nuclear deterrence, views sometimes adopted by some of his followers.

Niebuhr formulated a perspective on religion and social reform known as Christian realism in books such as *The Nature and Destiny of Man* (1941), *The Children of Light and The Children of Darkness* (1944), and *Man's Nature and His Communities* (1965). In the decade before 1950 Christian realism was an effective religio-political movement that provided a religious presence in American life, influenced a postwar political framework, and shaped the thinking of ecclesiastical and political bureaucracies. Felix Frankfurter, Walter Reuther, Adlai Stevenson, and Hubert Humphrey were among those who claimed the realist label.

In Charles W. Kegley's compendium *Reinhold Niebuhr: His Religious, Social and Political Thought,* historian Arthur Schlesinger, Jr., said that Niebuhr's reformulation of the Christian theory of man and history helped a distraught generation, many of whom were cultured despisers of religion, cope with the tragedies of the twentieth century. This theological perspective had an impact on mainline Protestant thinking about God, history, and the self, as it ushered in a postliberal era in American churches. Books such as Walter M. Horton's *Realistic Theology* (1934), Edwin Lewis' *Christian Manifesto* (1934), and George W. Richards' *Beyond Fundamentalism and Modernism* (1934) illustrated this change in mood. John C. Bennett, one of Niebuhr's closest colleagues, characterized the basic tenets of realism by pointing out that history has its tragic dimensions and human beings their finitude and sin, that individuals, however, have a capacity for fair-mindedness and selflessness which nations do not, and that political and social power offer temptations and responsibilities.

From the realist perspective, good religion includes mystery, ethics, and humility, and social reform consists of choosing between lesser evils in the pursuit of justice and equality, which are essentially love in action. Politics is the practical art of relating the human hopes for community to the real communities in which we live and of doing so in a way that reminds us of the human capacities for creativity and pride.

As a religious perspective on social reform, Christian realism corrected the naiveté of Protestant political philosophy, theories of international politics, and American foreign policy. It was the vehicle whereby European Neo-Orthodox theology was adapted to the American situation and made pertinent to social and political events. More important than the specific reforms it spurred was that realism provided an ethical perspective wherein the relevance of religion was understood. This relevance led some of Niebuhr's followers in the postwar years to an uncritical defense of democracy, whereas others who moved left received negative attention from Senator Joseph McCarthy.

After the mid-1960s, when Niebuhr's professional activity ceased, political conservatives and liberals debated the relevance of this ethic. On the one hand, Michael Novak, Princeton ethicist Paul Ramsey, and political philosopher Kenneth Thompson argued that realism necessitated the defense of traditional democratic values irrespective of the gap between those values and their implementation. On the other hand, John Bennett and Roger Shinn insisted that the tendencies of realism to become *Realpolitik* must be resisted, because realism is always a corrective ethic. This debate extended into the 1970s and 1980s and beyond the Niebuhrian circle, particularly in disagreements between neo-conservatives and traditional liberals over the role of the United States in international affairs.

RACE AND THE SOCIAL ORDER

In *The Souls of Black Folk* (1903) W. E. B. Du Bois stated that the problem of the twentieth century is the problem of the color line. In 1909 he helped found the National Association for the Advancement of Colored People, and in a *Christian Century* article in 1931 he said that the record of the church on race is an indictment of God. That criticism was a reminder that religion is a social phenomenon and that religious groups are voluntary social institutions. Religion's record on racial justice issues was no better or worse than that of American society's as a whole.

During and after World War I the dominant social patterns of racial segregation were generally accepted by the members of dominant religious groups. Those few who supported equal though separate facilities, the liberal view of the time, worked either through the efforts of the Young Men's Christian Association (YMCA), the Young Women's Christian Association (YWCA), or on secular interracial committees. The Federal Council of Churches established its Department of Race Relations after the war, and between then and the end of World War II that department advocated "a non-segregated church in a non-segregated society." This development was nurtured by extra-religious factors such as the publication of Stockholm University social economist Gunnar Myrdal's *An American Dilemma* (1944), commissioned by the Carnegie Corporation to study race relations in American society, President Harry S. Truman's establishment of the Commission on Civil Rights, and the inroads on racial segregation made in the military during his presidency.

In 1959 Yale University professor Liston Pope claimed that the church remained the most segregated institution in society, lagging behind most social institutions (for example, the Supreme Court, industry, and sports). The impetus that might have led to some change in that recalcitrance during the 1960s had occurred before Pope's assessment. On 18 May 1954, with the *Brown* v. *Board of Education* decision, the Supreme Court made school segregation illegal. Recognizing the limitations of the states' rights view in matters of civil rights, the Court declared that school discrimination was an abrogation of basic civil rights. From this landmark decision until the passage of the first Civil Rights Act in June 1964, racial protests and demonstrations increased, as did the participation in them of individuals and groups associated with religion. The Montgomery, Alabama, bus boycott in December 1955 drew attention to discrimination in public transportation and to a young black preacher, Martin Luther King, Jr., who two years later became the first president of the Southern Christian Leadership Conference.

In the late 1950s and early 1960s protest demonstrations in the South increased, the most notable of which occurred in Birmingham, Alabama, in the spring of 1963, during which King was jailed. There he wrote his famous "Letter from a Birmingham Jail," which led to the 1963 summer march on Washington, D.C., in which an estimated 40,000 white church members participated. The letter also precipitated the bombing of the Sixteenth Street Baptist Church in Birmingham, in which four young girls were killed.

In June 1964 the National Council of Churches established the Commission on Religion and Race; numerous member denominations followed by forming similar commissions. The Roman Catholic church followed the general trend by urging the desegregation of parishes and dioceses. This was the first time a direct action agency had been commissioned to provide leadership in the public sphere of racial conflict. The involvement of representatives and members of religious groups, such as William Sloane Coffin, Robert Spike, and Episcopal bishop Paul Moore, in the March on Washington, the passage of the 1964 Civil Rights Act, and the Selma, Alabama, March in 1965 was significant. In fact, not since Reconstruction and Prohibition had religious groups effectively involved themselves in social causes to this degree.

But 1965 was also the year of the Watts riots in California (an indication of racial protest moving west and north), increased talk about black power through spokesmen like H. Rap Brown and Stokely Carmichael (now Kwame Ture), and the repudiation of integration by some members of the black community—all illustrations of the growing discontent with gradualism. Add to this the assassination of King in 1968, the increasing influence of Malcolm X and the Black Muslims and Black Nationalists, the development of the Freedom Now Party and its visibility at the Democratic National Convention in July of 1968, James Forman's Black Manifesto of 1969 demanding $500 million in reparations from the white church for black injustice, and the focus of racial issues began to change. So did the activity of the Ku Klux Klan and White Citizens' Councils, organizations that claimed a share of the membership of religious groups. Racial polarization was apparent in society and churches.

Observers of the black church debated about its social role in the racial struggle. Was black religion assimilationist, compensatory, or communitarian? What they agreed upon was the close connection between black religion and social protest, believing that black religion provided a channel through which feelings about social injustice could be voiced and protest expressed in a systematic way. In the late 1960s black church ideology was reassessed, churches that did not support the black revolution were boycotted, and the issues of social justice and pride of race joined the moral, pietistic, and orthodox messages of many black churches.

In the late 1960s radical elements of the black church advocated an approach to racial equality and/or separatism and the criticism of white racism through black theology. This form of liberation theology, associated with James Cone, J. Deotis Roberts, Gayraud Wilmore, Albert Cleage, and others, was characterized by biblical interpretation wherein the exodus event is paradigmatic for the black racial struggle, by theology that focused on social justice and hope, and by an ethic that included activism, confrontation, and sometimes violence and revolution.

From the traditional black church, from black caucuses in white denominations, and from ad hoc groups of black church people came a series of statements on black theology. The National Committee of Black Churchmen, the National Conference of the Black Theology Project, and the Philadelphia Council of Black Clergy, all coalitions of black ministers, were among those groups advocating black theology. In the 1970s and 1980s the social and economic concerns of the black church often found expression in political activity, as was evident in the 1984 presidential campaign of the Reverend Jesse Jackson.

WAR AND PEACE

In his important survey *Christian Attitudes Toward War and Peace* (1960) Roland H. Bainton identifies three positions with respect to military conflict in the church's history: pacifism, the just war, and the crusade. These positions were still apparent in the twentieth century in secular and religious circles, and among Catholics, Protestants, and Jews, although there was no agreement on the application of these terms to any conflict by members of these groups. Despite the fact that the potential for nuclear war complicated ethical choices, religiously inspired social reform on war and peace still arranged itself around familiar alternatives.

During the 1920s, particularly in American churches, there were strong commitments to peace and a warless society, given the guilt engendered by the militarism of World War I and its mixed results. Pacifists like Sherwood Eddy and Kirby Page were regarded as prophetic voices. Consequently, church people were split over the entrance of the United States into the League of Nations, while there was considerable support for the Kellogg-Briand Pact (1928), which pledged that international war would be outlawed.

The attitude of America's mainline religious groups toward the issues of war and peace between 1936 and 1941 reflected attitudes prevalent during World War I and foreshadowed the Vietnam era. By 1936 Japan had occupied Manchuria; Mussolini and Hitler were in power; and Spain was rent by civil war. Pacifism was still a clear alternative because, as some argued, war was beneath civilized nations and the United States could ignore aggression in Europe. But the attack on Pearl Harbor soon split the churches on the issue of collective security as opposed to nonintervention. In *American Protestantism and Social Issues* (1958) Robert M. Miller describes this confusion over war and peace as "more starkly extreme in the Protestant

churches than in American society as a whole— and this is a damning comparison."

This split was widened by the first publication of *Christianity and Crisis* on 7 February 1941. Its editor, Reinhold Niebuhr, wrote that "those who exist like parasites on the liberties which others fight to secure for them will end by betraying the Christian ethic and the civilization which has developed out of that ethic." He had in mind primarily the editors and readers of *The Christian Century* and other liberal Protestants who viewed the war from a neo-isolationist perspective, and not just those affiliated with the historic peace churches (Church of the Brethren, Mennonites, and Quakers).

In retrospect, this realist argument, though it did not appeal to the just war theorists, revealed the impact that the Roman Catholic just war tradition had had on American religious thinking. As an ever-recurring "ideal" in Christian thought dating back to St. Augustine, the just-war view held that under the auspices of a legitimate state, a war designed to vindicate justice, and therefore to restore peace, could be fought if it did not violate ethical means. Although at the 1937 Oxford Conference, a precursor to the first World Council of Churches conference in 1948, war was condemned as "a particular demonstration of the power of sin," by 1941 European and American Christians were supporting the need for it. In the postwar years the deterrence strategies of the United States and the Soviet Union, the Korean War, and the concerns about the spread of communism all became controversial issues for American Christians.

Beginning in the mid-1960s religious groups were well represented in the protests directed at U.S. policy in Vietnam. Much of this activity was coordinated by Clergy and Laity Concerned about Vietnam, an interfaith group seeking to bring together the Catholic, Protestant, and Jewish communities to effect a change of policy. In 1966 alone, formal statements criticizing the United States were issued by the Synagogue Council of America, the Central Committee of the World Council of Churches, and the Roman Catholic Bishops. Early in 1967, Clergy and Laity convened a group of 2,400 clergy, seminarians, nuns, and laypeople in Washington, D.C., to urge that the war be ended and that senators and representatives press for a negotiated peace.

Though many of these persons were not just-war advocates, they used that position to argue that even on just-war criteria, Vietnam was immoral. Others, like Roman Catholic priests Daniel and Philip Berrigan and lawyer and ethicist William Stringfellow, expressed their criticism in social protests and civil disobedience, which led to confrontations with the FBI and subsequent jail terms.

In the 1960s Evangelicals in the United States were less inclined than mainline Protestants toward political participation, and in the 1980s they were more inclined. In the closing days of the 1980 presidential campaign between Jimmy Carter and Ronald Reagan, leaders of the mainline denominations signed a theological statement criticizing conservative evangelical groups for their support of Reagan. After the election, opposition to the strengthening of national defense came from these same leaders. But among evangelicals and the majority of those affiliated with mainline religion, the values of family, neighborhood, work, peace, and freedom as expressed in the Reagan administration were equated with the Protestant ethic. These values translated into wide public support for a strengthened military and a hardline policy toward the Soviet Union.

The Vietnam War and the debate over nuclear war converged in the 1980s to prompt action on the part of some mainline religious groups, among them the United Presbyterian Church (now the Presbyterian Church, U.S.A.). In 1975 the church commissioned an advisory council to reassess the concept of peacemaking. In a 1980 paper entitled "Peacemaking: The Believers' Calling," the council advocated that the church undertake a special emphasis on peacemaking for the 1980s, including elements of worship, study, consciousness-raising, witness, advocacy, and support for increased legislative action. Through this emphasis the mainline denominations incorporated the peace issue into the center of church life, a position that the Quakers and the peace churches had consistently maintained.

The theme of "peace and justice" also received increased attention by the World Council of Churches and liberation theologians of Africa, Asia, and Latin America. Robert McAfee Brown, a prominent North American theologian and social activist, interpreted this theme for the reli-

gious community of the United States. In *Theology in a New Key* (1978) and *Making Peace in the Global Village* (1981) Brown investigates the nature of peacemaking, the interconnections of peace and justice, and the proper perspective from which this social linkage must be viewed, arguing that Christian faith requires a commitment to radical forms of social change. Another expression of this interconnection was the Sanctuary Movement of the 1980s, an effort on the part of religious groups to provide asylum for refugees fleeing political violence in Central America. The National Conference of Catholic Bishops also addressed this theme of peace and justice in an important 1983 document, "The Challenge of Peace: God's Promise and Our Response," in which they criticize deterrence as a strategy for achieving a peaceful world, suggest that nuclear wars cannot be just, and urge that the conditions for peace be actively nurtured by the religious community.

THE ROLE OF WOMEN

One of the most significant developments in religion in the last half of the twentieth century has been the changing role of women. Especially after 1950, women in religion joined women in other American institutions in pressing for and achieving fuller participation in leadership and decision-making and in gaining status and recognition.

Although some Congregational, American Baptist, Disciples of Christ, Unitarian, and Universalist churches ordained women to the ministry in the nineteenth century, in the latter half of the twentieth century approval for the ordination of women was voted by such groups as the United Methodists (1956), Presbyterians (1956), Lutherans (1970), and Episcopalians (1976). These official actions were accompanied by growing numbers of women as students in theological seminaries, as candidates for ordination, and as ordained members of the clergy. Some denominations (American Baptists, United Methodists, and Presbyterians, for example) created permanent women's task forces or commissions within their ecclesiastical structures to promote the rights and participation of women in all areas of church life. Among American Jews, the Reform branch, which historically was the most sensitive to the woman's role in religion, began ordaining women as rabbis in 1972, and in 1985 the first woman was ordained into the Conservative rabbinate.

Opposition to full participation of women in religious institutions remained, and ordained women still faced resistance in churches and synagogues. For example, in 1984 the Southern Baptist Convention passed a nonbinding resolution opposing the ordination of women; the Missouri Synod Lutherans were also opposed to it. While the Roman Catholic church and the Eastern Orthodox churches provided greater opportunities for women to hold significant positions in the church (for example, nuns serving on parish pastoral teams), women continued to be denied ordination. The Orthodox branch of Judaism consistently refused to ordain women.

The greater involvement of women in church and synagogue life brought about significant changes, particularly in such areas as the content and method of theological education, the language of religious discourse and worship, and the content of and approaches to biblical study and theology (witness the writings of such scholars as Letty Russell, Rosemary Ruether, Elizabeth Schüssler Fiorenza, and Phyllis Trible).

In the 1970s and 1980s many religious feminists assumed one of three positions with reference to "patriarchal Judaism and Christianity": (1) a rejection of Jewish and Christian traditions in favor of nature and goddess-oriented religions; (2) an interpretation of Judaism and Christianity that focused on liberation theories; or (3) a more selective interpretation of the Bible in which inclusive themes of Jesus' disposition toward women were employed.

CATHOLICS AND THE NATION

The period from the Depression to the 1980s marked the coming of age of the American Catholic church. The church began to take its place as a major indigenous religious body. In the first few years of the twentieth century the church had grown rapidly following a large-scale immigration of European Catholics, which lasted until the 1920s, when restrictive laws drastically reduced the numbers of all immigrants.

Increasing organizational unity accompanied a larger membership. A major organizational step was taken in 1917, when Father John J. Burke helped to form the National Catholic War Council, which became the National Catholic Welfare Council (NCWC) after World War I. The council made a national commitment to social and political action. Father John A. Ryan, a professor at Catholic University of America, who had early established himself as a progressive with the publication of *A Living Wage* in 1906, was involved with the NCWC from 1919 to 1945 and was in charge of all aspects of the social action department after 1928. In 1919 he wrote a paper for the NCWC, "Social Reconstruction: A General Review of the Problems and Survey of the Remedies," which became known as "The Bishops' Program of Social Reconstruction." This essay, building upon the papal encyclical *Rerum Novarum* (1891), advocated minimum wage and child-labor laws, public housing, the right of labor to organize, and unemployment, industrial accident, and old-age insurance. Many of these recommendations later became part of President Franklin D. Roosevelt's New Deal.

The 1929 stock market crash and the subsequent Depression led to increased support for social reform. American efforts were undergirded by Pope Pius XI's encyclical *Quadragesimo Anno* (1931), issued forty years after Pope Leo's *Rerum Novarum*. The earlier encyclical asserted the right of workers to organize and established a role for government in creating economic justice; *Quadragesimo Anno* envisaged a social reconstruction based on justice and Christian principles, with restraints on free competition and economic domination. In 1935 the social action department of the NCWC issued an important pamphlet prepared by Father Raymond A. McGowan and Father Ryan entitled "Organized Social Justice: An Economic Program for the United States Applying Pius XI's Great Encyclical on Social Life." Its objective was a "new economic order" that would entail the elimination of existing economic disorder and violence. Through government initiative society would be further organized—greater unionization of labor, an increase in consumer and rural cooperatives, and even an ordering of urban middle classes, probably along vocational lines.

While there were conservative tendencies evident in the 1930s, some new organizations were formed to promote economic justice. In 1933 the Catholic Worker Movement was formed. Its two central figures were the French itinerant worker-essayist Peter Maurin, who became the chief theoretician of the movement, and the former Socialist and convert to Catholicism Dorothy Day, who served as chief polemicist and moving force behind *The Catholic Worker,* a publication designed to be the Christian alternative to the Communist *The Daily Worker.* Day singlemindedly gave papal social doctrines their most radical interpretation, proposing a blend of sacramental piety, voluntary poverty, and the founding of "houses of hospitality" in urban centers where Catholics could share life with the destitute. Her movement rejected the socialist concept of class struggle as well as the rugged individualism and inhuman mass production encouraged by middle-class capitalist culture.

In 1937 another group, the Association of Catholic Trade Unionists, was formed whose aim was to support responsible trade unionism. It conducted classes in the ethics of labor relations, labor law and history, and union procedure; published a newspaper, *The Labor Leader;* and endorsed those strikes that after investigation were deemed to be just.

A popular voice in the 1930s was that of Father Charles E. Coughlin of Royal Oak, Michigan, who became a famous radio personality. At first he spoke out for social and economic justice, emphasizing the criticism of unchecked free enterprise in the 1891 and 1931 encyclicals. He created his own lobby, the National Union for Social Justice (1934), and his own newspaper, *Social Justice* (1936), which sold outside Catholic churches each Sunday across the nation. Later he turned to the right, opposed Roosevelt and the New Deal, became anti-Semitic, and even favored the Nazis.

When Pope John XXIII called the Second Vatican Council (1962–1965) and issued his two encyclicals *Mater et Magistra* (1961) and *Pacem in Terris* (1963), he opened doors between the church and the modern world that had been closed for years. One of the most important documents of Vatican Council II was the "Pastoral Constitution on the Church in the Modern World," which addressed such areas as marriage and the family, economics, politics, peace, and international relations. In marriage, the centrality of conjugal love and a covenant relation be-

tween the partners is emphasized, rather than procreation and the nurture of children; in economics, the issues of inequalities, the "revolution of rising expectations," particularly among the poor, are stressed; on the subject of war, indiscriminate military destruction of cities and populations, as well as the arms race, is condemned.

Of particular importance to the American church was the leadership provided during Vatican Council II by Father John Courtney Murray in the drafting of *The Declaration on Religious Freedom.* Before 1965, when this declaration was issued, many non-Catholic Americans were suspicious that the church did not really believe in religious freedom. *The Declaration on Religious Freedom* announced to the world that no double standard existed, that "freedom for the church when Catholics are a minority, privilege for the church and intolerance for others when Catholics are a majority" was a myth.

The bishops of Vatican Council II in their pronouncements chose to ignore the contemporary debate over birth control, and merely repeated the official ban on artificial means of birth control. This view was upheld, with only a minimum of open dissent until 1968, when Pope Paul VI issued his encyclical *Humanae Vitae.* Many had hoped that the encyclical would contain a relaxation in the church's teaching on birth control, but the traditional view of contraceptive use was upheld. Negative reaction to the encyclical in the American church was immediate and massive.

Post–Vatican Council II Catholicism has proved to be more diverse than anyone might have imagined. If the church came of age in the mid- and late twentieth century, it did so amid the uncertainties and tensions of the times. While Pope John Paul II upheld many traditional teachings on such matters as abortion, contraception, clerical celibacy, and an all-male clergy, and even though he remained sharply critical of liberation theology, he declared many times that the struggle for social justice is an essential part of the church's work. The American bishops themselves continued to provide strong leadership in the effort to outlaw abortion and issued pastoral letters on the national nuclear arms policy and on Catholic social teaching and the economy of the United States. If all these moves were not made with complete and consummate ease, they were certainly made by a mature church confident of its place in a free society.

JEWS AND THE NATION

While Jews suffered severe economic hardship along with other Americans during the Depression, they were somewhat better prepared for the effects of the crash due to the well-established tradition of giving private assistance to needy members of their community. By 1936 there were 143 Jewish federations and welfare funds in the United States, 48 of which had been created after 1931. In addition to maintaining an exemplary record of providing relief to their own people, Jews have always contributed significantly to non-Jewish organizations promoting peace, civil rights, social justice, and other liberal causes.

A striking challenge to the American Jewish community was the need to settle approximately 110,000 refugees from Nazi Germany between 1933 and 1941, several thousand of whom were intellectual leaders. Among them were composer Kurt Weill, theatrical director Max Reinhardt, psychoanalyst Dr. Theodor Reik, and the best known of all, scientist Albert Einstein.

Jews proved to be very loyal to President Roosevelt and endorsed his New Deal program. To some degree certain Jewish efforts had already anticipated those of the New Deal. During the 1920s Jewish leaders in the garment unions had helped to create unemployment and pension funds to which employees contributed. Further, both the International Ladies Garment Workers Union under David Dubinsky and the Amalgamated Clothing Workers under Sidney Hillman had also convinced employers to contribute to workers' unemployment and pension funds. It was only a small step for Dubinsky and Hillman to become active in the New Deal's National Recovery Administration. Jewish support for Roosevelt became even more enthusiastic after 1941, when America entered World War II and the president led the war effort against Nazi Germany. For the most part Jews expressed such great confidence in Roosevelt because he embodied those liberal policies they had come to value. He also drew on the ideals of charity and brotherhood that were an integral part of Jewish religious teaching.

Zionism (a movement for creating a Jewish political or religious community in Palestine) had been a part of the American Jewish experience before the late 1930s; but as World War II approached, changes occurred in Jewish communal organization, pro-Zionist groups became stronger, and more Jews adopted the cause of creating a homeland for the Jews. Of the three branches in American Judaism, Conservative Jews were very supportive of the movement; some Orthodox Jews, who still retained the ancient hope that one day Israel might be restored, were sympathetic. At first Reform Judaism was anti-Zionist (see the "Pittsburgh Platform," a set of principles issued by a national meeting of Reform rabbis in Pittsburgh, Pennsylvania, in 1885), later slightly pro-Israel (the "Columbus Platform," issued at a national meeting of Reform rabbis in Columbus, Ohio, in 1937), and finally, strongly pro-Israel (see "Reform Judaism: A Centenary Perspective," issued by the Central Conference of American [Reform] Rabbis at their meeting in San Francisco, in 1976). When the State of Israel was finally established in 1948, American Jews extended their enthusiastic support and contributed large sums of money for the new nation through such agencies as the United Jewish Appeal.

Many prominent American Jews, both secular and religious, served in numerous Zionist organizations (the Zionist Organization of America had been formed in 1918) and helped to shape the views on Zionism of Jews and other Americans. One of these was Rabbi Stephen S. Wise, whose service to humanity went far beyond the concerns of Zionism and bounds of Judaism. For example, he was cofounder of the National Association for the Advancement of Colored People in 1909 and of the American Civil Liberties Union in 1920. He argued the Jewish cause before American presidents from Wilson to Roosevelt and was one of the first to raise warnings about the Nazi danger.

Another person active in Zionist and humanitarian work was Henrietta Szold, who wrote, spoke, and organized on behalf of establishing a safe refuge for world Jewry. In 1912 she founded and was the first president of Hadassah, a women's organization that was heavily involved in medical relief. Between 1933 and 1948 she directed the Youth Aliyah, under Hadassah sponsorship, which rescued some 30,000 young Jews from Germany and Poland.

After World War II, Jews, as well as other

Americans, enjoyed a time of prosperity and weakened anti-Semitism. In *A Certain People* (1985) social critic Charles E. Silberman, looking back from the 1980s, observes that since World War II there has been, with only a few exceptions (among blacks, as one example), a general "continuing decline in 'personal' as well as 'institutional' anti-Semitism." In the post–World War II period many Jews moved to the suburbs. New synagogues were built. Individual Jews such as writers Saul Bellow and Isaac Bashevis Singer achieved distinction and enjoyed wide acclaim. Still, some of the old agenda persisted—questions of identity, survival, and how to prepare for the future.

Jews in general were significantly more opposed to the Vietnam War than other ethnic groups (48 percent in a 1967 Stanford survey). Among Jewish young people, journalist Stephen D. Isaacs (*Jews and American Politics*, 1974) reports that a striking 20 to 50 percent, depending on the estimates, of the membership of the New Left, a loose confederation of radical political groups, were Jews (in the U.S. population Jews comprise less than 3 percent).

Although many Reform and Conservative Jews had been strong advocates of civil rights and black aspirations in the 1960s, in the next few years and into the 1980s they felt threatened by the animosity of more radical blacks and by what, from the Jewish standpoint, seemed to be a rebirth of the quota system. Some Jews, who had suffered much discrimination in the past from quotas, decided to oppose any affirmative action efforts that invoked quotas to advance blacks and other nonwhites in education and employment. In 1972 the American Jewish Congress announced an attack on quotas, which, in an attempt to right the wrongs of the past, it felt would discriminate against Jews and other whites. The AJC position remains the same in the 1980s; but it recognizes that in very limited situations, where there is a history of egregious discrimination, temporary and limited quotas may be appropriate.

As American Jews pondered their future, one program was proposed by Nathan Glazer in "The Crisis in American Jewry" (*Religion American Style*, P. H. McNamara, ed., 1974). Eschewing a simple one-directional identification of the Jewish "crisis," such as anti-Semitism or assimilation, he argued that in the late twentieth century American Jews could either look inward and become more ethnic or look outward and become more politically and socially liberal. Internally, this kind of liberalism included supporting the causes of civil rights, nondiscrimination, and equal opportunity; internationally, it meant peace, careful diplomacy, and alleviating the plight of Soviet Jews. Glazer did not see simply reverting to a traditional religious posture as an adequate answer, nor was he proposing a cold, disembodied humanism divorced from religion. Rather, recognizing that there was strength and validity in the ethnic-liberalism mixture, he argued that both would have to be humanized, or spiritualized, by association with Jewish religion. Following that program might then help answer the question, What is Judaism to be?

EVANGELICALS AND THE NATION

American revivals have long been viewed as containing an element of social control and reform of one kind or another. In the nineteenth century Dwight L. Moody, a revivalist whose audience included mainly middle-class Americans but not recent immigrants or poor Catholics, was supported by Evangelical businessmen who saw his revivals as a way of emphasizing the values that would produce conscientious, loyal, and honest workers and calm the anxieties of the unemployed. In the early twentieth century Billy Sunday used his revivals to denounce in colorful language a whole list of evils: corruption in politics, Darwinism, the new scientific theories, immigrants as a threat to the "American way of life," dancing, tobacco, and especially the "booze traffic."

For the next several decades, urban revivalism remained quiescent and muted. Concerns arising from the Depression and World War II occupied center stage. The beginnings of a new Evangelicalism can be marked from 1942, when the National Association of Evangelicals was founded, and 1943, when the Youth for Christ movement was inaugurated. After World War II and through the 1970s Billy Graham was the most public and persuasive symbol of this new form of Protestant conservatism and the new phase of American mass revivalism.

In *Revivals, Awakenings, and Reform* (1978) religious historian William G. McLoughlin characterizes Graham's stance as traditionalist, claiming that he aimed "to demonstrate that

Fundamentalism was not dead but in fact held the key to the return of law, order, decency, and national progress." While the thrust of Graham's sermons was an urgent appeal to repent of one's sins and make a decision for Christ, he usually started and often sprinkled his messages with references to social ills and national sins. His cure for America was a potent mixture of piety and patriotism. In the 1970s and 1980s he blunted some of the sharp edges of his Fundamentalist beliefs, visited Communist nations, and gave his support to nuclear disarmament. To his critics, however, Graham always lacked a truly prophetic understanding of the Christian faith and an appreciation of the ambiguities of modern life.

It was the election of Southern Baptist Jimmy Carter as president in 1976 that made *Evangelical* a highly visible word and movement, describing those believers in Jesus who had had a vital "born-again" experience. Even though the emphasis upon the born-again experience is personal and internal, the Evangelicals of the 1970s and 1980s, numbering perhaps as many as 40 million people and called the New Religious (or Christian) Right, moved away from a merely private faith into the public sphere to influence directly politicians, elections, and legislation. They were doing exactly what they had criticized the mainline and liberal denominations for doing in the 1960s. The New Religious Right agreed on certain goals: to fight against abortion, homosexuality, drugs, pornography, and the Equal Rights Amendment, and to advocate traditional marriage and family patterns, voluntary prayer in the schools, and a strong national defense.

Among others, the Reverend Jerry Falwell, a Virginia independent Baptist minister and television personality and founder of the Moral Majority, stood out as an articulate leader of the new conservatives in the 1980s. The Moral Majority and other Evangelical Protestant pressure groups, highly politicized and using the latest technology of mass communications, often overlooked theological differences when it came to political action and espoused causes common to conservative Jews, Catholics, and Mormons. It was plain that the Evangelicals had carved out a place for themselves in the national debate over values and were determined to impose upon the nation their vision of a better America.

In the twentieth century not all religious Americans have chanted the slogan "Deeds, not creeds." Many traditional Catholics, conservative Protestants, and Orthodox Jews have resisted collective efforts toward social reform, believing that religious organizations ought to be concerned with private piety and personal morality. But even among believers who feel an obligation to work for a better world directly, immediately, and corporately, consensus is often lacking regarding the kinds of social, political, and economic problems that ought to be faced, the priority of their importance, and the solutions that are feasible and enduring. Such disagreement is hardly surprising given the fact of American religious pluralism, which has been even more prominent in the late twentieth century. Nevertheless, the multifaceted character of religious approaches to society notwithstanding, an element of social reform appears to be a constant, vital feature of American religion.

BIBLIOGRAPHY

Aaron I. Abell, *American Catholicism and Social Action: A Search for Social Justice, 1865–1950* (1960); Roland H. Bainton, *Christian Attitudes Toward War and Peace: A Historical Survey and Critical Re-Evaluation* (1960); John C. Bennett, *The Radical Imperative: From Theology to Social Ethics* (1975); Neil Betten, *Catholic Activism and the Industrial Worker* (1976); Paul Blanchard, *American Freedom and Catholic Power* (1949); Donald G. Bloesch, *The Evangelical Renaissance* (1973); Robert McAfee Brown, *Theology in a New Key: Responding to Liberation Themes* (1978) and *Making Peace in the Global Village* (1981); Carol P. Christ and Judith Plaskow, eds., *Womanspirit Rising: A Feminist Reader in Religion* (1979); W. E. B. Du Bois, *The Souls of Black Folk: Essays and Sketches* (1903); Marshall Frady, *Billy Graham: A Parable of American Righteousness* (1979); E. Franklin Frazier and C. Eric Lincoln, *The Black Church Since Frazier* (1973).

Robert T. Handy, *A Christian America: Protestant Hopes and Historical Realities* (1971); Arthur Hertzberg, *Being Jewish in America: The Modern Experience* (1979); Susannah Heschel, ed., *On Being a Jewish Feminist: A Reader* (1983); Samuel S. Hill and Dennis E. Owen, *The New Religious-Political Right in America* (1982); Walter M. Horton, *Realistic Theology* (1934); Stephen D. Isaacs, *Jews and American Politics* (1974); Janet W. James, ed., *Women in American Religion* (1980); Charles W. Kegley, ed., *Reinhold Niebuhr: His Religious, Social and Political Thought* (1956, rev. ed. 1984); Martin L. King, Jr., *Where Do We Go From Here: Chaos or Community?* (1967); Edward C. Lehman, Jr., *Women Clergy: Breaking Through Gender Barriers* (1985); Edwin Lewis, *A Christian Manifesto* (1934); William G. McLoughlin, *Revivals, Awakenings, and Reform: An Essay on Religion and Social Change in America, 1607–1977* (1978); Donald

SOCIAL REFORM SINCE THE GREAT DEPRESSION

B. Meyer, *The Protestant Search for Political Realism, 1919–1941* (1960); Robert M. Miller, *American Protestantism and Social Issues, 1919–1939* (1958); Gunnar Myrdal, *An American Dilemma: The Negro Problem and Modern Democracy* (1944).

Reinhold Niebuhr, *Moral Man and Immoral Society: A Study in Ethics and Politics* (1932), *The Nature and Destiny of Man: A Christian Interpretation* (1941), *The Children of Light and the Children of Darkness: A Vindication of Democracy and a Critique of Its Traditional Defense* (1944), and *Man's Nature and His Communities: Essays on the Dynamics and Enigmas of Man's Personal and Social Existence* (1965); Michael Novak, *The Spirit of Democratic Capitalism* (1982); David J. O'Brien, *American Catholics and Social Reform: The New Deal Years* (1968) and, with Thomas A. Shannon, as eds., *Renewing the Earth: Catholic Documents on Peace, Justice, and Liberation* (1977); Mel Piehl, *Breaking Bread: The Catholic Worker and the Origin of Catholic Radicalism in America* (1982); Milton Plesur, *Jewish Life in Twentieth-Century America: Challenge and Accommodation* (1982); Liston Pope, *Millhands and Preachers: A Study of Gastonia* (1944); Charles Powers, *Social Responsibility and Investments* (1971).

Paul Ramsey, *War and the Christian Conscience: How Shall Modern War Be Conducted Justly?* (1961); Walter Rauschenbusch, *Christianity and the Social Crisis* (1907); George W. Richards, *Beyond Fundamentalism and Modernism: The Gospel of God* (1934); Rosemary R. Ruether, *Sexism and God-Talk: Toward a Feminist Theology* (1983); Charles E. Silberman, *A Certain People: American Jews and Their Lives Today* (1985); Robert W. Spike, *The Freedom Revolution and the Churches* (1965); Kenneth W. Thompson, *Interpreters and Critics of the Cold War* (1978); Melvin I. Urofsky, *A Voice That Spoke for Justice: The Life and Times of Stephen S. Wise* (1981); Judith L. Weidman, ed., *Women Ministers: How Women Are Redefining Traditional Roles* (1981); Gayraud S. Wilmore and James H. Cone, eds., *Black Theology: A Documentary History, 1966–1979* (1979); J. Philip Wogaman, *The Great Economic Debate: An Ethical Analysis* (1977); John H. Yoder, *The Politics of Jesus: Vicit Agnus Noster* (1972).

[*See also* BLACK RELIGIOUS THOUGHT; RELIGIOUS THOUGHT SINCE WORLD WAR II; SOCIAL REFORM AFTER THE CIVIL WAR TO THE GREAT DEPRESSION; SOCIAL REFORM FROM THE COLONIAL PERIOD THROUGH THE CIVIL WAR; *and* WAR AND PEACE.]

ETHNICITY AND RELIGION

Laura L. Becker

THE intermingling of peoples from a multitude of different ethnic backgrounds is one of America's most distinctive traits. Once viewed as inevitable ingredients in the great American "melting pot," ethnic groups are now acknowledged to be enduring and complex phenomena. Of particular interest is the relationship between ethnicity and religion. Both are major components within the structure of society and the identity of individuals, but they are not simply parallel. On the contrary, ethnicity and religion interact with and affect each other in a variety of ways. Ethnicity can reinforce religious identity, shape the style of religious behavior, divide religious groups that would otherwise be united, and compete with religion for an individual's loyalty and support. Religion, in turn, can have similar impact on ethnicity and can take on a decidedly ethnic character itself.

The term *ethnic* derives from the Greek *ethnos,* or nation, and an ethnic group is one that is basically delineated by cultural traits or national background. Race and religion may be distinguishing features, but the ethnic group differs in that the sense of peoplehood rests mainly on such things as language, customs, and the perception of shared ancestry.

At one time, national and ethnic groups were believed to be biological units, and their cultural peculiarities were perceived as innate. Growing understanding of the mechanisms of socialization has made it clear that nonphysical group traits are almost always learned, not genetic. But ethnicity is, in effect, inherited, in that it is to a large degree determined for the individual by the accident of birth. Thus an individual born into and raised by a Cuban-American family will be Cuban-American, not Greek-American. This makes ethnicity, along with religion, one of the "primordial attachments" that Clifford Geertz has asserted is a "given" in the way in which an individual perceives himself and is perceived by others.

Today, not all Americans maintain an ethnic identity. As we shall see, there is a clear tendency for attachments to countries and cultures based outside the United States to weaken over time, especially from one generation to the next. Nevertheless ethnic identity has been of great importance throughout American history because America is a nation of immigrants.

Prior to the Revolution, the majority of Americans were of English origin, with substantial minorities of Scotch-Irish and German settlers. From the Revolution until about 1880, more English and Germans came, along with Scots, Welsh, Dutch, Scandinavians, and large numbers of Irish. These people shared a Northern European and (except for the Irish and some of the Germans) a Protestant heritage. They are referred to by scholars as Old Immigrants, because the closing decades of the nineteenth century brought a marked change in the migratory flow.

Between 1880 and 1924, massive numbers of so-called New Immigrants came to America from Southern and Eastern Europe. They included Italians, Poles, Russians, Czechs, Slovaks, Hungarians, Greeks, Lithuanians, and dozens of smaller groups, most of whom were Roman Catholic, Eastern Orthodox, or Jewish. There were Chinese and Japanese immigrants as well, who adhered to non-Western religions. Restrictive national quotas were instituted in the 1920s, keeping immigration at a minimum until they were eased in 1965. Since then, large numbers of so-called Recent Immigrants from Asia, the Near East, the Caribbean, and Latin America have come, further augmenting America's ethnic diversity.

But ethnicity in America is not necessarily a direct product of foreign nationality. In the first place, political nationhood was not a prerequisite for the development of ethnic feeling. Many of the ethnic groups in this country, such as the Irish, the Germans, and the Czechs, arrived before national independence or consolidation had been achieved in their place of origin. Other groups, such as the Welsh, Croatians, and Armenians, have an ethnic identity despite the fact that their homelands have not had national status in modern times. Other ethnic groups did not feel kinship in their native land. Immigrants from Italy, for example, arrived as Sicilians, Neapolitans, and Calabrians, becoming Italians only as the various subgroups discovered their common language, customs, and interests here in America.

The immigrant generation almost always retained pronounced "foreign" characteristics and, in Milton Gordon's phrase, merely "accommodated" themselves to the new environment by adopting those forms of behavior that enabled them to get along. Some, however, eagerly embraced the mainstream American way of life, and ensuing generations were even more strongly subject to the process of acculturation, through which they became less distinctive in both their outward behavior and their inward attitudes and values. But true assimilation—the total blending of a group with the host society—did not necessarily follow. As Marcus L. Hansen noted, even where the children of immigrants sought to become totally Americanized, the grandchildren have often taken a greater interest and pride in their roots.

Thus, there was neither the "Anglo-conformity" many WASPs expected nor a true "melting pot" such as playwright Israel Zangwill extolled at the turn of the twentieth century. While intermarriage across ethnic lines has obscured the heritage of many Americans, recent census data reveal that a substantial majority still trace their ancestry or feel attached to at least one national origins group. We have arrived at a state of "cultural pluralism," an America that contains many identifiable ethnic groups. Ethnic group members are not necessarily recognizably "foreign," but they do share something special with fellow group members.

For many, one of the most important shared elements is religion. Indeed, religion and ethnicity reinforce each other in many ways. The most extreme case is that of the Jews, where they are more or less fused. America has witnessed, indeed fostered, wide variations and changes in Jewish beliefs and practices, including the emergence of new forms of Judaism (Reform, Conservative, Reconstructionist) to supplement the traditional Orthodox form and of people who consider themselves to be Jews despite the fact that they do not adhere to any form of Judaism. Nevertheless, the bounds of Jewish ethnicity are clearly demarcated by religion in that the voluntary adoption of any religion other than Judaism precludes an individual from being identified as a Jew in virtually all instances. The same is true of smaller sects such as the Old Order Amish, famous for their distinctive "Pennsylvania Dutch" way of life.

In the case of other groups, religion and ethnicity are not fused but have a very strong association. Episcopalians and Quakers are largely of British heritage; Irish-, Polish-, French Canadian-, Italian-, and Spanish-Americans are almost uniformly Catholic; Scandinavian-Americans are largely Lutheran; Greeks and Serbs are overwhelmingly Eastern Orthodox. Unlike the Jews, one can be an Italian Protestant, a Swedish Catholic, a Greek Muslim. But often such religious "deviance" leads to exclusion from the majority or at least doubts about such an individual is a "true" Italian, Greek, Swede, and so on. Indeed, scholars have claimed that a Serbian immigrant who becomes Roman Catholic "automatically becomes a Croatian," while Slovaks who were Greek Catholic rather than Roman Catholic were considered Ruthenians. Thus religion and ethnicity were for all intents and purposes coterminus for a number of immigrant groups and have remained strongly associated among later generations.

Whether or not ethnicity and religion are as intricately bound as in these cases, they almost always reinforce each other to some extent. Much of the groundwork for such reinforcement was laid in the old country, if not by religious homogeneity within the political nation, then by a sense of persecution from without. The Irish are a prime example of the latter, for they clung to Catholicism as both a comfort and a challenge in the face of English Protestant domination.

Scottish Presbyterianism was buttressed by English efforts to establish Anglicanism on Scottish soil, while Catholic French-Canadians were equally tenacious in the face of English Protestant domination in Canada. Many of the Orthodox peoples were beset by unsympathetic conquerers: the Catholic Austro-Hungarian Empire in the case of Serbs and Ukrainians, the Muslim Ottoman Empire in the case of Bulgarians and Armenians. Jews, of course, were a persecuted minority throughout much of the world.

In all of these cases, religion was one of the major ways in which a people kept itself a distinct entity while under "foreign" rule. When group members came to America, religion often served the same function, especially among those who faced prejudice here. Protestant nativism certainly led some non-Protestants to abandon their faith in order "make it" more easily in America, but for the majority, it probably strengthened their determination to cling to the faith of their fathers. In the case of certain groups, such as the Irish, the Jews, and the Armenians, continued concern for compatriots abroad has helped to keep this "resolve in the face of persecution" mechanism operative.

As Oscar Handlin and Timothy L. Smith have made clear, religious feelings were generally heightened to begin with among people who migrated to America. Part of this was due to selective migration, but much was the result of the migratory experience itself. This experience was traumatic to at least some degree for virtually all immigrants—an uprooting from one's hometown, kinfolk, the familiar round of existence. It engendered loneliness, a sense of loss, fear of the new and unknown. Under these conditions, people turned to their religion for comfort and guidance and were receptive to an image of themselves as seekers of the promised land, as lost sheep dependent on their good shepherd. The chaos associated with emigration often led to what Marcus L. Hansen has called Puritanization: an emphasis on strict theological and moral conformity to provide group stability in the face of the bewildering new array of choices and the absence of traditional institutions of control. Thus the migratory experience helped place religion firmly at the center of the immigrants' life, a pattern that often endured well beyond the immigrant generation.

Indeed, the church or synagogue generally became the center of the ethnic community in America, sustaining the mutual reinforcement of ethnicity and religion that derived from heritage and migration. In fulfilling its traditional role as a place of worship, the church helped preserve what Thomas Luckmann has called the "sacred cosmos" of the immigrants, their accustomed way of relating to the world and understanding the meaning of their existence. Religious institutions also played an important part in the perpetuation of language. Long after immigrants and their children were comfortable using English on a day-to-day basis, many clung to their traditional liturgies and hymns and Bibles. This was particularly noteworthy in the case of the Jews, for whom the use of Hebrew was a common bond, and in the case of the various Eastern Orthodox groups, where the entire service was in the native language. But it also applied to groups such as the Welsh Calvinistic Methodists, German and Dutch Reformed church members, Korean Presbyterians, Muslim Arabs, and many non-English-speaking Catholics. Over the years many churches and synagogues have provided religious schools where youngsters raised in America could study the language and the history as well as the religion of their forebears.

Churches and synagogues also supported the ethnic group by serving basic community needs —aiding the poor, arranging for the care of the sick and the orphaned when necessary, providing night classes for adults—and by functioning as a social center where ethnic group members could gather to share their memories of the past and discuss common problems facing them in the present. Regular worship, of course, provided regular opportunities for people to meet, but churches often sponsored various organizations as well, such as choirs, men's and women's clubs, and benevolent societies.

In these ways, religious institutions did much to further ethnic solidarity. Indeed, as W. Lloyd Warner and Leo Srole argued in their study of Yankee City, the church "serves more than any other structure to organize the group as a community system." After all, immigrants came as individuals or families or small clusters; they needed something to bring them together in their new settlements. This was especially important for groups where local or regional identities were strong, such as the Germans and Italians. The church provided common ground, a basis for forming a broader ethnic identity, which in turn helped them to deal more effectively with the outside world.

Religious institutions have also provided a key reinforcement of the ethnic-religious tie in the form of leaders. Pastors, priests, and rabbis have always tended to function as spokesmen for the ethnic communities because they have a better-than-average education, because Americans are generally deferential to "men of the cloth," and because they are usually concerned about the welfare of the ethnic group. This concern stems in part from clerics' natural interest in the living conditions and psychological well-being of their parishioners. But religious leaders have also recognized that ethnic identification helps draw and hold church members. Hence they have provided special church classes and organizations and sermons on ethnic themes as the second, third, and fourth generations grow up. Lay ethnic leaders likewise have used religious loyalties to strengthen their cause. Serbian organizers, for example, were careful to include the word *Orthodox* in the title of their national federation founded in 1901 to attract Serbs who had joined earlier Croatian or Slovenian (Catholic) benevolent societies and might not have been inclined to switch out of ethnic loyalty alone.

The religious and ethnic communities themselves operate in ways that strengthen each other. Pressure against marrying out of the faith narrows the range of potential interethnic possibilities to at least some degree, while pressure against marrying out of the ethnic group almost always narrows the range of potential interreligious mixtures. In communities where the vast majority of ethnic group members belong to one church, pressure to conform to both religious and ethnic standards is considerable. An English Quaker or Scotch-Irish Presbyterian who was denounced by his church in colonial rural Pennsylvania, for example, might have found himself with only German Lutherans to associate with.

Separation from either the religious or the ethnic group would lead to the loss of much of the richness in either, for yet another way in which they reinforce each other is through ritual. Many of the key ethnic rituals are at least partly religious in nature; Harold Abramson's list includes the Anglo-Saxon Protestant church supper, the Italian festa, the Irish wake, and the Jewish bar mitzvah. Viewed from the opposite

perspective, religious rituals provide a major means for second-, third-, and fourth-generation ethnics to keep in touch with their national heritage after they have acculturated in terms of language, dress, and general behavioral patterns. Holidays in particular are a time in which old traditions are lovingly practiced and passed on.

These traditions vary significantly among different ethnoreligious groups, because religion and ethnicity not only reinforce each other, they shape each other in important ways. The effect of religion on ethnic values and behavior is harder to document because it is less concrete, more a matter of a broad ethos. One could cite the notion of a Protestant ethic (shared by Jews) that treats work and one's general achievements in this life as important and pleasing to God, as opposed to the more otherworldly orientation of traditional Catholicism and Eastern Orthodoxy. Hand in hand goes the reforming instinct, the optimistic view that the quality of life on earth is worth efforts to improve it versus traditional Catholic fatalism. These differences are manifested in the degree of commercialization and industrialization in the immigrants' countries of origin, as well as the varying concern with social mobility and social change the immigrants and their children manifested in America, though the differences have been muted over time.

Protestants and Jews, of course, differ among themselves in these and other matters, such as the importance given to education for the laity. Some denominations or subgroups emphasize feeling, others emphasize rational understanding; some warn that secular knowledge can detract from religious faith, others argue that all knowledge can help one to be a better person. But for all their internal nonuniformity, Protestant and Jewish immigrants generally felt that secular education was valuable, while neither Roman Catholicism nor Eastern Orthodoxy encouraged it to the same extent, perhaps due to the priest-centered and ritual-oriented nature of their religious worship. Thus one can see overall differences in the educational backgrounds that immigrants of different religions brought with them, as well as in the interest in education they evinced once in the United States. Such differences often persisted through the second generation, though again they are less apparent by the third.

Still another aspect of religion that has had an

impact on ethnic values and behavior is Protestantism's rigid moral code, or "Puritan streak," which distinguished migrants from Protestant, especially Calvinist-influenced, countries. Catholic, Orthodox, and (to an extent) non-Calvinist Protestant cultures were generally more openly expressive: less likely to prohibit dancing, for example, more likely to encourage sacred art. Thus religion affected the general demeanor of a group, its characteristic style, on both the individual and the denominational level.

Broad differences also exist with regard to group governance. Protestantism and Judaism have always allowed more scope for equality and lay participation in decision-making. Boards of deacons, elders, governors, or directors help choose the clergyman in most Protestant and Jewish congregations, and they assist him in establishing institutional policies. Decision-making in Catholic and Eastern Orthodox churches has tended to remain more concentrated in the hands of priests and their clerical superiors. While lay influence has been largely male influence in the more conservative branches of *all* religious groups (Protestant and Jewish as well as Catholic and Eastern Orthodox), it is worth noting that women have made some inroads as clerics within liberal branches of Protestantism and Judaism, whereas they are still entirely excluded from the priesthood within the Catholic and Eastern churches. Such differences both manifest and reinforce broader attitudes toward authority and the proper role of men and women.

In sum, each different form of religion engendered a different ethos that affected the behavior of immigrants who adhered to it. But the impact of religion on ethnicity has had more tangible manifestations as well. In some cases—the Irish and Koreans, for example—the church hierarchy provided a major avenue of mobility and outlet for talented group members in the face of somewhat limited opportunities in this country. Religion has also affected the ability of certain ethnic groups to fit into mainstream American life. Traditional Jews, for example, have had to make special efforts to observe their dietary laws and the prohibition against travel and work on the Sabbath. Muslims, likewise, have had to adjust to the fact that Sunday is the "day of rest" in America, as well as to the fact that most Americans do not take time out for formal prayer during the workday. Both these groups, as well as adherents of Eastern Orthodoxy and non-Western religions, have found it difficult to celebrate their holy days in a country dominated by the calendar of Western Christianity. Not surprisingly, these obstacles have resulted in some decline in religious observance. Yet, as noted, religious celebrations, along with religious organizations, have been important elements shaping the life of virtually every American ethnic group.

Ethnicity, in turn, has had a major part in shaping the particular nature of group religious practice. Language is central, not only for the broad way in which it molds thought by providing the means through which individuals perceive and describe their world, but also for the way it influences liturgical style. Virtually all non-English immigrants worshiped in a language other than English for some time after their arrival in America. Jews used Hebrew rather than the language of their country of origin, while Catholics used Latin until official policy was changed by Vatican II in 1965. But even in these cases, sermons tended to be delivered in the group's native tongue, while among Protestant and Eastern Orthodox congregations, worship was entirely in the native language of the immigrants.

Indeed, a group's liturgy was often so highly language specific that the use of English in worship was a major source of controversy in most of the non-English denominations. Many individuals throughout our history, from Norwegian- to Armenian- to Mexican-Americans, have argued that a change in language would lead to an erosion of religious purity; that translating the rhymes and rhythms of the native words would inevitably damage either their meaning or beauty or both. Hence language was, and in many cases still is, a major element in an ethnic group's unique religious style.

Elements of "national character" or "national genius" have also affected religious style in America. Nathan Glazer contrasts the "dignified Orthodoxy" of the highly acculturated and successful Sephardic Jews with the less decorous Orthodoxy of the ghettoized and impoverished Eastern European Jews. Italian Catholics emphasized festivity and emotion, while German Catholics stressed the grandeur of the Mass, and Irish Catholics the mystical elements of the faith. Religious worship among Welsh Calvinistic Methodists and Czech Catholics in America included unusually extensive congregational singing in harmony, reflecting the strong choral traditions of their ancestral homelands.

National character aside, isolation and divergent experiences led to divergent religious beliefs and practices abroad that were perpetuated in America. Some of these fall into the category of folkways—traditions of unknown origin that came to be considered customary and "correct." Many are associated with holidays. Among Catholics, ethnic Poles traditionally placed hay under the tablecloth at home on Christmas Eve, while French families built elaborate crèches and Irish-Americans lit candles in their windows. Christmas was a strictly religious affair among Scottish Presbyterians (for whom New Year's Eve was the convivial part of the season), while German Lutherans traditionally celebrated on Christmas Eve rather than on Christmas, customary among Protestants of English heritage.

Traditional holiday foods and songs, of course, have varied greatly from one ethnic group to another. Many of the Christmas carols and dishes considered standard among Americans today originated in Great Britain and were entirely new to immigrants from other countries. While most descendants of these immigrants have adopted the Anglo-American customs, they have perpetuated their own songs and recipes as well. Holiday practices among American Jews likewise vary with ethnicity. Many Jews of Sephardic (Iberian, Balkan, Near Eastern, and North African) heritage, for example, eat foods that are not considered kosher for Passover by Jews of Ashkenazic (Central and Eastern European) heritage, and they conclude their seders with additional songs that are not part of the Ashkenazic Haggadah, or Passover liturgy, standardized in the Middle Ages.

Differences are not only manifested during holidays, of course. Lutherans from Germany, Norway, Sweden, Finland, and Czechoslovakia favored different forms of clerical dress, different altar arrangements, and different hymns. Weddings and funerals still vary in their degree of solemnity. And of course there are many ways in which pagan customs have become intertwined with or coexisted with organized religion. The use of amulets, potions, incantations, and other "special precautions" to cure illness or ward off "evil spirits" is most common among Americans of Caribbean or Latin origin, but al-

most all ethnic groups have some unique customs or superstitions that are not based on sacred texts or officially sanctioned tradition. Other religious practices that vary from one ethnic group to another are a matter of emphasis within established church tradition. A primary example is saints days among Catholic and Orthodox church members. Different countries acquired different patron saints—Patrick for the Irish, Stephen for the Hungarians, George and Elias for the Romanians, Juan for the Puerto Ricans—many of which have retained their importance among ethnic groups in America.

Attitudes toward clergy and formal worship among Americans also reflect the influence of ethnic background. In his *Ethnic Diversity in Catholic America,* Harold J. Abramson has argued that those from nations in which the church and clergy were leaders in the fight for political and/or cultural independence, such as Irish and French-Canadians, tend toward high levels of formal observance and high regard for clergymen. Those whose heritage lies in more religiously divided countries in which the clergy played a less significant role in national affairs, such as Germans, tend to be moderately supportive of institutionalized religion. And those coming from places in which the church was seen as part of an oppressive establishment, such as Italians and Mexicans, are generally the least likely to go to church regularly and to support parochial schools.

Religion among groups in this last category also took on a highly individual orientation. While Catholics from Southern Italy had relatively little regard for their priests, they needed religion to survive psychologically in the face of a precarious existence. Hence the evolution of what Rudolph Vecoli has called *clientismo.* This was a form of saint worship: the belief that particular saints had particular powers and that if one prayed to the right saint in the proper manner, the saint would grant one's wish. Such a perspective gave people some feeling of control over their lives, which Italians emigrating to the United States found comforting as well. Likewise, Puerto Rican Catholicism emphasized *personalismo*—shrines, candles, intimate relationships with saints. The Puerto Rican clergy were perceived as being tools of Americanization, unconcerned with the social needs of the people. Yet despite their anticlericalism, the people still felt a need for religious expression. In fact, many Puerto Ricans migrating to the mainland abandoned Catholicism entirely, joining Pentecostal churches instead because they offered a close personal relationship to Jesus and freedom from a hierarchy.

Intellectual trends in the country of origin also affected immigrant religious styles. Nationalism, rationalism, democracy, socialism, and communism are some of the secular ideologies that undercut obedience to established religious authority, promoting questioning or loss of faith in countries where they were prominent. Substantial numbers of Germans, Finns, Czechs, Russians, and Eastern European Jews came to America with little concern for religion of any kind, or at least hostility toward traditional institutions. Ironically, pietism, devotionalism, and similar religious revitalization movements taking place in the old country could also undercut established religious authority, producing schisms within denominations, as in the case of German and Scandinavian Lutheranism, or whole new denominations, as in the case of English Methodism and Hasidic Judaism. But pietism could also strengthen the established religion, as it did in Ireland during the "devotional revolution" of the mid-nineteenth century and in Serbia during the late nineteenth century. As with language, national character traits, folkways, and the traditional relationship between the laity and clergy, the effects of intellectual and spiritual experiences were brought over and passed on by those emigrating to America.

Given the formative influence of ethnic origin on religious practice, it is not surprising that ethnicity has been one of the most significant divisive factors within the American religious structure. As H. Richard Niebuhr pointed out in his seminal work *The Social Sources of Denominationalism,* America's religious pluralism is not simply the by-product of rampant American individualism, as European critics have often charged. Rather, much of it derives quite directly from European nationalism. Writing in the late 1920s, Niebuhr listed twenty-seven independent religious bodies whose direct ties to Europe appear in their titles, along with more than a dozen other synods or groups that were ethnically homogeneous. While there have been numerous mergers since Niebuhr compiled his list, the *Yearbook of American and Canadian Churches* still includes at least two dozen such "ethnic" churches or synods.

All of the broad religious groups in this country (Protestants, Catholics, Jews, Eastern Orthodox, Muslims, Hindus, Buddhists) and many individual denominations as well have been divided by ethnicity at one time or another. After the Reformation, Protestantism became closely associated with nationalism, rendering theologically similar peoples quite independent of each other. American Lutherans, therefore, have included German, Norwegian, Swedish, Finnish, Hungarian, and Slovak groups. The Reformed churches in this country were English, Dutch, German, Scottish, Scotch-Irish, Welsh, Hungarian, Armenian, and Korean. There were English, Welsh, German, and Russian Baptists. Many of these groups formed independent synods, and all maintained some independent churches, many of which still exist. Missionary work produced new ethnic Protestant subgroups in America, such as German Methodists, Italian Lutherans, and Japanese Congregationalists.

The Catholic church was more united in terms of structure, in that there was a single overarching organization for all Catholics (with the exception of a group such as the Polish National Catholic Church). But despite the broad organizational unity, American Catholics during much of the nineteenth century were largely divided into "national parishes" separate from the traditional territorial parishes, though controlled by the same bishops. National parishes were an accommodation to immigrants' demands that they be able to worship with their own kind in the style to which they were accustomed using priests of their own background, even if they lived in ethnically mixed neighborhoods. Such an arrangement was initially opposed by the Irish-dominated American Catholic hierarchy on the grounds that it would allow the perpetuation of diverse practices and inhibit Americanization. But the immigrants were insistent, and officials yielded.

After World War I had provided the Americanization movement with further impetus and mass immigration had ceased, the hierarchy began to dismantle national parishes. But they still exist throughout both urban and rural America, and have done much to prevent uniformity within the Catholic church. Indeed, it is the opinion of scholars such as Andrew Greeley that national parishes have functioned almost like the different Protestant denominations. The larger ones have often included auxiliary institutions such as fraternal organizations, sodalities, hospitals, and orphanages, while even the smaller ones sponsor parochial schools teaching the language and history of the ethnic group. All of this has perpetuated and heightened the divisive effects of ethnicity on Catholics and Catholicism.

So has the sheer number of countries represented by American Catholics. They include large numbers with Irish, German, Belgian, Austrian, Italian, Portuguese, Polish, Czech, Slovak, Slovene, Croatian, Lithuanian, Hungarian, French-Canadian, Mexican, Puerto Rican, Cuban, and Filipino backgrounds, along with smaller numbers having English, French, Dutch, Scandinavian, Spanish, and miscellaneous Asian origins. The situation is further complicated by the existence of various Uniate Catholic groups in America. These are descendants of churches that broke with Rome at some point in time and later reunited, yet maintained some distinctive traditions, such as married clergy and non-Latin liturgy. Among these are the Syrian Maronite and Melchite Christians and the "Greek Catholics" from the Ukraine.

Adherents of Eastern Orthodoxy are probably the most throughly divided religious group in America. The Orthodox church was bound up with the state from its inception, so as the Byzantine Empire dissolved, the church split into a series of individual national churches that developed independently, bound together only through the primacy they all accorded the patriarch in Constantinople. When immigrants from these countries came to the United States, they usually retained ties to the head of their church back in the old country, though some have formed independent "autocephalous" Orthodox churches here, and several banded together in 1970 under the umbrella of the Orthodox Church in America. Regardless of the path chosen, the various national churches have remained quite distinct from one another, maintaining their individual languages and liturgies. Thus, one can still identify Albanian, Armenian, Bulgarian, Greek, Romanian, Russian, Serbian, Syrian, and Ukrainian Orthodox churches.

Jews, too, came to this country divided by nationality. While their special status throughout Europe kept most of them somewhat apart from the life of the nation in which they lived, those in America were nevertheless well aware of their differences in origin, especially the three main divisions. There were Ladino-speaking Sephardic Jews of Spanish or Portuguese ancestry who had worshiped in secret as Marranos or settled in Latin America, Holland, Italy, Greece, and the Balkans following their expulsion from the Iberian Peninsula at the end of the fifteenth century. There were German-speaking Jews from Central Europe, especially Germany and Austria. And there were Yiddish-speaking Eastern European Jews, themselves divided into a number of groups, of which the largest were Russian, Polish, Lithuanian, Galician, Hungarian, and Romanian. Each of these groups tended to organize and worship in its own synagogues. Since World War II there has been a migration of sabras, native-born Israeli Jews, along with refugees from other Near Eastern countries, North Africa, and the Soviet Union.

American adherents of Islam and non-Western religions such as Hinduism and Buddhism are fewer in number but nevertheless divided. Recent research on the Muslim-American community identifies more than one hundred different national backgrounds, notably Syrians, Iranians, Turks, Egyptians, Palestinians, and Yugoslavians. Mosques are shared, but many Muslims prefer to worship among their own kind. Hindus have come to America not only from India, but from the many places Indians have settled over the years, including Uganda, Kenya, Guyana, and Trinidad. They often feel little sense of religious or social kinship with Hindus from other lands. Individual Buddhist temples likewise tend to be patronized by either Chinese, Japanese, or Korean worshipers.

Thus most American religious groups are ethnically divided. Some of the most pronounced divisions have social overtones reinforced by differences in the time of arrival among the various groups. The fact that the Irish were the first large group of Catholics to come to this country has had a profound effect on their relationship with the various ethnic groups who arrived later and resented Irish domination and sense of superiority. It also contributed to the superior socioeconomic achievement—higher average income and higher average educational level—the Irish still show relative to the Poles, Italians, and others. Likewise, German Jews on the whole arrived twenty to eighty years earlier than Eastern Europeans, so that by the time the latter came, the former were quite successful, assimilated, and more inclined to be hostile toward the poor, non-Westernized newcomers than they would have been on religious grounds alone.

Differences would have been present even if groups had arrived simultaneously, however. Scholars such as Andrew Greeley, Harold Abramson, Elmer Spreitzer, and Eldon Snyder have noted a variety of secular traits in which various ethnic groups of the same religion deviate from one another. Italian and Polish Catholics arrived during approximately the same period, for example, but Polish-Americans studied in the 1970s were noticeably less likely to be white-collar workers. Protestants of Scotch-Irish background, most of whose forebears arrived in this country during the mid-eighteenth century, today on average have a poorer education than Protestants of Scandinavian background, most of whose forebears arrived in the mid- to late nineteenth century. Socioeconomic differences such as these are important because they are one measure of distance between ethnic groups and often have a pronounced impact on social relationships, including the willingness of people to live and worship together, to merge, or remain divided.

One must reiterate, however, the importance of variations in religious style and practice. With the significant exception of language, none of these presents a major practical obstacle to unity among ethnic groups of the same religious persuasion. Yet, as noted, folkways tend to be seen as "right ways," especially when they are related to something as central and potent as religion. There is also the simple fact that people tend to be more comfortable with something familiar to them. Hence, differences in style, such as clerical garb, the mood of the service, and the inclusion or omission of certain prayers or songs, have served as divisive issues despite their dubious theological significance.

While acculturation has eroded some of these barriers, it has raised others, because disagreements over the use of English and the elimination of certain old customs created schisms within ethnic churches and denominations. German Lutherans, for example, were divided into four different synods as late as 1930, with the eastern synods more amenable to English and thus attracting older, more assimilated churches into their fold. When the Dutch Reformed Church dropped the word *Dutch* from its title, other Dutch Reformed Americans organized the True Dutch Reformed Church, determined to maintain the language and traditions of the old country more faithfully.

Thus, ethnic issues could actually divide members of the same ethnoreligious group in America. Language retention has been the most volatile issue, but political disputes have also played a part, especially among Eastern Europeans. Armenian-Americans split over their degree of militancy against the Turks. Greek Orthodox churches in this country divided during World War I into royalists who backed the king in his neutral stance and liberals who supported the prime minister in his call to join the Allies. Events following World War II created a series of crises within other American Orthodox groups by throwing into doubt the integrity of the various old-country patriarchs, now that they had to work with officially atheist communist regimes. Some Romanians, for example, remained loyal to Bucharest, while others joined the independent Orthodox Church in America. The Serbs underwent a major schism in 1963 over allegiance to the patriarch in Belgrade. For their part, Korean Presbyterian churches split over their response to South Korean leader Park Chung Hee during the 1970s.

In sum, ethnic identification, with all its political, social, and stylistic aspects, has been a major divisive factor within American religion. It has inhibited unity and even cooperation among members in almost every denomination and has actually caused dissension within religious groups that shared a common national heritage. Religion, likewise, has served to divide ethnic groups.

As noted earlier, certain peoples were quite uniform in their religious persuasion. But there are many more examples of national groups that contained members of many different religious groups. The British brought a wide range of Protestant denominations to this country: Episcopalian, Presbyterian, Congregationalist, Baptist, Quaker, to name a few. The Dutch were divided into Catholics and Calvinists. There were Catholic, Lutheran, Reformed, and Jewish Hungarians; Catholic, Greek Catholic, Greek

Orthodox, and Lutheran Slovaks; Orthodox and Congregationalist Armenians; Maronite, Melkite, Orthodox, and Muslim Syrians; Hindu and Sikh Indians; Protestant, Catholic, and Buddhist Koreans. Perhaps the most heterogeneous group of all were the Germans. They came as Catholics, Lutherans, Reformed, Jews, and a variety of sectarian groups, such as the Dunkers, Brethren, Mennonites, and Moravians. Once here, they splintered further, forming Presbyterian and Methodist churches, among others.

A number of these divisions were exacerbated by timing. Early Arab settlers in this country tended to be Christian, while more recent ones have been largely Muslim. In the case of the Japanese, generation is the main dividing factor, with most of the immigrant generation being Buddhist while half their children and most of their grandchildren have become Christian. The Japanese tradition of religious tolerance and openness has mitigated against problems in that group, but there has been a noticeable lack of unity in most other cases where religious differences exist within an ethnic group. It is worth noting, for example, that there is a Hungarian Catholic League of America, a Hungarian Reformed Federation of America, and a World Federation of Hungarian Jews. There is also an American Hungarian Federation open to all regardless of religion, just as there is a German-American National Congress, and so on. But pluralism still dominates.

As with ethnic issues, religious issues have even divided people who ostensibly share a common religious and ethnic identity. The Dutch Reformed who insisted on retaining the word *Dutch* in their title also insisted on adhering to closed communion and the use of psalms instead of hymns. Post–World War II Serbian immigrants have generally been more tenacious about maintaining the traditional Orthodox prayers and calendar than older Serbian-Americans. And while it was the newcomers who saw themselves as purer in these cases, sometimes it was just the opposite. Descendants of colonial German Lutherans felt that many nineteenth-century arrivals were contaminated by false ideas circulating in the fatherland. And again, Pietist–non-Pietist splits within many of the Protestant churches exacerbated differences between settlers from the same country and the same denomination.

The division of ethnic groups by religion and of religious groups by ethnicity has the advantage of providing the individual with a rather specific identity (e.g., Scottish Presbyterian) instead of merely the broad identity afforded by ethnic or religious affiliation alone. In a mass society, such a subidentity can have definite psychological and social utility. But insofar as religion prevents rather than reinforces a broad ethnic identity, and ethnicity prevents rather than reinforces a broad religious identity, the two can be said to work at cross purposes. While division by no means inevitably leads to demise, it often helps to weaken or fragment a group, sometimes to the point where it may be too weak to survive organizationally. This danger is enhanced by a fundamental aspect of American civilization: the lack of compulsion for the individual to join or remain a member of any particular group. It is a well-known fact that this has led to open competition among religious denominations. But competition for an individual's loyalty can also occur between ethnic and religious groups.

The notion that ethnicity can take precedence over religion has received less attention than its inverse, but a number of historical examples exist to illustrate that the possibility is more than theoretical. German and Czech freethinkers and Jewish and Finnish socialists were among those for whom ethnicity was more important than denominational affiliation, a clear alternative for their fellow immigrants to emulate now that they were free of old-country pressures to maintain religious allegiance. In another instance, ethnic pride assumed such importance that it prompted a group of Polish-Americans to break away from the Roman Catholic church, which declared that loyalty to the faith must come first. Father Francis Hodur formed the Polish National Catholic Church around the turn of the century, claiming that the Polish people everywhere needed their own church to support Poland's status as a truly independent nation. Such schismatic action was extreme, but German and Italian immigrants threatened and sometimes established their own churches without the authorization of the Roman Catholic hierarchy, and they might well have continued to worship independently had their demand for their own national parishes gone unanswered.

Ethnic needs or goals have also taken precedence over religion among groups that have felt that their survival was threatened. In colonial America, for example, German Lutherans were so concerned about the erosion of their language and culture that schools and newspapers were established as a cooperative venture with German Reformed and Moravian congregations. Indeed, German Lutherans prior to the Civil War often showed more affinity for members of other German denominations than for the theologically similar Episcopalians or even fellow Lutherans from Scandinavia.

A more recent case in point is the American Arab community. While Christians are divided into Maronite, Melkite, and Orthodox, researchers have shown that members of these groups have often ignored their differences in order to maintain ethnic endogamy. That is, many prefer to intermarry across religious lines than to maintain religious homogeneity by marrying outside the ethnic group. Likewise, Muslim Arabs in the United States downplay the Sunni/Shiite division. The Pan-Arab movement arising out of the Middle Eastern troubles of recent decades has even mitigated against long-standing barriers between Christians and Muslims, leading to some common organizations, such as the National Association of Arab Americans.

Ethnic organizations that deemphasize religion or cut across religious lines have existed for many other groups as well. Raised in environments with flexible religious boundaries, Chinese- and Japanese-Americans were often more loyal to clans and regional associations than to any religious group. Protestants of different denominations and ethnicities have long mingled in social clubs. Strictly secular organizations such as the German Turnverein, the Polish National Alliance of the U.S., the Lithuanian Alliance of America, and the Slovene National Benefit Society attracted many Catholics, sometimes more than the church-related fraternal organizations set up by a hierarchy anxious for parishioners to emphasize religious rather than ethnic fellowship.

For their part, sizable numbers of Jewish immigrants joined socialist clubs and landsmanschaftn (benevolent societies) and sent their children to secular Yiddish schools instead of religious schools. Today, philanthropy, interest in the state of Israel, and participation in Jewish social and cultural organizations are among the many ways for the individual to relate to other Jews without necessarily attending or supporting a synagogue. American voluntarism, of course, sets no limits on the number of groups that an individual may join or support. But the fact remains that time, resources, and perhaps even the capacity for psychological commitment are limited in all individuals. Thus, the existence of secular ethnic organizations alongside religious organizations is an important facet of the competition between ethnicity and religion.

Furthermore, it has been argued that ethnicity can to a degree take the place of religion in an individual's life by providing the meaning, belonging, and comfort that are the major functions of religion. Harold Abramson has suggested that the ethnic group can give the individual an understanding of his place and purpose on earth along with an outlook on the future, a set of norms and values to guide his behavior, and suitable rituals to give meaning to critical stages of the life cycle. The notion of ethnicity serving as "a religion" seems farfetched and perhaps even un-American, something akin to love of state replacing love of God in a totalitarian society. Yet, as noted, scholars have placed ethnicity alongside religion as a "primordial attachment" and have pointed out an increasing tendency for modern man to "lunge back to the tribal caves," as Harold Isaacs put it. The fact that ethnic identity has persisted and indeed reasserted itself in America since the 1960s lends at least some credence to the possibility that ethnicity could become a more major subfocus of individual identity and participation than religion.

It is the reverse, however, that has received far more attention: the idea that religious identification is submerging ethnic identification in America. In some cases there is little question; certain religions are so all-encompassing and distinctive that they constitute ethnic groups in themselves. One such group is the Mormons, who have a unique history, set of prophets, and sacred text, and readily assimilate people from many backgrounds. They have long been highly concentrated geographically and at times have functioned almost as a political and economic entity. They encourage active participation in the church's social as well as religious activities from an early age, and make intermarriage with non-Mormons very difficult. Many of the newer "religions" that have attracted Americans in the twentieth century likewise resemble ethnic groups.

While these examples may be said to be outside the religious mainstream, Andrew Greeley has asserted that even mainstream Protestant denominations function much like ethnic groups. He has highlighted some consistent differences in the way contemporary Baptists, Methodists, Lutherans, Presbyterians, Congregationalists, and Episcopalians think and behave, suggesting that they differ as much or more than ethnic groups differ, and he has underscored the importance of denominational identity. Indeed, Greeley asserts in *The Denominational Society:* "The secret of survival of the organized churches in the United States . . . is their ability to play an ethnic or at least quasi-ethnic role in American society." Belonging to a church, he continues, provides people with a sense of community, the "means of defining who they are and where they stand" (p. 108). Like ethnicity, he concludes, denominational identity helps fill the gap between family membership and one's identity as an American.

Greeley's contention that fellowship is more important than belief in determining the high rate of religious activity among Americans makes his thesis somewhat controversial. But the broader notion that Americans beyond the immigrant generation may come to have a stronger religious identity than ethnic identity achieved widespread publicity in Will Herberg's *Protestant-Catholic-Jew,* published in 1955. Taking a cue from Ruby Jo Kennedy's description of New Haven as a "triple melting pot," Herberg argued that ethnicity was a dying phenomenon, that distinctions between the various national origins groups within the United States were being blurred because Americans were intermarrying freely across ethnic lines. However, Herberg noted, such intermarriages almost always took place within the broad divisions of Protestant, Catholic, or Jew. Hence, he postulated that religious affiliation would remain a major source of stratification within American society, while ethnicity would lose its significance.

In the case of smaller ethnic groups, or those living among few of their own kind, this blending process had clearly been under way for a long time. Slovak Lutherans worshiped with German Lutherans in rural areas; Orthodox Serbs and Bulgarians scattered in small towns sometimes joined the larger Russian Orthodox organizations and today may even mix in cities. This melting process occurred more noticeably and more rapidly among Jews, though for reasons that went far beyond numbers. While Eastern European Jews of various national backgrounds set up their own congregations and clubs upon arrival, common economic and social problems encouraged a rapid blurring of ethnic divisions. Indeed, as noted, mistreatment and minority status in Europe had precluded most from forming deep national attachments to begin with.

Even the much more pronounced division between the wealthier, assimilated Sephardic and German Jews and the poorer, unassimilated Eastern Europeans broke down surprisingly rapidly. The rise of Conservative Judaism provided a middle ground in theology and religious style to which both groups could relate; the rapid economic progress of the Eastern European Jews and the universal impact of the Depression lessened the gap in wealth; anti-Semitism and the Zionist cause strengthened the sense of shared fate. By the 1930s intermarriage between Jews of German and Eastern European heritage was quite common. Indeed, with the exception of those newly arrived from Latin America and pockets of refugees from Arab countries, few Jews in America define themselves in terms of national origins. And despite large numbers who rarely or never participate in religious worship, most Jews still share the opinion sociologist Marshall Sklare found in the 1950s: that "religion must become the main expression of Jewish life."

While it is to be expected that smaller groups would deemphasize their differences in order to survive, larger groups have experienced the same kind of ethnic "melting." Various studies using data on British, German, and Scandinavian Protestants from the years 1900 to 1920 revealed an endogamy (inmarriage) rate 50 to 75 percent above what would be expected on the basis of the groups' proportion of the local population if ethnicity were not a determining factor. Studies made between 1950 and 1970 show that the rate had dropped to the vicinity of 25 percent in most cases. Thus, when Charles H. Anderson published *White Protestant Americans* in 1970, he used the subtitle "From National Origins to Religious Group." Turning to institutions, it is worth noting that the last Welsh Presbyterian Synod dissolved in 1954 and that a series of mergers between various national Lutheran synods has taken place since the beginning of this century, so that by the end of the 1960s the three large Lutheran organizations remained separated by theology but cut across ethnic lines. In 1984 two of the remaining three had plans for a merger that would include another smaller group as well.

Analyses of data gathered by the National Opinion Research Center (NORC) strengthens the notion of a Protestant melting pot. According to polls taken in the late 1960s, Protestants were crossing denominational as well as ethnic lines. Even members of the four largest Protestant denominations in America—Baptists, Lutherans, Methodists, and Presbyterians—who presumably had plenty of their own kind to choose from, were intermarrying with members of a different Protestant denomination at rates of 65 to 85 percent.

Catholics, too, showed much evidence of blending. Harold Abramson gathered data in 1968 and found that with the exception of the recently arrived Spanish-speaking and the highly clustered French-Canadians and Italians, most Catholic ethnic groups (Irish, German, Polish, other Slavic, English) had outmarriage rates of at least 50 percent. One generation earlier, all but English Catholics had been below 35 percent. Richard D. Alba confirms this trend toward change over time, citing a significant increase in the number of Catholics with multiple ancestry among those born after World War II, compared with those born before World War II. Indeed, writes Alba in "The Twilight of Ethnicity," "ethnicity appears to be nearing twilight among the Catholic ethnic groups" of America (p. 97).

The reasons for the growth of the "triple melting pot" are many. First, there is the sheer decline in ethnicity, independent of any religious developments. Its most basic cause, according to Herberg and others, is the decreasing use of foreign languages, which stood as both real and symbolic barriers between Americans of different national origins. This trend, along with other forms of acculturation, is closely related to the distance from the immigrant generation, a distance increasing due to the sharp curtailment of

immigration in 1924. Between 1930 and 1970 the proportion of Americans "of foreign stock" —that is, native or foreign-born with at least one foreign-born parent—dropped from 36 to 19 percent. Social and geographic mobility, major trends in modern American life, also play a role in the breakdown of ethnicity. They take individuals out of their old ethnic neighborhoods and bring them into contact with new ideas and people of different backgrounds, different values, and different behavioral patterns. The mass media has performed some of these same functions.

Furthermore, Protestants, Catholics, and Jews have each become increasingly aware of their special group concerns. For Protestants, lack of unity, both ideological and organizational, has been a consistent issue. And while a comfortable certainty that they are the "real" Americans persists among many, the transition from a clearly dominant to a less dominant position as determiners of American values and behavior has led Protestants to reassess—and in many cases reassert—their role in the life of the nation. Catholics have been collectively concerned with policies of the Vatican, the American church hierarchy, and the American government regarding issues such as abortion, divorce, the role of laymen, and aid to parochial schools. They have also sought to overcome the negative blue-collar, hard-hat image often attached to them, to forestall changes in their old urban neighborhoods, and to achieve a more prominent place in the national political scene. Jews have been brought together by a widely shared middle-class status and outlook, concern for the State of Israel, and a perceived need for continued vigilance against anti-Semitism here and abroad. Such shared concerns have helped each of the major religious groups to overcome and submerge their internal ethnic divisions.

Finally, the tendency for ethnic affiliation to take a backseat to religious affiliation has been aided by the fact that America has generally sanctioned the latter, but not the former. Religiosity has always been a much-admired trait in this country, but "foreignness" and "foreign loyalties," as defined by a variety of standard makers, have been discouraged by formal and informal devices throughout American history.

Yet despite the weight of logic and evidence suggesting that the "triple melting pot" is replacing ethnic diversity, many scholars have concluded that Herberg was wrong, or at least premature, in his redrawing of the divisions within American society. There was an "ethnic revival" in the 1960s inspired by the rise of black consciousness during the civil rights movement. Old customs were celebrated with new pride and openness, genealogy flourished, an Ethnic Heritage Week was established, organizations were founded, and research projects were undertaken to explore the "ethnic phenomenon" further.

Many of these projects have contributed to a new awareness of ethnicity in American life. Nathan Glazer, Daniel Patrick Moynihan, Michael Novak, Andrew Greeley, and Harold Abramson have demonstrated that many ethnics seem to be "unmeltable"; that they maintain their group loyalty and cultural traditions well into the third and fourth generation. Beyond ethnic identification lie the myriad of measurable socioeconomic differences alluded to earlier. Greeley and Abramson, who have done the most rigorous work, point out that Protestants and Catholics of different ethnic backgrounds differ in everything from wealth to family values, political participation to personality traits, regional concentrations to intermarriage rates. Greeley has even compiled statistics suggesting that German Catholics think and behave more like German Protestants than they do like Irish Catholics. This suggests that ethnicity may have a greater influence on life-style than religion.

While the ethnic revival was real, and continued immigration has kept the model of biculturalism alive for American ethnics of older ancestry, the salience of ethnicity remains unclear. Debate over this matter centers in part on the statistics used, which are not always as clear-cut as they purport to be. Some are based on small samples, others are not controlled for important intervening variables such as generation or region, and there is also that old question whether the glass is "half empty or half full." Is 40 percent endogamy a sign that Irish ethnicity is strong or weak? It certainly is lower than it used to be. Likewise, there is the question of what ethnicity means to the individual. Even if he shows some traits typical of his group, is ethnicity necessarily a major determining factor in his life, a central feature in his self-perception? Herbert Gans has argued that much of what passes for group membership is merely "symbolic ethnicity," an identifying label and a bit of "spice" or flavoring in personality and behavior.

In any case, it is clear that religious identification is higher than ethnic identification. NORC data from 1972 suggests that 78 percent of Americans identify with one nationality, but fully 95 percent of Americans polled the same year identified with one religion. Furthermore, rates of religious endogamy among Protestants, Catholics, and Jews are higher than those of most ethnic groups. NORC data from 1957 shows that 88 percent of Catholics, 81 to 83 percent of members of major Protestant denominations, and 94 percent of Jews were married to someone of the same religion.

Yet these rates, too, have been declining over time. Richard D. Alba's data from NORC surveys of 1973–1978 shows that among people born since World War II, 24 percent of Protestants and 44 percent of Catholics of European ancestry have married out of their faith. Recent data on Jews indicates a tremendous upsurge in exogamy: by the mid-1970s, nearly half the marriages taking place involving a Jew were interfaith marriages. While Protestants' rate may seem relatively low, it is worth reiterating that they are the largest religious group in America, giving them more potential for in-group marriages. Moreover they are now crossing denominational boundaries at high rates, which is a kind of intermarriage in itself given the history of antipathy between the various Protestant groups in America.

Does all this suggest that in the competition between religion and ethnicity for an individual's loyalty, the winner will be neither? Robert N. Bellah, Will Herberg, and others have made much of America's "civil religion"—democracy, free enterprise, idealism, plus a set of rituals and symbols associated with this nation—as the ultimate grounds for unity, the ultimate melting pot. But intermarriage does not necessarily signal the end of group identity. A majority of people of mixed ancestry choose to identify with one ethnic group or another, while an even greater proportion of those who marry someone outside their faith choose one denomination with which to affiliate. Indeed, the continuing strength of religious identification and the weaker but nonetheless persistent degree of ethnic identification suggests that both will remain important in American life for decades to come, reinforcing, shaping, dividing, and competing with each other as they have done since the founding of this nation.

BIBLIOGRAPHY

Harold J. Abramson, *Ethnic Diversity in Catholic America* (1973); Richard D. Alba, "The Twilight of Ethnicity Among American Catholics of European Ancestry," in *Annals of the American Academy of Political and Social Science,* 454 (1981); Charles H. Anderson, *White Protestant Americans* (1970); Jay P. Dolan, *The Immigrant Church: New York's Irish and German Catholics, 1815–1865* (1975); Joe R. Feagin, *Racial and Ethnic Relations* (1978; 2nd ed., 1984); Otto Feinstein, ed., *Ethnic Groups in the City* (1971); E. K. Francis, *Interethnic Relations* (1976).

Nathan Glazer, *American Judaism* (1957; rev. 1972) and, with Daniel P. Moynihan, *Beyond the Melting Pot* (1963; 2nd ed., 1970); Milton Gordon, *Assimilation in American Life* (1964); Andrew M. Greeley, *The Denominational Society* (1972), *Ethnicity in the United States* (1974), and *The American Catholic: A Social Portrait* (1977); Oscar Handlin, *The Uprooted* (1951); Marcus L. Hansen, *The Problem of the 3rd Generation Immigrant* (1938) and "Immigration and Puritanism," in John M. Mulder and John F. Wilson, eds., *Religion in American History* (1978); Will Herberg, *Protestant-Catholic-Jew* (1955; rev. 1960); Harold Isaacs, *Idols of the Tribe* (1975); Thomas Luckmann, *The Invisible Religion: The Problem of Religion in Modern Society* (1967); Martin E. Marty, "Ethnicity: The Skeleton of Religion in America," in *Church History,* 41 (1972); Randall M. Miller and Thomas D. Marzik, *Immigrants and Religion in Urban America* (1977).

H. Richard Niebuhr, *The Social Sources of Denominationalism* (1929); Michael Novak, *The Rise of the Unmeltable Ethnics* (1972); James Stuart Olson, *The Ethnic Dimension in American History* (1979); Timothy L. Smith, "Lay Initiative in the Religious Life of American Immigrants, 1880–1950," in Tamara K. Hareven, ed., *Anonymous Americans* (1971), and "Religion and Ethnicity in America," in *American Historical Review,* 83 (1978); Stephen Thernstrom, ed., *The Harvard Encyclopedia of American Ethnic Groups* (1980); Charles A. Ward et al., *Studies in Ethnicity: The East European Experience in America* (1980); W. Lloyd Warner and Leo Srole, *The Social Systems of American Ethnic Groups* (1945).

[*See also* BUDDHISM; CATHOLICISM FROM INDEPENDENCE TO WORLD WAR I; CATHOLICISM IN THE ENGLISH COLONIES; CATHOLICISM SINCE WORLD WAR I; COMMUNITARIANISM; DUTCH AND GERMAN REFORMED CHURCHES; EASTERN CHRISTIANITY; EMERGENCE OF AN AMERICAN JUDAISM; HINDUISM; ISLAM IN NORTH AMERICA; JUDAISM IN CONTEMPORARY AMERICA; LUTHERANISM; SECTS AND RELIGIOUS MOVEMENTS OF GERMAN ORIGIN; SHINTO AND INDIGENOUS CHINESE RELIGION; *and* SOCIAL HISTORY OF AMERICAN JUDAISM.]

THE SOUTH

Samuel S. Hill

THE South is a particular case in the study of American religion. While recognizably American, the religion of the southern region is distinctive owing to the special nature of regional culture and, in line with that fact, its singular religious history.

No other American religious region compares with the South in identifiability and distinctiveness, although up to the 1830s, New England did compare. Until then two Calvinist groups were consistently and prominently strong, Congregationalists and Presbyterians, with a sprinkling of Baptists. The early Middle West belonged to the Methodists and the Calvinist people who migrated there from New England and the Middle Atlantic states.

Immigration changed those relatively homogeneous conditions in New England and the Middle West. Beginning in the 1830s, Roman Catholics, Lutherans, and Jews, most notably, moved into those areas and altered the religious (and sociocultural) landscape. The entire society north of the Mason-Dixon line felt the impact of these new people and their ways from then on. Far less so did the South; in fact, the cultural solidity of the South increased throughout the nineteenth century. The salience of the immigration factor, its pervasiveness in the North and its scarcity in the South, is fundamental for understanding the distinctiveness of Southern history and culture. This is as true with respect to religion as to any other component of the culture.

The continuity of the South's history from the colonial period until the 1830s and much later is remarkable. British Protestantism was the South's religious mainstream—almost its only stream—from the settlement of Jamestown in 1607. The Church of England (later Episcopal) enjoyed establishment status throughout the colonial period. The fact that establishmentarianism was ill suited to American contours and temperaments, proving largely ineffective, does not detract from the pronounced British accent of colonial Christianity.

Protestant denominations that had spun off from the Church of England made up the balance, namely, the Quakers, the Baptists, and the Methodists. A small number of Congregationalists also turned up. Quite a few descendants of the other large British Protestant body, the Presbyterians, resided in the Old Dominion and the Carolinas and were prominent. (There were pockets of Lutherans, Moravians, and German Baptists.)

Only one major exception appeared, the Christianity of the slaves, but Europe's traditional faith was embraced by few of them until after independence. Moreover, its nomenclature was the same, Methodist and Baptist, and it was given little opportunity at first to develop a distinctive life of its own.

Thus the brands of Christianity with which the region began shifted slightly between 1607 and the 1830s, but the traditional approach held fast. The spectrum broadened as evangelical forms supplemented older British Protestant forms. Still, few Catholics or Jews, or Protestants of European origin, appeared on the scene. Some indigenous bodies, formed in the South or originating in the North, supplemented the transplanted British denominations. What they held in common was a commitment to the restoration of primitive Christianity, a goal they believed possible, necessary, and in fact realized in their own existence. The largest of these was the Disciples of Christ (or Campbellite or Christian) movement; a smaller one was the Christian Church of James O'Kelly, called at first the Republican Methodist Church, which merged with the Congregational Church in 1931. Less formal in its organizational existence, but powerfully influential and also restorationist, was the landmark movement among Baptists in Tennessee and Kentucky in the 1840s. This "Baptist successionist" theology insinuated itself into Southern Baptist Convention life, especially in its southwestern reaches, and plays a part in today's "moderate-inerrantist" conflict. "Successionist" in this context refers to the conviction that there have been Baptist churches straight through from the first century and that the only true churches are Baptist churches. Two landmark denominations have come on the scene in this century, the American Baptist Association (1904) and the Baptist Missionary Association of America (1905), both strongest in the Arkansas-Texas-Oklahoma area.

What impresses the observer is how homogeneous Southern religion was by the time the North had witnessed the era of immigration—which brought to Northern life diversity and a growing commitment to pluralism as a social value. Most Southern church people lived within the orbit of an evangelical version of the Christian faith, with the choices no greater than between Baptist and Methodist, "Christian" or Congregational. Presbyterianism stood just on the edge of this span. This left the Episcopal church as the only dramatic alternative. Most of the other groups were ethnic (non-British, that is) in one sense or another. That classification includes also black religion—black congregations and denominations were not a regular feature in the South until after emancipation. Black Southerners worshiped in white-led or white-monitored services for the largest part.

There is no compelling reason why the North's patterns of diversity and heterogeneity should be regarded as expected or normative for Southern regional developments. Nothing inherently proper or "superior" attaches to the way patterns shifted in the North from 1835 onward. The South had been a culture on a different course from the first settlement at Jamestown. That was predictable. A company of people with somewhat different animation settled in a territory characterized by a different climate and topography and under its own cultural conditions, economic, religious, and political.

What is astonishing is how a regional culture that had fostered the theory and practice of innovation, openness, and a bold daring in the public life of a society in the late eighteenth century became so fixed and parochial after 1830. The focus and concern shifted from the union of states to each state—in actuality, to each state that shared the prescribed vision of the good societal life. The career of John C. Calhoun reflects this transference with remarkable transparency from federalism to state's rights. Some promoters of the South's virtues, ways, and vision sought to export the region's model to other societies, George Fitzhugh being the most conspicuous. A Virginia lawyer and author, Fitzhugh justified slavery and Southern civilization and contended that the South was superior to the North. For the most part, however, the region was preoccupied with making the case for its ways in the national Congress and with bolstering those ways by laws and policies within its own jurisdiction.

At all events, as one region was being forced to loosen its forms of public life—sometimes kicking and screaming, to be sure—the other was holding on for dear life, in fact creating a degree of conservatism it had not practiced or promulgated earlier. The Southern region was born as a self-conscious general culture in this era—not earlier than the 1820s, really, although some of the seeds for its parochialism were present from the beginning. (Regional consciousness increased, reaching its apogee in the decades following Reconstruction.) From about 1830 a regional culture was drifting toward becoming a nation. As a separate state from 1861 to 1865, the South was closer to sham than to genuine independent poltical status, but its appearance revealed the devout and firm intentions of major regional leadership and broad consensus.

The region's religion was part and parcel of the enlarging and hardening regional culture. Already evangelical by momentum, it became more intensely so, partly because the denominations in that family added revivalism to evangelicalism's list of features. The number of denominations increased, but the range of options remained narrow. It is not so much that alternatives were prohibited from entering as that none was introduced since few new groupings of people were entering. Also, the conventional religious approaches had achieved a neat fit with the metaphors, values, and sensibilities of the region's culture, for example, reinforcing slavery. Evangelicalism was firmly planted as the standard religion of the American South by the 1830s. In concrete terms that meant that Baptists and Methodists and Baptist- and Methodist-like approaches to Christian faith dominated. Presbyterianism was there and coexisted with the definitively evangelical bodies, as did the Episcopal church, which enjoyed an enduring and influential presence. Most other bodies were either limited to their ethnic parameters—the Moravians, who were Czech and German and who spoke German, the Lutherans and Dunkers, who were German—or were dissident English Protestants, such as the Quakers.

In the South the widely diffused and theologically dominant evangelical party became identified with "what Christianity is all about." It is therefore imperative to understand the approach of that party. Setting it alongside the two other major parties of Protestantism, the liturgical and the classical (or Reformation), affords some initial insight. Liturgical Protestantism, epitomized by the Episcopal church, centers on the act of public worship. The service (literally, "service" or "the work of the people") of worship is prescribed, structured by a liturgy from which there may be no basic deviation, and regularly conducted by a priest who has been suitably trained and properly ordained. The people are meant to *participate* in the service by saying many of the words in the liturgy, by sitting, standing, and kneeling when each action is appropriate, and by going forward to the altar to commune directly, that is, to receive bread and wine in Holy Communion.

In order to compare the liturgical approach with the evangelical, three aspects of the liturgical must be highlighted. First, it lives *out of* something, a prescribed form of worship, rather than *by* something such as the biblical text or a theological creed. This means that it is not marked by precision or exactitude of belief, not preoccupied with the issue of authoritative teaching. Second, its central feature, the service of worship, is laid out, with the result that a quiet and gradual and even not conscious spirituality is characteristic. This is quite different from the evangelical form of Christianity in which spontaneity, personal expressiveness, and even overt manifestations of the conscious inner working of the divine spirit are typical and proper. Third,

the question of a person's own eternal destiny is recessive. Belief in the afterlife, heaven and hell, is affirmed, but no definite criteria are offered for determining "which way" one's destiny lies. Trust in God and participation in his presence in the life of worship, the sacraments, and prayer deflect one from asking directly, Am I saved? Sin and human sinfulness are taught; what they do in each person's life is to cause spiritual blindness. God is there, present all around for the seeing, if only people will open their eyes to see and act upon what they see. Blindness is a serious, life-depriving illness. But it is curable by the loving power of a God who is quite accessible and is continuously presenting himself.

Classical, or Reformation, Protestantism—the kind exemplified by Presbyterians (Calvinists generally) and Lutherans—is the other variety that preceded evangelicalism in the South and continues in strength as a moderate alternative to it. Here all attention is directed to the Word of God, the Christian message contained in the Bible. Preaching becomes the representative action of church life. People attend worship services mainly to listen, to hear the Word read and proclaimed. The minister functions, accordingly, as a student of the Bible and theology and as a preacher and teacher of the Word.

With respect to personal destiny, in classical Protestantism, as in liturgical, the matter is one of responsible indifference, of trusting God. This tradition then is not given to "saving souls," to generating the conversion experience, or to identifying "the lost" for special ministration. Instead, Christians listen, take to heart, heed, and put into practice the proffer of love and forgiveness from God to each and the responsibility of living in covenant with him and with fellow human beings. Calvinism in particular is a way of duty, of living out one's life in obedience to the Lord's commands. Whereas liturgical Christians centrally celebrate and see, classical Protestants hear and obey. Sin and sinfulness are basic teaching here as well but take the form of fallenness. All people are fallen (as is the whole created order), estranged from God, limited by their humanity, at odds with God's will. Each and all need to be forgiven, healed, and lifted by a power they cannot generate. Utter dependence on God's mercy is the deepest level of Reformation understanding. So dependent on the Lord are we all that it is in his hands to redeem us and, as he wills, to invite us to an eternal life with him in heaven.

Popular Southern Christianity, evangelical by major classification, has a closer kinship to the classical than to the liturgical variety. Its inclinations are to the Bible, correct teaching, preaching as the central act in worship, and response perceived in the terms of duty and obedience. With few penchants for seeing or regarding sin as blindness or believing that God is all around —in the sense of liturgical Christianity's "sacramental universe"—it veers sharply from that family of Christians. It also takes quite a different tack than the classical family about the nature of sin. No more is sin "fallenness" than it is "blindness." It is personal disobedience, willful rejection of God and his claims. But the practical impact of a person's sinfulness is even more important, namely, guilt. Being a guilty sinner before God comprises the heart of the evangelical message preached from thousands of Southern pulpits.

It is not that evangelical Christianity everywhere and in all its varieties views personal guilt as the essence of Christian teaching and responsibility. Indeed, most forms of it outside the South and some within it give greater stress usually to utmost devotion to the authority of the Bible and sound doctrine, but sometimes also to social responsibility and a disciplined personal spirituality. The South's representative form of evangelicalism is linked with its heritage of revivalism that has roots in the Great Awakening of the mid-eighteenth century but is really derivative from the Great Revival on the frontier between 1799 and 1810.

Thus, in the South's most popular type of Christianity "evangelicalism" connotes "evangelism." The former term is one party and family within the larger Protestant community and tradition; it has a common quality, commitment to the principle of authority and, at that, the authority of the biblical text together with the correct interpretation of it. Evangelism, itself a term with a range of historical usages, means in its own Southern setting the enterprise of converting the unsaved (the lost souls) to faith in Christ, thereby assuring them of pardon of their sins and everlasting life in heaven. This is accomplished through a convert's bearing witness and through "evangelistic preaching."

This way of understanding Christianity grows out of a specific world view. Its major components are the one God and the individual. At issue is the nature of their correlation. Related they are, ineluctably, inasmuch as God created the individual man or woman and has profound interest in and concern and plans for each person. In that sense no one is ever apart from God; through his creating each and all and also through Christ's offering himself as the sacrifice for the sins of the whole world, every person is bound to God. Yet, the relation can be lacking in relationship, that is, without activation in the dynamic qualities that link two personal entities. There is meant to be an awareness on each person's part of God's love for that person by name, as well as an acknowledgment of that "reaching down" that takes hold in the response of that person to God and his total claim upon one's life.

Something is wrong, lacking, amiss, however, in the design intended by the creating, redeeming God. A gulf separates the individual and God. Hostility or cross-purposes prevail instead of a binding reciprocity. Therefore, a bridge must be built. Peace must be declared. A harmony of wills must replace a discordant interaction. God, from his own initiative, offers pardon, new being, and the gift of eternal life. That presentation is directly affiliated with his setting the terms by which humankind is judged defective and deficient. This is a world view operating sub specie aeternitatis, by divine plan and authority. The whole world and the entire historical process—including every individual—is in his hands. He has every right to a total life commitment from every person.

Southern evangelicalism thus depicts a cosmic encounter between two personal entities, the demanding, requiring, self-sacrificial God and the defective, deficient, self-idolizing individual. The party of the first part defines the terms under which the party of the second part lives. Each has requirements placed on him or her, but each falls short, and each is held accountable. The shape of the failure is guilt. The bridge provided for redemption from failure is cruciform. Repeatedly, the message proclaimed is, first, that each person is sinful, guilty, and hell bound, and second, that Christ has died for the sins of everyone.

From the Great Revival to the present regional religion has been permeated by this outlook. To be sure, not all churches or Christians have viewed things this way; certainly not Episcopalians and Presbyterians, often not Methodists, sometimes not Baptists. But this depiction of the problem and the solution, most basically, the conviction that the message is couched in problem-solution terms, is the standard one for regional life. The burden of explanation lies—heavily—on any who differ from that perception of reality. Many who do not understand Christianity this way have trouble articulating the divergence.

Historically such a theology has produced a sense of aggressiveness and urgency. This ideological factor has played a role in the rapid growth and widespread expansion of nineteenth-century Methodism, the Southern Baptist Convention until the present, and for the lifetime of the younger denominations, most of them Pentecostal or Holiness. It has also equipped them with focused, limited missions; their task has been to convert the unconverted, to save sinners. Other denominations of Christianity may operate with diffused goals and they may have dissipated their energies on sundry causes, but the evangelistic bodies have pressed forward with single-mindedness and a remarkable efficiency.

Additionally, such a direct vision has prompted many regional bodies to structure their programs hierarchically, goal one ranking ahead of two, goal two before three, and so on. Evangelism has been accorded a primary position. While the claim has been made that other ministries, too, are important, for instance, education, feeding the hungry, and ridding the society of immoral influences, in practice they have taken a place well behind the first and sometimes are seen as instrumental toward the first. Traditional Christian approaches in Europe, the American North, and even in some quarters in the South, have arrayed their causes and concerns more in network fashion than hierarchically.

Perhaps few characteristics of Southern evangelicalism go further toward differentiating popular regional religion than this series of teachings: a theology of personal guilt linked with an evangelistic program resulting in a focused (and restricted) perception of Christian responsibility. Understanding this way of thinking sheds light on why the Social Gospel has occupied a minor role in Southern religious life.

That this way of understanding Christianity should have appeared in the South is hardly curious. Evangelistic evangelicalism was prominent elsewhere in America in the early national period down to about 1830, and, in a more diffused form, in the Great Awakening of 1725–1750. Moreover it has continued as "modern revivalism" or "mass evangelism" from Charles Grandison Finney through Dwight L. Moody and Billy Sunday down to Billy Graham and scores of other evangelists like them. It has enjoyed popularity at intervals and in a variety of forms in the British Isles. Overseas, theology accompanied by these means has been used very widely in an effort to confront non-Christians with the Christian message and convert them. The American South has no corner on evangelicalism.

What does demand explanation is the hold this form of Christianity has maintained on the South. Once the Great Revival had proved evangelicalism's effectiveness and sharpened its measures, it became standard. It remains the most popular.

The minimal impact of immigration upon Southern religion has been noted. A small number of European Jews, Italian and Latin American Catholics, German and Scandinavian Lutherans, as well as northern Adventists and western Mormons moved into the region. Recent scholarship has expanded our awareness of the ethnic component to the largely homogeneous population of the South. Before and after the Civil War in port and border cities such as New Orleans, Louisville, St. Louis, Baltimore, Charleston, Savannah, and Mobile, the French, Italians, Germans, and Latin Americans arrived. Jews, Germans (early), and a few eastern Europeans (later), were to be found in strength in Charleston and Savannah, especially, and generally scattered in towns and cities. The minimal impact made by these ethnic groups is suggested, however, by their typical concentration in a small number of places—port and border cities. It is demonstrated by the comparative ease with which Roman Catholics accepted regional attitudes on slavery and the place of Negroes. Most Jews also blended into the landscape rather readily. This state of affairs is by sharpest contrast with the effect Irish immigrants and, later, Italian and others, had upon Boston (and similarly on numerous urban areas in the North).

Even so, the absence of such a culturally altering factor cannot explain or typify the persistent hold of evangelicalism on the South. Moreover this persistent hold is more significant in the period following Reconstruction, the so-called New South period, than for the Old South era, the decades between the founding of the Republic and the Civil War, especially 1830 to 1861. In the early era the Southern population needed to be evangelized. Owing in part to the incapacity of the colonial establishment pattern, the region was very underchurched—it can be said, largely unchurched. When the Great Awakening of the 1740s and 1750s erupted, the people it claimed for the Christian faith were mostly outside the church and, more fundamentally, without connection to religion. Much the same was true of those reached by the Great Revival about 1800 on the Kentucky and Tennessee frontiers. Since towns were forming slowly and the prevalent style of farming placed families at remote distances from most neighbors, the spread of faith lacked networks and took place slowly. Camp meetings and local church revivals worked increasingly well for the garnering of souls. These were innovative mechanisms developed for reaching people with the message.

In sum, aggressive evangelistic programs fit the Southern social scene generally well down to midcentury. Evangelical Christianity of that particular stripe was suited to a population needing initial contact with Christianity and basic incorporation into its institutions. Putting the point in a comparative framework, the absence of centers of concentrated population marked off the South as distinctive. In the North villages and towns were culturally central from the colonial period forward. (The South's community patterns probably owed more to Welsh influence than to English and Scottish.) By the 1830s Northern social problems, ills, and needs were clamoring for and receiving attention from the churches. Immorality of various kinds was seen as a social disease, not simply the expression of an unregenerated individual's perversity. Hunger, war, slavery, and injustice were adjudged concerns of the Almighty and therefore concerns of his church. Recent historical investigation has disclosed the activity of national evangelical societies in the antebellum South, but their work dealt mostly with religious education. Social ministries were not their goal, and even these missionary, tract, and Sunday-school societies were tolerated and supported because they observed the distinction

between evangelism and "modern reform." In truth, many social problems were greater in the North because of the more rapidly growing, congested, and interdependent nature of life there. Yet one factor loomed very large to the Southern religious sensibility: the issue of slavery. The intrusion of that issue into any discussion or activity—or even the faintest idea that it might be introduced—struck fear and created barriers to social ministries. Never deeply involved in "kingdom" service, the South grew less so as sectionalism hardened and its need enlarged to defend its case by preserving its regional values and institutions. Religion, it was more widely and loudly trumpeted, was meant to be personal, not political. The world needing reforming was constituted of individuals needing regeneration. Evangelizing each and all of them would ensure a godly society.

Another factor was at work deepening the impact of evangelicalism in the antebellum period, namely, the religion of black Southerners, most of whom were slaves. Once the Methodist and (Separate) Baptist ways of carrying on church life became prominent among white Southerners, blacks became the subject of their evangelistic zeal. After nearly two centuries of Africans' presence in which little was ventured and little was realized, efforts were greatly stepped up. By the 1790s blacks were being evangelized in notable numbers. And the white churches devoted much of their zeal—and a great deal of self-scrutiny—to sorting out their policy concerning these transplanted Africans now very much a part of the American scene. In quite a structured fashion the Methodist denomination debated with moral intensity its obligation to the black people on its members' farms and plantations and in every neighborhood. Should the church work to eradicate slavery and emancipate the slaves? Or should it leave intact the institution of slavery and concern itself with the evangelization of individual slaves? Judgment shifted from the former policy of the 1780s to a clear preference for the latter by 1800, with the question no longer debated by 1820.

The abandonment of the eradication/emancipation cause did not mean overlooking the slaves' religious life—far from it. Evangelistic efforts were consistent and intense. The Methodists even developed a highly organized mission to the slaves. Baptists and Presbyterians joined the cause. Some Episcopal involvement occurred. What resulted was the steady Christianization of the Afro-American population. White Christians often shared in the joy of blacks' conversion. Sometimes, however, they were forced to set limits on the ways in which "getting religion" manifested itself. On plantations regular services were monitored. In states laws were passed prohibiting slaves from learning to read and write. In white churches, where slaves were present in special sections, white pastors and lay leaders directed the services.

Going to such lengths to keep matters in hand is a clue to the dynamics of the evangelical faith as it stirred black souls. The singing, testifying, unmistakable piety, devotional expressiveness, and (when it was allowed) preaching left an indelible mark on Southern Christianity. Had there been any disposition on the part of white Christians to move away from evangelical forms to something else, we may suppose that black involvement in them would have prevented it.

Evangelicalism among Southern blacks in the post–Civil War period weaves a very different story, but the point to be made here is that the continuing strength of evangelical Christianity in the regional population at large has roots in several causes, a major one of which was the dramatic responsiveness of blacks to the Christian faith so presented. Their participation served to reinforce the other factors at work: the kinds of residential and community patterns prevalent in the South; the absence of disruptive factors such as immigration; the continuing need to introduce a frontier people to the rudiments of Christianity; and so on.

Thus it was at the time of the brief life of the Confederate States of America. An originally loose and somewhat diversified culture had crystallized into a political state; but not for long, with virtually no chance—or desire—to remain so joined. In a great many respects the South and "the North"—the reality of the former produced the latter as a referent—had never been so close, so culturally united as in that era. Indeed the inextricability of the North and South made necessary their division into two separate states. Regionality, once a choice and the result of adventitious factors, became regionalism. The magnitude of this effectiveness peaked in the post-Reconstruction period, a time dominated by Jim Crowism and parochial Southernness.

Moreover, even when the secession of the one region from the Union was political in form, its deepest roots were cultural. What Emory M. Thomas has termed a "cultural nationalism" informed Southern outlooks in the period of political separation and, later, a brittle parochialism. Religion was that reality's glue. In Thomas' words, "Perhaps Southern churches are the best place to look for the origins of cultural nationalism in the Old South. There the Southern mind, conditioned by reverence for the concrete and characterized by assertive individualism, blended with a unique religious tradition to mold intellectual and cultural life" (*The Confederation Nation, 1861–1865*, 1979, p. 21).

True to its evangelical form, that religious influence both sought to revolutionize and left things intact. It challenged and it comforted, it transformed and it reinforced. At the personal level the Southern churches preached repentance and conversion. One was to turn from natural (evil) ways to the Lord's way. The moral inclinations of the human heart, being perverse, needed fundamental reorientation. At the same time the ethical values and practices of the society were held up as positive. Unlike its impact elsewhere, the religion of the South was not directed toward inspiring reform or creating in believers a zeal to perfect human society. The churches minded their own—spiritual—business. Once they stepped outside their proper boundaries of converting individuals and entered the arena of social justice, they had "quit preaching and gone to meddling."

A remarkable continuity of regional self-understanding and zeal linked the Old South–Civil War South with the South that emerged following Reconstruction. White Southerners remained as convinced as ever that black people were their inferiors and were inherently limited in capacity. In the 1880s and 1890s the laws and policies of the several states reflected that view. Taken all together, these were called Jim Crow laws. They provided for the segregation of life of the two races in every possible aspect: schools, public facilities and accommodations, streetcar seating, voting rights, cemeteries, and much more. Evangelical Protestantism continued as pervasive as ever. Baptists and Methodists, together with Presbyterians, the Campbellite tradition, and the nascent Pentecostal and Holiness groups, remained predominant. An important change did occur: the enlargement of evangelical membership. Throughout the nineteenth century no rival faith challenged evangelicalism (not even secularism, since it was unfashionable to be a religious outsider). But a minority of the white and the black population declared formal membership in a church. It is one thing for a faith to have sole currency and to be thoroughly legitimate in a society. It is something else for a large proportion of the population to be formally affiliated with it. Not until after 1880 did the white churches really burgeon in size; once that trend began, it was destined to continue. There had been some black churches earlier, but for the most part black congregations and denominations organized after the war—some even in the weeks and months following the peace of Appomattox in April 1865.

In other words, culturally little changed. No truly new options appeared. Nevertheless the expansion of church membership signaled a new phase in the relation between religion and culture in the American South. At the demographic level it meant that frontierlike conditions had been succeeded (in most places) by a pattern of living that featured networks of people, events, and activities. People saw each other more frequently, transportation was easier, access to church was greater, and a better availability of ministers to conduct services had opened up. This set of conditions on the local scene had its counterpart in the degree of organization at the denominational level. There were more publications, regular quarterly and annual general meetings, greater awareness of national and world events, more agencies to promote missions and social services, domestic and foreign, and so on. These modern developments made for keener denominational awareness. Now local congregations, whether Baptist, Methodist, or Presbyterian, black or white, were being included in causes, at home and abroad, using more modern means to expand their ministries. Competition among denominations, while hardly novel, increased. Appeals for donations to carry on various ministries became common. In the process those issuing the appeals, denominational boards, agencies, and personalities, became familiar. In some cases they acquired considerable power.

China, India, Africa, and Latin America emerged as places needing Christian personnel and funding. But this global outlook also included the North; not that missionaries were dispatched there, nor were Southern preseminarians encouraged to seek their theological education there. Instead, the North came to be seen as a less righteous society and as an alien land filled with alien peoples. Cosmopolitan vision may indicate deprovincialization, or it may make manifest a latent disposition to regard home base as superior and normative for other societies. Both consequences showed up in the Southern spirit.

A great deal had changed since the demise of the Old South. In other respects, however, the old nationalism had simply shifted into a new culturalism. The antebellum South had constructed its economic and ethical system, then defended it in both polemic and battle. The "New South" rallied to the "lost cause" by plumping for a godly, family-based, conservative society that should have been the envy of every other right-thinking society. Common Southern opinion held that the heathen in foreign lands needed the pure Gospel preserved by the South. The waverers of the North should have looked to Dixie's preserved forms as judgment on its apostasy and as resource for coming back to authentic Christianity. Mutatis mutandis, the post-Reconstruction South was as sure of the rightness of its cause as the prewar South had been. Only the context and particular manifestations had changed.

And religion played as integral a role—perhaps a larger role—in the Jim Crow era as it had in the rebellious Old South era. It had served as the cement in a "cultural nationalism" for a society preoccupied with its political rights and policies. Once the political issues had become recessive owing to the region's being willy-nilly a component of the nation, the region became a separatist and defensive culture. The Southern region was never as much "the South" as in the period between 1880 and 1930. Its reputation as a distinctive culture, out of step with general contemporary developments and described by many as "backward" or "benighted," derives more from the society of segregation than from the society of slavery. In this late nineteenth- and early twentieth-century culture, religion's role was no less significant, but it was somewhat different.

Religion helped legitimate Southern culture in the post-Reconstruction period. Something was needed to legitimate it. History had played cruel tricks on a region whose people were not more perverse than others and whose "peculiar institution"—a gradual evolution more than a deliberate system—was hardly a creation of any particular generation of them. An evil system it was, nevertheless, and one very much at odds with the rhythms and values of Western democracies in the nineteenth century. Moreover, they had instigated a war rather than abandoning their traditions, rights, and sense of honor and localism. Lacking a clear notion of the different ontologies of individuals and societies, they were incapable of facing causation—and guilt—squarely and accurately. At the social level the "religion of the lost cause" emerged in full strength during the 1890s. The antebellum Southern modus vivendi in politics and law, family and town, and race relations was held up as beautiful and ideal. The heroes of the South as a civic realm and as an embattled military force were apotheosized. A whole people and heritage were glorified. Statues were erected; societies were formed; a lore emerged; a period of history was remembered, its passing lamented, but informal efforts to recover it abounded. The South was exalted as a state of mind, a glorious place-time-cause society. That it could have been deficient, negligent, misguided, or culpable lay outside the moral perceptions of the great majority of Southerners, rank and file and elites alike. Thus, the celebration of the lost cause was a form of legitimation, and was itself a kind of "civil religion."

A similar dynamic operated at the level of the individuals who made up the society. They, too, were regarded as superior, religiously and morally superior to people elsewhere, in the American North and in foreign lands. Not all Southerners lived up to the regional standard, of course, but those who manifested the authentic way of life were seen as choice, the choicest of God's flock. They were good neighbors, a hospitable and thoughtful people. They were hard-working, provident mothers and fathers. They were civic-minded, attentive to the needs of "the home, the school, and the church"—although not typically involved in political affairs and even a bit suspicious of them. It is important to stress that participation in church was viewed as a civic responsibility. A good citizen was made such in part by taking his or her part in a church congregation. Not to

be a Christian, with attendant membership in a congregation, was increasingly a status others simply could not understand. Although not always judgmental about a friend or family member's failure to profess faith and join a church, they saw such behavior as suspect in others.

This attitude resulted in the growth of church membership and in the explicit assessment of Southern churches (and the total society) as the most righteous and faithful anywhere, in a sense as the hope of the world. Church roll figures did grow at a rapid rate beginning in the 1880s, both relative to percentage of increase in (all) previous decades and to general population growth. Earlier there had been simply no religious alternative to standard regional versions of evangelical Christianity. Increasingly there came to be no socially acceptable alternative to being a professing (or baptized) Christian. Additional factors beyond personal acceptability and social legitimation explain the heightened religiosity of white Southerners during the years before and after 1900—perhaps some of them are supernaturalistic—but those two figured prominently.

Needing bolstering in their own eyes and in the eyes of their fellow countrymen to the north and west, the South turned in part to transcendent frames of reference. Besmirched by slavery, defeated in war, and ravaged by war's wake for several decades, the regional culture looked upward to feel good about itself and to present itself to those beyond its cultural walls as a noble people. Benighted or backward it might seem to outsiders, but on its own terms it was a godly, righteous society, a holdout against social and moral erosions damaging a once godly society in the North. Southern Methodism, Southern Baptistism, and Southern Presbyterianism were different—here different meant better, truer to God's holy Word and to the sober, disciplined life called for by the Bible.

Black Southerners were as central in the regional picture as ever. Slavery had been abolished. While almost any condition improves upon human servitude, the segregationist attitudes and policies of the New South effectively shackled blacks' freedoms. The laws passed in the 1890s confirmed the North's worst fears about the South. They also consumed much of the white society's energies, then and later, while clamping the severest restraints on the opportunities of black men, women, and children. It is of the greatest significance that all this tightening of Southern society was occurring at the same time that the North was being transformed by forces of change, immigration, urbanization, industrialization, and modernization. Struggles constant and profound forced a social era new in contours and policies. In the South retrenchment occurred. The region was beset by dire economic conditions. Despair, defensiveness, and provincialism characterized its outlook. The place of black people revealed with crystal clarity how out of step with the time the South was.

For the South's black population this period was very bright in religion. From the rapid outcropping of new independent congregations once the war was ended, more and more churches of their own appeared. Whole denominations also became an aspect of the Southern scene. Two North-based Methodist bodies spread into the region, and an indigenous one sprang to life. Black Baptist life flourished; soon there were associations, boards and agencies, and (by 1895) a convention. From these religious concentrations the South's black people derived a great deal: faith and spiritual sustenance; a social and community center; awareness of controlling something that they knew a great deal about, that was in every sense their own; membership in a cause, even an organization, that had national and even worldwide significance.

Just as antebellum religion for all Southerners was shaped by black religious form and style, so the subsequent South could not overlook a strong and unique black religious presence. Separate from white churches, black churches organized in accordance with the canons and customs of a segregated society. But whites knew the black churches were there; Christianity was seen to be vital and integral to black people's experiences. On the whole white people approved of blacks' religious forms and expressions. In accordance with the perspectives of a segregated society such attitudes were partly condescending: Negroes are naturally religious and their services are typical of a primitive people. At the same time, affirmation of blacks' rights to express themselves in culturally unique ways was widespread, and appreciation that the church, not something else, was the center of black life was felt. For their own part black Christians went on being aware of such attitudes but not determined by them—and in many cases having accepted the white society's evaluation of their differences as pointing to their inferiority.

The prominent place of guilt in the popular religion of the South has long been widely recognized (if not always sensitively understood). In the popular evangelicalism of the revivalistic stripe that took hold from the Great Revival forward, blacks and whites alike emphasized guilt. Indeed, revivalistic evangelicalism in its "pure" form is built on a theology of the individual's personal sinfulness that renders each guilty before a wholly righteous and all-demanding God. Revivalistic sermons stirred hearers to face their own transgressions against a just and loving Lord and to cry out for mercy. Records of early black services and personal testimony reveal that conversion occurred in just such a fashion. White evangelists made the same plea and got comparable responses. Some scholars have conjectured that the moral influence of the peculiar biracial character of Southern society, white over black, made the popular religious sensibility vulnerable to a guilt orientation. This interpretation does not account for the centrality of that theme in the faith of antebellum Southern black people, however.

A drift toward distinctive approaches to Christianity, especially as regards the place of the conversion event, took place following emancipation. As newly freed blacks worked out their own style of church life, they reshaped patterns of religious association in the South. They developed a theology and practice that gave a modified role to the moment of entry (that is, the one-time event of datable, memorable conversion). Their faith affirmed that Christian liberation was communal and that Christian community was liberating. Each individual's need for the Savior and joyous gratitude for his forgiveness remained vital to black faith. But it was not so basically pegged to the dramatic, instantaneous moment of a person's seeing the light and experiencing pardon. Among white evangelicals, however, stress on the moment of entry, the conversion experience, became even more pronounced. In fact, in the practice of a great many churches the revivalistic slant had evolved from the occasional seasonal special emphasis on converting lost sinners to the standard theology of most Sunday sermons. The earlier Southern (and more classically evangelical) distinction between worship services and evangelistic services blurred. As time went on, evangelistic-style sermons became more and more common even in Sunday morning services described as "worship."

The shift of worship services to a predominantly evangelistic tenet in white religion may have roots in the guilt of a white society that lived with the reputation of being culpably racist through both slavery and segregation. Even in its own eyes it had to reckon with the lengths to which it found itself going to defend, insure, and preserve the segregation of the races. And all that for a sector of the population which lived nearby, some of whom were friends called by (first) name. That sort of social dynamic is the stuff of which guilt is made. Thus, it may well have contributed to the regularization of guilt-based preachments as the staple of white Southern religion. At any rate, a drift toward distinctive approaches by white and black churches did take place in the decades following emancipation. Only then did revivalistic evangelicalism acquire a pervasive presence in the white churches.

It must be recalled that guilt-oriented Christianity was a staple within revivalistic evangelicalism and not everywhere. Presbyterianism remained on a different course. It did show its Southernness, but in other ways; principally through its moralistic ethics and through its teachings about the "spirituality of the church" that the church was to mind its own (spiritual) business and steer clear of involvement in social problems. The Episcopal church provided a genuine alternative in worship styles, but its witness was far from prophetic. The ethnic churches, mostly of German descent, continued as such, their members being indistinguishably regional in outlook and custom. Even the Quaker community experienced some Southernization in that some of its meetings became revivalist. The pacifist and egalitarian motifs retained a certain formidability, however. Roman Catholics and Jews continued small and singular, although historians of both groups point out how acculturated their members were.

The Holiness and Pentecostal movements burst on the Southern (and national) scene between 1885 and 1915. In the South their impact was to intensify revivalistic evangelicalism's concern. Conversion was required, yet something else was added. For the Holiness groups each convert had to pass from conversion to entire

sanctification, to a condition of total righteousness or moral perfection in relationship with the Lord. In the Pentecostal case the saved person needed to progress to the baptism of the Holy Spirit, which provided the gift of speaking in tongues. Pardon from guilt was less the orientation with these groups than spiritual power and opportunity. What they shared—and still share—with the older Southern forms is a radically supernaturalist religious philosophy, and one in which the direction is predominantly vertical. Almost everything had to do with a proximate, accessible God, experience of him, empowerment by him, and responsibility to him. Any sense of vocation to address "the kingdom," the society and culture, and ordinary human need is recessive or minimal and always well down the list of hierarchically ordered values. The Holiness and Pentecostal bodies departed from the popular Southern mainstream in leaping regional and denominational boundaries in favor of identification with all those who shared their radical supernaturalism. This often included black people, even Southern blacks, some of whom were fellow congregants.

Diversity is as characteristic of Southern religious patterns as homogeneity—a condition as factual as it seems to be paradoxical. Such a large geographic entity inevitably witnessed different kinds and rates of development. The English and Scottish religious traditions prevailed in the colonial seaboard area, where they were later joined by small bands of German Protestants. In the southern part of Louisiana French Catholics predominated from the early eighteenth century. In those areas of Texas that were influenced by Mexico, Catholicism of a notably different sort continues to render those areas quite distinctive. The same is true of other portions of Southern territory, such as the southern half of the Florida peninsula, the counties of northern Virginia near Washington, and of Tidewater, Virginia, around Norfolk, and many others—but none so dramatically as the Southern highlands, so-called Appalachia.

The lands in southwest and western (West, after 1862) Virginia, eastern Kentucky and Tennessee, western North Carolina, and northeast Georgia comprise the heart of those Southern highlands. Euro-American settlers were moving into American Indian settlements by the late colonial period. A steady flow of lowland newcomers penetrated the challenging high country throughout the nineteenth century before railroads (and much later, highways) opened up the area to outsiders after 1880. Thus, an alternative culture took shape, one that retained its special character rather solidly through the 1930s and that persists in diluted form today.

Religion is one of the Appalachian culture's most noticeable dimensions. Although its hold is less firm than it was half a century ago, its imprint is impressive. A glance at the names of churches on modern highways, and back roads as well, emphasizes the point. More demonstrative is the particular nature of the sermons and music one hears on the radio in the mountain areas.

As for denominations, some are peculiar to Appalachia. In the Virginias, Kentucky, and northwestern North Carolina, especially, Baptists abound—all kinds of Baptists, it would seem. Old Regular ("footwashing," independent) Baptists, Primitive Baptists (Calvinistic), Free-Will Baptists, and Union Baptists are found scattered throughout. The last are a people who were formed in order to maintain loyalty to the Union (Northern) cause in the Civil War; while quite small now, their historic reason for existence is tied to their particular sympathies during that conflict. In addition, there are "missionary Baptists," who seek to evangelize the lost at home and abroad and organize societies to accomplish that goal. Some of these societies (still a minority) by now are churches belonging to the Southern Baptist Convention, a relatively new body in the area. It is important to stress that "Baptist" often does not mean "Southern Baptist" in the Southern highlands. And very rarely does it mean "black Baptist," since the number of black people in mountain counties is very small. (Being quite different from the coastal and Piedmont sections, the mountain agricultural economy had no plantations and thus no slavery.)

Farther south, the Holiness and Pentecostal movements originated and flourished. The Baptist tradition is far from absent, but the dominant bodies are the Pentecostal Holiness Church (and variations on it) and the Church of God. Greenville, South Carolina, and Franklin Springs, Georgia, are "sacred places" to the former. Cleveland, Tennessee, the historic "capital city" of the Church of God movement, continues to headquarter two organizations, the Church of God (Cleveland, Tennessee) and the Church of God of Prophecy. Several other groups stemming from the Camp Creek revival of 1886 and the Tomlinson roots are found in that general area. In fact, a kind of Southern highlands "burned-over district" exists there. Within a hundred miles of where the two Carolinas, Tennessee, and Georgia join, a great deal of conservative—typically sectarian and Fundamentalist—Protestantism originated and is vigorous today.

The issue of the exportation of Appalachian religion is a fascinating one. The several Baptist forms that emerged there have rarely taken root elsewhere. By sharpest contrast the Pentecostal and Holiness bodies and the groups they influence have spread broadly from their places of origin. Also, they have fused with similar products of the Spirit in other places. A related development occurred in the other regional highland area, the Ozarks of Arkansas and Missouri, when the Assemblies of God sprang to life in 1914. This too is a transregional body. Yet the impression must be avoided that the Southern highland territories are the only or the preeminent home of these late nineteenth- and early twentieth-century movements. Kansas and California also witnessed and implemented early Pentecostal stirrings and Anderson, Indiana, is the home of the Church of God, a denomination national in scope that is Holiness without being Pentecostal.

Other Christian bodies, of course, are in evidence. Presbyterians and Episcopalians maintain a presence, both having entered to establish missions and schools and the former, in addition, through early and enduring Scots-Irish settlement. Methodists are relatively numerous, as might be expected of the South's second-largest communion. Quakers, Brethren, Campbellites, and others are found here and there. The Roman Catholic church has attempted to extend its witness but without conspicuous statistical success. Jews, liberal Protestant bodies, and "Eastern religions" are scarce indeed. There are only a few hundred Snakehandlers anywhere; the origins and such "strongholds" as there are are located in Appalachia.

Footwashing, in line with the example of the humble servanthood of Jesus toward his disciples, is rather widely practiced. In fact, intimate, expressive, and communal practices are characteristic features of Appalachian religion. Homecomings, reunions, "all day preaching and dinner on the ground," and "gospel sings" are among those festive occasions. Music is a vital and much enjoyed aspect. Rarely are hymns sung; classical hymnody is not popular in the area nor is its more staid mode sufficiently expressive to suit Appalachian tastes. Gospel songs from "off" (the mountain) are common. But home-composed "mountain spirituals" are even more typical and regular. The guitar is a favorite instrument, quartets a much sought form of "special music." Pianos are found in the more "progressive" churches, organs in practically none. Town churches, especially "uptown" churches, of course, approach conservative Protestant worship in ways not markedly different from comparable congregations in other Southern towns and cities.

Vying with music for uniqueness is the peculiar style of preaching. Difficult to describe, it is readily recognizable to almost any ear. The delivery is rapid, "singsong" in an almost chantlike manner. Repetition of key phrases is a hallmark. The preacher's phrases and sentences are rarely discrete. Instead they are strung together by elongated inflections and strictly sonic transitions. Curious, unattractive, even offensive to the outsider's ears, this style of preaching is assessed by many Appalachian people as "real," all other modes being regarded as alien, perhaps also cold and unspiritual.

Appalachian religion is a variation on the evangelical Protestantism theme. It magnifies authority, that of the Bible read literalistically. It is typically evangelistic, except where Calvinistic views of election persist. It holds to the direct access of each person to the Lord, in prayer, for guidance and forgiveness, in the hope of heaven, and often for physical healing and speaking in tongues. Worship is informal, intended to respond to the Spirit's leading and certainly not bound to any forms. Organization of both congregations and associative bodies is loose. A highly democratic order of working together is practiced. Its ethics are "puritan," under a vigorous mandate high in principle and applied to individualistic and personal morality. Its denunciation of sin—particular sins especially—is vig-

orous and a standard feature. Explicit and demonstrative in nature, it is also communal and caring. Perhaps it is distinguished from mainline regional Protestantism by raising earnestness to an even higher power and by its unique styles in preaching and music.

One aspect of the story of Southern religion's diversity is its provincialism, even patterns of isolation within its provincialism. But another aspect is the ways in which the South is transcended. Obviously the South is and always has been an integral part of American society and culture. The thirteen colonies made up a unit. The Confederate States of America constituted a paradox: a separate nation whose people and culture remained a part of the nation withdrawn from. Secession dramatized how integrated all the states were; and the relative ease—hardly a smoothness—of reunion simply confirmed that the South was one part of a national unit. During the decades following Reconstruction a defensive and impoverished Southern region was thoroughly reincorporated into the nation at large. Thus, under a variety of conditions, the South was simply one unit within a large single political and cultural entity. Family metaphors suggest the relation: first cousins separated, third cousins alienated, brothers at war, strangers in the same household, and so on.

But what of religion? Is the general symbiosis of the nation at large and its Southern region—a sometime breakaway, typically eccentric subunit—also comprehensive? In the area of religion, too, the relationship shifts from era to era, but the two are recognizably related. During the 1980s the South's religious patterns more closely resemble the general American scene than they have in a long time. The big news in both places is the vitality of evangelicalism. In the South and North alike conservative (often sectarian and even Fundamentalist) bodies grow in size and social influence. Similarly, more staid denominations, both Catholic and classical Protestant, are experiencing revitalization, some of them in charismatic or even Pentecostal modes. Emphasis on the question of authority, on a meaning-specific (usually literalistic) biblical hermeneutic, and on a strongly personal sense of relationship with God prevails in evangelicalism in both regional cultures.

But there are important differences. They

center on the contrast between the two spans of culturally influential religious outlooks. In the South the span ranges from moderate to radical evangelicalism with the revivalistic type at the epicenter. This family of Christianity is the source of the region's conventional wisdom on the subject of religion. All the others are mildly marginal to revivalism, such as Presbyterianism; an alternative to it, Episcopalianism; or different, bordering on strange, Catholicism and Judaism. Thus, the center of gravity is on left-wing Protestantism—that associated with America as frontier history, rather than on the radical Protestantism of the Mennonites (continental) or Quaker (British). As such, the American South is unique in the history of Christendom. Never before has a version of that faith that is animated by the concern to bring outsiders to faith dominated a society already so thoroughly Christianized.

The span of religious patterns for the rest of the country is enormous. The result is that no geographic subculture is permitted the luxury of embodying conventional wisdom. In a great many states and communities most or all of this diverse array of religious groups is present—or at least the names are familiar: Lutheran, Roman Catholic, Presbyterian, Methodist, Congregational (United Church of Christ), Jewish, Baptist, Episcopal—and even (Dutch) Reformed, Unitarian, Mormon, and Mennonite. There are pockets of concentration: Catholics in many places, in some places Lutherans, Mormons, and Mennonites. Yet, with the possible exception of Utah, no consensus, certainly no basic cultural penetration, prevails. To repeat, the span is enormous; it issues in a climate that is as heterogeneous religiously as it is ethnically. In fact, when the vigorous impact of secularism is tallied, the likelihood of any widely held religious knowledge or persuasion or values is reduced to a very low level.

The South's unique religious character is dramatized by this comparison. A limited-option culture is present. A rather large amount of conventional wisdom—"what every schoolchild knows"—concerning basic religious teachings is found in most places, social classes, and age groups. In this secularist age there still is one Western culture convinced of, even shaped by, supernaturalistic perspectives on reality.

Interaction between the South and the rest of the country is somewhat greater than it has been. Several denominations have for long or always been national in organization and activity, for example, Roman Catholic, Lutheran, the Society of Friends (Quaker), the Disciples of Christ, and the Episcopal. There is a single United Methodist Church, called the United Methodist Church since 1968; the reunion of the old regional bodies occurred in 1939. In 1984 the historic "southern" and "northern" communions merged to form the Presbyterian Church (U.S.A.). The Southern Baptist Convention is as self-contained and nonecumencial as ever, although it is a constituent body in the Baptist World Alliance; it also has penetrated northern and western states with a moderate number of congregations.

Radical evangelicalism, some of it Fundamentalist, is by its nature cooperative, that is, cooperative with its own kind. Pentecostal peoples reach out for each other because their glossolalic experience supersedes regional accents or cultures, and their organized bodies are typically national. Similarly, there are independent, sectarian churches that form loose coalitions of Fundamentalism, for example, the Baptist Bible Fellowship and (in a political vein) the Moral Majority, Inc. Earlier we observed that often these kinds of conservative movements are interracial. To that feature must be added their tendency to be transregional.

Surprising to many is the notion that Fundamentalism is not the dominant position in the South's Christianity. Nor is the South the heartland of American Fundamentalism. Of course, a higher proportion of Christians of the South than of the rest of the country believe in biblical literalism. But literalism in biblical interpretation, while characteristic of Fundamentalism, is not all that distinguishes it from other forms of conservative Protestantism. It is a movement characterized by a high degree of certainty about certain positions tenaciously held and by a hostile or suspicious attitude toward "the world" with whose conventions it takes vigorous exception. On the whole the South is an evangelical territory of more moderate forms—Fundamentalism being the most extreme variety within that diverse family. Southern Fundamentalism certainly exists. Yet that approach to religion does not dominate the region nor serve as the central resource or axis for national Fundamentalism. The most important history of American Fundamentalism, George M. Marsden's *Fundamentalism and American Culture* (1980), contains (quite properly) scant reference to the phenomenon in the Southern region. After 1925 (the terminal date of Marsden's history), however, the movement's impact on the region and on the national scene has been enlarged. Fundamentalist evangelicalism flourishes especially west of the Mississippi. It must be noted, also, that the Bob Jones University orbit of influence (from 1927) is considerable if spotty. The "electronic church," to the degree that it is Southern in style, also bears these qualities, particularly in the ministries of Jerry Falwell, Jim Bakker, Jimmy Swaggart, and James Robison. A wing of Fundamentalist strength has emerged in the Southern Baptist Convention from the late 1970s. In sum, Fundamentalism has become more common in the South since the 1950s than it was previously. More now than earlier, the regional branches of this movement are involved with and giving leadership to national causes. Yet these churches are still off the cultural center. Mainline Southern evangelicalism continues to fear them and find them distasteful. Independence and cultural rejection are still not highly acceptable in a region where denominational loyalty and regional identification are old and strong traditions.

Finally, Southern evangelicalism has not been notably exportable. The revivalistic approach has had its inning in "the North," to be sure. Historically, that is where it commenced, in both its Great Awakening form—the "surprising" work of God, not a planned, organized effort—of the eighteenth century and as "modern revivalism." The latter was launched by Finney in the 1820s; its preeminent contemporary exemplar is Billy Graham. (In between, its most famous exponents were Moody and Sunday.) "Modern revivalism" is sure of its goal (the conversion of the lost) and is predicated on success in achieving it, and uses elaborate "measures" of organization and technique in pursuing it. That approach is current and still effective in cities throughout America and in foreign centers as well—especially in Graham's capable hands. But neither it nor smaller, less refined versions of it are very popular, much less standard, in evangelical circles outside the South. Evangelicalism

generally, and certainly Fundamentalism, operate differently elsewhere in the country. Where revivalistic concerns and styles are practiced, they are part and parcel of an indigenous tradition or an aspect of the ongoing approach of a particular denomination.

Northern evangelicals who move to the South are often hard put to find a familiar expression of Christianity. The dominance of revivalism in many Southern churches is one reason. A second is related, namely, that discipline is a regular ingredient in classical evangelicalism, less so in the South's more revivalistically inclined adaptation. Spiritual discipline refers to a more gradual, rather quieter, firm and determined approach, rather than to a mood. The Southern revivalistic version is more apt to be responsive to occasional appeals. It too produces genuine commitment, but its manner is episodic, more enthusiastic, and often quite demonstrative.

The South is indeed a particular case in the study of American religion. Its religious patterns and practices are distinctive, a fact that correlates with the region's distinctive history. While many of the movements and much of the theology parallel developments in standard Western Christianity, regional religious life follows a course of its own. So responsive to the culture has it been that it continues to have a powerful attraction for a majority of its population. The result is a religious consensus quite remarkable for a late twentieth-century society.

BIBLIOGRAPHY

Kenneth K. Bailey, *Southern White Protestantism in the Twentieth Century* (1964); Tod A. Baker, Robert P. Steed, and Laurence W. Moreland, eds., *Religion and Politics in the South* (1983); John B. Boles, *The Great Revival, 1787–1805: The Origins of the Southern Evangelical Mind* (1972), "Religion in the South: A Tradition Recovered," in *Maryland Historical Magazine*, 77 (1982); S. Charles Bolton, *Southern Anglicanism* (1982); John Lee Eighmy, *Churches in Cultural Captivity* (1972); David E. Harrell, Jr., *Quest for a Christian America* (1966) and, as ed., *Varieties of Southern Evangelicalism* (1981); Samuel S. Hill, Jr., *The South and the North in American Religion* (1980) and, as ed., *Encyclopedia of Religion in the South* (1984).

Rhys Isaac, *The Transformation of Virginia, 1740–1790* (1982); John W. Kuykendall, *Southern Enterprise: The Work of National Evangelical Societies in the Antebellum South* (1982);

Charles H. Lippy, *A Bibliography of Religion in the South* (1985); Donald G. Mathews, *Religion in the Old South* (1977); Liston Pope, *Millhands and Preachers* (1958); Walter B. Posey, *Frontier Mission: A History of Religion West of the Southern Appalachians to 1861* (1966); Albert J. Raboteau, *Slave Religion: The "Invisible Institution" in the Antebellum South* (1978); H. Shelton Smith, *In His Image, But . . .* (1972); Charles Reagan Wilson, *Baptized in Blood: The Religion of the Lost Cause, 1865–1920* (1980).

[*See also* BLACK CHRISTIANITY IN NORTH AMERICA; FUNDAMENTALISM; HOLINESS AND PERFECTION; NINETEENTH-CENTURY EVANGELICALISM; PENTECOSTALISM; RELIGION AND LITERATURE; REVIVALISM; *and* SOCIAL CHRISTIANITY.]

CALIFORNIA AND THE SOUTHWEST

Sandra Sizer Frankiel

THE religious culture of California and the Southwest, spanning the area from the Oregon border to western Texas, represents a diverse yet regionally distinctive development in American religion. The presence in some areas of strong Native American cultures, the different patterns of Spanish, Mexican, Anglo, and Asian entrance into the region, and the overall character of the Far West and its population have contributed to this distinctiveness.

NATIVE AMERICAN CULTURES

Native cultures in the area have been dated as old as 15,000 years; distinctive cultural developments have been traced back to about 3,500 years ago. The region has included enormous diversity. California alone is notable for the number of different linguistic and cultural groups: about 135 dialects were spoken there at the time of European conquest. These included not only the large Penutian, Hokan, and Shoshonean language families of the region, but also representatives of the Athapaskan and Algonquin families whose major representatives are to the far north and east. The West Coast thus was a settling place for distant peoples for centuries before European immigration. In the Southwest, diversity was less, as was population density due to the arid conditions of much of the region. Nevertheless, some highly distinctive cultures emerged there, while the many different California groups came to share, in broad configuration, cultural traits adapted to their common environment.

In general we can divide the native peoples of the region into four religiocultural groups. There were the northern Californians, culturally similar to the peoples of the Pacific Northwest; the central Californians, including most of the tribes of the central valley and coastal regions down to the Techahapi Mountains; the southwestern hunting peoples, including southern Californians; and the southwestern agriculturalists.

Northern Californians shared with their Northwest neighbors an economy focused on hunting and fishing and a religion centered on shamanism. Like the Northwest tribes, they emphasized the importance of wealth as a means to status; however, they had no potlatch (a ceremonial feast marked by the host's lavish distribution of gifts requiring reciprocation). They developed elaborate mythologies and rituals, although their artistic development was less pronounced than that in the Northwest.

Central Californians featured a village organization (populations averaging about 130 per village) that centered religiously around shamanism. California shamanism did not emphasize the idea of a guardian spirit or animal ally for the shaman, except for the grizzly bear shaman known to some tribes. Rather, the power of the shaman rested in power objects that he had obtained and carried in his own body. These had been acquired in his spiritual quests, sometimes as gifts from a spirit who then became relatively unimportant. Although shamans were primarily healers, weather shamans were also common.

Ceremonials important to the central California tribes were the sweathouse, regularly used by the men for healing and for social purposes; the girls' adolescence ceremony, which celebrated the fertility of the young women and was a major rite of moral significance for the entire village; and the "Kuksu cult," an initiates' society that included virtually all the men of the village. In the latter, participants engaged in masked dances, impersonating the divine and animal spirits. In general, the focus of these tribes was on healing and strength, with some development of communally oriented rituals.

Southwestern hunting peoples (including most southern Californians in addition to the Apache and Yuma tribes) shared many characteristics of the tribes of the Great Basin and the Plains. They were shamanistic and emphasized healing. Many practiced the art of sand painting. Religious interest centered, however, on the vision that came to an individual, bringing him (and sometimes her) a spirit ally, a song, and possibly a ritual. Among most of the southwestern hunters there was no arduous vision quest as on the Plains; rather the vision came in a dream or a waking trance. The southern Californians also employed for this purpose the powerful hallucinogen tolguacha (jimsonweed), which affected those taking it for several nights, its power increased by succeeding nights of dancing and a period of fasting. This cult spread northward from the San Diego area in the several generations before the Spanish entered California. While in general all the visions were considered by southwestern peoples to be individual possessions, rituals taught by a spirit ally could sometimes be passed on to others (usually in exchange for money or other compensation and with the approval of the spirit in charge). This gave rise to some group ceremonies, especially around the rites of the hunt. Other variants on the basic southwestern hunter pattern included the annual mourning for the dead in southern California, pilgrimage rituals such as the salt pilgrimage of the Papago (Arizona) and the peyote quest of the Huichol (northern Mexico), and the eagle killing or scalp taking of certain other peoples.

Perhaps the most famous of all the peoples of this region are the southwestern agriculturalists. They have been the most stable and in many ways the most resistant to European encroachment. Settled on the land, their civilizations extend back nearly 2,000 years. These peoples, called in modern times the Pueblos because they lived in villages (*pueblos* in Spanish), were not the only agriculturalists. But their way of life, symbolized by their white adobe villages on the high mesas, was the most distinctive. The term *Pueblo* includes both the eastern Pueblos along the Rio Grande and the high desert settlements of the Hopi and Zuni, in New Mexico and eastern Arizona, respectively. The Hopi and Zuni, because of their isolation from Europeans, have preserved more of their traditional culture down to the present.

The Pueblo peoples focused on the solar cycle, which was essential to the agricultural year; and virtually all of their rituals were calendrical. The coming and going of the rains, the cycles of the planting, maturity, and harvest of the maize dominated the symbolism and practices of their intense ceremonial life. Prominent in the symbolism were the kachinas: the spirits of ancestors and other great beings who brought blessings upon the earth, especially the rains and fertility. Represented by the kachina dancers with their elaborate masks and costumes, they entered a village in late winter, stayed for the cycle of spring rituals, and departed to the "other world" in late summer. The rites connected with the kachinas and the maize were in the charge of a mostly hereditary priesthood, whose members ensured the precisely correct performance of each ceremony. Through these rites, the life of the community was maintained; and this, for the southwestern agriculturalists, was the center of religious life.

Mention should also be made of the Navaho, for they are famous among the peoples of the Southwest and are often mistakenly identified as one of the Pueblo peoples. Rather, the Navaho were a northern hunting people (Athapaskan speaking) who migrated southward and gradually amalgamated with some Pueblo tribes and slowly adopted some of the settled life of agriculture and sheepherding. They are known for an extraordinarily rich aesthetic and ritual life; their sand paintings, hand-woven blankets, and songs have attracted the attention of numerous artists and anthropologists. In Spanish days they were also known as one of the more hostile and warlike tribes. Their religious life is replete with ceremonials conducted by (paid) specialists in a precise manner, not unlike the Pueblos. But the Navaho rites do not focus on the growth of crops; rather, like other hunting peoples, they work toward healing and strength. The ritual goal is the establishment of order and harmony, dealing with illness or crisis through the gentle integrative effect of elaborate ceremonies. Despite the incursions of Europeans and direct persecution by the American government, the Navaho have preserved much of their ceremonial and traditional culture down to the present.

SPANISH MISSIONS

All the native cultures of the region were deeply disrupted when, in the late sixteenth and seventeenth centuries, Spanish conquerors appeared, and missionaries emanated from Mexico to evangelize the Southwest. After an early Spanish expedition aimed at conquering the mythical "seven cities of Cibola" (which were believed to be the Zuni pueblos), the Spanish retreated from military exploits and left the task of reaching out to the frontiers to the friars. In 1581 Fr. Agustín Rodríguez began converting Pueblo Indians in the villages of New Mexico. After some early successes, he and his party were killed by the inhabitants of one village. Expeditions of adventurers in search of silver followed, but few missionary efforts were made until after the founding of Santa Fe in about 1610. For the next seventy years the Spanish Crown and the Franciscan order expended enormous energy and large amounts of money in evangelical missions and building churches. Extending even into eastern Arizona among the Zuni, the padres built churches and other structures in each pueblo and instructed the natives not only in the Roman Catholic catechism but also in Spanish, Latin, music, painting, and numerous practical skills like blacksmithing and carpentry.

While in many ways the friars were successful, they often offended the natives. For example, it was a Pueblo custom that while men hunted, wove, and made war, women built the adobe houses. When the padres tried to order men to build walls, the men were humiliated and became angry. Also, the padres often punished delinquent converts by shaving their heads, adding another humiliation, for in Pueblo culture long hair was valued. Further, the missionaries increasingly insisted that all converts give up their religious customs, such as their dances, songs, and masked celebrations for the old gods or spirits, and their use of sacred cornmeal. The Pueblo peoples believed they should keep these rites as

well as practice the new Christian ceremonies—all for the more complete harmony of the universe. For example, they made St. James, St. Isidore, and St. Rafael into kachinas.

The differences in viewpoint led to increasing conflict between the natives and missionaries. The friars after 1630 began to persecute Indian priests, accusing them of sorcery; they flogged many and hanged some. They raided the sacred chambers, defiling altars and murals and burning masks and prayer feathers in the plazas. Even so, the Pueblo peoples did not react immediately with violence; their villages were often divided into factions that favored or opposed the Christians. However, famines in the 1650s, followed by Apache raids, convinced more and more people that the Christian way of life was not bringing good results to their villages. In 1680 the Pueblos united in a great uprising against the invaders. They sacked and burned the missions, killed the governor in Santa Fe, and massacred large numbers of Spanish colonists and friars. Spain would soon recolonize the region in the "peaceful reconquest" of Diego de Vargas, but mission work among the native peoples progressed more slowly.

Missions in Arizona were fewer in number (except among the Zuni, who also rose up and destroyed the missions in 1680) and situated mostly in the south. In 1687 the Jesuit missionary Eusebio Francisco Kino was sent to the province of Pimería Alta, the far northwest corner of New Spain, which included part of Arizona. By 1690 two missions and eleven *visitas* (temporary mission stations, often simply chapels) existed in Arizona south of the Gila River. This work did not expand farther, although a few of the *visitas* became regular missions. When the Jesuits were expelled from New Spain in 1767, the Franciscans took over six Jesuit missions, and later established two more. All of these were in Papago territory, where the people seemed to be gentle and receptive. They were surrounded, however, by tribes hostile to the Spanish—the Yuma, Navaho, Maricopa, and Apache—who frequently attacked the missions. Thus the Arizona missions merely held their own until the revolutions began in Mexico in 1810.

In Texas a few missions existed in the El Paso area (in the southwest portion of the state) before 1700, but they did not survive. Most of the

Spanish work was done in eastern Texas, partly as a fortification against the nearby French who occupied Louisiana. Wars with the French, however, as well as Indian hostilities, limited the success of these missions. The Texas missions were led brilliantly for a decade by Fr. Antonia Margil, but after his death in 1726 they slowly declined until only the San Antonio area had flourishing establishments. In 1794 the Texas missions were secularized and their property distributed to settlers.

Thus the greatest successes of the Spanish missionaries were the early work in New Mexico, before the 1680 revolt, and the work among the Papago in Arizona shortly thereafter. Not until the late eighteenth century, in California, would another wave of great missionary work begin. In the mid-eighteenth century the Jesuits had established a chain of fourteen missions in Baja California. When the Franciscans took over these, Fr. Junípero Serra was put in charge. He conceived the next stage in the plan: to extend the missions into Alta California. His idea appealed to the Spanish Crown, for the king was concerned about possible Russian expansion down the coast of California from the north. Serra, a brilliant and vigorous missionary, personally established or supervised the founding of nine missions from San Diego to Monterey and then on to San Francisco, between 1769 and 1784, the year he died. His successor, Fr. Francisco de Lasuén, added nine more before 1803, while Fr. Estevan Tapis saw the completion of the chain of twenty-one California missions.

In this region, because of the success of the friars in attracting—or at least not alienating—most of the Indians, and because of the rich resources of California, the missions accumulated a good deal of wealth. They also had fair success at converting the natives. Uprisings occurred occasionally, but none was as serious as the Pueblo revolt in New Mexico. Native protests seem to have taken more individual forms, such as simply running away to an outlying village. Also, some of the friars seem to have learned the necessity of tolerance. While they persistently argued against "superstitions" and "idolatry," sometimes punishing converts who persisted in traditional practices, they also allowed a certain leeway, at least for recent converts. For example, some of the friars permitted their charges to return to their native villages for special ceremonial occasions. We may imagine that perhaps the girls' adolescence ceremony or the mourning ceremony among southern tribes may have been regarded as relatively harmless by the padres. In any case, although the friars remained insistent on educating the natives to be good Christians on the Spanish model, they also recognized that gradual assimilation was the best they could expect.

The Spanish policy was to educate the natives, encourage intermarriage, and establish missions near Spanish villages in order that the Indians would eventually become Spanish subjects in thriving provincial towns. But conditions were difficult. Disease and war undermined most native communities. The Pueblos, for example, had a population of perhaps 40,000 to 50,000 in the mid-sixteenth century; by the end of the seventeenth century there were no more than 14,000, and only half the villages still existed. California probably had a population of 130,000 before the beginning of Spanish contact; by the time the missions were secularized in 1821, the population may have been as low as 40,000, with about half of this number actually living at the missions.

Under such conditions, most natives did not become "Spanish"; they died, or they survived in their own societies, but in cultural forms sharply limited by Spanish influence. Only the presence of Pueblo cultures remained consistently strong in the Southwest. The more warlike tribes, such as the Apache, faced the same ultimate fate as Plains peoples: war with the Spanish and then Americans until they were defeated and placed on reservations. Most surviving peoples in this region went largely unnoticed until the revival of Native American ethnic and religious consciousness that began in the 1960s.

HISPANIC AND MEXICAN CULTURE

While acculturation of natives proceeded slowly, Spanish settlers began to create their own culture in the region. Early immigrants (other than missionaries) were either soldiers or settlers who came, with the encouragement of the Spanish Crown, to found agricultural villages. Often the soldiers intermarried with native women, creating a mestizo group that quickly assimilated Spanish culture. Nevertheless, Spanish settlements remained small and scattered; only in larger towns like Santa Fe, San Diego, and Monterey did they begin to produce a Spanish-Mexican culture. In the towns, society revolved around local and provincial life, led by the more wealthy ranchers and the powerful politicians (especially the military governors and their associates).

Catholicism was the univerally accepted religion, but it was more a background assumption than a distinct force in the regional culture. The church generally supported the secular government. There were numerous arguments between the Franciscans and the secular powers, for the missionaries often defended the interests of native peoples (viewing them through the lens of their becoming "Spanish"). These arguments sometimes limited the rights of the settled Spanish or Mexican Catholics, but otherwise had little lasting effect.

The Mexican war of independence from Spain in the nineteenth century changed the face of things—although in these northern provinces its effects were short-lived. In 1810 a revolutionary group overthrew the Spanish government in Mexico City. During the next eleven years the forces battled, until finally in 1821 Mexico became an independent state and Spain withdrew. One of the early moves of the new government was to secularize the Franciscan missions—disbanding them as missionary enterprises, taking over most of the property (which in California was considerable), and leaving only the churches as the centers of native "parishes." This effectively cut short the educational enterprises and the continuing efforts to convert the natives. Further, it undermined a significant power source of the church by taking away its wealth. Mexicans began to enter the area in greater numbers, receiving land grants from the new government. Thus, whereas the original intention of the missions was to have Hispanicized Indians reinherit their land when they were sufficiently "civilized" to manage it in a Spanish way, now the Indians were entirely disinherited by the new Mexican landowners.

Had Mexican dominance continued for a significant length of time, a new culture would have been established throughout the region. The enterprise was interrupted, however, by the war between Mexico and the United States in 1846–1848. The American victory resulted in Mexico's being forced to sell, for $15 million, a very large territory: California, Texas, Nevada, Utah, most of New Mexico and Arizona, and parts of Wyoming and Colorado. California and Texas became states almost immediately, each after flirting with total independence; New Mexico, Arizona, and the others entered the Union later. But the ties to Spain and Mexico were cut—the Spanish permanently, the Mexican changing from overt political connections to informal cultural ones, maintained and transmitted through the interaction of Mexican-Americans with families on both sides of the border.

As a result of a largely open border, Mexicans have often immigrated to the United States, temporarily or permanently, and have constituted a significant ethnic minority in California and the Southwest. Culturally, however, their influence has been minimal throughout most of the region; they have often suffered discrimination and pressure to assimilate entirely. Part of this tendency was already present in the Spanish-Mexican heritage: a class system evolved that valued Spanish over native bloodlines, and the more one assimilated European styles and values, the higher one could aspire. The wealthy Mexican hoped to become indistinguishable from the Spanish aristocrat, while the peasant of mostly Indian heritage remained at the lower end of the social scale.

In the Spanish context this class hierarchy became part of local culture, although it was certainly not equitable by modern standards. Then when Anglo-Americans in the Southwest and California added their own prejudices, especially against dark skin, the system became much harsher to the Mexican. Anglos also usually carried a proscription against intermarriage between Anglos and Spanish speakers. Thus the ordinary Mexican-American had virtually no leverage in Anglo society. Only in recent years, with the ethnic consciousness produced by the Chicano (an abbreviation of *Mexicano*) movement, has the situation begun to change. As for the upper-class Mexicans—the "Californios"—who owned the land when Anglos came to the West in the 1850s, they were honored and respected in the early years of Anglo settlement. The genteel, hospitable ranch owner became a mythical model for an easygoing way of life in California. But by the late nineteenth century the power of that segment of the population had declined as well, so that *Mexican* began to be a term for a group the Anglos considered homogeneous—poor, Spanish-speaking peasants.

It has been suggested that the Roman Catholic church might have taken the part of the disadvantaged Mexicans. However, the church in California and much of the Southwest was itself impoverished after the Mexican war for independence. Its lands and properties appropriated, it had virtually no resources other than what it could beg from the church in Europe. The small churches on the far rim of North American settlement did not carry much weight with the prelates of Europe, so they remained relatively poor well into the twentieth century. Religiously, they provided their people with church services and the celebration of feast days, but the Spanish-speaking American churches wielded little influence in the hierarchy of Roman Catholicism, either in this country or abroad. The officials supervising these churches often were not Mexican-American; indeed, it was not until 1978 that the first Mexican-American bishop was appointed, Patrick Fernández Flores of the diocese of El Paso. Thus the contribution of Mexican-American Catholicism to the general religious consciousness has been small. The subtle effects —the remains of Spanish architecture, copied in modern times, the model of the genteel Californio, the fiestas that attract tourists to staged celebrations of Mexican festivities—are mostly fragments of a mythological imagination of Mexico.

There is, however, one exception to the above generalizations, namely in New Mexico, centering around the city of Santa Fe. Hispanic consciousness has remained strong throughout most of the history of the area, even as the Anglo population has increased. New Mexicans have continually insisted on their uniqueness as a cultural region, distinct from both the East Coast and the West Coast. This sense of a subculture within the Southwest has been remarked upon by many observers, and most significantly explored in a study of public ritual in Santa Fe by Ronald L. Grimes.

In a predominantly Catholic city where religion has been linked to crucial historic events, the culture of the Spanish-speaking population has a greater influence than in the rest of the Southwest. The founding of Santa Fe and the reconquest of New Mexico by Don Diego de Vargas after the Pueblo revolt in 1680 are regarded as "founding" events in the mythical sense in a way that is not true of the founding of Mission San Diego in California, for example. In Santa Fe these events are symbolized and reenacted in the processions of La Conquistadora, the Virgin Mary in the form of a statue that has been crowned in a papal ceremony, and in the Fiesta of Santa Fe, in which de Vargas and his caballeros, together with a fiesta queen, are the central figures. The symbols and ceremonies represent, in the terms of a Hispanic Catholic tradition, the proper historical, spiritual, and social ordering of New Mexico society.

In Santa Fe, as in no other American city, the sense of history as the history of conquest, family and ethnic ties, and the spiritual reality of a kingdom of Christ (seen through the feminine icon La Conquistadora) is communicated through a Catholic, Mexican-American idiom. This sense of reality is at least partly accepted even by the Anglo population, even when they do not agree with Roman Catholic religious principles and practices, and their acceptance helps perpetuate New Mexico's sense of historical and cultural uniqueness.

ANGLO IMMIGRATION AND RELIGIOUS CULTURE

Northern California. After the Mexican War, which led to the admission to the Union of California and Texas, California rapidly developed into a populous state. The announcement of the discovery of gold at Sutter's Mill in 1848 brought thousands of adventurers and prospectors over the next few years. (Actually, gold had been discovered earlier in the state but, for reasons not entirely clear to historians, the news had been largely ignored by the American public.) The search for wealth brought a population mostly of young men who intended to make their fortune and return to the East. Many stayed, however, and the rapidly growing population attracted Christian ministers who hoped to save the souls of these materialistic Americans. In cities like San Francisco and Sacramento, as well as in the gold rush towns of the Sierra foothills, churches grew up beside the saloons and brothels.

Traditional Protestantism, mostly of the Evangelical denominations with a heavy accent from the Episcopal church, dominated the scene in terms of wealth and numbers of churches.

However, many observers noted that the religious attitudes of Californians were not the same as those of easterners and midwesterners. Californians seemed to shy away from enthusiasm and outward demonstrativeness in religion; and, while they contributed generously from their bulging pocketbooks, they seldom made strong personal commitments to any one church or tradition. They soon became known among missionaries as kind and generous, but also as independent and strong willed. The churches grew steadily, but proportionate to the population they were small compared to most areas of the Midwest, South, and East. Revivals made only a negligible impact—camp-meeting revivals failed to stir much interest, and only the A. B. Earle revival of 1866 and the Dwight L. Moody revivals of the 1880s received any mention in the annals of the times.

Religious groups and personalities that diverged from the mainstream did receive a hearing. Spiritualists were known from California's earliest days—indeed, one legend had it that John Marshall, the discoverer of gold, was a spiritualist and was led to his find by a message from the realms beyond. Seventh-day Adventists, beginning in 1868, attracted considerable attention in the towns north and east of San Francisco Bay. While they remained a small sect, Californians enjoyed their arguments against traditional Protestantism; and when spiritualists and Adventists held a debate in San Jose in 1874, it attracted crowds from all around the bay. Perhaps most influential among the unorthodox, however, was Thomas Starr King, the great Unitarian orator who preached all over northern California during the Civil War years.

Reared in New England on the works of William Ellery Channing, Ralph Waldo Emerson, and Theodore Parker, Starr King brought a vibrant transcendentalism to California. He preached of the glories of nature and of God's providence in creating California, in a message that went beyond all churches and denominations to what he called "spiritual Christianity." His lectures were always thronged with listeners; materialistic they might have been, but they yearned for a broad-minded Christianity such as he preached. Starr King was undoubtedly the most popular religious leader in the state's history.

Starr King left his mark on California by encouraging the expression of liberal religious views. In the years following his death in 1864, traditional church leaders brought a number of ministers to trial for heresies of a Unitarian or Universalist hue. Two Methodists, S. D. Simonds and D. A. Dryden, were brought to trial in their church; Simonds for questionable views on the doctrine of God, Dryden for a heresy about the afterlife. While Simonds was eventually reinstated, Dryden, though a popular Methodist preacher, had to leave the ministry. The best-known case, however, occurred among the Presbyterians. Laurentine Hamilton, a prominent minister in Oakland, created a controversy with his sermons on the nature of life after death, which contained unorthodox notions about the punishment, if any, of sinners after death. The secular papers took up his cause, extolling tolerance and criticizing narrow-minded traditionalism. Nevertheless, the presbytery excluded Hamilton, and he established an independent church. He maintained a fine reputation, and some regarded him as the carrier of Starr King's banner of liberalism.

Starr King and the other liberals represented a growing popular spirit of tolerance that, unwittingly, even the Seventh-day Adventists helped to encourage. Traditional Protestant ministers had been working to build a Christian California on the model of New England parishes or Ohio villages. They fought for their vision not only by building churches but also by starting moral reform organizations and campaigning for temperance and Sunday laws. In the 1870s the issue of the Sabbath became central for the traditionalists versus the liberals (who were joined by many secular merchants): Should California's Sunday law, passed in 1857, be liberalized or more strictly enforced? In the election year of 1882 the traditionalists forced the issue, persuading the attorney general to enforce the law. Jews, Chinese, and others were arrested, but some of the most notable were Protestants—namely the Seventh-day Adventists, who of course opposed the Sunday law. Even those who were prejudiced against ethnic minorities could not ignore that some of the finest Protestant citizens, including the president of Pacific Press Publishing Company, the Adventist press, were being hauled into court. Juries all over the state, even in highly Evangelical areas, refused to convict the Sabbath breakers. The Democrats with their liberal Sabbath plank won the election handily, and the new assembly in 1883 removed the Sunday law from the books, making California the first state in the Union to be totally without Sunday legislation.

Thus, although leaders of the mainstream denominations remained traditional—and indeed were known in the East for their strict conservatism—liberalism outside the denominations had, from the 1860s on, a strong position in northern California religious culture. From then onward the unorthodox often sought a haven in California. In San Francisco in the 1800s one could find not only spiritualists and transcendentalists but Gnostics, healers, and pagans of all kinds; twenty years later, Oriental religions were beginning to make their mark on the culture. In the southern part of the state, however, a different pattern emerged.

Southern California and the Southwest. Although miners in search of precious metals scoured the other western states, no other area, except Denver, Colorado, was colonized in such a rush as marked northern California with its rapid urbanization. Rather, slow infiltration first by miners, then ranchers, then health seekers, artists, retirees, and businessmen increased the population of southern California, New Mexico, and Arizona. Real estate booms accented the gradual growth when a railroad was completed or a new industry, such as oil drilling or filmmaking, began. Southern California moved ahead of the rest of the Southwest in growth, but even there the largest increase did not come until the period of the first great migrations by southerners and midwesterners, after 1910.

Miners left their mark on the culture of the region mainly in the ghost towns and their legends; dozens of such towns can still be found in Arizona alone. The tales of mountains and deserts include eerie stories of lost miners, secret treasures, and strange twists of nature. Often these build on earlier Indian legends—for example, the Superstition Mountains, near Phoenix, were feared by the Pima and Maricopa peoples because of the mysterious loss of 200 of their warriors there (a loss for which, however, the Apaches later claimed credit). Such legends have contributed to the southwestern sense of the land as a place of mystery or "enchantment."

Ranchers brought permanent Anglo settlement alongside the remaining Mexican ranches; they contributed to the culture in the lives and legends of the "cowboys." Early scouts like Kit Carson, outlaws of the range like Billy the Kid and Wild Bill Hickock, and lawmen like Wyatt Earp were among the many heroes bred by the early ranching era. These figures were latter-day manifestations of earlier frontier heroes like Davy Crockett—essentially loners and fighters by nature. The cowboy tales revived a familiar part of American character: the individual against the wilderness, and sometimes against society too, surviving the dangers of nature, conquering Indians, and remaining independent.

From the late nineteenth century on, the distinctive character of the environment—mild seasons, dry air, and striking landscape—attracted other Anglos. Health seekers began to move to southern California in the 1880s; not long afterward the rest of the dry Southwest was being prescribed for those with respiratory ailments. Also, artists and writers traveled through the region, many of them settling there. The journalist Charles Nordhoff, whose *California* became a publicity piece, was one of the early visitors. He settled on the island of Coronado, near San Diego, and remained there until his death. Novelists Zane Grey, Ross Santee, and Eugene Manlove Rhodes lived much of their lives in the Southwest and memorialized it in their fiction. Artists such as John Marin and Georgia O'Keefe were inspired by the landscape and local colors. These and the many other artists and writers attracted to the region did not often form a cohesive segment of southwestern society, but they contributed to the culture both by shaping a regional image and by creating a place for themselves in a society that, in its early years, was not especially artistic or intellectual. Some of them helped encourage tolerance for a more experimental side of culture, which later would provide a foundation for some of the new popular religions.

For the most part, however, the individualism of miners, ranchers, artists, and many health seekers was not conducive to the growth of any strong religious tradition. Religion was a matter to be settled between the individual and God. The constant presence of a striking and sometimes disturbing natural environment appears in the sense of awe and mystery we find in the writings and journals of many southwesterners; sometimes "God" is hinted at behind this sense of mystery. But the social life of the earliest Anglo settlers was not permeated by religion until the area began to be more settled by Protestants. When farmers moved westward after 1880, when real estate speculators, health seekers, and businessmen who ran the railroads and provided other services came to the area, a clearer religious pattern began to emerge. Then in the cities and larger towns a strong Protestant establishment began to emerge, either dominating or mingling with the Catholicism of Mexican-Americans and, with the implicit consent of the ranchers, giving a moralistic Protestant cast to southwestern life.

In New Mexico, as we have seen, Hispanic Catholicism remained strong, over 60 percent of the population being Catholic in 1906, while Protestants made up less than 7 percent. Of those, the majority were Southern Methodist or Southern Baptist, indicating the strong southern (and especially Texan) ties of the Protestant immigrants. In Arizona, church membership was much weaker overall, with about 35 percent of the state's population being Catholic, 6 percent Protestant (mostly Presbyterian and Methodist), and 4 percent Mormons, or Latter-day Saints. The strength of socially conservative sects like those from the South and the Mormons from Utah indicates that Protestantism in this region was, like its early manifestation in gold-rush California, highly conservative.

The best study of a city in this region has been of Los Angeles, and the results tend to support the generalizations just made. The Protestants who began arriving in numbers around 1880 established strong communities, some of them actually colonies. Pasadena, for example, became well known as a temperance town, while Long Beach, originally a summer church campsite, became a favorite place for Methodists to settle. With the establishment of the University of Southern California under Methodist auspices as the only significant institution of higher learning in the region, Protestant influence in Los Angeles was secure. Meanwhile, Protestants who occupied the upper ranks of religious and charitable organizations also began to be elected or appointed to most of the significant offices in the city of Los Angeles. The *Los Angeles Times* became the organ of the Protestant community—not in a sectarian sense, but in reflecting Protestant values and morals. This hegemony over the city's positions of power, with an informal interlocking directorate between government on the one hand and churches and charities on the other,

continued until about 1920. Although Los Angeles, with its large Mexican-American population and a growing segment of Orientals, was hardly a homogeneous community, Protestant control made it appear so for many years.

Los Angeles was the locus of a number of Evangelical movements that suggest the strength of Evangelical commitment in southern California. In 1895 Phineas F. Bresee, a regional leader in the Methodist Holiness movement, broke from Methodism to form the independent Church of the Nazarene. This church merged with other Holiness groups in 1908 to form the national Church of the Nazarene, destined to become one of the fastest-growing Holiness churches in the country. And, while Bresee was something of a liberal (his early associate in founding the church was Joseph P. Widney, later a liberal Methodist), southern California sprouted other Holiness groups that were much more conservative in their insistence on departure from the "establishment" churches. Moreover, urban Los Angeles became the site of the great Azusa Street revival in 1908, which attracted Pentecostals from all over the country. Actually Azusa Street did not initiate a strong Pentecostal movement in California, but it inspired many who went on to organize churches elsewhere. These examples suggest that, while the extreme wings of conservative Evangelicalism found only limited success in California before 1920, there was still a sufficiently strong Anglo-Protestant conservative culture to initiate and nurture such movements in their early years. Later, after 1920 and following upon strong waves of immigration from the South, Pentecostalism would take firm root. The sensational preaching and life of Aimee Semple McPherson ("Sister Aimee") would create a large church, the International Church of the Foursquare Gospel, as a center of conservative Evangelical religion. (Some have argued that McPherson's media-conscious approach was typically southern Californian, reflecting the new film industry that was transforming Los Angeles culture.)

Thus southern California and the Southwest created in various ways a strong conservative religious culture among most Protestants. As we will see, the region also nourished many alternative groups, especially in southern California. But the overall religious conservatism of both Protestants and Catholics is significant, especially in comparison with northern California, where conservatives were increasingly edged out by liberals espousing toleration.

ASIAN IMMIGRATION AND RELIGION

The presence of Chinese and Japanese immigrants in California dates back to the time of the gold rush. By the 1860s there were significant Chinese communities in northern California. The focus of missionary attempts by Protestants, Chinese immigrants soon became the object of prejudice and discrimination by many Anglos. A few Protestant ministers fought against discrimination, portraying the Chinese as bearers of a high and rational culture stemming from the great sage Confucius. For most Anglos, however, the Chinese were aliens with strange and repellent customs, such as wearing their long hair in "pigtails" and eating odd foods. As a source of cheap labor, the Chinese were exploited, especially in the railroad-building years, and their poverty and competition for scarce jobs made other Americans resent them even more.

Because of their low rank in the Anglo-dominated society, the Chinese had little immediate influence on American culture. They created their own communities, many of them keeping to the ways of their ancestors and continuing to practice their religious folkways.

Japanese immigrants fared somewhat better, not having to face the extreme discrimination that the Chinese had encountered. In large part this was due to the different attitude of the culture they entered. The Japanese came primarily into southern California and gradually into the north after 1920, when the region had become much more cosmopolitan. Among elite and liberal circles, religions of other cultures had become "interesting" and even fashionable, so Japanese Buddhism was accepted in a way that the earlier Chinese had not experienced for their religious traditions. Nevertheless, the Japanese were regarded as aliens, and as a result they also created their own subcultures that were distinct from the American mainstream. During World War II, the Japanese became the targets of the racism and persecution they had earlier escaped; many of them were put in internment camps as suspected traitors. Not until much later, in the late 1950s and 1960s, did either the Chinese or the Japanese traditions begin to be appreciated by a larger public and contribute directly to the culture of California.

JEWISH IMMIGRATION AND RELIGIOUS CULTURE

Jews joined the cosmopolitan immigration to California in the gold rush, and indeed were part of every subsequent wave of immigration to California and the Southwest. Mostly settling in the cities and larger towns, they created distinctive religious communities wherever they went. In part, communal tradition encouraged them to remain at least religiously separate from non-Jews; but anti-Semitism also contributed to their separation. In many towns and cities until the 1950s and 1960s, social clubs, employers, and property owners discriminated against Jews, thus forcing social segregation. As a result of these conditions and their small numbers, Jews did not in most areas make an obvious contribution to the region's religious life. Even in San Francisco, where a strong Reform Jewish community existed from early days, their influence on the culture was indirect.

The exception to that generalization is Los Angeles, where after 1900 Jews began to migrate in large numbers—including a significant number who moved from northern California after the San Francisco earthquake in 1906. In Los Angeles Jews created distinctive communities of many varieties, staying partly separate still, but present in such significant numbers as to exercise a strong influence toward cosmopolitan life and away from Protestant domination. Together with the alternative Anglo traditions to be discussed below, they provided an increasingly effective counterbalance to the Protestant hegemony over Los Angeles.

ALTERNATIVE RELIGIOUS STYLES

We have seen how northern California early became a haven for liberals, from Unitarians to Gnostics and mystics of various kinds. The strong Protestant establishment in the rest of the region (with the exception of New Mexico, where the establishment was strongly Catholic) meant that such liberal movements had more difficulty gaining ground, and they seldom became politically influential. Nevertheless southern California, and to a lesser extent the rest of the Southwest, had their share of unorthodox religious movements, mostly among the Anglo population.

From at least 1895, Christian Science, New Thought, and Theosophy were attracting members in southern California as well as in the north. These three movements, which together we may label the *metaphysical religions* of the time, were among the more popular new waves of religious thought on the urban East Coast and in urban centers like Chicago and Kansas City. They differed in many ways, both in their structures of authority and in their specific beliefs. Many of their goals and practices, however, were similar. They shared a focus on the rational and transrational mind as the means of approach to the divine, a more impersonal concept of God, a criticism of traditional Christian doctrine, and a faith in the inner power of the human being to achieve divinity. New Thought and Christian Science also held in common an interest in mental healing—indeed, they derived from a common source in the teachings of a mental healer, Phineas P. Quimby, in Maine. Theosophy venerated the teachings of the great "masters" in other religions, especially Hinduism; New Thought was eclectic and psychologically oriented; while Christian Science held that all perfect wisdom came from the writings of its founder, Mary Baker Eddy.

The growth of these groups in southern California was considerable. By 1906 California had the sixth largest Christian Science membership of any state. It has been estimated that in Los Angeles the metaphysical religions, taken together, had at least 15 percent of the membership of population of Protestant background. Moreover, some of the leaders of traditional Protestant churches, especially Congregationalist and Methodist, were becoming liberals and showing interest in the beliefs and practices of the metaphysical religions. Conservatives, of course, attacked them vigorously, but the more they attacked, the more the new religions seemed to grow.

One of the more interesting manifestations of the new religions in southern California was the Theosophical community venture at Point Loma, near San Diego. One wing of the American Theosophists, led by Katherine Augusta Tingley (who had broken with the movement's primary leader, Annie Besant), formed in 1895 the beginnings of the community. Dedicating themselves to humanitarian brotherhood and spiritual study for the advancement of the human race, they built housing, a Greek theater (still standing), and other facilities for a religious and cultural community. For a time, they were politically active, encouraging the formation of (Bellamy) Nationalist clubs up and down the coast. But largely they oriented themselves toward their internal work, including the educating of orphans and Cuban immigrant children, as well as providing lectures and cultural events for themselves and for visitors. Point Loma became known for its pageants, where in elaborate ancient costumes performers would recite, give dramatic performances, or hold religious services expressing the wisdom of ancient and exotic teachers. The community experienced internal and financial difficulties beginning in the 1920s, and in 1934 it disbanded.

Other metaphysical groups flourished in southern California as well. One of the more successful of New Thought groups was the Church of Religious Science, founded by Ernest Holmes in 1917. In the 1980s the charismatic minister at its San Diego branch, Terry Cole Whitaker, attracted hundreds to her Sunday sermons.

Rosicrucian groups, whose origins go back to secret orders in late medieval Europe, have also been represented in California, notably by the Rosicrucian Fellowship with its center in Oceanside (between Los Angeles and San Diego) and the Ancient Mystical Order Rosae Crucis, which in 1928 made its headquarters in San Jose. These groups combine elements of ancient mystical thought from Egyptian, Gnostic, and Jewish Kabbalistic sources with a general Theosophical emphasis, focusing on initiation into an awareness of divinity within oneself.

Unity and the Church of Divine Science, among others that have their main headquarters outside the region, have attracted adherents in the state. Most important is that all these groups together have imparted a particular flavor to religion in California. Except for the most conservative Protestant groups, metaphysical language, concepts, and attitudes are common currency among the religious portions of the population.

Moreover, such concepts have been adapted by otherwise quite conservative groups in certain instances. A significant example is the I AM movement begun in the 1930s by Guy and Edna Ballard in Los Angeles. Ballard claimed to have received revelations, along with gifts of gold, on Mt. Shasta from a figure called the Comte de Saint-German (the real Saint-Germain, an occultist who frequented the court of Louis XV, died in 1784). Ballard's messages combined Theosophical teachings with concentration and visualizations, such as instructing his followers to visualize a violet flame coming from above to surround them.

Calling on the Mighty I AM Power, Ballard's students learned positive affirmations not unlike those used in New Thought groups. Ballard's group, however, had a distinctive tone of militarism and superpatriotism. His followers were to "blast" the dangerous forces threatening America and always obey the Mighty I AM Power being channeled through Ballard himself. In some of his teachings, America was to be the home of the race of masters, once the sinister forces were destroyed. Ballard died in December 1939, and the coming of World War II channeled the patriotism of many cult members in other directions. The group still survives and holds yearly meetings on Mt. Shasta. The phase of Ballard's leadership shows, however, that metaphysical concepts could be construed and employed to support conservative as well as politically neutral or liberal causes.

Not all spiritual movements of the interwar period were politically oriented. In 1935 a new group started in Los Angeles that was to spread a message of spirituality and healing throughout the country: Alcoholics Anonymous (AA). This and its later offshoots (for drug addicts, overeaters, families of addicts, and others) offered a nondenominational, nonpolitical approach to spirituality as the foundation for developing a positive self-image and arresting the illness that was manifesting itself in compulsive behaviors. These Twelve-Step Programs, as they came to be called, offered the individual the opportunity to develop his or her own conception of a Higher Power, to build personal relationships, and to make a guided self-assessment so that major life changes could be made. In many ways a precur-

sor to the human potential movement discussed below, AA combined the California traditions of nondenominationalism, self-development, antiauthoritarianism, and healing, while providing a strong context of group support.

RECENT TRENDS

Since the 1960s California has become well known, if not infamous, as a haven for "new religions." Although other areas of the country and other parts of the West and Southwest also have housed communes, religious experiments, and strong alternative religious groups, California remains the leader in the number and success of its new religions. From a historical point of view, we can see that the liberal and tolerant ambience of the San Francisco Bay area, together with the amorphous tradition of the metaphysical religions in both southern and northern California, contributed to the creation of an environment where alternative religious styles might find a congenial home. It comes as no surprise, then, that the San Francisco Bay area would be described as one of the major centers of the "new religious consciousness" (as in the book of that title edited by Charles Y. Glock and Robert Bellah) that many saw emerging in the 1960s and early 1970s.

Many of the so-called new religions are not really new; they are usually offshoots of earlier alternative traditions, reworkings of familiar ideas by a particular leader, or American branches of ancient traditions from other cultures. As such they are often manifestations of what Robert S. Ellwood has called "emergent religion," largely noninstitutionalized and using different symbolic structures from those of established religions. Nevertheless there are a few new features relevant to understanding the regional culture.

First and most controversial is the fact that the followers of many of the new religions develop a strong attachment or devotion to the leader; in Hindu terms, the guru. This is a rare phenomenon in American religions. The few exceptions include Joseph Smith among the Mormons and Mary Baker Eddy in the Church of Christ, Scientist, who exercised virtually absolute control over their organizations during their lifetimes. They too were sharply attacked by outsiders.

Now many groups have such leadership structures, ranging in degree from the Unification Church under the Rev. Sun Myung Moon, who barely veils his claims to be the Messiah, to the somewhat more modest approach of A. C. Bhaktivedanta Swami Prabhupāda, founder of the International Society for Krishna Consciousness (ISKCON), whose followers believe him to be the direct link to the deity Krishna but whose explicit devotion is to Krishna alone. Some other groups do not focus so strongly on their leaders, regarding them more as spiritual guides or masters. Yet the followers regard them as rightly having authority over their spiritual lives, and in many cases over other aspects of their lives as well.

This development suggests that a significant experiment has been occurring in the attitudes of Americans toward authority. While bumper stickers often proclaim "Question Authority!" many people have been exploring the value of submission, in the most personal areas of their lives, to persons they regard as possessing higher wisdom or as being further along on the path of spiritual development. This is a departure from the trends of Protestantism since the Reformation as well as a sharp divergence from the traditional American ideals of democratic decision making and individualism. It is not, of course, alien to most traditional cultures elsewhere in the world or even to earlier pastoral traditions in Christianity or orthodox rabbinic traditions in Judaism.

A second important development is the growth of meditative traditions. Numerous Hindu and Buddhist groups teach meditative practices; a few, like the Transcendental Meditation of Maharishi Mahesh Yogi, have centered entirely around a simple meditation of concentration. The Divine Light Mission, led by the Guru Maharaj Ji, who became a nationally known figure at age thirteen, emphasized a form of meditation that generated a powerful experience of inner light, sounds, sweet tastes, and vibrations. Moreover, various forms of therapy have begun using meditation, trance, or visualization to aid clients. The use of concentration or contemplation is not entirely new to the metaphysical religions; New Thought's "affirmations" bear some similarity. But the religions imported from the Far East have amplified and deepened the use of meditation significantly.

Zen Buddhism is probably the most outstanding example of this trend. Buddhist teachers have been present in America since the turn of the century, of course; the appearance of the monk Soyen Shaku at Chicago's World's Parliament of Religions in 1893 is a useful symbol of the presence of Buddhism. Nevertheless serious Buddhist practice was largely limited to Asian-Americans and a few small elite groups, often from Theosophical backgrounds. In the 1950s Zen was popularized by the Beat poets, beginning with their readings at the Six Gallery in San Francisco in 1955. They appropriated some features of Zen, namely, its spontaneity, unconventionality, and espousal of the possibility of sudden enlightenment; however, few of them seriously undertook the discipline of Zen (Gary Snyder being the principal exception). They popularized an attitude, not a religious practice.

With the founding of Zen Center in San Francisco in 1962, a new era opened. This was the first major center organized by American students rather than founded on a Japanese base. Under the leadership of Shunryu Suzuki Roshi, a disciplined community formed whose influence would extend throughout the region. Zen Center's purchases of Tassajara Springs in 1967 and of Green Gulch farm (on the coast north of San Francisco) indicate both the strength of the movement and the commitment of members wanting to live in a fully practicing Buddhist community. The center of the practice was of course *zazen,* sitting meditation. For residents, there was a regular schedule of daily meditation plus occasional longer practices, or *sesshins,* with extensive meditation for days together. Nonresidents could come for instruction, too, on a regular basis or for weekend workshops.

Zen Center is but one of the leaders in a wide-ranging movement of practicing meditation. Throughout California one can find practitioners of *vipassana,* (a classic Indian Buddhist form), Tibetan meditation, and a wide variety of Hindu forms often combining meditation and the physical disciplines of yoga, which increase flexibility and enhance the flow of spiritual energy. Chinese teachers of Taoist meditation have also begun to pass on their tradition to Americans. What is notable about most of these is a strong emphasis on discipline, some of it strictly traditional and severe by American standards, and the founding of meditation on sophisticated philosophical traditions, thus combining serious learning with serious practice in ways that the earlier metaphysical traditions in America seldom did.

Still, the groups formed around gurus and the serious practitioners of meditation are rather few in number. A much larger, more eclectic, and somewhat less disciplined movement brings to light the third feature of the new religious spirit —namely, the "human potential movement." This movement is not explicitly religious, and many consider it secular, an extension of humanistic psychology. In recent years, however, various groups and practitioners within the movement have become more attentive to spiritual dimensions of their practice and have appropriated elements of religious traditions, such as meditation or ritual, for their purposes.

The human potential movement traces its roots to research in group dynamics in the 1940s at the National Training Labs in Bethel, Maine, where sensitivity training was first developed and from which "encounter groups" emerged. The primary thrust of the movement is still therapeutic, the goal being "transpersonal awareness" or "transpersonal experience," a development in the direction of mysticism. Were this the only development, we might regard it as an extension of the tendencies of New Thought, which also shared a border with the psychology of its time. Recent developments, however, show two important additions.

First, the human potential movement has emphasized interpersonal relationships, either as ends in themselves or as a foundation for higher experience. In group meetings of varying degrees of intensity, participants explore the possibility of greater openness in expressing emotions and often experience deep love and acceptance. The groups founded on these experiences stand in contrast with earlier New Thought developments, which were generally individualistic. Second, the human potential movement in recent years has included the integration of various kinds of physical therapy and "body work," as it is called colloquially, into the development of awareness. In contrast to the asceticism that has been prominent in some Asian religions and in many eras of Christian culture, the new personal-growth techniques regard the body as one means to self-transcendence. They hold that by releasing physical tensions, undoing repressions, and becoming aware of one's body

at deeper levels, one may achieve a new level of harmony with one's self.

Thus one finds in California numerous physical therapies, such as Rolfing, a deep muscle tissue massage designed to reintegrate the body's basic system, and Polarity, with an emphasis on balancing positive with negative energies. Also popular are spiritual healing practices by, for example, psychics who "see" and remove disruptive energies or Reiki practitioners who, using an originally Japanese art transmitted by initiation, lay hands on a person to communicate healing energies.

Eastern influence is also evident in acupuncture, acupressure, and shiatsu, while the Chinese and Japanese martial arts, particularly t'ai chi ch'uan and aikido, attract many who wish to combine development of the physical self with a tradition of spirituality. The Esalen Institute, a leading center in the human potential movement with headquarters in San Francisco and at Big Sur on the coast, which for two decades has attracted thousands per year to its programs, often includes training in various forms of massage, Sufi dancing, body movement, or t'ai chi. (Its hot tubs at Big Sur, overlooking the Pacific, are regarded by some as an experience in self-transcendence.)

These various features of the new religious movements in California suggest that two parallel developments have been occurring. One is the experimentation, by a small but significant number, with a disciplined religious life, often with submission to a strong authority. This has its precursors in some religious and communal groups in the nineteenth century, but it still goes against the grain of most American traditions. Second is the growth in meditative traditions and in integrating the body and physical experience into spiritual development, both of which are explorations into new fields of energy, new at least for Americans. Many individuals report that these practices yield a renewed sense of vitality, strength, and health, as well as spiritual aliveness in some cases. Research into these methods of transforming consciousness and opening energy fields may aid in understanding such experiences.

One more development deserves mention: the growth of religion among a newly conscious subculture, that of homosexuals. It was in San Francisco in the early 1950s that the first gay society for self-protection (the Mattachine Society) was formed, but it was wholly secular. Gay society centered mostly around private homes or taverns, being ostracized by churches and synagogues. The year 1964 marked a shift, however, when the Council on Religion and the Homosexual was formed out of a conference in Mill Valley (just north of San Francisco). This opened the way for some churches to accept gay caucuses or fellowships within their ranks.

In Los Angeles in 1968 Troy Perry, a Pentecostal minister, founded the Metropolitan Community Church as the first gay church; the group evolved from a local Pentecostal group to the wide-ranging and eclectic worship of the Universal Fellowship of Metropolitan Community Churches, encompassing nearly 100 churches across the nation. Other gay churches have been founded as well, and gay synagogues have appeared, especially in San Francisco and Los Angeles.

These groups are founded on the unity of the gay subculture as much as, or perhaps more than, on the theological or practical traditions of a religious mainstream. Among Christians, they usually have a strong element of liberation theology, while the Jewish groups usually take their guidelines from Reform philosophy. They often incorporate a metaphysical or mystical slant common to many California traditions. Their distinctive social base, however, gives them the character more of an ethnic culture than a reform movement, and their unique contributions will undoubtedly appear in the future.

It remains to be seen what structural changes in religion or society might emerge from all these new developments. What is clear is that the region is following a course set by its own tradition, established over a century ago when spiritualists held their séances and Thomas Starr King preached transcendentalism to crowded auditoriums. California and the Southwest still have, as always, a mainstream of Protestant, Catholic, and Jewish groups and its share of conservatives in religion and politics. Ethnic and local subcultures remain in many cases strong and distinctive. The liberal and metaphysical traditions, however, are the region's most characteristic contributions to American culture. As the adherents of these traditions move into new areas of exploration, we may expect these unusual contributions to continue.

BIBLIOGRAPHY

John E. Baur, *The Health Seekers of Southern California, 1870–1900* (1959); John W. Caughey, *California* (1940; 2nd ed., 1953); Robert S. Ellwood, Jr., *Alternative Altars: Unconventional and Eastern Spirituality in America* (1979); Charles Y. Glock and Robert N. Bellah, eds., *The New Religious Consciousness* (1976); Emmett A. Greenwalt, *The Point Loma Community in California, 1897–1942* (1955); Ronald L. Grimes, *Symbol and Conquest: Public Ritual and Drama in Santa Fe, New Mexico* (1976); Cleve Hallenbeck, *Spanish Missions of the Old Southwest* (1926); Robert V. Hine, *California's Utopian Colonies* (1953; repr. 1966); Thomas Starr King, *Substance and Show, and Other Lectures* (1877); Alfred L. Kroeber, *Handbook of the Indians of California* (1925).

Joan Moore, *Mexican Americans* (1970); Barbara G. Myerhoff, *Peyote Hunt: The Sacred Journey of the Huichol Indians* (1974); Jacob Needleman, *The New Religions* (1970); Leonard Pitt, *The Decline of the Californios: A Social History of the Spanish-speaking Californians, 1846–1890* (1966); Gladys A. Reichard, *Navajo Religion: A Study of Symbolism* (1950); Gregory H. Singleton, *Religion in the City of Angels* (1979); Kevin Starr, *Americans and the California Dream, 1850–1915* (1973); Ruth M. Underhill, *Ceremonial Patterns in the Greater Southwest* (1948); Francis J. Weber, *The Pilgrim Church in California* (1973) and, as ed., *The Religious Heritage of Southern California: A Bicentennial Survey* (1976).

[See also "CULTS" IN THE LATE TWENTIETH CENTURY; NATIVE AMERICAN RELIGIONS; NORTH AMERICAN INDIAN MISSIONS; RELIGION IN HISPANIC AMERICA SINCE THE ERA OF INDEPENDENCE; RELIGION IN THE SPANISH EMPIRE; and RELIGIONS OF MESOAMERICA.]

RELIGIOUS PREJUDICE AND NATIVISM

Leo P. Ribuffo

BEING an American means many things, but the meaning has always included the prerogative of calling others un-American. Countersubversive movements—movements dedicated to protecting the United States from allegedly dangerous foreign influences—have marked American history for more than two centuries. Following contemporary usage, "nativism" encompasses hostility to both immigrants and "alien" ideas. However, unlike many accounts in which Catholics and Jews appear largely as victims of Protestant harassment, this discussion of nativism also considers clashes between these two minorities as well as their treatment of less influential faiths. In a further departure from standard practice, religious prejudice here includes rationalist prejudice against religion in general or against particular religions.

Religious prejudice, nativism, and anti-Semitism, a special form of nativism, have rarely appeared in pure form. Rather, they have been mixed with disputes over class, ethnic, and denominational power and prestige, as well as with nationalism, imperialism, racism, rationalism, opportunism, and personal animosity. Furthermore, "prejudice," "nativism," and "anti-Semitism" carry enormous negative connotations. "Nativism" was first circulated in the 1840s by foes of "native American" political parties that specialized in attacking Catholics. "Anti-Semitism," coined abroad, was first used in 1879 by Wilhelm Marr, a proponent of Jewish disfranchisement in Germany. Marr wore the label openly, but Jew-baiters in the United States have often denied their anti-Semitism. Indeed, although various kinds of religious bias survive in America, almost no American defends prejudice in principle.

An understanding of American religious prejudice, nativism, and anti-Semitism first requires a sense of the very different world of mid-sixteenth-century Europe. That world could not conceive of the current American creed that all religions stand equal before the law and that all "mainline" faiths deserve equal esteem. In sixteenth-century Spain and France Roman Catholicism was synonymous with patriotism. In sixteenth-century England, although the established church that had separated itself from Rome embraced many discordant voices, all its members could agree that the pope was, in William Tyndale's words, the "devil's vicar." Antipathy to Catholicism and English imperial ambitions reinforced one another. Songs, plays, books, and engravings portrayed Spain as a bastion of autocracy, ignorance, and cruelty worthy of the Turks. In *Discourse on the Western Planting* (1584) Richard Hakluyt, an influential advocate of English expansion, urged colonization in order to save the New World from the Spanish "demie Saracine" and the Roman Antichrist.

"Plantings" first took root in Virginia, but the New England colonies developed faster, left larger legacies to nativist descendants, and better illustrate the danger of imposing modern conceptions of prejudice on previous eras. The Separatists who founded Plymouth in 1620 and their fellow Puritans who established Massachusetts Bay ten years later agreed that Roman Catholicism bore the "mark of the Beast." They considered the Church of England only slightly less tainted in the "image of the Beast" and so decided to keep their distance. Believing their own holy commonwealths among Satan's favorite targets, the Puritans vigilantly guarded against Catholic infiltrators, "popish" ideas, and other heresies. In 1647 Massachusetts Bay ordered "perpetual imprisonment" for any priest who entered the colony. Although Catholics rarely appeared, the Puritans found it difficult to maintain orthodoxy. Thriving New England settlements, "mixt assemblies" from the time of their founding, quickly attracted Anglicans, Baptists, and such unconventional Puritans as Roger Williams and Anne Hutchinson. In response Puritan leaders restricted the franchise to "visible saints" and banished, harassed, or executed the worst malcontents. When Baptists petitioned for religious toleration in 1681, Samuel Willard accused them of misunderstanding the "design of our first Planters, whose business was not Toleration; but were professed enemies of it, and could leave the world professing they died *no Libertines*" (quoted in William Marnell, *The First Amendment,* 1964). The Puritan organizers of communities that developed into New Hampshire, New Jersey, and Connecticut agreed.

Quakers seemed especially dangerous. They not only allowed women to preach but also sanctioned antinominan appeals to an "inner light," which John Higginson, a prominent Puritan, described as a "stinking Vapor of Hell." Stubborn and economically successful, the Quakers were hard to ignore. Between 1658 and 1661 Massachusetts Bay hanged four Quakers who had persisted in spreading their doctrines. Revulsion against this harsh punishment produced a brief respite. However, starting in the 1670s the Puritans reaffirmed their commitment to orthodoxy, partly in response to threats from local Indians and French Catholics in the North. Along with other religious dissidents, Quakers were frequent targets during the witch trials of the 1690s, according to Christine Heyrman ("Specters of Subversion," in David Hall et al., eds., *Saints and Revolutionaries,* 1984). Cotton Mather linked theological foes when he claimed that a bewitched girl unable to recite Scripture easily read a "Quaker or Popish book."

Quakers, Baptists, and heterodox Puritans found refuge in settlements that eventually coalesced into Rhode Island. Practices in this "haven" illustrate how little seventeenth-century conceptions of tolerance resemble the contemporary ideal. On the one hand, founder Roger Williams believed that orthodox coercion corrupted true faith; on the other, he denounced Quakers for doctrinal error, favored a moral code based on the Ten Commandments, and considered Catholics foreign agents. Thus, al-though the charter Williams acquired in 1663 promised liberty of conscience, the colony restricted activity on the sabbath and prevented Catholics and Jews from voting. Nevertheless, Jews began to arrive in 1658 and acquired the right to worship in public by the end of the century.

Only Pennsylvania and, briefly, Maryland and New York rivaled Rhode Island as enclaves of relative tolerance. Repeating the pattern of Rhode Island's experience, Pennsylvania's charter of 1682 did not interpret liberty of conscience as legal equality, since Catholics were forbidden to vote, hold office, or celebrate mass in public, and Jews, similarly disfranchised, also faced commercial restrictions. Like Pennsylvania's Quaker founder, William Penn, the Catholic founders of Maryland understood that tolerance of their own minority faith required tolerance of other faiths as well as considerable prudence. In 1663 proprietor Caecillus Calvert warned the first Catholic settlers against giving "offense" to Protestants. Within a decade disputes between the Catholic governors and the largely Protestant assembly had erupted into violence. The Toleration Act of 1649 embraced all Christians except non-Trinitarians. Temporarily gaining full control in the mid-1650s, the Puritans executed at least four Catholics and banned "popery, prelacy, and licentiousness of opinion." In 1648 a Jewish physician was indicted, but not convicted, for denying the trinity.

In New York the Dutch legacy and the lenient first English proprietor, James, Duke of York (later James II), undermined Anglican supremacy. Establishment of the Dutch Reformed Church in the New Netherlands had not prevented settlement by Quakers, Lutherans, and Jews. In several instances Dutch superiors had overruled Governor Peter Stuyvesant, who wanted to bar Jews, a "deceitful race" of "Christ's enemies," from trade if not from the colony itself. The 1664 pact that transferred the New Netherlands to England provided religious freedom for Dutch Reformed Protestants. In 1683 the predominantly Dutch assembly allowed tax-supported churches wherever two-thirds of the voters agreed but forbade persecution of any believers "in God by Jesus Christ." Governors appointed by James after his ascension to the throne in 1685 allowed Catholics to vote, hold office, and openly celebrate mass; lifted lingering restrictions on Jewish businessmen; and welcomed Huguenot refugees. In contrast, New Jersey and Delaware shunned such experiments in tolerance. Nonetheless, since the two colonies needed to accommodate diverse populations, they allowed liberty of conscience to most Protestants.

Throughout the seventeenth century the Anglicans who had settled Virginia managed to exclude all but a handful of Congregationalists, Baptists, Quakers, Catholics, and Jews. Even so, the understaffed Church of England hardly constituted a formidable establishment. In the early eighteenth century Scots-Irish Presbyterians became a powerful presence in the backcountry. Many Presbyterians also settled in the Carolinas, where the Church of England was even weaker than in Virginia. Georgia, chartered in 1732 as a buffer against Spanish Florida, established Anglicanism but accepted German Pietists, Jews, and virtually anyone else willing to settle in this beleaguered outpost.

England's long and tumultuous Reformation decisively influenced religious relations in the colonies. To govern the doctrinally divided Commonwealth established in 1649, Oliver Cromwell acquiesced in liberty of conscience for most Protestants. While the Crown and Parliament harassed their respective religious foes during the subsequent Stuart Restoration, alliances flourished among theologically incongruous groups. Edmund Andros, governor of the consolidated Dominion of New England, used tolerance as a weapon against Puritans and even allowed George Keith, a leading Quaker, to denounce Puritan "degeneracy" from the Boston Common. According to Cotton Mather, the "Bloody Devotoes of Rome had in their design and Prospect nothing less than the Extinction of the Protestant Religion" (quoted in Thomas Brown, "The Image of the Beast," in Brown and Richard Curry, *Conspiracy,* 1972). Flirtation with Rome ended when William and Mary overthrew James II in 1689. Although the Toleration Act allowed freedom of conscience, Catholics, Jews, and Protestant dissenters remained second- or third-class subjects. New England Puritans lost much of their power, and Catholics faced imprisonment even in Maryland for openly celebrating mass. As late as 1742 New York executed two suspect Catholics, one of whom was actually a nonjuring Anglican.

The patterns of belief and behavior created by the English Reformation long outlived the specific theological controversies of the time. Indeed, these patterns survived not only in England but also in America and shaped the contours of American countersubversion almost a decade before the colonies declared independence. Seventeenth-century Americans, like their more diverse successors, feared that alien ideas might infiltrate their communities, even if aliens themselves were barred. Similarly, when Cotton Mather discerned Catholic and Quaker elements in witchcraft, he illustrated the tendency to conflate incongruous adversaries that has prevailed until the present. Since the seventeenth century apocalyptic rhetoric and expansive categories like "popery" have coexisted with fine distinctions in the measurement of virtue. Nevertheless, one must beware of pronouncing ideas absurd or fears groundless simply because they are expressed in archaic or inflated language. In the seventeenth century Quakers did disrupt the Massachusetts social order, Spanish and French Catholic troops did encircle British North America, and occasional "papal plots" did arise in England.

Furthermore, words offer only imperfect indicators of behavior. Massachusetts Quakers, granted freedom of worship under the charter of 1692, still faced harassment for the next twenty years. In many colonies Jews and Catholics may have fared better than legal codes suggest. Lax enforcement allowed New York Jews to build a synagogue in 1685 and vote until 1737; elsewhere some Catholics voted and held local office after the Revolution of 1689. Incipient rationalism, which eroded the significance of theological issues, mitigated religious conflict in Philadelphia. Chronic labor shortages required concessions everywhere. In general, standards for naturalization were looser in the colonies than in England. By the early eighteenth century British North Americans were freer in their choice of religion and in politics than any other people in the Western world.

This religious equilibrium was disrupted by immigration, the Great Awakening, and the struggle between Britain and France. Roughly a quarter of a million Scots-Irish Presbyterians, two hundred thousand German Pietists and Lutherans, and sixty thousand French Huguenots immigrated before the War for Independence. Typically, cultural rather than theological differences between immigrants and natives prompted complaints that German and French settlers clung to their foreign ways. Benjamin Franklin underestimated the capacity of the dominant culture to absorb newcomers when he accused *"Palatine Boors"* of transforming Pennsylvania, "founded by *English* [into] a colony of *Aliens."* However, even during the eighteenth century the process of absorption was also changing the dominant culture. Furthermore, the influx of non-Anglicans strengthened the constituency that sought freedom of conscience. Paradoxically, after polemics between New Light advocates of the Awakening and their Old Light foes subsided, the revival also furthered toleration. Awakened Protestants felt a bond across denominational lines, New England Congregationalists became factionalized, and Presbyterians and Separate Baptists strengthened their positions. The French and Indian War intensified anti-Catholic sentiment and fostered Protestant militancy. The clergy adapted earlier invective against Spain and associated France with the Antichrist, papal power, and the scarlet whore of Revelation. Sometimes they also added that British victory might usher in God's kingdom. Less apocalyptic than the clergy, George Washington suspected Catholics of aiding the enemy and prohibited Catholic troops from celebrating Pope Day. In several colonies Catholics were disarmed.

Fear of "popery," which the colonists interpreted in broad terms, helped the movement for independence. As Bernard Bailyn has shown in *The Ideological Origins of the American Revolution* various revolutionaries viewed British efforts to govern the colonies as signs of a vast conspiracy intended to undermine colonial liberty. From this point of view the prospect of a resident Anglican bishop looked like "ecclesiastical slavery." Indeed, many dissenting clergy still viewed the Church of England as an example of thinly disguised "popery." The British cabinet prudently declined to dispatch a bishop but then erred by seeking accommodation with actual "papists." The Quebec Act of 1774 extended the French influence into the Ohio Valley and granted freedom of religion to Catholic settlers there who swore allegiance to the Crown. Many colonists shared Alexander Hamilton's fear that "priestly tyranny may hereafter find as propitious soil in

America as it ever had in Spain or Portugal." John Adams fused traditional Protestant antipathy with Enlightenment disdain for the Catholic "horror of letters and learning."

The War for Independence created few clear divisions along sectarian lines. Anglicans were disproportionately loyalist, especially in the north, while New Light evangelicals—Presbyterians, Congregationalists, and to some extent Baptists—were disproportionately revolutionary. Religious and cultural minorities tended to side with the Crown, although the approximately two thousand Jews provided an exception to this generalization. Two Jews acted as aides to General Washington. A Roman Catholic also served on Washington's staff, yet most Catholics probably preferred the Crown to a prospective evangelical republic. Similarly, Quebec declined to join the United States, even though a delegation from the Continental Congress promised religious freedom, a delegation that included John Carroll, who later became the first Catholic bishop in the United States. This unsuccessful diplomatic mission illustrates the colonists' willingness to subordinate anti-Catholic sentiment to the cause of independence. Vital assistance from France further challenged the colonists' ritual allegations of Catholic ignorance, tyranny, and disloyalty. In contrast, Quakers, German Pietists, and other pacifists who refused to pay war taxes or swear allegiance to the new government faced arrest, loss of political rights, or seizure of property.

In general, the revolutionary era accelerated the momentum toward religious toleration and liberty. On the eve of independence a majority of the thirteen colonies still retained religious establishments. However, as John Adams said in defense of Massachusetts, these were "very slender" establishments. In the five southern states Protestant dissenters usually voted, held office, attended their own services, and escaped taxation for the Anglican Church. Under New York's multiple establishment system most non-Anglicans could apply tax money to their own clergy. Massachusetts, Connecticut, and New Hampshire required each local jurisdiction to pay a minister—a system that benefited the Congregationalist majority and highlighted the burdens imposed by slender establishments. Baptists who refused on theological grounds to seek exemptions were badgered or imprisoned; Quakers and some Anglicans also suffered. Isaac Backus, a Baptist pastor, challenged state authorities with the question: if the Revolution opposed "ecclesiastical slavery," then how could the state privilege any one religion over any other? Such ideological inconsistency would have produced few legal changes unless dissenters like Backus, allied with Enlightenment deists, had pressed the point. Political, economic, and demographic factors also encouraged disestablishment. Southern Anglican establishments, tainted by Toryism, fell more easily than their Congregationalist counterparts in New England. Moreover, numerous Scots-Irish southerners joined Thomas Jefferson in scorning Anglicanism and its successor, the Episcopal Church, as "truly the religion of the rich."

During or soon after the War for Independence, some states abolished established churches, others forbade their creation, and still others moved from single to dual or from dual to multiple establishment. The new state constitutions that made these changes undeniably advanced the cause of freedom of conscience. Nevertheless, just as prewar establishments were weaker than the term implies, so disestablishment fell short of religious equality. Significantly, disestablishment did not necessarily prevent general assessments to support Christian, most often Protestant, churches. A majority of states still barred or restricted office holding by Catholics, and only New York placed no such limitation on Jews. Even Pennsylvania and Delaware, which had never established churches, required officials to affirm the trinity.

The Federal Constitution written in 1787 was much more liberal than those of most states. No delegate to the Philadelphia Convention proposed any sort of religious establishment. Article VI, section 3, banning religious tests for office, passed easily over objections by delegates from North Carolina, Connecticut, and Maryland. A handful of speakers at ratifying conventions agreed with David Caldwell, a minister who told the North Carolina meeting that the Constitution invited "Jews and pagans of every kind to come among us." The more frequent complaint that no bill of rights protected religious and other freedoms soon found remedy.

The First Amendment prohibits Congress from enacting any law "respecting an establishment of religion, or prohibiting the free exercise thereof." Interpreted in a minimal sense, the amendment bars the federal government from requiring compulsory church attendance or directly aiding any one denomination. However, after two centuries of debate scholars and jurists still have not reached a consensus on the outer limits of its interpretation. Although James Madison guided the measure through Congress, his own belief in the "perfect separation" of church and state probably represented only a minority opinion among his fellow legislators and countrymen at large. Debate over passage of the amendment in Congress as well as in state legislatures evidenced little concern for the protection of infidels. More often the debate focused on the potential threat to religion, and some proponents saw the amendment as a way to protect state establishments against federal encroachment.

The Federal Constitution set an example. In the decade following its ratification, Georgia and South Carolina abandoned preferential treatment for Christians, while Pennsylvania and Delaware dropped their respective New Testament and Trinitarian requirements for office. No state after the original thirteen required a religious test. Yet some faiths remained legally inferior to others. Multiple Protestant establishments lingered in Vermont until 1807, Connecticut until 1818, New Hampshire until 1819, and Massachusetts until 1833. New Jersey Catholics remained ineligible for high office until 1844; restrictions in New Hampshire lasted until 1876. In Maryland and Rhode Island analogous curbs on Jews survived until 1826 and 1842, respectively. North Carolina excluded Jews from the executive branch until Reconstruction. Even where these measures affected few if any citizens, they imposed a stigma, as a Catholic proponent of Jewish equality told the North Carolina constitutional convention in 1835. Campaigns to abolish religious tests often entailed bitter controversy. Foes of Maryland's "Jew bill" denounced its foremost advocate, a Protestant, as "Judas Iscariot."

If viewed in isolation, the controversy over religious tests exaggerates prejudice against Catholics and Jews during the early national period. For the most part these restrictions reflected pro forma affirmation of Protestant virtue or concessions to clerical suspicion rather than fervent hostility to Catholics and Jews. Thus eva-sions and adjustments could and did occur. The Massachusetts Constitution of 1780 permitted Catholics to hold office if they rejected papal authority "in any matter civil, ecclesiastical, or spiritual." New York dropped the ban on Catholic legislators when the first was elected in 1806. Dismissing tales of the "sordid ignorance" of "popery," some Protestants sent their children to Catholic schools. In the 1790s the Adams administration attempted to curb entry by Jeffersonian "wild Irish" (a category that included Catholics as well as Protestants), but thereafter immigration remained dormant as a national issue until the late 1820s. Similarly, rivalry between Protestant and Catholic clergy simmered without reaching a boil.

Restrictions on Jews were less the product of anti-Semitism in particular than wariness of non-Christians in general. Typical in this respect, a delegate to the Massachusetts Constitutional Convention in 1820 grouped "jews, mahametans, deists and atheists" among enemies of the "common religion of the Commonwealth." As early as 1809 the North Carolina legislature bent the law to seat a Jew. Although Maryland barred Jews from state office, one served as United States attorney in Baltimore. These incongruities symbolize a larger ambivalence. On the one hand, since the days of Cotton Mather and Roger Williams Protestants had viewed Jews as living links with Old Testament prophets; on the other hand, they held Jews responsible for crucifying Christ and rejecting his message. Nor were American Protestants and Catholics immune to the stereotypes long held in Europe of Jews as unusually greedy, cunning, and clannish.

The two decades following the Revolution were probably the least devout in United States history. Indeed, ministers fought to retain state support partly because voluntary contributions declined. Not only were many Americans unchurched, but a significant minority experimented with "rational religion." Enlightenment deists, whose intellectual contribution to the Revolution had eclipsed that of the clergy, held a broad spectrum of beliefs. For example, Washington remained within the Episcopal church, John Adams drifted toward Unitarianism, and Elihu Palmer, Ethan Allen, and Thomas Paine explicitly attacked Christianity. Nor were these attacks the only unsettling consequences of what Bernard Bailyn calls the "contagion of liberty."

The lower classes began to refuse deference even to their creditors.

These trends disrupted the coalition among evangelical, enlightened, and impious revolutionaries. The clergy who favored separation of church and state had never doubted that the United States must remain stable, moral, and, broadly speaking, Christian. Responding to the apparent decline of religious belief, they led a Second Great Awakening whose consequences dwarfed those of the first. By the time the last state-supported churches were disestablished in 1833, interdenominational evangelical Protestantism was already becoming, in William G. McLoughlin's phrase, a "new form of establishment" (1973). Until the eve of the Civil War this Second Awakening energized movements to uplift strivers or incarcerate malcontents, to abolish war or invade Mexico, to end slavery or extend its boundaries. Participants in such movements played variations on the central theme of revolutionary ideology—that hidden conspiracies threatened American freedom.

As early as 1798 militant Federalist ministers assailed what Jedidiah Morse called a "secret plan" to destroy American "liberty and religion." According to Morse, this conspiracy, which began in 1736 with the creation of the Bavarian Society of Illuminati, an international Enlightenment Fraternity, had already spread through European Masonic lodges and precipitated the French Revolution. Morse reworked English charges against the Illuminati in American terms. Prominent Protestant clergy, and at least one Roman Catholic priest, echoed his claims. Although these polemicists hesitated to condemn all Masons, they eagerly concluded that Jeffersonian Republican political clubs were the main source of domestic danger.

These allegations were only slightly more far-fetched than others routinely exchanged by Federalists and Democratic Republicans in the 1790s. Morse, Osgood, and their allies correctly believed that the foremost Republicans, Thomas Jefferson and James Madison, favored strict separation of church and state. Nevertheless, the notion of a conspiracy stretching from Bavaria to Monticello never took hold as a central issue in national politics. President John Adams hedged on the validity of Morse's claims, and the Masons enhanced their reputation by advertising George Washington as one of their own.

RELIGIOUS PREJUDICE AND NATIVISM

By 1820, however, fear of Masonic subversion had inspired a potent social movement and promising political party, the Anti-Masonic party. In 1826 Masons in Canandaigua, New York, apparently abducted and murdered William Morgan, one of the order's loudest critics. Masons impeded investigations of the crime, secured light sentences or acquittals for indicted brethren, and threatened newspapers covering the story. Incensed critics of Masonry interpreted Masonic cronyism as grand conspiracy. To expose the conspiracy, they ran candidates for the New York legislature and spread warnings to nearby states. Profiting from a political spectrum in flux since the Federalist collapse, the Anti-Masonic party influenced—and occasionally dominated—the politics of New York, Massachusetts, Vermont, Pennsylvania, and Rhode Island during the early 1830s.

Anti-Masonry grew strongest in New England, where Jedidiah Morse's message had seeped into political lore, and among transplanted New Englanders elsewhere. Unlike Morse's small band of Federalist clergy, Anti-Masonry organized a grass roots movement in the name of the common man. As Pennsylvania leader Thaddeus Stevens complained, Masonry fostered "hatred of democracy" while securing "unmerited advantage to members of the fraternity over the honest and industrious uninitiated farmer, mechanic, and laborer" (quoted in Michael Holt, "Antimasonic and Know-Nothing Parties"). Faith as well as fortune seemed at stake. Baptists, Methodists, and Presbyterians shunned Masonry as a rationalist alternative to religion. Quakers and German Pietists objected to the order's secret oaths, which sounded especially sinister in their retelling by apostate Masons. The Anti-Masonic party attracted men and women jealous of the highly successful Masons, including prosperous townspeople as well as poor farmers. Nor did such Anti-Masonic leaders as Thurlow Weed, William Seward, and John Quincy Adams emerge from society's fringes.

Although Masonry constituted no "secret government," as Seward contended, Anti-Masons had plausible reasons for viewing it with suspicion. The order had grown rapidly in size and influence since the War for Independence. Investigations of Morgan's disappearance were thwarted because two-thirds of New York state officials were members. The Masons' promi-

nence and influence, combined with their deviance from the prevailing ethos, made them appealing targets. In line with its Enlightenment origins the order purported to select a natural aristocracy rather than celebrating the common man. While many middle-class men considered play a threat to discipline, Masonic lodges sanctioned what a Connecticut Anti-Mason called "extravagant mirth." Middle-class women formed an important auxiliary to the Anti-Masonic party, prompted by their awareness that such playful sessions drew men away from the home. Perhaps the most important cause of anti-Masonic sentiment was that Masonry did serve as a religious surrogate and even conducted funeral services for members, thereby occasioning suspicion amidst an evangelical Protestant revival. In short, Anti-Masonic polemics were as deeply rooted in the reality of the 1830s as were denunciations of the "slavocracy," an international abolitionist conspiracy, or the "Hydra headed monster," the Second Bank of the United States.

Anti-Masonry achieved greater success as a social movement than as a party. Congressional representation never exceeded twenty-five party members. Although state legislatures investigated the Masons, revoked lodge charters, or banned "extrajudicial oaths," enforcement was lax. William Wirt, former U. S. attorney general and the reluctant presidential candidate for the Anti-Masonic party in 1832, won roughly 3 percent of the vote and carried only Vermont. Scorning his supporters as "fanatical fools," Wirt failed to see that Anti-Mason leaders had become less interested in uprooting Masonry than in opposing Jacksonian Democrats. By 1840 almost all the leaders as well as most of the rank and file had joined the Whig coalition to elect William Henry Harrison as president. Anti-Masonry became a victim not only of its own success but also of the successful recreation of a two-party system. At the grass roots level Masons were excluded from congregations and juries, rejected as suitors, and otherwise stigmatized. Verging on collapse, the order no longer looked threatening.

The Church of Jesus Christ of Latter-day Saints (Mormon) faced much harsher persecution than the surrogate religion of Masonry. This offshoot of evangelical Protestantism offered earthly community, an accessible afterlife, and the strong leadership of founder Joseph Smith,

Jr. Mormonism immediately attracted adherents and enemies. Within a year of the church's founding in April 1830 the main body of Mormons had moved from upstate New York to Ohio, while a second large contingent settled in Missouri. In both places Mormons suffered physical abuse, destruction of property, and occasional murders. Complying with the governor's declaration that they must be "exterminated" or driven from Missouri, militia massacred a Mormon settlement in 1838. Illinois provided temporary sanctuary. After Smith's arrival in 1839, Mormons transformed a swampy river town into a flourishing, nearly sovereign city of fifteen thousand and renamed it Nauvoo. Non-Mormons denounced Nauvoo's freedom from state control, Smith's autocratic manner, and the church's drift toward polygamy. In 1844 Smith suppressed a newspaper published by apostate Mormons. After complicated legal and paramilitary maneuvers, Smith and his brother Hyrum were indicted for treason, jailed in Carthage, Illinois, and murdered by a militia turned mob on 27 June 1844. Brigham Young reluctantly led the Mormons west from Nauvoo during the winter of 1845–1846.

Within three years the Mormons built a prosperous enclave around the Great Salt Lake, wrote a constitution, and sought admission to the Union. In 1850 a hostile Congress granted only territorial status to Utah, although President Millard Fillmore prudently appointed Young governor. There followed six years of acrimony between church leaders and non-Mormon Indian agents, federal judges, and surveyors. Embittered officials convinced President James Buchanan that the Mormon hierarchy fostered "open rebellion" against the United States. In 1857 Buchanan ordered the army to escort a new non-Mormon governor to Utah, expecting most Mormons to welcome this liberation from ecclesiastical tyranny. Instead, the Mormons, fearing another campaign of extermination, fortified mountain passes, raided army supply wagons, and, joining Indians at Mountain Meadows, murdered settlers bound for California. After federal troops encamped near Salt Lake City, the ignoble "Mormon War" ended in an ambiguous truce.

Antebellum persecution of Mormons was not limited to idiosyncratic agitators. The deadliest mobs consisted of militia acting with government sanction or acquiescence; mob leaders were often merchants or professionals. Economic grievances frequently fueled religious animosity. A Mormon bank failed in Ohio during the panic of 1837, and the Mormon migration to Illinois raised land prices. In general church members preferred to conduct business among themselves. Some assailants were prompted by the prospect of plunder. Furthermore, while Mormon prosperity elicited envy, church members were also scorned for their humble origins.

Anti-Mormon tracts, speeches, and press accounts appealed to Americans who had never met and surely had never competed with a Mormon. Affirming democracy and condemning secrecy, the main themes in this literature overlapped with earlier attacks on Masonry. Mormons were accused of treason, terrorism, importation of foreign "serfs," and a "grand conspiracy" with Indians to destroy white settlements. Even by antebellum standards anti-Mormon rhetoric displayed an unusually large proportion of misunderstanding, envy, and psychological projection. After all, though Brigham Young may have dreamed of divine judgment on the United States, he never seriously considered secession. With a few exceptions, such as the Mountain Meadows killings, Mormons resorted to violence only in self-defense. Mormon immigration totaled only twenty-two thousand by 1855, a small fraction of the nation's newcomers. To their credit, most Mormons agreed with Young that it was cheaper and more humane to feed Indians than to kill them. Nonetheless, anti-Mormon sentiment was so pervasive during the disintegrating 1850s that, as the *New York Times* editorialized, few Americans would have complained if they were "utterly exterminated."

Roman Catholics were too numerous and well-connected to exterminate. Yet, during the three decades before the Civil War Catholics encountered worse treatment than they have during any other period in United States history. The immigration of more than one million Catholics from the late 1820s raised simmering controversy to a boil. The new arrivals came primarily from Germany and Ireland and typically drank alcohol, supported urban political machines, slighted the sabbath, and disproportionately filled jails, asylums, and relief rolls. Protestants denounced "popery" in sermons, speeches, periodicals, novels, and children's books. Leaders of anti-Catholic movements included distinguished clergy, prominent politicians, and unemployed workmen as well as renegade priests, opportunists, and thugs. Their activities ranged from proselytism to arson.

Polemicists renewed traditional accusations that Catholicism fostered false faith, political tyranny, and sexual immorality. Although allusions to the "scarlet whore" were no longer de rigueur, the Presbyterian Assembly in 1835 declared Catholicism "essentially apostacized from the religion of our Lord." Seventh-day Adventists, a new religion that emerged from the Millerite fervor of the era, held Catholicism responsible for the sin of Sunday worship. Patrician historians presented the Catholic church as the prototypical enemy of liberty and progress. *Awful Disclosures of the Hotel Dieu Nunnery of Montreal* (1836) stands out among tracts alleging priestly lechery; ostensibly the confessions of "Maria Monk," a runaway nun, it actually combined the fantasies of a young woman who had never taken vows with the prose of several Protestant ministers. The traditional motifs of anti-Catholicism sometimes gave way to condemnations of immigrants who failed to meet evangelical standards of honesty, diligence, independence, and sobriety. The invective of skilled workers mixed economic self-interest with snobbery. Philadelphia carpenter Jacob Teck told a trades convention in 1847 that the glut of Catholic immigrants on the labor market threatened the American artisan's "boasted respectability and moral standing." According to *A Plea for the West*, a nativist classic published in 1835 by Lyman Beecher, European monarchs deliberately flooded the United States with docile immigrants who were dominated by priests and remained virtual soldiers in a foreign army.

The creators of public school systems usually conflated morality, patriotism, and Protestantism. The King James Bible served as standard fare for opening exercises, and sometimes it served as a primary textbook, too. Catholics protested that their children should be allowed to use the Douay Bible and requested public funds for their own schools. At times they succeeded and secured considerate treatment for Catholic pupils, local control in Catholic neighborhoods, and state funds for Catholic academies. More often they were thwarted by countercampaigns to save the classroom and state treasury from "popery." Moreover, the creation of two hundred Catholic academies by 1840 reinforced Protestant fears that Catholics intended to halt the westward march of their religious influence.

Anti-Catholic sentiment sometimes went beyond words. In 1834 solid citizens burned an Ursuline convent outside Boston. That same year a mob drove Irish Catholic workmen from New Hampshire. In Philadelphia conflicts over Bible reading in public schools exacerbated conflicts between unskilled Irish immigrants and evangelical artisans. Riots in July 1844 left two churches destroyed and twelve persons dead. Assaults on priests and Catholic laymen were legion throughout the 1830s and 1840s. In California, for example, harassment forced Hispanics from the gold fields. Although attacks on Catholics were less likely to receive official sanction than attacks on Mormons, militia in Philadelphia did sack churches or stood aside and watched others do so.

Catholics answered their foes in print, debated them in public, heckled, slugged, and sometimes killed them. Bishops in council formally repudiated political meddling for themselves and urged Catholics to refute nativist "babbling" by obeying the law. Nonetheless, John Hughes, the militant archbishop of New York, cultivated Whigs and Democrats, accused Protestant clergy of denouncing Catholics in order to "extort" money from gullible audiences, and rallied armed parishioners to protect his churches. Catholic politicians sometimes banned nativist meetings; a handful of priests publicly burned Protestant Bibles. Waging intermittent war, urban Protestant and Catholic gangs were less interested in theology than in wages, self-esteem, and turf.

The late 1840s brought a partial remission of anti-Catholic sentiment, partly because eleven hundred Catholics served in the Mexican War. But during the 1850s anti-Catholic acts spread again, prompted by increased immigration of Catholic workers, economic recession, the general decline of political civility, and errors committed by church leaders. In 1850 Hughes, no more tolerant than his evangelical enemies, proclaimed the "decline of Protestantism." When Pope Pius IX dispatched Bishop Gaetano Bedini to America in 1853 to settle controversies between laymen and clergy over church trusteeship, his visit drew attention not only to the volatile issue of trusteeship but also to the question of Vatican authority. Dubbed the "bloody butcher of Bologna," where he had served as governor, Bedini was physically attacked in Wheeling, and nearly shot in Baltimore. Elsewhere during the 1850s, mobs burned a dozen Catholic churches, beat priests, and sank the marble block donated by Pope Pius IX for the Washington monument in the Potomac.

Significantly, the 1850s produced a national political movement centered on opposition to Catholicism, the American party, or, as its members were generally called, the Know-Nothings. As early as the 1830s local "native American" parties had won control of several cities. Many of their constituents later filled Know-Nothing ranks. The Know-Nothing movement began in 1853 when the Order of the Star Spangled Banner, energized by new recruits from lesser nativist groups, entered a militant new phase and began secretly to back political candidates. Members used secret handshakes, passwords, and rituals; pledged to vote only for native-born Protestants "without regard to party predilections"; and responded to inquiries about their activities with an enigmatic "I know nothing." Such inquiries mounted as the order's covert support swung many elections in 1853 and 1854. By the time the Know-Nothing movement surfaced and held a national convention as the American Party in 1855, it already had elected at least seventy members to Congress.

The Know-Nothing party was comparable to the Anti-Masonic party a generation earlier in that it flourished briefly in the midst of a disintegrating party system, disproportionately attracted young voters and non-voters alienated from ordinary politics, nonetheless fell into the hands of political professionals, left a slim legislative record, and ultimately merged with a sturdier party—in this case, the Republicans. In several states Know-Nothing legislatures investigated convents and prohibited Catholic bishops from owning church property. Catholics continued to vote despite efforts of Know-Nothing rowdies and election day riots in St. Louis, New Orleans, and Louisville. The party failed to limit immigration or extend the period of naturalization. As it divided over slavery, the Know-Nothing presidential nominee in 1856, Millard Fillmore, won 21 percent of the vote, running

strongest in the South and border states although carrying only Maryland.

In retrospect the anti-Catholic upsurge is easier to understand than the crusades against Masonry and Mormonism, because hundreds of thousands of Catholic immigrants were changing what it meant to be an American. Since some states allowed immigrants to vote before their naturalization, Catholic ballots may have provided Democratic president Franklin Pierce's margin of victory in 1852. Not only did the mid-century papacy support reaction, but a majority of American bishops had been born abroad. Thus it is hardly surprising that Protestant heirs to suspicion of "popery" placed such facts into the omnipresent framework of conspiracy. In so doing, they underestimated the ways in which the United States changed Catholic immigrants. The Catholic hierarchy—ethnically divided, wary of the Vatican, and understaffed—could not effectively control immigrant behavior. And most immigrants voted Democratic because the Whigs were hospitable to nativism, not because the hierarchy told them to do so. Indeed, most of the bishops preferred the culturally conservative Whigs to the Democrats.

Before the Civil War Jews faced no comparable persecution, even though immigration from Germany increased the Jewish population to one hundred and fifty thousand by 1860. Jewish immigrants seemed less threatening than their Catholic counterparts because they were more prosperous. Nonetheless, instances of insensitivity to Jewish beliefs occurred. Governors alluded to Christ in Thanksgiving proclamations, and at least one treaty protected only Christian missionaries abroad. Two national groups spawned by the Second Awakening, the American Society for Evangelizing the Jews and the American Society for Meliorating the Condition of the Jews, tried to convert them. Along with Seventh-day Adventists and militant freethinkers, Jews were prosecuted for violating blue laws. Beyond insensitivity, notable cases of discrimination and prejudice also occurred. By the 1830s the infinitive "to Jew" connoted sharp dealing. Sermons, tracts, and Sunday school lessons held Jews responsible for Christ's crucifixion. Although Jews prospered in finance, none received a partnership in a gentile banking house. In the early 1800s Federalists, including John Adams and John Quincy Adams, scorned "alien Jew" Jeffersonians. Fifty years later, Judah P. Benjamin, senator from Louisiana, and chairman of the Democratic National Committee, August Belmont, encountered similar slurs.

This survey of antebellum countersubversion and religious prejudice risks oversimplification. In practice, conspiratorial motifs overlapped; comparisons of Brigham Young and the pope became commonplace. Furthermore, despite their interdenominational alliances, evangelical Protestants continued to disagree about theology, church polity, and prospective converts. Seventh-day Adventists and Campbellites (later known as the Disciples of Christ) faced particularly fierce opposition. Yet cooperation and even friendship sometimes transcended religious differences, especially if economic rivalry was minimal. Know-Nothings fared poorly in the old Northwest Territory where Protestants and Catholics lived in roughly equal numbers.

Furthermore, the antebellum era demonstrates that victims of prejudice in one context can become its perpetrators in another. John Floyd, a Catholic and secretary of war in James Buchanan's cabinet, dispatched troops against the Mormons. James Bennett, a Catholic and editor of the *New York Herald,* flayed "Austrian Jew banker" August Belmont, and Representative Lewis C. Levin, the premier Jewish nativist, defended anti-Catholic rioters. Strained relations between Catholic and Jewish leaders worsened during the 1850s as the result of an international controversy over Edgar Mortara, an Italian Jewish child apparently baptized in secret against his parents' wishes and forcibly raised a Catholic. Finally, the Second Great Awakening failed to eradicate anticlericalism, rational religion, and militant unbelief. Impious mobs occasionally disrupted revivals. Senator Richard M. Johnson led the fight for Sunday mail delivery, a government service anathema to evangelical Protestants, but nonetheless managed to win the vice-presidency in 1836. Freethinker Abner Kneeland was less fortunate and served a prison term for blasphemy.

In general, the Civil War marked no drastic transition in the history of nativism and religious prejudice. Thaddeus Stevens, formerly an Anti-Mason, later feared that "invisible powers" of Masonry might save Andrew Johnson from impeachment. Although after the war animosity to Mormons and Catholics declined from prewar peaks, neither faith was regarded yet as fully American. Abraham Lincoln ended the military occupation of Utah, but Congress upheld a Republican platform that paired polygamy and slavery and forbade plural marriage in the territories. The influx of non-Mormons into Utah exacerbated the acrimonious situation, which in turn prompted renewed hostility in the East. From the 1870s to the 1890s the State Department urged foreign governments to end emigration by "ignorant classes" drawn to Mormonism, while army officers blamed Mormons for Indian uprisings, and Protestant clergy condemned Utah as the national "brothel." Congress tightened control over the territory and refused to grant statehood until 1896, six years after the Mormon Church had forbidden further plural marriages. Then the House of Representatives refused to seat the polygamous Brigham Roberts, and the Senate investigated allegations of sub-rosa polygamy before seating monogamous Reed Smoot.

During the 1860s supporters of the Union ominously noted Pope Pius IX's tilt toward the Confederacy, most Know-Nothings found homes in the Republican party, and foes of William Marcy Tweed's Democratic machine in New York City routinely conflated Catholicism and corruption. From Reconstruction through the 1890s clashes persisted over Bible reading in public schools, appropriations to parochial schools, and denominational education of American Indians. Several states banned voting by non-citizens or vigorously enforced such laws that were already on the books. Bigots were not the only ones concerned about these issues, and even debates among responsible citizens almost always touched on nativist themes. In 1885 Josiah Strong published *Our Country,* the premier nativist tract of the late nineteenth century that updated the old theme of anti-Catholicism to fit the new theme of Social Gospel. According to Strong, Catholicism prevented immigrants from understanding representative government, a system that came "naturally" to Protestants. Also during the late 1880s, foes of "Romanism," less generous than Strong, revitalized venerable nativist organizations or built new ones. The most important group was the American Protective Association (APA), founded by Henry L. Bowers in 1887. APA members pledged not to vote for, strike with, or hire Catholics if non-Catholics were available. Former priests, ersatz nuns, and lurid tracts (including the *Awful Disclosures* of "Maria Monk") helped to spread the secret order's countersubversive message. By early 1895 the APA comprised one hundred thousand members and many more allies in proliferating patriotic societies. While leaders of the APA sometimes suspected the Catholic church of plotting insurrection, they were less likely than their Know-Nothing forebears to sanction violence. Compared to the 1850s, the 1890s produced few interfaith shoot-outs. But when violence did occur, recent immigrants were once again the favorite targets.

The war for and against the Union reinforced evangelical trends and catalyzed a rise in anti-Semitism. While Jews served disproportionately in both armies, they were often accused of profiting from the war rather than contributing to the fight. In the South, some Jewish merchants suffered boycotts. Judah Benjamin, first secretary of war and then secretary of state for the Confederacy, faced escalating anti-Semitic invective. The United States Congress hesitated to authorize Jewish chaplains, although it finally did so. Henry Wilson, one of the founders of the Republican party, was not alone in believing that productive citizens had arrayed against the "curbstone Jew broker." Ulysses S. Grant capped a series of anti-Semitic incidents in the Union officer corps when he barred "Jews as a class" from the military department of Tennessee in 1862. Several families were driven from their homes before President Lincoln revoked the order.

Suspicion of Jews increased during the late nineteenth century. Senator John T. Morgan reflected the heightened suspicion of Jews when he called one rival a "Jew dog" in 1878. Although relatively few Americans expressed hostility to Jews as bluntly as Senator Morgan did, most Christians continued to agree with Morgan Dix, the Episcopal minister of Trinity Church in New York, that the "judicial murder" of Jesus was a historical fact. Historical fiction, a thriving genre that included Lewis Wallace's *Ben Hur* (1880), treated Judaism as a legalistic faith inferior to Christianity. Patricians disdained upwardly mobile Jews as the quintessential parvenus of the

Gilded Age, and a few joined Henry Adams in fearing their imminent hegemony. Moved by personal dislike as well as by snobbery, Henry Hilton barred financier Joseph Seligman from his hotel in Saratoga Springs, New York, in 1877. Widespread restrictions against Jews soon followed at other resorts, clubs, and elite preparatory and finishing schools. Poor Jewish and gentile immigrants clashed over jobs, housing, and neighborhood boundaries. Especially during the depression of the 1890s, conflict went beyond insults and fist fights. For example, New Jersey factory workers rioted to prevent the hiring of Jews, and Mississippi night riders harassed Jewish shopkeepers. Meanwhile, unsympathetic Shylocks whined on stage, grotesque Jews inhabited serious fiction as well as potboilers, hook-nosed caricatures filled illustrated magazines, and Jewish pimps and arsonists were favorite subjects for investigative journalists.

The dissemination of unflattering stereotypes, and widespread social discrimination marked a new phase in American anti-Semitism. However, the late nineteenth-century shift should not be exaggerated. Hilton's ban on Jews elicited condemnation as well as emulation. Caricatures ranged from calumny to kidding. Some magazines both mocked the immigrants' imperfect adaptation to American ways and condemned anti-Semitic outbreaks abroad. Indeed, while explicitly anti-Semitic movements gained large French and German followings during the 1880s, none arose in the United States. Edouard Drumont's charge that Jewish conspirators controlled the French government helped bring down a prime minister, but an Americanization of this argument, *The Original Mr. Jacobs,* published in 1888 by Telemachus Timayenis, a Greek immigrant, attracted slight attention. In short, most Americans continued to hold mixed feelings about Jews. As the *Boston Transcript* mused, "It is strange that a nation [with] so many good traits should be so obnoxious."

After the Civil War nativism remained entwined with politics. Republicans could not resist temptations to ally quietly with foes of "popery." President Rutherford B. Hayes appointed James Wigginton Thompson, an anti-Catholic polemicist, as secretary of the navy. While James G. Blaine, Republican nominee for the presidency in 1884, vowed never to criticize the religion of his Catholic mother, a Protestant supporter's denunciation of the Democratic party of "Rum, Romanism, and Rebellion" cost Irish-American votes and contributed to Blaine's defeat by Grover Cleveland. Cleveland's victory, repeated in 1892, increased Protestant fears of immigrant voters and Catholic clerics. One Baptist writer surmised that a direct telephone line now linked James Cardinal Gibbons, archbishop of Baltimore, with the White House. The APA dominated Republican politics in several states.

Leaders of the insurgent People's party, founded in 1892, forcefully repudiated the APA, but they were less zealous in guarding against anti-Jewish innuendo in their rhetoric. For example, Tom Watson, a Populist representative from Georgia, linked the house of Rothschild with Cleveland's disastrous economic policies and charged Democrats with capitulation to "red-eyed jewish millionaires." Yet Populists in general were no more prone to anti-Semitism than other Americans, and such references comprised a minor part of their vocabulary. William Jennings Bryan, the Democratic Populist presidential candidate in 1896, shunned anti-Catholic and anti-Semitic appeals in his campaign. Bryan lost to William McKinley, the Republican nominee, who successfully courted both APA members and Catholic Democrats.

Between 1880 and 1930 the United States received twenty-seven million immigrants, most of them Catholics and Jews from eastern and southern Europe. Although references to papal conspiracies and Christ's crucifixion persisted in nativist rhetoric, racial and economic motifs became increasingly prominent. The "new immigration" consisted of "beaten men from beaten races," as Francis Walker, president of the Massachusetts Institute of Technology, summarized the emerging orthodoxy in the 1890s. While Josiah Strong worried that Catholics would escape church discipline and rush into radicalism, president of the Knights of Labor and himself a Catholic, Terence Powderly, feared that "foreign serfs" would depress wages. Neither fear was entirely groundless. Employers opposed restrictions on immigration and played ethnic groups against each other. Radical Irish Catholic coal miners took up arms against Welsh Protestant mineowners in Pennsylvania. The patrician organizers of the Immigration Restriction League, less concerned with cheap labor than with the preservation of "Anglo-Saxon" culture, campaigned to bar illiterate immigrants. While Brahmins and biologists sought such legislation, others took direct action in the name of Anglo-Saxon purity. The leader of a New Orleans mob that lynched eleven Italian prisoners in 1891 regarded his victims as "so many reptiles." Yet Italians, often called the Chinese of Europe, fared better than the Chinese themselves. Following decades of West Coast agitation fueled by missionaries' denunciations of "heathen" practices, Congress first curbed Chinese entry in 1882 and then virtually barred it in 1892.

Although broadly Protestant values remained dominant around the turn of the century, a majority of Americans still belonged to no church. Indeed, a significant minority of Protestants drifted toward casual agnosticism; some immigrant groups, notably the Czechs, strengthened the ranks of freethinkers; and militant agnostics like Robert G. Ingersoll denounced religion as "superstition" before large audiences. The revivals that originally were intended to bolster Protestantism now opened old wounds and inflicted new ones. For instance, instead of making common cause with the Mormons against Ingersoll's "ribald infidelity," Josiah Strong counted Mormonism on his list of national "perils." Protestants fought among themselves over Darwinism, biblical criticism, and missionary policy; in some denominations, these controversies resulted in heresy trials. In 1908, some orthodox churchmen pronounced William Howard Taft, a Unitarian who doubted Christ's divinity, unfit for the presidency. Despite their intramural disputes, Protestant theological liberals and conservatives generally shared prejudices against unconventional responses to the era's spiritual crisis, such as Christian Science, Pentecostalism, and the International Bible Students' Association (later known as Jehovah's Witnesses).

The two decades following the critical election of 1896 were marked by stirrings of reform that scholars subsume under the label "progressivism." A few progressives espoused cultural pluralism. By and large, however, reform continued to coexist with and often to reinforce prejudice. Translating old concerns into fashionable terms, journalists envisioned a conspiracy between Mormon leaders and corporate trusts. Similarly, the leading anti-Catholic periodical, the *Menace,* damned the Catholic church for thwarting unions as well as for plotting to kill "heretics." West Coast progressives extended the degrading images and legal disabilities formerly applied to the Chinese to the Japanese. With varying degrees of insensitivity and malice, muckrakers, municipal reformers, and purity crusaders warned against knife-wielding Italians, sullen Slavs, and drunken Irish. And as the most prosperous of the "new immigrants," Jews encountered special suspicion. While philo-Semites noted a "cousinly" affinity between thrifty Yankees and successful Jews, anti-Semites used this stereotype differently and attributed Jewish prosperity to chicanery, clannishness, and crime. In 1908 Theodore Bingham, police commissioner of New York, claimed that half of the city's criminals were "Hebrews." In fact, Jews were generally underrepresented among the criminal population.

After the turn of the century science buttressed bigotry. Typifying the relatively mild nativism of the 1880s, Josiah Strong not only believed that most immigrants could be assimilated, but expected them to help the United States fulfill its destiny as the "elect nation." By the 1910s, most geneticists, anthropologists, and psychologists maintained that the "races" originating in southern and eastern Europe were innately inferior to the old northern European stock and thus were incapable of assimilation. The leading popularizer of this notion, Madison Grant, published *The Passing of the Great Race* in 1916. According to Grant, although Sicilians and Polish Jews might steal "Nordic" women, heredity prevented them from displaying "Nordic" intelligence, courage, or idealism. Ironically, Americans were less tolerant on the eve of World War I, following twenty years of progressivism, than during the 1890s. Tom Watson epitomized this unfortunate transition as he left behind the mild nativism of his Populist phase during the 1890s and assailed the "parasite race" of Jews and the "jackassical" Catholic religion during the 1910s.

Restrictive legislation, job discrimination, and violence coincided with the harsher mood. Presidents Grover Cleveland, William Howard Taft, and Woodrow Wilson vetoed bills imposing a literacy test. But as immigration policy became increasingly nationalized and systematized, entrance requirements were tightened to exclude the "feeble minded," political dissidents, and those unable to pay a head tax. (In 1907 the tax amounted to four dollars, a significant sum for uprooted peasants). Upwardly mobile Jews deemed deficient in character or alien in temperament bore the brunt of discrimination in law, medicine, and other professions. In 1913 Harlan Fiske Stone, dean of the Columbia Law School, asserted that "oriental" Jewish minds betrayed a "racial tendency" to memorize instead of thinking creatively. Thinly veiled anti-Semitism marked much of the opposition to Louis Brandeis' confirmation as justice of the United States Supreme Court in 1916. The most infamous vigilante act committed during the progressive era also involved a Jew, Leo Frank. Convicted in Atlanta of a murder he did not commit, Frank was lynched on 17 August 1915 after his sentence had been commuted. Tom Watson's denunciations of Frank as a "satyr faced Jew" created an atmosphere congenial to his murderers and to vigilantes who harassed other Jews in Georgia. In November 1915 another Georgian, William J. Simmons, founded the twentieth-century version of the Knights of the Ku Klux Klan.

Nativist brutality must not obscure the continuing complexity of relations among and within religious and ethnic groups. To a greater extent than their antebellum counterparts, post-Civil War immigrants altered the economy, challenged social mores, and ultimately broadened the definition of what it meant to be an American. Consequently, it is not surprising that spokesmen for the prevailing Protestant culture reacted with alarm. Indeed, many Catholic priests shared Josiah Strong's suspicion of their Italian, Czech, or Polish parishioners. Similarly, the *Hebrew Standard* declared in 1894 that "thoroughly acclimated" American Jews bore no religious, social, or intellectual resemblance to "miserable darkened Hebrews" from eastern Europe. Epitomizing many Americans' mixed feelings, successful politicians preached Anglo-Saxon superiority and derided alien influences while soliciting votes from non–Anglo-Saxon aliens. For instance, President McKinley first accepted APA support and then placed a Catholic on the Supreme Court. Victims of prejudice continued to find their own scapegoats. Denis Kearney, a Catholic agitator, combined eclectic animosities when he accused "foreign Shylocks" of importing Orientals to "debauch" white women. While racism received scientific sanction and pressure mounted for immigration restriction, most Americans still expected immigrants already landed eventually to assimilate.

World War I ultimately encouraged religious prejudice, nativism, and, especially anti-Semitism. The war and the Red Scare of 1919–1920 institutionalized federal suppression of dissenters, heightened unfounded belief in conspiracies, legitimated violence against alleged subversives, and increased support for Prohibition and immigration restriction. The Wilson administration prosecuted religious objectors to war in general as well as radical protestors against the Great War in particular. Quakers and Mennonites who refused alternate service went to prison along with leading Jehovah's Witnesses. German-American Lutherans were subject to federal surveillance even though their church supported the war. False rumors, reminiscent of the Civil War period, accused Jews of evading combat in order to make money, and officials returning from Russia in 1919 repeated the royalist accusation that Communism was "Yiddish." Distrust of German-American brewers eased passage of the Eighteenth Amendment and the Volstead Act, commonly known as Prohibition. Growing hostility to immigrants facilitated the enactment of a literacy test in 1917 over Wilson's second veto. Nonetheless, six hundred thousand immigrants, one-sixth of whom were Jewish, arrived in 1921 during the postwar depression. In response Congress temporarily limited immigrants from outside the Western hemisphere to 358,000 annually. Three years later the permanent Johnson-Reed Act cut the figure to roughly 154,000 apportioned according to national origins, a system that blatantly discriminated against eastern and southern European Catholics and Jews.

The National Security League, American Protective League, and other self-designated patriotic societies preached "preparedness" during 1915–1917; harassed alleged slackers throughout the war, often with Justice Department sanction; moved on to "reds" after the armistice; and persisted in promoting "one hundred percent Americanism" throughout the 1920s. Although the Ku Klux Klan never enjoyed federal patronage, it flourished during the postwar depression and became the largest vigilante organization. At its peak in early 1924 the loosely organized Klan comprised at least two million members and perhaps as many as four million. Members included Republicans and Democrats, northerners and

southerners, strikers and strikebreakers, farmers and businessmen, con artists and zealots, genteel ladies and sadists. Support was strong in medium-sized cities where evangelical Protestants encountered sizable but not overwhelmingly large Catholic and Jewish populations. The Klan paid less attention to blacks than did its Reconstruction ancestor. Rather, as the *Fiery Cross* magazine explained in 1924, the Klan rallied "old stock Americans" against Jews, who "dominate the economic life of the nation," and Catholics, who "dominate the political and religious life." To counteract this twin menace, Klansmen marched, flogged, and occasionally killed.

Anti-Semitism operated in three broad areas during the 1920s. First, discrimination took a new turn with the adoption of explicit quotas on Jews at elite universities and professional schools. Columbia and Harvard, for example, cut their Jewish enrollment in half. Similarly, local legal covenants barred sale of residences to Jews (as well as to blacks and, less often, to Catholics). Such restrictions not only evidenced snobbery and religious prejudice but also served, in Carey McWilliams' famous phrase, as a "mask for privilege" that hindered economic competitors. Second, widespread popularizations of scientific racism treated eastern European Jews especially unfairly. Kenneth Roberts warned that these "human parasites" could not be assimilated in *Why Europe Leaves Home* (1923), a tract against "mongrelization." Third, *The International Jew,* a series of articles first published in Henry Ford's newspaper, the *Dearborn Independent,* placed Jews at the center of a conspiracy theory as farfetched as any in American history. Like Jedidiah Morse's Illuminati cabal propagated 130 years earlier, this comprehensive conspiracy theory came from abroad. It derived from *The Protocols of the Learned Elders of Zion,* putative records of the plotters but actually a fabrication by Russian anti-Semites. Elaborating on *The Protocols'* central theme that the elders manipulated both exploitative capitalism and subversive communism to undermine Christian civilization, Ford's staff added characteristic American touches. Jews were accused of spreading religious modernism, fixing the 1919 World Series, and founding farm cooperatives to corrupt the heartland. *The International Jew* won favor among some genteel anti-Semites as well as earthier Klansmen.

Polarization of Protestants accompanied World War I, and after the war the split within

Protestantism turned into a chasm. Theological conservatives (known as Fundamentalists after 1920) were victims of prejudice as well as purveyors of prejudice in the heresy trials, schisms, and polemics that followed the war. Theological liberals rarely understood the intricacy of Fundamentalist theology or the depth of Fundamentalist beliefs in original sin, inerrant Scripture, and Jesus' imminent return. When liberals charged them with stupidity, Fundamentalists countered with allegations of infidelity and subversion. Fundamentalists were more likely than liberals to hold Jews responsible for Christ's crucifixion and to condemn Catholicism in classic terms as the scarlet whore. Baptist, Methodist, and Disciples of Christ Fundamentalists disproportionately joined the Klan. Yet one must not exaggerate the connection between Fundamentalism and bigotry. Conservative clergy occasionally allied with Catholics to censor films or condemn birth control. William Jennings Bryan, the foremost Fundamentalist layman, denounced the libelous *The Protocols.* Whereas many Fundamentalists sympathetically interpreted Zionism as the fulfillment of biblical prophecy, Social Gospelers often derided it as the token of immigrant clannishness. Even the trial of John T. Scopes for teaching evolution cannot be reduced to a war between ignorance and wisdom. While Bryan volunteered to prosecute Scopes in order to uphold Christianity, Clarence Darrow, a militant agnostic in the fashion of his friend Ingersoll, joined the defense in order to uphold the surrogate religion of science. Looking on, secularists like H. L. Mencken, Sinclair Lewis, and Upton Sinclair portrayed Fundamentalism as a conspiracy of yahoos and hypocrites.

Religious and ethnic conflict was central to national politics during the 1920s. Indeed, the Democrats were virtually disabled by divisions over Prohibition, the Ku Klux Klan, and the presidential aspirations of Governor Alfred E. Smith, a "wet" Catholic champion of the "new immigration." Prohibition was not inherently nativist. Some Catholics had allied with the evangelical Anti-Saloon League, the lobby most responsible for the Eighteenth Amendment. Nonetheless, "dry" Protestants, including many League members, had long associated "Romanism" with "besotted ignorance." Furthermore, Catholics disproportionately violated the Volstead Act. In 1924 the Democratic convention rejected Smith and narrowly declined to condemn the Klan by name. After Smith's nomination in 1928, the Klan denounced him as a tool of Pope Pius XI, the "dago on the Tiber." Bob Jones, a prominent Fundamentalist minister, claimed to prefer a "nigger" president to Smith, while James Cannon, a Methodist bishop and leader of the increasingly nativist Anti-Saloon League, called Smith the spokesman for "dirty people" from the streets of New York. However, prejudice was confined neither to Klansmen nor to the broader community of Fundamentalists. In keeping with Republican tradition, presidential candidate Herbert Hoover acquiesced in party cooperation with anti-Catholic militants in his campaign against Smith. *Christian Century* magazine called Smith the representative of an "alien culture, of a medieval Latin mentality, of an undemocratic hierarchy and a foreign potentate" (quoted in Lichtman, *Prejudice and the Old Politics*). Smith responded with courage, common sense, and naiveté. He rightly stressed the compatibility of Catholicism and Americanism, but he understated the church's participation in politics, diplomacy, and the enforcement of Victorian morality.

Religious and ethnic issues from the 1920s persisted through the Great Depression and World War II. Franklin D. Roosevelt temporarily healed the Democratic party's cultural wounds and created a religious coalition that included Fundamentalists, Social Gospelers, Catholics, Jews, and former Klansmen. Catholics especially enjoyed unprecedented political power and legitimacy, winning one-quarter of all New Deal judicial appointments. For the first time two Catholics sat in the cabinet. Children of the "new immigration" helped to build the Congress of Industrial Organizations. Catholic clergy and laymen played a major role in imposing a prim production code on the film industry. Meanwhile, movies portrayed affable singing priests, all-American athletes at Catholic colleges, and fighting Irish regiments. Perhaps the most significant, if perverse, sign of Catholicism's growing acceptance was the career of Charles Coughlin, the "radio priest" who first supported Roosevelt's policies but later turned against him and became the nation's most powerful activist on the far right.

Numerous far right agitators regarded the New Deal as a bureaucratic threat to American individualism, scorned the Congress of Industrial Organizations as a Communist tool, and ultimately blamed national problems on an international Jewish conspiracy. (Coughlin himself began to publish *The Protocols* in 1938.) Supporters of the far right who agreed with this consensus nonetheless varied in background and attitude. Gerald B. Winrod, a Fundamentalist, compared the National Recovery Administration's symbol, the blue eagle, to the Satanic Beast of the Book of Revelation, expected Zionist elders to ally with the Antichrist, and traced the Zionist conspiracy back to apostolic times via the Bavarian Illuminati. Gerald L. K. Smith, theologically more liberal than Winrod and second in notoriety to Coughlin, mixed attacks on "New Deal Communism" with calls to redistribute wealth. Among paramilitary groups the Silver Legion under William Dudley Pelley made the most noise, and the Black Legion committed the most crimes per capita. Like their predecessors the nativist groups of the 1930s and 1940s attracted solid citizens as well as eccentrics. Moreover, Protestant bigots increasingly cooperated with their Catholic counterparts against Jews, radicals, and New Dealers, for they now perceived worse threats than the pope to disarm. Nonetheless, support for organizations on the far right never equaled support for the Klan at its peak. The Klan itself faded during the Depression and finally declared bankruptcy in 1944.

The far right's colorful countersubversion should not obscure less flamboyant bigotry. On the contrary, the conspiratorial anti-Semitism of Coughlin, Smith, and their fellows converged with mainstream prejudice. According to polls conducted during the late 1930s, at least one-third of the population thought Jews too powerful. A 1937 editorial in *Christian Century* complained that by failing to assimilate, Jews revealed an "unwillingness to submit . . . to the democratic process." Economic discrimination against Jews reached its zenith during the Depression. As had been the case since the progressive era, competition between Jews and Catholics, especially the urban Irish, sometimes degenerated into name-calling, street fights, and the desecration of synagogues. The Christian Front, founded in 1938, cited Coughlin's teachings to justify its members' assaults on "Christ killers." The response to these anti-Semitic incidents by Catholic politicians, policemen, and churchmen was less than evenhanded.

Catholic and Protestant leaders also allowed harassment of Jehovah's Witnesses, whose refusal to salute the "graven image" of the Ameri-

can flag and whose denunciations of rival faiths as "rackets" provoked vandalism, beatings, expulsions from schools, and removals from relief rolls. During World War II a capricious selective service system imprisoned half of the eight thousand Witnesses seeking exemptions. Despite their growing influence, Catholics themselves were still not fully accepted. Ethnic groups less prosperous than the Irish—Italians, Poles, and Hungarians—encountered more insults and discrimination. Protestant opinion strongly condemned President Roosevelt's appointment of a personal representative to the Vatican in 1940. According to a Gallup poll, 38 percent of the population would not vote for a Catholic presidential nominee.

The international advance of Nazism and debate over the United States' entry into World War II increased domestic religious tensions. A boycott of German goods begun in 1933 by a minority of Jews with slight gentile support prompted a counterboycott of Jewish businesses by ethnic rivals. Unlike most Jewish rabbis and Protestant clergy committed to the Social Gospel the majority of Catholic clergy favored Francisco Franco's insurrection against the Spanish Republic. The *Catholic World* was not alone in asking why liberals appalled by German anti-Semitism ignored the plight of Spanish Catholics. However, in general Christian denominations paid scant attention to Nazi persecutions. Only Quakers and Unitarians significantly aided Jewish or gentile refugees, and spokesmen on the far right such as Coughlin and Winrod lauded Nazism as a bulwark against Communism. Although reputable noninterventionist groups attempted to clear their ranks of bigots, Charles A. Lindbergh, a genteel anti-Semite and amateur race theorist, emerged as the anti-interventionist America First Committee's most visible spokesman. Typically exaggerating Jewish power, Lindbergh charged in September 1941 that Jews along with the British government and the Roosevelt administration led the movement toward war. Ironically, many interventionists at the State Department shared his disdain for Jews.

Throughout the 1930s nativist diplomats denied visas to victims of Nazism, especially Jewish victims. Fewer than thirty-two thousand immigrants arrived in 1935. Roosevelt ordered a more generous interpretation of the Johnson-Reed Act, but left enforcement to the State Department and never sought basic changes in the law. He believed that the refugee issue was politically explosive and that increased admission of Jews would further inflame anti-Semitism. He was right on both counts. In 1939 polls revealed that only 8 percent of the population welcomed more refugees. As late as June 1940 Breckinridge Long, assistant secretary of state and a genteel anti-Semite, instructed subordinates to "put every obstacle" in the path of prospective immigrants. By early 1943 reports of Nazi genocide had reached a skeptical, indifferent public. The Roosevelt administration still made no sustained effort to save European Jews. Indeed, the United States missed opportunities involving little risk: publicizing the atrocities, pressuring Germany through neutrals, and bombing the concentration camps. Certainly the depression, international *realpolitik,* military contingencies, and preoccupation with American casualties help to explain the United States' inaction. No doubt remains, however, that American anti-Semitism cost at least several hundred thousand lives.

During the fifteen years after World War II celebrants of the American way of life could—and did—point to much evidence of subsiding religious prejudice, nativism, and anti-Semitism. Attempts to revive the Ku Klux Klan met with ridicule; formerly prominent agitators like Smith and Winrod faded into obscurity; and Coughlin was silenced by his bishop in 1942, perhaps on orders from the Vatican, and conducted mass quietly in Michigan. Many theologically conservative Protestants moved from strident Fundamentalism to the stylish evangelism symbolized by Billy Graham. Psychologists, anthropologists, and geneticists now discredited the cult of Anglo-Saxon superiority that their predecessors had framed as science. Men and women, tempered by if not quite melted in the military pot, returned from service more tolerant than they had been before the war. President Dwight D. Eisenhower became the latest in a line of believers in belief as he made religious pluralism rather than "one hundred percent Americanism" synonymous with patriotism. "Our form of government has no sense unless it is founded on a deeply felt religious faith, and I don't care what it is," he allegedly said in 1954.

More ecumenical than earlier presidents who had routinely proclaimed patriotism synonymous with Protestantism or Christianity, Eisenhower broadened the American way of life to include the "Judeo-Christian tradition." By the mid-1950s Jews had achieved a level of acceptance accorded to Catholics in the late 1930s. This acceptance had not come easily. During the 1940s anti-Semitic incidents spread to the military, job discrimination persisted, and 55 percent of Americans polled still thought Jews exercised excessive influence. Late in the decade, however, several states outlawed employment discrimination, and the U.S. Supreme Court ruled restrictive covenants legally invalid. In 1948 the United States became the first nation to grant de facto recognition to Israel. Films such as *Crossfire* and *Gentleman's Agreement,* both released in 1947, dramatized the dangers of genteel as well as conspiratorial anti-Semitism. Protestant theological conservatives increasingly accepted a philo-Semitic interpretation of Zionism. In 1955 sociologist Will Herberg's *Protestant-Catholic-Jew* concluded that Protestantism, Catholicism, and Judaism had become equally legitimate variants of the "common culture religion."

Although Herberg alluded to cultural "competition" as well as to "coexistence," he underestimated the diversity, conflict, and prejudice within the "triple melting pot." The decline in anti-Semitism probably owed as much to Jewish activism as to gentile disgust with Nazi atrocities. Genteel anti-Semitism survived sub rosa, and ethnic competition still yielded epithets. In the same year that it passed a resolution endorsing Zionism, Congress enacted legislation on the treatment of displaced persons that de facto discriminated against Jews. Some elite colleges retained informal limits on Jewish enrollment until the 1960s. The McCarran-Walter Act of 1952 evidenced continued suspicion of "new immigration" groups and retained national origins quotas that favored "more readily assimilable" entrants. Relations between the predominantly liberal National Council of Churches (NCC) and the Conservative National Association of Evangelicals (NAE) rarely rose above coolness and often sank lower. Carl McIntire, a maverick Presbyterian and president of the Fundamentalist American Council of Christian Churches, chided NAE "quislings" for cooperating with the "Marxist" NCC. Moreover, from McIntire's Fundamentalist perspective the Catholic church still looked like the scarlet whore of Revelation.

From 1945 to 1960 controversy centering on Catholicism often brought the "triple melting pot" to a boil. Even more than the New Deal, the cold war legitimated the Catholic church, for Catholic clergy had rarely flirted with the leftist Popular Front, unlike many of their Protestant counterparts. Yet the Catholics' aloofness also signaled their divergence from the main currents of cultural liberalism. Similarly, Catholic leaders campaigned against birth control in New England, derided the separation of church and state a "shibboleth of doctrinaire secularism," and forced the removal of the anticlerical *Nation* from New York City schools. Doctrinaire secularists, liberal Protestants, and a few Jews joined Fundamentalists and evangelicals in attacking Catholic influence and insularity. In 1948 militants founded Protestants and Other Americans United for Separation of Church and State (POAU). Spokesmen for the group, led by general counsel Paul Blanshard, mixed fair criticism with clichés, pettiness, and cold-war agitation. For example, the group suspected nuns of "brainwashing" Catholic children, compared Soviet and Vatican "dictatorships," and suggested registering bishops as foreign agents. In 1951 POAU, along with the NCC and NAE, successfully fought President Harry S. Truman's appointment of an ambassador to the Vatican.

John F. Kennedy's 1960 race for the presidency bore superficial resemblance to Smith's race thirty-two years earlier, for both their candidacies followed controversies involving Catholicism and politics. Both Democratic nominees were opposed by some prominent Protestant theological liberals along with conservatives and conspiratorial bigots. W. A. Criswell, a Baptist Fundamentalist who feared the "death of a free church and a free state," sounded like Norman Vincent Peale, popular author of *The Power of Positive Thinking* (1952), who worried that "our culture is at stake." Yet differences between the campaigns of 1960 and 1928 outweighed their similarities. Open discussion of Senator Kennedy's faith was more decorous, and underhanded anti-Catholic slurs received no encouragement from his opponent, Richard M. Nixon. Kennedy was shrewder than Smith and conceded that some "legitimate questions of public policy" impinged on religion, and he specifically repudiated aid to parochial schools along with diplomatic ties to the Vatican. The Vatican obliquely criticized Kennedy's views, while Francis Cardinal Spellman visibly sup-

ported Nixon. Although Kennedy ran well among Catholics, he received a smaller percentage of their votes than Smith had. While his own Catholicism produced a net loss of support, he won by stressing issues unavailable to Smith in 1928: cold war, economic recession, and an opponent named Nixon.

During the fifteen years after Kennedy's election celebrants of rapid social change could—and did—discover much evidence that the United States was entering a "post-Protestant," perhaps a "post-Christian" era. The Immigration and Nationality Act of 1965 abandoned national origins quotas. Even more than his election, Kennedy's assassination, followed by his brother Robert's, discredited Catholicism as a reputable national issue. Between 1964 and 1984 five Catholics, including children of Polish and Italian immigrants, were nominated for the vice-presidency. Even McIntire mellowed sufficiently to praise Senator Barry Goldwater's "Romanist" running mate William Miller. Pope John XXIII and the Second Vatican Council that he convened further improved the reputation of Catholicism. Formerly despised "sects" achieved the standing of "churches," or at least respectable positions within churches. Both Protestants and Catholics welcomed Pentecostals, while Jehovah's Witnesses joined the ranks of socially acceptable conscientious objectors. Mormons, erstwhile symbols of treason and lechery, became unmatched symbols of patriotism and marital fidelity.

Yet predictions of a tolerant post-Protestant culture proved as unreliable as had earlier announcements of pluralist harmony. For example, movements seeking black equality generated anger as well as Christian love. In contrast to Martin Luther King, Jr., who preached a social gospel against prejudice, Malcolm X declared that the problem "most people face in the world is how to get freedom from Christians" and asserted that Jews had built Israel with money "taken out of the back of every black brother in the ghetto." Legislation, agitation, and judicial decisions widened the separation between church and state and prompted counterattacks in the name of the sacred. Many Fundamentalists left their devout isolation and turned to televised militancy. Furthermore, the growing cooperation between former religious and ethnic rivals often derived less from generous principles than from mutual enmity toward third parties. Placing white solidarity above all, the Ku Klux Klan even admitted Italian Catholics.

By the late 1970s religious issues had become central to national politics in ways that John F. Kennedy could not have imagined. In 1976, for the first time since 1896, two self-described born-again Christians—Jimmy Carter and Gerald R. Ford—ran against each other for president. Carter defeated Ford in part because he more effectively mobilized evangelicals and Fundamentalists than Ford did. Three years later Jerry Falwell, an independent Baptist, founded the Moral Majority to combat pornography, abortion, and homosexuality; restore prayer to the public schools; and elect political conservatives. In 1980 Falwell's constituency formed part of the coalition that placed Ronald Reagan in the White House. In 1984 black Baptist Jesse Jackson sought the Democratic presidential nomination. After Jackson privately called Jews "Hymies" and his ally, Louis Farrakhan of the Nation of Islam, deplored Jewish "gutter religion," Republicans labeled the Democrats a party of bigotry. Democratic nominee Walter F. Mondale countered that President Reagan would allow Reverend Falwell to name the next Supreme Court justices. In 1986 Pat Robertson, a Fundamentalist preacher with a large television audience, began campaigning for the 1988 Republican presidential nomination. Throughout this period abortion verged on becoming an issue as divisive as Prohibition had been during the 1920s. Now, however, theologically conservative Protestants, Catholics, and Jews coalesced against liberals in their own denominations.

The odyssey of American Jewry reveals the conflicting religious currents since 1960. On the one hand, anti-Semitism declined to the lowest point in more than a century, perhaps to the lowest point ever. During Kennedy's administration two Jews sat in the cabinet for the first time. The Second Vatican Council repudiated belief in collective Jewish guilt for Christ's crucifixion, Catholic orders ceased praying for the conversion of the Jews, and priests taught students about the horrors of the Holocaust. Ebbing economic competition between upwardly mobile Catholics and Jews improved relations on a less abstract level. Anti-Semitism within Fundamentalist and evangelical congregations sank to roughly the national average. A move rightward

against stereotype by prominent Jews, comparable to the development of a Catholic left, enhanced the image of Jewish Americanness.

On the other hand, Jews still encountered greater distrust than any other group associated with the "new immigration." A few Nazi-sympathizers continued to march, vandals defaced synagogues more often than churches, and farmers hard hit by recession in the 1980s flirted with conspiratorial anti-Semitism. Disagreements between Jews and non-Jews about mixed marriage, conversion, affirmative action, and Middle East policy sometimes slid into insensitivity or outright prejudice. In 1975 General George Brown, Chairman of the Joint Chiefs of Staff, declared that Jews controlled finance and the mass media. Later in the decade polls showed that 8 percent of Americans thought Jews too powerful and 25 percent considered them more loyal to Israel than to the United States. In 1980 Bailey Smith, president of the Southern Baptist Convention, lamented Jewish estrangement from Jesus and publicly doubted that God heard Jewish prayers. Smith apologized, as did Jesse Jackson in 1984. But Louis Farrakhan's reference to Jewish "gutter religion," coupled with his subsequent embellishments on the theme, highlighted disproportionate anti-Semitism among blacks. Like white Americans, black Americans had long viewed Jews as "Christ killers" and exaggerated their economic power. Some blacks also envied the Jewish community's achievement of both success and solidarity. Starting in the late 1950s competition between blacks and Jews for white-collar jobs and political influence, reminiscent of earlier rivalry between Irish Catholics and Jews, caused relations to deteriorate. This deterioration was augmented by black Muslim identification with Israel's Arab adversaries. In sum, black and white gentiles continue to view Jews with mixed feelings.

Prevailing interpretations of religious prejudice, nativism, and anti-Semitism in the late-1980s still rely on theories developed during the 1950s and early 1960s. At that time pluralist scholars such as Seymour Martin Lipset, Nathan Glazer, and Richard Hofstadter attributed most American countersubversion to "extremists" moved by mental aberration or social "status anxiety." They traced what Hofstadter called a "paranoid style" from Jedidiah Morse to Barry Goldwater via Anti-Masonry, Populism,

McCarthyism, and "political fundamentalism." Their work certainly represents an advance beyond the defenses of bigotry produced by an earlier generation of social scientists. As critics have noted, however, even sophisticated pluralists underestimated conspiratorial and xenophobic attitudes within the cultural mainstream, slighted economic origins of ethnic conflict, too neatly divided villains from victims, and missed continuities between psychological normality and abnormality. Nevertheless, commentators have applied pluralist formulas—albeit with decreasing acuity—to the latest surge in immigration, the rise of various unorthodox religions, and the revival of Fundamentalist controversies dormant since the 1920s.

By the late 1970s the "new immigration" from eastern and southern Europe had become one of several old immigrations. The residual ethnicity of the second and third generations was overshadowed by a large, newer immigration primarily from Asia and Latin America. Most commentators mistook the decline of bigotry against Jews and Catholics for the disappearance of nativism per se and exaggerated the hospitality extended to Hispanics and Asian-Americans. Indeed, these broad categories underscore the presumption that diverse nationalities should blend into manageable ethnic conglomerates. Although the foreign-born portion of the population now stands at its lowest level since record keeping began in 1850, the latest immigrants to some extent do change neighborhoods, alter the economy, and modify what it means to be an American. Hence, a nativist response is all but inevitable. The suspicion of prosperous Asian-Americans now resembles ethnic prejudice rather than the racist slurs against the "yellow peril." Like successful Jews in the 1910s, Asian-Americans are accused of insularity, aggressiveness, and an overdeveloped work ethic. Poor Hispanics face derision for exhibiting traits of preindustrial peasants, derision often voiced by the proud grandchildren of preindustrial peasants. Glib criticism of bilingual education, inflated estimates of illegal immigration, and a proposed constitutional amendment declaring English the official national language also mark political discourse. The Immigration Reform and Control Act of 1986, though liberal in some respects, nonetheless reflected exaggerated fears that undocumented workers, most of whom entered from Latin America, threatened American culture and prosperity. On the one hand, this legislation offered amnesty to many illegal aliens who came to the United States before 1 January 1982; on the other hand, by imposing penalties on employers of illegal immigrants, it made likely increased discrimination against—or at least increased humiliation of—all Hispanic job seekers. Except for occasional violence, hostility to legal immigrants pales beside that of the 1920s. But federal denial of asylum to illegal aliens from Haiti and Central America—political refugees in fact, if not in name—costs lives.

Contemporary invocations of the Judeo-Christian tradition, reminiscent of allusions to Christian nationhood 150 years ago, again exclude many believers and unbelievers. In general, these ritual references signal obliviousness rather than animosity. Muslims and Buddhists, for instance, are even less visible now than Jews were during the early national period. Yet many Americans remain eager to ridicule unorthodox faiths. Judges sanction forcible "deprogramming" of adolescent sectarians, media figures speculate on the neuroses of "Moonies," and erstwhile cultists have supplanted estranged Mormon wives on the lurid lecture circuit. Escaping Brigham Young's fate, Reverend Sun Myung Moon of the Unification Church nonetheless served a prison term for an irregular use of funds that would have passed without prosecution, perhaps without notice, in a "mainline" denomination. In short, a plurality of Americans still adhere to a de facto religious establishment, a bland combination of liberal theology and mild reform.

Renewal of the Fundamentalist controversy in the late 1970s centered on the new Christian right. Jerry Falwell, the movement's premier spokesman, has demonstrated the adaptability of contemporary countersubversives. Unlike his predecessors in the 1930s, Falwell shunned anti-Semitism and belatedly approved racial integration. In 1984 he barely protested the appointment of an ambassador to the Vatican. Yet, although they have courted Jews and Catholics, Fundamentalists and evangelicals on the far right have found new enemies: feminists, homosexuals, and "secular humanists." Ironically, the last label, which would have fit Ingersoll or Darrow, describes no major figure on the American scene. Co-opted by modernist theology, the community of militant freethinkers has shrunk to insignificance. The new Christian right's foremost critics are at least pro forma theists. Falwell, Robertson, and their colleagues, however, correctly sense that cosmopolitan understanding of Fundamentalism has improved little since the Scopes trial. Damning the new Christian right as the latest "paranoid style," liberals adopt an emotionally satisfying but politically ineffective strategy.

The labels "religious prejudice," "nativism," and "anti-Semitism" do not describe the same phenomena in the 1980s as in the 1880s, let alone the 1680s. Students of these subjects have uncovered, if not fully explained, the grand conspiratorial obsessions that have characterized these phenomena throughout American history. Now scholars must distinguish more carefully among varieties of bigotry and between bigotry and other conflicts of interest or opinion. Stereotypes can be flattering as well as derogatory, prejudices run the gamut from transitory misconceptions to implacable loathing, and discrimination ranges from snobbery to genocide. What one American considers religious prejudice, a biased judgment based on insufficient evidence, his neighbor may consider a sacred duty demanded by God. Unless scholars write with greater sophistication, they risk, on the one hand, ignoring prejudices couched in subtle idioms and, on the other hand, misinterpreting legitimate or inevitable conflicts over economic, cultural, and spiritual issues.

BIBLIOGRAPHY

Bernard Bailyn, *The Ideological Origins of the American Revolution* (1967); Ray Allen Billington, *The Protestant Crusade, 1800–1860: A Study of the Origins of American Nativism* (1938); Morton Borden, *Jews, Turks, and Infidels* (1984); Naomi Cohen, ed., *Anti-Semitism in America,* special issue of *American Jewish History,* 71 (1981); Richard O. Curry and Thomas M. Brown, eds., *Conspiracy: The Fear of Subversion in American History* (1972); David Brion Davis, ed., *The Fear of Conspiracy: Images of Un-American Subversion from the Revolution to the Present* (1971); Leonard Dinnerstein, *The Leo Frank Case* (1968); Henry L. Feingold, *The Politics of Rescue: The Roosevelt Administration and the Holocaust, 1938–1945* (1970); Norman F. Furniss, *The Mormon Conflict, 1850–1859* (1960); David A. Gerber, ed., *Anti-Semitism in American History* (1986); Nathan O. Hatch, *The Sacred Cause of Liberty: Republican Thought and the Millenium in Revolutionary New England* (1977); John Higham, *Strangers in the Land: Patterns of American Nativism, 1860–1925* (1955, 2d ed., 1963) and *Send These to Me: Jews and Other Immigrants in Urban America* (1975, rev. 1984); Michael Holt, "The Antimasonic and Know-Nothing Parties," in Arthur M. Schlesinger, Jr., ed., *History of U. S. Political Parties,* vol. 1 (1973).

Erling Jorstad, *The Politics of Doomsday: Fundamentalists of the Far Right* (1970); Donald Louis Kinzer, *An Episode in Anti-Catholicism: The American Protective Association* (1964); Allan J. Lichtman, *Prejudice and the Old Politics: The Presidential Election of 1928* (1979); Seymour Martin Lipset and Earl Raab, *The Politics of Unreason: Right-Wing Extremism in America, 1790–1970* (1970, rev. 1978); William G. McLoughlin, "The Role of Religion in the Revolution: Liberty of Conscience and Cultural Cohesion in the New Nation," in Stephen G. Kurtz and James H. Hutson, eds., *Essays on the American Revolution* (1973); Carey McWilliams, *A Mask for Privilege: Anti-Semitism in America* (1948); Albert J. Menendez, *John F. Kennedy, Catholic and Humanist* (1978); Robert Moats Miller, "The Ku Klux Klan," in John Braeman, Robert H. Bremner, and David Brody, eds., *Change and Continuity in Twentieth-Century America: The 1920's* (1968); David M. Reimers, *Still the Golden Door: The Third World Comes to America* (1985); Leo P. Ribuffo, *The Old Christian Right: The Protestant Far Right from the Great Depression to the Cold War* (1983); Mark Silk, "Notes on the Judeo-Christian Tradition in America," in *American Quarterly,* 36 (1984); Anson Phelps Stokes, *Church and State in the United States,* 3 vols., (1950); William Preston Vaughn, *The Antimason Party in the United States, 1826–1843* (1983); Robert G. Weisbrod and Arthur Stein, *Bittersweet Encounter: The Afro-American and the American Jew* (1970); David S. Wyman, *The Abandonment of the Jews: America and the Holocaust, 1941–1945* (1984).

[See also CATHOLICISM FROM INDEPENDENCE TO WORLD WAR I; CATHOLICISM IN THE ENGLISH COLONIES; CATHOLICISM SINCE WORLD WAR I; EMERGENCE OF AN AMERICAN JUDAISM; FUNDAMENTALISM; *and* JUDAISM IN CONTEMPORARY AMERICA.]

WOMEN AND RELIGION

Rosemary Skinner Keller

COLONIAL SOCIETY

The American colonies in the seventeenth and eighteenth centuries were the stage for a vast overseas expansion and settlement of European peoples. At the beginning of the seventeenth century, the Spanish and Portuguese held the upper hand, closely followed by the French. By the eighteenth century, English colonization was setting limits to the North American expansion of rival European powers. Cultural pluralism, religion, and women played an integral part, interweaving throughout the drama of colonization.

Native Americans of many tribes and cultures were displaced, Christianized, and destroyed not only culturally but also physically by the European expansion. Competing visions of Christian renewal—Spanish Catholic, French Catholic, Puritan, Quaker, and German Pietist—jostled to establish claims upon the New World. Meanwhile, black Africans, another conquered people, were being sent to the American colonies as slaves. Each European group claimed to be the divinely ordained instrument of God, both to settle and to evangelize the New World. Further, the dominant visions of religious renewal assigned women specific roles, sometimes offering them conflicting messages, at once encouraging and repressing new egalitarianism.

When travelers, settlers, and missionaries came to North America in the early colonial period, they confronted indigenous Indian cultures in which women played diverse roles in the religious life of the tribes. Each of the various competing Christian churches vied for the souls of American Indians and imposed upon them their disparate religious cultures. Thus Indians were not just Christianized. They were turned into Counter-Reformation French Catholics in Quebec, Counter-Reformation Spanish Catholics in Mexico, German-speaking Moravian Brethren in Pennsylvania, and English Puritans in New England. Indeed, Indian women went through an astonishing plurality of metamorphoses throughout the colonies as each religious group claimed success in evangelization by making Indians over into their own cultural image.

The convent life, brought by both French and Spanish nuns, offered Native American converts a sphere of assured social respect, comfort, education, and some autonomy—a larger scope than tribal life afforded for the talents of an independent woman who wished to pursue intellectual advancement, adventure, and high commitment to Christian ideals. The brilliant renaissance humanist, scholar, and poet Juana Inés de la Cruz lived most of her life as a professed nun in the Hieronymite convent of San Geronimo in Mexico City. She chose a religious life over marriage, believing that the former offered her a larger sphere for educational development than the latter—and her culture provided no other options for "respectable" women. But even the convent proved narrow and repressive for this truly gifted woman. The tragedy is that her culture had no place for a woman of her talents, nor would the story have been much different if she had been born in Puritan Massachusetts or colonial Montreal.

Most Native American women who were reached by European missionaries remained in their villages and grafted selective aspects of Christianity onto their own religious traditions, a process that continues even today. Many Indian women and men exhibited far more willingness to penetrate the mysteries of European Christianity than was true in reverse. A number

1547

of seventeenth- and eighteenth-century American Indian women turned to Christianity with a fervor and intellectual intensity so convincing as to astound European-American missionaries and lay observers. The Native Americans actively sought Christian understanding and grace, whether through a rigorous education under a priest, minister, or nun; self-mortification, fasting, and prayer culminating in a conversion experience perhaps akin to an Indian vision quest; vows of chastity; good works; a persistent attempt to convert family and friends; or a combination of all these.

Thus schooled in Christianity, the Indians were able to chide white settlers for many of the unchristian practices inherent to colonization. The story of several Indian women who spoke at the Council of the Six Nations in western New York State in 1794 is revealing. In response to an earlier visit to the council by preacher Jemima Wilkinson, in which she had called upon the Indians to repent of their sins, the women challenged the American government and colonists to cease oppressing the Indians and taking their lands.

The struggle for religious freedom was at the heart of the relationship between church renewal and the place of women in early Puritan society of seventeenth-century New England. Men and women of first-generation New England Puritanism were the products of a dissenting culture that was at war with the established Anglican church of the English Reformation. The splintering of the English Reformation into an array of competing sects reflected the conflicts of social classes as well as of religious viewpoints. In this atmosphere of incipient civil war in England, women often took the initiative to gather dissenting congregations, call ministers, and assert their own rights to preach and to administer churches. Dissenting ministers encouraged such independence in women when the foe was the established church.

Once the dissenting clergy became ministers of churches established according to New England laws, their view of religious liberty changed sharply. While still at sea before landing in the Massachusetts Bay, Puritan divine John Winthrop stated that the emigrants were to enjoy the liberties of the Gospel within a harmonious community. "Liberty" did not imply freedom of conscience in religious belief, however, but freedom to obey the will of God and to restore God's order in a chaotic world. Such a vision depended upon a highly structured hierarchical society in which all people knew their places and chose to stay in them.

Puritan theory assigned a positive but limited place to women as helpmates to their husbands and coauthorities over children and servants, under their husbands. It encouraged the active piety of laywomen as docile recipients of Puritan preaching and piety. Accommodation of women to their socially prescribed subordination was essential to maintenance of the Puritan order, and most females assumed that position without question. No space was available for the woman whose religious experiences bypassed ministerial authority and who sought to define her own faith. Yet the inherent tension in the Puritan view of women was illustrated in sermons preached by Puritan divines at the funerals of female parishioners. Characteristically, the godly woman was described as the dutiful daughter, submissive and faithful wife, wise mother, prudent household manager, and kind and charitable neighbor and friend. In her relationship with God, however, she was an autonomous being. Men and women were equal and independent before God in the next world, if not in this.

Strains in the social order occurred even within the first generation of Puritan settlement, because a considerable number of women applied the implications of radical equality and freedom voiced by Saint Paul to themselves. Their primary text, one that had empowered the radical sectarians of the English Reformation, was Galatians 3:28: "There is neither Jew nor Greek, there is neither slave nor free, male nor female; for you are all one in Christ Jesus."

The movement launched by Anne Hutchinson, which led to her trial and excommunication by civil and church officials in 1638, exemplified both religious and sexual insubordination by New England women. Hutchinson contended both that grace came to individuals directly from God and that New England clergy were not fit ministers of the Gospel. She then proceeded to hold private meetings in her home, in which she taught her beliefs to men and women of the Boston church. Her views and actions directly challenged the theological base and political power structure of the Puritan order and the Puritan meaning of religious freedom. Her bold and radical application of Puritan thinking—that spiritual equality and freedom before God sanctioned social equality and freedom of women alongside men on earth—resulted in her banishment from the colony. Her inquisitors felt that her behavior, in addition to being unfitting for her sex, was neither tolerable nor acceptable in the sight of God.

Anne Hutchinson was the symbol, and probably the impetus, for a larger number of women who challenged religious and sexual subordination whether in Boston, Salem, New Haven, or possibly other New England towns. Throughout the seventeenth century, women who dissented from the authority of minister, magistrate, or husband were branded heretics and often deemed witches as well. They were condemned as heretics because, according to religious leaders of the time, woman's place in society was divinely ordained and revealed in Scripture. They were believed to be witches because only the promptings of the devil could explain such insubordination in a woman.

Trials against women for heresy and witchcraft swept across New England from the mid-1600s until the end of the century. They abated perhaps less because their presuppositions were discredited than because the ministry had won its struggle to repress women and to assign them a subordinate position within society and the church. Puritan preachers increasingly encouraged the active lay piety of women in their congregations, as long as women took their cues from pastors and confined their evangelizing zeal to the private sphere of family and home.

The domestic piety of women characterized the world and vision of southern white women's religious life in the colonial period. Most of these women belonged to the established Anglican church, although there were also Catholic women in Maryland, Jewish women in the Carolinas, and an increasing number of women entering dissenting churches. They were encouraged to a devout but moderate piety within the limits of their homes as mentors of their children and servants. They were also instructed to discreetly evangelize their husbands. Wives were of course not to take authority over husbands but to patiently endure, even though their husbands might be impious, unfaithful, or even abusive.

By the eighteenth century southern women were clearly thought to have a more religious nature than men. This aspect of their personalities narrowly defined the boundaries of women's lives. Though religion did not offer most women an alternative to their inherited life cycle, it did provide them with opportunities to cultivate their individuality. Women were encouraged to have private devotions, to compose religious exercises, and to develop their own prayers. A diary could become both an expression of religious sentiment and an awakening of the self.

In addition to teaching their children catechism and prayers, many southern women, out of their own religious zeal, also instructed their slaves in Christian principles. If many white women were illiterate, black women had a much more difficult time obtaining any reading and writing skills unless they had a mistress who allowed it to happen—often in secret.

Black women, brought as slaves to North America in the seventeenth and eighteenth centuries, often came from cultures where women had responsibilities and privileges not always based on husbands' and fathers' patriarchal powers. In West African tribes, women controlled marketplaces, and their economic monopoly provided them with opportunities for autonomous activity and leadership. For instance, in religious ceremonies women frequently were priests and leaders of cults.

In North America, African women initially were excluded from church membership. The increasing tendency of colonial Christianity to idealize white women for their piety and morality seldom was extended to black women, who were regarded as immoral, subhuman, and little fitted to Christian religiosity.

Even before slavery gained official status in North America, an indentureship for a black person often became life servitude. The servant class came to be separated into "Christian" and "Negro" (implying non-Christian). Colonial plantation owners underscored the distinction by neglecting to bring "Negro servants" into the Christian church, by sometimes legislating against black church attendance, and by resisting the demands of churches and missionary societies to evangelize Africans because they feared that baptism would give the slave rights of emancipation.

For at least one black woman, Elizabeth Key, baptism brought freedom. She was the daughter of an Englishman, Thomas Key, and an unknown slave woman. In 1656 she brought suit in the Northumberland County Court, Virginia, for her freedom on the basis that her father was a free man, that she had been baptized a Christian, and that her contract as an indentured servant had been fulfilled. If the case had occurred six years later, there would have been no question about her status: she would have remained a servant. In this case, Elizabeth Key's Christian faith helped her to win her freedom.

By the early 1660s, however, Massachusetts, Virginia, and other English colonies had taken steps to make slavery a legal, self-perpetuating institution. Intending to settle the question of whether converted slaves should or could be freed, Virginia passed legislation in 1662 stating that children would inherit their mothers' social status—not their religious condition. Still not certain that Christians could be enslaved, however, for there was no English law positively stating that, Virginia enacted legislation prohibiting a slave's status from being altered because he or she was baptized. It remained for some Christian theologians to argue that the Scriptures allowed slavery and that it was compatible with Christianity to baptize a person and yet force that individual to remain in bondage.

Only in 1701 did the leadership within the Church of England form a united drive to evangelize colonists in America and teach among slaves. A missionary band, the Society for the Propagation of the Gospel in Foreign Parts, was formed that operated out of London and was financially independent of local church parishes. Although the Society for the Propagation of the Gospel owned slaves in its early years and took the position that emancipation was not a mandatory result of conversion, settlers were suspicious that the society ultimately intended to press for freedom for black slaves.

The Great Awakening, which highlighted American sectarianism and fragmented the activity of the Society for the Propagation of the Gospel around the mid-eighteenth century, also provided black people with their first virtually unrestricted participation in Christianity in North America. During the religious ferment and widespread conversion experiences, white antislavery sentiment and black assertiveness intensified. In 1743 in Bucks County, Pennsylvania, for example, a black woman and her husband sued a white man for trespassing upon her

character. They made clear their understanding that a Christian woman's moral reputation should not be impugned without legal challenge, regardless of the woman's race.

Popular Awakening evangelists, such as George Whitefield, commented on the enthusiasm with which black people, particularly women, received the Gospel and its messengers. John Wesley, himself an antislavery advocate, noted in his diary that the first Methodist convert in New York City was a "Negro Servant" named Betty. Nevertheless, sentiment against slave conversions still abounded, and circuit riders had to urge owners to send slaves for religious instruction and worship. At the same time Quakers and other antislavery groups increased their proclamations and other challenges to the institution of slavery.

African women adopted Christianity with alacrity. With the disintegration of African communal identity, Christianity offered the best hope for black mothers to find a new identity for themselves and their children. During the Great Awakening, blacks flocked particularly to the Baptists, attracted by the antislavery message that was at least hinted in these circles. Even the dissenting churches, however, seldom extended full and equal fellowship to their black converts. Consequently, by the early nineteenth century American black Christians began to break with these churches and to found black congregations and denominations in the North. Although preaching authority was not officially extended to women in black churches, black women began to find ministerial roles as missionaries, charity workers, and educators within black denominations.

The diverse religious scene of colonial America also included the heirs of the Radical Reformation. From seventeenth-century England there flowed Quaker missionaries, exponents of radical, spiritualist Puritanism. From Germany came a diversity of Pietist sects, which often adopted communal social forms and some of which even practiced celibacy. These groups were more experimental than mainline denominations in their theology and social practices toward women. The Quakers, through their cofounder Margaret Fell and her daughters, developed a theology and exegesis of women's spiritual equality. They advocated women's right both to preach and evangelize and to participate in church administration. The Quakers preserved and developed the emancipatory trends of dissenting Puritanism. Not surprisingly, they were drawn into confrontation with the Puritan authorities in Massachusetts who were engaged in repressing antislavery sentiment in their own Christian social order. Several Quakers were finally hanged because the Puritans believed their inspiration was from the devil rather than the Holy Spirit. The sufferings of Quaker women in this struggle with Puritan theocracy forms a heroic chapter of early Quakerism in America.

A controversial innovation in early Quakerism was the institution of women's meetings, which gave Quaker women an official role in the administration and government of the Society of Friends. Women's meetings both supervised internal morality and managed extensive works of external charity. They gathered and administered funds for the relief of the imprisoned, the poor, the sick, the widowed, the orphaned, and the aged. They organized projects, such as spinning groups, for unemployed women and placed orphans in apprenticeships. In addition, they supervised marriages and tithe-paying within the Society of Friends.

Among the German Pietist sects, the Ephrata community of Pennsylvania and the Moravian Brethren form two notable types. In both, women had a fixed and settled place. The forthright confrontation with religious authority found in the Puritan and Quaker contexts finds no echo among the German groups. Yet the German sects also extended a large sphere to women's religious and administrative abilities through their communal social order. Further, these sects experimented with the doctrines of God and human nature that have their roots in the Christian mystical and Gnostic traditions. God was believed to have a feminine as well as a masculine side, and celibacy was seen as restoring androgynous wholeness to fallen humanity.

The evangelical revival that swept the American churches in the eighteenth century from New England to the southern colonies revived some of the emancipatory potential of radical Christianity that was found earlier among the antinomian Puritans and the Quakers. Revivalism also bypassed established ecclesiastical authority by stressing direct personal experience of God's redeeming grace. In this drama of repentance and conversion, social distinctions melted away. Women, unequal in society, were spiritually equal before God as repentant sinners and as recipients of divine grace.

The evangelical and revival movements accentuated the trend toward increased emphasis on woman's spiritual and moral superiority that had originated in late-seventeenth- and early-eighteenth-century Puritan preaching. The religious image of women was shifting away from the late medieval emphasis on women's dangerously carnal propensities. Woman came to be seen as the more naturally religious gender, who must take the primary responsibility in the home for evangelizing children and "uplifting" her husband from the secular and impious influences of society. A new symbolism was beginning to attach itself to the growing separation between woman's domestic sphere and man's public sphere. The home and the female sphere became the realm of religion, and the outside world the realm of nonreligion—distinctions that would become increasingly prominent in the nineteenth and twentieth centuries.

This growing stress on woman's moral superiority, her greater religiosity, and her role as domestic evangelist created mixed messages for women in the evangelical movements. Woman was, at once, man's spiritual equal, even his superior, and yet his social subordinate. On the one hand, woman's piety was still seen as directing her to voluntary acceptance of her subordination in church and society. On the other hand, the stress placed on her religiosity and her evangelizing mission tended to break these limits and direct women's ministry into a widening sphere that led from the family circle into prayer circles of friends into mission and revival organizations.

The understanding of marriage experienced by the Great Awakening's leading theologian and preacher, Jonathan Edwards, and his wife, Sarah, demonstrates this legacy. Edwards deeply admired his wife's piety. She promoted the revival through her attendance at meetings, through her influence among women and youth, and, most significantly, through the magnetic pull her religious experiences exerted on her husband. Although he did not acknowledge its source, Edwards used her spiritual cleansing as a paradigm of God's mighty acts. Yet he unquestionably expected women to maintain Eve's subordinate status. He allotted reason to men and affection to women. In his treatise on marriage, *When Marriage Is According to Nature's and God's Designation,* undoubtedly a description of his own relationship with Sarah, Edwards said God had made women "weaker, more soft and tender, more fearful, and more affectionate as a fit object of [men's] generous protection and defense." His definition of women effectively removed them from leadership in the revival.

THE REVOLUTIONARY WAR AND THE EXPANDING REPUBLIC

The American Revolution had both far-reaching and immediate consequences for women. The revolutionary commitment and patriotism of the Founders was grounded in an image of the American nation as a divinely appointed instrument of political emancipation. Both the rationalist traditions of the Enlightenment and the evangelical fervor of revivalism transformed the war into a religious commitment, a battle in which God had ordained an American victory. As "Daughters of Liberty" who supported the army through sewing bees and fund raising, many women were enthusiastic supporters of the revolutionary struggle.

Yet again, as during the Reformation, the ideology of equality, shaped by men in their conflicts with established authority, was not intended to be extended to women and other minority groups. White propertied males were the subjects of that "equality of human nature" from which, according to the Declaration of Independence, there flows equal civil rights. The pleas of Abigail Adams to her husband, John, to "remember the ladies" went unheeded at the Continental Congress. John Adams' letters, however, indicate that he, like other Founding Fathers, realized the wide-ranging implications of religious freedom and human rights that they had written into the Declaration of Independence and the Constitution, and knew that these rights must one day be extended to disenfranchised individuals.

The most immediate implication of women's religious experience during the American Revolution and early nineteenth century was the development of the role of republican womanhood and motherhood. Such an understanding elevated public virtue, disinterested secular service

growing out of honesty, integrity, and moral values, to a religious principle. Women, as guardians of the home, became the primary bearers of republican ideals, responsible for inculcating virtue in their sons, daughters, and even husbands. Such a purpose for women justified a broader education for them but one that would focus on their purpose within the home, not in society at large.

Women had experienced conflicting realities of religious freedom in the seventeenth and eighteenth centuries. At first they had enthusiastically responded to and participated in renewal movements, and had helped evangelize Indians and settle a new continent. But the emancipatory messages of these experiences were contradicted by growing restrictions on the actual social mobility and economic roles of women. By the time the colonies became the United States of America, woman's life had become directed into narrower and more intensive functions as wife and mother. Religious piety had simultaneously exalted woman's place and sought to restrict her to a shrinking world.

On the other hand, the evangelical mandate to women and the revolutionary ideology of religious freedom and human rights had liberating potential for women. Throughout the nineteenth and twentieth centuries these ideals would provide the foundation for religious and secular movements that sought the attainment of women's rights in both the sacred and secular spheres and the private and public realms of life.

During the nineteenth century religion in America was redefined and reshaped. Changing definitions of maleness and femaleness were an important part of that reshaping. The location of religion and the definition of women in relation to it were shifting within the dominant Protestant ethos of American society. With the disestablishment of mainline Protestant denominations after the revolutionary war, religion officially became a private concern—plural, personal, and voluntary. All religions were potentially included, although Catholics and Jews experienced the American religious scene as it had been molded by Anglo-Saxon Protestantism.

Secularization of society meant that the religious leader lost something of his official standing as a public figure. The old Puritan union of minister and magistrate was broken. Ministers now exerted their influence primarily in voluntary assemblies, rather than in churches established by New England laws. The church became an extension of the home rather than the right hand of government. Predominantly female congregations, which already characterized Protestantism, continued to increase.

The location of religion in the domestic or personal side of life reinforced the tendency to see religion as a particularly feminine sphere. As in the past, women were viewed as normatively religious and men as preoccupied with the secular concerns of the "real world." Key Christian categories—sacrificial love, servanthood, altruism, and even redemptive grace—came to be identified as characteristically feminine. Piety, domesticity, and submissiveness also were seen as essential to woman's nature and contrary to man's.

In one sense, the feminization of religion strengthened the dominant social ideology concerning women's roles. Religion was a means of enculturating women to their domestic maternal role, to acceptance of powerlessness and dependency on men. When biblical texts were taken out of the context of larger scriptural understandings, they often became powerful tools with which to limit rather than liberate women's spiritual gifts.

The text of Ephesians 5:21–30 has often been distorted for such purposes. The verse "Wives be subject to your husbands, as to the Lord" provides powerful justification for the subordination of women to men when taken out of the context of its preceding verse, "Be subject to one another out of reverence for Christ," and a following verse, "Husbands, love your wives, as Christ loved the church and gave himself up for her." The passage, in its entirety, counsels both men and women to a partnership in love that avows mutuality of both affirmation and subordination to one another.

On the other hand, religion enabled women to expand their self-understanding and to break out of the traditional roles that society had long prescribed for them. The Bible itself provided the strongest justification for human liberation that nineteenth-century feminists could employ. Throughout the century, religion became an infinitely variable instrument for enlarging women's sphere through utopian movements, evangelism, ordination, missionary work, and social reform.

Revivals were the scene of the earliest organized participation of women in religious movements of the nineteenth century. The perfectionist view of femininity, suggesting that women uplift mankind and direct their husbands and children toward virtue, impelled women's participation in revivalism, both as subjects and as promoters of evangelicalism. Because women were understood to be more religious than men, they were seen as the natural subjects of revivalism and as more effective evangelists in their homes and communities. As revivalism flourished, women increasingly sought avenues of expression within the movement; they were no longer simply the objects of evangelization. Once converted they found ways to share their religious experiences: first leading female prayer meetings, then encroaching on mixed prayer meetings and claiming the right to active ministry. From there it was but a short step for women to preach in public assemblies, setting the stage for their efforts, later in the century, to be ordained.

Many women, whites as well as blacks, experienced the contagious effect of the message of spiritual equality preached by ministers of the Great Awakening. By 1800 a number of women, sometimes over husbands' objections, were participating in revivals and joining the Baptist and Methodist denominations. Membership of women in Evangelical churches increased markedly in the early nineteenth century, building on the momentum that had originated in the South during the revolutionary era. In revivals and Evangelical church services, women no longer played a secondary role but were on an equal footing with men.

The Evangelical denominations could provide women with an emotional outlet and identity that other groups could not. They could also bring black and white women together. A Presbyterian minister described one revival in North Carolina in 1802, where he walked near a black slave grasping her mistress's hand and thanking God that her mistress had prayed for her when she could not pray for herself. She praised God that she now was able to pray for her mistress and for everybody else.

The ambiguity of the relationship between white Christian women and black slaves was a reality of their religious experience. In theory, a white woman was expected to view her servants as members of her household and to extend her evangelizing nurture to them, so that mistress, children, and servants would kneel together in prayer at the close of the day. In fact, many slaves preferred to become Baptists or Methodists, attracted by the lively styles of worship and the great communal autonomy found in the dissenting churches. White women were caught between the male religious and social authorities and the enslaved black world. They were themselves subjects and victims of a patriarchal social order; they were also agents of the patriarchy who struggled, not always successfully, to enculturate their slaves in its values.

The perfectionist view of female nature was central not only to revivalism but also to much of nineteenth-century American religion. Among its most pronounced expressions were the early nineteenth-century utopian and millennialist sects. These sects saw themselves as the avant-garde of a dawning age of human perfection. Many of them viewed the reunion of masculine and feminine elements, or the recovery of human androgyny in the image of divine androgyny, as the key to redemption. Two female-founded sects, the Shakers, begun by Mother Ann Lee, and the Christian Scientists, started by Mary Baker Eddy, explicitly linked the perfection of humanity with the feminine as the higher element representing divine wisdom and love. The Shakers, however, comprised the only utopian community to develop a consistent theory of equal empowerment of women. Though elements of feminism are found in utopian communities, their beliefs did not consistently imply the leadership of women alongside men in all facets of community life.

The leadership of nuns in immigrant Catholicism demonstrates a more liberated view of their lives and work than has been recognized. Nuns possessed a mobility, autonomy, and control over their own organizations that could be claimed by few other American women at that time. Yet they were indoctrinated with the traditional view, linked to their separate and celibate female orders, of femininity as subservient to masculine clerical authority. In a predominantly Protestant society that linked female piety closely to marriage and maternity, the celibate woman was an object of superstitious fear; nuns therefore often received the brunt of anti-Catholic bigotry. They played a major role in

introducing Catholicism to America and in gaining greater public acceptance for Catholicism through their devoted service to the church and to civic and military institutions, especially through nursing and teaching. Nuns were not so much drawn to reflect on their role as women as to see themselves as representatives of Catholicism. While Protestant women who nursed soldiers in the Civil War saw their activity as claiming new roles for women, nuns saw their purpose as gaining acceptance for Catholics.

Roman Catholic nuns stand out in the history of women and religion in America, however, as major institution-builders for both their church and their sex. Through their sisterhoods, nuns staffed the vast network of schools, hospitals, and social service organizations endowed by the Roman Catholic church. Among the early founders of religious orders in America were Elizabeth Seton, who began the Sisters of Charity in 1809, the first American women's religious order, and Rose Philipine Duchesne, who sailed from France in 1818 to found the first American convents of the Sacred Heart. Frances Cabrini founded the Missionary Sisters of the Sacred Heart in Italy in 1880 and the first motherhouse in America. She became superintendent-general of her order for life, with eventual authority over 65 houses and some 1,500 daughters. In 1946 Mother Cabrini became the first American citizen to gain sainthood; Mother Seton was beatified in 1963 and canonized twelve years later.

Mainstream Christianity identified women within the home as the bearers of piety and religiosity. This was not true, however, of the heritage that immigrant eastern European Jews brought to America. In Jewish culture, godliness long had been defined as preeminently a male responsibility. The woman's work within the home was understood primarily as a secular activity that allowed her husband to withdraw into religious study and contemplation. One of the particular strains on Jewish communities, as they went through successive attempts to adapt to American middle-class society, was a cultural dissonance with their earlier traditions. By American standards, the traditional rabbinic male was not sufficiently secular and "masculine," while the traditional Jewish female needed to be more religious and "feminine." Developments within Reform Judaism in America encouraged and enhanced the woman's role in the synagogue, a process that served to expand her whole identity as a woman.

In mainstream Protestantism, vigorous debate over the right of women to preach and to be ordained set the state for the development of "ordination movements" in the twentieth century. Questions of female propriety were introduced as women took an increased leadership role in revivals during the early nineteenth century.

Women were often well received as evangelists—as long as they did not seek licenses to preach or to be ordained—because their preaching was powerful and seemed filled with the Holy Spirit. Probably the most distinguished female revivalist was Phoebe Palmer, a member of the Methodist Episcopal Church and called the mother of the Holiness movement. Her evangelistic tours, conducted with her husband, Walter, a medical doctor, took her throughout the United States and into Canada and the British Isles. Her 421-page *Promise of the Father,* published in 1859, presents a passionate defense of woman's right to preach, applicable even in the late twentieth century.

After the Civil War, scattered individual women began to seek licenses to preach and to be ordained. The proper role of women in the church—be it singing, teaching, praying, or preaching—became an issue of intense debate. Many of the arguments, which sought to reinterpret biblical authority to more strictly limit social prescriptions for women, remain prominent today.

Antoinette Brown was the first fully ordained woman in a recognized American denomination, the Congregational church, in 1853 in South Butler, New York, but almost no others followed in her footsteps during the nineteenth century. In Brown's ordination sermon, the Rev. Luther Lee of the Wesleyan Methodist Church invoked the two biblical texts that have continued to be basic sources for women's ordination. One was the aforementioned passage from Galatians 3:28: "There is neither Jew nor Greek, there is neither slave nor free, there is neither male nor female; for you are all one in Christ Jesus." The second was the prophesy in Joel 2:28 quoted by Peter in the Pentecost story in Acts 2:17: "Your sons and daughters will prophesy."

Though denied ordination and leadership in mainline Protestantism, women created parallel societies and sent deaconesses and female missionaries to mission stations throughout the world. These schismatic movements characterized the major activities of women outside the home in post–Civil War America, whether in religious or secular areas. The development of separate spheres of service for women in church structures had a dual potential: it could contain and isolate women's work from the major service of clergymen, or it could enable women to develop autonomous power and self-conscious sisterhood. In fact, women's separatist organizations produced both results. In addition, these associations became the first training stations for women, enabling them to move into wider fields of service in the church and in secular society by the end of the nineteenth century.

Social reform became a religious calling to a large and active segment of women in nineteenth-century America. Countless numbers of women found "fields of usefulness" in society as a fulfillment of their deeply felt religious calling. Anna Howard Shaw, the first woman ordained into the United Methodist tradition, typified those who moved from institutional church work into the women's rights movement. Shaw was ordained by the Methodist Protestant Church in 1880, but the denomination revoked her ordination four years later. The New York Conference of the Methodist Protestant Church defied the General Conference ruling, however, allowing Shaw to retain her membership in its conference. She continued to serve her congregation at East Dennis, Massachusetts, until she resigned her pulpit in 1885. She then moved toward involvement in the struggle for suffrage as "the great cause" of her day, and subsequently became president of the National American Woman Suffrage Association.

Female reformers not only worked for the rights of women but also entered all other areas of social action, including abolitionism, education, temperance, peace and arbitration, antilynching, prison reform, and professional social work. Religiously motivated women who became leaders in these fields include Sarah and Angelina Grimké, Catherine Beecher, Frances Willard, Hannah Bailey, Ida B. Wells-Barnett, Dorothea Dix, and Jane Addams. In the South, such women as Belle Harris Bennett, Lucinda Helm, and Laura Haygood began to move the churches toward social responsibility, particularly regarding racial justice. They were followed by Carrie Parks Johnson, Jessie Daniel Ames, and Dorothy Rogers Tilly, whose contributions dominated women's work in the Commission on Interracial Cooperation and its successor, the Southern Regional Council, in the twentieth century.

The question of how women should pursue social reform—within their homes or in the public arena—remained a vital issue. By the end of the nineteenth century, women had demonstrated that they could serve wherever their minds, bodies, and wills took them. While some women responded to the increasing secular needs of society at the turn of the century, many continued to act out of the strong theological motivations that had led their sisters into social reform throughout the preceding era.

A highly utilitarian motivation—that women should extend their "fields of usefulness" beyond the home into active service of the institutional church and society—pervades the writings of women preachers, lay workers, and social reformers. It was an extension of the perfectionist doctrine that women had a specially uplifting, even purifying, work that only they could contribute. By entering one of the helping professions, such as teaching or social work, or by volunteering in church missionary work and social reform movements, middle-class women justified their worth to themselves and to others in a day when society increasingly viewed females of their class as homemakers and ornamental appendages to men.

Of course, not all women—or men—viewed women as the proverbial "weaker sex." The utopian and perfectionist strain in American religious thought, with its suggestion of a redemptive uplift of the "carnal masculine" through the "spiritual feminine," hinted at a more exalted role for women. Indeed, militant feminists found it hard to be content with mere claims of equality. Some, such as Ann Lee and Mary Baker Eddy, suggested that women were superior and that through womanhood would come the redemption of the race. The attitudes of most nineteenth-century female leaders, whether of secular or religious persuasion, mingled elements of

both the egalitarian and the "higher feminine" traditions in their thought and action.

THE TWENTIETH CENTURY

Because the United States is predominantly a Protestant culture, the experiences of women leaning toward feminism in black and Indian subcultures, as well as in Catholicism and Judaism, have markedly differed from those of women in the mainstream culture.

Native Americans have sought to create an accommodation or syncretism between their own religions and Christianity. This syncretism represents an effort to relate to modern Western culture and yet retain traditional Indian identity. Indians of the Southwest plains are a case in point. The expropriation of their land and forced migration have reduced them to a impoverished and demoralized state. Nevertheless, native religion continues to thrive despite three centuries of Christian evangelization that included almost sixty years during which the practice of native religion was illegal. In traditional religion as practiced today, women concede the more prestigious roles to men, who have had more difficulty adjusting to the poverty and isolation of reservation life. Women often take the lead in Christian churches and are the more committed Christians, although Christianity generally succeeds among Indians only to the extent that it allows syncretism with native religion or provides analogues to it. The most recent development is Pan-Indian religions, such as the peyote cult or Native American Church, which emerged in large part to compensate for the loss of traditional Indian culture. Here again males play the predominant role, supported by women.

The role of black women in American religion in some ways parallels that of Indian women. As a conquered people brought as slaves to North America, Afro-Americans were almost totally deprived of their traditional culture and Christianized. Separate African syncretistic cults did not emerge in North America, as they did in Caribbean and Brazilian voodoo, although American blacks did create a distinct black Christianity that probably contains remnants of African culture. By breaking with white Christianity to form black denominations, Afro-Americans forged a black church that could provide a social and cultural base for black identity. Black women have generally viewed Christianity positively for that reason, despite its heavy patriarchalism.

As in the Indian case, the secondary and supportive role of black women in religion partly represents a concession to the ego needs of black males, who women perceive to be demoralized by white oppression. Playing the prestigious roles in the leadership of the black church, the primary social institution of black identity, helps to compensate for the status deprivation of the black male in the dominant culture. However, the apparent patriarchalism of the black church is somewhat misleading. One has to look beneath the surface to see how black women often wield the real power in local churches, although not the ascribed authority, through fund raising, education, and other supportive functions. By the early twentieth century, education became the particular focus of black women's ministry in local churches and was defined as the woman's sphere in contradistinction to the man's sphere of preaching.

Black women also built on the inspiration and experience gained in local churches to form many auxiliary denominational institutions, such as women's missionary societies and training schools. And they helped bring about social reform through black women's clubs, antilynching societies, schools, and service institutions such as orphanages. Black women in the twentieth century continue very much in the tradition of nineteenth-century Christianity, in which women's roles in the church became a launching pad for the formation of denominational organizations and religiously inspired but nondenominational philanthrophical and social reform movements.

Jewish women in America have experienced not only the feminist struggle but also crises of class, religious, and racial identity. As members of an immigrant group that entered America as oppressed workers, early-twentieth-century Jewish women in urban industry became important labor organizers, and many—particularly garment workers—joined the newly emergent labor unions. Jewish women also had to cope with the ways that Americanization altered the traditional roles of women in the Jewish family. Many Jewish women found emancipation through secular education, having been deprived of traditional Jewish religious education. As Americanization and economic prosperity increased, it became possible for Jewish women to reembrace their religious identity in a new way and to challenge Jewish men for an enlarged role in the practice of Judaism. Jewish women in the twentieth century also have been a part of the Zionist movement, which expresses the disenchantment of Western Jews with the experience of assimilation into secular nationalisms. As Zionists, Jewish women are reaching out to help shape a new Jewish identity that will be simultaneously ethnic and egalitarian.

Although they are Christians, Catholics also suffered religious discrimination when they began to settle in the American colonies. This discrimination intensified in the late nineteenth century, when Catholics from Ireland and eastern and southern Europe arrived in large numbers. There was little participation by Catholic women in the nineteenth-century feminist movement. As an embattled cultural group, Catholic women put their energy into affirming their Catholic identity and proving to the Protestant majority the compatibility of Catholicism with American values. Only when the battle of Americanization was won by midcentury, as exemplified in the election of John F. Kennedy to the presidency, did they turn to confrontation with the male hierarchy for enlarged roles in religious leadership.

This suggests that when a religious and ethnic subculture is oppressed by the dominant culture, as has been the case with American Indians, Jews, blacks, and Catholics, women put their ethnic identity first and concede leadership in the distinctive institutions of the subculture to men. Only when a certain cultural and social parity is established between the minority and majority communities do women turn their attention to feminist questions within their own communities. Accordingly, it is not surprising that the women's rights movement was dominated by middle-class Anglo-Saxon Protestant women in the nineteenth and early twentieth centuries. Only in the late 1960s, as Jews and Catholics emerged into cultural parity and middle-class status, have distinctive Catholic and Jewish feminist movements begun to arise that challenge the patriarchalism of Jewish and Catholic communal institutions. This process has only recently begun for a smaller group of middle-class black women, while it has scarcely started at all for Indian women, whose primary battle is still the survival of their people as a distinct cultural community.

Catholic women in the twentieth century also were faced with a militantly antifeminist hierarchy that opposed women's suffrage and reproductive rights and promoted traditional femininity, especially through the cult of Mary. This antifeminism was perceived by the Catholic hierarchy as a key element in its crusade to protect Catholicism from "modernity." The power of the hierarchy was consolidated in the early twentieth century as it moved to accommodate itself to the American situation. In the process, the limited autonomy enjoyed by Catholic laity in parishes and by women's religious orders was suppressed. Only in the 1950s and 1960s did the movement to form the conscious identity of Roman Catholic sisters begin to upgrade the educational skills of American nuns and in the process lay the foundation for the full-scale feminist revolt of American religious women in the 1970s.

Although Catholic women were seldom actively involved with the feminist movement, some outstanding laywomen were militant social activists. The work of "Mother" Mary H. Jones and of Dorothy Day was highly significant. In the late nineteenth and early twentieth centuries Mother Jones led nonviolent strikes for various labor groups, including railway and mine workers. Dorothy Day has been termed the most influential person in American Catholicism by Roman Catholic historian David O'Brien. Along with Peter Marin, she founded the Catholic Worker Movement in 1933. During her lifetime the movement grew to have more than fifty houses of hospitality and farming communes to provide relief and care for the hungry and homeless poor. Day also published the *Catholic Worker* newspaper, applying her prophetic understanding of the Gospel to economic, political, and social issues of the period.

The Evangelical, Holiness, and Pentecostal traditions represent those branches of American Christianity that are often stereotyped as conservative. This comes from the frequent confusion of Evangelical and Fundamentalist Christianity. Fundamentalism—which represents a reactionary attempt to preserve themes of classical Christianity—developed in the late nineteenth and twentieth centuries in response to liberal religious and secular culture. Like Catholic antimodernists, Fundamentalists saw reaffirming women's "place" in a patriarchal social order as the key to reestablishing "true" Christianity.

Yet the Evangelical, Holiness, and Pentecostal traditions diverge from Fundamentalism in that they derive from experiential and charismatic movements which included women precisely because their presence validated the existence of the Spirit. These movements found signs of the Spirit outside rather than within institutions. The tendency of these traditions to include women did not disappear but continued well into the first decades of the twentieth century. However, in the 1930s this charismatic tradition became more institutionalized, and women were shut out of many roles in religious leadership that they had held in earlier days. The emphasis on the subordination of women partly arose in reaction to women's expanding roles in politics and paid employment. Yet in the late 1960s a new evangelical feminism was reborn and revived the earlier struggle between a liberatory and patriarchal charismatic tradition.

In mainline Protestant churches, the predominance of women as directors of religious education at the local church level did not occur until the Depression, when money in churches was short and women were willing to work for small salaries. Religious education as a profession was pioneered by men and women who turned from the old model of evangelization to a system of proselytism based on education and personal growth. Drawing on theories of progressive education as well as on liberal concepts of historical-critical interpretation of the Bible, religious-education pioneers sought to ground their profession in sound modern knowledge and methodologies drawn from the fields of history and psychology.

Although most of the professors of Christian education at the graduate school and seminary level were male, the first women to join theological faculties in the twentieth century were generally limited to this area of specialization. Women as Christian educators also pioneered women's professional ministry in local churches. Yet by the 1980s they were becoming victims of their own success. As more and more women have become ordained, ordained professionals who specialize in education have displaced nonordained directors of religious education. Thus the future of religious education both as a profession in its own right and as an avenue of advancement for women in the church is in doubt.

From the late nineteenth century Protestant churches have followed a pattern in which women win laity-governing authority first at the local level and then at the level of conferences and synods. Only when women have gained full lay rights do these churches turn to the granting of ordained status to women. Here, too, there is a sequential process "up the ladder," as women are granted first deaconess status to serve as missionaries at home and abroad and then local pastor status. Finally, ordination, of which there may be one or two steps, is granted. After full ordination is gained, ranks within the clergy order, such as district superintendent, may follow. Accordingly, the United Methodists elected their first woman bishop, Marjorie Matthews, in 1980, twenty-four years after granting full status to women in the ordained ministry of the then Methodist church.

A few denominations, notably the Congregationalists, Unitarians, Universalists, and Methodist Protestants, progressed through this pattern of winning lay ministry in the nineteenth century. But this development was blocked in other mainstream denominations in the 1880s and partly diverted into deaconess orders for women. Consequently, this process of winning full lay rights and finally ordained ministry for women began for these Protestant churches at the end of the nineteenth century and did not progress to the granting of full ordination until the period from the mid-1950s to the 1970s.

For some churches progress initially was retarded by ecumenism, when the merger of ordaining and nonordaining churches was carried out by conceding to the nonordaining partner and refusing women ordination in the new united church. But dissatisfaction with this compromise often sparked a reaction within the new denomination, resulting in the ordination of women at some later time. This occurred in the Methodist church, where nonordaining Methodist Episcopals outvoted ordaining Methodist Protestants in the merger of 1939, yet in 1956 the resultant Methodist church voted to ordain

women. Occasionally ecumenical relations even hastened progress, as in the Lutheran churches that were pressed to ordain women because their parent bodies in Scandinavia had voted to do so in the 1960s. The Episcopal church, which in 1976 granted bishops the prerogative of ordaining women, has been caught in a crossfire of opposing ecumenisms: on the one side, momentum from mainstream ordaining Protestant denominations and, on the other side, pressure from the nonordaining Roman Catholic and Orthodox churches.

The ordination of women had become a critical issue in almost all religious bodies by the last quarter of the twentieth century. Both Reform and Conservative Jews now ordain women. The Unitarian Universalist Association has continued in the forefront of the ordination movement, as were its predecessor bodies in the nineteenth century. The Universal Fellowship of Metropolitan Community churches has the largest percentage of ordained women in its clergy of any denomination, though the total number is smaller than the actual number of ordained women in other denominations.

The winning of ordained status for many women by the mid-1970s has created a new era in the churches. Now those remaining Fundamentalist, Roman Catholic, and Orthodox churches that do not ordain women feel mounting pressure from within and without to reconsider their historic position.

Increasing numbers of women enrolled in theological schools in the 1970s. In the 1980s women comprise more than 50 percent of the students at many seminaries of liberal Protestantism, and their numbers are increasing even at the most conservative seminaries. This presence of women in turn has created a new base for criticism of the sexism of the theological tradition itself. Feminist studies in biblical, theological, historical, and practical fields have proliferated in the 1970s and 1980s. Courses such as biblical hermeneutics from a feminist perspective, feminist theology, women and religion in American history, women in crisis, and the pastoral care of women are offered at many seminaries, colleges, and universities. The churches have been challenged to rethink their religious culture from its very roots.

While feminism has created ferment within religious structures in the late twentieth century, the relationship between religious feminism and wider social structures has come under closer scrutiny. Christianity had provided a public base for women's progressive movements in nineteenth-century America that seemed to disappear in the twentieth century. In fact, the close identification between progressive feminism and progressive Christianity in social action and reform collapsed in the 1920s. When feminism reappeared as a movement in the 1960s, it was generally more secular and more suspicious of the positive character of Christianity.

The most telling explanation for this apparent change lies in the shifting boundaries between the religious and the secular in American society. In the nineteenth century men were beginning to enter a secular public culture and consequently religion was defined as the culture of women and the home. But this meant that religion, although privatized for men, remained a public culture for women. Women used the culture of the home to crusade out into the traditionally male domain and press their issues of women's rights and social reform. For mainstream Protestant women, the winning of the vote in 1920 also coincided with a shift in the boundaries between the religious and secular. Now women who entered into the male spheres of business, higher education, and politics accepted the assumption that they should do so on male terms; that is, with a secular and not a religious cultural platform. The women reformers of the 1920s and 1930s typically spoke the language of sociology rather than theology in order to advance themselves and their concerns. The efforts of Jane Addams to address the issues of urban dislocation and world peace are a notable example. For these women, religion had become a private culture that they did not take with them into the marketplace. Addams continued to be inwardly motivated by religious faith to perform social service. Others, however, found no place for piety in their lives.

For other groups of women, secularization took a different form. Evangelical and Roman Catholic women experienced growing conservatism from their churches on women's issues as both churches battled what they saw as the pernicious influence of secularism. Later in the century these churches would repoliticize their religious culture, but primarily as a platform against women's legal, social, and reproductive rights.

Women in the Pentecostal tradition provide a significant case in point. Among the most prominent twentieth-century representatives is Kathryn Kuhlman, the Pentecostal faith healer and evangelist who preached to millions at revivals for over fifty years. Many charismatics credit her with giving the movement greater respectability in mainline churches. Pentecostalists of a generation prior included Aimee Semple McPherson and Alma White, the most colorful female evangelists of the twentieth century. McPherson founded the International Church of the Foursquare Gospel and White, the Pillar of Fire church. White, consecrated by her church as the first American female bishop in 1918, led its members until her death at age eighty-four.

The equality of the sexes avowed by this tradition was undermined by restrictions on women's roles. While one calling to prophesy and eight to preach were recognized among women, the priestly functions of administering the sacraments were restricted among women. Even more widespread was the view, held by Kuhlman among others, that although women could be spiritual leaders in churches, they were their husbands' subordinates at home. A corollary belief was that women were God's second choice, called only when men were unavailable. Not surprisingly, women who accepted such teachings were more likely to win the approval of male church leadership than women who questioned such teachings. McPherson and White, however, had difficulty reconciling their public ministries with expectations of female subordination at home. McPherson was convinced that, had she not left her husband to begin her ministry as a traveling evangelist, he would have lost her anyway because she would have died of a broken heart from not following God's call. White spoke forcefully for women's rights in the church and in the larger society. She was joyful over passage of the woman suffrage amendment in 1920, but her marriage was marked by tension and even by separation for many years because of her husband's antagonism to her speaking publicly without his consent.

Jewish women were caught in a subculture that had accepted secularism and assimilation but that also sought to redefine the relation of religious and ethnic identity. Zionism had the potential to integrate religious and ethnic identity as part of a public and political culture for American Jews, yet the American Jewish community has not reached a consensus on foreign policy toward Israel.

Finally, for American Indians and blacks, the religious culture became a primary means for affirming the identity of the ethnic subculture against white domination. Consequently, the church has remained a base for political organizing for black civil rights and Indian autonomy—though not for expanding the role of women.

CONCLUSION

These shifting boundaries between public and private, religious and secular, partly explain the pendulum swing from a left-wing social and political movement for black civil rights, followed by struggles for women's rights and peace led by progressive clergy in the 1960s, to a right-wing political-religious movement led by opponents of secularism and modernity in the late 1970s and early 1980s that made antifeminism a key part of its ideology.

In both the left-wing and right-wing movements, political and religious forces already were intertwined in quasi-privatized subcultures that only needed a spark to call them back into the public arena as contending forces for the American budget and the American soul. Religious feminism began to emerge as a force with the historically proven power to challenge the wider society, as well as religious culture, to restructure its organization.

The last quarter of the twentieth century marks a major turning point in the relationship between women and religion in America. Only since the 1970s has the history of women and religion begun to be recovered on a broad scale and has an authentic female voice, individuated from men's, emerged through feminist theology. The themes and stories condensed into this chapter make one wonder how such a history and voice have been submerged over such a long time period.

In the latter part of the twentieth century, also, women are being integrated into mainline structures of religious institutions on a basis of more legitimate parity than has ever happened before. In the process, religious justifications constricting women to subordinate roles within the family and workplace are being overthrown by large numbers of women and men. Ethnic women also are discovering their own identity and interests, distinguished from that of men within their subcultures.

Efforts to subordinate women in religious institutions and in society, growing out of sacred justifications, will continue as they always have. The story of women and religion can never be a repeat of the experiences of the past three centuries, however. Recovery of the history of women and the voice of feminist theology growing out of it, coupled with the advances in the status and role of females in recent years, promise new issues arising from liberation in the twenty-first century.

BIBLIOGRAPHY

James Axtell, ed., *The Indian Peoples of Eastern America: A Documentary History of the Sexes* (1981); Charlotte Baum, Paula Hyman, and Sonya Michel, *The Jewish Woman in America* (1976); R. Pierce Beaver, *All Loves Excelling: American Protestant Women in World Mission* (1968); Elizabeth Cazden, *Antoinette Brown Blackwell: A Biography* (1983); Nancy F. Cott, *Root of Bitterness; Documents of the Social History of American Women* (1972) and *The Bonds of Womanhood: "Woman's Sphere" in New England, 1780–1835* (1977); John Demos, *A Little Commonwealth: Family Life in Plymouth Colony* (1970); Ann Douglas, *The "Feminization" of American Culture* (1977); Mary Ewens, *The Role of the Nun in Nineteenth-Century America* (1978); Rudolf Glanz, *The Jewish Woman in America: Two Female Immigrant Generations, 1820–1929* (1976); Philip Greven, *The Protestant Temperament: Patterns of Child-Rearing, Religious Experience, and the Self in Early America* (1977).

Nancy Hardesty, *Women Called to Witness: Evangelical Feminism in the Nineteenth Century* (1984); Edward T. James, Janet W. James, and Paul Boyer, eds., *Notable American Women, 1607–1950: A Biographical Dictionary*, 3 vols. (1971); Janet W. James, ed., *Women in American Religion* (1980); Rosemary Keller, *Abigail Adams and the American Revolution: A Personal History* (1982) and, with Louise Queen and Hilah Thomas, as eds., *Women in New Worlds: Historical Perspectives on the Wesleyan Tradition*, 2 vols. (1981, 1982); Linda Kerber, *Women of the Republic: Intellect and Ideology in Revolutionary America* (1980); Lyle Koehler, *A Search for Power: The "Weaker Sex" in Seventeenth-Century New England* (1980).

Asunción Lavrin, "Ecclesiastical Reform of Nunneries in New Spain in the Eighteenth Century," in *The Americas*, 22 (1965), "Women in Convents: Their Economic and Social Role in Colonial Mexico," in Berenice A. Carroll, ed., *Liberating Women's History: Theoretical and Critical Essays* (1976), and, as ed., *Latin American Women: Historical Perspectives* (1978); Anita Libman Lebeson, *Recall to Life: The Jewish Woman in America* (1970); Gerda Lerner, *The Grimké Sisters from South Carolina* (1971); Bert James Loewenberg and Ruth Bogin, eds., *Black Women in Nineteenth-Century American Life* (1976); Donald Mathews, *Religion in the Old South* (1977); Beatrice Medicine and Patricia Albers, eds., *The Hidden Half: Studies of*

Plains Indian Women (1983); Edmund Morgan, *The Puritan Family: Essays on Religion and Domestic Relations in Seventeenth-Century New England* (1944; rev. 1966); Raymond Lee Muncy, *Sex and Marriage in Utopian Communities* (1973); Mary Beth Norton, *Liberty's Daughters: The Revolutionary Experience of American Women, 1750–1800* (1980); Robert Peel, *Mary Baker Eddy,* 3 vols. (1966, 1971, 1977); James P. Ronda and James Axtell, *Indian Missions: A Critical Bibliography* (1978).

Rosemary R. Ruether and Rosemary S. Keller, eds., *Women and Religion in America: A Documentary History,* 3 vols. (1981, 1983, 1985); Anne Firor Scott, *The Southern Lady: From Pedestal to Politics, 1830–1930* (1970); Barbara Sicherman and Carol H. Green, eds., *Notable American Women, The Modern Period: A Biographical Dictionary* (1980); Kathryn Sklar, *Catharine Beecher: A Study in American Domesticity* (1973); Leonard I. Sweet, *The Minister's Wife: Her Role in Nineteenth-Century American Evangelicalism* (1983); Laurel Ulrich, *Good Wives: Image and Reality in the Lives of Women in Northern New England, 1650–1750* (1982); Barbara Welter, *Dimity Convictions: The American Woman in the Nineteenth Century* (1976); Bernard Wishy, *The Child and the Republic: The Dawn of Modern American Child Nurture* (1968).

[*See also* MISSIONARY ENTERPRISE *and* PROFESSIONAL MINISTRY.]

Part IX
THE DISSEMINATION
OF AMERICAN RELIGION

THE PROFESSIONAL MINISTRY

Charles E. Hambrick-Stowe

THE ministry has reflected American religion's pluralism and fluidity. The Catholic parish priest, the early circuit rider, the revivalist, the Presbyterian settled pastor, the urban black preacher, the rabbi in an alien land, and the men and women who preached in Pentecostal missions are widely disparate; yet, commonalities exist. The Russian priest John (Ioann) Veniaminov, who began work with Alaskan Native Americans in 1825, was cut from the same cloth as John Eliot in early Massachusetts. A 1960s activist complained, "From the conservative Frank Norris in Texas to the urbane liberalism of [Harry Emerson] Fosdick in New York, the role of the minister has remained essentially the same—preaching and counseling" (Charles Prestwood, *The New Breed of Clergy*, 1972, pp. 5–6). Notwithstanding diversity and change, the ministry developed an American character.

Washington Gladden embodied the clerical tradition as well as the drive for up-to-date relevance in an 1898 textbook. *The Christian Pastor and the Working Church* stands in a line back through Cotton Mather's *Manuductio ad Ministerium* (1726) to Richard Bernard's Old World classic, *The Faithfull Shepherd* (1607), and extending to the professional journals of the 1980s, the "evangelical" *Leadership* and the "liberal" *Christian Ministry*. The subject matter is remarkably similar, although theology, emphases, and particular topics change with time. The Social Gospel's Gladden, beyond pastoral and pulpit duties, explored ministry to the poor and women's work. Presbyterian Lloyd C. Douglas observed, "No vocation has created a more voluminous literature concerning itself than ours" (*The Minister's Everyday Life*, 1924, p. vii). From colonial days to the present, writers have expressed anxiety about secularization, decline of preaching,

and erosion of influence. The search for cultural identity and professional effectiveness, rooted in a call to mediate experience and understanding of God, shapes the minister's role.

The concept of profession or clerical office should not sever the clergy from popular religious history. Religious leaders have been popular figures emerging from the crowd. Ministerial history is not all of religious history, but one cannot comprehend American religion without it.

Books, magazines, and pamphlets over centuries suggest ongoing tensions between clerical self-image and lay expectations. At least six conceptions have vied for predominance.

First, the ministry is a (Protestant) calling or (Catholic) vocation from God. With Christian writers, a rabbi insisted, "the Rabbinate is a calling rather than a profession" (Israel Goldstein, *Problems of the Jewish Ministry*, 1927, preface). It differs from other occupations since its purpose is not to administer an institution but to inspire. The classic expression of God's primary action in raising up preachers was Gilbert Tennent's *The Danger of an Unconverted Ministry* (1740). A century and a half later another evangelical warned, "No man has any call to the Christian Ministry who has not with all his heart received the Holy Ghost" (James William Kimball, *The Christian Ministry*, 1884, p. 7). Books reminded ministers that their spiritual calling gave theirs a special status above other occupations.

Second, a minister is one ordained to pastoral office or holy orders. The priesthood embodies the church in traditional Catholicism; the church exists with a priest at the altar. In Protestantism the church is the people, but churches retained the office. The minister is "set apart" to perform liturgical tasks, especially the sacraments. Frontier leveling enabled anyone feeling God's call to preach, but respect for ordination survived. Generations of colonial Anglicans went unconfirmed for want of a bishop. New England Congregationalism maintained that only the ordained could preach, teach with authority, and administer sacraments. Missouri Synod Lutherans encouraged lay preachers, but insisted only pastors celebrate Communion. Even restorationist Alexander Campbell by the 1830s stressed the need for a clerical office. The laity could do everything "when circumstances demand it," but the advance of the Gospel required special evangelists. Lacking rabbis until 1840, hazanim (readers) and shohetim (slaughterers) carried out Jewish ritual. They worked at other occupations but filled the offices that preserved the community. Methodists and Catholics were ordained in stages, recognizing the need for training, probation, and regulation. If the ministry as calling elevates the God-ordained individual, the clerical office subsumes the ordained under the institution.

Third, the minister, despite separation of church and state, is a state licensee. The explosion of religious experience in America meant that established churches could not regulate preaching or new movements. The civil government sought to maintain order through licensing procedures. In the 1740s, Virginia evangelical preachers threatened the Anglican order. New Light Presbyterian Samuel Davies opened the door for legitimate pluralism by asking the governor for a license to preach. His deference purchased unharassed Presbyterian growth and a rise in its status. Pentecostals faced similar problems as dissenters in the 1910s. To perform marriages and qualify for the railroad clergy rate (essential for a burgeoning national movement), whites obtained licenses by affiliating with the incorporated black Church of God in Christ. After the Sixteenth Amendment ministers required civil recognition for tax purposes.

Fourth, the clergy has considered itself a social class. Cotton Mather was destined by birth for his role in colonial New England. As he graduated from Harvard College, President Oakes intoned: "COTTONUS MATHERUS. What a name! . . . If this youth bring back and represent the piety, learning, and graceful ingenuity, sound judgment, prudence and gravity of his reverend grandsires John Cotton and Richard Mather, he may be said to have done his part well." Except

for Catholic priests, ministers across the spectrum have tended to self-perpetuate through clerical families. Jewish rabbis and Eastern Orthodox priests expected sons or sons-in-law to follow them. In some established groups the clergy came from genteel families. Southern Presbyterians distinguished themselves from Methodists and Baptists in this regard in the early nineteenth century. As Methodists and Baptists rose on the social scale, a cultured southern urban class of "gentlemen theologians" developed. Ministers searched out youth of piety and intellect to cultivate for the profession. Similar recruitment obtained among teaching sisters with girls in Catholic schools. Clothing, a black robe or a collar, set clergy apart. The black pastor was the only man in a suit on weekdays. The publication of autobiographies and collections of lives of ministers fostered the sense of belonging to an elite of dignity, spirituality, and knowledge.

Fifth, the minister has been an individual, often independent, revivalist. From the Great Awakening's "grand itinerants," to nineteenth-century evangelists like Peter Cartwright and Charles Grandison Finney, to the rise of the great urban revivalists—Dwight L. Moody, Billy Sunday, and Billy Graham—and the ranks of modern "old-time" television preachers, the famous names typify an immensely popular figure. The revivalist might belong to a denomination, and serve it loyally, but it mattered less than saving souls and a personal following. Revivalism minimized class. Except for an exhibition of spiritual and oratorical gifts, the preacher was of the people. Education was unnecessary, even harmful if it led him to speak over people's heads, emphasize doctrine over experience, or identify with wealth and neglect the unlettered. William Warren Sweet expounded the thesis that churches which became the most influential in America were those that most successfuly met the religious needs of the frontier. The Yankee Flavel Bascom, a member of the American Home Missionary Society in Illinois, contrasts with the itinerant Methodist Peter Cartwright. Bascom wrote, "I endeavored to draw sound instruction from the Word of God . . . stimulate thought and study, and thus correct the erroneous notions so prevalent around us." He set himself against the "boisterous address" of "ignorant" preachers. Cartwright chided that eastern seminaries "manufacture young preachers like they do lettuce in hot-houses" and warned, "he must quit reading his old manuscript sermons, and learn to speak extemporaneously. . . . If he did not adopt this manner of preaching, the Methodists would set the whole western world on fire before he could light his match" (Sweet, vol. 3, pp. 257–258). Late-twentieth-century independent Fundamentalists repeat the argument, adding that liberals have abandoned "Bible preaching." The difference is more of form than of content. But with the revivalist, personality and form are almost everything.

Sixth, ministers identified themselves as professionals. As did lawyers and physicians, nineteenth-century middle-class ministers defined their role as a skilled and academically learned calling serving humanity, not to receive a wage but out of commitment to the social good. A professional was retained, not hired. Denominations requiring academic training led the way by establishing seminaries as graduate professional schools. Methodists and Baptists were not far behind. The concept meant that the ministry was one profession among others. Human skills were learned and had to be honored and remunerated. The ministry competed with other professions for the same bright youth. "Why is it," a Presbyterian lamented in 1846, "that while annually hundreds of our young men enter upon the professions of Law and Medicine so few turn their attention to the ministry?" To advance the profession, ministers recruited in evangelical colleges, sought higher salaries, and became community leaders. Professionalism, a defensive reaction to the shattering of organic colonial society, could be unpopular with parishioners. "Professionalism" itself was democratized, describing the aura of anyone with a desired skill. Billy Sunday was such a professional revivalist; indeed, he was a professional ball player before his call and transferred the marketing techniques of sports to his ministry.

The tension between "calling" and "profession" persisted. A manual explained that God's call alone is inadequate for "dealing with the problems which the Rabbi encounters in the practice of his ministry." Training in preaching, counseling, and management were needed, and in this "the Jewish ministry partakes of the character of a profession" (Goldstein, preface). "Professional" ministers modified their interpreta-

tion of "call." A Congregational seminary dean demythologized it as faith in God and a desire to serve. A Disciples minister wrote, "The call to the ministry is not greatly different from the call of duty and the call of opportunity anywhere" (Hampton Adams, *Calling Men for the Ministry*, 1945, p. 130). An Episcopal bishop, Stephen F. Bayne, cautioned, "How many . . . have missed their vocation because they waited for the imagined thunderbolt of a 'call' to strike" (Butler and Pittenger, p. 8). Professionalism has been a general trend as the ministry has defined its role. But the conviction that God calls leaders, that the ministry is unique among occupations, endured. Both the sacerdotal and the revivalist views distrust professionalism if it unduly emphasizes skill and reward. American ministers and believers have insisted that "no man taketh this honor unto himself, but he that is called of God" (Hebrews 5:4).

The ancient traditions of Judaism and Eastern Orthodoxy, ethnic identities foreign to Western Christianity, have lived with the tensions of preservation and accommodation. Catholics and Protestants (German Reformed, Lutheran, Mennonite) loath to adopt English faced the same challenges, but none of them were so alien. Some priests and rabbis saw their role as defending sacred tradition against dilution. Others saw it as mediating between tradition and American culture, to preserve tradition's essence but modify practice. There is no linear development from early "conservative" to modern "liberal," as the renaissance of Orthodox Jewry and Greek liturgy attests. The clergy worked between these poles.

That no clergy is needed for Jewish worship conditioned the American rabbi's role. No rabbis existed for the minyans (quorums of ten adult males, meeting in homes) and synagogues in colonial seaports like New Amsterdam and Newport. The European trait of lay congregational control thrived in this country. The first ordained rabbi, Abraham Joseph Rice, arrived in 1840 with missionary zeal but soon despaired of the lax German-American Jews. He became a grocer and bitterly conducted a private traditional minyan. Other mid-nineteenth-century rabbis met the challenge constructively. Isaac Leeser, reader of a Philadelphia congregation, though never ordained, was well educated and scholarly. He preached in English, edited a journal, and with reader Louis Salomon advocated "a federated union" of synagogues. Efforts to import rabbis for yoked synagogues, as in 1845 with Dr. Max Lilienthal in New York, were unsuccessful.

Rabbi Isaac Mayer Wise of Cincinnati was the driving force, from the late 1840s, of an American Reform Jewish movement. He published a simplified prayer book, substituted Judaism as a religious community for the concept of nationhood, called for the union of all "Ministers and Other Israelites," and founded Hebrew Union College in 1875 to train a rabbinate. Reform rabbis abandoned the rigors of the Torah and many observances, emphasizing the prophets. They presented themselves as ethical guides through the maze of American life. In this century second-generation Eastern European Jews entered the Reform rabbinate with a traditional orientation, reintroducing Hebrew, paying more attention to the Torah and ritual, and restoring Zionism.

Eastern European immigrants, from regions where rabbis venerated Yiddish and required strict ritual observance, overwhelmed the Reform impulse. Unfortunately, charlatan "rabbis" took advantage of the untutored. A professional rabbinate respectful of orthodoxy arose when Solomon Schechter, a Romanian who had studied in Germany and taught at Cambridge, became president of New York's Jewish Theological Seminary in 1902. Conservative rabbis, stung by Orthodox refusal to recognize their ordination, organized the Rabbinical Assembly and settled into denominational life. Emphasizing Judaism as a people, they expanded synagogues as community centers. Rabbis became institutional administrators as well as scholars and teachers.

Orthodox Judaism became the largest group with a resurgence of identity after World War II and the founding of Israel. Early leadership, including Rabbi Henry Pereira Mendes, formed the Union of Orthodox Jewish Congregations (1898) and the Union of Orthodox Rabbis (1902), Rabbi Isaac Elchanan Theological Seminary, and Yeshiva University. American-born rabbis trained in these institutions organized in the 1920s and formed the Rabbinical Council of America in 1935. A trend among ultra-Orthodox Jews to denigrate the role of the "professional pulpit rabbi" was offset by renewed emphasis on the rabbi as religious scholar. Orthodox synagogues and rabbis have excelled in establishing day schools.

The Central Conference of American Rabbis' *Report of Committee on Relation Between Rabbi and Congregation* stated in 1903 that "the spiritual welfare of the Jewish community depends upon the mutual relationship of rabbi and congregation." The relationship had qualities of professionalism: "The congregation employs the rabbi, and the rabbi serves the congregation, but the attitude of the one to the other is not that of employer to employee." The rabbi's first duty was preaching, and most texts stressed powerful preaching in the American scene. But unlike the Protestant view, "the Jewish conception of the rabbi is that he should be primarily a scholar, not a pastor. . . . Social calling that passes under the name of pastoral work is a sham and a delusion." Emphasis on numerical growth was "commercialism." The "evangelical conception of the ministry" nevertheless influenced at least Reform and Conservative rabbis. The introduction to a Detroit rabbi's book rejoiced that during his tenure the city grew by a factor of four while his synagogue multiplied by eight and built twice (Leo M. Franklin, *The Rabbi*, 1938).

In practical terms, the rabbi bent to the Protestant model. He (or she in Reform and, as of 1987, Conservative Judaism) compromises with wealthy lay leaders, has difficulty finding study time, and considers such time a luxury. "Although little change has been made in rabbinical training programs, the role of the rabbi has changed significantly; once he was professionally an interpreter of the laws, a legist, whereas now he is professionally a minister." The rabbi visits the sick, counsels, serves on community boards and Jewish agencies, plans worship, preaches, and so on. "The modern American rabbi leads an extremely busy and useful life, but it is not the life of the rabbi of old" (Blau, pp. 132–133).

The Eastern Orthodox priesthood's relation to American culture paralleled the rabbinate's. Orthodox have been a substantial ethnic group for a century, but churches and clergy remained on the sidelines of American culture, dismissed by Protestants and Catholics as anachronistic. The shift from an immigrant clergy to an American-born, seminary-trained professional priesthood was slow. During the American Bicentennial a writer asked, "Is our faith, which we claim to be true and universal, to remain a ceremonial and marginal accident in the texture of America, or is it, by the will of God, an essential event which is happening not only *in* America but also *to* America?" (Tarasar, p. 11). In the final quarter of the twentieth century, an educated and energetic priesthood led the church, traditions intact, into the mainstream of American life.

As Protestant ministers look to colonial beginnings for their self-image, many Orthodox priests look to Russian missionaries in Alaska, notably John Veniaminov (Bishop Innocent), as the "source and spiritual criterion of American Orthodoxy." Innocent, as Metropolitan of Moscow after 1868, took special interest in the North American diocese, moved the see to San Francisco to minister to Greeks and eastern Europeans (to New York in 1903), and supplied Russian-trained priests and monks. In 1891 scores of Eastern-rite "Uniate" priests, led by Father Alexis Toth of Minneapolis, left Roman Catholicism for Orthodoxy. Catholic bishops could not abide married priests, even with long-standing papal approval. Orthodox priests may marry prior to ordination. Since only celibates qualify for the office of bishop, ambitious young men prone to study often became monks (archimandrites) rather than priests to be noticed for advancement.

The 1917 Bolshevik Revolution transformed American Orthodoxy. Financial support for clergy dried up; Romanians, Serbs, Ukrainians, Syrians, and Greeks formed separate churches. American Russian Orthodox clergy declared independence from Moscow. Clergy were ill educated and professionally untrained. The functions of the priesthood as traditionally conceived required little training; the singing of the liturgy was the major activity. The priest was one of the people, laboring at farming or other employment. Since the laity did not expect professionally skilled priests, many resisted efforts to upgrade training.

Greek immigration paralleled the late-nineteenth- and early-twentieth-century Jewish influx, but the church grew slowly because males predominated and priests were scarce. Without a bishop until 1918, parishes began as lay societies. Archbishop Athenagoras organized the church and clergy (1930–1949), founding Holy Cross School of Theology (Boston) for clerical training and the advancement of Orthodox studies. Greek priests preserved ethnic and religious tradition. Indeed, in all Orthodox churches the priest played the role of cultural leader. While the (Russian) Orthodox Church in America long advocated an English liturgy, Greek priests continued to worship in Greek.

Formal Orthodox education began in 1905 when Bishop Tikhon opened a small seminary in Minnesota, but it did not flourish until the founding of St. Vladimir's (New York) in 1938. Seminarians received a bachelor's degree through Columbia University and the professional bachelor of divinity. By the 1960s students entered Holy Cross and St. Vladimir's after college for three years of graduate training. Patristics, Orthodox theology, and Bible were augmented by some homiletics and pastoral counseling. The immigrant period was complete by the 1950s as American-born seminary-trained priests came into leadership positions.

The Roman Catholic priesthood, as set forth at the Council of Trent (1545–1563), is a sacred order, set apart as a sacerdotal class distinct from the laity for the function of performing the Mass. Priests came to America with exploration and colonization. The legacy of missions run by Spanish Dominican and Franciscan friars remains in America's self-awareness. Maryland, in 1634 a Catholic haven, was a center through the eighteenth century, though Catholics became a disenfranchised minority. Leadership in Maryland and Pennsylvania, entirely Jesuit, was further crippled by the order's dissolution in 1773. A "Constitution of the Clergy" in 1782 to 1784 attempted to organize, but Marylander John Carroll was appointed superior without the priests' consultation. The pope elevated Carroll as bishop of Baltimore in 1790, however, after election by American priests. Tension between authority and democracy—clear in the trusteeism controversy (local lay authority, including calling priests) and the clash of ethnic loyalties—were constant themes. Carroll's challenge was to create "a permanent body of national Clergy." He imported a hundred French Sulpicians, the backbone of the clergy for several decades, who established churches and schools across the continent. He founded Saint Mary's Seminary in Baltimore, the nation's first. By the First Provincial Council of Baltimore in 1829 six seminaries existed. The consecration of John Hughes, an Irish-American diocesan seminary graduate, as bishop of New York in 1837 proved their effectiveness. Priests like Hughes helped the church respond to Irish immigration and anti-Catholicism.

Dominicans worked in Kentucky and the West; Ursuline sisters taught in New Orleans, New York, and Boston. John Carroll in 1790 welcomed houses of Carmelite nuns "to pray for the American missions," but he promoted teaching and nursing orders over contemplatives. Former Episcopalian Elizabeth Seton founded her Sisters of Charity and Saint Joseph's Academy in Emmitsburg, Maryland (1809). Mary Rhodes's new order, the Sisters of Loretto (1812), taught in Kentucky, joined by the Sisters of Charity of Nazareth under Mother Catherine Spalding. The Society of the Sacred Heart, under Mother Rose-Philippine Duchesne, began educational work in St. Louis in 1818. Other women's orders followed. The church created western dioceses as priests and nuns engaged in missionary work to Native Americans and began churches and schools. The first black priest, former slave Augustus Tolton, was ordained in 1888, and black orders were founded (the Oblate Sisters of Providence, 1829 in Baltimore; and the Sisters of the Holy Family, 1842 in New Orleans), but blacks were few. Liturgical style is one reason: the black preacher excels with verbal freedom incompatible with Catholic worship.

Irish-Americans soon dominated the diocesan priesthood and the orders. In the mid-nineteenth century, key Protestant converts, including Isaac Hecker, the founder of the Paulists Fathers, sought a style of priesthood within the mainstream of American life. The Americanist movement flourished, but conservative priests of Irish, German, and Polish extraction insisted on the gap between Catholic and American values. After the pope condemned Americanism in 1899, priests abandoned theology and focused on pastoral and institutional work.

In the twentieth century, the Catholic church was again transformed by immigration from Italy, Portugal, eastern Europe, Mexico, and Latin America. Still, Irish clerical hegemony prevailed, as relatively few Italian- and Spanish-speaking men and women found vocations. Recruitment strove to keep up with the growth of a diverse community.

Demand for up-to-date skills survived modernism. Some texts differed little from Protestant professional manuals. A bishop wrote in 1919, "A smattering of Theology and of Church History, a little piety, the observance of the commandments, and the ability to raise money, may have been all that was demanded of the American priest four or five decades ago. But that time is past" (George T. Schmidt, *The American Priest,* 1919, pp. 13–14). He called for a knowledge of sociology and urged priests to preach strong, well-crafted sermons, not "mere talks." Texts covered home visitation, parochial school administration, social work, evangelism of non-Catholics, and parish financial management. Other books sought to raise diocesan priests to the levels of professional competence associated with the orders.

Religious brothers and sisters, unordained, are technically not clergy, though considered so in the lay mind. Apart from teaching, brothers in large congregations were assigned work thought menial by worldly standards. Not surprisingly, in upwardly mobile America, parents objected more strenuously to sons becoming brothers than priests. Brotherhoods identified with a professional role, such as high school teaching, however, took on the social status of the occupation. The Sister Formation Conference (begun 1953) and other organizations of women religious fostered professionalism. As nuns became successful, with advanced degrees, priests advised them not to "outdistance spirituality." After 1960 vocations among women dropped sharply as other avenues of work opened. Nuns themselves changed, redefining the vows of poverty and obedience to include political action. Vatican II's revival of the married diaconate order expanded the church's corps of ministers and created new opportunities for men ordained especially to serve among the poor.

Priests developed new self-images. Through the first half of this century the priestly role taught in seminary was stable, conservative, and based on classical textbooks. Priests trained in the 1920s agonized little over identity or vocational definition, expressing it simply: "I wanted to do the work of a priest." Their most satisfying work was with the sick and youth, although Mass and confessions absorbed their time. Priests ordained from the 1960s on read broadly, including Protestant works. Lack of a fixed literature paralleled a shift in the seminary's spiritual life from the "Rule" to "regulations." The priest's role was in flux, which partly explains a compensatory renewal of interest in liturgy. Pastoral counseling gradually replaced the hearing of confessions and the sacrament of penance. Vatican II brought a shift in the priest's sense of servanthood, from cultic and hierarchical duty to serving the church as the people of God.

Ministry in the Anglican tradition shares common ground with the Catholic. Holy orders are conferred through episcopal ordination in hierarchical and traditional fashion. As expressed in nineteenth-century debates, "From the earliest writings of the Christians . . . there were three orders of ministers in the Church, Bishops, Presbyters, and Deacons," and "the Bishops alone ordained" (John Esten Cooke, *An Essay on the Invalidity of Presbyterian Ordination,* 1829, pp. 208–209). As in Catholicism, the central duty of the priest has been to celebrate the Eucharist, though Episcopal evangelicals emphasized the pulpit. Priests have been university educated and concerned with the dignity of the office. They retained a certain Englishness, responsive to such developments as the high church Tractarian movement.

In colonial Virginia, divinity and law epitomized learning; church and courthouse were gathering places. Clergy were few and scattered, however, with less than half the churches served. Local vestries, controlled by squires, held authority. When clergy arrived through the work of James Blair and the Society for the Propagation of the Gospel in Foreign Parts, they were made to feel like hired hands. In the Parson's Cause (1750s), they sued to secure dignity and remuneration as ministers of the establishment, a drive that was also a defensive reaction to popular sectarian preachers.

The revolutionary period produced a major crisis for Anglican ministers. In the early 1770s they petitioned for a resident bishop for institutional and ritual reasons, but patriots perceived a Tory plot. The Loyalist exodus decimated membership. The New England clergy (including Congregationalist converts) led the formation of the Protestant Episcopal Church in 1789. The consecration of the first bishops (Samuel Seabury by nonjuring Scottish bishops, William White and Samuel Provoost in England) revealed a high church/latitudinarian split of long duration among the clergy, but the church adopted a democratic style with elected bishops and strong vestries.

The church languished with too few ministers

and a Tory stigma until it was revitalized by the tension of evangelical and high church parties after 1811. Evangelical ministers favored extemporaneous prayer, quarterly celebration of a protestantized Lord's Supper, and strong preaching. Ministerial training centered at the Episcopal Seminary in Alexandria, Virginia (1823). The high church party founded General Theological Seminary in New York (1819). The church's march west failed to keep pace with revivalist denominations because of its formal worship and its inadequate recruitment for the new dioceses. In the late nineteenth century, ministers like William Augustus Mühlenberg of New York strove to be evangelical and catholic. He combined ornate liturgy with ministry to the poor, hoping to reduce the church's elitist reputation. But as ministers took up theological liberalism, their appeal remained strongest among the wealthy.

Episcopal priests loyal to a sacerdotal concept of their office were attacked by both secular rationalists and fundamentalists. "Nothing is so much opposed by what passes for 'the modern spirit' as that one thing which the Priesthood chiefly represents—Christianity as a supernatural force working through the Church continuously in history" (Abram Newkirk Littlejohn, *The Christian Ministry at the Close of the Nineteenth Century,* 1884, p. 27). With his church in numerical decline and priests as "religious functionaries" facing an identity crisis, Bishop George W. Barrett in 1969 argued for tradition:

> If worship is a valid occupation, if theology is a respectable discipline, if the Christian faith can be communicated through words and taught by disciplined educational methods, if pastoral care involves more than simple faith, common sense, compassion, and good will, then the professional, full-time ministry is not only valid but essential.
>
> (*Demands on Ministry Today,* p. 25)

More than two centuries after the frustrated Virginia parsons presented their cause, Barrett added, still "the priest confronts his impossible task, confronts it in faith, confronts it in awareness of God's mercy."

The Lutheran ministry for two centuries knew the dilemmas of Orthodoxy. Should the clergy protect ethnicity or help the church minister broadly in Anglo-America? Pastors were accustomed in Europe to state support, so like the Orthodox and Episcopalians—and New England Congregationalists—the transition to voluntarism altered their conception of the office. A lofty view of the pastor, inherited from Martin Luther, persisted. Luther first held a congregational and functional view of ordination and ministry, based on salvation by personal faith and the priesthood of the faithful. Preaching and teaching were delegated to those called and trained by the church itself. In the face of radical disorder, however, Luther saw the need for an order of ministry independent of congregational authority, derived from Christ, and controlled by the clergy.

Early colonial pastors (Swedish in Delaware, Dutch in New York) favored liturgical worship and presbyterial organization. William Christopher Berkenmeyer, who arrived in New York in 1725, recruited, examined, and licensed pastors to serve congregations over a vast area. The immigration of German Pietists to Pennsylvania created a leadership crisis; congregations petitioned for ministers from the University of Halle. After an unfortunate dispute over remuneration that revealed the strength of local ideas, Henry Melchior Mühlenberg committed himself to an American career (his foundation work was paralleled among the German Reformed by Michael Schlatter). He established distinctly Lutheran churches, weeding out followers of Count Nikolaus von Zinzendorf. Swedish and German pastors and lay delegates, who gathered to ordain a minister in 1748, fostered the Pennsylvania Ministerium. Churches formed a synod with Mühlenberg as overseer. He guided the church's ministry to embrace a formal liturgy with increasing use of English. As it evolved, "American Lutheranism" saw priestly authority in the congregation, with its public administration granted to the pastor.

Pennsylvania Ministerium pastors committed to the use of German blocked the trend to accommodate to American culture. They embraced Pietistism and revivalism, abandoned the high liturgy, cooperated with New Light German Reformed pastors, and proposed a seminary to stop the decay of evangelical faith. Samuel Schmucker led the consolidation of four synods into the General Synod of the Evangelical Lutheran Church, founded Gettysburg Seminary (1826), and (though an ecumenist) instituted a loyalty oath to Lutheran standards at ordination. Other pastors, especially 1840 to 1860 immigrants, insisted on Lutheranism's separate identity and formed new synods. As Wittenberg Seminary in Ohio trained "American Lutheran" pastors, Gettysburg and the Pennsylvania Ministerium's new seminary in Philadelphia upheld confessional standards. Tremendous German immigration in the late nineteenth and early twentieth centuries further complicated the situation. Branches included the Buffalo Synod, with an apostolic, sacerdotal concept of ordination and pastoral authority; the Wisconsin Synod, with authority passing to the clergy from the people; and the strictly confessional Missouri Synod. Lutherans formed Norwegian, Swedish, Danish, and Finnish synods, edging toward unity only in the twentieth century. Pressure to conform to biblical inerrancy at Missouri's Concordia Seminary in the 1970s led to an exodus of professors, pastors, and churches to form the Association of Evangelical Lutheran Churches. Women's ordination divided conservative and moderate Lutheran denominations in the second half of this century.

Lutheran clergy have been university trained, a tradition rooted in Luther's Wittenberg, with many through the last century educated in Europe. Seminaries established by factions ensured a learned pastorate and complicated negotiations among synods. A recent survey of Lutheran attitudes revealed that members sought firm personal faith in a pastor as one called by God. They revered the liturgy and expected a pastor to perform it well. Ironically, preaching rated lower in recognition of modern busy schedules. The ministry has two sides: the personal call from God and professional skill. Lutherans queried stated that "who a man *is*" matters more than "what a man *does*" (Milo L. Brekke et al., *Ten Faces of Ministry,* 1979).

The ministry of Reformed churches, heir of Zwingli, Calvin, and Puritanism, developed near the center of American society for three and a half centuries. Presbyterian, Reformed, and Congregational ministers were among the nation's religious leaders, a highly educated class, the first to consider themselves professionals. They founded institutions of higher learning and saw publication as part of their calling. Devoted to doctrine, they distinguished themselves from one another as often as they sought unity.

THE PROFESSIONAL MINISTRY

English Puritans in the 1600s expressed two simultaneous ideas of ministry. Local congregations chose and installed their own pastors, but God bestowed the clerical office. Presbyterians held that a minister received office when other clergy (presbyters) ordained him with laying on of hands. Although Congregationalists experimented with ordination by local laity, New England ordination (but not the call to serve) was soon a clerical affair. Anne Hutchinson and the Quakers challenged Massachusetts authority with a radical doctrine of free grace that rejected clergy and formal worship. Her banishment in 1638 signaled the clergy's consolidation of power through synods, control of entrance into the ministry, and the monitoring of congregational affairs. Orthodoxy upheld ministers as means of grace. The rise of ministerial associations and emphasis on favorable "terms of call" suggest that by 1700 something like professionalism had emerged. Congregationalists and middle-colony Presbyterians held similar views on the nature of the ministry by then. The 1801 Plan of Union made their ministries interchangeable and cooperative in the advance to the New York frontier and in foreign and home missions.

The Congregational ministers' social role from colonial days to 1850 changed "from office to profession." Weakened influence led them to promote revivals in the 1740s, but the Great Awakening only further diffused religious authority, and ministers shifted attention from status to local duties. Closeness to the people made possible a role in the American Revolution. The ministry remained a local "public office" through the eighteenth century; lifetime pastorates were the norm. After the Revolution partisan politics shattered the social order. Ministers worked for moral reform through nondenominational societies. Responding to the western call, regional and national agencies recruited candidates from evangelical colleges for standardized education in the new seminaries. Seminary training, and a career ladder of ever-larger congregations, professorships, editorships, or the bureaucracies of boards and agencies, created a national identity. The local pastor became a specialist in spiritual nurture, a professional whose identity and orientation derived from the profession itself, not from his role in a town.

With the "log colleges" of William Tennent and others and the College of New Jersey (1746),

Presbyterians committed themselves to an educated native clergy. Before Princeton (1812) and other seminaries, ministers attended a church-related academy and apprenticed with a minister. College and seminary had become the norm by the mid-nineteenth century. With such standards, Presbyterians were less prevalent on the frontier than Methodists and Baptists, and in the South they preferred urban churches. One accepted a call to Kentucky in 1783 only with "a written invitation . . . drawn up and signed by such only as were permanent settlers really desirous of constituting themselves into a church" (Sweet, vol. 2, p. 30). Presbyterian ministers started schools wherever they went—forty-nine colleges in twenty-one states by the Civil War. They held a high view of their status. A Presbyterian graduate of Congregationalist Andover Seminary and professor at South Carolina's Columbia Seminary wrote in 1844: "All the professions are advancing. We must at least advance with them, and if possible keep before them, or be despised" (Holifield, pp. 33–34).

Crises through the nineteenth and twentieth centuries forced ministers to modify further their self-understanding. Charles Grandison Finney's refashioned revivalism, the New School–Old School Presbyterian breach, and the antirevivalist Mercersburg movement in the German Reformed Church shattered the evangelical synthesis. Massive Roman Catholic immigration put Protestant ministers on the defensive. Identification of faith with northern or southern culture, the abandonment of revivalism, and the liberal transformation of Congregationalism put ministers at odds with one another. Henry Ward Beecher's genteel oratory created a new model for some, but Princeton-led Presbyterians reacted to liberalism by narrowing ministerial standards. Fundamentalist ministers withdrew to form new Presbyterian churches and seminaries. Reformed-tradition clergy competed not only as one profession among many in society, but with others within the profession. Facing numerical decline, they created new "united churches" by denominational mergers in the mid-twentieth century. Denominations ministered to their own ministers through career development programs and full-time regional executive ministers with counseling skills.

The Baptist ministry, seemingly indigenous to the South, stemmed from Puritanism. Experienced faith, the Reformed biblical plan of salvation, and separation from the world for new life bespeak the Baptist preacher's New England origins. Believer's baptism was the logical conclusion of the gathered church, Roger Williams pointed out. Dr. John Clarke, an English physician, assumed a thirty-year pastorate of the Particular Baptist Church in Newport, Rhode Island, in 1644. The congregation ordained his untrained successor, Obediah Holmes, on the basis of spiritual gifts and divine call. Harvard president Henry Dunster became a Baptist in 1653; Thomas Gould gathered a congregation in 1665, erecting a meetinghouse in Boston in 1680. Baptist influence spread to Connecticut in 1705 under the ministry of Valentine Wightman and his children. English Baptist ministers entered tolerant Pennsylvania. Elias Keach and Thomas Killingworth gathered numerous churches and organized the Philadelphia Association (1707), which in the 1750s sent missionaries to Virginia and North Carolina. The association promoted ministerial education by founding Hopewell Academy. One alumnus, James Manning, went on to the College of New Jersey and founded Brown University.

The Great Awakening was the decisive New England Baptist event. Isaac Backus is only the best-known New Light Congregationalist to take up the Separate Baptist standard. New Baptist churches sent zealous, freshly awakened preachers south. Shubal Stearns and his brother-in-law Daniel Marshall, 1745 George Whitefield converts, led with a church at Sandy Creek, North Carolina, that became the revival center. They set the pitch for southern and western preaching, according to Robert B. Semple in 1810:

> The *Separates* in N. England had acquired a very warm and pathetic address, accompanied by strong gestures and a singular tone of voice. Being often deeply affected themselves while preaching, correspondent affections were felt by their pious hearers, which were frequently expressed by tears, trembling, screams, shouts and acclamations. All these they brought with them into their new habitation. The people were greatly astonished having never seen things in this wise before. . . . From 16, *Sandy Creek Church* soon swelled to 606 members; so mightily grew the work of God!
>
> (*A History of the Rise and Progress of the Baptists in Virginia*, p. 4)

The "surprising elocution" of unordained Martha Stearns Marshall's "prayers and exhortations" often "melted a whole concourse into tears" (Semple, pp. 374–375).

Unlike Presbyterians who sought civil licenses, Baptists had no use for compromise. They formed an evangelical counterculture against the Anglican establishment. Neighbors gathered churches and simply "raised up" preachers. Anyone with a call, even slaves, could preach. Congregations licensed preachers and ordained after an evaluation period; preachers sought the regional association's favor. Biblical devotion and the structure of Reformed theology schooled them over time. Baptist preaching surged into the nineteenth century at the 1801 Cane Ridge Revival. The mobile farmer-preacher, promoting a religion of experience, ensured frontier success.

Professional education took root slowly. Baptists feared that formal training, even remuneration, would taint the ministry. Urban congregations, however, desired college-educated ministers. In the 1820s, Baptists began to found colleges and seminaries. Baptists in the North established Newton Theological Institution (1825) and Rochester Theological Seminary (1850). Southern Baptist Theological Seminary in South Carolina (1859; to Louisville in 1877) made professional training available among southerners after the church divided over slavery. Moral philosophy and rational exposition of Scripture taught by Baptists in the South differed little from that at other seminaries. With Presbyterians and Methodists, urban Baptist ministers wrote for publication and aspired to edit journals. Northern seminaries and clergy became open to biblical criticism, liberal theology, and the Social Gospel of Baptists Walter Rauschenbusch and Shailer Matthews. In this century Harry Emerson Fosdick was a leading light among pastors. Liberal clergy experienced opposition, with conservative secessions. The development of black pastors, meanwhile, was more bound up with race than polity.

Southern Baptists remained theological and social conservatives. Education never became an ordination requirement. Anti-intellectualism surfaced with Hard-Shell, Primitive, Landmark, and Fundamentalist movements. Experts at old-style evangelism, they expanded west and north. In 1955, 20 percent of ministers had only a high school education, but 62 percent had finished college and the denomination provided educational programs; of college graduates, most went on to seminary (Clifton J. Allen, ed., *Encyclopedia of Southern Baptists*, 1958, p. 859). By the 1980s most new ministers were graduates of college and one of five large seminaries. In the turbulent 1960s, Southern Baptists pursued work in a traditional manner. While 65 percent of young Methodist, Presbyterian, and United Church of Christ ministers agreed that "social service in nonchurch agencies may offer youth a better opportunity to render Christian service than the pastoral ministry," only 8 percent of young Southern Baptist Convention ministers agreed (Leiffer, p. 143). In the 1970s the convention initiated career guidance and counseling programs for ministers.

A book title encapsulates the history of Methodist ministry, *The Circuit Rider Dismounts.* The ordained minister of 1800 had a horse, Bible, Book of Discipline, and hymnal and preached at dozens of stations on a far-flung circuit. By 1900 he pastored an urban church and had a library in the parsonage and at least a college degree. Methodists were originally served by two ministries: ordained traveling ministers and local lay preachers. Some local preachers were ordained deacons, but only itinerants were elders and conference members. When itinerants settled in town churches, lay preachers abandoned their work. The language and accoutrements of itineracy persisted, with furnished parsonages provided and churches considered "stations." Apart from their appointment by the district superintendent and bishop, Methodist ministers were not distinct from Presbyterian or Baptist colleagues. John Wesley's vision—"all the world is my parish"—was domesticated.

In the 1760s Robert Strawbridge, a local preacher converted in Ulster by Wesley's itinerants, trained preachers in Maryland who later joined the organized itinerancy. Anglican-ordained preachers arrived to enjoy the Great Awakening's final phase. Wesley's denunciation of the American Revolution and the exodus of all preachers but superintendent Francis Asbury left Methodism in a shambles. The Southern Conference sought to ordain ministers to fill the void, despite Asbury's disapproval. The year 1784 marks the birth of a fully American Methodist ministry, originating not in local congregational authority but in the person of John Wesley. Wesley ordained two ministers and superintendent Thomas Coke "to go and serve the desolate sheep in America." Asbury gathered sixty preachers at the Baltimore Christmas Conference to establish the church as a hierarchy of superintendents (to Wesley's dismay, soon called bishops), elders, deacons, lay preachers, churches, and class meetings. By 1840 almost 4,000 ordained itinerants and over 7,700 local preachers ministered to a church of over 1 million members. The combination of itinerant and local preachers earned frontier success. Lay preachers not only kept the fire burning while itinerants were away, but often had laid it in the first place by gathering worshipers before a circuit rider appeared.

The connectional system bound itinerants to the denomination and also provided freedom to operate independently. A typical circuit in early-nineteenth-century western New York, Illinois, or Missouri was up to 500 miles, requiring fifty sermons in six weeks, plus class meetings and home visits. Asbury shifted preachers from circuit to circuit, usually every six months, though the general conference in 1804 approved two-year assignments. After the Civil War the tenure increased to three (North) or four (South) years. Short assignments were to avoid the settled ministry's shortcomings—popular disdain of "hireling" clergy, deference to the wealthy, diminished pulpit zeal, and narrowing of national vision. The system ensured a preacher for every congregation and station. When camp meetings achieved popularity, the Methodist Episcopal Church, with its army of itinerants, created a perpetually expanding revival. The Methodist preacher flourished as a frontier institution because he embraced camp meeting revivalism, including emotional displays, unreservedly.

The circuit system's difficulties became apparent, too. Constant travel was hard, and marriage usually resulted in location. By the 1840s bishops divided circuits into smaller units. Preachers taken with city life argued that the system was ill suited to upwardly mobile congregations. After the Civil War prestigious churches demanded a part in selecting pastors and protested reassignment, arguing that ministers, like college teachers or editors, were not to be moved. Methodists debated modifying the itineracy heatedly at conference and in the press. Modification proponents insisted they would just augment the bishops' authority to appoint without limitation. Traditionalists saw a fundamental change in the character of the ministry. Localized, if not "settled," ministry was an accomplished fact by 1900, due to the itineracy's success. The continent was settled and Methodist preachers had kept pace.

The ministers' educational level rose with that of their members. John Strange's eloquence came from a "Brush College, more ancient though less pretentious than Yale or Harvard or Princeton" (Sweet, *Circuit-Rider Days in Indiana*, 1916, p. 50), by which he meant apprenticeship on the circuit. No advocate of ignorance, Cartwright helped found three Methodist colleges and the University of Illinois. As the Methodist Episcopal Church, South, rebuilt after the Civil War, proponents of an educated clergy bucked popular opinion to establish a "Central University" with a theological seminary. Educator Landon Cabell Garland wrote, "It was never a sound policy to admit into the ministry men grossly ignorant, upon the plea that there were multitudes of ignorant people to be served." A bishop retorted: "The best preachers I ever heard had never been to college at all—hardly to school. . . . [E]very dollar invested in a theological school will be a damage to Methodism" (Hunter Dickinson Farish, *The Circuit Rider Dismounts*, 1938, pp. 264, 272–273). In 1873 the church moved ahead with financing by Cornelius Vanderbilt.

In 1944, with fewer ministers than in any year since 1900, the church undertook a recruitment program; by the 1950s seminaries were crowded. In the 1950s seminarians increased another 87 percent; by 1959, 82 percent of new elders had a degree. Methodist seminaries, even in the South, were open to biblical criticism and the Social Gospel. The ministry became more liberal than any save the Congregational, causing alienation between some pastors and congregations in the 1960s and 1970s. Churches were required to establish pastor-parish relations committees.

Two frontier movements, connected by a notion of "restorationism," illustrate America's democratizing influence on the role of the ministry. The "Christian" movement, which brought forth new denominations (notably the Disciples of Christ), and Joseph Smith's Church of Jesus Christ of Latter-day Saints (Mormons) both aimed to reestablish the primitive church. Both

groups outraged Baptists and Presbyterians by their use of the Bible. Both were anticlerical, convinced that churches were remnants of a corrupt Europe. Both claimed to have rediscovered God's plan of salvation. Both (in contrast to all Protestants) administered the Lord's Supper weekly. Both announced a millennium of unity and peace in America. The Disciples carefully limited the status and role of ministers; Mormons eliminated the professional ministry altogether, substituting a unique order of universal male lay priesthood.

Barton Stone, Presbyterian initiator of the Cane Ridge Revival, came to see that denominations were "traditions of men" and in 1804 claimed the name "Christian." Thomas and Alexander Campbell and other former Presbyterians formed the Disciples of Christ, incorporating the Stonites, in 1832. They denigrated the Old Testament and church tradition; the New Testament alone patterned Christian life. The church of Jesus must be restored in simplicity. Campbell condemned a clerical order set apart from (hence above) the laity and the perceived abuses of "hireling" clergy. Ordination was performed in a diminished Baptist style by the congregation. Titles ("reverend") were abandoned, and the minister's role was understood functionally. Campbell (with Reformed ministers) interpreted the scriptural orders of bishop, elder, and deacon as local offices. He came to accept the financial support of preachers, but maintained that ministers only did what God called every Christian to do. In many congregations, to demonstrate the priesthood of believers, lay elders officiated at the Lord's Supper. But preachers and editors—ordained ministers —spearheaded the denomination's expansion. They established seminaries where liberal theology, the ecumenical movement, and the Social Gospel elevated the ministers' awareness of their role in church and society. Conservatives separated to form the Churches of Christ early in the twentieth century.

The Disciples defended a professional concept of ministry:

> The Apostolic church established a constellation of offices or ministries which it laid upon persons it considered qualified to exercise them. Without derogating from the servanthood of the whole body, without implications of sacer-

1576

dotalism or hierarchy, that church regarded these persons as particularly deserving the title, "ministers" or "servants."

(Smith, pp. 80–81)

They even appealed to tradition; Campbell himself used the term "order of ministry."

Young Joseph Smith in central New York's "burned over district" in 1820 came to the conclusion, through a spectacular vision, that the churches were false. Like the Christian restorationists, he sought a fresh departure but differed by believing that the angel Moroni had given him a new revelation as prophet. His translation of the golden plates (1830) told of the lost tribes of Israel in America, an American visit by the risen Christ, and the promise of his restored church. Campbell bitterly attacked Smith, as some of his lieutenants converted to Mormonism. Undisputed leader of his growing but persecuted church, Smith augmented the Book of Mormon with revelations until his assassination in 1844 in Illinois. Brigham Young led the majority west to Utah to establish a theocratic society under a succession of prophets.

Mormonism was centralized in the office of the prophet, but everyday life in wards and congregations developed without clergy. All worthy male members were ordained to the priesthood. Youths were initiated as deacons and rose to become teachers and Aaronic priests; men were ordained to the offices of elder, seventy, and high priest in the Melchizedek priesthood. Men shared responsibility and authority in a highly sacerdotal religious life. The hierarchy appointed bishops from among high priests to oversee regional wards. The system expanded into new areas of ministry, education, and missionary and social work with great elasticity and high participation. Women, denied the priesthood, carried many responsibilities. A growing corps of professionals still work full-time for the church in Salt Lake City but are not considered a class of clergy.

The Holiness and Pentecostal traditions, emerging primarily out of late-nineteenth-century Methodism, were led by a grass roots ministry among marginal social groups. Female exhorters, such as Phoebe Palmer, played an important role at early Holiness camp meetings, expounding sanctification as a second blessing received in the experience of the baptism of the

Holy Spirit. Evangelists preached that believers could attain, by God's power, a state of perfection ("entire sanctification") in which the tendency to sin was eradicated. After the Civil War, Methodist ministers formed the National Camp Meeting Association for the Promotion of Holiness, with prayer meetings, publications, and educational work. Hundreds of evangelists, divinely called or self-appointed, led revivals, often with faith healing. When Methodist bishops condemned the movement in the North (1881) and South (1894), Phineas F. Bresee and other ministers of Holiness congregations formed groups that later organized as denominations. The Church of the Nazarene (1908) brought the ministry into a connectional system similar to Methodism. Until well into this century Holiness ministers held formal training in low esteem; no educational standard was ever set. The personal call from God to the preaching ministry was the prerequisite for ordination. Few were anti-intellectual (Nazarene colleges predate the denomination), but the establishment of a seminary (Kansas City, 1945) caused as much conflict as Vanderbilt had among southern Methodists. By the 1970s most young pastors had seminary training. This development could cause tension between a professionally minded pastor and a blue-collar congregation, but more generally it demonstrates the growth of the church.

Pentecostalism grew mainly out of the Holiness movement, but its evangelists understood the gift of the Holy Spirit as an endowment of power more than a change of heart. This "latter rain" (Joel 2:23), including speaking in tongues and faith healing, heralded the premillennial Second Coming of Christ. Participants felt that the miracle-filled life of the book of Acts was again possible, with speaking in tongues its normative mark.

In the Holiness revivals (1880–1900) evangelists like Mary B. Woodworth-Etter evoked extreme physical and emotional responses. Iowa preacher Benjamin Hardin Irwin in the mid-1890s taught a postsanctification "baptism of fire." Bishop Alma White's Pillar of Fire movement spread from Denver to Los Angeles. At the turn of the century many believers were waiting for a new outpouring of the Holy Spirit. It began with Charles F. Parham in Kansas, a licensed Methodist preacher who left the church disgusted at a salary raised by "suppers and worldly entertainment." He set out "on faith," typical of later Pentecostals, to found Bethel Bible School in Topeka. In 1900 Parham, evangelist Agnes N. Ozman, and others experienced speaking in tongues. A black Baptist preacher from Houston, William Joseph Seymour, heard of Parham from a black female evangelist and enrolled at his school. Parham dispatched Seymour to Los Angeles in 1906 with prayer and the laying on of hands. This commissioning shows that while Pentecostals emphasized a divine call, they held an organized and legitimized ministry.

Black churches barred Seymour, but he launched a mission on Azusa Street where the revival caught fire. Thousands attended the spontaneous, fervent services led by dozens of preachers. While some opposed formality, twelve elders organized Azusa into the "Apostolic Faith Gospel Mission." Of the three black elders, two were women, as were four of the nine whites. They published a periodical, issued ministerial credentials, and sent out evangelists with laying on of hands. Azusa participants included young Holiness ministers who flocked to Los Angeles to seek the experience or to correct Seymour's errors. Receiving the Spirit, they carried it to cities across America. Charles H. Mason transformed his Church of God in Christ and other southeastern black churches into Pentecostal churches. G. B. Cashwell, a Fire-Baptized Holiness Church preacher, won A. J. Tomlinson and the Church of God (Cleveland, Tennessee). Frank Bartleman's nationwide tour took Pentecostalism to the Christian and Missionary Alliance. In 1914 editor Eudorus N. Bell initiated the white Assemblies of God. Denominations were organized around some doctrinal point, usually on racial lines.

Patterns of professionalism emerged. Prominent preachers became Bible school administrators, denominational overseers, and magazine editors. But most itinerated, gathering small congregations and moving on. Few early congregations paid a full-time pastor, nor were salaries expected. Believers handed preachers envelopes privately. As evangelists fomented revivals—notably Aimee Semple McPherson, 1918 to 1921—churches institutionalized piety. Though only one early minister (Bell) was college educated, most studied at Bible schools. The ministry's rising educational level reflects these schools' upgrading; later, a seminary became available.

Churches exchanged the storefront and tent for large, increasingly impressive buildings. Many who had scorned the title "reverend" for "brother" or "sister" came to accept "pastor" and even "doctor." By the 1980s Pentecostals occupied a corner of American religion's middle ground. Ministers, with rising professional awareness, entered into fellowship with local colleagues.

The ministry of independent Fundamentalist and Bible churches—split from denominational churches or founded by forceful preachers—parallels the Pentecostals'. This ministry developed with a coherent biblical world view when John Nelson Darby's dispensational premillennialism was introduced to America in the 1870s. Darby's scheme influenced ministers from Pentecostal to Presbyterian, but took root at the Moody Bible Institute under Reuben A. Torrey, the mushrooming Bible colleges, and Dallas Theological Seminary. Cyrus Ingerson Scofield, who began the latter as a correspondence school, published his *Scofield Reference Bible* in 1909. Dispensationalist ministers saw the denominations as apostates under Antichrist, to be left behind at the rapture. They carefully guarded their own independence and that of their congregations. The personality and polished charisma of the preacher is at the center of the church. Jerry Falwell is the best known of the type, as he telecast his Lynchburg ministry nationwide and built a substantial college. At Thomas Road Baptist Church, by virtue of his pastoral office Falwell holds ecclesiastical authority as autocratic as that of a Roman Catholic bishop. While some independent church pastors serve under the governance of a lay board, others wield this power themselves. The successful Fundamentalist preacher is a builder of local institutions that focus the members' life on the church.

W. E. B. Du Bois described the black minister's role from slave days to our own: "The Preacher is the most unique personality developed by the Negro on American soil. A leader, a politician, an orator, a 'boss,' an intriguer, an idealist,—all these he is, and ever, too, the center of a group of men, now twenty, now a thousand in number" (*The Souls of Black Folk,* 1903, p. 190).

Slave religion, an amalgam of West African and southern evangelical elements, was a socioreligious means—free from white control—of personhood and hope. The preacher, heir of

African priesthood traditions, presided at fervent worship services. By the Great Awakening, Baptist revivalists influenced slave preachers, who were welcome at prayer meetings. George Liele and Andrew Bryan even institutionalized their Savannah following in 1788 as the first black Baptist church. White ministers encouraged black evangelism, but unsympathetic whites often persecuted the slaves' attempts to worship. Uprisings led by charismatic religious figures Denmark Vesey (1822) and Nat Turner (1831) turned slaveholders against evangelism and unsupervised services.

Blacks could preach at the "praise house" on the plantations of pious masters, but their role at secret nocturnal meetings was more important. The preacher developed a unique style echoing African rhythms and led the ecstatic "ring shout." The sermon built to a chanted crescendo and a spiritual. One preacher recalled how "my jaws became unlocked, and my tongue started to move so I could speak. I preached with no trouble, for I just said what the spirit directed me to say. This is why I don't prepare any sermons today. I just read the word and pray. God will do the rest." Converts expressed their response: "God struck me dead with his power" (Clifton H. Johnson, ed., *God Struck Me Dead*, 1969, pp. 23, 59).

In Philadelphia and New York free blacks organized religious societies, churches, and then denominations. Leaders like Richard Allen (a Methodist itinerant), Absalom Jones (a black Episcopal priest), and Peter Williams, Sr., became ministers with professional aspirations not unlike those of their white colleagues. Discrimination, which forced them from white churches, nevertheless required blacks to make their way independent from the white profession. Allen formed the first black Methodist church (Bethel in Philadelphia, 1794) and was ordained deacon by Bishop Francis Asbury. The new denominations, the African Methodist Episcopal Church (1816) and the African Methodist Episcopal Church Zion (1821), retained Methodism's tenets. They served broad social and educational functions; after the Civil War, African Methodist Episcopal missionary preachers moved south to organize churches and begin educational and humanitarian work.

Whether to require the ability to read the Discipline and the Bible before ordination agitated the church in 1843 before the standard was adopted. Daniel Alexander Payne, trained and ordained in a Lutheran seminary, led the education campaign. In 1850 the Baltimore church to which he was assigned turned him out; he had "too fine a carpet on [his] parlor floor, and [wouldn't] let them sing their cornfield ditties." Literate preachers going south found similar resistance from rustic African Methodist Episcopal blacks. Southern preachers feared the church would "gobble them up," reduce their ministerial standing, and eliminate "corn songs" and "ring shouts." The church did carry its requirements and decorum south. "We cannot expect the people to . . . reverence us unless we are able to repay them with that instruction and knowledge which our exalted position demands" (Walker, pp. 22, 75–77). Some blacks, such as Congregationalist Lemuel Haynes and Presbyterians James W. C. Plennington and Henry Highland Garnet, attained prominence in white churches.

After the Civil War, black churches proliferated, some separating from white denominations. Most blacks belonged to the Methodist and Baptist churches, though Holiness and Pentecostal preachers also commanded followings. The church was the major institution, the preacher the central figure, in segregated society. As churches were small and poor, many preachers worked weekdays. Barbering, for example, allowed daily contact with people. The preacher, the most respected of citizens, exercised a wide ministry of communications, social work, power brokering, legal and medical advice, and liaison work with the white community. The minister was better educated than most parishioners, but not professionally trained by white standards. Blacks who preferred "better educated" white lawyers and physicians rarely sought a white pastor. White preaching did not appeal to blacks. Parishioners referred with pride and affection to "my pastor," in a way they thought of no one else.

Black preachers were "self-reliant individualists," "self-made men," with personality, style, and money-raising ability as key ingredients of success (Hamilton, p. 200). The preacher presents himself as unique, distinct in some way from the many competitors. Eccentricity sometimes led to heterodoxy, as with Father Divine and Daddy Grace. Some embodied popular aspirations, for the poor "to identify with something larger, wealthier, more powerful, more articulate, and more flamboyant than themselves in order to obscure the poverty, insignificance, and powerlessness that dominate their lives" (Melvin D. Williams, *Community in a Black Pentecostal Church,* 1974, p. 51). Some accumulated authority and transferred it to the political arena, as did Adam Clayton Powell, Jr. Black ministers have also achieved national influence with sheer honesty and passion for justice, as did Martin Luther King, Jr.

Many black ministers gained professional competence without formal training. In the 1970s one in fifteen had attended seminary. Some denominations, and the many independent congregations, tolerated low ordination standards. According to Charles V. Hamilton, "Some recognize and believe that the ministry is a profession in the same sense as other professions, but the field itself has not insisted on it." With other professional opportunities recently available, ministerial status has declined somewhat. With black middle-class growth, large churches competed for educated ministers. Baptists joined the African Methodist Episcopal Church in perceiving professional training as a priority. Enrollment at black seminaries like Howard University and at integrated seminaries increased greatly in the 1950s. Theological education became more accessible with the civil rights movement. Black theology, political activity, and projects like the *Biographical Directory of Negro Ministers* (1965; 3rd ed., 1975) enhanced the ministry's self-awareness as a professional group. A Baptist wrote: "One ought to know Jesus intellectually as well as spiritually and emotionally. . . . We must take the best of our black culture, train it, polish it, learn to appreciate it, and then send it back into the black community to work for the empowerment of black people through the black church" (Hicks, p. 110).

The issue of women in the ministry is both current and historical. Religious orders have been noted. Early in this century sisters considered themselves "professional" at the same rate as teachers and nurses generally. Protestants and Catholics, however, shared a sense that women were assistants in ministry. Only recently are women rising in the ranks of denominations that ordain them, though most serve small churches or as low-salaried assistant pastors.

Several denominations developed a Protestant sisterhood of deaconesses in the 1850s, an idea imported from Europe by a Pittsburgh Lutheran pastor. Lutherans were not ordained but consecrated by laying on of hands, not paid but provided for. By 1889 twelve Lutheran deaconesses and twenty probationers, all but two of them immigrants, were at work. Episcopalians followed with deaconess institutions, beginning with St. Andrews Infirmary in Baltimore (1857), with women "designated to the work by prayer." The German Reformed Church opened a house in Hagerstown, Maryland, in 1866 with three women "ordained to the order of deaconess." The Methodist Episcopal Church began in 1885, establishing twelve houses in five years. Deaconesses did three kinds of work: hospital nursing, social work, and pastoral assistance. They received training at a "motherhouse" and were paid after the early years.

The movement imitated the Roman Catholic sisterhood, but Protestants spoke of reclaiming a biblical order. "Phoebe our sister, which is a servant [i.e., deaconess] of the church" (Romans 16:1) was the model in books and sermons and in the minds of the women. The Social Gospel inspired ministry to the poor, and women were called to work with children, indigent women, and the sick. The existence of many deaconess hospitals indicates their effectiveness. With the late-nineteenth-century rise in women's education and expectations, the office enabled women to serve, while allowing churches to avoid the ordination question. Deaconess organizations declined as other employment opportunities opened and the denominations that sponsored them began to ordain women.

Black women responded to God's call to preach. A woman known as Elizabeth, who itinerated for sixty years starting in 1799, answered a Virginia official's demand to know if she was licensed: "Not by the commission of men's hands: if the Lord has ordained me, I need nothing better." Richard Allen's preaching and an ecstatic experience awakened Jarena Lee to preach, but the conservative Allen denied permission. After a series of family tragedies she began preaching to black congregations; her ability won Allen's approbation. Unordained, she described herself as "the first female preacher of the African Methodist Episcopal Church." In the single year of 1827, she traveled 2,325 miles and preached 178 sermons. In this century charismatic black women have gathered their own congregations as well as serving denominational congregations.

The first woman ordained in a denomination was Antoinette L. Brown (Blackwell), locally ordained in a Congregational church in New York State in 1853, without ecclesiastical standing. Olympia Brown, ordained in the Universalist church in 1863, received her call while hearing Antoinette Brown at Antioch College. "It was the first time I had heard a woman preach, and the sense of the victory lifted me up. I felt as though the Kingdom of Heaven were at hand" (*Annual Journal of the Universalist Historical Society*, 1963, p. 24). In the second half of the twentieth century the United Church of Christ, American Lutheran, Methodist, Presbyterian, and Episcopal churches ordained women, though with turmoil and secessions in the last two. Holiness and Pentecostal but usually not other Fundamentalist churches have welcomed women preachers, though over time men predominated. Generally, churches emphasizing the Holy Spirit have recognized women; those tied to a literal reading of 1 Timothy 2:11 ("Let the woman learn in silence with all subjection") have denied women. Fifty-eight women had received ordination in Southern Baptist Convention churches by 1979, but few served churches, and at least one Kentucky association withdrew fellowship from a church for ordaining a woman.

In his classic essay "The Rise of the Evangelical Conception of the Ministry in America (1607–1850)" (in Niebuhr and Williams), Sidney E. Mead argued that a grand theme united the ministries of America's denominations. New World experience forced ministers to shift from static and hierarchical European clericalism to a democratic, practical, and charismatic model. His seminal study describes a general trend. But Mead overstated both European episcopal order and American democratic congregationalism (the latter, for example, by minimizing Methodist hierarchy). Ministers in some traditions became more sacerdotal and authoritarian in America over time. A fuller understanding of the development of the professional ministry in America would comprehend the ongoing tensions between formality and spontaneity, tradition and adaptation, learning and simple faith, hierarchical order and local exigency. Ministers in every tradition, in their own ways, defined their role in this dynamic context.

BIBLIOGRAPHY

Robert Mapes Anderson, *Vision of the Disinherited: The Making of American Pentecostalism* (1979); Leonard J. Arrington and Davis Bitton, *The Mormon Experience: A History of the Latter-day Saints* (1979); Joseph L. Blau, *Judaism in America: From Curiosity to Third Faith* (1976); Burton J. Bledstein, *The Culture of Professionalism: The Middle Class and the Development of Higher Education in America* (1976); William H. Brackney, ed., *Baptist Life and Thought: 1600–1980* (1983); John V. Butler and W. Norman Pittenger, *What is the Priesthood? A Book on Vocation* (1954); Richard R. Caemmerer and Erwin L. Lueker, *Church and Ministry in Transition* (1964); Daniel H. Calhoun, *Professional Lives in America: Structure and Aspiration, 1750–1850* (1965); Elinor Tong Dehey, *Religious Orders of Women in the United States: Accounts of Their Origins and of Their Most Important Institutions* (1913); Joseph H. Fichter, *Religion as an Occupation: A Study in the Sociology of Professions* (1961).

Harry G. Goodykoontz, *The Minister in the Reformed Tradition* (1963); David D. Hall, *The Faithful Shepherd: A History of the New England Ministry in the Seventeenth Century* (1972); Charles V. Hamilton, *The Black Preacher in America* (1972); Sara Harris, *The Sisters: The Changing World of the American Nun* (1970); James Hennesey, *American Catholics: A History of the Roman Catholic Community in the United States* (1981); H. Beecher Hicks, Jr., *Images of the Black Preacher* (1977); E. Brooks Holifield, *The Gentlemen Theologians: American Theology in Southern Culture, 1795–1860* (1978) and *A History of Pastoral Care in America: From Salvation to Self-Realization* (1983); Anne C. Loveland, *Southern Evangelicals and the Social Order, 1800–1860* (1980); Bert James Lowenberg and Ruth Bogin, eds., *Black Women in Nineteenth Century American Life* (1976).

Donald G. Mathews, *Religion in the Old South* (1977); Gerald O. McCulloh, ed., *The Ministry in the Methodist Heritage* (1960); Donna Merwick, *Boston Priests, 1848–1910: A Study of Social and Intellectual Change* (1973); Philip J. Murnion, *The Catholic Priest and the Changing Structure of Pastoral Ministry: New York, 1920–1970* (1978); H. Richard Niebuhr and Daniel D. Williams, eds., *The Ministry in Historical Perspectives* (1956; rev. 1983); Murray Polner, *Rabbi: The American Experience* (1977); Donald M. Scott, *From Office to Profession: The New England Ministry, 1750–1850* (1978); William Martin Smith, *Servants without Hire: Emerging Concepts of the Christian Ministry in the Campbell-Stone Movement* (1968); William Warren Sweet, *Religion on the American Frontier*, 4 vols. (1931–1946; repr. 1964); Constance J. Tarasar, ed., *Orthodox America: 1794–1976* (1975); Robert G. Torbet, *The Baptist Ministry: Then and Now* (1953); J. William T. Youngs, *God's Messengers: Religious Leadership in Colonial New England, 1700–1750* (1976); Clarence E. Walker, *A Rock in a Weary Land: The African Methodist Episcopal Church During the Civil War and Reconstruction* (1982).

[See also CALVINIST HERITAGE; CALVINIST THEOLOGICAL TRADITION; HISTORY OF PREACHING IN AMERICA; PASTORAL CARE AND COUNSELING; and WOMEN AND RELIGION.]

PASTORAL CARE AND COUNSELING

E. Brooks Holifield

THE changing styles of pastoral care and counseling in America have reflected a striking shift of emphasis in the mainline churches from a preoccupation with other-worldly salvation to a widespread interest in self-realization. And the "pastoral care movement" of the twentieth century, resting on foundations laid in an earlier era of revivalism and Pietism, helped to popularize a psychological vocabulary that has informed Protestant and Catholic reflection about preaching, religious education, and pastoral leadership, as well as private conversation between pastors and parishioners. Judaism, in its Reform and Conservative branches, has, to a lesser degree, absorbed much of the same ethos. The movement from salvation to self-realization illumines a complex history of changing relationships among theology, psychology, and institutional development in American religion and society.

The colonial clergy of the seventeenth century conceived of pastoral care, or "the cure of souls," as a method of diagnosing and treating sin and its effects and as a means of salvation. *Care* referred not simply to private counsel but also to public preaching, the administering of sacraments, the governance of congregations, and the cultivation of piety. But the religious traditions entertained diverse perceptions of sin and its cure. Roman Catholics, guided by the Catechism of the Council of Trent (1564), encouraged the enumerating of transgressions in the privacy of the confessional and the applying of sacramental remedies. Pietistic Lutherans thought of sin as faithlessness and practiced a method of "soul analysis," taught at the University of Halle, that interpreted feelings of despair as signs that the Word had begun to live within the faithless heart. The mainline clergy of the

Church of England learned, from such works as George Herbert's *Country Parson* (1652) and Gilbert Burnet's *Discourse of the Pastoral Care* (1692), that sin was a disruption of cosmic order that required the pastor to assume responsibility for every detail of life within the geographical parish. And the Reformed theologians in the tradition of John Calvin emphasized that sin was idolatrous disobedience, a misdirected consent of the will, that would yield only to divine grace and the probing of spiritual inwardness through introspective meditation.

The clergy learned their methods of pastoral counsel mainly by reading textbooks in "casuistry," or "case divinity," the application of general principles to particular "cases of conscience." The Catholic moral theologians of the sixteenth century, especially the Jesuits, elaborated a complex body of casuistry that promised to solve almost every spiritual dilemma that anyone could imagine. But the casuists who most influenced the early American tradition were such English Puritans as William Perkins, whose *Discourse of Conscience* appeared in 1596, and William Ames, whose *Conscience with the Power and Cases Thereof* (1643) remained in use at Yale College and other schools well into the eighteenth century.

The casuists described pastoral care with the aid of hierarchical images. The pastor's task was to understand and interpret the upper level of the hierarchy—the activity of God and the acts of supernatural beings. And pastors also worked with the assumption of a hierarchical psychology. The soul, like the cosmos, was a hierarchy; a person was a microcosm of the universe. The body participated in the world of material objects: the "vegetative soul," or ability to grow, marked each person's kinship with the world of plants; the "locomotive soul," or capacity to move, exhibited a point of commonality with the stars; the "sensitive soul," or capacity to perceive, think, remember, and feel, represented the proximity between human and animal life; and the "rational soul," or power of knowing, judging, and choosing, demonstrated the likeness between human beings and angels. A person was a hierarchy of powers, and each ascending stage integrated the lower stages into a higher unity. The highest was reason. And the pastor's task was to ensure that reason maintained its hegemony by using its two faculties of understanding and will.

Pastoral counseling, therefore, assumed the form of a straightforward appeal to logic and persuasive argumentation. The clerical casuists assumed that natural reason, aided by Scripture and divine grace, could unravel the mysteries of both divine and demonic activity. In New England, for example, the leading pastors constructed their pastoral methods with the aid of a logical system devised by the sixteenth-century logician Petrus Ramus (Pierre de La Ramée), whose analytical procedures taught them to reduce a pastoral concept, like "distress," into its two primary components, "fear" and "despair," and then to reduce each of those concepts to two more concrete terms, until finally producing a chain of logical dichotomies that could describe the various permutations of the distressed soul. Having used a logical method to diagnose the problem, the pastors then combined their findings with an appropriate biblical passage in a syllogistic form that could presumably convince the ailing parishioner that the pastoral insight was correct. Pastoral counseling consisted of questioning, logical analysis, and argumentation. And the pastor's exalted position in the social hierarchy accentuated the authority of the method. The casuists warned the pastor never to let the distressed soul question clerical wisdom; for unless the perplexed submitted themselves to wise counsel, they would remain uncomforted.

But what constituted wise counsel? By the eighteenth century the question divided the pastors. The "New Light" proponents of the religious revivals gave one answer; their "Old Light" rivals, another. The two groups disagreed about both psychology and theology. For the Old Lights the understanding was of higher value than the affections; they concluded that religious "rebirth" was a gradual process wherein God worked by rational persuasion. The New Lights believed that the affections were the deeper and more significant powers of the soul; they believed that rebirth therefore required a crisis that reached the depths of the nonrational self.

Both groups agreed that the pastor should "discern" the state of the distressed soul, but their psychological and theological differences led to conflicting proposals about pastoral discernment. The Old Lights decided that visible behavior was the only ground for pastoral evaluation. The New Lights preferred to probe beneath visible behavior to the hidden religious inclinations. The New Lights, moreover, thought that the most dangerous pastoral error was to offer premature comfort to persons under conviction of sin, thereby producing complacency at the wrong moment. The Old Lights replied that most of the souls who sought their advice needed comfort more than wary, cautionary silence or harsh judgments that could discourage the soul and cast it into despair.

The controversy produced the masterpiece of colonial writing on pastoral care when Jonathan Edwards defended the revivalist position in his *Treatise Concerning Religious Affections* (1746). Arguing that the affections were the springs of human actions, and that true rebirth produced a new "sense" for the beauty and excellency of divine things, Edwards provided a new form of casuistry to help pastors and others discern the hidden subtleties of true and false spirituality.

Similar debates divided other religious traditions. Orthodox Lutherans accused Lutheran Pietists of being too strict when they probed for feelings of despair. The Pietists charged that their critics remained on the surface when they limited their inquiries to matters of doctrine and behavior. Roman Catholic clergy chose between the positions of the rigorists, who imposed strict requirements for penance, and the laxists, who often saw confession itself as a sufficient medicinal cure for sin. Or they chose from among the doctrines of the "probabilists," who permitted Christians facing moral dilemmas to select the less demanding of two generally acceptable options; the "probabiliorists," who insisted that the stricter option must always be followed; and the "equiprobabilists," who tried to find a middle course.

Such issues persisted for decades, but by the early nineteenth century a transition in the American economy and social order began to produce a revised conception of pastoral care and counseling. The nation moved from a self-subsistence agricultural economy, organized in household industries, to a nascent industrial economy built on the factory. The change established more visible lines of division between town and country, for the new commerce required urban concentration, produced urban wealth, and exalted urban values. The townsfolk prided themselves on their culture and rationality and sought actively to distance themselves from the excesses of frontier religion. Hence they demanded a new style of ministry.

The change helped stimulate the emergence of a distinctive genre of theological literature—the textbook in "pastoral theology," which had already appeared in Europe and England. Even a sketchy listing of the most popular American texts locates their authors in an urban setting. In 1813 Ezra Styles Ely's anecdotal *Visits of Mercy* appeared while he was serving a fashionable Presbyterian church in Philadelphia. In 1827 Samuel Miller, a teacher at Princeton who had been a pastor in New York City, published his *Letters on Clerical Manners and Habits,* with instructions on proper decorum in pastoral conversation. The year 1842 saw the appearance of *Thirty-four Letters to a Son in the Ministry* by Heman Humphrey, a Presbyterian president of Amherst College. Two years later Enoch Pond, the editor of a Congregationalist journal, released his *Young Pastor's Guide; or, Lectures on Pastoral Duties.* In 1849 the Episcopal bishop of Virginia, William Meade, who lived in Richmond, published the *Lectures on the Pastoral Office* that he delivered to the seminary students in Alexandria. In 1850 Ichabod Spencer, a pastor in Brooklyn, published his famous *Pastor's Sketches,* of which 6,000 copies were soon in circulation in a nation with 27,000 pastors. The pastoral theologians in the urban seminaries soon began to publish their textbooks—like James Spencer Cannon's *Lectures on Pastoral Theology* (1853)—systematizing the lore and wisdom that was supposed to mark the educated pastor.

The course of study in early Protestant seminaries accentuated the growing importance of pastoral theology. The earliest teachers of the subject were usually church historians or systematic theologians. At Andover, founded in 1808, pastoral theology was part of church history. But by the time the Harvard Corporation formed its theological faculty in 1819, it seemed useful to plan for a separate chair of "Pulpit Eloquence and the Pastoral Theology," which came into being eleven years later. Other schools during the 1820s established chairs of pastoral theology and pulpit eloquence, designed mainly for instruction in preaching but including suggestions about the style and bearing of ministers in their more intimate relationships with individuals and small groups.

The handbooks and seminary courses advocated one overarching requirement: the physician of souls was to be a gentleman. They informed ministers how to visit families, how to conduct themselves decorously, how to temper their guidance to such disparate groups as refined ladies and ambitious young men, awakened sinners and the religiously indifferent. In accord with both religious tradition and the prevailing passion for Baconian induction, they taught pastors how to classify temperaments, spiritual states, and dispositions, and to outline the normal progression of inward religious experiences. And they urged the clergy to use such methods to appeal to the will through a balance of rationality and sentiment, argument and silence.

The emphasis on the will—on decision—reminds us that the pastoral manuals were not simply reactions to urban expectations. They were also the products of a revivalist piety that defined the principal work of the clergy as the "conversion of souls" and the reflections of a new devotionalism that had altered the organization of the churches during the Second Great Awakening. The revival brought increasing numbers of people together in small groups. The manuals taught the clergy how to conduct group sessions marked by free conversation and public confession, the expression of feelings as well as ideas, and a high valuation of self-criticism and mutual sharing.

The manuals almost created a Protestant consensus, except for the intense debates between high church pastors, who wanted to restore the Catholic practice of confession, and low church clergy, who did not. In the Episcopal church a burgeoning high church party began, early in the nineteenth century, to call for mandatory private auricular confession as the primary agency of pastoral care. A while later, high church Lutherans advocated a similar practice, and by the end of the antebellum era Lutheran immigrants were entangled in conflicts over confession and clerical absolution. Roman Catholics, in the meantime, were defending the confessional against ludicrous attacks by the Protestant Know-Nothing movement, which viewed the confessional booth as a place of sedition and seduction. Despite such attacks, the confessional served as the center of Catholic pastoral care, with most priests following the authority of the eighteenth-century Italian bishop Alphonsus de Ligouri, whose *Theologia moralis* (1748) and other writings offered pronouncements on over 4,000 pastoral questions, popularizing an equiprobabilist strategy within the American Catholic church.

The theoreticians of Protestant pastoral counsel drew on two intellectual movements. First, the educated clergy of all denominations assumed the truth of a "rational orthodox" theology according to which reasonable argumentation could not only demonstrate a host of "natural" theological conclusions about God and the soul but also prove the biblical revelation to be the unique Word of God. Second, the clergy appealed to the new texts in "mental philosophy" that outlined the differences among the will, the understanding, and the affections, and proceeded to define the minute shadings that distinguished sensations and perceptions; or emotions, desires, and volitions; or feelings of revenge, envy, and jealousy; or dispositions of pride, conceit, vanity, and haughtiness; or moods of penitence, discontent, sadness, mournfulness, and grief; or scores of other inner states.

Most authors of the mental philosophy textbooks were clerical disciples of the Scottish philosophers Thomas Reid and Dugald Stewart, and the clergy used their methods of introspective analysis to clarify the inner workings of the mind, the stages of grief, and the levels of spiritual growth. Such texts as the *Elements of Intellectual Philosophy* (1826), written by the Congregationalist minister Thomas Upham, or *Psychology* (1840), published by Frederick Rauch of Mercersburg Theological Seminary, affirmed the harmonious balancing of the will, the understanding, and the affections as an ideal of spiritual health. They assumed that such a balance usually resulted from some combination of divine grace and human decision. That assumption, and the mental philosophy underlying it, suggested a pastoral strategy: to convince the intellect, appeal to the affections, and persuade the will, thereby producing assent to the truth, while remaining within the boundaries of clerical gentility. Pastoral care was genteel argumentation.

After the Civil War, the vocabulary and methods of pastoral care rapidly changed, largely in accord with some momentous transitions in American culture. The war itself subverted much of the older sentimentalism; the shift of interest in the natural sciences from geology to biology brought into focus the untamed vitality of physical nature; the growing visibility of technology evoked a sensitivity to power and energy; the barons of capitalism provided an ideal of masculine power; and popular culture spawned a veritable cult of virility that worshiped boxers and football players, applauded philosophers who spoke of the "strenuous mood," and elected politicians who extolled the "strenuous life." One result of those trends was the growing popularity of "muscular Christianity," an insistence that faith required the heroic and masculine virtues.

In such a setting, some ministers lost interest in pastoral counsel, which they associated with decorous visits in Victorian parlors. To them pastoral care of the antebellum variety seemed threateningly "effeminate" and unmanly. But a new generation of pastoral writers assured the clergy that pastoral counsel could be effective and manly if only it were more "natural." In 1877 the Presbyterian Thomas Murphy published his *Pastoral Theology;* G. B. Willcox of Chicago Theological Seminary followed suit in 1890 with *The Pastor Amidst His Flock;* Washington Gladden wrote *The Christian Pastor* in 1898; and these popular texts had dozens of imitators, most of them praising the "muscular minister" who could organize effective groups as well as inspire dispirited souls through lively conversations.

By *natural* the postwar pastoral theologians initially meant little more than the cultivation of a manly, cheerful, informal, and therefore persuasive bearing. They advised ministers to be merry and winsome and to avoid suggestions of the morbid, even when visiting the sick and dying. They urged them to discard pomposity and unnecessary reserve; a hearty informality seemed more effective. The goal was still the same, namely, to move the will, but the style would be different.

The rhetoric of naturalness, cheer, and informality appeared even in the continuing arguments about penitential confession in the sacramental churches. The Roman Catholic bishop of Richmond, James Gibbons, insisted that a few moments in the confessional could elevate men and women from shame and confusion to quickness of step, joy of countenance, and brightness of eye. It could restore spiritual vitality. The Episcopalians were not so sure about that. The evangelicals among them complained that the confessional seemed to be a morbid instrument for lackadaisical men and "silly women," but the high church party insisted that private confession allowed ministers to deal with sins as physicians dealt with diseases. Underlying both assertions was a set of similar presuppositions about what was natural.

By the late nineteenth century, though, a psychological accent on subconscious vitalities and a theological emphasis on divine immanence complicated the simple association of naturalness with forceful informality.

When the clergy drew on the new psychology of such men as William James, Hugo Münsterberg, and Granville Stanley Hall, they preferred initially the "functionalist" emphasis on adaptation, action, habit, and will. It confirmed their conviction that the secret of character was self-mastery and self-control. The new psychologists were also the children of the masculine era. But soon they suggested, often reluctantly, that proponents of the natural should take into greater account the place of receptivity and surrender in the growth of the self. James insisted that an unremitting emphasis on the active powers led to a one-sided conception of the self. While continuing to accent the power of the will, he also called for repose and a toning down of moral and bodily tensions, and by 1890 he was becoming increasingly interested in the notion of a "subliminal self," a source of energy to which the conscious self could surrender and thereby achieve a deeper inner unity. That insight would appear repeatedly in early-twentieth-century efforts to reevaluate pastoral conversation.

The reevaluation drew also on the emerging traditions of psychotherapy within American medicine. Ever since the 1880s medical neurologists had assumed responsibility for healing maladies of the soul, but they found it difficult to transcend traditional antagonisms between the proponents of "rest cures" and those of "work cures" until such Europeans as Pierre Dubois, Pierre Janet, A. A. Liebault, and Sigmund Freud began to convince them of the plausibility of a "scientific mind cure" that could probe the hidden psychological sources of mental disorders. The Protestant churches were among the first American institutions to affirm the new psychotherapies. Freud's translator and interpreter in America, A. A. Brill, found himself in demand for lectures not only in the soirées of Greenwich Village but also in fashionable Episcopal churches in Boston.

Such ideas about subconscious and unconscious vitalities subverted, for only a few ministers at first, the old confidence in the rational dialectics of manly counsel. Nature itself seemed to demand surrender as well as assertion. The new notions found a hearing, first, among liberal theologians who were convinced that God was immanent in natural development. And the liberal preoccupation with religious experience helped spawn the "psychology of religion" as a potent, though transient, movement in the colleges and seminaries. Such psychologists of religion as Granville Stanley Hall, Edwin Starbuck, and James Leuba turned their attention first to the experience of conversion, interpreting it as a natural occurrence that usually accompanied the physical and emotional changes of adolescence. They eventually began to offer advice to the clergy, suggesting that they learn to identify the stages of natural religious growth (and hence refuse to press for premature religious decision) and to recognize the importance of self-surrender in religious experience. William James's *Varieties of Religious Experience* (1902) synthesized their findings into a complex of images and insights that would influence pastoral care for decades. His conclusion that men and women were in touch with a "wider self," through which they could be transformed, contained the seeds of a therapeutic enterprise.

The first serious efforts to transform the cure of souls in the light of such changes began in 1905 among some Episcopalians at the Emmanuel Church in Boston. Their Emmanuel movement attracted support and emulation in all the mainline Protestant denominations. By 1908 the movement had its own journal, *Psychotherapy,* which carried articles by theologians, psychologists, neurologists, and Freudian psychoanalysts. The founders, Elwood Worcester, the rector of Emmanuel, and his associate, Samuel McComb, believed that every minister practiced "psychotherapy," whether intending it or not, and they wanted clerical therapy to be guided by scientific wisdom.

Working with the neurologists Richard Cabot and James Jackson Putnam, the Emmanuel clergy conducted diagnostic sessions at the church, referring some cases to physicians, others to ministers, holding group sessions for therapeutic purposes, and proposing new methods of counseling. The central idea of the movement was that the "law" of effort and the "gospel" of relaxation belonged together. Relaxation was the prelude to self-control; a symbolic moral holiday served, as James had discovered, to reinvigorate the moral will. Hence Worcester and McComb taught ministers to interpret counseling as a process that began with techniques of relaxation, offered healing suggestions to the unconscious, and only then moved toward rational consciousness. The movement continued into the 1920s, though it soon lost the allegiance of the physicians and attracted the scorn of ministers. Yet it helped introduce the new psychology into the church at a time when it was barely understood within the hospital.

World War I introduced the masses to the mysteries of psychological testing, and the reaction against the war, and the society that had gone to war, transformed psychologists and psychoanalysts into symbols of cultural freedom. By the 1920s American journalists were writing of a "psychological revival" in the culture. But it was the "mental hygiene movement," founded in 1903 by a young businessman named Clifford Beers, that provided the main entrance for clergy into the new psychological ethos. Its theme of "adjustment"—to other persons, to society, and to "the whole of things"—coincided with a growing interest in the metaphor of adjustment among philosophers and liberal theologians.

John Dewey defined the meaning of adjustment for the pastoral care writers; his *Democracy and Education* (1916) might be described as a hidden classic of the pastoral care movement. He derived his idea of adjustment from Darwinism and functional psychology, and also from his assumptions that the achievement of selfhood was a "process" and that the self's greatest good was "growth." Such ideas found initial expression in the churches within the religious education movement, through its patriarch George Albert Coe, who in 1909 had become the professor of religious education at Union Theological Seminary in New York. Coe argued that religious education, by helping adjust the race to its divine environment, promoted self-realization. He pressed, therefore, for a functional interpretation of religious experience as a means of unifying the personality.

Long before there were chairs of pastoral counseling in the Protestant seminaries, religious educators taught the subject. At Union Theological Seminary in New York, for example, Harrison Elliott offered instruction as early as 1921, numbering among his students one Carl Rogers, who would become a dominant influence on the later pastoral counseling movement. To the religious educators, counseling offered a means of personality adjustment, and though they taught their students the ideas of Freud and the post-Freudian revisionists, they filtered those ideas through the lenses of an educational psychology that emphasized the plasticity of human nature and the possibilities of intelligent self-direction.

The idea of adjustment made sense in the liberal seminaries because it had permeated liberal theology so thoroughly. Such theologians as Douglas Clyde Macintosh at Yale and Henry Nelson Wieman at the University of Chicago made the notion of adjustment the bedrock of theological method. Macintosh believed that "right religious adjustment" could reveal the nature of the divine reality; Wieman defined God as the "character of events" to which men and women needed to adjust in order to avoid the loss and fragmentation of their selfhood.

The metaphor of adjustment therefore guided the pastoral theologians who published texts on the cure of souls during the early 1930s. In *The Cure of Souls: A Socio-Psychological Approach* (1932) Charles Holman of the University of Chicago urged the religious counselor to promote adjustment by encouraging devotion to noble causes and values, providing assurance of cosmic support in the struggle, and bringing people into the rich social environment of the Christian community. When Karl Stolz of the Hartford School of Religious Education published his *Pastoral Psychology* (1932), he explained that human life was a sequence of adjustments and that it was the pastor's responsibility to create in maladjusted persons the will and ability to reorganize themselves.

The publication of John Sutherland Bonnell's *Pastoral Psychiatry* in 1938 popularized the principles of the academic pastoral theologians. A Presbyterian minister in New York, Bonnell combined the ideas of the Viennese analyst Alfred Adler and those of the American psychological traditions in an argument that the goal of pastoral counseling was to bring about right adjustment to other persons and to God. By the late 1930s growing numbers of the liberal Protestant clergy were ready to listen to such arguments, partly because the celebrated preacher at Riverside Church in New York City, Harry Emerson Fosdick, had persuaded them to devote more of their time to pastoral counseling, even to refashion the sermon in the image of the counseling session.

By the 1930s, though, the notion of adjustment became subject to criticism among the clergy, particularly those who assumed the leadership in a program of professional training known eventually as clinical pastoral education —a long-term supervised encounter with men and women in crisis in hospitals, prisons, and social agencies. In 1925 Richard Cabot, a professor of medicine and of ethics at Harvard, published a "Plea for a Clinical Year in the Course of Theological Study." In the same year, the liberal clergyman Anton Boisen began, with Cabot's support, to train a handful of students at Worcester State Hospital. In 1930 Cabot and Boisen joined with others in the formation of the Council for the Clinical Training of Theological Students. They did not set out to train counselors; their intention was to reform the profession of ministry and the discipline of theology. Yet one important consequence of their movement was a shift in the understanding of pastoral care.

By 1932 the clinical educators divided into two mutually antagonistic groups, one with its headquarters in Boston, the other with its main offices in New York. Cabot mediated for a while, but he was soon ousted from the presidency of the New York council, whereupon the men and women who worked alongside him in Boston formed their own organization, the New England Theological Schools Committee on Clinical Training. The split resulted partly from personality conflicts, but the two groups also held differing views of clinical training and different ethical ideals: one accented the ideal of ethical formation, the other exalted freedom and autonomy. Underlying those disputes were deeper disagreements about human nature.

The Boston tradition initially tended to think that Cabot was correct when he insisted that "growth"—growth in such powers as sympathy, courage, honesty, tenacity, and knowledge—was the ethical absolute, and they therefore emphasized the goal of moral and spiritual "formation" in clinical training. Such clinical leaders as Austin Philip Guiles in Boston viewed clinical supervision as a disciplining that would produce competence, and his colleague Rollin Fairbanks of the Episcopal Theological School insisted that clinicians should make—and teach students to make—explicit moral judgments about imperative duties.

Underlying those assertions was an understanding of human nature that had some of its roots in the writings of Richard Cabot, who viewed ethical growth with the aid of biological imagery and with the assumption of purposeful order within the self. He hoped that clinical training would teach students to listen to "unspoken words" and thereby discern the "growing edge" of the self. Cabot derived the notion of a growing edge from physiology. The self was like a piece of human tissue, putting out new cells as it grew. Implicit in his depiction of growth was a vocabulary that defined the self with metaphors of purpose, rationality, order, effort, will, freedom, and cumulative experience.

In 1936 Cabot and Russell L. Dicks, a chaplain at the Massachusetts General Hospital, published a book that helped to change the understanding of pastoral care in American Protestantism: *The Art of Ministering to the Sick*. The book used Cabot's imagery of growth, assigning the minister the responsibility for finding and cultivating the growing edge of the ill person, largely through "good listening." Defining God as the power in ourselves that makes for health, they thought that ministers could enter the sickroom confident in a purposive force within each person. The pastor's task was to nurture an atmosphere in which healing growth could best occur.

The New York tradition derived its dominant metaphors initially from the liberal pastor Anton Boisen, who had begun his clinical work with the intention of studying "living human documents" as a means of understanding religious experience. A tortured soul who twice felt compelled to hospitalize himself, Boisen published in 1936 his *Exploration of the Inner World,* which advanced the notion that emotional collapse was a chaotic encounter with God which could lead either to a new integration of the personality or to a fall into total inner disarray. Schizophrenic torment offered a clearer insight into the personality than did biological growth in tissues and cells. Boisen found Freud useful but shortsighted. Boisen's heirs felt more at home with the depth psychologies. Implicit in their outlook, therefore, was an ethical and theological vision that defined the self with metaphors of struggle, conflict, impulse, nonrational feeling, and inner chaos.

The leader of the movement in New York was a psychiatrist, Helen Flanders Dunbar, who had worked with Boisen at Worcester State Hospital and had studied psychoanalysis in both Vienna and Zurich. Dunbar shared Boisen's hopes that the tortured symbolic visions of mental patients might provide a deeper understanding of both religion and the self, although she supplemented Boisen's ideas with psychoanalytic notions that distressed him.

It soon became clear that the New York tradition not only emphasized, in Freudian fashion, inner discord, but also shared a common ethical goal of freeing students and parishioners from a harsh moralism and authoritarianism. Their emphasis on "understanding" connoted tolerance, an acceptance of feelings, of the body, the senses, and sexuality, and an opposition to rigidity and condemnation. "Understanding" implied a willingness to sympathize with people rather than to idolize conventions and rules.

An interest in freedom was by no means absent from the New England tradition, and the New Yorkers also had some concerns about moral formation, but the differences in emphasis were pronounced, and not until 1967 did the two traditions form a united Association for Clinical Pastoral Education. Long before then, however, it was clear that the notion of "adjustment" no

longer commanded much attention. The acceptance of psychoanalytic teaching by both the Boston and New York traditions suggested an alternative metaphor for pastoral care and counseling: namely, "insight."

The notion of insight had proponents outside the clinical traditions, as well. During the early 1930s the "realist" theologians—H. R. Niebuhr, Reinhold Niebuhr, Paul Tillich, and others— thoroughly criticized the theological idea of adjustment. It took only a few years for theological realism to shape a new perspective on the cure of souls. In 1939 Rollo May, a young pastor who had studied both at Union Theological Seminary in New York and at Alfred Adler's Vienna clinic, published *The Art of Counseling,* a book consisting of lectures originally delivered to pastors' schools in Arkansas and North Carolina. May taught the pastors that human life was marked by an unending conflict between freedom and limits, and that the counselor was to help people maintain a healthy tension between their freedom and the demands of reality. The purpose of counseling was to offer interpretations that would provide understanding and insight, which were attained when the ego surrendered its pretensions and learned to trust the "structure" of reality.

World War II and the postwar economy helped to ensure that the ideal of insight would deeply influence pastoral care and counseling. The chaplains who marched with the soldiers discovered their failings as counselors and flocked into seminars on pastoral care throughout the war. A commission on ministry of the New York Academy of Sciences concluded during the 1950s that the experiences of the chaplains had helped to make pastoral counseling a "special part" of ministry in postwar America. The prosperity stimulated by the war then opened a new world of opportunity for ministers who sought self-improvement—precisely at the time that "insight" attracted the attention of the pastoral theologians. And the war also produced the greatest upsurge of interest in psychology in the nation's history. After 1945 psychological themes began to permeate American writing, films, education, business, and religion. By 1957 *Life* magazine could announce that "this is the age of psychology."

The movement to improve pastoral care became a veritable crusade. In 1939 few theological schools had even bothered to offer counseling courses that would introduce students to the latest psychological theories. By the 1950s almost all of them did, over 80 percent offered additional courses in psychology, and 80 percent could list at least one psychologist on their faculties. They could do so, for one reason: large foundations and the government provided direct and indirect financial help. And clinical educators refused to lag behind the seminaries. By the end of the 1950s they had established 117 regular centers for clinical pastoral education, formed alliances with more than 40 theological schools to offer clinical work, and cemented ties to such medical centers as the Washington School of Psychiatry and the William Alanson White Institute in New York.

The seminary courses and clinical centers were not able to meet the demand for training in pastoral care, and by the mid-1950s at least thirty-five institutes and seminars—such as Reuel Howe's Institute for Advanced Pastoral Studies near Detroit and Thomas Klink's Program in Religion and Psychiatry at the Menninger Clinic in Topeka, Kansas—met regularly to propagate the new methods. By 1956 the National Council of Churches established a Department of Pastoral Services; a broad grouping of religious leaders and psychiatrists founded the National Academy of Religion and Mental Health; and some ministers began to form centers for pastoral counseling outside the parishes. By 1960 there were at least eighty-four Protestant counseling centers staffed by ministers, psychiatrists, and social workers that promoted counseling on a large scale.

Pastoral writers produced a flood of books, articles, and journals. In 1947 the clinical educators founded a *Journal of Pastoral Care* and a *Journal of Clinical Pastoral Work,* and by 1950 a larger readership seemed ready for the periodical *Pastoral Psychology,* which attracted 16,000 subscribers, of whom about 14,000 were pastors. There were claims that pastoral theologians in the 1950s were publishing more in one month than they had published in a year during the 1930s.

Roman Catholics remained cautious until after World War I, and conservatives like Bishop Fulton J. Sheen criticized modern psychology, but in 1953 Pope Pius XII gave the church's approval to psychoanalysis and other forms of psychotherapy, and by 1957 more than one hundred priests belonged to an American Catholic Psychological Association. Such writers as Charles Curran and Gregory Zilboorg interpreted traditional Catholic notions of the cure of souls in the light of modern psychotherapy. By the end of the 1950s such Catholic schools as Fordham, Woodstock, St. John's, and Loyola offered training in "pastoral psychology." And in 1955 the Jewish Theological Seminary in New York inaugurated courses taught by psychiatrists to acquaint future rabbis with psychotherapeutic methods.

But the "pastoral care movement" remained largely a Protestant enterprise, reflecting postwar affluence and the "white collar" economy that sustained the prosperity. By 1956 white-collar occupations engaged more than half the working population. As a result, growing numbers of workers discovered that their economic success and social standing required skills in working with other people. Such an economy intensified popular interest in psychology, but also created among intellectuals an unease with the conformity supposedly imposed by a bureaucratic "mass culture." The writers who influenced pastoral care tended to envision self-realization as a process that stood in tension with both social conventions and the mass social structures of the society. Only in the light of two modern intellectual movements—the theological revolt against moralism and the sociological critique of mass culture—can one understand the appeal of the postwar counseling methods.

The revolt against moralism began before the war, both European and American theologians insisting that the content of Christian ethics must vary with varying circumstances lest the Christian become entrapped within an idolatrous legalism. It became a truism among many religious ethicists that the command of God was a call for free obedience that might well require the flouting of conventional ethical assumptions. The critique of mass society—mediated to the pastoral writers through the work of such social critics as Erich Fromm, Karen Horney, David Riesman, and William Whyte—proclaimed the message that the "bureaucratic" institutions of the postwar capitalist society had imposed coercive and alien expectations. It was no surprise that the pastoral theologians began during the 1950s to emphasize the tension between the current social order and the mental health of the people who lived in it.

Such an intellectual environment helps to explain the influence of the psychologist Carl Rogers on the first generation of postwar pastoral writers. Rogers believed that the human organism was marked by an inherent tendency toward actualization as a social and sociable person, but that the inner wisdom of the organism stood in tension with internalized patterns of interpretation imposed by other persons and social institutions. Authorities imposed rigid expectations that led to distorted self-perceptions and thus undermined self-acceptance. A counselor, by adopting an empathetic, nonjudgmental attitude of "positive regard," and trying simply to reflect and articulate the feelings of the client, could support the personality's innate forward movement and assist persons to accept themselves. Such a depiction of counseling seemed a useful counterweight to the glib advice and moralizing that often marked counseling in the institutional church. And it appeared to coincide with the theological criticism of legalism.

Four pastoral theologians assumed a position of intellectual leadership. Seward Hiltner, a Presbyterian minister teaching at the University of Chicago, drew on social and cultural anthropology in preparing his *Pastoral Counseling* (1949). Carroll A. Wise, a professor of pastoral psychology and counseling at the Methodists' Garrett Biblical Institute, based his *Pastoral Counseling: Its Theory and Practice* (1951) on theological personalism, dynamic psychology, and Rogerian theories of counseling. In *The Christian Pastor* (1951) Wayne Oates, a professor at Southern Baptist Theological Seminary, attempted to combine traditional Protestant language with a theory of psychosocial role behavior taken from the social sciences. And Paul Johnson, a Methodist professor of psychology at Boston University, drew on Rogerian methods, interpersonal psychology, and personalist theology for his *Psychology of Pastoral Care* (1953). All four, but especially Oates, had some reservations about Rogerian methods, and Hiltner developed an independent "eductive" approach that took into account the "precounseling" relationships between pastors and parishioners in congregations. But all four writers also propagated a Rogerian style to a generation of seminary instructors and pastors. One reason for its popularity, in fact, was that it could be taught within the crowded seminary curriculum; it offered a

relatively safe method for a counselor of limited training.

By the 1960s, though, the culture seemed awash in therapeutic possibilities. Exotic techniques that had once been known only to a few initiates became the objects of entertaining distraction in popular journalism. Disillusioned by the Vietnam War, racial tensions, and political ineptitude, many of the young, especially, began a search for new ways to "fulfill" themselves. In such an atmosphere, some pastoral writers had second thoughts. Partly troubled by the excesses of the new therapies, partly intrigued by the new methods, they searched for alternatives to Rogerian techniques. Some, to be sure, turned to the new "humanistic psychologies" that, by accenting the potentiality for growth, continued the older Rogerian themes. But others began to emphasize the "context" in which counseling occurred, and they decided that Rogerian methods could not entirely suffice for work within the churches and pastoral counseling centers.

They gave increasing attention, first, to the interpersonal context of pastoral care. The social psychology of the neo-Freudians attracted their attention, and they found guidance in the writings of Harry Stack Sullivan, whose book *The Psychiatric Interview* (1954) encouraged active intervention on the part of the counselor. One result of the interest in the interpersonal was a proliferation of small-group activity in the churches. As early as 1950 two brothers, Clinton and Clifton Kew—one an Episcopal rector, the other a psychologist—were advertising the possibilities of group therapy in church settings. But an equally important impetus came from the experiments in group dynamics that had grown out of Kurt Lewin's research at the National Training Laboratories in Bethel, Maine, where training groups (T-groups) were founded to study institutional change and interpersonal relationships. Small groups seemed to offer healing, community, and intense emotional experience, much in the fashion of an older Pietism.

The move toward interpersonal psychologies coincided with an interest in developmental stages of growth. As early as 1951 Lewis J. Sherrill at Union Seminary in New York was defining growth as a series of transitions through specifiable stages, but not until the pastoral theologians had time to assimilate the work of such developmental theorists as Robert Havighurst, Arnold Gesell, and especially Erik Erikson did they begin to ponder seriously the implications of "life stages" for understanding both human growth and pastoral counseling. In the late 1950s Oates, Hiltner, and others were emphasizing that development proceeded by means of painful inner conflicts. Other pastoral writers, such as Howard Clinebell and Paul Johnson, drew on the humanistic psychologies to argue that development was not so much a series of crises as an unfolding of inner potential. By the 1970s a few had turned to a slightly different developmental issue. Appropriating insights from recent studies in moral development, such scholars as James Fowler tried to describe the phases of "faith development," from literal and exclusive dogmatic belief to a trust and care that was universal in reach and vision.

The pastoral writers who were seriously interested in theology turned their attention also to contextual themes. They spoke of the need to locate interpersonal psychology within a "larger context," or an "ultimate context," and hence, in traditional language, to discover the meaning of God for pastoral counseling. As early as 1940 they began meeting in such groups as the New York Psychology Group, the Columbia University Seminar on Religion and Health, and the psychiatric institutes of the White Foundation. By 1950 a few theologians were ready to announce some conclusions. David Roberts of Union Theological Seminary published in that year his *Psychotherapy and a Christian View of Man,* insisting that psychotherapeutic theory enriched the theologian's understanding of Christian doctrine. Albert Outler at Yale responded in 1954 with his *Psychotherapy and the Christian Message,* in which he contended that theological insight should deepen psychological wisdom. But the theologians who were destined to have the greatest influence were Paul Tillich and the exponents of "process theology."

Tillich's "method of correlation," explicated in his *Systematic Theology* (1951–1963), provided a means of translating theological terms into a psychological vocabulary (so that the older doctrine of justification by grace, for example, became the affirmation that one could "accept one's acceptance"). And the process theologians, especially Charles Hartshorne at the University of Chicago, presented a doctrine of God that seemed to

afford numerous analogies to psychological processes. A few pastoral theologians tried, with limited success, to affirm the relevance of European Neo-Orthodoxy for pastoral counseling, but the liberal traditions, with their focus on religious experience, were more attractive to most counselors. Another small group of pastoral writers, led by Seward Hiltner, tried to find in pastoral work itself a source for theological assertions, but their project also attracted only limited support.

To some pastoral theologians, moreover, it seemed insufficient merely to discuss the interpersonal and theological contexts of counseling. What concrete difference did such discussions— or their results—make in the actual counseling sessions? Asking that question, they explored the institutional context of pastoral care: the local church. Beginning in 1956 Hiltner and Lowell Colston, an intern at the University of Chicago counseling center, tried to discover whether counseling conducted within a medical center differed (or produced different results) from counseling within a church. Their findings were inconclusive, but an increasing number of pastoral theologians became interested in the extent to which the physical setting of the church building, the network of continuing pastoral relationships, and the clients' special expectations of the pastor made pastoral counseling distinctive. One result was a spirited debate about the propriety of "private" pastoral counseling or independent counseling centers—a debate that accompanied the formation in 1963 of an American Association of Pastoral Counselors, which finally decided to support the centers but to discourage private pastoral counseling.

The interest in the context of pastoral care remained intense throughout the 1970s, as evidenced, for example, by the proposal of Don Browning at the University of Chicago that pastoral counselors give greater attention to moral guidance within a church conceived as a community of moral discourse. By the 1970s most pastoral writers were distinguishing carefully between pastoral care, as the dimension of ministry concerned distinctively with personal and interpersonal forms of human need within communities, and pastoral counseling, as one specialized expression of that broader enterprise.

The openness to psychology within the churches has helped the American clergy transcend the petty moralisms and exhortations of some of their predecessors. But the preoccupation with pastoral counseling became, for a time, so engrossing that it reshaped conceptions of the sermon, of theology, of religious education, of pastoral leadership, and of worship and piety. Hence the clergy often inadvertently consigned religious discourse solely to the sphere of the inward and private. In recent years they have recognized more clearly that pastoral counseling—a counseling rightly sensitive to psychological wisdom—can best flourish when it is not exalted as the paradigm of either clerical activity or communal relationships in religious institutions.

BIBLIOGRAPHY

Anton Boisen, *Out of the Depths* (1960); William Clebsch and Charles Jaekle, *Pastoral Care in Historical Perspective* (1964; repr. 1975); Simon Doniger, "Why Pastoral Psychology?—An Editorial," in *Pastoral Psychology,* 1 (1950); David Hall, *The Faithful Shepherd* (1972); E. Brooks Holifield, *A History of Pastoral Care in America* (1983); Rodney Hunter, ed., *Dictionary of Pastoral Care and Counseling* (1985).

John T. McNeill, *A History of the Cure of Souls* (1951); H. Richard Niebuhr and Daniel D. Williams, eds., *The Ministry in Historical Perspectives* (1956; rev. 1983); Philip Rieff, *The Triumph of the Therapeutic* (1966); Donald M. Scott, *From Office to Profession: The New England Ministry, 1750–1850* (1978); Allison Stokes, "Bibliographies of Psychology/Religious Studies," in *Religious Studies Review,* 4 (1978).

[*See also* HISTORY OF PREACHING IN AMERICA; PROFESSIONAL MINISTRY; *and* PSYCHOLOGY OF RELIGIOUS EXPERIENCE.]

RELIGIOUS EDUCATION

F. Michael Perko

IN many respects, the history of education in America until the turn of the twentieth century is the history of religious education. The public schools fostered a mainstream Protestant piety until their secularization at the end of the nineteenth century. Large numbers of Americans have continued to be educated in institutions that are denominationally sponsored or affiliated. Moreover, Sunday schools and religious education programs of a variety of kinds are themselves a major element in the American educational landscape. It is thus impossible to understand the history of education in America without significant reference to the role of religion. Only within the particular social and cultural ecologies of individual denominations and ethnic groups, however, can the religious influences on American schooling properly be studied and evaluated.

HISPANIC AMERICA

The formal history of education in North America begins with the publication in 1543 of the first textbook (a catechism) by Bishop Juan de Zumarraga of Mexico City. Ideally, the Indians of each village were to be given a rudimentary education that would aid in their Christianization and provide skilled labor for the Spanish empire.

In those sections of what later became the United States that were then under Spanish control, this model of the mission school predominated. From 1573 to 1763 Franciscan missionaries labored in Florida among the Indians with little success. Their work proved more fruitful among the Spanish, for whom they established a classical school and preparatory seminary at St.

Augustine in 1606. In the Southwest, educational activities were somewhat more promising. In the 1630s several Indian schools were founded in what is now New Mexico and in 1682 the first school in what later became Texas was established at the Indian mission of Ysleta near El Paso. By the middle of the eighteenth century, Texas had several Catholic schools for Indians, as well as a school for Spanish settlers that was founded sometime before 1789.

Perhaps the most extensive and best-known educational network in Spanish America was that of the California missions. In 1769, Spain occupied Alta (upper) California, and by 1772 five missions with schools had been established. Since these Spanish mission schools had religious proselytization and the teaching of vocational skills as their primary objectives, the emphasis was on the teaching of religion and manual education. Those children who wished to learn to read and write could do so. Most concerned with establishing the motherland's territorial rights, the schools nonetheless offered the beginnings of formal schooling to the original inhabitants.

FRENCH AMERICA

French educational influence in what is now the United States largely emanated from Quebec, founded in 1608. Between 1632 and the 1654 arrival of the English in what is now upper Maine, French Capuchins founded seven missions with schools. A mission that included schooling activities was begun among the Iroquois in New York in 1668 and was so successful that some 2,000 converts were made in the first ten years. In the early 1700s, French missionaries from Quebec provided basic education in what is now Detroit as well as rudimentary schooling at Kaskaskia, Illinois, by 1768.

Perhaps the greatest French success, however, was in the South, where efforts began after the early settlement by Sieur d'Iberville at present-day Mobile. In 1722 the Capuchins started a school at New Orleans; five years later the first permanent school in New France was opened by the Ursulines in the same city. A day and boarding school that taught reading, writing, and arithmetic along with catechism and vocational training, it was a largely white institution in which blacks and Indians were taught in small numbers. For the French as well as the Spanish, the extension of the empire was the primary motivation for educational formation.

ENGLISH COLONIES

The dominant influence in American educational development, however, was English rather than Spanish or French. The English, unlike the two other groups, regarded their colonial empire as a permanent extension of the motherland. Thus, settlers who came did so with the expectation of spending their lives in the New World and tended to emigrate as families. Schooling, as a result, was seen as important since it was the vehicle for the transmission of English culture to their children.

Schooling in England had traditionally been sponsored by religious groups, a pattern that was continued in North America. However, because of the different groups that settled in various regions of the country, divergent schooling structures developed. Colonial American schooling must be seen in the context of the three major regions of settlement during this period.

The South was the least educationally advanced region. Beginning with the foundation in Virginia of the Church of England in 1611—a pattern followed in the other southern colonies —education was viewed primarily as a responsibility of the family and the church. This individualistic understanding, together with an economy based largely on isolated plantations, tended to retard educational development. Perhaps the greatest influence on southern education was the Society for the Propagation of the Gospel in For-

eign Parts (SPG). Between 1702 and 1758 the London-based society sent 300 missionaries and more than 20 schoolmasters to the colonies. For the most part, the schools conducted by the SPG were charity schools, aimed at serving a poor clientele. Another innovation was the "old field school," frequently conducted by Anglican priests or lay readers. While these schools, along with a few sponsored by Roman Catholics, Quakers, and Presbyterians, served the region, they were few in number.

The most sophisticated region from an educational perspective was New England. The Puritans who settled the area brought with them a tradition of education as a vital component in their reformed faith. Moreover, the rapid growth of the population to 130,000 by 1700, along with the pattern of settlement near villages or in cities, tended to encourage school development. In 1635 the Boston Latin Grammar School was founded and in 1642 the Massachusetts General Court passed the colony's first education law, requiring parents and masters to see to the education of their children and apprentices. The same colony passed the "Oulde Deluder Satan" Law in 1647, which mandated education in order to counter the forces of the devil and Romanism. This law became the basis for further legislation in the other New England colonies.

The schools of these colonies were publicly supported and denominationally controlled. In the town schools, the curriculum was largely a religious one, with emphasis on the Bible and religious doctrine, reinforced by such texts as the *New England Primer*. The Latin grammar schools, a more advanced stage of education, offered Latin and Greek, but still emphasized religious training. While Enlightenment influences were felt in education by the eighteenth century, making colonial schooling more secular, New England's schools were pervasively religious into the national period.

Education in the Middle Colonies tended to be a hybrid of southern and New England patterns, mirroring the diverse ethnic and religious backgrounds of the region's settlers. In the 1620s the Dutch had settled what later became New York, establishing the Reformed Church in the colony. The foundation of the first school in 1638 marked the beginning of elementary schools that taught reading, writing, religion, and occasionally arithmetic. The schools were administered by the Dutch West India Company, which provided financial support, and the Classis of Amsterdam, which examined, licensed, and often selected schoolmasters. With the accession of the British, English schools under Anglican sponsorship came into being, generally in rural areas.

Education in New Jersey and Pennsylvania was sponsored by a wide variety of religious groups, including Lutherans, Presbyterians, Huguenots, German pietists, Roman Catholics, and Jews. The SPG operated charity schools in Philadelphia, as well as a school for blacks. The Quakers were especially prominent in education, opening a free public school in 1689 and carrying on educational work among blacks and Indians. The predominant form of education throughout the Middle Colonies was the private or denominational school.

THE COMMON SCHOOL CRUSADE

The period following the revolutionary war witnessed interest in the development of educational systems under state sponsorship. While Thomas Jefferson, Benjamin Rush, and Noah Webster all proposed national systems of education, none materialized. Only with the expansion of the population, largely as a result of immigration, and the rise of Jacksonian democracy in the 1830s, did sentiment for common schooling begin to build. A generation of common school pioneers operating from religious and patriotic motives sought to mobilize support for popular education. Horace Mann, a Unitarian Whig politician, was appointed the first superintendent of the Massachusetts State Board of Education in 1837. He began a national crusade for free common schooling.

One major factor in the rapid spread of common schooling was the support given by religious Evangelicals. Pulled by the millennial optimism of the early nineteenth century and pushed by fear of Catholic domination of the Mississippi Valley, they sought to make the nation godly through schooling, establishing in the process a Protestant *paideia* (cultural environment). Missionaries sent west by the American Home Missionary Society pioneered in the formation of common schooling, and at least one Methodist district required that its clergy preach yearly on

the efficacy of public education. Influential Congregationalists such as Lyman Beecher and Calvin Stowe carried the common school cause to a national audience, while the Presbyterian William Holmes McGuffey helped to shape generations of American students through the moralism of his *Reader*. In Kentucky the first three state superintendents were ministers, as was Sheldon Jackson, the first General Agent of Education for Alaska. A Methodist lay preacher, Samuel Lewis, filled a similar position in Ohio.

The first common schools were pervasively religious institutions. Avoiding sectarianism did not imply the absence of Christianity. Because their leaders believed that religion was necessary for the preservation of the republic and that Protestant Christianity was the national religion, the schools under their influence taught a common evangelical faith based on the Bible, avoiding potentially divisive doctrinal controversies. The King James Bible was universally utilized, while textbooks in history and geography propagated the view that the Protestant faith of northern Europe was intrinsically superior to the Roman Catholicism of the South and East.

Catholics and others objected to this Protestant tone in institutions that were supported with public funds. Their protests frequently took the form of legal and political action either to obtain state funding for denominational schools or to remove Protestant religious teaching from those supported with public monies. In 1840 Bishop John Hughes of New York unsuccessfully petitioned the city's common council to allow Catholic schools a share of the state school fund, much of which went to the institutions of the evangelical Public School Society. When this was refused, Hughes resorted to political action in subsequent city elections. Under this pressure, the state legislature in 1842 passed a bill that, while still denying funding to the Catholic schools, removed funding from the institutions sponsored by the Public School Society. Similarly, in 1852 Archbishop John Baptist Purcell of Cincinnati successfully challenged the use of Protestant textbooks in the common schools, but failed in his attempt to gain a share of the state school revenues by encouraging Catholics to vote as a bloc in the 1853 elections. A continual stream of court cases involving the Protestant tenor of the public schools and, specifically, the use of the King James Bible continued from a battle fought in Cincinnati in 1869 to the Edgerton, Wisconsin, controversy of 1888. The result was the gradual secularization of the common schools.

From the early seventeenth to the late nineteenth centuries, American schooling was a religious enterprise. Rooted in whatever the dominant religious tradition of a particular locale happened to be, it articulated the tenets held by the majority of the citizenry. Only as immigration changed the character of the nation and diversity of belief became increasingly acceptable within American culture did those schools that were publicly supported necessarily become religiously neutral.

CATHOLIC SCHOOLING

While Catholic schooling has existed in America since the early seventeenth century, its shape has changed several times. Initially, it provided education in the French and Spanish territories, serving a clientele of Indians and colonists. Elsewhere the minority status of Catholicism created different patterns of development. Maryland, which had been founded in 1634 as a Catholic refuge, witnessed the establishment of its first school by Ralph Crouch in 1640. After the 1692 establishment of Anglicanism in the colony, Catholic education went underground. In 1745 or 1746 the Jesuits founded a school at Bohemia Manor, in territory claimed by both Maryland and Pennsylvania. In Pennsylvania the situation was less difficult under the religious toleration offered by the Quakers. Around 1743 two Jesuits came from Germany and started schools for German immigrants near Conewago and at Goshenhoppen. Two more Jesuits, Ferdinand Farmer (Steinmayer) and Robert Molyneux, arrived from Germany in 1752 and founded schools at two Philadelphia parishes. Anti-Catholic laws prevented the establishment of Catholic schooling in the other colonies.

The period following the revolutionary war was the first meaningful establishment of Catholic schooling. The Sulpician priest Gabriel Richard labored at the edge of the northwestern frontier, founding a seminary and girls' school in 1804 at what would become Detroit and publishing the first American Catholic textbook, *The Child's Spelling Book,* in 1809. The major impetus for the foundation of parochial schooling, however, was provided by the formation of several American communities of religious sisters and the arrival of others from Europe. The sisters served as a source of inexpensive educational labor without which the extensive network of Catholic schooling could never have developed.

A number of attempts at school establishment by transient groups from Europe failed until the formation of a group of native-born "pious ladies" at Georgetown in 1814. This group eventually became the Visitation order, which founded a school that taught reading, writing, arithmetic, and geography. Despite a tenuous beginning, by 1832 the school was enrolling a hundred students. The foundation of another American sisterhood, the Sisters of Charity, by Elizabeth Bayley Seton in 1809 resulted in the formation of a school at Emmitsburg, Maryland, in 1810 and eight more by 1828. In 1812 two more communities of women were founded in Kentucky, the Sisters of Loretto and the Sisters of Charity of Nazareth, as well as a community of Dominican women in 1822. These groups established several schools in frontier Kentucky, especially near the Catholic center of Bardstown. European communities of women were also successfully established in America during this period with the arrival of the Sisters of St. Joseph in 1834 and the Sisters of Providence and Sisters of Notre Dame de Namur in 1844.

Most Catholic educational growth was an urban phenomenon. In 1820 the first Roman Catholic school in New England was founded by the Ursulines in Boston. This school, which was moved to Charlestown and then burned in anti-Catholic riots in 1834, enrolled over 100 girls in the first year and taught a curriculum consisting of both classical and practical subjects. Several day schools were also founded. In New York, which maintained anti-Catholic laws until 1784, the first Roman Catholic free school was founded in 1800 and had become the second largest denominational school in the city by 1806, enrolling 220 pupils at two sites. Besides the schools founded by Molyneux and Farmer, Philadelphia's German Catholic population also established a school at Holy Trinity parish in 1789. In the South, an academy and parochial school was established by the Religious of the Sacred Heart at St. Charles, Missouri, in 1818; a branch was founded at Grand Coteau, Louisiana, in 1821.

Generally, Catholic education during this period was a small-scale enterprise, characterized by poverty, teacher shortages (many teachers were expected also to function as sextons or organists), and a sparse and scattered Catholic population. Despite these difficulties, there were by 1840 at least 200 Catholic schools in the United States, about half of them west of the Alleghenies.

The years from around 1830 to the turn of the century witnessed rapid expansion of Catholic schooling in America, produced largely by extensive immigration. The Catholic population of the United States increased from around 500,000 in 1829 to 8 million in 1884, doubling each decade. This first wave of immigration included large numbers of Irish escaping the potato blight of 1821 and the famine of 1845, as well as Germans fleeing poor economic conditions or the abortive revolutions of 1848. Over forty new communities of religious women and eleven communities of brothers settled in the United States prior to 1884, providing still more educational laborers.

This combination of immigration and the availability of teachers helped to motivate the foundation of Catholic schools. Additional impetus was given by the failure of bishops to arrive at accommodations with the elites who controlled the developing common school system. Initially, American Catholics were successful in many locales in their quest to obtain state funding for Catholic schools. Illustrative of such arrangements were the Lowell Plan (1831–1852) in Massachusetts and the Poughkeepsie Plan (1873–1898) in New York, which provided state support for Catholic schools, including a subsidy for teacher salaries. As the common school movement developed, however, state funds began to be channeled exclusively into the public schools. Disillusioned by subsequent attempts to achieve state funding of Catholic schools or to merge them into the common school system, hierarchs turned increasingly to a separate network of schooling to provide for the maintenance of Catholic and ethnic culture. Beginning with mild exhortations in favor of parochial schooling at the First Provincial Council of Baltimore in 1829, Catholic hierarchs insisted with increasing frequency that an alternative system of schooling was the only viable option left open to them. As the era progressed, more and more pressure was placed on pastors and parents alike to found and support a separate network of schools.

The impetus given by these forces was reflected in the rapid growth in both quantity and scope of Catholic schooling. In the archdiocese of Cincinnati, for example, the number of children in Catholic schools had increased to around 15,000 by 1866, representing over 37 percent of all those attending school in the city. In New York, the "School War" of 1841 and 1842 fought by Bishop Hughes with the Public School Society had the effect of speeding the development of separate Catholic schools, while school formation was a regular event in the diocese of Philadelphia after 1830.

The late nineteenth and early twentieth centuries provided even stronger forces in support of Catholic schooling. The Catholic population swelled from 9 million in the 1890s to 20 million by the 1920s, this time as a result of immigration from southern and eastern Europe, especially Austria-Hungary, Italy, and Russia. Parochial education saw enrollments climb, too, as a result of the passage of child-labor legislation. Church officials were increasingly strong in their promotion of Catholic schools and condemnation of "godless" public ones. A high point in legislation concerning Catholic schooling was reached at the Third Plenary Council of Baltimore in 1884, which mandated the establishment of schools in each parish within two years. In several dioceses, synods were held in the following years that reinforced the plenary council's position to the extent of obliging pastors to establish schools under pain of removal.

Support for this position was not, however, universal, and patterns of growth differed markedly from diocese to diocese. In 1880, 22 percent of Chicago's schoolchildren attended Catholic schools, compared with 10 percent in Boston, a city with a proportionally higher Catholic population. The difference is explained by such factors as the ability of Catholics to co-opt the public school system more successfully in some cities (e.g., Boston) than others and the ethnic makeup of the Catholic population (Germans tended to be more school-oriented than the Irish and Italians). Many parents promoted public schooling as a better channel of upward mobility for their children. Important, too, were the attitudes of local bishops. Archbishop John

Williams of Boston, for example, did no more to promote such schools after the plenary council than before.

Archbishop John Ireland of St. Paul, while a supporter of Catholic education, was also in favor of Catholic attendance at public schools, which he praised in a speech given to the National Educational Association in 1890 that provoked considerable controversy. Ireland also came under fire for the compromise he approved in 1891 whereby two Catholic schools in the towns of Faribault and Stillwater were taken over by the local school boards, which provided public support while retaining Catholic teachers. This action seemed to gain Vatican support with the publication of Archbishop Francesco Satolli's *Fourteeen Points* in 1892, which both promoted Catholic schools and allowed for the existence of public ones. Bishops such as Bernard McQuaid in Rochester and Michael Corrigan in New York strenuously opposed this new direction. Finally, in April 1892 Vatican officials promulgated a decree allowing Ireland's experiment to continue but forbidding its extension to other dioceses. The results of this controversy did much to blunt whatever Catholic enthusiasm for compromise with public education still existed.

While such differences existed, the era was generally one of growth and consolidation for Catholic education. In 1908 America officially ceased to be a missionary country. The Catholic population by 1920 had reached over 19 million, with an increase in Catholic school attendance from around 400,000 in 1880 to 1.7 million. Administrative structures became more formalized with the foundation of the first diocesan school board in New York in 1886 and the formation of the Catholic Educational Association in 1904. The establishment of parochial secondary education began with the Catholic High School of Philadelphia in 1890. Teacher education, too, became a concern with the inception of the "Sisters' College," a summer program to provide pedagogical training for religious women at Catholic University of America.

The period between World War I and the Second Vatican Council was one of great growth for Catholic schooling: the number of Catholic schools doubled and the number of pupils tripled. In the peak years between 1950 and 1960 Catholic elementary education grew by 171 percent, compared with a 142 percent growth

rate for public schools. There were curricular changes as well. Initially, Catholic schools rejected both the Deweyian pedagogy that had become popular during the era and the newly developed testing movement, seeing both as potential threats to the primacy of the individual. Over time, however, educational psychology (though without psychoanalytic overtones) gained wide currency, and the curriculum itself became somewhat more social. Another major area of development was education for those outside the mainstream. In 1954 the National Catholic Educational Association organized a department of special education to deal with the lack of such facilities in Catholic education. Between the late 1940s and the mid-1950s a number of dioceses (among them, Washington, San Antonio, and St. Louis) racially integrated their schools. It is important to note, however, that even during these boom years, nearly half the Roman Catholic school-age population did not attend parochial schools.

After 1957 the course of Catholic parochial education changed drastically. The numbers of students entering Catholic schools dropped sharply, with some dioceses experiencing as much as a 20 percent decline in enrollment in a single year, the result in part of a drop in the birth rate. A decrease in the percentage of sisters in the teaching force (from 48.9 percent in 1968 to 21.9 percent in 1981) and the corresponding increase in the number of lay teachers substantially raised educational costs. Since the enrollment drop focused almost exclusively on primary education, however, the increased secularization of American Catholics may also have been a major factor. Such shifts in American Catholic culture were brought to the surface by the Second Vatican Council and encouraged critics like Mary Perkins Ryan, who argued in 1968 that Catholic schooling encouraged a "ghetto mentality," was inferior and anti-ecumenical, and consumed funds more profitably spent on broader areas of religious education. In a more muted vein, the 1966 book *The Education of American Catholics* by Andrew M. Greeley and Peter H. Rossi found no sociological evidence that schools were necessary for the survival of American Catholicism, but concluded that they had probably been worth the effort.

Catholic parochial schooling today continues its struggle to define its place on the educational landscape. While it is largely lay staffed and administered, control still rests primarily in the hands of clergy. Questions about the rights of Catholic schoolteachers to unionize raise new issues in finance and social justice. In urban areas, parochial institutions increasingly serve as alternative schools for the poor, many of whom are non-Catholic. While numbers have declined, the demise predicted by some has not occurred and the more conservative direction of American life in recent years may become a factor in the schools' continued existence.

PROTESTANT DAY SCHOOLS

Although Catholic schooling has provided the major alternative to public education in America, a number of Protestant denominations have strong traditions of school support, while the growing network of nondenominational schools is one of the more interesting features of the contemporary educational scene.

Various Lutheran groups have engaged in educational activities. Henry Melchior Mühlenberg, the "father of American Lutheranism," helped to organize a number of parochial schools, so that by 1820 the General Synod had 324 schools in its 700 congregations. After 1860, however, Sunday schools and weekday religious schools supplanted parochial education; by 1982 the 3-million-member Lutheran Church in America listed only 44 schools under its sponsorship. Among some German and Scandanavian Lutheran bodies the propriety of parochial schooling was hotly debated, with the Swedes and Danes accepting public education more readily than the Germans. The result was that in 1982 the 2.5-million-member American Lutheran Church, which was formed by mergers of several of these groups, had only about 375 schools enrolling 31,284 pupils, a set of statistics nearly identical to those of the fiercely conservative Wisconsin Evangelical Lutheran Synod with only 400,000 members.

The group that has most emphasized parochial schooling is the Missouri Synod. After the synod's foundation in 1847, its goal of a school in every congregation came close to becoming a reality, so that by 1872 the 472 congregations were able to boast 446 schools modeled on the German *Volkschule*. These schools both propagated conservative Lutheran doctrines and acted as agencies for the transmission of German language and culture. Changes in the pattern of German immigration, however, caused these institutions to fade in the period following the Civil War. Many of the newer immigrants saw little need for formal education, while those in favor of it differed on whether the schools ought to maintain their German character.

Legislative battles against the restrictive Bennett and Edwards laws in Wisconsin and Illinois in the early 1890s did much to force Missouri Synod Lutherans to reappraise and reform their schools. The former law stipulated that local boards of education were to enforce compulsory attendance at either a public or private school, and mandated the use of English in teaching reading, writing, arithmetic, and U.S. history. The latter required that all children between ages seven and fourteen attend the public school of the area in which they resided for at least sixteen weeks a year. However, the improvement in the quality of public education and anti-German popular sentiment, especially around the time of World War I, considerably slowed the schools' expansion, so that a 50 percent increase in denominational membership between 1896 and 1916 was matched by only a 12 percent increase in school enrollment. At the same time, the Lutheran schools were adapting to American culture, with nearly half conducting religious instruction in English by 1921. Administrative structures were also developing as the Missouri Synod created an office of superintendent of schools and established a school board. After 1936, as the Depression waned, the parochial schools experienced a resurgence. By 1961 the denomination sponsored 1,323 schools in North America, enrolling 150,440 pupils. Despite the questioning of educational values that occurred in the 1960s, the schools continue to be popular among both clergy and laity. One especially interesting feature is the increasing proportion of non-Lutheran students, 40.6 percent in 1982, which seems to indicate that these institutions, like their Catholic analogs, are functioning as alternative schools. The large proportion of such students, however, raises questions about the contemporary mission of Missouri Synod education as well as its shape in the future.

Another large system of parochial schools is that operated by the Seventh-day Adventist church. When the denomination emerged in the early 1840s as a result of the ministry of William Miller, a Baptist preacher, there was little concern for education since many believed in the imminence of the second coming of Christ. By the mid-1850s, however, some parents had begun schools in Buck's Bridge, New York, and Battle Creek, Michigan. These schools operated sporadically until the foundation of the first official Adventist school in Battle Creek in 1872. Caught in a war over curriculum, the school closed in 1882. After reopening the following year, it adopted a classical course of study. While two other secondary institutions founded in 1882 did emphasize manual labor and other aspects of the denomination's reformed curriculum, little was done in the church as a whole in the 1880s. Further reforms instituted by Ellen White after an 1891 educational convention, however, revitalized Adventist schooling. As religion rather than the classics became central in the curriculum, the number of secondary institutions increased, while elementary education grew from 15 schools in 1890 to 594 in 1910. Educational work was also begun among blacks in the South during this period.

While the years prior to World War II witnessed further expansion, there was also a movement away from the curricular extremism of the 1890s. The time since the war has been marked by both numerical and structural growth. In 1982 the Adventist church operated 1,106 elementary and 81 secondary schools in the United States with a total enrollment of 68,575. Since 1975 the church has had a director for elementary and secondary education for North America, and each of the eight union conferences also has its own educational director, with subordinate conference educational superintendents. Some of the unique characteristics of Adventist schools are their avoidance of highly competitive activities, a creationist approach to science, small size, and a tradition of opposition to state aid.

Calvinist education in America traces its present roots to the Calvinist revival begun in the Netherlands in the 1870s by Abraham Kuyper. Religiously, Calvinist schooling relies heavily on the doctrine of sphere sovereignty, according to which numerous social institutions operate independently in their own areas of competence. Since education is one of these, both the parochial school and public instruction are violations of the doctrine. A related teaching is that of the covenant, which carries with it the belief that God uses the institution of the family to carry forward the Kingdom. Calvinists thus see their education as different from that of secular public schools or denominational ones. These doctrines were held by immigrants who settled in western Michigan in 1847 and formed a classis that joined the Dutch Reformed Church in 1850. With the help of the larger church, an academy was founded at Holland, Michigan, in 1851, as well as other schools in subsequent years.

Most Calvinist educational development, however, was the work of the True Dutch Reformed Church (later called the Christian Reformed Church), founded in 1857, beginning with the 1856 school established at Grand Rapids by one of the seceding congregations that founded the new denomination. Theoretically, the schools were parentally controlled and sponsored, but in fact they were virtually parochial schools during these early days. The twenty schools were organized into regional groups called Alliances by the Society for the Promotion of Christian Education on a Reformed Basis, founded in 1892. This organization was replaced in 1920 by the National Union of Christian Schools, an organization of lay-member school boards rather than church officials as the earlier society had been. Thus the schools returned to the tradition of religious orientation without denominational administration. The union has recruited teachers, supported a journal, and published pedagogical literature. Two particular issues that face the Calvinist schools today are their ambiguous relation with the Christian Reformed Church and the continual quest for public funding.

The newest religious arrival on the American educational scene is the Christian day school. Since the 1960s Evangelicals and churches that are rarely part of mainline denominations have been establishing schools, according to some commentators, at the rate of two per day. While only 150 such schools were established between 1920 and 1960, between 9,000 and 11,000 have been founded since then, with an estimated enrollment of 1 million. Of these, about 70 percent are sponsored by individual churches. In large measure, their growth has been a measure of conservative dissatisfaction with public education, particularly in the areas of discipline and curriculum content. Like Catholics of an earlier generation, these conservative Evangelicals first tried unsuccessfully to co-opt the public institutions and ended by establishing their own. While some have been condemned as racist, the majority are not racially segregated. Other grounds for criticism have been the poor level of instruction in some, as well as a kind of "superpatriotism." The exact nature of their relationship with state and federal governments, particularly in the area of school regulation, has also been a matter of dispute.

JEWISH DAY SCHOOLS

Jewish education in America has included day schooling since its inception. Most early immigrants were Sephardic Jews from Spain and Portugal. In 1731 Yeshibat Minhat Areb, the school of Congregation Shearith Israel of New York, was founded; six years later, under the leadership of David Mendez Machado, it became a private religious school. There are also records of a school for the poor founded in the same city in 1758 and several in the Carolinas, but all of these seem to have existed only sporadically.

The massive immigration of central and eastern European Jews beginning in the 1840s (210,000 between 1840 and 1880) brought changes in patterns of community life. The cohesiveness of Jewish communities that had characterized the colonial era began to disintegrate, and other institutions besides synagogues became important in community life. Most large congregations of German Jews founded day schools such as New York's Talmud Torah and Hebrew Institute (1842), which taught English, Hebrew, and sometimes German. By the early 1870s, however, most of these had collapsed from a lack of students and funding, as well as opposition by some congregants. While a second wave of immigration brought 3 million Jews to the United States between 1880 and 1920, making it the home of 30 percent of world Jewry, there was little increase in day schooling. These immigrants generally favored public education because of their poverty, belief in the "melting pot" ideal, and desire for upward mobility.

The American Jewish revival that followed World War II helped to bring about a rapid growth in Jewish day schools. The greatest growth in Jewish education has been in this sector, with 95 percent of the present 360 day schools established since the 1940s. In 1982 about 13 percent of the Jewish child population attended these institutions, most of which are Conservative or Orthodox in character. Most include subjects such as prayer, the Torah and commentary, Hebrew, history, ethics, and Israel. Outside of New York, instruction in 90 percent of the schools is in Hebrew or a combination of Hebrew and English.

Reasons given for this rapid growth include the postwar surge of religious sentiment, the prosperity of American Jewry, the example of the early-twentieth-century pioneers, the events of the Holocaust and the establishment of Israel, the religiosity of the postwar immigrants, the perceived failure of public education, concern over the declining Jewish birthrate, and the supplanting of the melting pot ideal with one of ethnic diversity. Some, however, have opposed the schools as fostering anti-Semitism and endangering Jewish survival by removing Jews from the educational mainstream. Funding is accomplished by tuition (about 50 percent), endowments, federal aid, and assistance from congregations and federations.

PREPARATORY SCHOOLS

Religiously affiliated boarding schools have occupied a somewhat smaller place on the American educational scene. Although most of these are Roman Catholic, the best-known schools are under Protestant control and have traditionally provided secondary education to the nation's elites. Some preparatory schools descended from eighteenth-century academies (e.g., Andover, Exeter, and Deerfield) are nominally religious, and some nineteenth-century foundations (Lawrenceville, Choate, Middlesex) are explicitly nondenominational. However, a substantial number of schools (among them, St. Paul's, St. Mark's, Groton, St. George's, and Kent) have strong Episcopal traditions. St. Paul's, founded in Concord, New Hampshire, in 1855, was directed in its early years by an Episcopal priest, as were St. Mark's (1865) and Groton (1884) in Massachusetts. Even in 1916 the average tuition in fourteen of these schools was $950, guaranteeing a select clientele.

Emphasis has traditionally been on character formation in the context of a family environment that emphasizes classical academics and athletics. For many years, these schools served as "feeders" to Ivy League institutions. In 1907 about 40 percent of the Yale freshman class, for example, came from nine of these schools, while only 20 percent had attended public institutions. Initially having as their goal the production of Christian gentlemen and scholars, the preparatory schools after the turn of the twentieth century substituted a "muscular" faith leading to the ideal of the gentleman as a perfected public servant. Their success may be judged by the fact that one school, Groton, with fewer than 1,000 alumni out of college, had, by 1933, given the country a president, two secretaries of state, three senators, eleven ambassadors, and two state governors.

OTHER SCHOOLS

Only a few schools exist in the United States based on religious traditions other than the Judeo-Christian one. One example is the Gurukula, started in 1971 in Dallas by the International Society for Krishna Consciousness (ISKCON). Children born into the society are allowed complete freedom to the age of five and then are removed from their parents and sent to Gurukula, a primary school that by 1974 enrolled ninety-eight students, ages eight to fifteen. The pupils are required to study a curriculum that includes Sanskrit, English, geography, history, and basic mathematics six hours a day, six days a week. Girls are also taught cooking and sewing. All subjects are taught from the perspective of Krishna Consciousness and meet the Texas state requirements for the first six grades. The noncertified teachers, who are chosen by the headmaster, see themselves as giving practical instruction on how to live perfectly in the material world engaged in devotional service, thus fulfilling all of one's desires in this life and the next. While the philosophy of Swami Bhaktivedanta emphasizes the importance of devotion over knowledge and deprecates the importance of material learning, he nonetheless encourages his disciples to complete their education through high school. Those who wish to become ministers are given a two-and-a-half-year course, with the society teaching them to read and write first, if necessary.

LEGAL CONTROVERSIES

The relationship between the church and the state in matters related to education has at times been an uneasy one. Legal conflicts have centered on the three major issues of state regulation and funding of religious schools and the place of religion in public education, especially with reference to the legality of "released time" religious instruction.

The 1889 Bennett Law in Wisconsin required the local board of education to supervise attendance in religious schools and mandate that English be used in the teaching of reading, writing, arithmetic, and U.S. history. In the same year, Illinois went one step further by compelling all children between the ages of seven and fourteen to attend public schools for at least sixteen weeks a year. Efforts by Catholics and Lutherans in 1891 unseated the Republican legislatures that had passed the laws and led to their repeal. An Oregon law passed in 1922 requiring the attendance of all children in public institutions was declared unconstitutional by the U.S. Supreme Court in *Pierce* v. *the Society of Sisters* (1925).

The controversy over funding religious schools began in the nineteenth century with such conflicts as the 1840s "school war" in New York, in which Catholics sought to obtain a share of state school funds. In the twentieth century, *Cochran* v. *Louisiana Board of Education* (1930) and *Everson* v. *the Board of Education* (1947) began the development of the "child benefit theory," whereby state aid could be provided to parochial schools for materials and services such as textbooks, school buses, audiovisual materials, and testing services on the grounds that the child rather than the church was the beneficiary. This position was refined in further decisions so that by 1971 the Supreme Court had formalized the following triple criteria of secular legislative purpose, a primary effect that neither advances nor inhibits religion, and avoidance of excessive entanglement as the bases upon which constitutionality of state and federal aid would be decided. The seeming reversal of these criteria in *Mueller* v. *Allen* (1983), in which the Court found constitutional a Minnesota law that provides tax credits to the parents of children in tuition-charging schools, has left the future of these issues unclear.

The place of religion in public education has been a matter of dispute since the middle of the nineteenth century. Cases such as the Cincinnati "Bible War" of 1869 and the Edgerton, Wisconsin, case of 1886 successfully challenged the use of the King James Bible in the schools, bringing about the secularization of public schooling in the process. Twentieth-century cases such as *Engel* v. *Vitale* (1962) and *Abington School District* v. *Schempp* (1963) ended state-mandated school prayer. An Illinois school board regulation that allowed sectarian teachers to offer religious instruction once a week in public schools was declared unconstitutional in *McCollum* v. *Board of Education* (1948), but a "released time" program in New York in which the instruction was carried out away from school grounds was ruled constitutional in *Zorach* v. *Clausen* (1952). Since that time, organizations such as the National Council on Religion and Public Education have worked to develop curricula and materials for public schools to teach about religion without teaching religion itself. A 1984 attempt to mandate school prayer federally suggests that the issue of religion in public schooling is not dead and will become more complex as students from religious traditions other than the Judeo-Christian enter the schools in increasing numbers.

PART-TIME RELIGIOUS INSTRUCTION

Part-time religious programs for students in secular schools have flourished since the late eighteenth century. Among Christians, Sunday schools and the Catholic Confraternity of Christian Doctrine (discussed below) have been instrumental in the instruction of countless children. Young Men's and Young Women's Christian Associations (YMCAs and YWCAs) have also provided secular and religious education for adolescents and young adults. For Jews, religious education for children has been carried out in a wide variety of institutions, while the Young Men's and Young Women's Hebrew Associations (YMHAs and YWHAs) have served the needs of youth and young adults.

In 1780 or 1781 the English newspaper publisher Robert Raikes, concerned about the "morals of the lower classes," hired a teacher to set up the first Sunday school, which taught reading and religion. By 1787 about 250,000 children in Britain were enrolled in such institutions. The first official Sunday school in the United States was founded in Philadelphia in 1790 under the sponsorship of several religious leaders, including a Catholic priest. Less class-oriented than its British counterpart, the new institution promoted middle-class respectability. The interdenominational American Sunday School Union (ASSU), founded in 1824 to provide a national structure, immediately began to publish primers, spellers, hymnals, catechisms, Bibles, and tracts, and to make the Sunday schools centers of literacy. By 1859, 30,000 of America's 50,000 public libraries were housed in Sunday schools, and in many locales the Sunday school was a precursor of public education.

Fearing Roman Catholic expansion and committed to the missionary task of Christianizing the nation, in 1830 the ASSU opened its Valley Campaign, the goal of which was to establish "a Sunday school in every destitute place where it is practicable, throughout the Valley of the Mississippi," by 1832. Frontier agents such as Stephen Paxson, a convert of the Sunday school who in twenty years founded more than 1,200 such institutions, spread the new gospel throughout the Midwest. Only among urban immigrants and blacks were the Sunday schools a failure. Suspicion that the ASSU was dominated by Presbyterians led to the formation of still other organizations, among them the General Protestant Episcopal Sunday School Union in 1826 and the Methodist Sunday School Union in 1837.

After the Civil War, the Sunday school was transformed by Evangelicals such as Dwight Moody and William Reynolds. Touched by the urban revivals of the 1850s and believing in a literal interpretation of Scripture, they enlisted the support of business entrepreneurs like Henry Wanamaker and H. J. Heinz to produce a network that compared its educational attainments to those of Harvard and its organization to that of Tammany Hall. These largely Republican proponents of religious efficiency promoted a uniformity that reached its peak with the 1872 introduction of a standardized seven-year cycle of Scripture topics for every Sunday of the year. By 1900, 3 million students were studying these lessons, which could be presented by untrained instructors, giving rise to a populist vision of the world as one vast Sunday school.

Organized Roman Catholic efforts at religious education for those in American public schools began with the establishment of the Confraternity of Christian Doctrine in 1902.

While the beginning of the twentieth century seemed a dazzling time for Sunday schooling, problems soon appeared. Some objected to its quarterly lessons on temperance, while modern biblical criticism was beginning to create instructional problems. The advent of released time programs, family centered instruction, and vacation Bible schools was also weakening the influence of Sunday schools. Mocked by critics as old-fashioned, they began to wane. Convinced that professional leadership was the answer to the problem, a new generation of reformers founded the Religious Education Association in 1903. Based on liberal theology and the pedagogical theories of John Dewey, it developed new curricula based on the "graded lesson" approach and promoted the extensive use of professional directors. By the end of World War II, however, its approach had proved only moderately successful. Neo-Orthodox theologians successfully challenged the optimistic world view of the liberals, producing alternative religious education materials in the process. Between 1926 and 1936, Sunday school enrollments in the mainline denominations dropped by as much as 34 percent, while growing in more conservative groups such as the Assemblies of God and Pentecostal Holiness Church by as much as 300 percent. As for Catholics, the Confraternity of Christian Doctrine was established in most parishes by the 1930s, its more conservative approach supported by local bishops and church authorities in Rome.

More recent attempts to produce programs of a more pluralistic variety have spawned charges of blandness. Enrollments continued to decline in some liberal denominations by as much as 300,000 between 1970 and 1976; in the same period, more conservative denominations such as the Southern and Independent Baptists made rapid gains. Although some denominations have given up Sunday schools, they are still found in many churches. Materials continue to change toward a more psychological approach, but classroom practice still resembles that of fifty or sixty years ago in many schools. The Sunday school remains important as an incarnation of popular Protestantism and the transmitter of an optimistic vision of America.

The most prominent of the young men's societies established during the nineteenth century was the Young Men's Christian Association. Travelers to the London World's Fair of 1851 brought the idea back. The earliest foundation in Boston, unlike the London one, allied itself with the city's trinitarian denominations. By 1860 the nation's 205 associations enrolled 25,000 members. In addition to boarding facilities, these early associations provided religious lectures, libraries and reading rooms, and courses in languages, music, and gymnastics. In the years following the Civil War, the associations came under the direction of paid secretaries, frequently drawn from the ranks of business. Various training schools to provide secretaries were also founded during this era. Classes, including Bible study, became important to the degree that, by 1878, their attendance was greater than that at gospel services or tent meetings. In 1884–1885 the Boston association offered instruction in seventeen subjects to 1,014 men and 153 women; around 1890 industrial education classes were added.

During the 1870s and 1880s the work of the associations expanded to include activities for boys, as well as courses in Christian sociology, economics, and physical education. By 1916 some 83,000 students were being instructed in more than 200 YMCA courses by 2,500 instructors.

Growth and innovation have marked the associations since the 1920s. New theories of religious education have caused more emphasis to be placed on personal initiative, while Bible study has become a means to solving life problems rather than an end in itself. Between the world wars, attendance at physical education classes grew rapidly until, by 1936, about half those attending YMCA classes were in physical education. By 1940 the educational programs in ten associations had been transformed into colleges. During the Depression attendance swelled, though traditional religious activities went into decline. By the end of World War II, however, such activities again became popular, mirroring increased interest in religion across the nation. In 1950, 228 associations enrolled

33,000 students, most under the age of eighteen, in their Bible classes. There has been a membership growth of some 50 percent since that date; about 25 percent of the new members are girls and women. Today the YMCA continues to provide a wide variety of religious and educational programming for both children and young adults.

The Young Women's Christian Association developed out of a women's prayer meeting in New York City. Several members founded a Ladies' Christian Association at New York University in 1858, and in 1860, a boarding house for working girls. The first formal association was founded in Boston in 1863. By the late 1860s this organization and others like it had established boarding facilities, as well as classes in such subjects as astronomy, bookkeeping, physiology, and domestic science. By the 1870s the YWCA, like its male counterpart, was offering physical education classes and had expanded to midwestern cities. Bible classes were taught with attendances as large as 600 people. The first student association was founded at Illinois Normal School at Bloomington in 1872 and was followed by others in normal schools (teacher training institutes) and women's colleges. In the 1880s and 1890s leaders like Emily Huntington and Grace Dodge enlarged domestic education programs and established normal departments within the associations. In the present century the YWCA has expanded to a membership of about 2.2 million. It offers similar programs to those of the YMCA and, like it, opens activities to members of the opposite sex.

Most educational activities of American Jews have been carried out in part-time programs. In the colonial period Hebrew instruction and preparation for Bar Mitzvah were generally done by synagogue functionaries or independent teachers. In 1808 the foundation of the Polonies Talmud Torah in New York set the pattern for the Jewish school as supplement to secular education. The massive immigration of central and eastern European Jews beginning in the 1840s hastened the disintegration of the cohesiveness that had characterized Jewish communities in the colonial era, and other institutions besides synagogues became important in the preservation of Jewish religion and culture. Sunday schools were popular, as well as afternoon schools founded in response to Christian proselytization. Although 40,000 to 50,000 Jewish children lived in New York in 1880, fewer than 15,000 received some form of Jewish education.

After the second wave of immigration that began in 1880, diversity characterized Jewish education. The Talmud Torahs, founded by congregations and the Young Men's Hebrew Association, taught mainly poor boys on an afternoon and Sunday basis. Institutional schools run by charitable agencies were the best attended of all. But since they taught mainly religion and little Hebrew, many parents doubted the schools' Jewishness. Congregational schools, generally sponsored by Conservative or Orthodox communities, were in session several times a week, with a curriculum that consisted largely of translating prayers and Bible readings into English. Sunday school classes were frequently conducted by public school teachers who had little background in Jewish studies. In the *hadarim,* individualized instruction was given in fifteen-minute sessions and some instruction was still done by private tutors. Still, fewer than 21 percent of Jewish children in cities like New York received some form of Jewish education.

The foundation in 1910 of the Bureau of Education of the Jewish Community of New York signaled the beginning of organized concern for Jewish education. Along with similar agencies founded in other cities, the bureau helped to found schools, train and license teachers, and publish texts. Some cities began central Talmud Torahs. As Jews moved to suburban areas, however, congregational schools began to predominate, so that by 1928 they enrolled more pupils in New York than did Talmud Torahs. A new feature in Jewish education was the rise of Yiddish schools, including national-radical schools that taught religion and socialism, Shalom Aleichem schools that emphasized socialism and Zionism, and Arbeiter Ring schools sponsored by radical workers.

The experience of the Holocaust and the establishment of the state of Israel helped to fuel an American Jewish revival after World War II. Communities rallied in support of education with the result that school enrollments increased from 200,000 in 1937 to 553,000 by 1959. By the latter year about 80 percent of Jewish children attended some Jewish school, with the majority (88 percent) about evenly divided between weekday and Sunday schools. Education was increasingly centered in synagogue schools, a reflection of the need for group affiliation and a decrease in the home-centered character of American Jewish life. The curriculum, which focused on the Bar Mitzvah, emphasized customs and ceremonies, with less attention given to the Bible, history, and Hebrew. Hebrew study institutes also came into existence as a result of the foundation of Israel.

Other educational activities for young Jewish men and women have been carried out under the auspices of the Young Men's and Young Women's Hebrew Associations. The roots of the YMHA can be traced to the Jewish young men's literary societies of the 1840s. The first association was founded in Baltimore in 1854; another appeared in New York in 1874. In 1888 a women's auxiliary took the name Young Women's Hebrew Association for the first time and became independent in 1902, although eventually YMHAs and YWHAs merged into single organizations. The National Council of Young Men's Hebrew Associations and Kindred Organizations was founded with 175 members in 1913 and merged with the National Jewish Welfare Board (now known as JWB) in 1920. A significant educational contribution of the associations was the training of teachers for Jewish religious schools. By the mid-1980s the 275 Jewish community centers and YMHAs and YWHAs and camps enrolled some 1 million members in a variety of activities that included physical education and health classes, as well as lectures and forums.

THEORIES OF RELIGIOUS EDUCATION

American religious education has depended heavily upon the work of several theorists. The first of these, Horace Bushnell, challenged the traditional concept of regeneration, especially with respect to children, in his *Christian Nurture* (1847). Arguing from an almost forgotten Congregationalist covenant doctrine according to which children were presumed to be "federally holy" and baptized as infants, he insisted that faith might well develop in an evolutionary fashion as part of the child's growth rather than in a single moment of conversion. While this view was challenged by many, it served as the basis for

much later religious education theory. Influenced by Bushnell and the writings of John Dewey, George Albert Coe's *A Social Theory of Religious Education* (1917) became the classic progressivist treatise. Insisting over and over again on the social character of religious education, which he defined as the "growth of the young toward and into a mature and efficient devotion to the democracy of God, and happy self-realization therein," Coe argued for the professionalization of religious education so that it might become the ground for wider social reconstruction.

Coe's position was attacked by Neo-Orthodox and Catholic critics who found his liberal views suspect. The most reasoned reply to these objections was Harrison Elliott's *Can Religious Education be Christian?* (1940). For Elliott, religious education necessarily had to be based in experience: "God is manifest supremely in Jesus Christ, but . . . nature and history are also manifestations of God who becomes known only through the experience and the reverent search of man." Utilizing the research of educational psychologists and of the neo-Freudian Karen Horney, he went on to show how such an approach was both religiously and developmentally sound. Like Coe, he insisted that a democratic society demanded democratic forms of religious education based on a gradual development of Christian faith. The writings of progressive theorists like Coe and Elliott have had a dramatic effect on religious education even among the Neo-Orthodox. While not all subscribe to the democratic liberalism of these major theorists, the notion of Christian nurture as the basis for religious education is held even by many conservative denominations. The years since the Second Vatican Council have witnessed a shift in Roman Catholic materials from an approach characterized by Coe and Elliott as authoritarian to one more experiential and progressivist in nature.

CONCLUSION

Religious education has been a part of American life for nearly four hundred years, its role more complex than simply the transmission of faith or religious truth. Religion exists only as part of a broader social matrix within which persons are situated. It is within these contexts that religious education has always manifested its importance. It has served not only as a vehicle for the transmission of religious beliefs but also of language and culture, a fact that has made recent immigrants among its most ardent supporters. Those from the mainstream, too, have emphasized religious education as a vital component in the preservation of their own "ways of seeing" and of a single republican vision. If faith in schooling has become a dogma of American civil religion, it is only because the eighteenth and nineteenth centuries have shown how effective religious training is in the transmission of culture.

The very importance of religious education, however, means that it will continue to be an arena of religious development and conflict. Traditionally, those on the margins have felt themselves threatened by the culture propagated in mainstream institutions and have responded with attempts to co-opt public schools or found their own. Just as the nineteenth century witnessed the emergence of Catholic and Lutheran education, the twentieth is seeing the rapid growth of Jewish and Christian day schools, as well as the emergence of a small network of conservative Catholic institutions. Recent immigration from Asia is likely to produce similar effects, especially as models of cultural diversity replace the older emphasis on the melting pot. We can expect that the shifting cultural mainstream, which now includes Catholics and Jews, will regard such new institutions with the same mistrust that characterized earlier Protestant views of Catholic schooling. Such conflict is inevitable, since the struggle is not only over the souls of children, but also over which cultures will survive into the next generation. Religious education is not simply of historical interest, but continues to function as a potent force in cultural transmission and, as a result, in the ongoing development of religion in America.

BIBLIOGRAPHY

Donald E. Boles, "Did the Walls Come Tumbling Down? Tuition Tax Credits in Minnesota," in *Religion and Public Education*, 11 (1984); Harold A. Buetow, *Of Singular Benefit* (1970); James C. Carper and Thomas C. Hunt, eds., *Religious Schooling in America* (1984); George Albert Coe, *A Social Theory of Religious Education* (1917); Lawrence A. Cremin, *American Education: The Colonial Experience* (1970) and *American Education: The National Experience* (1980); Robert D. Cross, "Origins of Catholic Parochial Schools in America," in *American Benedictine Review*, 16 (1965); Harrison S. Elliott, *Can Religious Education Be Christian?* (1940); Ruth Miller Elson, *Guardians of Tradition* (1964).

Andrew M. Greeley and Peter H. Rossi, *The Education of Catholic Americans* (1968); C. Howard Hopkins, *History of the Y.M.C.A. in North America* (1951); Thomas C. Hunt, "The Edgerton Bible Decision: The End of an Era," in *Catholic Historical Review*, 67 (1981) and, with Marilyn M. Maxson, eds., *Religion and Morality in American Schooling* (1981); J. Stillson Judah, *Hare Krishna and the Counterculture* (1974); Marvin Lazerson, "Understanding American Catholic Educational History," in *History of Education Quarterly*, 16 (1977); Robert W. Lynn and Elliott Wright, *The Big Little School* (1971; rev. 1980).

James McLachlan, *American Boarding Schools* (1970); Robert Michaelson, *Piety in the Public Schools* (1970); Judah Pilch, ed., *A History of Jewish Education in the United States* (1969); James W. Sanders, "Roman Catholics and the School Question in New York City: Some Suggestions for Research," in Diane Ravitch and Ronald K. Goodenow, eds., *Educating an Urban People* (1981); Stephen A. Schmidt, *A History of the Religious Education Association* (1984); H. Shelton Smith, ed., *Horace Bushnell* (1969); Timothy L. Smith, "Protestant Schooling and American Nationality, 1800–1850," in *Journal of American History*, 53 (1967); David Tyack and Elisabeth Hansot, *Managers of Virtue* (1982); Elizabeth Wilson, *Fifty Years of Association Work Among Young Women, 1886–1916* (1916).
[*See also* CHURCH AND STATE *and* CHRISTIAN THEOLOGICAL EDUCATION.]

RELIGION AND COLLEGIATE EDUCATION

F. Michael Perko

IN many respects, the history of the higher learning in America until very recent times is largely one in which religion and collegiate education are inextricably bound. In colonial America, religion served as a driving force in the formation of the first collegiate institutions, designed to produce both a learned clergy and an educated gentry. The early years of the nineteenth century witnessed the foundation of a host of institutions with specific denominational characters as American education expanded westward onto the frontier. After the Civil War, sectarian rivalries became even more pronounced, resulting in denominational founding and sponsorship of numerous institutions. Religious collegiate expansion continued well into the twentieth century, a situation attested to by the fact that the 1950 U.S. Census is the first that records a student population in publicly supported institutions equal to that in the private sector.

In addition to those schools with denominational affiliations, religion also found a place in secular institutions. Many of the early state universities were highly religious in tone. As campuses became more secularized in the later years of the nineteenth century, university pastors and chaplains were appointed to foster belief and observance. Later, denominational organizations such as the Jewish Hillel Foundation and the Roman Catholic Newman Clubs were organized as religious centers for students at state colleges and universities or for those attending institutions established by religious groups other than their own. Fueled by a discontent with the liberalization of American Protestantism in the last years of the nineteenth century, conservative Evangelicals and Fundamentalists developed organizations such as the Intervarsity Christian Fellowship and, later, Campus Crusade for Christ to evangelize the campuses and provide religious support for students from conservative Christian backgrounds.

THE COLONIAL ERA

Collegiate education in what is now the United States began with the establishment of an institution with a deeply religious character, Harvard College. Founded in 1636, it received its name as the result of a 1638 bequest of the Reverend John Harvard. The college was cast in the evangelical model of Emmanuel College of Cambridge University, one of the strongholds of English Puritanism. The curriculum, typical of the era, emphasized the study of classical and biblical languages, "catechetical divinity," and rhetoric. Virtually all of the college's administrators and tutors, as well as many of its overseers, were ministers. Just under half of the alumni between 1642 and 1689 entered the ministry. What is interesting is that just over half did not, suggesting that Harvard, from its earliest days, was also engaged in the education of gentlemen.

The second collegiate institution, William and Mary, existed in a very different ambient. As early as 1619 the Crown had appropriated 9,000 acres of land for a college, but an Indian massacre in 1622 eliminated many of the college's friends, as well as the Privy Counselor sent over to get it going. Finally, in 1693, William and Mary was founded to provide a literate clergy (in this case, Anglican) and to educate the colony's future leaders. A religious atmosphere less intense than Harvard's was a result of both the more traditionally English culture of Virginia and the Anglican "via media."

RELIGION AND COLLEGIATE EDUCATION

The role that sectarian conflict played in the formation of colonial collegiate institutions is illustrated by the history of the founding of the third college, Yale. By the end of the seventeenth century, conservative Congregationalists were wary of the atmosphere at Harvard. Increasing liberalizing influence there fueled the insistence of these divines that some more orthodox alternative was necessary. The Collegiate School in Connecticut was chartered in 1701, but only in 1716 settled in New Haven. A disgruntled fellow of the Harvard corporation, Cotton Mather, recruited Elihu Yale, a Boston-born Englishman living in London, as its first benefactor. In return for about £550 worth of dry goods, the college was renamed in his honor.

Religious disagreement produced another collegiate institution in 1746. The Great Awakening had swept through Yale in 1740 and was accorded a positive reception by both Thomas Clap, the rector, and the students. After an inflammatory sermon by Gilbert Tennent, however, the attitude rapidly changed. Yale became increasingly closed to the revivalists and their ideas. Some twenty years earlier, William Tennent, Sr., had formed the "Log College," an academy to train young men for the evangelical ministry. Like the Congregationalists, however, the Presbyterians were split into Old Side and New Side factions. After their 1738 expulsion from the New Brunswick Presbytery, the New Side party began to look in the direction of a more permanent collegiate institution than the "Log College." Their efforts culminated in the 1746 establishment of the College of New Jersey (renamed Princeton in 1896). Rather than having roots in the English universities, however, Princeton was grounded in the tradition of the dissenting academies of England and the Scottish universities.

While King's College (later Columbia University) in New York had initially been under the control of Anglicans, a revolt by Presbyterian and Dutch Reformed interests resulted in a new charter in 1754 that provided seats on the board of trustees for the senior Anglican, Dutch, French Calvinist, and Presbyterian ministers of the city. The cosmopolitan atmosphere of New York encouraged a religious diversity unique among the colonial colleges.

The growing strength of other religious groups resulted in the formation of several additional colleges. Arising out of the Hopewell (New Jersey) Academy founded in 1756 by the Philadelphia Association of Baptist Churches, a collegiate school eventually established itself in Rhode Island and was chartered in 1765. The College of Rhode Island was renamed in honor of its major benefactor, Nicholas Brown, in 1804.

Ethnicity and religious conflict motivated the founding of Queen's College (later Rutgers University) by the "New Light" faction within the Dutch Reformed Church in 1766. So strong were the ethnic ties that the first president, Jacob Rutsen Hardenberg, had little familiarity with English despite a family history of more than one hundred years in North America.

Dartmouth College arose out of the transformation of the Reverend Eleazar Wheelock's academy at Lebanon, Connecticut, originally established as an Indian school, into an institution of higher education. Wheelock, a "New Light" minister who fell under the spell of George Whitefield, was committed to the evangelization of Indians. A talented fund-raiser, he spent considerable time soliciting money in the British Isles, with the result that the £12,000 he gathered between 1766 and 1768 was probably more than was raised by any other colonial school or college in the years preceding the Revolution.

The patterns of collegiate formation before the Revolution illustrate the pervasive influence of religion. Of the nine colleges founded before 1776, only the University of Pennsylvania had nonreligious origins. Even it, however, soon passed into the hands of powerful Anglicans. By the Revolution, all nine of the colonial colleges were tied to religious interests.

Sectarian rivalry played a key role in collegiate formation. As an entire religious group, or one party within it, felt constrained by the available educational resources, it frequently moved to establish its own college. Higher education in a particular theological tradition, especially for future ministers, was seen as a vital part of the religious enterprise.

Relations both with denominations and the state were more ambiguous than would later be the case. While some of the early institutions (among them, the College of New Jersey and Queen's) were tied to denominational structures, others such as Dartmouth were essentially private enterprises in which the religious ties were more in the area of tradition than of financial support. Few, if any, required a religious test or evidence of denominational affiliation as a prerequisite for matriculation. Similarly, all of these institutions were beneficiaries of public revenues. Harvard, for example, received over $115,000 from Massachusetts prior to the Revolution. William and Mary, starting with a royal grant of £2,000, later received duties on skins and furs, and still later the proceeds of a tobacco tax. During the Revolution, Yale received a French prize of war brought into New London. Virtually all of the colonies allowed colleges to run lotteries, and Rhode Island exempted Brown's faculty from taxes.

PROTESTANT HIGHER EDUCATION, 1776 TO 1860

The revolutionary war resulted in the devastation of several American colleges. The College of New Jersey, having served at various times as a billet for British and Continental troops, as a military hospital, and as the temporary capitol of the Continental Congress, was left in shambles. Yale was forced to close for lack of food, while William and Mary's Wren building was accidentally burned to the ground by French troops quartered there during the siege of Yorktown. Financial hardships were also wrought by the loss of Crown subsidies. During the years following the war, individual states moved to disestablish religion, creating difficulties in Massachusetts, Virginia, New Hampshire, Connecticut, and New York, where colleges were tied to the established church. Generally the transition to completely private status was a gradual one; and Harvard continued to enjoy a virtual monopoly on higher education in Massachusetts until the 1852 founding of Tufts by Universalists.

In spite of these reverses, the period from the Revolution to the Civil War was one of massive collegiate growth: over 250 new colleges were founded, in contrast to the 9 of the colonial era. The reasons for this dramatic expansion were varied. American faith in the future and the conviction that an educated citizenry was necessary to national preservation played a major role. Sectional rivalries and the perception that the presence of a college enhanced the prestige of local communities also served as motivating forces. As curricula broadened, students began

to perceive that college education had an economic purpose. Legally, the Dartmouth College case decided by the Supreme Court in 1819 established the right of chartered private institutions to conduct instruction without state interference, encouraging institutional formation.

Religious factors also played a major role in the expansion. The Second Great Awakening in the early decades of the nineteenth century produced a religious fervor that found expression in a marked acceleration of new college foundations during the 1830s, rising to a high point between 1856 and 1861. Competition among denominations spurred higher educational development, as did fear of the rising network of Roman Catholic schooling on the frontier. The conviction was strong that the evangelization of the frontier required literate ministers who could best be trained in western institutions. The commitment to this enterprise was such that of some 40,000 pre-1860 college graduates examined in one study, 10,000 had entered the ministry. An illustrative result was the formation of eleven religiously affiliated colleges in Kentucky, twenty-one in Illinois, and thirteen in Iowa before 1870.

A key institution in this educational expansion was the Society for the Promotion of Collegiate and Theological Education at the West (SPCTEW), a pan-Protestant agency founded in 1843 that solicited funds and provided moral support for college foundation and development while muting some of the worst features of denominational zeal. Although some eastern colleges were aided by the society, the main thrust of its effort was collegiate education on the frontier. With the 1887 establishment of Pomona College in California, institutions aided by the SPCTEW stretched from coast to coast, and the support given totaled as much as $74,000 in a single year. Although theological education was to be the priority of these new institutions, they quickly began to devote themselves to broader constituencies.

Perhaps the most prominent educational groups in the antebellum period were Presbyterian. These accounted for forty-nine colleges. The reasons for this Presbyterian domination, especially on the frontier, involved high standards of ministerial education and willingness to enter into cooperative collegiate ventures via the SPCTEW. Common efforts with the Congregationalists, for example, resulted in the establishment of colleges in twenty-one of the thirty-four states prior to the Civil War.

Congregational interests were responsible for the establishment of twenty-one colleges, either exclusively or in cooperation with other religious groups (most notably, Presbyterians). Initially, the tendency was to found these in the East. After the failure of the Plan of Union, however, Congregationalist missionaries followed the natural patterns of migration from New England into the Midwest and established eight colleges in the upper Mississippi Valley. At least one college, Wheaton, was founded in protest to perceived Presbyterian domination of Knox and Illinois colleges, which had been joint ventures. Two colleges on the West Coast, including the College of California (1855)—which became the secular University of California in 1868—were Congregationalist-related prior to the Civil War.

Initially, Methodists had little impetus for sponsoring higher education. Because of an emphasis on personal conversion rather than intellectual questioning, education beyond the basic level was regarded as largely unnecessary. The 1784 *Book of Discipline* commented, "Gaining knowledge is a good thing, but saving souls is better." It was not until the 1830s that real advocacy of higher educational standards for the ministry began. As a result of this shift, Methodists, like other evangelical Protestants, moved to found colleges to train future clergy. Their efforts, which reached a peak in the 1850s, culminated in the foundation of some thirty-four institutions by 1860.

The pattern of collegiate development among Baptists was similar. After the establishment of the College of Rhode Island in 1765, largely as the result of local interest, it was nearly fifty years before the foundation of the second Baptist college, Colby, in 1813. Like the Methodists, the Baptists had no tradition of an educated ministry, and tended to recruit their membership from the lower socioeconomic strata. As the denomination became more stable and wealthy in the 1820s, and as a result of concern over competition with other groups, higher education began to develop. During the next forty years, some twenty-five Baptist institutions were established. The emergence of the Disciples of Christ cost the Baptists some of their most ardent educational advocates, and the church was rent again, like the Methodists, by the Great Schism of 1844.

Several other denominations were also active in collegiate formation, although to a lesser extent. Episcopalian interests in education resulted in the foundation of about ten colleges in the antebellum period. A number of these, such as Columbia, Pennsylvania, and Charleston, passed out of Episcopal control fairly quickly, however, while others, such as Kenyon (1824), remained denominational. Beginning with Gettysburg (1832) and Wittenberg (1845), Lutherans established colleges for the promotion of faith and ethnic culture. The first Disciples college, Bacon (1837), became the University of Kentucky, and was followed by four others. German Reformed interests were served by the formation of four colleges, Universalists by four, and the Society of Friends and Unitarians by two each. Single colleges were founded by the Christian Church and United Brethren, and the Dutch Reformed continued with their one institution, now named Rutgers.

While individuals belonging to all of these denominations were active in college formation, caution must be exercised in stressing the ties between various denominations and colleges. Recent research suggests that while most of the newly formed institutions could be identified with one tradition or another, few had the strong denominational ties and sponsorship that would later be the case. Most were the results of a kind of religious boosterism that sought to improve the local community by establishing higher education. These institutions might best be characterized broadly as Christian colleges, spreading pan-Protestantism to the expanding population of the West, rather than as strictly denominational ones.

As we have seen, one of the great periods of expansion for religious higher education in America occurred between the Revolution and the Civil War. Most of these colleges were small (the average enrollment of Ohio's twenty-two colleges in 1859 was eighty-five students) and as likely to fail as to succeed (one estimate places the number of failures by 1860 as high as 700). Religious factionalism frequently weakened support and denominational rivalry promoted an oversupply of colleges. Given these handicaps, their establishment was frequently a near-miracle. Horace Mann's snide remark that "The Great West has been conquered, religiously speaking, from Black Hawk to John Calvin" contained more than a grain of truth, and the

Protestant colleges were major vehicles of this conquest.

While most of American collegiate education was religiously based during the antebellum era, a new form of higher education was also emerging. Beginning with the University of Georgia in 1785, state-sponsored education entered the marketplace. By 1800 institutions had been founded in North Carolina, Tennessee, and Vermont; and by 1861 twenty of the thirty-four states were sponsoring institutions of higher education.

These public institutions were not secular in the contemporary sense. In 1840, 67 percent of the state universities had clergymen as presidents. Religious interests dominated the formation of several of these institutions. The University of North Carolina, Delaware College, and Indiana State University were only a few of the schools under Presbyterian control, while Mississippi College (1830) passed from state to Presbyterian to Baptist control before permanently becoming a state institution in 1844. The distinction sometimes made between religiously affiliated colleges and those founded according to secular "revolutionary" principles is not generally meaningful during this period. Both were religious in orientation, administered by clergy, and governed by the religious leaders within the community.

PROTESTANT HIGHER EDUCATION, 1860 TO 1940

The Civil War era witnessed profound changes in American collegiate education. The alliance of East and Midwest, the promotion of westward expansion, and the sweeping away of the old planter aristocracy were all felt in higher education and combined with missionary zeal to encourage the continued establishment of religious colleges on the frontier. The departure of southern legislators from Congress made possible the passage of the Morrill Act in 1862, which gave federal land to the states in support of technical and agricultural education. Since the monies derived from the sale of these lands could be distributed in a variety of ways, a number of private colleges with religious roots, including Yale, Dartmouth, Rutgers, and Transylvania, became "land grant" schools.

A major institution that arose after the war was the research university. Patterned loosely on the model of the German university, it concentrated on the education of graduate students and the production of research. Beginning with the 1874 to 1876 formation of the Johns Hopkins University, the research universities came to exercise an increasing prominence in American society. Their professional emphasis and later their skepticism about the compatibility of science and religion served to separate them from the religious colleges of the day with their emphases on broad liberal education for undergraduates and the development of piety and virtue. Even institutions that began with strong religious ties, like the Baptist-related University of Chicago (1888), quickly moved in directions that took them far from those of their co-religionists.

A drift of four-year colleges out of explicitly religious orbits began to occur in the postwar period. Among Presbyterians, colleges such as Princeton, Western Reserve, and New York University disaffiliated, while by 1884, eighty-four directly related and fifty-eight indirectly related institutions lost their Methodist affiliation. Vassar and George Washington lost their Baptist affiliation during this era, while Harvard, Yale, and California severed their Congregationalist ties. These shifts can be attributed to several causes, among them the evolution of some religiously affiliated institutions into public ones and conflict among denominations. The incorporation of the Carnegie Foundation for the Advancement of Teaching in 1905 also tended to encourage secularization since colleges had to sacrifice most denominational ties in order to allow their faculties to qualify for Carnegie pension benefits. While this influence has probably been overstated, some fifteen colleges (e.g., Dickinson and Goucher) of the first fifty accepted by the foundation officially severed denominational links to do so. The fact, too, that several denominations began to strengthen their links with collegiate education may have influenced them to end their relationships with institutions having only nominal affiliation.

The increased self-definition of American religious bodies is seen in their moves during this period to establish national boards or agencies to deal with higher education. In 1893 the Congregationalists established the American Education Society and, in the following year, the Congregational Education Society. These were followed in 1921 by the Congregational Foundation for Education, which took over responsibility for church-related colleges and provided over $200,000 in aid during the first year. Among Presbyterians, the most strenuous efforts were those of the Presbyterian Church, U.S.A., which founded the Presbyterian Board of Aid for Colleges and Academies in 1883 to take responsibility for raising funds and allocating territories to the Presbyterian colleges for their own fund-raising efforts. In 1905–1906 contributions amounting to over $1.5 million were made. Rising denominational concern for more direct relations with affiliated colleges is seen in this board's policy of providing aid only when a college was either organically connected with the church or when the charter provided for a board of trustees with a two-thirds Presbyterian membership.

Two Lutheran bodies, the Lutheran Church in America and the Norwegian Lutheran Church of America, exercised similar control. Initially the Lutheran Church in America's Board of Education, founded in 1887, was empowered to select sites and open colleges. After 1907 it was able to give financial aid to schools besides the struggling western institutions. To receive aid, however, institutions were required to be connected to a synod or have a board consisting of two-thirds church members. The Norwegian church controlled only two colleges, St. Olaf and Luther, but did so directly since the church convention was also the corporation that governed the colleges.

Perhaps the most direct control was asserted by the Methodists, who founded a Board of Education in 1868, partially out of a concern for the proliferation of colleges. While this board initially did little but provide loans to ministerial students, an 1892 reorganization established a University Senate mandated with the task of setting uniform degree standards and classifying institutions. This was the first use of such a board as a de facto accrediting agency, since this function was generally carried out by state agencies.

Because of traditions of local control among Baptists and Disciples of Christ, denominational agencies exercised far less control. Anyone could become a member of the American Baptist Education Society, founded in 1888, by contributing $10. This agency sought to secure sites and buildings, contribute to operating expenses, and support teachers' salaries. Its chief enter-

prise in the early days was the University of Chicago, but aid was also given to a number of other colleges. The society consisted largely of one man, John D. Rockefeller, who contributed $1.9 million of the $3.4 million given by the mid-1890s. When he turned his attention elsewhere, the society foundered. It was reconstituted in 1920. While there had been early insistence on denominational control of institutions, this changed rapidly since the agency had no real control over either state conventions or the individual colleges. Among the Disciples of Christ, a similar lack of power retarded the formation of any board, until the Association of Disciples Colleges, rather than the denomination, formed a Board of Education in 1914.

The increased denominational interest in higher education, mirrored in the establishment of educational agencies, resulted in a wave of college formations. Among the northern Presbyterians, the loci of attention were the midwestern and border states. The southern branch of the church continued its development of colleges throughout the South and in the border states. Among the other denominations of Calvinist origin, the Congregationalists started colleges in the Midwest, as did the German Reformed, Christian Reformed Church, and the Reformed Church in America.

Especially prominent in college formation during the post–Civil War era were the Methodists. Between 1860 and 1940 over thirty new schools were established, largely in the midwestern and southern states. Lutheran bodies such as the Lutheran Church in America and the Norwegian Lutheran Church took advantage of increases in strength from immigration to develop collegiate education in the upper Midwest and Pacific Northwest. Perhaps the most concerted Lutheran efforts were those made by the Lutheran Church—Missouri Synod. A need to staff parochial schools motivated the establishment of an extensive network of at least seven teachers' colleges in the last years of the nineteenth and first years of the twentieth centuries.

The movement for women's collegiate education, which had begun before the Civil War, resulted in the foundation of schools by most major denominations. Even those schools that were not under denominational control, moreover, were highly religious in tone. Institutions such as Vassar (1861), Wellesley, and Smith (both 1875), to cite only a few examples, offered curricula that consisted of both classical learning and Protestant religious culture.

The greatest Protestant collegiate advances of the period, however, were made by the more conservative denominations, as well as by new groups that had only begun to emerge during the latter half of the nineteenth century. As these became more stable and their members prospered economically, they turned their attention toward higher education.

Within the conservative wings of major denominations, Southern Baptist Convention educational foundations were among the most extensive. Between 1860 and 1945 at least twenty new institutions, such as Stetson University (1883) and Blue Mountain College (1873), were begun, largely in southern and border states. Typically, schools were affiliated with the various state Baptist conventions. Various Mennonite bodies founded at least five colleges around the turn of the century, while the Church of the Brethren was responsible for at least four more. The Free Methodist Church of North America and the Wesleyan Church founded at least four colleges, while the Reformed and Associate Reformed Presbyterians also became involved in higher education. Even the small Wisconsin Evangelical Lutheran Synod established several institutions, including Northwestern College (1865) and a collegiate pre-seminary.

A number of the newer denominations established institutions of higher education. After some initially rocky starts, the Seventh-day Adventists developed a nationwide network of colleges, including schools in California, Maryland, Massachusetts, Michigan, Nebraska, Tennessee, Texas, and Washington. Because of Adventists' religiously based interest in health, these schools quickly developed programs in education, nutrition, and medicine. Between 1899 and 1920 the Church of the Nazarene also established at least five colleges. The Churches of Christ started several institutions, mainly from 1900 to 1940, including the moderately large Pepperdine University (1937), while the Churches of God of Anderson, Indiana, and Cleveland, Tennessee, started schools in Ohio, Oregon, Tennessee, and Texas, largely out of roots in former Bible colleges (discussed below). Two schools sponsored by the Assemblies of God, Southern California College (1920) and Northwest College

(1934), also had Bible college origins. The Church of Jesus Christ of Latter-day Saints formed Brigham Young University (1875), while the Reorganized Church of Jesus Christ of Latter-day Saints established Park (1875) and Graceland (1895) colleges in Missouri and Iowa.

The Civil War period also marked the beginning of religiously based education for blacks. An effort by the African Education Society, an auxiliary of the American Colonization Society, resulted in the establishment of Pennsylvania's Ashmun Institute (later Lincoln University) in 1854. Two years later Wilberforce University of Ohio was founded. These institutions were initially under Presbyterian and Methodist auspices.

The era from 1865 to 1900 witnessed the creation of forty four-year private black colleges, including Livingston College (1879) and Morris Brown College (1881). Among the white or integrated denominations and agencies that participated in this effort were the American Missionary Association, American Baptist Home Missionary Society, Disciples of Christ, Methodist Episcopalians, Presbyterians, Seventh-day Adventists, Episcopalians, and Congregationalists. Almost an equal number of black colleges were the product of black churches such as the African Methodist Episcopal, African Methodist Episcopal Zion, and Christian Methodist Episcopal Churches, as well as several black Baptist groups.

Also beginning to offer post-secondary instruction during these years were the new institutions known as Bible institutes or colleges. As conservative Evangelicals became increasingly disillusioned with the religious and theological education available in the major denominations, they moved to found these separate institutions whose goal was to produce a cadre of biblically literate and religiously mature lay people for work both in home and foreign missions. Some Bible schools were supported by conservative denominations such as the Churches of Christ, Free Will Baptists, Assemblies of God, Christian and Missionary Alliance, and Christian Reformed. The majority, however, were interdenominational institutions that attracted students from a wide variety of religious backgrounds, including mainstream Protestant ones. A partial list of the schools founded by 1945 includes over 100 entries, an indication of their rapid rise on the higher educational landscape. Over time, a number of them became accredited four-year colleges.

The curricula of these colleges deviated markedly from that provided in more traditional institutions. Frequently, the lack of adequate student preparation necessitated remediation in basic skills. The study of the English Bible dominated the program of instruction. As these schools developed, they began to offer instruction in classical and biblical languages, theology, and, in the more liberal ones, social sciences. Specialized vocational education was also provided for those who wished to become church pastors, Christian educators, church musicians, or missionaries. An emphasis on "practical work" and field-based instruction sent students into a wide variety of social, philanthropic, and church institutions to learn by doing.

The students themselves tended to come from lower-middle-class backgrounds. Males were frequently in the minority, making the Bible schools a vehicle for women's education. The students also tended to be older than traditional undergraduates and many had worked in a variety of secular occupations before entering the school.

The funding of these schools was generally the result of small donations from individuals, congregations, and graduates, with occasional larger donations. Operating expenses were low, since faculty initially received little or no remuneration while serving several functions. In their early days, there was a general reluctance to obtain endowments or construct new buildings since many of those responsible were premillennialists who believed in an imminent Second Coming. In time, however, the institutions responded to pressures urging them to stabilize.

Perhaps the most famous and prosperous of these schools is the Moody Bible Institute. Founded by Dwight L. Moody, a successful shoe salesman who abandoned his career to become a full-time evangelist, it began in 1889 in a single three-story building and by 1927 occupied another thirty-three. In the latter years of the 1920s, the combined enrollment in its day and evening schools usually exceeded 2,000, with many more in the correspondence division; the school owned over $4.5 million in property; and its leaders raised more than $400,000 annually to meet expenses.

Most Bible colleges, however, were more modest. The Boston Bible School (1897), for example, rarely had more than 20 students at any time until the 1930s, and never more than 100. In its fourth year, the budget was only $780, and it struggled throughout the era to survive. The Missionary Training Institute (1882) founded in New York City by A. B. Simpson, a Presbyterian minister, had only around 200 students during the early 1900s.

Besides training workers for the growing Fundamentalist movement, the Bible colleges also served as quasi-denominational unifying centers. Establishing reputations as centers of piety and sound doctrine, they educated the young, sponsored conferences, and published a wide range of literature. For many of their alumni, the Bible college served as the community of primary allegiance in a religious movement that tended toward radical congregationalism.

PROTESTANT HIGHER EDUCATION, 1940 TO THE PRESENT

While few colleges were formed during World War II, the postwar years saw the growth of denominational higher education. Fueled by veterans returning to school under the Servicemen's Readjustment Act (GI Bill of Rights) of 1944 and, later, by the postwar "baby boom," many colleges increased in size and complexity, with many doubling in size. In several instances, mainline denominational institutions merged, while in others, denominations cooperated in the establishment of new colleges. Most new institutions, however, were the product of efforts by conservative religious groups. The Church of God of Cleveland, Tennessee, Churches of Christ, Christian Reformed, and Pentecostal Holiness churches all began schools in these years. Among the Southern Baptists, there were at least five new schools. One individual congregation, Thomas Road Baptist Church, and its pastor, the Reverend Jerry Falwell, assumed responsibility in 1971 for the establishment of Liberty Baptist College in Lynchburg, Virginia.

Some 400 to 600 Protestant colleges and universities are in operation today; it is difficult to accurately determine their number since the relations between colleges and their associated religious groups vary, and since nondenominational institutions are usually counted as nonsectarian. A 1966 Danforth Foundation study showed that over 66 percent were associated in ways that included at least five of the six criteria of control of board membership, ownership by religious body, financial support by religious group, religious statement of purpose, and preferential hiring of faculty and administrators. Baptists and Lutherans tend to have the strongest relationships, and Presbyterians the weakest.

Academic programs also vary by denomination. About 33 percent of all religious (including Roman Catholic) doctoral-granting institutions are under Methodist auspices. Of Presbyterian schools, 75 percent are four-year undergraduate colleges.

Overwhelmingly, America's Protestant colleges are two- or four-year institutions. Curricula tend to be fairly standard and resemble those of secular institutions, though conservative groups tend to stress the study of philosophy and religion more than others. The colleges are for the most part in the middle of the academic marketplace. On the one hand, they are underrepresented on a Danforth list of the top fifty American institutions based on entrance of their alumni into first-rank Ph.D. programs and acquisition of prestigious fellowships. On the other hand, these schools are well represented by physicians and college teachers. Not surprisingly, they are the greatest producers of clergy.

Within the colleges, values and perceptions vary by institutional type. Students in Evangelical and Fundamentalist schools tend to value propriety, community, and practicality of education more highly, while those in mainline denominational institutions place more stress on scholarship. Mainline students seem more oriented toward liberal-arts values while those in evangelical and fundamentalist schools are more directed toward vocational ones. In one study cited by Bowles and DeCosta (1971), Protestant college graduates ranked higher on scales of aesthetics, awareness of differing life-styles, interest in politics, and appreciation of individuality than the national average, but were below the national average on appreciation of vocational training and understanding of science and technology.

The major problems for many of the Protestant colleges involve finance. Salaries continue to be lower than the national average, and the lack of library holdings is among the greatest weaknesses. While most of the physical plants are adequate, a lack of funding for faculty research and continuing education makes it difficult to attract the best professors. The vast majority of colleges receive some denominational funding, with the Lutheran Church—Missouri Synod among the most generous.

CATHOLIC HIGHER EDUCATION

The development of Catholic higher education in America follows the same general patterns as that of the Protestant colleges, but with a time lag. Only after the foundation of sixteen other institutions was the first American Catholic college, Georgetown, established in 1786. In large measure, this was a result of the paucity of American Catholics. As late as 1770 there were no more than 22,000 Catholics in the country, and only after the late 1830s did the number top 500,000. Even after Catholics began to arrive in greater numbers several factors served to retard institutional growth: their comparative poverty, the popular sentiment that religious education necessarily involved yet unavailable clergy and religious, and a reluctance on the part of bishops to support colleges under lay control.

The schools were founded for reasons comparable to those that motivated Protestant collegiate establishment. Concern for preliminary education for seminary students, the desirability of such stable institutions as centers for missionary activity, and the need to inculcate moral values were all articulated as reasons for school formation. While the focus of attention in Catholic colleges was on support of the growing Catholic community, significant numbers of Protestant students also matriculated, especially in those locales with few other educational alternatives.

About half of the forty-two Catholic colleges established between 1786 and 1850 were founded by bishops, with an equal number started by religious congregations and a few by priests as venture (for profit) schools. After 1850 religious communities dominated institutional formation. Most prominent among these were the Jesuits, who had established thirteen schools by 1850, and doubled that number by 1916.

Like many of their Protestant counterparts, these fledgling Catholic schools frequently suffered from a lack of funding and enrollment. Only ten of the forty-two founded before 1850 have survived, and only 30 percent of those established between 1851 and 1899. Only as American Catholics became both more prosperous and more attuned to the value of higher education did the rate of failure go down.

Unlike the Protestant colleges, the model of organization for the early Catholic schools was generally Continental rather than English. Frequently this meant that students were enrolled after the completion of primary schooling and graduated six years later with a bachelor's degree. Only after the late-nineteenth-century Committee of Ten Report (issued by the National Educational Association in its efforts to establish a formative high school curriculum) did many of the schools adopt the more typical model of a four-year high school followed by a college course of the same length. The curriculum itself was similar to that of the Protestant college, stressing classical languages and philosophy, and underwent a similar evolution in the second half of the nineteenth century, broadening to include English and scientific studies. While commercial courses were offered after the Civil War, students taking them received no degree.

The faculty before 1900 were generally clergy, who comprised nearly 90 percent of most nineteenth-century teaching staffs. The problem of finding qualified instructors was especially acute for diocesan institutions. Those under the sponsorship of religious communities could generally bring personnel from Europe. Since many of the clergy were also involved in parochial ministry, teaching staffs were augmented frequently by impressing seminarians into service. Lay teachers were viewed as second-class citizens, required to keep all of the religious rules of the school but kept in insignificant positions. Salaries were low, contributing to perennial problems in recruiting an adequate faculty.

The major administrators of Catholic colleges throughout the nineteenth and early twentieth centuries were ideally priests who were good preachers and visionary builders. As was also the case in most Protestant schools after the early years of the colonial era, Catholic colleges were administrators' schools, and presidents had near absolute power. Most, however, were young and inexperienced, contributing to the problems of their fragile institutions. Since most were also the superiors of their religious communities, there was frequent turnover. While Charles W. Eliot ruled Harvard for forty years in the late nineteenth and early twentieth centuries, Loyola University of Chicago had fourteen different presidents during the same period.

The finances of many of these institutions were tenuous throughout their histories. While some bishops gave land and buildings to orders for colleges, many schools were founded with little or no aid. The primary source of income was instructional, and endowments were generally nonexistent. The Jesuits experienced a special problem since they were forbidden by rule to require fees for their teaching.

Generally, Catholic schools were not coeducational. The admission of women to previously all-male colleges frequently began with summer sessions designed for sisters and other teachers, as was the case at Marquette in 1909. Very few traditionally men's schools, however, admitted women on an equal basis until after 1960. Education for women was provided in separate institutions that paralleled the Protestant women's colleges. These Catholic schools began comparatively late, with the College of Notre Dame of Maryland (1896) probably being the first. By the 1930s some twenty had been started. They offered a curriculum similar to that of the men's colleges, but with the addition of domestic departments. One of their earliest functions was the training of teachers.

Catholic institutions also lagged in the development of graduate and professional education. The late 1870s saw the beginnings of graduate programs only at Georgetown and St. John's (later Fordham University). Only with the 1889 opening of the Catholic University of America, the result of a $300,000 bequest, was there an attempt to parallel the secular Johns Hopkins. In most cases, it was the 1930s before serious masters' programs emerged, and it was nearly thirty more years before even a few Catholic schools developed doctoral programs.

In the area of professional education, a few Catholic institutions quickly emerged. In the early years of the twentieth century Creighton, St. Louis, Marquette, and Loyola of Chicago added medical schools; St. Louis, Notre Dame, Georgetown, and Catholic University had become involved in legal education a generation earlier. This rapid expansion into medical and legal education was not so much the result of creating new schools as of affiliating free-standing institutions that were seeking stability and respectability. Among other areas of professional education that Catholic schools entered before World War II were engineering, nursing, education, and dentistry.

Today's roughly 240 Catholic colleges are characterized by a diversity nearly as wide as that of their Protestant counterparts. Varying in size from under a hundred students to over 16,000, they serve a wide variety of constituencies. A few large institutions enroll a disproportionate number of students. The twenty-eight Jesuit colleges and universities, for example, represent less than 10 percent of Catholic institutions of higher education, yet serve over 30 percent of the students. Colleges sponsored by communities of religious women, on the other hand, comprise the largest group of institutions but enroll fewer students than the Jesuit schools.

Recent shifts within Catholicism and American society have had profound effects on the colleges. A combination of demographic factors and a more pronounced theology of the laity has resulted in more lay participation in the colleges, and has helped to change their character in the process. Decreasing numbers of clergy and religious to staff institutions have raised costs and threatened many small schools. At a time when the population of college-age students is decreasing, funding has become a more serious problem, since Catholic colleges continue to depend more on tuition income than do colleges at large. The general inability of Catholic schools to develop outstanding graduate programs has prevented their movement into the first rank of American universities. Increased professionalization and secularization have created identity problems for many institutions, while pressure to specialize has destroyed the ideal of an intellectual synthesis on which most Catholic education was based.

Catholic alumni are as likely to succeed at good secular graduate and professional schools as are alumni of other institutions, and they enter these at a rate proportionate to their numbers in the collegiate population. There is no evidence that attendance at Catholic colleges is either an economic or an academic handicap. According to Greeley (1969), Catholic students who have gone to Catholic schools tend to view the church more positively and are more likely to remain in the church than Catholics who attend secular institutions. The success of American Catholic higher education, which currently enrolls over 500,000 students, appears to be greatest on the level of four-year undergraduate schooling.

JEWISH HIGHER EDUCATION

While Jewish groups in the United States have not been heavily involved in the establishment of colleges and universities, there are nonetheless examples of Jewish higher education. In the late 1850s Isaac M. Wise established Zion Collegiate in Cincinnati as a preparatory school for a planned rabbinical seminary. Although this effort failed after one year, it established a pattern by which secondary and, occasionally, higher education was conducted under the auspices of noncollegiate institutions. Several of the ten yeshivas (schools of Talmudic learning) founded between 1908 and 1959 in New York, Baltimore, Detroit, and Cleveland engaged in collegiate as well as rabbinical education. The seminaries also became involved.

The Jewish Theological Seminary of America (1886) developed programs in Hebrew literature and religious education and, in 1947, founded the University of Judaism in Los Angeles to promote Jewish education among the laity and encourage youth to enter Jewish teaching and other professions. After its 1948 merger with the Jewish Institute of Religion, Hebrew Union College also began preparing teachers. Perhaps the most extensive programs of college education developed out of the Rabbi Isaac Elchanan Seminary in New York (1897), which began a Teachers Institute for Men in 1917 and, in 1928, was given state permission to conduct a college of arts and sciences along with rabbinical work and to give a secular bachelor's degree. These programs became the basis in 1945 for the foundation of Yeshiva University.

Another institution that has entered the field of Jewish post-secondary education is the teachers college. The first of these, Gratz College of Philadelphia, was founded in 1894; by 1928, another six were started. The period since World War II has seen the development of four more. All of these began as training schools for teachers but eventually became involved with advanced studies and adult education. Several have developed cooperative ventures with secular institutions.

The only independent Jewish graduate school in America that has been devoted exclusively to Jewish scholarship is Dropsie College for Hebrew and Cognate Learning (founded in 1907). Its programs in rabbinics, Scripture, language and history, philosophy, education, and Middle Eastern studies were developed to meet the particular needs of its constituency. Recently, however, the college changed its name to the Annenberg Research Institute, and is no longer accepting incoming graduate students.

Other religious groups besides Christians and Jews have entered higher education, though in small numbers. The followers of an Eastern guru established Maharishi International University in 1972, utilizing the plant of a failed college in Iowa. A more recent development was the foundation in the early 1980s of the American Islamic College in Chicago, which has specialized in Arabic language and culture and Islamic religion.

RELIGIOUS MINISTRY IN SECULAR HIGHER EDUCATION

In addition to sponsoring religious colleges, various groups have attempted to establish a presence on the campuses of secular institutions or those of other denominations. Initially there was little effort among mainline Protestants and Catholics to provide religious ministry in a collegiate setting. While Yale appointed the Reverend Naphtali Daggett as Livingston Professor of Divinity in 1755, making him in the process America's first college chaplain, it was more than a century before the example was emulated, and in 1920 there were fewer than twenty full-time college chaplains in the United States.

What explicit religious organization was done tended to occur in student voluntary organizations. One of the first attempts at a national grouping came with the establishment of the Young Men's Christian Association. Brought from England by a New York University student in 1851, the organization quickly established its interest in college students. In 1857 the first campus YMCA was founded at the University of Virginia. Fifteen years later, at the Illinois State Normal School, the first campus Young Women's Christian Association was formed. Over the years, YMCAs and YWCAs have provided a wide range of classes and support services for Christian students on both denominational and secular campuses.

A variety of factors motivated the development of chaplaincies on Protestant campuses around the turn of the twentieth century. Since fewer administrators and faculty were clergy, there was a growing inability to meet religious demands. The demise of compulsory chapel at institutions such as Harvard in 1887 and Dartmouth in 1920 created a feeling that some replacement was necessary. As various functions within the colleges became more specialized, the desirability of an explicitly religious pastor and counselor became clear. By this time, too, many denominations were in a financial position to make support of such positions more likely.

The period from 1880 to 1910 was one of local experimentation. Only the Presbyterian Church in the United States of America moved to define a long-term policy. During these years Presbyterians, Baptists, Methodists, and Congregationalists all established full-time campus pastorates at secular universities, while Lutherans and Episcopalians began a policy of trying to make the local parishes centers for student ministry. The Disciples of Christ concentrated on the teaching ministry, establishing Bible chairs at five state universities by 1909. Roman Catholics founded the Melvin Catholic Club at the University of Wisconsin in 1880, and in 1894 the first Newman Club was established at the University of Pennsylvania.

The next ten years saw denominational action on a large scale. Northern Baptists, Lutherans, Episcopalians, and Congregationalists all established national agencies or supplied national funding for campus ministry. Methodist activities began more slowly, largely as a result of concerted opposition by the supporters of denominational colleges. The Federation of Catholic College Clubs, while not a national agency, served to coordinate Newman Center activities. These national actions were mirrored by an increase in personnel, so that, by the early 1920s, there were over 125 full-time chaplains of various denominations in secular colleges and universities.

Expansion continued in the years prior to

World War II. Denominational expenditures for college work rose, generally peaking between 1925 and 1930. Despite a sharp decline as a result of the Great Depression, support began to rise again after 1935. Campus ministry activities were begun by the Presbyterian Church in the United States, Southern Baptist Convention, and Southern Methodists. Many groups drew up plans to supply religious support not only to those enrolled in state schools but to all students belonging to the denomination. Unitarians, Mormons, and Christian Scientists also created programs. Jewish ministry to students began with the establishment in 1925 of the first Hillel Foundation, sponsored by B'nai B'rith, at the University of Illinois.

Developments since World War II have taken a somewhat different form. While the goal of many denominations had been to place a minister on every campus, the dramatic increase in students, coupled with a lack of funding, has encouraged interchurch ventures. Groups such as the United Church of Christ, Presbyterians, American Baptists, Disciples of Christ, and Episcopalians frequently have banded together to provide services. Denominational colleges, including Catholic ones, have begun to provide ecumenical campus-ministry staffs, and the utilization of lay ministers has increased. Even where cooperative ministry has not taken hold, coordination among campus religious groups has proved highly effective.

The percentage of full-time campus clergy has increased at a significantly faster rate than that of the clergy at large. Although the number of campus ministers has grown, many centers are still understaffed. Full-time workers also tend to be concentrated in church-related colleges and large public universities, with few in community colleges and urban universities.

The style of campus ministry has also broadened. Many ministry settings provide not only counseling and worship, but also educational programming, student residences, and social-action projects. About fifty Bible chairs have been established in state schools, largely as a result of Disciples of Christ activities, and campus pastors in many other settings teach on a part-time basis. An increasing number of colleges, including secular ones, employ coordinators of religious affairs on their student-personnel services staffs.

The same era that has seen the development of campus ministry as a profession has also witnessed the strengthening of student-led religious groups. The alliance of the YMCA and YWCA with liberal Protestants in the 1920s made these organizations increasingly unacceptable to the growing numbers of Evangelicals and Fundamentalists interested in higher education. Unsuccessful attempts were made to provide support for Evangelicalism in the colleges with the formation in 1925 of the League of Evangelical Students and the Intercollegiate Gospel Fellowship in 1939. Meanwhile, the Intervarsity Christian Fellowship had established itself in Great Britain. In response to a call from several academics and wealthy businessmen, Intervarsity sent a medical student to Canada in 1928 to begin programs. In 1939 the Canadian fellowship sent three workers to the United States. They established a students' residence and twenty chapters of the organization in the first year. Over the years, the number of chapters has increased significantly, as have the organization's financial resources. Mergers in 1945 with the Students Foreign Mission Fellowship and in 1948 with the Nurses Christian Fellowship have given Intervarsity an orientation toward mission and broadened its scope to include students in nursing schools and training hospitals.

Utilizing an itinerant staff, the focus of the organization is on giving students the responsibility for local evangelism. While Intervarsity has no systematic doctrine, its working theology may be characterized as one of Calvinism, modified by revivalism and pietism. All of its founders were premillennialists and some were also dispensationalists. Its program includes prayer, Bible study, and fellowship in order to help students mature evangelically, provide a Christian context for their lives, and reinforce confidence in the authority of Scripture. Over 75 percent of Intervarsity members come from Methodist, Presbyterian, and Baptist backgrounds, and the tendency has been to rely on upon religiously conservative students entering college rather than on conversions to make up membership. Intervarsity groups tend to be concentrated in the Middle-Atlantic, East-Central, West-Central, and Pacific-Southwest regions, with comparatively few in the South and in New England.

A second major evangelical organization is Campus Crusade for Christ, founded in 1951 by

Bill Bright. A former businessman who was then a student at Fuller Seminary in Los Angeles, Bright moved to a house near the University of California at Los Angeles campus and held religious meetings for students, making a special effort to attract fraternity members and athletes. His initial success resulted in requests to do similar work at other institutions, and he recruited his first staff of six young men. By 1952 Campus Crusade had spread to four other western campuses. In 1956 Campus Crusade acquired five acres of land in Minnesota and began a training center. Four years later there were 109 staff members active on forty campuses in fifteen states. In 1962 headquarters were moved to Arrowhead Springs in San Bernardino, California, which in 1978 became Campus Crusade's Great Commission School of Theology.

Unlike Intervarsity Christian Fellowship, Campus Crusade has tended to rely heavily on trained leadership. Some of its activities have included campus revivals, the formation of the Christian World Liberation Front as an alternative to radical organizations, and the use of magicians, lecturers, and entertainers to spread its message. Seven Athletes in Action teams perform in ten sports. Campus Crusade underwent a complete reorganization in the late 1960s involving the establishment of a "working" board of trustees, and the central administration was restructured by several Harvard business students with ties to the organization.

RELIGION AND HIGHER EDUCATION: AN EVALUATION

American higher education has had strong historic ties with religion. With the exception of the University of Pennsylvania, all of the colonial colleges were themselves religious institutions. Throughout the nineteenth century, educational Evangelicals labored to establish religious colleges as bases for missionary activity and as bulwarks against other denominations. Even the state universities founded in the nineteenth century were highly religious in tone and curricular content. Teachers and administrators were frequently members of the clergy. Only in this century has religion ceased to dominate higher education, and only since World War II has the majority of students not studied in religious colleges. Thus for more than two-thirds of the history of American higher education, religious schools have predominated.

The last forty years have been difficult for religiously affiliated higher education. Small size has made schools especially vulnerable in times of economic difficulty, and the necessity of depending heavily upon tuition for operating funds has both taxed their resources and made it difficult to compete with the less costly state schools. Institutions have also faced crises of identity in trying to determine what their role ought to be in a secular society in which higher education is increasingly specialized and professionalized. Changes within the churches have increased the difficulties.

In spite of these problems, though, religious higher education continues to occupy an important place in the ecology of American schooling. Large numbers of students continue to study in religious institutions and seem to reflect these schools' values. Even critics of religiously based higher education admit that it also serves the purpose of acting as a countervailing force to publicly supported colleges and universities. Because it responds to somewhat different stimuli and has different goals, religiously based education offers a contrasting vision of what higher education can be and provides options that otherwise might not be available.

Organized ministry to students outside of religious institutions continues to carry spiritual values to students in secular educational settings. Besides reinforcing the faith of students and providing them with opportunities for worship, campus ministries have been effective critics of social structures, both within higher education and on the political level. As campus ministry has taken on an increasingly prophetic role, it has had a disproportionate influence on the life of the nation. The activity of campus pastors in protests over the Vietnam War is only one example.

Both for historical and contemporary reasons, religion's influence on the life of the nation through higher education is evident. Responding to different social, political, cultural, and theological forces at various times, it has been an enduring thread running continuously through the tapestry of American collegiate and university education.

RELIGION AND COLLEGIATE EDUCATION

BIBLIOGRAPHY

Horace M. Bond, "The Origin and Development of the Negro Church-Related College," in *The Journal of Negro Education*, 29 (1960); Frank Bowles and Frank A. DeCosta, *Between Two Worlds* (1971); Virginia L. Brereton, "Protestant Fundamentalist Bible Schools, 1882–1920" (Ph.D. diss., Columbia Univ., 1981); Lawrence A. Cremin, *American Education: The Colonial Experience* (1970) and *American Education: The National Experience* (1980); Andrew M. Greeley, *From Backwater to Mainstream* (1969); Robert Hassenger, ed., *The Shape of Catholic Higher Education* (1967); Lawrence N. Jones, "The Inter-Varsity Christian Fellowship in the United States" (Ph.D. diss., Yale Univ., 1961); Paul M. Limbert, *Denominational Policies in the Support of Higher Education* (1929).

George M. Marsden, *Fundamentalism and American Culture* (1980); Natalie A. Naylor, "The Ante-Bellum College Movement: A Reappraisal of Tewksbury's Founding of American Colleges and Universities," in *History of Education Quarterly*, 13 (1973); C. Robert Pace, *Education and Evangelism* (1972); Robert R. Parsonnage, *Church Related Higher Education* (1978); Manning M. Pattillo, Jr., and Donald M. Mackenzie, *Church-Sponsored Higher Education in the United States* (1966); Judah Pilch, ed., *A History of Jewish Education in the United States* (1969); David B. Potts, "American Colleges in the Nineteenth Century: From Localism to Denominationalism," in *History of Education Quarterly*, 11 (1971); Edward J. Power, *A History of Catholic Higher Education in the United States* (1958).

Richard Quebedeaux, *I Found It!* (1979); Frederick Rudolph, *The American College and University* (1962); Ernest R. Sandeen, *The Roots of Fundamentalism* (1970); Clarence P. Shedd, *The Church Follows Its Students* (1938); Seymour A. Smith, *The American College Chaplaincy* (1954); Donald G. Tewksbury, *The Founding of American Colleges and Universities Before the Civil War* (1932); Kenneth Underwood, *The Church, the University, and Social Policy* (1969); Timothy P. Weber, *Living in the Shadow of the Second Coming* (1979).

[See also RELIGION AS AN ACADEMIC DISCIPLINE.]

CHRISTIAN THEOLOGICAL EDUCATION

Glenn Miller and Robert Lynn

NEITHER history nor contemporary use provides a single, sufficient definition of Christian theological education. In common usage the term includes three related topics: the academic, or technical, study of theology; the preparation of ministers for their vocation; and the institutions devoted to the academic study of theology, the preparation of ministers, or both. In any given period academic theology, the need for ministerial preparation, and the places where such education occurs interact to produce a specific understanding of theological education. These need careful definition.

Academic theology is the application of a specific scholarly method—whether literary, historical, or philosophical—to the Scriptures, teachings, or traditions of the Christian faith. It is a technical skill that requires considerable resources, including scholars who devote most of their time to study, provisions for publication, and large libraries. Normally this craft must be learned under the guidance of an established master.

Most theological thinking in Christian history has not been academic. While virtually all Christian leaders have been required to do some theological work during their ministry, this work has typically taken the form of sermons and catechetical lectures, books written in response to specific events, polemics against heretics, devotional writings, and other nontechnical tracts. Christianity has been more a religion of teaching. Nonetheless, academic theology informs nontechnical theology. Technical theology is often seen as part of the preparation of ministers who may or may not use the tools of scholarship directly in their subsequent work, but whose standards of critical thought can be raised by exposure to a technically oriented environment.

From the first to the twentieth century the Christian church has demonstrated concern for the preparation of ministers for office. However, preparation has varied from age to age according to the church's expectations of a minister, the specific nature of a given minister's duties, the class structure of church and society, and whether the minister is seen primarily as a priest, shepherd of souls, or preacher. For example, while the formal requirements for a priest in the Middle Ages were often meager—the ability to say the mass in Latin and to read and write—his informal learning from, say, service as an acolyte was expected to be considerable. In contrast, bishops were expected to have an education equal to that of the aristocracy and, frequently, some university training.

To cite another example, in the Reformed tradition the minister was expected to be a resident pastor-theologian whose work primarily took place in the study, and formal qualifications—including the knowledge of classical languages and Hebrew—predominated. In contrast, the original Methodist circuit riders, whose work was primarily evangelistic, did not need formal training as much as they needed to experience conversion for themselves.

A full history of preparation for ministry is beyond the scope of this essay. However, general patterns and expectations for ministers will be discussed in order to highlight the description of technical theology and of theological institutions.

The complexity of technical, or academic, theology requires institutions for its communication. At a minimum a school needs teachers, students, and libraries, although most are multifaceted structures that issue degrees, schedule classes, follow detailed curricula, have formal and informal relationships to other schools, and have public means of governance. Schools of theology are not value-free, but shape the way in which both technical theology and preparation for ministry occur within them. Institutional forms, in other words, are a very important element in theological education.

In addition, each school has its own ethos that influences learning and teaching. An individual who learned or taught at the University of Chicago at the height of the Progressive movement inhabited a world of optimism and confidence. The school, the nation, and the culture were seen as rushing headlong into their greatest adventure—a "Christian Century" of promise. On the other hand, a student at Princeton Seminary in the same period lived in an atmosphere in which the great Reformed tradition was under assault by modernity, and learning thus took place in a defensive atmosphere.

BACKGROUNDS

England was the most important influence on the development of American theological education during the sixteenth and seventeenth centuries. The collegiate structure of the English university magnified the impact of Renaissance humanism. Since the colleges were free to determine their own course of study, independent of the medieval requirements for degrees, they were able to take as their standard the "learned person"—one who was thoroughly familiar with classical literature, knew some mathematics, and was able to express himself well. At the same time other forces in English life were separating professional education from the universities. Civil or Roman law, taught on the Continent by faculties of law, did not have normative standing in England where common or customary law governed in criminal and property cases. Training in the common law centered in the Inns of Court, located in London; medicine, likewise, took a more practical turn in England, where the guilds of physicians had more influence than the universities over admission to practice. Thus, the full European university never flourished in England. This had consequences for all aspects of theological education, as did the nature of the relationship between church and state, clergy and laity.

The English Reformation began with Henry VIII. Although scholars find dating the Reformation difficult, the main outlines of the new church were evident after Elizabeth I had secured the primary ecclesiastical laws: the Act of Supremacy (1559), the Act of Uniformity (1559), and the Thirty-nine Articles (1563). The king or queen, although a non-ordained person, held the highest office in the church. Despite clerical representation in the House of Lords, Parliament was largely composed of laymen, who determined articles of faith, established the *Book of Common Prayer* (1549; final revision, 1662), and made laws of worship and ritual for the realm. The cooperation between laity and clergy in the governance of the church continued down to the local level. Appointment to ecclesiastical office was through patronage, a species of real property in common law. A patron was a layman who owned the right to present or nominate the minister of a particular parish.

The squire (as the largest landowner in a community was called) and the parson shared the burden of local government and, as on the Continent, the resident minister had an array of non-priestly functions, including managing the parish's "glebe" (farm), acting as surveyor, and, frequently, practicing rural medicine. The classic theology of the Church of England stressed the lay character of ecclesiastical authority. The only distinction between priest and layman was in office or function. In theory a layman could be authorized to serve as priest and a priest could be assigned lay duties. Both were part of the governing order, which was supreme over all areas of common life.

The theology of Anglicanism, the collegiate system of education, and the secular form of church government conditioned the English understanding of preparation for the ministry. Since both clergyman and layman were members of the approximately 10 percent of the population who ruled, both were expected to receive the same education. The primary literary training of the colleges was supplemented by very limited programs in theology designed to provide a basic knowledge about the Christian faith, a program of chapel, and some personal counsel on religious matters. The same program prepared the student to become either squire or parson.

The medieval program in theology was never legally discontinued at either Oxford or Cambridge. Despite the continuation of the Regius and Lady Margaret professorships in divinity (which remained sinecures until the nineteenth century), the traditional divinity program was quietly superceded by college programs of literary study. These trends in education contributed to the style of English theology. Theological writing was done by bishops and rectors of large parishes often in response to specific occasions, such as the publication of a heretical work, problems in the relationship between church and state, the advent of a new philosophy, or another new intellectual trend. The classic form of such theology was the printed debate in which one individual sought to refute another's assertions. The various publications, perhaps because of the heavy emphasis on literacy and humanistic influences in the colleges, displayed considerable literary skill and masterful use of quotations from ancient sources.

The English reliance on pastor-theologians, who did theology in the public forum, meant that England did not develop a technical or academic theological tradition until the late nineteenth century. The colleges did not provide a place for such a tradition; the strongly humanist flavor of English intellectual life discouraged it; and it was rarely needed in the churches.

The Catholic church in England was excluded from the universities not only by law but by custom. The English system of education was designed to produce a particular type of public servant who was thoroughly integrated into English life. To provide their own learned leadership, Catholics established colleges at Dounai in Flanders after 1568. Although very important in English Catholic life, the Dounai schools had little influence on the United States.

COLONIAL AND EARLY NINETEENTH-CENTURY THEOLOGICAL INSTITUTIONS

The English tradition of ministerial preparation was the most common in America during the colonial period. Unlike the European university, the college with its fellows and tutors was an institution easily planted throughout an empire. Trinity College, Dublin, established in 1592, was the first attempt to establish a college in a colonial context.

The New England Puritans were as devoted to the English method of ministerial preparation as the Anglicans. In New England a marked aversion to establishing schools to provide strictly technical or scholastic theological training was characteristic until the end of the eighteenth century. Instead, both Harvard and Yale were directed toward the education of leaders for church and state. Both schools, like the English colleges on which they were modeled, provided enough theology for a public leader, whether minister or layman, and left more technical study for the individual to pursue after graduation. The appointment of the Hollis Professors of Divinity at Harvard in the eighteenth century was only a very slight departure from this general pattern.

New England theological writing was occasional and was done by individuals engaged in the day-to-day work of the churches. This pastoral style of theology was not an unintended by-product of New England's colonial and provincial location but a matter of choice. New England was never more English than in its style of theologizing in the public forum.

Jonathan Edwards (1703–1758), one of the leading figures of the Great Awakening that occurred in the colonies from 1734 to about 1749, was the American master of this form of theological labor. The revival was both a cause for wonder and a movement that had to be defended. When critics such as Charles Chauncy assailed the strict doctrine and emotionalism of the revival, Edwards responded with carefully reasoned treatises that answered their objections. The more formal treatises, which he wrote after his dismissal from Northampton in 1750, followed a similar form. Edwards' works are marked by the spirit of public debate, often beginning with an analysis of a discussion and then moving toward the resolution of the issues. His writings are also characterized by the absence of the technical forms of exegesis and dogmatics common on the Continent. Theology, for him as for other New Englanders, was more the art of rational discourse about religion than it was a scientific method to be followed.

The College of William and Mary in Virginia was the most important exception to the general pattern of the English-style college in the colonies. Established by the Scotch Anglican James Blair and chartered in 1693, the school's course of study was based on the Scottish tradition of a two-year program in philosophy leading to the B.A., followed for clerical candidates by study with the divinity faculty. The advanced program included technical biblical studies and Hebrew. The Divinity School at William and Mary was closed by Thomas Jefferson in 1779 as part of his program of separation of church and state.

The Middle Colonies lacked the religious and social homogeneity that had sustained the classical English college elsewhere, but the institution proved flexible enough to adapt to the situation. Between 1745 and 1760 such schools as the College of Philadelphia (today the University of Pennsylvania), the College of New Jersey (Princeton), and King's College (Columbia University) were governed by boards of trust which by law had to be composed of members of different denominations. The student body was legally open to members of any Christian group. The only place where the influence of a sponsoring denomination was assured was in the office of president or rector, for which the charter might stipulate a clergyman of a particular denomination.

With the significant exception of the Lutheran immigrant churches, which continued continental patterns of theological training, American Protestants tended to accept the classical English collegiate program as proper and sufficient preparation for ministers until the late nineteenth century. Even the seminary-building Presbyterians estimated in 1924 that only a quarter of their ministers had seminary degrees in addition to their college degrees. Every major nineteenth-century denomination constructed colleges, and the Methodists in particular dotted the landscape with hundreds of small church-related schools.

The persistence of the college as the standard for ministerial preparation was not owing to the college's role as theological educator. If anything, nineteenth-century colleges grew less theological as time passed, although some did establish departments of the Bible to aid students planning work in the ministry. Instead, the secular values taught by colleges were held by American Protestants to be important for their own sake. Generally, these were the values of English humanism and of the Greek and Roman classics, including a knowledge of history and literature, a worldly-wise tolerance, and a deep sense of personal honor and patriotism. But social values were equally important. In England a college degree made an individual legally "a gentleman and a scholar" with the right to the social status of "mister," and such customs as common meals taught students middle- and upper-class standards of behavior and manners. Although Americans did not continue all of the English tradition of the gentleman, in part because the United States lacked a legally recognized aristocracy, Americans prized "gentlemanly" social graces and socially recognized status. The ideal minister was a gentleman first, a theologian second.

After the establishment of the seminaries, beginning in 1808, much American theology continued to be practiced in the English mode. The debate, whether written or oral, was more important than the learned treatise or the massive compendium of dogmatics. With the exception of a handful of technical journals, the bulk of American theologizing before the twentieth century was conducted in the larger marketplace of ideas.

The Early Seminary Movement. Reformed faith, as expressed in the Westminster Confession (1646), the standard confession of British Calvinism, implied the academic study of theology, since the doctrine of Scripture contained in the confession was stated in precise and technical language. The Bible was seen as the sole authority in matters of faith and practice and as inspired by God. The only authoritative version of the Scriptures, moreover, was that in the original languages. Ministers acted as teaching elders charged with the accurate presentation of the contents of Scripture. Despite the rich academic tradition of the European Reformed churches, including the Church of Scotland, the logic of Reformed theology was not compelling to New England. Instead, New England churches moved toward academic theology by a circuitous route.

The theology of Jonathan Edwards, which had been inspired by the Great Awakening, stressed a Calvinism that required a public account of conversion before full membership in the church could be extended. Further, each church was the judge of its own faith and practice and, at least in theory, had its own confession of faith. Perhaps because Edwards investigated the problems of the relationship between the divine and human will in salvation and used an extensive and idiosyncratic theological vocabulary, the Edwardsean corpus contained a number of difficult and largely unsolvable intellectual puzzles. Pastors such as Samuel Hopkins and Nathaniel Emmons, who developed Edwards' theology, diligently searched for new metaphors and arguments to interpret their master. Already complex, Edwardseanism became laden with such terms as "disinterested benevolence." So confusing was the resultant admixture of logic, rhetoric, and technical terminology that few nonspecialists can read Edwardsean works today.

The methods and conclusions of Edwardsean theology were too intricate to be transmitted without specific instruction. Students needed masters and libraries. When Charles Backus and other clergymen became known as theologians, young Edwardseans moved into their manses for a season of study. After several student generations, pastor-teachers became experienced and developed programs of study that included set readings and set topics for essays. In effect these successful teachers established small, private divinity schools, which tended toward greater sophistication and higher standards as time went on.

Following the election of Henry Ware, a Unitarian, as Hollis Professor of Divinity at Harvard in 1805, orthodox New Englanders became concerned with the doctrinal integrity of their tradition. To the orthodox, the Unitarian's denial of the divinity of Christ, original sin, predestination, and the trinity was heresy or, worse, blasphemy. Eliphalet Pearson, Harvard's Hebraist, resigned his position in 1806 and retreated to Phillips Academy in nearby Andover to devise an alternative way to train ministers. Jedidiah Morse, a Charlestown minister and overseer of Harvard, became the leader of the anti-Unitarians and aided in planning the new educational institution. Meanwhile, Leonard Woods, representing the Edwardsean wing of New England orthodoxy, communicated to Morse and Pearson a desire to establish a theological school. Delicate negotiations for union of the two proposed institutions followed, and after several compromises—including agreement on a creed—the two parties established the Theological Institution in Andover Academy in 1808.

The new school was dedicated to technical theology. Declaring that only college graduates would be admitted, the founders proposed to offer courses in the various fields of theological study, including systematic theology, the Bible, and ecclesiastical history. Each field was to be taught by an instructor who made the study of that field his life work. Moses Stuart (1780–1852), a self-trained biblical scholar, exemplified these standards. From 1810 until his death Stuart focused the resources of Andover seminary on exegesis, developed a program for resident licentiates (graduate students), and had his best students appointed as instructors or sent to Germany for further training. Finally, he secured a second professor in biblical studies from among his students. The professional biblical scholar was now part of the American landscape, and as new schools were founded such technicians were avidly sought or, like Stuart, raised from the ranks.

The development of Princeton Seminary was equally complex. The theological direction that was characteristic of the school was introduced by John Witherspoon (1722–1794), the Scottish divine who became president of the College of New Jersey in 1768. Witherspoon taught common sense realism, a system of thought that stressed that humans reasoned inductively. According to common sense realists, the mind began with data, organized that data into hypotheses, and then devised tests to see whether the hypotheses were accurate. When this system was applied to Christian theology, the Bible became the storehouse of the most important data about God, and theologians were charged with the use of scientific method in its explication. What Witherspoon did was a theological transposition. He used the new philosophy where the older orthodoxy had preferred the thought of Aristotle. The result was a new scholasticism, closely related to traditional patterns of thought, yet differing significantly from them in emphasis and tone.

The theological development of the College of New Jersey was slowed by the chaotic events of the revolutionary and early national periods. Although Witherspoon educated a significant number of ministers in his first years as president, fewer candidates were trained in succeeding years. Witherspoon's successor, Samuel Stanhope Smith, was unable to attract many prospective ministers to the struggling college. In the early 1800s, partly in reaction to Smith's failure to educate ministers for the denomination, New York Presbyterian Samuel Miller, a leading pastor and author, launched a drive for a new theological institution. He was joined by Ashbel Green, the pastor of the largest church in Philadelphia and trustee of Princeton College, and Archibald Alexander, the church's most influential theologian and formerly president of Hampton-Sydney in Virginia. The new school, which was located at Princeton after delicate negotiations, was originally a creation of the General Assembly, the governing body of the church and legally a corporation in Pennsylvania, and only later became a semi-independent school with its own board.

The Theological Seminary of the Presbyterian Church, as it was originally called, was different from Andover in its program and ethos. Unlike Andover, which was the child of the Awakening, Princeton had a distinctly ecclesiastical character. The students were submerged in the Reformed tradition and common sense philosophy, and were taught the value of a common (churchwide) confession of faith. From its earliest days Princeton was a confessional institution tied to the Presbyterian church in ownership and spirit. The school's goal was to produce church leaders who were thorough masters of the tradition of Reformed theology.

In addition to their need to elaborate all of the details of the confession of faith in such a manner as to leave no conceivable question unanswered, the first instructors at Princeton were fascinated by technical Bible scholarship, and they granted their promising young colleague Charles Hodge a leave of absence to study in Europe. Hodge returned a master of European theological science, which was developing scholarly methods for the examination of the Scriptures, especially in such specialized fields as the study of Hebrew and the cognate languages. While impressed by this type of study, Hodge rejected the historical criticism of the Bible that was becoming a characteristic of German university theology. Both of Alexander's sons, who served as teachers for a period, went to Germany for similar training.

The founding of Andover and Princeton inspired the further development of seminaries. Harvard and Yale, which had earlier hoped to expand their informal programs into full divinity faculties, moved quickly to establish divinity schools or departments. At Harvard, where liberal Christianity (the term Unitarians used for their own position) was dominant, the divinity school resolved to use the standards of contemporary scholarship as part of its definition of a nonconfessional seminary.

Yale's Department of Theology, which was established after the official separation of church and state in Connecticut, was part of the college's attempt to find a new means to carry out its original task of training ministers. The faculty of Yale believed that the older, legally established faith could be transformed into a new Christian America united by a basic faith that was larger than any one denomination. The school, consequently, resolved to support the evangelical revival and elected a theological position that, its teachers believed, would sustain revivals and voluntary societies. Theologian Nathaniel Taylor, who attempted to reconcile predestination and original sin with an optimistic view of the human condition, was the best symbol of the early Yale divinity department.

The Anglicans moved early toward seminaries. The Revolution ended the denomination's southern establishments and the church's hopes for a dominant position in the middle and northern regions. But if the Church of England in America was now simply a denomination among denominations, what did it mean to be Anglican? In England, despite the often fierce fighting between Whig (Low) and Tory (High) churchmen, the church sought to be as inclusive as possible. In America, however, Anglicanism had to exhibit its unique qualities over and against other Christian groups. Bishop William White of Philadelphia began the process of Anglican self-definition by preparing in 1811 a Bishop's Course of Studies, a list of key texts to be studied by prospective clergy. The founding of General Seminary in New York in 1820 marked the beginning of an Anglican academic tradition in America.

Lutherans had also been examining their place in the American religious scene. During the colonial period Lutherans had relied on pastors from abroad, especially from Germany, and, increasingly, on men trained in various reading programs (private programs of study). The traditional dogmatic substance of Lutheranism, including the doctrine of the real presence of Christ in the Eucharist and belief in the details of the Book of Concord and Augsburg Confession, had eroded, and some congregations were finding the Anglican tradition more congenial. Samuel Schmucker, a graduate of Princeton Seminary, was acutely aware of these problems, and under his leadership both Gettysburg College and Gettysburg Seminary were founded in 1826 to further the Lutheran faith. Schmucker's acceptance of the prevalent American pattern of college and seminary was a significant departure from the European tradition of study in an approved university. He wanted young American Lutheran pastors to be part of the American tradition of learned gentlemen more than the German tradition of the pastor as a "resident theologian."

Discord. The new theological seminaries had a difficult time fulfilling their task in the middle decades of the nineteenth century. At least three factors helped to create an atmosphere of discord that substantially slowed American mastery of technical theology. First, American Protestants in the nineteenth century participated in a movement of church renewal that featured the revival, a type of church service designed to encourage conversions, new missionary movements, and a drive, more pronounced among some denominations, for personal holiness and commitment. Often, the individual was brought to an intense experience of conversion or renewal that was believed to mark a new stage in life (he or she was "born again"). This movement, which was deeply influenced by the ideals of the new American republic, posed many questions for American theologians, including such vexing puzzles as the ability of the will to overcome original sin, the need for any system of sacraments not directly related to a person's own decision, and the validity of the doctrine of the persistence of sinfulness in an individual. The seminaries, which were closely related to the churches, had to deal with these issues, and yet the American theological community had not matured sufficiently to provide intellectually compelling solutions.

Second, European theology—the model for the new American theological professionals—was spawning new movements. In addition to advances in technical biblical study and the early liberalism of such teachers as Friederich Schleiermacher, who had located religion in the emotional depth of the person rather than in revelation, a new conservativism (called "Neo-Orthodoxy" in most European histories of theology) was winning advocates in the Old World. In Germany confessionalism, a movement that hoped to return the churches to the theological standards of the sixteenth century, was increasingly important. In England the Oxford movement was hoping to find the essence of the Church of England in its more Catholic traditions, especially apostolic succession and sacramental efficacy, and in Scotland the Evangelical party slowly gained strength and finally left the established Kirk in order to enjoy a Presbyterianism free of patronage. These new ideas came to the United States in different ways. Some were espoused by immigrants, some by American scholars who had spent time abroad, and some through European books and journals.

Third, American cultural and political life was alive with the spirit of party and of movement. By the time of Andrew Jackson, democracy meant taking sides, finding a way to power through a group, and enjoying the fruits of that power. In the churches competing theologies became the rallying cries of factions. The seminaries and divinity schools, young, freshly created institutions, were overcome by the combination of theological problems and this new spirit of partisanship. Seminaries became citadels for this or that movement in the church. If conquest of an existing school by a particular faction was not possible, a new seminary was founded to support its position. The schools were involved in almost constant theological controversy.

The case of Lane Seminary in Cincinnati is an excellent illustration of the crisis. Founded in 1829 in response to the duty of evangelizing the West, the school had elected Lyman Beecher, one of the strongest advocates of western missions, as president and the highly skilled technical critic Calvin Stowe as professor of the New Testament. The prestige of Beecher and the hope for success in the West attracted a significant number of students from the Oneida Manual Labor Institute in New York, an experimental school for ministers that attempted to combine both liberal arts and theology in a single program. The future seemed bright: a good faculty, sound finances, and a substantial student body.

However, controversy began even before Beecher assumed office. The first chairman of the board, Joshua Wilson, witnessed a split in his own congregation, as part of the church withdrew and called the charismatic young evangelical Asa Mahan as their pastor. Wilson, shocked by the defection, became an ally of Ashbel Green, the leader of what became known as the "Old School" party of the Presbyterian church. Seeing in Lane Seminary an outpost of the opposition (later "New School") party, Wilson resigned and planned to try Beecher for heresy. Generally speaking, the Old School held to a rigid interpretation of the Westminster Confession, especially of the doctrines of predestination and man's inability to aid in his salvation, while the New School tended to soften these doctrines and allow some role to the will in salvation.

While Wilson's plans were maturing, the young idealists from Oneida carried out their own program of reform. Led by Theodore Weld, they held a debate on the subject of slavery and declared themselves in favor of immediate abolition. In itself the debate caused few problems, but the students, following the logic of their position, established missionary programs in the black community. In the belief that these activities harmed Lane's position in racially volatile Cincinnati, the trustees ordered the students to concentrate on their studies. In response the students withdrew to a new seminary, Oberlin, where Charles Finney, a famed evangelist who believed that revivals could be produced by human means, had recently been elected professor of theology. By the time Wilson formally charged Beecher with heresy, Lane was a small, underattended seminary. The school finally failed in the 1920s.

Similar, although less dramatic, confrontations happened elsewhere. The Reformed churches (Presbyterians, German Reformed, and Congregationalists), if only because they had the largest number of schools, were most affected. Princeton Seminary, proud of its mission to the whole Presbyterian church, was forced by its wealthy contributors and by the existence of newly established rival New York (later Union) Theological Seminary to choose between the Old and New Schools. It elected to become Old School, resulting in Princeton's theologians becoming the primary defenders of the Old School position. All theological subjects were taught from that point of view.

Presbyterian Columbia Seminary in South Carolina (now located in Georgia), which was chartered to meet the special needs of the South, became an outpost of the Old School. Union Seminary in Virginia, whose faculty and financial supporters were divided between rival factions, was almost destroyed by the animosity between the two groups. It only recovered when the North-South tensions in the nation allowed it to redefine its goals in terms of southern regionalism.

Yale found itself facing competition from a new, more orthodox school at East Windsor, Connecticut, which later moved to Hartford. Debates between 1844 and 1860 over the Mercersberg theology, a high church form of reformed religious thought that stressed the corporate nature of Christian faith and emphasized the sacraments, greatly weakened the small seminary maintained by the German Reformed church at Mercersberg, Pennsylvania. When the battle ended, the school had only a few students who were taught in the home of the remaining instructor, Philip Schaff. Schaff himself left in 1863.

New York's General Seminary (Episcopal) found itself at the center of the debate over the Oxford movement, which stressed the importance of apostolic succession and the objective efficacy of the sacraments. Tiny Virginia Seminary in Alexandria became the base for the evangelical reaction. When the Civil War erupted, the northern evangelical bishops in Massachusetts, Connecticut, and Pennsylvania established their own schools, while new Anglo-Catholic schools, beginning with Nashoda House in 1841, were formed in the West.

The Lutherans, who did not have a united church in the nineteenth century, were split further by ethnic diversity as new immigrants came from Germany and the Scandinavian countries. The European controversy over the nature of the confession of faith as well as over the objective presence of Christ in the Eucharist caused discord as well. Lutherans struggled unsuccessfully to find some grounds for unity. As in other denominations, these theological differences contributed to the establishment of new seminaries based on a school's relationship to the new conservatism, and inspired those excluded from these institutions to found yet more schools to teach their position.

The seminary movement lost its focus in the midst of these struggles. There came to be too many schools, staffed by too few qualified teachers, devoting too much energy to issues that proved to have little significance for the overall development of American religion. The greatest loser in these battles was theological scholarship. Although some American theologians, such as Moses Stuart and Charles Hodge, struggled to follow the unfolding debates in Europe over the historical method of biblical interpretation, newer philosophical trends, and fresh views of the inherited faith, most were content with more parochial issues. As a result, American Christians were by and large surprised by Charles Darwin's new understanding of natural selection, published in 1859, and even more confounded by radical theories about the authorship of biblical books. Ironically, the growth in the number of seminaries from 1830 to 1860 did not produce an equal growth in theological acumen. The full consequences of this lack of focus and resolution were felt after the Civil War, when the American theological community's poor acquaintance with the changing European context set the stage for a period of radical readjustment of the seminary tradition.

Baptists and Methodists. The early nineteenth century was a period of vigorous numerical and intellectual growth for Baptists and Methodists. In a dramatic institutional shift, these churches moved rapidly from being almost sectarian bodies, primarily lower and lower middle class, to the point where they commanded the allegiance of almost half the Protestant population of the new nation.

Although both Baptists and Methodists attracted new members as a result of the emotional revivalism that was common on the frontier, both denominations possessed definite theological traditions that they believed deserved scholarly consideration. Although anti-intellectualism was common on the frontier, neither religious group was primarily anti-intellectual. However, they shared a resentment at the tendency of Congregationalists, Presbyterians, and Episcopalians to monopolize teaching positions in the nation's colleges.

The origins of Baptist theological education lay in the church's sectarian past. After a brief period of toleration under Oliver Cromwell, English Baptists were excluded from the universities by law, and most were unable, because of either geography or social class, to attend the more tolerant Scottish universities. The Baptists responded by founding a small dissenting academy at Bristol, England, near the Welsh heartland of the Calvinist branch of the denomination. This academy, whose faculty rarely had more than two members, was neither a European school of theology nor an English college. The curriculum varied with the instructor. The most serious limitation of the Bristol school was that it could not issue degrees, and its graduates could not legally become "gentlemen and scholars."

When the Great Awakening increased American Baptist resources, the denomination made plans for a chartered (degree-granting) school. Led by the Philadelphia Association, the College of Rhode Island (present-day Brown University) was established in 1764 under a charter that made Baptists share control with other denominations but specified a Baptist president. Shortly after it was established, the school began to confer honorary degrees on prominent, scholarly Baptists in England.

The need for public recognition of achievement was one element in the Baptist drive to establish liberal arts colleges in the antebellum period. Although the schools were mainly intended to prepare ministers, their broader purpose was to prepare a Baptist public equal in attainments to those of the other churches, but many of these schools were poorly financed and later drifted from denominational control.

The establishment of Baptist schools devoted entirely to teaching theology (i.e., Baptist seminaries) was part of the denomination's response to the revival of missionary interest that began with the sending of William Carey to India in 1793. The conversion of Luther Rice and Adoniram Judson to Baptist principles in 1812, while they were serving as missionaries of the Congregationalist American Board of Commissioners, caused a flurry of activity within Baptist churches. Organizations, including national and state conventions, were founded to help support foreign and home missions, education, and publications.

Richard Furman, pastor of the First Baptist Church of Charleston, South Carolina, invited William Staughton, a graduate of Bristol, a highly qualified scholar, and a master educator, to come to America in 1793. His involvement with Baptist education in the New World began with a small school in his parsonage in Philadelphia where a number of Baptist leaders received their training. These leaders included John Mason Peck, who later served as an educational missionary for the Triennial (national convention) and established several small academies in the West.

Led by Staughton and Rice, the Baptists planned a national university to be located in the nation's capital. The school was to combine a liberal arts program with separate faculties for each of the learned professions. Staughton moved to the new institution as president. The Baptist leadership, however, had overestimated its financial and political support. The denomination, bitterly divided between advocates and opponents of missionary efforts, was unable to sustain the venture. Columbian College became a private school under Baptist influence, and the theological faculty moved to Newton, Massachusetts, where the Newton Baptist Theological School was located. Partly as a result of regionalism, schools were subsequently founded in Hamilton and Rochester, New York.

By the 1840s Baptists were locked in controversy over slavery. Furthermore, Baptists in the South and West had grown more numerous and powerful than those in the East and wanted a more centralized denomination. Either the slavery or the centralization issue alone might have been enough to split the relatively unstable denomination, and it divided in 1845 into two separate conventions. Southern Baptist leaders began advocating the establishment of their own seminary shortly after the division. Although two small divinity departments had been started at Furman University in South Carolina and Mercer University in Georgia, neither represented the whole convention in faculty, student body, or support.

The individual responsible for the establishment of a convention-wide seminary was James P. Boyce (1827–1888), the son of a wealthy planter and a graduate of Princeton Seminary. Boyce believed that a Southern Baptist school had to maintain theological purity, provide advanced technical training, and prepare persons both with and without college degrees for careers in the ministry. The new Southern Baptist Theological Seminary opened in 1859 at Greenville, South Carolina. Headed by Boyce and John A. Broadus, the school followed the University of Virginia in the use of an elective program. In the post–Civil War period, financial crises forced the school to move to Louisville, Kentucky.

Methodist development was similar to Baptist. The denomination began as an evangelistic movement within the Church of England and separated only after the church proved unresponsive to its ministry. Methodism grew out of the theology of the "High" or "Tory" churchmen of the eighteenth century, who stressed the human response to God in worship and devotion, combined with an emphasis on holiness and perfection. John Wesley (1703–1791), the founder of Methodism, was a highly skilled theologian, but he was not a theological innovator. His religious philosophy was a practical application of themes that had been common in English theology since the early seventeenth century. The high church or Tory party stressed the human response to God in worship and devotion, which they combined with an emphasis on holiness. What Wesley did was to take these common themes and develop them in a practical direction. He did, however, have certain emphases. According to Wesley, God in Christ had created a plenitude of grace, both for salvation and for holy living, that man had only to accept in order to begin his pilgrimage toward perfection.

The early Methodists had little time for theological reflection. Wesley kept his preachers moving and provided them with a sound grounding in his own principles. Methodist class meetings and annual conferences reinforced Wesley's educational program. He took men from such occupations as soldiering, baking, and shoemaking and made them effective communicators of the Gospel.

Wesley had always assigned his own books to the circuit riders, hoping that they would, as he had, learn to read on horseback. After his death, his followers recognized the intellectual treasure their founder had bequeathed to them, and some became interested in a systematic study of Wesley's theological views. Richard Watson, among others, completed studies that, when compared to similar works written by theologians of other denominations, might be called Methodist dogmatic or systematic theologies. These Methodist studies followed a method similar to that of the Protestant scholastics and often used the scholastic pattern of organization. The scholastic period in Methodist thought was very significant for later Methodist theological education, because it convinced Methodists that their own heritage had a unique and valuable theology that ought to be taught to later generations.

Methodist education in America took the form of the traditional college. From the Christmas Conference, held at the Lovely Lane Chapel in Baltimore in 1784, to the end of the nineteenth century Methodists strove to establish liberal arts schools, especially in the Midwest. This commitment to the college grew out of the conviction that Wesleyanism was a simple set of doctrines that could be easily understood and defended by any individual who would candidly examine its claims. The college and university were thought to be the most appropriate places for such examination.

Methodist critics of theological schools, such as Peter Cartwright (a college founder himself), have often been misunderstood on this point. Beneath their vitriolic language and appeals to popular sentiment were an affirmation of the public character of Wesleyan theology and a belief that Methodists were to be masters of a practical divinity.

The Methodist fascination with the college and its potential did not disappear when the church gradually came to realize the value of the advanced professional training for its ministry. The course of study, a list of required books adopted by the bishops, remained the foundation of Methodist theological education until comparatively recently. When Methodists established a seminary, the school found it difficult to exist apart from a college. For example, Garrett Biblical Institute in Chicago was on the campus of Northwestern, and the pattern has continued. Even in the twentieth century, Methodism has few freestanding seminaries.

Catholics. At the beginning of the nineteenth century American Catholics were a small minority, largely centered in Maryland and mostly of English descent. By the end of the century, the Catholic church was the largest single religious organization in the United States and was composed of all the major European nationalities. The rapid growth of the American Catholic church provided the context for the development of American Catholic education. Confronted by a constant shortage of priests, only partly alleviated by the immigration of European clergy, the church had to recruit a ministry, create a hierarchy, and conduct a mission to a nation that was predominantly Protestant.

The first American bishop, John Carroll (1735–1815), had begun his ministry as a member of the Society of Jesus, or Jesuits. Tradition-

ally, the Jesuits had used education as a means of countering Protestant influence, and Carroll shared the belief that education was an effective means of evangelization. Accordingly, in 1790 he established Georgetown College in Washington, D.C., which was placed under Jesuit control after the Papal Act suppressing the order was repealed in 1814. But, unlike most Protestant college founders, Carroll did not believe that the university was the best way to train secular (not members of a religious order) priests. To train the needed parish ministers, he invited the Sulpicians (Society of St. Sulpice) to found a seminary. They established their school, St. Mary's, at One Mile Tavern, near Baltimore, in 1792.

Carroll's invitation to the Sulpicians was the beginning of a French tradition of priestly formulation in the United States that with few exceptions continued into the 1960s. Together with the Vincentians, another French order, the French educational orders sponsored most of the schools that trained secular clergy in the United States.

French Catholic theological study had been shaped by the seventeenth-century revival of faith in France. During that crucial century the French church, led by strong bishops and preachers, had attempted to bring its ministry up to a new spiritual standard. At the center of the French reform was Saint Vincent de Paul, who presided over a number of significant ecclesiastical developments: the establishment of a system of charities, the founding in 1634 of the Sisters of Charity—the first noncloistered order for women—and the preaching of missions to the rural areas. In 1625 he established the Lazarists (Vincentians) to continue the rural mission and, more importantly, to work for the spiritual improvement of the French clergy.

Jean Jacques Olier also made major contributions to the new style of French Catholicism. After successful preaching missions to Auvergne and Brittany, he moved to the urban parish of St. Sulpice in Paris. His energetic ministry to this church (which included the Sorbonne) attracted a number of priests to his side. With their support he established the Sulpicians as a society to train priests. Significantly, all members of the order were diocesan priests bound to their own bishops.

Partly because of their origins in a revitalization movement, the French orders had a particular style of theological education emphasizing the formation of personal piety and character. The intellectual life, while not discouraged, was not stressed, and much of the work consisted of the recitation, often from memory, of safe theological manuals. The Sulpicians believed, for example, that the young candidate needed to live in the closest possible relationship with his confessor. The retreat before ordination, originated by Saint Vincent, also reflected this emphasis. Neither order placed an emphasis on learned priests. A good priest was to be pious, concerned about his charge, and orthodox. These qualities, not an adventuresome intellectual spirit, were to be instilled in the candidate.

Bishop Carroll's invitation to the Sulpicians was not the only reason for the early French influence on American priestly training. The excesses of the French Revolution, especially the Reign of Terror, drove many priests into exile. The young United States was a natural place for French priests to settle. They played a significant role in the early hierarchy, as many of the first bishops in the American church were French.

The rapid expansion of the church and the pressing needs of each diocese contributed to a pervasive localism in Catholic theological education. Wherever possible the ordinary (the bishop charged with the administration of a diocese) attempted to keep the training of his clergy under his own personal control. Although Benedict Fenwick, the bishop of Boston, advanced the idea of a national seminary as early as 1829, there was little support for it among the American hierarchy. As in the case of Protestant localism, the slender resources of the numerous schools significantly weakened their quality.

THEOLOGICAL EDUCATION AFTER THE CIVIL WAR

The Civil War is a useful event to mark changes in American life. Although the outlines of postbellum American society could be discerned as early as the 1820s and 1830s, the great conflict intensified those developments and made them evident. The America that entered the war had been rural, small-town, and agrarian; the America that ended the war was clearly becoming urban and industrial. The social context that had supported the antebellum seminary passed rapidly from the scene.

The changes in American society were more important for theological education than were the immediate losses of some seminaries from wartime damage. The most serious loss came from declining enrollments, but since most schools charged no tuition, this meant largely the loss of nominal fees for room and board. The seminaries lost little because they had little to lose. They had little property to maintain and few salaries to pay. The southern schools fared worse than their northern counterparts. Many, like Southern Baptist in Greenville, South Carolina, had put their endowments in Confederate securities that were worthless after the war, but even these schools found that their marginal economic character enabled them to survive the loss of endowment and revenue.

The 1860s to 1880s also marked a change in the educational context of theological education. The seminaries had been established with the hope, not always realized, that their matriculating students would be graduates of traditional B.A. programs. Students were presumed to know Latin thoroughly and to have at least the rudiments of Greek and some philosophical training. Languages and philosophy played different roles at various institutions. For Andover and similar schools, the languages were the necessary preparation for the biblical programs; at Princeton the philosophical background was more important. But there was a logic to the pattern of college B.A. studies followed by the seminary that was intuitively obvious.

The post–Civil War period saw preseminary education change radically. Liberal arts schools expanded their curricula and offered programs of study in major and minor fields. While classics and philosophy continued as majors, they were no longer the center of the curriculum. Colleges also began to move away from literary subjects. The B.S. degree, which concentrated on science and higher mathematics, changed from an experimental and somewhat suspect alternative to the B.A. to a major and popular educational program. While seminaries formally insisted on a B.A. background, the pressure for more students meant that the B.S. was increasingly accepted as adequate.

Further, the new college was a complex institution. The small faculties and limited offerings of the antebellum college had made it possible for a single faculty member to administer a school in addition to teaching. The duties of the president's office consisted of little more than correspondence and presiding at meetings of the faculty. The new system demanded more officers such as deans, registrars, and department chairmen.

In the same period, the modern university became a significant part of American higher education. William Rainey Harper received the first American Ph.D. from Yale in 1875, and in 1876 Johns Hopkins University was established with research as its primary objective. Encouraged by the Morrill Act of 1862, a law that provided land as an endowment for universities offering studies in engineering and agriculture, numerous state-supported universities were established. The new universities were more than colleges on a grand scale, for they featured progressive stages of scholarship from undergraduate majors through advanced research degrees as well as a number of professional schools.

By 1880 new fields of study—economics, psychology, sociology, and education—were being offered by these colleges and universities. Two decades later schools of social work and education, in which the social sciences were applied to new professions, were common.

In an attempt to adjust to the new style of education, the seminaries adopted more elaborate administrations, developed programs with electives, and expanded their faculties. In short, they began to take on the institutional form of graduate schools. The new Ph.D. degree was particularly valuable inasmuch as it provided a better way of preparing and certifying teachers than the programs of self-education or foreign study.

But a difficult issue lay beneath these surface changes: where did the seminaries and divinity schools fit into the new educational order? A symptom of this problem was the academic degree. With few exceptions—such as Chicago Theological Seminary—antebellum seminaries had not offered degrees. The schools had difficulty securing charters that granted them the right to award degrees; some states felt that legal incorporation might violate their mandated separation of church and state, and in others seminaries were originally chartered as benevolent institutions or charities. In any event, the right to grant degrees was not needed in the antebellum world. The bachelor of arts, followed at many

schools by an almost automatic master's degree, made the minister "a learned gentlemen." Further, the churches, which had the right of ordination, believed that their own endorsement of a program was all the certification that a program needed.

Nonetheless, the new order in university education was based on a degree system, with a hierarchy that reached from the bachelor's, which indicated a novice, through the master's and doctor's, which signified specialized research capabilities and systematic study. By contrast, the degree nomenclature of the seminaries did not become uniform until well into the twentieth century. Some schools elected to use disciplinary degrees modeled on those conferred in the arts; hence, bachelor of theology (Th.B), master of theology (Th.M), and doctor of theology (Th.D). Other institutions used or resurrected the pre-Reformation British degree of bachelor of divinity (B.D.), to be followed by other titles for more advanced study, including master of sacred theology (S.T.M.).

The seminary degree structure, which was chaotic until the 1930s when the Association of Theological Schools mandated the use of the bachelor of divinity as the first theological degree, was rarely understood outside of the circle of professional theologians. Neither the adoption of the bachelor of divinity standard in the 1930s nor the master of divinity in the 1960s has made the seminary degree structure more comprehensible to people habituated to the more usual university rankings.

As in the colleges, the changing meaning of the degrees accompanied deeper changes in the nature of seminary education. The traditional pattern of residence and curriculum was replaced by a new, quantifiable pattern of required courses, credit hours, quality points, and research projects. While the early seminary had been a group of students who shared quarters and ate together in the commons, an approach that excluded most married men and almost all women from study, the new degree structure made flexible institutions possible. Although schools were slow to take advantage of these new opportunities, married students became increasingly common after World War I and constituted a majority after World War II. Women were not a significant proportion of the student body until the 1960s.

The development of the seminary toward a college and university form created a major problem for the teaching of a unified theology. The earlier seminaries had operated out of a clear understanding of theological encyclopedia (the theoretical interrelationship of the different theological disciplines). Although there were variations, the basic fields of the standard curriculum were the Bible, theology (and philosophy of religion), history, and preaching.

The tendency of the seminary to model itself on the college, however, meant that each field or discipline came to be taught as a specialized series of courses with some studies for beginners and others for more advanced students. In other words, each of the theological disciplines became something like a separate undergraduate department. The richer seminaries and the divinity schools further enhanced this model by introducing doctoral programs in the various theological sciences, replete with special seminars and dissertation standards.

For most schools, the problem of program quality was complicated, rather than solved, by these changes. While the richer institutions were able to keep up with the demands of the new context, the poorer lacked the necessary resources to maintain the new standards and found themselves worse off than in the antebellum period. Yet the obvious solution—a reduction of the number of seminaries in each denomination by one or two—was not considered by the largest denominations.

Theological Changes. In the period from 1860 to 1914 the seminaries had a difficult enough time adjusting to formal educational changes alone. However, these were also years of rapid theological transformation. The most important changes were in biblical studies where "higher" criticism, the examination of the literary and cultural history of the Scriptures, and "lower" criticism, the critical examination of the textual tradition of the Bible, were changing the contours of Scripture. In Old Testament studies, the crucial issues were the basic outline of Hebrew history and the proper ordering of biblical texts. Since the meaning of a text changes dramatically depending on whether it was written in the eleventh century B.C. or the sixth, much of traditional exegesis was at stake. The questions of New Testament criticism also concentrated on when and where the books had been written and what they meant in their original contexts.

By 1880 the critics had tentative solutions to these basic questions. The Pentateuch was shown to be a late redaction of a number of earlier sources, and such books as Isaiah were believed to have been composed over long periods of time. The postexilic period, traditionally seen as an era of literary inactivity between the great prophets and the New Testament, was now deemed the most creative period of all. The New Testament puzzle came together more slowly, despite the almost continual production of scholarly lives of Jesus, but by the late nineteenth century Mark had come to be seen as the oldest Gospel and most of the non-Pauline writings, including the Gospel of John, the Letters of John, Revelation, Hebrews, and Luke, had been assigned to the period after A.D. 70.

The new biblical history tended to place the supernatural elements of the biblical story on a naturalistic level. Miracle stories were presumed to be the outgrowth of ancient world views and not part of authentic history. As their historical validity came into question, the cultural context of such stories became an increasingly important key to their interpretation.

Early nineteenth-century exegesis had rested primarily on the mastery of linguistics, some knowledge of antiquities, and ordinary grammatical analysis. Although many students were bored by this curricular routine, the skills were not difficult to teach. The new biblical studies, in contrast, were the product of extensive scholarship and of a type of literary analysis that was not easily taught. Despite efforts by some schools, such as Union Theological Seminary in New York, to sustain the expectation that every seminary graduate would be a biblical scholar, the increasingly technical character of biblical studies made that impossible. Only those students who saw their future in research and teaching were willing to sacrifice the time and effort needed for modern critical studies.

By World War I a new teaching approach had been developed. Biblical studies began with a course in *Introduction* modeled on the German *Einleitung* in which the professor reported the results of his and others' research and gave advanced and doctoral students the opportunity to pose questions about prevailing theological positions. One sign of the change was the gradual abandonment of compulsory Hebrew in many of the more advanced schools. Furthermore, as biblical studies ceased to dominate the time of students who did not intend to teach or do research, the seminary program made room for a number of new disciplines, including religious education, sociology of religion, and Christian social ethics.

The late nineteenth century saw another new style of biblical study, dispensationalism, evolve on the right of the religious spectrum. Originally advocated by John Nelson Darby, a former priest of the Church of Ireland and a Plymouth Brethren preacher, and refined through a series of Bible and Prophecy Conferences (public meetings devoted to the exposition of the prophetic passages in the Bible, usually led by a noted clergyman), the new system stressed historical interpretation and saw God as working through a series of covenants (dispensations) and prophecies yet to be fulfilled. While biblical criticism was very hard to teach, dispensationalism, which professed to need no other tool of interpretation than the Bible and which often used language that was readily understood, was easily taught and mastered. By 1900 dispensationalism was the favored hermeneutics of professional evangelists and many popular Bible teachers.

Catholic Education. The intellectual ferment in Protestant schools in the late nineteenth century was not to be found in the nation's Catholic seminaries. In the wake of the French Revolution, the Roman Catholic church had withdrawn into itself to prevent the contamination of the faith by contact with modern thought. A new centralizing movement (often called Ultramontanism) sought to tie the administration of the church more tightly to Rome. The highlights in this development were the declaration of the dogma of the Immaculate Conception in 1854, the publication of the Syllabus of Errors in 1864, the First Vatican Council (1869–1870), and *Aeterni Patris* (1879), a papal pronouncement on doctrine which made Thomism the normative theology of the church.

The Congregation for the Propagation of the Faith (usually called the Propaganda) had authority over all churches that were technically still missionary areas. The church in the United States was a missionary church until well into the twentieth century, which meant that decisions reached in Rome were more immediately applicable to America than those decisions were in Germany, where the church was governed by a publicly recognized canon law and various concordats with the state. The tenure of American pastors, for example, was at the pleasure of the bishop and not for life as under the established church canons. This made the Catholic church in the United States more responsive to Rome than the European Catholic churches.

Many priests in the United States, like their parishioners, were immigrants from Europe, whose education probably reflected the prevalent educational standards of their homelands. The Irish Catholic church in the nineteenth century was just emerging from a period in which English domination had restricted its educational and pastoral ministry by such means as the enforcement of the penal laws, limiting Catholic civil rights, establishing Protestantism as the legal religion of Ireland, and passing laws prohibiting certain Catholic institutions, particularly schools, from operating. Seminary education in Ireland, for example, dates only from 1795, and the early Irish schools were—like their American counterparts—often staffed by French immigrants fleeing the Revolution. Men educated in these schools consequently brought with them to America very similar ideas to those taught in the American schools, including the belief that priestly formation (a technical term for the style of piety in which the priest was "formed" into the image of Christ) and rigid orthodoxy were the goals of theological education.

German Catholic immigrant priests came from a different tradition. Diocesan and monastic schools existed in Germany, but the university remained a primary center for the education of priests. Although never as attracted to the newer historical studies as the Protestants, Catholics had begun such work in Germany, particularly in the area of church history.

The rise of modern Germany from 1860 to 1890 under Bismarck had its effects on German Catholic education. The new German government in its *Kulturkampf* (struggle for civilization) required that new priests be trained exclusively in the universities in an effort to expose the church to new trends, especially nationalism and science, and to secure a more loyal church. Many religious orders, including the Jesuits, were expelled.

The *Kulturkampf* served to reinforce the conservative side of German Catholic life. Once Bismarck had been forced to retreat from the position taken in the *Kulturkampf*, German Catholics became more devoted to those elements of the old system that had been under attack. Paradoxically, a series of laws designed to produce a more modern church had the effect of producing the opposite. Since many American Catholics of German descent avidly followed events in Germany, similar attitudes became common among them.

A new departure in training priests for the United States was the establishment of an American college at Louvain, Belgium, in 1857. The new school sought to recruit candidates from all of the nations of Europe and to train them to serve specifically in American parishes. The school had the further advantage of providing a place where American priests could study in a Catholic cultural context (the United States was believed to be Protestant) and pursue advanced studies.

Ultramontanist theology, a movement that sought to reverse the eighteenth-century trend toward national Catholic churches directed by civil authorities, inspired some seminarians to travel "over the mountains" from France to Rome for their studies. Originally, Americans were trained at the College of Urban, which was directed by the Congregation for the Propagation of the Faith. In 1859, on the suggestion of Pope Pius IX, the North American College in Rome was founded to train priests for America, and an American rector was installed. The new school quickly became an elite institution that trained many of those who later became bishops.

In Roman seminaries students were taught primarily from approved doctrinal manuals, with a strong emphasis on the importance of the Roman See for the whole church. Rather than providing an alternative model for American priestly education, especially the tendency toward an unquestioning orthodoxy, Rome reinforced the same tendencies found at home.

The Third Plenary Council of the American Catholic Church met in Baltimore in 1884 to discuss, among other topics, the training of priests. The council largely followed the doctrinal and educational philosophy contained in *Aeterni Patris,* although there were some provisions for broadening minor seminary education.

The council's most significant act was its reaffirmation of the educational structure of minor seminary and major seminary. The resultant system of schools took a young man from about the age of fourteen and kept him in semi-cloistered schools until he was ready for full ordination. During this period the student was immersed in priestly culture and separated from nonministerial peers. Both in curriculum and in periods of study this structure varied from the pattern of college and graduate study that was becoming increasingly popular in American education as a whole. The effect was to reinforce the separateness of Catholic seminary studies, even to the extent that those who had already attended college were encouraged to complete the seminary course. The Council recognized the complex task of the modern ministry by requiring young priests to take examinations after five years in the seminary and to attend clerical conferences four times a year.

The size and ethnic complexity of the Catholic church in America makes generalizations about it suspect. A strong minority in the church, primarily second- and third-generation Irish, wanted the church to move more into the mainstream of American life. At the Third Plenary Council these clergymen, led by John Lancaster Spalding, made plans to establish a school to acquaint young priests with the general intellectual culture. Despite considerable opposition, Catholic University opened in Washington, D.C., in 1889. Pope Leo XIII urged the various seminaries and colleges to affiliate with the new school. While few such affiliations followed, a conference of seminaries was established that in 1904 became part of the National Catholic Educational Association.

Catholic University was almost immediately involved in the Americanism crisis. Like so many American Catholic issues Americanism had its genesis abroad. The French edition of Walter Elliot's *Life of Isaac Thomas Hecker* (1898) implied that the American Catholic church had found a means of accommodating its message and its structure to the realities of modern democratic life. Since separation of church and state was the pressing issue facing French Catholics, the book's message was that the French church ought to follow the American example. Pope Leo XIII, who later made his peace with French developments, addressed the encyclical *Testem benevolentiae* (1899) to the American hierarchy. James Cardinal Gibbons denied that such a heresy existed, but the charge brought the new school under suspicion and encouraged it to take a conservative stance.

American Catholic education was plagued by other events in Europe as well, the most serious being the modernist controversy. Catholic modernism, led by distinguished scholars such as the French priest Alfred Loisy and the Irish-born British priest George Tyrrell, stressed the adoption of the historical-critical method of biblical study, the repudiation of scholasticism, and the primacy of development in the history of dogma. To Pope Pius X modernism was heresy, and he prohibited its teaching by Catholics in his 1907 encyclical *Pascendi.* In 1910 an oath was imposed on suspect clergy requiring them formally to renounce modernist teachings. Bishops were instructed to cleanse their schools of all hints of the heresy.

Few modernists existed in the American church, so American schools were by and large uneffected by the papal pronouncements. However, professors were discouraged from venturing forth in the future, and the oath against modernism added the weight of conscience to the requirements of church law. Faced with dismissal or even excommunication, teachers naturally stayed with the safe conclusions of the sanctioned manuals and shied away from ambitious biblical studies. However, the rapid development of American Catholic theology after the Second Vatican Council (1962–1965) suggests that Catholic scholars had continued to read modern theological literature in spite of the papal ban.

The Protestant Ministry. The antebellum Protestant minister gradually came to spend more time in active ministry and less in the study, where the pastor had written his sermons, held catechism classes, and received parishioners for the care of souls. Local congregations developed mission societies, small Sunday schools, young people's societies, specialized classes, and discussion groups. Equally important, Americans had begun to tire of distant, authoritarian pastors who issued calls for close examination of the soul and threats of damnation. As Washington Gladden, one of America's leading liberal theologians and an authority on the modern church, said in the 1890s, the new expectation was for the minister to be a friend and confidant. In addition, the sermon was expected to be shorter and in popular language.

The latter part of the nineteenth century was also the great age of Christian lay activism. The Young Men's Christian Association, the Sunday school, various foreign and home missionary societies, and the new city missions all sought workers to aid them in bringing the nation to Christ. The revivals of Dwight L. Moody, which were both cause and effect of this new activism, were highlighted by Moody's call for recommitment of the faithful—as important to his crusades as his call for converts. Indeed, many other Protestant evangelists and pastors issued a similar challenge to their audiences.

An increasing number of new Protestant leaders were female. Women had traditionally been deeply involved in Protestant benevolent work, and the new activism provided more opportunities for female leadership. Temperance, a movement that was particularly attractive to women because of alcohol-related abuse of wives and children, opened a new sphere for the concerned Christian woman.

The need for schools for Christian workers was deeply felt among Protestant activists, and a number, including Moody (Chicago) Bible Institute and Philadelphia Bible Institute, were founded near the turn of the century. These schools had no formal entrance requirements, very low fees, and—especially in cities—evening as well as day classes. They often became dispensationalist in doctrine, partly because of the convictions of their founders and partly because dispensationalism could be easily taught to those with little formal training.

The Bible schools pioneered new forms of ministry for both home and abroad, including the professional Sunday-school worker, the evangelistic song leader, the revivalist, and the missionary pilot, who often flew other missionaries into remote areas. The Bible schools' early interest in Christian journalism broadened in the twentieth century to include the evangelistic use of radio and television. Despite initial reticence, the Bible schools also developed courses of study—almost always briefer than college and seminary—for pastors.

The existence of the Bible schools may have encouraged the seminaries to find a place for specialized ministries, including directors of religious education, Christian social and settlement workers, and others. The most favored new ministry, religious education, found a place—and its own degree structure—in many institutions. Hartford Seminary, a school originally founded as an orthodox alternative to Yale, was a pioneer with its School of Religious Education and its preparation of missionaries. New schools—such as Southwestern Baptist Seminary, established in Fort Worth, Texas, in 1908—were more willing to admit these new ministries than older, more established institutions. As a general rule a seminary's openness to new forms of ministry and to the admission of women were directly correlated. However, this very openness had unintended consequences for women, as many of the leadership posts, including jobs as director of religious education, professor of religious education in seminaries, and denominational positions came to be filled by men in the 1930s, 1940s, and 1950s.

THEOLOGICAL EDUCATION, 1900–1945

By 1900 the Progressive impulse had begun to permeate American life. Progressivism, which had roots in earlier evangelical social causes—especially antislavery—and was inspired in part by rapid progress in science and technology, envisioned an America in which the problems of the large city, the corporation, and the working class would be solved. What the engineer accomplished in industry, the Progressive hoped to accomplish in society.

During this period theological education was effected by the settlement house movement, which had originated in England where Toynbee House was founded in 1884 by university students. Jane Addams visited Toynbee House and established Hull House in Chicago in 1889, and from there the concept spread. Schools in or near large cities—such as Andover (located near Boston) and Union Seminary in New York—established settlements in the hope that students, living among the poor, would come to appreciate the needs of the urban slum dweller.

A more important shift occurred in seminary curriculum. The social sciences were seen by Progressives as a means to practical reform, and most schools began to add courses, such as sociology, applied Christianity, psychology of religion, and religious education, that attempted to apply new theological and social scientific methods to the work of the ministry. These new disciplines emphasized practical experience, as did other new forms of professional education. Union Seminary in New York established an ex-

perimental religious education program in which students both observed and participated in the religious development of other individuals. The most important system-wide innovation was the employment of students in local churches. Although less than fully realized, the goal of this new approach was for the student to work with an experienced minister and to have the school evaluate his performance. The question of the student's remuneration by the local church was particularly troublesome, as such payments were very important to the individual seminary's economics.

The New Professional. The Progressive movement, the increasing variety of religious workers, and the new social sciences pointed to a different way of understanding theological education and a new type of graduate: the professional religious worker. William Rainey Harper, the first president of the University of Chicago, was one of the first to introduce this new understanding into the curriculum. While traditional seminaries had attempted to produce resident theologians for local churches, Harper was willing to abandon that goal. To be sure, he felt that students ought to know the Christian faith, its doctrines, and its Scriptures, but these were secondary to students' mastery of their work in the world. According to Harper, students should study in the controlled environments of theological clinics or laboratories in which they could learn from experience. Theological education and ministerial preparation were to be almost identical.

Harper's view of theological education grew out of American liberal theology. Although liberalism was a diverse movement, it had common emphases: modern knowledge, especially as revealed in the application of the scientific method to all areas of human inquiry, should be incorporated into theology; Christianity was nondoctrinal and nondogmatic; God was immanent (within the natural order) rather than transcendent; and the potential of humankind was undetermined but greater than realized. For Harper the ideal religious professional was educated in these tenets. The minister was to be trained in modern methods, in knowing how to discern and experience the movement of the spirit (or the spirit of the age, which Harper may have considered to be the holy spirit), and in helping humanity to reach its highest potential.

Hartford Seminary became the classic institutional expression of the new professional ideal. The seminary was divided into schools devoted to specific religious professions—pastoral ministry, religious education, missions, and graduate studies. Few other institutions were able to afford the luxury of separate schools, but the newer ideals influenced their programs in other ways. Especially after publication of the work of the great ecumenical missionary conference at Edinburgh in 1914, a special professor of missions was common at most institutions alongside special professors in religious education and pastoral administration. Field education became almost universal.

The concept of the religious professional was not limited to liberalism. As Americans came to see professionalism as a value in itself, various occupations struggled to be seen as professions. Americans used "professional" loosely to mean anyone who was good enough to earn his living by means of a particular skill or who had mastered a body of knowledge. The list of professions included barbers and photographers as well as lawyers and doctors. Given this general social premium on professionalism, many who never understood either the social scientific or theological bases of Harper's ideas nonetheless found them congenial. Even the Southwestern Baptist Seminary, although conservative in theological orientation, used the professional ideal to structure its institutional life.

By 1914 seminaries and Bible schools had adopted somewhat similar understandings of their task. If the Bible schools tended to educate people for less prestigious positions, they differed from seminaries more in terms of class, wealth, and types of supporters than in their concept of general educational mission.

Pastoral Counseling. The original interest in the pastor as counselor was a product of the Progressive movement. Liberal theology assumed that religion was to promote social and individual health. By the early 1960s pastoral counseling was becoming almost identical with such specialized ministries as hospital chaplaincy, and training for counseling (which had stressed on-the-job training since its inception) moved increasingly out of the seminary context and away from seminary control. Program standards were determined by the centers themselves with the seminary's role restricted to the approval or disapproval of those programs. In addition, in-ternships, professional societies, and various forms of peer evaluation came to be the primary means of certifying new professionals in the counseling field.

Neither the seminaries nor the churches have subjected the new ministry of counseling and the new institutions of theological education to sufficient review. Serious questions remain, including the issue of the legal accountability of pastoral counselors for malpractice.

Evaluation: The Great Seminary Surveys. In 1924 Robert Kelly, working under the auspices of the Institute of Social and Religious Research, published *Theological Education in America.* This work, inspired by the revolutionary Flexner Report (1910), which revealed serious problems among the nation's medical schools, surveyed 100 of the nation's 140 seminaries. The report demonstrated that few of the seminaries studied had the resources to conduct an academic program on either the older model of the pastor-theologian or the newer model of the religious professional. The schools were marginal in almost every respect: out-of-date, poorly staffed, poorly attended, and with scant resources in the way of books, funds, or friends. Only a small group of seminaries were successful institutions.

There was little reason to doubt Kelly's findings, since the conditions he described had existed since at least the 1840s. American theological education was historically a two-tiered system. The best seminaries offered instruction equal to that given in university graduate schools; the worst were barely on the level of Bible schools. Structural problems, especially in the area of finances, were chronic. Nonetheless, the Kelly survey angered many in American theological education who believed that it had not told the whole story. The 1920s were a difficult period for the nation's religious leaders, and they feared the report would damage support for schools. They began pressing for a more extensive study. The Institute of Social and Religious Research responded by commissioning a new survey under the leadership of William Adams Brown with the research to be done by Mark May. Brown, a professor at Union Seminary, was one of the country's most trusted liberal leaders and an important figure in the ecumenical movement.

The Brown-May Report, published in 1934 in four volumes, suffered from its format. In an effort to avoid the criticism that had greeted Kelly, the more reproving passages of the work were so carefully nuanced that they lost their impact. However, two aspects of the report were very important. First, the report argued that the concept of the minister as an engaged religious professional was the norm by which education should be judged. A seminary was to be a place where ministers were prepared for specific church-related vocations. The ideal curriculum had to be correlated with the actual work of the ministry, and while much Bible study, history, and theology were to be continued in the program, their inclusion was justified by their value in pastoral work.

Second, the Brown-May Report was the first systematic reflection on "field education" (supervised work in churches). Mandated by the concept of theological study as preparation for ministry, field education was often simply doing tasks that the minister did not want to do. In theory, it was ministry under a seasoned pastor's or church worker's guidance; in fact, it often entailed the less rewarding aspects of parish life. The Brown-May report showed that much of the language used by schools to describe their programs of field education had little to do with the programs as they were actually administered.

After World War II a third survey was undertaken by H. Richard Niebuhr, James M. Gustafson, and Daniel Day Williams. This survey was prefaced by a series of essays on the development of different types of ministry and bore the optimistic title *The Advancement of Theological Education* (1957). In the midst of a postwar boom and an apparent religious revival, the seminaries were basically satisfied with their overall approach to their work. With a classical turn of phrase, Niebuhr saw the modern minister as a "pastoral director."

Accreditation: The Rise of the ATS. Movements toward the accreditation of institutions of higher learning began in the 1870s and 1880s. State legislatures, with the exception of New York, had been free with their charters, and the American educational landscape was cluttered with schools that possessed the right to grant degrees. Accreditation was a formal way in which universities and colleges could voluntarily establish minimal standards. Characteristically, accreditation agencies began with easily met standards and slowly raised them year by year.

The seminaries stood apart from this development originally. In most cases a seminary was content to judge itself by the internal standards of its relationship to a particular denomination, its theological positions, and its educational expectations. For instance, as late as World War II Southwestern Baptist Theological Seminary believed that it needed no other approval than that of the Southern Baptist Convention.

Accreditation of seminaries was eventually instituted to serve two purposes. First, it provided a means for other educational institutions to evaluate seminary work. Since advanced study in theology was often conducted in universities, a student's seminary work had to be evaluated against a common standard of performance. Secondly, accreditation was a means of seminary reform. By holding out the carrot of approval, an accrediting association could secure compliance with minimum standards and definitions and the weaker schools could thus be improved.

The American Association of Theological Schools (ATS) became an accrediting agency after the publication of Brown-May in 1934. It began with only forty members and grew very slowly, despite the fact that its standards were lax, compared with those of colleges or universities. The ATS was initially a guild of the liberal schools and some of the better confessional schools, such as Southern Baptist Theological Seminary and Princeton.

World War II provided a great impetus toward making accreditation mandatory. The military set the standard for membership in the chaplain corps by analogy with medicine and law. Just as a military lawyer had to be a graduate of an accredited law school, so a Protestant chaplain was expected to have graduated from an accredited seminary. As a result most of the schools affiliated with the major demoninations joined the ATS.

In the 1960s and 1970s the more conservative Protestant and the Roman Catholic seminaries sought membership in the ATS. This expansion in turn resulted in new interest in the formal standards of theological education. By the 1970s accreditation procedures were often jointly conducted by regional accrediting bodies and the ATS, with schools shaping themselves as much to the expectations of the regional bodies as to those of the association. This innovation signaled a new awareness of the place of the seminaries within the American educational system by formally accepting their understanding of themselves as graduate professional schools.

The ATS also succeeded in bringing together theological educators for discussions, conferences, and the publication of the journal *Theological Education*. The association's role in helping promote faculty scholarship changed the American style of theological education by spreading new ideas, locating areas where changes needed to be made, and by providing statistical information that could inform decisions.

Evangelicalism. Storm clouds had begun to gather in Protestantism as early as the 1880s when considerable controversy erupted among northern Protestants over higher criticism and Darwinism. The 1890s were a season of heresy trials of such noted scholars as Charles Augustus Briggs of Union Seminary, who was accused and convicted of teaching a doctrine of Scripture contrary to that found in the Westminister Confession and catechisms. Despite repeated attempts to stop the spread of liberalism, the movement continued to grow as did a complex antiliberal movement.

By 1920 meetings of the national denominations, especially the Northern Baptist Convention and the Presbyterian General Assembly, were marked by intense debate over what standards of belief in the Scriptures ought to be followed. The conservatives or Fundamentalists argued that Scripture had to be seen in terms of the doctrine of plenary verbal inspiration and, hence, contained no errors of fact, while the liberals maintained that critical scholarship had to be free to examine all of the biblical materials. In addition, there was considerable discussion as to whether the churches ought to work actively for laws prohibiting the teaching of evolution in the public schools.

Liberalism and Fundamentalism were loose alliances containing many shades of opinion and political orientation. Many liberals, for example, while willing to follow the conclusions of scholarship wherever they might lead, nonetheless held quite conservative views on particular doctrines. Fundamentalism was even more divided. Most Fundamentalists believed in traditional Christian orthodoxy and saw themselves continuing a tradition of teaching that reached back to the Reformation and beyond. For them nondogmatic Christianity was a contradiction in terms. Other Fundamentalists were deeply influenced by dispensationalism or by radical an-

ticommunism. And some, like William Jennings Bryan, believed Scripture to be the source of the best American values.

The controversy within the various denominations often ended with an emerging bureaucracy —a group that claimed to represent all sides— firmly in control of each church. As happened after the Oxford movement, there was a separation of local churches into liberal or conservative congregations. The seminaries did not participate in these developments nor—outside of such staunchly conservative bodies as the Southern Baptist Convention or the Missouri Synod Lutherans—were they integrated into the denominational bureaucracies. Nevertheless, the schools tended to become identified with one faction or another and to be supported by the churches identified with that faction. The close link between liberal theology and contemporary scholarship led many of the older institutions— Union, Crozer, Andover, Newton, Chicago, Yale —into the liberal camp. Princeton, once the citadel of the right, found itself moving after a long struggle toward a more moderate position.

Conservatives felt excluded from these arrangements and occasionally founded new seminaries. But the cost of establishing schools to replace those that they believed had fallen to the enemy was high. The new model of professional training for ministry required greater resources than did the earlier model of a school of theology. The academic standards of the new conservative schools suffered as a result of limited finances for books, faculty, and student aid—a problem that persisted into the 1950s and 1960s. Conservative educators resented what they believed to be an unfair division of resources.

Not all conservative schools originated in antiliberalism. Despite the apparent victory of religious moderates in the 1920s and 1930s, there was a continuing evangelical movement. Evangelicalism had always founded schools as part of its pattern of ministry, and twentieth-century evangelicalism was no exception.

POST-WORLD WAR II THEOLOGICAL EDUCATION

World War II and the immediate postwar period were very important in the history of theological education. Funds from the G.I. Bill made it possible for returning military personnel to take the full course in secondary education. As a result the pattern of four years of college and three years of seminary, long the goal of seminary educators, became the norm in the larger denominations. The postwar interest in religion further increased the seminary rolls.

New resources and students made the 1950s and early 1960s times of prosperity for most theological schools. New faculty were added, and areas of the curriculum previously ignored were given a new emphasis. Prosperity did not mean doctrinal innovation—the conformity of the Eisenhower years mitigated against basic change—but the opportunity to attain certain long-held organizational goals.

Neo-orthodoxy. The Neo-orthodox movement in American theology is still too recent to have been subjected to rigorous historical and critical analysis. "Neo-orthodoxy," as many American theologians called the movement that was more adequately described by its European proponents as the theology of crisis or dialectical theology, was an expression of a style of theology associated with Karl Barth, Emil Brunner, Karl Heim, and such biblical critics as Rudolf Bultmann and Oscar Cullman. In America the movement was epitomized by Reinhold Niebuhr, his brother H. Richard Niebuhr, and Paul Tillich.

American Neo-orthodoxy, despite its often vivid condemnations of its liberal predecessors, continued many characteristic emphases of old liberalism. This was particularly true in biblical studies, in which the historical-critical approach to Scripture was affirmed, and in social activism. If the Neo-orthodox were not sure that modern biblical study yielded the whole truth about Scripture and became significantly chastened in their optimism about social Christianity, they had no intention of retreating from either position. Nor were the Neo-orthodox any less committed to a scientific view of the world or to the social sciences.

Thus, the lines between liberalism and Neo-orthodoxy were blurred. The primary differences were in Neo-orthodoxy's interpretation of the role of tradition as containing, if not objective truth, at least valuable insights into the human condition and, thus, an existential or personally valid view of human nature. The Neo-orthodox saw in such doctrines as original sin and justification by faith important ways of speaking about the human situation. In contrast, liberals argued that the classical definition of original sin as an inherited aspect of life that separated an individual from God was both in error and, perhaps, a block to human progress.

Given the continuity with older liberalism, it is not surprising that American Neo-orthodox theologians were content with the contemporary model of professional education. The primary effects of Neo-orthodoxy were to increase the sense of vitality within the older fields of theology and to reaffirm their place in the schools. Theology, like social science or psychology, was seen as a valuable tool for the analysis of the human condition.

Both Neo-orthodoxy and liberalism were closely allied with the ecumenical movement, which contributed substantially to all theological schools by bringing together students and teachers from different traditions and encouraging them to exchange points of view and to learn from one another. Even in denominational schools, the movement brought about depths of insight and of churchmanship new to the American scene.

The primary contribution of Neo-orthodoxy was what might be called an ecumenical style. Since theological pronouncements were broad expressions about human existence to Neo-orthodoxy, these statements could be analyzed for insights which, even if they were not ultimately acceptable in their formulations, might add to the appreciation of humankind's religious experience. It was possible intellectually and imaginatively to enter into various, even alien, Christian perspectives.

Neo-orthodoxy also bridged theological schools of different persuasions. Very conservative and southern theological schools moved closer to the discussions of the larger theological community. The nature of Neo-orthodoxy was such that the position could be used as a way of continuing many traditional emphases while appreciating more modern approaches, especially in biblical studies. The Neo-orthodox movement did not end the older battle between liberalism and conservatism but provided many with a needed middle ground.

Catholicism and the Second Vatican Council. American Catholic theological education changed dramatically as a result of the Second Vatican Council (1962–1965). The council's theme was reconciliation between the church and the modern world, and a new spontaneity and freedom in the Catholic church and Catholic theology resulted from its decisions, which affirmed the right of Catholics to be full participants in modern culture, called for the celebration of Holy Communion in the language of the congregation attending the service, and replaced the traditional Catholic advocacy of a state-supported church with an acceptance of the religious civil rights of non-Catholics, including Jews. American Catholic theological education changed as many practical courses were added that had long been associated with Protestant schools, including religious education, field education, and pastoral psychology, and the reading of Protestant theology (occasionally under Protestant faculty) was encouraged. The traditional spirituality of the seminary also underwent significant modification. Students were entrusted with more freedom in their spiritual and personal life and, occasionally, were allowed a voice in school governance.

The newly felt need for accreditation prompted the schools to ensure that students were candidates for degrees and to have the requirements for those degrees published in school catalogs. Libraries were upgraded, and lay people were invited to take courses offered in the evening. In short, between 1965 and 1970 the Catholic seminary, which had resolutely remained outside of mainstream American education, moved just as determinedly into that mainstream. The new seminary, which seemed so exciting to those outside organized Catholicism, did not always inspire the same devotion within the church. By the 1970s Catholic seminaries suffered from a decline in enrollments that pushed some schools to the edge of financial disaster and forced others to close.

Vatican II and Protestant Theological Education. Protestant theologians followed Vatican II and its aftermath with interest, and began to incorporate some of the newer Catholic theology into their own positions. Not only were Catholic theologians read but, especially on the doctoral level, large numbers of Catholics enrolled in traditional graduate programs. At the same time Catholic scholars began to be called to Protestant faculties to teach in such areas as biblical studies. Although the movement was less dramatic in the other direction, Catholic institutions also sought Protestant scholars, and Protestants studied in Catholic graduate programs.

One sign of the fruitfulness of this exchange was the widespread popularity of the Latin American theologians of liberation in the 1970s, who sought to reinterpret traditional theology in such a way as to make it available to those struggling for freedom (both economic and personal) in Latin America. Just as American theologians were forced by changes in their own culture to consider the ethical meaning of such events as the civil-rights struggle, the women's movement, and United States foreign policy, they found unanticipated dialogue partners in the third world. While liberation theologians in the United States, Catholic and Protestant, were substantially different from those of Latin America, North American theologians were deeply influenced by their readings of the works of third-world Christians, by their discussions with them in such interdenominational organizations as the World Council of Churches, and by lectures delivered by third-world theologians in North American seminaries.

Another crucial aspect of Protestant seminary life deeply affected by contact with Roman Catholicism was spirituality. The Catholic concept of spiritual formation as a natural part of a sound educational program suggested and almost demanded new efforts in this area. With the exception of the evangelical and Anglo-Catholic seminaries, American Protestant schools had largely relinquished the task of directing the student's spiritual life to the individual student or to the churches. Although chapel services continued— as much from habit as conviction—the seminaries in the twentieth century tended to believe that piety was too closely identified with the private realm to be a subject of public discourse.

While most Protestant institutions have not yet determined what specific form efforts at enhancing spirituality will take, new sources in spiritual direction have been added and faculty, often in discussions in small groups, recognize the need for more personal counsel in this area.

Contact with Catholicism has also tended to deepen the Protestant seminary's appreciation of the role of the sacraments in church life and in ministry. Although the understanding of the minister as a professional religious leader has been retained, more emphasis has been placed on the minister's liturgical role.

CHRISTIAN THEOLOGICAL EDUCATION

The 1960s. The turbulence and creativity of American life in the 1960s contributed to some significant and apparently permanent changes in society addressed by theological schools. By 1968 mainstream theological schools were enrolling an increasingly large number of blacks, women, and representatives of other minority groups. In part these trends were attributable to changes in local churches and in American society as a whole. As the nation's general economy became more open to minorities, so did the seminaries. The change in constituency also reflected a shift in the understanding of theological education itself. Seminaries began to see themselves as one of the means by which positive social change could be accelerated. This understanding grew out of the protest movements of the early 1960s and 1970s in the areas of civil rights and in American foreign policy. The goals of the protesters enjoyed strong support at most seminaries.

The image of the seminary as a place of liberation was new to theological education. While previous Protestant activists had seen the seminary as a platform for their position or as a place of indoctrination, the advocates of the new perspective envisioned the institution as a means of transforming church and national life. Schools such as Intermet in Washington, D.C., trained students in reform work in the midst of the community. The goal of creating a liberating institutional environment became as important as more traditional goals of scholarship and professional expertise.

The protest movements also created new directions in governance that involved students in different levels of school administration. Often students were given representation on faculty committees and other policy-making bodies, and students were given greater freedom to shape their own educational programs. The number of required courses at most schools fell drastically, and in a few institutions even biblical studies were made optional. But by the mid-1970s many of the more radical experiments in governance and curriculum had begun to recede as both universities and seminaries became more concerned about their institutional survival.

The most pressing problem of seminaries in the twentieth century has been how to finance their academic programs. As the curriculum expanded and libraries added new services, particularly audiovisuals and, by the 1980s, computer laboratories, costs increased proportionately. Financial problems were one of the reasons why some seminaries attempted to establish consortia or cooperative programs among schools, and, in some cases, actually reversed the historical trend of establishing new schools by uniting similar institutions under one name and joining their faculties. The Graduate Theological Union and the Boston Theological Union are examples of consortia that have worked, while such schools as Andover-Newton demonstrate the viability of formal unions. The faculties and administrations of these "united" seminaries believe that they have enriched the programs of their schools by bringing the insights of more than one theological tradition to bear on contemporary theological questions.

Academic Changes. The Doctor of Ministry (D.Min.) program, instituted at many schools of theology during the 1970s, has helped provide needed revenues by attracting new students. Indeed, some financially pressed schools may have begun D.Min. programs before they had acquired sufficient resources to meet the standards that the degree structure imposed.

The educational problem that the D.Min. degree sought to solve was one implicit in twentieth-century expectations of seminary education. The Doctor of Ministry degree was to be built around evaluated experience, often demonstrated by a successful project in ministry, as well as sufficient supervised experience and advanced professional training in such areas as counseling. The best secular comparison is with the program of studies for a certified public accountant. However, since the schools also had to train students in Scripture, church history, and systematic theology, there was often no room in the program for the needed supervision. At some schools, the D.Min. degree became a part-time program, often taken in the summer months, with the classroom component somehow fitted into the pastor's busy schedule. Some schools located D.Min. centers far from their campuses and staffed them with faculty who flew in for one-day seminars. The programs were (and still are) criticized by many who believe that they have not attained the standards of doctorates in other fields or professions.

Departments of Religion. Most church-related

schools had long maintained a religion or Bible department as part of their responsibility to their denominations, and some university theology departments operated on a Ph.D. level. In the 1960s and 1970s, however, university religion departments began to develop their own methodology and to play an increasingly important role in theological research.

The religious studies departments broke what had been a long-standing monopoly of theological schools: technical theological studies. Although many in the new departments insisted that their academic work had its own theoretical basis, apart from theology, many religious studies professors were teaching traditional theological disciplines, including Bible studies, contemporary religious thought, and church history, in a new secular setting. The effect of the discussions of method, however, was to free the religion departments from the task of ministerial preparation and to enable them to pursue scholarly goals on their own terms.

The consequences of this spectacular change for divinity schools and seminaries are not yet completely clear. The better students, who might have seen seminary education as a means to a scholarly career, can now attain the same goal with greater specialization through a university program with a more prestigious degree. Seminaries have begun offering their own Master of Arts in Religion (M.A.R.) degrees in response to this competition.

Evangelicalism. In the 1970s and 1980s a strong evangelical movement became more prominent in American theological education. In part this was because the evangelical theological schools narrowed the financial gap between themselves and the more liberal institutions. Evangelical faculties included individuals who had advanced degrees from highly respected universities and seminary graduate programs and who were beneficiaries of the general prosperity of their institutions. Consequently, academic productivity on the right increased as evangelical professors adopted a more mature professionalism. By the early 1980s discussions between evangelical and mainstream theologians were increasingly common. Although some of the older tensions between Fundamentalists and liberals have persisted, there has been a new tone of cooperation and respect.

Traces of the older Fundamentalist movement continued. In 1976 Harold Lindsell, former dean of Fuller Seminary, published *The Battle for the Bible,* in which he claimed that evangelical seminaries were moving toward theological liberalism, especially on biblical issues. Lindsell believed that conservatives should rally behind the doctrine of inerrancy and remove all instructors from evangelical seminaries who were not orthodox on that point. In short, he called for a new Fundamentalist-modernist controversy.

Among Missouri Synod Lutherans, the battle over the teaching of the Bible resulted in a change in the denomination's leadership and a small split within the denomination. Concordia Seminary, the denomination's principal school, experienced considerable disruption when its faculty, searching for greater academic freedom, founded Seminex Seminary to compete with the conservative parent institution.

The Southern Baptist Convention, which had largely escaped the early liberal-Fundamentalist split, found itself involved in an internal theological struggle. As in the Missouri Synod dispute, the issue was whether or not modern critical methods should be used in the schools. No one is sure which direction southern Baptist seminaries will take (or might be forced to take), although in the late 1980s conservatives appeared to be in control.

The Future of Christian Theological Education in America. No historian is a good prophet, but certain trends seem likely to continue. Although a few theologians, including Edward Farley of Vanderbilt, have raised serious questions about the theoretical foundations of theological education in the 1980s—including the question of how the goals of traditional theology can be attained—no fresh suggestions for reform have been made. There are, however, some serious problems on the horizon. If the demographic projections of a decline in the number of Americans between twenty and thirty are accurate, then the schools will face increasing difficulties in recruiting sufficiently large student bodies to maintain their programs. The financial problems caused by the increasing cost of modern education will probably continue to plague theological schools, with the most serious difficulties occurring in those schools with smaller endowments that serve smaller publics. Catholic seminaries, which have reported declines in the number of vocations for a decade, may expect their financial situation to be more critical.

It is possible that these pressures will contribute to some new experiments and forms of theological education. For many Catholic and Protestant schools, the only solution to what appears to be a bleak financial future seems to be consolidation of institutions. While some of the values that graduates of smaller schools found significant may be lost, especially the deep sense of community and common purpose engendered in a society of less than 200, this may be the only way in which the churches can continue to meet the standards that their seminaries have accepted as norms for their own teaching.

The hope for the future of religious education lies in a regeneration of American theology. If American theology can find new and fresh formulations, it can then find sources of institutional renewal and real alternatives to the present situation. One hopes that this may result in a new relationship between academic theology, the preparation of ministers, and the schools in which they are educated.

BIBLIOGRAPHY

William Adams Brown, *The Education of American Ministers* (1934); Heather Day, *Protestant Theological Education in America: A Bibliography* (1985); John Tracy Ellis, "The Formation of the American Priest: An Historical Perspective," in John Tracy Ellis, ed., *The Catholic Priest in the United States: Historical Perspectives* (1971); Edward Farley, *Theologia: The Fragmentation and Unity of Theological Education* (1983); E. Brooks Holifield, *A History of Pastoral Care in America: From Salvation to Self-Realization* (1983); Robert L. Kelly, *Theological Education in America: A Study of One Hundred Sixty-One Theological Schools in the United States and Canada* (1924); H. Richard Niebuhr, Daniel Day Williams, and James M. Gustavson, *The Purpose of the Church and Its Ministry: Reflections on the Aims of Theological Education* (1956) and *The Advancement of Theological Education* (1957); H. Richard Niebuhr and Daniel Day Williams, eds., *The Ministry in Historical Perspectives* (1956); Mark A. Noll, "The Founding of Princeton Seminary," in *Western Theological Journal*, 42 (1979); Timothy L. Smith, *Uncommon Schools: Christian Colleges and School Idealism in Midwestern America, 1820–1950* (1978). [See also HISTORY OF PREACHING IN AMERICA; PASTORAL CARE AND COUNSELING; *and* PROFESSIONAL MINISTRY.]

RELIGION AS AN ACADEMIC DISCIPLINE

*Harold E. Remus, F. Stanley Lusby, and Linda M. Tober**

PART I: ORIGINS, NATURE, AND CHANGING UNDERSTANDINGS

The phrase *religion as an academic discipline* refers to the study of religion for other than professional, confessional, proselytizing, or apologetic purposes. A number of differentiae define this twentieth-century phenomenon. By contrast with theological education, which provides professional preparation for service in a particular religious tradition and generally presupposes or requires religious commitment of some kind, the academic study of religion is viewed as part of a liberal education that seeks both critical and sympathetic understanding of religious phenomena from the whole spectrum of religious traditions without presupposing or seeking the student's commitment to those traditions or preparing the student to serve within them in a professional capacity. By contrast with religious education, whether in confessional elementary or secondary schools or in church-related colleges and universities, the academic study of religion does not seek to inculcate religious doctrines or specific religious values, to strengthen or win commitment to a religious tradition or institution, or to provide instruction preparatory to professional training for the ministry or rabbinate. The professional competence of scholars and teachers of religion as an academic discipline is judged not on confessional grounds but with respect to knowledge of their field. The academic study of religion is commonly designated as *religious studies* or *religion* or (often in Roman Catholic schools) *theology.*

PRECURSORS

While religion as an academic discipline has its own distinctive configurations in America, it is deeply indebted to centuries of reflection on and study of religion in both the West and East for crucial elements of theory and practice.

One such element is textual criticism, the establishing of the best text of religious documents that may exist in many translations and in many manuscripts copied over many centuries. The development of a science of textual criticism to establish the best text of the New Testament writings, for example, drew on critical study and collation of Greek texts at the library in ancient Alexandria, on the efforts of early Christian scholars like Origen and Jerome, on the Renaissance focus on the classics of Greece and Rome and the Reformation stress on the Bible in the original languages, and on the nineteenth-century discovery and editing of manuscripts and papyri and formulating of principles of textual criticism. Similarly, since the Buddha, like Jesus, taught only orally, his sayings being recorded by disciples and then assembled in collections in various languages, textual criticism of these collections has been essential and has been carried out by the Pali Text Society (London), beginning in the late nineteenth century and continuing to the present.

The development of the science of philology in Europe in the nineteenth century placed study of these ancient texts on a sound linguistic basis. Closely related was the emergence of anthropol-

*Part I of this essay was written by Harold E. Remus and Part II was written by F. Stanley Lusby and Linda M. Tober.

ogy, archaeology, and ethnology as independent disciplines in the eighteenth and nineteenth centuries, which aided in understanding the roots of world religions such as Hinduism, Buddhism, Judaism, and Christianity and also opened up the study of the religions of prehistoric and preliterate peoples. Psychology and sociology, which developed in the same period, very early made a significant impact on the study of religion.

The development of these various disciplines has been influenced by social and cultural changes. Reflection on and study of religion are also responsive to such changes and have been, accordingly, sometimes explicative or apologetic —seeking to explain or defend a particular religious tradition—sometimes critical, and sometimes all of these at once in the search for reinterpretations of religion to suit new situations. Inasmuch as such reflection and study tended to distance the person engaging in them from unexamined practice and belief, they adumbrated the modern academic study of religion. Among the ancient Jews and Romans, for example, the authority and consent attaching to religious laws and customs were undermined and/ or underwent changes as a result of various encounters with Hellenism and the customs of the many peoples of the Hellenistic and Roman empires. Among the Greeks, during the revolution in thought and belief associated with the Ionian philosophers of the seventh and sixth centuries B.C.E. and the changes in the climate of opinion that were part of the Sophistic age (fifth century B.C.E.), a number of influential thinkers and writers came to regard traditional religious laws and customs as strictly human creations. Others sprang to the defense of tradition; in either case there were distancing and reinterpretation.

Something similar is observable in treatments of extraordinary phenomena, or miracles. Augustine and Aquinas, in defending Christian miracle claims, manifested an awareness that education and culture affect one's judgment of such claims; on the other hand, thinkers in the Enlightenment tradition, such as David Hume, pointed to the social conditioning of miracle claims in order to discredit them or reduce their number. Such reflections on the nature of religious laws and customs and on miracle claims vaguely anticipate the findings of modern scholarship but develop practically none of the implications. These are systematically developed, however, in modern approaches to religious phenomena such as the sociology of religion and the philosophy of history, both of which figure in the academic study of religion. While the latter is a recent development, therefore, it is also evident that it is deeply rooted in the past.

STUDY OF RELIGION IN AMERICAN SCHOOLS AND COLLEGES

Until well into the twentieth century the study of religion in American schools and colleges meant instruction *in* religion rather than study *of* or *about* religion(s), and the religion taught was either Christianity or Judaism. The change from instruction in to study of or about religion(s) and the broadening of the denotation of religion beyond Christianity and Judaism reflected changes in the Western world generally and in American society and culture specifically: the expansion of knowledge beyond medieval and Renaissance curricula to include the new sciences—natural and social—and their applications in technology; industrialization and capitalism, with the attendant need for training in practical skills and technique; the transformation of schooling, once the privilege of the few, into the prerogative of all; an ever-increasing sense of nationhood and democracy as well as increasing attention to the demarcation of civil and religious spheres; specialization of knowledge, especially as taught and practiced in German universities and imported to the United States; and new currents in thought such as Hegelianism, Transcendentalism, and pragmatism. These changes affected the ownership and control of schools and colleges, the aims and theories of education, and the understanding of the nature of religion and how and where it was to be studied and taught.

To be specific, for a good part of American educational history it was assumed that curricula at every level of schooling would include instruction in religion or religious values and that teachers and students would reflect that instruction in their lives. The highly influential elementary textbooks *The New England Primer* (ca. 1690) and McGuffey's *Eclectic Readers* (six editions, 1836– 1857) tied religious and moral teaching to instruction in the alphabet and reading. In the earliest colleges, which modeled their aims and curricula after the ancient English universities and in turn became the models for much collegiate instruction in America, each student was to "consider the main End of his life and studies, to know God and Jesus Christ which is Eternal life" (Harvard Statutes, ca. 1646), and all were to "live Religious, Godly and Blameless Lives according to the Rules of Gods [*sic*] Word" (Yale laws, 1745).

Underlying these aims and provisions for instruction in religion were certain understandings of human nature and society and the role education played in forming them. If human nature was predisposed to evil, then instruction in religion and morality was essential both to the eternal bliss and earthly good of individuals as well as society. This social view appears prominently in early statements of the purposes of schools and colleges. Harvard was to be "a nursery for . . . Men" (Cotton Mather, 1702)—ministers as well as gentlemen who would occupy public office. Yale was to train up "many worthy persons for the service of God in the state as well as in church" (charter, 1745). The College of William and Mary was founded so "that the Church of Virginia may be furnished with a Seminary of Ministers of the Gospel" but also so "that the youth may be piously educated in good Letters and Manners, and that the Christian Faith may be propagated amongst the Western Indians" (charter, 1693). The Northwest Ordinance of 1787, which set aside income from public lands for schools, justified that provision by linking education to religion and morality: "Religion, morality, and knowledge being necessary to good government and the happiness of mankind, schools and the means of education shall forever be encouraged." So, too, the charter of the University of Georgia (1785) linked civic good to education, "the forming hand of society, that by instruction they [the youth] may be moulded to the love of virtue and good order."

When earthly good—as an end in itself or as proof of eternal divine election—came to weigh equally with eternal bliss as the end of religion, or often even to outweigh it, the place and purpose of religion in education changed, too. Alexis de Tocqueville's observations that "the Americans not only follow their religion from interest, but they often place in this world the interest which makes them follow it" and that "it

is often difficult to ascertain from their [American preachers'] discourses whether the principal object of religion is to procure eternal felicity in the other world or prosperity in this" (*Democracy in America,* 1835) were illustrated in an elementary textbook published in the same year. In a chapter on "How to Make Money," John McVickar's *First Lessons in Political Economy; for the Use of Primary and Common Schools,* proclaimed that "even the poorest boy in our country," possessed of good health, industry, education, practical skill, "and add to this, moral habits and religious principles, so that his employers may trust him and place confidence in him . . . certainly has as good a chance of becoming independent and respectable, and perhaps *rich,* as any man in the country."

This stress on earthly good accorded with the growing industrialization and commercialization of American society and the extension of schooling to increasing numbers and different social strata. These changes are reflected in curricula at all levels. One consequence was that religion, though still generally included in some way, increasingly lost ground—along with the other traditional subjects of the classical curriculum—to courses in the modern languages, commercial subjects, the new sciences and their practical applications, and various other vocational and professional skills. Benjamin Franklin's proposed curriculum for an academy in Philadelphia (chartered 1753) included history of religion—but no instruction in religion—as one of some two dozen subjects both traditional and modern. Franklin's proposal was both symptomatic and prophetic, as were William Smith's curriculum for what became the University of Pennsylvania (chartered 1755), which included instruction in the Bible but no courses in religion, and Thomas Jefferson's plans for the University of Virginia (chartered 1819), which made no provision whatever for instruction in religion. The state universities and land grant colleges established as a result of the Morrill Act (1862) at first offered religion courses like those taught in denominational colleges, but multiplying of courses to keep pace with new knowledge and new needs, introduction of the elective system, public ownership of these institutions, and new currents of thought and scholarship meant that such courses were increasingly viewed as both otiose and suspect.

The suspicion focused on the nature of courses in religion and the propriety of studying religion in public institutions of learning. Religion, for most Americans, meant Christianity, but the varieties of American Christianity engendered strife that affected the study of religion in both public and private institutions.

Another central issue was the question of ownership and control. The tradition, established in the early colonies, of ecclesiastical ownership and control of schools and colleges gained impetus in the later colonial and post-Revolutionary periods when the Great Awakenings brought many new members into the churches and, with them, the desire and means to establish denominational schools and colleges. In the nineteenth century virtually all the Christian denominations sought to keep pace with westward migration by establishing colleges to provide general education as well as instruction in religious (that is, denominational) traditions. Demarcation of the line between public and private or ecclesiastical control was a source of recurring controversy. Before the Civil War, denominations controlled at various times a number of state universities, and they sometimes tried to hinder establishment of state universities or to channel public funds and land grants to denominational colleges. Even under state control, the ethos of state universities in the eighteenth and nineteenth centuries was commonly religious, with proprietary rules, compulsory chapel attendance, and courses in religion. State universities could therefore argue that they had the advantage of being Christian without being sectarian and at times were able to hinder the founding of denominational colleges.

Whether in public, denominational, or private nondenominational schools, the study of religion occasioned heated controversy over which—if any—of the varieties of Christianity represented in America was to be studied. Decades of strife led eventually to certain principles regarding the study of religion in secondary schools and institutions of higher education.

First, given the First Amendment prohibition of establishment of religion, the religious pluralism of American society, and the voluntarism of American religion, religious groups were free to establish their own schools offering courses in religion. Indeed they often saw this as the only way for instruction in religion to play a role in education. At the elementary and secondary levels, public schools in the nineteenth century were often Protestant in ethos and, alongside reading of the King James Bible without comment or interpretation, offered instruction in a generalized Protestantism. When these elements were increasingly, and then decisively, excluded from the public schools, a few Protestant denominations (such as the Lutheran Church—Missouri Synod) established their own schools, offering instruction in their traditions. Roman Catholics, who early on had started their own schools, now established schools on a large scale in which instruction in religion was offered. Some Jewish communities also founded schools in which instruction in Jewish tradition formed part of the curriculum.

At the post-secondary level, denominational institutions commonly required courses in religion. Their nature and quality varied widely since instructors were often hired on the basis of religious profession and for the purpose of inculcating particular religious traditions. For example, a textbook entitled *Elements of Religion* (1894) by H. E. Jacobs was in fact a popular exposition of Lutheran teaching for use in Lutheran colleges.

Today, religion courses continue to be offered in denominational colleges and universities. But increasingly they have become elective and represent study of or about religion rather than instruction in religion, and *religion* has come to denote both non-Christian and non-Western religions. Moreover, the instructors do not necessarily belong to the denomination that owns or controls the school.

Second, the Dartmouth College case (1819), protecting private colleges from government encroachment, and the Supreme Court ruling of 1925 striking down an Oregon law requiring attendance at public elementary and secondary schools safeguarded the right to establish private schools, whether under religious auspices or not. Most private schools, at every level, were founded by religious groups. Such ties became increasingly tenuous in the nineteenth and twentieth centuries, and today many such schools retain only a loose or historical affiliation with their founding religious groups. These private, non-denominational colleges and universities have increasingly moved from required instruction in religion to elective courses in the study of religion, Western and non-Western, as part of a liberal education.

Third, a number of controversies and court cases in the nineteenth and twentieth centuries led to the principle that, whereas public institutions of learning might not offer instruction *in* religion, they might legitimately offer teaching *about* religion. Philip Lindsley, president of Cumberland College (a public institution, now the University of Nashville), very early (1829) voiced a view that later became court doctrine: "A *public* college—that is, a literary and scientific college designed for the public generally—ought to be independent of all religious and sectarian bias, or tendency, or influence." In practice, however, the University of Michigan was more representative of state schools in the nineteenth century: the presidents, faculty, and regents were Christian and fostered a Christian ethos, and the university offered instruction in Christianity. In the twentieth century the stance of the University of Oregon was for a time typical of the state institutions: it refused to create a chair of religion in the Department of Philosophy for fear of violating its religious neutrality, and it excluded religious facilities and exercises from university premises.

Neutrality left unanswered, however, the questions posed in 1932 by Robert Sproul, president of the University of California: "Is religion itself a legitimate field of learning in the university? Is it a specific experience of the race, a necessity for each growing citizen, and a way of cultural growth for the future, or is it only a vestigial activity, and an antiquated pre-scientific anachronism?"

One way of including religion in university curricula, while avoiding university involvement in denominational rivalry and without contravening the First Amendment prohibition of the establishment of religion, was Thomas Jefferson's response to the charge that the University of Virginia was "an institution, not merely of no religion, but against all religion." Jefferson proposed (in a letter to Thomas Cooper in 1822) that

> . . . the different religious sects . . . establish, each for itself, a professorship of their own ten-

ets, on the confines of the university, so near as that their students may attend the lectures there, and have the free use of our library, and every other accommodation we can give them; preserving, however, their independence of us and of each other. This fills the chasm objected to ours, as a defect in an institution professing to give instruction in *all* useful sciences. . . . And by bringing the sects together, and mixing them with the mass of other students, we shall soften their asperities, liberalize and neutralize their prejudices, and make the general religion a religion of peace, reason and morality.

This proposal for denominational professorships of religion was prophetic of an arrangement sometimes employed in the twentieth century in order to allow the study of religion on state university campuses. The instruction offered, however, was still largely instruction in Christianity and/or denominational traditions.

Somewhat similarly, at the elementary and secondary school level an arrangement known as "released time" that was initiated early in the twentieth century and became widespread allowed use of a portion of the school day, on or off the school premises, for instruction in religious traditions of the denominations involved. Another plan, instituted in North Dakota in 1912 and adopted in other states, offered credit for courses in the Bible. Although these courses gave instruction in (rather than about) religion, and specifically in Christian traditions, they foreshadowed later academic study of religion in high schools in that they were offered for credit and were sometimes taught by public school personnel.

One by one Supreme Court decisions in the 1940s disallowed, on First Amendment grounds, the use of public funds, personnel, and facilities for instruction in religion. The landmark ruling for academic study of religion in public institutions came in the Schempp case (1954). Although ruling that school-sponsored prayer and devotional Bible reading were unconstitutional under the First Amendment, the Court recognized, also under the amendment, "the teaching *about* religion, as distinguished from the teaching of religion, in the public schools." The Court's rationale is important in understanding the rationale for the academic study of religion in public institutions:

It might well be said that one's education is not complete without a study of comparative religion or the history of religion and its relationship to the advancement of civilization. It certainly may be said that the Bible is worthy of study for its literary and historic qualities. Nothing we have said here indicates that such study of the Bible or of religion, when presented objectively as part of a secular program of education, may not be effected consistently with the First Amendment.

This ruling brought full circle, but with some significant changes, what had obtained in the colonies and until well into the twentieth century and had been voiced as a desideratum even by Jefferson: study of religion was to be included in curricula as part of a liberal education. In the words of one informed mid-twentieth-century observer, "religious phenomena constitute so large a segment of human experience" that without study of them "a college or university could scarcely be regarded as offering a liberalizing education." The purpose of offering such study "is not that of making the university religious, but to assist the university to be itself in the fullest and best sense" (Holbrook, 1963, pp. 68–69, 174).

The Supreme Court's specification that religion as taught in public institutions of learning was to be "teaching *about* religion" accorded with sweeping changes in scholarship and higher education in the nineteenth and twentieth centuries. These had a deep and lasting effect on religion scholarship and teaching, beginning in divinity schools located in centers of learning. These schools gave a hearing to new thought and were ready to try the new methods in research that had drawn American students in all fields to German universities and had revolutionized the study of religion and theology there.

German theology and methods, focusing on primary sources and employing critical historical and philosophical approaches to religious traditions, were introduced at Harvard Divinity School in the early decades of the nineteenth century, and, with the revitalization of the school under President Charles W. Eliot after 1880 the faculty, most of whom had studied in Germany, were committed to historical scholarship. At Yale, too, philological and critical historical scholarship won an early foothold and gradually gained ascendancy. When William Rainey Harper, who received his Ph.D. from Yale in 1875, became president of the new University of Chicago in 1891, he assembled a faculty committed to the new methods and ideals of research. The new academic disciplines that emerged at the end of the nineteenth century also affected the way religion was studied in these centers of learning. The social and psychological approaches to religion, for example, are reflected in such Ph.D. dissertation titles as: "Japanese Phallicism" (Chicago, 1894) or "Semitic Phallicism" (Harvard, 1908), "Historical Illustrations of the Psychology of Religious Belief" (Harvard, 1905), and "A Consideration of Prayer from the Standpoint of Social Psychology" (Chicago, 1908). Religion scholarship itself occasionally led to new disciplines in the university, as when Francis Peabody's courses in social ethics at Harvard Divinity School resulted in the establishment of the university's Department of Social Ethics (a title suggested by William James).

The new disciplines were fruitfully applied by historians such as Bartold Georg Niebuhr, anthropologists such as E. B. Tylor, psychoanalysts such as Sigmund Freud and Carl Jung, and sociologists such as Émile Durkheim and Max Weber, not only to the study of Judaism and Christianity, but also to non-Christian, non-Jewish, and non-Western religions, including preliterate (so-called primitive) religions. Such cross-cultural, comparative study stimulated similar studies by scholars in traditional areas of religion scholarship, such as biblical studies, and led eventually to the development of an academic field commonly designated *religion* or *religious studies* that was dedicated in principle to the academic study of religion of all times and places.

This development had significant implications and ramifications for the institutional embodiment of the academic study of religion, the mode of such study, and the ways that professors or students were trained in it. By the end of the 1960s most of the accredited four-year colleges and universities in the United States were offering courses in religious studies. About two-thirds of these schools had a special program in religious studies, and of them about two-thirds offered an undergraduate major. Not surprisingly, most religiously affiliated schools have such programs, but half of the private, nondenominational schools and a third of the state schools do as well. In the latter the increase was most dramatic in the 1960s and early 1970s, in the wake of the Schempp ruling and in the context of the social and intellectual unrest of that period. Religious studies courses offered students opportunities to pursue some of the basic human issues—such as freedom, justice, love, evil, death—that universities were often bypassing in favor of technical and analytical study. A decline in institutional religions has also been a factor in enrollment in religious studies courses. As Robert A. Spivey observes, "when church and synagogue are weak, then religion study will be strong because people will be questioning and thinking about traditional religious roots," as well as searching for meaning in life and examining other religious traditions (1968, pp. 9–10).

The academic study of religion has come to have a recognized place in the liberal arts curricula of the majority of two-year colleges. In general, such study parallels that in four-year schools but with some important differences. The courses are fewer and introductory, while instructors are often part-time or have major teaching responsibilities in another area and have less graduate training and little or no special training in religious studies; on the other hand, the teachers are apt to have more training in pedagogy or are expected to develop such skills.

At the secondary-school level, the study of religion has been introduced in a number of places, according to certain principles and models. One principle is that the curriculum materials employed should represent the best of religious studies scholarship and lead to understanding rather than commitment. At the same time, students' religious commitments are not to be undermined. Such study is generally elective rather than required. Skilled teachers with some training in the religious traditions they teach and in methodologies appropriate to teaching *about* religion are required. In developing materials and preparing teachers, state departments of education and school boards that have inaugurated such programs have drawn on faculty resources in university religious studies departments. One model is to study religious texts as literature as part of the English curriculum and taught by English teachers. Another approach is to include the study of religion in the social studies curriculum. The Public Education Religious Studies

Center at Wright State University in Dayton, Ohio, provided a focus for research in this area in the 1970s.

ADVANCED EDUCATION IN RELIGION AND THE TRAINING OF A PROFESSORIATE

The course of the advanced education in religious studies that was developed to train scholars and teachers competent to take their place alongside those in other fields is related to the cultural changes and the changing understandings of the study of religion outlined above. In the colonial period advanced or specialized education in religion meant the training of clergy; it took place in several ways. Many of the clergy were educated in Europe. Those educated in American colleges began concentrated study of theology after completing undergraduate work by reading in theology with a faculty member. A third, very common means to acquire the specialized education in religion necessary for the ministry was to read under the tutelage of a clergyman, either after or in place of college.

The Revolution and independence meant that for some churches, especially those that had supported the losing side in the Revolution, the supply of clergymen who had received their professional training in Europe diminished or ceased, at least for a time. The other ways of educating an indigenous clergy were also proving inadequate. Formal graduate study in religion began to replace the system of apprentice training; in some colleges it gradually came to be distinct, though not separate, from the rest of the school. There was also a movement to establish seminaries separate from the colleges since the ethos and the education the latter offered were often viewed as inimical to religion. Establishing of seminaries was sometimes confessionally motivated; the price of confessionalism was repeated involvement of seminaries in the incessant doctrinal controversies of the nineteenth century, with consequent strain on academic energies and resources.

In the colonial period strictures on religious freedom had kept Roman Catholics from founding their own schools. After American independence, Catholics began to establish seminaries to train an indigenous clergy, and by 1868 fifty seminaries had been started, generally in isolation from institutions of higher learning.

Prior to the last quarter of the nineteenth century, then, the institutions committed to advanced or graduate education in religion lacked basic elements now commonly regarded as requisite to such study. First, owing to their relatively large number, these institutions were small in size and possessed inadequate resources. Second, the majority of seminaries were situated apart from centers of learning, often in out-of-the-way places largely cut off from the intellectual currents of the day. Third, the professors called to labor in such circumstances were overworked and underpaid. To be sure, some were men of considerable intellectual powers and with academic backgrounds comparable to those of the best college professors of the day. Alongside their teaching they were able to produce respectable works of scholarship. But others brought to the task only the education acquired in colleges or seminaries as ill equipped and poorly staffed as those in which they themselves now taught. Fourth, many of the students, even at the old, established schools, came without college degrees, and the time that teachers might have devoted to graduate education in religion had to be given over to collegiate instruction.

It was in the late nineteenth century that graduate education at the doctoral level began to develop, in religion as well as in other fields. In 1861 Yale granted the first Ph.D. in the United States. By 1900 the university as a center of research offering graduate education in a multiplicity of fields had assumed the lead in higher education, displacing the college of twenty-five years previous with its traditional classical curriculum and unearned master's degrees. In this same period, concluding with the end of World War I, the first doctoral degrees in religion were awarded and the first doctoral programs specifically in the field of religion were established.

Divinity schools connected with universities were at first content to have their students or graduates pursue doctoral studies in various departments of the university graduate school, such as philology or philosophy. Gradually, however, these and other divinity schools began to develop doctoral programs of their own or in cooperation with universities. In 1914 Harvard, for example, authorized the Divinity School to grant the Th.D. (Doctor of Theology); twenty

years later the Graduate School established a Ph.D. in the history and philosophy of religion for persons who wished to teach religion courses in colleges and universities. In 1913 Garrett Biblical Institute announced an arrangement by which its students could pursue a Ph.D. program at Northwestern University in Evanston, Illinois. At Yale graduate study in religion other than or beyond the professional kind was recognized in 1920 when a Department of Religion was established in the Graduate School to offer (with the Philosophy Department) the Ph.D. in philosophy of religion and, as an exclusive charge, in historical and contemporary religion, with specialization in comparative religion, Christian origins, biblical theology, history of doctrine, contemporary theology and theological ethics, and the psychology and philosophy of religion.

Ecclesiastical doctoral programs were instituted under church auspices at several other institutions in this period—at Southern Baptist Theological Seminary in Louisville in 1892 and somewhat later at Union Seminary in New York (first Th.D., 1924). Among Roman Catholics a strong desire to elevate the quality of Catholic higher education and to increase the church's leadership in the intellectual life of the country led to the opening of the Catholic University of America in Washington, D.C., in 1889 exclusively as a graduate school of theology with the authority to confer the doctoral degree. By the beginning of World War I nine had been conferred. Some of the forty Ph.D.'s granted by other departments of the university in this same period were in the field of the Bible and religion. In the years since, many students at Catholic University have pursued Ph.D. study in the area of religion in various departments of the Graduate School. A Ph.D. program was established in the Department of Religion and Religious Education in 1940; the present School of Religious Studies is made up of five departments and an interdepartmental program in liturgical studies.

By 1880 the tiny Jewish population of the American colonies had swelled to a quarter of a million and twenty years later to a million. Until well into the nineteenth century synagogal and communal affairs were handled by the laity, while intricate questions of the law were referred to the rabbis of Europe. When synagogues became more numerous and some were able to provide for a rabbi, they sent to Europe. When the stream of immigration became a flood, however, the Jewish communities began to train an indigenous clergy. The first permanent rabbinic school, Hebrew Union College, was established in Cincinnati in 1875 and graduated its first rabbis in 1883. Three years later representatives of Historical (Conservative) Judaism founded the Jewish Theological Seminary in New York. The strong impetus given to Orthodoxy by immigrants from eastern Europe resulted in the establishment in 1897 of the school for the study of the Torah and the training of rabbis that eventually developed into Yeshiva University (New York).

The Jewish scholarship that developed in the United States in the second half of the nineteenth century was pursued by rabbis of European origin and training. With the establishment of the seminaries and of Semitics chairs in universities, a tradition of indigenous American scholarship began to develop. In 1905 Jewish Theological Seminary instituted a program leading to the D.H.L. (Doctor of Hebrew Letters). Dropsie College (Philadelphia, Pennsylvania), chartered in 1907 as a graduate research institution, conferred its first Ph.D. in 1912. Further proof that Jewish scholarship was taking root in this country was the succession of professors by their pupils and the publication of scholarly works such as *The Jewish Encyclopedia* (1961).

Semitics chairs or departments were established in a number of America's foremost universities in the late nineteenth century: Columbia, Johns Hopkins, Harvard, Pennsylvania, and Chicago. The incumbents of these chairs were sometimes Christian scholars, but many were Jewish. The titles of graduate courses in these Semitics programs sound much like those in doctoral programs in religion today; the methods were those of modern scholarship and the doctoral students thus trained often went on to teach religion courses in colleges or to accept appointments in seminaries. An important event for the development of Judaic studies in their own right was the appointment at Harvard in 1915 of Harry A. Wolfson as instructor in the Semitics department and then, in 1926, as the first Nathan Littauer Professor of Jewish Literature and Philosophy.

After World War I serious efforts were made to build on the foundations for graduate education in religion laid prior to the war. Of the various attempts to establish the teaching of religion at state universities, the only one to develop a doctoral program in this period was the School of Religion founded in the 1920s at the University of Iowa. Seen from the standpoint of the academic study of religion today, the school was a transitional institution: the faculty were hired with a view both to academic competence and to confession—Protestant, Catholic, Jew—and were paid by the denominational constituencies. After foundation grants expired, the university assumed the school's administrative costs, and over the years it has increasingly contributed to the payment of faculty salaries; today the burden of the funding is carried by the university.

Whereas the School of Religion was organized on the principle of cooperation between university and religious communities (with equal representation for the three major faiths) and was active in campus religious life, the plan drawn up at Princeton University in 1935 called for a program administered and funded exclusively by the university and clearly distinct from campus religious activities. The religion professor was to be trained specifically in the field and was to employ the historical method. The first incumbent was appointed in 1940 and, with flourishing enrollments, a department was established in 1946, followed in 1955 by a Ph.D. program, preparation for which was to be the equivalent of "that required for the Bachelor's Degree in the Department of Religion at Princeton."

With the introduction of Ph.D. programs in religion at state and private universities, accepting an undergraduate major in religion in place of the traditional requirement of a seminary degree, a new pattern in graduate education in religion was established. Meanwhile, older patterns, presupposing seminary training, persisted and developed further. The Yale Ph.D. program, established just after World War I, has already been noted. In 1923 the Columbia-Union Ph.D. program was announced, and prior to American entry into World War II the Harvard, Duke, and Catholic University Ph.D. programs came into being. In addition, at least eight programs leading to the Th.D. or S.T.D. (Doctor of Sacred Theology) were inaugurated before the war came to an end.

The time was ripe for evaluation and standardization. These came from the Conference of Theological Seminaries that had been formed in 1918; in the mid-1920s the conference inaugurated a major self-study that included doctoral programs (Ph.D. as well as Th.D.) in its purview. From the study emerged a statement on degree nomenclature and standards that was adopted by the conference in 1932. In its list of accredited schools the conference (later reconstituted as the American Association of Theological Schools) annually or biennially noted the schools with doctoral programs or resources that did not conform with the standards. In 1942 a much longer statement of standards for doctoral degrees offered by theological schools was adopted by the AATS.

In the period following World War II several features characterize graduate education in religion in the United States. One is the proliferation of doctoral programs in religion, corresponding to a dramatic increase in undergraduate programs in religion. From 1931 to 1960 twenty doctoral programs were established at universities and seminaries. From 1961 to 1970 twenty-three more were added. Whereas doctoral programs in religion had previously been located predominantly in seminaries, of the forty-three doctoral programs established between 1931 and 1970 twenty-seven were in private universities and three in state universities. The contraction of the job market for humanities professors in the 1970s and 1980s, however, has meant that new doctoral programs in religion are now uncommon.

The trend to locate religion doctoral programs in universities is reflected also in the doctoral curriculum and the preparation for doctoral study. Whereas the traditional subjects of the academic side of the seminary curriculum, such as biblical studies, history of Christianity, and theology, were once the staple of doctoral study in religion, there has been a concerted effort to restructure doctoral curricula along comparative, phenomenological lines. And whereas entering students were formerly largely seminary graduates, they now commonly matriculate with bachelor's degrees in religious studies.

In this period Roman Catholic biblical scholarship won recognition from even the most Protestant scholars, and the Second Vatican Council (1963–1965) produced a considerable change in the way religion and theology are studied in the Roman Catholic doctoral programs, with names like Karl Rahner, Bernard Lonergan, and Pierre Teilhard de Chardin figuring as prominently as Aquinas.

The destruction of the traditional centers of Jewish learning in Europe before and during World War II made it necessary for the Jewish community in America to put forth greater and special efforts to train its own scholars. At Jewish Theological Seminary the number of D.H.L. degrees granted increased, and in the 1960s a Ph.D. degree was instituted. The number of doctoral degrees granted by Dropsie College also increased. The Orthodox seminary in New York, which in the 1920s had become first a college and finally Yeshiva University, inaugurated a D.H.L. program that in 1970 was discontinued in favor of the Ph.D. Hebrew Union College instituted a Ph.D. program in the late 1940s. In addition, university Ph.D. programs in Judaic studies increased. Over 80 percent of the professors surveyed in Arnold J. Bard's 1966 study had received their graduate training in the United States. Many of these scholars were teaching in departments of religion—"a sign of our times: religion is studied as a historical phenomenon in these departments, and not as a truth to be propagated" (p. 12).

Increasingly, graduate education in religion is more accurately viewed not in confessional or even in ecumenical terms, but rather in relation to common scholarly endeavors cutting across, or even independent of, the lines of religious traditions. The styles of the most recent period recall patterns that were first urged early in the century and are now coming closer to embodiment.

LEARNED SOCIETIES, RESEARCH, AND PUBLICATIONS

Learned societies to foster scholarship in religious studies began to be formed in the late nineteenth century. The Society of Biblical Literature and Exegesis was established in 1880 and the American Society of Church History in 1888. As new disciplines developed in religious studies or in other fields and as the field of religious studies expanded, new societies were formed, sometimes by members of existing societies, and the older societies themselves underwent considerable change.

The Society of Biblical Literature is illustrative. At its first formal meeting in 1880, eighteen persons attended and six papers were presented. At the fiftieth anniversary of the Society in 1930 members numbered 449 and 45 papers were presented. At the centennial celebration membership exceeded 4,500 and 294 papers were presented across a broad spectrum of disciplines, subdisciplines, and interdisciplinary research, organized under more than forty sections, seminars, groups, and consultations. This reorganization of the society's annual meeting as well as its regional meetings—away from the previous format of a small number of papers presented to plenary sessions of Old and New Testament sections—was effected in 1969. It resulted from a desire to decentralize meetings and provide greater opportunity, especially for the increasing number of younger scholars, to engage in discussion of current research that would lead to publication either in advance of or subsequent to the meetings. Publication possibilities were enhanced when the society, along with the American Academy of Religion, formed Scholars Press in 1974 to disseminate the results of research rapidly and economically using new technologies.

In 1964 the National Association of Biblical Instructors, founded in 1909 out of a concern for the quality of biblical teaching in colleges and universities, was reconstituted and renamed the American Academy of Religion. It now meets annually with the Society of Biblical Literature. Other societies came into being to advance scholarship in specific areas of study: the National Association of Professors of Hebrew, the International Association for Septuagint and Cognate Studies, the Society of Christian Ethics, the American Society of Missiology (founded 1973). Others such as the Catholic Biblical Association of America (founded 1936), the Catholic Theological Society of America (founded 1946), and the National Association of Baptist Professors of Religion (founded 1927), developed within confessional families but grew to include scholars outside these confessions. The Society for the Scientific Study of Religion was founded in 1949 by religion scholars and social scientists to stimulate research on religious institutions and religious experience, while the Institute on Religion in an Age of Science (1954) has brought together natural scientists, social scientists, philosophers, and religion scholars to engage in dialogue about the relationship between contemporary scientific theory and religious and philosophical traditions.

A number of these societies publish their own journals; the larger ones sponsor publishing programs that may include monographs, dissertations, texts, and translations. Members of the Society of Biblical Literature played prominent roles in the successive revisions of the King James Bible and in work on the *American Jewish Version* (1917) and the *New Translation of the Torah* (1963). The Catholic Biblical Association of America was responsible for the revision of the Challonier-Rheims New Testament (1941) and for a new critical translation, *The New American Bible* (1970).

In 1969, following consultations called by the American Council of Learned Societies, the Council on the Study of Religion was formed as a federation of learned societies in the field of religion to foster communication among the societies, to help eliminate redundancies in function and action, and to identify unmet needs. Among the results has been the publication of a common newsletter, a review journal, a job registry, and a directory of academic departments and programs of religious studies. A conference in 1978, sponsored by the council and funded by the National Endowment for the Humanities, sought to assess the state of the art in religious studies scholarship and to identify new fields and areas of study (a report on and papers from the conference appeared in the *Council on the Study of Religion Bulletin*, 1978).

As in the past, these new fields, methods, and approaches point to changes in culture and society at large. Women's studies in religion began in the late 1960s by documenting sexism and androcentrism in canonical literatures, moved to searching out female symbolism and positive images of women, and then to investigating the images and religious experience of women outside mainstream religious and scholarly traditions. Scholars of American religion have been turning their attention to Native American religions, departing from evolutionary conceptions of them as "primitive," "low," or "archaic" and according them a more prominent place in American religious history. The study of that history itself is moving away from institutional, denominational, and elitist models of historiography to include popular religion as well as "new religions." The latter, though seemingly novel, may more accurately be termed "emergent religions" (Robert S. Ellwood, Jr.) inasmuch as many of them have roots in and affinities with earlier religious currents in America.

RELIGION AS AN ACADEMIC DISCIPLINE

The many new approaches in recent historiography and in disciplines such as sociology, anthropology, and hermeneutics are also being applied to the study of religious phenomena. Study of the social world of Israelite religion and of early Christianity, for example, gives new perspective to these histories and literatures and places their relations to neighboring and rival religions in a different light. The relation of religion to literature and the arts, a concern of a subfield in the academic study of religion that originated in the twentieth century, has recently been studied with reference to the hermeneutical theories of H. G. Gadamer and Paul Ricoeur and the work of structuralists, deconstructionists, and comparativists. The study of ritual, which until recently meant primarily the study of Christian liturgies, has now been established as a distinct field that draws on a variety of disciplines and includes in its purview non-Christian rituals as well as a full spectrum of symbolic acts ranging from ritualistic behavior in animals to extremely complex religious liturgies and civil ceremonies.

The academic study of religion in the last quarter of the twentieth century reflects both the pluralism of American society and of the "global village" and the steady expansion and specialization of knowledge in academia. The study of religion is thus moving away from definitions and conceptions of religion and attendant methods of study inherited from Christianity, particularly from the Protestant seminary curriculum. Increasingly, therefore, it is characterized by comprehensiveness of subject matter and, because religion itself ranges across so many areas of life, it draws on a variety of methodologies and approaches in order to understand and interpret religious traditions without violating their integrity.

The question of what teaching *about* religion means has engendered some debate among religion scholars. Generally, their aim in research and teaching has been to approach and understand religious traditions without bias and to interpret them to others in a way that seeks neither to inculcate nor to disparage them but rather to understand them. "Neutrality" and "objectivity" are words commonly used to characterize this stance. Some scholars have objected, however, that strict neutrality is unattainable—in *any* discipline—and that lively engagement by scholar, teacher, and student with their subject matter is unavoidable and, indeed, essential to understanding it. Sensitivity to personal biases and personal reactions to one's subject matter can enhance research, and neutrality or objectivity would mean, not lack of passion or personal concern, but rather being "open to a plurality of viewpoints, and pledged to none." (Whittaker, 1981, p. 131).

CONCLUSION

The question Robert Sproul posed in 1932, "Is religion itself a legitimate field of learning in the University?" has in recent decades been answered in the affirmative: departments and programs of religious studies are standard fixtures even in private non-denominational and public institutions of higher learning; thousands of scholarly books and journals in religious studies are published every year; meetings of learned societies bring together thousands of religious studies scholars across a broad spectrum of fields and subfields. "Religion," then, is after a long hiatus once again part of the American academic scene, even to some extent at the secondary-school level. But in contrast with the seventeenth, eighteenth, and nineteenth centuries, "religion" has come to mean not only Christianity and Judaism but a variegated plurality of religious traditions, including "civil" religion; "secular" religions such as National Socialism, Marxism, and "democracy"; and "invisible religions" (to use Thomas Luckmann's phrase), such as sports and consumerism. The methods employed in the study of religion are like those in other academic disciplines, and the aim is not the practice of religion or even indoctrination but rather understanding of religion in its various manifestations past and present.

PART II: THEORIES AND METHODS

As a relatively new academic discipline with theories and methods distinct from those that are employed in the study of a particular religion and those that aim to increase and deepen religious and moral sensibilities, the academic study of religion recognizes the breadth and diversity of the religious dimension of human life. As such it includes methods appropriated from the human sciences as well as approaches emerging from studies of specific religious traditions, especially Christian theological studies, and from scholarly attempts to account for the distinctive character of the phenomena of religion.

Among the most influential of methods in the history of the academic study of religion have been those developed in connection with clergy education and Protestant theological studies. One legacy of the adoption of methods appropriate to the study of Judaism and Christianity particularly has been the tendency to understand all religious expressions in terms of the structures and forms of scholarship emerging from the theological developments of these traditions. So, for example, as the methods of biblical criticism and the history and thought of Western institutions developed, religions came to be evaluated in terms of the degree to which they had moved from oral traditions to a sacred text or of the degree to which religious institutions and doctrinal interpretations had been developed. From this way of understanding religions, we have theories of primitive and civilized religions, high and low traditions, and the hierarchical consideration of religions.

Among the notable exceptions to these approaches was the work of George Foot Moore at Harvard. Moore was the first Christian scholar in America to so thoroughly master the study of Jewish sources that his *Judaism in the First Centuries of the Christian Era, The Age of the Tannaim* (1927–1930) became the definitive work in its field. He also produced a two-volume *History of Religions* (1913–1919) that was informed by the most competent scholarship of specialists in each tradition and demonstrated the great potential of pursuing work in the history of religions. Largely free from apologetic purpose, Moore's work extended to each religion equivalence of treatment, historical description, and analytical criticism.

After World War II and especially with the growth of the Neo-orthodox movement in Christian theology—with its concern for the social order and its recognition of the claims of science in the natural world and of the historically conditioned character of the products of religions—new methodological possibilities were discovered in the academic study of religion. For example, Reinhold Niebuhr's thesis of the distinction between religion and culture and the discontinuity of the claims of each brought renewed concern for issues of social and cultural existence (e.g., war and peace, political and racial justice) and a renewed sense of the obligation of religious traditions to address them. In part stemming from the non-creedal and tolerant character of Neo-orthodoxy, there is now what is referred to as "religious ethics" in contrast to "Christian ethics." This movement is especially concerned with the multiplicity of religious and cultural contexts, and so employs the insights of comparative religious studies as well as those of philosophical studies to address issues of social and moral concern.

Emerging from the same movement, Paul Tillich's work served to underscore the contributions of Christian theological reflection to the academic study of religion. His method of correlation, which aims at discovering the relation between dilemmas of the contemporary world and the answers to questions of existence offered in the Christian message, as well as his understanding of the relation of religion and culture, the role of myth and symbolic language, and the import of the claims of the world's religions for the task of the systematic theologian, have all contributed to current methods and approaches employed in the study of religion. Areas of study such as religion and culture and broadened concern for the study of the myths, symbols, and rituals of the world's religions testify to Tillich's impact. Although his work has not established a uniform method in the academic study of religion, it has served to place the Christian theologian's reflections among the diversity of religious insights and has thus contributed to the employment and transformation of theological methods in the study of religion.

While the methods of Christian theological studies have been fruitfully employed in the academic study of religion, scholars of the comparative study of religions and the history of religions have sought to articulate methods and approaches that are appropriate not simply to a particular tradition but emerge from investigations of the diversity of religious expressions and traditions. The comparative study of religions originated in nineteenth-century European scholarship, especially that of thinkers such as Friedrich Max Müller and C. P. Tiele, who established a theoretical framework that maintained religion was a general capacity of human beings, a dimension of human existence that could not be understood in terms of only one form of its expression. In many ways Max Müller's famous dictum "Those who know only one religion, know none" inaugurated what is today called the history of religions. Although this, like many other approaches to the academic study of religion, had European beginnings, the greatest contributors have for the last half-century been American.

The American origins of this approach can be traced both to the first meeting of the World's Parliament of Religions (predecessor of the International Association for the History of Religions) held in Chicago in 1893 with the aim of fostering understanding and cooperation among the varied religions of the world and to the early scholars in comparative studies who sought an "objective" and historical approach to the study of religion. Exemplary of scholars who contributed to this development was Morris Jastrow, Jr., who defined the aim and scope of the systematic, scientific, and historical/critical study of religion, delineated a method appropriate to the new discipline, and set forth a comprehensive and coherent program for its pursuit. In *The Study of Religion* (1901), Jastrow endorsed the historical study and classification of the many religions that he understood to be an objective and unbiased foundation for studies in the philosophy and psychology of religion. In addition, he urged colleges and universities to include the historical study of religions in their curricula as an essential element of liberal education. Contemporary history of religions methods, however, have been most influenced by the scholarship of Joachim Wach and Mircea Eliade.

Joachim Wach, thoroughly acquainted with European scholarship in the study of religion, exerted a major influence on the history of religions following his move to America from Germany in 1935. While recognizing that the study of religion had important relationships to philosophy, theological studies, and the social sciences, Wach insisted that the history of religions was a distinctive field of study with three main divisions: hermeneutics, which focuses on the fundamental conditions for understanding and interpretation; the study of religious experience and its expression in a variety of forms and traditions; and the sociology of religion, which focuses on types of leadership and on institutional and structural forms of religions in their concrete social and cultural contexts.

Proceeding from his understanding of religion as sui generis, Wach defined the essential characteristics of religious experience as necessarily including a response to what is experienced as Ultimate Reality, the engagement of the totality of one's being in this response, a profound feeling of intensity, and action that issues from the experience. In addition, he delineated what he understood to be the universal modes of its expression as theoretical (myth, doctrine, dogma, and theology), practical (cultic or ritual expression in worship and service), and sociological (types of religious leadership and structural formations of religious communities). Although Wach recognized the necessity of grounding work in the history of religions in careful historical scholarship dealing with the data of the various religions, most of his own work was morphological and typological, cutting across particular traditions with analysis and comparison of varying modes of religious experience and the diverse forms of its expression. The expansion of programs in religion in North American colleges and universities following World War II involved to a large extent the addition of courses and faculty reflecting the methods of the history of religions and, more directly, carrying Wach's approach and commitment.

Mircea Eliade has frequently been identified with the phenomenology of religion, a movement within the broader history of religions. Basic to this approach is the recognition that religion is diverse and that any attempt to understand it requires empathetic investigation of this plurality. Empathy, in turn, requires the historian or phenomenologist of religion to maintain an attitude of openness toward the varied religious expressions and experiences and to self-consciously leave behind all preconceived ideas about the nature of religion as well as any commitments to a particular religion. This does not mean that historians of religion are not or cannot be believers or participants in a religious community, but that these commitments should be suspended in the inquiry into the characteristics of religious manifestations. In the phenomenology of religion this methodological step is known as the application of the epoche, or "brackets." Once prior commitments and understandings of religion are put aside, it is possible to discover similarities and differences among the many religions. Generally this method is characterized by attempts to discover patterns or types of expression and experience that appear throughout various religious traditions, and in areas of experience that might not have been considered religious, through the construction of morphologies. From analysis of these patterns of religious expression the phenomenologist of religion then identifies what is typical and fundamental to all religious traditions and defines the general structures of religion.

Yet another approach is exemplified by the work of Wilfred Cantwell Smith. Although most scholars agree that the methods of the history of religions necessarily include the historical study of the concrete forms and structures of particular religions, Smith shifts the focus from "religion and religions" to the "faith" of persons whose lives are informed and nurtured by the various religious traditions. He insists that the subject matter of the study of religion "is . . . not merely the overt manifestations of man's religious life, but that life itself."

Taken on the most general level, the method of the history of religions is, on the one hand, held to be a corrective to those approaches that maintain religion be understood in terms of the claims and features of one particular religion and those approaches that understand religions as nothing more than forms of cultural expression, forms of social organization, or psychological projection. And, on the other hand, methods of the history of religions seek to disclose the multifarious character of religion and religious experiences as they are manifested throughout history and throughout the world.

The subject matter of the academic study of religion is illuminated by those methods of inquiry appropriate to a single tradition, by approaches that display the multiplicity of religious manifestations, and, because of the significance of religion in every aspect of human experience, by the methods of the human sciences. So one finds among the theories and methods in the study of religion those that propound the social (Robert Bellah) and the cultural (Clifford Geertz, Victor Turner) dimensions of religious life and expression.

Since Émile Durkheim, a dominant sociological approach views religion as fundamentally a resource for social cohesion. Religious symbol systems have accordingly been analyzed within their respective sociocultural contexts in relationship to and in differentiation from other social structures. Appropriating such an approach, Bellah has delineated stages in the evolution of religious symbol systems. In another use of this theoretical approach to religion, Bellah has characterized a "civil religion" that has been a basis for social and cultural cohesion in United States history.

Clarifying the symbiotic relationship between religion and culture that has been a characteristic interest of twentieth-century cultural anthropology, Geertz has explicated a theory of religion that understands it to be a cultural symbol system that "tunes human actions to an envisaged cosmic order and projects images of cosmic order onto the plane of human experience." A case study in which this approach is applied to the analysis of a specific religious tradition is his *Islam Observed: Religious Development in Morocco and Indonesia* (1968). Likewise, anthropologist Turner's theory of the primary role of religious rituals as complex systems of meaning within which dominant symbols communicate the major aspects of human life includes both the emotional (or unconscious) life and the social and moral life. His analysis of the dynamic character of ritual symbols in *The Forest of Symbols* (1967) illuminates the ways in which they act as forces moving participants to "social action" while at the same time serving to communicate both principles of social organization and the highest norms and values in a culture.

Related to these fields of the study of religion are the "dialogal" areas that explore the relationship between the study of religion and related subject matters. These approaches adopt the methods and procedures developed in one field of study and apply them as a mode of entry to the academic study of religion. In this area we find use of the methods of the natural sciences (religion and science), the humanities (religion and literature), and the social sciences (sociology and psychology of religion). The value of these kinds of studies lies in their capacity to illuminate the data of religions and thus to supplement and enrich the work of the academic study of religion with its primary emphasis on exploring the essential integrity, dynamics, and character of religion and religions.

All of these approaches will continue to contribute to the academic study of religion as this new discipline seeks further theories and methods that are appropriate to its subject matter and that will clearly establish it as a distinctive discipline.

BIBLIOGRAPHY

Origins, Nature, Changing Understandings

John Badertscher, "Response to Sinclair-Faulkner," in Peter Slater, ed., *Religion and Culture in Canada/Religion et culture au Canada* (1977); Arnold J. Band, "Jewish Studies in American Liberal-Arts Colleges and Universities," in *American Jewish Yearbook*, 67 (1966); David Barr and Nicholas Piediscalzi, *The Bible in American Education: From Source Book to Textbook* (1982); Robert N. Bellah, "Civil Religion in America," in Donald R. Cutler, ed., *The Religious Situation* (1968) and "Confessions of a Former Establishment Fundamentalist," in *Council on the Study of Religion Bulletin*, 1 (1970); John P. Boyle, "Paradigms for Public Education Religion Studies Curricula: Some Suggestions and Critique," in *Council on the Study of Religion Bulletin*, 12 (1981); Carol P. Christ, "The New Feminist Theology: A Review of the Literature," in *Religious Studies Review*, 3 (1977); William A. Clebsch and Rosemary Rader, "Religious Studies in American Colleges and Universities: A Preliminary Bibliography," in *Religious Studies Review*, 1 (1975).

Roy J. Deferrari, "The Origin and Development of Graduate Studies under Catholic Auspices," in Roy J. Deferrari, ed., *Essays on Catholic Education in the United States* (1942); Robert Detweiler, "Recent Religion and Literature Scholarship," in *Religious Studies Review*, 4 (1978): James E. Dittes, "Confessing Away the Soul with the Sins, or: The Risks of Uncle Tomism among the Humanists," in *Council on the Study of Religion Bulletin*, 2 (1971) and "The Investigator as an Instrument of Investigation: Some Exploratory Observations on the Compleat Researcher," in Donald Capps et al., eds., *Encounter with Erikson: Historical Interpretation and Religious Biography* (1977); Jim Freedman, "Will the Sheik Use His Blinding Fireballs? The Ideology of Professional Wrestling," in Frank Manning, ed., *The Celebration of Society* (1983); Ronald L. Grimes, *Symbol and Conquest: Public Ritual and Drama in Santa Fe, New Mexico* (1976) and *Research in Ritual Studies: A Programmatic Essay and Bibliography* (1985); Karl Hartzell and Harrison Sasscer, eds., *The Study of Religion on the Campus Today: Selected Papers from the Stony Brook Conference on Religion as an Academic Discipline* (1967); Clyde A. Holbrook, *Religion, A Humanistic Field* (1963); William James, "The Canoe Trip as Religious Quest," in *Studies in Religion/Sciences Religieuses*, 10 (1981); Gilbert Klaperman, *The Story of the Yeshiva University: The First Jewish University* (1969); Ernest B. Koenker, *Secular Salvations: Rites and Symbols of Political Religions* (1965).

Thomas Luckmann, *The Invisible Religion: The Problem of Religion in Modern Society* (1967); Martin E. Marty, "The Altar of Automobility," in *Christian Century* (22 Jan. 1958); George W. MacRae, ed., *Scholarly Communication and Publication* (1972); Neil G. McCluskey, ed., *The Catholic University: A Modern Appraisal* (1970); Milton McLean, ed., *Religious Studies in Public Universities* (1967); Robert Michaelsen, *The Scholarly Study of Religion in College and University* (1964), *The Study of Religion in American Universities: Ten Case Studies with Special Reference to State Universities* (1965), and *Piety in the Public Schools: Trends and Issues in the Relationship between Religion and the Public Schools in the United States* (1970); Robert N. Minor and Robert D. Baird, "Teaching About Religion at the State University: Taking the Issue Seriously and Strictly," in *Council on the Study of Religion Bulletin*, 14 (1983); Hans Mol, *Faith and Fragility: Religion and Identity in Canada* (1985).

Jacob Neusner, "Judaism within the Disciplines of Religious Studies: Perspectives on Graduate Education," in *Council on the Study of Religion Bulletin*, 14 (1983) and "Why Religious Studies in America? Why Now?" in *Journal of the American Academy of Religion*, 52 (1984); Laurence J. O'Connell, "Religious Studies, Theology, and the Humanities Curriculum," in *Journal of the American Academy of Religion*, 52 (1984); Paul Ramsey, ed., *Religion* (1965) and with John F. Wilson, eds., *The Study of Religion in Colleges and Universities* (1970); Harold E. Remus, ed., *Council on the Study of Religion Directory of Departments and Programs of Religious Studies in North America* (1978, 1981, 1985); Philip Boo Riley, "Teaching About Religion at the Religiously Affiliated University: Taking the Issue Seriously and Strictly. A Reply to Robert Baird and Robert Minor," in *Council on the Study of Religion Bulletin*, 14 (1983); William C. Ringenberg, *The Christian College: A History of Protestant Higher Education in America* (1984).

C. Freeman Sleeper and Robert A. Spivey, eds., *The Study of Religion in Two-Year Colleges* (1975); Gerard S. Sloyan, "The New Role of the Study of Religion in Higher Education: What Does It Mean?" in *Journal of Ecumenical Studies*, 6 (1979); Robert A. Spivey, "Modest Messiahs: The Study of Religion in State Universities," in *Religious Education*, 43 (1968); Douglas Sturm, "The Learned Society and Scholarly Research: Models of Interaction," in *Council on the Study of Religion Bulletin*, 12 (1980); Claude Welch, "Why a Council on the Study of Religion?" in *Council on the Study of Religion Bulletin*, 1 (1970), *Graduate Education in Religion: A Critical Appraisal* (1971), and *Religion in the Undergraduate Curriculum: An Analysis and Interpretation* (1972); John R. Whitney, "Introducing Religious Literature in Pennsylvania Secondary Schools," in *Religious Education*, 63 (1968); John H. Whittaker, "Neutrality in the Study of Religion," in *Council on the Study of Religion Bulletin*, 12 (1981); Paul J. Will et al., eds., *Public Education Religion Studies: An Overview* (1981).

Theories and Methods

Robert Bellah, "Religious Evolution," in *The American Sociological Review*, 29 (1964) and "Civil Religion in America," in *Daedalus*, 96 (1967); Walter H. Capps, ed., *Ways of Understanding Religion* (1972); Mircea Eliade, *Patterns in Comparative Religions* (1958) and *The Sacred and the Profane: The Nature of Religion* (1959); Edward Farley, *Theologia: The Fragmentation and Unity of Theological Education* (1983); Clifford Geertz, "Religion as a Cultural System," in Donald R. Cutler, ed., *The Religious Situation* (1968); Giles B. Gunn, ed., *Literature and Religion* (1971); Morris Jastrow, Jr., *The Study of Religion* (1901).

Joseph M. Kitagawa, ed., with Mircea Eliade, *The History*

of Religions: Essays in Methodology (1959) and "Humanistic and Theological History of Religions with Special Reference to the North American Scene," in Numen, 27 (1980); Reinhold Niebuhr, Love and Justice (1957); Wilfred Cantwell Smith, The Meaning and End of Religion: A New Approach to the Religious Traditions of Mankind (1962); Paul Tillich, The Future of Religions (1966); Victor Turner, The Forest of Symbols: Aspects of Ndembu Ritual (1967); Joachim Wach, Sociology of Religion (1944) and The Comparative Study of Religions (1958).

[See also CHRISTIAN THEOLOGICAL EDUCATION; HISTORIOGRAPHY OF AMERICAN RELIGION; RELIGION AND COLLEGIATE EDUCATION; and SOCIOLOGICAL STUDY OF AMERICAN RELIGION.]

NORTH AMERICAN INDIAN MISSIONS

Henry Warner Bowden

HUMANS came to the Western Hemisphere approximately forty thousand years ago, possibly much earlier. They entered what is now North America in pursuit of game animals that wandered across the Bering Land Bridge when ice ages exposed tundra there. As centuries went by, these people dispersed to all regions southward, adapting to different climates and developing a remarkable variety of cultural patterns. Many civilizations emerged, flourished, and waned in the millennia before contact with Europeans. At the beginning of what some call "the historical period" because no written documents existed prior to that time, there were at least 2,000 separate native cultures in the New World. The territory north of Mexico contained over 300 cultures, made distinct by language, social customs, and religious ceremonies. When Christopher Columbus encountered one of these indigenous groups in 1492, he referred to them as "los Indios" because he insisted that his ships had reached the Asian subcontinent.

SIXTEENTH-CENTURY MISSIONS

Further exploration disproved Columbus' claim, but his inaccurate label for natives remained. Spanish authorities thought of Indians as new imperial subjects; other Spaniards valued them as cheap labor for mines and plantations. Ecclesiastical and royal officials in Spain also gave high priority to Christianizing the natives, at least in principle. But support from a distance seldom produced vigorous or sustained evangelical activity on the local level. Missionary work was impeded by harsh realities such as military expeditions and the *encomienda* land system, which allowed owners to exploit native popula-

tions. The most vigorous champion of Indian rights was Bartolomé de las Casas, a tireless Dominican priest whose writings influenced legal reforms and heightened respect for the natives' human rights. With his advocacy, missionary efforts went slowly forward despite secular opposition, and within a generation of discovery supervisory districts had been established in what are now Haiti, Cuba, Mexico, Nicaragua, Honduras, Venezuela, and Peru.

Caribbean islands and wealthy lands in the central Americas were not the only objects of Spanish imperialism. Royal ambitions extended around the globe in the sixteenth century, centering on the Philippines while focusing on China. Missionary interests tended to follow suit, and most volunteers considered American posts secondary to prized assignments in the Far East. Nevertheless evangelical work developed in the Americas with considerable vigor. Religious orders rather than the secular priesthood contributed personnel, and of the many communities involved none was more active in converting natives than the Franciscan.

This monastic order built a wide network of mission stations in Mexico and established precedents there that prevailed when the friars moved northward later. Franciscans had become accustomed to close cooperation with governmental officials. After a few experiences in which missionaries were killed in areas without military protection, Franciscans rarely initiated missions in unpacified regions. They chose rather to represent Christianity as complementary to Spanish civilization, embodying religious presence as part of an overall social, economic, military, and political amalgam. The forces of church and state became components of a unified program intent upon "reducing"

Indians to both "civilized" behavior and "the true faith."

Missionary attitudes toward native religions were decidedly negative. As soon as the Franciscans saw pagan images and sacrificial pyramids in Mexico, they denounced all forms of Indian worship in the most uncompromising terms. Beginning in the 1520s they put forth a continuous stream of invective against native practices and beliefs. Indians were seen as benighted by polytheism, idolatry, and devil worship; their rites were reviled as barbarous because they involved human sacrifice and cannibalism. While few native cultures actually shared these specifically Aztec rituals, the Franciscans indiscriminately and zealously condemned all of them.

Missionary attitudes were the theological manifestation of a pervasive Spanish scorn for every aspect of native life. As emissaries of Iberian culture, the Franciscans simply perpetrated their own version of European arrogance toward indigenous patterns. They saw nothing salvageable in native religions and believed that the first step in rectifying the situation was to crush them. Franciscan missions sought to save souls by filling a vacuum after destroying Indian faiths and to build churches on the ruins of razed native foundations.

In 1513 Juan Ponce de Léon discovered the Florida peninsula, and several attempts followed to secure its riches and convert its natives. Nothing of lasting significance occurred until 1565, when Spanish ships expelled French Huguenots and established St. Augustine at the mouth of the St. Johns River. This first permanent white settlement in what became the United States served as the base for missions to the interior. Between 1566 and 1571 members of a new monastic order called the Society of Jesus (Jesuits) attempted to plant missions in the Carolinas and Virginia, but all such ventures failed. The Franciscans concentrated on the immediate Florida peninsula and succeeded far better. Through painstaking dedication friars mastered native languages and influenced religious habits among, for example, the Timucuan and Apalachee tribes. Tangible indications of their success occasioned an episcopal visit in 1606; one year before the foundation of the first English colony at Jamestown, the bishop of Havana, Cuba, confirmed more than 2,000 native converts and ordained over twenty white residents to the priesthood. Florida missions slowly declined from this apogee over the next century. The young churches were too remote from supply depots and ecclesiastical authorities to sustain themselves. Increased hostilities from nearby English colonies also hastened their collapse.

Exploration into what became known as the American Southwest began in 1540, and subsequent missionary work there produced more lasting results. Following earlier reports of riches and advanced civilizations, Francisco Vásquez de Coronado traversed much of Arizona and New Mexico, establishing sustained contact with Pueblo natives of the region. Parties searched for wealth from the Grand Canyon to central Kansas, but they discovered little of practical value. A Franciscan, Juan de Padilla, remained in Kansas to preach among the local inhabitants. Evidence shows that the isolated monk was soon executed, and, though no lasting mission stemmed from his efforts, Padilla is regarded as a proto-martyr in the history of American evangelical activities.

There were other attempts to explore the northern frontier of Spanish domains—some legal, some illegal, all abortive. Finally in 1598 an *hidalgo,* or aristocrat, named Juan de Oñate received royal permission to colonize land along the upper stretches of the Rio Grande. Instead of concentrating exclusively on easy money from mines, Oñate sponsored the slower process of steady growth in cattle and crops. He led four hundred settlers into New Mexico to begin farming and also subsidized ten Franciscans to spread the Gospel among the thousands of natives who lived there.

SEVENTEENTH-CENTURY MISSIONS

Missionaries in New Mexico enjoyed the advantage of dealing with native peoples whose cultures were more stable and continuous than those of most others in North America. The fact that these Indians lived in permanent towns led to the collective Spanish name "Pueblos," but actually they comprised several different groups separated by language and cultural nuances. Having settled residences, a dependable agricultural economy, and cohesive social leadership, the Pueblos offered a promising field for evangelical endeavors.

Spanish governors built the town of Santa Fe for political administration of the area, but missionaries used a native pueblo renamed Santo Domingo as their base of operations. From there they sent preachers throughout a region covering almost 90,000 square miles. The Franciscans, rarely exceeding a total of forty missionaries at any time, labored to baptize and train converts. At first the missions were an apparent success. Natives had been trained from childhood to conform to dominant social pressures, and they seemed to find no difficulty in adding the Spanish deity to gods of precontact origin. Since their own religion involved priestly societies and sacramental rituals, they readily understood the forms of Franciscan Catholicism. Some contemporary observers claimed there were many thousands of native believers in dozens of towns, but the actual number was probably far lower.

Two difficulties impeded missionary progress. The Franciscans clashed continually with Spanish administrators over prerogatives and policy and failed in many cases to convert Indians thoroughly. The latter problem doomed their efforts. Few missionaries learned native dialects or lived among the people; none translated the precepts of Christianity into a local tongue or stayed in New Mexico more than ten years. Instead of building on common religious principles, the Franciscans denounced local gods and used repressive force, such as closing native worship chambers, burning Indian ritual objects, and whipping persistent leaders. By 1680 these forceful measures produced an armed rebellion in which the Pueblos successfully expelled all colonists, killed most Franciscans, and burned their churches. Spanish armies eventually recaptured the territory in 1696, but returning missionaries made little headway with natives after that. Their subsequent effectiveness in the region lay in ministering to an increasing Hispanic population rather than to natives, who clung tenaciously to precontact folkways.

The southwestern missions of the Jesuits followed a different pattern. A good example of an alternative evangelical method was that of Eusebio Kino, who produced lasting results in Sonora. Failing to receive his desired appointment to China, Kino conducted a hapless mission in Baja California until he was sent to northwestern Mexico in 1687. Instead of condemning local natives and their religions, he took pains to befriend the Indians, especially the Yaquis and Pimas, smoothing preliminary conversations with small gifts of fruit and trinkets. His gentle interactions with native leaders had a cumulative effect, and Kino is thought to have baptized well over 4,000 converts. He explored much of the surrounding region, blazing trails for later Jesuits to continue important work in southern Arizona. Kino also improved the subsistence patterns of natives by introducing cattle and European grains to supplement their economy. His cartographical interests proved useful as well, showing that California was not an island and opening the way for Franciscan missions there in the eighteenth century.

In New France (now Canada), far to the northeast, Jesuits were also active in spreading Christianity to native tribes. A small group of Franciscans (Récollets) made initial attempts, but it was the Jesuits who in 1626 began living with the Hurons, one of the most powerful confederacies in the Great Lakes area. Missionaries were allowed to live there because of a stipulation in the 1608 trading alliance concluded by Samuel de Champlain. Occasional difficulties between Jesuits and native leaders might have led to bloodshed had it not been for this treaty. The epitome of Jesuit missionary zeal was Jean de Brébeuf, whose tolerance, patience, and wisdom placed native churches on a solid foundation of reciprocal goodwill. He lived with natives in their own semipermanent villages, learned their language, lived on their diet, and shared their hardships. Brébeuf adjusted his preaching to local cultural values in order to perpetuate Jesuit missions among vigorous new adherents to the Catholic faith.

Jesuit missionary techniques followed a similar pattern around the world. Believing that God had not completely abandoned sinful humanity, Jesuits tried to find common denominators for discussions with natives in every culture. They used precontact religions as a preliminary basis to discuss faith and then tried to develop ideas that led to Christian formulations. This process retained native languages and symbols, so the resulting versions of native Christianity exhibited Catholic expressions in indigenous forms. Moreover, in pursuing such dialogues, Jesuits preferred to work among natives where no other Europeans could interfere. Whereas Franciscans rarely operated without the comforting presence of secular power, Jesuits chose to have as little contact as possible with their countrymen. In that way they could bring evangelical influences to bear without economic, political, or military considerations coming into play. The work of individuals such as Matteo Ricci in China and Robert de Nobili in India, as well as the successful mission constructed along these lines in Paraguay, served as models for this independent type of evangelical approach. Jesuits in North America sought to reproduce the model wherever they were assigned.

A few dozen "blackrobes," as Jesuits were often called, joined Brébeuf in his isolated freedom and gradually won the trust of a growing minority of Hurons. Indian Christians did not subscribe wholly to French Catholicism but developed instead their own selective blend of native expressions and Gospel emphases. Some converted because of material interests, hoping that baptism might protect them from disease or secure trading privileges. Others seem to have been drawn to the theological cogency of Christian concepts as an improvement over native ideas. While never a dominant group in the 1630s or 1640s, Huron Christians continued to develop as a distinctive faction, using their own language and liturgical symbols within broad latitudes of the Christian heritage. Jesuits built Sainte-Marie as headquarters for mission stations throughout Upper Canada, and monastic fathers served as pastors to their charges in native villages.

In 1648 disaster struck, not from antagonistic Hurons but from their traditional enemies. Sporadic warfare had for centuries plagued relations between Hurons and the Iroquois, a league of tribes in New York that shared virtually identical cultural patterns. For unknown reasons the Iroquois switched in that year from occasional raids to a full-scale war of attrition. As villages fell before the onslaught, missions were destroyed in the general debacle. The invaders wintered in Huronia and renewed their attacks in the spring. Early in 1649 Brébeuf was captured and executed after hours of torture. Following months of ultimately futile resistance, the Hurons fled to an island in Georgian Bay during the next winter. By 1650 the mission was at an end, the Huron nation a broken and scattered remnant. When the Jesuits retreated to Quebec, many native Christians followed them and established a town called Jeune Lorette. Other than a few pockets of Hurons who appeared as "Wyandots" in eighteenth-century American history, this Canadian settlement is all that remains of the native Christian state that the Jesuits originally envisioned.

There were other French blackrobes who made notable attempts to evangelize groups of native Americans. Isaac Jogues worked among the Hurons for five years and then opened a new station at Sault Ste. Marie, where several tribes met for summer fishing and trading. In 1642 Jogues was captured by the Mohawks, a tribe in the Iroquois League, but he managed to escape the following year. In 1644 he returned to New France and received permission from both civil and ecclesiastical authorities to open a mission in Mohawk villages. He was killed shortly after entering their territory again, offering fellow missionaries an example of self-sacrificing dedication. Jacques Marquette inspired others in a different way. His pioneering work on Lake Superior and later at Mackinac Island illustrated Jesuit willingness to take the Gospel to isolated areas. He helped explore the Mississippi River Valley with Louis Jolliet and planned to build a large mission among the friendly Illinois natives. But his health failed, and his death exemplified the fate of those who spent all their energies in pursuit of evangelical ideals.

English Protestants contributed far less in missionary efforts than did Spanish Franciscans or French Jesuits in the seventeenth century. Puritans in New England accomplished more than colonists farther south, but even Puritan missions were meager and began only after local tribes had been influenced by explorers, soldiers, traders, and farmers. Of the few who manifested any concern for natives, John Eliot was the best known. Retaining his ministry to a white congregation at Roxbury, in 1643 he began learning the Massachuset language, a dialect of Algonkian linguistic stock. By 1646 he was delivering rudimentary sermons in the acquired tongue and proceeded to interest a few Massachusets in conversion. Over several decades Eliot gathered them into Christian communities and persuaded them to associate only among themselves. When they began to live apart from non-Christian natives, their settlements were called "Praying Indian" towns.

Praying Indians exhibited a thoroughgoing conversion to new standards, due possibly to a decline in their own cultural integrity and to the pressure of high Puritan expectations. These native Christians turned away from a life-style dependent on hunting and began to live and farm in fourteen permanent towns. Many learned to read in order to grapple with Protestant theology, and Eliot supplied translations of edifying works, an effort that culminated in 1663 with a Massachuset version of the Bible. Several native converts became ordained ministers themselves and worked to spread the Gospel, advising tribesmen on ways to regulate their lives as examples of godly living. These efforts touched only a handful of natives but indicate the extent to which Christian Indians wished to emulate both English culture and the new religion.

In 1675 warfare erupted between natives and colonists. The missions became indirectly involved and were damaged beyond repair. A neighboring tribal leader known as Metacomet, or King Philip, became prominent in overt retaliations against white encroachment. King Philip's War unleashed latent colonial suspicions against all natives, and Christian Indians were unjustifiably accused of complicity with the enemy. Eliot's converts were herded together in Boston Bay, where many died from exposure and malnutrition. After Philip was killed in 1676, few Indian Puritans remained to resume their adopted way of life. As the tribal base for converts dwindled through the rest of the century, Eliot's work reflected proportionate loss. By 1700 aboriginal culture along the seacoast had been obliterated, as had all vestiges of Praying Indian towns.

EIGHTEENTH-CENTURY MISSIONS

During the colonial period European powers viewed North America as part of an international chessboard where local events contributed to maneuvers for wider spheres of influence. Alliances and missionary contact with native tribes were affected by these larger considerations. Spanish authorities had little concern for upper, or Alta, California until 1769, when they heard that Russian contingents had begun explorations from Alaska down the Pacific Coast. In that year an expedition under Gaspar de Portolá left Mexico to secure the land for Spain, and Franciscan missionaries accompanied soldiers to make sure the natives became Catholic rather than Eastern Orthodox. Junipero Serra, the friar who inaugurated California missions, was a dedicated administrator whose zeal led to the establishment of nine evangelical settlements for Native Americans. Serra employed more gentle and tolerant methods than his order had used in the previous century: he didn't whip backsliders or force natives to settle around the mission. He provided for material improvement in the lives of converts, too, teaching them the rudiments of agriculture and the advantages of a settled way of life. By the end of his mission Serra had baptized 6,000 natives, confirmed 5,000, and linked the mission chain into an effective ecclesiastical presence.

French missionaries worked in many parts of the Mississippi Valley during this era, but their efforts produced little of significance. Jesuits in Canada staffed missions around the Great Lakes while members of the same order gradually assumed responsibility for missions upriver from New Orleans. While they performed some notable work among the Natchez and Kaskaskia peoples, no single evangelist distinguished himself, nor did the work endure for many generations. Gallic territorial holdings declined through the years, falling to Spanish control in the Gulf region and to British domination in the north after the fall of Quebec in 1759. English interests increasingly controlled affairs in the interior as well as on the eastern seaboard. Consequently most eighteenth-century missions were the efforts of English-speaking agents.

The ecclesiastical counterpart to British royal authority was the Church of England, and in 1701 it set up mechanisms for missionary activity abroad. Thomas Bray, colonial commissary for the bishop of London, founded the Society for the Propagation of the Gospel in Foreign Parts (SPG). He hoped funds provided by that organization would subsidize missionary work among Native Americans and also among the increasing number of African slaves in the colonies. Bray also thought that ministers from his own church might counteract the presence of Congregationalists and Presbyterians, who were successful on the seacoast.

The SPG supported more than 300 missionaries, but few of them pursued contact with Indians for any length of time. None lived with a tribe; a few taught in schools where an occasional native youth learned English speech and habits. Most of them gravitated toward white parishes and conventional clerical routines. Whenever SPG men dealt with Indians, they tried to enlist native cooperation in serving both God and king by opposing Britain's enemies. This form of mixed evangelism took shape first against the French and then against republican advocates during the Revolution.

Much more vigorous activity emanated from those Congregational and Presbyterian colonists whom the SPG had hoped to curtail. Eleazar Wheelock developed a new approach to missions while continuing his Congregationalist ministry at Lebanon, Connecticut. Having established a preparatory school for young men of pre-college age, Wheelock decided in 1743 to train Indian youths as well. He thought his small academy, Moor's Charity School, could ingrain the essentials of Gospel thought and practice in native students, allowing them to return as missionaries to their tribes where they would be more welcome than white ministers. During the next two decades almost fifty young Indians, some Iroquois but mostly Algonkians, attended Wheelock's academy. Few graduated, and fewer accepted missionary assignments. The difficulties of a classical curriculum, the unfamiliar demands of physical labor and discipline, as well as the rigors of orthodox doctrinal catechizing, proved insurmountable obstacles. The plan in its ideal form might have yielded results, but Wheelock's applied regimen produced more disappointment than success.

The single bright spot in Wheelock's experiment was Samson Occom, a Mohegan Indian who excelled in the school's program of studies and later shone as the most outstanding American Indian clergyman. Eyestrain coupled with precarious health made college impossible for Occom, but in 1747 he received a Presbyterian license to preach and settled in eastern Long Island. Full ordination did not come until 1759, but the native evangelist used the intervening years to practical advantage among the Montauks with whom he lived. Occom conducted regular preaching services, taught school, and performed marriages and funerals. He also served natives in more traditional ways by advising on practical matters and adjudicating personal disputes. In 1766–1768 Occom traveled to England and solicited funds for Wheelock's mission school. He received great public acclaim there and embodied for British audiences the best of Christian scholarship and piety. The funds he collected went to the founding of Dartmouth College, much to Occom's later dismay because it attracted few Indian students.

In 1784 Occom was instrumental in conducting the remnants of his and other New England tribes across the Hudson to New York. From a base at Brothertown he conducted itinerant preaching tours, much like a circuit rider, holding six or seven services a week. We know little about the content of his sermons or how many converts he baptized, but it is noteworthy that whites as well as Indian parishioners accepted his leadership. Strangely enough, Occom did not cultivate a successor. As much as he must have appreciated the advantages enjoyed by native clergy among their own people, he did not recruit or train any Indians to continue the leadership he exemplified so well. Still, his solitary eminence indicated the extent to which evangelical influences could sustain an individual career.

The missionary who expanded on Occom's task in New York was Samuel Kirkland, a dedicated worker among the Oneidas, one of the principal tribes in the Iroquois League. In 1766 Kirkland received Congregationalist ordination and a commission from the Society in Scotland for Propagating Christian Knowledge (SSPCK). With that foreign aid he lived with the Oneidas as an adopted kinsman for most of his remaining four decades. In addition to preaching, baptizing converts, and conducting worship in native longhouses, Kirkland urged his friends to accommodate to white practices. He persuaded them to build a meetinghouse, a sawmill, and a blacksmith shop. Diversified farming and draft animals helped Christian Indians cope with modern conditions. But Kirkland's objectives, put forth with unobtrusive methods, came to grief after the revolutionary war. Most Iroquois had supported the British cause, and vindictive Americans indiscriminately pushed the league's tribesmen into Canada. Kirkland stayed behind and spent the last years of his life establishing a school that became Hamilton College.

David Brainerd, another missionary funded by the SSPCK, had a brief career among the Delaware Indians of New Jersey and Pennsylvania. During the last three years of his life Brainerd preached to Delawares through an interpreter and sought additional ways to communicate his personal piety to native audiences. He ranged through territory surrounding the Lehigh and Susquehanna rivers, but the site of best native response was Crossweeksung, New Jersey. There Brainerd formed the nucleus of a church, baptizing twenty-five converts and celebrating their first Lord's Supper in 1746. Often despairing of his own unworthiness, Brainerd sought reassurance through frequent visits to white friends. He died at the home of Jonathan Edwards on one such trip, and the great New England theologian memorialized the young missionary by using his influence to have his journal published in 1748. That book inspired others to volunteer for missionary endeavors and to accomplish more than this famous but ineffectual evangelist ever did.

David Brainerd's brother John was his immediate successor. He received SSPCK support in 1748 to minister among Delaware converts for almost three decades. Unlike his brother, the younger Brainerd did not travel erratically or entertain grand evangelical schemes. He acted instead as pastor to Christian Delawares, advising them on mundane matters and suggesting ways in which they might improve the quality of their spiritual lives. One of his strategic contributions lay in protecting what remained of native culture. In 1758 the colonial legislature bought all Delaware land claims and established Brotherton, a reservation where natives could live undisturbed. Brainerd acted as superintendent, minister, and guardian, but the Delaware population dwindled because of disease and cultural disintegration. By 1801 the survivors moved to New York and joined other tribes in their slow sequence of removals to land beyond the Mississippi. Brainerd gave them a Gospel heritage that remained with successive generations throughout that despairing journey.

Missionaries from another evangelical tradition and a different ethnic background produced more numerous and durable Delaware converts. The United Brethren, or Moravians, came from Germany and shared their form of Christian piety with Indians around their central town of Bethlehem, Pennsylvania. Several Moravians worked with the Indians, but the most outstanding individual was David Zeisberger. After ordi-

nation in 1749 and several frustrating years with an Iroquois tribe, Zeisberger turned in 1756 to a life's work with the Delawares. He lived with native converts in the Lehigh Valley and helped them build model communities that featured houses, schools, chapels, and farms. Zeisberger also instructed his charges in Moravian pacifism and persuaded them completely to abandon warlike habits. During the 1763–1765 frontier scare known as Pontiac's Rebellion, Zeisberger protected his followers from widespread white hostility that resembled anti-Indian racism. After 1765 he resettled with them in more remote territory and then moved westward several times in attempts to escape the pressure of land-hungry whites.

By 1772 Zeisberger and his peaceful church members moved into Ohio to establish Christian towns along the Muskingum River. There they built villages called Schönbrunn and Gnadenhütten, where Zeisberger lived with native constituents, rejecting the physical comforts of white civilization. Delaware spokesmen and German Moravians preached the Gospel to the many different tribes collected in Ohio at that time, but outside events did not let missions follow an untroubled course. Revolutionary war sentiments polarized tribesmen, and the pacifist Delaware Christians were suspected of opposing sympathies by both sides. In 1781 British forces compelled native converts to spend the winter on the shores of Lake Erie, while Zeisberger was kept in a Detroit prison. When a party of ninety Christian natives returned to Gnadenhütten in the spring to retrieve food supplies, they were captured and massacred by American troops. After the war, few Moravians showed much interest in continuing Zeisberger's mission. The only lasting evidence of his many sacrifices is a contingent of Delaware Moravians who survive in Canada today.

The Revolutionary period physically crippled several missions and ended a historical era in the perennial enterprise. By securing political independence, the American government removed foreign interests from much of North America. During the century coming to a close European powers had used Native American groups for leverage in their own imperial struggles. When citizens of the United States looked westward at what they considered their own country, Indians seemed simply obstacles in the path of American pioneers. Federal officials faced no serious foreign rivals in territorial expansion, and Native Americans had to choose between assimilating to white culture or fleeing its advance. When national policy rather than foreign diplomacy became the key factor in treatment of the Indians, that change greatly affected the theory and practice of subsequent Christian missions.

NINETEENTH-CENTURY MISSIONS

Missionaries and politicians shared common assumptions about American culture in the early days of the republic. National spokesmen believed that agricultural economy, public education, and Protestant religion were fundamental supports of democracy, and in 1803 the Louisiana Purchase doubled the land base on which to extend those principles. Federal authorities never settled on a consistent way to treat Indians in the context of this dominant view of American life. Some wanted to exterminate the natives or banish them from white jurisdiction, while others sought to incorporate them after they had been converted to white Protestant values. Advocates of the latter policy began in 1819 to provide annual funds for instructing Indians in agriculture, literacy, and other beneficial pursuits. This federal "civilization fund" became the means for sending church-nominated governmental representatives to various tribes, spreading a gospel of salvation and civilization for the purpose of making natives both Christians and citizens of the country. Despite formal declarations about the separation of church and state, ecclesiastical and governmental agents cooperated closely to achieve common objectives.

Military leaders were no less active in pursuit of the opposite policy with respect to Indians. In 1809 William Henry Harrison, governor of the Indiana Territory, negotiated the Treaty of Fort Wayne that isolated natives in small districts and opened most of the Midwest to whites. Two years later he defeated truculent Shawnees at Tippecanoe Creek and in 1813 ended all native resistance in the region. The following year Andrew Jackson cleared much of the Southeast by defeating hostile Creeks at Horseshoe Bend and then forcing natives to evacuate much of the territory. Missionaries worked with Indians during those times, but few were successful because of

the deteriorating circumstances. Isaac McCoy, a Baptist, and James B. Finley, a Methodist, were representative figures who labored among groups scattered through the Midwest. Both individuals continued the old pattern of attending to natives while serving white congregations at the same time. McCoy persevered longer than others; then, in 1830, he followed his Illinois charges westward to a reservation in Kansas.

The most efficient agency to direct evangelical activity in this period was the American Board of Commissioners for Foreign Missions (ABCFM), an interdenominational organization begun in 1810. Most of its workers came from Congregational and Presbyterian churches, but they pursued essentially the same goals as all Protestant missionaries. The ABCFM secured most of each year's federal appropriation and with it sent people to establish model farms and exemplary households amid Indian settlements. Christian emissaries may have given slightly more emphasis to expounding the Bible than to inculcating civilized behavior, but their schools and workshops also stressed the qualities of industry and order. Their attempt to exhibit religious piety involved a concomitant effort to display sobriety and discipline. They hoped that this blend of virtues deemed essential to civilized life would gradually transform Indians into churchgoing citizens of the new nation.

ABCFM hopes were best realized among the Cherokees, a tribe inhabiting eastern Tennessee, western North Carolina, and northern Georgia. Missionaries from a variety of denominations worked with different Cherokee groups, but the most prominent among them was Samuel A. Worcester, whom the board appointed in 1825. With Worcester's encouragement and that of Galagina, a native minister renamed Elias Boudinot after schooling in New England, the Cherokees quickly adapted to most aspects of white culture. In 1828 missionaries provided funds for a printing press, and the *Cherokee Phoenix* became the first native language newspaper in the country. Worcester also translated portions of Scripture, tracts, hymnbooks, and other religious literature into the Indian tongue. Cherokees built numerous schools and churches, absorbing lessons on farming, education, trade, and politics with great attentiveness. Their tribal government patterned after the American Constitution, their bicameral legislature, supreme court, tax system, permanent residences, intensive farming, domestic herds—all these pointed up missionary success at inculcating aspects of Christian civilization. Cherokee life was the showcase of what missionaries in every region sought to accomplish.

But success was only temporary because Cherokees could not follow Gospel precepts without white interference. Georgia authorities had been urging natives since 1802 to relinquish their lands. After 1829 President Jackson pressed even harder to make Indians accept white government or else move beyond the Mississippi. The next year he pushed the Indian Removal Bill through Congress and began transferring all southeastern tribes to Indian Territory (present-day Oklahoma). Missionaries initially stood beside native converts against white encroachment, but eventually all of them yielded. In 1830 Worcester went to prison as a result of his defiance of new laws engineered to dispossess Cherokee landholders. His case later achieved a favorable ruling in the Supreme Court, but the 1832 decision did little to relieve natives, who were increasingly victimized by greedy whites. Remaining Cherokees were forcibly removed from their traditional surroundings in 1838–1839, and Worcester followed them west, trying to embody Gospel precepts that were belied by the actions of most of his countrymen.

Evangelical work among trans-Mississippi tribes took another form under the guidance of Pierre Jean De Smet, a Belgian Jesuit based at St. Louis. Flathead Indians in Montana had made numerous requests that Catholic missionaries live among them, and in 1840 De Smet finally responded. He traveled to the Bitterroot Valley and installed personnel at St. Mary's Mission, the first of a large network in the Northwest. De Smet spent most of his time publicizing missions and recruiting volunteers in Europe. He became more widely recognized as an advocate of the cause than for conducting evangelical operations in person. Still, Jesuit work among the Coeur d'Alenes after 1841, the Blackfeet after 1845, and the Kalispels in 1845 benefited from his logistical support (i.e., the procurement, maintenance, and replacement of materiel and personnel). During the 1850s and 1860s he served as peacemaker and trusted friend to the Osage and Dakota peoples, but his missionary impact there was minimal.

The Dakota Indians, more generally known as the Sioux, consisted of many separate groups scattered between Minnesota and Montana. Catholic missions to them began in 1841, when Augustin Ravoux went to live among the Santees, an eastern Dakota tribe. He had no immediate successor, though, and most subsequent missions in Minnesota were Protestant. Methodists and Swiss Reformed initiated some short-lived evangelical programs in Dakota territory. Oberlin College also sent a few Congregationalist representatives to the Ojibwas, Algonkian neighbors of the Dakotas, but the most durable Christian activity came from Episcopalians. James L. Breck began Episcopalian work among the Ojibwas, and in 1860 Bishop Henry B. Whipple expanded it. During the remainder of the century Whipple championed Indian causes, becoming nationally prominent as a lobbyist with the federal government in pursuit of equitable treatment of Native Americans.

Missions among the Dakotas received steady support from the ABCFM. Several individuals worked for the board during the middle decades of the century, but the best known was Stephen R. Riggs, who arrived in the region in 1837. Riggs helped compile a Dakota grammar and dictionary, collaborating also on a native translation of the Bible, elementary readers, catechisms, and hymnals. He stressed civilized habits alongside religious conversion and acceded to native preferences only in language. In 1856 Riggs built a mission station named Hazlewood that realized most of his ideals. Native Christians became resident farmers there, making the difficult transition from precontact behavior that featured a nomadic, hunting way of life. At Hazlewood converts also abandoned war, polytheism, and plural marriages to embrace literacy, diligence, and private property.

But here, too, promising evangelical efforts were disrupted by events beyond missionary control. In 1862 desperate bands of Dakota warriors began fighting federal agents who could not deliver promised food allotments. The violence quickly escalated, and soon open warfare spread through half of Minnesota. Most Christian Dakotas refused to engage in bloodshed, and prominent Hazlewood citizens were conspicuous in showing humanitarian concern for whites. But the missions were wrenched out of their setting because all Dakotas were confined indiscriminately after government soldiers quelled the uprising. Many imprisoned natives at Mankato and Fort Snelling accepted baptism as a badge of defeat, but Riggs stayed with his group of lifetime converts. He moved with them first to Nebraska and then to Flandreau, South Dakota, where the community still exists.

After the Civil War federal officials took various steps to reform policies regarding Native Americans, and this in turn seriously affected missionary activity. The Bureau of Indian Affairs had been transferred from the War Department to the Department of the Interior in 1849, but little materialized from that cosmetic alteration. President Ulysses S. Grant attempted serious improvement in 1869 when he created the Board of Indian Commissioners to root out corruption in the government's procurement system and reorganized appointment of missionaries to reservations. Sometimes labeled the Quaker plan because the Society of Friends had suggested it to the president, Grant's so-called Peace Policy allowed clergymen of only one denomination on designated reservations. Missionaries whose church had enjoyed long contact with particular tribes—Roman Catholics, for example—were summarily dismissed, and representatives of some other church were arbitrarily put in their place. Catholics ultimately received assignments on only seven reservations, an injustice that led to their founding the independent Bureau of Catholic Indian Missions in 1874. Methodists, as another example, had no real experience in native evangelism, but they were given responsibility for fourteen reservations. The good intentions behind such major realignments could not compensate for resultant inequities, and the plan was soon abandoned. But dislocation, confusion, and denominational rivalry caused unmeasured damage.

A more lasting federal action attempted to take government entirely out of Indian affairs by abolishing the reservation system. American politicians had made reservation treaties with Indians since the 1750s, confining them to small parcels of land while opening the rest to white settlement. A century later the national government began to break up even those holdings, allowing no collective ownership whatsoever. In 1887, again in the name of reform and with the support of advocates who expressed altruistic motivations, Congress passed the General Allot-

ment Act. That bill authorized the president to carve up reservation land and distribute a quarter-section (160 acres) each to heads of families. Surplus land was available for white use. Natives were thus pushed toward separate ownership and deprived of the communal property that had formed a basic foundation of Indian culture and cohesion. Between 1887 and 1934 whites acquired more than 60 percent of the remaining land held by Indians. The measure failed to make private landowners and middle-class capitalists of Native Americans. Instead it impoverished them and further accelerated their downward psychological and cultural spiral.

TWENTIETH-CENTURY MISSIONS

The uneven struggle between minority cultures and assimilationist pressures continued into the 1930s. As always, the majority of missionaries sided with those who wanted to repress Indian vitality, reduce tribes to individual components, and incorporate them into a national homogeneity. Few whites appreciated cultural pluralism as an alternative to destroying native ways of life. One individual who wanted to reverse assimilationist trends, however, was John Collier, appointed Commissioner of Indian Affairs in 1933. By that time all Indians had been enfranchised by the Citizenship Act of 1924, but government research showed that they had not benefited from or assimilated to white socioeconomic standards. Collier took steps that eventually helped to restore tribal lands and invigorate Indian cultures. In 1934 he influenced passage of an omnibus bill called the Indian Reorganization Act (IRA) that provided for greater home rule on reservations and allowed traditional religious leaders to hold worship services despite missionary opposition. Since then the contest between diversity and uniformity has been more balanced.

Christian opposition to resurgent native religious expression was deep-seated. As late as 1958 the National Council of Churches published a study showing that only 22 percent of Protestant missionaries to Indians involved native leadership in their work; no more than half of the Catholic missionaries did so. The vast majority of such Protestants as Baptists, Reformed, and Presbyterians considered Indian spirituality and rituals to be almost entirely irreconcilable with Christianity. Evangelists from Episcopalian, Congregationalist, Catholic, and Methodist perspectives thought that some elements of Native American religions were complementary to Christian teachings. Less than half of all missionaries knew a native language, and only a very small percentage indicated openness to cultural diversity. Although a small number had become less antagonistic to indigenous cultures and their spiritual values, missionaries generally resisted the revival of native rituals. Collier's plan for religious toleration found little welcome among those who condemned any reappearance of precontact religious traditions.

Revitalized Indian spirituality seemed all the more disturbing to Christian evangelists because it had recurred throughout the American past. Independent religious vitality had expressed itself repeatedly whenever white domination had threatened to deprive natives of their cultural autonomy, and its potential resurgence under IRA protection drew strength from those previous occasions. One of the earliest on record involved a shadowy figure known as the Delaware Prophet, who pitted Indian religious values against white standards during Pontiac's Rebellion. In 1805 Tenskwatawa, revered as the Shawnee Prophet, preached against liquor, intermarriage, and the use of white trade goods. He promised that if natives returned to their forefathers' ways, divine spirits would restore the happiness known before white settlers had come. A Seneca visionary named Ganiodaio (Handsome Lake) called for the establishment of a new Iroquois religion around 1800. During the 1880s a Paiute seer named Wovoka announced a similar vision for Plains Indians. This pan-Indian phenomenon, generally known as the Ghost Dance, stressed peace and loyalty to precontact traditions as a means of restoring native vitality. The Ghost Dance marked the end of one phase of Indian revitalization because it contributed to the massacre of 200 Dakotas at Wounded Knee, South Dakota, in 1890. But the longings that it symbolized have persisted into the present century.

Other forms of native spirituality have been syncretistic, blending traditional activities with Christianity in ways that technically are not revitalization efforts. The most widespread of these involves the use of peyote. Peyote is a cactus indigenous to the Rio Grande Valley and northern Mexico. The crown, or "button," of the plant heightens perceptions of sound and color when eaten. Ceremonies utilizing peyote retain a distinctive Indian emphasis on visions. Early Spanish documents indicate that natives used it in northern Mexico, but it did not spread into the United States until the 1880s. When Ghost Dance popularity subsided, peyote apparently filled the vacuum in many disintegrating cultures. By 1910 users were prevalent on reservations in Oklahoma, and converts could be found in most western states. In 1918 they chartered the Native American Church to secure freedom of religion for themselves. Despite white harassment, the church has expanded to include approximately 300,000 members. It is one of the best examples of native ritualism wedded to Christian tenets and ethical behavior.

Other resilient forms of native spirituality have self-consciously rejected association with Christianity. These traditional practices are supported by Indians who blame white religion as well as other white values for devastating their precontact cultures. Most vital among these renewed forms is the Sun Dance, a Plains Indian liturgical act of tremendous power. This sacred ritual was virtually extinguished by governmental fiat in 1890, but it has rebounded since then to embody a spiritual energy denoting resistance to cultural domination. The modern Sun Dance does not contain all of its precontact elements, which included self-inflicted pain. But contemporary expressions retain emphases on stoicism, endurance, and selfless dedication to a high god of the native community. They also highlight the place of visions as spiritual guides while enhancing the general well-being of communities oppressed by outside influences.

After almost 500 years evangelical efforts have not created a flourishing Christian enclave in any culture indigenous to the New World. To be sure, missions never existed in a context where conditions allowed them to develop their inner potential to a complete outcome. Outside influences always interfered with evangelical efforts and changed them before they could operate as intended. Diseases, warfare, white encroachment, and governmental removals took their toll before Gospel communities could mature. Nevertheless, converts were never numerous in any specific tribe, and native Christians rarely achieved the status of leaders equal to their white supervisors. Missionaries who interacted with Indians did so with the conviction that they brought something to improve life, saving souls and reforming social behavior. The evidence from almost half a millennium shows that Christian ideology did not attract many natives. It shows rather that Gospel messengers together with other whites produced more negative than positive effects in Indian cultures. By all these criteria Christian missions have been a failure.

In accounting for this failure, one must allow for a disparity between good intentions and eventual outcomes. It is also important to bear in mind that vast cultural differences have separated Indian and white protagonists. At times missionaries aimed at a high ideal but employed methods that contravened it by violating native social values and character traits. At other times the Gospel itself fell on uncomprehending ears. Doctrines such as monotheism made little sense to peoples accustomed to a division of labor among spirit-beings. Concepts of sin and salvation astonished natives who gave no ontological status to wrongdoing and who expected reunion with all tribesmen in the afterlife. Ethical codes that extended to clothing, capitalist economy, and family arrangements seemed too oppressive to those who prized individual expression and freedom to follow private inclinations.

Considering all these incompatibilities, perhaps the remarkable thing about American Indian missions is not that they failed in most cases but that they succeeded at all. The Christian Gospel has claimed sincere converts since the time of discovery; believers continue to appear. Many now stand on traditions built by generations of believers, and they often comprise Indian churches with leadership drawn from their own people. In light of the vast population of precontact times or even the few survivors now, they are not many. But despite hardships and disappointments, they embody perhaps the best witness to lasting truths that people have discerned in the Bible.

BIBLIOGRAPHY

Robert F. Berkhofer, Jr., *Salvation and the Savage: An Analysis of Protestant Missions and American Indian Response, 1787–1862* (1965, 1972); Henry W. Bowden, *American Indians and Christian Missions: Studies in Cultural Conflict* (1981); Edmund A. de Schweinitz, *The Life and Times of David Zeisberger: The Western Pioneer and Apostle of the Indians* (1870, 1971); John Tracy Ellis, *Catholics in Colonial America* (1965); Grant Foreman, *Indian Removal: The Emigration of the Five Civilized Tribes of Indians* (1932); William T. Hagen, *American Indians* (1961); Francis Jennings, *The Invasion of America: Indians, Colonialism, and the Cant of Conquest* (1975); Alfonso Ortiz, *The Tewa World: Space, Time, Being, and Becoming in a Pueblo Society* (1969); Francis P. Prucha, *American Indian Policy in Crisis: Christian Reformers and the Indian, 1865–1900* (1976).

Neal Salisbury, *Manitou and Providence: Indians, Europeans, and the Making of New England, 1500–1643* (1982); James S. Slotkin, *The Peyote Religion: A Study in Indian-White Relations* (1956); Edward H. Spicer, *Cycles of Conquest: The Impact of Spain, Mexico, and the United States on the Indians of the Southwest, 1533–1960* (1962); Carl F. Starkloff, *The People of the Center: American Indian Religion and Christianity* (1974); William C. Sturtevant, ed., *Handbook of North American Indians* (1979–); Reuben G. Thwaites, ed., *The Jesuit Relations and Allied Documents*, 73 vols. (1896–1901); Bruce G. Trigger, *The Children of Aataentsic: A History of the Huron People to 1660* (1976); Alden T. Vaughan, *New England Frontier: Puritans and Indians, 1620–1675* (1965); Anthony F. C. Wallace, *The Death and Rebirth of the Seneca* (1970); Wilcomb E. Washburn, ed., *The American Indian and the United States: A Documentary History*, 4 vols. (1973).

[See also GREAT AWAKENING *and* NATIVE AMERICAN RELIGIONS.]

THE MISSIONARY ENTERPRISE

Patricia R. Hill

THE American missionary enterprise, although largely a creature of nineteenth-century religious culture, had roots in the colonial period. Converting American Indians had been avowed, at least peripherally, as a goal of all colonizing efforts in North America. The missionary work of Catholic priests in the French and Spanish territories of the New World was extensive and assiduous in comparison to that of Protestant missionaries in the British colonies. But the Puritan colonists, too, had their missionary heroes in John Eliot and David Brainerd. Despite such sporadic interest—and some limited success—in converting Native Americans, Protestants in the New World did not conceive of their errand into the wilderness primarily as the expression of missionary fervor. The main function of the church in Puritan eyes was not to convert the heathen without but to regulate the spiritual lives of the saints; outreach ordinarily did not extend much beyond unconverted members of saints' families. Anglicans manifested even less concern with conversions to Christianity, although dedicated missionaries sent out from England by the Society for the Propagation of the Gospel in Foreign Parts (SPG) in the eighteenth century did provide the ministrations of the church to those not living in established parishes. The real missionaries of the colonial world, however, were the Quakers, whose radical teachings and still more radical style offended Puritan and Anglican authorities alike. Yet by the end of the seventeenth century, even the Quakers had largely settled into their own insular communities and began to focus their energies on commerce rather than conversion.

Eighteenth-century Americans evinced little interest in missions, either to Indians or to the unconverted among them. There were some ex-

ceptions, of course. Cotton Mather was an advocate of missions to Indians, Catholics, and Jews; he applauded the missionary work of European Pietists. Jonathan Edwards, one of the principal architects of the Great Awakening and the friend and memoirist of Brainerd, served a stint as missionary to Indians living near Stockbridge, Massachusetts. The Society in Scotland for Promoting Christian Knowledge, chartered in 1709, was rather more successful in the American colonies than the SPG; an organization modeled on it was incorporated in 1787 as the American Society for the Propagation of the Gospel. Moravian settlers in the Middle Colonies were consistently faithful to their conception of the Christian life as a missionary enterprise. And a variety of Dissenters came as missionaries to the colonists. Scottish Presbyterians worked among the unchurched Scots-Irish in the frontier regions; itinerant Baptist preachers made substantial gains in the same areas among Anglo settlers. After mid century, Methodist lay preachers itinerated in the colonies, laying the groundwork for Methodism's massive expansion in the nineteenth century. For American Protestantism generally the colonial era was spent in establishing and gathering congregations rather than converting the heathens—European, African, or Indian. The evangelical fervor aroused in the Great Awakening marked the nearest approach in colonial America to later missionary enthusiasm.

Activism in missions, with which American Christianity has been associated, dates from the early years of the republic. The New York Missionary Society (1796), composed of Presbyterians, Baptists, and Dutch Reformed, was the first mission organization established in the new nation; local and regional missionary mite societies proliferated in the years that followed. These early associations, while occasionally devoted to work among Native Americans, were primarily purveyors of the Gospel to the unchurched in the West and in the seaboard cities. The Second Great Awakening spawned a host of religious organizations and societies designed to carry forward the work of the revival. Wide interdenominational cooperation was characteristic of such early voluntary groups as the American Bible Society (1816), the American Colonization Society (1817), the American Sunday School Union (1824), and the American Tract Society (1825). Manifestations of the American propensity in the postrevolutionary period for forming voluntary associations, these societies supplemented and supported the church extension efforts of denominational missionary societies. Both kinds of associations, like the various reform groups formed in the 1840s and 1850s, were grounded in the Hopkinsian principle of disinterested benevolence, which was the logical extension by the New Divinity men of Jonathan Edwards' definition of the nature of God as benevolence to being in general.

A commitment to foreign missions required, however, even more disinterested benevolence than the Second Awakening fostered. American foreign missionary societies had European antecedents in the Continental Pietists' missions and, more immediately, in the English society formed by Baptists in 1792, the Anglican's Church Missionary Society (1799), and especially in the London Missionary Society (1795). To a large degree, however, America's foreign mission enterprise owes its existence to a handful of students at the Andover Theological Seminary who as undergraduates at Williams College had joined a secret Society of Inquiry concerning missions and had—at the now famous impromptu prayer-meeting in the shelter of a haystack—dedicated their lives to taking the Word overseas. Their commitment took institutional form in the American Board of Commissioners for Foreign Missions, established in 1810; the first group of missionaries under ABCFM auspices sailed for India in 1812. En route two of the party, Adoniram Judson and Luther Rice, became convinced of the theological necessity of adult baptism and transferred their allegiance to the Baptists. Their widely publicized conversion and Judson's presence in Burma virtually embarrassed American Baptists (who had been sup-

porting English Baptist missions) into forming the Baptist Board of Foreign Missions in 1814. Other denominations followed suit.

Old School Presbyterians withdrew their support from the ABCFM in 1837 to form their own society; Methodists and Episcopalians organized in 1819 and 1821, respectively. Nevertheless, interdenominational cooperation in mission work was more typical in the first half of the nineteenth century than in later years, when separate denominational mission boards proliferated. In the early years denominational societies were more loosely affiliated to the institutional structures of the various churches than was the case during the high imperialist era of foreign missions, when mission boards became official arms of the churches. While even denominational societies operated as voluntary associations among a minority constituency of like-minded clergy and laity, it was easy for those with doctrinal affinities to form joint ventures like the United Foreign Missionary Society established by Presbyterian, Dutch Reformed, and Associated Reformed churches in 1817 and the American Home Missionary Society (1826), in which Presbyterians and Congregationalists cooperated. An even wider spectrum of denominations worked cooperatively in the Bible and tract societies.

American Protestants, buoyed by the heady optimism of national Manifest Destiny, came to believe that American Christians had a special responsibility for the salvation of the world as well as of the American continent. Their ready belief in the efficacy of human agency in the divine work of salvation reflects not only the general cultural climate but the theological revolution implicit in the Second Awakening and Finneyite revivalism. It was not primarily Edwardsean Calvinism but Wesleyan Arminianism that fueled the missionary activism of evangelical religion in nineteenth-century America. The theology of evangelical revivalism proved potent; by the onset of the Civil War, American Protestants were supporting missions in India, Burma, Southeast Asia, the Sandwich Islands (Hawaii), South America, China, Africa, Palestine, the Turkish Empire, and Catholic Europe. There was a degree of cooperation among the various societies in dividing the world into spheres of influence. Such cooperation was hampered, however, not only by doctrinal differences but by debates over mission policy that created divisions within as well as between societies.

The most intractable problem confronting the foreign mission movement at mid century was the debate over English language instruction. Rufus Anderson, longtime senior secretary of the ABCFM, led the fight to abolish English in the schools and missions supported by the ABCFM. His position, shared by his friends Henry Venn of the British Church Missionary Society and Francis Wayland, president of Brown University, was that the missionary's task was to evangelize, not to Westernize other peoples. They had come to believe that sending farmers and craftsmen, not to mention teachers and doctors, was a misapplication of all-too-scarce mission resources. Missions should, in their opinion, be focused on the more directly evangelical work of preaching and translating the Bible.

The establishment of permanent mission stations tended, in any case, to defeat what Venn had formulated as the "three selves" goal of foreign missions: the creation of self-governing, self-supporting, self-propagating native churches. This conception of the missionary task constituted a departure from long-established mission strategies; Jonathan Edwards' memoir of Brainerd makes it clear that setting up schools and introducing farming as a way of life were elements integral to mission work. Those who opposed Anderson and Venn were advancing traditional wisdom when they argued that Christianization must be accompanied—or even preceded—by "civilization." They believed that evangelization involved the renovation of heathen cultures as well as the salvation of individual souls. Anderson prevailed in his efforts to redirect ABCFM policy in the 1850s, but the "civilizers" controlled the shape of the Protestant missionary crusade of the late nineteenth century.

Although supporters of foreign missions had established a firm institutional base within the American churches before the Civil War, foreign missions remained the primary concern of only a small minority of both clergy and laity. The evangelical press focused attention on the dramatic stories of missionary heroes and heroines, like the harrowing tale of Adoniram Judson's lengthy imprisonment in Burma, an ordeal he survived only because Ann Judson importuned the authorities into allowing her to make daily visits to his prison with food and medicine. But if melodramatic publicity made a handful of missionaries' names household words, it did not generate a commensurate amount of financial support. By mid century the Americans still lagged far behind the British in resources, both human and monetary, devoted to foreign missions. And the Civil War forced a reduction in overseas mission work. After the war, foreign missions languished; receipts did not reach prewar levels for several years, and the overseas mission stations were understaffed.

The tendency of American churches to channel money into church extension and home missions was reinforced by the call to work among the freedmen in the South and with Indians in the South and West. The federal government's willingness to delegate to the churches responsibility for educating freedmen and Indians made such work especially attractive to patriotic Christians. The temperance movement, particularly the Woman's Christian Temperance Union (WCTU), placed enormous demands on the time and energy of concerned Protestants. And, with the New Immigration of the late nineteenth century breaking in a wave over the nation's cities, a whole new realm of home mission work opened up with the establishment of city missions. The Salvation Army, imported from Britain in 1880, was soon engaged in rescue work among the urban poor in major American cities. And it was the need in the industrial cities that stimulated the emergence of both the Social Gospel and the phenomenon of the institutional church, which offered a program of vocational training and recreational facilities for immigrants. Competition within denominations between advocates of home and foreign missions was, under the circumstances, inevitable; what is surprising is that foreign missions not only survived but burgeoned after 1880, becoming one of the dominant features of American Protestantism.

The distinction between home and foreign missions was not always entirely clear. Some denominations combined both in a general missionary organization; others, like the ABCFM in its early years, considered missions to Native Americans as foreign missions. The foreign language missions to immigrants in the cities also fell into ambiguous territory. Work among the Chinese on the West Coast counted as foreign mission work while that carried on among European ethnic groups in eastern and midwestern cities was more often considered home mission activity. This division reflects prevalent racial theories in the post–Civil War period, which placed the races on an ascending evolutionary scale with Anglo-Saxons at the top.

The degree to which "scientific" theories of Anglo-Saxon superiority reinforced and even fueled a sense of mission among American Protestants cannot be ignored. Josiah Strong's *Our Country* (1885) popularized the idea that Anglo-Saxon superiority carried with it a responsibility to assume the burdens of leadership in evangelization as in all other endeavors. Christianity, according to his view, represented the highest form of religion—purest in its Protestant version—just as democracy—purest in its American version—represented the highest form of political culture in the world. The implications of this assessment of religion and culture for home missions are evident in unabashed efforts to Americanize immigrants. For foreign missions it meant the triumph of the civilizers; Christianization was inextricably linked to Westernization. American Protestants embarked upon a course of religious and cultural imperialism that paralleled the economic and political imperialism of the age. While recognizing the racism that pervaded mission theory, one must in fairness note that the mission movement often provided strong opposition to the economic and political exploitation of immigrants and of the non-Western world. And in abandoning the narrow definition of evangelism to which Rufus Anderson wanted missionaries to adhere, the churches launched a broadened program of social service, providing educational, medical, and industrial aid in America and around the world. Benevolent imperialism cushioned the shock of adjusting to a new reality dominated by Western industrial civilization.

Conceiving of social service as a legitimate facet of mission work had the added advantage of justifying a continued expenditure of energy and resources in fields where the harvest of souls had been meager. Even before the Civil War the ABCFM had closed missions, like those in Thailand and among Native Americans, where the results had been most disheartening. But with the exceptions of Fiji, Hawaii, and among the Karens of Burma, no American missions had, judged by numbers of converts, been particu-

larly successful. The tangible achievements of Western missionaries lay in their work as linguists, translators, lexicographers, and amateur anthropologists and ethnographers; of enormous scholarly value, this work was only tangentially important to supporters of evangelical foreign missions. When success could be measured in terms of schools and hospitals established and numbers of pupils taught or patients treated, the impact of America's foreign missions would seem much more significant. So, too, would effective campaigns to urge social reforms: an end to footbinding in China, suttee (the practice of immolating widows on their husbands' funeral pyres) in India, and polygamy in the South Seas.

The broadened definition of evangelism adopted in the imperialist era by the mainline Protestant denominations, whose combined missionary activity accounted for the bulk of America's involvement in missions until well into the twentieth century, cannot be traced simply to its pragmatic appeal. Theories of racial superiority played a role as did—more benignly—the influence of the liberal theology that underlay the Social Gospel. Perhaps equally important was the increasingly active part taken by women in mission work after the Civil War. Deaconesses and Salvation Army lasses who served as social workers in city missions that were the religious equivalent of social settlements and women doctors who volunteered as medical missionaries to the secluded women in non-Western cultures forced a change in the definition of evangelism through their very presence. Denied ordination, women necessarily served as teachers, nurses, doctors, and social workers rather than as preachers of the Word.

The participation of women in the massive foreign missionary crusade mounted by America's Protestant churches in the late nineteenth century did more than ensure that cultural imperialism accompanied religious imperialism. The missionary revival that swept through the established churches toward the end of the century was generated by a complex matrix of theory and circumstance, not least of which was the existence of a woman's foreign mission movement. Foreign missions gripped the imagination of hundreds of thousands of American churchwomen in the years after the Civil War. A Woman's Board of Missions (Congregational) was organized as an auxiliary to the ABCFM in

1868. Methodist, Presbyterian, and Baptist women formed their own denominational foreign missionary societies in short order—and in the face of considerable opposition from those who feared that the women would divert funds from existing missionary societies and who felt they could detect the taint of women's rights in the movement.

Denominational women's foreign missionary societies proliferated rapidly; by the eve of World War I more than 3 million American women were enrolled in some forty societies. Considered, as it was by participants, as an interdenominational movement, the woman's foreign mission movement was the largest of the great nineteenth-century women's movements. Its impact on the churches in championing the cause of foreign missions and generating giving for missions was phenomenal. The missionary magazines published by various women's societies and the study materials they produced in the early years of the twentieth century kept the cause before the eyes of churchwomen who, after all, made up the bulk of church membership rolls.

The emphasis that the movement placed on missionary education for children trained a generation ready to believe in the importance of foreign mission work and provided a model for the mission study courses that became popular among college students in the late nineteenth century. Plans were laid at the Ecumenical Missionary Conference held in New York in 1900 to systematize mission study among women; a Committee on the United Study of Foreign Missions was named. Beginning in 1901 the committee commissioned and published mission study texts annually through the 1930s. The women's United Study was a model for the Missionary Education Movement established in 1902 to produce and distribute study materials on both foreign and home missions.

Other factors complemented and reinforced the enthusiasm generated by the women. The British example continued to wield enormous power. The publicity given Henry M. Stanley's search through darkest Africa for David Livingstone excited popular interest in missionary adventures. Millennialist expectations, so important to mission theory early in the century, were revived as a wave of premillennialism, accompanied by a dispensationalist theory of history that argued the Second Coming was imminent, lent a new urgency to the task of evangelization as preparation for Christ's return. This new brand of premillennialism, which figured largely in the holiness theology associated with J. N. Darby and the influential Keswick Conference in Britain, was spread widely in the United States through the agency of the *Scofield Reference Bible.* It became—appropriately enough, since the organizers of the Keswick Conference had been inspired by Dwight L. Moody during one of his revival campaigns in England—a staple of the Bible Institute movement modeled on the Moody Institute in Chicago. Premillennialists were often attracted by faith missions (like Hudson Taylor's China Inland Mission) that concentrated on evangelical preaching, but those premillennialists influenced by the Keswick view that sanctification was empowerment for service were in surprisingly large numbers quite prepared to accept educational and medical missions as strategies for evangelization. Arthur T. Pierson, whose *Crisis of Missions* (1886) had a formidable effect on American mission advocates in colleges and seminaries, was a premillennialist of the latter type. A more liberal postmillennialism, which marked the attitude of Social Gospelers intent upon ushering in the Kingdom, proved an equally powerful motive for evangelism broadly defined. The two approaches coalesced in support of urban revivalism and city missions in America, which in turn, somewhat paradoxically, generated volunteers for foreign missions.

The career of Dwight Moody, the preeminent urban revivalist of the post–Civil War years, illustrates the paradox. Moody himself was interested not so much in foreign mission work as in city missions. His support for the Young Men's Christian Association (modeled on the British organization that worked with young men living on their own in cities) led him to sponsor summer conferences for students involved in YMCA work. At the first of these, held at Mount Hermon School, Northfield, Massachusetts, in 1886, leaders from college branches of the YMCA—at the instigation of Robert Wilder, a recent graduate of Princeton Seminary and son of the editor of the *Missionary Review of the World,* and Luther Wishard, secretary for the YMCA's college work—organized the Student Volunteer Movement for Foreign Missions (SVM), which became American Protestantism's most influential instrument for recruiting volunteers for overseas fields. Like the woman's foreign mission movement, the SVM is a prime example of the great lay movements that shaped the particular character of mission activism in America in the late nineteenth century.

The SVM was important not only for its work among college students but as an organizational base for the remarkable career of one of its founders, John R. Mott, who became the foremost missionary statesman of the twentieth century. Mott was the great ecumenist of missions, a force for interdenominational and international cooperation. His was the hand that wrought the World's Student Christian Federation (1895). Chairman of the World Missionary Conference in Edinburgh in 1910, Mott extended the conference's influence—and his own —through the agency of a Continuation Committee that organized the International Missionary Council (IMC). This council, together with the Federal Council of Churches formed in 1908 to address the problems of industrial society, served as a model for other ecumenical organizations. Ultimately, the international Faith-and-Order and Life-and-Work movements established after World War I combined with the International Missionary Council and the World's Student Christian Federation to constitute the World Council of Churches in 1948.

Ecumenical cooperation through these councils became the hallmark of liberal Protestant missions. Such missions were called conciliar and the theology that informed them was labeled conciliar theology to distinguish it from the alternatives promulgated by more conservative evangelical groups after World War I. In the prewar era, however, the lines between liberal and conservative were not so clearly drawn. The organizers of the SVM, which was to be bitterly attacked by Fundamentalists in the 1920s, were, for example, deeply influenced by Arthur Pierson. In fact, the coining of the SVM's watchword, "The Evangelization of the World in this Generation," should probably be credited to Pierson rather than to John Mott. And a moderate like Robert E. Speer, the great Presbyterian mission statesman who saved his denomination's mission operation from being wrecked upon the shoals of Fundamentalism in the 1920s, can be found along with Pierson among the contributors to *The Fundamentals* (1910–1915).

The relative harmony among evangelicals holding widely divergent theological positions makes it possible to generalize about the nature and course of the Protestant missionary crusade before the Great War shattered the progressive optimism of American culture. While denominational loyalties governed giving for missions and denominational differences determined mission policies in such things as the polity of churches established among converts, there was sufficient unity of purpose and method to encourage considerable cooperation among most of the denominational sending agencies. Overseas, annual interdenominational conferences were instituted on several mission fields. The beginnings of international—or at least Anglo-American—cooperation can be traced to the Centenary Conference on Protestant Missions of the World held in London in 1888. Five years later the major (and many minor) denominational missionary societies in the United States and Canada organized themselves into the Foreign Missions Conference of North America, for the purpose of triennial consultations on mission methods.

America's Protestant mission establishment became increasingly professional in the years that followed. Mission administrators began to put their multimillion-dollar enterprise on a businesslike footing. Postgraduate work was required of candidates for mission service; professional training schools for Christian workers were established. Some of the training schools, like the Moody Bible Institute and the Chicago Training School for City, Home and Foreign Missions, were independent; in other instances missionary training programs were established as separate departments of denominational colleges or seminaries.

The Ecumenical Missionary Conference of 1900 reinforced the call for a "science" of modern missions. It also continued the tradition of Anglo-American domination of international missionary councils, a disturbing development for Continental mission leaders troubled by the social activism associated with Anglo-American missions. The reservations they expressed were later echoed by American Fundamentalists in their postwar critique of liberal Protestant missions, but in 1900 it still seemed possible to unite behind the goal enunciated in the watchword of the SVM. Charts and tables were prepared that compared the numbers of the unevangelized with the membership statistics for the various Protestant churches. The share that each church—and each member—would need to contribute if the world were to be evangelized in one generation was calculated in numbers both of missionaries and of dollars. The mathematical precision in such calculations of Christian duty appealed to a generation of church members caught up in Progressive America's characteristic enthusiasm for the application of science to social problems. It became fashionable to speak of the sociology of modern missions. In the years between 1897 and 1906 James Dennis produced his three-volume survey of the world mission situation under the title *Christian Missions and Social Progress: A Sociological Study of Foreign Missions;* it catalogues the introduction of the blessings of Western civilization in virtually every corner of the globe.

The successive opening of new fields to missions over the course of the nineteenth century was read as a sign of the approaching millennium. Consequently, there was a tendency among mission advocates to view European and American imperialists as partners in the evangelization of the world. Certainly missions followed the course of empire. British and European sending agencies established missions in colonial territories claimed by their governments. Since the United States engaged, until the very end of the century, mainly in commercial rather than political colonialism, American mission societies operated in countries like Japan, Korea, and China, with which the United States had trade treaties, places like Samoa, where the United States had negotiated for naval bases, or in territories where the colonial government was tolerant of if not sympathetic to missions.

Partly because no language barrier existed between British colonial regimes and American missionaries, Americans were particularly active in British colonies. After the East India Company lifted restrictions in 1833 on missionary activity, India became, for much of the nineteenth century, the focus of America's missionary fervor. Other places within the British sphere, notably Egypt and Palestine, were also among the early targets of American sending agencies. As various Asian nations were forced or cajoled into opening trade relations with the West, American missionary interest in the Far East expanded. When the United States itself acquired colonies in the Spanish-American War, missionaries flooded into the Philippines and other Pacific islands—even where the indigenous populations had already been converted to Catholicism.

Americans always took a special interest in the fields opened to missions by American commercial contact; Hawaii and Japan, for example, fall into this category. With the enunciation in 1900 of the United States' Open Door policy for China—a plan designed to prevent any one Western power from exercising colonial control, thus ensuring equal commercial access for all—the focus of American missionary interest shifted decisively to China. While there had been a tacit although not entirely exclusive division of fields by denomination earlier in the century, China offered sufficient scope for all comers. Indeed, the task was so overwhelming—and efficiency so stressed in the current cultural climate in America—that evangelizing China evoked a marked increase in interdenominational cooperation. Joint ventures in establishing Christian colleges were inaugurated; successful experiments in setting up national Christian churches in mission lands were cited as lessons for American Protestants on the true spirit of a Christianity not marred by petty denominational divisions.

The nature of America's missionary crusade in the era of modern missions, which coincided with the opening years of the twentieth century, is exemplified in the Laymen's Missionary Movement (LMM). Founded in 1907 by Samuel Capen, a Boston carpet store owner who was president of the ABCFM, the LMM typifies the modern mission movement in its lay leadership and in its adaptation and application of the advertising and public relations strategies developed by consumer capitalism to religious philanthropy. The LMM's object was to persuade businessmen to interest themselves in foreign missions. The approach used was pragmatic; missions were presented as a growing concern well worth the investment of time, energy, and capital. Strategies adopted by the movement ranged from prayer breakfasts for businessmen to interdenominational cooperation on a city-wide basis in "every member" canvases soliciting funds for foreign missions. Their fund-raising campaigns were successful on a scale equaled (and exceeded) only by the woman's foreign mission movement during the 1910–1911 celebration of its jubilee. The leaders of this lay movement were anxious to establish themselves as peers of the nation's business and political leaders; the cultural climate made it possible for them to do so. It was in this period that John R. Mott solidified the reputation that made him a world figure in the first half of the twentieth century, an intimate of prominent statesmen and capitalists as well as churchmen, an apparently natural choice of President Woodrow Wilson for delicate diplomatic negotiations in Mexico and Russia.

The professionalization of mission administration and the "secularization" of missions (implicit in a definition of evangelism that included social service) occurred in the context of Protestant cultural hegemony. The missionary enterprise itself—despite professionalization in recruitment and training—was largely dominated by a missionary subculture, a network of families and individuals within particular fields or within particular denominations whose names became identified with missions. The Judsons of Burma were virtually synonymous with Baptist missions for many years. The Thoburns and Scudders of India loomed equally large in the Methodist and Reformed churches, respectively. The Mateers and Luces of China were not only familiar names to mission supporters in the Presbyterian denomination, but also participated in the web of mission field connections that produced the old China hands who manned the East Asian desk in the State Department and established East Asian studies programs in major American universities in the twentieth century. Individual missionaries, most often single women, came to symbolize whole fields for some denominations: Lottie Moon represented China to Southern Baptist Convention members, and Jean Kenyon Mackenzie became, for Presbyterians, the voice of African missions.

Interdenominational conferences held annually in many mission fields reinforced more casual links between missionaries. Retreat centers both overseas and in the United States helped maintain ties between missionaries on vacation or on furlough. Denominational homes and schools for missionary children, often located— as were retirement homes for missionaries— near denominational colleges, provided yet another dimension to the shared experiences that set the children of missionaries apart. This sub-culture persisted well into the twentieth century, long after the mainline Protestant groups had radically reduced their commitment to overseas missions. But since the subculture produced the historians of Protestant missions, it also engendered a distorted perception of the changing nature of American missions after World War I. The historical focus has been on a decline in foreign mission activity that has in fact characterized only liberal Protestantism, not American religion more widely.

As American culture became increasingly secular after 1920, mainline Protestant domination of American religion was challenged. The pluralism that came to characterize the American religious scene in the twentieth century is mirrored and even exaggerated in America's foreign mission enterprise. The mushrooming of Evangelical and Pentecostal churches has been accompanied by an aggressive expansion of overseas outreach by these groups. The spectacular growth of the the Southern Baptist Convention has made it not only the largest Protestant denomination in the United States, but also the fielder of the world's largest Protestant missionary operation. Often considered by historians as a peculiarly American religion, the Church of Jesus Christ of Latter-day Saints (Mormons) has since mid century experienced a worldwide expansion of phenomenal proportions; its overseas missionary force, consisting almost entirely of short-termers rather than career missionaries, now numbers in excess of 30,000. American Catholicism has also come of age as a missionary force in the twentieth century. Curiously, the story of American Catholic missions recapitulates and echoes the history of mainline evangelical Protestant missions in a number of respects.

The Catholic church in America was officially designated by Rome as a mission church until 1908. European missionary societies channeled millions of dollars to the American church in the course of the nineteenth century. While the Society for the Propagation of the Faith was established in some American dioceses, contributions from American Catholics to the SPF for the whole of the century amounted to little more than $1 million. The missionary work engaged in by American Catholics was mainly limited to equivalents of Protestant home missions and church extension. Catholic revivalism in the nineteenth century took the form of parish missions, which promoted a Catholic version of experiential religion and fostered—somewhat ironically—a puritanical morality condemning card-playing, dancing, and alcohol. The WCTU had its parallel in the Catholic Total Abstinence Union. Catholic missions to American Indians were accorded national recognition in the establishment of a Bureau of Catholic Indian Affairs when the federal government handed the management of Indian affairs over to the churches after the Civil War.

By the turn of the century, American Catholics were organizing institutional counterparts to Protestant home mission boards. An American Catholic Missionary Union was formed in the 1890s to engage in parish mission work. The Catholic Church Extension Society (1905) organized missionary congresses in 1908 and 1913 to promote mission efforts in rural areas. A National Conference of Catholic Charities was formed in 1910 to coordinate Catholic social work. The largest Catholic home mission enterprise had, however, no Protestant parallel in size or function: the parochial school system operated on a scale larger than the most ambitious dreams of Protestant home missions. And the establishment of charitable and teaching orders of men and women religious had no domestic equivalent among Protestants, with the possible exceptions of the Salvation Army and a quite small cadre of Methodist deaconesses. American Catholics, however, made no significant contributions of either money or personnel for overseas missions until the twentieth century.

American financial support for Catholic foreign missions increased rapidly after the turn of the century. European mission leaders pressed the increasingly affluent American church to shoulder its share of the expense of international missions; annual giving for overseas work passed the $100,000 mark early in the century and had topped $1 million by the 1920s. American Catholics have since become the primary sustainers of the church's worldwide missions. The actual sending out of substantial numbers of missionaries lagged behind monetary support. A handful of priests and sisters were working overseas in the late nineteenth century, but the first American order specifically devoted to foreign missions, the Catholic Foreign Mission Society (Maryknoll), was not established until 1911 and did not send its first missionaries until 1918.

Maryknoll has remained a center for Catholic foreign missions, but the number of Maryknoll fathers and sisters serving overseas was soon surpassed by that of Jesuits, who have made up the bulk of American Catholic missionaries ever since. By mid-century, the American Catholic mission force was several thousand strong and constituted nearly a tenth of the world total of Roman Catholic missionaries.

The growing wealth of American Catholics was only one factor in the transformation of the American Catholic church from a mission church to a missionary church. World War I had interrupted the flow of immigrants; after the war, restrictions on immigration reduced the flow from Catholic countries of southern and eastern Europe to a trickle. No longer essentially an immigrant church divided by language and ethnic barriers, American Catholicism entered a period of national consolidation. The war itself facilitated Americanization; the formation of a National Catholic War Council both demonstrated Catholic patriotism and marked a new level of national organization among American Catholics.

The National Catholic Welfare Conference (NCWC), approved by Rome in 1923 as a permanent replacement for the National Catholic War Council, parallels the interdenominational Protestant Home Missions Council organized in 1908. The NCWC coordinated work previously done independently by each diocese, just as the Home Missions Council encouraged coordination of denominational efforts. The departments into which the NCWC was divided echo Protestant concern with education, publications, social action, and laity involvement as important corollaries to successful mission efforts.

Education, of course, had a much broader meaning in the context of the Catholic parochial school system than it had for Protestants, who launched their Missionary Education Movement in 1902 primarily to promote foreign missions and whose post–World War I Christian education programs were limited to religious education. Within the parochial school system, the habit of supporting missions was instilled by some of the same strategies that Protestants used with children; schoolchildren were offered the opportunity to take responsibility for individual "heathen" orphans. There was not, however, a Catholic equivalent to the SVM, since Catholic missionaries were drawn from the ranks of religious. Vocations were certainly encouraged, but lay volunteers for overseas mission work were not widely recruited.

Publications, ranging from translations of the Bible to monthly missionary magazines and covering an eclectic spectrum in between, had been at the heart of Protestant mission work since the organization of Bible and tract societies in the early nineteenth century. The production of missionary literature for domestic consumption and for distribution in mission fields was considered so vital to the movement that reports of denominational boards and women's societies devoted a separate section to reviewing the year's efforts in these areas; special sessions at national and international missionary meetings focused on missionary literature. Circulating mission libraries were established in many local churches, and mission materials were placed in public libraries. Curriculum materials that promoted home and foreign missions were developed during the phase of professionalization that marked the heyday of mainline Protestant missions. Controversies between liberals and conservatives were aired in the pages of religious journals.

After the Civil War, American Catholics embarked on a publishing spree similar to the one Protestants had launched in the early nineteenth century. Catholic journals and newspapers multiplied rapidly in the postwar years. The Paulists' Catholic Publication Society produced everything from prayer books and hagiography to curriculum materials and instruction manuals. Like the Protestants, American Catholics published periodicals devoted to advancing particular factional views on matters of social justice and political action that fell within the purview of home missions broadly construed; by the 1930s, such publications ran the gamut from Dorothy Day's left-wing *Catholic Worker* to Father Coughlin's proto-Fascist *Social Justice*. On the foreign mission front, the Maryknoll society carried on an extensive publication program ranging from tracts and promotional literature to scholarly treatises on mission history and theology, and the Jesuits published their own missionary magazines.

Social service has been a component of American Catholic mission work at home and abroad from the beginning. The social action program of the NCWC called for much of the same social legislation advocated by Progressives and endorsed by Protestant home mission societies. The suggestion has been made that John Ryan, whose 1919 pamphlet was the basis for the Bishops' Program of Social Reconstruction, was truly the father of the first New Deal. On a less progressive plane, the Legion of Decency had its Protestant counterpart in the motion picture censorship advocated by home mission boards. And just as the Protestant churches through their home mission organizations finally took the lead in campaigns for social justice and minority rights, so too the Catholic Interracial Council began to push for integration as early as the 1930s. American Catholic foreign mission work always included orphanages, hospitals, and schools.

As they did in the Protestant missionary enterprise, women played an important role in Catholic missions. Sisterhoods staffed schools and hospitals. Laywomen, first through the women's committee of the National Catholic War Council and then through the National Council of Catholic Women, opened and supported the National Catholic School of Social Service, which trained social workers for war work and later for missionary service overseas. In general, however, lay involvement in Catholic missions has never matched the prominent role played by lay movements in the Protestant missionary enterprise. The Catholic lay movements that emerged in the 1940s and 1950s were oriented toward neither social action nor missions; the more recent Catholic charismatic revival has not stimulated the aggressive missionary outreach characteristic of Protestant holiness and Pentecostal groups.

The coupling of social service with evangelism did not engender the debate within Catholic circles that it did among mainline Protestants after World War I. Within the Catholic context, social service was seen as entirely compatible with the largely conservative theology that informed Catholic missions until the post–Vatican II era.

The social work of Catholic missions was not linked, as was similar work done by Protestants, to a liberal theology tending toward ecumenism and religious relativism. These liberal tendencies intensified among Protestants after 1920, after eventually precipitating a crisis within the Protestant establishment. Building on the momentum of the immediate prewar years and the experience of cooperative war work, liberal Protestants launched an ambitious ecumenical program for the support and coordination of home and foreign missions. The Interchurch World Movement of 1919–1920 not only failed to realize its goals; it provided a focus for growing Fundamentalist discontent with missions grounded in Social Gospel theology.

Fundamentalists within the mainline Protestant denominations were particularly unhappy with foreign mission operations that in their eyes offered material aid in place of saving truths. They argued that, in the drive for ecumenical cooperation, doctrinal integrity had been sacrificed and that a watered-down Christianity scarcely distinguishable from secular humanism had been substituted for the blood of Christ. The battle between Fundamentalists and liberals for control of denominational mission operations was particularly hard fought within the Northern Baptist Convention and among Presbyterians; campaigns were conducted on three fronts—in the seminaries, on the mission field, and at the denominations' annual general assemblies or conventions. The religious press published charges and countercharges from all quarters. The furor even surfaced in secular publications. By the mid-1920s, moderates and liberals had won the war within the mainline denominations, but their victory did not improve their fortunes. Fundamentalist dissenters created independent mission-sending agencies. Support for the Protestant establishment and its missions declined throughout the decade. One measure of this trend is a steady falling off in giving for foreign missions; another is the dramatic drop in SVM recruits, from 2,700 in 1920 to barely 250 in 1928.

If Fundamentalists had their doubts about liberal Protestant missions, so, increasingly, did liberals themselves, for a rather different set of reasons. The war had exposed the hypocrisy of the so-called Christian West and shattered the evolutionary optimism associated with theories of Anglo-Saxon superiority. Nationalist revolutions and anticolonialism made liberals question the assumptions that underlay the seemingly benign cultural imperialism of Protestant missions. The most liberal mission theorists moved from ecumenism to cultural and religious relativism. More moderate mission advocates recognized their failure to include representatives of the "younger" churches of the non-Western world

in international missionary consultations. An effort was made to rectify this omission at the Jerusalem Conference of the International Missionary Council in 1928, but delegates from the new national churches challenged the Western mission establishment to accept them as full partners in mission rather than to treat them as neophytes.

It was in this climate of questioning that prominent Protestant mission leaders, at the instigation and with the financial backing of John D. Rockefeller, launched in 1930 the exhaustive assessment project known as the Laymen's Foreign Missions Inquiry. William Hocking, professor of philosophy at Harvard, headed the inquiry and wrote, under the title *Re-Thinking Missions* (1932), an introduction to the multivolume report issued in 1933. Hocking pointed to a number of shortcomings in the actual work of missions, from inadequately trained staff and shortages of equipment to wasteful duplication of services. These criticisms generated, from some quarters, a defense of the quality of mission personnel, but the deeply controversial aspect of the report was the suggestion that collaboration replace conversion as the goal of missions in relation to other world religions. The mainline Protestant denominations were unwilling to accept a radical religious relativism that reduced Christianity to one among many versions of divine revelation. They were, however, increasingly ready to adopt the position, articulated by Venn in the nineteenth century, that the successful mission would render itself obsolete.

As the Protestant establishment in America became convinced that its mission operations must be handed over to the control of native churches around the world, the overseas mission force of mainline American churches was steadily reduced. Financial support for the younger churches, rather than the maintenance of large mission stations, has become the pattern for what the denominations associated through the National Council of Churches call their overseas ministries. Personnel sent abroad by these churches now ordinarily go as fraternal workers who cooperate with and are under the supervision of local church leaders. This pattern, however, characterizes what has become in the course of the twentieth century a small—and declining—segment of America's overseas mission operations.

Conservative evangelical groups, both denominations formed by Fundamentalists who left mainline churches and the proliferating holiness and Pentecostal churches, organized after World War I to send out missionaries who would carry with them a saving faith. Individual conversions were the clear and overriding goal of such missionary activity. Ironically, the decisive separation of church and state that came with the secularization of the dominant culture in America provided a rationale for arguing that social and political ends were not the proper business of religion. The churches' responsibility for the social order was not considered the significant issue that it had been for those liberal Protestants who formulated the Social Gospel. This is perhaps only natural; the demographic profile of Fundamentalists and Pentecostals shows a group, in contrast to liberal Protestants, not largely drawn from among the movers and shakers in American society. Not accustomed to controlling their culture, they made no assumption of a right to decide social and political questions—and their assurance that religious salvation took precedence over such issues bolstered the comfort they took from their own faith.

Dispensational premillennialists and holiness adherents had, since the first days of the China Inland Mission in the 1860s, been attracted by the concept of faith missions—missions not attached to and dependent on support from any denominational structure, but reliant on intercessory prayer and a God who met all needs through providentially inspired gifts from the faithful. But these independent faith missions came to recognize the advantages to be gained from the mutual support and cooperation that the mainline Protestant agencies achieved through the Foreign Mission Conference of North America. In 1917 a group of faith mission agencies organized the Interdenominational Foreign Mission Association (IFMA).

Many of the growing number of conservative evangelical churches, holiness denominations like the Christian and Missionary Alliance and the Pentecostal Assemblies of God, established mission boards and sent out missionaries under denominational auspices. These churches, disaffected from the Protestant establishment that controlled the Federal (after 1950, National) Council of Churches, the IMC, the SVM, the YWCA–YMCA, and the WSCF, began in the 1930s and 1940s to develop interdenominational networks of their own. The Intervarsity Fellowship formed in England in 1928 provided a model for the Intervarsity Christian Fellowship introduced to college campuses in the United States in 1940. A small cadre of Fundamentalist groups formed an American Council of Christian Churches in 1941. A broader spectrum of conservative evangelicals joined together in the National Association of Evangelicals in 1942; the missionary arm of the NAE was organized as the Evangelical Foreign Missions association in 1945. The EFMA works jointly with the IFMA on a variety of matters ranging from publications to personnel. Together these associations represented the sending agencies and denominations that were, by 1960, fielding the majority of America's overseas missionaries.

The story of America's foreign mission enterprise in the twentieth century is, then, not a history of decline but of displacement. The size of America's mission force has, with the exception of a slight falling off from the early 1920s through the early 1930s, increased throughout the century. Indeed, it was only after 1950 that a majority of the world's Protestant mission force came from North America.

The home mission efforts of the new evangelicals has focused on personal conversion. The social action and social justice issues that were the common concerns of both liberal Protestant and Roman Catholic home missions—in the 1930s in response to the Depression and even more markedly in the civil rights struggles of the 1960s—were not a part of the agenda for evangelical home missions. The evangelical churches employed Billy Graham–style revival crusades as a primary strategy for domestic outreach and evolved in the Church Growth movement an equivalent of nineteenth-century Protestant and Catholic church extension efforts. As the evangelical churches broadened their base in American society in the 1950s, they became increasingly sophisticated in the use of the media to convey their gospel. Radio and television broadcasts as well as publications like *Christianity Today* (founded in 1956) reached a broad audience.

By the mid-1960s, the evangelical dissenters from the conciliar theology that informed the work of the Division of Overseas Ministries of the National Council of Churches and from the liberation theology that informed a growing number of post–Vatican II Catholic missions recognized the need to articulate an evangelical strategy for missions. In 1966 the IFMA and the EFMA sponsored, at Wheaton College in Illinois, a Congress on the Church's Worldwide Mission that issued the Wheaton Declaration, a statement of evangelical mission principles. In the same year, *Christianity Today* sponsored a World Congress on Evangelism that met in Berlin. In a move consistent with their long-held view that the mainline Protestant churches had abandoned the central truths and the true mission of Christianity, the new evangelicals meeting in Berlin adopted the goal of the SVM's watchword as their goal for missions.

Trends since the late 1960s indicate that the torch of missions has passed to the new evangelicals. The number of American Roman Catholic missionaries peaked in 1966 and has since declined steadily. In part, of course, this decline mirrors the drop in vocations and the exodus of religious from orders. But it also reflects a response, not unlike that of liberal Protestants to burgeoning nationalism in the 1920s, to the church's confrontation with the issue of the indigenization of Christianity in the non-Western world. The liberation theologies that emerged in Latin America in the 1960s had a profound effect on the style of American Catholic missions; the engagement in political struggles abroad, like the involvement with racial struggles at home, made missionaries particularly sensitive to questions of religious and cultural imperialism. Worker priests—and sisters—and lay missioners are creating collaborative models for missions, but, as with liberal Protestants, the appropriateness of providing support for local church leaders rather than providing leaders has encouraged the reduction in numbers of missionaries.

The Division of Overseas Ministries of the National Council of Churches reported a reduction during the 1970s in the size of the mission force fielded by its member denominations. The United Methodists' Commission on Relief and their Board of Global Ministries were, along with the NCC's own Church World Service, the only exceptions to this general pattern of diminishment. It is revealing that the United Methodists have been deeply committed to the same kinds of relief, refugee assistance, disaster aid, and economic development that fall within the purview of the Church World Service. Liberal Protestants remain committed to a model of social service as

Christian witness; receipts for overseas ministries of the churches of the National Council dropped slightly at the beginning of the decade, but rose slowly throughout the remainder of the 1970s. Nevertheless, the receipts for missions among the agencies associated with the NCC at the end of the 1970s represented only about 15 percent of the total income reported by Protestant mission agencies in North America. And their overseas personnel were a mere 10 percent of the North American total.

While the number of missionaries supported by the EFMA and the IFMA grew throughout the 1970s, and the EFMA agencies experienced a surge in income, the most dramatic development of the decade was yet another major shift in the overall composition of the North American overseas mission force. By 1980 the unaffiliated sending agencies dominated the picture. They sent out approximately three-fifths of all American personnel, and their income amounted to more than half the total for all Protestant missions. The largest of the unaffiliated agencies, the Foreign Mission Board of the Southern Baptist Convention, accounts for about a tenth of the total income and personnel reported by unaffiliated agencies. The remainder, which now constitutes the bulk of the Protestant missionary enterprise, is made up of such a large number of diverse agencies that generalizations about policies and mission strategies are difficult if not nearly impossible to make.

For the affiliated evangelicals, those associated with the NAE and the EFMA/IFMA connection, the 1970s were a time of change. Both at home and abroad the new evangelicals evinced a greater openness to combining evangelism with social action. In the Chicago Declaration (1973), Ronald J. Sider, a prominent leader of the new evangelicals, argued for the inseparable link between evangelism and social action. At the Lausanne (Switzerland) International Congress on World Evangelization in 1974, John R. W. Stott urged a change in rhetoric that would replace "evangelism" with "mission." Matched by a countervailing trend on the liberal Protestant scene—a renewal of interest in spirituality—the willingness of evangelicals to incorporate social goals into their mission aims has resulted in a partial and very tentative rapprochement between these evangelicals and the conciliar Protestants. But if liberals and conservatives have drawn closer in their interpretation of Christ's great commission to "go . . . and teach all nations" as it applies to overseas missions, they remain deeply divided over appropriate social goals for the churches at home. Leaders of the National Council of Churches are among the severest critics of the social and legislative program promoted by evangelical lobbies such as the Moral Majority.

Perhaps the most striking feature of the history of America's missionary enterprise in the twentieth century is the movement's virtual loss of visibility as a cultural phenomenon. In the late nineteenth century, foreign missions were celebrated as manifestations of America's national beneficence as a Christian and democratic society. Missions were intimately linked to commerce and foreign policy. Missionary statesmen wielded enormous social and political clout. Turn-of-the-century presidents publicly prayed for and applauded missionary endeavors. After World War I, the popular press followed the disputes between Fundamentalists and liberals over missions. But as the culture itself ostensibly grew more secular—and as the mainline Protestant churches reduced their missionary force—missions lost both their public dimension and public attention. The steady growth and particular character of America's missionary enterprise over the course of the twentieth century has remained a largely invisible and unexplored facet of American religion.

BIBLIOGRAPHY

Wade Crawford Barclay, *History of Methodist Missions*, 3 vols. (1957); Rodger C. Bassham, *Mission Theology: 1948–1975, Years of Worldwide Creative Tension—Ecumenical, Evangelical and Roman Catholic* (1980); R. Pierce Beaver, *All Loves Excelling* (1968; rev. as *American Protestant Women in World Mission*, 1980); Thomas A. Breslin, *China, American Catholicism, and the Missionary* (1980); Arthur Judson Brown, *One Hundred Years: A History of the Foreign Missionary Work of the Presbyterian Church in the U.S.A.* (1937); Joan Jacobs Brumberg, *Mission for Life: The Story of the Family of Adoniram Judson* (1980); Charles L. Chaney, *The Birth of Missions in America* (1976); Torben Christensen and William R. Hutchison, eds., *Missionary Ideologies in the Imperialist Era, 1880–1920* (1982).

Jay P. Dolan, *Catholic Revivalism: The American Experience, 1830–1900* (1978); John Tracy Ellis, *American Catholicism* (1956; rev. 1969); John K. Fairbank, ed., *The Missionary Enterprise in China and America* (1974); Arthur F. Glasser and Donald A. McGavran, *Contemporary Theologies of Mission* (1983); James Hennesey, *American Catholics* (1981); Patricia R. Hill, *The World Their Household: The American Woman's Foreign Mission Movement and Cultural Transformation, 1870–1920* (1985); C. Howard Hopkins, *John R. Mott* (1979); Jane Hunter, *The Gospel of Gentility: American Women Missionaries in Turn-of-the-Century China* (1984); William R. Hutchison, *Errand to the World: American Protestant Thought and Foreign Missions* (1987); Irwin T. Hyatt, Jr., *Our Ordered Lives Confess* (1976).

Kenneth Scott Latourette, *A History of the Expansion of Christianity*, 7 vols. (1937–1945); John Patrick McDowell, *The Social Gospel in the South: The Woman's Home Mission Movement in the Methodist Episcopal Church, South, 1886–1939* (1982); Helen Barrett Montgomery, *Western Women in Eastern Lands* (1910); Stephen Neill, *A History of Christian Missions* (1964); Clifton Jackson Phillips, *Protestant America and the Pagan World* (1969); Valentin H. Rabe, *The Home Base of American China Missions, 1880–1920* (1978); Robert G. Torbet, *Venture of Faith: The Story of the American Baptist Foreign Mission Society and the Woman's American Baptist Foreign Mission Society, 1814–1954* (1955); Samuel Wilson, ed., *Mission Handbook: North American Protestant Ministries Overseas* (12th ed., 1980).

[*See also* ECUMENICAL MOVEMENT; GREAT AWAKENING; HOLINESS AND PERFECTION; NINETEENTH-CENTURY EVANGELICALISM; NORTH AMERICAN INDIAN MISSIONS; SOCIAL REFORM AFTER THE CIVIL WAR TO THE GREAT DEPRESSION; SOCIAL REFORM FROM THE COLONIAL PERIOD THROUGH THE CIVIL WAR; SOCIAL REFORM SINCE THE GREAT DEPRESSION; *and* WOMEN AND RELIGION.]

THE RELIGIOUS PRESS

Martin E. Marty

THE religious press in America consists of a network of magazines, journals, newsletters, and other printed materials that supplement the spoken word, books, and electronic media as means of communication. Most of that communication consists of messages between the leadership of religious groups or movements and their constituencies. On occasion, there have been and are periodicals designed to cross denominational boundaries and to make a direct impact on the larger, in part secular culture. Yet the majority of the tens of thousands of publications that have existed and still exist do not aspire to general circulation. They are instruments of religious institutional promotion and of the development and informing of the faithful.

The popularity and prevalence of the printed word results from at least two factors in American religion. First is the nature of that religion, the vast majority of whose professors are of biblical heritage and are Jews or Christians. These are "people of the Book," themselves trained in literacy in order to understand messages conceived to be revealed by God. They apply this literacy to other areas, to enhance their grasp of the essential book, the Bible. Most advocates of a religious press see it as an endeavor to make the Word applicable to contemporary situations.

In Judaism, Catholicism, and Protestantism, verbal communication focuses on the reading of Scripture, the celebration of liturgy, and, for Protestants in particular, the act of preaching. Yet oral communication, in which the presence of God may be recognized, is by its nature ephemeral and focused. People leave the weekly gathering after having heard a message and offered prayers. Yet in such a gathering there can have been little opportunity to discuss details of family living, personal devotion, the causes of the organization, human need, world affairs surrounding the religious institution, or dimensions of the culture. These must all be supported in some other way, and this will not be done by the public. The secular press, being secular, keeps most religious news at some distance and, even with the best intentions, could not cover the materials relevant to members of all groups.

Reference to the groups points to the other dimension of American religious life that has encouraged the religious press. This is its pluralism. *The Yearbook of the American and Canadian Churches* lists well over 200 denominations, and encyclopedias of religion have no difficulty locating 1,000 religious groups. Most of these include a variety of boards, bureaus, educational agencies, and often factions or movements. Individuals or small groups who would like to change denominations or form transdenominational movements find the press an efficient instrument. There is no efficient means, however, to employ the secular press to such an end. Newspaper and magazine publishers know that the vast majority of religious news and information concerns only a small minority of their readership. A story favorable to Mormons may put off Baptists, while a story relevant to Baptists may not concern Methodists.

For those reasons, the religious press rarely has a truly mass character. A nation in which general circulation magazines like *The Saturday Evening Post* or *Life* and *Look* cannot prosper, but in which periodicals directed to owners of yachts or Scottish terriers or classic cars do, is a pluralist world well adapted to the needs of religious groups. A Roman Catholic who cares for "liberation theology" and Latin American progressivism will have little interest in a periodical designed for Methodist devotions. So the *Upper*

Room (circulation 3 million) will go unread by him. Yet his cherished *National Catholic Reporter* will have no attractions for a conservative Roman Catholic who favors *The National Catholic Register* or for the charismatic Catholic who relishes periodicals devoted to the life of the Spirit in the experience of people.

To these two features, the reliance on the word for religion and the pluralism of interests, one may add a third. The American religious landscape has always presented ecological niches in which new growths can appear. There is always room for the entrepreneur, the individualist, the person of vision and experience who has a new idea and would like to attract a new clientele or circle of interest. How shall such a person spread the word and gather people or nourish them? The circuit-rider or traveling evangelist knew the value of personal contact, but there were limits. The most economical means was to start a paper or a magazine. It serves as an attention-getting device in the hands of early converts who spread it to others. Then it serves as a magnet to attract those who show some interest, a definer for those who need to know the new boundaries of the group, an articulator and ideological regulator, and a sounding board for response.

For all these reasons it is clear why the religious press in America, whatever its aspirations to being part of "mass media of communications" may be, has to content itself and draw excellence from its intention to be a form of privileged communication with access to special groups. At the same time, this means that there will normally be a limit to the direct impact of the religious press on the culture itself. It may help form a movement or direct an impulse that "makes news" and the secular media may pick it up. Thus the religious press in the 1960s, through the years of the civil rights struggle, could support—or, in some cases, could criticize —the movement as led by the Rev. Martin Luther King, Jr. *The Lutheran,* the Catholic diocesan press, and the quarterlies issued by the three major branches of Judaism were there, free to take up the pros and cons of such a movement in a way that individuals in pulpits might not have been able to do. The periodical was the gatekeeper to a world larger than the parish. It helped form a cohort to support King or a force that opposed him. When King marched and religious leaders marched with him in support of civil rights—or when others stayed home to jeer those who marched—then the television networks or *Newsweek* or the Associated Press took up the religious issue and made it a mass item. Most viewers of television or readers of a newspaper would not know how the constituencies had been formed by a press that was, to them, invisible.

Given the nature of American pluralism and the difficulty of amassing resources for expensive ventures or finding enough news to interest broad readerships, it is understandable why the religious press has been a weekly, monthly, or quarterly phenomenon and rarely a daily one. There have been very few experiments with a daily religious newspaper. Some European nations, like Germany or Holland, have religious dailies, the instruments of Christian-based political parties or movements. Without such parties in America, there was no market for such semisecular newspapers.

Shortly after the Second Vatican Council (1962–1965), there was talk that Roman Catholicism was so full of vitality, controversy, and news that it could sustain a daily. Robert Hoyt, who took the *Kansas City Reporter,* a diocesan paper in Kansas City–St. Joseph, Missouri, and turned it into a very controversial liberal weekly on a national basis, probed the possibility seriously. His failure to find a market or enough material has ever since been taken as a sign that the 50-million-member church, the largest religious group, could not promote such a paper. From time to time there is talk within the burgeoning Protestant conservative movement, which has prospered in the use of television in an era when such prosperity was not envisioned, of beginning a daily newspaper, but by the mid-1980s nothing had come of it.

One grand if partial exception has been *The Christian Science Monitor,* founded by Mrs. Mary Baker Eddy and the leadership of the Mother Church of the Christian Science movement in Boston. The *Monitor* is a highly respected paper with a national circulation. The kind of mutation that few envision happening twice, this newspaper began by holding the loyalties of Christian Scientists who welcomed its special perspective. Thus its reportage and editorial comment on death and disease reflect Christian Science's attitude toward the material realm, where mortality and disability, while real events that have to be covered, are also treated as somehow illusory. Similarly, Christian Scientists welcomed the daily editorial that spoke more directly to their own spiritual needs. Yet the paper could not survive only on institutional loyalty and won its following through general excellence in reporting and editorializing. To non–Christian Scientists, then, it is merely a highly respectable paper, not a sectarian one, and they can easily either overlook or assent to the mild statements of denominational views given their interest in the rest of the paper. By no means, however, is *The Christian Science Monitor* in any full sense of the term a religious paper devoted to news of religion. *The Washington Times,* financed by the Unification Church, is even more concerned to appear to be a secular newspaper that simply does not offend its "Moonie" investors; and it would offend its general readers if it devoted too much attention to Unification Church news. Such examples as these two simply prove the rule: the religious press in America makes little use of the daily newspaper.

Colonial America did not have, properly speaking, a religious press. Journals like *American Magazine,* founded in 1757 by the Rev. William Smith, were exceptional and hardly representative of the religious complexity of colonial life. In nine of the thirteen colonies religion was established by law. Thus the secular press in the northern colonies reflected the privileged world of New England Congregationalism just as instinctively as the legislative assemblies turned to a Congregationalist for Fast Day or Election Day sermons. Church and state were interwebbed, and non-Congregational churches were relatively few until late colonial times, so the religious outlook reflected the Congregationalist world as a given. Editors being what they have usually been, independent and critically minded people, they might criticize activities of religious leaders as well as praise them or merely report on them. Such activities were parallel to those of national newspaper editors who criticize nation, parties, and individuals, all against the background of general support for America itself. For this reason the papers were not and did not look religious, and no religious press can be said to have existed on a large scale.

In the southern colonies a similar situation prevailed in respect to Anglicanism, the officially established Episcopal church. In those colonies the church was often quite passive and quiescent. It attracted only a minority of the population and the nature of parish life was such that it rarely made news. So the colonial press in Virginia and the Carolinas was not a religious press and there was little religious news in its columns. Each parish communicated with its own faithful in direct ways, but there was little colony-wide dissemination.

In the Middle Colonies, the pluralism of religious interests kept the secular press from being devoted to religious news and inspiration. Meanwhile, the religious forces were themselves too dispersed or too lacking in imagination to see the potential of the printed word in their ministry.

The great change came early in the nineteenth century in Protestantism, toward the middle of the century in Catholicism, and a bit later in Judaism. During the Second Great Awakening and the expansion of religious energies into the West, Protestants discovered or invented a press to accompany their efforts. The churches were engaged in competition for the loyalties of people on the frontier and there was not enough manpower to reach all the settlers on a regular basis. For those among them who were literate, the religious press was an excellent instrument. Most of the competing denominations, in this case led by Methodists, Baptists, and a new group called the Disciples of Christ, began to encourage local and statewide papers and, particularly in the case of the Disciples of Christ, the journalist was to assume a very powerful role. Alexander Campbell used his *Millennial Harbinger* to rally people and explain his cause, offering religious "intelligence" to the people. Generations later, battles within the Disciples of Christ were to be fought through periodicals.

The press was not only an instrument in denominational competition and evangelization or the nurture of the converted. In this period there were interdenominational, often lay-led agencies that partook of what historian Charles Foster called an Anglo-American "Errand of Mercy." By such terms he and other chroniclers refer to a complex network of voluntary religious associations, usually Protestant based, designed to reform America, to address problems, to serve humanity. These agencies would not rely on the denominational leadership to propagate their causes, causes that such leaders often supported but also found distracting from other purposes. Instead, interlocking directorates of lay elites in Philadelphia, Boston, New York, and other centers raised money, stimulated support, and preached reform and welfare.

To illustrate the scope of these periodicals and their foci, Foster lists numbers of them. The most important was *The Quarterly Register of the American Education Society,* which flourished in Boston between 1827 and 1831. There were also a *Youth's Friend, Sunday School Journal, American Tract Magazine,* and any number of more general-sounding papers with names like *The American Christian Record.* That some of these had polemic interests can be safely deduced from two journals from 1828–1829 and 1830 in Lockport, New York, and New York City: *Priestcraft Exposed and Primitive Christianity Defended* and *Priestcraft Unmasked.* Between 1825 and 1849, from Washington, D.C., there issued the *African Repository,* promoting the energetic American Colonization Society, which tried to raise motivations and money for sending freed slaves back to Africa. In Boston from 1840 to 1849 *The Peace Advocate* promoted Christian pacific interests. The dates on these magazines point to another feature: their ephemeral nature. They rose and fell with causes that were in and then out of favor. They often expressed the dreams of amateurs who were overextended and underequipped for their tasks; yet they served vital purposes.

It might be said that for almost every Protestant cause in that era of the new voluntary organizations, there was a periodical. Just as some promoted revivals and social reform, others engendered interest in the foreign missionary activities that quickened American Protestantism after the second and third decades of the nineteenth century. It became urgent to raise pennies in Sunday schools and churches to train and support agents of religion in the Sandwich Islands, or the Middle East, or wherever. So *The American Biblical Repository* (New York, 1839–1850), *The American Missionary* (New York, 1857–1860), *The Massachusetts Missionary Magazine* (Salem and Boston, 1803–1808), *The Sailor's Magazine, and Naval Journal* (New York, 1828–1840), and scores of others filled the need.

Home missions, the development of churches in newly settled or underchurched areas, as well as the mission to Native Americans, were promoted through specialized journals. The role of the religious press in support of southern slavery and northern abolitionism is well known. While the slave religion of the American South had no religious press because literacy was formally discouraged or forbidden on the plantations, black freedmen and their churches relied on their own press. Some, like the pioneer *Freedom's Journal,* were generally secular but, churches being a thriving institution among freedmen, religious news was prominent. The "Bethelites," of the African Methodist Episcopal Church, had a paper of their own, the *Christian Recorder,* in Philadelphia between 1854 and 1862. After emancipation and with the spread of black churches in an age of increasing literacy, the church paper was the common instrument of dissemination.

Simple registers of religious newspapers in the pre–Civil War period run to book length. Thus historian Wesley Norton in his 1977 study of religious newspapers in the Old Northwest included an eighteen-page bibliography from that region alone. A sample from one page of titles will best make the point about diversity and the impossibility of even beginning to account here for all the major and some of the minor papers. There was the *Israelite* of Reformed Judaism in Cincinnati, and then a *Journal and Messenger* of Ohio Baptists. Following these and suggesting ethnic diversity were the *Journal de L'Illinois, Katholisches Wochenblatt,* and *Kirke Tidende fur Den Skandinavisk Evangelisk-Lutherske Kirke,* issued by French and German Catholics and Norwegian Lutherans in Illinois. *Licht-Freund* was a Cincinnati Universalist semi-monthly; after two mainstream Lutheran magazines, one in English and one in German, there follows the *Medium,* a Michigan Swedenborgian semi-monthly, followed, in turn, by Methodist magazines. Where subscription numbers are known, they are printed: 2,000 for the *Israelite,* 500 for the Norwegian Lutheran paper and that of the Universalists—signs that one did not need large constituencies in order to be motivated to issue a paper.

By the time of the Civil War the pattern was set: Protestant jurisdictions, Catholic dioceses, and Jewish movements, before there were denominations, would each encourage a house organ. Second, voluntary associations needed a periodical to promote their interests. Third, pioneers, innovators, and inventors of new sects or movements used the press to spread their causes. And finally, the press came to be the reflector and instigator of intradenominational conflict as well. The pattern having been set, it is more valuable to reflect on the scope and function of papers than to try to list more.

A historical notice of Catholic papers helps locate the functions. Historians conventionally date the birth of the Catholic press to 1807–1808 in Detroit. Since then hundreds of periodicals have been issued under Catholic auspices. Most widespread and influential have been the papers published by dioceses, the regional jurisdictions made up of a number of parishes and presided over by a bishop. The bishop tends to take ultimate responsibility for such papers, but through the years an elite of editors, often lay people, has been given wide responsibility for making their products solvent, faithful, lively, yet not departing from Catholic consensus. At their worst they simply and duly reflect an official line; at their middling and best they offer semi-independent editorials and more than one point of view on issues that Catholics may debate.

Such diocesan papers depend upon advertising and in many cases on a rather coerced parish support. Advertising deals not so much with goods for churches as for services performed by Catholics: funeral homes, tuxedo rentals, and flower shops; sometimes political candidates offer their products and services on the pages. Advertisers expect thereby to reach a Catholic community that is far less defensive than it had to be in the nineteenth century, that cannot depend as much as before on harassment and condescension by non-Catholics to hold the loyalties of the faithful.

A convenient and intentionally non-controversial *Catholic Digest* on the model of the *Reader's Digest* prospers. *Extension* magazine promoted the outreach of the Catholic Extension Society. *America,* sponsored by the Jesuits, has given a range of opinions about the shape of the church and came to be regarded as progressive during the Second Vatican Council. Beyond these are scholarly journals like *Thought* and *Theological Studies* or independent culture quarterlies like *Cross Currents,* which is ecumenical but operates from a Catholic basis.

Some religious orders develop publishing complexes. The Claretians, a small group that does most of its work in Latin America, poured energies into *U.S. Catholic,* a perennial prize-winner in the general readership category. Mixing interviews, polls, editorials, and long features of interest to Catholic families and inquirers, it was the flagship for an order that published a number of newsletters and *Salt.* This social justice magazine, like its counterparts, nudged the church from the left and contented itself with fewer subscribers than the general magazines could reach. On the Catholic left, however, none gained fame to match that of *The Catholic Worker,* founded by Peter Maurin and Dorothy Day in 1933.

Before the Second Vatican Council almost the entire Catholic press saw its role as defending the church, informing the faithful, building loyalty, and transmitting church teaching without question. After the council, all the independents and even many diocesan papers gave reflection to the new pluralism within the church. An impressive set of lay editors, among them James O'Gara at *Commonweal* and Robert Burns at *U.S. Catholic*—plus the stormier Robert Hoyt, who moved from *The National Catholic Reporter* to *Christianity and Crisis*—set the terms for the public side of the parochial press. Secular media came to quote these journals and thus greatly to enlarge their scope.

Normative has been the denominational paper that has taken on a house organ character. This aspect has made the journals both more credible to their sponsors and less credible to critical readers. The notion of a house organ is not surprising or unique. The secular society's agencies and businesses tend to use their own press to present the best possible images of their endeavors. Seen as public relations, they confirm the positive images of those who are already favorable to an organization and try to lure new people.

As house organs, the periodicals historically have been assigned the task of fulfilling denominational purposes. For some this has been a confessional one. The conservative Lutherans, for instance, who defined themselves doctrinally, would issue *Der Lutheraner* or *The Lutheran Witness* as expressions of the intransigent Missouri Synod Lutherans. The by-laws of the denomination stipulated that these organs must be censored, their doctrinal material approved; thus the reader was assured that all theological expression in the magazine's pages was reflective of the official position and was thus unassailably true. More liberal denominations might use their columns, on the other hand, to foster debate over the tradition and its contemporary expression. This meant that the periodical then presented the good image of a church body secure enough to allow diversity or dedicated to free debate.

Doctrine has not been so much the issue in the moderate, liberal, or internally diverse denominations. Sidney E. Mead has shown that the denomination in America has been used less to propagate creedal and confessional views than to express common goals, purposes, and programs. In those cases, and this would be fairly typical in the complex of *Advocates* put out by regionalized Methodism, doctrine would be muted, while devotion and the works of reform and welfare or service would be prime. In such cases, *house organ* usually does not mean a doctrinally cramped press but instead one designed to fulfill its responsibilities to support clienteles, stimulate more good works, and advertise the values of churches that "do things."

To say *house organ* does not mean, however, that all editors always agree completely with their sponsors. For one thing, not all sponsors can state clearly what it is that editors should agree about. Others encourage many kinds of questionings and disagreements as signs of vitality. Third, there is something about the vocation of editor that leads many away from contentment with simply echoing or parroting a party line. Often the editor is chosen for literary skills and a gift of expression that makes him or her stand out—sometimes as a maverick and sometimes more predictably to the left or right of most members of the supporting denomination. If an editor is too far out of step, this usually leads to restraint, modification, or loss of a job. Rather than use editorial energies to question denominational doctrinal positions or purposes, those responsible for publication more often become controversial by using the press as an instrument to enlarge the world of readers. Thus they may, in recent times, depict aspects of religious life in the Third World, where anti-Americanism is sometimes reflected in church life. Sometimes controversial men and women who represent frontier positions in the denomination are featured. Often editors will make use of a tradition against itself and alienate readers who have accommodated themselves to more recent unfold-

ings of the tradition. In other words, just as theologians have often moved from being custodians of a heritage to stimulating innovation, so more often than not, editors of house organs engage in house cleaning and *aggiornamento,* a creative "shaking up," usually taking care not to shake up the readership so much that they be dismissed.

A typical denominational periodical will include several feature articles, usually with a personal interest, demonstrating the life of faith through personalities. Others may deal with issues of church and world. Along with these will be some editorials on denominational and cultural themes. Toward the back of such a magazine will be news of the denomination: ordinations, moves of clergy, starting of new churches, dedication of buildings, anniversaries, deaths. In large national groups such news is sometimes regionalized in a supplement. Finally, book reviews encourage reading of books supportive of religious purposes or may criticize alien ones; in modern periodicals, there may be television or movie and record reviews as well. In other words, there is an eye on the surrounding world. In most cases, advertisements of religious books, furnishings, articles, or life insurance and representational advertising completes such a periodical. Whether the periodical represents Protestant denominations or Catholic dioceses, the format does not vary much.

The impact of such periodicals depends on several factors. First is the ability of the editors to present materials that will interest significant numbers of readers. Often periodicals make their way to homes through parish distribution, so that every member-unit receives them; readership may be much smaller than circulation. Equally important as a test of effectiveness, it must be said, is the intactness of the supporting group. Mainline Protestant and Catholic magazines and papers have experienced difficulties as they have moved into open acceptance of ecumenism and pluralism. The house organ may not capture as much reader interest as does the organ of a defensive and aggressive group. Thus a subscriber to *The Episcopalian* might more readily read *The Atlantic* or *Harper's* or get religious news from the religion sections of *Time* and *Newsweek.*

The journal of a conservative denomination, on the other hand, tries to provide cradle-to-grave coverage for its members. It publishes negative views of secular media and literature and critical opinions of all denominations but its own. The clergy are seen as mediators between the interests of the denomination and headquarters. These publications are concerned with boundary maintenance. Readers are more likely to get all their religious news except for momentary and accidental intrusions from this one source than from, say, television. Such high-walled and bounded groups have the advantage of promoting status within, thus leading to curiosity about fellow members. A Seventh-day Adventist or a member of the Christian Reformed Church will be interested in learning that a member received a civic award or made a professional football team. A Presbyterian or Roman Catholic whose life is less bounded by the denomination will find little of his or her world confirmed by such attention and will take sports news from *Sports Illustrated* or civic news from secular papers.

To focus on the denominational house organ, however, fails to do justice to another very vital band of publications, those that are ecumenical, interdenominational, or focused around purposes and viewpoints. They have the liability of having no automatic assent group and must work hard to keep circulation lists large. On the other hand, their asset is a plausibility that comes with the lack of an automatic constituency. Such journals, therefore, usually have much smaller circulations but relatively larger influence.

To illustrate this, without being wholly arbitrary, we shall concentrate on periodicals alphabetized under *C.* For a time in the 1960s, the secular Columbia University School of Journalism invited three other *C*'s to discuss issues of common concern at "Four C's Conferences": *Commonweal,* a lay Roman Catholic weekly; *Commentary,* a monthly sponsored by the American Jewish community and reflecting Jewish concerns but not confined to a representational viewpoint; and *Christian Century,* a liberal Protestant journal. To this list we shall add *Christianity Today,* an evangelical weekly, and *Christianity and Crisis,* another Protestant journal. These five can represent a larger class of independents.

Commonweal was founded in 1924, at a time when Catholics were moving from sheltered immigrant and ethnic life into the cultural mainstream. Michael Williams, a contentious and cre-

ative editor, saw a need to give expression to a culturally vital world Catholicism. He was more interested in Catholic philosophy than in the day-to-day life of the church. For that reason he resisted close institutional church ties and instead relied on wealthy backers who shared his vision. Some of the magazine's energies went into giving coherence to a Catholicism that was still highly particularized and dispersed. At other times Williams' staff presented the positive face of Catholicism in the face of lingering Protestant anti-Catholicism. The magazine was usually regarded as more congenial to the political left than was the rest of Catholicism, and its high-brow interests left it with a circulation of 15,000 to 30,000 in a church in which college graduates were very much the exception.

Through the mid-century years *Commonweal* became an instrument for defining the positive place of Catholicism in American literary and political culture. This alienated conservatives who wanted to preserve Catholic boundaries, but attracted those Catholics who welcomed the papacy of John XXIII and the ecumenically minded Second Vatican Council. The magazine opposed the tactics of Sen. Joseph McCarthy, a prominent Catholic right-wing ideologue, and came into its own during the presidency of John F. Kennedy, who seemed to mark the maturation of the Catholic presence in America. As post-conciliar Catholicism entered a period of chaos, the role of the *Commonweal* seemed a little less clear than before.

A partner in "Four C's" and other dialogues was *Commentary,* which came to be one of the most respected and controversial literary and political magazines in the nation. This well-subsidized high-quality journal was founded by the American Jewish Committee and was edited first by Elliot Cohen and then by Norman Podhoretz. Cohen was not expected to give day-to-day comment on Jewish life but to discuss the Jewish presence in a larger world view. He edited *Commentary* during a period of interest in other faiths and in the recovery and expression of Jewish theology. *Theology,* a Greek term, is not always a natural or congenial notion to American Jewish thinking. Yet in the 1950s, led by Abraham Joshua Heschel and Will Herberg and influenced by world figures like Martin Buber and Franz Rosenzweig, Jews at Reform's Hebrew Union College or Conservatism's Jewish Theological

Seminary and in rabbinates were exploring Jewish existentialism. The impact of the Holocaust had not yet been internalized in Jewish theology, but there was a recovery of biblical thought and attention to lore like that of Hasidism, a quasi-mystical branch popularized by Buber and others. The magazine reflected the generalized liberalism typical of Judaism shortly after mid-century.

In a changed world and under the editorship of Podhoretz, *Commentary* took a drastic turn, one that illustrates the ways in which the ecumenical religious press is often very much the reflection of the position of its editor-in-chief. For a time there was a significant decrease in Jewish interest. Then, after the Six-Day War in 1967 and the Yom Kippur War in 1973 and with increased interest in the Holocaust and after the suburban dispersal of ghetto Jews, real concern for Jewish survival led Podhoretz to question the relativism, pluralism, and relaxed character of Jewish life. He selected writers who were more conservative, just as he distanced himself from many of the more congenial ecumenical contexts that had been espoused earlier. By no means uncritical of Israel itself, the magazine was critical of those who wavered in support of Israel. There was some distancing from other racial groups; *Commentary* began to oppose quota systems that promoted access to American institutions by previously underrepresented groups, such as the blacks or Hispanics. Hard-line military support of Israel and anti-Sovietism attracted writers who were reacting against their own earlier socialist commitments. *Commentary* became a neoconservative leader in American politics and the arts.

Third of the religious three of the "Four C's" was *The Christian Century,* born among the Disciples of Christ and edited for thirty-nine years by Charles Clayton Morrison, who dominated it as Podhoretz later dominated *Commentary.* Morrison, who bought the magazine in 1908, turned it rather militantly into an "undenominational" and his successors named it an "ecumenical" weekly. Widely read in libraries and on campuses, indexed in the standard access guides to periodical literature, *The Christian Century* exercised influence far beyond the circle of its 30,000 to 40,000 subscribers. Morrison made it an instrument of the Protestant Social Gospel and strenuously promoted church unity. It must be said, however, that almost until the Second Vatican Council the magazine was anti-Catholic. It used a model of interfaith cooperation that stressed assimilation to an "American" and universal model and it feared Catholic particularism. On similar grounds, it was grudging in its support of Israel, which seemed to deny the assimilative models of Reform Judaism that Morrison had always supported. Pluralism was a problem for this liberal expression of an expansive Protestant outlook.

The Christian Century made its way in a time when denominational magazines seemed too sectarian, too cramped to comment on movies, general books, and affairs beyond their borders. As denominations opened up and enlarged their concerns, *The Christian Century* found new missions, prodding the churches and attracting controversial authors who won readership by the way they said things. The magazines became more of a forum and less ideological than it had been earlier. Under Harold E. Fey it altered its anti-Catholic and anti-Israeli stances; Kyle Haselden helped it become an instrument for racial concord and social justice; Alan Geyer stressed international peace during the Vietnam War era; James M. Wall guided it in a period when mainline Protestantism was on the defensive and needed new morale.

The Christian Century was squeezed, as it were, by a small magazine on the Protestant left and a large and prosperous one on the right, both also beginning with C. *Christianity and Crisis* was born before World War II under the leadership of Reinhold Niebuhr, a stellar contributing editor to the *Century* through the 1930s. Niebuhr repudiated that magazine's general pacifism, its reluctance to use military might against the threat of Hitler. *Christianity and Crisis* under Wayne Cowan and his associates became a more focused and less critical advocate of radical causes after the mid-1960s and consistently supported "liberation theology." Nondenominational and independent, the biweekly presents the liberal voice of Protestantism.

On the right was a much more powerful development. A schism had begun in Protestantism late in the nineteenth century. The ecumenical forces, symbolized by the Federal Council of Churches in 1908 and its successor after 1950, the National Council of Churches, stressed social action and justice but neglected evangelism and were liberal in doctrinal outlook. During the

1940s the more moderate heirs of Fundamentalism, the right-wing faction in denominations or the progenitor of smaller conservative denominations, regrouped in the National Association of Evangelicals and similar organizations. The prominence of evangelist Billy Graham in the 1950s led to high morale and expansiveness in this "Neoevangelical" front.

To further the movement, a number of progressive leaders chose Carl Henry to found *Christianity Today* in 1956. This fortnightly magazine was often belligerent toward liberal Protestantism, but in contrast to Fundamentalism was more open-minded about the culture. Henry wanted to stimulate "the uneasy conscience" of evangelicals to turn again to the social scene they had abandoned. His positions were generally quite conservative, supportive of presidents like Eisenhower, Nixon, and, under his successors, Reagan—though *Christianity Today* did not engage in formal endorsements. Editors opposed radicalism in the peace and civil rights movements, the feminist and homosexual rights movements, and in theology; and they rather consistently criticized the economic policies of the World Council of Churches, critical of capitalism as these were.

The original sponsors of *Christianity Today*, prosperous conservative Protestant lay people such as J. Howard Pew of the Sun Oil Company, may have had some natural influence on editorial policy. Yet it must also be said that the editors gave voice to the more intellectual and progressive sides of an otherwise extremely conservative movement. While *Christianity Today* could attack *Christian Century* and *Christianity and Crisis,* it was attacked, as was Billy Graham, from the Fundamentalist right for too much accommodation to moderates. This left a void to be filled by other magazines, including *The Fundamentalist Journal,* published by evangelist Jerry Falwell.

This sampling of five independents suggests several common features. In each case, the editor-in-chief is charged with the responsibility of setting terms, carving a space, attracting loyalties, and winning a place for the magazine's viewpoints. Second, with varying degrees of enterprise and energy, the magazines set out to nudge, not to represent, the formal organizational life of Protestantism, Judaism, and Catholicism. They are free to take up topics that house organs less easily address. They gain plausibility by the intrinsic contributions of their editorial work to the debates of a pluralistic, secular society in which religion has much influence. In all cases, they tend to have more cultural scope than do the ecclesiastical groups from which they draw readers. It should also be said that their existence is always a bit precarious, though less so when they have financial backers, as do *Commentary* and *Christianity Today.*

Reference having been made to a Protestant right-wing, brief mention of the Catholic right is in order. Before Vatican II it would not have been as relevant to type Catholic journals according to political or theological ideology. *Commonweal* and *The Catholic Worker* aside, the Catholic press was generally viewed as theologically conservative and politically moderate. In 1907 the Vatican had condemned modernism in theology. The American church, hardly touched by that movement but just beginning to encourage theological exploration, turned timid and for almost a half century gave little encouragement to experiment. Most Catholic theology was safe and conservative. The exception came to be the Jesuit journal, *Theological Studies,* which in the 1950s began to publish work on American pluralism by such outstanding figures as Gustave Weigel, S.J., and John Courtney Murray, S.J. Their views were vigorously opposed by the Vatican traditionalists of the *American Ecclesiastical Review.*

After Vatican II, progressives found voice in *The National Catholic Reporter* and, durably, in *Commonweal,* while many diocesan journals, edited by competent lay leaders, always under official auspices, supported the more "open" aspects of *aggiornamento,* that is, shaking up and reform. Surveys of editors of the diocesan papers suggest that they believe their readers think of the Vatican and the world church as "conservative" and the American church and its bishops and journals as "liberal." *Liberal* is a relative term, of course, but it is safe to say that in many dioceses, editors tilted toward liberal social programs, the civil rights and peace movements, criticism of social injustice and extravagant military defense expenditures, and the like. In this respect they were more liberal than many lay people on selective issues.

Reaction to post–Vatican II excesses inevitably set in, giving new life to some conservative papers. Already mentioned is *The National Catholic Register,* a weekly whose columnists stressed the cautious aspects of the council and published the works of the more traditionalist bishops and theologians. They cheered Pope Paul VI for his 1968 anti-birth-control encyclical *Humanae Vitae* and scorned the theologians who resisted it. The columnists were critical of Catholics who were not strenuously in the anti-abortion camp, who used historical-critical methods for interpreting the Bible, or who supported theological questioners like the German Hans Küng.

The accession of Pope John Paul II gave these conservatives new impetus to stress his conservative side, just as they downplayed his more controversial economic and social justice expressions. *Our Sunday Visitor,* more moderate than *The National Catholic Register,* was a defender of the papacy in such controversies. *The Wanderer,* the most extreme among conservative papers, successor to a German *Der Wanderer,* published in Minnesota, took an extremely hard-line position against moderates. Conservatives in the vatican highlighted this element of the American religious press, and Vatican officials gained much of their view of the state of the American church from such publications. This meant that attitudes toward doctrine and practice in America came not from the mainstream or the progressive papers but through the eyes of those who constantly looked for and pointed to what they regarded as deviation from the formal Catholic line.

Judaism has nothing quite like this situation of denominational and interdenominational contention through the press, although there are quarterly journals like *Tradition* for Orthodoxy, *The Journal of Reform Judaism* for Reform, and *Conservative Judaism* for Conservatism. Of course, they disagree with each other—otherwise, why three main "denominational" branches in Judaism? Yet these quarterlies tend to have more scholarly or rabbinic purposes, and while they are by no means uncontentious, they are less poised than the weekly, fortnightly, and monthly "throwaway" magazines to engage in battles over every cultural, political, and theological turn.

It is more difficult also to sort out what is the religious press in Judaism because of a more webbed relationship between religion and ethnicity. Most American magazines of the nineteenth century were edited by and for Protestant stock, but one would never think of listing *Harper's Weekly* or *The North American Review* as religious magazines. Chicago newspapers may pay great respect to the power of a 2-million-member Catholic diocese, but even if edited by Catholics they are not part of the religious press. Yet the great numbers of Jewish immigrants who fled the pogroms in eastern Europe after 1880 were served by Yiddish and other papers often listed as part of the Jewish press; but are they the religious press?

The answer should generally be "no," since the American Yiddish press usually was inspired by explicitly anti-religious forces: they may have been Zionist, socialist, or merely progressive. Yet in almost all cases they were aggressively secular; synagogue was something that one moved beyond, for the most part. There was respect for tradition and perhaps for High Holy Days and some kinds of observances that kept the Jewish community intact. But, as many observers pointed out, within a generation the people who moved from the European *shtetl* to the American ghetto left religious belief behind, and the papers reflected this.

Therefore, to read that at its peak in the decade after 1914 there were five Yiddish dailies in New York alone is not to counter our earlier generalization that religion news does not produce religious dailies. These were literary quasi-magazines that ministered to the needs of people who could not read English, preferred Yiddish, and had community concerns that metropolitan papers overlooked—yet were a highly literate group who could support such dailies. Best known of these papers was Abraham Cahan's *Jewish Daily Forward,* which the novelist founded before the turn of the century on New York's Lower East Side. Cahan was a gifted writer who attracted blue-collar and elite audiences alike. His paper had an anti-Zionist outlook for two decades, then it moderated; after Hitler came to power, it was pro-Zionist.

Under Cahan the *Forward* was militantly anti-religious, a viewpoint less fashionable in later decades. Yet, as late as the 1960s, it still on occasion published old-fashioned, anti-religious diatribes. Countering the *Forward* on the right was the more religious and much more conservative *Tageblatt,* which also had less influence. Also the *Morgen-Zhurnal,* while not being a religious publication, did promote Orthodox Judaism alongside its general "Americanism." The Yiddish press in any case was doomed to die with the disappearing language and new sets of concerns of fourth-generation Jews.

The American Jewish Year Book annually publishes lengthy lists of local or regional "Jewish Periodicals," many of them weekly and some monthly. Readers of these will find notices of religious services, editorials concerning religious dimensions of community life, and the like. For the most part, however, the communitarian and ethnic side of Jewish interests is what motivates publication, and the formally religious side, as expressed at synagogue, is muted.

This means that English-reading Jews, who make up the vast majority, are served more by a handful of quarterly journals than by weeklies or monthlies, and these journals tend to be directed more toward rabbis than to the general population. Reform's *American Judaism,* Conservatism's *United Synagogue Review,* and the Orthodox *Jewish Life* were monthlies with content of interest chiefly to the laity, while the *CCAR Journal, Tradition,* and *Judaism* look more like journals issued in Protestant and Catholic seminaries than like opinion or news journals. All of them find coherence in their support of Israel and their struggle against anti-Semitism, yet they tend to go denominational ways in interpreting Jewish practice and theology. Since the American Jewish community is much smaller than the Catholic and Protestant, and since the rabbinate numbers only a few thousand compared with the hundreds of thousands of Christian clerics, the boundaries of the Jewish publishing market are confining, with manifest limits to subscriber potential and, thus, futures.

Concentrating as we did on the tri-faith expressions in the religious press does a disservice to forces beyond them. American pluralism has always made room for great numbers of movements outside Protestantism, Catholicism, and Judaism. Thus Jehovah's Witnesses propagate their millennial vision through *The Watchtower.* Witnesses are expected to devote time each week selling this magazine on street corners, thus making it one of the more visible if, to outsiders, arcane expressions of the religious press in America. Christian Science has not only the semi-secular *Monitor* but also the *Christian Science Sentinel,* which is much more devoted to Christian Science healing testimonies and doctrines than is the daily; the *Sentinel* is featured in the windows of the Christian Science Reading Rooms.

From the first, the Church of Jesus Christ of Latter-day Saints, the Mormons, used the press to build loyalties if not to represent itself. In recent decades the *Ensign* has served Mormon adults; its glossy format cannot be matched in, say, Episcopalianism, where readers are more likely to get along without so much church news. The Mormons perfectly illustrate a case in which peoplehood matches denomination—the Mormons make up a distinct, unblended "people," who need and welcome a journal that helps define and motivate them. *The Deseret News,* the major Salt Lake City, Utah, newspaper, is owned by the church and has a "Church News" section that gives more prominence to Mormonism than the *Monitor* does to Christian Science. Yet it defines itself as and desires to be simply the metropolitan newspaper. Here, as in the case of Judaism, it is hard to see where the "people" stop and "religion" starts, though it must be said that *The Deseret News* is wholly favorable to the church while the Yiddish press was generally opposed to the synagogue.

More modern spin-offs from conventional Christianity also use the press, sometimes aggressively, to spread their message. Thus the Worldwide Church of God, founded and headed by Herbert W. Armstrong, produces the glossy *Plain Truth* and makes it available free of charge at many airport and supermarket newsstands. *Plain Truth* appears to be a magazine of general comment on world affairs, but it is always informed by and promotes the distinct millennial views of Armstrong, and has given visibility to his group far beyond its number of actual supporters.

Similarly, religious groups not of Christian provenance are more strenuous than the conventional groups in using the press for outreach. The sight of members of the Society for Krishna Consciousness selling *Back to Godhead* and other Hare Krishna periodicals is familiar at airports, and few must be the regular travelers who have not at least paged through these journals representing a form of religion from India, imported to and transmuted in America.

The Unification Church founded by Dr. Sun Myung Moon widely circulated *Unification News,* just as "anti-cult" parents have a set of journals to disseminate their views of the dangers associated with such intense religious groups.

THE RELIGIOUS PRESS

The organization of the religious press differs widely from magazine to magazine, group to group. Because they have limited circulations, most operate with low budgets, and editorial staffs must make their work part of a religious vocation: salaries are ordinarily lower than in the secular press. Yet most of the established religious journals have no trouble finding people eager to pursue the vocation. Many of them combine an interest in writing or editing with a religious vision and are willing and eager to work where there are fewer opportunities for economic advancement. The editorial personnel of religious publications are often trained at journalism schools; many, like Carl Henry, had experience in the secular newspaper world before undertaking religious publication. The talent is extensive; the limitations come from a lowering of imagination because of real or presumed constraints by easily offended sponsors or clienteles and from budgetary constraints.

The survival of the myriad religious publications was made possible in part by the fact that, as products of nonprofit institutions, religious journals were long subsidized by drastically reduced postal rates. Efforts by the postal service and the Congress to change this pattern led publishers and editors to unite across religious boundaries as never before to engage in rearguard, defensive, and more or less futile efforts to stave off new commercial rate schedules. The coming together, however, demonstrates that there are resources among organizations for common action. The Associated Church Press was historically largely Protestant but came to be more pluralist; the Catholic Press Association serves Catholics; an Evangelical Press Association attracts journals with attention focused on conservative Protestants, but many of the editors are also in the ACP. The Religious News Service issued for decades by the National Conference of Christians and Jews was rescued in the early 1980s, in a time of financial travail, by an agency of United Methodism. The news service serves a transdenominational purpose and supplies religious news to the secular press, on the model of the wire services, through daily bulletins. At the same time, the National Council of Catholic Bishops (formerly the National Catholic Welfare Conference) sustains a press service for the many diocesan papers, just as a Baptist agency serves the Southern Baptist Convention papers of each state. Such services make possible the coverage of news, a far too expensive venture for all but a few magazines to undertake on their own.

A balance sheet on the religious press suggests a spectrum of opinions as broad as the spectrum of publications. The general public is usually not aware of the religious press, except when an occasional story is picked up by secular wire services. Members of denominations or supporters of causes read their own journals, but might ignore alternatives. Public and college libraries catalogue numbers of religious journals, and scholars can draw upon those that are indexed. Indeed, most works of American history that feature religion are dependent in no small measure on the thousands of religious periodicals that advocate various causes. The letters to the editor, news items, editorials, and articles serve as one of the more efficient and relatively representative means of access to the mentality of church members. In this way, otherwise forgotten journals gain a second life and a hearing far beyond their original clienteles.

The periodicals live between two extremes. Those that service mainstream constituencies tread a fine line between denominational or movement features that provide the rationale for the magazines' existence and the secular environment in which members live. To be too "churchy" would lose the attention of the members, but to be too "worldly" is to attract them to areas where they could be lured and distracted from these churchly concerns. The mainline church magazines have suffered as their members live ever more exposed existences in the general culture. United Methodism saw its general magazine *Together* succumb, as did *A.D.*, a joint magazine of the United Church of Christ and the largely northern United Presbyterian Church in the U.S.A. The Episcopalian in the 1970s became an inexpensive, lightly subsidized shadow of its glossier former self. In contrast, *The Lutheran, The Lutheran Standard,* and *The Lutheran Witness* counted on long-held loyalties and retained impressive circulations into the mid-1980s.

Away from the mainline, another set of periodical editors, standing on the same boundary, have an easier role in that, literarily, many of their members "have no place else to go." That is, they are trained to hold negative and suspicious views of the approach of secular media to religion, to be wary of a conspiracy of humanists who would undercut religion. Most secular journals are to be avoided or read only critically. Meanwhile, readers are encouraged to view all of life through the norms of their own group. These publications tend to have less positive views of other religious groups and of the pluralist and secular cultures. They contribute to sheltered lives, cognitive minorities, the creation of "life-worlds," and structures of plausibility that can be called sectarian and can lead people far from the general concerns of the Republic. This is not the place to judge who has the bigger problems, since theological norms would have to be brought to bear to resolve them. They are brought up instead to illustrate the vocation and location of the religious press.

Almost all critics of the religious press criticize it for lack of imagination, trivialization, and the like. Satirists like to point to headlines such as TORNADO KILLS OKLAHOMANS, NONE OF OUR CHURCHES DAMAGED. Religious periodicals can make relatively captive audiences of their constituencies and engage in distortion of their worldviews, at some expense to the common religious and national or international life. They can deprive readers culturally by publishing shoddy writing and selecting weak topics.

On the other hand, while the scholarly and elite religious press sets out to raise professional standards, it must also be said that defenders find plenty to defend. The secular society does not and will not feed the legitimate religious needs of Americans; they have to provide their own sustenance. Pluralism can be a very confusing concept, one that starves by offering a buffet of equidistant options among which selectors have difficulty choosing. The common aspects of life that do so much to humanize the world—the calendar of events, the rites of passage, the achievements of ordinary people, the heroism of those who serve others—would go unreported in an ever more impersonal society, did the religious press not go out of its way to call attention to examples.

If theological and denominational prejudices or narrowed visions of social thought are often prevalent in the American religious press, it also has often served as an ecumenical agency, promoting understanding and empathy. If the religious periodicals have often been house organs, they have more often than not served to open windows to the outside and, at their best, to open doors so that people learn of a bigger world than they would otherwise have known. In any case, so long as religious groups and entrepreneurs have visions and causes, there is no stifling the impulses that give rise to the use of the printed word.

BIBLIOGRAPHY

Associated Church Press, *Directory* (1951); Eleanor Blum, *Basic Books in the Mass Media* (1980); Clarence S. Brigham, *History and Bibliography of American Newspapers, 1690–1820*, 2 vols. (1947); Catholic Press Association, *Catholic Press Directory* (1923); Harold E. Fey and Margaret Frakes, *The Christian Century Reader* (1962); Paul J. Foil, C.S.C., *Pioneer Catholic Journalism* (1930); James L. C. Ford, *Magazines for Millions: The Story of Specialized Publications* (1969).

Winifred Gregory, ed., *American Newspapers, 1821–1936: A Union List of Files Available in the United States and Canada* (1937); Howard Eikenberry Jensen, "The Rise of Religious Journalism in the United States . . . ," Ph.D. diss. (Chicago, 1920); Joseph T. Klapper, *The Effects of Mass Communication* (1960); Martin E. Marty, John G. Deedy, Jr., and David Wolf Silverman, *The Religious Press in America* (1963); Thomas F. Meehan, "Catholic Periodical Literature in the United States," in *Catholic Encyclopedia* (1911); Frank Luther Mott, *American Journalism: A History: 1690–1960* (1941, and later editions); Wesley Norton, *Religious Newspapers in the Old Northwest to 1861: A History, Bibliography, and Record of Opinion* (1977); Theodore Peterson, *Magazines in the Twentieth Century* (1964); Warren C. Price and Calder M. Pickett, *Journalism, An Annotated Bibliography, 1958–1968* (1970).

Mary Lonan Reilly, *A History of the Catholic Press Association, 1911–1968* (1971); John Tebbel, *The American Magazine: A Compact History* (1969); Mary Patrice Thaman, C.PP.S., *Manners and Morals of the Religious Press* (1954); Edna Brown Titus, ed., *Union List of Serials in Libraries of the United States and Canada*, 5 vols. (3rd ed., 1965); Rodger Van Allen, *The Commonweal and American Catholicism: The Magazine, the Movement, the Meaning* (1974); James Playsted Wood, *Magazines in the United States* (3rd ed., 1971).

[*See also* MASS COMMUNICATIONS.]

MASS COMMUNICATIONS

William Martin

THE "electronic church," though prominent in the national secular media only since the mid-1970s, is as old as radio itself. The first broadcast of a human voice, in 1906, was of a Christmas service that included the singing of "O Holy Night" and a reading from the Gospel according to Luke. And on 2 January 1921, just two months after KDKA in Pittsburgh became the first licensed radio station in America, the Calvary Episcopal Church began broadcasting its regular Sunday evening service. Religious leaders quickly recognized radio's potential as a tool for teaching and evangelism and, by 1925, approximately one-tenth of the more than 600 radio stations in America were owned and operated by churches and other religious organizations.

Almost from the beginning, the more liberal denominations tended to cooperate in their broadcast efforts. The Federal Council of Churches of Christ (FCCC), representing twenty-five denominations, began developing religious programs as early as 1923. A year later, the Greater New York Federation of Churches launched a program that became, when the NBC network was established in 1926, the "National Radio Pulpit." The first speaker of this distinguished series, Dr. S. Parkes Cadman, was followed by such masterful preachers as Harry Emerson Fosdick, Ralph Sockman, and David H. C. Read.

The decade of the 1920s, of course, was a time of great animosity between liberal and Fundamentalist Christians. To avoid involvement in this conflict or other forms of competition between various religious groups and factions, NBC invited the FCCC to serve as its sole source of Protestant programming, for which the network would give free time. Delighted with the arrangement, the FCCC formulated a policy whose first principle was that religious groups have a right to expect such free time, as part of the obligation of a station or network to offer public-service programming. Unofficially, but quite effectively, it also managed to cut Fundamentalist broadcasters off from access to the network. CBS, formed in 1927, accepted paid religious programming until 1931, at which time it followed NBC's lead, thus shutting another door to broadcasters whose theology or style might prove controversial or offensive.

Fundamentalists, accustomed to adversity, did not hang back, waiting for an invitation to preach. In 1922 evangelist Paul Rader began airing the services of his Chicago Gospel Tabernacle over his own station, WJBT ("Where Jesus Blesses Thousands"), and quickly saw his crowds swell mightily as people came to see in person the man they had heard on the radio. The following year, Omaha's WOW ("Woodmen of the World") began carrying the "Radio Chapel Service," a nondenominational program that continued until 1977. R. R. Brown, the program's principal speaker until his death in 1964, was known as the "Billy Sunday of the Air," at least in part because his distrust of microphones led him to shout and gesture at his listeners as if they were in the studio with him. Brown seems to have been the first radio preacher to have formalized the concept of the electronic church, inviting listeners to join the World Radio Congregation and issuing official membership cards.

Aimee Semple McPherson also moved quickly to take advantage of the new medium's power. In 1924 she observed that "it [has] now become possible to stand in the pulpit, and speaking in a normal voice, reach hundreds of thousands of listeners . . . [and] to carry on the winged feet of

1711

the winds, the story of hope, the words of joy, of comfort, of salvation'' (Ellens, 1974, p. 28). Coupled with her skills for promotion and drama, McPherson's use of radio made her one of the best known religious personalities of her time and the first nationally known Pentecostal evangelist.

Other noted preachers also proved successful in using radio as an extension of their pulpits. In 1927, John Roach Straton began, from New York's Calvary Baptist Church, what is today the nation's oldest continuing radio ministry. In 1928, Donald Grey Barnhouse, pastor of the Tenth Presbyterian Church in Philadelphia, became the first religious broadcaster to buy network time when he began airing the church's evening services over a hundred CBS stations. "The Lutheran Hour," which eventually became a major staple of religious broadcasting, soon joined Barnhouse on CBS, with Dr. Walter A. Maier as its speaker. And in Chicago, the Moody Bible Institute's WMBI, which received its license in 1927, not only aired an ambitious mixture of Christian programming that included music and drama as well as preaching, but developed many productions that it made available to other Christian stations.

A medium as powerful as radio, of course, was subject to exploitation and abuse, even from religious broadcasters. In Los Angeles, "Fighting Bob" Shuler reached estimated millions with broadcasts that often included sensationalist moralizing and racy exposés of corruption and wickedness among Los Angelenos, Christian and otherwise. Shuler helped elect a reform mayor, imprison a district attorney, and force a police chief out of office. It was said that no politician dared oppose him, particularly if his personal life was not free of taint. In 1931, Shuler's questionable tactics cost him his radio license and with it his popularity and power.

Another colorful maverick in religious radio's early history was Dr. John Romulus Brinkley, the father of "border radio." The "Doctor," who received his diploma-mill certification from "The Eclectic Medical University of Kansas City, Mo.," specialized in rejuvenation operations that involved replacing worn-out human testicles with those of a three-week-old goat. In 1923, Brinkley built radio station KFKB near his clinic in tiny Milford, Kansas, and began hawking patent medicines and extolling the wonders of his

operation. KFKB had one of the strongest signals in the nation, and Brinkley's four daily broadcasts raked in millions of dollars in the next seven years. When he was not on the air himself, he sold time to a variety of gospel singers and preachers, who also enjoyed good returns on their small investment.

In 1930, KFKB was voted the most popular station in the nation and Brinkley narrowly missed being elected governor of Kansas; in fact, had not so many ballots been discarded because his name was misspelled, it is probable he would have won the election. That same year, however, after an intensive campaign by the American Medical Association, which denounced him as a quack and a charlatan, Brinkley lost both his medical and radio licenses. Never one to accept impotence, he quickly bought a station in Villa Acuña, Coahuila, Mexico, just across the border from Del Rio, Texas. With 500,000 watts of power, this new station, XER (later changed to XERA), was ten times as powerful as the strongest U.S. stations, which were restricted by law to a maximum of 50,000 watts, and the second most powerful station in the world.

Much as he had done in Milford, Brinkley supplemented his own broadcasts with those of anyone willing to pay for the time. Because, under good conditions, XERA could be heard "from border to border and coast to coast," it attracted evangelists, naturopaths, country and western musicians, right-wing hatemongers, and hucksters who sold everything from amplified harmonicas ("Take it with you and play it right there in church. It sounds like a mighty organ") to gold-mine stock, rose bushes, and penny-a-day burial insurance. The good doctor and his fellow broadcasters prospered mightily until 1941, when U.S. pressure finally moved the Mexican government to revoke XERA's wave-length assignment and to dispatch soldiers from the Mexican Army to tear down the station and its towers. Brinkley was indicted for mail fraud but died in 1942, before he could be brought to trial. In 1947, "Mexico's radio outlaw," now renamed XERF, but reportedly owned by some of Brinkley's former associates, went back on the air. Its format, which had been adopted by other border stations, was not remarkably changed.

In Royal Oak, Michigan, Father Charles Coughlin expanded a children's story program, begun over one station in 1926, into a nationally heard and highly controversial mix of religious, economic, and political comment that moved his listeners to write and to send money to support his broadcasts. As his eloquent preaching drew larger audiences, Coughlin formed the Radio League of the Little Flower (named for his tiny parish church), added stations in Chicago and Cincinnati, and, in 1930, signed a contract with the CBS network. With the onset of the Depression, Father Coughlin began to criticize "unregulated capitalism" and to castigate people of wealth and power who were "dulled by the opiate of their own contentedness." His attacks on President Herbert Hoover led CBS to ease him off the air in 1931, but he quickly developed a network of independent stations that carried his program throughout the eastern half of the United States. Air time alone cost him $14,000 a week, but his audience was estimated at a phenomenal 45 million. One sermon alone drew a response of 1.2 million letters.

Coughlin used his tremendous popularity and brilliant rhetorical skills to achieve great political power. He was credited with being the one man most responsible for the election of Franklin D. Roosevelt to the presidency. He organized a political lobby of 5 million members, and in 1934 he got his listeners to flood Congress with 200,000 letters in a protest against the establishment of the World Court. By this time, Coughlin was receiving more mail than any other individual in the world, and that mail contained more than $500,000 a year. As the 1930s progressed, Coughlin grew increasingly intemperate and began to engage in personal attacks, particularly against President Roosevelt, on whom he had cooled considerably. He began to characterize the president as "Franklin Doublecrossing Roosevelt" and threw his support behind the unsuccessful Union party in the 1936 election. When Roosevelt appointed former Klansman Hugo Black to the Supreme Court, Coughlin denounced the president as "stupid," a remark that led to a reprimand from the bishop of Detroit and the cancellation of his broadcasts. Late in 1938, however, Father Coughlin returned to the air, but instead of moderating his approach, he became even more radical, speaking out in sympathy for Nazis, blaming Jews for economic problems in the United States and the war in Europe, and, in his newspaper, *Social Justice,* calling for Roosevelt's impeachment. This time,

Coughlin's excesses cost him his audience. Income dropped precipitously and, under pressure from the National Association of Broadcasters, most stations refused to sell him any further time. In 1942 the government threatened to charge him with treason, and his bishop offered him the choice of keeping silent on social issues or leaving the priesthood. Coughlin chose to remain a priest and continued to serve his parish until his retirement in 1968, but he was never again involved in politics, even on a local level.

Several more conventional ministries still in operation in the mid-1980s were begun in radio's pioneer period. Herbert W. Armstrong established his "Radio Church of God" in 1934, J. Harold Smith launched the "Radio Bible Hour" in 1935, M. R. DeHaan inaugurated the "Radio Bible Class" (forerunner of the "Day of Discovery" television broadcast) in 1938, Theodore Epp began the "Back to the Bible Broadcast" in 1938, and Harry Schultze, followed soon by Peter Eldersveld and later by Joel Nederhood, launched the Christian Reformed Church's "Back to God Hour" in 1939. But none of these men was more successful in his time than Charles E. Fuller, founder of "The Old Fashioned Revival Hour."

Fuller began teaching Bible lessons during the 1920s over a station owned by the Bible Institute of Los Angeles (BIOLA). In 1930 he started airing services from his independent Calvary Church in Orange County and included a phone-in segment, one of the first audience-participation talk shows in radio. Though Fuller was its founder, the Calvary Church did not approve of his broadcasts, and he left the church in 1933 to enter a full-time radio ministry, supported solely by contributions from listeners. Despite the fact that this was the low point of the Depression, contributions ran ahead of expenses and Fuller began to add stations. By 1937, "The Old Fashioned Revival Hour," originating in Long Beach, was being aired coast-to-coast on thirty stations of the new Mutual Broadcasting System, which had departed from the precedent set by NBC and CBS and was selling large blocks of prime Sunday evening time to religious broadcasters. By the middle of 1943, "The Old Fashioned Revival Hour" and a second Fuller program, "The Pilgrim's Hour," were being heard over a thousand stations at an annual cost of $1.5 million for air time alone, and Fuller's Gospel Broadcasting Association was buying 50 percent more time than the secular company in second place. His success soon led him to found Fuller Theological Seminary, one of the most respected of all evangelical schools today.

Fuller's preeminence among evangelical broadcasters gave him, without his having sought it, a central role in shaping the strategy virtually all electronic ministries would eventually use in getting their programs to the public. Since approximately one-fourth of its total revenue was coming from religious broadcasting by 1943, the Mutual System resisted the recommendation of the Federal Council of Churches against selling time to media ministries. But, with added blandishments from national advertisers who coveted the choice time periods used by the electronic evangelists, the network did relegate such broadcasts to the less favorable Sunday morning slots and set a half hour as the programs' maximum length. Rather than accept the switch, Fuller lined up a makeshift network of independent stations and sent them recordings of his programs, which they could play at whatever time was available. This same procedure is now used by most contemporary religious broadcasters heard on more than one station.

In 1949 the American Broadcasting Company, which had donated time to representatives of the three major faiths since it was formed in 1943, began losing advertising revenue to television and invited Fuller to purchase time for a transcribed program to be aired over its 280 stations every Sunday morning. The shift brought a drop in listener response, but in 1950 a live afternoon broadcast achieved a Nielsen ranking as the third most popular daytime program on radio. Fuller continued his radio ministry until a few months before his death at age 80 in 1968.

After two decades of infancy and adolescence, religious radio reached a kind of maturity in the 1940s. This was manifested primarily in a recognition of the strength that comes from unity and numbers and also of the need for what amounts to a trade association to help encourage high standards, curb excesses, serve as a clearinghouse for information and a forum for the exchange of ideas and concerns, and represent broadcasters' interests in dealings with the Federal Communications Commission and other governmental bodies. For Evangelicals, the key organization has been the National Religious

Broadcasters, chartered in 1944 and closely aligned with the National Association of Evangelicals, which had been formed in 1941 in an effort not only to promote conservative Protestant Christianity but also to overcome the divisive spirit often present in Fundamentalist and evangelical circles. The Federal Council of Churches continued to play that role for most mainline churches, but several denominations—specifically, Congregationalists, Methodists, the (mostly northern) Presbyterian Church in the U.S.A., Evangelical and Reformed, and the United Church of Canada—banded together in 1944 to form the Joint Religious Radio Committee (JRRC). Led by Everett C. Parker, the JRRC experimented with a variety of non-preaching formats and with tape syndication of its programs. In 1948 it merged with the FCCC, and, when the Federal Council changed its name to the National Council of Churches in 1950, what had been the JRRC became the NCC's Broadcast and Film Commission.

In 1945, several denominations, including the Southern Baptist Convention, the Methodist Church, the Protestant Episcopal Church, and the Presbyterian Church in the United States, moved to initiate or enhance their broadcast ministries through formation of the Southern Religious Radio Conference, which also encouraged non-preaching formats, airing mostly on free time provided by networks or local stations. Two years later the Southern Baptist Convention, which had been involved in local and denomination programs for many years, withdrew from the conference to form the Radio and Television Commission, which remains one of the most important and innovative forces in religious broadcasting today. With the exception of "The Catholic Hour," a national broadcast promoted by laymen, Roman Catholic religious broadcasting during this period was limited to local efforts.

By 1950 the foundation and framework of the radio division of the electronic church were well in place, so that most of the changes that have occurred since then have been changes of enormous growth, notable technological developments, and concomitant pressures for improvements in quality. The essential features of large-scale radio ministries remain quite similar to what they were at mid-century: evangelists record their programs, buy time on stations that will play their tapes, and pay their bills by requesting contributions from their audiences, whether on the air, in personal appearances, or by direct mail. Since the evangelists pay a fee roughly equivalent to the costs of air time plus the revenue that would be earned if the station sold advertising, station owners are freed not only from the burden of selling advertising, but even from worrying about whether or not anyone is actually listening. Further, since the programs are taped, personnel needs are significantly reduced; often, a single technician and announcer can handle most of a day's broadcasting chores, and even the announcer's contributions can be taped and simply inserted between programs. As case after case has demonstrated, these factors make it possible to convert a money-losing secular station—whether already owned or picked up at a bargain price—to a religious format and to show a profit in a matter of months. Though some religion-oriented stations are nonprofit and others appear to operate from motives that are predominantly religious, at least one reason for the proliferation of such stations is that they are a dependable, relatively trouble-free source of substantial gain for their owners.

In addition to broadcasts on local stations and fledgling attempts to establish Christian radio networks by means of satellite and cable technology, many ministries make extensive use of super-power stations in their efforts to reach foreign countries, some of which will not allow Christian broadcasts to originate within their borders. In 1984 some 60 organizations were operating over 125 transmitters internationally. Several important organizations stand out: the World Radio Missionary Fellowship of Miami, Florida, which operates HCJB, a 500,000-watt installation in Quito, Ecuador; the Far East Broadcasting Company of La Mirada, California, with 28 stations in various parts of the world; Trans World Radio of Chatham, New Jersey, which operates six transmitters with a combined power of 5 million watts and broadcasts in 73 languages; and ELWA ("Eternal Love Winning Africa") in Monrovia, Liberia, which holds the distinction of broadcasting in the largest number of languages (almost 50) from a single location.

As this abbreviated sketch makes clear, the electronic church has a long and vigorous history and has proved to be an extraordinarily durable aspect of both religion and radio in America.

Still, religious broadcasting would probably never have become a topic of wide discussion and concern in recent years had it not been for developments in television, whose kingdom, power, and glory were just beginning to be understood as radio religion achieved stability at mid-century.

As had been the case with pioneer radio, early experiments in television included religious programming. When NBC began limited telecasting in 1939–1940, the Federal Council of Churches assisted in arranging for productions aimed at Protestants, Catholics, and Jews. Its first production, "I Believe," featured a discussion by noted theologians of the relationship between religion and everyday life. This was soon followed by a children's show that used puppets to dramatize biblical stories. These programs, and such later NCC productions as "Directions," "Lamp Unto My Feet," and "Frontiers of Faith," proved a welcome change from the rather stodgy preaching format of FCCC radio programs and helped inspire other religious organizations to more imaginative use of the new medium. The Seventh-day Adventist Church began its innovative and flexible "Faith for Today" program in 1950 and its star, William A. Fagal, became the first television pastor. In 1951 the Missouri Synod Lutherans inaugurated the dramatic series "This Is the Life."

In similar fashion, the Southern Baptist Convention launched its national television ministry in 1954 with a series of films based on the parables of Christ. From that beginning the SBC's Radio and Television Commission produced an impressive array of dramas, documentaries, biographies, cartoons, musical productions, and other films designed for television. Another denomination active in television in the 1950s was the (mostly southern) Presbyterian Church in the United States, with a fifteen-minute interview program called "Layman's Witness" and other efforts that featured more conventional preaching and teaching. In the mid-1960s the United Church of Christ presented a provocative series called "Tangled Web," consisting of lectures on the applications of Christianity to major social problems.

While these pioneers experimented with approaches and forms they felt television not only made possible but required, the most successful religious telecast was a Catholic program whose set consisted of a chair, a blackboard, a table, and a Bible, and whose entire cast was a single preacher. The preacher, of course, was Bishop Fulton J. Sheen, and that made all the difference. Though what a biographer described as his "wanton arrogance" made him unpopular among his priestly colleagues, Sheen was already widely known to Americans as a popular author and as the speaker on "The Catholic Hour" radio program since 1930. When he made the switch to television in 1951, his carefully prepared sermons, a commanding physical presence that was magnified by his black cassock and red cape, a speaking manner that combined humor, drama, and classical rhetoric, and the impression of absolute confidence in what he was saying won him an ecumenical audience that responded to his messages with as many as 6,000 letters a day at the height of his popularity. Sheen's success, however, did not sit well with his superior, Cardinal Spellman, and the program was cancelled in 1957. An unsuccessful attempt to revive it in 1959 demonstrated that preachers, like other entertainers, can fall from public favor with disheartening suddenness.

Bishop Sheen's success notwithstanding, the greater expense and expertise required for television, the lack of access to the major networks, and a recognition that the people from whom they drew most of their support were underrepresented among set owners combined to make most evangelical preachers wary of embarking on a television ministry. The first of the independent electric preachers to utilize the new medium as a significant aspect of his ministry was Rex Humbard, who began telecasting services from his church in Akron in 1952. "I saw this new thing called television," he recalled, "and I said, 'That's it.' God had given us that thing . . . the most powerful force of communication to take the Gospel into . . . every state in the union."

Three years later Oral Roberts exploded assumptions of what could and could not be done on television by bringing the heat and sweat and tension and excitement of his miracle healing services right into the living rooms of hundreds of thousands of people who had little previous awareness of or experience with such phenomena. Roberts continued to use this tent-service format until 1967, when he terminated his crusade ministry and his program; he returned to television in 1969 with the variety show/interview/low-key preaching format that has become a trademark for him. For a short while in the early 1950s, Billy Graham hosted an interview program on ABC-TV, but he admits somewhat ruefully that he has never met a single person who saw one of the programs. A studio program was also undistinguished. For Graham, the real entry into television came with ABC's coast-to-coast broadcast of his 1957 New York crusade from Madison Square Garden.

Despite these beginnings, Evangelicals found television difficult to crack until the latter part of the 1960s. The National Council of Churches was still adhering to its official policy of refusing to pay for air time and to its unofficial practice of keeping Evangelicals out of the time it did receive. On the other side, both the networks and major local stations preferred to donate time to religious organizations as part of their FCC obligation to present public service programming, and the organizations they chose to benefit were seldom evangelical ones. The breakthrough for Evangelicals, particularly the independent religious broadcasters—i.e., those who, like Graham, Roberts, and Humbard, were neither sponsored by nor answerable to denominational authority—came with the rise and near fall of independent UHF (ultra high frequency) television stations.

As the struggle with the better reception, superior programming, and established reputations of VHF (very high frequency) network affiliates pushed UHF stations to the brink of bankruptcy, the latter began selling time to religious broadcasters just for the financial security offered by 52-week contracts. Owners of UHF stations soon discovered what some of their colleagues in radio had long understood: that the electric preachers, who buy an entire hour or half hour, thereby removing pressure to sell advertising, can be a godsend. To make this arrangement even more appealing to the owners, the FCC ruled in 1960 that a station's public service obligation could be met by paid religious broadcasts as well as by those for which time was given free. Given the choice between donating time and being paid for it, more and more station owners quite understandably opted for "doing well by doing good." This situation not only fostered the growth of evangelical programming on secular stations, but contributed significantly to the birth (or rebirth) of television stations with a religion-oriented format. Increased availability of Christian programs and the demonstrable existence of a relatively small but fiercely loyal audience for such programs have led individuals and organizations with religious as well as economic motives to realize that a commercial station that has lost money or gone bankrupt with a predominantly secular format might succeed as a tax-free, nonprofit station with a predominantly religious format.

A further important result of the acceptance by stations of paid religious broadcasts has been the diminution of the role of mainline denominations in such broadcasting. Since most mainline churches have regarded air time as a right rather than as a commodity for which they should be expected to pay, and since even those that were willing often had neither the money to pay nor the desire to engage in the kinds of solicitation most evangelical broadcasters used, Evangelicals have gained a virtual monopoly in religious radio and television, purchasing over 90 percent of all broadcast time devoted to religion. The remainder is divided among those Roman Catholic and mainline Protestant churches whose members constitute approximately 70 percent of American Christianity. Mainline groups have manifested great concern over this situation, but have been unable to devise an effective counterattack. In 1980, for example, the United Methodist Church announced a $25 million plan to purchase a major television station that would serve as a production and broadcast center for the denomination. A few months later, after fund-raising efforts had not only fallen far short of the goal, but had forced cutbacks in other aspects of the denomination's work, the television project was severely curtailed. Sobered by this experience, other major religious bodies have been reluctant to launch similar efforts.

The development of religiously oriented UHF stations has been accompanied and enhanced by the advent of communications satellites, cable, and various low-power television devices that have made national networks of Christian broadcast facilities both technically and economically feasible. Communications satellites such as RCA's SATCOM, Western Union's WESTAR, and Southern Pacific's SPACENET are placed into space at such a distance from the earth that they rotate in a geosynchronous orbit; that is, they maintain a fixed position in relation to the

earth, so that they seem to be "parked." Signals bounced off them from earth-station transmitter stations, commonly referred to as "uplinks," return to a specific coverage ("footprint") area that may be as large as the entire United States. The satellite-relayed signal can then be picked up by earth-station dishes anywhere in the coverage area and transmitted to local viewers either by the airwaves, on standard or low-power transmitters with a radius of 10 to 25 miles, or by cable. Organizations such as the Christian Broadcasting Network, the PTL Network, the Trinity Broadcasting Network, the National Christian Network, the Southern Baptist Convention's American Christian Television System (ACTS), the Roman Catholic Eternal Word Television Network, the Catholic Telecommunications Network of America, and the Jewish Television Network have all used some combination of these methods to establish religious television systems that offer a full or partial schedule of religious and family-oriented programs as an alternative to the fare available on the major networks.

The most successful of these networks has been the Christian Broadcasting Network (CBN), headquartered in Virginia Beach, Virginia. Begun by Yale Law School graduate M. G. "Pat" Robertson in 1960, CBN has grown from a single UHF station, the first television station ever to devote more than 50 percent of its air time to religious programming, to the second largest cable operation in America. In addition to a variety of preaching and teaching programs and the "700 Club," a talk show that serves as the network's anchor program, CBN offers a twenty-four-hour lineup that includes news, sports, movies, adventure programs, and situation comedies. To make sure the Lord's vineyards will have plenty of qualified workmen to trample out the vintage, in the fall of 1978 Robertson founded CBN University, which offers training in communications, education, law, theology, and various other disciplines.

The North Carolina–based PTL network, headed by Jim Bakker until he resigned early in 1987 amidst charges of sexual irregularities and financial corruption, and the Trinity Broadcasting Network, led by Paul Crouch and headquartered in Santa Ana, California, are smaller versions of CBN. The National Christian Network, begun in Cocoa, Florida, is even more a product of new developments in communications technology than its three forerunners; however, it serves primarily as a distribution service for broadcasters who wish to utilize its satellite channel and uplink facility. After several years of severe financial difficulties, this cable operation was purchased in 1986 by Jerry Falwell, the leader of the Moral Majority. His nonprofit umbrella group, Old Time Gospel Hour, Inc., has renamed it the Liberty Broadcasting Network.

The most ambitious effort yet undertaken by a denomination is the Southern Baptist Convention's American Christian Television System. In the spring of 1984, ACTS began transmitting a mixture of religious and "wholesome" secular programs via satellite to a hybrid network whose main component is more than a hundred low-power stations scattered throughout the nation. To spare viewers the annoyance of appeals for funds by stations or program producers, each station is financed and supported primarily by local churches in its broadcast area. The Catholic Telecommunications Network of America launched a more modest effort in 1982. This network transmits specialized programming to receiving dishes owned by local dioceses; the programs may then be recorded and used in schools and hospitals or broadcast over local cable or commercial facilities. Another Catholic effort, the Eternal Word Television Network, operated by Mother Angelica and nuns from the tiny Our Lady of the Angels Franciscan monastery in Birmingham, Alabama, resembles a miniature version of CBN or PTL. Finally, though Jews in America have shown little interest in either evangelism or religious broadcasting, the small Los Angeles–based Jewish Television Network uses cable systems in an effort to provide religious and traditional cultural programming for Jews unaffiliated with temples or other Jewish organizations.

In the mid-1980s the bulk of religious telecasting consisted of four major components. In the first category, and comprising an ever-diminishing segment of air time, are long-running ecumenical and denominational programs: the NCC's "Lamp unto My Feet," the Lutherans' "This Is the Life," the Seventh-day Adventists' "Faith for Today," the Paulist production "Insight," the Church of Christ's "Herald of Truth," and a few others. The audience for these programs is modest, typically between 200,000 and 500,000 viewers for the entire nation. Like most religious broadcasting, these programs serve mainly to nurture those already adhering to the sponsoring faith.

The second component consists of weekly worship services televised over local stations by individual congregations. The number of these has also shrunk in recent years as stations have begun to charge churches for air time they once donated. Because of small audiences, most of these broadcasts probably have little impact beyond making local pastors and congregations feel they are doing something significant. But some such programs—mainly those with outstanding preachers—have unquestionably fostered notable growth in the sponsoring congregations, and a few have been so well received that they have moved to syndication on local stations and cable systems.

The third major component of televised religion is comprised of syndicated programs, produced by Graham, Humbard, Roberts, and more recent televangelists such as Jimmy Swaggart, Robert Schuller, Jerry Falwell, Pat Robertson, Jim Bakker, James Robison, Kenneth Copeland, and Charles Stanley. The efforts of these men, brought to national attention by the involvement of Falwell, Robison, and Robertson in the 1980 elections, generated much of the enormous media attention devoted to religious broadcasting and gave rise to the term *electronic church*.

The fourth component consists of the cable and satellite networks mentioned above. There is, of course, considerable overlap between these components, particularly in the placing of local and syndicated programs on the schedules of cable and satellite networks. Because of the increased cost of time on local secular stations, it seems likely that most of the new growth in religious telecasting will occur in the realm of cable and satellite technology. Local churches will probably be offered access to channels on some new cable systems, but lack of experience, lack of confidence in the usefulness of the enterprise, and the cost of providing cameras and other production equipment will likely combine to discourage extensive use at this level, at least until experimental efforts prove it can be successful and guidelines and methods are established for more effective employment.

Another intriguing but little-discussed possibility would be the establishment of electronic churches whose reality would match the metaphor. Evangelical entrepreneurs have laid the groundwork for such institutions by merchandising videocassettes of sermons, lectures, and other instructional materials. Some denominations, such as the Assemblies of God, have begun beaming programs via satellite to receiving dishes attached to church buildings, so that congregations all over the nation could watch the same programs simultaneously. Though most of the independent ministers profess to be supporters of the local church, it would be rather simple for them to set up "franchise" churches. A man or woman approved by the evangelists, perhaps trained at their colleges or institutes, could serve as pastor or administrator. By using videocassettes and satellite technology, classes and worship services could be led by the media ministers themselves. Such a vision has ominous overtones, but it is plausible that a franchise pastor might be a good one, that the preaching and teaching in many churches might be improved by such measures, and that a polity might be worked out that would avoid some of the potentially corrupting tendencies inherent in a religion centered around a media "star." On this and other matters, the future of the electronic church is difficult to predict, but it seems likely that religious broadcasters will continue to seek bold and inventive ways to exploit every form of communications technology in their efforts to expand their ministries and to preach the Gospel to the whole creation.

Though the future of religious broadcasting is unclear, the accumulation of reliable data during the 1980s has made it possible to provide reasonably confident answers to some recurring questions about the present scope and impact of broadcast ministries. Perhaps the most basic of these questions pertains to the size and composition of the audience for religious broadcasting. Who actually watches and listens to television and radio preachers? When national media became fascinated with the electronic church during the election campaign of 1980, most—including the *New York Times*, the *Wall Street Journal*, *Newsweek*, *U.S. News and World Report*, and various other secular and religious journals—credited the electronic evangelists with audiences ranging from five to more than a hundred times their actual size, stirring unrealistic alarm or false hope, depending on one's point of view. Some media ministers avoided such claims, but others

gave new meaning to the phrase "evangelistically speaking," which refers to the tendency to count arms and legs instead of heads. However much these estimates by news media and religious broadcasters differed from one another, they shared one feature: they all were absurd.

In contrast to these extravagant and divergent claims, over a decade of audience surveys, including not only the regular reports of the Arbitron and Nielsen rating services, but also studies conducted by the Harris and Gallup organizations, by market research companies hired by broadcasters, and by various academics, have provided a more modest and remarkably uniform picture of the audience for religious broadcasts. This picture was further reinforced by a major study, completed in 1984, that was funded by a consortium including the National Council of Churches, the National Religious Broadcasters, leading denominational bodies, and several major broadcast ministries, and conducted jointly by the Gallup Organization and the Annenberg School of Communications at the University of Pennsylvania. Based on the findings of these studies, it appears that approximately 13 million people (6 percent of the national television audience) watch religious television on a regular basis.

A 1985 study commissioned by the Christian Broadcasting Network and conducted by the A. C. Nielsen Company, using a metering system in which individual television sets were wired to computers that automatically recorded the channels to which the sets were tuned, reported a significantly larger audience for religious broadcasting than other studies had found, claiming that 40 percent of the nation's households (approximately 61 million Americans) tuned in a religious broadcast at least once a month. Closer analysis, however, revealed that households were counted as viewers of religious broadcasts if their sets received such broadcasts for as little as six minutes a month. Researchers involved in the Annenberg/Gallup study contend that most of the larger audience claimed by interpreters of the Nielsen study disappears when the criterion for viewership is raised to the extremely modest figure of fifteen minutes a month, and that when more plausible criteria were used, they could find no evidence of an audience for religious television significantly larger than the one reported in their study.

According to most studies, no religious broadcasters attract even an average 2 percent of the viewers in the markets in which their programs are aired. Almost two-thirds of the audience are over fifty; only about 15 percent are under thirty-five. Over 60 percent are female, with black women more likely to watch than white women. Less than 10 percent report a total household income in excess of $25,000, and 41 percent report less than $10,000. Predictably, this lower income level corresponds to modest educational and occupational attainment; a Gallup study entitled *The Christian Marketplace* found that only 15 percent of those who express a strong preference for televised religion have attended college, and 26 percent did not complete high school. The same study found that laborers are more than four times as likely to view religious programs as professional people. Thus, the audience for religious television is drawn predominantly from the lower middle, working, and lower classes.

The audience also manifests distinct regional patterns, with southerners four times more likely to watch than easterners and three times more likely than westerners. In fact, over 80 percent of those who prefer religious shows live in the South or Midwest; and nine of the ten top syndicated television ministries draw at least half their audiences from twelve southern states, Texas, Oklahoma, New York City, and Los Angeles. Only Robert Schuller enjoys a more evenly spread distribution. Residents of rural areas and small towns with a population of less than 2,500 are eight times more likely to watch such programs than are dwellers in cities with a population of more than 1 million, and almost 60 percent of the audience is found in cities with fewer than 25,000 inhabitants. The audience for religious radio is similar to that for religious television in most respects; one interesting difference is that black males are more likely to listen to religious radio than to view religious television, probably because radio offers far more broadcasts by black ministers.

This composite picture bears a striking resemblance to the demographic portrait of Protestant evangelical Christians in America and, indeed, no single factor is more strongly associated with viewing religious programs than belief in the tenets of evangelical Christianity. With the exception of certain subgroups such as the elderly, the handicapped, and recently divorced people, regular viewers are also likely to be at least moderately active members of a local congregation. For them, religious broadcasts constitute a fairly stable component of religious expression, not a substitute for other forms of religiosity.

Much of the attention given to religious broadcasting since the 1980 election campaigns has focused on the efforts of some television evangelists to mold this audience of churchgoing Evangelicals into a powerful political force. In considering the impact of religious broadcasting on politics, it is important to remember that only a small number of its practitioners have participated in these efforts. Some of the most popular television preachers—Robert Schuller, Oral Roberts, and Rex Humbard, for example—carefully avoid identification with political figures or causes. A few others make occasional statements that have political overtones, particularly about Israel, but only three televangelists with a wide following had much to say about electoral politics in 1980: Jerry Falwell, James Robison, and Pat Robertson. Since then, Robison has reduced, but not ceased, his activity in the political arena and Jimmy Swaggart has become much more involved. Others may well enter the ranks, but there is no clear trend in this direction. So it is largely with the work of a small, but nevertheless notable, minority of religious broadcasters that the following remarks are concerned.

In 1976, New Right political leaders Richard Viguerie, Paul Weyrich, and Howard Phillips announced that they planned to involve evangelical Christians in their activities in future elections. When Robison and Falwell joined them in a variety of organizations and causes in 1979 and 1980, while Pat Robertson sounded many of the same notes without actually joining their band, it appeared they had succeeded impressively. Then, when Ronald Reagan won the presidency and six New Right candidates unseated established senators in the 1980 elections, many people, including major media representatives, assumed that television preachers represented a new and enormously powerful political force, with Falwell's Moral Majority serving as its most visible symbol. A closer analysis of election statistics, however, has called that interpretation into question.

Even the most optimistic estimates place the total audiences for Falwell, Robison, and Robertson at no more than 6 or 7 million people. When children, shut-ins, die-hard Democrats, and the politically apathetic are subtracted, the number of people who pay close attention to the television voices of the New Right is substantial but hardly astonishing, a conclusion supported by post-election polls. An ABC-Harris Poll, for example, credited followers of the television preachers with giving Reagan approximately two-thirds of his 10 percent margin over Jimmy Carter. In other words, Reagan would have won without a single vote from any of them. Still, these men do in fact have regular contact with several million people who are accustomed to calling and visiting and talking to others in efforts to change their minds or enlist their support and who are willing to give generously of their time and their money, if convinced they might make a difference. Further, the Annenberg/Gallup study showed that they are more likely than non-viewers to vote, to be politically conservative, to oppose a nuclear freeze, to hold traditional attitudes about sex roles, and to be more concerned about evangelism than about social justice. When harnessed to the technological sophistication and tactical expertise of veteran New Right political organizers, they did make a difference in several close races in 1980. In 1982 their impact seems to have been minimal, and may even have been negative in some cases. In 1984 the television evangelists took a lower-key approach to electoral politics, but local evangelical pastors, stirred by their example, worked avidly to register voters in their congregations and urged them to participate in the political process, almost always on the side of traditionally conservative issues. Finally, although Reagan may not have needed them, the 5 million votes evangelical Christians are credited with giving him in 1980 would have been sufficient to have changed the outcome of seven of the eleven previous presidential elections. Thus, even though claims of past impact have been overstated, there is little question that television preachers and their flocks can and may exert considerable influence on American politics.

Another set of issues focuses on the effects of the electronic church on the local church. Does it bring people into the church, or keep them out? Is it taking money away from the church, or increasing contributions by stimulating the habit of giving?

Predictably, most religious broadcasters view their ministries as increasing church membership. Almost without exception, they justify the enormous sums of money they spend by pointing to the effectiveness of television as an evangelistic tool. They produce "trophy letters" from people who claim to have been saved while watching their programs, and their publications contain impressive statistics on the number saved each year or in response to a given program. A closer look at these statistics, however, usually proves disappointing. As difficult as it may be to accept, there is considerable evidence, much of it gathered by evangelicals themselves, that the electronic mass media, as they are currently being used, at least in America, are not particularly effective instruments of evangelization.

As noted above, the audience for religious broadcasts is composed overwhelmingly of people who are already Christians. Repeated studies, whether conducted by respected evangelical researchers or by non-partisan groups, as in the recent Annenberg/Gallup collaboration, reveal that a high proportion of those who claim to have been converted by a media minister later acknowledge that they were, in fact, already Christians and attending church on a regular basis at the time of their "conversion." Though George Gallup, Jr., has been an advocate of increased use of television by the churches, the summary report of the Annenberg/Gallup study acknowledged that "religious broadcasters *rarely* speak to audiences outside their natural constituency, that they attract only an audience that is already convinced or already highly religious." Further, despite the claim of some television preachers to be great supporters of the local church, that message is seldom emphasized in their telecasts, their publications, or their fund-raising letters. The Annenberg/Gallup study found that only 13 percent of all religious broadcasts urge viewers to attend local churches.

In short, it is doubtless true that some people are converted and brought into the church as a consequence of religious radio and television programs. It appears, however, that their number is not great. In America—the situation may be different in other countries—religious broadcasting, as conducted in the mid-1980s, is not a cost-effective evangelistic tool. Most people come into churches over natural bridges; specifically, at the invitation and urging of relatives and friends. The only exceptions may be local programs and spot announcements tied to specific churches, particularly when these churches have a program and minister that listeners find appealing.

Addressing the issue from a different angle, some critics of the electronic church have expressed fear that, by encouraging viewers to sit at home and watch instead of involving themselves in a real church, television preachers are depriving people of the spiritual and emotional growth that comes from engagement with live people and tangible problems, leaving them without the succor and aid of the church when they are in need. At the same time, the critics charge, the electronic church injures real churches by diminishing their numbers and, therefore, their capacity to function as effectively as they ought.

These charges have a surface plausibility, but are not supported by available data. The 1980 study *Profile of the Christian Marketplace* reported that 9.1 percent of the general public indicated their involvement in the church had lessened as a result of viewing religious television programs, but half of that group had no affiliation with a Christian church, and a clear majority were not avid fans of religious programming, indicating that it may have been hostility rather than devotion to the preachers that kept them away from church. The Annenberg/Gallup study showed that although 18 percent of the viewers of religious television said it contributes more to their spiritual life than does the church, and 14 percent said that viewing religious programs is in fact a substitute for going to church, viewers of these programs are no more likely than nonviewers to express dissatisfaction with their churches, and only 3 percent say viewing has actually decreased their involvement in church. Further, when religiosity and other factors are held constant, viewing religious television does not seem to be associated with lower levels of attendance or volunteer work. In fact, most viewers report that religious television does not detract from but enhances their church participation. Among those for whom viewing religious programs is correlated with lower religious involvement when subjective religiosity is held constant, people over fifty, divorced, of low levels of education, or requiring assistance in going

places are overrepresented. In short, for all but a tiny segment of the audience, listening to or viewing religious programs is a component of religious expression, not a substitute for other dimensions of religiosity.

The fear most often expressed by critics from liberal denominations—namely, that the electric preachers are inducing people to stay home from church—appears to stem at least in part from concern over the precipitous decline in membership within their own churches during the 1970s. Perhaps, they imagine, the missing sheep are staying home and watching television preachers, transferring into one of the evangelical denominations whose membership is staying even with or even running ahead of population growth. Again, such suspicions seem plausible, but extensive research on "unchurched Americans" indicates the decline in liberal churches is less a matter of members dropping out than of a failure to attract new members to replace those lost by death and other normal forms of attrition. The mainline churches are holding onto older members reasonably well, but they are not attracting young adults under forty in anything like the numbers they once did, especially those educated in secular colleges and universities and therefore fully exposed to the sweeping value shifts that surfaced in the 1960s. These young people, whose value packages include emphasis on personal freedom, acceptance of diversity, resistance to authority, and distance from traditional institutions, feel little need to belong to any church, much less to a conservative church espousing values so opposed to theirs. And they give little evidence of paying much attention to religious broadcasters. Less than 5 percent of the 61 million unchurched Americans who were the subject of a landmark study by the Gallup organization in 1978 could recall ever having watched a television preacher other than Oral Roberts (12 percent) or Billy Graham (11 percent).

Nevertheless, both mainline and evangelical church leaders have manifested concern over the economic effects of the electronic church on local churches. Estimates of the costs for all religious broadcasting vary widely, but several of the leading broadcasting are known to have annual budgets of well in excess of $50 million, so that an overall figure of $1 billion is not incredible. Since virtually all of whatever money is involved comes from contributions by listeners and viewers, most of whom are church members, it seems almost fatuous to suggest that this would not have an adverse effect on local church budgets; in fact, however, that may indeed be the case.

The key to making sense of such an apparently illogical assertion is to remember that we are not dealing with a zero-sum situation, in which a certain amount of money is set aside for contributions to various recipients, and any amount given to one diminishes the amount available to another. Instead, we are dealing with a donor pool comprised of people known not only to be generous in their contributions to churches and related causes, but also willing to make cuts in other areas of their budgets to enable them to give more to causes they feel are particularly worthwhile. While it is obviously true that money sent to an electronic evangelist *could* have gone to a local church, it is not at all clear that it *would* have. The money garnered by media ministers does not just fall into their laps. It is cultivated and harvested with some of the most sophisticated fund-raising techniques known, and there is no overriding reason to believe the money would have gone to local churches, or to any other charitable causes, had these techniques not been used.

Perhaps more important, what little evidence exists on the question does not provide much cause for panic on the part of the churches. In the *Christian Marketplace* study, only 1.5 percent of the public named religious radio or television as their first choice for a charitable donation, in marked contrast to the 43.1 percent who named churches or mission efforts. Further, only 2.3 percent said they contributed to religious radio or television more than once a year. In the Annenberg/Gallup study, nearly one-third of all viewers had made financial contributions to the programs they watched, with 40 percent of regular viewers giving to three or more programs. But the median amount contributed during the previous year was only $30. It appears, then, that the bulk of the support for religious broadcasting comes from a dedicated corps of 2 to 3.5 million donors, some of whom doubtless give in a manner that is truly sacrificial. The Annenburg/Gallup study found no evidence that contributions to broadcast ministries diminish contributions to local churches. It is even plausible that broadcast ministries raise the level of awareness of the need for giving and thereby improve

rather than impede contributions to the local church.

The final set of issues to be considered here pertains to the impact of religious broadcasting on the central components of the electronic church: the evangelists themselves, the message they preach, and the audience they reach. Since, as we have seen, the most significant segment of the electronic church is composed of the television ministries produced and viewed by Evangelicals, it is primarily these ministries with which the following observations are concerned. To a greater extent than is true of the preceding portion of this essay, these remarks are based less on hard data than on personal opinion, but that opinion is based on fifteen years of careful observation, on extensive files of materials produced by dozens of media ministries, and on interviews with well over a hundred people involved in religious broadcasting, including most of the major radio and television preachers themselves.

At least two key factors have been crucial in creating the conditions that currently prevail in religious television. The first is economic. A major television ministry is an expensive enterprise. In the mid-1980s most of the major television ministries were spending more than $20 million each a year, and the annual budgets of the five or six largest ministries ran well in excess of $60 million each. Further, several appeared to be running quite close to or below the edge of true financial solvency. A second important factor is that, in addition to genuinely believing in the worth of what they are doing—an assumption they should be granted until there is strong evidence to the contrary—the evangelists themselves are, almost without exception, men and women of enormous ego and ambition who subscribe enthusiastically to the basic American values of success, competition, and progress. For them, simply holding one's own, by achieving a level of operation and maintaining it without attempting to extend and expand it, is virtually unthinkable.

These two factors combine to exert considerable shaping pressure on the content and mode of television ministries. Both to satisfy their own aspirations and to bring in enough money to keep their operations afloat, media ministers must create and sustain an impression of success, growth, and momentum that will attract viewers, win their loyalty and enthusiasm, and motivate them to provide a dependable financial base for the ministry. This usually means establishing colleges, elaborate churches, training institutes, hospitals, satellite earth stations, retreat and vacation centers, orphan homes, and foreign mission programs. It almost always means getting on and staying on as many stations as they can possibly afford and, to raise the money this costs, subjecting their supporters to an unrelenting barrage of fund-raising efforts on the air, through the mail, and, sometimes, over the telephone. This, in turn, has important effects on the message, the ethics, and the independence of religious broadcasters.

As noted earlier, many station owners have gladly accepted religious programming because it provides them with income they might otherwise have lost. At the same time, they do not want broadcasters to do anything that will harm their stations' images or in any other way lessen their attractiveness to viewers or advertisers. This has two immediate results. Except for daily programs like the "700 Club" and the "PTL Club" which appear mainly on the Christian satellite and cable networks or during the late-night or early-morning hours, most syndicated programs air during the Sunday-morning hours, when the fewest number of people are watching any kind of television program. Station owners are also aware that the audience for religious programming is quite small. Therefore, even if the religious broadcasters could pay the much higher fees for time slots when more people are watching television, owners would be reluctant to sell them this time, since the programs that followed them would have a minuscule holdover audience and might well suffer in the ratings, thus lowering the prices stations could charge other programmers and advertisers. If they sell them the Sunday-night time slots, as some stations do, they are likely to be in a sequence with other religious programs, so that the holdover effect is financially unimportant to the station.

The second result is that, just as the networks originally managed to exclude broadcasters who might prove offensive to listeners or sponsors, so local station managers are likely to sell time only to those evangelists whose programs are relatively innocuous, at least to the people likely to be watching them. Thus, when a preacher attacks groups such as homosexuals or Roman Catholics

on his telecasts, he runs a real risk of being taken off the air, a fate that has befallen several evangelists in recent years.

The intrinsic nature of television and its audience also affects the content of the programs. Television specializes in messages that can be grasped easily by people giving less than full attention and that, if not grasped and accepted, can be tuned out in an instant. This tends to lead away from systematic, in-depth analysis to oversimplification of issues and sensational accounts of putative solutions, and away from an emphasis on discipline or sacrifice or self-denial—all elements that had an important role in Jesus's ministry—to an emphasis on instant gratification, material success, and celebrity. These traits, it seems fair to say, are no less true of religious television than of secular television.

The preachers insist that the Gospel was never intended to be an abstruse message apprehendable only by the intellectually sophisticated. On the contrary, it is explicitly the "simple Gospel," the "old, old story," the "foolishness of God" that destroys the wisdom of the wise and thwarts the cleverness of the clever. But critics of the electronic church insist that, in their desire to attract and hold an audience, televangelists have not just simplified the old, old story; they have changed its essential nature, offering cheap grace, salvation without sacrifice, the crown without the cross.

Without question, the electronic church is vulnerable to these criticisms. The emphasis of many programs on slickness, success, and celebrity often stands in garish contrast to the biblical picture and proclamation of the prophets and of Jesus and his apostles. Television is not solely to blame, of course, nor are these the first preachers to tickle the ears and delight the eyes of their congregations. Almost all major American evangelists have been skilled actors and showmen and have heeded nineteenth-century evangelist Charles Grandison Finney's dictum that "the commonsense people will be entertained." They have drawn their crowds not simply with the preaching of the Gospel but with stories that tingled the spine and tugged at the heart, with choristers who imitated locomotives and played the trombone, with prominent politicians and fabled tycoons, and, long before television, with entertainers and athletes and reformed scoundrels and heroes of every sort. If they have reflected long enough to ask how Jesus would react to such tactics, they have allayed misgivings with the conviction that he would delight in the crowds. The crowds, in turn, have delighted in the tangible evidence that it is possible to enjoy the pleasures of the world and to move up with the Master. Still, the involvement of evangelists in a medium designed primarily for entertainment and financial gain has no doubt contributed significantly to their collective rush toward celebrity and consumer religion.

The demand for success, growth, viewers, and money also places evangelists' ethical integrity under heavy strain. Despite the presence in their ranks of some notable profligates, as revealed in lurid detail during the scandal that rocked the PTL network and related ministries in 1987, most religious broadcasters appear truly to believe in what they preach, to believe they are serving God when they preach it, and to believe it is God's will that their ministries grow and prosper. Still, the driving force of their ambition and the insatiable financial demands placed on them by growing staffs, high interest rates, inflation, increased time charges levied by station owners who know they can get whatever they ask, enormous debts incurred in a time of great growth but payable when that growth has slackened or ended, the demand for programming that will outstrip the competition, and the increasingly high costs of fund-raising itself serve to take a significant toll on the integrity of all too many television preachers. It may lead them to believe that, because the technology exists to make a mass-produced letter appear to be a personal one, it is ethically acceptable to send such a letter to unsophisticated supporters. It may lead them into cut-throat bidding wars with rival preachers in attempts to obtain favorable time slots on local stations. It may cause them, as in readily documentable cases, to misrepresent their effectiveness, their needs, and the ways in which they plan to spend the money they are soliciting. It may delude them into actually believing, as they often imply and sometimes explicitly claim, that their prayers on one's behalf are somehow worth more than those of a more ordinary friend or pastor or deacon or elder, and that fantastic hundred-fold, heaven-sent returns on all donations to their ministries will actually occur. It may seduce them into speaking of secular humanists and political liberals as moral

equivalents to robbers, murderers, rapists, and perverts. One can understand and sympathize with men and women under such pressures of time and money that they do not have the opportunity to consider the propriety of every action, but one need not approve of those actions when they fall so far short of what we should be able to expect from those who claim to speak for God.

To say that religious broadcasters manifest ethical shortcomings and that their broadcasts are evangelistic tools of limited effectiveness for American audiences is not, however, to say that media ministers bring no benefits to the evangelical community. In numerous ways, they doubtless strengthen and deepen the faith of listeners by providing them with instruction, exhortation, inspiration, hope, encouragement, entertainment, example, and opportunity for service. They also serve a symbolic function of considerable importance. Evangelical Christianity has experienced real growth in recent years, to be sure, but a high proportion of the estimated 35 to 50 million Evangelicals were present and active before pollsters and the mass media discovered them.

When the Jesus Movement, the charismatic movement, and Jimmy Carter's announcement that he had been "born again" brought Evangelicals more publicity than they had known since the dark days of the Scopes trial, they burst out of the closet with an energy and enthusiasm that surprised everyone, including themselves. The enormous surge in religious broadcasting not only reflects this aggressive spirit but helps maintain it, as Evangelicals note well that virtually all the religion on radio and television is their kind of religion, that the secular media are fascinated with it, and that liberal Christians are panicked by it. The buoyant confidence produced by the realization that they are no longer a beleaguered backwater minority but a significant and thriving part of mainstream American Christianity has led to a greater willingness to share their faith with others. It has generated increased efforts to strengthen and consolidate their gains by such means as the establishment of Christian schools to control the socialization of evangelical children, the publication of Christian Yellow Pages to encourage Evangelicals to support each other economically, and the formation of such organizations as Moral Majority, Christian

Voice, and the Religious Roundtable to influence elections and legislation.

It would be difficult to determine precisely what effect the electronic evangelists have on these processes, but the prominence of their participation in them is such that they surely deserve a significant share of the responsibility for them. Thus, even though they may produce few direct conversions, their role in the growth and apparent robust health of evangelical Christianity may be quite significant indeed. And that, for a long time, may well assure the media ministers a congregation sufficient to keep those cards and letters coming in.

BIBLIOGRAPHY

Ben Armstrong, *The Electric Church* (1979); Erik Barnouw, *A Tower in Babel* and *The Golden Web*, vols. I and II of *A History of Broadcasting in the United States* (1966); Bill Brammer, "Salvation Worries? Prostate Trouble?" in *Texas Monthly* (March 1973); David W. Clark and Paul H. Virts, "Religious Television Audience: A New Development in Measuring Audience Size," paper presented to the Society for the Scientific Study of Religion, Savannah, Ga., Oct. 25, 1985; J. Harold Ellens, *Models of Religious Broadcasting* (1974); Daniel P. Fuller, *Give the Winds a Mighty Voice* (1972); George Gerbner et al., *Religion and Television,* summary report of the Annenberg/Gallup Study (1984); Jeffrey K. Hadden and Charles E. Swann, *Prime Time Preachers* (1981); David Edwin Harrell, Jr., *All Things Are Possible* (1976); Peter Horsfield, *Religious Television in America: Its Influence and Future* (1983).

William G. McLoughlin, *Modern Revivalism* (1959); William Martin, "The God-Hucksters of Radio," in *The Atlantic* (June 1970) and "The Birth of a Media Myth," in *The Atlantic* (June 1981); Virginia Stem Owens, *The Unchurched American* (1978), *The Total Image, or Selling Jesus in the Modern Age* (1980), and *Profile of the Christian Marketplace* (1980); Bernard A. Weisberger, *They Gathered at the River: The Story of the Great Revivalists and Their Impact Upon Religion in America* (1958); "The World, the Viewers, and the Lessons of Religious Television." the report of the Annenberg/Gallup Study (1984).

[*See also* CATHOLICISM SINCE WORLD WAR I; FUNDAMENTALISM; PENTECOSTALISM; RELIGION AND FILM; *and* RELIGIOUS PRESS.]

POPULAR CULTURE

Wayne Elzey

SCHOLARS who attempt to assess the relationship between religion and popular culture encounter several difficulties, for in America there are many religious groups, several levels of culture, and remnants of many cultures. Further, the religious responses to popular culture range from rejection to eager acceptance and often change in accord with the success of a religious movement.

Popular, moreover, is as elusive a term as *religion* or *culture.* Most of the small sects described by Elmer T. Clark in *The Small Sects in America* (1937) or by Robert S. Ellwood, in *Religious and Spiritual Groups in Modern America* (1973) could be classified as popular in the sense that they originated and developed among the common people rather than among a culturally sophisticated and theologically educated elite. But none are popular in the sense that they have attracted a large following. Indeed, to the extent that small sects are labeled "cults," many belong with some of the most unpopular religious movements in the United States.

Even when scholars restrict their discussion to the ways in which Protestant piety has appropriated popular culture for its own ends, as in the present case, they encounter difficulties. Scholars of modern Protestantism stand in a different role vis-à-vis the issues of religion and culture than do their colleagues in other fields. Anthropologists and scholars of comparative religion study the religions of preliterate and non-Western cultures because they believe that an understanding of other ways of being human enriches and broadens their own culture. The same holds true for historians who investigate premodern cultures and for sociologists and folklorists who inquire into the religions of folk and peasant cultures. From the religious side, cultural theologians such as Paul Tillich have looked to the literary and artistic creations of high culture as a means of recovering the "depth dimension" in modern society.

The religious appropriations of popular or mass culture, by contrast, hardly seem worthy of serious attention. Oscillating wildly between lurid exaggeration and watered-down homogenization, the cadaverous "praying hands," the modern cathedrals that resemble gigantic greenhouses and hockey arenas, the Born-Again belt buckles and Bible-quoting comb and brush sets seem to be bizarre confections of the sacred and the profane, mistakes that should not have happened.

When measured against the creative and reforming impulses in the Protestant tradition, much of middle-class Protestantism is ordinary, everyday, humdrum religion. It no longer seems to function as an active and independent creator of popular culture. It is derivative and unoriginal and often self-consciously so. Viewed as a set of religious beliefs or political opinions or as a body of literary and artistic accomplishments, much middle-class Protestantism is as Sydney E. Ahlstrom described it: "a kind of 'Christianity of Main Street,' a farrago of sentimentality, moralism, democracy, free enterprise, laicism, 'confident living,' and utilitarian concern for success."

Ahlstrom has a point. One wonders, for example, if any appreciation remains for the historic tensions and paradoxes inherent in the relationship between Christianity and culture when Fuller Theological Seminary advertises its graduate program as "CHRIST CULTURE: It Doesn't Have To Be Either/Or." Is there any continuity between St. Augustine's *Confessions* and the free-verse poem in *Inspiration* magazine that compares conversion to opening a new can of tennis balls? ("Becoming a Christian is like being PSSCHT . . . Released! 2 Cor. 5:17.") Some semblance of discipleship may persist in Christians Are Preferred, a dating service located in Mt. Laurel, New Jersey. But does grace survive only in the Christian Charm Course dreamed up by Manna Publications? And has the prophetic tradition, so outspokenly critical of "niceness" and polite adjustment, deteriorated into the song ministry of "The Astonishing, Outrageous, Amazing, Incredible, Unbelievable" recording artist Gary S. Paxton? "God likened his church to a body with each member fulfilling his or her function," explain the liner notes to Gary's 1977 album *More*. "Gary likes to say he's an armpit."

One of the central problems facing the student of popular religion is trying to decide whether American Christians are innocent as doves or wise as serpents. In "How to Tell a Story," Mark Twain wrote, "To string incongruities and absurdities together in a wandering and sometimes purposeless way, and seem innocently unaware that they are absurdities, is the basis of the American art." Twain was describing American humor, but the description fits American piety equally as well.

A strain of sage naïveté in American piety explains puns, rhymes, non sequiturs, and incongruities in ways that almost defy scholars to pass judgment on the level of rational self-awareness present in popular religion. Is there really a Christian commune called The House of the Rising Son? A Christological treatise titled *No Nous Is Good Nous?* "Five Wonder Bulbs" (*Crocus zonata*) sold by the Greenhouse Division of the House of Wesley in Bloomington, Illinois? A singer named Chris Christian who records on Myrrh Records? What is real and what is parody? The Badge-A-Minit hand die press with a color-coded die set for stamping out Jesus-Saves pin-backed badges? Or Ann Elizabeth Wade's Praying Hands Tele-Dial Pen Set that promises to save fingernails as well as souls? Any regular "Praise The Lord" program telecast on Trinity Broadcasting Network and hosted by the network's bumblingly earnest founder who looks like a pious clone of humorist Steve Martin? Or a *real* parody of an *imaginary* "Saturday Night Live" parody of "Praise the Lord" written by humorist Stan Frieberg and telecast on a *real* "Praise The Lord" program on Saturday, February 18, 1984?

The sense of incongruity that so much of popular religion engenders in the outsider and the insider, in different ways, is significant. One source of the sense of incongruity is the discovery that two or more things sharing no intrinsic or familiar relationship have been combined. The perception of incongruity may produce laughter, tears, moral outrage, blank astonishment, fear, or even reverence.

The uses of incongruity are an important but neglected dimension of American piety. The evangelist who juggles the testimony of the quadriplegic artist with a humorous parody of the ultraliberal minister who joined two men in matrimony—and that with a description of the living death that awaits those who have not accepted the God-man as their personal Savior—is drawing on a formulaic and rationalized pattern of incongruities in order to evoke a sequence of predictable emotional responses in his audience. Part of the charisma of popular preachers derives from their ability to combine aristocratic elegance with a down-home, backyard folksiness. In April 1981 the most aristocratic of all the national ministers, Robert Schuller, asked for volunteers for the Beverly Hills Garage Sale and Auction. Among the articles donated were a putter autographed by Gerald Ford, a waterskiing boat, a Rolls Royce, and a condominium. Religious how-to-do-it manuals are filled with positive advice and instruction. But they also provide vivid reminders of how-*not*-to-do-it. "You may have the measurements of a Jayne Mansfield," Ethel Marbach noted in *A Do-It-Yourself Guide to Holy Housewifery* (1964). "But without that hardcore inner valiancy you're just a big bust."

The incongruities are not all on the side of the religious. Historians of American Protestantism have adopted a point of view that seems only slightly less incongruous than that of the believers they study. Just at the time that scholars of non-Western religions began purging their discipline of theories that reduced religion to idolatry or credulousness or an anxiety response, leading scholars of American religion began applying similar explanations to middle-class Protestantism, and the results were devastating.

"Every culture religion is a form of idolatry," Reinhold Niebuhr proclaimed, and those words echoed through scholarly surveys of American religion for the next half-century. As a result, scholars dismissed periods during which religion enjoyed its greatest popular success as the nadir of authentic faith. "It would be difficult to find a decade in all American history when religion wore a face more appealing to American culture than it did in the 1950s," William A. Clebsch wrote. "It is impossible to find a decade when its leading interpreters so nearly approached unanimity of concern for religion's failure." The first irony here is the conclusion that the more religious Americans appear to be, the less religious they really are. The second irony is that such a conclusion utilized theories of religion that no longer were respectable in dealing with any form of religion except middle-class Protestantism, where they were lauded as revolutionary.

The result has been that a two-sided misunderstanding has grown between religious people and the people who study them. Each group views the other as accomplishing roughly the reverse of its intentions. Academic scholars pride themselves on their objectivity and openness to diverse viewpoints. They are careful lest any personal bias, religious belief, or unconscious cultural presupposition contaminate their research and their conclusions. To the scholars' bewilderment, believers then attack them as propagandists for an immorally permissive and doctrinaire relativistic secular humanism. From the scholars' viewpoint, pious and thoughtful students of the Bible who diligently peruse the Scriptures—armed with meticulously detailed concordances, lexicons, handbooks, and harmonies—look like customers ransacking a Sears catalog for clues proving that the blue flannel bathrobe described on page 9 foreshadows the appearance of the eighty-four-piece socket wrench set on page 1142.

One major source of incongruity in popular religion lies in its attempt to solve a logically insoluble problem: How can everything be kept up-to-date in the timeless and unchanging Kingdom of God? The project has been pursued nowhere with more diligence and ingenuity than with regard to that most important product of popular piety—the Holy Bible.

Modern Bibles represent America's best effort to abolish the bothersome distinction between the sacred and the profane, once and for all. Modern Bibles are objects of devotion and practical how-to manuals. They combine Victorian elegance with space-age technology. The Bible is a private family icon, but it also serves as a portable shrine for the inauguration of public officials. It remains the source of the paradigmatic symbols defining American destiny and identity, and yet it is full of advice about salesmanship and dieting. The Bible is an anthology of sentimental stories that touch the will through the avenue of the heart, but it demands the application of complicated and intellectually taxing schemes of interpretation. The Holy Bible is a cosmos in miniature.

Bruce Barton—popularizer of biblical scholarship, author of a best-selling life of Jesus, senior partner in the advertising firm Batten, Barton, Durstine and Osborn—obtained the account for the Revised Standard Version of the Bible in the early 1950s. He first suggested the advertising slogan "The Bible Jesus Would Have Loved," before settling on the "Biggest Bible News in 341 Years." Some advertisers continued to follow Barton's lead. The New International Version of the Bible (1978) claimed to be "The Greatest Publishing Event Since 1611." By and large, however, Bible advertisements like the Bibles themselves have shifted the emphasis from the Word to the feelings of the reader. The Jerusalem Bible (1966) promised "The Most Satisfying of All Translations," while the Good News Bible (1976) joined in with a breathless "This Can't Be The Bible—I Can Understand It." All references to the Bible finally disappeared in the ads for the phenomenally successful Living Bible (1967), which read simply "The People's Choice."

Nearly 2,600 editions of the Bible and the New Testament were published in the United States during the first 180 years of independence. Between 1949 and 1953 the distribution of Bibles increased by 140 percent. Public opinion polls in the mid-1950s reported that 90 percent of all Americans believed the Bible to be the revealed Word of God. "Bible and bubblebaths are an unbeatable box-office combination," lamented the editors of the *Christian Century,* dismayed by a public who flocked to watch *Sodom and Gomorrah* (1952), *Samson and Delilah* (1949), *Solomon and Sheba* (1959), *The Robe* (1953), and other biblical spectaculars.

Americans had come to view the Bible as an anthology of anecdotes and sentimental human-interest stories about the most unforgettable characters they had ever met. Fulton Oursler of

Reader's Digest composed what immediately became the best-selling life of Jesus written in America, *The Greatest Story Ever Told* (1949). His popularization of the Old Testament, *The Greatest Book Ever Written* (1951), also sold well. The Revised Standard Version, despite the controversies surrounding its revision, remained atop the best-seller lists for three years and opened the way for a flood of new editions of the Bible over the next three decades.

By 1980 Americans could choose from a list of Bibles including not only the KJV or AV, the ASV and RSV, but also the NEB, MLB (or BV), NIV, NASB, NKJV, NAB, ICV, RDB, TEV (or GNB), NWT, IV, at least four AB's and two CB's, an IB, JB, LB (and its variants CLB, RLB, TW), an OB, and a host of other editions and reference Bibles. There were even a TB and a TNT, "talking" versions of the Bible and New Testament.

The trend toward colloquial permissiveness evident in *Webster's Third New International Dictionary* (1961) also affected Bible publishers. "Yea" and "lo" and "beseech" went the way of cursed Jezebel "who tired her head." *Christianity Today* compared the language of the King James Version (KJV) to that of a federal income tax form. Country and western singer Jeannie C. Riley attributed her conversion to a Bible that finally made sense. In 1976 Pat Boone called the Living Bible "the single most important contribution America has made to the world."

Although the King James Version remains the most popular and best-selling version, its hard-core defenders have come to appear irrelevant or intemperate. "What would Shakespeare or Milton studies be if people used half a dozen versions?" one scholar complained. From the other direction, Dr. Peter S. Ruckman, notorious watchdog of the KJV, dismissed the Living Bible in *The Bible Babel* (1981) as "about as alive as a pile of grade 'C' lumber." That was more than could be said for the products of the Catholics ("the Douay-Rheims-Christopher gang") and those of liberals and pseudo-Fundamentalists ("the Paine-Voltaire-Rosseau-Russell-Berkeley-Gibbon-Possum-Freud-Nietzsche-RV-Hobbes-Piltdown-Schweitzer group"). The latter group also included the Lenins (the Bolshevik and John), the NCC, Bob Jones University, the ACLU, Jerry Falwell, OSHA, Tobit, Moffit, Maggie and Jiggs, and "superstitious idiots like

Sophocles and Tillich." "Not all the loonies are in the bin," explained Dr. Ruckman. "All the boobies are not in the hatch."

Modern Bibles are worldly Bibles. They are a blend of glory and glitter and look for all the world as though William Tyndale were still alive and living in Las Vegas. As the internal parts of the Bible were being simplified, paraphrased, condensed, and made to sound more plain and natural, the exteriors were being grained and gilded and marbled and stained and lacquered and civilized in every way conceivable. Bibles come today in a wide assortment of colors ranging from plain black, brown, and white to Blueberry Blue, Chocolate, Indigo, Marbled Crimson, Snow White, and Lollypop. And in at least eight shades of black (Jet Black, Midnight Black, Traditional Black, Ceremonial Black, Licorice Black, Liturgical Black, Executive Black, and Dark Black).

Since the popular evangelists' Bibles first were bound in limp leather during the 1850s, Bibles have appeared bound in sealskin, cowhide, goatskin, horsehide, kidskin, calfskin, sheepskin, pigskin, leopardskin, camel's hair, and water buffalo hide. Recently Bibles have appeared bound in the skins of animals showing up later on the prophetic timetable—the Brown Buksyn, the Black Skivertex, the Velva-Gilded Moroccograne, and the Flush Cut Kivar. Utilitarian Bibles are covered in easy-washable see-through vinyl or in metal, for the serviceman. Inexpensive ($2.95) but long-wearing and stylish is a kind of designer Bible from Thomas Nelson in "real bluejean denim, with simulated stitched pockets and a 'Good News' patch on the front."

In form as well as content modern Bibles meet every need. There are award Bibles, executive Bibles, picture-book Bibles for children, pink or blue New Testaments for the nursery, and special Bibles for the blind and the deaf. Since 1915 there has been a Runner's Bible. Large family Bibles include a domestic intertestamental period for recording births, deaths, marriages, and, since World War II, service records. Wide-margin, loose-leaf Bibles appeal to the Bible student. White, zippered Bibles or white Bibles with metal locks and button flaps are targeted at brides and unwed females.

"A large Bible can have the same effect as a .45 revolver," D. James Kennedy warned house-to-house evangelists in *Evangelism Explosion*

(1977), reflecting the current trend to downsize the Bible. Moody Press's lightweight Thinline Bible ("But Inside It's a Heavyweight!") competes with Tyndale's Smallest Bible, with Collins' Ultra-Thin Bible, and possibly with the Micro Mini Bible. In a different way all compete with the Reader's Digest Condensed Bible and the Bible in Basic English. The latter restricts itself to 1,000 common English words, while the New Life New Testament ("The World's Most Understandable Bible") uses only 850 words. The final word in biblical reductionism to date is the Living Word Pendant Bible (1984) from J.C. Penney. All 1,148 pages of the Old and New Testaments (KJV) are reduced 300 times and reproduced on a 2″ × 2″ space-age microfiche chip delightfully fashioned in the shape of a cross electroplated in fourteen-karat gold and accompanied by a gold-rope chain, for $19.95 (microscope not included).

In 1983, the National Year of the Bible, Bible sales exceeded $170 million. In a cover story on "The Bible in America" *Newsweek* reported that *Books in Print* took fifty-five pages to list Bibles and Bible-related entries, compared with fourteen for sex and fifteen for food; that Gideons International had distributed over one million free Bibles in the past year; and that the American Bible Society had just passed the 100 million mark in Bible distribution. The 1980 catalog of the Nazarene Publishing House listed over 430 different editions of the Bible and New Testament.

But that is just the beginning. Unreported was the mass of bonus Bibles sent out by radio and television ministers and editors of religious magazines. For $200 cash (or twelve payments of $17 each) one can purchase a membership in the Rex Humbard You Are Loved Club and receive a Rex Humbard Family Life Study Bible (RHFLSB) free of charge. Half that amount enrolls one as a Life-Line Partner and entitles him or her to one of the 200,000 Rex Humbard Prophecy Bibles now in print. Cash-and-carry customers can purchase a Rex Humbard KJV with olive-wood covers for $15, exactly the same price as the nubby blue-and-white Rex Humbard Doormat. Other national ministries offer similar plans.

Also unreported were the numerous high-tech Bibles. The New Testament (KJV) recorded on twelve cassettes from Reneco Electronics

runs from $30 dollars, and the New Testament (NIV), from Living Water, runs from $50. The Dramatized Bible ("It's Happening Right Before Your Ears!") provides a you-are-there immediacy with music, varied speaking parts, and sound effects. Read by Alexander Scourby, the entire KJV costs only $25 more than the New Testament read by Efrem Zimbalist, Jr., and $10 less than selected Old Testament Passages read by Sir Laurence Olivier. The KJV on 2,700 2″ × 2″ slides retails for about $300. Engineers at Bible Research Systems in Austin, Texas, recently developed THE WORD Processor, the KJV on eight floppy discs initially priced at $162.95. Space-age Bibles may, nevertheless, face their time of tribulation. Radio pastor David F. Webber of the Southwest Radio Church in Oklahoma City noticed that if numerical values are assigned to each letter of the alphabet such that *A* equals 6, *B* Equals 12, *C* equals 18, and so on, then the numerical value of *C-O-M-P-U-T-E-R* is 666 or the same as *K-I-S-S-I-N-G-E-R*. Customers eyeing THE WORD Processor might double-check with the Anti-Christ Information Center in Alta Loma, California.

Top of the line in contemporary Bibles is not the $3,500, three-volume, gold and leather edition reported in *Newsweek*. It is the New Media Bible. Beginning in 1976 plans were made to film the entire Bible, book by book, over a period of thirty-three years. Subscribers would pay $2,500 per year, or $82,500 for the entire set.

Second only in importance to the Bibles are the reference works and manuals for studying the Bible and for applying it to the problems of everyday life. American Protestants have shown a staunchly ambivalent attitude toward biblical scholarship. Born in the land of all the Kaiser's men, Higher Criticism of the Bible seemed irrelevant to the business of saving souls and improving moral character. At its worst, Higher Criticism was a frontal attack on the authority and inerrancy of the Scriptures.

But an independent tradition of popular Bible study did develop, nurtured by Sunday schools, church camps, vacation Bible schools, and neighborhood study groups. Teachers in Bible colleges and participants in Bible conferences perfected Bible study and disseminated the practice through reference Bibles and periodical literature. Bible study has produced a multitude of spiritual artifacts: multiribboned Bible bookmarks, Bible stands, Bible rests, Bible cases, Bible workbooks, Bible coloring books, Bible games, Bible crossword puzzles, Bible rulers inscribed "Let the Peace of God Rule In Your Hearts, Col. 3:15," and Bible Guidance Dialers that "tell you what to read in time of need."

From the inception of Bible publishing in the United States at the beginning of the nineteenth century, Bibles contained explanatory and expository notes. Colored maps pinpointed the settlements of the descendants of Noah. Genealogical charts traced lineages from Adam and Eve to Jesus, highlighting key family groups. Time lines followed world history from the Past through the Present, the Rapture, Tribulation, Armageddon, and on to the Millennium. Scriptural coins and money terms were listed along with their equivalents in United States currency. Tables organized the five "woes" in Habakkuk 2, the seven "blesseds" and eight "overcomes" in Revelation, and the five "much mores" in Romans 5. Classification tables cataloged the Names and Titles of Jesus Christ from Genesis through Revelation, as well as Great Men of the Bible, Great Women of the Bible, Animal Kingdom of the Bible, Vegetable Kingdom of the Bible.

During the 1890s popular scholarship took on color-coordinated tones. Usually the words of Jesus were printed in red. One variation was the 1913 Precious Promise New Testament: With All The Promises in Red. Another is the KJV from Collins with the words of Jesus in green, "the color of renewal." Salem Kirban, advertising himself as "a converted ARAB," put together Salem Kirban's Reference Bible. Judgment verses are in red, promises in blue. More complicated is the so-called Rainbow Bible. First published in 1928 as The Marked Bible, a current edition from Zondervan rightly divides the words of truth into pink (salvation), green (the Holy Spirit), brown (temporal blessings), and Hawaiian Blue (prophetic subjects).

Languages have not been neglected. The 107 editions of the English text of the Polyglot Bible published between 1825 and 1881 stand as a landmark of popular philology. Currently in print are at least three new-style polyglot New Testaments containing six English translations. Tyndale offers a New Testament with eight English translations, and its People's Parallel Bible incorporates the texts of the KJV and the Living Bible within a single volume.

Daily Bible study plans link faith with knowledge (Phil. 4:8) and wisdom with the house (Proverbs 9:1). The Scriptures are scanned systematically, verse by verse and chapter by chapter. Assistance is offered with difficult passages, daily duties are set forth, and a miscellany of information is gathered relating to world affairs: "Pray for: St. Kitts: mean temp. 78°, pop. 45,000, 92% Protestant, 2% Roman Catholic." In order to reach a larger audience and provide closer supervision, Bible study also takes the form of radio and television courses and home-study programs. Jerry Falwell, chancellor of the Liberty Baptist Schools, offers "the most comprehensive Bible correspondence course available in America." The program of study, outlined in the pamphlet "A Brand New Look At The Grand Old Book," consists of a four-semester curriculum, a broad range of electives and 300 hours of taped classroom lectures, leading to a General Bible Course Diploma.

Although he promises no degrees, five days a week since 1967 "your Bible bus driver," Dr. J. Vernon McGee, has conducted students on "thrilling five-year trips from Genesis to Revelation, threading back and forth between the Old and New Testaments." He does offer sightseers on his "safari through the Scriptures" a kind of Fodor's guide to the Bible, a blue, genuine-leather, $50 Through the Bible Bible along with a twelve-volume set of "Through the Bible Cassettes," 266 of them, for $725. "All aboard the Bible bus," calls out Dr. McGee. "And leave the teaching to us."

There are two sides to Bible study, one pure and the other applied. One part of Bible study is devoted to the memorization of Bible verses and biblical trivia. The well-versed student should know that there are 773,693 words and 3,566,480 letters in the KJV. He or she should demonstrate an ability to keep Uz and Buz separate from Ahijah and Abijah or Bedad and Hedad while remembering that 1 Chron. 1:25 and Isaiah 8:1 contain, respectively, the shortest verse ("Eber, Peleg, Reu") and the longest word ("Mahershalalhashbaz") in the Old Testament.

Much of this is kid stuff, as it is on "The Bible Bowl," a Christian quiz show telecast from Dallas, Texas, that features competing squads of Gospel Girls and Bible Boys. But in mature Bible study the Bible is approached as a system of interconnected meanings in which everything refers to everything else. At first glance Genesis 1:3 ("And God said, Let there be light") appears to be only a simple reference to one event in the creation. With the help of concordances and commentaries, however, the full meaning becomes clear. The verse also refers to the reign of Jesus during the millennium. See Luke 2:9, where it says that *light* shines around the shepherds at the birth of Jesus; see Col. 1:16–17 where it says that all things were *created* in Him, through Him, and for Him; and see Psalms 104:21–22 where it says that when the sun *shines*, lions lay down in their dens. Compare with Isaiah 45:7 and Revelation 20:3.

Despite their colloquial styles, modern Bibles are scholarly Bibles. In addition to the text, they contain a full complement of footnotes, subscripts, superscripts, center-column cross-references, condensed glossaries, lexicons, short concordances, and running scholarly commentaries. "In the beginning," the Amplified Bible starts out, "God (prepared, formed, fashioned) and created the heavens and the earth [Heb. 11:3]." Study Bibles atomize the Scriptures, exhaustively cross-filing, indexing, analyzing, and cataloging individual words. The Word Study Bible, for example, renders Acts 3:1 as "Now Peter and John went up together into the temple at the hour of prayer. . . ." The numbers refer the reader to entries in a companion concordance that lists every appearance of the Greek word in the New Testament, gives citations in the context of the relevant verses, and provides cross-references by page number to the lexicons, dictionaries, and concordances of Kittel, Strong, Moulton and Geden, and Arndt and Gengrich, "making page flipping and reference collecting obsolete."

Befitting a holistic institution, popular study of the Bible contains built-in protection against the humorless and literalistic drudge. Everyone knows about the peculiar genealogy of parentless Joshua, the son of Nun, Dr. Charles Francis Potter admitted in *Is That In The Bible?* (1933). But who was the smallest man in the Bible? Was it Knee-High Miah or Bildad the Shoe-Height? Probably Peter, who slept on his watch.

Popular Bible study also has its practical side. Religious literature abounds with claims that "it pays to read the Bible," that the Bible is "God's How-To Book," "the Great Manufacturer's Handbook," or for sports fans, "God's Playbook." "Ten times a day practice the following affirmation, repeating it out loud if possible," instructed Dr. Norman Vincent Peale. " 'I can do all things through Christ which strengtheneth me' (Philippians 4:13). Repeat those words NOW." Protestantism, with its this-worldly asceticism, has added emphasis to the practical relevance of the Bible. If everyone is his own priest and if all vocations are to be regarded as religious callings, then the Bible is directly applicable to the work not only of the smith, the cobbler, and the baker, but also of the hairstylist, the professional athlete, and the construction worker.

And the weight watcher, to cite another example. "Now some are puffed up," St. Paul preached to the church at Corinth (1 Cor. 4:18), provoking the current flood of books on Christian dieting. In 1977 Neva Coyle founded Overeaters Victorious, a ministry to fools filled with meat (Proverbs 30:22) and based on the methods outlined in Frances Hunter's *God's Answer to Fat: Lose It!* (1976) and Joan Cavanaugh's classic *More of Jesus, Less of Me* (1976). Hunter, who also authored *Hang Loose With Jesus* and once described herself as the Phyllis Diller of theology, claims to have lost more than 20,000 pounds (not all at one time). The Bible warned us long ago, Hunter said, that Satan haunts the pastry shops and the delis: "Be not desirous of his dainties; for they are deceitful meat" (Proverbs 23:3). Hunter continues, "Only buy foods that Jesus, John or Peter would buy. I can't imagine Jesus Christ coming out of the supermarket with twelve bags of chips —one for each disciple." Cavanaugh, confessing that she steadfastly ignored Deuteronomy 32:15 ("you became fat, you grew thick") ballooned to 230 pounds and displaced the water in the baptistery one Sunday before learning, like Job, to esteem the words of the Lord more than her necessary food (Job 23:12). The urgency of the crusade against fat is apparent in *Fed Up With Fat* (1983). The authors, Jim Tear and Jan Houghton, persuaded apocalyptist Hal Lindsay to write the foreword.

Cherry Boone O'Neill argued in *Starving for Attention* (1982) that the Bible also has much to say to the Christian anorectic or sufferer from bulimia, whose only food is sighs and whose groans pour out like water (Job 3:24–25). Underweight Christians can prepare the recipes of

Graham Kerr, those outlined in Eileen Gaden's *Biblical Garden Cookery* (1976) —try, for example, Corinth Tongue—or Maxine Fritz's *With an Oriental Flavor* (1976). Exhibiting the penchant of popular religion to link up heterogeneous areas of experience, the latter was advertised as "a unique combination of devotional insights and Chinese recipes."

Christian men and women can pursue physical as well as spiritual fitness by using any of several Bible-based jogging and aerobics manuals. Any woman who has been compared to a mare of Pharaoh's chariots (Song of Solomon 1:9) might purchase a copy from one of the more than twenty-two printings of Joyce Landorf's *The Fragrance of Beauty* (1973), a Christian beauty manual based on an application of 2 Cor. 2:14: "He uses us to tell others about the Lord and to spread the Gospel like sweet perfume."

Taking advantage of the premium Bible study places on memory and ferreting out hidden connections, former NBA star Jerry Lucas created the Bible Memory Verse Cards. How can one remember to hook up the story of Noah with the Gospel of Mark? Visualize Noah's beard with a lot of little marks running up and down it, explained Lucas, whose success led to the formation of Memory Ministries and to the purchase of the 400-acre Fruit of the Spirit Ranch north of San Francisco. Vacationers memorize between fifty and one hundred chapters of the Bible during a two-week stay and may also explore the fascinating world of "theomatics," one of many numerical schemes for interpreting the Bible. One reviewer summarized the method as follows: Hebrew and Greek use the first nine letters of the alphabet for the numbers 1–9, the second nine letters for the numbers 10–90, and the remainder for 100, 200, 300, etc. On this basis a theomatic analysis of the New Testament reveals that "Jesus" (in the nominative), "Christ" (in the accusative), "God" (in the accusative and with the definite article), and "Lord" (in the genitive and without an article) all share the common multiple 111, a trinitarian number divisible by three.

Modern Bibles are compromises. They hitch a state-of-the-art technology to a state-of-the-heart theology. They market a condensed, lushly bound, color-coded, eminently practical, but highly abstract scholasticism in the vernacular, highlighting minor product differences in jingles so catchy they are easily taken over by a Japanese manufacturer of pickup trucks—"All The KJV (or Truck) You'll Ever Need."

There have never been as many Bibles and kinds of Bibles as there are today. But never has the Holy Bible so incongruously mirrored and appropriated the secular world. And if popular religion has directed much energy toward the creation of many versions of the same thing—the Bible—it also has directed much energy in the opposite direction toward the creation of a single version of everything—a totally sacred world of profane things.

At the center of American Protestantism stands the ideal of a world free from evil and corruption, sacred in all its dimensions. The separation of church and state established boundaries between the government and religious groups, but it did not deny the government a religious dimension. "American civil religion," based loosely on biblical salvation histories, has conferred a transcendent meaning on American history and created a panoply of national holy days, pilgrimage sites, national temples, enthronement ceremonies, and quasi-sacred lore about founders and martyrs.

If the separation of religion and government did not deny the government a religious dimension, neither did it, as Karl Marx predicted, relegate Protestant Christianity to being one of many elements in the world of private competition, where the churches compete with each other for souls and with business for property and capital. American Protestants instead have sought to confer a religious meaning on nearly every dimension of the private sector, creating, as it were, a sacred world from the bottom up. Émile Durkheim's insight that "anything can be sacred" could be updated to read "everything should be sacred," for each and every creation of popular culture there ought to be a religious equivalent.

In modern America nothing has been too trivial, too frivolous, or too profanely utilitarian to serve as a vehicle of Christian witness. There are Gentle Witness drinking mugs, Witness Watchband calendars, and Silent Witness eyeglasses with a logo of a fish on the frame. Christian games run the gamut from Social Gospel learning-simulation games like CENTER CITY: A Simulation of Urban POVERTY ("when players cross ethnic lines they are awarded maximum points") to compatible cartridge games like the one set in Agapeland. Christians still wedded to board games can turn from the older Bible Baseball and Football to Noah's Ark Lotto, Christian Keno(sis), or Eternity, a stewardly version of Monopoly. A Christian Mother Goose trilogy recently appeared, and Zondervan publishes a religious version of Harlequin Romances in its Serenade Books series. An evangelical crusade reenacted the Berlin airlift ("Jesus '81 Berlin Airlift"), and more than thirty international gangs of Bible smugglers carry the Lord in their luggage behind the Iron Curtain. Nearly 250 Christian retirement communities are scattered across the nation, along with several Christian nightclubs.

While the franchised Christian massage parlor or the evangelical distillery has not yet made an appearance, American Protestants have appropriated popular culture with remarkable zeal since World War II. Earlier they tended to view gambling, the novel, the theater, jewelry, sexually titillating literature, Catholics, and bowling alleys as inherently evil. Modern Protestants have come to view such phenomena at best positively, at worst neutrally, considering such practices not inherently evil but rather under the control of the wrong leaders. A measure of the change is the fact that one could gain a rather accurate sample of the issues and opinions of religious groups today by reading the comic books they produce.

During the 1950s those still too hesitant to view the latest biblical spectacular at their local theater had a number of alternatives. World Wide Pictures, the production arm of the Billy Graham Evangelistic Film Ministries, offered viewers religious musicals in the style of *Oklahoma (Oil Town U.S.A.)* and tales of rebellious youth modeled on *Rebel Without A Cause (The Restless Ones)*. Some viewings took place at drive-in churches. Similar duplications appeared in the record and television industries. By 1984 the Christian Broadcasting Network (CBN) was the third largest cable system in the United States. In addition to the traditional religious programs, CBN broadcasts Christian versions of soap operas, talk shows, cartoon shows, and cooking classes, along with daily reruns of situation comedies and westerns produced for commercial television in the 1950s.

This new inclusive and ecumenical outlook easily assimilated tabooed peoples. The Protestant rehabilitation of the non-Protestant began during the 1940s and has proved largely successful. Hollywood contributed stories of kindly priests and troubled nuns. In 1949 three of the top ten best-selling fiction titles were *Seven Storey Mountain, Peace of Soul,* and *The Greatest Story Ever Told;* two years earlier *Peace of Mind* was the best-selling work of nonfiction, and *Miracle of the Bells* the best-selling work of fiction. The five books were written by, respectively, a Catholic monk, a Catholic bishop, a Catholic layman, a rabbi, and a Jewish newspaperman (about a Catholic priest).

Since World War II a host of religious organizations has emerged, divided along profane vocational lines. "For virtually every professional and scholarly organization in America, there exists an equivalent," James Davison Hunter observes, listing "the American Scientific Affiliation, the Christian Association for Psychological Studies, the Christian Medical Association, the Christian Businessman's Association, the Christian Veterinarian's Fellowship, and the Fellowship of Christian Athletes to name a few." Ernest Sandeen coined the term "parallel institutions" to refer to these and other organizations that were, he argues, compromises, ways of enjoying the benefits and prestige that accompany success in a secular culture without totally identifying with that culture. Such parallel institutions combine the best of two worlds. While most center on vocations of prestige and influence, some recent ones more closely resemble Thomas Nelson's blue-jean Bibles: the Hardhats for Christ (a subdivision of the Christian Construction Workers), the Association of Christian Truck Drivers, and (Holy Hell's Angels!) the Christian Motorcyclists Association.

But it has been with the printed word that the Protestant impulse to convert the world has had its greatest successes. Here too is a religious equivalent for practically every form of secular writing—not only Christian books and magazines but also Christian postcards, greeting and sympathy cards, newspapers, posters, maps, stamps, instruction manuals, mail-order catalogs, cartoons, badges, plaques, telephone directories *(The Christian Yellow Pages Service)*, billboards, advertisements, decals, tracts in the form of traffic signs ("One Way" and "Do Not Enter —Hell"), crests, pennants, and trademarks

("Jesus Jeans"). Nor should one forget the numerous religious book-of-the-month clubs or the Christian Bookseller's Association.

Next to the Bible, the tract has served as the most important distinctively religious form of literature in America. According to E. Brooks Holifield, the American Tract Society within two years of its founding in 1825 "had printed 3,815,000 copies of 200 separate tracts designed to appeal both to the 'lower' ranks and to 'the intelligent and discerning.'" Although drab in appearance and inexpensive, the tracts attempted to "emulate the style of the popular gilt-edge gift books that graced the parlor tables of Victorian homes." The illustrated tracts cited verses of Scripture, issued warnings, reprinted sermons, but above all dealt in "heartwarming narratives. They told stories of *The Dairyman's Daughter, The Blacksmith's Wife,* and *Jonathan Brown the Bargeman.*"

The older tracts linger on in reprints from the Old Style Tract Society. For over a century the condensed story and anecdote have been a staple of popular preaching and religious writing. Even the self-help literature written in the genre of "How to Repair Your Carburetor" is thoroughly anecdotal. Peale's *The Power of Positive Thinking* (1952) is typical. The book contains more than 160 anecdotes taking up more than 80 percent of the text.

The anecdote, further condensed and compacted, becomes the icon. The modern tract represents the complete synthesis of religious content with secular form. The financial industry alone has provided a host of models for modern tracts. There are Bank on Christ Cards, dollar bills marked "Blood Money" with a picture of Jesus in the center, checks drawn on the Bank of Heaven ("Resources Unlimited") or on your local bank with an appropriate verse of Scripture, Christian Gift Certificates ("Pay Bearer on Demand According to His Riches in Glory"), and insurance policies drawn up by the Eternal Life Insurance Company, "the best in the universe." Forward Movement Publications, masquerading as the research division of the Christian Instrumentation Corporation, distributes "A Catalogue of Christian Instruments for the Space Age," advertising "One Trans-Galactic Space Ship, Multi-Passenger; Anti-Gravity Drive; When Ordering, use Code Word: CHURCH." Other tracts take advantage of the hair-of-the-dog-that-bit-you view of salvation common in Protestant piety:

X-Pressway to Hell
Rated X
Adults Only

Coming Soon
Heaven and Hell
Starring YOU

It is the story, however, that has fascinated pious Americans. Apart from providing a wealth of new information, pious literature teaches its readers little that is novel, nor does it challenge them to confront the world in ways that are radically new. But to dismiss popular pious literature as the substitution of sentimentality for ideas overstates the case. For this literature does provide a paradigm for proper thinking. It spurs its readers to remember, to assimilate new situations to older categories, and to modify the latter to include new experiences. In a fashion altogether appropriate for a religious tradition that takes feeling as its privileged mode of knowing, American piety has tended to organize the world on a continuum where uncontrolled passions and no passions at all stand at opposite extremes.

Sandra Sizer has compared the function of the gospel hymns and revivals of Dwight L. Moody to that of a thermostat which maintains a proper balance between an overheated and a cold or lukewarm emotional life. By dialing the right temperature, a solution emerges for every problem. Nearly everything in the profane world possesses some sensible quality by which it can be manipulated toward one end or the other of the continuum. Properly balanced, all profane things are transformed into sacred things.

America's first widely popular religious novel, Harriet Beecher Stowe's *Uncle Tom's Cabin* (1852), appeared originally in forty installments in the *National Era.* James D. Hart estimates its sales at the end of the first year as the equivalent of a book selling 3 million copies in 1947. The novel presently is available in ten paperback editions. It remains the best example of a genre of pious literature that Stowe created—the encyclopedic, episodic, and anecdotal cosmological tract.

By drawing on the biblical symbols of bondage, exile, the promised land, a chosen people, suffering, and redemption, Stowe lifted the issue of slavery from the profane realm of economics and politics to the timeless realm of myth and epic. With an attention to detail as exacting as that of Cecil B. deMille or a modern study Bible, Stowe pieced together odds and ends from the Bible, newspaper clippings, fragments from the lives of Christian saints, frontier lore, and allusions to Lord Byron. She laced these with puns and ironic wordplays about the Sin- and Saint-Claires, the legalistic Dr. Botherem, "Miss Feeley" (who was anything but), and many more.

The Christian allusions predominate but hardly in their original form. Tom "looked respectable enough to be a Bishop of Carthage," but so in a different way does his master, Augustine St. Claire. Augustine's daughter Eva resembles both Eve and Christ as well as her saintly namesake, Saint Clara. Augustine's twin brother, Alfred, is, like his namesake, knowledgeable in all matters pertaining to the English, while his son Henrique bears a startling resemblance to the sociopathic king of kings in the New World, Henri Christophe of Haiti.

Stowe's morally riddled geography, for which the travels of St. Augustine may have served as model, provides the context for exploring nearly every possible contrast of black/white, young/old, Protestant/Catholic, soldier/Quaker, action/passion, backwoods/cities. Stowe portrays a world torn in half. One half consists of the model family, precisely balanced between warm affection and cool efficiency, sensibility and rationality. The other half, the world of America outside the home, is a welter of incongruities. Human beings are sold and families separated without a flicker of emotion by the same individuals who, in other circumstances, explode in rage at the slightest provocation. Despite first appearances, the neurasthenic wife possesses no more real sensibility than the Calvinist spinster possesses true moral impulse. Slavery, the cold business of treating human beings like animals, finds its perfect complement in liquor, an impersonal agent that also transforms human beings into animals.

Stowe's twin stories, centering on Tom and George Harris, were taken to opposite conclusions. The first, taking its cue from the lore of Christian martyrs, shows that the deep divisions in American society between black and white (but also between young and old, male and female, Protestant and Catholic, North and South)

could only be healed in another world, heaven. The second story took its cues from Christian militancy and shows that integration in this world could occur only in another nation, Liberia. Stowe's conclusion achieves an integration of symbols perhaps unmatched in American literature. A reunited mulatto holy family—husband, wife (dressed as a man), and son (dressed as a daughter)—escapes from the American South into Canada. They plan to travel east and settle on the occidental coast of an Oriental continent in an independent black nation, a new nation dependent on white assistance and situated in the region where, according to the preface, human civilization first began.

This basic model by which evil is allotted to excessive passion, no passion at all, or to some incongruous combination of the two, has been a persistent one. Focused in one direction it resulted in T. S. Arthur's temperance-tract melodrama, *Ten Nights in a Barroom and What I Saw There* (1854). Simon Slade, previously the miller in a small and homey village eager for culture and status, builds the Sickle and Sheaf saloon. The judge who bought his mill turns it into a distillery. Soon even innocent children take on "gross sensual expressions." Obscenity and vulgarity replace normal conversation, and "greasy Irish girls" serve dissipated, hiccuping customers whose shattered nerves and cadaverous faces belie the uncontrolled animal passions they have let loose on the villagers.

In Elizabeth Stuart Phelps's *The Gates Ajar* (1868), the pattern of violence and impersonality was focused in the opposite direction to unmask a judgmental and unfeeling Calvinist theology in a world where war, fire, and disease separate families and remove loved ones. Mary Cabot, whose brother Royal was "shot dead" in the war, cannot find comfort from the Dr. Blands, Deacon Quirks, and Meta Tripps who only prolong her agony in "the most exquisite of inquisitions, the condolence system." She discovers comfort and enlightenment in the household of Winifred Forceythe, a farsighted modern version of St. Boniface, and her unpredictable daughter Faith. "A happy home is the happiest thing in the world," muses Mary, dreaming of a heaven filled with red balloons and pianos. "I do not see why it should not be in any world."

"But what can any individual do?" the narrator asks at the end of *Uncle Tom's Cabin.* "Of that every individual can judge. There is one thing that every individual can do—they can see to it that they *feel right.*" Charles M. Sheldon, a Congregational minister, agreed in his series of anecdotal Sunday-evening sermons, later serialized and reprinted as *In His Steps* (1896) and eventually made into two movies. The most popular of all Social Gospel novels is a how-to book set in the form of a story. Several prominent members of a wealthy and respectable church take a pledge to preface every decision with the question "What would Jesus do?" As the novel makes clear, no one can decide for anyone else, but guided by right feeling they all come to the same conclusion: If Jesus were alive today, He would use his wealth and talents to minister to the poor.

The world now only extends to the city limits, but within these confines Sheldon found room for the contradictions that had bothered his predecessors. Above live the upper-class citizens in their mansions—powerful, educated, cultured, wealthy, and efficient, but also uncaring, unfeeling, and thoroughly unfulfilled. Below live the poor in the slums—dirty, ignorant, ragged, unduly intimate with one another, and stirred into mob frenzies by liquor. More important than the minimal successes of Sheldon's urban missionaries in converting and helping the poor are the conversions experienced by the missionaries themselves. Something of the naturalness of the poor and their capacity to feel rub off on the rich. "Business," observes the aptly named Mr. Wright, "should be run on some loving family plan." In Sheldon's novel the viewpoint of middle-class consciousness organizes the world.

The Social Gospel tradition in which salvation comes to the preacher continues to be a prominent strand in religious literature. In *Christy* (1967) Catherine Marshall sends one of her heroines into the hills of Appalachia to teach school. An idealistic but impatient nineteen-year-old from a "highfalutin' home," Christy finds herself among a topsy-turvy people ravaged by exotic diseases, poverty, ignorance, feuds, and moonshine. Yet they are sympathetic, caring, and loyal to a fault. They speak in phrases "straight out of Shakespeare and Spenser," insist that Latin be at the center of the curriculum, and generally are "as healthy as the pigs" who sometimes snuggle on their laps during mealtime. Like her namesake, Christy returns from the dead in a scene near the end of the book, a more complete per-

son. In *The Cross and the Switchblade* (1975) David Wilkerson travels from his insulated pastorate in upstate New York to minister to the street gangs in New York City only to discover nearly identical circumstances to what Christy encounters. Ruth Carter Stapleton measures parents by a similar standard in *The Gift of Inner Healing* (1976). What else could one expect from the typically incongruous family with its cold and distant father and "smother mother" but the emotionally mixed-up, grown-up children of today?

And don't forget husbands! Marabel Morgan chimed in with her best-selling *The Total Woman* (1973). The anomalies populating the works of medieval teratologists—tribes who lived upside down or who slept in their ears or who had eyes in their stomachs—exemplify ordinariness when compared to that oxymoron, the normal husband. Cold when he should be hot and hot when he should be cold, he is oversexed at the office and comatose in bed with his wife; verbal and articulate at work but struck dumb the minute he walks into the house—that active outdoorsman slumped motionless over there for the last two hours watching football on TV. Employing over 130 anecdotes and examples, Morgan argues that only the wife can be a total human being. Without any sense of incongruity the wife blends together the best of *The Sensuous Woman* and "the organization woman" who efficiently plans her meals while scrubbing out her refrigerator. "Sex," Morgan comments, "is as clean and pure as eating cottage cheese."

A significant part of contemporary devotional literature differs from the earlier literature in one respect. Marabel Morgan's book is an example. The suggestion of actually trying to *change* things, in this case the husband, is repeatedly cited as a chief cause of divorce and ruin of the home and family. This is the literature of consolation, the chirpy sympathy card.

The peace-of-mind movement that surfaced after World War II superficially resembled the positive-thinking movement popularized by Peale. But there were major differences. Peale considered the personality a tabula rasa and preached habituation and conditioning as the means for creating a positive outlook on a world that was largely neither good nor evil. Such an outlook, in turn, was praised as leading to power, confidence, success, a longer life, and a better world. In contrast, the peace-of-mind movement saw little that was positive and optimistic at all, apart from a vague sense that the universe, excluding most of the human race, was blandly benign.

Fulton Oursler's *The Greatest Story Ever Told,* set as an historical-biblical romance, first appeared as a radio program in 1947. The book, published two years later, has sold more than 4 million copies, has been translated into fifteen languages, and has been made into a Hollywood film. According to Alice Payne Hackett's survey of best-sellers, within a quarter-century of its appearance, Oursler's tale of "the Great Psychologist" with His "eight rules for sound mental health" was the best-selling nonfiction title ever published in America, excluding Bibles and reference works.

Oursler's numerous character studies show that the world of the New Testament was no different from the world of today. Then as now, there were "scientific Christians" (Thomas the Apostle), nagging housewives and "modern women" (Martha and Mary), "nympholeptics" (Salome), "professional pickets," "displaced persons," "lawyers," and "divorcées." But what most attracted Oursler's attention were the leaders. "The trouble is," Jesus Barabbas confides to Joseph at the beginning of the book, "we have no leaders." "Here were the leaders," Oursler comments, "spiritually ill and dying yet wielding power over the minds of the common people." Thus the overarching question, "Is life worth living?"

Oursler proves it was by detailing archetypally maladjusted personalities, all of whom had risen to positions of leadership. Taking the liberty to "fill in the chinks left open in the biblical accounts," he modeled political leaders in the time of Jesus according to the sources of evil he saw in the twentieth century. Too much feeling and the lack of feeling again served as diagnostic instruments for assessing the shape of reality.

There were four typical kinds of maladjusted leaders. The first, the slot for sex and violence, was filled by the two Herods. Herod the Great, a maniacal psychopath "with the bulging eyes of a hyperthyroid victim," caged his enemies in "concentration camps." He was an animal who stole his throne "like a tiger, ruled like a fox and died like a dog." The hedonistic, "fat and pursy" Herod Antipas was "a typical oriental who lived fatly for the full pleasure of his passions," principally for food and sex. The Zealots and especially their leader, Jesus Barabbas, exemplify misdirected passion of a second kind, similar to juvenile delinquency today, a theme that Oursler addressed in other works such as *Father Flanagan of Boys Town* (1949). In *The Greatest Story Ever Told* Oursler implies that today's moral crusaders and revolutionaries are only aging juvenile delinquents who continue to act out the childish games of cowboys and Indians. Communism is juvenile delinquency on an international scale.

On the passionless side were two groups, the Sadducees and the Pharisees. Herod the Great acted like an animal. Annas, "the political boss of Jerusalem," treated the people like animals. And whereas the Zealots acted like children, the Pharisees treated the people like children, badgering them with a legalistic moralism that looks suspiciously like a stereotype of American Fundamentalism.

According to Oursler, moralism, amoralism, moral crusading, and immorality account for evil. Salvation lies in morale, the truly "revolutionary message of Jesus." Oursler and the other peace-of-mind authors hardly preach social adjustment. Joshua Loth Liebman's *Peace of Mind* (1946), which in many respects resembles Oursler's popularizations of the Bible, describes an "at-oneness with the universe" that enables "us to accept disappointment, failure, rejection, even death with adult peace of mind." Oursler writes in a similar vein that "all Jesus had to offer was happiness. This was a state of mental well-being by which a man could remain tranquil and yet with an eager zest for life, no matter how poignant his loss, how deep his sorrow, how excruciating his pain." The New Testament instructs readers about how to be a happy victim. "Hyacinths for the landlord," Oursler wrote elsewhere. "Coffee for the sheriff, a smile even for the executioner." In her formula for holy housewifery Marbach puts it simply: "Cheer up! Tomorrow may be worse."

The happy victim is closely allied with an even more effective symbol, the religious idiot-savant. Dale Evans Rogers wrote the best-selling *Angel Unaware* (1953) as an informal diary. The supposed author is an astonishingly precocious and athletic two-year-old Mongoloid child who has died and gone to heaven after completing a well-planned mission to the people Down There.

"Heroes of the Spirit, Masters of the Palette" is the title of an illustrated essay published by *Reader's Digest*. "All the artists here represented suffer from a grievous handicap," the article begins. "Through illness, accident, birth defect or warfare, they have been deprived of the use of their hands. But through zest for life—and by dogged determination—they have transformed their personal disasters into triumphs we can all enjoy."

During the late 1970s and 1980s millions experienced secondhand the disaster of Joni Eareckson, as related in *Joni* (1976). Paralyzed from the shoulders down in a diving accident at age seventeen, she woke up in a hospital bed meditating on Lamentations 3:4 (Berkeley Version), "He has made my skin and flesh turn old; He has crushed my bones." Franz Kafka's *The Trial* and Viktor Frankl's *Man's Search For Meaning*, dropped off by a well-meaning friend, were no help, but the writings of C. S. Lewis and Francis A. Schaeffer were. So was the Bible, where Eareckson found the verse that directly addressed her quadriplegic condition: "We are handicapped on all sides, but we are never frustrated," 2 Cor. 4:8 (Phillips). "I don't know *why* I was paralyzed," her book admits. "But I wouldn't change my life for anything. I even feel privileged." Joni learned to draw with a pen in her mouth and gained national attention with numerous exhibitions of her art, the publication of three books, frequent apperances at Billy Graham rallies, an interview with Barbara Walters on the "Today" show, the formation of a Joni's Family Club, a "Joni Sings" single from ABC Sanctus Records with a 5" × 7" glossy of Joni inside, and a *Joni's Family Newsletter*. In January 1978 she completed a successful screen test for the motion picture *Joni*. "As she began to deliver her lines," one observer recalled, "tears came to the eyes of the men and women of the crew. . . . This was somehow different. This was real."

John William Ward points to one perennial source of popular religion's appeal in his analysis of Harriet Beecher Stowe's classic: "If one of the tests of the power of fiction is the way in which a novel provides images that order the confusing realities of life, then *Uncle Tom's Cabin* ranks high." Popular religion insists that even though the world often works at cross-purposes and seems organized in contradictory ways, reality is finally neither unpredictable nor confusing. The images and constructs upon which popular religion relies are not those of the scholar and scientist who probe for invisible causes and intangible connections. Instead popular religion works by reminding believers that meaning resides in the logical affinities one dimension of sensible experience has with another. There *is* a certain persuasiveness to the opinion that peoples living in tropical climates tend to be dark-skinned, politically volatile, eat spicy foods, and have hot tempers. Such a way of thinking is even more compelling once one recognizes that it is neither narrow nor closed to new information nor intolerant of diversity. Peoples living in hot climates, like businessman-historian H. H. Bancroft's pale and effeminate natives of Hispaniola, may well loll away the days somnolent under their bananas trees.

Popular religion deals eagerly in such discoveries, in Claude Lévi-Strauss's words, "those which nature authorized from the starting point of a sensible organization and exploitation of the sensible world in sensible terms." Connections discovered at the level of sense experience appear to be timeless and ahistorical. Individuals and societies do not seem to change, nor do the persistent patterns of disharmony and evil. People today are as they were in biblical times. But since things *do* change, the project of modernizing the Kingdom of God never ends. Popular religion appropriates the latest advances in technology and the recent fads and shifting tastes in popular secular culture as proof that things are as they always have been.

Historian Paul A. Carter cited with approval the observation that during the Gilded Age segments of American culture "were getting more religious and more secular at the same time and through the operation of the same forces." The same observation fits contemporary America. Scholars may puzzle over it, but Christians can cite the biblical warrant of Ephesians 5:31–32: "And the two shall become one. This is a great mystery."

BIBLIOGRAPHY

Daniel J. Boorstin, *The Americans: The Democratic Experience* (1973); Paul A. Carter, *The Spiritual Crisis of the Gilded Age* (1971); William A. Clebsch, *From Sacred to Profane America: The*

Role of Religion in American History (1968); Ann Douglas, *The Femininization of American Culture* (1977); Mircea Eliade, *The Sacred and the Profane: The Nature of Religion* (1959).

James D. Hart, *The Popular Book: A History of America's Literary Taste* (1950); Margaret T. Hills, *The English Bible in America: A Bibliography of Editions* (1961); E. Brooks Holifield, *A History of Pastoral Care in America: From Salvation to Self-Realizatin* (1983); James Davison Hunter, *American Evangelism* (1983).

Claude Lévi-Strauss, *The Savage Mind* (1966); H. Richard Niebuhr, *Christ and Culture* (1951); Sandra S. Sizer, *Gospel Hymns and Social Religion: The Rhetoric of Nineteenth-Century Revivalism* (1978); Peter W. Williams, *Popular Religion in America: Symbolic Change and the Modernization Process in Historical Perspective* (1980).

[*See also* Bible in American Culture; Folklore and the Study of American Religion; *and* Mass Communications.]

ALPHABETICAL LISTING OF ARTICLES

ALPHABETICAL LISTING OF ARTICLES

ALPHABETICAL LISTING OF ARTICLES

ALPHABETICAL LISTING OF ARTICLES

ALPHABETICAL LISTING OF ARTICLES

LIST OF CONTRIBUTORS

LIST OF CONTRIBUTORS

Catherine L. Albanese
University of California, Santa Barbara
TRANSCENDENTALISM

Leonard E. Barrett
Temple University
THE AFRICAN HERITAGE IN CARIBBEAN
  AND NORTH AMERICAN RELIGIONS

Laura L. Becker
University of Miami
ETHNICITY AND RELIGION

Newell S. Booth, Jr.
Miami University
ISLAM IN NORTH AMERICA

Henry Warner Bowden
Rutgers University
THE HISTORIOGRAPHY OF AMERICAN
  RELIGION
NORTH AMERICAN INDIAN MISSIONS

Glenn R. Bucher and L. Gordon Tait
The College of Wooster
SOCIAL REFORM SINCE THE GREAT
  DEPRESSION

Donald E. Byrne, Jr.
Lebanon Valley College
FOLKLORE AND THE STUDY OF
  AMERICAN RELIGION

Debra Campbell
Colby College
CATHOLICISM FROM INDEPENDENCE TO
  WORLD WAR I

Lino Gómez Canedo
Academy of American Franciscan History
RELIGION IN THE SPANISH EMPIRE

Donald Capps
Princeton Theological Seminary
THE PSYCHOLOGY OF RELIGIOUS
  EXPERIENCE

Mary K. Cayton
Miami University
CONGREGATIONALISM FROM
  INDEPENDENCE TO THE PRESENT
SOCIAL REFORM FROM THE COLONIAL
  PERIOD THROUGH THE CIVIL WAR

J. E. Robert Choquette
University of Ottawa
FRENCH CATHOLICISM IN THE NEW
  WORLD

Milton J. Coalter, Jr., and John M. Mulder
Louisville Presbyterian Theological Seminary
DUTCH AND GERMAN REFORMED
  CHURCHES

James H. Cone
Union Theological Seminary
BLACK RELIGIOUS THOUGHT

LIST OF CONTRIBUTORS

Walter H. Conser, Jr.
University of North Carolina, Wilmington
RELIGION AND SCIENCE

John W. Cook
Yale University
MATERIAL CULTURE AND THE VISUAL
    ARTS

John Corrigan
University of Virginia
THE ENLIGHTENMENT

Paul A. Crow, Jr.
Council on Christian Unity
THE ECUMENICAL MOVEMENT

Robert Emmett Curran
Georgetown University
AMERICAN CATHOLIC THOUGHT

Robert S. Ellwood
University of Southern California
OCCULT MOVEMENTS IN AMERICA

Wayne Elzey
Miami University
POPULAR CULTURE
RELIGIONS OF MESOAMERICA

Melvin B. Endy, Jr.
Hamilton College
THE SOCIETY OF FRIENDS
WAR AND PEACE

Eldon G. Ernst
Graduate Theological Union
THE BAPTISTS

John Y. Fenton
Emory University
HINDUISM

Deane William Ferm
RELIGIOUS THOUGHT SINCE WORLD
    WAR II

Sandra Sizer Frankiel
University of California, Berkeley
CALIFORNIA AND THE SOUTHWEST

Paul D. Garrett
Antiochian Village
EASTERN CHRISTIANITY

Edwin S. Gaustad
University of California, Riverside
GEOGRAPHY AND DEMOGRAPHY OF
    AMERICAN RELIGION

Sam D. Gill
University of Colorado
NATIVE AMERICAN RELIGIONS

Stephen Gottschalk
CHRISTIAN SCIENCE AND
    HARMONIALISM

John Webster Grant
Emmanuel College
PROTESTANTISM AND SOCIETY IN
    CANADA

C. Carlyle Haaland
Wagner College
SHINTO AND INDIGENOUS CHINESE
    RELIGION

Charles E. Hambrick-Stowe
Church of the Apostles, Lancaster,
    Pennsylvania
THE PROFESSIONAL MINISTRY

David Edwin Harrell, Jr.
University of Alabama, Birmingham
RESTORATIONISM AND THE
    STONE-CAMPBELL TRADITION

James Hennesey
Canisius College
CATHOLICISM IN THE ENGLISH
    COLONIES

Stuart C. Henry
Duke University
REVIVALISM

Henry Herx
Catholic Communications Office
RELIGION AND FILM

Patricia R. Hill
Wesleyan University
THE MISSIONARY ENTERPRISE

LIST OF CONTRIBUTORS

Samuel S. Hill
University of Florida
THE SOUTH

E. Brooks Holifield
Emory University
PASTORAL CARE AND COUNSELING

David L. Holmes
College of William and Mary
THE ANGLICAN TRADITION AND THE
EPISCOPAL CHURCH

Daniel Walker Howe
University of California, Los Angeles
THE IMPACT OF PURITANISM ON
AMERICAN CULTURE

Donald G. Jones
Drew University
CIVIL AND PUBLIC RELIGION

Abraham J. Karp
University of Rochester
THE EMERGENCE OF AN AMERICAN
JUDAISM

Deborah B. Karp and Abraham J. Karp
University of Rochester
JEWISH LITERATURE AND RELIGIOUS
THOUGHT

Rosemary Skinner Keller
Garrett Evangelical Theological Seminary
WOMEN AND RELIGION

William McGuire King
Albright College
LIBERALISM

Christa R. Klein
Religion Division, Lilly Endowment, Inc.
LUTHERANISM

William B. Lawrence
Owego United Methodist Church, Owego,
New York
THE HISTORY OF PREACHING IN
AMERICA

Henry Samuel Levinson
University of North Carolina, Greensboro
RELIGIOUS PHILOSOPHY

Charles H. Lippy
Clemson University
COMMUNITARIANISM
MILLENNIALISM AND ADVENTISM
SOCIAL CHRISTIANITY

Lawrence H. Mamiya and C. Eric Lincoln
Vassar College
Duke University
BLACK MILITANT AND SEPARATIST
MOVEMENTS

Stephen A. Marini
Wellesley College
THE GREAT AWAKENING

George M. Marsden
Duke University
FUNDAMENTALISM

William Martin
Rice University
MASS COMMUNICATIONS

Martin E. Marty
University of Chicago
FREE THOUGHT AND ETHICAL
MOVEMENTS
THE RELIGIOUS PRESS

John A. Mayer
St. Francis College
SOCIAL REFORM AFTER THE CIVIL WAR
TO THE GREAT DEPRESSION

Glenn Miller
Southeastern Baptist Theological Seminary
CHURCH AND STATE

Glenn Miller and Robert Lynn
Southeastern Baptist Theological Seminary
Lilly Endowment, Inc.
CHRISTIAN THEOLOGICAL EDUCATION

Deborah Dash Moore
Vassar College
SOCIAL HISTORY OF AMERICAN
JUDAISM

LIST OF CONTRIBUTORS

James H. Moorhead
Princeton Theological Seminary
THEOLOGICAL INTERPRETATIONS AND
    CRITIQUES OF AMERICAN SOCIETY
    AND CULTURE

Jacob Neusner
Brown University
JUDAISM IN CONTEMPORARY AMERICA

Mark A. Noll
Wheaton College (Illinois)
THE BIBLE IN AMERICAN CULTURE

Jaroslav Pelikan
Yale University
LUTHERAN HERITAGE

F. Michael Perko
Loyola University of Chicago
RELIGION AND COLLEGIATE
    EDUCATION
RELIGIOUS EDUCATION

Charles S. Prebish
Pennsylvania State University
BUDDHISM

Richard Quebedeaux
CONSERVATIVE AND CHARISMATIC
    DEVELOPMENTS OF THE LATER
    TWENTIETH CENTURY

Albert J. Raboteau
Princeton University
BLACK CHRISTIANITY IN NORTH
    AMERICA

**Harold E. Remus, F. Stanley Lusby, and
    Linda M. Tober**
Wilfred Laurier University
University of Tennessee
University of Tennessee
RELIGION AS AN ACADEMIC DISCIPLINE

Leo P. Ribuffo
George Washington University
RELIGIOUS PREJUDICE AND NATIVISM

Russell E. Richey
Duke University
INSTITUTIONAL FORMS OF RELIGION

Thomas Robbins and Dick Anthony
"CULTS" IN THE LATE TWENTIETH
    CENTURY

Lynn Ross-Bryant
Occidental College
RELIGION AND LITERATURE

Robert F. Sayre
University of Iowa
RELIGIOUS AUTOBIOGRAPHY

Jean Miller Schmidt
Iliff School of Theology
HOLINESS AND PERFECTION

Jan Shipps
Indiana University/Purdue University at
    Indianapolis
THE LATTER-DAY SAINTS

George H. Shriver
Georgia Southern College
ROMANTIC RELIGION

William K. B. Stoever
Western Washington University
THE CALVINIST THEOLOGICAL
    TRADITION

Leonard I. Sweet
United Theological Seminary
NINETEENTH-CENTURY
    EVANGELICALISM

Edwin E. Sylvest, Jr.
Southern Methodist University
RELIGION IN HISPANIC AMERICA SINCE
    THE ERA OF INDEPENDENCE

Baird Tipson
Gettysburg College
CALVINIST HERITAGE
NEW ENGLAND PURITANISM

Harold Y. Vanderpool
Institute for the Medical Humanities,
    University of Texas
MEDICINE AND MEDICAL ETHICS

Dennis N. Voskuil
Hope College
NEO-ORTHODOXY

LIST OF CONTRIBUTORS

Grant Wacker
University of North Carolina, Chapel Hill
PENTECOSTALISM

Charles I. Wallace, Jr.
Willamette University
WESLEYAN HERITAGE

Earle H. Waugh
University of Alberta
DIVERSITY AND PLURALISM IN
  CANADIAN RELIGION

Mary Jo Weaver
Indiana University
THE ROMAN CATHOLIC HERITAGE

Louis Weeks
Louisville Presbyterian Theological Seminary
PRESBYTERIANISM

Paul Westermeyer
Elmhurst College
RELIGIOUS MUSIC AND HYMNODY

James F. White
University of Notre Dame
LITURGY AND WORSHIP

Peter W. Williams
Miami University
CATHOLICISM SINCE WORLD WAR I
RELIGIOUS ARCHITECTURE AND
  LANDSCAPE
UNITARIANISM AND UNIVERSALISM

John Wilson
Duke University
THE SOCIOLOGICAL STUDY OF
  AMERICAN RELIGION

Don Yoder
University of Pennsylvania
SECTS AND RELIGIOUS MOVEMENTS OF
  GERMAN ORIGIN

Charles Yrigoyen, Jr.
Drew University
UNITED METHODISM

INDEX

INDEX

INDEX

Apache, 149b, 1511b, 1512a

Apalachee Indians, 1672a

apartheid, 1464b

apocalypticism, 831a–b

Apology for True Christian Divinity (Barclay), 596b, 602a

Apology of the Augsberg Confession, 421a,b

Apostle of Burma, *see* Judson, Adoniram

Apostles' Creed, 421a, 508b

Apostolic Faith, 934b, 937b, 939b, 941a,b

Apostolic Faith Gospel Mission, 1578a

Apostolic Overcoming Holy Church of God, 941b

Appalachia, 1504a–1505b

Appeal to the Coloured Citizens of the World (Walker), 112a, 1178a

Application of Redemption, The (Hooker), 1041a

Aquarian Gospel of Jesus Christ, 716b

Aquinas, Thomas, 160b, 161a, 1006a, 1654a

Arabs, 1487a

Arada sect, 181b

Aragón, 191b

Arbeiter Ring schools, 1607b

Arcana School, 719a

archaeology: and study of religion, 1654a

architecture, *see* Religious Architecture and Landscape

Are Parochial Schools the Answer? (Perkins), 387b

Argall, Samuel, 226a

Argenteum Astrum, 720b

Arian heresy, 748b

Arichat (Canada), 236a

Arieli, Yehoshua, 1399a, 1403a

Aristotle and Aristotelianism, 1090a,b–1091a

Arizona, 198b, 360b, 1511a,b, 1517a, 1673b

Arlington Street Church (Boston), 1673b

Armenian Apostolic Church of America, 343b

Armenians, 326a, 343a

Arminianism, 393b, 399a, 464b–465a, 467b, 478a, 483b, 487a,b, 513a, 556b, 563b–565a, 779b, 793b, 800b, 875b–876a, 1045a,b, 1684b

Arminian Magazine, 535b

Arminius, Jacobus, 458a, 459a, 464b, 513a, 556a–b, 580b

Armstrong, Herbert W., 1707b, 1713b

Army, United States, 694a

Arnauld, Antoine, 1090a

Arndt, Karl J. R., 625b

Arnold, Eberhard, 626a

Arnold, Gottfried, 620b

Arrow, Lucy, 826b

art, *see* Material Culture and the Visual Arts

Art as Experience (Dewey), 1201b

Arthur, T. S., 1737b

Articles of Faith (Talmage), 662b

Articles of Faith of the Evangelical Church, 551a

artificial insemination, 1262a,b, 1263a

Art of Counseling (May), 1590b

Art of Ministering to the Sick (Dicks), 1589b

Arunduell, Sir Thomas, 345a

Arya Samaj, 689a

Asbury College (Maryland), 544a

Asbury, Francis, 540b, 541a,b, 542a,b, 543b, 795a, 796a, 846a, 879a, 889a, 1255b, 1308a, 1312a, 1315b, 1575a–b

Asbury Theological Seminary (Kentucky), 827a, 828a

Ashanti-Fanti, 172a, 175a, 176b–177a, 179b

Asher, Jeremiah, 638a

Ashkenazi, 274a, 292b, 1015b, 1016a, 1303a

Ashmun Institute, *see* Lincoln University

Asia, 990a–b, 1167b–1168a; *see also* Far East

Asian-Americans, 674b–675a, 1545a

Asian religions: Hinduism, 690a–b; Hispanic America, 202b; Shinto and indigenous Chinese, 699a–709b

Asians: Baptists, 570a–b; California, 1518a–b; Moorish Science, 756b, 757a

Asian studies, 673b

Aspirations of Nature (Hecker), 1003b

Assemblies of God, 933a, 939b–940b, 941a, 942b, 967a,b, 1264a, 1422b, 1504b, 1578a, 1606a, 1617a,b, 1694a

Assistant, The (Malamud), 1025a

Associated Church Press, 1708a

Associated Jewish Charities of Chicago, 1454b

Associated Parishes, 1271b

Associate Presbyterian Church (Seceders), 501b

Associated Reform churches, 501b, 506a, 507a, 508a, 510a, 1684b

Association for Clinical Pastoral Education, 1590a

Association for Research and Enlightenment, 719b

Association for the Sociology of Religion, 19b

Association of American Hebrew Congregations, 277b

Association of Catholic Trade Unionists, 1471a

Association of Disciples Colleges, 1616b

Association of Evangelical Friends, 610a–b

Association of Evangelical Lutheran Churches, 444b, 1572b

Association of Evangelicals for Italian Mission, 570a

Association of Motion Picture Producers, 1355a

Association of Muslim Scientists and Engineers, 727a

Association of Muslim Social Scientists, 727a

Association of Pentecostal Churches of America, 823b

Association of Southern Women for the Prevention of Lynching, 1450a

Association of Theological Schools, 1639b

associations (Chinese religion), 708a–b

Assumption, 326b

INDEX

INDEX

Carpatho-Russian Orthodox Greek Catholic Church in the U.S.A., 336b, 342a

Carranza, Pedro de, 193b

Carranza, Venustiano, 215b, 216a

Carrasco, David, 129b

Carrera, Rafael, 209a

Carroll, Charles, II (of Annapolis), 351a–b, 354a

Carroll, Charles, III (of Carrollton), 351a, 357b–358a, 359a,b, 360b, 998a

Carroll, Daniel, 350b

Carroll, Henry K., 5b

Carroll, James, 351a

Carroll, John, 75b, 351a, 354a, 359b, 366b, 645a, 998a–999a, 1082a, 1280b, 1314a,b, 1383a, 1528b, 1569b, 1637a–b

Cartagena Colombia de Indias, 192b

"Cart and Whip" Act (1661), 597b

Carter, Jimmy, 573b, 972b, 973a, 1074a, 1075b, 1469a, 1474a, 1544a, 1725b

Carter, Paul A., 494b, 1740b

Cartesianism, 1090a,b

Cartier, George Étienne, 265a

Cartier, Jacques, 225a, 256a

Cartwright, Peter, 795b, 805a–b, 1227b, 1231a, 1308a, 1312a–b, 1566b–1567a, 1637a

Cartwright, Thomas, 462b

Carus, Paul, 671b

Casas, Bartolomé de las, 1671b

Case, Shirley Jackson, 567b

case divinity, *see* casuistry

Case of the Episcopal Churches in the United States Considered, The (White), 395b

Cashwell, Gaston Barnabus, 826b, 939b, 1578a

Casimir, Johann, 457b

Castañeda, Carlos E., 198a

Castro, Emilio, 989a

Castro, Fidel, 218a, 219a

casuistry, 1583b–1584a,b

Cathedral of Saint John the Divine (New York City), 1364a

cathedrals, 1325b–1326a

cathedra Petri (seat of Peter), 329a

Catholic Advocate, 1250a

Catholic Apostolic Church, 1275a

Catholic Art Association, 382a

Catholic Association for International Peace, 1422b

Catholic Biblical Association of America, 1008b, 1083a, 1663a,b

Catholic Biblical Quarterly, 1008b

Catholic Central Verein, 371b

Catholic Church Extension Society, 1691a

Catholic Columbian, 925b

Catholic Confraternity of Christian Doctrine, 1605a, 1606a

Catholic Daughters of America, 372a

Catholic Digest, 1701a

Catholic Educational Association, 1600a

Catholic Film Newsletter, see Film and Broadcasting Review

Catholic Foreign Mission Society (Maryknoll), 1691a–b, 1692a

Catholic Herald, 925b

Catholic Historical Review, 378a, 1007a

Catholic Hospital Association, 1260b

"Catholic Hour, The," 1007b, 1714b, 1716a

Catholic Interracial Council, 387a, 1692b

Catholicism, Roman: abortion, 1258a; African heritage, 184b–185a; Americanization, 45a–b; Anglican Reformation, 391a–392b; architecture, 1333b, 1326b–1327a, 1328a, 1335b–1336a,b, 1337a–b, 1338a; autobiography, 1232b–1233b; Bible, 1076b, 1078b, 1081b–1082a, 1085a–b; birth control, 20b; blacks, 645a–646a; broadcasting, 1714b, 1715b–1716a, 1717a,b, 1718a; California and Southwest, 1513a, 1514a–b, 1517a; Canada, 242a, 244a, 247a, 249a, 250a, 251a–b, 254a,b; capitalism, 1464a; church and state, 1375a, 1376b, 1383a–1385a,b, 1386a, 1388; church attendance, 83a; and civil religion, 1407a; conscientious objectors, 1424b; Cuba, 183a; desegregation, 1467a; divorce, 21b; and Eastern Christianity, 332b; ecumenism, 980b, 981b, 991a,b–992b; education, 1619b–1621b, 1622b, 1623a; and Episcopal Church, 409b, 411a, 412b, 415a; ethnicity and, 1478b, 1480b, 1481b, 1482a,b–1483a, 1483b–1484a, 1486b, 1489a; evangelicalism, 880b–881b, 885b, 973a; feminist theology, 1166a; fertility rate, 21b; films, 381a, 1343a, 1540b, 1542b; folklore and folk belief, 91b, 95b, 98a, 99b; free thinkers, 736b–737a; French in New World, 223a–238b; and Fundamentalism, 957b; geography and demography, 72b, 74a–b, 75a,b, 77b, 80a,b, 83b; German immigrants, 615b; German Reformed churches, 519a,b; Hispanics, 80a, 201a–222b; historiography, 4b, 6a–b, 11b, 13a, 14b–15a; hospitals, 1260a–b; Italians, 406a–b; Jehovah's Witnesses, 838a–b; laity, 36a; liturgy and worship, 1280a–1281a; and Lutherans, 420b, 421a, 422b, 446b–447a, 449b; marriage, 27b; material culture and visual arts, 1360a–b, 1364b; medicine and medical ethics, 1256b–1257a, 1260a–b, 1261b, 1263b; Métis movement, 269b; ministry, 1566a, 1569b–1571a; missions, 1673a,b, 1674a, 1679a–b, 1680a,b, 1681a, 1690b–1691a, 1692b, 1694b, 1695a; music, 1285a–b; Native Americans, 263b, 1457b, 1673a,b, 1674a, 1679a–b, 1680a–b, 1681a; nuns, 1554a–b; Oxford movement, 401b–402b; pastoral care, 1583a, 1584b, 1586a, 1591a–

INDEX

Christian Arbitration and Peace Society, 1419a, 1459a

Christian Attitudes Toward War and Peace (Bainton), 1468a

Christian Baptist, 848b

Christian Beacon, 959b

Christian Beliefs and Anti-Semitism (Glock and Stark), 20a

Christian Bookseller's Association, 1736a

Christian Broadcasting Network, 1717b, 1719b, 1735a

Christian Catechism (Schaff), 1113b

Christian Century, 853a, 933a, 1149b, 1540b, 1541a, 1703a, 1704a–b

Christian Church (Disciples of Christ), 249a, 502b, 544b, 846a–b, 857a, 1273a, 1493b–1494a, 1614b

Christian Commission, 1445b

Christian Conference of Asia, 989b

Christian Connection Church, 588a, 849a–b, 850b, 854b

Christian Endeavor Society, 924a

Christian Evangelist, 852b–853a; see also *Christian*

Christian Faith and Life curriculum, 506a

Christian Front, 1541a

Christian Fundamentals Association, 955a

Christian History, 795b

Christian Holiness Association, 813a, 828a

Christianity, Social, *see* Social Christianity

Christianity and Barthianism (Van Til), 1156a

Christianity and Crisis (Niebuhr), 1465b, 1701b, 1703a, 1704b

Christianity and the Social Crisis (Rauschenbusch), 109a–b

Christianity as a Purely Internal Principle (Francis), 1122b

Christianity in Culture (Kraft), 971b

Christianity Today, 960a, 964a, 965a–b, 966a, 1168a, 1694b, 1695a, 1703a, 1705a,b, 1730a

Christian Labour Union, 922a

Christian Library (Wesley), 528a

Christian Lyre, The (Leavitt), 1285a, 1294b

Christian Manifesto, A (Lewis), 1152b, 1466a

Christian Marketplace, The, 1720a

Christian Messenger, 847b

Christian Methodist Episcopal Church, 547a, 641a, 648a, 1177a, 1444a, 1617b

Christian Ministry (Abbott), 1144b, 1565a

Christian Missions and Social Progress (Dennis), 1689a

"Christian" movement, 1576a–b

Christian Nurture (Bushnell), 489b, 1053b, 1109a, 1385b, 1608a

Christian Oracle, see Christian Century

Christian Pastor and the Working Church, The (Gladden), 1144b, 1565a, 1586b

Christian Philosopher, The (Mather), 781a, 1043a–b, 1090b, 1238b

Christian Recorder, 1700b

Christian Reformed Church, 514b–515a, 515b–516a, 1275b, 1602b, 1616b, 1617b, 1713b

Christian Science and Harmonialism, **901a–916b;** California, 1519a; campus ministries, 1623a; medicine, 1258b, 1259b; publishing, 1698b–1699a, 1707a–b; science and, 1249a; Transcendentalism, 1127a; women, 1448b–1449a, 1554a

Christian Science Monitor, 914b, 1698b

Christian Science Sentinel, 1707a–b

Christiansen, F. Melius, 1302b

Christians in the American Revolution (Noll), 14a–b

Christian Socialism, *see* Social Gospel

Christian Socialist Fellowship, 922a

Christian Social Union, 408b, 922a

Christian Sociology, *see* Social Gospel

Christian Standard, 852b, 853a, 856b

Christian Standard and Home Journal, 816a

Christian Theological Education, **1627a–1652b**

Christian Theology in Outline (Brown), 1134a

Christian Voice, 1725b–1726a

Christian Watchman, 363b

Christian Woman's Board of Missions, 1446a

Christian World Liberation Front, 840a, 969a, 970b, 1624a

Christian Worship, 1301b

Christian Yellow Pages, 1725b, 1735b

Christ in Theology (Bushnell), 1110a

Christmas, 1364b–1365a

Christocentric motifs, 1137b

Christology, 160a, 1137a–b

Christopher, Saint, 225b

Christ Seminary-Seminex (Seminary in Exile), 444b

"Christ the Lord Is Risen Today," 533b

Christ the Saviour Seminary (Pennsylvania), 336b

Christus, 1343a

Christy (Marshall), 1738a–b

Chronicon Ephratense, 624b

Chronological History of New-England (Prince), 3b

Chrysostom, Saint John, 164a–b, 1281b

Chubb, Thomas, 1045a

Church Against the World, The (Muller), 1153a

Church Against the World, The (Niebuhr), 1153b

Church Amish, 619a

Church and State, 1240b, **1369a–1391b;** Canadian Protestantism, 243b–244b; Catholicism, 157a,b, 370b, 371a, 384a, 998b, 1004b, 1009a–b; disestablishment, 485a; Eastern Christianity, 328a; ecumenism, 985b; Enlightenment, 1099a; France, 223b–224a; Islam, 724a–b; Lutheranism, 435a; Mexico, 216b, 217a; Puritanism, 1061b–1062a; religious education, 1599a, 1604b–1605a; Spanish empire, 191b; U.S. Constitution, 1529b

Church and State in the United States (Schaff), 4a

Darrow, Clarence, 738a, 956b, 1249b, 1387a, 1420a, 1540a

Dartmouth College (New Hampshire), 795b, 1063b, 1612b, 1613b, 1615a, 1676b

Dartmouth College case (1819), 1656b

Darwin, Charles, and Darwinism, 1244a–b, 1245a–1246a,b, 1247a, 1248a, 1249a–1250b; and Africans, 173a; Bible, 1085b; church and state, 1386b–1387a; Congregationalism, 491b–492a; Episcopal Church, 410b; free thought, 735a,b; Fundamentalism, 956b, 1456a; liberalism, 1134b, 1135b–1136a; romantic religion, 1110b; theological education, 1635a

Darwinism, Social, *see* Social Darwinism

Daughters of Sarah, 973b

Daughters of the American Revolution, 1405b

Daughters of Zion, 303b

Dauversière, Royer de la, 227b

Davenant, John, 462b

Davenport, James, 780a,b, 790a

David, Samuel, 334b, 341a

David and Bathsheba, 1349b

David Lipscomb College (Tennessee), 855a

Davidson, Israel, 1017b

Davies, Horton, 1269a

Davies, Samuel, 500b, 791b–792a, 795b, 1096a, 1374a–b, 1566b

Davis, Alexander Jackson, 1334a

Davis, Andrew Jackson, 903b

Davis, Jackson, 716a,b

Davis, Jefferson, 404a, 1084a

Davis, Ossie, 769a

Davisson, Ananias, 1297b

da'wa (call to Islam), 729b

Dawes Act of 1887, 1458a

Dawn, 917b, 925b

Dawn Horse Fellowship, *see* Primitive Church of Divine Communion

Dawson, Sir J. William, 246a

Day, Dorothy, 167a, 169b, 379a, 388b, 1007b, 1233a–b, 1471a, 1558a, 1701b

Day, Stephen, 1286b

"Day of Discovery," 1713b

Day of Doom, The (Wigglesworth), 833a

Day of Judgment, 723b

Day of Wrath, 1346b–1347a

day schools, 1602b–1603b

Dayton, Donald W., 828a

deaconesses, 548a, 630a, 1559a, 1580b, 1686b

deacons, 452b, 512a

deadly sins, 65b

death carts, 1360b

death imagery, 1360b

Death of a Salesman (Miller), 1023a

death of god, 114b, 674a–b, 1162b–1163a,b

DeBenneville, George, 630a

Deborah, 1019a

Decision, 876b

"Declaration of Evangelical Social Concern" (1973), 970b, 1168b

Declaration of Independence (Trumbull), 1363b

Declaration on Religious Freedom (1965), 111a, 157b, 384a, 1162a, 1471b

DeConcini, Dennis, 274a, 277a

De Conscientiae (Ames), 1040b

"Decree on Ecumenism," 1162a

Dedham case (1820), 583b, 1379a–b

Deep River (Thurman), 1180b

Defender, 958b

Definite Synodical Platform, 441a,b

DeHaan, M. R., 1713b

Deism, 531b, 732a, 733a–b, 1099b, 1100a, 1101a–b, 1212b, 1214a, 1256b

Deistical Society of New York, 1101a

deities, 258b–259a

De La Motta, Jacob, 278b, 279b

Delannoy, Jean, 1350b

Delany, Henry, 405a

De la recherche de la verité (Malebranche), 1090a

Delaware, 500a, 513b, 1527a

Delaware College, 1615a

Delaware Indians, 148a, 1676b–1677b

Delaware Prophet, 1681a

De Legibus (Suarez), 206a

Delgado, Richard, 743a, 752a

Deluge (Allston), 1362b

Demby, Thomas, 405a

DeMille, Cecil B., 1344b–1345a, 1349b

Democracy and Education (Dewey), 1588a

Democracy in America (Tocqueville), 362a

democratic faith, 1402b

Democratic party: Catholics, 376b, 383b; evangelicalism, 895b; Jews, 298b, 309a; Pentecostals, 943b; religious prejudice, 1537a, 1540a,b, 1544a; social reform, 1450b; sociology of religion, 23a,b

Democratic-Republican party, 482a,b, 1378b, 1530b

Democratic Vistas (Whitman), 1226b

democratization, 36a, 1080a

Demoglou, Alexander, 335a

demographics, *see* Geography and Demography of American Religions

Dempster, John, 814b

Denck, Hans, 616b

Denison University (Ohio), 562a

Dennis, James, 1689a

denominationalism: Canadian Protestantism, 241b–242a; Congregationalism, 485b, 488a–b, 489a, 490b–491a, 493b; ecumenism, 981b; ethnicity,

INDEX

Elliott, Walter, 371a, 1642b

Ellis, John Tracy, 11b, 382a, 1008a, 1161a

Ellison, Ralph, 1220a

Ellwood, Charles A., 19a

Ellwood, Robert S., 15a, 682a, 1520b, 1727a

Elmer Gantry (film), 1348b

Elmer Gantry (Lewis), 112b

Elmhurst College (Illinois), 521a

El Salvador, 221a,b; *see also* Religions of Mesoamerica

Elson, Edward R., 964a

El Tajín, 120a

ELWA ("Eternal Love Winning Africa"), 1715a

Ely, Ezra Styles, 1585a

Ely, Richard T., 409a, 920b–921a, 1248a, 1449a

emancipation (Judaism), 273a–b

Embarkation of the Pilgrims (Weir), 1363b

Embury, Philip, 540a

Emergence of an American Judaism, The, **273a–290b**

Emergence of Liberal Catholicism in America (Cross), 15a

Emergency Peace Campaign, 1423a

emergent religions, 1520b

Emerson, Ralph Waldo, 105b, 585a, 683b, 734a,b, 903a, 913b, 1064a, 1065a, 1070b, 1106b, 1107a–b, 1108a, 1117a,b, 1120a–b, 1122a–b, 1123a, 1124a,b, 1125b, 1126b, 1131b, 1191b, 1192b–1193a, 1214a–1215a, 1221a, 1225b–1126a, 1231a, 1239a, 1243a,b–1244a, 1273a–b

Emerson v. *Board of Education* (1947), 1386a

E-meter, 749b

Émile (Rousseau), 1104a

Emmons, Nathaniel, 1631a

emperor: Shinto, 700b–701a, 702a–b, 705a

Empire Strikes Back, The, 842a

empiricism, 779a–b, 1089b, 1102a, 1139b–1140a,b, 1141b–1143b, 1190b, 1192a, 1199a–b

Enchiridion, *see* Small Catechism

encomienda land system, 1671a–b

end-of-inquiry realism, 1194b

endogamy, 1488b–1489a, 1490a,b

endowments (Mormonism), 659b

Endy, Melvin B., Jr., 14a

Engel v. *Vitale* (1962), 1386a, 1605a

England: anti-Catholicism, 1525b; Anglican tradition and Episcopal Church, 391a–392b; Calvinism, 456b–457a, 461a–463a, 464a–465b; Canada and French Catholicism, 228b–229a; colonies and Catholicism, 345a–355b; Jews, 292a, 295a; Wesleyanism, 529b–530a

England, John, 363b, 366b, 886b, 999a–1000a, 1314a, 1384a

English Synod of Ohio, 442a

Enlightenment, The, **1089a–1102b;** church and state, 1374b–1376a; civil religion, 1398a,b,; free thought and ethical movements, 732a–733a;

Great Awakening, 775b, 779a–b; Hispanic America, 195b, 205b–206a; history of American religion, 3b; Judaism, 273a–b, 292a, 1381b; literature and religion, 1213b; liturgy and worship, 1271a, 1273a, 1277b; Lutheranism, 429a; medicine, 1256a–b; occultism, 714a–715a; Roman Catholic theology, 157b, 161a; science and religion, 1239a–1242a; religious studies, 1654a; theological interpretation of America, 103b–104a; Transcendentalism, 1118b

Enquiry Concerning the Human Understanding (Hume), 779b

Ensign, 1707b

Enthusiasm Described and Caution'd Against (Chauncy), 790a, 1093a

entire sanctification, 814a,b, 815a, 817a,b, 819a, 935a–b, 936a, 938b, 1577b

Ephrata Community, 624a–b, 1293a–b, 1373b, 1551a

epidemics, 1255b–1256a

episcopacy, 395b–396b, 458b

Episcopalian Church Association for the Advancement of the Interest of Labor, 922a

Episcopal Church of Saint Clement (Virginia), 1338b

Episcopal Divinity School, *see* Episcopal Theological School

Episcopalian, The, 1702b, 1708b

Episcopalianism, 481a–b; Anglican tradition and, 391a–418a; architecture, 1338b; bishops, 358b; blacks, 638a, 1444a–b; California, 1514b; Canada, 240a, 268b; Catholicism, 364b; church and state, 1378a; collegiate education, 1614b, 1617b, 1622b, 1623a; disestablishment, 485a; divorce, 21b; and Eastern Christianity, 333b; ecumenism, 982b, 986a, 991b; ethnicity and religion, 1478b; and Fundamentalism, 955b; geography and demography, 77b; laity, 36a; liberalism, 1129a; and Lutherans, 432b, 449b; Mexico, 1571b; missionaries, 1684b; music and hymnody, 1291b–1292a, 1293b; Native American missions, 1679b, 1681a; on nuclear war, 1427a–b; pastoral care, 1585b–1586a, 1587b–1588a; politics, 23a; prejudice, 1529a; and Puritanism, 1060b; religious education, 1603b; social reform, 1438b; South, 1495a, 1496b–1497a, 1503a, 1504b, 1506a,b; South Africa, 1464b; on war, 1415b, 1416a, 1417a, 1419b, 1425b; women, 1469b, 1559b, 1580b, 1581a

Episcopal League for Social Action, 408b

Episcopal Pacifist Fellowship, 411b

Episcopal Society for Cultural and Racial Unity, 412b

Episcopal Theological School (Massachusetts), 407b, 408a, 416a–b

"Epistle to the Hebrews" (Lazarus), 1019a

Epitome Doctrines Moralis (Golius), 1190b

INDEX

INDEX

Formula of the Mass (Luther), 428a

Fort Wayne Gospel Temple, 836a

"forty-eighters," 736b

Forum, The, 750a

Forverts, see Jewish Daily Forward

Forward Movement Publications, 1736a

Fosdick, Harry Emerson, 505b, 572a–b, 588b, 955b, 1149a, 1304a, 1319b–1320b, 1323a, 1574b, 1589a, 1711a

Foster, Charles I., 14b, 1699b–1700a

Foster, George Burman, 567b, 1141a

Foster, John, 1101b, 1359b

Foster, Lawrence, 659a

Foster, Randolph S., 818a

Foundations of Belief (Dewart), 1169b

Four Gallican Articles (1682), 224a

Fourier, Charles, 861a

Fourierism, 861a, 1124a, 1125b, 1126a

Four Noble Truths, 669a

Four Quartets, The (Eliot), 1231b

Foursquare Gospel Church, *see* International Church of the Foursquare Gospel

Fourteen Points (Satolli), 1600a

Fowler, James W., 66a, 67b–68a

Fox, George, 595a–b, 597a–b, 598a, 608b, 610a, 1275b

Fox, Margaretta and Catherine, 716a–b

France: Catholicism, 223a–255a, 1525b; church and state, 1383b; Jews, 292a; medicine, 1257a; Mexico, 211a; Reformed churches, 457b–458a; slaves, 171b; Spanish-America missions, 197b, 1512a; theological education, 1637b–1638a

Francis I, King, 223b

Francis, Convers, 1117b, 1122b

Franciscans, 168b; art, 1360a; colonial Maryland, 350a; education in Spanish America, 192b, 193a; French colonies, 229b–230a; Hispanic America, 201b, 360b; hospitals, 194a; Mexico, 121b, 122b, 210b; missions, 75b, 361a, 1511a, 1512a, 1513a, 1569b, 1595a–b; Native American missions, 1671b–1672a,b, 1673a,b, 1675b; Our Lady of Guadalupe, 205a; Spanish missionaries, 187b, 188a–b, 189a,b–190a, 197a–198b

Francis of Assisi, 168b

Francis of Sales, 224b

Francke, August Hermann, 434a, 778b

Franckean Synod, 440b, 441b

Franco, Francisco, 379b, 1541b

Frank, Leo, 1538b

Frankean Evangelical Lutheran Synod, 1438b

Frankel, Zacharias, 273b, 277b, 1030b

Frankfurter, Felix, 1455a

Franklin, Benjamin, 358b, 714a, 732a, 785b, 852b, 1062b, 1067b, 1068a,b, 1091b, 1213a,b, 1223b, 1256b, 1289a, 1376a, 1398a,b, 1528a, 1655b

Franklin College (Indiana), 562a

Franzmann, Martin, 1304a

Fraternal Appeal (Schmucker), 437b

fraternal orders, 1405b

Fraternitas Rosae Crucis, 719b

Frazier, Edward Franklin, 15a, 174a

Frederick William III, 457a, 512b, 520a, 981b

free blacks, 206a, 367a, 492a, 638b–639a, 871a,b

Free Church, 243b, 244b, 1269b, 1270a–b, 1272a–1274a, 1276a, 1279

Freed-Hardeman Junior College (Tennessee), 855a

Freedman's Commission, 404b

Freedman's Savings and Trust Company, 1443a

freedmen, 1442b–1443b, 1700b

Freedmen's Aid Society, 547b

Freedmen's Bureau, 1442b, 1443a

Freedom Church, *see* African Methodist Episcopal Zion Church

Freedom Now, see Other Side, The

Freedom Now party, 1467b

freedom of religion: and cults, 751b

Freedom's Ferment, 1331b

Freedom's Ferment (Tyler), 656a

Freedom's Journal, 1700b

freehold, 1370a

free love, 734b

Freeman, George Washington, 603b

Freeman, James, 580b, 1095a, 1098a

Freemasonry, 515a, 628a, 714b, 733a

Free Methodist Church of North America, 818a–b, 828b, 1617a

Free Presbyterian Church, 1438b

Free Religious Association, 586b, 587a,b, 735b, 736a, 737b, 739b, 1247b

Free Serbian Orthodox Diocese, 340a, 342b

Free-Soil party, 1072a

free speech, 1387b–1388a

Free Synagogue, 1320b

Freethinkers of America, 738a, 739a

Free Thought and Ethical Movements, **731a–740b**

Free Thought Society of America and Other Americans, Inc., 739a

free will, 1098a

Free Will Baptists, 481b, 495a, 563b–564a, 1439a, 1504a, 1617b

Frelingheusen, Jacob, 500b

Frelinghuysen, Theodore Jacob, 514a, 782a–b, 788b, 799a–b, 807a, 1374a

French-Canadians, *see* French Catholicism in the New World

French Catholicism in the New World, **223a–238b,** 254a, 357b; and English colonies, 343a,b; geography and demography, 75b; religious education, 1595b–1596a

French Prophets, 626a

French Revolution, 1105b

Freud, Sigmund, and Freudians, 60b–61b, 63a, 1258a, 1587b, 1658b

Freylinghausen, Johann Anastasius, 436a

Frick, Henry Clay, 810a

Friedlaender, Israel, 283a, 1017b, 1030b–1031b

Friedensbote, 521a

Friends, *see* Society of Friends

Friends, General Conference, 608b, 611a

"Friends of Truth," 595b

Friends United Meeting, 610b–61a

Frisbee, Lonnie, 969a

Frisco Kid, The, 1345b

Fritchman, Stephen, 590b

Fritz, Maxine, 1734a

Frobisher, Sir Martin, 239a

From Luther to Hitler (McGovern), 424a

Fromm, Erich, 1591b

From Puritan to Yankee (Bushman), 13b

From the Manger to the Cross, 1343a

Frontenac, Louis de Buade de, 228a

frontier: Catholics, 362a; communitarianism, 861a–b; demography, 76a–b; folklore, 91b–92a; historiography, 6b–7b; religious buildings, 1331a; revivalism, 804b–805b

"Frontiers of Faith," 1715b

Frontier Spirit in American Christianity (Turner), 6b

Frost, Robert, 1065a, 1218b

Frothingham, Octavius Brooks, 586b, 736a, 1247b

Froude, R. H., 1114b

Fruitlands, 1123b, 1124a–b, 1439a

Fruit of Islam, 765b, 769b

Fruit of the Spirit Ranch, 1734a

Fry, Daniel, 717b

Fry, Franklin Clark, 444b, 998a

Fuenleal, Sebastian Ramirez de, 196b

Fuenmayor, Alonso de, 196b

Fugitive, The, 1348b

fuguing tunes, 1291a

Funita, Terumi, 704b

Fullam, Terry, 415b

Fuller, Charles E., 958b, 1713b–1714a

Fuller, Margaret, 592b, 1108a, 1117a, 1122b, 1124a,b, 1126a–b, 1243a

Fuller, Robert C., 903a, 905a

Fuller, William E., 941a

Fuller Theological Seminary, 960a, 970b, 1714a, 1727b

Full Gospel Businessmen's Fellowship International, 967a

Full Gospel Tabernacles, 942a

Fulton, Robert, 1100b

Fundamentalism, 810a, **947a–962b**, 1071a, 1159a, 1160b; abortion, 1263b; and Baptists, 571b– 572a; Bible, 1081b, 1085a; biblical inerrancy, 1320a; broadcasting, 1711a–b; Canada, 247b– 248a, 251b; and Catholicism, 376a; collegiate education, 1618b, 1623b; divorce, 21b; electronic church, 82a; Episcopal Church, 410b; folklore, 99b; free thought and ethical movements, 738a,b, 739a,b; liberalism, 1145a, 1148a; literature, 1220b; ministry, 1573b, 1574b, 1578b; missions, 1688a,b, 1693a, 1694a,b; Neoevangelicalism, 963a, 965b, 969b; New Christian Right, 973b– 975a; post-World War II, 1168a–b, 1169a; preaching, 1567a; prejudice, 1540a,b, 1542b, 1543a,b, 1545b–1546a; and Presbyterians, 505a– b; publishing, 1705a; Quakers, 610b; science, 1248b–1250a; social reform, 1441b, 1456a; South, 1506b–1507a; theological education, 1647a–b, 1651a–b; theological interpretations of America, 109b–110a; women, 1558a–b, 1581a

Fundamentalism and American Culture (Marsden), 14b, 1507a

Fundamentalist Journal, 1705a

Fundamentalist Phenomenon, The (Falwell), 974b

Fundamentals, The: A Testimony to the Truth, 1081b, 1248b

fund-raising, 304a–b, 316a, 410a

Funes, Dean, 195b

Furfey, Paul Hanley, 1997b

Furman, Richard, 1635b

Furman University (South Carolina), 562a, 1636a

Furness, William Henry, 1118a, 1122b

Future of an Illusion (Freud), 1258a

Future of Belief, The (Dewart), 1169b

G

Gaba, Christian, 175b

Gaceta de Guatemala, 205b

Gabriel, Ralph Henry, 1318a, 1399a

Gadamer, H. G., 1664a

Gaden, Eileen, 1734a

Gage, Charles, 352a

Galagina, *see* Boudinot, Elias

Galambos, Louis, 39b

Galicians, 266a, 333b, 343a

Galileo, 1237a,b

Gallicanism, 223a–224a, 225a

Gallup Organization: on Canadian religion, 253a; church membership, 83a; Episcopal Church, 417a; religion's influence, 285a–b; religious broadcasting, 1719b, 1721a,b, 1722a,b; religious preferences, 83b

galut (exile), 111b

INDEX

Glasgow Colonial Society, 241a
Glas, John, 845a
Glatzer, Nahum N., 1034a
Glazer, Nathan, 12a, 1473a–b, 1544b
Gleaner, The, 1019a
Gleason, Philip, 11b, 45a
glebes, 394a, 1370a, 1378a
Glennon, Joseph Cardinal, 387a
Clock, Charles Y., 20a, 745a, 1520b
Glorious Revolution, 599a, 1375a–b
glossolalia (speaking in tongues), 81b, 82a, 643b,
    763b, 826a–b, 933b–934a, 966b, 968a, 1279b,
    1506b
Gloucester, Stephen, 638b
Glover, Ann, 352b
Glueck, Nelson, 1018a
Gnadenhütten (Ohio), 1677b
Gnosticism, 719a–b
Godard, Jean-Luc, 1354a
God Deals with Us as Rational Creatures (Colman), 1090b
Goddenough, Erwin, 60b
God in Christ (Bushnell), 1109b
God in Christ (Nevin), 1053b
God in You, The (Eby), 621b
God Needs Men, 1350b
God of the Oppressed (Cone), 1185b
Go Down, Moses and Other Stories (Faulkner), 1219a
Godoy, Manuel de, 206b
gods, Mesoamerican, 120b, 122a,b, 123a, 124a–126b,
    127a–128a, 131a
"God's Coward" (Hennacy), 1233b
God's New Israel (Cherry), 1399a
Godspell, 1349b–1350a
"God's White House" (Washington, DC), 764b
God That Failed, The (Wright), 1234b
Goebel, Max, 513a
Gogarten, Friedrich, 1150b
Going, Jonathan, 561b
Going My Way, 1348a
Gold, Herbert, 1024a
Gold, Michael, 1022a
Golden Age, The, 1352b
Golden Censer (Bradbury), 1295a
Golden Chain (Bradbury), 1295a
Golden Shower (Bradbury), 1295a
Goldman, Emma, 1455a–b
Goldmark, Josephine, 1455a
Gold Mountain Dhyāna Monastery, 681a
Goldstein, David, 371b–372a
Golem, The, 1347a
Golius, Theophilus, 1190b
Gomar, Francis (Gomarus), 1459a–b
Gompers, Samuel, 1455a
Góngora, Antonio Caballero y, 195b, 196b

"Goodbye, Columbus" (Roth), 1025a
Goodhue, Bertram Grosvenor, 1336b, 1337a, 1339a,
    1364a
Goodman, Christopher, 456b
Good News Bible, 1076b, 1729b
Goodpasture, Benton C., 855a
Goodspeed, Edgar J., 567b
good works, 167b–168a
Gopi Krishna's Kundalini Research Foundation, 698a
Gordis, Robert, 1017b, 1172a
Gordon, Adoniram J., 935b, 936a, 950b
Gordon, Albert I., 285a
Gordon, George, 1145a
Gordon, Milton, 1478a
Gordon College of Theology and Missions, 959a
Goshen College (Indiana), 618a
Gospel: films, 1343a; Presbyterianism, 502b
Gospel According to St. Matthew, 1353b
Gospel Advocate, 582b, 855a, 856b
Gospel Broadcasting Association, 1713b–1714a
Gospel Guardian, 856a
gospel hymnody, 1298b–1299a
Gospel Hymns (Sankey and Bliss), 1298b
Gospel Hymns Nos. 1 to 6 Complete, 1298b
gospel music, 96a–b, 98a, 646a–b, 883a, 1296b–1297a
Gospel Messenger, 621b
gospel of wealth, 1318a
"Gospel of Wealth, The" (Carnegie), 1968a,b
gospel of the Kingdom, *see* Social Gospel
Gospel Road, 1350a
"gospel rock," 968b
gospel songs, 819b–820a, 1505a
Go Tell It on the Mountain (Baldwin), 1234b
Gottheil, Richard, 301b, 1017a
Gould, Thomas, 1574a
Goupil, René, 227a
government: Dutch and German Reformed, 511b–
    512a; Puritanism, 1058b–1059b, 1060b–1061b;
    Quakers, 602b; *see also* Church and State
Government of the Tongue, The (Perkins), 459b
Govorukhin, Hieromonk Juvenaly, 330b
Graca, Marcelino Mancel de, *see* Daddy Grace
Grace, Charles Emmanuel, *see* Daddy Grace
Graceland College, 1617b
Grace Magazine, 764a
Graduate, The, 1349b
Graduate Theological Union, 1650b
Grafstein, Laurence, 743a
Graham, Billy (William Franklin Graham), 573b,
    576b, 811a–812a, 957b, 959a, 960a, 963b–964b,
    965a, 966a, 970a, 973b, 1071a, 1322b, 1473b–
    1474a, 1507a, 1542a, 1716b, 1722b
Graham, Dom Aelred, 676a
Graham, Sylvester, 836a, 1259a

INDEX

INDEX

Holy Cross Greek Orthodox School of Theology (Connecticut), 336a

Holy Cross School of Theology (Boston), 340b, 1569a,b

Holy Cross University (Massachusetts), 365b

Holy Koran (Moorish Science), 757a

holy land: Judaism, 319b–321b

holy man, *see* rabbi

Holyoke, Edward, 1238b

Holyoke, Samuel, 1291b

holy people, 317b–319b, 322b

"holy rollers," 643b–644a

Holy Shankaracharya Order, 697a

Holy Trinity Monastery, 338b

Holy Trinity parish (Philadelphia), 359b

Holy Ukrainian Autocephalic Orthodox Church in Exile, 340a

holy war, 1409a,b–1410a, 1411a; Civil War, 1417a; and social reform, 1468a; Spanish-American War, 1419b

holy way of life: Judaism, 315b–316b

Hombre-Dios, 124b

Home Missions Council, 1691b

Home of the Heron (Inness), 1363a

homeopathy, 906a

home talks, 866b–867a

homsexuality, 386b, 414a–b, 592b, 930b, 1263a, 1264a, 1388b, 1522b–1523a

homily, 1314a

Honduras, 209a,b, *see also* Religions of Mesoamerica

Honest to God (Robinson), 1162a

Honey Out of the Rock (Deutsch), 1023a

Honpa Buddhist Church of Alberta, 268a

Hood, Fred J., 14b

Hooft, Willem Adolph Visser't, 427a, 984a, 987b, 989a

Hooker, Richard, 1059a

Hooker, Richard J., 1224b

Hooker, Thomas, 465a, 473a, 474b, 476a, 477b, 1041a

Hoover, Herbert, 376b, 1385a, 1540b, 1713a

Hope College (Michigan), 515a

hope, 1164a–b, 1165a, 1173b–1174a, 1182b

Hopedale Community, 1418b, 1439a

Hope Publishing Company, 1304a

Hopewell Academy, 1574a, 1612b

Hopi, 142a, 148a, 1510b

Hopkey, Sophia, 526b

Hopkins, Emma, 909b, 911b

Hopkins, John Henry, 403b, 404a, 1271a, 1333a

Hopkins, Mark, 491b, 1192a

Hopkins, Samuel, 484a, 503a, 796a, 1048a–b, 1431b–1432a, 1631a

Hopkinsians, 484a, 487b

Hopkins Latin School of New Haven, 1063a

Horace Bushnell (Smith), 10a

Horney, Karen, 1591b

Horning, Moses, 617a

Horning Mennonites, 617a

horror films, 1347a, 1350a

Horowitz, Irving, 744a

Horton, Walter Marshall, 1143b, 1147b, 1148b, 1150a, 1152a–b, 1154b, 1466a

Hosier, Harry, 544b

Hosmer, George W., 588a

Hospital of Nuestra Senora de los Desamparados, 194b

Hospital of San Andres (Lima), 194a

Hospital of San Hipolito (Mexico City), 194b

hospitals, 194a–b, 1257a, 1260a–b

Hôtel Dieu Hospital (Montreal), 227b

hot-gospelers, 800a

Hotovitzky, Alexander, 333a

House of Acts commune, 968b

House of Miracles comune, 969a

house organs, religious, 1701b–1703a

Houston Ministerial Conference, 383a

Hout, Robert, 1698b, 1701b

Hovey, Alvah, 567b

Howard, Oliver, 1442b, 1443a

Howard, Simeon, 1094b

Howard University, 1443b

Howe, Daniel Walker, 584a

Howe, Eber D., 656a

Howe, Frederic C., 1230b

Howe, Irving, 1171b

Howe, Julia Ward, 107b, 592b, 1086a, 1299b, 1446a

Howe, Reuel, 1591a

Howe, Samuel Gridley, 588b, 1434b

Howells, William Dean, 1229b

"How I Served My Apprenticeship" (Carnegie), 1228a

Howl (Ginsberg), 1232a–b

"How My Mind Has Changed" (Morrison), 1149b

How to Live and That Well (Perkins), 459b

Hromadka, Josef, 988a

Hsüan-Hua, 672a, 681a

Huaxtecs, 119a

Hubbard, L. Ron, 749a

Hubert, Jean François, 231a

Hubmaier, Balthasar, 1272b

Hudson, Hugh, 1350a

Hudson, Winthrop S., 9a, 12b, 449b, 1399a, 1403a

Hudson River school, 1363a

Huehueteotl, 124b

Huehuetlatolli, 125b

Huerta, Victoriano, 215b

INDEX

INDEX

Kazin, Elia, 1356b
KDKA, 1711a
Keach, Benjamin, 1290b
Keach, Elias, 1574a
Keane, John, 368b, 370a,b, 371b, 1004a,b, 1451a
Kearney, Denis, 1538b
Keble, John, 401b, 1114b
Kedrovsky, John, 337a, 338a
Keen, Benjamin, 121a
Keep America Out of War Crusade, 1423a
Kegley, Charles W., 1465b
kehillah (community), 200a–b
Keighley, William, 1347b
Keil, Wilhelm, 625b
Keith, George, 597b, 599b, 1527a
Kelley, Dean M., 80b–81a, 1168a
Kelley, Florence, 1449b, 1455a
Kellogg, John Harvey, 836b, 1259a
Kellogg-Briand Pact (1928), 1468a
Kelly, Robert, 1645b
Kelpius, Johann, 1292b
Kemp, Peter, 542b
Kemper, Jackson, 397a, 398a,b
Kenkel, Frederick, 924a, 1452a
Kennedy, D. James, 1730b
Kennedy, Edward M., 386b, 975a
Kennedy, John F., 383a–b, 1087a, 1385a, 1405a, 1425b, 1543a, 1703b
Kennedy, Robert F., 389a
Kennett, Jiya, 671a
Kenrick, Francis Patrick, 359b, 365a, 370a, 1085a
Kensett, John F., 1363a
Kensington (Pennsylvania), 364a
Kent, Charles Foster, 1204b
Kent, Corita, 385a
Kentucky, 360a, 502a,b
Kentucky Harmony (Davisson), 1297b
Kenyon College (Ohio), 399b, 416a, 1614b
Kern, Hendrik, 673a
Kerouac, Jack, 673b
Kerr, Graham, 1734a
Kershner, Frederick C., 1151b
Kes, 1357b
Keswick Conference, 1687b
Keswick movement, 610a,b, 820a–821a, 952a–953a, 954b
Ketocton Association, 792a
Kett, Joseph F., 69b
Keuka Lake community, 863a
Kew, Clifton, 1592b
Kew, Clinton, 1592b
Key, Elizabeth, 1549b–1550a
KFKB, 1712a–b
Khomiakov, Alexis S., 981b

Khrapovitsky, Anthony, 337b
Kierkegaard, Søren, 1150a, 1154b–1155a
Ki Fanah Yom (The Day Wanes), 1021a
Kilgore, Charles Franklin, 846b
Killingworth, Thomas, 1574a
Kimball, J. Golden, 97a
Kimball, Spencer W., 665a
Kinetoscope, 1342a
King, E. J., 1297b
King, George, 717b
King, Henry Churchill, 920b, 1130a–b, 1131b, 1132a, 1133b, 1136a, 1138b, 1140a, 1144b, 1349b
King, J. E., 826b
King, Martin Luther, Jr., 114a–b, 572b, 575a,b, 576b, 646b–647b, 684b, 767b, 839b, 930b, 969b, 988b, 1071a, 1085a, 1164b–1165a, 1180b–1182b, 1183b, 1234b–1235a, 1322b–1323a, 1425b, 1426a, 1467a, 1543b, 1580a, 1698a–b
King, Thomas Starr, 582a, 587b, 1515a–b
Kingdom, 925b
Kingdom of God, 109a–b, 113a,b
Kingdom of God in America, The (Niebuhr), 8b, 1153b
King James Version of the Bible, *see* Authorized Version of the Bible
King of Kings (1927), 1344b–1345a
King of Kings (1961), 1349a
King Philip's War (1675–1676), 1675a
King's Chapel (Boston), 471a, 580b
King's College, *see* Columbia University
King's Daughters, 924a
King's Farm (New York), 352a
Kingston (Canada), 231b
Kino, Eusebio Francisco, 198b, 1511b, 1673a–b
kinship, 144b
Kiowa Indians, 147a–b
Kirchen-Ordnung of 1748, 517a
Kirchenverein, 520a–b
Kirchoff, Paul, 119a
Kirke Tidende fur Den Skandinavisk Evangelisk-Lutherske Kirke, 1700b
Kirkland, John Thornton, 484a
Kirkland, Samuel, 1676b
Kirtland (Ohio), 655b–656a, 657a, 658a–b, 659a
Kirtland Temple, 658a
Kito no Michi, 702b
Kittamaquund, Chief, 348a
Klein, A. M., 1023b
Klein, Felix, 371a
Kleine Gemeinde, 617b
Klein-Nicolai, George, 582a
Klink, Thomas, 1591a
Knapp, Martin Wells, 820a, 823b
Kneeland, Abner, 734b, 1535a
Knights of Columbus, 369a, 371b, 372b, 378b, 1421b

INDEX

Lamy, Jean-Baptiste, 360b

Lancaster (Pennsylvania), 274a, 618a–b, 619a, 624b, 632a

Lancelot du Lac, 1351b

Landman, Isaac, 1018a

Landmarkism, see Old Landmarkism

Landmark movement, 1574b

Landorf, Joyce, 1734a

Landsberg, Max, 281b

landscape, *see* Religious Architecture and Landscape

landsmanshaften, 282a,b, 293b, 300b

Land Without Bread, 1352b

Lane, Charles, 1124a

Lane Seminary (Cincinnati), 817a, 1437a, 1633b–1634a

Lang, Fritz, 1347a

Langlois, Richard, 670b

language: ethnicity and religion, 1481b, 1485a,b; liberalism, 1131b–1132a; Native American religions, 138b, 140a–b

Language of Canaan, The (Lowance), 14a

Lankford, Sarah, 813a, 814b, 815b

Lanman, Charles Rockwell, 673a

Lansing, Robert, 1459a

Lao-tzu, 706b

LaPorte, Roger, 388b

Large Catechism (Lutheranism), 421a

La Salle, Robert Cavelier de, 229b–230a

Las Casas, Bartolomé de, 188b, 192a

Lasko, Stephen V., 340a

L'Assomption parish (Canada), 235a

Last Days of Pompeii, 1349a–b

La Strada, 1353b, 1356b

Last Will and Testament of the Springfield Presbytery (Stone), 847a, 983a

Lasuén, Francisco de, 198b, 1512a

La Symphonie Pastorale, 1350b

Late Great Planet Earth, The (Lindsey), 969a

Lathrop, Julia, 1449b

Lathrop, Rose Hawthorne, 369a

Latin America: African beliefs, 1174b; Baptists, 570b; Catholics, 1481b; church and state, 1381a; liberation theology, 1167a–b, 1649b, 1695a

Latin American Council of Churches, 989b

Latin American Episcopal Conferences, 201b–202a, 217b, 221a–b

Latitudinarianism, 779b

Latourette, Kenneth Scott, 572b

Latrobe, Benjamin Henry, 624a, 1333a

Latter-day Saints, The (Church of Jesus Christ of Latter-day Saints), **649a–665b,** 1309a, 1576a–b, 1577a; abortion, 1263b; architecture, 1331b–1332b; California and Southwest, 1517a; campus ministries, 1623a; Canada, 241a,b, 268b; church

and state, 1389b–1390a; collegiate education, 1617b; communitarianism, 873a; Episcopalian converts, 405b; ethnicity and, 1487b–1488a; folklore, 97a–b, 99a; folk songs, 96b; geography and demography, 76a–b, 77b; medicine, 1258b–1259a; missions, 1690b; music and hymnody, 1298a–b; prejudice, 1531b–1532b, 1535b, 1537b, 1543b; publishing, 1707b; restorationism, 846a; South, 1506a; theological interpretation of America, 106a–b

Laubervière, François-Louis de Pourroy de, 228b

Laud, Samuel, 462b

Laud, William, 462b, 464a–b, 465a, 467b–468a

Laughton, Charles, 1348b

Laurier, Wilfrid, 267b

Lauterbach, Jacob Z., 1017b

La Valette, Antoine, 226a

Laval, François de, 227b–228a

Lavanoux, Maurice, 1280b

La Venta, 120a

LaVerne College (California), 621a

law: African, 175b; and Canadian religion, 254b–255a

Law, Andrew, 1291a

Law, William, 780a,b

Lawrence, Charles, 353b

Lawrence, D. H., 1225b, 106a

Lawrence, William, 1318a

Lawrie, Lee, 1337a

Laws, Curtis Lee, 571b, 974b

Layman, Emma, 675a, 676a–b, 679b, 681a

"Layman's Witness," 1715b

Laymen's Foreign Missions Inquiry, 1693b

Laymen's Missionary Movement, 1689b–1690a

"lay renaissance," 369b

Lazarists, *see* Vincentians

Lazarus, E. S., 1015b

Lazarus, Emma, 1019a, 1020a–b

Lazar, Theodosius, 341b

Leadbeater, Charles W., 718b

Leade, Jane, 620b

Leadership, 1565a

League for Social Service, 493a

League of Catholic Unity, 493b

League of Evangelical Students, 1623b

League of Nations, 410a, 506b, 1069b, 1459b, 1468a

League of Nations Non-Partisan Association, 1459b

League of Universal Brotherhood, 1616a

learned societies, 1662b

Leaves from Satan's Book, 1346a

Leaves of Grass (Whitman), 1226b

Leavitt, Joshua, 1285a, 1294b

Lebanon, 267b, 327a,b

Le Blanc, Edouard, 236b

LeBuffe, Francis, 1250b

INDEX

Le Caron, Joseph, 226b
Le Conte, Joseph, 1136a, 1244b–1245a
Le Loutre, Jean-Louis, 226b
lecture days, 472b
Lectures (Witherspoon), 1095b
Lectures on Moral and Political Philosophy (Smith), 1096a
Lectures on Pastoral Theology (Spencer), 1585a
Lectures on Revivals of Religion (Finney), 804a, 876b
Lectures on the Moral Government of God (Taylor), 1049a
Lectures on the Pastoral Office (Meade), 1585a
Leddra, William, 597b, 1372a
Lee, Ann, 863b–864a, 1298a, 1554a
Lee, Ivy, 1320a
Lee, Jarena, 638b, 1580b
Lee, Jesse, 879a
Lee, Luther, 816a–b, 825b–826a, 1555a
Lee, Robert, 1275a
Lee, Robert E., 404a
Leeming, Bernard, 992a
Leeser, Isaac, 275a–276a, 280a, 297a, 298b–299a, 1015b–1016a, 1016b–1017a, 1018b, 1315a, 1567b–1568a
Lefebvre, Marcel, 384b
Legba, 178a, 182a
legends: folk religions, 91a, 92a–b, 99a
Legends of the Jews (Ginzberg), 1017b
Legion of Decency, 1692b
Lehigh University (Pennsylvania), 416a
Lehman, Herbert, 1454b
Lehmann, Paul, 1164a
Leibniz, Gottfried Wilhelm, 981a–b
Leigh, Charles, 239a
Leiper, Henry Smith, 987b
Leisler, Jacob, 352b
Leivick, Halper, 1021a
Leland, John, 560a, 795b, 1376a
Lemmons, Reuel, 855b
Lemon v. *Dicenso* (1971), 1386a
Lemon et al. v. *Kertzman et al.* (1971), 1386a
Lenski, Gerhard, 22b
Leo I, Pope, 155a
Leo III, Pope, 155b
Leo X, Pope, 189b, 223b
Leo XIII, Pope, 111a, 161b, 214b, 368a, 370b–371a, 372a, 375a, 928a, 1004b, 1642b
Leon, Count de, *see* Müller, Bernhard
Leone, Mark P., 15a
Léon-Portilla, Miguel, 129a–b
Leopoldine Foundation, 361b
Lerner, Max, 1404b
Leroux, Pierre, 1001b
Les Anges du Peche, 1351a
Les Dames du Bois de Boulogne, 1351a
Les Passions de l'âme (Descartes), 1090a

Les Ruines (Volney), 1100b
Lessing, Gotthold, 1089a
Lethbridge (Canada), 268a
"Letter from a Birmingham Jail" (King), 1467a
"Letter from a Region in My Mind" (Baldwin), 1234b
Letters and Papers from Prison (Bonhoeffer), 1160b–1161a
Letters on Clerical Manners and Habits (Miller), 1585a
Letters to the Hon. John Forsythe on the Subject of Domestic Slavery (England), 366b
Leuba, James, 54b, 1587b
Levadoux, Michael, 361a
Leverett, John, 1090a–b
Levi, Eliphas, 720a
Levin, Lewis C., 1535a
Levin, Meyer, 1022a
Levinson, Daniel, 66b
Lévi-Strauss, Claude, 1740b
levitation, 695a
Lewger, John, 348b
Lewin, Kurt, 1592b
Lewis, Clarence I., 1204b
Lewis, C. S., 248b
Lewis, Edwin, 1147b, 1148b, 1149a, 1150a, 1151b, 1152b, 1204a, 1466a
Lewis, H. Spencer, 719b
Lewis, John, 354a
Lewis, Joseph, 738a
Lewis, Samuel, 1597b
Lewis, Sinclair, 112b, 1540a
Lewisohn, Ludwig, 1022a–b
Leyburn, James G., 180b
Liberal, 1705b
Liberal Catholic Church, 718b
Liberalism, **1129a–1145b,** 1159a; California religions, 1515a–1516a, 1519a; Calvinism; 1053b, 1055a; Catholic thought, 1004a–1005a, 1007a, 1010b, 1011b; church and state, 1377b, 1379a; Congregationalism, 483b–484b; Enlightenment, 1094b; evangelicalism, 972b–973b; Free Religious Association, 736a; Fundamentalism, 949a, 953b, 954a,b, 955b; medicine, 1260b; Methodist churches, 550b; ministry, 1573b; missions, 1692b–1693a, 1695a–1696a; Neoevangelicalism, 965b, 966a; Neo-Orthodoxy, 1147a–b, 1149a,b, 1152b; Puritanism, 1070b–1071a; religious philosophy, 1189b; religious press, 1705b; romantic religion, 1110b–1111a, 1115a; science and religion, 1247b–1248a; Social Christianity, 920b; theological education, 1644b–1645a, 1647a–b, 1648a–b, 1651a–b; theological intepretation of America, 109a, 110a, 111a; Transcendentalism, 1127a; Unitarians and Universalists, 580a–593a
Liberal Theosophy, 718b

INDEX

Lyman, Eugene, 1141b, 1204a
Lynch, Frederick, 1420a
Lynch, John, 235b
lynching, 1444b, 1450a
Lyrical Ballads (Wordsworth), 1105b

M

Maccabean, The, 1019a
Macdonald, John, 353b
Macedonian-Americans, 340a
MacFarland, Charles, 1420a
Machado, David Mendez, 1603a
Machado, Gerardo, 218b
Machen, J. Greshem, 505b, 953b, 959a–b, 1204a, 1249a
Maciel canon, 195b
Macintosh, Douglas Clyde, 1142b–1143a, 1152b, 1204a, 1588b
Mack, Alexander, 782a
Mack, Alexander, Sr., 620a,b
MacKenna, John, 352b, 358a
Mackenzie, Jean Kenyon, 1690a
Mackenzie, William Lyon, 232a
Mackenzie River, 262b–263b
Mackinac, 360b
Maclear, James, 1403a
MacRae, George, 1010a
Madero, Francisco, 214a–b, 215a–b
Madison, James, 1061b, 1099a–b, 1377b–1378a, 1529b, 1530b
Madison, Reverend James, 1098b
madness, 1256b
Maezumi, Taizan, Rōshi, 671a
magazines, *see* Religious Press
magic, ritual, 720a–b
"Magic, Science, and Religion" (Malinowski), 1237a
magisterium, 158b
Magnalia Christi Americana; or, The Ecclesiastical History of New-England (Mather), 3a–b, 1042b, 1209a, 1310b
Magoon, E. L., 1363b
magus, 712a
Magyar Reformed churches, 424a
Mahabodhi Society, 670a, 671b
Mahan, Asa, 813a, 814b–815a, 816b–817b, 820b, 821a, 877a–b, 952b, 1634a
Maharaj Ji, Guru, 695a,b, 1521a
Maharaj Ji, Shri Hans Ji, 695a
Maharishi International University (Iowa), 694a, 1622a
Maharish Mahesh Yogi, 693b, 694b, 695a, 1521a

Mahāvīra, 687a
Mahāyana Buddhism, 669b
Mahoning Baptist Association, 849a
Maier, Walter A., 1712a
Mailer, Norman, 1023b
Maillard, Pierre-Antoine, 226b
Maimonides College (Philadelphia), 276a
Main Currents in American Thought (Parrington), 7b
Maine, 226a, 353a, 481b
Main Street (Lewis), 112b
Maisonneuve, Paul de Choatédy de, 227b
maize, 132a, 1510b
Makemie, Francis, 499b–500a
Making of a Counter Culture, The (Roszak), 674a, 1252a
Making Peace in the Global Village (Brown), 1469b
Maksimenko, Vitaly, 338b
Malamud, Bernard, 1024a
Malcolm X, 79a, 647b, 755b, 760b, 766b–769a,b, 1165a, 1183a–1184a,b, 1234b–1235b, 1467b, 1543b
Male and Female, 1344b
Malebranche, Nicolas de, 1090a,b
Malinowski, Bronislaw, 1237a
Mallett, Sarah, 825a
Malthus, Thomas, 1244a
mambo, 182b
Man Becoming (Baum), 1169b
Mance, Jeanne, 227b
Manchester College (Indiana), 621a
Man for All Seasons, A, 1357b
Manheim camp meetings (Pennsylvania), 819b
Manifest Destiny, 255a, 833b, 879b–880a, 1070a, 1207a, 1684b
Man Is Not Alone: A Philosophy of Religion (Heschel), 1036b, 1037a
Manitoba (Canada), 234b–235a, 267b, 268a
Mann, Arthur, 13a
Mann, Horace, 588a, 1062b, 1063a, 1125b, 1434b, 1597a, 1614b
Mann, N. M., 281b
Mannheimer, Isaac Noah, 1315a
Manning, James, 559a, 1574a
Manoogian, Torkom, 343b
Mañosca, Juan de, 196b
manse, 426b
Manson family, 746b
Man's Quest for God (Heschel), 1036a
mantra, 692a,b, 695a–b, 697b
Manu, Laws of, 683b
Manual of the Mother Church (Eddy), 912a
Manual of Theology (Dagg), 562b
Manuductio ad Ministerium: Directions for a Candidate of the Ministry (Mather), 1043b, 1310b, 1565a
Man Without a Country (Hale), 1229b

INDEX

media: evangelicals, 973b–974a; Graham, Billy, 811a–b; Methodist churches, 551a; millennialism and adventism, 841b–842a; *see also* Mass Communications

medicalization: cults, 751b–752a

medical schools, 1259b–1260a

Medicine and Medical Ethics, **1253a–1265b**; African, 175b; church and state, 1390a–b; Native Americans, 143a; *see also* healing, mind-cure

medicine, folk, *see* folk medicine

medicine bundle, 140b

Medellín conference of 1968, 220a, 221a

Medina, José Toribio, 194a

meditation, 471b, 691b, 693b–695a, 697b, 1521a–b, 1522a,b

Medium, 1700b

Medulla Theologiae (James), 1040b, 1091a

Medurot Do'akhot (Dying Campfires), 1020b

meetinghouse, 658a, 1327b, 1328a, 1329b, 1362b

Meetinghouse and Countinghouse: The Quaker Merchants of Colonial Philadelphia (Tolles), 14a

meetinghouse hill, 1328a

meetings (Puritans, Quakers), 472b, 600a–601a, 606a

Meharry Medical College (Tennessee), 547b

Meher Spiritual Center, 696a

Meidung, see shunning

Meishu-sama, 705b

Melanchthon, 980b–981a

Melanchthon, Philipp, 421a, 453a

Meland, Bernard, 1189b, 1202b, 1204a

Mélanges Religieux, 232b

Melchizedek priesthood, 650b, 653a, 659a, 1577a

Méliès, Georges, 1342a

Melkites, 327b, 333b, 342b–343a, 1281b

Melton, J. Gordon, 717a

Melville, Andrew, 458b

Melville, Herman, 106b, 112b, 734b, 880a, 1065a, 1075b, 1111a, 1227a, 1228a

Melvin Catholic Club, 1622b

membership, church, 20b, 22a, 80b–81a, 82a–83a; Baptists, 555a; blacks, 648a; Buddhists, 677a; Canadian Protestants, 249b; Church of the Nazarene, 823b; Congregationalists, 496b, 497a; Episcopal Church, 417a; holiness groups, 824a, 828b; Japanese-Americans, 705b; Jehovah's Witnesses, 838b; Methodists, 544b, 546b, 547a, 551a, 552a,b; New England Puritanism, 469a–471a, 478a, 479a–b; Quakers, 610b–611a; and religious broadcasting, 1721b, 1722b; restorationist churches, 853b–855a, 857a–b; South, 1501b; *see also* Geography and Demography of American Religion

membership, synagogue, 285b, 315b

Memoirs of a Catholic Girlhood (McCarthy), 1233a

Memoirs of American Jews, 1775–1865 (Marcus), 12a

Memorial and Remonstrance (Madison), 1377b

Memorial Day, 1400a

Memorial de los remedios (Las Casas), 192a

Memory Ministries, 1734a

Memphis Theological Seminary, 508a

Men and Religion Forward Movement, 1448a–b

Mencken, H. L., 112b, 738a, 1540a

Mendes, Henry Pereira, 277a–b, 1568a

Mendieta, Gerónimo de, 122b, 126a

Mendoza, Rodríguez de, 195b

Mennonite Brethren Church, 617a–b

Mennonite Brethren in Christ, *see* United Missionary Church

Mennonite Encyclopedia, 618a

Mennonite Hymnary, 1301b

Mennonite Quarterly Review, 618a

Mennonites, 616a–618a, 631a,b, 632a; art, 1362a–b; Canada, 240a, 244b, 250a, 267a; church and state, 1373b, 1376b–1377a; collegiate education, 1617a; geography and demography, 73a, 78b; music and hymnody, 1292b; pacifism, 1414a,b, 1418a,b,, 1422a, 1423a, 1424a,b; Pennsylvania, 432b; prejudice, 1539a; South, 1506a; worship, 1272b

Mennonite Youth Hymnal, 1302a

Men of Boys' Town, 1348a

Menorah, 1365a

Menorah Journal, 1019a

Mental Cure, The (Evans) 904a

mental healing, 1127a; *see also* mind-cure

mental hygiene movement, 1588a

"mental malpractice," 910b

mental philosophy, 1586a–b

Mercedarians, 190a

Mercersburg Review, 1113a–b

Mercersburg Seminary, 1313b

Mercersburg Theology, 519a–b, 523a, 1052b, 1111b–1112a, 1275a

Mercer University (Georgia), 562a, 1636a

Merchants' Hope Church (Virginia), 1329a

Meredith, James, 1183b

Merrill, William P., 1304a

Merritt, Timothy, 813a

Merton, Thomas, 167a, 169b, 381b, 388b, 1161a, 1232b–1233a, 1426a

Merwan Sheheriarji Irani, *see* Bābā, Meher

Merz, Georg, 1150b

Merzbacher, Leo, 1016a

Meshchersky, Evdokim, 333b, 334a, 337a

Mesmer, Franz Anton, 715b–716a, 1259b

mesmerism, 715b–716a, 902b–903b, 904a, 910b, 1258b, 1259b

Mesoamerica, *see* Religions of Mesoamerica

Message to the Black Man (Muhammad), 766a
Message to the Mother Church (Eddy), 902a
Messara, Gerasimos, 334b
Messein, Charles-Francois Bailly de, 231a
Messenger, 760a, 1122b
Messenger of Peace, 521a
Messiah (Handel), 427b
messianism, 234a–b, 264b, 832b
mestizo, 206a, 210a, 1512b
Metacomet, *see* King Philip's War
Metaphysical Club, 912b
metaphysics, 1089b, 1192a–b, 1195a, 1519a–b, 1520b
Metaxakēs, Meletios, 335a
Methodist Book Concern, 544a
Methodist Church, 539a, 550b, 551a–b, 552a
Methodist Church Music Society, 1301a
Methodist Episcopal Church, 540b, 542a–b, 543a,b, 546a,b, 547a,b, 548a–b, 549a, 550a; Canada, 240b, 241b; German-language missions, 629b–630a; holiness and perfection, 814b, 816a,b, 818a, 819b, 822a; itinerants, 1575b; Sunday schools, 884b; union, 539a; women, 825a, 1580b; worship, 1278b
Methodist Episcopal Church Conference, 1447b–1448a
Methodist Episcopal Church, South, 546a–547a, 549a, 550a; holiness movement, 822a–b; ministry, 1576a; union, 539a
Methodist Hymnal, 1278b, 1301b
Methodist Protestant Church, 495a, 539a, 550a, 1555b
Methodist Publishing House, 246a
Methodists: African slaves, 180a; architecture, 1330b–1331a; blacks, 404a, 636b–637a, 637b–638a, 1443b, 1444a, 1579b; broadcasting, 1714b; California, 1517a; camp meetings, 889a; Canada, 240a, 241a,b, 242a,b, 243a, 245a,b, 246b–247b, 254b, 268b; and Catholics, 991b; civil rights movement, 1180a; collegiate education, 1614a, 1615b, 1616a,b; common schooling, 1597a; conscientious objection, 1424b; denominational history, 32a; disestablishment, 485a; Evangelical Association, 628b; folklore, 92a, 94a; folk music, 96b; Fundamentalism, 949a, 952a–b, 955b; German language, 629b–630a; Great Awakening, 784a,b, 795a–b; holiness and perfection, 813a–828b, 1577b; laity, 36a; liberalism, 1129a; liturgy and worship, 1277b–1279a; and Lutherans, 443b; Mexico, 212a; ministry, 1566a,b, 1573b, 1575a–1576a; missionaries, 398b, 1683b, 1684b, 1687a; music and hymnody, 1920b; Native American missions, 1679b, 1680a, 1681a; New England, 482a,b,; politics, 23a; preaching, 1312b, 1315b–1316a; and Presbyterians, 502a,b; publishing,

1699b, 1700b, 1702a; retention rate, 21a; revivalism, 806b; romanticism, 1105b; slavery, 1438a, 1439a–b; social reform, 1443b, 1455b; social service, 494a; South, 1493a, 1494a, 1495a, 1497a, 1498b, 1499b, 1501b, 1502a, 1504b, 1506a; theological education, 1630a, 1635a, 1636b–1637a; United Brethren, 628a; on war, 1415b, 1417a, 1419b; Wesley, John, 393b–394a,b; westward migration, 75a, 77b, 80b; women, 1446b, 1447b, 1448a,b, 1450a, 1553b, 1559a–b, 1581a; *see also* United Methodism; Wesleyan Heritage
Methodists, The, 1783–1840 (Sweet), 7a
Methodists Associated Representing the Cause of Hispanic Americans, 552a
Methodist Youth Fellowship, 551a
Métis movement, 269a–b
Metoyer, Nicholas Augustin, 367b
Metreaux, Alfred, 180b
Metropolia, 337a, 338a–339a, 341b
Metropolis, 1347a
Metropolitan Community Church (Los Angeles), 1523a
Metz, Christian, 867b
Metz, Johannes, 162a, 1164a
Metzger, Max Josef, 992a
Meurin, Sébastian, 358a
Mexican-Americans: California and Southwest, 1512b–1514b; Indian Hindus, 685a
Mexican Revolution, 213a–218a, 379b
Mexican War, 1416a
Mexico: Catholics, 388a; education, 192b, 193a; Episcopal missionaries, 401a; hospitals, 194a,b; independence, 207a–208a,b, 209b–210b; Inquisition, 192a–b; medicine, 1257a; missions, 1671b, 1672a, 1673a; music, 1285a–b; Our Lady of Guadalupe, 205a–b; Presbyterian missions, 504a; religious education, 1595a; Southern religions, 1503b; Spanish clergy and government, 196b; Spanish missionaries, 188a, 189b, 190a; *see also* Religions of Mesoamerica
Meyer, Lucy Rider, 548a
Miami (Florida), 205 (table), 306b
Michael, 1346b
Michaelius, Jonas, 513b
Michaelson, Robert, 1403a
Michel, Virgil, 381b, 1007b, 1280b, 1337a–b
Michigan, 229b, 514b, 725b–726a, 737a–b
Michigan City (Indiana), 725b
Michigan Synod, 442a
Mictlantecuhtli, 124b
Mictlantecuhtli-Mictecacíhuatl, 127a
Middlebury College, 1063b
Middleditch, Robert, 882a
Middle East Council of Churches, 989b

INDEX

Missionary Sisters of the Sacred Heart, 1554b

Missionary Society of Connecticut, 482b–483a

Missionary Society of St. Paul the Apostle, 1003b

Missionary Society of the Evangelical Association of North America, 544a

Missionary Training Institute, 1618b

Mission Journal, 856b

Mission San Diego, 198a

Mission San Francisco de los Tejas, 197b

Mission San Jose y San Miguel de Aguayo (San Antonio), 1326a, 1360a

Mission San Xavier del Bac (Arizona), 198b

Mission Sonoma (California), 198a

Mississippi College, 1615a

Mississippi River, 229b, 230a

Missouri, 655b–656a, 657a,b, 658a

Missouri Synod Lutherans (German Evangelical Lutheran Synod of Missouri, Ohio), 438a, 439a,b, 440a,b, 442a,b, 443a, 444a,b, 445a,b, 446a,b, 447a, 971a; Bible, 1081b; broadcasting, 1715b; collegiate education, 1616b, 1619b; ministry, 1566a; publishing, 1701b; religious education, 1601a–b; religious studies, 1656b; theological education, 1647b, 1651b; women, 1470a

Miss Sadie Thompson, 1348a

Mistapeo, 259b–260a

"mite" societies, 489b

Mitchell, Henry, 185b

Mitla: Town of Souls (Parsons), 134a

Mitropolsky, John, 331a

mitzvot (holy actions), 315b

Mixtecs, 119a, 121b

Mixcóatl, 131a

Moberg, David O., 971b

Mobil Oil Corporation, 1465a

Moby-Dick (Melville), 106b, 1217a–b, 1228a

Moctezuma Ilhuicamina, 130a

Moctezuma Xocoyotzin, 122a

Mode, Peter G., 6b–7a

Models of the Church (Dulles), 1170a

modernism, 496a; Bible, 1081b; biblical inerrancy, 1320a,b; Catholicism, 161a–b, 371b, 375a,b, 1005b, 1006a, 1250b, 1643a; Episcopal Church, 410b; Evangelicalism, 975a, 976a; Free Religious Association, 736a; and Fundamentalism, 955a, 956a–b, 958a,b,; Judaism, 318b–319a,b, 1026b; liberals, 1139a; Neo-Orthodoxy, 1148a, 1149a; religious philosophy, 1189b; social reform, 1441b

Modernist Impulse in American Protestantism, The (Hutchison), 14b

modernization, 1066a–1068a

Modern Priest Looks at His Outdated Church, A (Kavanaugh), 384b

Modern Revivalism: Charles Grandison Finney to Billy Graham (McLoughlin), 14b

Mohammed, Farrad, *see* Muhammad, Elijah

Mohammed, Wallace Fard, 726b

Mohawk Indians, 400b, 1674b

Möhjer, Johann Adam, 981b

Moise, Penina, 1020a

Moiti, John S., 175b

Moldovan, Andrei, 339b

Molina, Francisco, 194a–b

Molly Maguires, 368a

Moltmann, Jürgen, 1164a

Molyneux, Robert, 1598a

Momaday, N. Scott, 147a–b, 1234a

monasticism: Anglo-Catholicism, 402a; Catholicism, 155b, 168a–b; Buddhism, 676a, 677a; Eastern Christianity, 327b; Hinduism, 691a

Moncton (Canada), 236b

Mondale, Walter F., 1544a

monism, 28b, 745b–746b

Monk, Maria, 363a, 881b, 1533a

Monophysite Armenians of Syria, 327a

Monophysites, 266a, 326a, 327a, 980a, 1281b

monotheism, 139a,b–140a, 699b, 705a, 987b

Monothelitism, 327a

Monsieur Vincent, 1350b–1351a

Montagu, Richard, 464b, 467b

Montague, William P., 1204a

Montañes, Juan Ortega y, 196b

Montanism, 979b

Monte Alban, 120a

Montgomery, Helen Barrett, 567b, 572a

Montgomery, James, 1294b

Montgomery (Alabama): civil rights, 647a, 1467a

Montreal, 227b, 228b, 231a,b, 232b, 246a, 267a,b

Monts, Pierre du Gua de, 239a

Mont-Saint-Michel and Chartres (Adams), 1229a

Montúfar, Alonso de, 192a, 205a

Moody, Dwight Lyman, 606b, 807a–809a, 820b, 821a, 897b, 935b, 936a, 949a, 951a, 952a, 954b, 983b, 1071a, 1298b, 1318a–b, 1334b, 1456a, 1473b, 1515a, 1605b, 1618a, 1643b, 1687b

Moody Bible Institute, 809a, 840b, 951a, 957b, 958b, 1298b, 1456b, 1578b, 1618a, 1643b, 1687b, 1688b, 1712a

Moody Monthly, 840b

Moody Press, 1731a

Moon, Lottie, 1448a, 1690a

Moon, Sun Myung, 115a, 747a–748a, 840a, 1521a, 1545b

Moonies, *see* Unification Church

Moon Is Blue, The, 1356b

Moore, Benjamin, 397a

Moore, George E., 1200b

Newton Theological Institution (Massachusetts), 562a, 1574b, 1650b

Newton Manor School (Maryland), 350a,b

New Translation of the Torah, 1663b

New Views of Christianity, Society, and the Church (Brownson), 1122b

New York, 240b; Anglicanism, 393a,b, 395b; church and state, 1378b; Catholicism, 352a–b, 360a; Congregationalists, 482b, 483a, 487a, 488a; Dutch Reform, 513b, 514a,b; Eastern Christianity, 337b; Episcopal Church, 397a, 400b; French missions, 227a; German Reformed, 516b; Jews, 296b; Presbyterians, 500a,b; prejudice, 1526b, 1527a,b, 1528b, 1529a, 1530a, 1531a

New York Association for Improving the Condition of the Poor, 363a

New York Association for New Americans, 304b

New York City: Catholicism, 352b, 358b, 362a, 363a, 366a, 1598b; Eastern Christianity, 331b, 332a, 334b; Episcopal Church, 406b; Hispanic Catholics, 387b–388a; Jews, 274a, 279a,b, 281a,b–282b, 284b, 295 (table), 297a–b, 299b, 301b, 302a,b, 308b; Methodism, 540a; Social Christianity, 920a

New York City Antislavery Society, 1436b, 1437a

New York Ecclesiological Society, 1271a

New York Federation of Reform Synagogues, 284b

New York Geeta Temple, 687b–688a

New York International Bible Society, 1076b

New York Jew (Kazin), 1232a

New York Kehillah, 304b

New York Manumission Society, 1430b

New York Ministerium, 440b

New York Missionary Society, 1683b

New York Observer, 363b

New York Peace Society, 1420a, 1435b

New York Psychology Group, 1593a

New York Public School Society, 366a

New York Review, 1005a, 1006a

New York Sunday School Union, 1434a

New York Synod, 442a

New York University, 1615b

New World, 1207a–b

New Vrindavan (West Virginia), 693b

Nez Percé, 147b

Niagara Bible and Prophecy Conferences, 246a, 936a, 950b

Niagara Movement, 1445a

Niblo, Fred, 1345a

Nica, Antim, 339b

Nicaragua, 209a, 220b–221a, 221b–222a

Nicene Creed, 326b, 328a, 392a, 421a, 508b, 979b–980a

Nichirien Shōshū Buddhism, 675a, 677a, 678a–b, 746b

Nichols, James H., 1113b

Nichols, Mike, 1349b

Nicholson, Henry B., 124b–125a

Nicholson, Joseph W., 1180b

Nichomachean Ethics (Aristotle), 1190a

nickelodeon, 1342b

Nicole, Pierre, 1090a

Niebuhr, Bartold Georg, 1658b

Niebuhr, H. Richard, 8b, 24a, 42a–43a, 113a–b, 496a, 842b, 1143b, 1147b, 1150a, 1151b, 1152a, 1153a–1154a, 1157a, 1160b, 1204a, 1483a, 1590b, 1646a

Niebuhr, Reinhold, 113a–b, 248b, 496a, 505b–506a, 521a–b, 523a, 929b, 930a, 988a, 1147b, 1148b, 1150a, 1151b, 1152a, 1153a–1154a, 1155a,b, 1156a, 1160a, 1204a, 1319a–b, 1423a, 1464a, 1465b–1466a, 1468b, 1590b, 1665a–b, 1704b, 1728b

Niebuhr: His Religious, Social and Political Thought (Kegley), 1465b

Nielsen, A. C., Company, 1719b

Nigeria, 172a

Night (Wiesel), 1024b, 1036a

Night of the Hunter, 1348b

Nights of Cabiria, 1353b

Niles, D. T., 988b

Nilsson, F. O., 569b

Nineteenth-Century Evangelicalism, **875a–899b**

"Ninety and Nine," 808b

Ninety-Five Theses or Propositions for Disputation by Dr. Luther of Blessed Memory, . . . , 420a–b

nirvāna, 669a,b

Nishijima, Kakuryo, 671b

Nityānanada, Bhagwan Śrī, 696a–b

Nixon, Richard M., 573b, 964a, 965a, 969b, 970a, 1086b, 1402a, 1543a

Niza, Marcos de, 197a

Noah, Mordecai Manuel, 296b, 2020a

Noah's Ark, 1345b

No and Yes (Eddy), 908a–b

Nobel Prizes, 609b, 1024b, 1025b, 1186b, 1424b

Nobili, Robert de, 1674a

Noble, T. Terius, 1302a

No Foreign War Crusade, 1423a

Noise of Solemn Assemblies (Berger), 1399b

Nol, Fan, 334a–b, 340a, 342a

Noll, Mark A., 14b

Nonconformists, 530a

nonviolence, 647a, 1181a–b, 1425b

Nordhoff, Charles, 622b, 1516b

Norfolk (Virginia), 359a

Norris, J. Frank, 957b, 958b, 959a

Norris, John, 1091b

North, Frank Mason, 926a

North American Baptist Conference, 569a

North American Christian Convention, 853b, 856b

North American College in Rome, 375b, 1642a

North American Indian Missions, **1671a–1682b,** 1683a–b, 1685b, 1686a, 1691a; *see also* Native Americans

North American Shinto Church, 702b

North American Zakah Fund, 728b

Northampton (Massachusetts), 782b–783b, 799b–800a

North Carolina, 296b, 393a,b, 395b, 502a, 516b, 603b, 1381b, 1529b, 1530a

North Carolina Baptist State Convention, 565a

Northeast Kingdom, 752b

Northern Baptist Convention, 555a, 566a, 567b–568a, 560a,b, 570a,b, 571a, 572a, 573b, 629b, 955b, 959a, 1647a, 1693a; *see also* American Baptist Churches in the U.S.A.

Northern Illinois Synod, 439b, 441b

Northern Ireland, 499b

North Market Sabbath School (Chicago), 807b

Northrop, F. S. C., 1204a

Northwest College, 1617a

Northwestern College (Iowa), 515a, 1617a

Northwest Ordinance of 1787, 1655a

Northwest Territory, 360b

Norton, Andrews, 585a–b, 1082a–b, 1119a

Norton, Charles Eliot, 584b

Norton, John, 1041a

Norton, Wesley, 1700b

Norwegian churches, 439b

Norwegian Evangelical Lutheran Church in America, *see* Norwegian Synod

Norwegians, 426a, 437b, 443b, 446b, 569a–b

Norwegian Synod (Norwegian Evangelical Lutheran Church in America), 439b, 440a,b, 442a,b, 443a, 444a, 1616a,b

Notes on Virginia (Jefferson), 1240a–b

Notre Dame University (Indiana), 365, 386a

Nouvelles de la Republique des Lettres, 1089a

Novak, Michael, 1011a–b, 1406a, 1465a, 1466a, 1490a

Nova Scotia (Canada), 226b, 230b, 231a, 241a, 242a, 244a, 267a, 266b, 353b

novels, 1021a, 1023b–1025b, 1111b

Noyes, John Humphrey, 76b, 817a–b, 865b–867b, 1439a

nuclear war, 389a, 1426b–1427a, 1468a, 1469b

Nuestra Señora del Rosario University (Santiago de Chile), 193b

numbers, archetypal, 62a

nuns, 168b, 170a, 1349a, 1554a–b, 1558a, 1570a,b

Nun's Story, The, 1349a

Nurses Christian Fellowship, 1623b

Nyankopon, 176b–177a

Nygren, Anders, 1150b

Nyingma Institute (California), 680a

O

Oates, Wayne, 1592a, 1593a

Oahspe, 717a

Obatala, 177b

Obeah, 1174b

Oberammergau Passion play, 1343a

Oberholtzer, John H., 617a

Oberlin College (Ohio), 490a, 492a, 617a, 816b–817a, 1063b, 1443a, 1634a, 1679b

Oberlin Evangelist, 817b

Oberlin Perfectionism, 803b, 817a–b, 952b

Objections Answered Touching Maryland, 346a,b

Oblate Sisters of Mary Immaculate, 232b

Oblate Sisters of Providence, 263b, 367b, 645a, 1570a

Obregon, Alvaro, 215b, 216a, 217a

O'Brien, David J., 11b, 13a, 1558a

O'Brien, Hugh, 368a

O'Brien, Pat, 1348a

Observations on Man, His Frame, His Duty, and His Expectations (Hartley), 1097b

Observations on the Growth of the Mind (Reed), 1120a

Occident and American Jewish Advocate, 1018b–1019a

Occident, 297a

Occom, Samson, 1676a–b

Occult Movements in America, 655a, 664b, **711a–722b,** 902b, 910b

occupations, 22b, 98a

Ockenga, Harold John, 960a, 963a

O'Connell, Daniel, 367a

O'Connell, Denis, 370a, 371a,b, 1004a–b, 1005a

O'Connell, William Henry, 371a,b, 385a

O'Connor, Edwin, 382b–383a

O'Connor, Flannery, 382b, 1220b

O'Connor, John J., 386b

O'Dea, Thomas F., 44a–b, 382a–b, 1008b, 1161a

Odets, Clifford, 1022b

Odiyan, 680a

Odum, Howard W., 19a

Oecolampadius, *see* Huszgen, Johann

Oellers, James, 359b

Ofiesh, Aftimios, 334b

"O, for a Thousand Tongues to Sing," 533b

Of Plimoth Plantation (Bradford), 3a

O'Gara, James, 1701b

Ogden, Schubert, 612b, 1162b

Oglala Indians, 142a

O'Gorman, Edmundo, 137a

Ogun, 177b, 178b, 182a

O'Hair, Madalyn Murray, 739a

O'Hara, Edwin V., 381b

Oh, God!, 1350a

Oh, God! Book II, 1350a

Ohienko, Ilarion, 340b

Ohio, 74b, 332a, 518a,b, 657a

INDEX

250a, 253b, 268b, 269a; and Catholics, 991b; church and state, 1376b, 1378a; collegiate education, 1613b, 1615a,b, 1616a,b, 1617a,b, 1619a, 1622b, 1623a,b; colonies, 350a, 778a, 779a,b; and Congregationalism, 483a, 495a; demography, 73b, 75a, 77b, 80b; ecumenism, 983a; and Episcopal Church, 409b; ethnicity and, 1479a; and Fundamentalism, 953a–954a, 955b–956a, 959a; German language, 629b; German Reformed, 519b; Great Awakening, 781a, 782a,b, 785b, 786b, 788a,b, 791b–792a, 795a, 797a; laity, 36a; liberalism, 1129a; liturgy and worship, 1273a, 1274b–1275b; and Lutherans, 449b; Mexico, 212a; ministry, 1566a,b, 1573a,b; missions, 398b, 1684b, 1687a, 1690a, 1693a; music and hymnody, 1290a; Native American missions, 1676a–b, 1680b–1681a; Neoevangelicalism, 963b; on nuclear war, 1427a–b; Plan of Union of 1801, 486a, 487a,b–488b; prejudice, 1527a,b, 1528a; politics, 23a; Puritanism, 471a, 1060b; restorationism, 847a; social reform, 1432b, 1433a, 1436a, 1438a, 1443b, 1455b; South, 1493a, 1494a, 1495a,b, 1497a, 1498b, 1499b, 1501b, 1504b, 1506a; theological education, 1630a, 1633b; on war, 1415b, 1416a, 1419b; women, 1448a, 1469b, 1581a; *see also* New School Presbyterianism; Old School Presbyterianism

Presbyterians, The, 1783–1840 (Sweet), 7a
presbyterian system, 458b
presbytery, 486b, 499a–b, 500a, 501a, 502a, 512a
"Presbytery, The," 499b
Prescott, William Kickling, 584a
presidential address, 1404b
Presidential Prayer Breakfasts, 963b
Presidential Succession of 1910 (Madero), 214a
press, religious, *see* Religious Press
press, Yiddish, *see* Yiddish press
Preus, J. A. O., 444b
Pribilla, Max, 992a
Price, Richard, 1069b, 1099b
Price-Mars, Jean, 179a, 180a–b, 181b–182a,b
Priestcraft Exposed and Primitive Christianity Defended, 1700a
Priestcraft Unmasked, 1700a
priestesses, 179b
priests, 179a,b, 512a, 653a, 1480a, 1565b
Priestley, Joseph, 1069b, 1097b–1098a, 1256b
priestly philosophers, 132b–133a
Primary Association (Mormons), 622b
Primitive Advent Church, 836a
Primitive Baptist Associations, 848b, 1504a
Primitive Church of Divine Communion, 696b

Primitive movement, 1574b
Primitive Physick (Wesley), 528a, 1254b
primitive religions, 176a
Prince, Joseph, Jr., 795b
Prince, Thomas, 3b
Prince Edward Island, 231a–b, 241a, 353b
Prince of the Ghetto (Peretz), 1022b
Princeton Sunday School Union, 884b
Princeton Theological Seminary (New Jersey), 508a, 953a–b, 1050a–1052a, 1055a, 1628a, 1631b–1632a, 1634a, 1638b, 1646b
Princeton theology, 504b, 505a, 1095b
Princeton University (New Jersey), 500b, 501a, 792b–793a, 1063b, 1095b, 1375b, 1612a, 1613a, 1615b, 1630a, 1661b
Principia (Newton), 1090b
Principle of Protestantism (Schaff), 4a, 1112b
Principles of Nature, Her Divine Revelation and a Voice to Mankind (Davis), 716a
Principles of Nature (Palmer), 1101b
Principles of Psychology (James), 1198a
printing, 193b–194a
Private Life of Henry VIII, 1356a
privatization, 27b–28b
"probabiliorists" and "probabilists," 1584b
Problem of Christianity (Royce), 1197b
"Problem of God—Yesterday and Today" (Murray), 1169a
Problems of Religious Progress (Dorchester), 5a
Proceedings of the American Academy for Jewish Research, 1019b
process theology, 1102a, 1162a–b
Proctor, H. H., 643a
Production Code Administration, 1355b, 1356a
Prodigal, The, 1349b
Professional Ministry, **1565a–1581b;** electronic church, 1723b–1724a; pastoral care, 1583a–1594b; secular education, 1622b–1624a; theological education, 1627a–1652b
Profile of the Christian Marketplace, 1722a, 1723a
Profiles of Belief (Piepkorn), 10b
Program in Religion and Psychiatry (Topeka), 1591a
Progress and Prospects of Christianity in the United States of America (Baird), 4a
Progressive Friends, 1438b
Progressive Movement, The, 1900–1915 (Hofstadter), 13a
Progressive National Baptist Convention, 567a, 575b, 648a
Progressive Orthodoxy, 1133b
Progressive movement, 494a
progressivism, 3b–4a, 39b–40a, 928b, 930a, 1451b–1453a, 1459a, 1644a–b
Progressive party, 1072b

INDEX

Roman Catholic Volunteers, 358a

Romances de los Señores de la Neuva España, 121b

Roman Empire, 1396a–1397a; Christianity, 154b–155a; Eastern Christianity, 325a

Romanian Orthodox Episcopate of America, 339b, 342b

Romanian Orthodox Missionary Archdiocese in America and Canada, 339b

"Romanism," 1113a

Roman Martyrology, 1280a

Roman Missal, 1280a

Roman Pontifical, 1280a

Roman Ritual, 1280a

romanticism, *see* Romantic Religion

Romantic Religion, **1103a–1115b;** Catholicism, 161; art, 1363a; historiography, 3b; religious philosophy, 1204a; science and, 1242b–1243a, 1245b

Romero, Oscar, 221b

Roncalli, Angelo, *see* John XXIII, Pope

Roochamah: Devotional Exercises for the Daughters of Israel, 1016b

Roosevelt, Eleanor, 380a,b, 1159a

Roosevelt, Franklin D., 305b, 378b–379a, 411a, 914b, 928b, 1388b, 1472a, 1540b, 1541b–1542a, 1713a

Roosevelt, Theodore, 733a, 810a, 1072b

Root, Elihu, 1420a, 1459a

Roots of Fundamentalism, The (Sandeen), 14b

Roozen, David A., 81a

Rosales, Diego, 194a

Rosecrans, William, 364b

Rosemary's Baby, 1350a

Rosenberg, Jack, *see* Erhard, Werner

Rosenberg, Julius and Ethel, 306b

Rosenfeld, Alvin, 1231b

Rosenfeld, Morris, 1021a

Rosenwald, Julius, 1454b

Rosenzweig, Franz, 287a, 1034a, 1703b

Rosicrucian Fellowship, 719b, 1519b

Rosicrucianism, 713b, 714a, 719b–720a, 1519b

Rosier, James, 345b

Rossellini, Roberto, 1353b

Rossi, Peter H., 1600b

Roszak, Theodore, 674a, 1252a

Roth, Henry, 1022a

Roth, Philip, 1025a

Roumanian Baptist Association of the United States and Canada, 570a

Rourke, Constance, 89b–90a

Rousseau, Jean-Jacques, 1089a, 1104a, 1105b, 1393a,b, 1396b, 1397a,b, 1402

Routley, Erik, 1304b

Rouvroy, Claude Henri de, Comte de Saint-Simon, 17b, 1001a

Rowe, Henry K., 6a

Rowe, Peter Trimble, 400b–401a

Rowlandson, Mary, 1224a

Rowntree, John Wilhelm, 608a

Royal Dutch Shell, 1464b

Royal Indian Patronage, 191a

Royal Society of London, 1238a,b

Royce, Josiah, 1064a, 1189a, 1193a,b, 1194a, 1196a–1197b, 1204a, 1247a

Rozhdestvensky, Platon, 332b, 333b, 334b, 337a–338b

Rubens, Peter Paul, 1361b

Rubenstein, Richard, 1035a, 1163a, 1171a

Rubinow, I. M., 1455a

Ruckman, Peter S., 1730a–b

Rudd, Daniel A., 645b

Rudolph, Albert, *see* Rudrānanda, Swami

Rudrānanda, Swami, 696b

Ruether, Rosemary Radford, 162a, 1166a–b

Ruhani Satsang, 697b

Rukeyser, Muriel, 1023a

"rule egoism," 745a

"Rules of the Band-Societies, drawn up December 25, 1738," 536a

Rumanians, 332a, 333b, 334a, 339b, 341b, 342a

Rus', Kievan, 327b

Rush, Benjamin, 501a, 582b, 632b, 1096a, 1097a–b, 1100b, 1241a, 1258a, 1434a

Rush, Christopher, 638a–b

Ruskin, John, 1333b

Russell, Mrs. Alexander, 670a

Russell, Archibald, 1442b

Russell, Bertrand, 1200b

Russell, Charles Taze, 630b, 837a–b, 843a,b, 1264a, 1390a

Russell, Letty, 1166b

Russia, 266b–267a, 299b, 330a–331a, 332b–333a, 334a,b, 335a, 336b–339a

Russian Imperial Missionary Society, 331a

Russian Mennonites, 617a–b

Russian Orthodoxy: Canada, 266b; clergy, 1569a,b; geography and demography, 80a; liturgy and worship, 1281a–b; music, 1302b–1303a; Tanaina, 263b

Russian Orthodox Church Outside of Russia, *see* Synod in Exile

Russian Orthodox Greek Catholic Church of America, 336b–337a

Russian-Ukrainian Evangelical Baptist Union of the U.S.A., 570a

Rust College (Mississippi), 547b

Rusyns, (Carpatho-Russians), 332b, 333b, 336b, 337a, 343a

Rutgers University (New Jersey), 514a, 515a, 1612b, 1615a

INDEX

Swing, David, 504b, 1130b, 1132b–1133a
Swiss Anabaptist, 616a
Swiss Brethren, 616a,b
Swiss Mennonites, 616a
Swiss Reformation, 451b, 511a–b
Swiss Calvinists, 456a–b
Sword of the Lord (Rice), 958a
Syllabus of Errors, 214b
symbols, religious, 62a, 140a–141b, 172b, 178a, 971a, 1207a, 1366a–b
Symmes, Thomas, 1287b
synagogue, 83a, 273a,b, 274b, 278b–287b, 297b, 315b, 322a, 1608a
Synagogue Council of America, 1468b
Synanon, 744a, 750a
Syncretistic Zen, 675a
synechism, 1195a
synod, 499a, 500a, 501a
Synodical Conference, 447b
Synod in Exile, 337b, 339a, 340a, 341b, 342b
Synod of Barmen, 423a
Synod of Dort (1618–1619), 459b, 512b, 513a
Synod of the East, 520b
Synod of the Free German Reformed Congregations of Pennsylvania, 518b
Synod of the Reformed German Church in the United States of America, 517b–518a
Synopsis Purioris Theologiae, 459b
Syrian Church of Antioch, Archdiocese of the, 343b
Syrian Jacobites, 343b
Syrian Orthodox Church of Malabar (India), 343b
Syrian Orthodox Youth Organizations, 341a
Systematic Theology (Hodge), 504b, 1050b
Systematic Theology (Strong), 1053b
Systematic Theology (Tillich), 1160a, 1593a
System of Doctrines (Hopkins), 1048a
Szold, Benjamin, 277b, 1017a
Szold, Henrietta, 303b, 1472b

T

Taché, Alexandre-Antonin, 234b–235a
Taft, Robert, 411a
Taft, William Howard, 1459a, 1537b, 1538a
Tageblatt, 1706b
t'ai chi ch'uan, 707a, 1522b
Tail of the Tiger (Vermont), 680b
Taishakyo (or Raikyo), 702b
Taiwan, 401a
Tajín, 124b
Takach, Basil, 343a
Talbot, George, 351a

Talbot, Gilbert, 351b
Talking God Seminary (California), 696b
Talladega College (Alabama), 492a, 641a, 696b
Talmage, James E., 662b
Talmud Torah (New York), 1603a
Talmud Torahs, 1607a,b
Talon, Jean, 228a
Tamaroas, 230a
Tamashchyk, Vasily, 340b
Tamayo, Alvaro, 59b
Tanaina, 263b
"Tangled Web," 1715b
Tannenberg, David, 1291b, 1292a
Tant, Yater, 856a
Tanyra, 679b
Taoism, 706b–707a, 1521b
Tapis, Estevan, 1512a
Tapp, Robert B., 592a
Tappan, Arthur, 806b, 817a, 1072a, 1434b, 1436b
Tappan, John, 1434b
Tappan, Lewis, 817a, 895a,b, 896b, 1072a, 1434b, 1437a
Tarascans, 119a
Tassajara, *see* Zen Mountain Center
Tassajar Springs, 1521b
Tatham, John, 352a
Tavibo, 839b
tax-exempt status, 1387b
Taylor, Edward, 780b, 1208b
Taylor, Graham, 1449a, 1461a
Taylor, Hudson, 1687b
Taylor, J. Randolph, 509a
Taylor, Joshua, 1362b–1363a
Taylor, Nathaniel William, 487b, 503a, 562b, 796a, 801b–802a, 807a, 876a, 881a, 1048b–1054a,b, 1108b, 1632b
Taylor, Thomas, 540a, 1120a
Tawil, Joseph, 343a
Teachers Institute, 303a
Teaching for the Lost-Found Nation of Islam in a Mathematical Way, 765a–b
Teaching Spiritualism, 717a,b
Teague, Collin, 564b
Tear, Jim, 1733b
Tecciztecatl, 128a
technology: and ecumenism, 986a
technometry, 1090a, 1091b
Teck, Jacob, 1533a
Teilhard de Chardin, Pierre, 161b, 169a, 382a, 1161a, 1250b, 1662a
Tejada, Sebastian Lerdo de, 211a
television, 82a, 380b, 741a, 841b, 842a, 943b, 944a, 973a,b–974a,b, 1168b–1169a, 1323b, 1341a,

INDEX

Union Theological Seminary (New York), 503b, 972b, 1147b, 1464b, 1634a, 1640b, 1644a–b, 1660b, 1661b

Union Theological Seminary (Virginia), 508a, 1634b

Union Theological Seminary School of Music, 1301a

Unitarian Christianity, 1070b

Unitarianism and Universalism, **579a–593b**

Unitarians, 531b, 1094b–1095a, 1192b; architecture, 1338a; and Catholicism, 364b; church and state, 1379a–b; and Congregationalism, 483b, 484a–b; Enlightenment, 1098a; Free Religious Association, 736a; free thought and ethical movements, 737b; geography and demography, 78b; Hinduism, 683b; liberalism, 1129a; ministries, 1623a; Puritanism, 1070b–1071a; religious prejudice, 1541b; social reform, 1432b, 1433a,b, 1434a,b, 1438a, 1443a; South, 1506a; theology, 1631a; Transcendentalism, 1118b–1119b, 1125a, 1243a–b; on war, 1416a, 1419b; women, 1445b, 1559a

Unitarians Face a New Age, 590a

Unitarian-Universalism, 592a–b, 991a

Unitarian-Universalist Association, 590a, 591b, 1559b

Unitas Fratrum, 517b, 622b, *see also* Moravians

United Artists, 1348a

United Baptists, 559b

United Brethren, *see* Moravians

United Christian Church, 628a

United Church Board for Homeland Ministries, 496a

United Churches of Christ in America, 522b

United Church of Canada, 247a–b, 248a, 249a,b, 251a,b–252a, 253b, 917b, 926a, 929a, 990a, 1714b

United Church of Christ, 495b–497a, 523a, 854b, 991a, 1274a, 1465a; broadcasting, 1715b; campus ministries, 1623a; geography and demography, 77b; on nuclear war, 1427a–b; religious press, 1708b; women, 1581a

United Church Women of the National Council of Churches, 496b

United Episcopal Church of America, 415a

United Evangelical Church, 550a, 628b

United Evangelical Synod of the Northwest, 520b

United Foreign Missionary Society, 1684b

United Hebrew Charities, 1454a,b

United Hebrew Trades, 301a

United Holy Church, 941a

United House of Prayer for All People, 763a–765a

United Jewish Appeal, 304b, 1472b

United Lutheran Church in America, 443a, 444a, 449a,b

United Methodism, **539a–553b**, 628a, 629a, 827a–b; missions, 1695a; on nuclear war, 1427a–b; reli-

gious press, 1708a,b; South, 1506b; television broadcasting, 1717a; women, 1469b, 1559a

United Methodist Board of Missions, 1464b

United Methodist Church, *see* United Methodism

United Missionary Church, 716a

United Nations Meditation Group, 698a

United Palestine Appeal, 304a,b

United Pentecostal Church International, 940b–941a

United Presbyterian Church in the United States, 507b, 508a–509a, 551b, 1275b, 1708b

United Presbyterian Church of North America, 501b, 504a, 506b, 507a,b, 508a

United Presbyterian Church of Scotland, 241a

United Presbyterian General Assembly, 1355b

United Provinces of Central America, 208a–209b

United Reform Church of the United Kingdom, 990b

United Secession, *see* United Presbyterian Church of Scotland

United Secularists of America, 739a

United States Catholic Miscellany, 363b, 1000a

United States Sanitary Commission, 1445b

United States Temperance Union, 1436b

United States v. *Seeger* (1965), 1389a

United States v. *Welch* (1970), 1426b

United Synagogue Review, 1707a

United Synod, South, 443a

United Way, 304a–b

unity: ecumenical movement, 977a–993b

Unity and Progress movement, 217b

Unity Church, 269b

Unity School of Christianity, 909b–913b

Unity Temple (Illinois), 1337b

Universal Brotherhood of Faithists, 717a

Universal Christian Council for Life and Work, 985b

Universal Fellowship of Metropolitan Community Churches, 930b, 1523a

Universalism: geography and demography, 78b; German language, 630a–b; and Lutherans, 437b; religious press, 1700b; social reform, 1433a, 1434a, 1439a, 1443a; women, 1445b, 1559a, 1581a; *see also* Unitarianism and Universalism

Universalist Church of America, 579a

Universal Jewish Encyclopedia, 1018a

Universal Negro Improvement Association, 644b, 758a–760b

Universal Peace Union, 1420a, 1457a, 1458b, 1459a

Universal Society, 733b

universities: free thought and ethical movements, 735a

University of California, 1614a

University of California at Berkeley, 1064a

University of Chicago, 562a, 1268a, 1615b, 1616b, 1658b

INDEX

INDEX

Winrod, Gerald B., 958b, 1541a,b, 1542a
Winston-Salem (North Carolina), 623a
Winter, Gibson, 41b, 412a
Winter Light, 1352a
Winthrop, John, 102a–b, 349a, 475b, 477a,b, 832b, 1058b, 1086a, 1209a,b, 1212b, 1223b, 1255a, 1307a–b, 1430a, 1548a
Winthrop, John, the Younger, 1255b
Winthrop, Professor John, 1092b
Wisconsin, 229b, 360b, 402a,b
Wisconsin Evangelical Lutheran Synod, 442a, 443a, 445a, 1572b, 1601a, 1617a
Wise, Carroll A., 1592a
Wise, Isaac Mayer, 275a–276a,b, 298b, 1016a, 1019a, 1028a,b, 1030a, 1282a, 1315b, 1454a, 1568a, 1621b
Wise, John, 1061a–b
Wise, Stephen S., 305a, 930a, 1320b–1321a, 1323a, 1454b, 1472b
Wise, Ted, 968b
Wishard, Luther D., 983b, 1687b
Wislerites, 617a
Wissahickon Pietists, 1291b, 1292b–1293a
witchcraft, 134a, 711a, 713b–714a, 720b–721a, 1527b, 1549a
Witchcraft Through the Ages, 1347a
Witherspoon, John, 501a, 1095a–1096a, 1242a, 1375b, 1631b
Wittenberg College, 1614b
Wittenberg Seminary (Ohio), 1572b
Wittenburg Door, The, 973b
Wittenmeyer, Annie, 1446b
WJBT ("Where Jesus Blesses Thousands"), 1711b
WMBI, 958b, 1712a
Woelfkin, Cornelius, 567b
Wojtylla, Karol, *see* John Paul II, Pope
Wolf, Eric, 134b
Wolf, Jacob, 1172a
Wolfson, Harry Austryn, 1018a, 1661a
Wollaston, William, 1096b
Wollebius, Johannes, 459a
Woman in the Nineteenth Century (Fuller), 1108a, 1122b, 1226a–b
Woman in the Wilderness, 625a
Woman's American Baptist Home Missionary Society, 1446a
Woman's Auxiliary, 1432b, 1446a,b
Woman's Baptist Foreign Missionary Society, 567a, 1446a
Woman's Bible, The, 1166a
Woman's Board of Foreign Missions of the Reformed Church in America, 1446a,b
Woman's Board of Home Missions, 1448b

Woman's Board of Missions (Congregational), 492a, 1446a, 1686b–1687a
Woman's Christian Temperance Union, 446a, 1419a, 1446b, 1447a–b, 1448b, 1449a–b, 1459a, 1685b
Woman's Department of the Commission on Interracial Cooperation, 1450a
Woman's Executive Committee for Home Missions, 1446a–b
Woman's Foreign Missionary Society, 1446a, 1448b
Women's Foreign Missionary Societies of the Presbyterian Church, U.S.A., 1446a
Woman's Home Missionary Society, 1446b
Woman's Missionary Society of the Evangelical Lutheran Church, 1446b
Woman's Missionary Union, 1446b, 1448a
Woman's Parent Mite Society, 1446a
Womanspirit Rising: A Feminist Reader in Religion, 1167a
Women and Religion, **1547a–1562b;** Antinomian Controversy, 475b; black clergy, 638b; blacks, 1580b–1581a; Catholicism, 365b, 369a,b, 381b, 834b–385a, 1012a; church and state, 1387b; clergy, 1481a; collegiate education, 1616b–1617a, 1620b, 1621a; communitarians, 622b; Congregationalism, 489b–490a, 492a–b, 496b; Episcopal Church, 413a–414a; evangelicalism, 893a–b; holiness movement, 814b, 815b, 825a–826a, 877b; Islam, 724a, 729a; Judaism, 288b, 300a,b, 302a, 308a,b, 310a, 1016b, 1282b, 1283a; Krishnas, 693a; Lutheranism, 446a–b, 1572b, 1580b; Methodism, 535b, 548a–b, 551b, 552a; missionaries, 1317a, 1686b–1687a, 1692b; Mormons, 653b, 664b–665a, 1577a; Native American religions, 144b; Neoevangelicals, 971b; nuns, 1570a,b; Oneida community, 866a; ordination, 1572b, 1580a,b, 1581a; post-World War II feminism, 1165b–1167a; Presbyterians, 504a, 507a–b; Protestant ministry, 1643b, 1644a; Puritanism, 457b, 1060a; Quakerism, 600b–601a, 1276a; religious life, 168b, 170a, 1571a, 1580a; religious studies, 1663b; scientific psychology, 1258a; seminaries, 886a; Shakers, 864a,b; Social Christianity, 924a, 925a,b, 929b; social reform, 1437b–1438a, 1442a–b, 1445a–1450b, 1469b–1470a; sociology of religion, 21b–22a; Sunday schools, 884b; temperance movement, 1458a; textbooks, 1387a; theological education, 1639b; Unitarians and Universalists, 592b; witchcraft, 712b; Zionism, 303b
women religious, 365b–366a
Women's American ORT, 306b–307a
Women's Baptist Home Mission Society, 567a
Women's International League for Peace and Freedom, 1426a, 1459b
Women's Missionary Societies, 1432b

INDEX

Ysleta Indian mission, 1595b
Yukon Indians, 261a

Z

Zablocki, Benjamin, 859a, 860b
Zacharias, Metropolitan, 334b
Zahm, John A., 371a, 1005b–1006a, 1250a–b
Zahn, Gordon, 1426a
Zakkis, Nestor, 331a–b
Zanchi, Girolama (Zanchius), 457b
Zangwill, Israel, 1478a
Zapata, Emiliano, 214a–b, 216a
Zapotecs, 119a, 120a–b, 134a
Zara, Louis, 1022a
Zaretsky, Irving I., 15a
Zayek, Francis M., 343a
Zeisberger, David, 1677a–b
Zen Buddhism, 670b–671a,b, 673a,b, 677a, 1365b, 1521b
Zen Center of Los Angeles, 671a
Zen Meditation Center (Rochester, New York), 671a
Zen Mountain Center (California), 679a
Zen Studies Society of New York, 670b
Zerbe, Alvin Sylvester, 1151a, 1155b
zero population growth, 309a
Zhitlowsky, Chaim, 283a, 1031b

Zilboorg, Gregory, 1591b
Zinnemann, Fred, 1341b
Zinzendorf, Count Nicholas Ludwig von, 434a, 517b, 622b–623a,b, 624a, 784a, 787b, 1293b
Zion City (Illinois), 936a
Zion Collegiate (Cincinnati), 1621b
Zionism, 287b, 288b, 291b, 300b, 303a–304a,b, 305b–306a, 320a, 321b, 322b–323a, 1472a–b; Jewish thought, 1029b–1030b; preaching, 1320b; prejudice, 1540a, 1541a; publications, 1019a,b, 1706b; rabbis, 1568a; women, 1557b, 1560b
Zionist Organization of America, 1472b
Zion's Camp, 657b
Zion's Harp, 1294b
Zion's Herald, 877b
Zion's Watch Tower Society, 630b
Ziorov, Nicholas, 332b, 333a
Zoarites, 870b–871a
Zorach v. *Clausen* (1952), 731a, 1386b, 1605a
Zoroastrian tradition, 832b
Zuk, Joseph A., 336a, 340b
Zukunft, 1020a
Zuloaga, Félix, 210b
Zumárraga, Juan de, 192a, 193a,b, 194a, 195b, 204b, 1595a
Zundel, John, 1301b
Zuni Indians, 144b, 146a–b, 149b, 1510b, 1511a,b
Zunser, Eliakum, 1021a
Zurich (Switzerland), 456a–b, 511a
Zwingli, Huldreich, 451b, 511a, 616a, 980b, 1274b